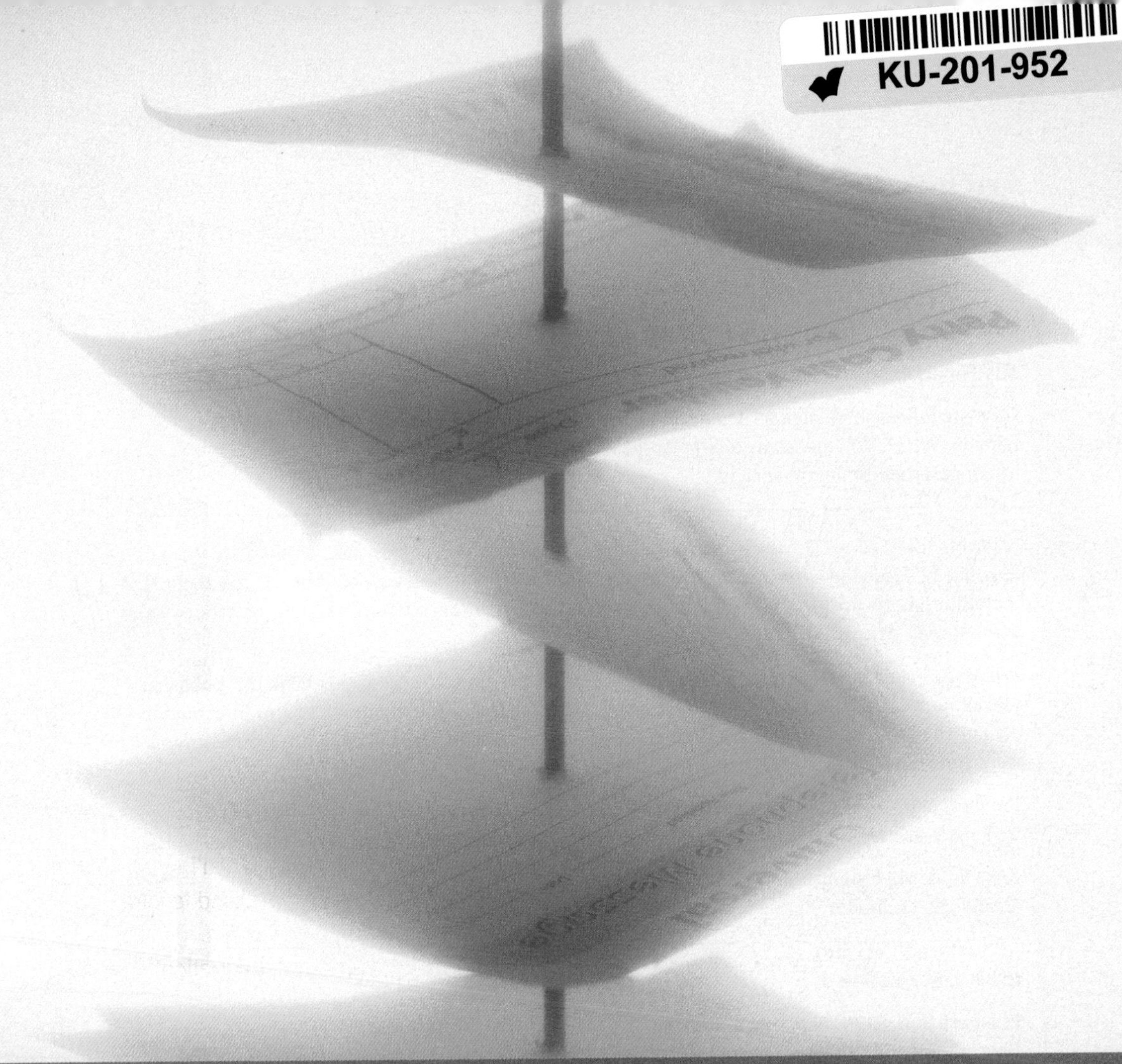

Organizational Behaviour and Management

THIRD EDITION

John Martin The University of Hull

THOMSON

Australia • Canada • Mexico • Singapore • Spain • United Kingdom • United States

THOMSON

Organizational Behaviour and Management, Third Edition

For more information, contact Thomson Learning, High Holborn House, 50–51 Bedford Row, London, WC1R 4LR or visit us on the World Wide Web at:
http://www.thomsonlearning.co.uk

British Library Cataloguing-in-Publication Data
A catalogue record for this book is available from the British Library

---

ISBN 1-86152-948-1

First edition 1998, reprinted 2000
Second edition 2001, reprinted 2002
This edition 2005

Text design by Design Deluxe
Typeset by Saxon Graphics Ltd, Derby
Printed in Italy by G. Canale & C.

Brief Contents

Full Contents

List of Features

Management in Action panels

List of Employee Perspective panels

List of Case Studies

Guided Tour

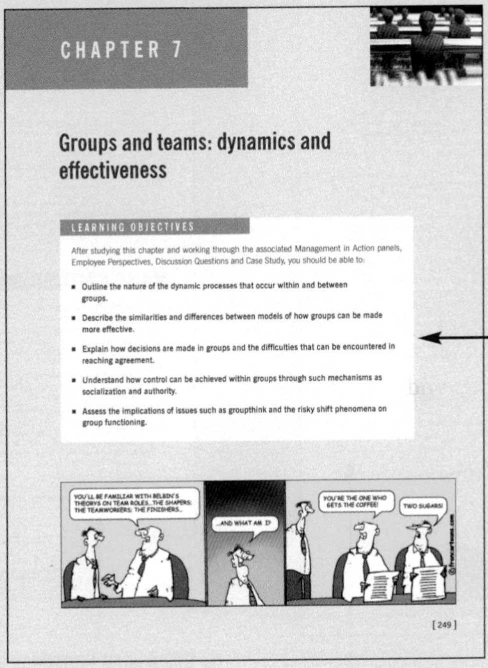

CHAPTER 7

Groups and teams: dynamics and effectiveness

LEARNING OBJECTIVES

After studying this chapter and working through the associated Management in Action panels, Employee Perspectives, Discussion Questions and Case Study, you should be able to:

- **Outline the nature of the dynamic processes that occur within and between groups.**
- **Describe the similarities and differences between models of how groups can be made more effective.**
- **Explain how decisions are made in groups and the difficulties that can be encountered in reaching agreement.**
- **Understand how control can be achieved within groups through such mechanisms as socialization and authority.**
- **Assess the implications of issues such as groupthink and the risky shift phenomena on group functioning.**

[249]

Learning Objectives to be achieved appear at the start of every chapter to help you monitor your progress. Each chapter also ends with a conclusion section that recaps the key content for revision purposes.

Key Terms are highlighted in the text where they first appear and defined in the margin. All the terms are collated in a Glossary at the end of the book, allowing you to find explanations of key terms quickly.

Employee Perspective – this new feature looks at what OB means in practice from the perspective of the *employee* – rather than the employer – in order to provide as complete a picture of the organizational experience as is possible.

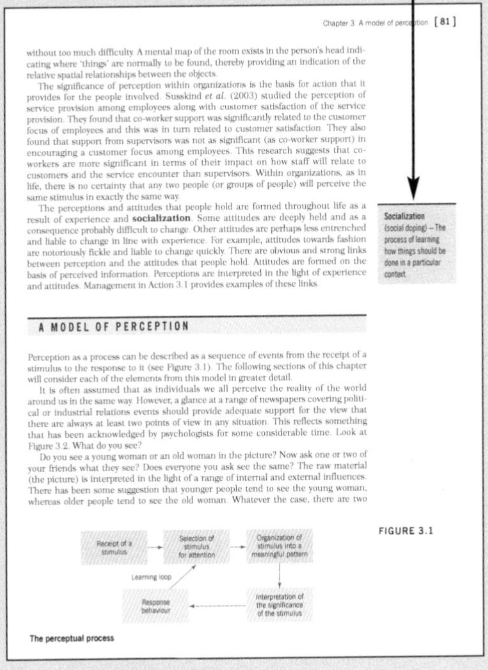

Chapter 3 A model of perception [81]

without too much difficulty. A mental map of the room exists in the person's head indicating where 'things' are normally to be found, thereby providing an indication of the relative spatial relationships between the objects.

The significance of perception within organizations is the basis for action that it provides for the people involved. Susskind *et al.* (2003) studied the perception of service provision among employees along with customer satisfaction of the service provision. They found that co-worker support was significantly related to the customer focus of employees and this was in turn related to customer satisfaction. They also found that support from supervisors was not as significant (as co-worker support) in encouraging a customer focus among employees. This research suggests that co-workers are more significant in terms of their impact on how staff will relate to customers and the service encounter than supervisors. Within organizations, as in life, there is no certainty that any two people (or groups of people) will perceive the same stimulus in exactly the same way.

The perceptions and attitudes that people hold are formed throughout life as a result of experience and **socialization**. Some attitudes are deeply held and as a consequence probably difficult to change. Other attitudes are perhaps less entrenched and liable to change in line with experience. For example, attitudes towards fashion are notoriously fickle and liable to change quickly. There are obvious and strong links between perception and the attitudes that people hold. Attitudes are formed on the basis of perceived information. Perceptions are interpreted in the light of experience and attitudes. Management in Action 3.1 provides examples of these links.

Socialization (social doping) – The process of learning how things should be done in a particular context.

A MODEL OF PERCEPTION

Perception as a process can be described as a sequence of events from the receipt of a stimulus to the response to it (see Figure 3.1). The following sections of this chapter will consider each of the elements from this model in greater detail.

It is often assumed that as individuals we all perceive the reality of the world around us in the same way. However, a glance at a range of newspapers covering political or industrial relations events should provide adequate support for the view that there are always at least two points of view in any situation. This reflects something that has been acknowledged by psychologists for some considerable time. Look at Figure 3.2. What do you see?

Do you see a young woman or an old woman in the picture? Now ask one or two of your friends what they see? Does everyone you ask see the same? The raw material (the picture) is interpreted in the light of a range of internal and external influences. There has been some suggestion that younger people tend to see the young woman, whereas older people tend to see the old woman. Whatever the case, there are two

FIGURE 3.1

The perceptual process

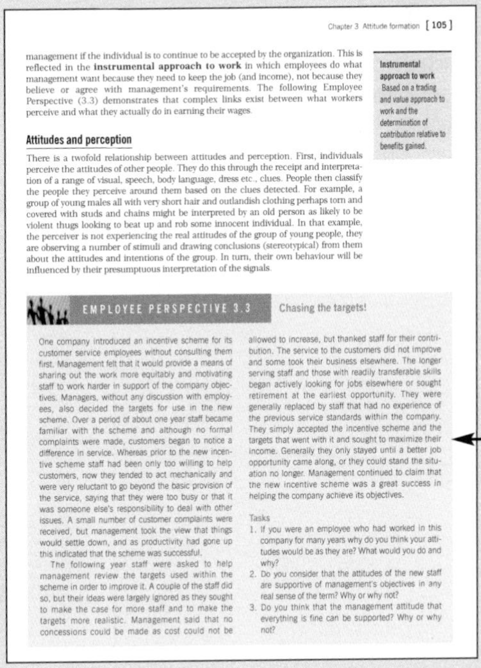

Chapter 3 Attitude formation [105]

management if the individual is to continue to be accepted by the organization. This is reflected in the **instrumental approach to work** in which employees do what management want because they need to keep the job (and income), not because they believe or agree with management's requirements. The following Employee Perspective (3.3) demonstrates that complex links exist between what workers perceive and what they actually do in earning their wages.

Instrumental approach to work Based on a trading and value approach to work and the determination of contribution relative to benefits gained.

Attitudes and perception

There is a twofold relationship between attitudes and perception. First, individuals perceive the attitudes of other people. They do this through the receipt and interpretation of a range of visual, speech, body language, dress etc., clues. People then classify the people they perceive around them based on the clues detected. For example, a group of young males all with very short hair and outlandish clothing perhaps torn and covered with studs and chains might be interpreted by an old person as likely to be violent thugs looking to beat up and rob some innocent individual. In that example, the perceiver is not experiencing the real attitudes of the group of young people, they are observing a number of stimuli and drawing conclusions (stereotypical) from them about the attitudes and intentions of the group. In turn, their own behaviour will be influenced by their presumptuous interpretation of the signals.

EMPLOYEE PERSPECTIVE 3.3 Chasing the targets!

One company introduced an incentive scheme for its customer service employees without consulting them first. Management felt that it would provide a means of sharing out the work more equitably and motivating staff to work harder in support of the company objectives. Managers, without any discussion with employees, also decided the targets for use in the new scheme. Over a period of about one year staff became familiar with the scheme and although no formal complaints were made, customers began to notice a difference in service. Whereas prior to the new incentive scheme staff had been only too willing to help customers, now they tended to act mechanically and were very reluctant to go beyond the basic provision of the service, saying that they were too busy or that it was someone else's responsibility to deal with other issues. A small number of customer complaints were received, but management took the view that things would settle down, and as productivity had gone up this indicated that the scheme was successful.

The following year staff were asked to help management review the targets used within the scheme in order to improve it. A couple of the staff did so, but their ideas were largely ignored as they sought to make the case for more staff and to make the targets more realistic. Management said that no concessions could be made as cost could not be allowed to increase, but thanked staff for their contribution. The service to the customers did not improve and some took their business elsewhere. The longer serving staff and those with readily transferable skills began actively looking for jobs elsewhere or sought retirement at the earliest opportunity. They were generally replaced by staff that had no experience of the previous service standards within the company. They simply accepted the incentive scheme and the targets that went with it and sought to maximize their income. Generally they only stayed until a better job opportunity came along, or they could stand the situation no longer. Management continued to claim that the new incentive scheme was a great success in helping the company achieve its objectives.

Tasks

1. If you were an employee who had worked in this company for many years why do you think your attitudes would be as they are? What would you do and why?
2. Do you consider that the attitudes of the new staff are supportive of management's objectives in any real sense of the term? Why or why not?
3. Do you think that the management attitude that everything is fine can be supported? Why or why not?

Management in Action provide applied examples of aspects of OB as experienced by managers in a *real* organizational context.

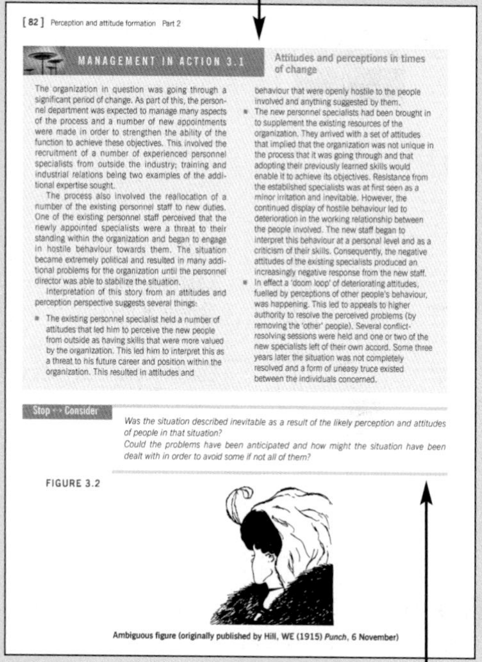

[82] Perception and attitude formation Part 2

MANAGEMENT IN ACTION 3.1

Attitudes and perceptions in times of change

The organization in question was going through a significant period of change. As part of this, the personnel department was expected to manage many aspects of the process and a number of new appointments were made in order to strengthen the ability of the function to achieve these objectives. This involved the recruitment of a number of experienced personnel specialists from outside the industry; training and industrial relations being two examples of the additional expertise sought.

The process also involved the reallocation of a number of the existing personnel staff to new duties. One of the existing personnel staff perceived that the newly appointed specialists were a threat to their standing within the organization and began to engage in hostile behaviour towards them. The situation became extremely political and resulted in many additional problems for the organization until the personnel director was able to stabilize the situation.

Interpretation of this story from an attitudes and perception perspective suggests several things:

- The existing personnel specialist held a number of attitudes that led him to perceive the new people from outside as having skills that were more valued by the organization. This led him to interpret this as a threat to his future career and position within the organization. This resulted in attitudes and behaviour that were openly hostile to the people involved and anything suggested by them.
- The new personnel specialists had been brought in to supplement the existing resources of the organization. They arrived with a set of attitudes that implied that the organization was not unique in the process that it was going through and that adopting their previously learned skills would enable it to achieve its objectives. Resistance from the established specialists was at first seen as a minor irritation and inevitable. However, the continued display of hostile behaviour led to deterioration in the working relationship between the people involved. The new staff began to interpret this behaviour at a personal level and as a criticism of their skills. Consequently, the negative attitudes of the existing specialists produced an increasingly negative response from the new staff.
- In effect a 'doom loop' of deteriorating attitudes, fuelled by perceptions of other people's behaviour, was happening. This led to appeals to higher authority to resolve the perceived problems (by removing the 'other' people). Several conflict-resolving sessions were held and one or two of the new specialists left of their own accord. Some three years later the situation was not completely resolved and a form of uneasy truce existed between the individuals concerned.

Stop ↔ Consider

Was the situation described inevitable as a result of the likely perception and attitudes of people in that situation?

Could the problems have been anticipated and how might the situation have been dealt with in order to avoid some if not all of them?

FIGURE 3.2

Ambiguous figure (originally published by Hill, WE (1915) *Punch*, 6 November)

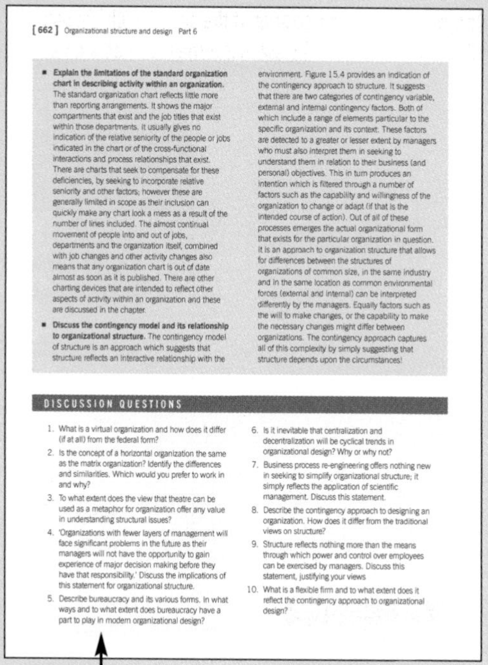

[662] Organizational structure and design Part 6

- **Explain the limitations of the standard organization chart in describing activity within an organization.** The standard organization chart reflects little more than reporting arrangements. It shows the major compartments that exist and the job titles that exist within those departments. It usually gives no indication of the relative seniority of the people or jobs indicated in the chart or of the cross-functional interactions and process relationships that exist. There are charts that seek to compensate for these deficiencies, by seeking to incorporate relative seniority and other factors; however these are generally limited in scope as their inclusion can quickly make any chart look a mess as a result of the number of lines included. The almost continual movement of people into and out of jobs, departments and the organization itself, combined with job changes and other activity changes also means that any organization chart is out of date almost as soon as it is published. There are other charting devices that are intended to reflect other aspects of activity within an organization and these are discussed in the chapter.
- **Discuss the contingency model and its relationship to organizational structure.** The contingency model of structure is an approach which suggests that structure reflects an interactive relationship with the environment. Figure 15.4 provides an indication of the contingency approach to structure. It suggests that there are two categories of contingency variable, external and internal contingency factors. Both of which include a range of elements particular to the specific organization and its context. These factors are detected to a greater or lesser extent by managers who must also interpret them in seeking to understand them in relation to their business (and personal) objectives. This in turn produces an intention which is filtered through a number of factors such as the capability and willingness of the organization to change or adapt (if that is the intended course of action). Out of all of these processes emerges the actual organizational form that exists for the particular organization in question. It is an approach to organization structure that allows for differences between the structures of organizations of common size, in the same industry and in the same location as common environmental forces (external and internal) can be interpreted differently by the managers. Equally factors such as the will to make changes, or the capability to make the necessary changes might differ between organizations. The contingency approach captures all of this complexity by simply suggesting that structure depends upon the circumstances!

DISCUSSION QUESTIONS

1. What is a virtual organization and how does it differ (if at all) from the federal form?
2. Is the concept of a horizontal organization the same as the matrix organization? Identify the differences and similarities. Which would you prefer to work in and why?
3. To what extent does the view that theatre can be used as a metaphor for organization offer any value in understanding structural issues?
4. 'Organizations with fewer layers of management will face significant problems in the future as their managers will not have the opportunity to gain experience of major decision making before they have that responsibility.' Discuss the implications of this statement for organizational structure.
5. Describe bureaucracy and its various forms. In what ways and to what extent does bureaucracy have a part to play in modern organizational design?
6. Is it inevitable that centralization and decentralization will be cyclical trends in organizational design? Why or why not?
7. Business process re-engineering offers nothing new in seeking to simplify organizational structure; it simply reflects the application of scientific management. Discuss this statement.
8. Describe the contingency approach to designing an organization. How does it differ from the traditional views on structure?
9. Structure reflects nothing more than the means through which power and control over employees can be exercised by managers. Discuss this statement, justifying your views
10. What is a flexible firm and to what extent does it reflect the contingency approach to organizational design?

Stop-and-Consider appear at the end of each Management in Action panel and help the reader actually *think* and *reflect* on the case material in some depth. This feature also identifies alternative perspectives and links with other concepts.

Discussion Questions at the end of each chapter help reinforce and test your knowledge and understanding, and provide a basis for group discussions and activities.

Conclusions provide a thorough re-cap of the key issues in each chapter, explicitly linked to each chapter's learning objectives, helping you to assess your understanding and revise key content.

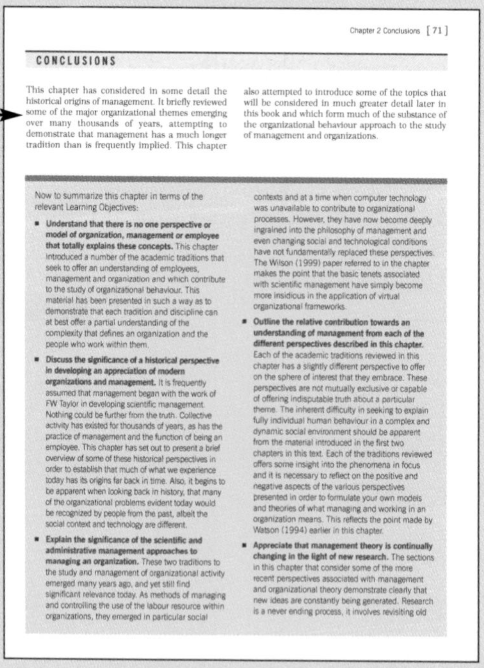

Chapter 2 Conclusions [71]

CONCLUSIONS

This chapter has considered in some detail the historical origins of management. It briefly reviewed some of the major organizational themes emerging over many thousands of years, attempting to demonstrate that management has a much longer tradition than is frequently implied. This chapter also attempted to introduce some of the topics that will be considered in much greater detail later in this book and which form much of the substance of the organizational behaviour approach to the study of management and organizations.

Now to summarize this chapter in terms of the relevant Learning Objectives:

- **Understand that there is no one perspective or model of organization, management or employee that totally explains these concepts.** This chapter introduced a number of the academic traditions that seek to offer an understanding of employees, management and organization and which contribute to the study of organizational behaviour. This material has been presented in such a way as to demonstrate that each tradition and discipline can at best offer a partial understanding of the complexity that defines an organization and the people who work within them.
- **Discuss the significance of a historical perspective in developing an appreciation of modern organizations and management.** It is frequently assumed that management began with the work of FW Taylor in developing scientific management. Nothing could be further from the truth. Collective activity has existed for thousands of years, as has the practice of management and the function of being an employee. This chapter has set out to present a brief overview of some of these historical perspectives in order to establish that much of what we experience today has its origins far back in time. Also, it begins to be apparent when looking back in history, that many of the organizational problems evident today would be recognized by people from the past, albeit the social context and technology are different.
- **Explain the significance of the scientific and administrative management approaches to managing an organization.** These two traditions to the study and management of organizational activity emerged many years ago, and yet still find significant relevance today. As methods of managing and controlling the use of the labour resource within organizations, they emerged in particular social contexts and at a time when computer technology was unavailable to contribute to organizational processes. However, they have now become deeply ingrained into the philosophy of management and even changing social and technological conditions have not fundamentally replaced these perspectives. The Wilson (1999) paper referred to in the chapter makes the point that the basic tenets associated with scientific management have simply become more insidious in the application of virtual organizational frameworks.
- **Outline the relative contribution towards an understanding of management from each of the different perspectives described in this chapter.** Each of the academic traditions reviewed in this chapter has a slightly different perspective to offer on the sphere of interest that they embrace. These perspectives are not mutually exclusive or capable of offering indisputable truth about a particular theme. The inherent difficulty in seeking to explain fully individual human behaviour in a complex and dynamic social environment should be apparent from the material introduced in the first two chapters in this text. Each of the traditions reviewed offers some insight into the phenomena in focus and it is necessary to reflect on the positive and negative aspects of the various perspectives presented in order to formulate your own models and theories of what managing and working in an organization means. This reflects the point made by Watson (1994) earlier in this chapter.
- **Appreciate that management theory is continually changing in the light of new research.** The sections in this chapter that consider some of the more recent perspectives associated with management and organizational theory demonstrate clearly that new ideas are constantly being generated. Research is a never ending process, it involves revisiting old

Annotated Further Reading at the end of each chapter allows you to explore the subject further, and acts as a starting-point for projects and assignments.

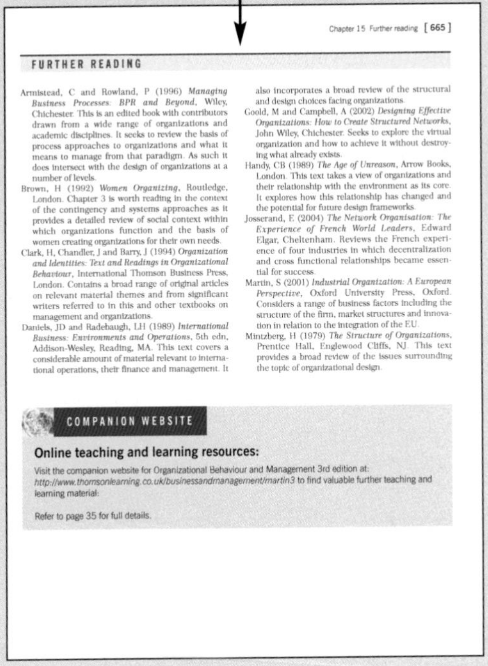

Chapter 15 Further reading [665]

FURTHER READING

Armistead, C and Rowland, P (1996) *Managing Business Processes: BPR and Beyond*, Wiley, Chichester. This is an edited book with contributors drawn from a wide range of organizations and academic disciplines. It seeks to review the basis of process approaches to organizations and what it means to manage from that paradigm. As such it does intersect with the design of organizations at a number of levels.

Brown, H (1992) *Women Organizing*, Routledge, London. Chapter 3 is worth reading in the context of the contingency and systems approaches as it provides a detailed review of social context within which organizations function and the basis of women creating organizations for their own needs.

Clark, H, Chandler, J and Barry, J (1994) *Organization and Identities: Text and Readings in Organizational Behaviour*, International Thomson Business Press, London. Contains a broad range of original articles on relevant material themes and from significant writers referred to in this and other textbooks on management and organizations.

Daniels, JD and Radebaugh, LH (1989) *International Business: Environments and Operations*, 5th edn, Addison-Wesley, Reading, MA. This text covers a considerable amount of material relevant to international operations, their finance and management. It also incorporates a broad review of the structural and design choices facing organizations.

Goold, M and Campbell, A (2002) *Designing Effective Organizations: How to Create Structured Networks*, John Wiley, Chichester. Seeks to explore the virtual organization and how to achieve it without destroying what already exists.

Handy, CB (1989) *The Age of Unreason*, Arrow Books, London. This text takes a view of organizations and their relationship with the environment as its core. It explores how this relationship has changed and the potential for future design frameworks.

Josserand, E (2004) *The Network Organisation: The Experience of French World Leaders*, Edward Elgar, Cheltenham. Reviews the French experience of four industries in which decentralization and cross functional relationships became essential for success.

Martin, S (2001) *Industrial Organization: A European Perspective*, Oxford University Press, Oxford. Considers a range of business factors including the structure of the firm, market structures and innovation in relation to the integration of the EU.

Mintzberg, H (1979) *The Structure of Organizations*, Prentice Hall, Englewood Cliffs, NJ. This text provides a broad review of the issues surrounding the topic of organizational design.

COMPANION WEBSITE

Online teaching and learning resources:

Visit the companion website for Organizational Behaviour and Management 3rd edition at: *http://www.thomsonlearning.co.uk/businessandmanagement/martin3* to find valuable further teaching and learning material:

Refer to page 35 for full details.

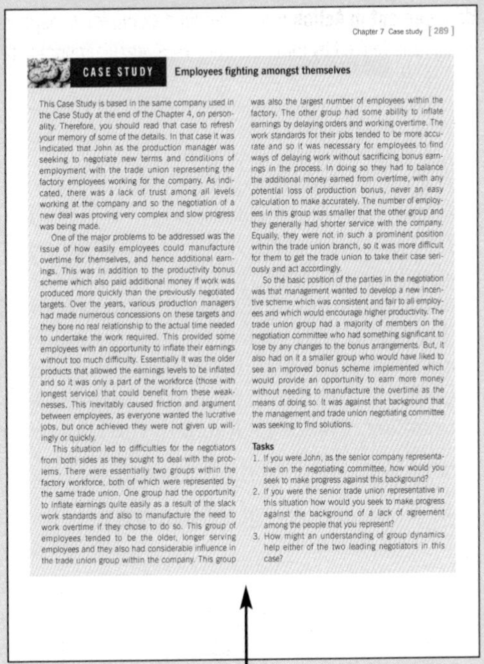

Chapter 7 Case study [289]

CASE STUDY **Employees fighting amongst themselves**

This Case Study is based in the same company used in the Case Study at the end of the Chapter 4, on personality. Therefore, you should read that case to refresh your memory of some of the details. In that case it was indicated that John as the production manager was seeking to negotiate new terms and conditions of employment with the trade union representing the factory employees working for the company. As indicated, there was a lack of trust among all levels working at the company and so the negotiation of a new deal was proving very complex and slow progress was being made.

One of the major problems to be addressed was the issue of how easily employees could manufacture overtime for themselves, and hence additional earnings. This was in addition to the productivity bonus scheme which also paid additional money if work was produced more quickly than the previously negotiated targets. Over the years, various production managers had made numerous concessions on these targets and they bore no real relationship to the actual time needed to undertake the work required. This provided some employees with an opportunity to inflate their earnings without too much difficulty. Essentially it was the older products that allowed the earnings levels to be inflated and so it was only a part of the workforce (those with longest service) that could benefit from these weaknesses. This inevitably caused friction and argument between employees, as everyone wanted the lucrative jobs, but once achieved they were not given up willingly or quickly.

This situation led to difficulties for the negotiators from both sides as they sought to deal with the problems. There were essentially two groups within the factory workforce, both of which were represented by the same trade union. One group had the opportunity to inflate earnings quite easily as a result of the slack work standards and also to manufacture the need to work overtime if they chose to do so. This group of employees tended to be the older, longer serving employees and they also had considerable influence in the trade union group within the company. This group was also the largest number of employees within the factory. The other group had some ability to inflate earnings by delaying orders and working overtime. The work standards for their jobs tended to be more accurate and so it was necessary for employees to find ways of delaying work without sacrificing bonus earnings in the process. In doing so they had to balance the additional money earned from overtime, with any potential loss of production bonus, never an easy calculation to make accurately. The number of employees in this group was smaller that the other group and they generally had shorter service with the company. Equally, they were not in such a prominent position within the trade union branch, so it was more difficult for them to get the trade union to take their case seriously and act accordingly.

So the basic position of the parties in the negotiation was that management wanted to develop a new incentive scheme which was consistent and fair to all employees and which would encourage higher productivity. The trade union group had a majority of members on the negotiation committee who had something significant to lose by any changes to the bonus arrangements. But, it also had on it a smaller group who would have liked to see an improved bonus scheme implemented which would provide an opportunity to earn more money without needing to manufacture the overtime as the means of doing so. It was against that background that the management and trade union negotiating committee was seeking to find solutions.

Tasks

1. If you were John, as the senior company representative on the negotiating committee, how would you seek to make progress against this background?
2. If you were the senior trade union representative in this situation how would you seek to make progress against the background of a lack of agreement among the people that you represent?
3. How might an understanding of group dynamics help either of the two leading negotiators in this case?

Case studies at the end of each chapter show how each chapter's main issues are applied in real-life business situations in different types of organizations. Each case study is accompanied by questions to help you test your understanding of the issues.

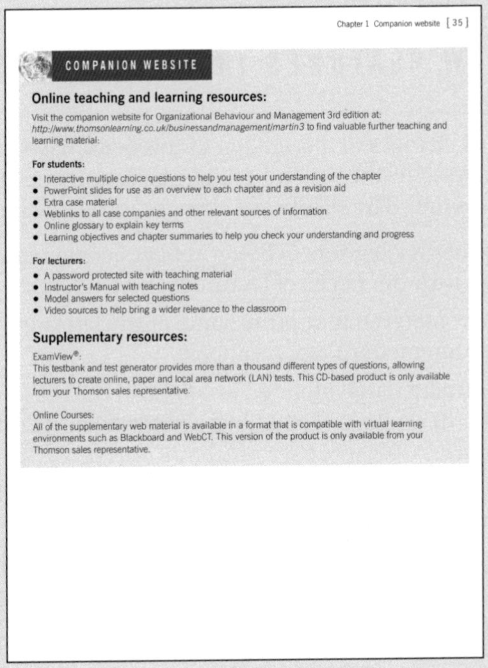

Chapter 1 Companion website [35]

COMPANION WEBSITE

Online teaching and learning resources:

Visit the companion website for Organizational Behaviour and Management 3rd edition at: *http://www.thomsonlearning.co.uk/businessandmanagement/martin3* to find valuable further teaching and learning material:

For students:

- Interactive multiple choice questions to help you test your understanding of the chapter
- PowerPoint slides for use as an overview to each chapter and as a revision aid
- Extra case material
- Weblinks to all case companies and other relevant sources of information
- Online glossary to explain key terms
- Learning objectives and chapter summaries to help you check your understanding and progress

For lecturers:

- A password protected site with teaching material
- Instructor's Manual with teaching notes
- Model answers for selected questions
- Video sources to help bring a wider relevance to the classroom

Supplementary resources:

ExamView®:
This testbank and test generator provides more than a thousand different types of questions, allowing lecturers to create online, paper and local area network (LAN) tests. This CD-based product is only available from your Thomson sales representative.

Online Courses:
All of the supplementary web material is available in a format that is compatible with virtual learning environments such as Blackboard and WebCT. This version of the product is only available from your Thomson sales representative.

Preface

This preface introduces the major features of the third edition of this book, along with suggestions on how students and lecturers might make use of the content. Another important feature of this book available to both lecturers and students is the accompanying website, which is also described in this preface. Specifically for lecturers who adopt this text will be a hard copy of a lecturers guide intended to support the use of the book in a wide range of teaching arrangements.

This book is intended for those people who seek to gain an insight into the world of people and their association with the organizations that form an integral part of their experience. This book is therefore intended to appeal to anyone who seeks to better understand this important aspect of human life. Topics included in the book include:

- A reflection on the nature of organizations and management.
- Consideration of those aspects of individuals and groups that form the human face of organizations.
- A review of processes such as motivation, learning, communication, decision making and negotiation that takes place within organizations.
- Management and leadership.
- The structure and design of organizations.
- The nature of work and its relationship to the technology used by organizations.
- Organization culture.
- Stress.
- Ethical perspectives within organizations.
- Power and control, conflict and organizational politics.
- Managing change.

CHANGES AND NEW FEATURES IN THE THIRD EDITION

There have been a number of changes to this edition of this book, based on a comprehensive review of the strengths and weaknesses of the second edition by a number of anonymous reviewers, to whom a great debt of thanks is due. The significant changes introduced in this edition include:

- Restructuring of some of the chapters to better reflect people management practice within organizations, together with the needs of lecturers and students.
- The introduction of new material to capture some of the latest trends in people management issues within modern organizations.
- The creation of part introductions intended to establish the reason for inclusion of the material in that part in the context of what has already been studied and what is yet to be developed.
- The introduction of a completely new feature – Employee Perspective panels – to capture this aspect of the human experience within organizations.
- The introduction of another completely new feature – a Case Study – at the end of each chapter in order to provide practice opportunity in dealing with organizational behaviour issues.

- A number of new Management in Action panels have also been introduced in this edition.
- The specific inclusion of international perspectives to many of the Management in Action panels, Employee Perspective panels and Case Study material.
- In-chapter tasks have been provided for almost all Management in Action and Employee Perspective panels.
- New to this edition is a Glossary designed to provide a reference point for the key terms used in the book.
- The introduction of more tightly structured learning objectives at the start of each chapter along with another new feature – an outline of the key learning points associated with each learning objective placed in the Conclusion for each chapter.
- An updated Further Reading section for each chapter.
- The Discussion Questions at the end of each chapter have been reviewed and some new ones added.
- A considerable number of new reference sources have added to the text in order to ensure that it is as current as it can be in terms of research and practice in this area.
- The website and lecturer support material has been completely updated to better reflect the needs of adopters and students.

THE AUDIENCE

There are many courses and degree programmes that contain aspects of organization, management or the people issues associated with running public or private sector businesses. These can include undergraduate degree programmes in management and business studies or those degrees with management as a minor component, as well as postgraduate degrees and other post-experience qualifications such as the Diploma of Management Studies, MA and MBA programmes. There are also the many professional qualification schemes in management, accountancy, engineering and related disciplines that include behavioural, managerial and organizational modules, for whom this book would be an important contribution. Such courses are invariably offered on both a full- and part-time basis and many self-study or distance learning approaches to these routes to personal development also exist. This book together with the associated support material is designed (based on the author's considerable experience in teaching the subject to all of these groups and using each of the forms of delivery indicated) to be a valuable asset in the delivery of the subject.

Specifically, this book will appeal to a wide range of people including:

- Undergraduate students on a wide range of organizational behaviour, introduction to management or people management modules.
- Practising managers who seek to develop an academic understanding of the topics through which to interpret their experience, perhaps as part of a diploma or degree programme.
- A second category of reader would be those with an academic background in either business or management who, having gained some management experience, have returned to higher education to further their development through an MBA or other masters' programme.
- A third group of readers would include those without formal management experience, but perhaps with some employment experience, who are studying aspects of human behaviour and management within an organizational context, perhaps as part of a part-time degree programme.
- A fourth category of reader would have an academic background in either the social sciences or one of the science disciplines, and have some subsequent organizational

experience. Such individuals would be likely to study this book in seeking to further their studies in the business, organizational or management fields through one of the many masters' programmes intended to achieve this objective.

- A fifth category of reader would include those individuals studying for the professional qualifications offered by the professional associations and who inevitably include aspects of organization, management and behaviour within the syllabus.
- Another category would be those people who work in organizations and who are undergoing some form of in-company or in-service training in managing people or organizational behaviour topics.

The blend of theory, critical perspective and practical application is balanced throughout the book in an accessible and engaging writing style. This will appeal to the wide cross-section of individuals indicated, offering challenges to each, without oversimplification or obfuscation and in each case seeking to further the understanding of the individual in this challenging and exciting field.

OBJECTIVES OF THE BOOK

It is human beings who both design organizations and work within them. Human beings, therefore, determine both what is done and how it is to be achieved. Against this background the purpose of this book is to develop an understanding of the most important features of this aspect of human experience, including:

- What defines organizations and management.
- The nature and impact of individuality on work activities.
- The ways in which groups form and interact as they carry out much of the work undertaken within organizations.
- The influence of technology on work organization.
- The nature of processes such as motivation and decision making on the functioning of organizations.
- The design and structural determinants of organizational form.
- Management issues such as leadership and ethics.
- The nature and impact of change on people and organizations.
- The power, political and control dimensions of organizational activity.
- The nature and impact of stress on people and organizations.

Specifically in relation to this purpose, the text sets out to achieve a number of objectives:

- *Provide an introduction to organizational behaviour*. While offering an up-to-date and reflective perspective, the text does not seek to be of interest only to readers seeking to develop their existing knowledge in this area. It is intended to be of interest to those readers who need to develop the breadth and depth of their understanding of what makes an organization function. Such readers will find that the clearly presented theoretical material, supported by the applied illustrations, will effectively meet their development needs.
- *Include a critical perspective*. In addressing the first objective the text goes beyond the purely descriptive and introduces a critical perspective to the material, by seeking to recognize the embedded nature of much theory and the underlying power dimensions to management activity. A critical perspective suggests that knowledge as well as organizations

are grounded in the social context that created them and any real understanding must take that into account and this text seeks to achieve that perspective while not losing sight of the other objectives.

- *Demonstrate an applied relevance*. To be of any value the study of organizational behaviour needs to retain a relevance to actual organizations and the experience of those within them. This is achieved in a number of ways, including the incorporation of applied research studies, the Management in Action panels, the Employee Perspective panels and Case Study at the end of each chapter.
- *Provide a basis for further study*. The reference sources used as well as the Further Reading are intended to provide a basis for readers to take their interest in particular topics further. This is an objective that can also be achieved through the use of the links indicated in the web pages associated with this book.
- *Provide a student-centred perspective*. There are a number of student-centred devices that have been used in the text as an aid to encouraging learning. These include the Part summaries and Learning Objectives at the beginning (and Conclusion) of each chapter, frequent headings and the introduction of a Glossary to the text, the Management in Action panels, Employee Perspective panels and the Discussion Questions and Case Studies at the end of each chapter.
- *Encourage students to develop research as well as practical and theoretical understandings*. The inclusion of Research activities on the website, Stop and Consider, and Tasks associated with the Case Studies, Management in Action panels, Employee Perspective panels and Discussion Questions will all encourage students to become actively involved in their own learning in relation to the subject matter. It will also help them to understand the difficulties of carrying out field and desk research as a necessary part of creating understanding in the management and organizational field.
- *Interactive approach to learning*. The use of group activities as part of the activities in each chapter allows students to develop collaborative skills in seeking to explore relevant features of the subject matter.
- *Learning support*. The website at *http://www.thomsonlearning.co.uk/businessandmanagement/martin3* provides students and lecturers with extensive support material directly linked to topics in the text.

To cater for this breadth of audience, the material is presented as both academic and practical in nature. It is also presented in a way which encourages students to interact with the material. For students studying alone, perhaps on a distance learning programme, the website should be particularly useful in helping to offset the feeling of isolation that often accompanies such study patterns.

THE STRUCTURE OF THE BOOK

Each chapter is essentially self-contained but inevitably forms part of an integrated whole. For example, the groups that form part of every organization are made up of individuals, they are also part of the organizational hierarchy and there will be some degree of organizational politics displayed within them. However, for ease of research, study and book organization these issued have to be compartmentalized. Students should recognize that much of the richness and complexity of organizational behaviour arises from the multiple elements active in any particular situation. This should become evident as students work through the book and it is reinforced through the Management in Action panels, Employee Perspective panels and Case Studies throughout the text.

Chapters 1 and 2 serve as an introduction to the study of management and organizations along with an overview of the evolutionary development of management across history. This and the subsequent material provides the following framework:

- Introduction to management and organizational behaviour
- Individuals within organizations
- Groups and teams within organizations
- Managing organizations
- Managing people within organizations
- Managing work design, technology and structure
- Managing the processes and dynamics of organizations.

KEY FEATURES

- *Part summary*. Each part or group of chapters begins with a brief outline of the content which is intended to provide a clear indication of the range of material included and how it fits in with the material that went before and the material that is to follow.
- *Learning Objectives*. The Learning Objectives for each chapter provide a clear statement of what students should expect to master by the end of their work on that material. The main points implied by each of the Learning Objectives are summarized at the end of each chapter in the Conclusions. Progress in achieving the objectives can be assessed by individuals as they work through the Discussion Questions; as well as the Stop and Consider topics and Tasks associated with the Management in Action panels, Employee Perspective panels and Case Studies.
- *Management in Action panels*. These are included to provide an indication of aspects of organizational behaviour as experienced by managers in a real organizational context. They also provide the basis for Stop and Consider activities as a means of reflecting upon the material in some depth and also identifying alternative perspectives and links with other concepts.
- *Employee Perspective panels*. There are inevitably more employees in most organizations than there are managers. The inclusion of this feature is intended to specifically introduce this perspective to the understanding of what organizational behaviour means in practice, often in an international context. Of course most managers are employees and so some of these panels provide illustrations of their perspective as employees, being managed by more senior managers in order to provide as complete a picture of this aspect of organizational experience as it is possible to do.
- *Case Study*. In order to allow an in-depth review of the chapter material in an applied and often international context each chapter contains a Case Study with associated tasks that will allow students to explore the complex implications associated with organizational behaviour.
- *Further Reading*. These suggestions provide students with a wide and diverse range of additional sources of material on aspects of the topics discussed within each chapter.
- *Discussion Questions*. A range of questions that could be used as the basis of discussion, essays or exams is provided to allow students to test and further their understanding of the material covered.
- *Research activities*. This feature is provided on the website for the book and is intended to provide more specific field- and library-based research opportunities to individuals and groups of students. They are the type of activity that would be most appropriate to block-teaching activities as research inevitably takes time to set up, carry out and be interpreted.
- *Website*. This represents an innovative feature for this book and provides extensive on-line support for lecturers and students.

HOW TO USE THE BOOK

Everyone has their own preferred way of studying. Most courses differ in the way in which they approach a topic and the emphasis given to particular perspectives. It is, therefore, not practical to offer precise advice on how to use this book and the available support material for every situation. There are, however, a number of general pointers that may be of use in seeking to gain maximum advantage from this book and your study of organizational behaviour. They include:

- *Recognizing that this book is not attempting to provide you with a formula through which to manage other people or guarantee organizational success*. That 'holy grail' does not exist; individuals and situations are too complex and dynamic for that type of simplistic approach to be credible.
- *Evolution of knowledge is occurring all the time*. New ideas, perspectives and interpretations are emerging almost every day. The study of organizational behaviour is not a fixed event. It is for that reason that monitoring appropriate sections of the business press and the management and academic journals and magazines pays dividends.
- *Resources exist to be used in support of your study*. This book is not a novel, but it does represent a major resource for your journey of discovery in organizational behaviour. The Part summaries and Learning Objectives are intended to guide you in your travels. Also the Glossary, Discussion Questions, Tasks and Further Reading act as pointers, maps and guides to help you gain the maximum benefit from the minimum effort en route. They are there as a help, not a hindrance or a chore; do use them. During your course you will be examined or tested in some way. The resources provided through this book attempt to prepare you for that process as well as ensure a fuller understanding of the subject. For example, the Discussion Questions at the end of each chapter are designed to assist in your development of a breadth and depth of understanding of the theoretical material as well as the practical implications of it. Through discussion with other people of your collective views about these questions you will become better able to develop your understanding of them along with the ability to address any assignment or examination questions.
- *Personal experience*. Every student reader has had direct experience of organizational behaviour in some capacity. It may have been extensive through working in organizations as a paid employee or even a manager. It could have been a vacation job as a student. However, it may also have been through school, or membership of a sports or youth club. The important thing to keep in mind throughout your study of this book is that you will have seen many of the concepts in practice, whether you realize it or not. Consider for a moment a primary school and the way the total activity is organized (structure), the way teachers lead the learning process (leadership, management and control) and the interpersonal behaviour of the children (individuals, groups, power, etc.). Reflect on your experience and its ability to enhance and illustrate this subject.
- *Networking is an important aspect of any manager's experience*. The same is true in your study of organizational behaviour. Every student will know many people who have been or are currently involved in organizations. Parents, grandparents, family members, friends, other students and lecturers are all likely to have had direct experience of a wide range of organizations across a considerable period of time. These are all valuable sources of material, examples and illustrations of organizational behaviour in practice.
- *When studying each chapter consider the integrated nature of human behaviour*. It is not possible to consider each chapter as an isolated 'chunk' of material than can be ignored once it is finished. Look for and consider the links between ideas and concepts as you work through the book.

SUPPORT MATERIAL

Organizational Behaviour website

The supporting website for the new edition of *Organizational Behaviour* is at *http://www.thomsonlearning.co.uk/businessandmanagement/martin3*. This comprehensive resource provides open access learning materials to students of *Organizational Behaviour*, including chapter overviews, links to the home pages of companies discussed in the cases, extra essay-style questions and a full list of organizational behaviour definitions from the Thomson Learning Pocket IEBM (*International Encyclopedia of Business and Management*). Students and lecturers can contact John Martin through the site to post their comments and queries about the book and the website.

The lecturers' area of the site is password protected and the password is available to lecturers who recommend the book on their courses. Please register through the website for your password. There will be no printed manual provided with this edition but all resources which previously appeared in the printed manual will now be provided online. The extensive lecturer resources include teaching notes, PowerPoint slides, extra case materials, and suggested course outlines.

The research activities are designed to further students' understanding of the material through library, Internet and field research activities. These should be used to further a student's understanding of, and practice in, research in this field.

The website is a totally optional resource. Use of the book is not dependent in any way on the website. Full value can still be obtained through the many excellent features included in the book. However, the Internet provides an opportunity to enhance the level of support and understanding in ways not available though the medium of the printed word. For example, the website offers students the opportunity to explore the enormous potential of the Internet in their study of organizational behaviour. The primary links have been selected because of their relevance to the subject matter and potential interest to readers. The website resource will be regularly updated so that it retains its value to students and lecturers as the most appropriate starting point on the Internet for organizational behaviour topics.

A further benefit of the website is the opportunity to update illustrative examples of organizational behaviour and learning materials after publication of the book. This will ensure that the book retains its currency and freshness throughout its life – a major benefit to both lecturers and students. Users can send comments back to the author about the book and the website, as well as interesting examples of organizational behaviour in practice that they have encountered.

The *Organizational Behaviour* website is a valuable resource that highlights the importance of *Organizational Behaviour* as a book and as a subject at the heart of the management of organizational endeavour. It also demonstrates the commitment to keeping this book at the forefront of both teaching and debate in this area. Why not visit the website and experience this for yourself?

Lecturers will have their own ideas on how they will use this book and the support material provided in delivering their modules. The Lecturers Guide is being provided to assist in the process of achieving the best match between the needs of lecturers and students on the one hand and the material provided through this learning package on the other. It provides a number of features that will assist lecturers to make the most of the book and web based support material in supporting a wide diversity of module designs and delivery patterns.

The Lecturers Guide will consist of a number of elements including:

1. Outline teaching plans for a number of different module lengths and delivery patterns.
2. Ideas for lecturers on how to use on the book in different ways in support of module learning objectives.
3. Suggestions to provide students with additional ways of enriching their study of material in the book.
4. Ideas for each chapter on how lecturers could encourage students to reflect on the key learning objectives and ideas from the chapter and seek out further study opportunities.

Acknowledgements

Any organizational activity inevitably reflects the efforts of a great many people. Writing a book is no exception. It is not possible specifically to mention everyone who played a part in helping to create this text.

The following people were particularly generous with their time and talent in reviewing material and offering advice on the content of the first edition of this book.

- Professor Michael Brimm, Professor of Organizational Behaviour at INSEAD (Fontainebleau, France).
- Professor Gordon C Anderson, Principal of Caledonian College of Engineering, Sultanate of Oman and Visiting Professor of Business, The Philips College, Nicosia, Cyprus.
- Professor Derek Torrington, Emeritus Professor of Human Resource Management, UMIST.
- Professor Eugene McKenna, Professor Emeritus, University of East London, Chartered Psychologist and Director of Human Factors International Ltd.
- Professor Dave Tromp, Professor of Industrial Psychology and Chairperson of Industrial Psychology, University of Stellenbosch, South Africa.
- Dr Jim Barry, Reader in Organization Studies, University of East London.

The contribution of the above people played a significant part in making the first edition of the book the success it was which helped to create the opportunity to develop the second and third edition. In addition, may I offer my deepest thanks to the panel of anonymous reviewers who offered their time and talent in reviewing the second edition along with the proposals for the third edition. Their comments were both helpful and appropriate. The end result can only be described as a considerable improvement as a consequence of their efforts. I can but hope that they feel justified in devoting the time that they did when they inspect the finished third edition. The responsibility for any mistakes, errors or omissions remains, however, firmly my own.

At Thomson Learning a number of people have been supportive of the whole project and of invaluable help in attempting to steer the work in appropriate directions. Worthy of particular note in this context are Geraldine Lyons, Marie Taylor and James Collins. Without them this edition would never have happened.

There are many academics, managers, bosses, subordinates and colleagues with whom I have had the pleasure (and sometimes pain) of working over the course of my career. Individually and collectively these have all played a considerable role in shaping my fascination with, and views on, organizational life and behaviour. The benefits and effects of their impact on me are in no small way reflected in the views and perspectives offered in this book.

Finally, and by no means least, I would like to place on record the support and interest of my wife, family and friends, who tolerated the time spent on the project as well as continually showing interest in how it was progressing.

I would also like to place on record my appreciation to the many copyright holders who have given permission to use material for which they hold the rights. Every effort has been made to identify and contact all copyright holders, but if any have been inadvertently omitted the publisher will be pleased to make the necessary arrangement at the earliest opportunity.

PART ONE

Management and organizational behaviour

The purpose of this section of the book is to introduce the reader to organizational behaviour as an area of academic and practical study of vital importance to those who work in organizations and particularly those who aspire to manage them.

It sets out to prepare the ground for the more specific sections that are to follow and which will explore some of the major issues associated with the study of how human beings interact with organizations and how in turn humans are impacted upon by the organizations that they work within.

This section will review issues such as the nature of research in the social world in which organizations and the people who work in them exist. It will also take a preliminary look at what an organization is; together with some consideration of the nature of management and what defines the role of an employee. This will be followed in the second chapter by consideration of how management has evolved over the course of history and of how academic thought has developed to create the different disciplines that now contribute to the understanding of how organizations function and interact with the human resource available to them.

This section seeks to establish the background for the next section which will explore the fundamental unit within any organization – the individual.

CHAPTER 1

Organizational behaviour today

LEARNING OBJECTIVES

After studying this chapter and working through the associated Management in Action panels, Discussion Questions and Case Study, you should be able to:

- **Understand the distinction between research in the natural and in the social sciences.**
- **Explain the particular difficulties involved in studying and developing theories in the area of management.**
- **Outline the essence of the relationship between organizations, managers and employees.**
- **Appreciate that the concept 'organization' incorporates many different forms.**
- **Discuss how the study of organizational behaviour can contribute to an understanding of management.**

INTRODUCTION

Organizations are an inescapable feature of modern social experience for all human beings. From the remotest village high in the Himalayan foothills to life in a large metropolis, organizations impact on all aspects of the human experience. Everyone experiences organizations in a number of different ways. We are the customers of organizations when we purchase goods in a supermarket or other shops; we are the employees of organizations when we work for them; we might be a manager within an organization. Consequently, we are heavily dependent upon organizations in all aspects of our lives. We certainly spend a great deal of our working lives in them as employees and managers. It makes sense therefore to develop some understanding of the things that go on inside organizations. This chapter begins that process by exploring what constitutes organizational behaviour and then introduces the major themes of the rest of the book, namely, management, employees and organizations.

WHAT IS ORGANIZATIONAL BEHAVIOUR?

Organizational behaviour
Approach to the study of management and organizations incorporating anything relevant to the design, management and effectiveness of an organization.

Hawthorne studies
A series of research studies exploring aspects of group working, carried out during the late 1920s and early 1930s.

Organizational behaviour provides one of the mainstream approaches to the study of management and organizations. Its main sphere of interest is anything relevant to the design, management and effectiveness of an organization, together with the dynamic and interactive relationships that exist within them. It drew some of its main inspiration from the human relations school of thought that emerged from the **Hawthorne Studies**, which were directed by Elton Mayo during the late 1920s and early 1930s. These studies first highlighted the complexity of human behaviour in an organizational setting. This in turn led to recognition of the importance of the social context within which work occurred and of the ways in which groups become a significant influence on individual behaviour.

However, organizational behaviour incorporates many more features than might be considered at first glance appropriate to a behavioural approach to human activity within an organization. The study of organizational behaviour involves two distinct features:

1. *Interdisciplinary*. There are many areas of study that can be integrated into organizational behaviour. It involves aspects of psychology, sociology, anthropology, political science, philosophy, economics and the systems sciences. Each of these disciplines has something to offer through a contribution to the human, structural, work, interactive and dynamic aspects of the human experience of working in an organization. To this wealth of base material can be added a critical theory perspective on the embedded nature (accepts the context) of much mainstream literature. Critical theory seeks to emancipate people from existing constraints and power relationships. Yet in so doing it invariably imposes another reality, albeit a different one, on the situation.
2. *Explanatory*. Organizational behaviour sets out to explain the relationships between variables. However, it does not provide an intention to prescribe the relationships or interactions between variables that should exist. This distinction is inevitable because when dealing with human behaviour at any level one is concerned with probability rather than certainty. In other words, no two people would react to a situation in exactly the same way, and even the same person might react differently on different occasions.

The areas of interest falling within the subject of organizational behaviour can be most easily reflected in a diagram, Figure 1.1. Rather than make Figure 1.1 look a complete mess with lines going in every direction, this has been shown as two-way lines between individual boxes and the linking theme box of organizational behaviour. Each section within this book takes as its focus one aspect of organizational behaviour. Compartmentalization is a convenient means of considering complex material from a teaching and learning perspective. However, the reality of organizational behaviour is that there are considerable and significant interdependencies and interrelationships between all the topics discussed.

FIGURE 1.1

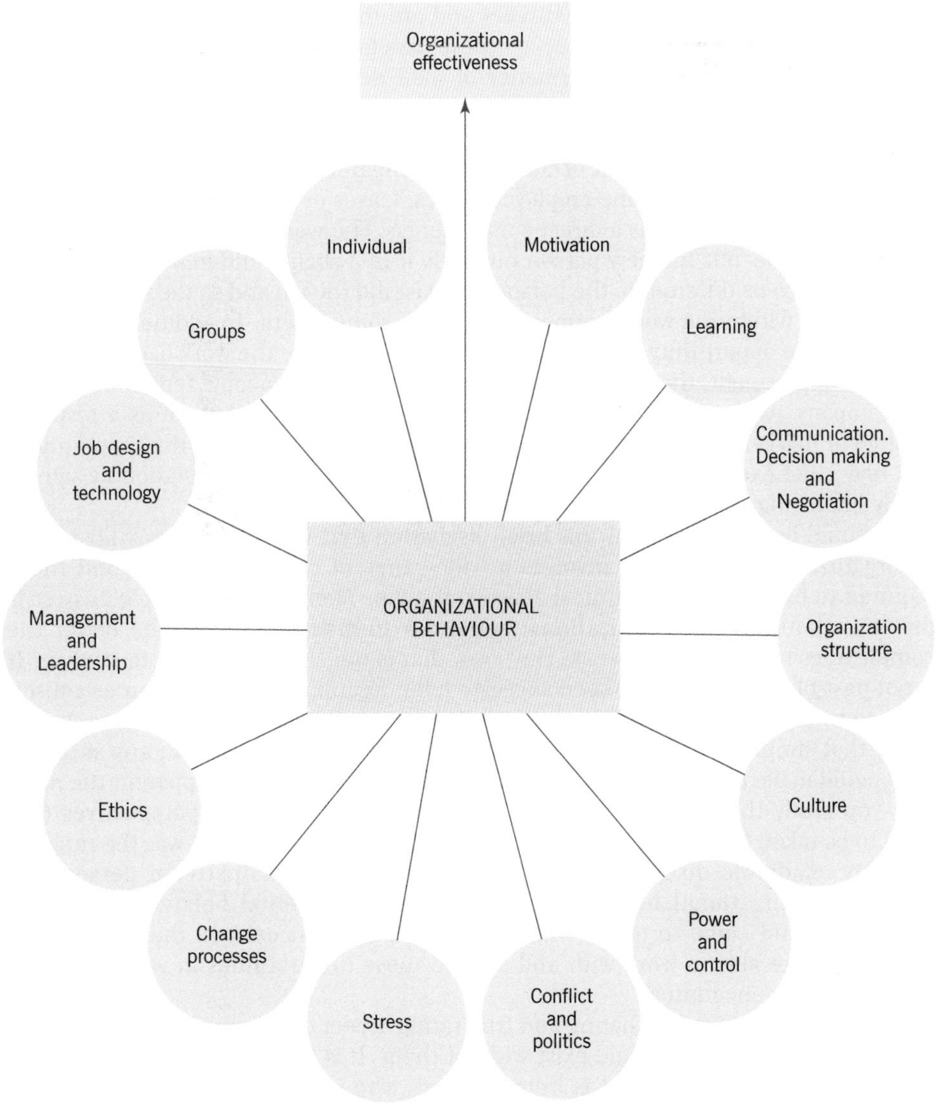

The world of organizational behaviour

WHY STUDY ORGANIZATIONAL BEHAVIOUR?

People within an organization are invariably trained to carry out their specific job responsibilities. But this tends to be a practical or technical process, involving learning how to do the job, whether that be in sales, marketing, finance, computers or whatever. But the technical aspects of any job represent only a small part of any work activity. Very few people have no contact with other people as part of the work that they do. People work in teams, or small groups within a department; they have customers and suppliers (inside and outside of the organization) and they have superiors and subordinates to report to and control. The resulting webs of relationships can be both formal and informal in nature, but they all involve other people. Most jobs involve some degree of persuading people to co-operate with some priority, action, or request involving a degree of inconvenience to themselves. As a manager it is necessary to deal with problem employees (not everyone co-operates all of the time), or with other managers who are seeking to advance their careers and are therefore in competition for more senior appointments. It is also necessary these days for managers to be able to improve consistently the operational performance of their departments in the constant drive for higher productivity.

The world of work is constantly changing. This is an ongoing process and is unlikely to end. The actual changes that occur within an organization might be large or small, but they are all changes. If one employee retires, leaves or is promoted to another job several things will change as a direct consequence. The work to be done will probably remain the same, but the new person might do it in a slightly different way. The new person will also be different to the person who last did the job and so the interpersonal relationships within the work group will change to some extent. In addition, managers might take the opportunity of someone leaving to restructure the work being done and even the department, thereby creating major change for the people remaining within the company. At an organizational level, change can be brought about as a result of product or market activity, mergers or acquisitions, or simply through the appointment of a new chief executive officer who will want to establish their reputation by significantly improving profit levels.

It should be apparent from this brief discussion that working successfully within an organization at any level involves a wide range of competencies beyond those required to carry out the technical aspects of a job. Therefore, the simple answer is that you should study organizational behaviour in order to understand better the complexities of the world of work. However, that is not the only reason to study it. It is not possible, as has already been suggested, for organizational behaviour as a discipline to be prescriptive in setting out exactly what to do in specific situations. Life is never that simple and there are always many more variables active in any situation than could make that a realistic possibility. Equally, as will become apparent the more that you study the subject, there are many different theoretical perspectives that need to be taken into account. One example of this indicated earlier was the range of separate academic disciplines that help to inform the mainstream perspective termed 'organizational behaviour'. Studying organizational behaviour helps to understand and come to terms with the ambiguities that exist in the social world and to be more able to work with and around those uncertainties in whatever work experience you encounter.

People are the most fascinating and frustrating aspect of any organizational experience, yet no organization could exist without them. It is human beings who establish organizations and run them; it is human beings who work inside them and who are the customers and suppliers of these same organizations. We cannot escape organizations or other people at any stage of our life, indeed it would not be a real life if we were able to do so. Therefore, it is an area worth studying for its own interest in order to understand better how human beings interface with organizations as well as to be able to better survive the experience of doing so.

HOW TO STUDY ORGANIZATIONAL BEHAVIOUR

Get involved is the short answer!

It is not a passive subject, it responds to involvement and active participation. Do not expect to be able to simply read the chapters and 'know' what it is all about. Think about the organizations that you have encountered in your life. They include, schools, colleges, shops and supermarkets, television and other media publishers including, newspaper, magazine and book publishers, cinema and theatre production companies, mobile phone companies to mention just a few. They all have people working within them, including managers and employees. They all impact on you in some way or another. For example, schools 'process' you as a pupil in a way which enabled you to pass examinations and learn those skills and facts that society deemed it necessary for you to acquire. In so doing you encountered the school staff who taught you, but the system also included the local authority support staff and education department managers who were responsible, along with the head-teacher, for ensuring that the school met the objectives set for it.

Think about the jobs that you have had during your career. As such you were (or are) an employee, or an associate as some organizations now prefer to call employees. Perhaps you were one of the special category of employee called a manager. Whatever your experience of organizations, you have more direct experience than you perhaps realize. Consider the experience that you do have and bring it with you when you read and interact with the material in this book. For example, did you manage other people if you were a manager; or how were you managed if you were an employee? Was it simply a process of giving and following orders, or did it involve more subtlety than that? What about any experience as a student working part-time in a supermarket. Perhaps you have had several such jobs, was the style of management different across the organizations that you worked for? If so why and what difference did it make to how you worked and how effectively the customer was served? These experiences can all add to the material that is presented to you in this book, and which will be introduced to you by the staff teaching your particular module. Also consider examples of management practice that you read about in magazines and the press. For example, Management in Action 1.1 represents aspects of staff involvement in Pret A Manger, a large sandwich and snack retail operation in the UK.

Also consider the movies, computer games, novels and magazines that you read. The stories and games that you read and engage in are usually based around some form of organization. What can you learn about the ways in which human beings interface with organizations from these sources? For example, a spy thriller might include aspects of how the undercover agent has not only to deal with danger and opponents who are trying to kill them, but also how to deal with the civil service bureaucracy in obtaining new gadgets and equipment for use in field operations. The biography of a political leader might also provide interesting insights into the politics and power issues that inevitably need to be dealt with by any manager seeking to compete with other managers for scarce resources.

So many parts of your life involving both current and previous experience, have prepared you to study organizational behaviour. Actively bringing this prior knowledge and experience to your study of it will enable you to better understand the processes

MANAGEMENT IN ACTION 1.1

Pret A Manger staff help choose the new recruits

Esther O'Halloran, recruitment and retention manager at Pret A Manger reported to the Chartered Institute of Personnel and Development's 2002 Human Resource Development conference that enabling staff to become involved in the recruitment of colleagues had reduced employee turnover in the company. As part of the second interview process, job candidates are expected to work in a shop for part of the day. The team that they work with then make the decision as to whether the candidate should be offered work. Ms O'Halloran believed that this approach was directly responsible for a threefold reduction in staff turnover to less than 100 per cent, which compared well to an industry average of about 150 per cent.

Reducing labour turnover had many advantages, but chiefly it would allow the growth in the number of retail outlets owned by the company from 118, employing 2300 people in 2002 to 163 shops employing about 3400 staff by 2005. O'Halloran indicated that getting the teams in the shops involved in the recruitment process meant that the staff felt responsible for the new recruit and would help them become an effective part of the team more quickly. That in turn meant that the new recruit would be more likely to stay with the company for a longer time.

Other tactics used by the company include giving staff who are promoted £50 vouchers, which they can then pass on to colleagues who have helped them gain promotion. This is intended to encourage team building and a mutually supportive working environment in the shops. Staff are also allowed to audit the performance bonus of managers as part of a process of encouraging good staff relations. Senior managers are also required to spend 10 days each year working in the shops making sandwiches to ensure that they stay in touch with the basics of the business and to experience the daily challenges facing shop staff.

Adapted from: Nelson, P (2002) Pret A Manger staff help choose the new recruits, *Personnel Today*, 23 April, p 4.

Stop ↔ Consider

What does this example suggest about the differences between being a manager and being an employee, together with the relative responsibilities of both in running a business?
Would this approach work successfully in all organizations? Why or why not?

involved when people and organizations interact, and more effectively prepare you for your future career, in whatever form that might be.

RESEARCH AND ORGANIZATIONAL BEHAVIOUR

The discussion so far has provided an introduction to organizational behaviour that suggests a high degree of complexity as well as high levels of interdependence between the active components. This provides a fertile basis for research activity as well as the opportunity for the parallel existence of competing explanations. The main research approaches will be explored more fully in Chapter 2, but it is worth considering for a moment the main research approaches that are available through which to create knowledge and theory.

In attempting to understand organizations as entities in their own right and management as one form of human activity within that context, it is necessary to be able to offer explanations that stand up to critical evaluation and replication. The natural sciences have developed mechanisms over many centuries that are able to meet that need. However, the primary difficulty for organization or management research is that it is not possible to isolate the key variables and replicate organizational functioning in the laboratory. Study of these phenomena therefore rests firmly within the social science arena.

It is frequently suggested that the study of organizations and management provides many competing theories but is unable to offer clear guidance to practitioners. For example, there are many theories of motivation, but on what basis should a manager choose between them? It is only within the last 100 years that writings in management encompassed more than merely a reflection of the experience of practitioners offering their own recipes for success or an intuitive analysis of organizational functioning. It is hardly surprising that the study of management and organizations is still comparatively unsophisticated and crude in its ability to offer comprehensive explanations.

The study of people and organizations is different from the study of the physical properties of metal or chemical reactions. However, that does not mean that it is impossible to apply the principles of scientific enquiry into social areas. For example, there are many psychologists working at the micro level of human behaviour that provide robust scientific explanations for aspects of it. Theories developed in this way are frequently based on laboratory studies in which much care is taken over the control of variables and other conditions. The difficulty comes from the need to extrapolate adequately from laboratory conditions to the complexity and richness of human experience within an organizational concept.

Consider as an example a laboratory experiment in which decision-making strategies among managers were to be investigated. Variables such as the decision-making topic, characteristics of the individuals concerned, restrictions on extraneous factors and time limits could all be controlled and accounted for. Equally, the measurement of the process could take a number of forms. For example, the actual decision made, time taken to reach a decision, individual interaction patterns and information used in the process. However, it is difficult to be certain what such an experiment indicates about decision making by real managers in real organizations in real time and, perhaps more important, dealing with real problems with real outcomes. There are so many additional variables that can influence decision making in practice. Power, control, politics and the dynamics of organizational experience cannot be totally accounted for in a laboratory experiment.

The experience of the world around each and every human being is dependent upon their ability to undertake three activities:

1. *Detect*. It is first necessary to be aware of the objects and situations outside the individual that provide the form for reality. This requires the input of information to the individual through the senses of hearing, sight and so on. However, the human senses are not aware of all possible stimuli available. For example, we cannot detect radio waves or see very well in the dark.
2. *Interpret*. Having detected the existence of things around the individual it is then necessary to impose meaning onto them. As a simple example consider the act of seeing a motor car. The reality of its being a motor car comes from the ability of the individual to add meaning and significance to the visual image from past experience and learning. The problems and consequences of this inability to apply an existing **frame of reference** to reality has been the basis of many science fiction books and films.
3. *Predict*. Having perceived a motor car then the implications arising from it can be predicted. For example, if the individual is attempting to cross a busy street then it should be avoided, as it could do great harm to them. So it is

Frame of reference
Internal frameworks held by an individual that informs their understanding of the world and how to relate to it.

> necessary (or at least sensible) to wait for a more appropriate time to cross. Without prior knowledge and experience of the object it would not be possible accurately to predict possible outcomes or develop an appropriate behavioural response.

From that basis it is clear that reality is not something that exists in a purely physical form outside the individual, but as a social construction experienced within the mind of each individual. The physical objects may be identical for all individuals in that situation, but their experience of them may be very different. Figure 1.2 illustrates this point by showing that two people looking at the same solid object will experience very different representations of it. Each person has only partial insight into the whole.

One of the most frequently referenced works in this field is that of Berger and Luckmann (1967) in which they explore the sociology of knowledge. Much of the possible variation in interpretation of stimuli is eliminated by the education and socialization processes to which all human beings are subjected as they develop within a particular society. In effect, we are **conditioned** how to see and interpret the world around us. This forms the justification for induction courses which provide new employees with the organization's preferred ways of seeing (and responding to) the world.

Conditioned
The behaviour of an individual which results from the application of behaviourism techniques.

When social scientists attempt to theorize about the world inhabited by human beings they are, to a very real extent, researching themselves as well. When attempting to understand an interpretation of the social world offered by a researcher it is important to consider their perspective in relation to it. However, this is able to offer only a partial insight into the perspective of the individual in question. Figure 1.3 attempts to illustrate this phenomenon by showing that it is never possible fully to understand another's perspective because in observing it only provides a partial view of the target person's overall perspective.

The scientific process that forms the basis of the natural sciences is described in Figure 1.4, adapted from Wallace (1971). It demonstrates a circular process that allows for hypotheses to be developed from existing theory (or understanding of the world). In turn, these must be operationalized and subjected to some form of testing in order to verify or refute the theory being examined. A cyclical process of identifying and testing hypotheses leads to more generalizations about the world, which in turn leads to the development of more theory.

The process reflected in Figure 1.4 is frequently described as the positivist approach to research or, more accurately, logical positivism (Remenyi *et al.*, 1998, p 32). In this **paradigm** the researcher would hold the view that an observable social reality existed and that the end product from the research would be the creation of law-like generalizations, applicable in every organizational and human context. This is the perspective that suggests that the real world exists outside each human being and the laws that govern the social world are simply out there, waiting to be discovered. The researcher is, therefore, 'an objective analyst and observer of a tangible social reality' (p 33).

Paradigm
A model based on particular assumptions about the nature of social science and of society.

This can be contrasted to the paradigm that holds that the real world exists only in the mind of the individuals perceiving it. This is the phenomenology perspective and

FIGURE 1.2

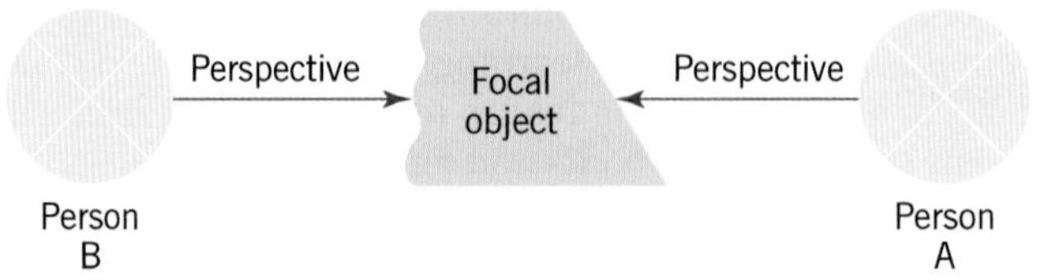

Different perceptions of the same focal object

holds that the social world is different for each person experiencing it, as they will interpret their perceptions of it in line with their internal schemas (mental models), based on past experience, socialization, education, etc. In that sense there will be considerable degrees of overlap in understanding between some individuals in the same situation, but there will also be considerable degrees of difference. For example, the workers' view of a proposed 5 per cent pay rise would probably not be the same as their bosses'. 'To the phenomenologist the researcher is not independent of what is being researched but is an intrinsic part of it' (Remenyi *et al.*, 1998, p 34). The world is socially constructed and meaning can only be identified in terms of the understandings of the actors in that situation. Experiments and the attempt to create law-like generalizations simply will not work in this paradigm.

The debate between these two paradigms can get acrimonious at times as the protagonists view research (and the world in which it functions) from diametrically opposing positions. The debate is not just academic in essence, although that is the arena in which it is carried out. For if either side of the debate is ultimately correct, in the sense that the other is wrong, then a significant aspect of research becomes inappropriate and of no value in helping to explain or run organizations. The debate also impacts on the choice of research approach that could and should be adopted. For example, the positivist tends to favour the use of scientific method

FIGURE 1.3

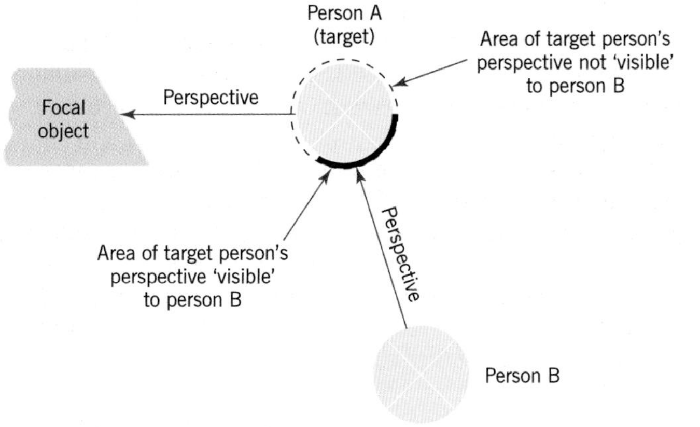

Understanding the perspectives of others

FIGURE 1.4

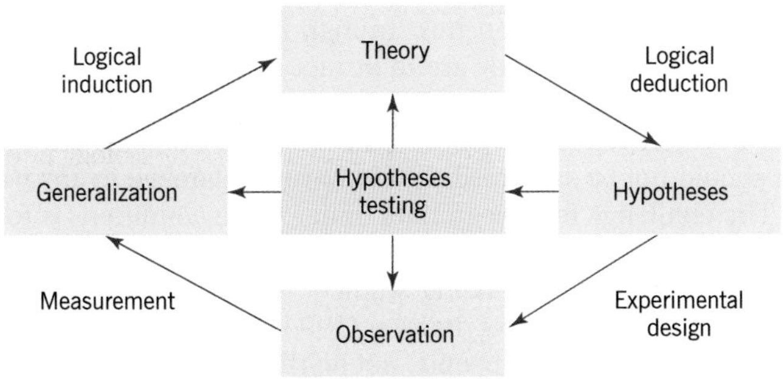

Scientific research processes (*adapted from:* Wallace, W (1971) *The Logic of Science in Sociology*, Aldine-Atherton, Chicago)

based on hypothesis and a deductive research process (Gill and Johnson, 1997, p 28). The deductive approach is based on the development of conceptual and theoretical structures before testing begins as a process of empirical observation through questionnaires, surveys, experiments, etc. By comparison, induction moves from observation to the provision of explanation. It reflects the ethnographic, case study and participative enquiry (Reason, 1994) approaches to research methodology.

Another important feature of social science research is the level at which it is being carried out. Essentially, the level in this context can be described as a scale running from macro to micro issues. There are five levels as follows:

1. *Individual*. This represents the micro level and takes as its focus of attention the individual within an organizational setting. This field is predominantly based on the work of psychologists. Issues such as perception, attitude formation, individual difference and motivation are common topics under this heading.
2. *Group*. Most human behaviour within an organization takes place in a group. It is important therefore to understand how groups form and perform the work expected of them.
3. *Managerial*. Managers are individuals and they also operate in groups just like other employees. However, there are a number of distinctive features associated with management activities that make it worthy of special categorization. For example, the nature, act and process of managing others are major areas of study.
4. *Organizational*. Typically, this would seek to address issues such as job design, structural frameworks and technology.
5. *Societal*. Issues such as power, control, politics, conflict and change fall under this umbrella heading. They represent part of the dynamic of the ways in which organizations function as a small-scale version of society. They also reflect the environmental forces that act upon any organization and within which it must function.

In addition to the obvious differences between the natural and social sciences there is the ethical issue of carrying out research on human subjects. Any of the research fields which involve human beings are faced with ethical problems. For example Finch (1993) discusses the need to be sensitive to how any output might be used in unintended ways (which might betray the implied trust between researcher and subject) when carrying out research grounded in the feminist tradition with other women. From another field, chemists working in the field of new drug treatments inevitably reach a point at which they must be tested on human beings, which of course raises ethical issues.

There are research guidelines on how human beings should be studied and by which researchers must abide if they are to attract funding and recognition for their work (see, for example, the British Sociological Association, 1973). The primary difficulty presented by such requirements is that research subjects should knowingly participate and should not be subjected to risk, harm or damage in any way as a result of the process. The challenge for researchers under these conditions is to develop and test theory (or otherwise create understanding) in such a way that it is not affected by the subjects knowing that they are being studied, or at the very least that they give their informed consent to the process. Reason (1994, p 1) goes so far as to suggest that research should be carried out with people, not on them. The basic problem is how the behaviour of the subjects might have changed as a result of knowing that they were being studied. This however is only one of the problems in the research process. For example, how might the presence of the researcher influence the behaviour that they are seeking to record and understand? Again, to what extent does any response from a subject simply reflect what that person feels the researcher wishes to hear, rather than their true opinion?

A FIRST LOOK AT ORGANIZATIONS

When asked to describe what is meant by the term organization, most people indicate the many public and private sector bodies that provide the goods and services necessary for life and employment. However, there are many bodies that bear a strong similarity to commercial organizations but which are undeniably different in function or purpose. For example, is the Church of England (or any other religious grouping) an organization in the same way that IBM is? Is a trade union, a students' union or a sports club an organization in the same sense of the term as a university or hospital?

No two commercial organizations are the same. Figure 1.5 identifies some of the major variables that influence the physical manifestation (profile) of individual organizations.

A number of the variables identified in Figure 1.5 are relatively obvious, others less so. Although there is a degree of interrelationship between the variables, there is scope

FIGURE 1.5

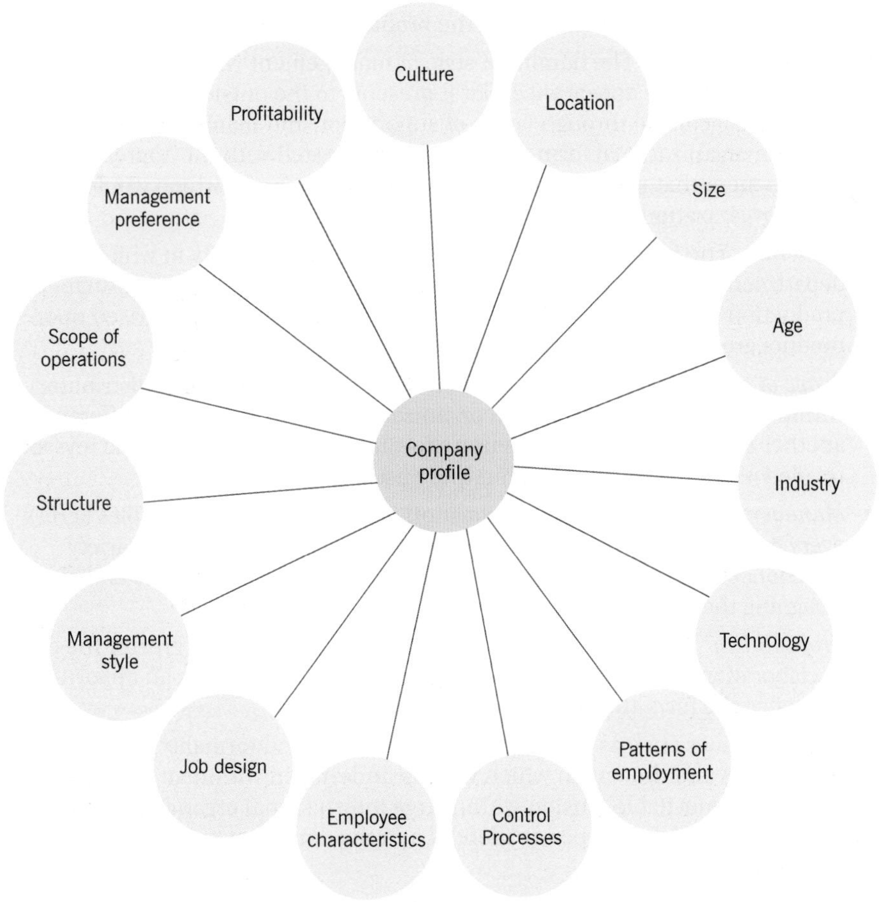

Determinants of organizational form

for management choice. For example, it is not unusual for some owners to restrict the growth of their organization deliberately in order to retain direct involvement in running the business. Taking each variable in turn:

- *Size.* The physical size of an organization is a major determinant of how it appears. The small corner shop selling a range of grocery items and sweets, employing two people would be vastly different in appearance from a large national supermarket chain with many thousands of employees. The size of an organization could also influence many of the other variables, such as the level of technology that it is able to support.
- *Age.* There is an apparent stability and security that comes from the appearance of age – financial institutions deliberately create this image. The age of an organization could also be expected to impact on many structural and functional issues.
- *Industry.* The nature of the product or service from which the organization derives its income is another primary determinant of its form. A company engaged in quarrying minerals would be expected to differ in many ways from a bank of roughly similar size and age.
- *Technology.* The type and level of technology used by an organization is another variable that is both influenced by and influences the organization. The use of robotic assembly processes has reduced human involvement in the assembly of products such as motor vehicle and other consumer goods, thereby driving up productivity as well as influencing the profile of the organization.
- *Management style.* The dominant style of management within the organization also influences the appearance that it presents to the outside world. The use of hierarchical control through layers of supervision and management produces a tall, thin organizational form. This can be contrasted with the approach to management that relies on self-managed work teams and which would provide a flatter organization as a consequence.
- *Structure.* The functional approach to organizational activity in which departments are organized around job expertise such as personnel, finance and production provides a very different appearance to one which is based upon product groupings with mixed operational teams.
- *Scope of operations.* A wholesaler of children's toys is acting as a distributor within the supply chain. Such an organization would appear very different to another organization in the children's toy industry which made some toys and retailed a much wider range directly to customers.
- *Management preference.* The application of the same set of principles across every organization is doomed to failure because of the situational variety experienced in practice. Managers exercise a degree of preference and choice in designing their organizations.
- *Profitability.* The larger the monetary resource available, the greater the degree of elaboration possible. The scale of finance available provides an opportunity to influence the form that individual organizations take.
- *Culture.* Issues such as the degree of individuality and formality influence work preferences and the way in which work is undertaken within an organization. There is an inevitable tension within large international organizations between the need for a global corporate identity and the dominant culture within local operating environments.
- *Employee characteristics.* The employees available to be employed within the organization also bring with them a wide range of variable characteristics that

will influence the nature and profile of it. For example, education levels within the general population influences a broad range of issues including the way that high technology might be used. The general experience of what work means within a society will influence expectations in relation to job design, management style and work ethos.

- *Job design*. There are many choices available in relation to how the work will be organized. For example, the degree of automation adopted, the involvement of employees in the full range of work activities and job flexibility all influence the combination of tasks in the jobs actually carried out.
- *Patterns of employment*. Attitudes and conventions with regard to the length of the working day, number of days worked each week, holidays, shift working and religious festivals all influence the way in which the workforce and organizations interact. Equally issues such as equality of employment opportunity, attitudes towards family and responsibilities for caring for the old and young can all influence the patterns of employment undertaken within a particular context.
- *Location*. There are cultural, legislative and dominant business practice issues that vary across the world and which shape organizations within each national border. Aspects such as communications and transportation also influence activities significantly. For example, mining operations are frequently carried out far from the location of the users of the extracted minerals and the company head office.

Management in Action 1.2 demonstrates some of these issues as identified by a Japanese company setting up business in the UK during the 1980s.

So far the discussion has not provided a clear differentiation of the parameters of an organization. How can a commercial organization be differentiated from a social club? The ultimate answer is that there is no clear distinguishing criterion as all forms of social grouping contain elements of similarity in terms of purpose, structure, people and systems. A number of writers offer definitions of an organization that offer broad similarities, including:

A. 'Organizations are collections of people working together in a coordinated and structured fashion to achieve one or more goals', Barney and Griffin (1992, p 5).
B. Organizations are 'consciously created arrangements to achieve goals by collective means', Thompson and McHugh (1995, p 3).
C. 'Organization: a social arrangement for achieving controlled performance in pursuit of collective goals', Huczynski and Buchanan (2001, p 884).

Each of these definitions is able to segregate out the more obvious non-organizational forms such as friendship groups. But what of other organizations such as youth clubs or pressure groups? A club with specific goals for the social development of members, or a pressure group to fight the building of a new road could easily fall within these definitions and yet would be of little interest to management and organizational researchers. Yet to incorporate terms such as 'profit', 'budget' or 'commercial' into the definition would cut out many non-profit organizations that do form a legitimate focus of study. The short answer is that there is no single definition that draws a boundary tightly around the notion of an organization. There is a wide range of research activity which seeks to explore different aspects associated with the concept of an organization and which consequently uses slightly different meanings. This is just one level of complexity in attempting to understand organizations, the managers who run them and the employees who work within them.

MANAGEMENT IN ACTION 1.2 Implementing Japanese management methods

Yuasa Battery was set up in the early 1980s in Wales to make sealed lead-acid batteries. It fell to the Japanese Managing Director, Kazuo Murata, to build and establish the factory as a viable operation. Two important lessons were learned from the experience of opening Yuasa Battery:

- Do the simple things right.
- Create conditions for improvement.

In seeking to establish the company, a number of problems endemic to western companies were identified. They included:

- Worker attitude to the wage/work bargain.
- Lack of the strict application of company rules.
- Workers not involved in determining improvements in productivity and working practice.
- Individualism emphasized within western culture.

Kazuo Murata, began the process of unlearning the 'bad habits' and creating the improvement necessary. This included:

- *Fairness*. The strict application of rules, procedures and standards in a fair manner resulted from this strategy. Rules are intended to benefit the organization and they should be applied consistently and fairly if they are to have any value.
- *Discipline*. Consider a sports team or a military force. Each must exercise a disciplined approach to its task if it is to be successful. This implies a controlled approach to work and getting the basics right.
- *Improvement*. The two earlier points are the basics of good organization, but to become a world-class organization continuous improvement is also necessary. Everyone must feel challenged by this necessity every working day. This implies critical self-examination and the development of better ways of working.

Based on: Harrison, A (1994) Implementing Japanese management methods, *Professional Manager*, January, pp 10–12.

Stop ↔ Consider

To what extent does the approach adopted by Kazuo Murata at Yuasa Battery provide an example of seeking to adapt the organization to the people and context, or does it reflect a desire to change the people to match the needs of the organization?

To what extent is it likely that people can be changed to meet the preferred requirements of the organization?

A FIRST LOOK AT MANAGEMENT

Managers are, by definition, the individuals that organize and control the organizations that employ them. In a small company they may actually own the organization itself, but usually they run an organization on behalf of the people to whom the organization legally belongs. It is the task of the management of the organization to operationalize and achieve the objectives of the beneficial owners. As Stanley (2002) puts it, managers are stewards of the business and therefore need to exercise great care in administering the resources of the organization. It is from those requirements that their decision-making functions and powers originate.

However, even in that simple paragraph there are a number of assumptions that when examined create complexity for the research into management. For example, it assumes that it is the beneficial owners of an organization who should have the primary say (or influence) on issues such as how the company is run. That is a viewpoint that can be questioned from many different perspectives. For example, a Marxist point of view would fundamentally bring into doubt the idea of capitalism, suggesting in turn that common ownership requires that everything is owned by the state in trust for the people. Consequently, a different approach to the determination of primacy in decision making must apply under that model.

Equally, it could be argued from a capitalist perspective, that in seeking to maximize returns to shareholders in the long run it is necessary to gain the highest levels of commitment from all employees. In so doing, if their interests are not put first, then they will not be motivated to produce the best returns for all concerned. This approach led to the **stakeholder** perspective on organizations. Stakeholder is defined as any group or individual who can affect, or is affected by, the activities of the organization (Freeman, 1984). The best levels of success can only be achieved by balancing the needs and contributions from each of the possible stakeholder groups, of which the shareholders represent only one category. For example, Henry Ford was famous for developing the assembly line approach to manufacturing motor cars in the early 1900s. His efforts achieved considerable success in developing production technology, cheap mass-appeal products and profits for the company. However, in 1913 labour turnover was 380 per cent. In order to keep 15 000 positions filled management had to recruit 50 000 people each year. In order to achieve a net increase of 100 people in the factory they had to recruit 963 people, because so many would not be able to stand the pace and conditions of work on the assembly lines (Losey, 1999). Management did not integrate the worker group as a significant stakeholder in their planning of the factory process. Management in Action 1.1 from earlier directly addresses these issues in one modern organization.

Stakeholder
An individual or group with some form of association or an interest in the organization.

It is only over recent years with the **delayering** of organizations that managers have seen their own position come under threat. Prior to this form of cost cutting, managers tended to have a much higher degree of job security than other categories of employee. They also enjoyed higher pay, better benefits and greater career opportunities. As a consequence, their primary loyalty was to the absentee owner, from whom these benefits accrued. However, in the search for ever higher levels of productivity and cost efficiency senior managers (and owners) found that, having reduced the numbers of employees significantly, the only areas left within which to seek dramatic cuts in cost were the previously protected management areas. This trend was also fuelled by the desire of organizations to 'get closer to the customer' by seeking to become more horizontal and less vertical. This delayering process created a situation in which managers began to experience high levels of stress and job insecurity, the result being the emergence of feelings of alienation and an increase in trade union membership among managerial employees. In short, they were recognizing the need to find ways of looking after their own interests in response to the employer not being willing to do so. The employer in this case being more senior managers. Therefore, the idea that management represents a single group or category of employee is not tenable. A point which is frequently missing from the literature.

Delayering
The act of removing layers from an organization thereby making it 'shorter' in the vertical dimension.

Management is a strange type of work in that it is an activity in which an employee, no different in principle from any other employee, is expected to act *in loco-parentis* for the owner. It is expected in principle that the manager should act in ways that may be to their own disadvantage in pursuit of the objectives of the owner. The delayering of organizations is a clear result of this requirement of managerial activity. It is because managers have traditionally become so personally and closely aligned with the objectives of the beneficial owner that the implications of delayering and related forms of cost saving produced such a traumatic shock. Managers are paid by the owners of the organization to act on their behalf. Managers forget at their peril that the basis of that relationship is contractual, not automatic! Equally, among the implications of that situation is that the interests of managers and beneficial owners can (and sometimes do) conflict. Because it is managers who run the organization on a day-to-day basis they may be tempted to favour themselves over the interests of the organization's owners in some of their actions. There is an inherent conflict of interest in terms of the expectations and requirements of the owners and those of the manager as an employee. It is for that reason that it is difficult in practice for the stakeholder concept to be fully implemented in running an organization. While the rhetoric may be evident in the sense of talking partnership etc., the dominance of hierarchical thinking and shareholder primacy is deeply ingrained, if difficult to guarantee.

It is difficult to be precise about management in theoretical or practical terms because it does not represent a homogeneous activity. There are two major differences identifiable in management activity:

- *Level.* There are many different ways to describe the level of management activity, the most common being a reflection of seniority. For example, director, senior manager, junior manager and supervisor. While that approach provides a useful basic reference criterion, it also contains considerable ambiguity. For example, simply knowing that an individual is a chief executive provides no clue to the level of responsibility involved. The company might employ ten people in one location, or many thousands in locations throughout the world.
- *Job.* The second major difference in managerial activity refers to the work of the individual. A manager might be responsible for the work of a personnel department, an engineering department, an accounting department, or a production department. They might even be a general manager, responsible for the work of several functions and having specialist managers reporting to them. In this last case the manager will be responsible for activities in which they have no direct experience, which in itself creates complexity.

Figure 1.6 reflects these two variables and their impact on jobs.

In addition to the two determinants of management activity just described, many of the variables described in Figure 1.5 also impact on management work. For example, the industry is a significant factor in this respect. Consider the very obvious differences between the job of a branch manager of a major bank and the job of a departmental manager in a manufacturing company. Both are responsible for the operational aspects within a defined part of the business, yet in other respects the jobs are very different as a result of the manufacturing/service nature of the organization.

Individual preference is another major influence on the actual job of a manager. In many management jobs there is a high level of opportunity to shape the actual work undertaken by the individual holding that position. A personnel manager has some degree of freedom to determine what tasks to delegate and which to retain for their personal attention. They also have considerable latitude to practise a style of management that they as individuals feel comfortable with, which can influence their own job activities and those of their subordinates.

The conclusion from this first look at management is that the practice of management reflects a complex process involving level, job, personal and professional variables. This process is carried out in a complex organizational environment. The result being that it is not possible to talk of either organization or management as single entities. Management in Action 1.3 reflects one person's view of the skills needed by future generations of managers.

FIGURE 1.6

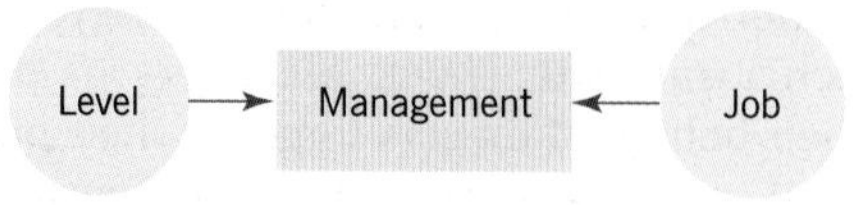

Major influences on management activities

MANAGEMENT IN ACTION 1.3 Survival skills for a new breed

The manager of the future will need different skills, it was argued by Karen Clarke in the essay that won first prize in an Institute of Management competition.

The skills required of managers in the past were decision making, expert (in their field), boss and director. This is progressively being replaced by three roles as organizations begin the twenty-first century. They are:

- *Leader*. The person setting the future direction for the business and concentrating on the wider picture (not day-to-day activity). The role of the leader becomes one of ensuring that progress towards the goal is maintained.
- *Coach*. The job of a coach is one of encouragement and of ensuring that everyone is pulling in the same direction. It is a process which allows empowerment and change to flourish.
- *Facilitator*. This is the process of identifying continuous improvement and encouraging a self-critical evaluation of work activity and performance.

It is argued by Clarke that it is now essential to achieve strategic positioning and operation of the business through the effort and ability of the staff employed within it. In order to achieve the world class service and manufacturing levels increasingly necessary for survival, staff must be committed to meeting the needs of customers. Consequently, delegation and empowerment are key factors in employee work activities of the future.

The desirability for managers to be the decision makers is increasingly being questioned. In the face of global competition, there is simply not the time for employees to pass decisions back in the system for someone else considered more appropriate to decide on. It is employees who are closest to the needs of customers and they must be allowed to operate as the customers' representative within the organization.

Adapted from: Clarke, K (1993) Survival skills for a new breed, *Management Today*, December, p 5.

Stop ↔ Consider

Do you agree with Karen Clarke's analysis that the roles she describes reflect different skills from those required in the past, or do they represent the same skills but expressed in a different social context?

Think about any organization that you have worked for in the recent past. Do the claims proposed by Clarke reflect your experience or not? If not, why might that be so?

Organizations are the entities that require the skills that managers possess, to perform the roles involved in managing as an active process. Management can therefore be described in terms of three main functions:

1. *Direction*. Before any work can be done, there is a need for a plan of action. It is necessary for management to decide what the organization should do and how it should achieve those objectives. Once done at the level of the organization, this process can be broken down into the strategies and goals to be achieved by each sub-unit within the company. For example, once a chocolate manufacturer has decided that it will make Easter eggs in particular varieties and sizes, it is then the job of the various section managers to set about determining the production schedule and other operational parameters so that the sales and profit objectives can be met.

   In practice, this top-down approach is much too simplistic as there may well be constraints in the system that limit the ability to achieve the overall objective. For example, the chocolate company may not have the warehouse capacity to store the volume of Easter eggs produced. Therefore, the development of strategy at any level of the organization is based on an iterative process and contains elements of bottom-up determination.

2. *Resources*. Another important function of management is to provide the resources to enable the desired task to be achieved. There are many resources necessary, including money, organization structure, job design, technology, procedures, systems and appropriately skilled people.
3. *People*. In all but the very smallest of organizations managers do not physically produce whatever it is they are responsible for. One way of conceptualizing management is to think of it as a series of subcontracting arrangements. The owners subcontract the running of the company to the board of directors. The board of directors in turn subcontracts the departmental work to line managers. This process cascades down to the people who actually make the products or deliver the service. This demonstrates that managers achieve their objectives through the efforts of other people. Therefore, in order to achieve their goals, managers find themselves in the position of having to manage the people rather than the operational process.

One of the other major aspects of organizational activity that managers are having to come to terms with is the effect of globalization. Even very small companies are experiencing some form of global activity. This might include selling products made by the company through a sales agent in another country. At the other end of the spectrum it could involve a very large organization operating across several national boundaries and with a truly multinational workforce and global perspective on its operations. Organizations need to develop an expertise in operating in locations that may have cultural and operating conditions very different from those prevailing at home. Individual managers need to develop the skills and ability to deal with governments, customers, suppliers, employees and colleagues from different countries.

Why organizations need managers

Managers plan, organize and control the acquisition, disposal and application of resources within the organization in pursuit of the goals determined by the owners. That view reflects the classical model described by Fayol (1916). From that perspective management is a very rational process and one category of employment within the organization. As such it requires someone to undertake specific duties associated with managing, just as a cleaner in a factory undertakes that particular job. One implication of this view is that being a manager confers no special status or rights over any other form of employment. Yet in practice (as was suggested earlier) one of the major functions of management is to act *in loco-parentis* for the absentee owner, which implies going beyond the wage/work bargain that forms the basis of most paid employment relationships.

There are other fundamental differences between the jobs of managers and those of most employees. Most employees are engaged to undertake a range of duties associated with the creation of the product or service that forms the rationale for the existence of the organization. Even employees who act as a support to the creation process contribute in a very necessary way by preventing the waste of productive resource. Managers, for the same reason, do not do that. They are specifically tasked to direct, organize and control the activities of others. They represent the most indirect of all operational jobs. It is this remoteness from direct operational activity and their agency function *(loco-parentis)* that sets them apart from other employees.

The type of work expected of managers is different from that of other employees. The impact of management's activities on other employees fundamentally influences the relationship with them. For example, it is management that decides who to recruit and who to dismiss. The power to take away someone's job is a particularly powerful weapon, right or responsibility, irrespective of how it is defined. It is such a potent tool that it is a right not usually given to every level of management. Managers are able to direct, channel and change the organizational experience for employees. Employees are not able to impact on managers in the same way. That is not to suggest, however, that employees are powerless within the organizational context. Indicated below are the main features that one magazine in the management field thinks are the main elements of a management job (*Supervision*, 2003, p 9). You might like to consider whether you agree with this list or not, based on your experience so far:

- They routinely enable people to work together productively and in a timely manner.
- They are ready to tackle the unexpected.
- They tap into people's self-motivation.
- They create opportunities and solve dilemmas at any hour. They get involved in the job of managing, even when they are not at work.

Why managers need organizations

Perhaps a more interesting question to ask is why do managers need organizations? At first it would appear to be a nonsensical question based on the assumption that organizations created the need for managers. However, there are a number of issues that suggest that the relationship between management and organizations is more complex than would at first appear to be the case.

One common joke in management circles suggests that there are only two skills in management. One is to create enough problems to justify the need for the job to exist. The second is not to create more problems than make for an easy life. This may be a cynical view of managerial activity but it does reflect aspects of the power and influence that managers have. This view of management can be reinforced by the shock that was experienced by many managers as organizations began to downsize and delayer. Up to that time redundancy was something that happened to other employees, not managers. The basis of the **psychological contract** between employer and managers had been fundamentally changed. The basis of the 'old contract' was that managers put their best efforts into furthering the interests of the capital owner in return for a career and the appropriate status. Frequently the best efforts willingly contributed by managers involved long working hours with no additional payment, taking work home and generally putting the job before family.

Psychological contract
The nature and boundaries of the employment relationship prescribed through the unwritten and unstated rights and obligations of both parties.

Organizations are having to seek new ways of achieving that level of management involvement in conditions which are fundamentally different and less directly beneficial to the individual. A new rhetoric is evolving about portable careers and related ideas to suggest that uncertainty and insecurity should not be considered as negative events. Worrall and Cooper (1999) report from the *Quality of Working Life* survey (the third year of a five-year tracking study) a number of interesting results that suggest that managers are changing their working patterns in response to the new business enviornment. They are beginning to move away from a reliance on the company as the source of all things and in some cases see the need for a better balance between home and work lives. Some of the relevant results are included in Table 1.1.

So what are the significant factors that create a reciprocal need between managers and organizations?

Career Individual managers expect to have a career. Organizations need managers for more senior positions. Performance appraisal systems, career development and succession planning all provide a basis for career development.

Status/power With a managerial position comes status and power and hence the ability to have other people do what the individual manager wants. Being considered as a significant member of the local community can also reflect the status of a manager.

Work preference Being a manager gives the individual some degree of choice in their work activities. They can delegate aspects of their work. They are able to shape events and the direction of work under their control.

Professionalization There is an increasing trend to professionalize management. The professional associations to which managers belong and the educational establishments offering management training are making efforts to raise the status of the job, thereby making it more attractive as a career option. It is not just the law and accountancy that can now lay claim to be a profession.

Self-interest Management is a political process as much as it is a decision-making one. There are few managers who are as quick to take responsibility when something goes wrong as there are when accolades are being handed out. The question to be answered is not does self-interest feature in management practice but to what extent will a manager put self-interest ahead of other criteria in any given situation?

Lifestyle A higher salary, better benefit package, and so on, generate a whole range of lifestyle differences. Not that all managers earn more than those whom they supervise. Frequently, for first-line managers the opposite is true as a result of the loss of bonus or overtime payments. However, there are differences in the social groupings in which people mix and the leisure activities that they undertake that create a raft of lifestyle differences.

Expectation Individuals are conditioned to expect differences as a result of becoming a manager. They expect respect, a higher income and greater freedom to influence events around them. Consequently, having experienced some of these benefits the result is an expectation (and desire) that they don't lose them, leading to a need to perpetuate such positions. For example, it is not in the interests of most managers to

Working hours reduce	1997 1999	38% work more than 50 hours a week 32% work more than 50 hours a week
Working weekends	1997 1999	13% always work weekends 8% always work weekends
Relationships with children	1999	41% of junior managers express concern
Balance between work and home life	1997 1999	25% feel work is less important than home 30% feel work is less important than home

TABLE 1.1 Managers' changing attitudes (source: Worrall, L and Cooper, CL (1999) *The Quality of Working Life: The 1999 Survey of Managers' Changing Experiences*. Institute of Management and UMIST, London)

see too many management jobs disappear or for radical alternatives in the form of self-managed teams to be developed. It would simply eliminate much of the opportunity and potential benefits available and require individuals to seek other forms of employment.

Many of these issues are generalizations which interlink and reinforce each other. For example, career and expectation are strongly linked together, as are the status and lifestyle benefits that result from promotion. The line of argument here is not that managers originally created organizations because they needed them, but that once in existence there is a reciprocal dependency that perpetuates a need for organizations to exist in order to continue to fulfil a broad range of needs including personal and professional.

A FIRST LOOK AT EMPLOYEES

Organizations do not exist in any real sense of the word. They exist as legal and financial entities on paper, but it is people that breathe life into the formal documents. Management in Action 1.4 illustrates some of these people perspectives within organizations in the context of the introduction of **business process re-engineering (BPR)**.

Business process re-engineering (BPR)
Reorganization of the business by the elimination of extraneous activity and the rapid transformation to a process focus.

The earlier discussion on management stated that the manager is acting on behalf of an absentee owner. This view is usually referred to as an agency perspective – the manager acting as an agent of (on behalf of) the owner. The clear implication being that most managers are in fact employees, just like every other type of worker. From a different perspective, as early as 1964, Cyert and March were writing about coalitions and Rhenman was writing about stakeholders in the running of organizations. Networks and coalitions formed between the many internal and external stakeholder groups linked with the organization are implied by these views. Figure 1.7 illustrates some of the primary stakeholder groups that can be identified in relation to any organization.

Each one of the stakeholder groups identified in Figure 1.7 has an interest in some aspect of the focal organization. Owners are interested in a financial return for their money; employees might be interested in a secure and interesting job that pays a realistic wage; suppliers in the opportunity to create long-term strategic alliances for commercial benefit; government as a source of employment and taxation. Internal to the organization some of the stakeholder groups will be temporary and seek to achieve specific goals.

Stakeholder groups are essentially people-oriented and so provide a basis for analysis. Human beings are complex as individuals and even more so in collective situations. Each person has many similarities with other humans, but, critically for organizational purposes, also a great many differences. Personality factors differ, as do the education level and life experience of each person. These form the basis of how individuals interpret and relate to the world in which they live. People can be unpredictable, which makes consistency of behaviour in an organizational setting difficult to achieve. Illness, mood and temperament are just some of the variables that can affect how each person will behave on any particular day. This does not just affect employees, it affects managers as well. No individual can be expected to function consistently and at peak performance all day, every day – even if business process re-engineering (or any other model) assumes that they can or should.

Employees are generally described as the non-management workers within an organization. However, as we saw in the previous section, many managers are also employees. But for the purpose of this aspect of our discussion, we shall stick to the predominant view that the classification 'employee' refers to those workers who are not managers. It is the management group who are supposed to function in the best interests of the beneficial owners of the business by directing the activities and behaviour of the 'employees' in order to achieve the business objectives. From that perspective, it suggests that employees exist to be manipulated (or directed) by managers in pursuit of organizational objectives. They are not therefore expected to think or to have any interest in the business beyond selling their labour to be used at management's behest. At least that represents the classic capitalist view of how labour is positioned relative to management and the owners of capital. However, it is being increasingly recognized that it is necessary for managers to acknowledge the fundamental nature of the human employee if they are to be able to manipulate (or harness effectively as managers would prefer it to be described) the employees available to them. For example, Management in Action 1.1 describes the effects of employee involvement in what would previously be regarded as a management domain – the recruitment of new employees. The *Harvard Management Communication Letter* of December 2002 addresses another aspect of this issue by setting out a strategy for managers to ensure that employees adapt more readily to changes decided upon by the company. It is premised on the ideas that change alters how employees define themselves and also that change creates uncertainty. There then follow a number of prompts intended to help managers raise employee concerns in a way which allows the employees to address their concerns.

Writers such as Fox (1985) suggest that the employment relationship in Britain is based on the traditional relationship between master and servant as a reflection of the

FIGURE 1.7

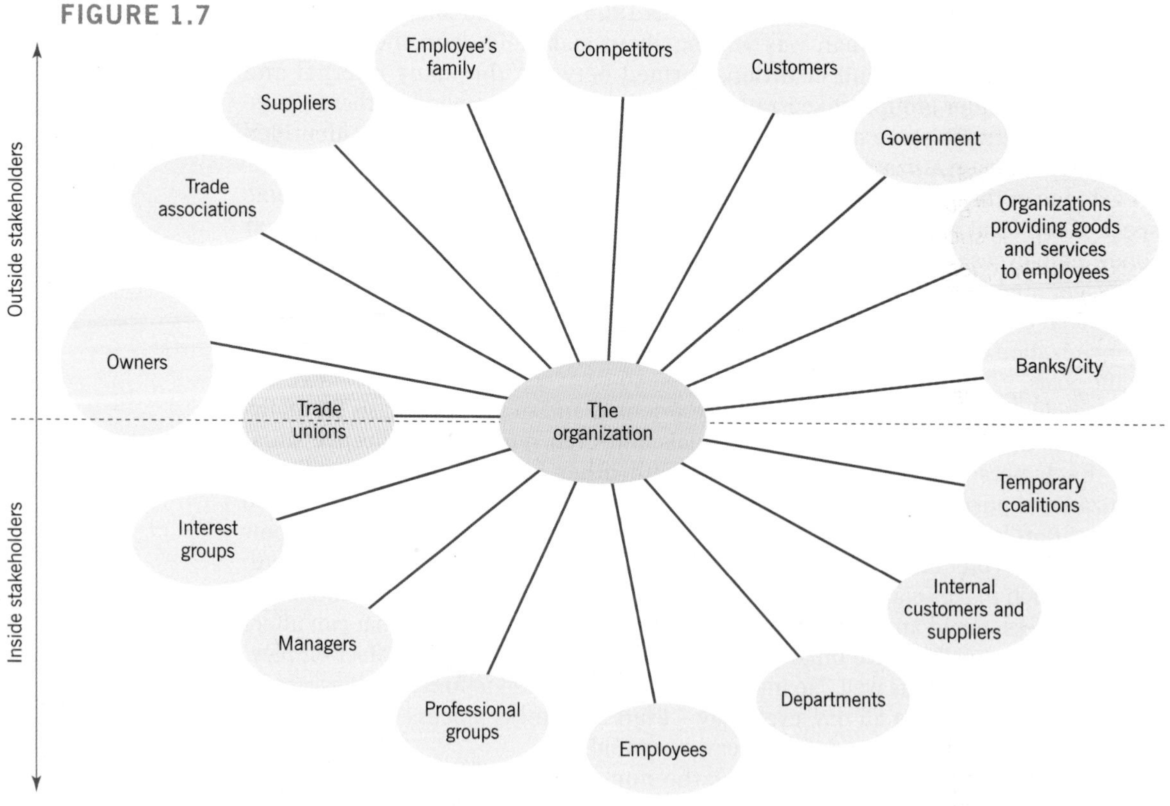

Primary stakeholder groups

MANAGEMENT IN ACTION 1.4 Cut out the middlemen

The techniques and formulas that are used as the basis of seeking out the best way of working and the lowest cost of operation are often silent on the human impact of their activity. At best these approaches assume a rationality in the way that human beings can easily be fitted into any organizational design or that communication can overcome any unwillingness on the part of employees to accept the need to produce more for less.

Business process re-engineering is the latest in a long line of approaches to attempt to ensure that organizations become truly efficient. Michael Hammer is one of the leading gurus in this field and insists that it is a process that is about eliminating work, a process that should not be considered as the same as eliminating people (simple downsizing). The net result, however, is the same, but it is argued that by concentrating on the fundamental redesign of the business process an effective organization will then result and one into which the people can be accommodated. The major area of impact for this approach to efficiency is the middle manager levels, what Hammer calls the 'death zone'. Re-engineering he describes as a process intended to replace the organizational forms that emerged during the Industrial Revolution when workers needed to be closely supervised for many reasons, including low levels of trust.

In the re-engineered company, teams are essential and a customer rather than boss focus is required. This invariably leads to the notion of self-managed teams with a much-reduced role for managers in the traditional sense of the job. Management becomes a role requiring lead-and-enable skills rather than those of command and control. It also reduces the ratio of managers required from approximately 1:7 to anything approaching 1:50. As an indication of the impact of re-engineering, Taco Bell moved from 350 area supervisors for its 1800 fast food outlets in 1988 to 100 market managers responsible for 2300 outlets a few years later. The effect on sales was an increase (on average) of 22 per cent per year and profits by 31 per cent per year.

Based on: Flood, G (1994) Cut out the middlemen, *Personnel Today*, 22 March, p 36.

Stop ↔ Consider

Is business process re-engineering (BPR) yet another attempt to find the elusive formula that would guarantee the success of a company?

If BPR were to be successful would every company follow it and therefore find the same solutions to the question of minimal cost with maximal customer focus? What might this imply?

What do you think about the view that a process focus should predominate with the human workforce being fitted around that?

How might employees and middle managers react to BPR approaches and what might the long term effect on organizations be?

relative status of both parties. It can be argued (for example, Beardwell and Holden (2001, pp 456–9) that much of the recent move towards human resource management and away from personnel management, is governed by the desire to 'go beyond the contract in getting better value for money from the employee resource. The traditional **compliance**-based authority structures of organizations are being replaced with an emphasis on **commitment**-based work organization. However, writers such as Sisson (1994) suggest that much of the difference between these two positions is rhetoric rather than reality, reflecting an attempt to, '... mask the reality of the harsh face of managerial prerogative in the service of capital.' Legge (1995, p 314). Management in Action 1.5 clearly indicates that the relationship between some

Compliance
Employees follow the rules precisely, paying only 'lip service' to the underlying aims and objectives sought by management.

Commitment
Employees internalize management's values and norms and in so doing commit themselves to management's aims and objectives.

management and employee groups can be exploitative in nature, far from harmonious and on occasion can lead to physical violence.

The reality of the precise nature of the relationship between managers and employees, is therefore open to question, and will depend to some extent on the views of the debaters. Some will argue that the relationship of old has changed and now is based on commitment rather than compliance. Others will argue that it is not really a commitment-based relationship as it is based upon fundamental inequality. Capital can take its need for labour elsewhere and indeed dispense with it altogether through the use of technology. Employees are very much dependent upon the work opportunities that exist in order to earn the money that they need in order to survive in modern society. The debate goes on, and will undoubtedly do so for some considerable time into the future. The major consequence of this is that it is not possible to assume that employees will have the same perspectives on anything relating to what happens within an organization as the managers. Indeed, it is not possible to assume that all managers will have the same perspective as each other. Both of these situations arise because the perspective and attitudes of each individual are determined by many factors, including personality, experience, education, objectives status, information available and peer group pressure. These are all factors that will be discussed at various points throughout the book. Consequently, the employee perspective will be introduced where it can be expected to have a pertinent contribution to make to the discussion.

The relationship between individual employees and the organizations that employ them is a complex one. At a basic (and perhaps cynical) level, the human employee is simply a flexible alternative to a machine or computer; to be replaced as soon as a more reliable and cheaper alternative becomes available. However, that view is overly simplistic. As the technology associated with work activity evolves, some jobs are eliminated, but new ones are created. The jobs created tend to be more cerebral than manual as machine-minding tasks are eliminated, and so the skill levels and education levels required to perform them also increase. During the transition period when new jobs are being created there are inevitably shortages of appropriately skilled and trained employees and so wage costs increase, bringing with it increased numbers of people willing to undertake the training required. There are of course many other forces acting upon the job choices that people make. For example, social and peer pressure can make some jobs more attractive than others, as can parental influence. Government policy can encourage (or inhibit) people to stay on at school and university, thereby channelling young people in certain directions. Government (and company) policy and grants can also encourage the retraining of older employees into new skill areas.

Metaphor
The explanation of something complex through reference to something simpler, but which conveys additional meaning.

Human behaviour also influences the perception and understanding of organizations themselves. Morgan (1986) and Gharajedaghi and Ackoff (1984) both describe organizational activity in terms of the differing **metaphors** that can be employed by people to understand it. They represent the ways in which an individual interprets an organization, which determines the characteristics that will be attributed to it and assumptions about how it functions. For example, considering an organization in metaphorical terms as a brain or as a machine bestows on it qualities associated with those structures. The metaphor adopted also conditions how individuals will assume that an organization works. The decisions and expectations of individuals in relation to the organization are also influenced by the metaphor adopted.

Whatever the situation, the position and perspectives of employees are fundamentally different to those of managers, even though many of the latter are also employees. The metaphor adopted by each category is inevitably different. It is to influence the metaphor held that so much management effort goes into seeking to influence the ways in which employees think about their role and responsibilities within

MANAGEMENT IN ACTION 1.5

Misery of rag-trade slaves in America's Pacific outpost

The capital of American Samoa, Pago Pago is home to a number of high volume garment factories, all with the right to claim that the goods are made in the USA. However, as a recent court heard from US attorney general (John Ashcroft) conditions in some factories were 'nothing less than modern-day slavery'. In a particular court case it was said that the 251 Chinese and Vietnamese workers at one factory paid £126 per month for room and board, which consisted of a bunk in a 36 bed dormitory and three meagre meals each day. The pay for the workers was routinely withheld and when workers went on strike to recover lost earnings, the managers turned off the electricity making the conditions in the living areas unbearable. During one of these disputes one of the women workers was dragged from her machine by several men and had one eye gouged out with a plastic pipe.

The clothes being made were for large name retail stores such as Sears and JC Penney as well as for the MV Sport and Spalding brands. Only JC Penney agreed to pay the workers the back pay owed to them. Workers are attracted to work at the factory by the higher wages available than could be earned in Vietnam. Sewing jobs paid $400 each month compared to the average in Vietnam of $30 per month. However, it was necessary to pay $4500 to a local labour export company in order to get a job in Pago Pago. The parents of one worker had to remortgage their home in order to guarantee the fee. One worker earned only $672 during her nine months employment at the factory before it was closed down and could not pay off her debts unless she got more work in a similar factory.

Charles Kernaghan, Director of the National Labour Committee in Washington said that the situation in American Samoa made it a perfect location for exploitation of labour. It was a US territory with an economy in desperate need of stimulation and it had no import tariffs in relation to mainland USA, looser immigration laws and tax incentives to encourage inward investment. Being eligible to display the 'Made in the USA' symbol on the labels of goods made there, it even implied that quality and labour practices were as they would be everywhere else in the USA, a distinct sales advantage. However, being more than 7000 miles from Washington it was in practice only lightly regulated, with government labour inspectors saying that they do not have a budget for travel to such remote locations in order to monitor working conditions.

Similar conditions apply to Saipan, another US territory in the Northern Mariana islands. But here workers have brought a class action case against leading American clothing and retail companies for alleged exploitation and sweatshop employment conditions.

Adapted from: Fickling, D (2003) Misery of rag-trade slaves in America's Pacific outpost, *The Guardian*, Saturday 1 March, p 20.

Stop ↔ Consider

What does this example of the treatment of people at work suggest about what customers, managers, governments and consumers actually think about employees?

organizations. Managers are also employees with one major distinction; they are supposed to act in the interests of the beneficial owner of the business, while ordinary employees have no such special status. At best they are one of the stakeholders within the organization, at worst a necessary resource to be manipulated in pursuit of organizational objectives and replaced whenever practical. The behaviour and attitudes of employees towards work and organizations also reflects the diversity of perspective about them. Sometimes it reflects favourable attitudes and underlying values, sometimes an open hostility and rejection of organizational purpose and management objectives. It all depends upon a wide range of factors, including the individuals themselves and their prior experience of how organizations and managers actually treat them.

There exists a view among certain academic writers and practising managers that the world of work has changed, bringing with it the need for employees to change as well. It has already been suggested earlier that the relationship between managers and organizations has changed with the introduction of downsizing and other cost reduction initiatives. This represents an example of what is termed the psychological contract. This represents the largely unwritten expectations that exist between employee and employer. It establishes the basis of what each can expect from the other. It has been argued that in the past this was based on the individual giving their full support to the company in return for career and regular wage increases etc. Whilst this may have been true in the case of administrative, technical and managerial positions, it would not be a common experience of most manual workers, unless they worked in the public sector. It is now argued by writers such as Hiltrop (1995, p 286) that:

> There is no job security. The employee will be employed as long as he or she adds value to the organization, and is personally responsible for finding new ways to add value. In return, the employee has the right to demand interesting and important work, has the freedom and resources to perform it well, receives pay that reflects his or her contribution and gets experience and training needed to be employed here or elsewhere.

The extract form Hiltrop is interesting in that it suggests that there still exists a balance of give and take in the employment relationship, albeit in different form to that existing previously. It suggests a personal career in which each individual takes responsibility for themselves and their own development in order to be marketable now and in the future in an increasingly uncertain world. But is such a rosy perspective part of the real experience of most employees? Consider the case study included at the end of this chapter in this context and a slightly different psychological contract appears to exist. Equally, Management in Action 1.5 presents a different perspective on the employment relationship. Perhaps the psychological contract described above represents an ideal type of relationship that might be hoped for among some categories of employee in some organizations, but not all. As is evident in the case study for this chapter, the real experience for some employees can be very different.

It is the predictable consistency in operation provided by computer-based technology that makes it such an attractive option in most work settings. It is not possible for human beings to match the unfailing and relentless consistency of performance achieved by robots in a factory, for example. However, human beings do have some advantages over computer technology. They are adaptable, flexible and can demonstrate a level of initiative beyond that available through any computer. Consequently, there is still a need to employ and a benefit to be gained from, that unpredictable but fascinating beast of burden – the human being. Call centres represent a modern organizational development in which new patterns and forms of work are emerging based on computer and telecommunications technology. As such, new ways of work are evolving in these environments and as a consequence some people refer to these as the modern-day equivalent of the 'sweatshops' of old, with demands for high work rates over extended periods, highly repetitive work of a low level, constant management monitoring of work and high labour turnover. During November 1999 the first major strike of employees in call centres was organized by the Communications Workers' Union in the UK over what were described as an 'oppressive management style' and 'persistent under resourcing' (Lamb, 1999a). This action demonstrates the difficulty facing managers in effectively blending together the opportunities available between new technology and human beings. Also, consider the experience of lower level employees working in call centres, who now find their jobs being transferred to India in the search for cost reduction made possible by using the latest technology and wage-based economies of scale, why should they be supportive of management objectives? For example, the scale of the potential savings is evident from research by Deloitte Touche Tohmatsu (reviewed by Crabb, 2003) which indicates that the top 100 financial services companies could save between £432 million and £618 million each over a five year period by switching operations to the developing world.

It is people who create organizations, either as a source of income or in response to a perceived social, political or personal need. It is people who operate the organization, taking decisions and physically arranging to produce the products or services. It is yet more people who regulate the organization in terms of safety, taxation, financial matters and fraud. Even more people are the suppliers and customers of the organization. Within the organization, careers are worked out and living standards are determined, individuals seek to advance their own position and status at the expense of others. On occasions they also seek revenge for some real or imagined injury or hurt from the past. In short, the human aspect of organizations is the story of human life and experience plus that of society, albeit writ small!

THE CHALLENGES FACING ORGANIZATIONS, MANAGERS AND EMPLOYEES

The basic challenge facing all organizations, managers and employees is that of change. The world is constantly changing and that rate of change is now becoming faster. Some of this change is evolutionary and other revolutionary. For example, the development of computer technology is subject to continual refinement. This is something that is evolutionary in nature. A change process experienced as a series of small frequent (incremental) amendments to the existing situation. Considering this type of change on a daily basis would offer no noticeable difference, but over a period of years considerable change is achieved.

Revolutionary change, in comparison, is a sudden and dramatic process that fundamentally alters the situation. One example of this is the arrival of the out-of-town shopping and leisure complex. Over a relatively short period of time town centres have become deserted as people find it more convenient to drive to one of these centres. The effect has been to force many town centre businesses either to relocate to a new complex or to close down altogether.

Change has always been a part of life. It has been argued by many writers that the pace of change impacting on organizations is occurring ever more rapidly. So much so that one catchphrase over recent years has been an exhortation to 'innovate or die'! This carries the clear implication that unless change becomes institutionalized the organization will not stay in business for long. There is a counter-argument to this view which suggests that by forcing change into an organization, managers are creating the very instability that can inhibit their ability to survive. Inevitably, change within an organization impacts on all the people within it. Change means different things to different people within the organization. To a significant extent the perspective on change depends upon the implied impact for the individual or group. So for a main board director it may mean growth of the company, a big merger deal bringing personal reputation and kudos. For the senior managers a particular change may mean additional resources to enhance the service they provide, or less resources through which to provide an enhanced service. To junior managers it might simply mean more work and having to ensure that lower level employees adopt new working practices that mean they have to do jobs differently to the way they were done in the past. For the lower level employees it may mean job losses and uncertainty as to how many jobs will exist after the change has been made. In addition it may well require remaining employees to undertake the work previously done by their displaced colleagues, leading to increased pressure and stress. In short, change is something that at the lowest levels of an organization is invariably viewed in negative terms because it usually means having to learn new things and do more with fewer resources, or at least that is the general perception of the impact. The challenge, particularly for managers, is to find ways of embracing change that do not engender negative and hostile reactions among employees.

There are many ways of categorizing change. Johnson and Scholes (1999) describe a PESTLE analysis process that provides a systematic basis for considering the environmental influences surrounding an organization:

- *Political.* Factors influencing the organization from surrounding political sources. For example, the political orientation of the government in power.
- *Economic.* These reflect the economic conditions and trends that can influence the environment within which the organization must operate.
- *Social/cultural.* Changes to the populations (customer and workforce) surrounding the organization can also have a significant impact on its functioning. For example, in Europe there is an expectation among employees that they are entitled to increasing levels of involvement in company decision making.
- *Technological.* The changes to the technology available to organizations affects both the products and services available and also the ways in which companies operate.
- *Legal.* The legislative rules may change. For example, increases in fuel tax may increase transport costs causing an increase in cost of operations and reductions in profit.
- *Environment/ethical.* There is pressure on all organizations to reduce damage to the environment and to act in an ethical way. Pressure groups constantly monitor company statements on their performance in these areas and often hold managers to account in public to demand action where it can be argued that not enough is being done.

Asch and Salaman (2002) draw together a wide range of variables to demonstrate that the problems facing managers in relation to the challenges of the future are based upon the interaction of two factors:

- The changing nature of complex and unpredictable environments.
- The plethora of (often competing) advice and exhortations of how to deal with such unpredictable environments.

In addition to the processes identified, there are the political reasons that lead managers to seek change within their organizations. For example, new managers often seek to make change in order to demonstrate a clear break with what existed previously. Equally, managers can attempt to enhance their own career prospects by seeking to be regarded by senior managers as proactive in pursuing change.

CONCLUSIONS

This chapter has introduced organizational behaviour together with the concepts of organization, management and employee, which form the basis of much of the emphasis in the rest of this book. It has also included some of the research orientations and approaches for the study of these issues in the real world by real people. The purpose of this chapter has been to set the scene for much of the later work in the book. It also set out to provide readers with some background to the research issues and approaches that are used to inform thinking in this and other areas of the study of management and organizations.

Now to summarize this chapter in terms of the relevant Learning Objectives:

- **Understand the distinction between research in the natural and in the social sciences.** This chapter has sought to introduce the distinction between natural and social science research. In the natural sciences, it is possible to utilize the scientific method of research and to seek to control closely each of the variables active in any situation in laboratory-based experiments. In the social world it is not often possible to provide such control and equally behaviour is an interactive, dynamic process occurring in real time and with many other variables influencing events. Consequently different research methods have to be employed to illuminate such events and equally it is rarely possible to offer definitive explanations of particular behaviours.
- **Explain the particular difficulties involved in studying and developing theories in the area of management.** The previous outline has provided a brief explanation of this objective. There are so many variables at work in even the simplest forms of human behaviour in an organizational context that it is very difficult to provide complete explanations or theories that might explain them. Therefore any theory is at best simply reflecting a probability that certain behaviours will occur in certain situations, given a range of other prerequisites. This is particularly true when considering management as a separate activity within organizations.
- **Outline the essence of the relationship between organizations, managers and employees.** There exists a complex relationship between the three main terms indicated. Each needs the other to a significant extent in order to produce whatever product or service is offered by the organization. It is not simply a one-way relationship. Organizations create goods and services, people are needed to achieve that. Absentee owners fund large organizations, therefore, they need managers to realize the objective of making money from the capital. Equally, managers need the organization to provide job opportunity, status, and career possibilities. Both managers and employees need the money earned from work to purchase the goods and services that make life meaningful and enjoyable. This creates a reciprocal need between organizations and the people who work in them.
- **Appreciate that the concept 'organization' incorporates many different forms.** The definition of an organization covers many different types. Not all organizations are of interest to every researcher, teacher or student of management. In some situations, the focus of interest will be management in a large multinational organization, in others management of small owner-manager companies. The public sector and voluntary sector are also significant types of organization that form the focus of interest in particular situations. Therefore, there are many forms of organization and it is frequently unstated or assumed that private sector large commercial organizations are the model on which all theory and explanation should be based.
- **Discuss how the study of organizational behaviour can contribute to an understanding of management.** The study of organizational behaviour is about understanding how people and organizations interact. As has already been suggested this represents a complex relationship with many factors active in any situation. The purpose of studying organizational behaviour is to begin to understand the variety of forces influencing behaviour within an organization, including the behaviour of other people, the design of organizations, the role of technology, political forces and stress. Management requires the achievement of objectives through other people at all levels both inside and outside of an organization. Therefore organizational behaviour seeks to illuminate the nature and responsibilities of management (among those of other stakeholders) in running organizations more effectively.

DISCUSSION QUESTIONS

1. Management represents the combination of experience and practical skill, it cannot be taught. Therefore there is no point in studying management. Discuss this question and in so doing justify the study of organizational behaviour.
2. 'Management is a manipulative process.' Discuss the extent to which you agree with this statement and explain why.
3. 'It is not possible to generate robust social science theories because there are so many variables at work. It requires the development of a totally new science.' To what extent would you agree with this statement and why?
4. 'There is no such thing as a typical organization or management job therefore it is pointless attempting to theorize about them.' To what extent would you agree with this view? Justify your answer.
5. 'Managers need organizations.' To what extent do you agree with this view and why?
6. To what extent and why should employees be regarded as one of many resources available to the organization, providing managers with the necessary labour needed to achieve objectives?
7. 'Because employees actually do the work of the organization they are in a stronger position than managers to know how to do things more effectively.' To what extent might this be taken to imply that if employees could be motivated more effectively, most management jobs could be eliminated?
8. Why do you think that people seek jobs as managers?
9. 'The study of organizational behaviour enables managers to become more effective at their job.' Discuss this statement.
10. Change can be equated with the challenges facing organizations and managers. Is this a valid comparison to make? Examine both sides of the argument and justify your own point of view.

CASE STUDY The reality of management life!

The case study is based in a large multinational service organization operating in the UK, although the parent group is based in the USA. The company makes and supplies office equipment and maintains existing equipment in client premises under service agreements. It also refurbishes equipment as clients need it updating or changing. The specific incidents reflected in the case study occurred in the refurbishment division of the company in the UK. The refurbishment division was headed by a manager (Mark) who had reporting to him seven field managers, each responsible for up to seven engineers who carried out any refurbishment and commissioning of equipment on client premises. Each field manager was responsible for a refurbishment in a specific geographic location of the UK. In addition, the refurbishment manager had reporting to him seven sales managers, one in each geographic area as indicated for the field managers; and a number of other senior technical and administrative staff, including a planning manager, secretary and two administrative assistants. The refurbishment manager reported to the director of operations for the UK company.

The case study is based on a situation that developed involving one of the field managers. The individual concerned (James) was 63 years of age and had worked for the company for 35 years, beginning as a service engineer and working his way up to the position of field manager. He had always worked in the same geographic area of the country and was well known and respected by both clients and fellow engineers. He had held his present position for three years at the time of the incidents described. At the time that James was appointed to his current position the company had undertaken a major reorganization of its activities. He along with all of the other managers had to undergo a recruitment and selection process involving interviews, psychometric tests and assessment centres intended to select the best candidates for the reduced number of management jobs within the new organization structure. James met the appropriate criteria and was appointed to the position of field manager (refurbishment). This itself was a new department within the company as previously refurbishment had been undertaken as a service activity within the company.

As a consequence of the reorganization the refurbishment department was created from among existing employees brought together with the intention that a viable team and working unit would emerge over time. In some cases line managers within the company had engineered situations in which a number of their weaker employees were transferred over to the new department as a way of getting rid of low performing individuals, those with less capability and those regarded as lazy or simply trouble-makers. Whilst there was no suggestion that James was one of these employees, some of his engineers fell into that category, as did some of the support staff moved into the department.

The refurbishment manager (Mark) was moved into the department from the position of area sales manager, having gone through the internal recruitment process and being identified as a high-flyer within the company. The brief that Mark was given was to generate increased sales of 10 per cent in the first year, to reduce customer complaints by 10 per cent over the same period and to create an effective refurbishment department across the entire UK operations. Not surprisingly there were many teething problems in the new department and Mark spent the first year fire-fighting in an attempt to limit the damage and achieve the objectives set whilst maintaining effective customer relations. He spent much of his time on the road visiting his managers, the worksites and customers. It quickly became apparent that the difficulties with the new department went further than a few underperforming employees. It was clear that prior to the change-over to the new structure a number of managers had either deliberately or accidentally allowed jobs to become seriously delayed or badly planned. Also a number of unrealistic promises (and quotations) had been made to clients and potential customers. This situation increased the pressure on everyone in the refurbishment department, particularly the managers.

A broad sweep of measures was instigated by Mark to improve the effectiveness of the new department, including team meetings and team building activities. This was on top of Mark spending a considerable amount of time with each team in order to monitor their work and ensure that they were working to the new procedures and requirements. It quickly became apparent to Mark that the department did not have enough people to undertake all of the work expected of them. The sales engineers were able to bring in enough orders, but the engineering side were unable to carry out the refurbishment work fast enough. This was partly due to the lack of engineers, partly due to the inexperience of some of the field managers, partly due to the quality of some of the staff (as implied earlier) and partly due to the need to improve team working across the new department. One particular area of difficulty was in the area under the leadership of James. He had considerable experience of the company, its products and the engineering processes involved, but there always seemed to be more problems in his area than in the others. Mark tried several ways to overcome the difficulties. He spent more time with James than with any of the other field managers; he helped James to plan his work and to deal with problem engineers. However, nothing seemed to work. One of the major problems was that James was finding it particularly difficult to use the new company computer-based systems. He did not like to use the email system and was not comfortable with the inevitable politics that accompany management activity. For example, the sales engineers in his area were becoming so frustrated with the lack of completed work for their clients that they had taken to emailing James to complain on a frequent basis, at the same time circulating the email to Mark and even his boss (the director) for information. This inevitably resulted in questions being asked of Mark and pressure being put on him to take action.

Mark eventually sat James down and had a frank discussion with him about what was going on. Eventually during the discussion, it emerged that James was very unhappy with the new job. It was completely different to his previous managerial task and required him to do jobs and tasks that he did not enjoy or feel competent to do. He even admitted that it was getting him down so much he was being physically sick most mornings before leaving home to go to work. He just felt so helpless and out of his depth in being able to do the job expected of him. Mark was taken aback by this revelation, not having suspected the personal nature of the situation. Thinking about the meeting afterwards, he decided to speak to his boss about a number of options. These included the possibility of reassignment within the company and giving James an early retirement package to allow him to leave work with some dignity. In speaking to his boss, it quickly became apparent that these were not going to be options that would be considered. Mark's boss said that James was not up to the job and should either be forced to resign or should be dismissed. It was not going to be possible to find James alternative work within the company that would make use of his considerable experience and knowledge about the company, its products, processes and customers. No enhanced retirement or other package would be made available in his case. The management view was that the company should get tough with underperforming employees and they should be made to perform by the threat of dismissal without any compensation. The fact that James had very long service with the company and had always been a good employee was deemed to be irrelevant.

Mark was appalled by what he was told by his boss. It represented a completely different attitude by a senior manager to that common before the reorganization. Clearly, a new get tough approach was to be the new way of managing people within the company. Mark pushed as hard as he could within the company for a special case to be made for James, but to no avail. Mark was essentially told that if he did not deal with James he would be replaced as well. Mark arranged to see James, told him of the situation, and suggested that he would have good ground for legal action against the company if they dismissed him. James said that such an approach was not his style and that he was going to resign and walk away with his dignity intact. He handed Mark a letter of resignation and left the office. Mark felt so angry at how James had been dealt with that he also began to look around for another job and left the company about three months later.

Task

What does this case suggest to you in relation to:
What management is?
What being an employee means?
The nature of the psychological contract?
How managers manage?
The signal that management's behaviour might send to other employees?
What an organization is and how they change over time?

FURTHER READING

Burrell, G and Morgan, G (1979) *Sociological Paradigms and Organisational Analysis: Elements of the Sociology of Corporate Life*, Ashgate, Aldershot. A classical review of the different ways of seeing things in organizational theorizing.

Clark, H, Chandler, J and Barry, J (1994) *Organization and Identities: Text and Readings in Organizational Behaviour*, International Thomson Business Press, London. Contains a broad range of original articles on relevant material themes and from significant writers referred to in this and other textbooks on management and organizations.

Clegg, SR and Palmer, G (eds) (1996) *The Politics of Management Knowledge*, Sage, London. This text explores the relationship between management knowledge, power and practice within an increasingly global organizational environment.

de la Billière, General Sir P (1994) *Looking For Trouble*, HarperCollins, London. An autobiography of a senior military officer, this book provides an insight into the nature of leadership as well as military organization.

Gunn, C (1993) *Nightmare on Lime Street*, 2nd edn, Smith Gryphon, London. This book provides a perspective on the possibility of malpractice in Lloyds of London. It reflects the possibility that not all employees can be trusted to act in the best interests of the owners.

MacGregor, I with Tyler, R (1986) *The Enemies Within*, Collins, London. This is the story of the miners' strike in the British coalfields during 1984 and 1985 written from the perspective of the Chairman of the then National Coal Board.

Mills, AJ and Murgatroyd, SJ (1991) *Organizational Rules*, Open University Press, Milton Keynes. This text introduces the existence of the formal and informal rule frameworks that guide much of the human activity within organizations.

Needle, D (2000) *Business in Context: An Introduction to Business and its Environment*. Thomson Learning, London. Provides an introductory text on what business is and how it functions within its ever changing environment.

Potter, J (1996) *Representing Reality*, Sage, London. This book provides a review of various constructionist views of scientific knowledge as well as providing examples from conversations and other interactions.

Turner, J (2002) *How to Study*, Sage, London. Provides a broad range of material and ideas on study at university level.

COMPANION WEBSITE

Online teaching and learning resources:

Visit the companion website for Organizational Behaviour and Management 3rd edition at: *http://www.thomsonlearning.co.uk/businessandmanagement/martin3* to find valuable further teaching and learning material:

For students:

- Interactive multiple choice questions to help you test your understanding of the chapter
- PowerPoint slides for use as an overview to each chapter and as a revision aid
- Extra case material
- Weblinks to all case companies and other relevant sources of information
- Online glossary to explain key terms
- Learning objectives and chapter summaries to help you check your understanding and progress

For lecturers:

- A password protected site with teaching material
- Instructor's Manual with teaching notes
- Model answers for selected questions
- Video sources to help bring a wider relevance to the classroom

Supplementary resources:

ExamView®:
This testbank and test generator provides more than a thousand different types of questions, allowing lecturers to create online, paper and local area network (LAN) tests. This CD-based product is only available from your Thomson sales representative.

Online Courses:
All of the supplementary web material is available in a format that is compatible with virtual learning environments such as Blackboard and WebCT. This version of the product is only available from your Thomson sales representative.

CHAPTER 2

Management and organizations – evolution and academic perspectives

LEARNING OBJECTIVES

After studying this chapter and working through the associated Management in Action panels, Employee Perspectives, Discussion Questions and Case Study, you should be able to:

- **Understand that there is no one perspective or model of organization, management or employee that totally explains these concepts.**
- **Discuss the significance of a historical perspective in developing an appreciation of modern organizations and management.**
- **Explain the significance of the scientific and administrative management approaches to managing an organization.**
- **Outline the relative contribution towards an understanding of management from each of the different perspectives described in this chapter.**
- **Appreciate that management theory is continually changing in the light of new research.**

INTRODUCTION

This chapter is intended to continue the introductory perspectives begun in Chapter 1. The purpose is to establish a historical and evolutionary perspective to the development of management and organizational theory. Organizations, the managers and employees working within them are not a new or recent phenomenon; they have all been around for many thousands of years. Many of the practices that we think of as modern and recent innovations have their origins far back in the mists of time. The purpose of this chapter is to introduce and reflect upon this perspective.

This chapter attempts to encourage you to reflect on where organizations and management originated from and by what routes they arrived at the present day practices that are taken for granted. In doing so, it is also possible to give due recognition to some of the considerable achievements from both the ancient and more recent past, together with the people who provided the theories and practices still in use today. Similar points can be made in relation to the research traditions that exist in relation to the study of organizations and management. Research into these topics has unfolded in many different directions and is a relatively recent phenomenon. Each academic approach claims to offer illuminating insights and a theoretical base for the understanding and practice of management and organizational functioning. Some of these traditions offer contradictory explanations and some seek to illuminate perspectives missing from other schools of thought. This chapter seeks to introduce the major academic disciplines and schools of thought that are active in this area, together with an indication of their history and particular focus on organizations and management. This review is necessary as the remainder of the book will draw on material from many of these disciplines in seeking to explore the topics under discussion.

EARLY ORGANIZATIONAL AND MANAGEMENT PRACTICE

Organizations have always existed in one form or another. When human beings began to develop collective activity as a means of improving their chances of survival and quality of life, the basis of the social organization was formed. This form of activity is still evident today in the many thousands of small family businesses (Bork, 1986). There is evidence of early forms of organization not based upon the family unit being used by the Sumerian people who settled around the River Euphrates approximately 3500 years BC (McKelvey, 1982). Of course, many organizations during that period continued to be family run. For example, the leadership of the state was based upon dynastic family groupings. By the time of the Roman Empire (around 300 BC) there was a significant banking and insurance industry in existence to support international trade and commerce.

The study of early management activity is difficult in that there are few specific writings or records that have survived. For example, archaeologists and historians still argue about how the pyramids in Egypt were actually constructed and so it is equally as difficult to understand how the work was organized and managed. Very often, the understanding of how management was practised in ancient times comes from scraps of writing about events, society or trade practices in general. It is therefore included either as an incidental description, or as part of the background for the main discussion. Management in ancient times does not seem to have commanded the special place in either academic or social circles that warrants the separate and detailed consideration evident today.

Most texts in the business field provide the distinct impression that management as an activity and topic of interest originated around the turn of the twentieth century with the emergence of FW Taylor and **scientific management**. While this may be true in terms of the volume of academic study and published work, it is far from the truth in terms of the practice of management. This section is therefore intended to provide a general and chronological introduction to the practice of management prior to the twentieth century.

Scientific management
The application of work study techniques to the design and organization of work in order to maximize output.

Management in the ancient world

The first point to be made in this section is that chronologically the ancient world covers many thousands of years and geographically the entire world. It embraces the evolving nature of society from the food-gathering Mesolithic family groupings, moving around with the seasons, to the great Roman Empire, covering much of the then known world. Parallel developments were also taking place in China, India and other parts of the world.

Even in those very early, and by today's standards primitive, days, knowledge and information passed between locations and civilizations. Trade and people movement was taking place in an increasingly sophisticated manner. With this movement, some cross-fertilization of thinking and ideas was inevitable. However, this was very limited by today's standards and probably occurred only across restricted geographical areas. In effect there was incremental development across time and space. Over the course of the generations covered by this section of this chapter it is possible to detect an ever-increasing complexity of organization (in both form and functioning) together with managerial practice. Much of this development would seem to be based upon trial and error methods driven by organizational need and previous failure, rather than theory development and formal training. Table 2.1 identifies some of the major developments identified during the ancient times covered by this discussion.

Approximate year	Individual or group	Contribution
5000 BC	Sumerians	Written documents, records, taxation
4000 BC	Egyptians	Planning, control, organizing
2600 BC	Egyptians	Decentralization
1800 BC	Babylonians	Business, law, minimum wage, responsibility
1600 BC	Egyptians	Centralization
1500 BC	Hebrews	Management by exception, chain of command
1100 BC	Chinese	Planning, organizing, directing, controlling
600 BC	Nebuchadnezzar	Production control and wage incentives
500 BC	Chinese	Job specialization
400 BC	Xenophon	Recognition of management as separate activity
175 BC	Cato	Job descriptions
900 BC	Alfarabi	Traits of leader
1100 BC	Ghazali	Traits of manager

TABLE 2.1 Selected management concepts in ancient times (*source*: George, CS (1972) *The History of Management Thought*, 2nd edn, Prentice Hall, Englewood Cliffs)

There are a number of striking elements incorporated into Table 2.1. Many of the contributions indicated in it would be familiar in management circles today. For example, the circular processes of centralization and decentralization undertaken by the Egyptians over some 600 years. This involved the system of government in the empire being decentralized and then becoming centralized again as the administrative weaknesses and consequent threats to the rulers were identified. The same cycle of centralization and decentralization is evident in many organizations in modern times.

The argument in relation to the existence of cycles of centralization and decentralization within an organization runs approximately thus. As a company grows in size from its very small beginnings, it tends to be organized in a centralized way, that is, under the close control of the central manager or perhaps a small team of managers. However, this eventually leads to slow decision making, high central administrative costs and lack of innovation in the sub-units of the company. Therefore, in response to this tendency to lethargy and high cost, a decentralization process begins in which freedom of action and responsibility for results is delegated down the organization to unit managers or section supervisors. However, over time this too begins to create problems in that duplication of effort can arise (every sub-unit lays claim to require its own accounting function in the search for better and more timely pricing and cost-control data for example). Restrictions in the ability to take advantage of opportunity because of the need to compete for resources with the other sub-units also arise.

In extreme circumstances, decentralization can lead to the break-up of the organization as managers seek to buy out their sub-units in the belief that they could do better as an independent company. As a consequence of the duplication of effort and lack of ability to tap into the opportunity for synergies within the organization cost begins to increase and the need for increased efficiency emerges and becomes ever stronger as leaner and fitter competitors gain advantage in the market place. Inevitably, the pressure to centralize grows in order to capture the benefits of administrative cost reduction and co-ordinated operational activity. Therefore, the cycle begins once again. This process has also been seen over recent years in the political sphere with the attempts to break up the Soviet Union, as the individual countries within it sought to become independent and therefore responsible for their own destiny.

The leaders in ancient Egypt recognized that neither centralization nor decentralization offers the perfect form of organization as they experienced the realities of running their vast country. It is a lesson that has had to be learned anew by every generation of managers since then. This perhaps justifies the view that humans learn very little from history. It is also justification in itself for looking back to see just how much progress has been made in understanding organizations and management practice across the centuries. Organizational control during the ancient world period tended to take the form of direct control of labour and the passing on of advice from father to son. For example, the Egyptians had laws preventing tradesmen from practising any trade other than that passed down by parents, or from engaging in political activity (Wilkinson, 1842).

It was recognized by the Babylonians by around 1800 BC that although work can be delegated, responsibility cannot. Contenau (1954) describes the building of a canal around that time in which it was made clear in a letter from the king that if the work was not acceptable the supervisor would be punished, not the workers. This is another aspect of ancient organizational life that finds many examples today. The captain of a ship is held responsible for any accident, even if he is not on the bridge at the time. However, it is a responsibility that many managers are not keen to accept. It is not uncommon to find that individual managers are very willing to accept responsibility when things go well and praise is being handed out, but they can be very quick to seek a scapegoat if something goes wrong! Management in Action 2.1 identifies a number of Babylonian management practices that retain a modern parallel.

MANAGEMENT IN ACTION 2.1 Babylonian management practice

The following extracts from the Code of Hammurabi, originating from around 1800 BC, demonstrate many management concepts as familiar today as they were at the time that they were written:

- Minimum wages:

  'If a man hires a field labourer, he shall pay him 8 gus of grain per year.'

- Control:

  'If a merchant give to an agent grain, wool, oil or goods of any kind which to trade, the agent shall write down the value and return the money to the merchant. The agent shall take a sealed receipt for the money, which he gives to the merchant. If the agent be careless and do not take a receipt for the money which he has given to his merchant the money not receipted for shall not be placed in his account.'

- Responsibility:

  'The mason who builds a house which falls down and kills the inmate shall be put to death.'

  'If a wine merchant allows riotous men to assemble in his house and does not expel them, he shall be killed.'

  'If a doctor operates on a wound with a copper lancet, and the patient dies, or on the eye of a gentleman who loses his eye in consequence, his hands shall be cut off.'

Adapted from: George, CS (1972) *The History of Management Thought*, 2nd edn, Prentice Hall, Englewood Cliffs.

Stop ↔ Consider

Compare and contrast the issues identified above with modern management practice. To what extent do you consider that the concepts and practices described are essentially the same across the centuries, but that it is the social context within which they are carried out that changes?
What does your answer to the previous question imply about the understanding and practice of management today?

The Confucian perspective in China emerged around 500 BC and produced a different basis for running organizations and society (see, for example, Chen, 1995). At about the same time Sun Tzu wrote a military textbook on the *Art of War*. It set out the basis of military campaigning and, in the process, identified many key management tactics. Described from a military perspective are issues such as planning, control, directing and military tactics intended to win battles. As a book it has recently been rediscovered and now appears in new translations and amplified form, Griffith (1971), Clavell (1983) and Wee (1991) being just some of them. There are even texts which bring together a number of the ancient military writings from China in an attempt to illustrate and understand what are thought to be different ways of thinking about leadership and management. (See, for example, *The Seven Military Classics of Ancient China*, Sawyer, 1993.) By about 1 AD it is thought that China had developed a factory-based system of production with departments reflecting the specialization of labour involved (Collons, 1971). Management in Action 2.2 illustrates a small range of Sun Tzu's ideas.

Ancient Greece and Rome saw yet more aspects of management develop that would be familiar in today's organizations. Socrates suggested, for example, that management skills were transferable between public and private sector organizations. The only difference, he claimed, being one of scale. Aristotle was also recorded as saying that before becoming a leader an individual should first learn how to take orders. In Rome there existed the regulation of many aspects of organizational activity to prevent a threat to the government's influence and control over society, as well as to

MANAGEMENT IN ACTION 2.2 Sun Tzu – The art of war or management

The following extracts reflect the views of a Chinese military leader writing about 500 BC:

- The establishment of an effective military leadership depends upon five *spheres*:
  1. Leadership – causes people to follow their superiors willingly; therefore, following them in death and in life, the people will not betray the leader.
  2. Cyclical natural occurrences – include yin and yang, cold and heat and the seasons and lunar periods.
  3. Geographic factors – the high and low, the wide and the narrow, the far and the near, the difficult and the easy, the lethal and the safe.
  4. Commandership – requires wisdom, credibility, benevolence, courage and discipline.
  5. Rules – are in regulations for mobilization, official duties and the management of material.
- All generals have to learn about these five spheres in their entirety. To know them is to be victorious, those who do not know them will fail.
- Each of the five spheres is evaluated through survey (research and planning).
- Military leaders who do not understand the five spheres and who do not heed the surveys will fail and should be dismissed.

It does not take much imagination to make the switch from the military leadership described above to the commercial practice of management. The need to understand and plan in relation to the market, customer needs, employee requirements and the use of rule and procedures to control the business are all as evident today as they were 2500 years ago. Equally, the need to train and evaluate leaders (managers) in relation to the role expected of them and to remove inefficient people are also described in graphic detail. It would appear from the translation used that Sun Tzu considers leadership and commandership to be related processes but consisting of different spheres. Perhaps similar to the distinctions between leadership and management as the terms would be used today.

Stop ↔ Consider

To what extent do you agree with the view expressed that leadership and commandership in ancient military times can be equated with the distinction in modern organizations between leadership and management?

protect the stability of society. These form part of the legal and organizational legacy handed down over the centuries. For example, the emergence of a joint stock company in which capital was raised from private individuals to make goods for sale was limited in size to that necessary to supply the government under a specific contract. However, the Roman government introduced several innovations that were beneficial to management activity. For example, the guaranteeing of weights and coins helped trade flourish (Wren, 1994). Slavery was a common form of employment in ancient time and is commonly regarded as an oppressive form of forced labour. Consider the following Employee Perspective (2.1) which suggests a different view by implying that some slaves had wealth and status.

Management in the medieval world

After the fall of Rome and during the 'Dark Ages' that followed there is little recorded material on the subject of management. Of the few sources available, two of the more notable are identified in Table 2.1, concerning the characteristics of leaders and managers in 900 and 1100 AD respectively. The Dark Ages are characterized as a period when feudalism was the predominant form of social organization with most

EMPLOYEE PERSPECTIVE 2.1 Slaves or masters?

Alberge (2003) describes a remarkable Roman find unearthed in the City of London during 1996. It was a wooden tablet that would have been covered in wax to enable a scribe to write on it with a metal stylus. The wax had long disappeared, but with the help of infrared imaging, the original words that had been inscribed in the wax could just be read. It was originally written between 80 and 120 AD and was a legal document setting out the terms under which one slave was arranging to buy another. The inscription reads:

> Vegetus, assistant slave of Montanus the slave of the August Emperor, has bought the girl Fortunata, by nationality a Diablintian [from near Jublains in France], for 600 denarii. She is warranted healthy and not liable to run away.

Given that the price paid for the girl was about twice the annual salary for a legionary soldier, Vegetus must have been a wealthy person, even though a slave.

Task

What might this suggest about the position, role and management of slaves in the Roman Empire?

people being forced into working on the land owned by other people. The tithe system forced a significant part of the production of agricultural labour to be used in support of the lifestyle for the church and secular rulers over some 400 years from about the time of the fall of the Roman Empire. A tithe is a form of taxation that requires a proportion of the goods made, cash earned, or food grown to be handed over to the feudal lord or local church.

With the fall of the Roman Empire the large organizations that had existed to facilitate trade disappeared. Smaller, more locally focused organizations emerged. During the Middle Ages the guild became a significant force in controlling organizational activity. Craftsmen from a particular trade would band together and regulate entry to that trade, the number of people allowed to practise the craft and other aspects of the work such as pricing. In that sense, they were the early forms of the trade unions and trade associations found today. Table 2.2 identifies some of the key contributions that occurred during what can loosely be described as the medieval period, which followed the Dark Ages.

Approximate year	Individual group	Contribution
1340	Venetians	Double-entry bookkeeping
1395	Francisco Di Marco	Cost accounting practice
1410	Soranzo Brothers	Journal entries and ledgers
1436	Venetians	Assembly line production techniques, inventory and cost control, personal management
1468	Friar Johannes Nider	Rules of Trade, business ethics
1500	Sir Thomas More	'Sin' of poor management, job specialization
1525	Machiavelli	Politics and power in achieving control, mass consent, leadership qualities

TABLE 2.2 Selected management concepts in the medieval period (*source*: George, CS (1972) *The History of Management Thought*, 2nd edn, Prentice Hall, Englewood Cliffs; and Wren, DA (1994) *The Evolution of Management Thought,* 4th edn, John Wiley, Chichester)

The Crusades from Europe began as a religious enterprise to retake Jerusalem, but they ended in failure. However, what did emerge was recognition of organizational differences between Europe and the Muslim-centred Middle East. There was also, in many ways, a grudging recognition of superiority in the ways of doing things in the Middle East. New trade routes and opportunities were also opened as a result of the two centuries of military activity in an attempt to achieve Christian dominance over that part of the world. In parallel with these activities, Marco Polo had been exploring the Far East, comprising China, India, Tibet and Burma. As well as the new trade routes that opened as a result of his travels, in the last years of the thirteenth century he brought back to Venice information on how organizations operated in the places to which he had travelled. For example, one piece of information that he provided was in relation to how the armies that he had seen were organized using the principle of a unit of ten at every reporting level. This created a workable hierarchy in which no manager needed to control and integrate the activities of more than ten subordinates.

Across Europe in the Middle Ages, trade was split into two broad categories of activity. There were the craft guilds, which were responsible for the manufacture of goods, and the merchant guilds, which were responsible for the sale and trade in goods. The craft guilds were the groups of people from a particular craft who organized the work and running of that craft in order to protect it from dilution or erosion. They determined the number of people who could practise a craft in a particular place, how many apprentices could be trained and the boundaries between crafts. The merchant guilds were the buyers and sellers who facilitated trade and production. They would buy raw material for sale to producers (both craft guilds and domestic producers) and they would then buy the finished goods for sale in markets both at home and abroad.

Domestic producers were the forerunners of the factory production system. They were based on a family unit and worked in their own home. Raw materials would be delivered to them, the family would produce goods from the material supplied (using their own tools) and the completed articles would be collected by the supplier when more raw material would be left. Typical examples of this type of work would be weaving and spinning. Domestic production is also known as outworking, putting-out or homeworking and is still found today. Addressing envelopes at home for mass mailing and advertising is one example.

The Venetians were well placed to take advantage of the opportunities for trade that became available in the Middle Ages. By the early 1300s a form of double-entry bookkeeping had been developed, which was published by Pacioli in 1494. The use of joint ventures and partnerships as a way of increasing capital and spreading risk also became widespread. The use of selling agents was common during this time. The process involved a merchant selling goods to an agent who had the rights to sell those goods to particular markets in return for either a share in the profit or, more latterly, a percentage of the value of the transaction (Lane, 1944).

Among the most fantastic aspects of Venetian management practice are those found in the records from the Arsenal of Venice. This was a government-owned shipyard, operational from about 1436. Its purpose was to build naval ships in order to protect the Venetian merchant fleet. Lane (1934) provides a detailed review of the running of the Arsenal and this is summarized in George (1972). The ships built were perhaps small by most standards. They were about 106 feet long and approximately 20 feet wide. Each ship was divided into three sections: fighting platform at the front, space for the oars down the middle and a command centre at the stern. The purpose of the Arsenal was not just to build the ships but to make arms and other military equipment, to store such equipment and ships until needed and to refit ships as necessary. To do so required a workforce of some 2000 people and a site of around 60 acres.

George (1972) identifies seven main points from the Lane (1934) text that are worthy of mention (pp 36–41). To this can be added the management requirements of the operation, making eight in all. They are as follows:

1. *Management.* The political and commercial importance of the Arsenal required that the state be involved in the management of it. In addition, the sheer size of the operation required a sophisticated form of management control. Many of the issues discussed in the following paragraphs form part of the management activities associated with the running of the shipyard. Three lords of the Arsenal, who reported to the commissioners – the link between the Arsenal as an operational unit and the Venetian Senate – officially headed the operation. Reporting to the lords of the Arsenal were the foremen and technical experts responsible for aspects of the production and design process. Among the specialist support functions available to the lords of the Arsenal were the bookkeepers and pages, who had the responsibility of creating and reconciling the financial aspects of the running of the shipyard.
2. *Warehousing.* Because of the need to be able to store and repair ships as well as build them it was necessary to have available a wide range of components that could be found and used at short notice. Components held in warehouses included rudders, benches, oars, pitch (for sealing joints in the wooden ships) and masts. These were held in specified quantities in specific locations so that they could be found, used and replaced quickly. It took several years to be able to introduce an equivalent system for raw material such as timber. This control of raw material became necessary because of the high cost involved in sorting through the vast stocks of timber scattered throughout the shipyard in order to find appropriate pieces.
3. *Assembly.* In order to be able to complete ships quickly a system of assembly line based production tasks were instituted. Ships in reserve were not held in a completed state but required the joints to be made watertight (caulking) and fitting out to be done. The hull of a ship, once in the water, was towed along a canal past warehouses which would pass over the designated components (oars, masts, stores, weapons, etc.) until at the end it was ready for active service. Management in Action 2.3 describes the report of one visitor in 1436 who saw at first hand the assembly line technique associated with the finishing of a galley. It was not unknown for important visitors to be treated to a spectacular event by having a ship 'built before their very eyes'. For example, Henry III of France visited Venice in 1574 and during dinner one evening saw a vessel built, finished and armed within one hour.
4. *People management.* A number of modern people management practices can be found in the records of the Arsenal of Venice. Recruitment was controlled in key crafts with admission tests being required before young people could become apprentice carpenters, for example. Wages and quality were also closely controlled in the manufacturing and assembly shops. Both piecework and day rates were used in appropriate situations. The making of oars was based on piecework with credit being given only for those finished pieces that were acceptable to the supervisor. Day wages (no bonus) were paid to those employees who could (or should) not be encouraged to produce faster – for example employees fitting exposed timbers to the hull. Each year a merit review of the master craftsmen was undertaken in order to evaluate performance and other contributions as the basis of wage determination and advancement. Starting and finishing times were also tightly managed as was the potential theft of timber or other useful components from the shipyard. Individual managers were able to delegate some of their duties (such as

MANAGEMENT IN ACTION 2.3 The Arsenal of Venice

The following quotation provides some insight into what must have been a truly magnificent sight. The clear description of an early assembly line in which the galley was towed past several work stations, each adding to the completion of the ship until by the end of the process it was ready to sail:

And as one enters the gate there is a great street on either hand with the sea in the middle, and on one side are windows opening out of the houses of the Arsenal, and the same on the other side, and out came the galley towed by a boat, and from the windows they handed out to them from one cordage, from another the bread, from another the arms, and from another the balistas and mortars, and so from all sides everything which was required, and when the galley had reached the end of the street all the men required were on board, together with the complement of oars, and she was equipped from end to end. In this manner there came out ten galleys, fully armed, between the hours of three and nine.

Written by Pero Tafur in 1436 after visiting the Arsenal. Taken from Lane, FC (1934) *Venetian Ships and Shipbuilders of the Renaissance* Johns Hopkins Press, Baltimore. *Quoted by*: George, CS (1972) *The History of Management Thought*, 2nd edn, Prentice Hall, Englewood Cliffs, pp 37–8.

Stop ↔ Consider

The assembly line approach to building ships must have been an impressive sight. Why then do you suppose that it was approximately another 450 years before Henry Ford developed the idea into the factory approach as we would recognize it today?

discipline and record keeping) so that they could concentrate on the major issues such as volume of production, cost and quality. Employees were also entitled to a number of wine breaks (5 or 6) each day in order to allow some recovery of energy and to maintain productivity.

5. *Standardization*. In order to be able to mass-produce anything a high degree of standardization is required. The Venetians recognized this and decreed that aspects of the design and manufacture of ships should be capable of standardization. The stern of each ship was to be identical so that rudders could be mass produced and fitted with ease to any ship, without the need for customization. Deck fittings and rigging was also to be standardized in order to allow uniformity and pre-manufacture of appropriate components, ropeworks, sails and other parts. Bows were to be of a standard design and size so that all arrows would fit them. This created the first true fleet rather than a collection of individual ships sailing as a fleet.
6. *Accounting*. The control of the operation required a strict accounting of the money involved in building the ships. This involved an accounting of money, material and time. By 1370 the accounts comprised two journals and one ledger. One journal was kept by the lord of the Arsenal responsible for cash transactions. The chief accountant kept a ledger from a journal produced by his deputy. At frequent intervals the journal kept by the lord of the Arsenal responsible for cash transactions was reconciled against the ledger produced by the chief accountant. Every year the account books were balanced and sent to the treasurer's office for storage and audit. Several accounting innovations were introduced over the years. For example, the notion of splitting accounts into fixed expenses, variable expenses and extraordinary expenses was introduced during 1564.

7. *Inventory control.* There were a number of inventory control procedures implemented within the Arsenal. Some have already been implied in that effective warehousing required a system that recorded the number and location of items. In addition, the control of inventory requires the recording of withdrawals and of quality. The quality and quantity of raw material and purchased components arriving at the Arsenal was checked by inspectors who reported back to the lords of the Arsenal on how actual arrivals compared with purchase intentions. These same inspectors were also responsible for inspecting finished goods to ensure that they were of an acceptable standard. Goods leaving the Arsenal were the responsibility of doorkeepers whose duties were to prevent anything leaving without proper authorization.
8. *Cost control.* It became apparent to the managers of the Arsenal that not all aspects of the operation were as tightly controlled as others. For example, the cost of finding an appropriate log was found to be three times as expensive as the log itself was worth. This formed the basis of a management initiative to improve the ability of the shipyard to store, retrieve and process wood. Piles of wood had to rummaged through before appropriate pieces could be found. The wood itself was also left lying around the shipyard, getting in the way of smooth operations. Stacks of timber even had to be moved from the slipways before ships could be launched. This illustrates an early example of problem solving through the application of cost control techniques.

The name Machiavelli is synonymous with the mischief and evil doings of people in power, or those intent on achieving it. The truth about him is, as is ever the case, more complex. For example, in a recent review of his life and work De Grazia (1989) finds him to be a character in search of how to justify to both the leader and the led the need for a new statecraft in the rapidly changing world of the late 1400s. George (1972), quoting from the first edition of Jay (1967) identifies four main themes identified by Machiavelli (pp 45–46):

1. *Mass consent.* Machiavelli recognized that ultimately power rested with the masses. Princes, kings and other leaders may enforce their own will on the people for a while, but if they are to achieve effective control, the masses must support them. This is a very early expression of the acceptance theory of power. In practice, power flows from the bottom up, not from the top down. Managers who lose the confidence and active support of their subordinates find themselves in a very difficult position. It is almost impossible to achieve any reasonable level of efficiency or effectiveness under such circumstances. The subordinates inevitably adopt an instrumental approach to their work and minimize the contribution that they make. He went so far as to suggest that given a choice of acceding to power through the support of the people or through the nobles, a prince should always choose the support of the people.
2. *Cohesiveness.* There exists an organizational and state need for unified operations and continuity of management and government. Machiavelli argues that a prince should 'manage' his subordinates and friends in a positive way in order to retain their support in running the organization or state. This can be interpreted as a form of manipulation in seeking to exercise control over those governed. It was the job of the prince to provide clear leadership and guidance in letting everyone know what policies, laws and practices were to be followed. A lack of clarity in these matters would lead to demoralization and lack of control.
3. *Leadership.* Machiavelli recognized two forms of leader. The first was a natural leader who enjoyed an instinctive ability to rule and exercise control. The

other type of leader had to learn the skills necessary to undertake their duties effectively. There are several characteristics of good leadership identified by Machiavelli, including the need to mix with subordinates, but not to the extent of losing dignity or compromising authority. Another area of advice offered is in the use of incentives to encourage citizens to contribute to society to the maximum extent possible in terms of skill and ability. An effective leader should also be adaptable, being sensitive to the changing moods and wishes of the people and society.

4. *Survival.* Every organization, be it state, church, department of state or commercial organization, appears to have an inbuilt desire to survive. In this context, the end justifies the means. A leader has a duty to ensure the survival of state and as such has the responsibility to seek out and deal decisively with all threats to it. Similarly, a manager has a duty to ensure the survival of the organization for which they have responsibility.

Although Machiavelli was writing about the affairs of state and of the tasks of rulers in the political context, his ideas have many parallels in the commercial world of management. It was, however, later generations who identified the similarities between the task of running a country and that of running a business.

Management during the Industrial Revolution

The emergence of Protestantism as conceived by such individuals as Luther and Calvin created a new situation in which it was possible for scientific enquiry to flourish. It has been argued by writers such as Weber (1905) that it was the possibilities that became available during the Reformation that allowed the emergence of the Protestant work ethic and so encouraged the rapid development of capitalism. Equally, his critics have argued the opposite, that capitalism was the creator of Protestantism (Tawney, 1926). Mastenbroek (1996) reviews features of organizational and management evolution around this period that ignore the religious aspect altogether. He emphasizes the developments between the networks of relationship in the social context, and the need to solve particular organizational problems.

The essential line of argument in support of the Protestant work ethic was the rejection of the Roman Catholic Church's insistence on subsistence standards of living and aspiration to the monastic style of life. This was replaced by the Protestant notion of stewardship and responsibility for maximizing the contribution from each individual and unit of resource. This, it was argued, provided the basis for the development of the capitalist ideology and form of organization. Each Protestant had a moral and God-given responsibility to work hard in the pursuit of maximizing their skill and return on capital employed, whether that capital be money, skill or some other resource. The counter-argument was that capitalism had already emerged before the Reformation and that having done so it laid the groundwork for individuals across Europe to seek to change the dominant religious beliefs to those supportive of the emerging commercial reality.

Whatever the truth, the emergence of the Protestant religions paved the way for a number of other changes over time. For example, Locke writing about political theory in 1690 provided part of the intellectual basis of the later civil revolution in England. This provided a basis for many other writers, most notably Adam Smith who published *Wealth of Nations* in 1776. This work argued that the 'invisible hand of the market' ultimately determined the most efficient utilization of resources. The application of self-interest at a personal level produced a situation (multiplied by the number of people exercising that right) in which everyone gained as resources would automatically follow higher prices and better rewards. Smith recognized the benefits of allowing the free market to determine economic and business activity, but he also recognized some of the potential problems. Part of his approach was to encourage the specialization of work, while recognizing that taken to extreme and for too long it would have a deleterious effect on the worker.

The use of forced labour in various forms was prevalent prior to the Industrial Revolution. The use of slavery and forms of compulsory labour on behalf of a feudal lord such as the practice of serf labour in England has been common across much of history and in most parts of the world. Even during the Industrial Revolution slavery managed to continue in the deep south of the United States of America until the mid-1800s. However, forced labour has still not been completely eliminated in all its forms and has recently been identified by the International Labour Organization to exist even now in parts of the modern economies of India, Pakistan and Peru (reported in Nolan, 1999).

Up to the beginning of the 1700s, the guild system had been the predominant system of manufacturing, supported by the domestic production of the goods and food necessary for personal use. The development of the putting-out system was introduced prior to the Industrial Revolution as another way of producing goods for sale. It required families to use their own equipment, tools and skill to work on components provided to them by manufacturer and merchants who then paid for the completed work when it was collected. While such practices were attractive, they also had many drawbacks. Quality control was difficult, as the agent had no direct control over the way the work was undertaken and only saw the finished products. Equally, agents could not control the pace of work as the piecework based payment system encouraged the family to fit such jobs around other work. Unless the agent provided the tools and equipment, there was also considerable variation in the ways in which the work was undertaken and hence standards of completed work. As the workers were very vulnerable to price fixing by the agent, it was also common to find the theft of components from one agent, in order to sell them to another in order to gain a better income. This created a perceived need for tighter control of operational activity (including people) and encouraged the introduction of factory-based production.

The development of factory-based production became possible through engineering developments and the invention of new machinery. The emergence of the factory system during the Industrial Revolution again changed the nature of organizational activity. Large-scale factory-based production became the normal working experience for many people. The creation of factory-based systems of production required different types of jobs to be designed in order to capture higher and more consistent productivity and quality from the workers. It also led to the development of new forms of hierarchical management practice and the creation of new technical specialisms. This approach formed the basis for most modern large-scale organizations. Table 2.3 identifies some of the leading contributions made in the management and organizational areas from the late 1700s to mid-1800s.

Wren (1994) brings together a number of sources and identifies various problems that arose in the early factory system and which had not been encountered previously. They were:

- *Suitable labour*. With the introduction of the factory system, it was necessary to find appropriate labour to operate the machinery and prepared to adopt the regulated working practices to obtain the best return from the investment. This was not easy as many people were drifting into the cities from the rural areas and found it difficult to adjust to the new ways of life. Many skilled workers were not prepared to give up their craft and guild-based work security for employment in a factory. Factory employment inevitably required the worker to engage in a narrow range of tasks repeated at high frequency over long periods

Approximate year	Individual group	Contribution
1767	Sir James Stewart	Source of authority and impact of automation
1776	Adam Smith	*Wealth of Nations*, specialization, control
1799	Eli Witney	Scientific method, quality control, span of management
1800	James Watt	Standard operating procedures
	Matthew Boulton	Planning, work methods, incentive wages
1810	Robert Owen	Personnel management, training, workers' housing
1820	James Mill	Human movement at work
1832	Charles Babbage	Scientific approach to work organization
1835	Marshall Laughlin	Relative importance of management aspects of work

TABLE 2.3 Selected management concepts from the Industrial Revolution (*source*: George, CS (1972) *The History of Management Thought*, 2nd edn, Prentice Hall, Englewood Cliffs)

of time and under close supervision when compared with the worker's previous experience. With the development of new machinery came the need for new skills and these were inevitably in short supply. Those with scarce skills could easily transfer allegiances to other employers for higher wages or better conditions. In short, it was a period with unstable workforce conditions in which there was considerable social as well as employment-based change.

- *Training*. Having obtained workers the employer was faced with the problem of how to ensure that they did the necessary jobs. This created a training need of considerable proportion. Education levels were relatively poor and engineering skills were in short supply. Even within the factory it was difficult for managers to achieve the consistency of work necessary for mass production operations. In small workshops or individual craft-based work, individualism had been acceptable, indeed something to be encouraged. However, in a factory in which standardization and uniformity are essential ingredients in being able to mass-produce goods to an acceptable and identical quality this poses severe difficulty. Employers found it necessary to begin to educate employees in the very basic mathematical and reading skills necessary to interpret orders and drawings. The application of job simplification to create specialized work activities was also used to simplify and reduce the job instruction needed.
- *Discipline and motivation*. For workers unused to the routines demanded of factory-based operations the strictures of regular attendance and controlled work activity came very hard. Absence was a regular feature of the work pattern of many employees as they sought to exercise some degree of control over their lives by taking time off work to celebrate holidays and feast days. Employers attempted to counter this by institutionalizing holidays and by offering company outings and feast days.

  Sabotage was another common problem in factory operations. Employees would smash a piece of machinery in response to attempts to increase the rate of production or the introduction of more efficient work practices. The Luddite movement came to epitomize these machinery-destroying episodes, as it was thought that new equipment would be the cause of unemployment. The cause of these events appears to be many and varied, not always linked to the introduction of new equipment. It is also apparent that there was not a single movement of Luddites but isolated and separate incidents that have been linked together under a common title. Several episodes of Luddite behaviour resulted in the perpetrators being hanged for murder around 1812. It is hardly surprising that it soon died out for lack of any leadership prepared to organize a systematic revolt.

Motivation appears to have been based upon three broad categories of activity (much as today). The first represents the use of positive reinforcement and inducement to encourage particular behaviours (the so-called carrot approach). The second involves the opposite approach – the stick is applied if something undesirable occurs. This is intended to reduce the likelihood of something happening as a result of the application of punishment. The third approach involved the attempt to win over the hearts and minds of employees so that they supported the aims and objectives of management. This approach attempts to internalize management values in the minds of employees so that they adopt a management preferred perspective towards their work. The use of various incentive options in support of these approaches appears to have been common across many factories. Piecework plans to encourage higher output, corporal punishment of child labour and fines for adults appears to have been widespread. In seeking to change the moral ethos of workers, the call to regular church attendance and to avoid the pitfalls of drink etc. appeared regularly.

- *Management*. The introduction of new factory methods of work created a need for a new breed of worker – the manager. The ability of the owner of a business to manage directly every aspect of it became less viable as the Industrial Revolution progressed. The scale of operations as well as the complexity involved required the delegation of part of the responsibility for managing a factory to other specialists. Wren (1994, p 45) suggests that the people appointed to these positions were generally illiterate workers who demonstrated a high degree of loyalty and ability to perform the job for which they were to be responsible. Pay was not much better than it was for the workers and the motivation in seeking out such positions was the opportunity to exercise nepotism in recruiting family members and thus enhance their own standard of living. Owners tended to employ family members in positions of power, presumably based on trustworthiness, protecting the family fortune and to develop business expertise for future generations of owner.

There were few opportunities to learn about management from books, even if people in the target market could read, and so experience tended to be handed down from person to person within a very restricted number of people. Problems tended to be relatively unique and so there was little by way of precedent to help solve them. So it was a time of experiment, effectively, making it up as they went along. A man called Montgomery produced the first guides to management for the spinning trades in about 1832. So much was he in demand that he moved to USA and was able to undertake a comparison between British and American management practices which was published in 1840.

With the generally improving standards of education and organizational practice, the standard of manager began to rise during the Industrial Revolution and it became easier to find suitable candidates prepared to take up the challenge. George (1972) describes in some detail an early factory operation in 1800, which demonstrates that the foregoing discussion of factory operations was by no means universal. Originally established by James Watt and Matthew Boulton to make steam engines in Soho, in

MANAGEMENT IN ACTION 2.4 The Soho Foundry

The Soho Foundry was among the first major applications of scientific management in England. It took place about 100 years before Taylor began his work in America. The factory began operations to make the steam engines designed by James Watt and by 1800 it had been taken over by the sons of the two founders. Expansion of the business inevitably required larger factory premises and considerable effort went into its development. Among the ideas incorporated into the new factory were:

- Product forecasting and production planning. Sales intelligence was systematically gathered both at home and abroad so that production plans could be made.
- Machine speeds were calculated and systematically varied according to the job being performed.
- Production processes were broken down into small parts and specialization of components introduced as well as job specialization among workers.
- A mixture of piecework and day rates was used as appropriate to the type of work involved. The use of standard job times was introduced as the basis of output evaluation.
- Entertainment was provided for employees on special occasions. Christmas gifts were given to workers and their families. Wage rises were also applied at Christmas time.
- Housing was provided for workers and considered as part of their wage.
- Overtime wages were paid for excess hours worked each day. Working conditions were considerably improved by such initiatives as frequent painting of the walls to make the foundry clean and pleasant to work in.
- The company also set up a Mutual Assurance Society – a form of insurance scheme for the workers – largely administered by the workers.

Adapted from: George, CS (1972) *The History of Management Thought*, 2nd edn, Prentice Hall, Englewood Cliffs, pp 59–62.

Stop ↔ Consider

To what extent might it be that the employment practices described were noteworthy because they were different from the norms of the time?

Might they have been introduced because they represent good practice or because they provided a benefit to managers by helping to motivate workers?

London, it provides a model example of its day in the application of planning, organizing, cost control, work-study and employee welfare programmes to achieve a factory-based production of steam engines. Management in Action 2.4 illustrates some of the initiatives adopted by Watt and Boulton.

Many other issues could be introduced in the discussion of the early factory system during the Industrial Revolution. The use of child and female labour, living conditions, education standards and the work of some of the pioneers of early human relations applications through the Quaker movement such as Rowntree and Cadbury, represent just some. However, space precludes consideration of the vast amount of social, economic and organizational material available.

Bureaucratic
An approach to organization which involves specialization of task, hierarchy of authority and decision making.

The **bureaucratic** approach to organizational activity began to emerge during this period as a result of the need to have large-scale administrative structures to run both commercial and public sector organizations. This was necessary in the days before computer technology. The bureaucratic form of organization began to be expensive to run, slow to respond and unable to meet the needs of customers effectively. Consequently, over recent years many organizations have developed alternative structural forms in an attempt to make themselves cheaper to run and more responsive to ever changing consumer demand. This process is creating circumstances that allow small organizations to flourish, as large companies outsource much of their activity (Wood, 1989).

STUDYING ORGANIZATIONS AND MANAGEMENT

The study of organizations

The study of organizations as institutions takes many different forms. Accountants, lawyers, economists, strategists, marketers, human resource specialists, operations managers are all disciplines that seek to offer some insight into the functioning of organizations. Sociologists, psychologists and critical thinkers from various traditions also have an interest in attempting to theorize about organizations. It is difficult to be specific when describing what defines the study of organizations; it means many different things depending upon who uses the phrase and for what purpose they use it.

However, simply because something is complex does not mean that it could not or should not be studied. Indeed, it is that very complexity that makes situations attractive from a research point of view. Thompson and McHugh (1995) provide a means of defining what they term as the mainstream and critical approaches to the development and interpretation of organizational theory. The main domain assumptions made in each tradition are identified in Table 2.4.

The assumptions identified in Table 2.4, from the mainstream approach to the study of organizations, emphasize a very rational view of the attribution of the qualities indicated. In short, they imply the application of the scientific method in the search for explanation and a science of organizations. The critical tradition, in contrast, requires approaches to the study of organizations to be:

- *Reflexive*. This implies that any approach to the study of organizations should attempt to ensure that the underlying values, practices, knowledge and expectations are not taken for granted.
- *Embedded*. This element insists that organizations need to be considered as part of a total environment. They are embedded in a context and that context needs to be understood and incorporated into any explanation.

Domain assumptions of mainstream approaches	Domain assumptions of critical approaches
Organizations as goal seekers	Reflexivity
Search for rational-efficiency-based order and hierarchy	The embeddedness of organizations Multidimensionality
Managerialism	Dialectics and contradiction
Search for organizational science	Social transformation

TABLE 2.4 Domain assumptions of the mainstream and critical approaches to the study of organizations (*source:* Thompson, P and McHugh, D (1995) *Work Organizations*, Macmillan, London)

- *Multi-dimensional*. The people dimension of an organization needs to be explained in terms of the multi-dimensional nature of human beings. Individual behaviour is formed in both a contextual and family setting, for example.
- *Dialectical and contradictory*. There are many inherently contradictory and inconsistent patterns of organizational functioning. For example, control of operational activity is a necessary aspect of managerial activity. However, this directly impacts on employee behaviour either in the form of work regulation or social control. In either case it is likely that employees will resist attempts to prescribe levels of control that they find unacceptable. This inevitably leads to attempts to increase the level of control and so a cycle of reciprocal behaviours is set up.
- *Socially transforming*. Critical theory seeks to empower all members of an organization. This notion, sometimes referred to as *praxis*, holds that individuals can be encouraged to see beyond the existing constraints and to be able to reflect on and engineer a reconstruction of their 'reality'.

The study of management

Prior to the twentieth century the management literature tended to be based around the writings of individuals who brought to the attention of a wider audience their own perspectives. For example, Babbage (1832), a mathematician by training, attempted to offer ideas on how to improve the efficiency of operational activity. One of the first teachers of management was Andrew Ure who taught in Glasgow in the early seventeenth century (Wren, 1987). However, it was not until the beginning of the twentieth century that the study of management began to feature systematically as a major activity in its own right.

Just as with the study of organizations described earlier the study of management can be broken down into two broad classification types. They are the mainstream perspectives and the critical perspectives (Alvesson and Willmott, 1996). Griffin (1993) identifies a number of what could be described as the mainstream perspectives to management theory as shown in Table 2.5.

Not every writer would agree with every entry in Table 2.5. For example, it could be argued that the inclusion of operations management is wrong because it represents a particular function within management – the management of production or service activities. Equally, some systems theorists would argue that they go beyond the mainstream perspective and attempt to incorporate a critical perspective into their work. Some (for example, Alvesson and Willmott, 1996, pp 10–11), argue that the mainstream perspectives are limited in their ability to offer a comprehensive explanation of management because they ascribe to it the qualities of a technical activity which underplays the social relations and political dimensions involved. They describe the critical perspective on the study of management as incorporating the following characteristics (pp 38 and 39):

- *Management is a social practice*. The evolution of management reflects a practice that emerged within a social, historical and cultural context. It cannot be separated from that context if it is to be understood properly.
- *Tensions exist in management practice*. The experienced reality of management as a political and social process is different from that postulated in the mainstream perspectives as a rational process seeking to apply impartial and scientific techniques to the problems of managing.

- *Critical studies are themselves embedded.* Although critical studies attempt to acknowledge the existence of the tensions inherent in management, they are themselves embedded in a particular context. Consequently, they need to incorporate a measure of reflexivity in them.
- *Critical studies seek to illuminate and transform power relations.* Critical studies attempt to transform the practice of management as well as illuminate it.
- *Critical theory contains an emancipatory intent.* One of the purposes of critical theory is to provide a basis for individuals within organizations to become free from the constrictions implicit in mainstream views.
- *Critical analysis is concerned with the critique of ideology.* It is implied that modern forms of control and domination are maintained through the theories and ideologies that underpin and inform the running of society and organizations. The questioning of received wisdom on how things should be provides a basis for liberation and emancipation.

Classical perspectives

- Scientific management. Concerned with the systematic evaluation of work and the search for higher productivity
- Administrative management. A forerunner of the systems approach, attempting to identify ways of managing the whole organization

Behavioural perspectives

- Human relations. An approach to management based upon the importance of groups and the social context
- Organizational behaviour. A holistic approach to managing organizations incorporating individual, group and organizational processes

Quantitative perspectives

- Management science. The development of mathematical models as the basis of decision making and problem solving
- Operations management. That areas of management attempting to produce the goods or services more effectively

Integrating perspectives

- Systems theory. A range of approaches to the study of organizations and management that attempt to cast these issues as an interrelated set of elements which are able to function as a whole
- Contingency theory. An approach which views the behaviour in any given context as a function of a wide set of contingent factors acting upon that situation

Contemporary

- Popularism. This reflects the wide variety of fads and fashions that gain rapid credence and just as quickly fade into obscurity. Only a few approaches in this category ever last longer than a few years or become a sustainable basis for actual managerial behaviour

TABLE 2.5 Mainstream management perspectives (*adapted from:* Griffin, RW (1993) *Management*, 4th edn, Houghton Mifflin, Boston, MA)

- *Critical theory implies more than a reconstruction of mainstream perspectives.* Critical thinkers seek to achieve fundamental change in the essentially power-based nature of management.

The study of management is a complex process and there are many different perspectives that could be adopted. Yet, for all the research that has been undertaken into management, we are no more able to practise it effectively than in years gone by. As Mant (1979) said: 'We do not, it seems to me, require one penny more spent on fundamental research into the "unknown", but to understand why we are so bad at putting to use what we already know' (p 207, quoted in Watson, 1994, p 11).

SCIENTIFIC AND ADMINISTRATIVE MANAGEMENT

Scientific management

The application of science to the running of organizations can be found in some of the very early sources identified in Tables 2.1, 2.2 and 2.3. The development of scientific management as an approach to the exercise of management is widely credited to FW Taylor (1911), who brought together several strands of thinking into a single methodology for applying scientific principles to the design and organization of work. The scientific management approach advocates the use of work-study techniques in the systematic investigation of work and the subsequent matching of worker to job requirements. The basis of this perspective had existed for many centuries in one form or another. For example, there is evidence of the use of time study to determine the length of time needed to undertake tasks within factory operations well before Taylor used it. Currie (1963) indicates that a Frenchman (Perronet) was using time study as early as 1760 to record the length of time needed to make pins. He also records the application of similar techniques in England around 1792.

The approach to scientific management as developed by Taylor involved the systematic identification of what each job involved in terms of the demands made on the individual worker. The design of appropriate tools and equipment, the selection and training of appropriate employees capable of doing the job, the encouragement of high productivity through the use of incentive-based wage structures and the appropriate management of work all followed from that start. Taylor began to apply his ideas on work that was routine and repetitive. The example always quoted is the loading of iron slabs that each weighed 92 pounds onto railroad trucks. This was carried out within the Bethlehem Iron Company, in which he had been employed to improve output. Through the systematic study of what was involved in the work, Taylor identified what he termed as the 'one best way' of performing the task. He then recruited men with the appropriate physical characteristics to undertake the heavy transportation task, taught them exactly what was required of them and paid them on a piecework basis. Piecework is an incentive wage system that pays a sum of money for each unit of output produced. The higher the output achieved, the higher the wage earned. By using this combination of factors, he was able to increase the daily output by a factor approaching 400 per cent.

There is also evidence that other people were interested in the application of work-study techniques at about the same time that Taylor was developing his ideas. For example, in England, Jevons (1888) describes the use of different sizes of spade for different material densities and the effects on worker effort, fatigue and productivity. Babbage (1832) also predates Taylor with many ideas on the application of systematic methods to understand work activities and the application of a strict division of labour, the use of incentive payments to encourage higher productivity and many other elements of scientific management.

There were many organizational and economic factors in the USA at the time that Taylor was working and which increased the impact of his ideas over those that had existed before. It is not possible to know just how much Taylor knew of the work of the other people who had been involved in early scientific management types of application. It is likely, however, that he was significantly influenced by Henry Towne, who in 1886 delivered a paper to the American Society of Engineers setting out his own approach to modern management within the Yale and Towne Manufacturing Company. Whatever the true extent of Taylor's use of other people's ideas he was keen to claim originality for his views. He was also responsible for making the most systematic and significant impact through the application of scientific management principles to industry.

It was an approach not without its critics and the strict application of its tenets was not possible in many situations. Industrial unrest and management hostility both conspired to undermine the basis of its potential contribution to what Taylor claimed was his intention – the creation of a more harmonious employment environment in which managers and workers co-operated in achieving mutual gain. However, press stories of the time suggested that high unemployment would follow the application of his ideas. A number of strikes followed the application of scientific management principles and it was eventually banned from use in the American defence industry during World War I. The following Employee Perspective (2.2) asks you to consider the employee view in this situation together with the management implications for today that arise from it.

It was left to the people who followed Taylor to develop his ideas and approaches so that implementation could be achieved. Names such as Gantt and Gilbreth are among the most famous who developed aspects of his work and formed the basis of much modern industrial engineering practice. Wheatcroft (2000) for example, provides a brief overview of the trends in scientific management practice during the twentieth century. Taylor's ideas also found support in the fledgling Soviet Union as the country sought to develop the centralized approach to the mass production of goods and utilities with little by way of skilled labour to call on. Scientific management is a topic that will reappear in several chapters of this book. It has obvious relevance to topics such as motivation, job design and management practice for example. Scientific management is also an area of interest for some economists, for example, Bruce and Nyland (2001) seek to explore the dominant approach to economics at the time that Taylor was developing his ideas together with the subsequent interaction between the two disciplines. Essentially, Taylor proposed a science of management based on empirical investigation rather than a reliance on 'rule of thumb' or tradition. This found favour

EMPLOYEE PERSPECTIVE 2.2

Being on strike against Scientific Management

Some of the workers employed under the scientific management approach went on strike against the application of Taylor's methods. Think about what that might mean to you personally if you had been a factory worker at that time and in that situation. You would have no wages or financial help from any source, and you may not ever get your job back.

Tasks

1. Why might you have taken such action, after all you could be financially better off as a consequence of the piecework payments that you could earn if you produced higher levels of output?
2. What lessons could be learned by modern managers from your answer to the previous task?

with the members of the institutionalist school who held misgivings about the deductivist method and *laissez-faire* underpinnings prevalent in economics of the time. Subsequently, Taylor, in collaboration with other economists, sought to better understand and manage issues such as the business cycle through empirical evaluation of problems such as stock control and stabilization of volatility.

Administrative management

Administrative management Considers management as a whole process aimed at running the organization.

Classical management theory An approach to structure based on the application of a number of principles regarding form and function.

Bureaucracy see Bureaucratic (p.52).

Human relations movement Originated from the work of Elton Mayo in recognizing the organizational significance of social groups and processes.

Another stream of thinking emphasized the view that management as an activity involved the undertaking of tasks relative to the running of the organization as a whole. Individuals such as Weber, Fayol and Barnard would be considered to fall within this general category. Many terms have been used to classify this approach to management thinking and the one preferred here is **administrative management**. The other major title used in this area is **classical management** both titles reflecting a view of what has been described as a traditional perspective on organizational functioning.

In combining the ideas of the three writers just indicated, there is no attempt to suggest that they collaborated with each other or that they were even aware of each other's work. They were in practice separated by time, language and location. The justification for grouping them together is that the ideas that they were discussing offer a broadly similar perspective on aspects of organizational activity. Weber was writing in Germany and publishing around 1905. Fayol was French and publishing around 1916, while Barnard was in America writing around 1938. The English translations of Weber and Fayol did not appear for many years after the original publication of their work. For example, Fayol did not appear in English until 1930 although it was not widely published until another translation appeared in 1948 (Wren, 1994, p 182).

The ideas developed by these writers are discussed in detail in subsequent chapters and so will not be covered in depth here. Weber's ideas on **bureaucracy** were developed at a time when size and complexity of organizations were increasing rapidly and there was no computer-based technology to assist with the routine processing of administrative work. Fayol identified functions such as planning, organizing and controlling associated with the management process. He also indicted 14 principles of management which, if applied in a common sense manner, could be beneficial to the managing activity. He also suggested that management could be taught in the classroom in order to improve the exercise of it in practice.

Barnard was a practising manager (like Taylor, Fayol and many of his predecessors) and his contribution to management and organizational thinking was to describe an organization as a co-operative system. In this view, he was hinting at much of what was to follow in the **human relations movement** in which the people aspects of the organization feature more strongly. It is also an early recognition of the systems view of organizational thinking in which the integrated nature of many aspects of organization and environment are postulated to form an integrated, interactive and mutually dependent entity.

THE HUMAN RELATIONS AND QUANTITATIVE SCHOOLS

There is a very strong emphasis on the task aspects of organizational functioning in much of the earlier work already discussed, particularly scientific management. In addition, there was the general unrest among workers and managers that followed from the attempts to direct and control work activity. It is hardly surprising, therefore, to find a counter-trend emerging. This developed with the human relations approach to understanding behaviour within an organization. Equally, the emphasis on the soft issues associated with people and work relationships was followed in time by the emergence of a hard approach based on numbers and data – the **quantitative school**.

Quantitative school
Uses mathematical models of the relationships between organizational variables so that causal relationships can be identified and predictions made.

The human relations school

Early research on the human relations aspects of work activity revolved around the nature of groups and the interactive functioning of group effort. There were two broadly parallel initiatives underway, one in England, the other in America. In England towards the end of World War I a series of studies was set up by the Industrial Fatigue Research Board into aspects of working conditions. One report from that research programme, published in 1928, identified the existence of a slight benefit when operatives worked in groups (Huczynski and Buchanan, 2001).

In America during 1921 a Christian-based church group held a conference on human relationships with a special reference to industry. This led to a research process involving the examination of the effects of groups in a work setting. Due to financial difficulties this work ended in 1933. At about the same time sociometry was developed (a mechanism for recording, analyzing and determining group composition and interaction) thus providing a research technique appropriate to group activity (Wren, 1994, p 276).

The Hawthorne Studies are widely claimed to be the forerunner of the human relations movement. But, as we have just seen, there were other research activities involving groups going on at around the same time. The Hawthorne Studies gained the widest recognition as the most significant research base on group activity within an organizational setting. The studies are discussed in greater detail in a number of later chapters and so will only be introduced here. They began in 1924 with the simple objective of discovering the effects of illumination on worker productivity and ended in 1933 with research output describing the importance of groups and group-based behaviour on activity at work. The Gillespie (1991) book identified in the Further Reading section in this chapter is strongly recommended as an authoritative source on both the research itself and the organizational, social and academic conditions under which it was undertaken. From a reading of this work, it is quite clear that it is difficult, if not impossible, to separate research and the interpretation of its output, from the organizational, social, political and personal surroundings in which it takes place. The following Employee Perspective (2.3) asks you to consider the relationship between a happy work-setting and productivity.

EMPLOYEE PERSPECTIVE 2.3 Good time workers

One of the challenges that some managers respond to is the desire to create a happy, fun and positive social context in the work-setting in the belief that a happy employee will be more productive.

Tasks

1. As an employee, what would make you happy at work all day every day? To what extent is this ever possible?
2. To what extent (and why) might it be possible to create such an enjoyable working environment that employees actually produce less output?
3. How might an effective balance between an enjoyable work experience and high productivity be achieved and maintained?

The results of the Hawthorne Studies were to fuel many other initiatives in an attempt to understand individual and group behaviour in an organizational setting. Developments in motivation theory and group dynamics are just two of the areas that emerged as a consequence of this work.

The quantitative school

The quantitative school approach attempted to define management problems in numbers terms and sought to find ways of modelling relationships so that causal relationships could be identified and predictions made. World War II provided a significant impetus to the development of this approach with the creation of many operations research techniques in Britain which spread to America shortly after the war. The military need to move vast quantities of people, equipment, military supplies, food, and clothing was a large-scale problem not encountered before. The development of mathematical models that allowed variables to be quantified and the relationships between them identified, helped to plan and execute these logistical necessities. The development of consulting practice as a means of adding to the problem-solving expertise and management capabilities of an organization became widespread during this period and the creation of operations research techniques further aided this development.

The techniques developed under the management science umbrella impacted significantly on issues such as quality, through the introduction of statistical process control methods. This allowed the establishment of systematic methods of measuring product quality and of identifying acceptance and rejection criteria for product management. Production planning techniques also emerged during this period as did forecasting methods and scenario planning. Scenario planning allowed the setting up of operational models that could have their parameters systematically varied in order to evaluate different decision options.

SYSTEMS APPROACHES TO MANAGEMENT

Systems approach to management
Systems contain strong self-regulation tendencies and can be separated from other systems by a boundary of some description.

The **systems approaches to management** developed from early work in the biological sciences. Boulding (1956) and von Bertalanffy (1968) introduced the phrase 'general systems theory' as part of the view that there were common characteristics of the systems that were found across all disciplines and that these systems contained strong self-regulation tendencies. In simple terms, a system is something that can be separated from other systems by a boundary of some description. It can be argued that the world is made up of hierarchies of interconnected sub-systems, systems and supra-systems. In management terms, this perspective was adapted by the 1960s to reflect the view that the earlier academic perspectives (scientific management, human relations school etc.) were lacking in not being able to offer comprehensive explanations of management and organizational phenomena. These limitations can be described as follows:

- *Scientific management*. Concentrated on the tasks necessary in pursuit of the objectives to be achieved and on how to control employee activity within that process. As such it ignored the social and organizational factors associated with work and the people employed within it.
- *Administrative management*. Emphasized the structure and design of organizations together with the needs of the management process in running them. It generally ignored the worker, job and task aspects of organizational activity.

- *Human relations school*. This concentrated on the people aspects of work, the social conditions under which it was undertaken and the group dynamics involved. It paid scant attention to the organizational aspects relevant to work or the job design and environmental circumstances surrounding the work. It also ignored the technological and economic issues surrounding work and organizational functioning.

The systems approach led to a recognition of the existence of a continuum of complexity in systems development, from the very simple biological organisms through to complex social systems such as an organization. The approaches adopted attempted to capture an understanding of the breadth of factors and influences impacting upon the system under enquiry. These included aspects of the environment with which a system needed to interact in order to survive. This led to the description of an organization as an **open system** (see Figure 2.1). In this context, an open system is one that is integral to and dependent upon the environment of which it is part. This conception of an organization implies that it is not just a collection of individuals or groups that meet together for particular purposes. It is a social structure that is part of the environment around it and that needs the environment as both recipient of output and provider of input.

Open system
Representation of an organization existing within an interactive environment producing outputs from inputs.

There are several systems approaches to management and some of the ideas originated from studies during the 1940s on coal-mining practices in England. Originally coal mining was a team-based activity in which groups of men would share the work and arrange the rewards accordingly. With the introduction of coal-cutting technology productivity improvements were possible but the consequence was a fundamental change to the existing working practices. Miners became tied to specific mechanically paced jobs and less opportunity for social interaction existed. Increased accident and absence rates resulted and these became a focus for study. As a consequence, Trist and Bamforth (1951) described the socio-technical nature of effective job design. In this approach, the social as well as the technical aspects surrounding the work were combined into the design of the work activities. In turn this formed an early stimulus to the further development of the systems approaches to management and work organization. For a more detailed review of the origins and philosophy associated with systems thinking see, for example, Stacey *et al.* (2000).

One of the difficulties in attempting to apply systems ideas to organizational and management issues is in defining the system under investigation. A system is

FIGURE 2.1

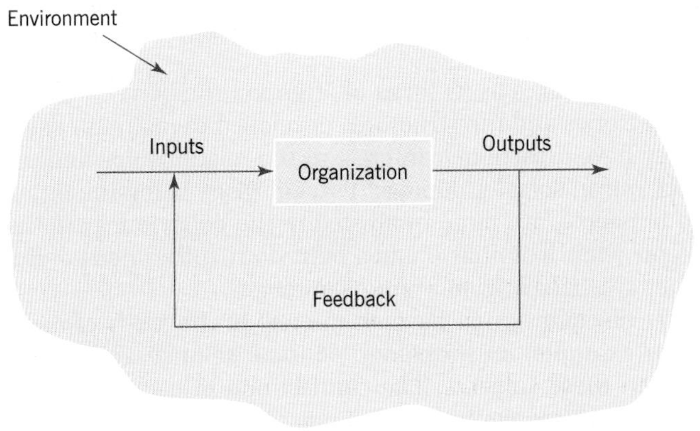

Open systems model of an organization

composed of many subsystems and is itself part of a larger system. Consider, for example, a school class. It is probably made up of family and friendship groups, teacher and pupil groups and ability groups. However, it is also part of a school, which in turn is part of the education system and a town and a country, and so on. Therefore, a network of systems exists in an exceedingly complex interactive and mutually dependent set of relationships.

In addition, the environment is also very difficult to define in relation to any system. Consider the school class just introduced. The environment consists of family members, friends, other classes, teachers, educationalists, employers, government officials (national and local), building and equipment suppliers, taxpayers, media providers, authors and so on. The short answer is that a system and its environment can only be defined in the particular circumstances in which it is being considered. There is not just one system or environment in existence in any specific context. As an approach this has both advantages and disadvantages. It avoids the problems of generalizing and it allows a personalized approach to particular situations. Nevertheless, by way of contrast, it makes communication difficult as it is not possible to offer general observations and can therefore sound trite and crass when attempting to suggest that everything depends upon the circumstances!

This foregoing discussion could imply the existence of a considerable degree of uncertainty and ambiguity within the systems approaches. They frequently claim to offer an emancipatory perspective to analysis and decision making through the involvement of stakeholders in creating an analysis of the system and the forces acting on it. It can, however, be argued that as an approach, systems thinking also provides a manipulative opportunity to managers. It is the people who define and control analysis about the systems in focus who are creating the reality within which others must function and these are, by definition, managers. Conversely, it can be argued that systems thinking is something that everyone can become involved in and that everyone can therefore assist in constructing the reality, analysis and the subsequent action plans. In the end it is managers who have most to gain from these interventions; they control the information, and the access to it that can create the reality understood as a system. Also, involvement can be used as a means of persuading (or forcing) employees towards a management determined agenda and viewpoint, thereby providing a means of control through absorption and reframing the reality within which employees work (Townley, 1994).

SOCIOLOGICAL AND OTHER PERSPECTIVES ON MANAGEMENT

As a discipline sociology takes as its focus of attention the behaviour and interactions between groups, societies and the structures developed to maintain control and order within them. They have a particular interest in the relationships and mechanisms of control and order within social groupings. Psychologists, being the other major discipline interested in people, are more interested in the behaviour patterns of individuals. They focus on what it is that creates behaviour differences among individual people even if they are 'behaving' in a group context.

There are other disciplines that have an interest in the study of management and organizations. For example, anthropology, political science and economics have a degree of interest in these subjects. The contribution of each of the disciplines can produce contradictory interpretations and perspectives on particular items of interest. For example, in studying management, the disciplines indicated might emphasize the following factors and influences:

- *Psychology*. The personality and other characteristics of effective leaders, their decision-making styles and communication patterns.
- *Sociology*. Sociologists might concentrate on the result of management decision making in terms of the impact on power and control relationships in the workplace. For example, the effects of technology on the reinforcement of managerial status in relation to subordinates. They might also analyze the structures and ideological basis of control mechanisms introduced by managers.
- *Political science*. Researchers from this background might take an interest in the strategies and tactics that managers and trade unions engage in as they attempt to achieve their objectives.
- *Anthropology*. These specialists might consider aspects of culture and how managers seek to create (or change) an organizational culture. They might also examine the symbols, roles and rituals that are used by managers to reinforce the cohesiveness of the organization.
- *Economics*. Economists have as their sphere of interest the working of the organization as a medium of exchange and of the application of market principles. They might well examine the efficiency of management decision making in terms of established economic theory and its possible impact on the future well-being of the organization. They would also take an interest in issues such as pay-bargaining strategies and outcomes, as well as product-pricing policies on profitability etc.

Each of these disciplines is offering a series of perspectives on the topics of organizations and management, and yet they do not, of themselves, provide a complete explanation. It was suggested in Chapter 1 that any individual's perspective offers only a restricted understanding of a particular focal object, an issue that will arise in every subsequent chapter of this book. The advantage of a sociological perspective to organization and management is that it introduces a critical perspective to the otherwise individual perspective of psychology. It considers the context in which the behaviour takes place, not just the behaviour itself. In reflecting upon the context, sociology takes account of the history of social organizations and of the structures of control under capitalism and other economic systems.

Marcuse (1964) provides a seminal work in the field of analyzing the unfolding of modern capitalist society and the implications for organizations and the people living in such a society. He demonstrates the possibility that the use of certain terminologies and practices associated with the concepts of 'freedom' and 'democracy' can, in reality, repress individuality and disguise exploitation. The changes in terminology from boss and owner to bureaucrat, manager and company hide the nature of the control of the working masses by masking domination and encouraging the creation of 'false needs'. These false needs would now be described as consumerism, reflecting products and services that are not essential for a decent life, yet are marketed (and sought after) as essential items and symbols of achievement and meaning. Employees therefore become trapped in a never-ending cycle of the need to work to earn the money to acquire the socially valued items offered by organizations seeking ever more opportunity to profit on behalf of capitalist owners.

In a much later work Reed (1989, Chapter 1), identifies three strands of sociological perspective on management that have evolved over the course of the twentieth century:

1. *Technical perspective.* A means-oriented approach to management in which it is regarded as a rationally designed 'tool' intended to achieve objectives through the co-ordination of social action.

2. *Political perspective.* Regards management as a social process intended to resolve conflict and difference between interest groups in order to allow the achievement of particular objectives.
3. *Critical perspective.* This approach regards management as a mechanism of control and domination. Management is the representative of the owner and as such is intended to achieve results beneficial to that group. It is therefore an instrument of the owners in pursuit of their interests.

NEW THINKING ABOUT ORGANIZATIONS AND MANAGEMENT

The application of the disciplines already introduced does not embrace every possible way of considering management and organizational issues. As Jacques (1996) points out there are no business problems in academic study and teaching, there are only finance problems, human resource management problems and organizational behaviour (OB) problems. However: 'Nobody in business has an OB problem. There is an OB aspect to every problem, but there is also an accounting aspect, a policy aspect and so forth' (p x). He then goes on to explain the realities of academic experience in creating the framework within which business and management is studied and taught, which at one point he describes as producing the 'emotionally laden fault lines in academia' (p xii).

Part of the reason behind the compartmentalization of the study of management and organizations is the need to teach the wealth of subject matter involved. Another represents the need to identify research issues that can be isolated and examined in detail. There is also an element of reflecting the largely functional arrangement of activity within the business world. People are originally trained as accountants or engineers etc. It is only much later in a career that someone will encounter responsibility for functions or areas of expertise other than the one for which they originally trained.

The growing recognition of the difficulties and relative artificiality created by compartmentalization has created a number of multidisciplinary initiatives in both business and academia. Within many large organizations the use of cross-functional project groups provides exposure to other ways of thinking and interpreting issues. At the university level and in terms of professional development there is usually some inclusion of modules in which the individual is exposed to other ways of thinking, interpreting and developing action plans. The use of multifunctional case study analysis would be one example of this approach. Compartmentalized surroundings lead to security in being able to develop a high degree of expertise and specialization in a relatively small area of knowledge. Emerging from this are the advantages (and disadvantages) of job specialization found in the job design options for any factory floor job. The advantages lie in the realms of productivity, skill level and training time. The disadvantages arise in the lack of ability to map research, knowledge and worker expertise onto the experience of real organizational functioning and associated human experience.

There are individuals and groups who recognize the relative limitations in the traditional way of constructing an understanding of management (and organizational theory). Jacques (1996), for example, sets out to describe and analyze the history of management in America using a variety of perspectives and seeks to evaluate it in historical and predictive terms. Thompson and McHugh (1995) provide an excellent review of the trends over recent years in theorizing about organizations and management (their Chapter 12) and in so doing recognize that the activities within the organization are carried out in a particular social context. Managers are free to shape their organizations in ways they feel necessary, but freedom in any context is restricted by any imposed conditions and the prevailing norms of the day.

Thompson and McHugh (1995) identify a number of themes across time that in part run parallel with each other. In doing so they identify a number of themes and approaches that will be dealt with either later in this chapter or elsewhere in the book. They introduce **modernism** and **postmodernism** as alternative formulations of social reality. Modernism is the representational aspects of the 'grand narrative, a coherent story about the development of the social and natural, revealed through the application of reason and science' (p 378). Postmodernists, in comparison, reject that cohesion, arguing that reality is made up of a differing range of realities and that it is constructed by our ability to express (or formulate) it. It is a view that holds that the 'truth is a product of language games' (p 379).

Watson (1994) argues that there will never be a single overall organization theory and that every practitioner, researcher, teacher and consultant will create their own, based upon a distillation of ideas from learning and experience. He goes on to suggest that the lack of a single theory does not mean that individuals cannot develop shared interpretative schemes containing common elements. Therefore, new ways of thinking and theorizing about organizations and management emerge as time goes by, based on critical evaluation of what is already understood, or taken for granted.

Modernism
An approach to management based on an understanding of the world through the application of reason and science.

Postmodernism
An approach to management based on reality being comprised of many different versions and the human expression of them.

Postmodernism

In attempting to understand organizations and provide theoretical frameworks many different approaches have been developed. These are inevitably given titles in an attempt to both differentiate them from other perspectives and to encapsulate some of the essence of the underlying thinking. Titles are simplifying devices, intended as a form of shorthand to compress meaning into bite-size chunks of information. For example, scientific management and **Fordism** are two terms used to describe approaches to organization that are based upon work fragmentation, de-skilling, machine-paced work and alienated labour. This level of categorization is rather specific but there are terms which attempt to stand further back from the specific. Carter and Jackson (1993) for example use the terms pre-modern, modern and postmodern to describe periods of trends in dominant approaches to what defines rational. The typical basis of organizational rationality in each epoch is identified in Table 2.6.

Fordism and post-Fordism
Refers to the way scientific management contributes to the running of organizations.

The general trend evident in the epochs identified in Table 2.6 is essentially one of an increasing reluctance to accept the given and assumed natural order of things, towards one of uncertainty and an acceptance of a rule-of-thumb rather than formula management. This is reminiscent of the point made by Watson (1994) indicated above.

These epochs or trends are intended to represent indications of how organizations function and how researchers theorize about them. Research as well as organization are integral parts of the broader social milieu and are as much influenced by,

Pre-modern	Modern	Postmodern
Diagnostic rationality based on theo-logic	Objective rationality based on scientific logic	Subjective rationality based on mytho-logic

TABLE 2.6 Epochs of organizational rationality (*source:* Carter, P and Jackson, N (1993) Modernism, postmodernism and motivation, or why expectancy theory failed to come up to expectation. In Hassard, J and Parker M (eds) *Postmodernism and Organizations*, Sage, London)

as influencing within it. Postmodernism, therefore, is meaningful in terms of its juxtaposition with modernism and it is useful to begin by attempting to provide an indication of the modernist view. Gergen (1992, p 211), identifies modernism as being characterized by:

- *Reason and observation*. The basis of understanding and survival emanate from an ability critically to observe, develop testable hypotheses and refine knowledge.
- *Fundamentalism*. That there are underlying principles and rules governing the universe and everything in it.
- *Universal design*. That there is a growing ability to master the universe through the identification of fundamental principles. Through this improved control will emerge better organizations, societies and standards of life.
- *Machine metaphor*. Take any machine and consider it as a system. It requires inputs of power and raw material, then transforms that input into some useful activity or product and spews out the end product (output) back into the environment. It also wastes some of the input during the process. Organizations can be described in similar terms, as can people. Therefore, if a machine system provides a useful model through which to represent other entities, this metaphor can be taken further and regarded as an essential building block of how things should be.

This rather simplistic view of the universe and how to discover it has been brought into question. For a number of writers the use of language to describe the observations from a modernist perspective became problematic. Even if the things being observed and described formed the basis of the essentials of the universe, the language used to articulate them did not. It is the actual pen that creates the writing not the term 'pen'. The term 'pen' conveys nothing about the nature of writing, communication or the intended purpose of the individuals involved. So if there is a distinction between thing and symbol, how accurate can the symbols be and how accurate can any inferences and conclusions that are based upon them be? Reality and the language used to construct it are, in effect, separate entities.

Hassard (1993) brings together the work of a number of writers in order to identify the distinguishing features of postmodernism as a basis for understanding management and organizations. They are:

- *Representation*. Rather than reflecting facts though language and forming ever clearer understandings, research is suggested to represent several different agendas. For example, it reflects the pre-existing knowledge base used to create understanding and it represents the professional standing of the people involved. Language represents social, political, personal, access/exclusion and control purposes as well as descriptive needs.
- *Reflexivity*. This requires a reflection on the assumptions made as part of the creation of knowledge. If language is not the slave of facts then its use must be questioned on every occasion.
- *Writing*. It could be assumed that language should be considered 'as a sign system for concepts which exist in the object world' (p 13). This is not so; postmodernism would see writing as a means by which the symbols of language can be separated from the objects themselves, yet remain linked through the spatial and temporal reality of experience for individual people.
- *Difference*. This concept is related to the need to both separate and join. In postmodernism it is necessary to deconstruct knowledge. In the foregoing discussion it is apparent that knowledge is constructed from the social context

and by the language used. In attempting to create real understanding it is first necessary to deconstruct these issues.

- *De-centring the subject.* Most of the knowledge created takes the individual as its basis and perspective. It is the human perspective and interpretation that contains the significant focal direction. That should not be the case, according to postmodernism. For example, sitting on the floor and looking at the world from a child's height would give the impression of a different world from that of the adult. Therefore, no one view has the claim to complete understanding of the world.

Using this thesis, postmodernism sets about questioning the place of reason and 'methodological unity' (Hassard, 1993, p 1). From its origins as a perspective on culture and art this approach has been used in an attempt to provide meaningful interpretation on organizations as they exist in real time and space. Postmodernism would suggest that it is only by exploring the paradoxes that exist that the otherwise hidden assumptions begin to emerge. It even makes an appearance in management science areas as writers such as Whalen and Samaddar (2001) suggest that developments in issues such as soft computing and knowledge management (in converting tacit knowledge to explicit knowledge for example) will significantly influence the research and practice of management science.

However, not everyone would support the basic approach suggested by postmodernism. It may be interesting to question rationality and to engage in deconstruction, but some experiences are very real, no matter how they are described. For example, as Tsoukas (1992, p 644) argues:

> It is because actions are not taken and voices not uttered in a vacuum that not all accounts are equally valid. No matter how much I shout at my bank manager he is not likely to lend me money if I am unemployed. This is not a figment of my imagination. Others also tell me they have had similar experience.

The point being that this experience is common to many people and that as part of organizational activity and the human experience it cannot be explained away as simply a figment of imagination or language symbolism.

LOOKING INTO THE 21ST CENTURY

It is notoriously difficult to predict the future. Opinions vary and estimates of what the future might hold can be overly optimistic or pessimistic. The history of organizations and management is littered with fads that were supposed to offer a universal panacea to revolutionize some aspect of business to the benefit of all concerned. Making the point that the shelf-life of fads seems to be getting shorter and shorter, Benjamin (2003) asks whether the trend in business trends is itself coming to an end? His conclusion is that there is no utopia in the basic business need to balance people, profits and technology in the search for maximal productivity, but that new ways (including revisiting old ways) of doing so constantly emerge.

One person's light-hearted view of what the future might be like for a board of directors in the not too distant future is outlined in Management in Action 2.5. Whilst this might be technically feasible, it is not very likely to occur in the timescale indicated. However, it does introduce the possibility of thinking just how different things might be over the next 100 years. The only thing that can be said with any certainty is that it will be different, just as how organizations and management function now is different to that common 100 years ago. However not everything is different today; there are

MANAGEMENT IN ACTION 2.5 Beam yourself up to the boardroom

The future of management is something that is of interest to many people, not least managers themselves. With the development of technology and globalization moving ahead at an ever faster pace it is possible to consider what might be available only a few short years from now. Lynn does just that in considering how a board of directors might operate in the year 2020.

The starting point for the review is to note that a board of directors still exists and has broadly the same responsibilities as today. It is largely the ways in which they function that change as well as the people themselves. For example, face-to-face meetings are rare, the virtual meeting house being the norm, based on the Internet ability to telecommute using electronic imaging. In the mythical company created by Lynn to illustrate his view of the future, the use of 'flesh time' (the term for a meeting between human beings actually in the same physical space) is regarded as an eccentricity by the young career executives and perhaps something that would be phased out. It is also regarded as a potential risk to the company as the need to travel across the world for meetings is dangerous as the volume of sky traffic is rocketing with the associated accident rate.

Equally, the need for 'real' meetings is unnecessary as at least one of the directors is said to be technically dead. However, the ability of computer systems to simulate a particular human being's thinking processes is used to retain the value of that particular individual for the board. Equally the company has been able to scale down much of its administration functions as a result of the opportunity to base itself on a space station out of earth orbit. Technically, therefore, it is not liable to the requirements of the earth's legal and taxation systems. One of the key items for discussion is the issue of the possible cloning of the group's star salesperson. Given that cloning becomes permissible under certain conditions, for example not being able to find an equivalent person without it, it is a viable option as a means of company growth.

Adapted from: Lynn, M (1999) Beam yourself up to the boardroom, *Management Today*, May, 61–5.

Stop ↔ Consider

How realistic is this view of the future of the board of directors?
Search out the article that it is based on and read the complete piece. Now formulate your own view of what the future might hold and compare it with the views of other students. Discuss the differences and similarities in each other's ideas, exploring the reasons for any variations. What does this tell you about the future of management?

still many similarities with organizational practice from the past, that much was identified earlier in this chapter. The question is how different will the future be?

One of the most common forms of picturing an organization is to use a triangle as a representation of the shape as in Figure 2.2. The chief executive is represented as the apex of the triangle with the departments and functions cascading down from that level to the lowest level of employees represented by the base of the triangle. The increasing width of the triangle as it goes from top to bottom represents the increasing number of employees at the lower levels. It represents the classic bureaucratic organizational form.

It is sometimes argued that the changes that are being experienced today and which it is predicted will continue in the future fundamentally challenge that traditional conception of an organization. Increased competition, customer expectation and the search for the high performance organization mean that it is necessary to reformulate the organization to capture and delight the customer in order to obtain and then retain their business. This leads to the traditional triangle being turned upside down, so implying that the front-line workers are the most important level (as they are then at the top) and that more senior team leaders and managers are there to support this front-line activity as in Figure 2.3.

The implied new responsibilities of the major levels within the upside down organization are indicated in Figure 2.3. However, much as Figure 2.3 might suggest that front-line workers are the most important level within the organization, managers retain their seniority and the traditional hierarchy usually remains intact. Consider for a moment the opportunity to gain promotion from front-line employee to team leader involving a demotion with less pay, status and authority as the reward. Not many people would seek promotion on that basis. Therefore, such representations inevitably do not mean what they could mean. At best, they reflect recognition that it is the front-line staff that meet and deal with customers; therefore they are fundamental to the continued success of the organization. Nevertheless, it does not mean that such realities fundamentally change the conventional hierarchy; it might adjust them slightly in the attempt to get closer to the customer, but not so much as to

FIGURE 2.2

The organizational pyramid

FIGURE 2.3

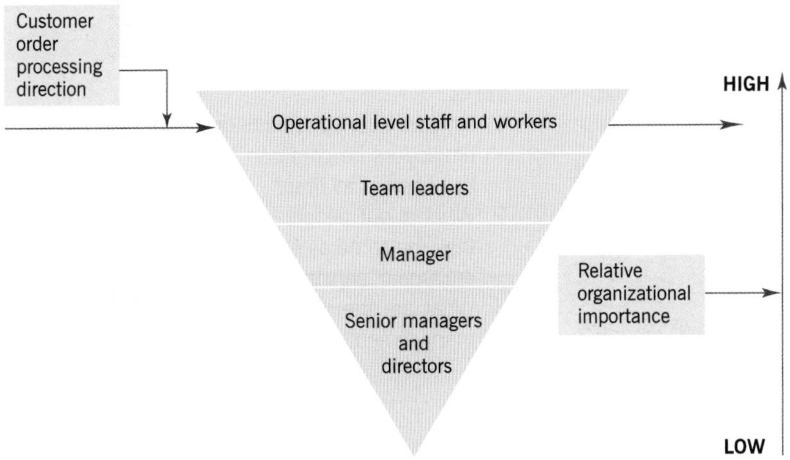

The upside-down pyramid of organizational functioning

change the dominant paradigm. It is in this context that Covey (2001) argues that the old command and control models of management must be replaced with leadership based on moral authority, if staff are to be guided in appropriate ways. So perhaps over the next century, more appropriate ways of leading and managing will be developed in the search for more appropriate organizational forms to enable employees to make the upside down triangle a reality.

There are a number of organizational forms that have emerged over recent years that seek to make use of the latest technology in finding ways of more effectively meeting customer needs in the evolving competitive environment. One of these is the **virtual organization**, in which a network or loose coalition of manufacturing and administrative services is formed using integrated computer and communications technology to link differing groups of personnel for a specific business purpose, disassembling when that purpose has been met, Wilson (1999). The point is made that such organizational arrangements require a shift in emphasis from audit and control to trust in employment relationships. Wilson goes on to argue that far from changing the nature of the management technologies, such innovations as the virtual organization actually produce an enhanced, more insidious form of technical and cultural control designed to engage the acquiescence of employees. The following Employee Perspective (2.4) introduces the notion of Generation X employees and their approach to work, and seeks to encourage a discussion about the implications of this within the totality of life.

Virtual organization
A metaphor for an organization that is capable of delivering more than its resources would allow.

Contrary to the optimistic view of employment presented through the Generation X perspective, some evidence suggests that many people leave school without achieving their potential or the objectives set for success in the educational system. For example, Thurow (1992) identifies that a significant number of high school graduates in America join the labour force with basic skill deficiencies in maths, writing and reasoning. This inevitably creates limitations for their job and career opportunities and places a burden on the organizations employing them. This is likely to have a significant impact on the future evolution of both organizations and management.

EMPLOYEE PERSPECTIVE 2.4 Generation X employees

Workers are also suggested to be changing as well as the organizations that employ them. For example, Generation X workers (born between the mid-1960s and the mid-1970s) were originally identified by Douglas Coupland and are said to be represented by the following:

> [They] do not appear to have any particular interest in climbing corporate ladders or in spending their careers in one type of work or job. Instead they want to explore and do different kinds of work in order to learn about themselves and to express their individual values ... [They] don't care about fancy titles, are unimpressed with the need to do specific tasks in specific ways merely because their boss wishes them to, and want their work to have meaning. (Brousseau and Driver, 1996, p 53)

Tasks

1. To what extent could the description of Generation X employees be common to some people in all locations across all time?
2. What about people born after the mid-1970s, are they the same as Generation X, or are they a different type of person? Why or why not?
3. What are the implications of your conclusions for management in the future?

CONCLUSIONS

This chapter has considered in some detail the historical origins of management. It briefly reviewed some of the major organizational themes emerging over many thousands of years, attempting to demonstrate that management has a much longer tradition than is frequently implied. This chapter also attempted to introduce some of the topics that will be considered in much greater detail later in this book and which form much of the substance of the organizational behaviour approach to the study of management and organizations.

Now to summarize this chapter in terms of the relevant Learning Objectives:

- **Understand that there is no one perspective or model of organization, management or employee that totally explains these concepts.** This chapter introduced a number of the academic traditions that seek to offer an understanding of employees, management and organization and which contribute to the study of organizational behaviour. This material has been presented in such a way as to demonstrate that each tradition and discipline can at best offer a partial understanding of the complexity that defines an organization and the people who work within them.
- **Discuss the significance of a historical perspective in developing an appreciation of modern organizations and management.** It is frequently assumed that management began with the work of FW Taylor in developing scientific management. Nothing could be further from the truth. Collective activity has existed for thousands of years, as has the practice of management and the function of being an employee. This chapter has set out to present a brief overview of some of these historical perspectives in order to establish that much of what we experience today has its origins far back in time. Also, it begins to be apparent when looking back in history, that many of the organizational problems evident today would be recognized by people from the past, albeit the social context and technology are different.
- **Explain the significance of the scientific and administrative management approaches to managing an organization.** These two traditions to the study and management of organizational activity emerged many years ago, and yet still find significant relevance today. As methods of managing and controlling the use of the labour resource within organizations, they emerged in particular social contexts and at a time when computer technology was unavailable to contribute to organizational processes. However, they have now become deeply ingrained into the philosophy of management and even changing social and technological conditions have not fundamentally replaced these perspectives. The Wilson (1999) paper referred to in the chapter makes the point that the basic tenets associated with scientific management have simply become more insidious in the application of virtual organizational frameworks.
- **Outline the relative contribution towards an understanding of management from each of the different perspectives described in this chapter.** Each of the academic traditions reviewed in this chapter has a slightly different perspective to offer on the sphere of interest that they embrace. These perspectives are not mutually exclusive or capable of offering indisputable truth about a particular theme. The inherent difficulty in seeking to explain fully individual human behaviour in a complex and dynamic social environment should be apparent from the material introduced in the first two chapters in this text. Each of the traditions reviewed offers some insight into the phenomena in focus and it is necessary to reflect on the positive and negative aspects of the various perspectives presented in order to formulate your own models and theories of what managing and working in an organization means. This reflects the point made by Watson (1994) earlier in this chapter.
- **Appreciate that management theory is continually changing in the light of new research.** The sections in this chapter that consider some of the more recent perspectives associated with management and organizational theory demonstrate clearly that new ideas are constantly being generated. Research is a never ending process, it involves revisiting old

ideas and exploring them in current situations, questioning the philosophical underpinnings of existing theory, and looking at social phenomena in new ways in order to better understand the processes involved. Usually it is not an explosive process of developing 'big bang' models; there is a considerable time lag between ideas being developed and them being published. There follows an iterative process of debate and discussion in the academic journals as the ideas are tested and challenged in order to refine them. This process can take many years, and old ideas long forgotten can suddenly resurface as researchers seek to further the knowledge available.

DISCUSSION QUESTIONS

1. Management is about managing in the present, within the constraints imposed by the past, whilst seeking to prepare for an unknowable future. It is therefore an impossible task. Discuss this statement.
2. To what extent and why might an improved historical understanding of management and organizations improve the performance of current practising managers?
3. 'The only thing that people learn from history is that people learn nothing from history.' To what extent does this statement explain why some of the management and organizational issues identified in history still have relevance today?
4. If research is a social process fixed in time and space by the prevailing beliefs and norms, can history ever be effectively understood and incorporated into a theoretical framework for modern management and organizations?
5. The ancient Egyptians learned by experience that neither centralization nor decentralization on its own allowed them to manage their empire effectively. To what extent can this knowledge help evaluate organization design today?
6. Is the functional approach to managing, teaching and research in the organizational field an effective option for preparing people to manage in the real world? Justify your answer.
7. To what extent does the postmodern perspective demonstrate that the notion of progress in society and organizations is an illusion?
8. Scientific management postulated that it was a management responsibility to identify the 'one best way' for the workers to undertake their tasks, and it was the employee's responsibility to follow the prescribed method of work. To what extent can this approach ever identify the most effective means of meeting customer needs?
9. The Human Relations School views the social context surrounding the work being done as very important in determining the results achieved by employees. Why might this be more important than how the work is carried out in determining the overall results achieved?
10. Reed (1989) identifies the Technical, Political and Critical perspectives to management. What are these perspectives and why are they significant in understanding what management is and how it is practised?

CASE STUDY To lie or not to lie, that is the question?

The company employed about 800 people and was a large engineering manufacturer based in the North of England. The products made were precision automotive components, used in top of the range motor vehicles, predominantly bought as company cars for senior managers. There was an economic recession at the time of the case study and so the market for large, expensive company cars was rather depressed with orders from the car makers having reduced significantly. It was not anticipated that the market conditions would improve for some time and so the company decided that it needed to reduce its workforce by about 15 per cent.

The company had a good reputation as an employer in the area and was well respected for the quality of its training of shop-floor workers and the generosity of its pay levels. There were no other employers in the area that required the same high standard of engineering skill that those working at the company possessed. Neither were the rates of pay as generous in other organizations. Being a caring employer the company proposed a voluntary severance scheme to the trade union representing the engineering workforce on the factory floor. This would provide volunteers leaving with double the financial compensation that the company were required to pay to them under employment legislation. One of the scheme conditions was that if enough volunteers to leave were not found then compulsory termination of employment would be implemented with only the statutory compensation being paid. This was intended to encourage more people to volunteer to leave and so avoid the need to dismiss people who did not want to leave. Management retained the right to refuse to accept any particular person volunteering, and to select any people for compulsory termination if it were needed. Of course the trade union had the right to be consulted and to make representations to management on the selection criteria and in seeking alternatives to compulsory termination of employment.

The voluntary scheme was agreed by the trade union and notices placed in the factory. These set out the basic terms of the scheme and asked people interested in applying to make informal enquires of the personnel manager before deciding whether to apply formally for voluntary termination. A steady stream of people made appointments to talk to the personnel manager about their circumstances, and to find out what the level of compensation would be in their particular situation. Behind the scenes line managers were making contingency plans to decide who they would dismiss should enough volunteers not be forthcoming. However, this process had to be secret as by law any possible compulsory terminations through redundancy must be discussed with the trade union before selection rules are developed and people are selected.

One of the longer serving employees made enquires of the personnel manager about their situation. However, they eventually decided that the money on offer was not enough to tempt them to apply for voluntary redundancy. The individual made the point to the personnel manager that they were not certain to get another job at their age (56 years old). Even if they could get another job, it would not provide the same level of income. Also with such long service at the company (40 years) they only had a few years to go until retirement and so would decline the offer and stay put. They also said that with such long service they would be very unlikely to be selected for compulsory termination within the present company. However, what the personnel manager knew, and the employee did not, was that the selection criteria for compulsory termination was going to be based on a range of work-based factors such as productivity, timekeeping, attendance, range of skills, etc. Even though the precise nature of the compulsory selection criteria would not be known until discussions were held between the company and trade union, the management had decided that contribution to the business in one form or another would be the only acceptable way forward. Also what the employee was not aware of, was that if it became necessary to compulsorily select employees, then his overall performance was such that he was definitely going to be selected, irrespective of his length of service.

The personnel manager explained to me that he felt very guilty about the position that this particular employee was in. In essence, the employee was turning down the offer to go voluntarily with a generous financial settlement, when it was certain that within a few weeks he would be compulsorily dismissed with about half of the financial compensation. The personnel manager could not make the position clear to the individual because of the legislative requirements, but could only gently encourage serious consideration of the terms offered through the voluntary scheme. After several attempts to encourage the employee to volunteer, he refused saying that he had always been happy at the company and the company would look after him in the future, until he retired. About three months later the employee was compulsorily made redundant and was personally devastated and left very bitter by the experience.

Tasks

1. Given that the example represents a real set of circumstances that occurred in one organization how might it be interpreted through each of the academic disciplines introduced in this chapter?
2. Is it acceptable to tell lies in this type of situation? Why or why not?
3. What would you have done had you been the personnel manager faced with that situation?
4. How might the study of organizational behaviour help you deal with such situations if you were the personnel manager?

FURTHER READING

Chen, M (1995) *Asian Management Systems* Routledge, London. This text considers the similarities and distinguishing features between the approaches to management in Chinese, Japanese and Korean businesses. As such it provides a balancing perspective with the Western-based views adopted by most textbooks.

Clark, H, Chandler, J and Barry, J (1994) *Organization and Identities: Text and Readings in Organizational Behaviour* International Thomson Business Press, London. Contains a broad range of original articles on relevant material themes and from significant writers referred to in this and other textbooks on management and organizations.

Clegg, SR (ed.) (2001) *Central Currents in Organization Studies 1, Volume 1, Historical Perspectives and Emergent Tensions. Volume 2, Laying the Theoretical Foundations.* Sage, London. Both volumes provide a detailed review of material relevant to this chapter.

Cooper, CL (ed.) (2002) *Fundamentals of Organizational Behaviour, Part 5, Methodologies in Objectives.* Sage, London. An academic review of the underlying perspectives on which much of the theory in this field is based.

Gillespie, R (1991) *Manufacturing Knowledge: A History of the Hawthorne Experiments*, Cambridge University Press, Cambridge. The Hawthorne Studies represent the most famous and often quoted large-scale research carried out this century. It began the human relations movement and spawned many later initiatives into worker motivation and group working. It therefore represents an important piece of management history. This book looks behind the scenes at the research process and critically examines it, bringing out a number of political and ideological features that shaped the conduct and interpretation of the research. It is therefore about the process of creating knowledge in the real world by real people.

Jones, G (1996) *The Evolution of International Business: An Introduction*, Routledge, London. Management is increasingly carried out in an international context. This text introduces readers to the study of how organizations have evolved internationally since the nineteenth century. As such it provides a background to the context within which management is carried out on an international scale.

Stewart, R and Barsoux, J-L (1994) *The Diversity of Management: Twelve Managers Talking*, Macmillan, Basingstoke. This book offers an interview-based perspective on what being a manager involves. As such it provides a perspective to be compared with the insights gained from theory development and other research approaches.

Watson, TJ (1994) *In Search of Management: Culture, Chaos and Control in Managerial Work*, Routledge, London. This book draws on participative research techniques to identify the reality of management in one organization. It reflects in depth how managers attempt to control their own lives while at the same time shaping the direction of organizational activity.

Wilson, JF (1995) *British Business History, 1720–1994*, Manchester University Press, Manchester. This text concentrates on the history of British manufacturing industry over the past three centuries. In this analysis the author argues that organizational culture is the most important component in business organization and management practice during that period.

COMPANION WEBSITE

Online teaching and learning resources:

Visit the companion website for Organizational Behaviour and Management 3rd edition at: *http://www.thomsonlearning.co.uk/businessandmanagement/martin3* to find valuable further teaching and learning material:

Refer to page 35 for full details.

PART TWO
Individuals within organizations

This section begins the more detailed exploration of organizational behaviour topics alluded to in the previous section. It takes as its focus the basic unit of human connection with any organization, the individual. Every human being is different in various ways compared to every other human being and therefore it is never possible to achieve total uniformity in how individuals behave and therefore how they can be managed within an organizational setting.

This section will introduce a number of features that contribute to the individuality of people, beginning with the topic of how they make sense of and come to relate to the world around them, otherwise known as perception. Individual differences between people are obvious in many ways, but not all are relevant to their connection with organizations. It is the study of personality in the next chapter that seeks to explore just how people differ in important ways and which might impact on their work and how they interact with the people with whom they come into contact. The final chapter in this section is about how people learn, together with the implications of this for the provision of training and development events within organizations. This is significant because it is through these processes that managers seek to provide employees with the practical and social skills necessary to be effective in their jobs. Also it is through the socialization processes in an organization that individuals learn what is expected of them and what they need to do to be successful in that context.

The themes covered in this section represent the basic building blocks of any organization. It is therefore important to understand the major variables at work at this level of analysis. It is individuals that make up the teams and groups that work in the departments and sections that actually deliver the results achieved. The next section of the book moves up a level, building on the individual dimension in considering the nature and functioning of groups and teams within an organization.

CHAPTER 3

Perception and attitude formation

LEARNING OBJECTIVES

After studying this chapter and working through the associated Management in Action panels, Employee Perspectives, Discussion Questions and Case Study, you should be able to:

- **Describe the processes of perception and attitude formation.**
- **Explain the links between perception, attitude formation and impression management.**
- **Understand why employee perceptions and attitudes are difficult for managers to influence.**
- **Discuss the issues surrounding organizational attempts to shape the perceptions and attitudes of employees.**
- **Assess the significance of person perception in the behaviour of managers and employees.**

INTRODUCTION

Perception can be described as a process of simplification. There are a vast range of stimuli (sensations or pieces of information) impacting upon the human senses all the time, even when we sleep. Because of the volume and range involved, it is not possible for anyone to pay attention to every stimulus and still be able to cope with the most simple of tasks. Imagine for example, trying to cross a busy street in the centre of a major city while listening intently to every sound, smelling every odour, feeling the clothes worn press onto the body and watching every other person, etc. A sure scenario for an accident! In addition to this volume-based need for simplification, human beings need to be able to classify the sensations that are experienced in order to make them meaningful. For example, the classification of a particular visual image as a motor car is necessary to be able to identify the benefits and hazards associated with it.

Two concepts related to perception are those of attitude and impression management. Human beings have attitudes about all manner of things and these impact on behaviour in relation to the focal object. Attitudes are partly formed by the perceptual process. Equally, the attitudes that a human being holds will influence the perception of the focal objects to some extent. This circular process between attitude and perception is evident in many aspects of human behaviour, not least discrimination against particular groups of people. Impression management reflects a deliberate attempt by one individual (or a group) to seek to convey particular perceptions to other people. For example, in a job interview the applicant would seek to convey a 'good' impression to the interviewer in order to improve their chances of being appointed. Good impression in that context refers to the desire to appear to be the type of person that the company is seeking. Children seek to give a particular impression to their friends by having the latest toy or clothes. They seek to be perceived in a particular way by their friends thereby creating particular attitudes towards themselves and gaining higher status within the group.

THE SIGNIFICANCE OF PERCEPTION AND ATTITUDE

To survive, humans must become aware of what is 'out there'; the vast range of 'things' that are external to themselves. They must then be able to decide what is significant (and why) in any particular context. This is necessary before the individual can then determine how to respond to the 'it' that has been perceived. This is the basis of the process referred to as **perception**. Most of the time people are not aware of the psychological process of perception. They simply become aware of the things going on around them that attract their attention. The process is generally subconscious. The following list contains some of the main human senses representing the detection systems for external stimuli which impact on people and in which some form of perception occurs:

Perception
A psychological process which enables individuals to make sense of the world external to themselves, necessary to determine response behaviours.

- Vision
- Temperature
- Sound
- Taste
- Pain
- Touch
- Smell.

In addition there is an eighth sense: an ability to be aware of spatial relationships. For example, a blindfolded individual could probably find their way around a familiar room without too much difficulty. A mental map of the room exists in the person's head indicating where 'things' are normally to be found, thereby providing an indication of the relative spatial relationships between the objects.

The significance of perception within organizations is the basis for action that it provides for the people involved. Susskind *et al.* (2003) studied the perception of service provision among employees along with customer satisfaction of the service provision. They found that co-worker support was significantly related to the customer focus of employees and this was in turn related to customer satisfaction. They also found that support from supervisors was not as significant (as co-worker support) in encouraging a customer focus among employees. This research suggests that co-workers are more significant in terms of their impact on how staff will relate to customers and the service encounter than supervisors. Within organizations, as in life, there is no certainty that any two people (or groups of people) will perceive the same stimulus in exactly the same way.

The perceptions and attitudes that people hold are formed throughout life as a result of experience and **socialization**. Some attitudes are deeply held and as a consequence probably difficult to change. Other attitudes are perhaps less entrenched and liable to change in line with experience. For example, attitudes towards fashion are notoriously fickle and liable to change quickly. There are obvious and strong links between perception and the attitudes that people hold. Attitudes are formed on the basis of perceived information. Perceptions are interpreted in the light of experience and attitudes. Management in Action 3.1 provides examples of these links.

Socialization
(social doping) – The process of learning how things should be done in a particular context.

A MODEL OF PERCEPTION

Perception as a process can be described as a sequence of events from the receipt of a stimulus to the response to it (see Figure 3.1). The following sections of this chapter will consider each of the elements from this model in greater detail.

It is often assumed that as individuals we all perceive the reality of the world around us in the same way. However, a glance at a range of newspapers covering political or industrial relations events should provide adequate support for the view that there are always at least two points of view in any situation. This reflects something that has been acknowledged by psychologists for some considerable time. Look at Figure 3.2. What do you see?

Do you see a young woman or an old woman in the picture? Now ask one or two of your friends what they see? Does everyone you ask see the same? The raw material (the picture) is interpreted in the light of a range of internal and external influences. There has been some suggestion that younger people tend to see the young woman, whereas older people tend to see the old woman. Whatever the case, there are two

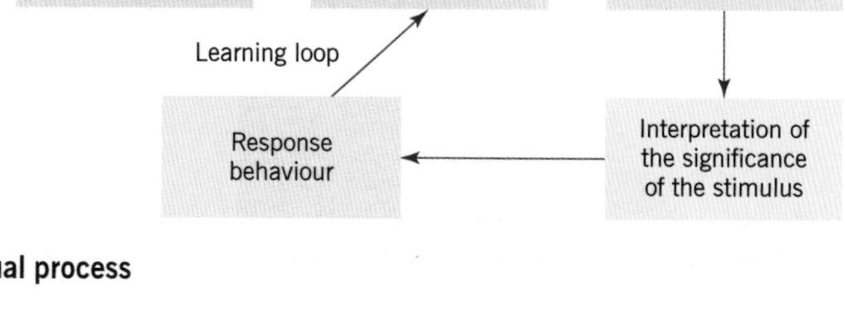

FIGURE 3.1

The perceptual process

MANAGEMENT IN ACTION 3.1

Attitudes and perceptions in times of change

The organization in question was going through a significant period of change. As part of this, the personnel department was expected to manage many aspects of the process and a number of new appointments were made in order to strengthen the ability of the function to achieve these objectives. This involved the recruitment of a number of experienced personnel specialists from outside the industry; training and industrial relations being two examples of the additional expertise sought.

The process also involved the reallocation of a number of the existing personnel staff to new duties. One of the existing personnel staff perceived that the newly appointed specialists were a threat to their standing within the organization and began to engage in hostile behaviour towards them. The situation became extremely political and resulted in many additional problems for the organization until the personnel director was able to stabilize the situation.

Interpretation of this story from an attitudes and perception perspective suggests several things:

- The existing personnel specialist held a number of attitudes that led him to perceive the new people from outside as having skills that were more valued by the organization. This led him to interpret this as a threat to his future career and position within the organization. This resulted in attitudes and behaviour that were openly hostile to the people involved and anything suggested by them.
- The new personnel specialists had been brought in to supplement the existing resources of the organization. They arrived with a set of attitudes that implied that the organization was not unique in the process that it was going through and that adopting their previously learned skills would enable it to achieve its objectives. Resistance from the established specialists was at first seen as a minor irritation and inevitable. However, the continued display of hostile behaviour led to deterioration in the working relationship between the people involved. The new staff began to interpret this behaviour at a personal level and as a criticism of their skills. Consequently, the negative attitudes of the existing specialists produced an increasingly negative response from the new staff.
- In effect a 'doom loop' of deteriorating attitudes, fuelled by perceptions of other people's behaviour, was happening. This led to appeals to higher authority to resolve the perceived problems (by removing the 'other' people). Several conflict-resolving sessions were held and one or two of the new specialists left of their own accord. Some three years later the situation was not completely resolved and a form of uneasy truce existed between the individuals concerned.

Stop ↔ Consider

Was the situation described inevitable as a result of the likely perception and attitudes of people in that situation?

Could the problems have been anticipated and how might the situation have been dealt with in order to avoid some if not all of them?

FIGURE 3.2

Ambiguous figure (originally published by Hill, WE (1915) *Punch*, 6 November)

possible interpretations of the same stimulus and it is not possible to state with certainty that one perception is right and the other wrong. Given that perception represents a simplifying process intended to allow (among other things) individuals to identify significant issues, previous experience in defining what is significant, plays an important role. As life experience differs for every individual, it is hardly surprising that the perception of stimuli also differs. Parents, friends, location, relative wealth are just some of the factors that might be expected to play a part in developing the experience and socialization of individuals and hence their perceptions.

Receipt of a stimulus

It is easier to illustrate the many aspects of the perceptual process using visual examples. Readers should understand, however, that similar perceptual processes are at work in all the human senses. For example, Figure 3.3 illustrates an experiment in which a pair of coiled but separate tubes have cold water passed through one and warm water passed through the other. If the temperature of the cold water is between 0–5° Centigrade and the warm between 40–44° Centigrade a subject taking hold of the coil will experience a hot, burning sensation. It is thought that the perception of this sensation occurs as the result of the simultaneous stimulation of warm and cold sensation receptors in the skin. This example illustrates a feature common to all sensory receptors: that raw data, or energy from the environment, impacts on one or more of our senses and stimulates a physical reaction at that particular location.

The fact that our senses play tricks on us is even more apparent in the world of visual illusion. Indeed, magicians rely on just this phenomenon to amaze audiences during stage and television performances. Another aspect of this is demonstrated in the impossible figure, which at one and the same time exists and yet cannot exist in Figure 3.4.

FIGURE 3.3

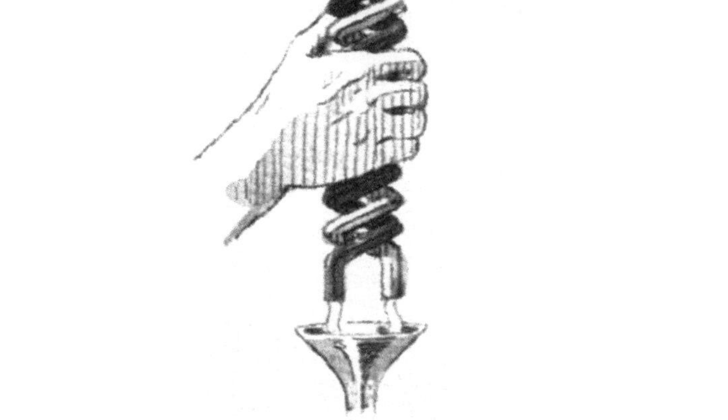

Perception of 'hot' as a result of the simultaneous stimulation of warm and cold receptors (*source:* Hilgard, ER, Atkinson, RC and Atkinson, RL (1971) *Introduction to Psychology*, 5th edn, Harcourt Brace Jovanovich, New York)

In this particular case, the difficulty lies with the ability of the eye to see two dimensions from the image presented and the perceptual system's ability to construct three dimensions from that data. Most of the time perceptual processes work consistently in creating meaning for the individual, but in this particular example the two systems provide contradictory messages and reality breaks down. In human terms, when such contradictions arise they force a slowing down in the ability to process information, while clarification is sought and the ambiguity resolved. While this might be acceptable in some situations, it could be dangerous if, say, the pilot of a passenger aircraft has to take valuable time to resolve conflicting images presented to them at a critical moment during a flight.

SELECTION OF STIMULI FOR ATTENTION

The selection of which of the many simultaneous stimuli impacting on the senses to pay attention to allows the individual to identify the most significant events. This could be either those that need to be attended to or those that are of most interest. This is a decision-making process and a function of three main elements: the circumstances, external and internal factors.

The circumstances

Circumstances can have a direct impact on the selection of the stimuli to which attention will be directed. For example, senior managers of a company experiencing financial difficulties would pay more attention to every item of expenditure than when a healthy profit was being made. Also, people in expensive business suits walking around a factory floor can create a wide variety of rumours because they stand out as different from the people usually found in that context. By comparison in a head office environment it would be people walking about in boiler suits who would attract attention.

Factors external to the individual

There are a number of factors external to the individual that can impact on the selection of a stimulus for attention. Hyrkäs and Appelqvist-Schmidlechner (2003) for example identified that a wide range of factors impacted on the perception of both positive and negative effects of multi-professional group working in the medical field. For example whilst communication and mutual understanding had improved across the teams, the frankness and tensions that resulted offended some members, who reacted negatively as a consequence. There are also features associated with the

FIGURE 3.4

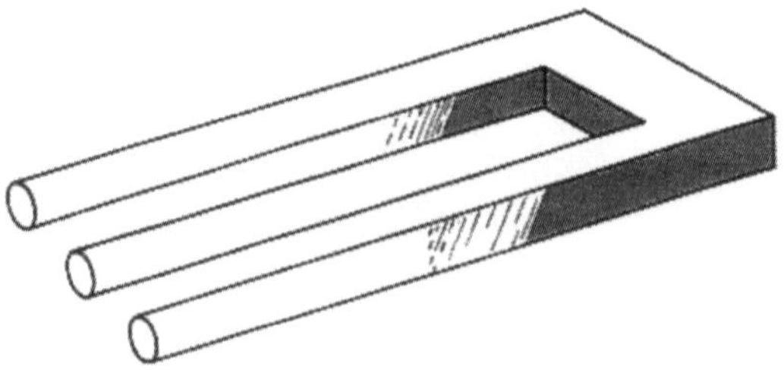

An impossible figure (*source*:Hilgard, ER, Atkinson, RC and Atkinson, RL (1971) *Introduction to Psychology*, 5th edn, Harcourt Brace Jovanovich, New York)

stimuli themselves that influence the process. Certain features of a particular stimulus might make it more likely to stand out from those around it and therefore attract attention, including:

- *Repetition*. The more often something is repeated the more likely it is that the message gets through to the level of consciousness. Advertising and public relations often apply this principle to increase the awareness of a particular product or brand name. However, repetition can also lead to the senses turning off from the awareness of the presence of a stimulus. This is called **habituation**. This can create hazards in a working environment if individuals frequently ignore warning signs that are always present for example.
- *Size*. It is perhaps obvious, but the larger a particular stimulus is, the more likely it is that it will attract attention.
- *Contrast*. The relative size (and other features) of events placed near together can influence a perception. For example, consider Figure 3.5.

Habituation
Constant repetition of a stimulus can lead to the senses turning off from the awareness of it.

Do you see:

A. Two figures, one a large circle surrounded by small ones, and a small circle surrounded by large ones?
B. Two figures, each with a same size of circle in the centre but surrounded by different sizes of circle?

Option B is a more accurate reflection of the two diagrams. However, many people report that option A is correct! The relative circle sizes influences the perception of the figures.

- *Novelty*. The presence of the unusual (in a particular context) tends to attract attention. Marketing specialists in designing advertising campaigns also use this aspect of perception.
- *Intensity*. The brighter or louder a particular stimulus the more likely it is to attract attention.
- *Motion*. Something which moves is more likely to attract attention than something which is stationary. Predatory animals use this feature when hunting their prey in moving very slowly to get close without being detected.
- *Familiarity*. For example, humans find it very easy to spot a familiar face among a crowd of strangers.

Factors internal to the individual

There are a range of factors internal to the individual that influence which stimuli are likely to be attended to as in Figure 3.6.

Taking each factor in turn:

FIGURE 3.5

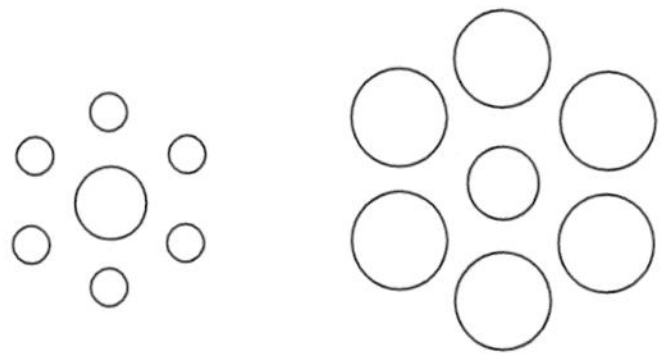

Contrast effect on perception (*source:* Hilgard, ER, Atkinson, RC and Atkinson, RL (1971) *Introduction to Psychology*, 5th edn, Harcourt Brace Jovanovich, New York)

FIGURE 3.6

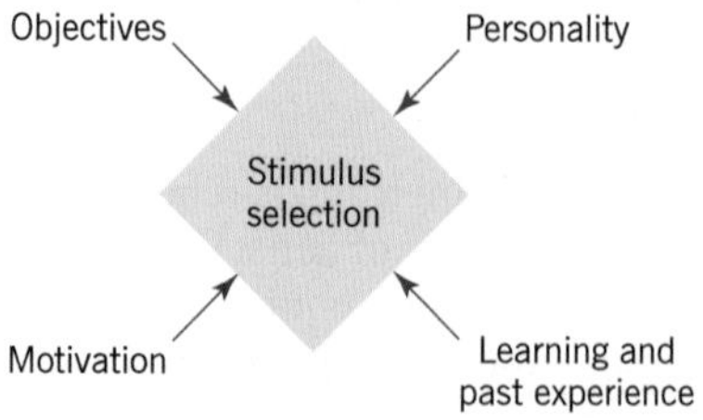

Internal factors influencing stimulus selection

- *Personality*. The personality characteristics of individuals influence the way that they predispose themselves to seek information from the environment (Witkin *et al.*, 1954).
- *Learning and past experience*. Young children and animals become aware of relevant stimuli very early on. Figure 3.7 shows that a toddler faced with crossing a visual cliff will hesitate. The same pattern is used for the 'ground' on both sides of the central island. Both sides are covered with thick glass; however, the 'cliff' side is much lower. Although it would be perfectly safe for the infant to crawl out over the 'cliff' it is reluctant to do so, suggesting that depth perception develops very quickly after the infant begins to move around (Gibson and Walk, 1960). In an organizational context Oliver and Wilkinson (1992) provide a detailed review of Japanese management practices, including the emphasis on socialization and training. Through these processes, employees are exposed to the issues that management consider important. Management seeks to shape their perceptions and attitudes. Of course, there is a debate about the extent to which employee perceptions and attitudes are actually shaped by these processes. Employees may be simply complying with the requirements of the job.
- *Motivation*. Both the physical and social needs that influence an individual at any point in time will influence which stimuli attract attention. For example, an employee paid a bonus based on the number of units of output is likely to pay much closer attention to events that impact on the volume of output.
- *Objectives*. People seek out those things and situations which are of value to them. Individuals have goals, intelligence and ability, which they utilize to their advantage in interacting with their environment. Consequently, stimuli which

FIGURE 3.7

The visual cliff

may be relevant within that framework will be scanned for relevance before being rejected or processed further. For example, an individual with shares in a particular company may well scan the newspapers for any snippet of information which might suggest a potential change in the share price.

ORGANIZING STIMULI INTO MEANINGFUL PATTERNS

Infants are born with no direct experience of the world. Their understanding is based on the genetic material which they inherit from their parents and their experience while in the womb. Understanding, based upon the process of grouping stimuli from the environment into meaningful patterns is one that develops in the child through early experience. The most important aspects of this process appear to be:

- *The figure–ground principle*. This principle is all about the process of perceiving a stimulus in a background context. Figure 3.8 illustrates the principle. Do you see a chalice or two faces in profile? Which you perceive depends upon what you identify as background and what as foreground. This particular example also illustrates another facet of perception – that of culture. The use of a chalice in Figure 3.8 is only meaningful in those cultural contexts where such drinking vessels are known. In other cultural situations, the illusion might not work at all.
- *The principle of continuity*. This relates to the tendency to detect continuous patterns in groups of individual stimuli. However, a row of numbers may be just that, they may not be related in a meaningful way. The daily sales returns from each of the outlets of a national retail company may not be related in any way, yet management frequently attempt to identify patterns from such data.
- *The principle of proximity*. Proximity refers to the perceptual process of creating association simply on the basis of nearness. For example, Figure 3.9 indicates how lines could be assumed to be associated, yet with a little more information a different relationship is suggested.
- *The principle of closure*. The principle of closure is all about making a whole out of the parts available. Figure 3.10 is a series of dark shapes; what does it suggest to you? In an organization this could be reflected in the need to detect what marketing strategy a competitor is about to embark upon from only partial information available such as rumour and customer feedback.

Perhaps Figure 3.10 appears to you to represent a dog? If it does, then it is doing so not because of the actual drawing, but because your perceptual system is seeking to draw together the available information and enclose it into a known and familiar image.

FIGURE 3.8

Reversible figure

FIGURE 3.9

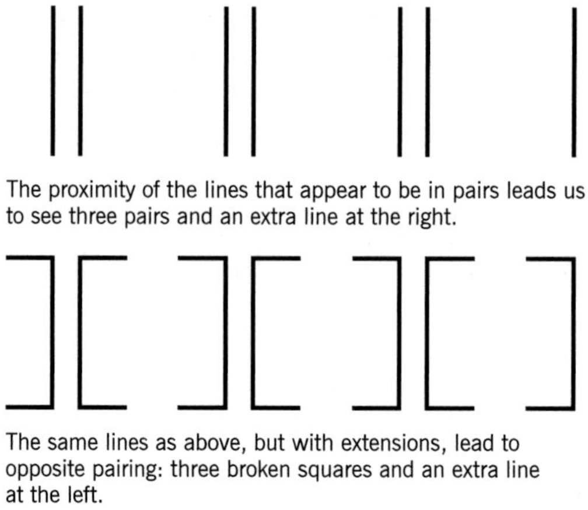
The proximity of the lines that appear to be in pairs leads us to see three pairs and an extra line at the right.
The same lines as above, but with extensions, lead to opposite pairing: three broken squares and an extra line at the left.

The principle proximity (*source*: Hilgard, ER, Atkinson, RC and Anderson, RL (1971) *Introduction to Psychology*, 5th edn, Harcourt Brace Jovanovich, New York)

FIGURE 3.10

The closure principle (*source*: Coon, D (copyright © 1985, 1991) *Introduction to Psychology: Explorations and Applications*, West Publishing Company. By permission of Brooks/Cole Publishing Company, Pacific Grove, CA, a division of Thomson Publishing Inc)

- *The principle of similarity*. This concept relates to the grouping together of stimuli based on similar characteristics. For example, 'all workers are lazy' might be the view of a particular manager. Consequently, such a manager seeing a worker standing around and not working might not recognize that the individual could be waiting for a machine to be repaired and therefore not able to work.

INTERPRETING THE SIGNIFICANCE OF A STIMULUS

The significance of a particular stimulus will be judged against a range of criteria. For example, it will depend upon prior experience, together with the physical and mental state of the individual at the time. An individual feeling thirsty is likely to become more aware of stimuli that have a refreshment theme. This process within the perceptual model can be thought of as a filtering mechanism. It is a process that is subjective and goes beyond the information contained in the stimulus itself. It is to a discussion of the major factors and processes involved in interpreting the significance of a stimulus that we now turn.

Language and perception shaping

The interpretation of a particular stimulus is dependent on many factors including prior understanding. This is also referred to as the individual's frame of reference. Many possible illustrations can be used to demonstrate the need for a high degree of contextual understanding before meaning can be understood. For example, imagine a situation in which an individual were able to travel backward or forward in time. The sites and scenes experienced would be truly shocking as the individual would not have the prior knowledge (frame of reference) on which to function effectively in what would be an alien context. The reaction from a person living some 2000 years ago to seeing an aeroplane for the first time can barely be imagined. Their frame of reference would be based on completely different understandings. The creation of understanding in any context is partly based on the use of language.

Language is a form of communication and creates meaning for users through the signals and information that it contains. However, language contains many levels of communication within it, not just the words and their associated meaning. There is the tone of voice and body language, which accompany the spoken words. Equally, in the written form of language a skilled writer can create word pictures to convey additional meaning to the readers. The role of language in creating perceptions for people has long been recognized. For example, there is an interesting review of the work of Max Weber in relation to the discussion of the Protestant ethic in Ray and Reed (1994, pp 23–32), in which the use of language to create perceptions of heaven and hell within Protestantism and its role in relation to the development of capitalism is explored.

Lothian (1978) reviewed the use of language in relation to understanding the published accounts of companies. He concluded that the difficulty for private shareholders in understanding published accounts lay with the accountants who used complex professional language to explain non-complex ideas. He goes so far as to suggest that much of the accountancy profession's language was bogus and intended to impress the innocent and unwary, while drawing a boundary around the members of the profession. Also, Whitmore (1994) discusses the ability of a university researcher to interact effectively with groups of people in receipt of welfare payments who were always worried about being reported to the authorities for some breach of the rules. She reports that:

> In spite of the fact that I was acutely aware of talking in 'academese' and tried not to use jargon or big words, my small words were often their big words. What I assumed was 'normal talk', they saw as 'professor words' ... The way we organized our thinking, how we expressed ourselves, both cognitively and emotionally, were different. The verbal and non-verbal meanings were simply not understood in the same way. (p 95)

In this review, Whitmore is describing how the perceptions of both groups (researcher and subjects) were linked to the language used and the interpretation of the other group's actions and words as a way of creating and reinforcing meaning. Therefore, language created a group differentiator, based on perceptual frameworks and experience. These guided the future actions of the subjects towards the researcher (a perceived outsider).

Perceptual errors

Perceptual errors
The mistakes of judgement or understanding that can occur during the process of interpreting stimuli.

Perceptual errors reflect the mistakes that can occur during the process of making sense of perceptual information. They can be mistakes of judgement or in understanding. One form of perceptual error has already been introduced in Figure 3.8 which can be interpreted in two distinct ways. Of course, the use of the term error in this context is interesting in that it depends on the intention of the provider of the stimulus, not the perceiver. Therefore, if the provider of the drawing in Figure 3.8 intended a chalice to be seen then the 'error' would arise if the perceiver saw two faces.

In an organizational context, the fact that it is possible to experience errors in perception can be problematic from several perspectives. Perceptual error could be accidental. For example, management might keep repeating the mantra that the 'customer is king' in seeking to focus employee attention on providing the highest standards of customer service. However, employees might interpret the intention as being a clear signal that market forces dominate management thinking and that future employment is based upon achieving targets, and therefore far from secure. Employee reaction to the management intentions might be negative, not what was intended at all. The following Employee Perspective (3.1) considers the reality of one aspect of customer contact for many employees working in front-line jobs in the retail and service sectors.

However, perceptual error can be used with more sinister intent. For example, management might actually be thinking about cutting the workforce, but be seeking to achieve this by indirect means. Perhaps, they might seek to hide their real intentions behind a subterfuge. For example, claiming that the introduction of new technology is intended to improve quality, whereas its real purpose is to reduce the number of employees. Previous experience by employees of management actions may lead them to the conclusion (perception) that any proposed action is unlikely to benefit them. Therefore this forms a significant part of the perceptual framework through which stimuli (messages) from that source will be interpreted.

There are a number of categories of perceptual error, some of which have already been introduced. Areas of perceptual error not already introduced include (the last two are discussed in greater detail later in this chapter under person perception):

EMPLOYEE PERSPECTIVE 3.1 Dealing with the customer!

Call centres are used to dealing with a wide variety of order taking and customer service activities over the telephone. The employee is supposed to engage the customer in a seamless conversation, guided by the computer generated script. However, things do not always go according to plan. Kathleen, a call centre employee based in Scotland told of one incident, quite common it was suggested, in which a very short pause in the employee speaking occurred while they were typing a reply from the customer. The customer (also a woman) was distinctly heard to pass the following comment to someone else in the background.

'The bitch, she's gone and ******* well cut me off!'

Of course the employee had not done so and replied, 'I'm sorry, what did you say?'

The person on the other end of the phone then hung up.

Tasks

1. How would you have reacted to such a comment if you were Kathleen?
2. Does this experience suggest that the customer is 'king' in all circumstances?
3. To what extent should employees have to put up with bad or inappropriate behaviour from customers?
4. As the manager of a call centre, what would you want your staff to do in such circumstances, and why?

- Expectancy
- The halo (and horns) effect
- Perceptual defence mechanisms
- Stereotyping

Expectancy

The expectations that exist prior to an event can significantly influence behaviour relative to that event. Being told that a new boss is temperamental and a stickler for accuracy will lead to a different reaction and perception of their actions to being told that they are friendly with an informal style.

Halo and horns effect

Halo (horns) effect
Positive (or negative) bias introduced when attributing all of the characteristics of a person (or object) from a single attribute.

The **halo effect** is the bias introduced when attributing all of the characteristics of a person (or object) to a single attribute. For example, a person who is a good time-keeper may be claimed to be a high-performing employee in all other respects. This has obvious dangers in forming judgements and deciding actions about other people. In seeking to reduce the number of employees, managers deciding who should stay only on the basis of (say) attendance records might result in the loss of more highly skilled and productive workers who have a less 'perfect' attendance record.

The opposite of the halo effect is sometimes referred to as the **horns effect**. This takes the view that everything about a person is bad on the basis of a single instance. It can be just as damaging to individuals and organizations as the halo effect. Consider that a department has an urgent customer order to complete and that the supervisor is under considerable pressure to get as many people as possible to work overtime in order to meet the order. Perhaps one of the best employees in the department has an important family event on that particular evening and so flatly refuses to stay at work and help out. As the supervisor is under pressure they may try and force the employee to work, which may simply make the employee more direct in their refusal. This will irritate the supervisor and it is likely that their judgement of the employee will become negative as a consequence. The fact that a broad range of aspects of the employee's work behaviour will subsequently be regarded as less valuable than before as a result of the one incident is an example of the horns effect.

RESPONSE BEHAVIOUR TO A STIMULUS

Individuals react to the perceptual world depending upon their needs at the time. In the usual course of events the stimuli that will gain attention at any point in time depends on a balance of forces active at that time. These include:

- Pressure to achieve a particular objective
- Interest in the task in hand
- Distraction opportunity
- Consequences of failure to achieve the end result
- Physiological state

The actual behavioural response to a perceived stimulus can fall into one of two main categories. They are:

1. *Internal behaviour shapers*. These response categories are not observable behaviours themselves. They are, however, the motivations, attitudes and feelings that help to determine much of the observable behaviour in people.

2. *Observable behaviour*. This refers to the actual behaviour that would be seen by other people. It is the tangible and physical expression of the underlying behaviour shapers. It is the reactions such as leaving a building when the fire alarm sounds, or work activity following job instruction from a supervisor.

Perceptual defence

Perceptual defence
A process that protects the individual against information or ideas that are threatening to an existing perception or attitude.

Another aspect of how responses are determined is the notion of **perceptual defence**. This process provides a measure of protection for the individual against information, ideas or situations that are threatening to an existing perception or attitude. It is a process that encourages the perception of stimuli in terms of the known and familiar. For example, a manager having taken the decision to introduce a new product into the company is likely to search out information that reinforces the validity of the decision and also interpret information received in a light favourable to that decision. Information that is contradictory to the validity of the decision is likely to be seen as a challenge, requiring the decision to be proved correct rather than negating the decision itself. This partially reflects the view behind the often-heard statement that problems are opportunities in disguise.

THE LEARNING LOOP

The role of learning on the perceptual process itself is something that the model described in Figure 3.1 recognizes as feedback. This is intended to indicate that individuals learn from experience. The person involved will perceive the consequences of their behaviours and as a result adjust their subsequent perceptual frameworks and behaviour. An individual who is disciplined by their manager for being late for work will, hopefully, change their future behaviour and arrive punctually. Similarly, an employee praised for good work will be more likely to repeat it in the future.

The effect of learning on the perceptual process can be demonstrated through a number of illusions. Figure 3.11 is the Müller–Lyer visual illusion (named after the originators) which, it has been suggested, has a basis in the prior learning of individuals. Which of the two vertical lines is the longer? In practice, they are the same length. It is suggested that the illusion of differing line length occurs through an association with rooms and buildings with corners based on these models. Individuals, therefore, attempt to place a perspective or context onto the shapes through their prior learning.

PERSON PERCEPTION

Person perception is of particular interest in organization behaviour because of the significance of interpersonal interaction within a work setting. How individuals perceive managers, subordinates and fellow workers is the basis of the effectiveness of any organization. Much of the day-to-day activity in employee relations is concerned with the management of perceptions and subsequent attitudes relative to the work setting. Warr (1971) offers a detailed schematic model of person perception, which has been simplified below as Figure 3.12.

The model comprises five sets of components, all interlinked in a complex array of information flow and decision making. They are:

FIGURE 3.11

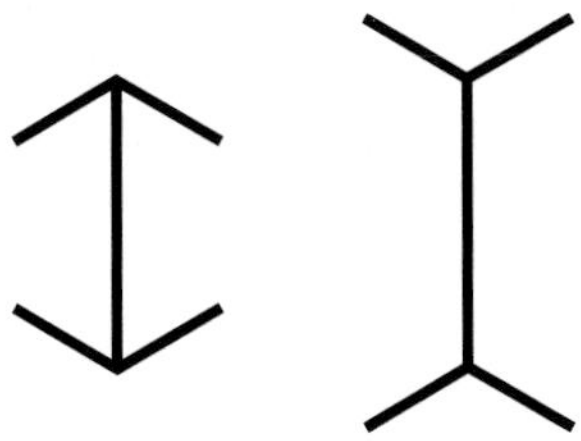

The Müller-Lyon illusion

FIGURE 3.12

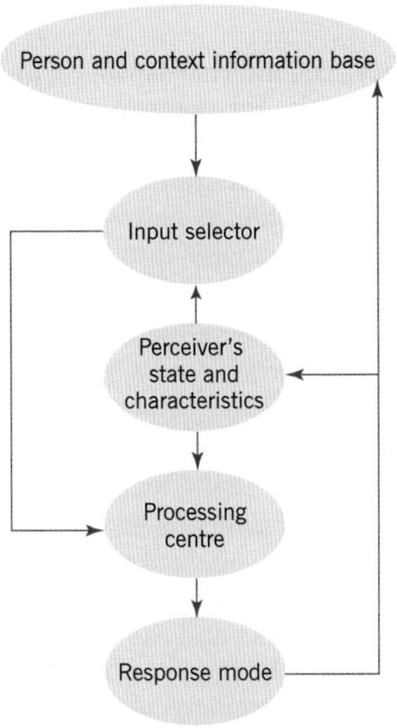

Model of person perception (based on Warr, PB (1971))

1. *The person and context information base.* These provide the current and previously acquired information on the target person and the context within which the perception is set.
2. *Input selector.* This refers to the process by which the vast array of current and previously obtained information is to be sifted. The assumption being that it is not possible to process all available information and that a filtering device is needed to weed out unnecessary information.
3. *The perceiver's state.* This is intended to provide for the variable effect on perception of the perceiver. Their current physical, psychological and emotional state will influence their perceptions, as will their underlying personality characteristics.
4. *The processing centre.* This is a series of decision rules built up over time from the experience of interacting with people. It therefore allows output probability options to be identified from the available data. This is reminiscent of attribution theory, discussed later.
5. *The response mode.* Having developed a profile of the target person in terms of the attributes and expectations, the perceiver will develop an appropriate

response. This will not just be in terms of actual behaviour, but will include attitudes such as liking, respect and interest, for example. These judgmental facets to person perception all feed back to the other levels, as the process is cumulative over time. The stored information is updated by current events and the entire process is interactive in real time.

A simplified form of person perception is to envisage it as a three-factor process, involving the characteristics of the perceiver, the characteristics of the perceived and the situational variables. Figure 3.13 illustrates the main features of this approach to person perception.

The model of person perception reflected in Figure 3.13 also has strong links with attribution theory to be discussed later. Taking each determinant from the model in turn:

- *Perceiver characteristics*. The internal aspects of an individual that determine perception about other people. For example, personality, motivation, objectives, learning, past experience and the individual's value system. Working with someone from another culture is a useful way of experiencing the scope of a value system on person perception as new ways of thinking about people and their characteristics and traits emerge through the exposure.
- *The characteristics of the perceived person*. When we meet someone, there is a wide variety of clues available. Their physical appearance, skin colour, gender, age, general appearance, voice, behaviour and apparent personality all provide information to the perceiver (DePaulo *et al*., 1987). Although the characteristics of the perceived person can make a positive contribution to the process of person perception, there is also a danger that it may lead to **stereotyping** (see below).
- *Situational variables*. Meeting someone for the first time in the company of either a friend, or someone that you dislike, would be likely to influence the initial perception of the new individual. Social, business or other contexts with their differing degrees of formality and ritual are also likely to influence initial perceptions. The room in which a meeting takes place, its standard of decoration and the general atmosphere all produce stimuli, which influence perceptions about the people found there.

Stereotyping
The tendency to attribute everyone (or thing) in a particular category with the characteristics based on a single example.

Table 3.1 provides an illustration of person perception in action. It reflects the perceptions of supervisors and subordinates about each other. The perception that was being

FIGURE 3.13

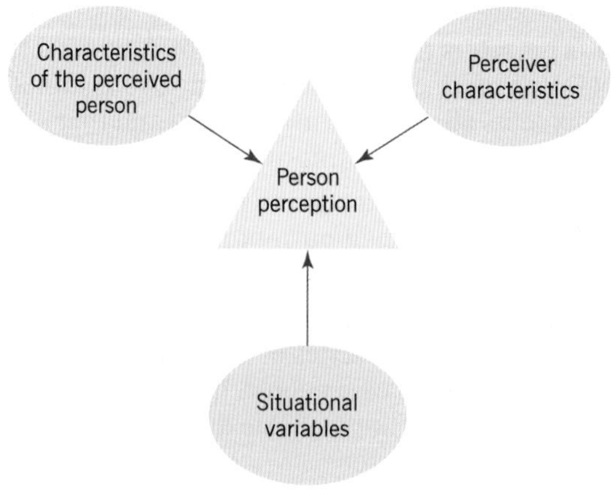

Person perception: a simplified model

examined related to the views that each group held about the other in terms of recognition for good performance.

Table 3.1 indicates a clear difference in perceived behaviour between the two groups. Supervisors perceive that they provide a much more positive response to good performance than do their subordinates. The difference between the two groups is startling, not just marginal. The perceptions of the subordinates about the supervisors are clearly different from the supervisors' perception of their own behaviour. One implication of this is that managers in general need to be much more aware of the signals that they give out if they are to avoid misunderstandings. But, can the responses be relied upon as an accurate reflection of the true perceptions of the two groups? Might the supervisors indicate positive views compared to their actual behaviour because they feel they would be expected to be more supportive of employees than they actually are? Might employees undervalue what supervisor support is available in reaction to unrelated management actions?

The Transamerica Centre for Retirement Studies undertook research into the perceptions of managers and workers in small businesses on the value of pension provision in reward packages (Ogden 2002). It found that over 70 per cent of employers believed that employees wanted high salaries most of all, and that employees preferred not to think about retirement planning until they neared retirement age. However, by comparison only 29 per cent of employees admitted giving little or no thought to retirement until later in life. Clearly there are widely differing perceptions of the same situation between the people involved. This result is also found in other areas of life requiring the interpretation of other people's motivations or actions. For example, Hastorf and Cantril (1954) studied the reaction to an American rules football game between two university teams. The subjects of the research were students from the universities concerned, Princeton and Dartmouth. General reports about the game suggested that both teams had engaged in rough play, but that Dartmouth had been the more aggressive. From a film of the game both sets of students were asked to score the number of fouls committed by each side (see Table 3.2).

The Princeton students saw a much larger number of fouls being committed by the Dartmouth team than the Dartmouth students did. They perceived the situation in a different light, based on their attitudes towards their own team. However, this would

Table of recognition	**Frequency with which supervisors say they give various types of recognition for good performance (%)**	**Frequency with which subordinates say supervisors give various types of recognition for good performance (%)**
Gives privileges	52	14
Gives more responsibility	48	10
Gives a pat on the back	82	13
Gives sincere and thorough praise	80	14
Trains for better jobs	64	9
Gives more interesting work	51	5

TABLE 3.1 Person perception in the context of recognition behaviour (adapted from: Likert, R (1961) *New Patterns in Management*, McGraw-Hill, New York)

not explain why the Princeton students did not significantly under-report their own team's performance. There are many possible explanations for this result, including the extreme behaviour of the Dartmouth team, causing the need to sanitize their misdeeds by their supporters. This implies a group reaction to the result, the game being the same perceptual stimulus for each observer, the stimulus being interpreted in the light of the attitudinal model. It would also be possible to argue that the attitudinal frameworks influence the perception itself, making the game different for each observer. The observer would therefore see only that which had meaning and significance for that individual. It is in this form that the significance for organizations becomes apparent. Individual perceptions and attitudes are informed through group interaction and therefore managers need to function at both levels in understanding and seeking to shape appropriate behaviours.

Stereotyping and projection

Stereotyping and projection were originally introduced in the section on perceptual errors above, they are discussed in detail here as they are also relevant to person perception and in order to avoid duplication of material. Stereotyping is the tendency to attribute everyone (or thing) in a particular category with the characteristics from a single example. For instance, one common stereotype suggests that all trade union members are anti-management and will go on strike with any excuse in order to get time off work. This is a factor of person perception that is frequently seen in the area of race relations and discrimination, but it also has very direct links to the general organizational world. For example, some managers would claim that all workers are lazy and some workers would claim that all managers search for ways to exploit them. These can be clear perceptual stereotypes in which every member of a category of employee or manager is being described in the terms found only in a small number of individuals. Crisp (2002) suggests that increasing the complexity in the way that people categorise others might help to reduce negative reactions to them. This might imply that the more managers and employees understand each other, the more the level of mistrust and number of problems will reduce. However, as the following Employee Perspective (3.2) demonstrates, different perceptions can exist between managers and employees in relation to delegation of decision making which can lead to misunderstandings and conflict.

Not all information perceived could be expected to be either supportive or contradictory to a particular stereotype. For example, an employee might find that not all managers were seeking to exploit them. The employee must somehow deal with this apparently contradictory information. It has been suggested that information which supports a particular stereotype is processed more intensively than information which is inconsistent with it (Bodenhausen, 1988). This builds on an earlier study, which demonstrated that students presented with contradictory information in relation to a stereotype (Haire and Grunes, 1950) adopted various denial or protection

	Average fouls committed by	
	Princeton team	**Dartmouth team**
Dartmouth students (48)	4.4	4.3
Princeton students (49)	4.2	9.8

TABLE 3.2 Observed fouls in the Princeton and Dartmouth football game

EMPLOYEE PERSPECTIVE 3.2 Perceptions about empowerment

Geraldine worked in a large car tyre factory in Italy. The factory employed approximately 500 people across a range of shifts covering the full 168 hours each week. The company had just introduced a total quality management (TQM) scheme within the factory that among other things was intended to allow the delegation of many routine operational decisions to factory employees. However Geraldine, along with many other employees, considered that the new TQM scheme was nothing more than an attempt to make the job of management easier by pushing responsibility down to employees, to make employees work harder, to allow the punishment of employees if things went wrong and ultimately to reduce the total number of workers.

The management of the company however perceived (and claimed) that the introduction of the TQM scheme was intended to engage employees in the operational activities of the organization to a much higher level than before and therefore to improve job satisfaction, productivity and customer service.

Tasks

1. Could Geraldine be right in her perception? How could you make certain one way or the other?
2. Why might these different perceptions have arisen, and could they be prevented or overcome?

devices. The purpose being to sustain the original stereotypical image, rather than accept the disconfirming evidence about the target.

The benefits of stereotyping are associated with its ability to allow categorization of people into groups. This could, assuming that the basis of stereotyping were correct, be a simplifying process. It could significantly reduce the need for mental processing of people as individuals and therefore free mental capacity to deal with issues that are more important. However, in doing so there is a real danger of missing important aspects of individuality within the people being stereotyped. For example, sex, race, disability and age discrimination are commonplace in the organizational world. However, adopting these common stereotypes into decision making about people usually introduces an irrelevant aspect to the process. For example, older people are frequently regarded as slower, less flexible, less adaptable and with lower computer capability than younger people. This is, however, a generalization which ignores any compensating strengths such as experience and stability. Management in Action 3.2 considers some current organizational practices with regard to this issue.

Projection implies that others possess the same characteristics as ourselves. In other words, we tend to assume that everyone thinks and behaves in the same way that we do. This is a potentially dangerous assumption for managers to make in relation to their employees. Managers invariably express surprise when employees react in a way that was not anticipated or when they refuse to agree with management's point of view. However, there is no reason why employees should perceive the world the same way that managers do, that much should be obvious from the discussion in this chapter so far. Equally, managers who describe the behaviour of other managers as power- and politically motivated might actually be inclined to behave in such ways themselves and be seeking to protect themselves by projecting these characteristics onto other people.

Projection
A psychological process of projecting onto others characteristics that we see in ourselves.

Body language and perception

Body language is a form of communication parallel to the spoken word. It includes a wide range of features associated with the ways in which people interact with each other. For example, posture, tone of voice, gestures and facial expression are common examples. Each of these aspects of communication provides additional signals to the

MANAGEMENT IN ACTION 3.2 The wonder years

Over recent years many organisations have downsized, or reorganised, frequently resorting to early retirement schemes often on generous terms as a way of significantly reducing the numbers of people employed by the business. This can lead to reduced levels of talent and skill together with an unbalanced workforce in terms of age. It is forecast that by 2010, nearly 40 per cent of the UK population will be over 45 years old. Research carried out by the Employers Forum on the experience of adults shows that more than one in five people had been unfairly treated at work because of their age, mostly during the recruitment process. Twenty five per cent also experienced it within the promotion process and 16 per cent in relation to training and development activities.

However, there is also a form of reverse age discrimination. Younger people can also find themselves being discriminated against. This is often dressed-up in terms of inexperience, unreliability, irresponsibility and being more likely to take time off work. So being too old or too young can lead to age related discrimination. There are a number of organizations that seek to champion ageless recruitment. For example, Tesco ASDA, and B&Q in the retail sector and HBOS in banking.

European legislation will outlaw age discrimination by 2006 and so employers need to be planning ahead for this issue. The British Government encouraged organisations to prepare effectively through Age Positive week in December 2002, intended to raise awareness about the issue of ageism at work. Good examples included organizations such as HBOS, which adopted several initiatives into its own activities:

- The Age Positive week was promoted on the company intranet.
- The revised code of practice issued by the government was issued to all HR teams within the company.
- The company introduced a flexible retirement policy (allowing people to stay on beyond normal retirement age, subject to business need).
- The inclusion of age related questions into staff opinion surveys.
- Individual business areas holding staff events, such as quizzes, 'buddying-up' younger and older workers in mixed age teams.

Adapted from: Higginbottom, K (2002) The wonder years, *People Management*, 5 December, pp 14–15.

Stop ↔ Consider

Age discrimination (as with all discrimination) is about the assumptions that people make about other people.

Is it possible that the process of decision making about people can become objective enough to avoid discrimination?

spoken words that are uttered by an individual. It is from the wealth of information available through body language that perceptions are formed about what a person has actually said. It is possible for a person to lie easily, but it is very difficult for them to be able to eliminate the body language signals that would allow another person to become suspicious.

Morris (1982, pp 160–71) describes situations in which people engage in the process of lying or otherwise attempting to deceive other people. Examples that he quotes include the defendant in a murder trial who knows that he is guilty yet seeks to maintain his innocence, another example being that of a bereaved mother seeking to 'put a brave face' on things for the sake of the children. In discussing these and other situations, Morris refers to the body language evident from the principal actors as 'non-verbal leakage', in other words, the means through which the individual's true feelings leak out into the observable domain. In the case of the bereaved mother, the 'brave face' must not be too convincing or she would be accused of being unfeeling, but equally it must be apparent or she would be accused of lacking courage and control. Morris describes this as pseudo-deception as compared with the attempts to deceive totally on the part of the murderer seeking acquittal. In that example, the body language must seek to reinforce the verbal lies.

Morris suggests that it is possible to control some aspects of body language such as smiling, frowning and other facial expressions, but that some body posture, hand gestures and leg movements will be directly controlled to a lesser degree. Therefore, these are more likely to provide clues as to the true feelings of the individual, hence the term 'non-verbal leakage'. The individual is not completely able to prevent clues emerging about their true feelings. However, other people have to be able to read the clues available. In both these illustrations above, attempts are made by the 'actors' to influence other people's perceptions of them and their feelings or truthfulness.

There are a number of cultural aspects associated with body language. For example, Pease (1984) draws attention to a number of hand gestures which have different meanings in different cultural contexts, including the thumbs-up sign, the OK ring and the V sign. For example the thumbs-up sign usually refers to an OK signal in English-speaking countries, but can be an obscene response in Greece for example (pp 12–13). In pages 23–26, Pease reflects on cultural differences in preferred spatial zones between people. He describes his observation of a Japanese and an American slowly moving around a room as they conversed. In Japan it is normal to operate on a 25-centimetre 'intimate' zone for conversations, but the American was more comfortable with a 46-centimetre zone and so kept backing away, only to be followed by the Japanese colleague seeking to get closer. Clearly, such events can influence people's perceptions of each other. Invasions of personal space can be interpreted as threatening or indicative of a desire for a more intimate relationship. They are signals that can be easily misinterpreted.

Self-perception

Having introduced a number of features associated with the perception of other people, there is one further aspect that is important in the process. That is the perception of the self. In Figure 3.13, the perceiver's characteristics are suggested to impact on their perception of other people. However, these characteristics tend to be classified either in physical terms or as experience, motivation, personality, etc. Just as important to the process of perceiving other people are the self-perceptions of the individual perceiver. Each person thinks of themselves in particular ways; they hold a perception of themselves. For example, an older person might consider that they are mature, successful, affluent, sociable, knowledgeable, worthy of respect, a pillar of the community, youthful and able to relate to young people. That defines their self-perception and it will to some extent impact on various aspects of that person's behaviour, including their perceptions of other people.

ATTRIBUTION THEORY AND PERCEPTION

Attribution theory attempts to provide a model of the way in which we make sense of other people's behaviour. Using ideas from perception it can be envisaged how we attribute various characteristics to other people. We also interpret their behaviour in comparison with others and in terms of past experience. This forms the basis of attribution theory. It is about the causes of behaviour in others, as perceived by ourselves. For example, Vaidyanathan and Aggarwal (2003) suggest that price increases can be seen as unfair even when they are justified by cost increases, if the justification is not

Attribution theory
Suggests that leaders vary their reactions to subordinates based on observation of their behaviours.

MANAGEMENT IN ACTION 3.3 The new manager's tale

The manager had been in his post for about three months at the time of the interview. He was in his early twenties and it was his first managerial appointment. He had been employed by the organization for about two years prior to the interview and had been working in an administrative capacity during that time. The individual had been promoted to the new position from within the team that he was to manage. The office was small with about six people working in it. The main activities within the office were the administration associated with sales planning and customer service on an international scale. As a result there was a considerable amount of information and paperwork flowing through the office at any one time. Customer records had to be kept up to date, as had the information flow to other departments and sections within the organization. A considerable proportion of the time was spent in liaison with customers and dealing with their queries. This process was made more difficult because of the different time zones involved.

During the interview it became clear that the quality of administrative systems was not of the highest order, in terms of records, accuracy and information content. The department had grown very quickly and the previous manager had not been thorough in ensuring that the systems introduced were adequate. In addition, staff had been recruited without any previous experience in that type of work, neither had they been trained adequately in customer care and the work of the department. Consequently, a 'slack' attitude to work existed and the unit creaked along rather than playing its full part in supporting the aims of the company. As might be expected, a crisis occurred and senior management had been forced to take action by replacing the previous manager. The new manager was judged capable of making the changes necessary to the operational frameworks of the department. Unfortunately, he was resented by the other staff, who saw him as a threat to their old, easy-going ways.

Senior management did not wish him to take a hard line with the staff in order to implement change, and thought that things would eventually calm down and that the staff were good at their job (if they were given good procedures to work within and so on). Consequently, pressure was put on the new manager to make the situation work. Unfortunately, the staff became more entrenched in their views and openly hostile towards him – at one point saying to his face that he was the problem in the office and that they hated him. Repeated requests to his boss for help produced little action. By this time, the new manager was of the view that even if the other staff were capable of doing the work, they were not acceptable to him. This inevitably made the situation even worse.

The new manager's boss would not take action against the other staff; neither would he take action against the new manager. After a couple of months the staff went over the head of the new manager and his boss to the sales director and complained that the new manager was no good and that the more senior manager was showing favouritism by supporting the new manager. They claimed to have no confidence in either manager. When the new manager's boss found out that the other staff had gone to the director without telling him first he was furious. At that time, his view of them changed and they suddenly became less than acceptable for the work within the department. What was previously the result of inadequate staff training and procedure design was now the fault of the staff themselves. He was attributing the behaviour of the staff to new causes, they did not want to co-operate with management and were trying to hide incompetence. Previously, his view was that they felt threatened by the situation and needed help to provide the expected service.

Stop ↔ Consider

To what extent does the situation described reflect perception in action or simply poor management? Justify your views.

seen as reasonable, or competitors hold prices steady. Management in Action 3.3 illustrates these experiences in a newly appointed first-line manager.

Kelley (1973) is credited with developing the theory of attribution. The central principle is that of covariation. A causal relationship is said to exist between two events if they occur together. If a particular outcome occurs only when a specific situation exists, then the situation is said to covary with the effect. For example, on a car assembly line good quality output is observed to occur when supervisors are walking the line; it is also noted that when they are absent from the line (say, at meetings) an increase in quality defects occurs. In this situation it would be natural to suggest (attribute) that close supervision is the cause of good quality output.

Kelley suggests that individuals attempt to identify covariance relationships through a number of devices. The criteria used include:

- *Distinctiveness*. If the particular event is not distinctive then it becomes pointless to imply a specific attribution as its cause. For example, a manager considered it her responsibility to improve the standard of English in reports produced by her staff. On one occasion a report was allowed to be issued without being vetted. That was distinctive behaviour in that context and therefore worthy of further consideration by staff as to the cause of the change.
- *Consensus*. If the particular event produces the same effect on other people then a degree of consensus is said to exist. If a manager who is always rude and bad tempered is suddenly friendly, and if other people are also more friendly than usual, then there is consensus between reactions. This implies that something common to both reactions exists.
- *Consistency*. The sameness of reaction and behaviour over time and situations. If a manager is always rude and bad tempered it would not seem to suggest anything unusual if they are abusive in a particular context. However, if the same manager were to praise, thank, or be pleasant on a particular occasion then it would become distinctive behaviour and worthy of further consideration.

Arriving at the attributions for particular behaviours is an important process as the subsequent responses depend upon how individuals interpret the original causes. In the instance described above, when the manager returned a report marked up for correction it did not cause offence or a problem. The reaction would be different where demands for reworked reports were the exception. Weiner (1975) developed a framework for determining a classification for different types of attribution and therefore appropriate response behaviours, (see Figure 3.14).

FIGURE 3.14

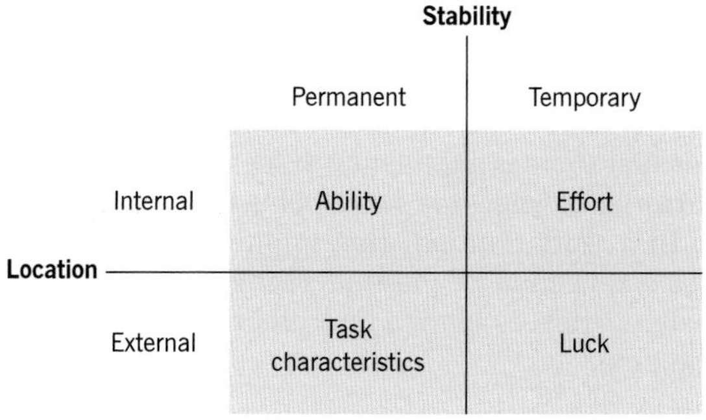

Attributions and response determinants (*source*: Weiner, W (1975) *Achievement, Motivation and Attribution Theory*, General Learning Press, Morristown, NJ)

The diagram is designed assuming that the purpose is to identify the attributions of, and provide a response to, a subordinate's performance. The diagram is built up from two axes, location and stability. Location can be determined from the perceived source of the behaviour:

- *Internal*. Based on the attributes of the individual in terms of ability, motivation, skill and effort for example.
- *External*. Based on the factors outside the individual, such as family circumstances, company policies and the attitudes of managers.

Stability is determined on the basis of the perceived degree of permanence of the attribute:

- *Permanent*. This reflects an enduring feature, something that is ongoing and which will remain a force in the future.
- *Temporary*. A transient feature, something that is likely to change over time. An example would be someone who is late for work one morning as a result of their car breaking down.

Each of the four cells in the matrix has been given a title that represents the underlying characteristics of behaviour that fall into that area. Consequently, the response to the attributions implied by those concepts will also differ:

- *Ability*. This implies that the problem is the inability of the individual to do what is expected of them. If a subordinate were to produce a performance that implied this cell of the matrix, then retraining might be appropriate.
- *Effort*. This implies that the subordinate is capable of doing what is expected of them, but did not apply themselves adequately to the job. Under these circumstances, a telling off or some other punishment might be considered.
- *Task characteristics*. This implies that the subordinate had little direct control over what happened, therefore putting it right would also be beyond their control. Consequently, an appropriate response might be to seek ways of improving their ability to deal with the situation in future. This might include redesigning the work or procedures.
- *Luck*. There are occasions when things do not go according to plan. The subordinate in question may have experienced difficulties in obtaining information from another department because it was busy or short staffed.

  Whatever the attribution, the appropriate approach will be to overcome the problem quickly. For the future, any lessons should be learned to prevent reoccurrence.

Attribution theory does not identify the actual cause of behaviour. What it does provide is the perceiver's view of the cause of the behaviour. This provides the essential foundation for what is called the fundamental attribution error (Harvey and Weary, 1984). This holds that there is a tendency to see others' behaviour as the result of stable, internal characteristics while one's own behaviour is a function of temporary, environmental forces. In a work context, this implies that managers tend to see employees' behaviour as a reflection of the underlying characteristics of the person (good or bad). Conversely, employees tend to interpret the same events as a feature of the circumstances at the time.

ATTITUDE FORMATION

Attitude
Predisposed feeling, thought or behavioural response to a particular stimulus.

The term **attitude** has entered everyday usage in that some people are described as having 'attitude'. At work, managers frequently look for a 'good attitudes' in potential recruits. Therefore, attitude clearly reflects a potent force in dealing with people.

The basis of attitudes

Attitudes are linked with many other aspects of behaviour. They have traditionally been considered to be relatively stable dispositions to behave in particular ways towards objects, institutions, situations, ideas or other people. They are also usually considered to develop as a result of experience. In other words, they influence an individual's response to something or someone. All people have attitudes towards things – school, university, parents, work, politics, sport, religion and other people. Some attitudes are deeply held and difficult to change, while others are more superficial and easy to drop or amend.

In one approach to the study of attitudes (Rosenberg, 1960) suggests that to change an attitude it is necessary to change either the underlying feelings or beliefs. This approach relies on a model of attitudes based on that shown in Figure 3.15.

Looking at each of the three components from Figure 3.15 in turn:

1. *Cognitive component*. This refers to the beliefs and values that the individual holds, perhaps in terms of support for a football club, say Sunderland AFC. One belief related to support for the club might be that it is the best football club in England. A related value underlying support for the club would perhaps be that it is important to the individual supporter to have something from their home town that provides a source of pride. The important point to note from this analogy is that beliefs are evaluative in nature, for example the 'best' football team. Values, by the way of contrast, tend to be the judgmental criteria against which beliefs are measured. For example, an individual may need something from their roots to cling onto as a way of providing meaning in their life. The football team may or may not serve these purposes, depending upon its success.

FIGURE 3.15

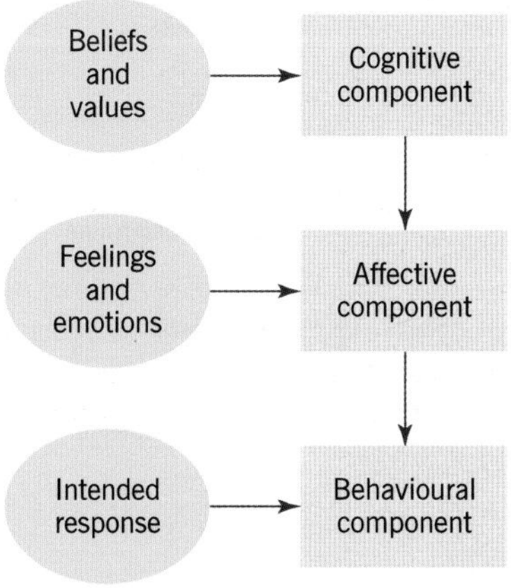

Construction of an attitude

2. *Affective component*. The feelings and emotions that make up the affective component arise from an evaluation between the two elements within the cognitive component. A supporter of the football club just mentioned could be expected to develop feelings and attitudes according to the success of their team related to the underlying beliefs and values about it. The affective component of an attitude tends to be socially learned. We acquire the ability to express our reaction to the balance between the cognitive elements in ways that align with our social environment.
3. *Behavioural component*. This reflects the outcome of the process. It is the actual or intended behaviour. In the case of support for a football team that is not performing well, an individual could continue support and hope for better results in future, change their allegiance to another club, or give notice that if losses continue they will stop supporting them. The behaviour resulting from the affective component would also be influenced by the importance of the attitude for the individual and the degree of intensity with which it was held.

The description of attitudes provided so far assumes a dispositional perspective. Another approach from Salancik and Pfeffer (1977) suggests that attitudes develop from the social frameworks and experiences encountered. In diagrammatic form, this process would be as shown in Figure 3.16.

By means of the socially derived cues and markers, an individual is sensitized to the prevailing attitudes and behaviours in particular contexts. The pressure is then on the individual to reach an accommodation between their previously held attitudes and behaviour norms and those expected in the current context. From this perspective attitudes are suggested to be situation specific rather than reflecting underlying frameworks within the individual.

Of course, these two approaches to attitude are not necessarily mutually exclusive. In some contexts it would be possible for deeply held attitudes and beliefs to become apparent, for example during a family discussion. Whereas in other situations it may be necessary to suppress one's own feelings and values if continued acceptance by the group is to be maintained. For example, in a work context employees are primarily employed to undertake the tasks demanded by management. From that point of view, the personal beliefs and values of the individual have to be subjugated to those of

FIGURE 3.16

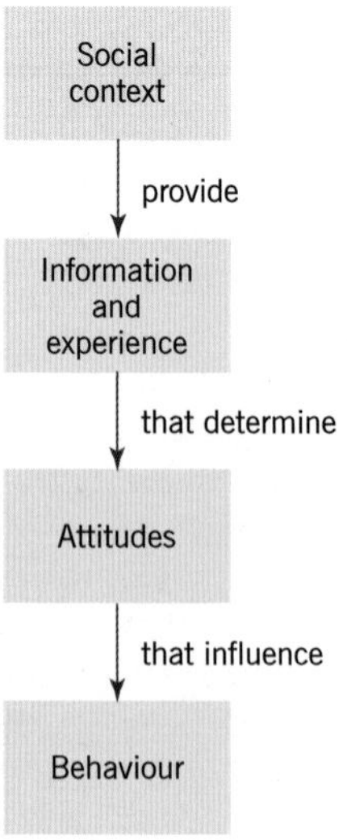

Situational construction of attitudes

management if the individual is to continue to be accepted by the organization. This is reflected in the **instrumental approach to work** in which employees do what management want because they need to keep the job (and income), not because they believe or agree with management's requirements. The following Employee Perspective (3.3) demonstrates that complex links exist between what workers perceive and what they actually do in earning their wages.

Instrumental approach to work Based on a trading and value approach to work and the determination of contribution relative to benefits gained.

Attitudes and perception

There is a twofold relationship between attitudes and perception. First, individuals perceive the attitudes of other people. They do this through the receipt and interpretation of a range of visual, speech, body language, dress etc., clues. People then classify the people they perceive around them based on the clues detected. For example, a group of young males all with very short hair and outlandish clothing perhaps torn and covered with studs and chains might be interpreted by an old person as likely to be violent thugs looking to beat up and rob some innocent individual. In that example, the perceiver is not experiencing the real attitudes of the group of young people, they are observing a number of stimuli and drawing conclusions (stereotypical) from them about the attitudes and intentions of the group. In turn, their own behaviour will be influenced by their presumptuous interpretation of the signals.

EMPLOYEE PERSPECTIVE 3.3 Chasing the targets!

One company introduced an incentive scheme for its customer service employees without consulting them first. Management felt that it would provide a means of sharing out the work more equitably and motivating staff to work harder in support of the company objectives. Managers, without any discussion with employees, also decided the targets for use in the new scheme. Over a period of about one year staff became familiar with the scheme and although no formal complaints were made, customers began to notice a difference in service. Whereas prior to the new incentive scheme staff had been only too willing to help customers, now they tended to act mechanically and were very reluctant to go beyond the basic provision of the service, saying that they were too busy or that it was someone else's responsibility to deal with other issues. A small number of customer complaints were received, but management took the view that things would settle down, and as productivity had gone up this indicated that the scheme was successful.

The following year staff were asked to help management review the targets used within the scheme in order to improve it. A couple of the staff did so, but their ideas were largely ignored as they sought to make the case for more staff and to make the targets more realistic. Management said that no concessions could be made as cost could not be allowed to increase, but thanked staff for their contribution. The service to the customers did not improve and some took their business elsewhere. The longer serving staff and those with readily transferable skills began actively looking for jobs elsewhere or sought retirement at the earliest opportunity. They were generally replaced by staff that had no experience of the previous service standards within the company. They simply accepted the incentive scheme and the targets that went with it and sought to maximize their income. Generally they only stayed until a better job opportunity came along, or they could stand the situation no longer. Management continued to claim that the new incentive scheme was a great success in helping the company achieve its objectives.

Tasks

1. If you were an employee who had worked in this company for many years why do you think your attitudes would be as they are? What would you do and why?
2. Do you consider that the attitudes of the new staff are supportive of management's objectives in any real sense of the term? Why or why not?
3. Do you think that the management attitude that everything is fine can be supported? Why or why not?

Second, individuals seek to give out particular perceptions through the impression that they seek to create, perhaps by their dress code, attitudes or other signals. For example, a group of young people dressed as indicated above might be seeking to convey a particular image of themselves as a group or as followers of a particular fashion. Equally, it would not be expected that a bank manager would dress casually in jeans and sweater for an important business meeting, as to do so would give completely the wrong impression (or perception) to the clients.

Attitudes and behaviour

Attitudes have an influence on behaviour, but it is a complex relationship. Katz (1960) suggests that attitudes serve four main functions:

1. *Adjustment.* They allow the individual to adapt to the environmental circumstances that they encounter. This contains elements of rationalization and justification by the individual for the behaviours in which they engage.
2. *Ego defensive.* By adopting particular attitudes, individuals allow themselves to protect their self-esteem from potentially threatening situations or knowledge. For example, the 'fact' that an employee was sacked from their job was nothing to do with their incompetence, but was because the manager hated them personally.
3. *Value expressive.* This allows the individual to externalize the important values that they hold. Young people frequently express their rebellion against the control of parents by adopting individual and sometimes shocking clothing styles. Johnson (1999) reports a survey indicating that only 8 per cent of employees in the UK felt that their values and those of their employers were very similar, only 14 per cent felt that they were very proud of their organization and only 30 per cent felt any strong loyalty towards it. All these data reflect clear attitude patterns expressing the underlying values associated with work.
4. *Knowledge.* This allows the individual to provide structure to the world around them. It allows the individual to group together facets of the world into a common category each with attitude-based response patterns for ease of working within a complex environment.

Cognitive dissonance
Used to explain behaviour in an individual in situations where conflict exists between attitudes or beliefs.

Festinger (1957) and Festinger *et al.* (1958) developed the concept of **cognitive dissonance** to explain behaviour in situations where conflicts existed between attitude components. It contains three main elements:

1. There may exist dissonant or 'non-fitting' relations among cognitive elements.
2. The existence of dissonance gives rise to pressures to avoid any further increases in it and actively to seek reductions in the level experienced.
3. Manifestations of the operation of these pressures include behaviour changes, changes of cognition and circumspect exposure to new information and new opinions.

Essentially, Festinger describes a mechanism that seeks to provide consistency between perceptions, attitudes and actions. A feeling of anxiety is produced when there is a contradiction or incongruity between the components of an attitude and behaviour. An employee may hold an opinion that they are a good worker and indispensable to the organization. The manager of that same individual may perceive that the person is a poor employee and barely acceptable. If the manager tells the employee of their opinion then the employee will be in possession of two sets of contradictory information. In order to deal with the dissonance created by that knowledge and to be able to rationalize the discrepancy the individual may adopt a number of strategies.

These could include working as the manager expected, suggesting that the manager does not have the knowledge to form a correct judgement, or implying that the manager was biased and unreasonable.

Another area in which attitudes and behaviour are linked emerges through the spiritual side of human nature. Attitudes towards the role of spirituality within organizations vary tremendously. However, there is a developing awareness that it is not possible to keep driving for ever higher performance from each individual without some negative consequences. A feeling is growing that there is a role for organized religion, poetry, yoga etc. to offer opportunities for people to find peace within themselves, together with an improved balance between the various components of life, including work. Welch (1998) illustrates this through the example of a Benedictine monk offering residential weekends on meditation and discussions on spirituality as a way of helping individuals search for meaning in their lives. Another example refers to a firm of solicitors that recruited a poet in residence. As well as writing officially for the company, they hosted workshops for all staff on poetry writing as a way of creating connections between individuals. The basis of this type of initiative is the recognition of a need for balance in life and the development of sustainable values, attitudes and beliefs in relation to work if sustained success is to be achieved. Attitudes towards work can change and Management in Action 3.4 provides an illustration of this from Japan.

IMPRESSION MANAGEMENT

So far in this discussion, perception has been described as a phenomenon in which the individual learns to make sense of the world in which they live. This is a unidirectional view of the topic. Recognizing that humans undertake a judgmental and categorized evaluation of the people and events around them provides an opportunity for individuals to present a particular image to the world around them and so encourage a desired response.

Impression management is something that all actors and politicians become very familiar with in the course of their work. An actor has to be credible in the part they are playing and they use a variety of techniques including make-up, lighting, costume and set design to create the illusion that they are the character they are playing. Politicians similarly must present themselves as credible, honest and trustworthy if they are to be elected or hold one of the offices of state. Public relations and media consultants are widely used to assist in the development and presentation of particular impressions for individuals in the public domain.

Within an organization there are several aspects associated with impression management in addition to the public relations perspective indicated earlier, including:

- *Career strategies.* In order to enhance prospects of promotion (and limit the likelihood of dismissal) it is necessary to create particular impressions to those able to deliver the desired result. Giacalone (1989) identifies a number of what he describes as demotion-preventing and promotion-enhancing strategies. These include being associated with the right people at the right time and providing plausible excuses for particular courses of action. The following Employee Perspective (3.4) demonstrates one of the negative political and impression-management labels that some people attract when working in an organization and they engage in what other people view as hostile behaviours.

MANAGEMENT IN ACTION 3.4 More than the job's worth

In Japan it is the devotion to duty of the salaryman that is responsible for much of the economic growth that turned the country into an economic superpower since World War II. In return for devotion to the interests of the employer, the salaryman was guaranteed both a career and a job for life.

However, there was a high price to pay for the lifetime job protection and the very people who were thought to be benefiting most from it are increasingly calling it into question. There are an estimated 10 000 deaths each year from *karoshi*, literally meaning sudden death from overwork. There is a growing willingness to take employers to court over infringements of employee treatment and human dignity. For example, Mr Haruo Kawaguchi sued his employer (Teikoku Hormone Manufacturing) for compensation for a six-year separation from his family because of a job transfer to another location.

Employees are slowly beginning to rethink their perceptions about the nature of work and its role in their lives. In a poll of 1600 executives, the values that made Japan successful such as efficiency, growth and competition were thought to be least important to the future of society. Creativity, fairness and symbiosis were identified as the most important qualities for the future development of society. Individuals are also beginning to shun the pursuit of career progression in favour of performing an interesting or worthwhile job. For example, Mr Tetsuro Handa moved from being a high-flying section manager in the export department with Mitsubishi to their environmental affairs department because he felt that it would be more important and rewarding in his life, irrespective of promotion opportunity.

This shift in perception is being fuelled by the worst recession in Japan for over 20 years and by early retirement or semi-redundancy among salarymen. During the recession in the early 1990s Japanese companies had to make strenuous efforts to cut back on labour costs, putting the notion of lifetime employment for salarymen under threat. To get round the difficulties that would have resulted from dismissing many thousands of such employees a number of measures were introduced by companies. These included unpaid (or reduced pay) leave, enforced holidays, early retirement and compulsory transfers to remote satellite operations. It has been estimated that there are about 1 million surplus workers on the books of Japanese companies because of this recession. One of the consequences to emerge is an adverse impact on the health of individuals. Increased incidence of mental health problems (such as depression and loss of confidence) and being afraid to tell their families of their true position are common examples. Under these conditions, it is hardly surprising that traditional loyalties are being questioned and a new perception of the way that life and work interact is being formed.

Adapted from: Dawkins, W (1993) More than the job's worth, *Financial Times*, 16/17 October, p 9.

Stop ↔ Consider

Does the situation suggest that it is possible to have too much of a 'good' attitude towards work?

Argue the case from both management and employee points of view.

EMPLOYEE PERSPECTIVE 3.4 Teflon worker!

There is a new term that has made an appearance in management circles over the past few years. A particular person might be referred to as either 'Teflon man' or 'Teflon woman', depending upon their gender. Teflon is a material that is used in cooking equipment to make it non-stick, applied to people it is a term that means that nothing sticks to that particular person; the individual is always able to avoid responsibility for any mistake, error or failure that they make. Some employees claim the credit for projects and activities once they are certain to be successful, even when they played very little part in the process. Also, such people frequently seek to lay the blame and responsibility at someone else's door very quickly when things go wrong, often producing just enough evidence to hide the real situation. It is generally a term with negative connotations; used by fellow employees to identify someone who is usually very ambitious and has to be watched carefully as they seek to advance their position in the company. It is also used to warn everyone in the company to be careful in their dealings with such people or they might be blamed for something that they did not do, or have the credit for the good things that they do stolen.

Task

1. As an employee how might you seek to maximize the likelihood of being well regarded by superiors by making obvious, and elaborating, your contribution to successful activity and reducing your apparent responsibility for failing activity without earning the title 'Teflon' from colleagues?
2. As an employee, how might you try to deal with the behaviour of such people if they are firstly colleagues, and secondly if they are your boss?

- *Public image*. The use of corporate identity symbols can include a badge or logo of some description, but it can also be taken further through the design of company premises and staff dress codes. Many fast food chains have a house-style for their restaurants that allows instant recognition anywhere in the world. Rafaeli and Pratt (1993) for example, regard this as such an important issue that they developed a model for comparing organizations based on requirements for dress codes among employees.
- *Managerial*. In industrial relations situations for example, it is necessary for the management team to present a unified front and to create an image of the organization that supports the public stance adopted during negotiations. Attempts to hold down pay increases by suggesting difficult financial conditions, while at the same time allowing managers to continue to spend heavily on entertainment is unlikely to be accepted willingly by the workforce and leads to claims of double standards and the use of the 'fat cat' label. Rankine (2003) makes just this point in relation to pension provision of senior executives.

There is some evidence of a growing trend for impression management within organizations; that of a management-imposed requirement for particular appearance characteristics. This is not a new phenomenon, for example a number of airlines have recruited only young attractive people to work as cabin staff for many years. However, this is now beginning to resurface in a number of ways that has led researchers at Strathclyde University to coin the term aesthetic labour to describe the management-determined mix of appearance, age, weight, class and accent characteristics. The researchers describe the trend using the example of a hotel seeking to project a total image concept, with the hotel building representing the hardware and the staff the software. Once recruited by such organizations, staff would experience pressure to mould themselves into the desired characteristics in order to provide the total experience sought by managers (Lamb, 1999b). In the same article it is reported, by way of example, that three teenage girls were replaced with 'models' by a night club because they were described as too ugly.

PERCEPTION AND ATTITUDES WITHIN AN ORGANIZATIONAL CONTEXT

Perception, attitudes and organizations

Organizations have many aspects of perception and attitudes to contend with:

A. *The attitudes and perceptions of actual customers.* A considerable proportion of company marketing effort goes towards encouraging particular attitudes and perceptions in their customers. The effort of organizations to achieve this are not restricted to an advertising or marketing approach. The results that a school achieves in examinations taken by its pupils will do much to encourage parents to send their children to it. Cameron *et al.* (2003) for example, identified that liking the music being played in the background influenced customer perception of waiting-time length (and mood) during service delay. However, it was mood alone that contributed to the customer evaluation of their experience. The cartoon included as Figure 3.17 provides an illustration of the negative attitudes and perceptions of customer care which organizations attempt to prevent, yet is all too familiar to the customer, which is why the humour works.

B. *The attitudes and perceptions of potential customers.* This category represents the people who do not currently buy the product or service offered by the organization. Much organizational effort goes into attempting to understand the characteristics of this group, their attitudes and buying habits.

C. *The attitudes and perceptions of the wider community.* Public relations is the discipline involved with the presentation of the organization's perspective. Either this can be an attempt to optimize positive value from an organization's activities, or it can be in response to a negative situation (bad publicity). It is frequently a discipline associated with spin and half-truth, but Kim and Choi (2003) found that the older practitioners with an ethical ideology based on idealism and relativism demonstrated a higher level of agreement with professional ethical standards than those with different ethical ideologies.

D. *The attitudes and behaviours of employees.* Management in Action 3.5 illustrates the management reactions to an employee who developed what could be described as deviant behaviour patterns. Deviant, that is, in terms of the norms expected by managers and delivered by most employees in that situation.

FIGURE 3.17

Attitudes and perception

MANAGEMENT IN ACTION 3.5

Have long holiday, will travel nowhere in job

The perception and attitude towards work in Japan is noticeably different to that in the West. Employees are expected to place the interests of the employer above personal interest. This is taken to such a level that it is not uncommon to find that individuals introduce themselves in terms of their company first. The same level of dedication applies to the time spent at work and the taking of holiday. The director of one government ministry retired after 35 years' service and proudly announced that he had never asked for any time off work other than for public holidays and that he had accumulated two years' worth of time off, which he could not now take as he was retiring!

One employee of the Ministry of Health dared to break this unofficial code of honour and his story became a best-seller as a popular book. However, it did nothing for his career prospects. Mr Masao Miyamoto lived and worked in America for 11 years after initially studying medicine in Japan. On moving to America, he undertook postgraduate work at Yale University and subsequently practised psychiatry. Upon his return home, he was appointed to a position in the Ministry of Health. He found the work culture and attitude of long hours spent at the office difficult to accept after living in America for so long. It was common for staff not to leave before 7pm, even if there was no work to do; they would not seek more than about four days' holiday a year; and would work for seven days each week.

Each year a holiday request chart was circulated and junior staff were expected to apply for holidays for that year by filling in the desired spaces on the form. No one ever applied for their full allowance and people always applied for fewer holidays than their superior. Mr Miyamoto applied for two weeks' holiday and began a controversy that sabotaged his career and resulted in his being exiled to a menial job, checking sailors for cholera in Yokohama. Mr Miyamoto's immediate boss attempted to persuade him to withdraw his application but after much debate (and *sake* drinking) agreed with his holiday request. However, the director of the section was less amenable and although the holiday was eventually agreed, Mr Miyamoto was accused of selfishness, causing disruption and of dishonouring his position. It was also suggested that he might like to resign rather than remain in such a difficult situation.

However, it was only after Mr Miyamoto applied for a holiday the next year to visit Tahiti that he was transferred to Yokohama. It was then that he wrote his book poking fun at the bureaucratic nonsense that he perceived around him. This further infuriated his superiors and some of his colleagues, but others quietly began to voice some measure of support for his personal stand. His bosses still find ways of undermining his confidence and of pointing out that he does not fit in. Even in a suit and tie, just like his colleagues, it is pointed out to him that he does not dress in a way that conforms to the dress code usually adopted within the Ministry. A high price for taking a holiday, to which by law he was entitled.

Adapted from: McCarthy, T (1993) Have long holiday, will travel nowhere in job, *The Independent*, 12 August, p 11.

Stop ↔ Consider

Which attitudes were wrong and why?
To what extent (and why) should employees conform to management expectations in relation to behaviour and dress code?

E. *Supplier attitudes and perceptions*. The purpose of seeking to influence the attitudes and behaviours of suppliers is to provide the organization with a favourable basis for trading. This could involve obtaining extended credit terms, rapid and frequent delivery patterns or improved quality at a reduced price.

F. *The organization's competitors*. The relationship between competitors is a complex one and needs to be managed carefully. Most organizations watch their competitors very carefully for any sign of activity that could influence positively or negatively the market or themselves. The recent battle for the takeover of the Safeway supermarket chain in the UK is one example (Bawden 2003). It began with a bid from Morrison's group, only to be quickly to be followed by bids from each of the other chains. They had been 'caught napping' by the initial bid and were determined to join in the action in order to maintain or improve their relative positions in the industry. This process involved much public relations activity to influence the perceptions, attitudes and actions of shareholders, the public, regulators and competitors.

G. *Regulators*. The power of regulators to control organizational activity through legislation and other rules tends to subject them to attempted influence by many pressure groups. This is done in an attempt to channel the future direction of legislation and policy. This is usually an area shrouded in mystery and behind-the-scenes activity, rather than direct intervention. Study tours, lectures, seminars, reports and fact-finding visits are just some of the 'tools' adopted by the professional lobbyist on behalf of clients. Of course sometimes this approach goes beyond the lawful attempt at influencing perceptions and attitudes and becomes bribery or corruption in one of its many forms.

H. *Shareholders*. These are, technically, the owners on whose behalf managers run the organization. In the public sector, it is the members of the general public, through parliament, who are the owners. There is a need for organizations to develop approaches to the presentation of shareholder information in such a way that the individuals and institutions involved are encouraged to maintain their investments. In the financial markets, a considerable number of analysts are employed to get behind the public output from organizations and identify the true position. It is, therefore, a game of cat and mouse with the stock market value of the organization being the prize.

Perception, attitudes and control

Whatever the ownership structure of the organization, managers find themselves having to achieve objectives through other people. Therefore, managers need to shape the behaviour of other people in order to direct them towards the goals sought. In order to control behaviour within the organization, managers have to either:

- Order others to carry out management wishes, or
- Persuade individuals willingly to undertake what is required of them.

The first option implies force and coercion by managers while the second implies rationality, linked to the exercise of free will on the part of the employee. In practice, managers utilize a mixture of both approaches. The use of excessive force and direct orders is unlikely to produce a willing response among those subject to them. Neither is it likely to produce the high levels of productivity required of organizations these days. Perception and attitudes provide the concepts through which managers attempt to control the behaviour of employees. If successful, this could encourage employees to be more compliant in doing management's bidding. Also, employees would be encouraged to see themselves as stakeholders in the organization, and thereby, through association and commitment, encouraged to positively invest in helping management to achieve its objectives.

Garrahan and Stewart (1992) provide a review of Japanese management practices in a car assembly plant located in the North of England, in which the whole question of participative management practice as a control process is explored. From that discussion it becomes apparent that careful initial selection of employees is reinforced through subsequent employee training and management practice. Employees therefore have their perceptions and attitudes towards work shaped into a management-preferred model. However, located in an area of relatively high unemployment there is inevitably an unanswered question as to the degree of success in actually shaping employee perception and attitude. It could simply reflect a compliance response based on the lack of alternative work options. Employees who need the job might be expected to adopt whatever attitudes are expected, in order to earn a wage. This results in an instrumental approach to work.

PERCEPTION AND ATTITUDE FORMATION: AN APPLIED PERSPECTIVE

The world is constantly changing and managers must manage in that dynamic situation. Perceptions are a constant source of information to each individual as they attempt to make sense of the world in which they live. As a continuous process, perception is potentially amenable to adjustment in the light of new information and through attitude changes. For example, finding out that a previous attitude about certain people is wrong could change future perceptions about them. Because perceptions and attitudes are interactive and dynamic, this implies that either they change in the light of experience, or that behaviours become increasingly detached from appropriate interaction with the experienced world.

Part of the purpose of perceptual and attitudinal mechanisms is to introduce the familiar into an uncertain world. They allow the individual to filter out the unnecessary and concentrate on significant events. Employees and managers are not likely to interpret the facts in the same way, or even in a consistent way across time. It is these dual aspects of uniqueness (each person is different) and variable interpretation (of the same stimuli) of the familiar that creates the difficulties for managers. Managers attempt to operate in a three-dimensional world in this context as in Figure 3.18.

Taking each dimension in turn:

- *Time*. Managers are constrained by events in the past. The size, culture and organization of the company were all determined in the past. Managers must work in the present time but within these constraints in attempting to ensure that the organization is able to meet its present and future commitments. They are of course entitled to make changes to the constraints, but this invariably takes time.
- *Locus*. Managers deal with internal and external events. The locus of emphasis can either be internal or external (or both) depending upon the circumstances.

FIGURE 3.18

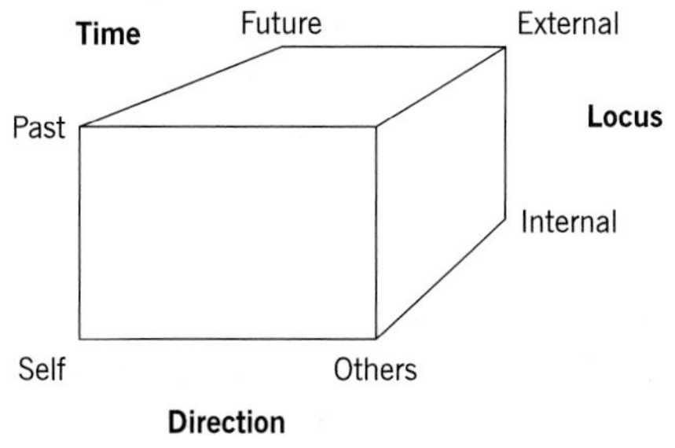

Three-dimensional view of management activity

For example, a hostile takeover in the City will force an external perspective as managers attempt to fight off the raiders. Of course, much of the impact of the action will be felt within the organization as costs are cut in an attempt to win the support of existing shareholders through improved returns on their investment.

- *Direction*. This dimension in the model attempts to reflect the degree of introspection in the process. Managers will be forced to consider either their own perspective or that of others, not necessarily within the organization. Managers can either operate according to their own agenda or can find it necessary to function according to the dictates of others. In seeking to defend against a hostile takeover, the agenda is largely determined by the raiders.

Managers attempt to extract the maximum utility from these concepts in manipulating the perceptions and attitudes of others. Many managers might find the use of the word manipulation in this context difficult to accept. It is a word with connotations that imply an approach to making people do things against their will. However, efficiency can only be achieved if employees and managers work in unison towards the same objectives and with the same vigour. In that sense employee behaviour must be manipulated (or directed, or channelled) into appropriate patterns. It is in achieving that particular synergy that Japanese organizations have been particularly successful (Oliver and Wilkinson, 1992). The needs of the organization are determined by managers largely as a result of their interpretation (or perception) of the situation, (see Figure 3.19).

From Figure 3.19 it can be seen that managers receive a great many stimuli from a variety of sources, all of which are interpreted through the managers' psychological make-up. The result is a response-set that directs subsequent action in the running of the organization. For example, if a manager interprets the business environment as hostile, they may well use the situation to force changes or concessions from an otherwise unwilling labour force. It is the formal role that managers play within an organization that makes their perceptions of particular importance. Managers are charged

FIGURE 3.19

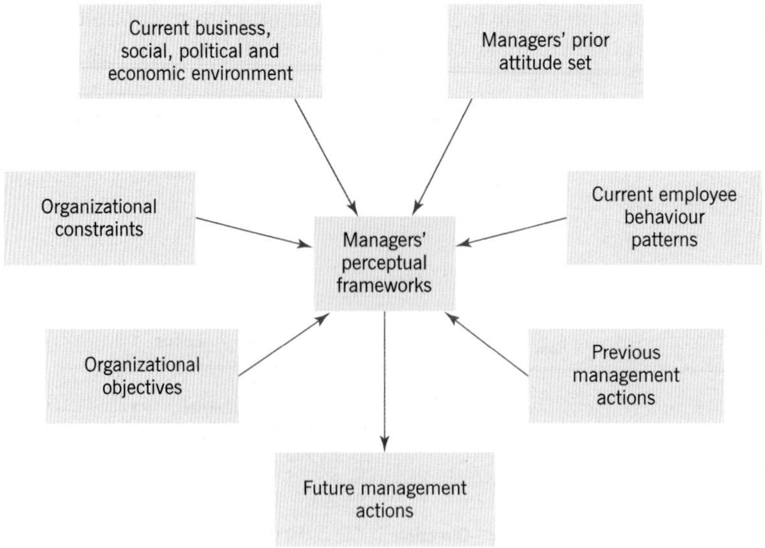

Managers' perceptions and the impact on subsequent actions

with the responsibility of running companies, therefore their perceptions and attitudes, linked to their subsequent behaviours, influence the direction of the organization and the manner through which it is achieved. That is not to suggest that employees have no influence on the process, simply to state that the ultimate influence rests with managers. It is they who take the credit for success, and they who must also accept responsibility for failure.

Part of the perceptual selectivity process directs individuals to give credence to information provided from sources that are regarded as authoritative. This helps to explain why employees in some organizations do not believe management when they attempt to communicate particular points of view. Previous management messages may not have been reliable; therefore employees come to rely on what they might regard as more credible sources. This demonstrates the concept of **perceptual set**, or the predisposition to perceive what we expect to perceive. Employees expect to see a management that is consistent with previous experience. They respond accordingly. They may receive the signals telling them how desperate the situation is, but simply read them as more of the same, and therefore ignore the message.

Perceptual set
The predisposition to perceive what an individual expects to perceive.

This phenomenon also influences how men perceive women. Deaux and Emswiller (1974) demonstrated that men interpreted competence in women as the result of luck rather than skill. Given that most managers are male; this approach provides a mechanism to inhibit the progress of females by attributing any success to chance factors. It also provides an opportunity for men to reinforce the solidarity of their male identity by maintaining a perceived superiority over women. Ragins and Sundstrom (1990) studied the perceived power of male and female managers by their subordinates. They found that generally there were no differences between the sexes in this context, although women managers were suggested to display higher levels of expert power than their male counterparts.

Direct attempts to influence attitudes and perceptions are not common. Clearly, any direct or obvious attempt to influence either would run a high risk of failure. The process of influence adopted in an organizational context is usually much more subtle. It can be detected indirectly through many activities associated with management control and authority, including:

- *Conflict determination and resolution*. What is perceived as acceptable behaviour by the organization is based on the attitudes and perceptions of managers. By taking disciplinary action against particular behaviours or work attitudes a signal is given indicating those that management consider inappropriate. Conversely, what is perceived by employees to reflect acceptable management behaviour is based on the attitudes and perceptions of the employees. Employee difficulties with regard to management's attitudes and behaviour can usually be referred to a grievance procedure for resolution. The purpose of these procedural mechanisms is to provide an institutionalized process for exploring the immediate problem and arriving at a mutually agreeable solution. Another way of describing this process would be as arriving at a better perception of the other person's point of view.
- *Culture*. This represents another area with which perception and attitudes are strongly associated. If culture is defined as 'the way that we do things around here' then it should be apparent how particular perceptions and attitudes could support it. Equally, by implying that 'inappropriate' attitudes and perceptions might undermine a desired culture or encourage a counter-culture it is easy to understand why they might be defined as hostile to management.
- *Communications*. The communications frameworks of the organization can educate, inform and persuade and so influence attitudes and subsequent perceptions. It is for this reason that managers can find themselves at odds with

trade unions over who has the right to communicate directly with employees. Communication is much more than the actual words used to convey the message.

- *Management style*. The way in which managers go about their tasks provides a clear signal to everyone as to what is regarded as important. This provides clear insights or clues to employees on what management is seeking so that an appropriate reaction can be determined. A workforce that perceives management pushing for higher worker productivity while enjoying long lunch breaks itself will generate cynical attitudes.
- *Work organization, job design and satisfaction*. The way in which work is organized, planned and designed also provides a clear signal to employees about the professionalism of managers and the degree to which they are serious about the business. Job satisfaction is an important attitude indicator, employees who perceive that their work is boring, menial and of little worth are likely to react accordingly.
- *Participative management*. Such practices provide for the perceptions of employees to be taken into account in the decision-making processes of the organization. This not only provides a clear signal on what is seen as important within the organization, but it allows the differing perceptions to be taken into account. It also provides the opportunity to influence attitudes and perceptions through discussion.
- *Power and control*. Managers assume the right to manage and, therefore, to control the activities of others. This task is made much easier if the individuals to be controlled are compliant and amenable to the process. To achieve this requires that their perceptions and attitudes be shaped accordingly. An extreme form is found when the search for power over another leads to **bullying**. Bullying involves influencing another person through the application of force, violence or intimidation. Research by NOP found that 10 per cent of people had actually been bullied at work and that the majority of the cases were within management and professional groups (Walsh, 1998). Non-management employees tended not to be bullied as often. The following Employee Perspective (3.5) demonstrates the effect of the power and control balances between managers and doctors in the dynamic and complex context of health care provision.

Bullying
The act of intimidating or forcing someone to do something by seeking to undermine their confidence and self-esteem.

- *Reward structures*. Pay is the most obvious reward. Basic wages or salary are often supplemented with bonus payments for extra output or performance. In addition, promotions, access to development opportunities and praise or punishment are all elements of the reward structures available for managers to use in encouraging appropriate behaviour. It can, however, be argued that reward structures do not produce fundamental changes in attitudes or perceptions. It is possible to achieve the desired reward through compliance behaviour, an instrumental approach to work. In other words, employees deliver what is expected without changing the underlying attitudes or perceptions. Rambo and Pinto (1989) demonstrate the complex interactions between variables in the creation of perceptions about a pay increase. In reaching this perception, it is not just the scale of money that is taken into account; many other variables influence the decision, future promotion opportunities and size of the current salary being just two. Highhouse *et al.* (2003) demonstrate similar complexity in the perception of fairness in starting salary.

EMPLOYEE PERSPECTIVE 3.5 Doctoring the health service

Higginbottom (2002) reported that during October 2002, 66 per cent of the hospital consultants (senior medical specialists) working in England and Wales voted against new working arrangements that would have tied them to a 40 hour working week within the National Health Service (NHS). The key element in the proposed contract was that the NHS would have first call on their time before they would be allowed to undertake any private work. The British Medical Association (BMA), which represents doctors, said that it had been rejected because of the fear that such working arrangements would give too much power to NHS managers, threatening the independence of hospital consultants. It also referred to a deep-seated mistrust between managers and consultants. In effect, it would give managers more control over the working lives of senior doctors. In addition, the government emphasis on the use of performance targets as the way of managing also detracted from the clinical need of patients which was the emphasis preferred by doctors.

Tasks

1. Should senior doctors act in this way? Why or why not?
2. Can health care be provided in a cost effective way if the perceptions and attitudes of managers do not prevail over those of medical staff? If you agree how might this be achieved whilst allowing doctors to retain control over medical treatment? If you do not agree how could health care provision be managed in terms of the balance between medical specialists and managers?

CONCLUSIONS

The subjects of perception and attitude formation are key aspects of management. They raise issues of ethics as a result of the potential for managers to seek to influence others in an attempt to manipulate events. They are processes that involve every individual all the time. They are dynamic processes and are of value in helping to simplify the complexity of the world as it is experienced. Unfortunately, by so doing they also make people vulnerable to mistakes in classification by creating illusions and encouraging other errors. The challenge facing managers is to make positive use of these concepts while not becoming so cynical that individuals simply become pawns in the game of life, there to be manipulated at the whim of the master. Perception is one of the fundamental ways in which attitudes are formed and it provides the basis of creating the perceptions of the self by others and of the desire to create particular impressions.

Now to summarize this chapter in terms of the relevant Learning Objectives:

- **Describe the processes of perception and attitude formation.** The perceptual process is described in basic terms in Figure 3.1. Attitudes reflect predispositions to behave in particular ways. So for example, a positive attitude demonstrated towards a company and a job opportunity, is often thought a necessary pre-requisite to being offered work. Figure 3.15 reflects the component parts of an attitude, although is has also been suggested that attitudes are socially constructed. In both possibilities, there are strong links between attitudes and perception as the means by which sensory information is captured and processed into meaningful information by the individual.
- **Explain the links between perception, attitude formation and impression management.** The relationship between these concepts is a complex and dynamic one. Perception is a process of making sense of the world around us and as such influences the attitudes that we hold. However, the attitudes that we hold also influence the perceptions that we make. For example, a customer will interpret the actions of an employee through the filter of their attitudes about the organization and its products and

services. Impression management is a process that also links to attitude and perception in that it reflects the attempts of an individual to present a particular image to the world, which will in turn influence (or so it is intended) the perceptions of that persona and the attitudes held about them.

- **Understand why employee perceptions and attitudes are difficult for managers to influence.** The processes are unobservable being inside the head of each individual. So managers cannot detect in absolute terms if employees have adopted the desired attitudes and perceptions, or if they are simply complying with the requirements for some private purpose. Public relations, internal marketing, reward systems, discipline systems, training, procedures, employee communications and involvement are all used to give out and reinforce the desired attitudes and perceptions that management seek. These processes all channel employee behaviour either directly or indirectly, and so allow managers to claim that the organization is unified in its pursuit of objectives. However, the degree to which that is actually the case is much more difficult to establish.
- **Discuss the issues surrounding organizational attempts to shape the perceptions and attitudes of employees.** There are many issues that impact on management's attempts to shape employee attitudes and perceptions. There is the ethical issue about how far it is right to go in seeking to create particular ways of interpreting and relating to the world in other people. There are the practical issues surrounding the degree to which it is possible to actually shape the attitudes and perceptions of others. There is also the problem of knowing which attitudes and perceptions are the most appropriate for employees to hold. For management to determine the preferred attitudes and perceptions reflects a 'top-down' perspective which ignores the potential benefits from 'bottom-up' or reciprocal influence. In addition, the attitudes held by employees can become so entrenched and strong that if the market moves on and they become outdated they can become a liability for the organization, but difficult to change.
- **Assess the significance of person perception in the behaviour of managers and employees.** The significance of person perception is that it provides the basis for the understanding and interpretation of other people. In an organizational context that is important because it determines the ways in which managers and employees relate to each other and it informs how each interprets the behaviours and intentions of the other. This is significant as it consequently forms the basis of the actions that each party takes in relation to the other which forms the dynamic and interactive behavioural patterns making up organizational experience. For example, an employee who perceives their manager to be exploitative and self-seeking will not be fully committed to supporting the manager. Equally, managers who perceive employees to be lazy and not interested in the long term future of the organization will tend to adopt a more directive and authoritarian style.

DISCUSSION QUESTIONS

1. Employees are never going to perceive the actions of managers in the way that managers would like because employees are subject to management direction. Discuss this statement and in so doing explore how this situation might be overcome.
2. Describe the perception process and explain the organizational significance of each stage in the process.
3. 'Impression management is the process by which human beings seek to influence the perceptions and attitudes of other people towards them.' To what extent would you agree with this statement and why?
4. To what extent are attitudes based on perception?
5. Provide an explanation for the expression, 'Beauty is in the eye of the beholder.'
6. Why might perception be described as an active process rather than a passive one?
7. Why might different people interpret the same situation differently? Provide examples from your own experience.
8. To what extent can managers influence the attitudes and perceptions of their subordinates? How could they set about doing so?
9. 'Management reflects the exercise of power and control, which is why employees tend to hold negative attitudes towards managers. Managers should pay more attention to the impression management aspects to their work.' Discuss this statement in the light of your experience and work on this chapter.
10. 'Attribution theory reflects the application of perception and attitude processes to other people.' To what extent and why would you agree with this viewpoint?

CASE STUDY The promotion

Richard was promoted to a new position within his company in Singapore. He had been a very successful sales manager for about two years and senior managers within the company wanted to make use of his talents in a more senior position. He had shown that it was possible to motivate a team of field sales staff who were much older than he was, all of whom had worked for the company for many years. Richard was regarded as a high-flyer and the early death of the regional sales manager created an opportunity to test out his capabilities in a much larger job, based in the company regional headquarters in Singapore.

Although Richard was only just 30 years of age, he was keen and ambitious, and had just added an MBA degree to his membership of the Chartered Institute of Marketing (UK), and his first degree in management science. He had performed well in his previous posts as a sales executive and sales team leader and was always among the top achievers in winning orders. He was also good at motivating his subordinates and cultivating new clients for the company, which specialized in the business-to-business sales of computer equipment. He was always making suggestions to his bosses about how he thought sales could be increased and the sales team made more effective. Richard did not suffer fools gladly and he was known to be a team leader who would encourage individual subordinates, but if they did not respond positively to his guidance, he would encourage them to move jobs or leave.

Although Richard had delivered impressive results in his time with the company (4 years in total) he had not had the managerial experience on a regional scale that he now faced in his new job. He was responsible for all field sales activity throughout the Asia-Pacific region, reporting to the marketing director of the company. At the same level as Richard were an export sales manager, a marketing manager and a sales administration manager, all of whom were older than Richard and had been with the company for more than 10 years.

The brief that Richard was given was simple, to increase the sales performance by 10 per cent each year for the next five years. Richard, based on his previous experience with the company did not regard this as a difficult problem as he had achieved more than 10 per cent annual growth in his previous jobs. However, it very quickly became apparent to Richard that things were not going according to plan. A couple of the specific country managers reporting to him made it clear that it was not going to be possible to achieve such growth in their areas. Another long serving manager said clearly that he should have been the one to be promoted to Richard's position as he had the longest service and therefore experience. A small number of the field sales staff were suspected of doing behind the scenes deals with the largest customers as a way of winning orders. These deals reduced the overall margin achieved on sales and were strictly against company policy. Richard was told that the previous regional sales manager had sanctioned these special deals in order to maintain sales volume and keep the key accounts. The director claimed that he was not aware of these arrangements.

Richard made plans to deal with the situation in a structured way, which involved providing training, recruitment of new staff, disciplinary action for breaches of company policy and closer management scrutiny of sales activity. However, although the director was prepared to go along with the general approach, he was not prepared to sanction any action to actively encourage certain individuals to leave the company, or to replace particular people if Richard deemed it necessary. Richard made the point that such an approach would inevitably impact on the ability to achieve the desired sales targets. The director indicated that he accepted this to a degree, but that significant improvements must still be made. After all, the director indicated, the sales force had long experience and had delivered in the past. They could do so now given effective leadership and positive support of the type that Richard had proved himself capable of.

Tasks

1. If you were Richard, what would you do in response to the situation?
2. In what ways could an understanding of perception, attitudes and impression management assist in helping to deal with the situation?

FURTHER READING

Ajzen, I and Fishbein, M (1980) *Understanding Attitudes and Predicting Social Behaviour*, Prentice Hall, Englewood Cliffs, NJ. A thorough review of the attitude literature and its implication for social behaviour.

Bromley, DB (1993) *Reputation, Image and Impression Management*, John Wiley, Chichester. A social psychological review of the subject of impression management in a variety of forms.

Cialdini, RB (1985) *Influence: Science and Practice*, HarperCollins, London. An interesting and readable text covering the psychology of influence and related behaviours. As such it covers many of the issues relevant to the behavioural consequences of attitudes and perception.

Clark, H, Chandler, J and Barry, J (1994) *Organization and Identity: Text and Readings in Organizational Behaviour*, International Thomson Business Press, London. Contains a broad range of original articles on relevant material themes and from significant writers referred to in this and other textbooks on management and organizations.

Fenton-O'Creevy, M, Nicholson, N, Stone, E and Willman, P (2003) Trading on illusions: Unrealistic perceptions of control and trading performance, *Journal of Occupational and Organizational Psychology*, 76, pp 53–68. Reviews research on traders working in investment banks in the City of London in which the relationship between perception and performance was investigated.

Pease, A (1981) *Body Language: How to Read Others' Thoughts by Their Gestures*, Sheldon Press, London. A practical guide on the interpretation of body language. Not an academic book but it does offer a wide-ranging review of areas that form a significant stimulus input to the perceptual system.

Segall, MH, Dasen, PR, Berry, JW and Poortinga, YH (1990) *Human Behaviour in Global Perspective: An Introduction to Cross-cultural Psychology*, Allyn & Bacon, Needham Heights. Offers a broad review of the subject matter. There are a number of references to attitudes and perception, but Chapter 4 is of particular relevance.

COMPANION WEBSITE

Online teaching and learning resources:

Visit the companion website for Organizational Behaviour and Management 3rd edition at: *http://www.thomsonlearning.co.uk/businessandmanagement/martin3* to find valuable further teaching and learning material:

Refer to page 35 for full details.

CHAPTER 4

Personality and individual difference

LEARNING OBJECTIVES

After studying this chapter and working through the associated Management in Action panels, Employee Perspectives, Discussion Questions and Case Study, you should be able to:

- **Outline the concept of individual difference.**
- **Describe the major theoretical approaches to the study of personality.**
- **Understand the strengths and weaknesses of each of the major theories of personality.**
- **Discuss the basic process involved in the development of psychometric tests.**
- **Explain the significance of individual difference as a basis for taking decisions relating to people within organizations.**

INTRODUCTION

Human beings as individuals are unique and psychologists have long sought to explain what that actually means. The psychological construct that has been used to embrace the features of individual difference is that of **personality**. The concept of **individual difference** has a long tradition within psychology and can be traced back to the early Greeks. For example, Theophrastus (a philosopher) was asking 2000 years ago why it was that with a common culture and education system people displayed different characteristics (Eysenck, 1982).

Personality eludes precise definition. As far back as 1937, Allport identified about 50 different interpretations of the concept. Since then many writers have attempted to define personality and Hall and Lindzey (1970) suggest that the definition preferred by each writer reflects the theoretical perspective adopted by that person, rather than any underlying conceptual insight. In other words, the definition of personality used by a particular writer becomes apparent through the description and justification of a particular theory.

Personality
The personal characteristics such as extroversion and stability that result in consistent patterns of behaviour over time.

Individual difference
See Personality (above)

THE STUDY OF INDIVIDUAL DIFFERENCE

The problem underlying the level of ambiguity in definition arises because personality (the construct that defines individual difference) cannot be directly observed. Some of the ways in which individuals differ can be described through obvious characteristics such as height, gender, etc. However, people also differ in less tangible ways, for example in intelligence and temperament which are much less clear in terms of meaning. Consequently, psychologists have concentrated on part of the overall meaning of individual difference, namely the underlying psychological structures that make up what has become known as personality. Consider for a moment two friends and how they differ from each other. Perhaps a description would include some of the following:

- *Physical description*. Height, weight, build, hair length and colour.
- *Emotional description*. Gushing, withdrawn, nervous or manipulative.
- *Sociability description*. Friendly, generous, giving, likeable and 'nice'.

These factors, along with many more, reflect ways in which people can be differentiated from each other. However, they are not all aspects of personality. Some characteristics reflect ability or physical qualities; others are probably a reflection of transient emotional states.

There is no single definition of personality that would be accepted by all theorists. In one common view, personality is considered to represent those personal characteristics that result in consistent patterns of behaviour (Burger, 1986). This rather loose definition provides some insight into the concept, but leaves many issues undecided. For example, an individual has many characteristics (say, the ability to drive a motor car) which provide the basis for a wide range of behavioural activities, yet they would not usually be regarded as personality characteristics. Also ignored in this definition is any reference to the source of personality. Is personality something that each individual is born with, or does it develop over time with experience? The answer is, probably, both. The relationship between these variables is shown in Figure 4.1.

We will now look at each element in turn.

FIGURE 4.1

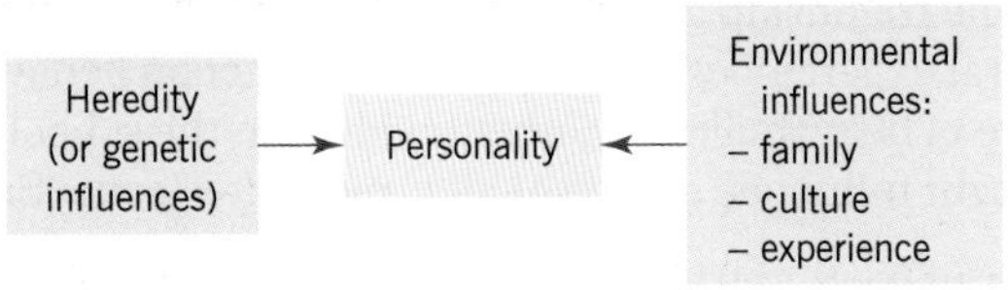

Relationship between the determinants of personality

Genetic influences It is not absolutely clear how much of the personality is determined by the genetic inheritance of the individual. In common expression there are many examples of heredity being used to justify behaviour. For example: 'That [particular behaviour] is just like your father [or mother].' However, an equally strong case has been put forward for the lack of genetic determination of personality, suggesting that it develops through interaction with people and events. This is the so-called nature–nurture controversy.

More recently it has been suggested that both nature (genetics) and nurture (environment) play a part to varying degrees in the determination of personality. For example, that genetics determine the range of possible development for a particular characteristic, but that environmental influences determine the actual degree achieved (Pervin, 1984). There is also some recent evidence from studies on twins by Holden (1987) that the genetic determinants of personality are more significant than previously thought. Research also demonstrates some interaction between the personality traits and job choices for young people at age 18 together with subsequent changes to personality traits by age, Roberts *et al.* (2003).

Environmental influences include:

- *Family*. When we are born we become part of a family. In our early years we are socialized into a family group and by that family into the wider society. Parents and siblings all have parts to play in introducing the individual to the behaviour patterns accepted within those cultures. Family in this context includes grandparents, aunts, cousins, and so on, as all have a part to play in establishing behaviour patterns in the child.
- There are many ways in which the family influences the development of the individual's personality. They include:
  - The process of interaction with children which will encourage particular behaviour patterns.
  - Older members serving as role models for the younger members to imitate.
  - The circumstances surrounding the family, including family size, economic status, religion and geographic location.
- *Culture*. The culture that an individual is born into has a considerable influence on the behaviour norms to which they are exposed. For example, Western cultures tend to emphasize individual characteristics while Asian cultures tend to emphasize collective values. Consequently, appropriate personality characteristics will be encouraged (through socialization) in individuals within each culture. One of the difficulties with the concept of culture is that it can lead to the assumption that all individuals within a specific context will display the same characteristics. The concept of culture is an **ideal type**. That is, the characteristics implied by a specific culture will be found to a greater or lesser extent in each individual within that context.

Ideal type
A model which would be identifiable only to a greater or lesser extent in practice.

- *Experience*. The friendship and other groups to which individuals belong, together with the general experiences of life all have an effect on behaviour. For example, the experience of being bullied by other children in the school playground can have a significant influence on personality and self-esteem (Bradshaw, 1981).

Nomothetic theories These offer an approach based upon the identification and measurement of characteristics through psychometric tests.

Idiographic approaches Are based upon the uniqueness of each individual and reject the use of psychometric tests.

There are a number of ways in which the subject of personality has been studied. The two major theoretical approaches can be described as the nomothetic and idiographic approaches. **Nomothetic theories** offer an approach to the study of personality based upon the identification and measurement of characteristics. This is achieved through the application of personality tests and tends to assume that the genetic determinants of personality are the most significant. A recent approach to using the nomothetic perspective on 'personality types' in relation to teamwork is reflected in Management in Action 4.1.

Idiographic approaches, in contrast, claim that it is necessary to take into account the uniqueness of each individual in describing their personality. It claims that tests are of limited value in measuring personality because it should be defined in terms of the self-concept of the individual. As such within the idiographic tradition, personality is largely a function of the dynamic interaction between the individual and the environment in which they live.

As with many other areas of psychological research, this classification scheme does not account for all the theories that have been developed. There is a third approach to the understanding of personality that combines elements of both the idiographic and nomothetic approaches. The approaches from this perspective are not easy to integrate into a single classification scheme because they are essentially individual contributions to the field.

One challenge in the organizational application of personality refers to the desire to identify which of its many dimensions are the most significant. It is argued that organizational success requires people with particular personality characteristics in order to provide the necessary drive, cohesion and support for the management agenda. It is assumed for example, that intelligence is necessary for success – but is it? Furnham (1993) argues that common sense is a far more important issue from an organizational point of view.

Another way in which the context and individual difference links together is through the notion of an internal or external locus of control. Individuals vary in the degree to which they consider that they are subject to control by forces internal or external to themselves. This does not refer to the direct control of behaviour or thoughts through hearing voices etc. It simply indicates the degree to which an individual considers that they are in charge of their own destiny. In many ways this is based around the individual's expectations. Human beings are predictive organisms in that we tend to learn from experience and predict future events based upon them. Individuals tending towards an internal locus of control would rely more heavily on their own capabilities and behaviour in seeking success. Kuratho and Hodgetts (1989) for example, suggest that successful business leaders fall into this category, relying on a belief in success being created by their personal ability to control events, not through the contribution of others. Employee Perspective 4.1 illustrates some of the practical issues that arise from the relationship between personality and work.

NOMOTHETIC PERSPECTIVES

The nomothetic approach concentrates on the identification and measurement of those dimensions that are generally considered to be the common characteristics of personality. This approach is based on the analysis of data obtained from research

MANAGEMENT IN ACTION 4.1 Personality and teams

Team working is a major part of the organizational experience for most people. Yet in many cases the team members are selected by virtue of the job that they do, or self-selection. There are models that suggest how to measure the individual differences between people in order to be able to ensure a balance of 'styles' that will hopefully ensure that the team functions effectively. Tony Alessandra puts forward the following four styles that he claims will help design effective teams:

- *Directors*. Driven by the twin needs to control and to achieve, these people are goal oriented and like to be in charge. Directors like challenge, are not afraid to bend the rules, are easily annoyed by delay, can be stubborn and insensitive.
- *Socializers*. This style is typified by people who are friendly, enthusiastic and thrive on admiration. Socializers are charismatic, optimistic and good at building alliances. They can be impatient and have a short attention span.
- *Thinkers*. These individuals are analytical, persistent and systematic people who enjoy problem solving. Thinkers have high expectations and can be over-critical, slow and deliberate.
- *Relaters*. This style reflects people who are good listeners, loyal employees and who develop networks of mutually supportive and reliable people. Relaters are good team players and become distressed by disruption and conflict.

Alessandra also explains how each personality style brings different strengths to a group activity. For example, he identifies the following aspects of a group activity:

1. *Communicating*. Directors tend to use short, task oriented comments and follow a clear agenda. Socializers tend to use humour, ask clarifying questions or generally act as go-betweens in seeking harmony.
2. *Using influence*. Directors tend to use the formal agenda processes and their leadership position as the means of exercising power and control. Relaters seek to maintain progress by elaborating what others say and encouraging everyone to contribute. Thinkers use information and logic to influence the process.
3. *Involving others*. Socializers like to be involved in the give-and-take of group discussion. Thinkers prefer to have much of the detail done before a meeting, but will get others involved in obtaining additional information.
4. *Decision making*. Directors like to have clear results with specific outcomes the result. They might even act unilaterally in this process. Socializers and Relaters prefer consensus decisions through compromise and conflict reduction. Thinkers prefer rational decisions dictated by fact or logic.

The aim is to be able to match the needs of the group activity with the strengths of each of the styles in order to produce synergy and the best outcome in terms of decision and job satisfaction.

Adapted from: Alessandra, T (2001) Team meetings, *Executive Excellence*, December, p 17.

Stop ↔ Consider

To what extent do the four styles reflect personality factors identified in the research? Is it likely that any individual can be described by one of the styles, if not what does this imply for the model?

carried out on large numbers of individuals, the purpose being to develop measurement scales for each characteristic. This approach provides the measurement of personality profiles and therefore allows comparison between individuals. So for example, person X has Y level of the introversion characteristic, a score which is similar to the vast majority of the population of which person X forms part. There are many personality tests of this type, but the best known were those developed by Eysenck and Cattell. This has been followed by more recent work, commonly referred to as the 'Big Five' model.

EMPLOYEE PERSPECTIVE 4.1 Personality or achievements?

Imagine you have been asked the following question by a friend:

> I am a quiet person, yet I work hard and get good results. In a recent discussion about a possible promotion, I was told that to stand a chance of getting the post, I needed to be more "lively" and "outspoken". I am perturbed that my work doesn't speak for itself, and convinced that my employers seem to want me to become a different person before I can move forward. Should I try to change my behaviour, or are they asking too much?

Tasks

1. The employee asking the question talks about 'changing their behaviour' and 'becoming a different person'. Does being asked to become more 'lively' and 'outspoken' refer to behaviour or personality and why?
2. How would you reply to your friend and why?

Now read the answer that was provided by Bullmore, J (2002) What's your problem? *Management Today*, December, p 77 when he was asked that question.

Eysenck and the study of personality types

As far back as Galen, the so-called classical temperaments of sanguine, phlegmatic, melancholic and choleric were being used to describe basic personality types (Eysenck, 1965). Quoting a source first published in 1798, Eysenck described the four temperaments as follows:

1. *Sanguine*. A person 'carefree and full of hope; attributes great importance to whatever he may be dealing with at the moment, but may have forgotten about it the next. ... He is easily fatigued and bored by work but is constantly engaged in mere games – these carry with them constant change, and persistence is not his forte.'
2. *Phlegmatic*. A person who displays a 'lack of emotion, not laziness; it implies a tendency to be moved neither quickly nor easily but persistently. ... He is reasonable in his dealing with other people and usually gets his way by persisting in his objectives while appearing to give way to others.'
3. *Melancholic*. A person who will 'attribute great importance to everything that concerns them. They discover everywhere cause for anxiety and notice first of all the difficulties in a situation, in contradistinction to the sanguine person. ... All this is not so because of moral considerations but because interaction with others makes him worried, suspicious, and thoughtful. It is for this (reason) that happiness escapes him.'
4. *Choleric*. A person 'said to be hot-headed, is quickly roused, but easily calmed down if his opponent gives in; he is annoyed without lasting hatred. Activity is quick but not persistent. He loves appearances, pomp and formality; he is full of pride and self-love. He is miserly; polite but with ceremony; he suffers most through the refusal of others to fall in with his pretensions. In one word the choleric temperament is the least happy because it is most likely to call forth opposition to itself.'

Eysenck was a prolific writer and produced many books and papers over the years. His 1967 and 1971 texts provide a good overview of the development of his work. His research approach to the study of personality involved both the rating of individuals by skilled raters and the completion of questionnaires by subjects. Eysenck carried out his research on people in the UK, USA and Europe. The results were subjected to factor analysis in order to identify the underlying dimensions of personality. Factor analysis is a statistical 'technique used to locate and identify fundamental properties underlying the results of tests or measurements and which cannot be measured directly' (Remenyi *et al.*, 1998, p 222). The outcome of the factor analysis was the identification of two dimensions along which personality could be said to vary:

- *Extroversion*. Measured on a scale running between the extremes of **extroversion** and **introversion**. The extrovert likes excitement, is sociable and lively. The introvert, by comparison, has a quiet and retiring aspect to their personality.
- *Neuroticism*. This implies a scale running from **neurotic** to stable in personality characteristics. The neurotic person tends to worry, is anxious, moody and unstable. The stable person tends to be calm, even tempered, carefree and reliable.

Extroversion
The qualities of excitability, sociability and liveliness in an individual.

Introversion
An introvert has a shy, quiet and retiring aspect to their personality.

Neuroticism
An aspect of personality reflecting a person who worries, is anxious, moody and unstable.

The two personality dimensions identified by Eysenck and the relationship between these and the much older temperaments are reflected in the main axes and quadrants of Figure 4.2. This figure also indicates the main characteristics of each of the 'types' of personality in the words around the perimeter of the outer circle. For example, someone who was unstable would also score highly on tests measuring the concepts of touchy, moody, etc. These also reflect the concepts upon which the factor analysis indicated earlier was carried out. The angle between the basic characteristics (passing through the centre point of the circle) is a reflection of the relationship between them. For example, there are about 90° between the characteristics of 'sober and rigid' and 'aggressive and excitable', implying that there is little or no correlation between them. Between the characteristics of 'sober and rigid' and 'lively and easygoing', however, there are 180°, implying a negative correlation. More of 'sober and rigid' means less of the opposite characteristics.

FIGURE 4.2

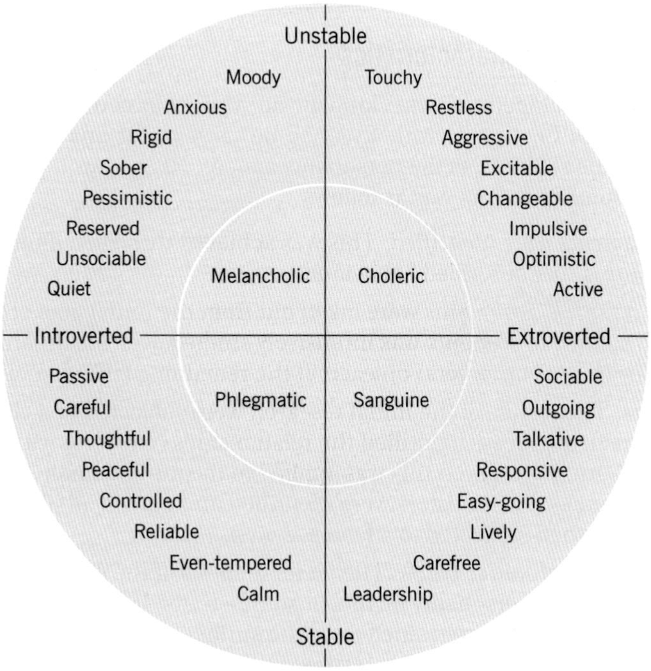

Eysenck's model of personality (*source*: Eysenck, HJ (1965) *Fact and Fiction in Psychology*, Penguin, Harmondsworth)

Conditioned
The behaviour of an individual which results from the application of behaviourism techniques.

Assessment of the theory Eysenck claims that the two main personality dimensions are linked to physiological functioning in the human body. For example, neuroticism is (he suggests) positively linked with those aspects of the autonomic nervous system that control body temperature, heartbeat, etc. He has attempted to use his theory to explain criminal behaviour and mental illness. For example, criminals are said to be highly extroverted, which, he claims, means that they are slow to condition and any **conditioned** behaviour is quickly extinguished. Essentially, conditioning represents a process of linking stimuli and responses as a basis of acquiring patterns of human behaviour. For example, employees generally do not absent themselves from work for long periods without good reason as they learn from experience that it leads to disciplinary action being taken against them and a loss of income. (Conditioning is discussed more fully in Chapter 5 in relation to learning.)

In linking extroversion with conditioning in the way he does Eysenck is suggesting that criminals are not conditioned into the patterns of behaviour that would be expected in normal society. The extrovert continually seeks novelty and stimulation which can be achieved through the criminal experience. However, there must be many extroverts who do not become criminals. Equally, it could be argued that much criminal behaviour reflects a conditioned response as the individual gains some reward from it.

There have been many criticisms of Eysenck's work, including the role that nature and genetics is said to play in the development of personality. Also, that having a theory based on just two dimensions is overly simplistic when considering the complexity of human personality and behaviour. However, his work has been based on a considerable amount of detailed research and so has strength. Eysenck himself does not claim that there are only two dimensions associated with personality, simply that they account for most of the published research. By implication, therefore, they are the most significant in the description and understanding of personality and individual difference.

Cattell and personality characteristics

Cattell (1965) developed a test known as the 'Sixteen Personality Factor Questionnaire', *(16PF)*. Just as with Eysenck he used factor analysis to sample the variables in what he refers to as the personality sphere. His research process in identifying the 16 personality factors was as follows:

1. *Trait elements were identified.* This was achieved through a dictionary search for all words that described behaviour.
2. *Initial research.* Synonyms were taken out from the initial pool of words. A small sample of students was intensively studied over a six-month period and rated (by trained observers) on each of the remaining trait elements.
3. *Analysis.* The results of the initial research were subjected to a cluster analysis. This statistical process identified the relationships (clusters) within the base data. In Cattell's research this was applied to the ratings obtained from the student studies. Fifty clusters were identified and named as surface traits. These were then subjected to a factor analysis.
4. *Identification of source traits.* The factor analysis of the surface traits produced the 16 personality factors or source traits. It is claimed that because the source traits are determined from the surface traits, which in turn were identified from the trait elements, they account for the whole personality. In short, the trait elements represent all the words developed to account for behaviour, so they must between them embrace every aspect of it, so the

research that follows must therefore define individual difference. It is these that became the factors in the 16PF questionnaire.

In developing the theory Cattell made use of three sources of information:

- *L-Data.* This refers to information, or ratings, obtained through the use of trained observers. The 'L' stands for life. For example, the initial research programme of student rating described earlier.
- *Q-Data.* This refers to questionnaire responses. An example of these would be the 16PF. He also developed tests of personality for other groups, including:
  - child's personality quiz (CPQ), for children aged from 6 to 11 years
  - high school personality questionnaire (HSPQ), for young people aged between 12 and 15 years.
- *T-Data.* This refers to data obtained through test applications. The results are obtained from the performance on tasks specifically designed to measure personality. These objective tests, as Cattell referred to them, were carried out when the subject had no knowledge of their true purpose. Cattell and Warburton (1967) describe over 200 such devices, including:
  - a chair that recorded the movement of anyone sitting in it, the purpose being to record the 'fidget' score for each person.
  - as part of a paper and pencil test the inclusion of two sets of identical questions, separated by a few pages. Included in the second presentation was some visually distracting material (say, cartoons). The difference in time to complete the two sets of questions measured the person's distractibility score.

Using the original factors and definitions for the 16 source traits from his 1960s research Cattell carried out another round of factor analysis. From that he identified eight second-order factors. However, it was the original 16 source traits that were used as the factors in the commercial form of the test. Over the years the original test created by Cattell has been subjected to development and the latest version of the 16 factors used in the 16PF questionnaire are as shown in Figure 4.3.

The scale for each bipolar factor ranges from one to ten, thus allowing each individual completing the questionnaire to have their results plotted onto the score sheet. The actual questionnaire used by someone completing the 16PF test contains a number of questions appropriate to each of the factors. After completion by the individual the results for each question are converted to a score on the scale of one to ten by comparison with published norms for the population to which the subject belongs. The individual scores for each factor can be plotted on the scale to provide a profile of the individual's personality. To illustrate this point, Figure 4.4 shows the 'average' profile of managing directors obtained by Cox and Cooper (1988) using an earlier version of the 16PF questionnaire than that shown as Figure 4.3. The test result for a specific managing director could be plotted on the same chart in order to show a comparison with the average for that population. This could be used as the basis of formulating a development programme for that individual, or as the basis for discussing their suitability or readiness for holding such a position.

Assessment of the theory The approach adopted by Cattell depends very much on the first step in his research process. If he has been able to identify all the possible trait elements in the personality sphere, then the rest must follow. The statistical tests carried out on his findings are such that the surface and source traits must account for the variation in behaviour. The basis of the claim is that because the behaviour

FIGURE 4.3

← **Scale of measurement runs from 1–10** →

Factor	Left Meaning	Right Meaning
Warmth	Reserved, impersonal, distant	Warm, outgoing, attentive to others
Reasoning	Concrete	Abstract
Emotional Stability	Reactive, emotionally changeable	Emotionally stable, adaptive, mature
Dominance	Deferential, cooperative, avoids conflict	Dominant, forceful, assertive
Liveliness	Serious, restrained, careful	Lively, animated, spontaneous
Rule-Consciousness	Expedient, non-conforming	Rule-conscious, dutiful
Social Boldness	Shy, threat-sensitive, timid	Socially bold, venturesome, thick-skinned
Sensitivity	Utilitarian, objective, unsentimental	Sensitive, aesthetic, sentimental
Vigilance	Trusting, unsuspecting, accepting	Vigilant, suspicious, sceptical, wary
Abstractedness	Grounded, practical, solution-oriented	Abstracted, imaginative, idea-oriented
Privateness	Forthright, genuine, artless	Private, discreet, non-disclosing
Apprehension	Self-assured, unworried, complacent	Apprehensive, self-doubting, worried
Openness to Change	Traditional, attached to familiar	Open to change, experimenting
Self-reliance	Group-oriented, affiliative	Self-reliant, solitary, individualistic
Perfectionism	Tolerates disorder, unexacting, flexible	Perfectionistic, organized, self-disciplined
Tension	Relaxed, placid, patient	Tense, high energy, impatient, driven

Catell's 16PF factors. Copyright © 1993 by the Institute for Personality and Ability Testing, Inc, Champaign, IL, USA. All rights reserved. Reproduced from *16PF 5th Edn Administrators Manual* by special permission of the publisher. Further reproduction is prohibited without permission of IPAT Inc.

exists, a verbal label is necessary to describe it. If no label exists then the behaviour cannot exist. This, of course, raises many questions relating to behaviour, language and the way in which personality interacts with both.

Words are used to describe ideas and feelings as well as behaviour, needs and wants. Consequently, the words identified might not reflect individual difference characteristics alone. There is also a complex relationship between the observable behaviour of individuals and the underlying personality characteristics that help to shape that behaviour. The links between what is observable, the words used to describe it and the associated psychological structures are far from clear.

FIGURE 4.4

Scale		Scale of measurement	
A	Reserved, detached, critical, aloof	1 2 3 4 5 6 7 8 9 10	Outgoing, warm-hearted, easygoing
B	Less intelligent, concrete thinking	1 2 3 4 5 6 7 8 9 10	More intelligent, abstract thinking
C	Affected by feelings, easily upset	1 2 3 4 5 6 7 8 9 10	Emotionally stable, calm, mature
E	Humble, mild, comforting	1 2 3 4 5 6 7 8 9 10	Assertive, competitive
F	Sober, prudent, taciturn	1 2 3 4 5 6 7 8 9 10	Happy-go-lucky, enthusiastic
G	Expedient, disregards rules	1 2 3 4 5 6 7 8 9 10	Conscientious, moralistic
H	Shy, timid	1 2 3 4 5 6 7 8 9 10	Socially bold
I	Tough-minded, realistic	1 2 3 4 5 6 7 8 9 10	Tender-minded, sensitive
L	Trusting, adaptable	1 2 3 4 5 6 7 8 9 10	Suspicious, hard to fool
M	Practical, careful	1 2 3 4 5 6 7 8 9 10	Imaginative, careless
N	Forthright, natural	1 2 3 4 5 6 7 8 9 10	Shrewd, calculating
O	Self-assured, confident	1 2 3 4 5 6 7 8 9 10	Apprehensive, troubled
Q1	Conservative, respects established ideas	1 2 3 4 5 6 7 8 9 10	Experimenting, radical
Q2	Group dependent, good 'follower'	1 2 3 4 5 6 7 8 9 10	Self-sufficient, resourceful
Q3	Undisciplined, self-conflict	1 2 3 4 5 6 7 8 9 10	Controlled, socially precise
Q4	Relaxed, tranquil	1 2 3 4 5 6 7 8 9 10	Tense, frustrated

16 PF profile of managing directors (after Cox, CJ and Cooper, CL (1988) *High Flyers*, Basil Blackwell, Oxford)

The 'Big Five' model

Research carried out on the traits proposed by many of the nomothetic approaches suggested that five were common to most of them, see for example McCrae and Costa (1989), Digman (1990). The five major factors are as follows, each containing six separate scales of measurement giving a total of 30 traits that are reflected in the model:

1. *Extraversion*. Ranging from outgoing and assertive at one extreme, to reserved and shy at the other.
2. *Emotional stability*. Ranging from secure and self-assured at one extreme, to anxious and depressed at the other.
3. *Agreeableness*. Ranging from co-operative and trusting at one extreme, to quarrelsome and hostile at the other.
4. *Conscientiousness*. Ranging from dependable and responsible at one extreme, to unreliable and disorganized at the other.
5. *Openness to experience*. Ranging from imaginative and broad-minded at one extreme, to disinterested and closed-minded at the other.

Research has shown that this model has some universal applicability. Also that Conscientiousness produces the strongest positive correlation with job and training performance, with Extraversion being associated with success as a manager and salesperson, see for example Barrick and Mount (1991), Hogan and Holland (2003). Conscientiousness has also been shown to be a significant factor in predicting pre-clinical success in medical training (Ferguson *et al.*, 2003). However, it was also found to be related to worse performance in clinical assessment, perhaps as that involves a different type of learning together with strategic problem solving. However, others have criticized it using broadly similar arguments to those levelled

Metaphor
The explanation of something complex through reference to something simpler, but which conveys additional meaning.

against other nomothetic approaches. The following Employee Perspective (4.2) seeks to show how personality can be used to support particular **metaphors** on how management should be practised.

IDIOGRAPHIC PERSPECTIVES

The idiographic perspective emphasizes the development of the self-concept aspects of personality rather than concentration on the measurement of common characteristics. There are difficulties for the test-based approach of Eysenck and Cattell as a result of the imposition of the researcher's frame of reference on data collection and analysis. Eysenck and Cattell reflect the positivist approach to epistemology in research. Epistemology is the branch of philosophy that debates the ways in which individuals begin to understand the world and communicate that knowledge to others (Burrell and Morgan, 1979, p 1). Positivists hold that the social world consists of cause and effect relationships, just like the world of the natural sciences and that the role of social science is to discover these causal connections (Kolakowski, 1993). Inevitably therefore, positivists tend to follow the experimental and scientific tradition in the search for underlying regularities laws that create the social world.

However the interpretivist tradition takes the opposing perspective and suggests that the social world is fundamentally different from that of the natural sciences. Therefore, the underlying laws implied by positivists do not exist as such. Interpretivists hold that the social world is created (or given meaning and substance) within the minds of the people who live in it. Consequently, there will be differences in how individuals conceptualize the social world in which they live. Therefore, understanding the individual and their view of the social world is necessary in seeking to understand individual behaviour. In relation to individual difference, idiographic theorists argue that in order to understand unique personality characteristics it is necessary to understand how the individual relates to the world in which they live and the individual qualities that make each person different from every other person.

Cooley, an American psychologist, introduced the concept of the looking-glass self to the debate on personality. He draws attention to the interactive nature of much behaviour and the development of self-image as a result of this process. We begin to see ourselves as others see us through the responses that we generate from others. This is the looking-glass, or mirror, that reflects a perspective back to us. Through the interactions with the people around us we come to understand who we are and so learn to adapt our personality to accommodate our environment.

Mead (1934) added to this approach through the concept of the generalized other. This concept is intended to reflect the existence of two components in the 'self'. They are:

- *I*. The unique, spontaneous and conscious aspects of the individual.
- *Me*. The internalized norms and values learned through experience within society.

The generalized other refers to the understanding that the individual develops of the expectations that society has of them. It is in the 'me' element of the 'self' that this evaluation takes place. The 'I' component is the aspect of personality that attempts to ensure that the individual meets their own expectations, rather than becoming a creature totally of the 'me' component. It also allows the opportunity to provide for evolu-

EMPLOYEE PERSPECTIVE 4.2 Organizations are zoos!

Risner (2003) suggests that people in the workplace fall into four main categories of personality type:

- *Lions*. Head straight for the end result doing almost anything to get the job done. They need achievement to measure success.
- *Monkeys*. Place high value on recognition and measure success through the amount of acknowledgement and praise received. They gravitate towards popularity, friendliness and prestige, whilst avoiding rejection, negativism and argument.
- *Dolphins*. These are steady, co-operative types placing a high value on sharing and trust. Routine and predictability make them feel safe, unplanned change makes them feel unhappy.
- *Elephants*. More concerned with content than congratulations. They need to know how things work and this can lead to paralysis by analysis and following every rule in the book. Speed is never an issue with these types of people.

Risner makes the point that good managers need to act like good zookeepers – understanding the animals in their zoo and communicating with them in appropriate ways to achieve effective team goals.

Tasks

1. As an employee would you be happy with this approach to classifying you? Why or why not?
2. What does this approach suggest about how people should be managed? Is such an approach likely to be effective? Why or why not?

tion in society through the adaptation of social norms to meet the needs of the individuals within it. Rogers (1947) proposed that the main objective of personality is a desire fully to realize one's potential. Like Mead, he also used the two components of 'I' and 'me' in describing the self-concept. His view of the linkages between 'I', 'me' and the 'self-concept' is illustrated in Figure 4.5.

One implication of this model of the self-concept is that the personality will be subject to change as the underlying personal self and social self change due to experience. This linkage is demonstrated in the model by the connections between the elements and the relationship implied by them. If this change did not occur then a tension would be created which could lead to the emergence of personality disorders within the individual.

Erikson (1980) considered the personality to be continually developing throughout life. His view was that as the individual passed through the various life stages

FIGURE 4.5

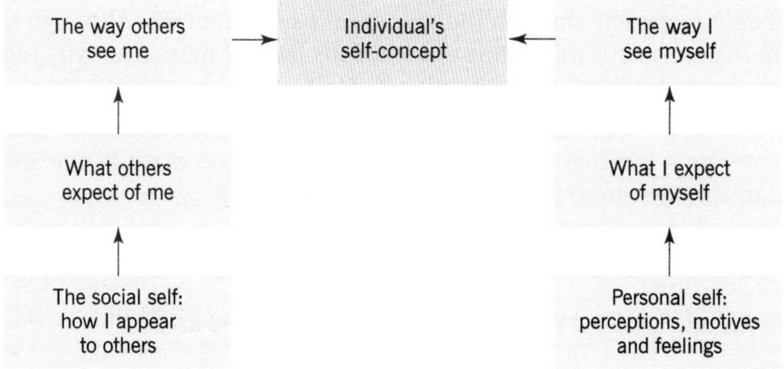

Rogers' view of the 'I' and 'me'

tensions and conflicts arise which have to be dealt with. For example Erikson's fifth life stage covers the years from 12 to 18 years of age when an individual experiences tensions between identity and role. In dealing with these conflicts the individual who successfully negotiates a resolution achieves healthy personality growth, whereas unresolved conflicts can lead to problems in later life. In this model there is a clear link between the concept of individual difference and the development of the 'self-concept' in a dynamic and ongoing relationship over time.

OTHER PERSPECTIVES ON INDIVIDUAL DIFFERENCE

Freud and psychoanalysis

Free association
The right of employees to associate with whom they choose; in psychoanalysis a process encouraging unprompted responses to a stimulus.

Sigmund Freud lived from 1856 until 1939 and spent most of his life in Vienna. He trained as a physician and then specialized in neurology. He originally worked with Josef Breuer who specialized in the use of hypnosis in the treatment of hysteria. However, about 1895 Freud began to use **free association** in the treatment of hysteria and stopped working with Breuer. The use of free association was the critical step in the development of psychoanalysis.

Free association is a process that begins with an item of emotional significance for an individual. The initial task of the psychoanalyst is to identify these items of significance through discussion with the patient. Freud suggested that dreams were a potent source of items of emotional significance with which to begin the process. The individual is then encouraged to talk about their ideas and thoughts in relation to these items of emotional significance until for whatever reason they stop. In technical terms they break off from the chain of association. This process is then repeated for other items of significance for the individual.

The points at which the individual broke off the thought chain were held to be major points of psychological resistance. Freud claimed that this occurred when the individual's internal psychological processes attempted to protect them from bringing out into the open those things which the individual wished to be protected from. It was these resistance points that became the focus for Freud's research and central to the development of psychotherapy.

Freud was a prodigious writer and his collected papers amount to some 24 volumes (Strachey, 1953–66). His theorizing was complex and covered many aspects of life, from cannibalism to the choice of career. According to Freud, there are three levels of mental activity:

1. *Unconscious*. This refers to mental activity that is inaccessible, deeply hidden and only accessible through the process of psychoanalysis. Although hidden from the conscious mind, this unconscious level of mental activity motivates much human behaviour.
2. *Pre-conscious*. This level refers to ideas that are unconscious, but unlike the unconscious category, they can be recalled when necessary. People's names and telephone numbers often fall into this category.
3. *Conscious*. This refers to the thoughts and ideas that we are aware of in the normal course of activity.

In addition, Freud classified the mind as consisting of three areas:

1. *Id*. The id is the area of the mind that contains all the inherited information available to the individual. It is the cauldron of our very being. It is the part of

our mind that follows the pleasure principle in seeking immediate gratification and satisfaction regardless of the consequences.

2. *Ego*. The ego develops during childhood and serves to balance the demands of the id. In doing so the ego follows the reliability principle in assessing the consequences of behaviour originating in the demands of the id.
3. *Superego*. This becomes the internalized version of parents. The superego becomes the observer of the ego and controls it through the same devices as would be adopted by the parents. Freud claimed that the superego had developed by about the age of five.

According to Freud, detectable behaviour in an individual is a balance between these three components of the mind. A well-adjusted individual will be controlled by their ego, a neurotic (driven by anxiety about the imposition of external control) through their superego, and the psychopath (driven by their own desires) through the id. The intention of psychotherapy as used by Freud is to restore the natural balance between the three components of the mind and so produce a 'healthy' individual in terms of personality.

In terms of individual difference, Freud described a process of development lasting from birth through to early adult life. The development of personality was the outcome of internal struggles and involved passing through a number of stages:

- *Oral*. The initial stages of life lasting from birth to about the age of two years. It reflects the importance of feeding, pleasure achievement and bonding with the mother.
- *Anal*. Lasting from about two years of age until four. It reflects the focus of attention shifting from the 'input' to the 'output' aspects of life.
- *Phallic*. At about the age of four the child enters the final stage of development which ends with puberty. This reflects the development of the individual in terms of the growing initial awareness of genital significance in subsequent sexual activity.

It is through the id, ego and superego that adults manage their interaction with the world around them. Freud described a number of defence mechanisms adopted by the ego in order to maintain the balance between the id and superego. Defence mechanisms protect the individual from the 'damage' that could result from unresolved internal conflict. The main forms of ego defence mechanism are:

- *Sublimation*. This allows the desires emerging from the id to be expressed in an acceptable manner. For example, pottery making and painting can be described as sublimation for the anal drives to handle and smear faeces.
- *Repression*. This describes a process where the existence of something is deliberately kept hidden from the conscious thinking level because it might be too painful.
- *Denial*. This is a defence mechanism in which the ego alters the perception of a situation in order to maintain a balance in the mind.
- *Projection*. The transmission of feelings and motives to other people. A manager might seek to justify their own political activity on the basis that others began such behaviour first.
- *Reaction formation*. This produces the opposite feelings and behaviour at the conscious level to those held at the unconscious level. So for example, unrequited love can become hate.

- *Regression*. The avoidance of problems between the id and superego through the adoption of patterns of behaviour that once produced satisfaction. For example, an older child may suck its thumb when being scolded by its parents.
- *Isolation*. This results in a separation of feelings and emotions from the experiences that normally produce them.
- *Undoing*. This attempts to 'undo' something from the past. The obsessional washing of hands, over and over again, could reflect a person attempting to cleanse themselves in a deeper way.

Assessment of the theory Freud's approach to personality is not a single theory as such. It is a complex model, including aspects of intellectual and sexual development, training, education, mental structure, social process and the dynamics of interaction. As such it is difficult to offer specific criticisms and equally difficult to defend it against any that are raised. Eysenck (1953) sets out the major objections to the theory, essentially on the basis that it was not scientific:

- *Lack of data and statistical analysis*. The data were not subjected to the processes considered acceptable by psychologists trained in the 'scientific method'.
- *Sample base*. The samples for his theory were mostly private patients, middle class and female. Furthermore, they put themselves forward for his treatment. They are not a representative sample of the entire human population and claims for a universal theory must therefore be open to question.
- *Inadequate definition of terms used*. The terms used to define Freudian theory are ill defined and consequently it is not possible to be absolutely certain of the meaning or even of their existence.
- *Lack of 'testability'*. Because of the 'richness' and complexity of Freudian theory it is not possible to falsify it. The scientific method involves a reductionist approach. Freud adopted a holistic model and attempted to reflect the complexity of life in a complex model.

The arguments raised by Eysenck are those that would be expected from a positivist when commenting on the work of an interpretivist (see, for example, the discussion in Henwood and Pidgeon, 1993 on this type of debate). The exponents from these two traditions talk past each other in deciding what offers an acceptable basis for explaining the social world. They therefore criticize each other's work largely because it does not fit into their preferred paradigm.

Other arguments against Freud's work include that it offered circular arguments to support the ideas in it and that by emphasizing early childhood it produces a model that is deterministic and ignores the possibility of subsequent individual development (see, for example, the work of Erikson outlined earlier). However, Freud's model offers 'richness' in attempting to encompass the whole of personality in a grand theory. Parts of the theory have been subjected to a more rigorous form of testing with some success (Kline, 1972). The following Employee Perspective (4.3) seeks to link Freudian ideas with the practice of human resource management by classifying the types of people who work in that field.

At a practical level Freud's work led to other research on the complexity of personality. Freud was interested in understanding the whole person and the part that early development played in the formation of the adult personality. The theory can be seen in some behaviour at work. For example, employees and managers often display 'temper tantrums' when things do not go according to plan, perhaps reflecting the ego defence-mechanism of regression.

EMPLOYEE PERSPECTIVE 4.3 **The personality of HR people**

Wilson (2003) using Freudian psychology and his consultancy experience, suggests that HR people tend to fall into one of the following types:

- *All wisdom and gravitas*. From a very stable family background and perhaps the youngest of two same sex siblings. They learn early in life about the value of harmony and stability and that they are only a small cog in a large machine. As children they become adept at spotting what authority figures expect and are able to coerce others into falling in line, thus earning praise.
- *The consummate professional*. From a confused lower middle class family background and may describe themselves as working class. Became aware early that life was unfair. Brought up to respect authority, parents became anxious when exam results were not as expected. Feels honoured by the challenging projects given to them by the company, but confused as to why reward involves being given more challenges to deal with.
- *HR supercharger*. Usually an only child on whom parents lavished conditional love providing the child was busy and involved with things around them. Parents worried about such children retreating into their rooms on their own. In early adolescence they tended to have many hobbies, but were expert in none of them. At school, they learned the power of communication as the way to get others to do things.
- *Maximum impact*. Perhaps the youngest of three or four siblings and always had to compete. They were always being compared unfavourably with the other children. They learn early on that the only way to compete against older and stronger siblings is through measurement – by outperforming them in times, grades, etc. They tend to be on the fringes and never part of the in-crowd.

Tasks

1. If you were an HR specialist, which category would you prefer to be and why?
2. To what extent do you consider that you could change the type of person that you are (perhaps in order to gain promotion) within that classification?
3. Could this approach offer any value in categorizing people that work in HR? Why or why not?

Jung and the cognitive approach

Jung was a close associate of Freud for a while, but the relationship was destined not to last for long and they parted company in 1913. Jung developed an approach to personality based on Freudian theory, but which incorporated aspects of the future goals held by an individual rather than simply emphasizing the past (Jung, 1968). It postulated three levels of personality:

1. *A conscious level*. This aspect of personality allowed for reality to be incorporated as a result of the everyday experience of the individual.
2. *An unconscious level*. This makes up the individuality of each person and is composed of the complexes and facets within individual difference.
3. *A collective unconscious*. This is the pool of inherited and socially derived universal experience that each person carries with them inside their personality.

Personality differences were reflected by a number of dimensions within Jungian theory, including the use of the extroversion and introversion. Another dimension was that of cognitive style, reflecting four different approaches to information gathering and evaluation:

1. *Sensing*. People who prefer to deal with hard information in a structured context.
2. *Intuiting*. People who dislike routine activities, but who prefer to deal with possibilities rather than certainty.

3. *Thinking*. People who prefer the use of logic and rationality as the basis of problem solving, without the feelings of others entering into the process.
4. *Feeling*. People who prefer to have social harmony around them, get along with others and have sympathy for those around them.

From this description it might be apparent that there are two dimensions involved in this framework: sensing and intuiting are at opposing ends of a continuum as are thinking and feeling. This is reflected in Figure 4.6.

The main personality characteristics for each cell in the matrix shown in Figure 4.6 are described in Table 4.1. This indicates the application of Jung's theory in differentiating personality and in describing the consequences of that approach for job preferences.

Assessment of the theory The theory developed by Jung lends itself more easily to testing than that of Freud. The Myers-Briggs Personality Indicator (referred to as the MBTI) is based on Jung's view of personality, to which was added a dimension reflecting lifestyle (Myers-Briggs, 1987). This is now a well-established psychological test and

FIGURE 4.6

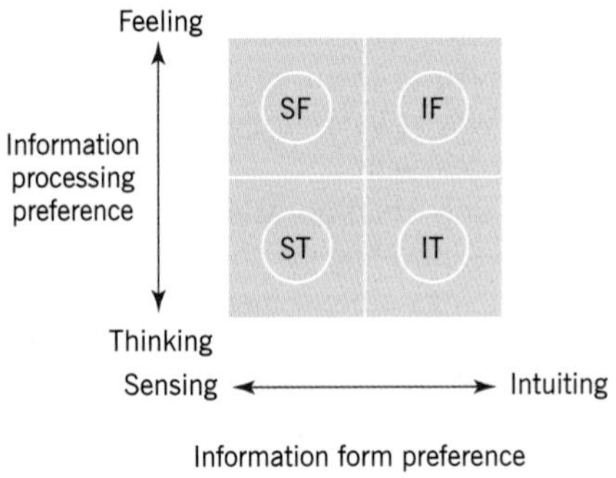

Jung's cognitive styles

	Jung's cognitive style			
	Sensing/thinking (ST)	**Intuiting/thinking (IT)**	**Sensing/feeling (SF)**	**Intuiting/feeling (IF)**
Prefers	Facts	Possibilities	Facts	Possibilities
Personality	Pragmatic, down-to-earth	Logical, but ingenious	Sympathetic, sociable	Energetic, insightful
Work preferences	Technical skills	Theoretical solving problem	Providing help and services to others	Understanding and communicating with others
	Physician accountant, computer programmer	Scientist, corporate planner, mathematician	Salesperson, social worker, psychologist	Artist, writer entertainer

TABLE 4.1 Differences between Jung's cognitive styles (*adapted from*: Vecchio, RP (1991) *Organizational Behaviour*, 2nd edn, Dryden Press, Hinsdale)

is widely used by organizations as an assessment tool and by researchers interested in occupational choice, personality and management style. There is also support for this model from research into personality characteristics and the successful adoption of Total Quality Management (TQM) practices in the USA and Taiwan, Yen *et al.* (2002).

However, the work of Jung has not gone without criticism. Eysenck (1965) for example, claims that the concepts of extroversion and introversion were already in existence. However, it must be remembered that Eysenck is generally dismissive of approaches based on a holistic perspective.

Murray and personology

Murray was another writer who attempted to reflect the whole individual in the theoretical model. Indeed, he preferred the term 'personology' to psychology as a description of his work. He emphasized the study of personology as the 'science of men taken as gross units' (1938). Murray worked intensively with a small number of subjects. The potential advantage of this was a fuller understanding of each individual person, with, potentially, generalizable theory resulting from the in-depth analysis.

Murray identified a total of 44 variables in his approach to individual difference, including:

- *Needs*. These form the main motivating factor in behaviour. He identified 20 manifest and eight latent needs. Manifest needs he described in familiar terms, for example, play, achievement, understanding and autonomy. Latent needs he described as being inhibited and usually expressed in fantasy rather than overt behaviour.
- *Presses*. These are the external determinants of behaviour. Presses operate on the needs of the individual, depending upon the circumstances. For example, successful organizations are able to create environments and cultures which in turn encourage an achievement orientation behaviour among individuals.
- *Internal states*. Murray identified four internal states that are capable of influencing behaviour, for example the ego ideal. The ego ideal refers to an aspect of personality that reflects an unrealized achievement drive based on a high level of, as yet unmet, aspiration.
- *General traits*. Murray listed 12 of these, including anxiety, emotionality and creativity. They are intended to embrace the broad characteristics that influence much behaviour. They can be seen as qualifiers to the other variables. For example, a person with a high level of anxiety will respond differently to the need for play than will a highly creative person.

Murray developed his theory over a number of years, through the application of a range of measurement devices. He tested his subjects on 24 different test applications in a single 36-hour period. This inevitably placed his subjects under considerable strain. Among the tests used were:

- *Autobiographies*. Subjects wrote about their lives and this was analyzed to identify any of the 44 variables already described. Particular emphasis was placed on childhood events.
- *Interviews*. Murray and his team interviewed each subject about issues such as their memories of childhood, family relationships and problems currently being experienced.
- *Experiments*. A number of tests were used to measure specific aspects of the theory. For example, one test required subjects to print words quickly using a hand-printing set.

Projective text
Ambiguous images are presented to an individual for interpretation; responses provide an insight into attitudes and personality.

- *Projective tests.* A **projective test** is an ambiguous stimulus and subjects are asked to describe what is happening. The interpretation of the picture is considered to reflect something about the individual's life and inner thinking processes. Figure 4.7 is similar to those used by Murray in that the events in the picture could be interpreted in many different ways.

Assessment of the theory Murray drew heavily on the work of Freud and Jung as his inspiration, but he provided a broad range of measurement to support his work. Eysenck (1959) claimed that there is almost no validity for the projective technique and that testers do not agree with each other on the interpretation of test protocols. He goes on to claim that projective tests are the vehicles for the riotous imagination of clinicians.

Murray was not the first to use the projective test as a means of gaining insight. Leonardo Da Vinci was the first person to record that paint smudges tended to be interpreted differently depending upon occupation and experience (Rabin, 1958). In more recent times there is the Rorschach test, named after the Swiss psychiatrist who developed the approach. They are also frequently referred to as 'inkblot' tests, as they are created from a series of shapes formed from inkblots. Figure 4.8 is an example of an inkblot shape as used in this type of test. This type of test requires subjects to answer the question, 'What might this be?' This is then further probed through three sub-questions, the answers being subjected to detailed analysis using a computer program:

1. What is it?
2. Where on the card do you see that?
3. What makes it look like that?

FIGURE 4.7

Ambiguous picture

FIGURE 4.8

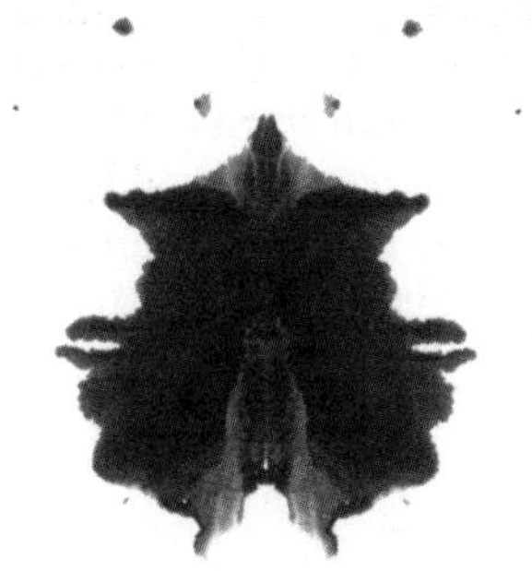

An 'inkblot' figure like that used in the Rorschach test

The type of projective test used by Murray differed from the Rorschach test in that he required subjects to create a story from an ambiguous drawing, rather than responding to a shape such as Figure 4.8. He went further than many of his contemporaries in providing a scientific basis for his work. However, it is still susceptible to the claim that it is weak in the level of scientific method adopted.

Kelly's personal construct theory

Kelly suggested that every human being was a scientist in the way in which they developed the ability to interact with the environment (Kelly, 1961). This view implies that human beings are predictive in their approach to identifying appropriate behaviour within a particular context. The scientific process involved in identifying appropriate behaviour patterns reflects a process of reformulating hypotheses about the world in the light of new information and consequently adjusting the behavioural repertoire.

Human beings develop a series of constructs through which to view the world around them. These form the basis of the ability to categorize the similarities and differences in events as they occur in the environment. A construct in this context is a bipolar continuum of extremes. For example, happy–sad; I am now–I would like to be; friendly–hostile; work I enjoy–work I hate. Such constructs are arranged into a complex internal mental framework, referred to as the individual's personal construct system. It is described as a hierarchical network as they interlink in a web of expectation and relationship. For example, an individual classified as trustworthy will be expected to display other related behaviours such as honesty, reliability, friendliness and so on. For Kelly, the personality reflects the way in which the individual experiments with and develops a framework for their world.

This approach to the study of personality implies that the personal construct theory can account for individual difference. It allows for two individuals to respond differently to the same situation because the network of constructs is unique for each individual. Therefore the experience of a situation will be different for each individual exposed to it. There are a number of characteristics relating to the way in which individuals utilize their network of constructs and the dynamics associated with the process, including:

- Individuals develop a personal prediction model for future events based on the identification of a replication of patterns in past events.
- Individuals differ in the networks of constructs that they develop. One of the consequences of this is that it produces a unique interpretation basis within each person.

- The constructs that people develop have a limited range of application. Every construct contains a field of relevance. This is psychologically based and meaningful only for the individual concerned.
- Construct systems are dynamic. They are essentially a basis for effective functioning in the future. The frameworks are liable to modification in the light of the feedback obtained from the responses to particular behaviours.

Kelly developed the 'repertory grid' as a means of identifying and measuring the constructs utilized by an individual. The process for developing a repertory grid is as follows (Kelly, 1961):

- The individual is asked to identify an important way in which two significant people (to the testee) are similar, but differ from a third. These two opposing features are the construct dimension underlying the channel of thought used by the individual.
- This process is repeated (not necessarily based on the same people) until between 20–30 separate distinguishing features are identified.
- A matrix is formed with the significant names along the top and the constructs identified listed down the side.
- A binary number (zero or one) would be entered in each cell of the matrix, based on the subject's assessment of whether each named person was more like one extreme of the construct or the other.
- The completed matrix can then be factor analyzed to identify the similarities and differences between the constructs identified. The cell entries can be examined to identify patterns among relationships. Figure 4.9 is an example of a repertory grid indicating the basic appearance of the matrix and constructs identified.

Assessment of the theory The personal construct approach to personality allows the development of an understanding in terms that are meaningful for the individual. The repertory grid mechanism allows the identification of how the individual construes the world and how they set about interacting with it. From this perspective it is grounded in a broader interpretation of personality than many of the other theories. Kelly suggests that personal construct theory is relevant to an understanding of an individual's perceptual frameworks and attitudes as well as personality and its development. It is a theory concerning the way in which an individual makes sense of their world and experiments with it.

FIGURE 4.9

Significant people

Constructs	Self	Father	Mother	Brother	Friend A	Friend B	
Loving	1	1	1	0	0	1	Cold
Friendly	1	0	1	1	0	1	Unfriendly
Trustworthy	1	1	1	1	1	1	Untrustworthy
Helpful	1	0	1	0	1	0	Unhelpful
Like me	1	0	0	0	1	1	Not like me

Simplified repertory grid

This notion of experimenting with the world has lead to some criticism of the theory. It is often assumed by scientists that they are the people who experiment and that only they are in a position to utilize the scientific method effectively. But, of course, this need not be the only definition of experimentation. Young children experiment with the world around them when they are engaged in play activities. They are learning the skills needed to manipulate aspects of their environment and how to behave towards it. This approach continues in adult life, reflecting a form of life and behavioural experimentation. The theory provides an explanation of personality that takes the whole person into account. It provides a means of developing an understanding of personality in a way that is relevant to the individual being studied. It does not force the person into a framework developed on other people.

MEASURING PERSONALITY AND INDIVIDUAL DIFFERENCE

Psychometrics

Several ways in which personality can be measured (tested) have been introduced earlier in this chapter, for example, the 16PF personality inventory. A psychological test is usually defined as a set of tasks presented in a standard form and which produce a score as the output, allowing for comparison with population norms. This is called **psychometrics**, the process of mental measurement. The application and interpretation of psychometric tests is a skilled job. Over recent years the British Psychological Society, the professional body representing psychologists, has developed and introduced a series of qualifications for those people seeking to use psychometric tests. This was done in response to a widespread concern that anyone could use, or more accurately misuse, these tests and in so doing inflict considerable damage on individuals, organizations and the psychology profession. One criticism of much psychometric testing lies in its use of linear or bipolar scales of measurement; more of one thing implies less of the opposite. For example, a higher level of extroversion means less introversion. Trompanaars and Woolliams (2002) argue that this is not appropriate to much human experience, particularly team working within organizations and leadership. They argue that new ways of interpreting and relating to combinations of events are needed in understanding leadership and preparing people for it.

Psychometrics
The process of mental measurement through the application of tests of personality or characteristic such as ability or aptitude.

There are two main reasons that psychometric tests are used. The first is to undertake scientific research into particular characteristics of people, for example to understand personality. The second is to enable decisions relating to people to be made, for example, who to appoint to a particular job. In both of these examples there is a need for accurate information in relation to those aspects of people that are important to the purpose. There are many tests available that can offer insights into aspects of individual difference. They include tests of particular skills, abilities, intelligence, aptitudes, job preferences, psychological functioning and extroversion/introversion. Test batteries such as the 16PF introduced earlier seek to test a broad range of dimensions of individual difference within the one instrument.

There are three ways in which tests can measure individual difference:

1. *Comparison of performance against a standard.* Response times to undertake a particular task being one example.
2. *Norm-referenced measurement.* This compares an individual's performance on a test with that of a peer group.

3. *Criterion-referenced measurement*. This compares performance on a test with an 'ideal' result.

The basis of a psychometric test is that the responses given by the testee can be interpreted as an indication of an underlying characteristic. Therefore, a test is claimed to be valid if it measures what it claims to measure. That does not mean, however, that there is a direct link between the test question and the underlying characteristic. The question asked may bear no apparent relationship to the characteristic itself. It is, however, necessary that the question elicits responses that can discriminate between those people with the underlying characteristic and those without it. In addition a test needs to be reliable in consistently producing the same result across time. There are different forms of validity and reliability, including:

- *Face validity*. This refers to the degree to which a test appears as if it ought to measure what it sets out to measure.
- *Predictive validity*. This reflects the ability of tests to predict future events. A test would have predictive validity if high-scoring individuals were successful, while low-scoring individuals performed badly in the job for which the test was being used.
- *Construct validity*. This refers to the extent that a test can be related back to a theory.
- *Test/retest reliability*. This reflects the ability of a test to produce the same score when it is administered on two different occasions.
- *Alternative form reliability*. Some tests are developed in two or more different forms. All the forms available should produce the same results.
- *Split half reliability*. This reflects the internal consistency within a particular test. Splitting the test up and comparing the results from the various combinations of questions or activities within it measures this form of reliability.

Developing psychometric tests

Psychometric tests go through a considerable development process before being accepted as usable for general application. The process of test development can be summarized as follows:

- *Step 1*. The initial ideas for a test often emerge from a practical need, for example, assisting personnel managers to identify the most appropriate job applicants. Tests can also originate from a theoretical need to measure some characteristic of individual difference as part of theory development.
- *Step 2*. The development of appropriate test items is a creative process. Many items generated will be unsuitable for any number of reasons, chiefly that they do not contribute to measuring the intended characteristics. It takes a considerable amount of time and ingenuity to identify an appropriate range of test items suitable for use.
- *Step 3*. The final forms of the test are developed and the administration arrangements designed. Attempts to prevent 'faking' an answer are built into the test. As far back as 1956 William H Whyte was offering advice on 'How to cheat on personality tests', see Management in Action 4.2.
- *Step 4*. The 'standardization' and 'norming' process. The populations for whom the test is intended to be used must be identified and statistically valid test scores collected for them. These results are used to calculate the standard scores or profiles against which a particular individual will be compared. These provide the basis of comparison between an individual and the population of

MANAGEMENT IN ACTION 4.2 How to cheat on personality tests

As early as 1956 one author was offering the following advice on how to approach answering the questions in a personality test. The advice is premised on the view that while there are some tests in which a high score would be beneficial to the individual, many require the individual to demonstrate that they are broadly similar to everyone else. So, for example, if the test were intended to identify who would make a 'good chemist' then a high score in comparison with the population at large would be beneficial to the career prospects of the testee. By way of contrast, in a test of personality, it would be beneficial to produce results that indicate a 'normal' individual – one that displays characteristics in common with the bulk of the population.

To quote specifically from the advice offered by the author when taking personality tests:

By and large, however, your safety lies in getting a score somewhere between the 40th and 60th percentiles, which is to say, you should try to answer as if you were like everyone else is supposed to be. This is not always easy to figure out, of course [...]. When in doubt, however, there are two general rules that you can follow: (1) when asked for word associations or comments about the world, give the most conventional, run-of-the-mill, pedestrian answer possible. (2) to settle on the most beneficial answer to any question, repeat to yourself:

(a) I loved my father and my mother, but my father a little bit more.
(b) I like things pretty well the way they are.
(c) I never worry much about anything.
(d) I don't care for books or music much.
(e) I love my wife and children.
(f) I don't let them get in the way of company work.

The rationale behind this advice is that psychometric tests are intended to identify the presence of those characteristics desired by organizations. The feeling emerging from the above quotation is that the individual so described would be an 'organization man' of the highest order. Someone who would not think too much and would not be distracted from the task in hand. Performing the tasks identified by management in a way which would not question them or pose a threat to the position of management. The main point that emerges from considering this advice is that tests are intended to identify those characteristics deemed important by the test creators. That is as true today as it was when they were first written.

Taken from: Whyte, WH (1960) *The Organization Man*, a Penguin special, Penguin, Harmondsworth.

Stop ↔ Consider

This implies that it is easy to 'fake' test results in the sense of being able to present a particular image of the 'self' in an attempt to conform to the management desired profile. Do you think this is possible? Does it matter?

which they form part. For example, Figure 4.4 demonstrated the 16PF profile of managing directors, against which particular managing directors could be compared. This stage provides the basis (once the test is published) for conclusions to be drawn about an individual.

- *Step* 5. At this stage, the data will be subjected to the various reliability and validity analyses described earlier. This is done in order to establish the credibility and value of the test for the user markets.

At this point the test becomes available for use and enters the commercial market. However, it is not the end of the process. Norms for other populations may be developed if the test were thought to be useful for purposes or groups other than those for which it was originally designed. Also the test could be subjected to criticism from other test designers, academics or users. Management in Action 4.3 illustrates how one organization has utilized psychometrics in its recruitment process.

MANAGEMENT IN ACTION 4.3 Psychometrics on-line for B&Q

DIY giant B&Q recently spent £120 000 on developing and installing an on-line psychometric test to be used as the first part of the company recruitment processes. It was initially used only for management positions, but has been so successful that it is to be extended to cover shop-floor jobs as well. It was developed over seven years by Colin Gill, chief psychologist at Psychological Solutions and much of the research was carried out on B&Q staff. So far it has cut the cost of recruitment by 60 per cent in terms of time and 30 per cent in terms of cost.

Candidates can access the test through the B&Q web site (**www.diy.com**). They answer a range of questions and then receive feedback on the result immediately. Candidates displaying appropriate characteristics are then invited for interview in the conventional way. With about 15 000 jobs being available in the company each year (with about 60 per cent of the 1000 new management appointees coming from outside the company) it is clearly important for the company to have a cost effective recruitment process. The test not only identifies appropriate characteristics but also identifies what the company describe as 'triple A' candidates – those who match exactly the requirements for management jobs. This process identifies these individuals with the potential talent for rapid development and success within the company.

Conventional personality questionnaires tend to use statement-based questions, for example, 'Do you like meeting people at parties?' Not surprisingly, the perception of the last party attended can have a significant impact on the answer. The B&Q questionnaire uses only adjectives, for example, 'Are you outgoing?', within a definite occupational framework. It is also able to take into account that candidates' perceptions of themselves might differ drastically from reality.

One of the potential disadvantages of the new system is that it requires access to the internet which not all potential candidates have. Consequently, a telephone version will be made available when the system is extended to cover shop-floor positions. Because the scoring of the questionnaire is done automatically within the computer system it should be free of bias, particularly age, gender and ethnic background.

Adapted from: Davidson, E (2003) You can do it, *People Management*, 20 February, pp 42–3.

Stop ↔ Consider

It is suggested that the test is free of age, gender or ethnic bias. Why might this statement be incorrect?

To what extent and why do you agree with the view that such tests are a valuable aid to the recruitment of shop-floor workers?

Graphology

Graphology
The study of handwriting to identify personal characteristics.

Graphology refers to the study of handwriting. It is one of a number of alternative forms of personality assessment with a long, if not scientific tradition. For example, there is the study of the shape of the so-called bumps on the head, in practice the shape of the bones forming the skull and face. This is called phrenology and examples of the assumed significance of the various 'bumps' can still be found on pottery heads with the areas of personality they were thought to influence marked. Graphology takes as its area of interest the writing of an individual and subjects it to analysis by a trained person. Supporters of graphology would claim that it is a branch of behavioural psychology, with no connections with astrology or intuition. Opponents would argue that it has no basis as a reliable form of assessment (Klimoski and Rafael, 1983).

Among the qualities 'extracted' from a sample of handwriting would be the size, slant, pressure, spacing of letters and words and the beginnings and endings of words, see for example Ashworth (2003). It is suggested by graphologists that someone who leaves a wide spacing between the lines of writing is an independent person who prefers to limit their contact with other people. As a technique for assessing the personality characteristics of people graphology might not gain the support of many psychologists but there is evidence that even during the 1980s just under 3 per cent of the top 1000 UK companies always used it for the assessment of management recruitment as reported in a survey by Robertson and Makin (1986). It is also widely used in Germany, Switzerland and France (Ashworth, 2003). Ashworth also reports an interview with John Crump of Kaisen Consulting who carried out research among their own employees using graphology and then subjected the results to scientific analysis. The results suggested that graphology produced a good historic snapshot of the person, but could not predict how they would react to future events such as a management crisis or an overseas posting. Crump suggests that it provides an effective way of narrowing down a group of candidates before resorting to the use of more sophisticated techniques.

EMOTION, INTELLIGENCE AND EMOTIONAL INTELLIGENCE

The role that emotion plays in organizational activity represents a growing area of research. For example, Fineman (1993) produced an edited book drawing on the work of several leading thinkers in this area to explore how emotion impacts on aspects of the experience for many people. Emotion is generally regarded as feelings and generally the management and organizational literature ignores such human aspects. If they are considered at all they tend to be incorporated as reflecting culture, commitment or perhaps the reactions to being managed or something similar. However, people have feelings (or emotions) regarding many aspects of the events, people and things that they experience in their lives; and organizations together with what occurs within them are a significant aspect of that experience. There are links between the feelings that people hold and the personalities that exist in all of the actors in a particular context. For example if two people do not get on as a result of what would commonly be called a 'personality clash', it will inevitably impact on the feelings that they have towards each other. Flam (1993) argues that the individual comprises several distinct 'selfs' – the emotional, rational and normative – all of which play a different part in the totality of human behaviour within an organizational setting. One way in which this approach to incorporating emotion into the use of personality has been through the development of the concept of emotional intelligence. The following discussion introduces intelligence first and then goes on to explore emotional intelligence.

Intelligence is a common term that is frequently associated with the achievement of academic success. But is that what the concept refers to and if so how does it relate to individual difference? Thurstone (1938) developed a model of **intelligence** based on a number of primary mental abilities such as verbal comprehension, word fluency, number ability and perceptual speed. Alternatively, Phares (1987) defines intelligence in terms of an ability to adapt to a variety of situations both old and new, a capacity for learning and the ability to make use of a wide range of symbols and concepts in relating to the world. From that perspective the concept of intelligence represents a broad range of factors and embraces many aspects of what would be classed as individual difference.

Intelligence
Described by a number of primary mental abilities including verbal comprehension, number ability, or and capacity for learning.

There are many theoretical approaches to the study of intelligence. These have included the development of the IQ concept in which the mental age of the testee was calculated from an intelligence test and compared with their physical age to give a scale of relative intelligence. So someone of average intelligence would score a mental age equivalent to their actual age and someone of higher than average intelligence would achieve an age score greater than their actual age. More recently, Guilford (1967) proposed a model of intelligence consisting of three dimensions (contents, products and operations). Each of these dimensions comprises a number of different abilities (4, 6 and 5 respectively). The model can be drawn as a cube with each of the three dimensions representing one of the three principal dimensions of the cube. Each of the individual intelligence abilities within the now three-dimensional model would intersect with the others, creating a total of 120 possibilities in intelligence variation (4 × 6 × 5). The three dimensions within the model are:

1. *Contents*. The four elements within this dimension reflect the base information on which subsequent actions are formed. For example, the semantic and symbolic meaning of numbers.
2. *Products*. The six elements within this dimension reflect the form in which information is processed. For example, the relationship between the weight and price of goods in a supermarket.
3. *Operations*. The five elements within this dimension reflect what the person actually does. For example, solve a problem or evaluate alternative courses of action.

Sternberg (1985) proposed an information processing-based theory of intelligence. In this model it was proposed that there exist three ways in which intelligent behaviour is evident:

1. *Components*. This aspect reflects the analytical abilities possessed by an individual.
2. *Experiences*. This aspect reflects the creative abilities that an individual has in being able to combine the things that they experience into novel patterns.
3. *Context*. This aspect reflects the ability of an individual to be aware of contextual circumstances and to exhibit an ability to utilize the environment to their own advantage.

John D Mayer and Peter Salovey first developed a theory of *emotional intelligence* during the 1980s which Mayer defines as, 'the ability to perceive, to integrate, to understand and reflectively manage one's own and other people's feelings' (Pickard, 1999, pp 49–50). This model was not directly intended to address the issue of success in an organizational context, as it originally emerged from an interest in how emotion and cognition could be used to influence individual thinking processes. It was Goleman (1996) who first popularized EQ (as emotional intelligence has become known) as an aid to organizational functioning. This has been expanded by a number of writers including Dulewicz and Higgs (Pickard, 1999) from the Henley Management College who have developed a model consisting of three main components and a total of seven elements of EQ in relation to organizational success. Their model is as follows:

- *The drivers*. The two traits of motivation and decisiveness are responsible for energizing individuals to achieve their goals.
- *The constrainers*. The two traits of conscientiousness and integrity, and emotional resilience perform the function of modifying the potential of the drivers to push to excess or in the wrong direction.
- *The enablers*. The three traits of sensitivity, influence and self-awareness help to ensure that the other traits operate in the social context involving the individual and other people.

It has been shown that men and women have different EQ profiles, with women displaying stronger interpersonal skills, and men showing higher levels of independence and a sense of the self (Lucas, 2000). A number of organizations have used the EQ concept to review individual difference profiles among work groups and claim to have had some success in changing behaviour patterns at work. It is, however, early days for this relatively new model in terms of its replacement for conventional models of intelligence.

Dulewicz and Higgs (as described in Pickard, 1999) argue that for organizational success to be achieved it is also necessary for an individual to have what they describe as intellectual intelligence (creativity and external awareness, for example) and managerial intelligence (delegating and business sense, for example) in addition to EQ. Management in Action 4.4 suggests that multiple intelligences exist within an organizational context and that they should be actively developed.

Wisdom is another facet of human beings that is often aligned with intelligence. Wisdom has been defined as, 'expert knowledge and judgement about important, difficult and uncertain questions associated with the meaning and conduct of life'. Baltes and Kunzmann (2003). Wisdom in this sense is thought to be different to both intelligence and personality as it reflects the end point of a developmental process that can go on throughout life. It is, however a relatively recent phenomenon in research terms and there is much more to learn about wisdom, what it is and how it develops.

INDIVIDUAL DIFFERENCE, PERCEPTION AND ATTITUDES

The previous chapter discussed the topics of perception and attitude in considerable depth. It should have been clear from that discussion that individuals vary in the way in which they interact with the world around them as expressed through their perceptual and attitudinal frameworks. Individual difference also influences how people interact with the world around them and consequently there are also links between it, perception and attitudes.

Perception

There exist at least two ways in which perception and individual difference could be associated. First, perceptions could be influenced by factors located within the personality. Second, personality could at least in part be formed by the ways in which people perceive and interact with the world around them. Figure 3.13 in describing a simplified model of person perception reflects the first of these possibilities. One of the factors influencing the perception of other people is indicated as the perceiver's characteristics. In other words, who we are influences the ways in which we relate to and interpret other people. The second possibility is identified earlier in this chapter through environmental influences on personality development.

Another way in which individual difference and perception are linked is through what Witkin (1965) defined as field dependence. This concept reflects the degree to which an individual is influenced in their perceptions through the surroundings associated with a particular stimulus. For example, the field-independent individual has the capability to separate the background from the stimuli more effectively and so interprets events in a clear, detailed and dispassionate way. Such individuals also have a clear perspective on their own characteristics, beliefs, needs and differences with other people. The perceptual impact of field dependence has been measured through

MANAGEMENT IN ACTION 4.4 Developing multiple intelligence

Based on the work of a number of writers, Lucas makes the case for their being ten intelligences of relevance to workforce activity:

- *Linguistic*. The use of words and stories to express clearly and with style.
- *Mathematical*. The use of figures, with a preference for evidence, categories, systems and abstract problems.
- *Visual*. The use of pictures, shapes diagrams and maps, with a good eye for colour.
- *Physical*. Preference for being active, expressive, quick to get on their feet, and enjoys new experiences.
- *Musical*. Preference for sound and rhythm, mood is affected by music.
- *Emotional*. Know how to manage emotions and their impact on others. Constantly seeking self-knowledge.
- *Social*. Preference for being with other people, showing empathy and helping them to solve problems.
- *Environmental*. Preference for the natural world, seeing patterns in nature that pass others by.
- *Spiritual*. Preference for dealing with the key questions in life and constantly explores the principles and values in life.
- *Practical*. Full of ideas and prefer to make things happen. Practical people enjoy finding workable solutions to everyday problems.

Lucas also suggests five ways to develop the fullest range of intelligences in the workplace:

1. *The environment (physical, musical and social).* Review of the environment and possible provision of a gym and use of music and encouragement of social interaction and knowledge sharing.
2. *People and learning (visual, spiritual and practical).* Recognize the feelings and values of employees. Build in good quality training provision and action learning activities.
3. *Communication (visual, mathematical and social).* Review internal communications in terms of the range of intelligences present in the organization.
4. *Rewards (linguistic, emotional and practical).* Make sure reward systems acknowledge the full range of talent used. Reward more than the achievement of results, perhaps managing difficult situation with sensitivity. Reward means more than money, for example recognition and family-friendly policies.
5. *Management structures (visual, emotional and spiritual).* Make the structures apparent through a range of visual devices, not just a chart. Encourage the use of emotional intelligence among managers.

Adapted from: Lucas, B (2002) Developing multiple intelligence, *People Management*, 26 December, pp 40–1.

Stop ↔ Consider

Are the intelligences indicated aspects of intelligence, or simply aspects of personality? To what extent and why should organizations be expected to adapt themselves to the supposed needs of people?

an embedded figures test in which figures are hidden within a larger picture. The time taken and number of embedded figures found reflecting the field dependence score. Variation in field dependence scores were partly explained through cognitive style differences and so became linked to personality factors.

Attitudes

Attitudes are also influenced by individual difference factors. It has been suggested that extroversion or introversion creates a favourable or unfavourable disposition towards the acceptance of particular attitudes (McKenna, 1994, p 256). This same source also quotes the work of Eysenck who demonstrated that introverts are more susceptible to socialization and the acceptance of the dominant values of society (and hence the associated attitudes) than are extroverts. There is also evidence that those with an authoritarian personality are likely to have attitudes that display subservience to superiors at the same time as hostility towards inferiors.

ORGANIZATIONAL APPLICATIONS OF INDIVIDUAL DIFFERENCE

The study of personality has concentrated on providing mechanisms for describing characteristics that allow differentiation between individuals. However, there is an interesting paradox involved in this. The measurement process provides a basis of comparison of the individual with a group of others – a population. This very approach allows a subtle shift in emphasis in the organizational application of personality measurement away from the identification of individuality, towards the identification of individuals with characteristics acceptable or desirable to management.

Recruitment and selection

The most obvious application of individual difference within an organization is recruitment and selection. In advertising a vacancy externally the organization is seeking to encourage people not currently associated with it to come forward for consideration and selection. In such situations there is a need to find out as much as possible about applicants so that a decision can be made. While information can be obtained from application forms, references and through interviews there is much debate about the accuracy and relevance of such methods. For example Webster (1964) found that interviewers made decisions about a candidate in the first few minutes and spent the rest of the interview attempting to confirm their original view of the candidate.

More recent reviews of the role of the interview in selection suggest that it has an important part to play as a final review of the individual and as a basis for negotiation of the relationship between the parties. This places it beyond simple validity based judgements (Anderson and Shackleton, 1993). The use of tests within the selection process appears to be increasing in parallel with this changing view of the interview. For example, Shackleton and Newell (1991) report that the use of personality tests increased to 37 per cent from 12 per cent over a five-year period. The following Employee Perspective (4.4) illustrates what can happen when personality tests are used as part of a recruitment process.

At one time personality tests were used for management positions and ability or aptitude tests were the preserve of manual jobs. This is now being questioned in some quarters. Some managers feel that the use of personality tests provides the opportunity to identify individuals who will 'fit' more effectively into the organization. In effect, managers argue that they can achieve organizational objectives more easily if they can identify individuals with the 'approved' characteristics. Research by Newell and Shackleton (1994) would seem to support this trend, at least in respect of management level jobs, in that they report levels of test use in approximately 75 per cent of managerial jobs, but only 20 per cent of manual jobs. Management in Action 4.4 provides a review of the appropriateness of tests in the recruitment processes of one large retail organization.

EMPLOYEE PERSPECTIVE 4.4 Shona's personality did not match

Shona graduated from a good university with a good first degree in history. She applied for several graduate training schemes and was interviewed for a few of them. For one job she was asked to take a personality test. The test lasted about one hour and Shona was told that she would be told the outcome in a few days. A few days later she was telephoned by the company and told that they would not be taking her application any further as the test result had indicated that she did not match the expected profile for graduate trainees. She was told that she had interviewed well and was clearly intelligent and quick to work through problems. But the test results indicated that she was not an assertive personality and did not have the group leadership qualities that they expected of high flyers. They apologized and wished her well for the future.

Tasks

1. How would you react if you were Shona?
2. If you were Shona, would you try and change yourself to present more of the desired image that was suggested as important for graduate employees? How might you do this?

Development

Psychometric tests can also be used to provide a profile of the people already in the organization. This can be used to provide a basis of control through access to promotion, development and related organizational 'rewards'. People with 'approved' characteristics, or prepared to develop or adopt them will be the ones who find advancement within the organization. Thus management may be able to achieve its objectives more easily as employees align themselves with the managerially preferred behaviours. That is, always assuming that managers know which characteristics are the best – a major assumption!

The development of technical specialists and managers is another area where testing has been used as the basis of reflecting personality characteristics. Tests such as the Occupational Personality Questionnaire (the OPQ) have been developed by the SHL Group plc (a firm of occupational psychology consultants) to enhance this very objective. It utilizes a series of 32 dimensions, or scales, to reflect the profile of an individual's personality. Examples from the OPQ32 questionnaire are shown in Table 4.2.

This particular questionnaire can be used in a number of ways including management selection and/or development. In selection terms it could be used as a means of providing the profile of an individual, which could then be used to make a decision, or as recommended by the professional associations, used as the basis of an informed discussion. The profile, or score of the individual on each of the 32 scales, would be compared against the ideal profile for the job for which they were being considered. The OPQ can also be used for determining development programmes. Based on the questionnaire results the individual would be offered advice and support in undertaking training or development to change their work performance and/or career options. The questionnaire could also be used where jobs were expected to change significantly in the future. The intention being to identify appropriate training for the individuals concerned or to identify alternative job opportunities.

As with all instruments that measure personality, the OPQ as a single instrument does not intend that it should be the only basis of a decision in relation to selection and development. Indeed, research by Blinkhorn and Johnson (1990) using three of the most widely used psychometric tests (including the OPQ) found little evidence of a long-term relationship between test results and performance at work. There are other factors to be taken into account, and there is no substitute for seeking a variety of information inputs to any decision about people in relation to their work activities.

Persuasive:	comfortable using negotiation, enjoys selling, likes to change other people's views
Controlling:	likes to be in charge, takes the lead, takes control
Competitive:	has a need to win, enjoys competitive activities, dislikes losing
Decisive:	makes fast decisions, reaches conclusions quickly, less cautious
Innovative:	generates new ideas, enjoys being creative, thinks of original solutions
Optimistic:	expects things will turn out well, looks to the positive aspects of a solution
Achieving:	ambitious and career centred, likes to work to demanding goals and targets
Conscientious:	focuses on getting things finished, persists until the job is done

TABLE 4.2 Examples from the SHL® OPQ32® (SHL and OPQ32 are registered trade marks of SHL Group plc, ©SHL Group plc. All rights reserved)

The British Psychological Society website (**www.psychtesting.org.uk**) also contains a comprehensive and accessible review of these issues.

Assessment cemtre
Group based recruitment or development using tests, interviews, group and individual exercises evaluated by a team of assessors.

Assessment centres were first used during World War II as a means of selecting officers for the military. Since then they have evolved to the point where many organizations use them for selection and development purposes. Assessment centres are events that are made up of a range of different activities, requiring individual and group performance. Individuals are observed by assessors and scored on their performance on each activity. At the end of the process the scorers pool all the information gained from the activities and decide on the outcome. The justification for this assessment being that the tasks can be designed to reflect real work activity. Performance is assessed in a live situation, multiple measures of personality and performance are obtained and the results are the combined effort of a number of trained assessors. Management in Action 4.5 provides an indication of assessment centres and how they could be designed.

Marketing

Marketing specialists are always seeking to understand consumers so that they can align the organization's offerings more appropriately. Equally, of course, an improved understanding of the consumer should allow for the design of more appropriate products and services. From those perspectives individual difference is an important concept in the marketing vocabulary. Several studies have been conducted over the years which seek to determine how potential customers perceive the characteristics of individuals who actually purchase particular items. One early study (Haire, 1950) compared the responses of housewives in describing the type of people who might have one of two variations of shopping list. The difference between the shopping lists was the inclusion of either ground or instant coffee. Some 48 per cent of housewives indicated that the shopper who bought instant coffee was a lazy person who did not plan ahead, whereas only 12 per cent of the people who bought ground coffee were described in the same way. This study has been repeated several times over the years with some moderate support.

MANAGEMENT IN ACTION 4.5 How to plan an assessment centre

There are three main types of assessment centre used by organizations. They are graduate recruitment, job selection (usually managerial or technical specialist) and for internal or development purposes. Each is different and requires a specific design of assessment centre. For example, graduate recruitment would need to assume much lower levels of company knowledge and work experience than a centre designed for internal promotion purposes.

The key features in the design of an assessment centre are:

- *Skills and competencies.* It is necessary to begin with a clear idea of the important skills and competencies being sought. For example one organization assumed that sociability was a key quality required among sales personnel. Only later was it discovered that this was irrelevant and that independence and persistence were much more significant qualities in relation to success.
- *Tests and techniques.* Given that most assessments last about two days a variety of activities and tests is common. They might include structured interviews, self-assessment questionnaires, psychometric tests, in-tray exercises, group discussion, group problem-solving exercises, job simulation exercises and job-related role play.
- *The assessment process.* In designing an assessment centre there are three main elements to consider. First, the qualities and competencies being sought and how they are to be measured. Second, the weighting to be applied to each element of the process. For example, should the psychometric tests be more highly rated in the overall result than the group discussion? Third, the form of assessment used in order to ensure consistency of judgement between raters and the avoidance of discrimination or stereotyping of participants.
- *Assessors.* The selection of assessors can be difficult in that a mix of specific training and experience is often needed. Specialist training is required in the application and scoring of psychometric tests, for example. Line managers have the experience in work practicalities but might not have the ability to rate individuals on group discussions consistently. Generally, a mix of assessors is used in a centre and training provided for them as necessary.
- *Feedback.* Decisions need to be made about the level and form of any feedback to participants. Clearly, the more participants the more difficult and costly in time and money it is to provide detailed feedback. However, delegates frequently appreciate some indication of their strengths and weaknesses. If a development centre is being run then its whole purpose is to provide feedback to individuals on their future needs. There is always a difficult area in relation to the creation of management reports from assessment centres. Participants frequently feel uneasy at the thought of managers being provided with information about them, particularly if this is not released to the participant.
- *Validation.* Any assessment centre is only as good as its ability to contribute to the effectiveness of the people working within the organization. There is little point in undertaking lengthy and costly procedures if they add little to the quality and performance of staff. Consequently, a process of monitoring and evaluating the assessment centre needs to be developed so that the impact on the business can be reviewed and corrective action taken as necessary.

Adapted from: Fowler, A (1992) How to plan an assessment centre, *PM Plus*, December, pp 21–4.

Stop ↔ Consider

Think about your future career. Design an assessment centre intended to identify your strengths and weaknesses in relation to your plans.

Who would you seek to be the assessors and fellow subjects of the centre and what skills would you expect the assessors to have?

Another aspect of individual difference in marketing is the ascription of personality factors to brands. Branded products contain both the physical properties that make up the product and its symbolic meaning for the direct consumer and wider population. For example a Rolls-Royce is not just another form of personal transport. It makes a statement about the owner in terms of wealth, lifestyle and status. These factors have significance for both the consumer and among the wider community. They allow other people to 'know' who the driver is and to encourage a particular impression to flow from those connections (real or imagined). To 'know' the characteristics of people in the intended market for products and services is to enable organizations to provide offerings that will gain acceptance quickly. Consequently, considerable effort goes into defining the profile of consumers and what defines their individual preferences.

Discrimination

Discrimination occurs in many forms. Women, ethnic minority groups, older people, younger people, religious groups, gay men and lesbians represent just some of the people who have found themselves discriminated against throughout history. Discrimination is associated with the attitudes (usually negative) of one group of people towards another. For example, women find it difficult to break through the 'glass ceiling' and obtain the highest positions within organizations. Studies of the influence of personality factors on negative attitude formation have a long history. For example, Adorno *et al.* (1953) demonstrated that people displaying the highest levels of prejudice towards other groups also had strongly authoritarian personalities.

Stress and bullying

Stress exists in many jobs and arises from a number of sources. One of the causes of susceptibility to stress in people is the nature of the individual. Rosenman *et al.* (1964) considered the possible relationship between personality characteristics and tendency to experience heart disease. They classified people as either Type A or B (see Table 4.3). They concluded that people with Type A personalities are more at risk from coronary problems. Type A people place a high emphasis on work at the expense of other aspects of their lives, frequently work at home and are less interested in exercise, for example. This finding has been substantiated a number of times over the years, see for example Friedman and Booth-Kewley (1987).

Type A personality characteristics	Type B personality characteristics
High need for achievement	Low need for achievement
Aggressive	Passive, doesn't lose temper
Competitive	Laid-back, enjoys leisure time
Restless	Easy-going, slow paced
Alert	Relaxed
Constantly feeling under pressure	Not usually feeling under pressure
Impatient	Patient

TABLE 4.3 Type A and Type B personality characteristics

Another aspect of stress at work arises through the phenomenon of bullying. Bullying has probably always existed, although there is a growing recognition that it is becoming more significant in its impact both on people and on organizations. Cooper (1999) reports a survey indicating that 18 per cent of respondents had been bullied during the previous year, while another 43 per cent had witnessed bullying over the same period. Adams (1992) draws attention to organizational bullying in all its forms. The case studies that she provides also give clear indications of the stressful impact of the experiences for the victims. Also included is a review of a number of the components of individual difference that contribute to the exercise of bullying (or victim) behaviour by individuals.

The testing business

Another organizational effect of personality is the growth of an industry around the measurement of it. There are a considerable number of psychologists and consultancies that offer services to organizations based on the existence of personality and the measurement of it. Naturally, it is in the business interests of those practitioners to ensure that the opportunities for the application of personality are brought to management's attention. This includes the training of company staff to use and interpret particular instruments, the development of new tests and the application of the tests in organizational activity. The difficulties that can arise from poorly trained individuals applying psychometric tests has long been recognized and has led the British Psychological Society to introduce formal accreditation training. In addition the Institute of Personnel and Development has introduced a Code of Practice on Psychological Testing.

INDIVIDUAL DIFFERENCE: A MANAGEMENT PERSPECTIVE

Managers are supposed to have particular personality characteristics in order to be successful; intelligence and initiative are often quoted as examples. Managers can also be affected by the application of personality testing through the development and promotion opportunities that they provide. Within an organizational setting the concept of personality is inseparable from the opportunities that it provides. It is not that the identification of personality is a management activity in its own right, but it allows managers to take decisions about other people. It is a concept that serves a **gatekeeper** function. The argument goes as follows; individual difference can be defined in terms of certain characteristics, some of which are helpful to managers, which in turn leads to the conclusion that if appropriate characteristics can be identified then the best candidates can be selected. Consequently, who is selected for training or promotion and how far they progress in the management hierarchy can be strongly tied to the various forms of testing available. In addition, the consequences are influenced by the willingness of an individual to take action based on test results. For example, being prepared to accept the offered definition of their personality and accepting the need for particular development.

Gatekeeper
Person within an organization able to grant or restrict access to a more senior person.

Social engineering
An attempt to create particular attitudes, practices, relationships or social structures by a dominant group.

The process of testing allows managers to specify the characteristics that they consider as important in employees of the organization. It is therefore a process of **social engineering**. A model employee is identified and individual candidates measured against that particular standard. This could relegate into second place the ability to perform the job by the individual as managers seek personality fit with their ideal employee. In an extreme situation this would allow managers systematically to manipulate the shape and form of the organization in terms of the people characteristics. This is reflected in the suggestion that recruitment should be based on 'organizational fit' not just job requirements (Bowen *et al.*, 1996). However, this does not account for the inevitable impact of change as a feature of organizational life. Change can include personnel changes, product changes, market changes, economic changes and legal changes. Among the consequences of change are the influences on the people employed. As the organization changes so do the jobs within it and therefore the abilities of the people performing those jobs also needs to change. There is a danger that taken too far the desire to match personality factors to the present situation may become a liability as circumstances change. The following Employee Perspective (4.5) demonstrates what can happen if change is avoided for too long and then happens on a large scale.

There are a number of situations where the application of personality concepts could be of value within an organization. For example, there are obvious links between extroversion and jobs which require a high level of interpersonal activity, such as sales, hospitality and public relations. There are also links between aspects of personality and organizational objectives. For example, as managers seek to improve effectiveness through initiatives such as employee empowerment, there is a need to tap into different human attributes than if employees are simply regarded as a 'pair of hands'.

EMPLOYEE PERSPECTIVE 4.5 Change and its effects

One large company prided itself over the years that it attracted and recruited the brightest and the best staff all of whom broadly met the particular personality requirements set by management to be customer oriented and accepting of the paternal and hierarchical style of the company. The company used the same formula for many years and was very successful. However, the market changed and customers began to buy from newer entrants to the market, all of whom offered better value for money. The company began to lose market share, profits dropped significantly and the share price soon followed. Major change was needed and new senior managers were brought in, who tinkered with the culture and the way that business was done, all to no avail. Eventually in order to save the company a completely new board of directors was appointed from outside the company and large scale change was undertaken. This inevitably included a large number of personnel changes. Many staff and managers who had worked loyally for the company for many years felt bitter and let down as the old ways of doing things were completely overturned and what had previously been valued was now rejected as worthless. Morale among existing staff dropped and customers began to complain of poor service. It took the company five years to turn the situation around and begin to make a small profit. Labour turnover also increased and at the end of the five years only about 15 per cent of the original workforce remained.

Tasks

1. Does it matter that most of the longer serving employees had left over the five year period?
2. Could the use of more formal personality testing in this company have helped to prevent the problems from becoming as serious as they did?
3. Might more employees have been retained in the longer term if testing had been systematic?

CONCLUSIONS

The concept of individual difference is a difficult one for managers to deal with. It operates at many different levels within the organization and has a number of different theoretical roots along with many different measurement mechanisms (over 5000 are available). At a common-sense level personality is something that most people, including managers, would claim to recognize. It reflects how people get on with each other including features such as sociability and intelligence. It is only when an attempt is made to be more precise in the definition of individual difference and its measurement, followed by establishing specific links with work activities that the real difficulties emerge. The links between personality and particular jobs are an area where managers might be expected to show interest, but there is little by way of agreement about the precise nature of that relationship.

Now to summarize this chapter in terms of the relevant Learning Objectives:

- **Outline the concept of individual difference.** There are many ways in which individuals differ from each other. Many are obvious such as gender or height and of little value in organizational terms. However, the use of personality implies certain characteristics that reflect psychological processes and orientations which determine how people differ from one another in ways which could impact on the way that they work and the type of work for which they may be best fitted.
- **Describe the major theoretical approaches to the study of personality.** There are two major approaches to the study of personality. One approach, the nomothetic, is based on the existence of characteristics such as extroversion and neuroticism which can be measured using a variety of tests. Understanding personality therefore becomes a process of measuring the degree to which these characteristics exist in an individual person, creating a personality profile. The other approach, the idiographic, is based on seeking to understand the individual in terms of how they relate to the world in which they live. The argument being that the real world exists in the mind of the individual and it is they who construct the reality that they react to. Consequently, in seeking to understand the individual it is first necessary to understand how they relate to and construct the social world around them. In addition there are models which do not neatly fall into either of these two classifications.
- **Understand the strengths and weaknesses of each of the major theories of personality.** Each of the theoretical models discussed in this chapter contains strengths and weaknesses. To a significant extent the views about the relative strengths and weaknesses of each is determined by the epistemological views of the reader. Positivists tend to the view that the laws of natural science can be applied to the social world, leading them to hold that the nomothetic models have more value than the ideographic. Interpretivists, would tend to hold the opposite perspective, believing that in the social world each individual constructs reality for themselves within their minds and that consequently the normal rules of science cannot apply. Each of the models discussed in this chapter has a brief review of the theory attached to it. Without repeating that material here, it provides the essential answer to this objective.
- **Discuss the basic process involved in the development of psychometric tests.** Development tests go through a number of stages, as follows:
  Step 1. The identification of a practical or research-based need.
  Step 2. The development of appropriate test items.
  Step 3. The final forms of the test are developed and the administration arrangements designed.
  Step 4. The 'standardization' and 'norming' process.
  Step 5. Reliability and validity analyses.
- **Explain the significance of individual difference as a basis for taking decisions relating to people within organizations.** There are a number of ways in which personality is used within organizations, and in relation to the people who work in them. There are the marketing related uses in terms of characterizing the customer (or potential customer). There are also the recruitment related uses in which potential candidates are screened for the existence

of desirable characteristics. There is also the opportunity to create work teams with a blend of particular characteristics and the identification of training and development needs based on the desire to encourage particular traits among employees. Such processes also signal the desired characteristics for those hopeful of promotion to more senior positions. There is a potential downside for these possibilities; that of socially engineering a particular type of workforce, which over time as conditions change cannot adapt to the new situation. There is also a question about the degree to which it is possible to socially engineer personality or workforce with any degree of success.

DISCUSSION QUESTIONS

1. Psychometric tests make it easy to sell consultancy services to senior managers and that is the only value that they have. Discuss this statement.
2. To what extent does personality explain individual differences between people?
3. Describe the genetic and environmental origins of personality. Which do you consider the most important to the development of adult personality? Why?
4. Would it be desirable for all the employees within an organization to have similar personality characteristics? Why, or why not?
5. To what extent do you consider that it might be possible to use graphology to understand the personality characteristics of an individual?
6. In what ways might personality and perception be linked?
7. Can personality be measured accurately by any form of psychometric test? Why or why not?
8. It has often been suggested that Freudian theory tells us more about Freud than it does about personality. Discuss.
9. Kelly's personal construct theory provides a useful theory of personality. However, it is not practical to use the repertory grid technique in an organization as it is too complicated. Discuss.
10. 'Any organization needs "different" people within it in order to optimize performance and effectiveness through the unique contribution of each individual.' Discuss.

CASE STUDY John and the sales administrator

John was the production manager in a medium sized manufacturing company in the South East of England. The company produced black plastic rubbish sacks from recycled plastic waste. John was in his late 30s and had been recruited by the chief executive to be the production manager/director designate about one year earlier. His background was that of an industrial engineer and the brief given to him was to increase the productivity of the production unit through modernization, improved planning and control systems, together with better supervision and employee management.

The general atmosphere within the company was one of hostility between management and the workforce at all levels. No one trusted anyone else and disputes were common. Deliveries were invariably late; this was used as a pressure point by supervisors and employees as a way of getting overtime as, and when they wanted it. In return management did not respect the non-management employees and would frequently threaten them with the sack or total closure of the company. When John was brought into the company it was hoped that his professional background and production experience would help to improve matters.

John began by spending most of his time in the factory 'walking the job' and speaking to employees and supervisors as often as possible. The poor performance of the factory was well known by all concerned and everyone would claim to have an interest in sorting it out, but nothing actually changed. A similar state of affairs existed in the administrative offices, where it was not uncommon to find staff saying to customers that it was 'Them in the factory' that were responsible for the late delivery and they were 'Just being awkward as usual'. The sales director was a remote individual and not a well integrated member of the senior management team, which also consisted of the chief executive, production manager (John) and the finance manager. The sales director had worked for the company the longest and spent most of his time away from the office visiting his favourite customers (current and potential) and supposedly helping to develop new products. His staff had to contact him by phone most of the time if they needed him as he was only in the office about one day each week. Consequently, most of the sales activity was effectively controlled and managed by the sales office manager.

John was making slow progress in the factory. New planning methods and supervisor training had been introduced, as well as some of the human resource practices improved. For example, attendance control procedures had been tightened and employees having time off work for any reason were interviewed on their first day back at work. Discussions were underway with the trade union over changes to the terms and conditions of work, but this was only making very slow progress. Some impact was evident on delivery schedules, although not enough to deal with the major problem of delays being used to manufacture the need for overtime.

One of the key working relationships that existed was between John as the factory manager and Ann, the sales office manager as she was the most common point of contact between customers and the company. The working relationship between these two was particularly important when orders were delayed or changed for any reason. Unfortunately, Ann and John did not get on at either a personal or professional level. Ann considered that the customer was right every time irrespective of the effect on the factory and that the factory had a duty to accept that a customer might change their minds and quietly fit in with her 'demands' on behalf of the customer. These demands were inevitably passed on as instructions over the telephone, even though Ann was junior to John in the hierarchy. This was not John's preferred way of working and if there was a problem from his side of the company, he inevitably went to see Ann to explain what the situation was and to see if some form of compromise could be arranged. This approach was usually brushed aside with comments such as, 'It's your problem, what am I supposed to tell my customer? You have let me down again. You and your factory people are hopeless.' If pushed she would ring the customer to see if alternative delivery times could be agreed, but this was inevitably couched in terms of, 'The factory have let us down again by failing to produce when they should and they want you to compensate by changing delivery times'.

On one occasion, a customer had rung to change an order and Ann rang John to instruct him as to what he should do. John was in the middle of a production meeting and had all the supervisors and production planning staff in his office discussing the next week's activities when the phone rang. He picked it up and heard Ann begin to lay down the law as to what needed to be changed, which he realized would significantly change the plans so carefully worked out for the next week. So he simply said that he was in a meeting and put the phone down. Well slammed it down might be a more accurate description!

Ann was shocked at this disrespect of her and her position as she saw it and immediately rang the sales director to tell him that John had been very rude to her etc. After speaking to him, she immediately went directly to see the chief executive and complained that she was too important to the company to be treated as she had been and that she expected the chief executive to immediately discipline John in order to put him in his place. John was subsequently asked to go and see the chief executive to provide his side of the story.

Tasks

1. In what ways and to what extent does this case study reflect issues of personality?
   How would you deal with this situation if you were the chief executive?
2. Could John have dealt with things differently and reduced the likelihood of this problem arising?
3. How might knowledge of personality theory have helped John to prevent the situation arising, or deal more effectively with the crisis?

FURTHER READING

Bartram, D (1992) The personality of UK managers: 16PF norms for short-listed applicants, *Journal of Occupational and Organizational Psychology*, 65, pp 159–72. This is a study which examines the 16PF test results of 1796 managers applying for jobs. From the analysis the 'norms' are developed, against which to compare individual manager's test results. As such it provides the basis for interpretation of the results for UK managers.

Boyatzis, R, Goleman, D and McKee, A (2002) *Primal Leadership: Realizing the power of Emotional Intelligence*, Harvard University Business Press, Boston, MA. A review of leadership and its relationship with EI and personality generally.

Clark, H, Chandler, J and Barry, J (1994) *Organization and Identities: Text and Readings in Organizational Behaviour*, International Thomson Business Press, London. Contains a broad range of original articles on relevant material themes and from significant writers referred to in this and other textbooks on management and organizations.

Donnelly, J (2003) Blot on the landscape, *The Psychologist*, May, Vol 16, no 5, pp 246–9. This article reflects upon the current use of the Rorschach test.

James, LR and Mazerolle, MD (2002) *Personality in Work Organizations*, Sage, London. Reviews the literature on personality and its application to organizational practice and research.

Ridley, M (2003) *Nature via Nurture: Genes, Experiences and What Makes Us Human*, Fourth Estate, London. Explains complex science in an accessible, anecdotal style. Shows how genes switch themselves on and off at different times throughout our development in response to outside stimuli and other genes. Takes a pure reductionist stance and is dismissive of interpretivist contributions.

Robertson, IT and Kinder, A (1993) Personality and job competencies: the criterion-related validity of some personality variables, *Journal of Occupational and Organizational Psychology*, 66, pp 225–44. This is a classic example of a research paper which examines the issue of the validity of psychometric tests.

Woodruff, C (1992) *Assessment Centres; Identifying and Developing Competence*, Institute of Personnel Management, London. This is intended for the practitioner market, but does provide an excellent insight into the assessment centre process, as used in selection and development.

COMPANION WEBSITE

Online teaching and learning resources:

Visit the companion website for Organizational Behaviour and Management 3rd edition at: *http://www.thomsonlearning.co.uk/businessandmanagement/martin3* to find valuable further teaching and learning material:

Refer to page 35 for full details.

CHAPTER 5

Learning within organizations

LEARNING OBJECTIVES

After studying this chapter and working through the associated Management in Action panels, Employee Perspectives, Discussion Questions and Case Study, you should be able to:

- **Describe the major theoretical approaches to learning.**
- **Outline the concept of a learning organization.**
- **Discuss the links between learning and the control of people within organizations.**
- **Detail the relevance of knowledge management for an organization.**
- **Explain why the styles of learning are relevant to understanding how people learn.**

INTRODUCTION

Within an organizational setting learning most frequently finds expression in the form of training and development. Organizations are faced with constant changes to trading and economic conditions requiring new skills and flexibility from existing workers. Therefore it becomes essential to train and retrain employees in order to retain organizational viability. In some locations skill imbalances exist, with unfilled vacancies coexisting alongside high unemployment. This leads to a range of (usually) government sponsored initiatives to retrain unemployed workers thereby enabling them to meet the skill requirements of the available jobs. In some countries or job sectors skill shortage and high employment levels coexist which can create high labour turnover as employees 'job-hop'. In this context, learning through training and development has an important role to play in helping to retain staff that might otherwise leave.

The opportunities for personal and professional development are important 'weapons' in management's attempt to attract and retain good staff, as well as the means of enhancing organizational performance. There are also benefits to be garnered in terms of improved levels of control (achieved through socialization) that management gain from the application of training and development processes. Governments are also interested in training and development for economic, political and social reasons, in addition to their role as a very large employer. A healthy economy (as a result of many factors including training and development) frequently reflects political and social stability which is to the benefit of both individual citizens and the dominant political rulers. For example, in 1993 a national initiative by the UK government attempted to place work-based training on a par with academic qualifications in order to enhance its value, transferability and perceived significance (Wood, 1993).

Clearly, the processes supported by learning have considerable significance for individuals, managers, governments and society. It is therefore useful to begin this chapter with an in-depth review of the similarities and differences between the main concepts to be discussed.

LEARNING, TRAINING AND DEVELOPMENT

It is perhaps useful to begin with a brief review of the concepts that are supported by a learning process. The terms training and development are often used in practice as if they were interchangeable. Education is another term that is commonly used and which has a strong association with training and development. The *Oxford Dictionary* defines these three concepts in the following way:

- *Educate*. To bring up so as to form habits, manners, intellectual and physical aptitudes.
- *Train*. To instruct and discipline in or for some particular art, profession, occupation or practice; to make proficient by such instruction and practice.
- *Develop*. To unfold more fully, to bring out all that is potentially contained within.

From these definitions the obvious similarities and differences between the concepts and their application to an organizational setting become apparent. The concept of education would seem to be a general process representing the basic preparation for adult life in a specific environment. In an organizational setting, this would equate with the socialization or induction process for new employees to a company, examples of which would include meeting appropriate managers and colleagues, and learning about the basic rules, procedures and product range of the company.

Training is described as a job-specific form of education. It could either be organization-specific or general. For example, a company might train its staff in the particular word processing package that it uses. This training would be specific to that particular organization, but could also be transferable to other companies (if they used the same package).

Development reflects a less specific activity which relates to potential. Development is about the future. It does not necessarily relate to the job an individual presently undertakes. It could be a set of experiences that provide the individual with a basis for future career moves. It could also be used to enhance the skill levels of an individual in anticipation of future change in the nature of work or products. For example, the planned introduction of high-technology equipment is frequently preceded by introductory courses for those affected. Development is being increasingly used to describe the full range of training and development activity, the argument being that it is a less restrictive term than training, does not preclude the use of training activities within its sphere of influence and is more easily associated with the concepts of individual and organizational growth. This is often associated with the notion of human resource development, in which individual; career and organizational development are brought together in an integrated approach to mutual benefit (Beardwell and Holden, 2001). However, the following Employee Perspective (5.1) demonstrates that sometimes learning, in whatever form it takes, and organizations are uneasy bedfellows!

Each of the terms education, training and development assumes that some form of **learning** takes place within the individual. This can be reflected as a mutually dependent set of relationships as shown in Figure 5.1.

Learning
The relatively permanent change in actual or potential behaviour that results from direct or indirect experience.

The *Oxford Dictionary* defines the term 'learn' as to 'get knowledge of or skill in by study, experience or being taught'. In other words, the individual is affected in some way or other as a result of the process. Learning can also be defined as the relatively permanent change in behaviour or potential behaviour that results from direct or indirect experience (Hulse *et al.*, 1980). The major elements in these definitions are that:

EMPLOYEE PERSPECTIVE 5.1 To develop or not to develop, that is the question?

Sarah, a junior manager with a British subsidiary of an American company decided that she wanted to develop her career by taking an MBA. The programme she selected was based on the executive model, requiring attendance on campus for four days every three months over a two-year period. In addition, occasional study group sessions required attendance for one half-day between each residential period. The application for company sponsorship was supported by her manager and the company HR department. Her application to join the MBA programme was successful and arrangements were made to join the next intake.

On the second morning of the first residential study period Sarah had a call on her mobile phone from her boss. The essence of the call was that because of financial constraints the company had undertaken a major rethink of its support for development programmes and had decided to cancel all support for MBA programmes. As a consequence, she would not have the fees for the programme paid (a total of £15 000 for the fees, plus hotel and other expenses) and neither would she be allowed time off work for the residential sessions at the university. Sarah was instructed to leave the programme immediately and return to work that day.

Tasks

1. As Sarah, what would you do next, and why?
2. How would such an action be likely to be interpreted by other managers (and employees)?
3. If you were a senior manager faced with the need to cut cost how would you have dealt with the situation?

FIGURE 5.1

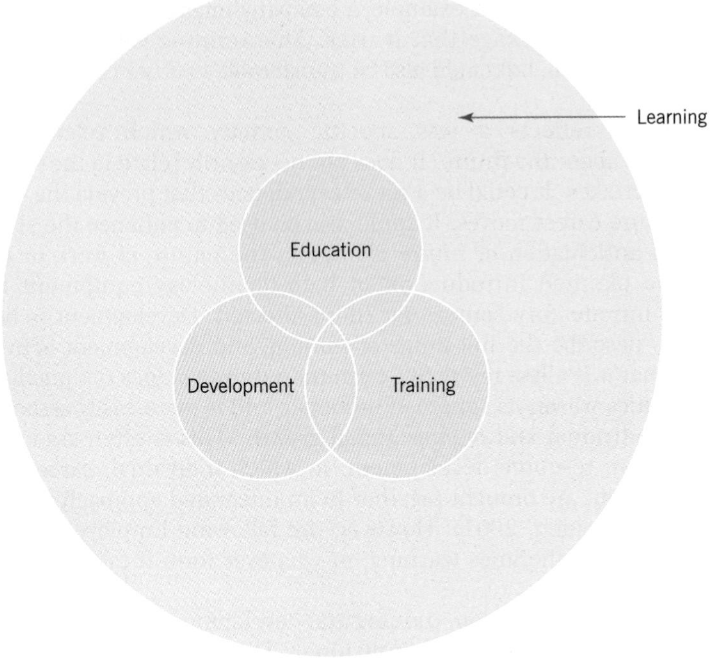

Learning, education, training and development

- *Learning implies change.* The acquisition of a new skill suggests that the individual will be different by comparison with before. For example, if an employee learns a new skill, that person can undertake a different range of tasks. The change becomes more difficult to detect, however, when the learning is cognitive in nature. For example, how will you be changed as a result of reading this chapter? You will have increased your level of understanding in the organizational behaviour field. In that sense your potential will have changed. But such changes might not be easily detectable as behaviour.
- *Learning implies sustained change.* The definitions of learning suggested earlier imply a long-lasting change consequence. Conversely, anything that produces a short-term effect is not true learning. So, for example, a student who learns the appropriate material for an exam and then puts it from memory has not learned anything.
- *Learning influences behaviour.* In some instances this is comparatively easy to see. For example, acquiring the skill of being able to drive a car. In other cases, the individual is learning to influence future behaviour. Your course in organizational behaviour is intended to introduce you to the behavioural and other issues associated with the human dimensions of organizations and consequently to influence your future management style and decision-making abilities.
- *Learning results from experience.* Some form of direct experience is necessary in order to produce learning. In the case of learning to drive a car, it is necessary at some point actually to get behind the steering wheel and drive on public roads. Indirect experience leads to vicarious learning. For example, an employee cheating on their time sheet and so earning more bonus will frequently be following (learning from) the example of other employees.

The learning process is outlined in Figure 5.2. This indicates the relationship between the learning process itself and the purpose to which it is being put. Equally, the impact on learning of past learning events is recognized in the model through the feedback loop. So for example, bad experiences in the formal school education system might negatively impact on an individual's willingness to expose themselves to learning opportunities in the future.

Also indicated in the model are those elements that precede learning, but which influence it:

- *External factors*. For example, the pressure placed on individuals to undergo learning. For example, children must by law be educated in an approved manner.
- *Internal factors*. For example, mood, intelligence, ability, personality and motivation all influence the learning process.
- *Learning experience*. A poorly designed learning event may result in the trainees not learning that which they were intended to learn.

The process by which people learn has long been an area of interest in psychology. There are three main approaches that have emerged over time, each one adding to the understanding of the process by building on top of the earlier approaches and accounting for different learning experiences. Subsequently, other perspectives on learning will be introduced. The three main approaches to learning are:

- Behaviourist theories
- Cognitive theories
- Social learning theories.

FIGURE 5.2

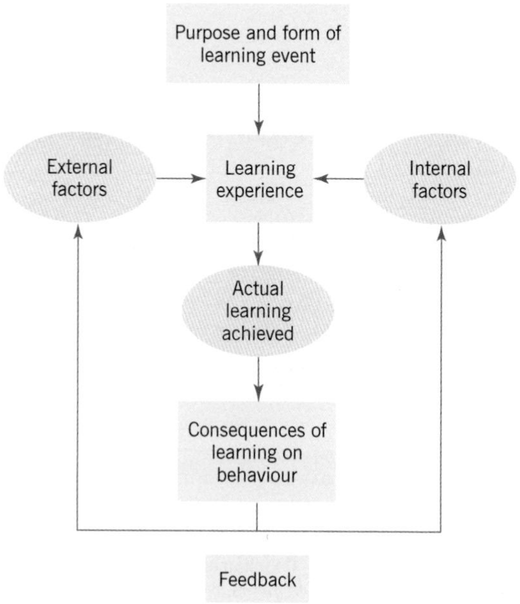

The learning process

BEHAVIOURIST THEORIES OF LEARNING

Classical conditioning
Learning based on links between conditioned stimulus and unconditioned stimulus established over several repetitions producing a conditioned response.

Instrumental conditioning
An approach to learning based on the shaping of particular behaviours by a trainer through reinforcement.

The behaviourist school of psychology has enjoyed a long and illustrious tradition. The two best-known names from this field of psychology are Pavlov, who developed the theory of **classical conditioning**, and Skinner, who developed the theory of **instrumental conditioning** as an approach to learning.

Pavlov and classical conditioning

Pavlov carried out his research in Russia and was concerned with how dogs learned their natural reflexes. Pavlov noticed that whenever his laboratory dogs were given food they salivated (1927). This was a natural reaction in the dogs, to which he gave the term 'unconditioned response'. This became the first step in the conditioning process. The second step was to link what Pavlov termed the unconditioned stimulus (food) with a conditioned stimulus (the ringing of a bell). This was done by ringing the bell on each occasion on which food was presented. Pavlov was trying to get the dogs to learn that the sound of the bell was associated with the appearance of food. After several repetitions, the dogs salivated automatically when the bell was rung. This was the third step in the conditioning process, the conditioned response. A direct link between the stimulus (bell sound) and the response (salivation) had been made. This series of steps can be shown as a diagram, Figure 5.3. In the classical conditioning model, the salivation was conditioned to occur as a result of the previously established association between the bell and the food.

The conditioned response is a relatively simple reaction when compared with the behaviour of humans, particularly in a social setting. This theory was able to explain some of the simpler forms of learning but the conditioned response quickly died away if it was not frequently reinforced. This feature of the model was referred to as an extinction response and makes it more difficult to explain how classical conditioning could build learning opportunities from the spontaneous, dynamic and random nature of much human interaction and experience. Pavlov was also able to make his

FIGURE 5.3

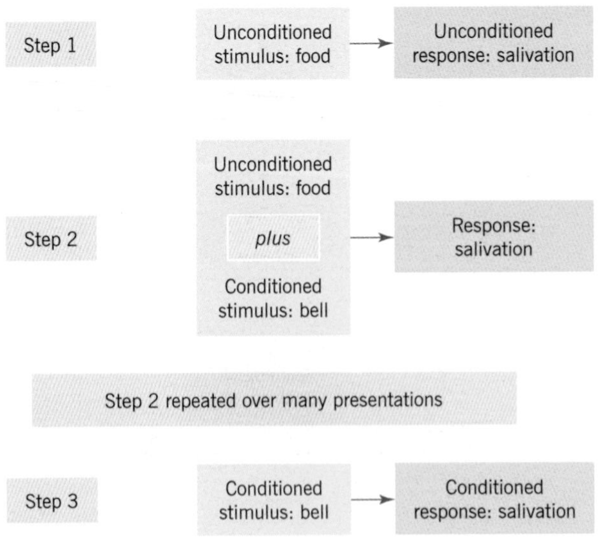

Pavlov's classical conditioning model

experimental dogs respond to a wide range of bell-related variables, so demonstrating a generalizable stimulus dimension which might help explain some of the links with real experience.

The work of Pavlov was running in parallel, although independently, with a number of American theorists. They included Watson, who coined the term 'behaviourism' to describe the emphasis on observable behaviour rather than the introspective approaches common in psychology at that time. Watson believed that learning in the environment was responsible for almost all development in the growing child. He introduced the concept of stimulus–response association (conditioning) as the basis of much routine human behaviour (Watson, 1924). For example, a manager who sometimes shouts at employees to ensure that instructions are followed might discover after a while that employees do not respond to instructions that are not shouted.

Thorndike (1932) built on this stimulus–response model through his studies of the ability of cats to escape from puzzle boxes. From these observations he concluded that the cats could learn by trial and error (slow learning). Thorndike suggested that what was happening was a slow strengthening of the stimulus–response connection through a number of repetitions of the cat being placed in the puzzle box, being allowed to escape and receiving a food reward immediately afterwards. The reinforcement offered by the food made it more likely that the cat would repeat the same behaviour next time it was placed in the puzzle box.

With the linking of the early behaviourists and Pavlov's classical conditioning the groundwork had been established to allow the introduction of this approach to more complex forms of learned behaviour. The stimulus–response model is good at explaining the simple cause and effect relationships evident in some activities. However, it is difficult to use the model to explain the wide variety of conscious purposeful human behaviour. The classical model as it became known does not allow for choice in the response options available to humans and experienced in everyday interactions. The actual behavioural responses occurring will depend upon a wide variety of factors acting on the individuals in that situation. The following Employee Perspective (5.2) demonstrates that people can act out of character if they are pushed too far or feel the need to do so.

EMPLOYEE PERSPECTIVE 5.2 Valerie shouted back!

In one factory department the supervisor was known to have a quick temper and had been known to shout at employees with little provocation. However, he also quickly calmed down and would soon be laughing and joking with employees. One of the factory workers was called Valerie who was usually very quiet and just got on with the jobs she was told to do. If she was shouted at by the supervisor she simply became even more quiet and withdrawn for a few hours and then returned to her normal pattern of behaviour.

However, on one particular day something that Valerie did was not to the supervisor's liking and he shouted at her. But unlike her normal reactions, this time she looked him straight in the eye, her own eyes blazing with anger and she slapped him across the face hard. That stopped the supervisor in his tracks. He just looked at her with his mouth wide open and said nothing with his hand on his now very red cheek, after a few seconds he just turned around and walked away silently. He did not venture out onto the shop floor for the rest of the day.

What he did not know at the time was that Valerie had left home that morning having had an argument with her children about their homework for school, her car would not start and the bus to work had been late and she had left her packed lunch at home!

Task

Try and explain Valerie's behaviour using the Classical model of learning.

Skinner and instrumental conditioning

Skinner is associated with the instrumental approach to conditioning, but he was not the first person to be associated with it. Instrumental in this context refers to behaviour being 'instrumental' in producing an effect. For example, a hungry rat can be conditioned to press a lever to obtain food. Pressing the lever (behaviour) releases the food and allows feeding (the effect). Pressing the lever is therefore instrumental in obtaining food.

Skinner put forward a distinction between two types of behaviour, respondent and operant (1953). Respondent behaviour was said to be under the direct control of a stimulus. This was the stimulus–response relationship in classical conditioning, for example, salivation in response to food presentation. Operant behaviour, conversely, was seen in terms of spontaneity, with no direct or obvious cause. A stimulus controlling operant behaviour is referred to as a discriminative stimulus. An example would be the knocking on your front door, which tells you that someone is trying to see you for some purpose, but does not force you to answer the door. In this way the concept is synonymous with the term 'instrumental' in that the behaviour (answering the door) is instrumental in producing an effect (finding out why someone was knocking on it). It is for this reason that the term 'instrumental conditioning' is used to describe this form of learning.

The best-known experiments in this area involve laboratory rats being placed in a Skinner box (named after the designer). There are many variations of this type of experiment and so only a simple generalized account will be provided here. Imagine a small cage, bare except for a feeding tray, a lever and a light source. Figure 5.4 is a schematic diagram of a Skinner box.

A hungry rat is placed in the box and left to explore its new surroundings under the watchful eye of the experimenter. As the rat approaches the lever in the box a pellet of food will be made available in the food tray. After a few repetitions of this, the rat may accidentally touch the lever and again food will be made available. From then on, only touching the lever will produce a food pellet. Eventually, this is also replaced with the

FIGURE 5.4

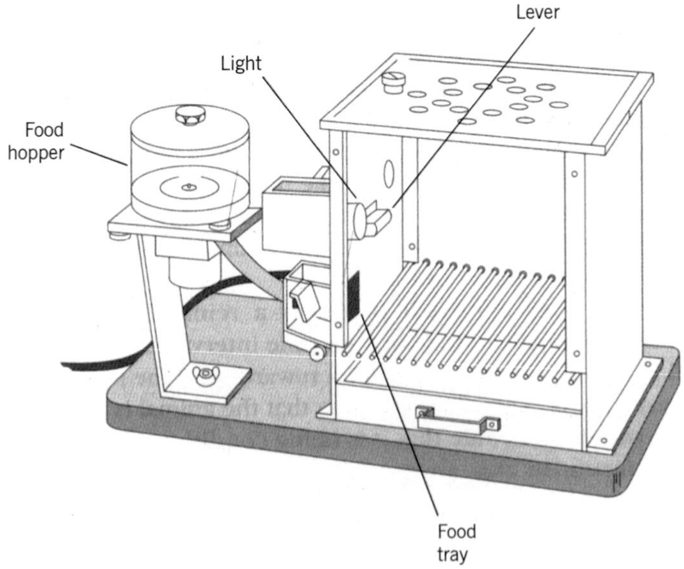

A Skinner box

actual pressing of the lever being required to obtain food. The lever pressing is reinforced by the presentation of food. There are an enormous range of variations that can be introduced to this basic process and it has been used on a wide range of animals. Pigeons have been taught to recognize colours and play table tennis, whales and dolphins trained for wildlife shows and dolphins trained to hunt for underwater mines in a war context.

The process of **reinforcement** is used to **shape** the behaviour pattern desired. Over many cycles of repetition only behaviours closer and closer to the desired outcome will be rewarded until the actual behaviour presented matches that desired by the trainer. Once established, it is not necessary to reinforce every occurrence of the desired behaviour in order to maintain it. There are four types of reinforcement schedule that can influence the level and rate of continued repetition of the desired behaviour. They are:

Reinforcement
The encouragement of particular behaviours through the application of positive and/or negative rewards linked to a reinforcement schedule.

Shape
To create or encourage particular behaviour patterns in another individual through the principles of reinforcement.

1. *Fixed ratio*. Reinforcement occurs after a fixed number of repetitions of a particular activity. For example, one pellet of food every 20 lever presses. This tends to produce a consistently steady rate of response in order for the respondent to be able to maximize the reward.
2. *Variable ratio*. This also provides reinforcement after a number of repetitions of the desired behaviour. However, unlike the fixed ratio, this time the number of repetitions required to produce the reward is randomly varied. This produces a consistently rapid rate of response as the respondent (rat in a Skinner box) has no way of predicting which response (lever press) will produce the pellet of food.
3. *Fixed interval*. This approach produces a reinforcement following the first appropriate behaviour after a set time interval. The behaviour pattern under this regime almost stops after a reward until the next time interval is due, when it starts again. This suggests that the animal is able to judge time and work out the schedule that it is being conditioned to.
4. *Variable interval*. In this approach the time interval at which food becomes available is randomly varied between upper and lower parameters. Under these conditions, the animal responds with a consistently rapid rate of lever pressing. This type of response would be expected as there is no way for the animal to know which lever press will activate the food delivery. The animal may be able to judge that time is involved, but it will be unable accurately to gauge the random variation in trigger intervals. It must respond at a rapid rate in order to obtain the food as soon as possible after it becomes available.

It is the partial reinforcement schedules just described that produce the most sustained and rapid response rates and are therefore the most effective in maintaining the desired behaviour. In one experiment a pigeon was 'reinforced' on average once every five minutes. That equates to 12 times in every hour. Yet it sustained a pecking rate of approximately 6000 per hour. In human terms this is the form of reinforcement used by gaming machines, lottery and other form of gambling to 'hook' the participants into continually spending their money, because the next bet might be the one that wins.

So far in the discussion we have described only positive reinforcement. That is, the subject being rewarded for doing something that the designers of the conditioning programme seeks. Other reinforcement options available include (also see Figure 5.5):

- *Negative reinforcers*. This refers to an unpleasant event that precedes behaviour and which is removed when the subject produces appropriate behaviour. For example, a torturer may stop beating up a prisoner if they confess to a crime.
- *Omission*. This refers to the stopping of reinforcement. Naturally, it leads to a reduction and eventually the extinction of the particular behaviour. For

example, employees who do an excellent job may stop doing so if managers do not reinforce the behaviour by acknowledging the contribution.

- *Punishment*. This relates to an unpleasant reward for particular behaviours. The slap on the leg of a child who does something wrong would be an example. This form of reinforcement decreases the occurrence of the behaviour in question.

Many experiments have been carried out on the conditioning of human behaviour. For example, Verplanck (1955) carried out a reinforcement exercise during an informal conversation with a student. The student was not aware of the reinforcement process being carried out. It is worth noting that the experiment as described would not meet the ethical standards required of research today. The reinforcement schedule designed required the experimenter to reward all statements of opinion made by the student. These included phrases such as, 'I believe', 'It is my opinion', 'I think', when used by the student within the conversation. The reinforcement was in the form of positive feedback to the student through the experimenter using phrases such as, 'I agree', 'You are right', 'That is so'. The use of this verbal reinforcement increased the number of statements of opinion used by the student. In another part of the same experiment, extinction was also demonstrated. This was achieved by the experimenter failing to reinforce any statement of opinion (by remaining silent) when the student made one. Not surprisingly, the use of these statements by the student reduced under this regime.

The process of instrumental conditioning has a wider application than the classical approach. It provides for the shaping of behaviour into particular patterns. It has also been used to account for many of the beliefs and superstitions that pervade human life. Examples include blowing on the dice to make them lucky; putting on a particular item of clothing before an exam in order to guarantee success; and never watching a favourite football team live on television to improve their chance of winning. The difficulty arises in being able to explain how reinforcement operates in the everyday exposure to multiple and random experience. The experiment described earlier might explain how one lecturer can influence the behaviour of one student. But is it adequate in explaining how an entire (and probably) large class learn successfully or perhaps conversely fail to learn as intended? The answer is clearly no. Also if reinforcement is delayed then it may become associated with other behaviour and there are also factors such as perception and memory which impact on how individuals interpret situations.

The conditioning approach to learning cannot explain all the thought and behaviour patterns evident in people. Individuals have objectives and purpose behind many of their behaviours which do not easily fit into a model based on the principles of conditioning. However, instrumental conditioning does have a place in the management of people as Management in Action 5.1 demonstrates. This case illustrates complexity in the real world and how instrumental conditioning can be used to influence behaviour.

FIGURE 5.5

	Stimulus given	Stimulus taken away
Pleasant stimulus	Positive reinforcement	Omission
Unpleasant stimulus	Punishment	Negative reinforcement

Reinforcement framework

MANAGEMENT IN ACTION 5.1 The domestic supervisor and conditioning

The domestic supervisor in a university hall of residence had been appointed to the job following the retirement of the previous incumbent, who had held the job for approximately ten years. With the change in supervisor, management had decided to restructure the duties of the post and take the opportunity to increase the level of direct supervision of the domestic staff working in the hall. At the same time the job title was changed from housekeeper to domestic supervisor. Previously, direct supervision of the domestic staff had fallen under the responsibilities of a supervisor who looked after two halls specifically for these activities.

The new domestic supervisor described how she was initially concerned about how to approach the job to ensure that she obtained a positive response from the staff. It was necessary to increase the level of direct supervision of the staff, which inevitably meant increased levels of work inspection. Given that the staff had all been in the same jobs for many years and worked under a different regime, this could have become a problem.

The new domestic supervisor had held supervisory jobs previously and at one time ran her own business. Calling on this wealth of experience she decided on the following course of action. The first stage was to let the existing staff get to know her and that 'things' would inevitably change. This involved several actions, including the provision of a bag of sweets on the desk from which all could help themselves, 'for a bit of energy to start the day'; frequent visits to each worksite to get to know the job and meet the staff on their own territory; only gradually over the period of a couple of weeks to begin to offer advice and suggestions on what needed to be done. This was usually done in terms of 'would it not be easier to try it this way?' or 'why not do this job when you have finished that one?' The 'suggestion' would only become more like an instruction if the individual would not enter into the spirit of the process and did not take the hint.

This approach began to create a team in which the individual employee did not feel threatened. This was important as a number of them had applied for the domestic supervisor's job when it was advertised and felt some resentment at being rejected. They began by resisting the approach. Not in a serious way, but by finding excuses for not doing things that the domestic supervisor wanted, or doing them in the old way. This required the most tact on the part of the domestic supervisor as she attempted to change the behaviour patterns of the staff. The approach adopted was to keep a 'light touch' in the way that issues were raised by making a joke or a light-hearted comment about something. For example, it was pointed out to the staff, while laughing, that they should clean the light fittings on their way to their longer than strictly allowed tea break as they had said that they did not have time to do this job. The point was made in such a way that it could not be seen as a direct order, given in an offensive manner. But it was a clear signal of what was expected and the possible next step if it was not implemented. This was followed by frequent and obvious checks on that particular job, with comment on the result. Praise if it had been done, a jocular, 'not had time to do these yet?' if it had not. The staff were unaware that their behaviour was being shaped. They thought that they had gone through a period of getting used to working with a new boss.

Stop ↔ Consider

If you were the new domestic supervisor described how would you have gone about establishing your credibility with your staff? How would you set about carrying out your new responsibilities in such a management job?

Would your approach contain any degree of conditioning in it? Why or why not?

In this particular case, it is apparent that the reinforcement process was combined with many other aspects in order to achieve the requirements of the job. The management control issues, the need to work within set procedures and guidelines together with the opportunity for operational managers to use some discretion when interpreting policies are all incorporated into the approach. The approach adopted in Management in Action 5.1 is an informal version of what has generally become known as behavioural modification, the basis of the approach being that managers should seek ways of maximizing appropriate behaviours among employees through the application of a range of reinforcement principles. Figure 5.6 is a representation of the behavioural modification process as it might be applied by a manager.

The model is self-explanatory in that it begins with a systematic review of the requirements and actuality of behaviour in the specific situation. This is then followed by a decision-making process which results in the identification of the appropriate reinforcement approach to be adopted. Once selected and operational, the results of the reinforcement approach would then be regularly monitored and any remedial or follow-up action taken. Among the criticisms of this type of approach to the organization of human behaviour is that it is managers who decide what defines appropriate behaviour and it therefore forms part of a social engineering or management control process. Also the range of rewards available within organizations is limited and needs to be controlled in ways which limit fraud, favouritism, discrimination and unfairness. This inevitably restricts the ways in which behaviour modification can be used in practice.

COGNITIVE APPROACHES TO LEARNING

The basis of cognitive approaches to learning is that an individual develops internal (cognitive) frameworks that allow them to interact more effectively with the environ-

FIGURE 5.6

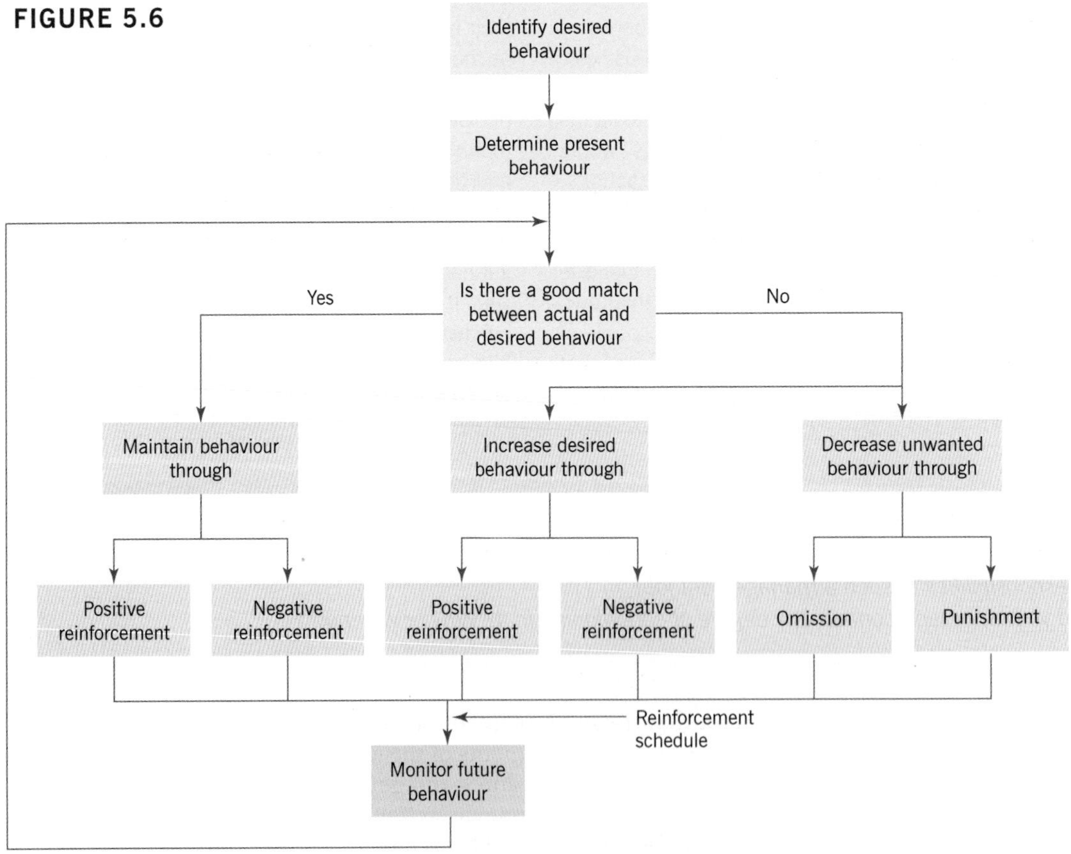

Behavioural modification (*adapted from:* Luthans, F (1985) *Organizational Behaviour*, 4th edn, McGraw Hill, New York)

ment around them. Therefore this approach creates a need to study the working of the mental processes involved in learning.

The early work in this field was carried out on animals and was based on the behavioural model already introduced. Kohler describes an experiment in which a chimpanzee demonstrated insight as a learning process (1925). Sultan (the name of the chimpanzee) was placed in a cage and given a short stick. A piece of fruit was placed outside the cage and beyond the range of the short stick. A longer stick was also placed outside the cage, but within range of the short stick. After a few attempts at obtaining the fruit by using the short stick, Sultan began to seek other ways of obtaining the fruit. After a number of false starts, he paused for a lengthy period and just looked around him. Suddenly, he jumped up, used the short stick to pull the long stick into range and thereby obtained the fruit. This suggested to Kohler that the chimpanzee was using cognitive processes to create insights into the problem and how it could be solved, in effect learning through problem solving. This approach to learning would seem to differ from the trial and error process described by Thorndike (1932) in that a sudden insight is apparent in finding a solution to the problem of obtaining the fruit.

This led to a number of other approaches to the development of cognitive learning. Essentially, this approach assumes that people are actively involved in the process of learning. They are not simply at the mercy of outside forces and internal drives. A simplified way of thinking about this cognitive approach is shown in Figure 5.7.

A more recent approach to the cognitive perspective on learning is based on information processing as a psychological process. According to Fitts and Posner (1967) the three primary characteristics of skilled performance are:

1. Organization
2. Goal directedness
3. Utilization of feedback.

The process of providing feedback enables the individual to more effectively and quickly achieve the goal being sought. There are many obvious examples of feedback in action. Central heating and air conditioning systems function through feedback, based on the thermostat. The most easily understood form is negative feedback. Negative feedback allows the system being controlled to remain on target (see Figure 5.8).

Essentially, negative feedback reduces the gap between the current and intended situations. So, in a central heating system, the feedback process measures the actual room temperature, compares it with the desired temperature and switches the boiler on if the room is too cold. In an organizational setting, a manager will usually receive monthly financial reports setting out actual expenditure against the budgeted level. This form of feedback is a budgetary control system. If the manager is spending more money than is provided for under the budget, they will be able to seek ways of reducing future expenditure, the intention being to utilize the principles of negative feedback to ensure that actual costs do not exceed the planned level over the year.

FIGURE 5.7

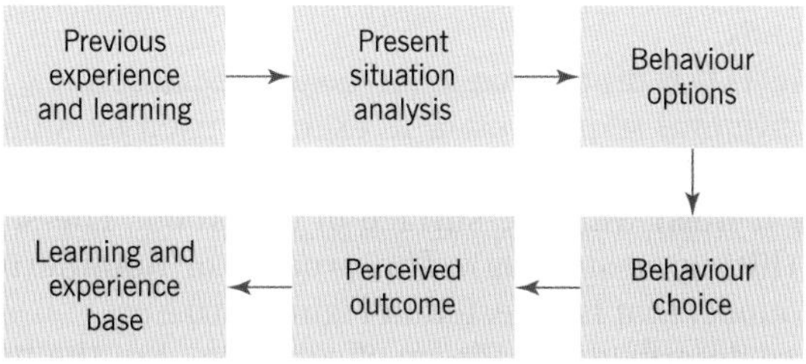

A cognitive model of learning

FIGURE 5.8

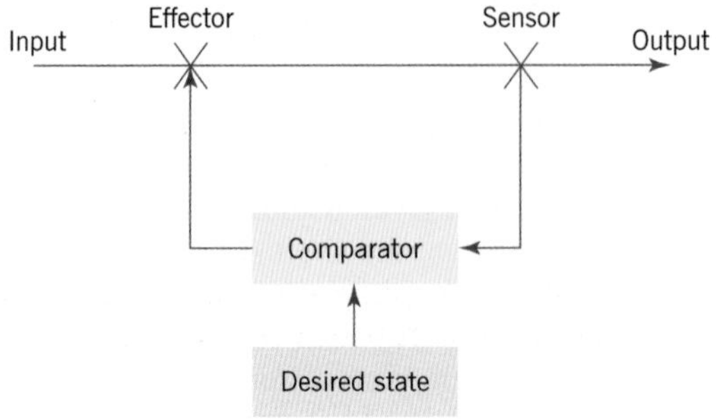

Negative feedback

Feedback within the cognitive model of learning can originate either from within the individual or from the environment around the individual. For example, a child learns that touching hot objects is dangerous from the pain suffered; while budgetary control systems are usually managed by finance departments on behalf of line managers. Feedback can also arrive at the same time as the originating event, for example, a room thermostat constantly responds to room temperature. It can also be delayed, as in the case of the financial information that is published after the end of the reporting period. Delayed feedback is of no value in maintaining current performance, but can be of value in influencing future behaviour. By the time the financial reports reach a manager the money is spent and nothing can change that situation. However, the manager can adjust spending in future financial periods and in that sense learn about financial management and to anticipate expenditure patterns.

Feedback, as described, is a useful means of controlling activity and providing learning opportunities in the dynamic world in which we live. However, it is rare in behaviour that a simple chain of events is the major determinant of behaviour. Take, for example, driving a car. This involves a co-ordinated set of feedback loops (visually searching the road around the car, listening to noise from the engine, sensing the feel of the road, judging speed and direction and so on) arranged into a framework which allows priority to be given to particular behaviours. This prioritization process can produce braking at one moment, accelerating at another, steering, etc. all included in the dynamic activity that we call driving. This much-simplified description of driving reflects the concept of prioritization and the hierarchical notion of response habits within the stimulus–response model. One way that the concept of feedback has been combined with the hierarchical notion of response habits is in the application of a *TOTE* unit.

TOTE refers to a **t**est, **o**perate, **t**est, **e**xit sequence and was first described by Miller *et al.* (1960). The TOTE model is shown in Figure 5.9. In essence the test phase of the model reflects a feedback loop in that if a mismatch between plan and goal is detected then the operate phase is activated. This sequence is repeated until a match between actual and goal is identified, when the cycle ends and that particular behaviour also ends.

The benefit of the TOTE unit is that it can be used to describe a series of hierarchically organized behavioural sequences. The example used by Miller is hammering a nail into a piece of wood. One phase is the identification of the position of the nail, the goal being to make it flush with the surface of the wood. The second phase is the hammer position (lifting or striking). The process of hammering the nail, then, consists of a TOTE model that is reflected in Figure 5.10.

The TOTE unit so described is made up of sub-units. But the hammering of a nail into a piece of wood may in itself be part of a much larger set of goals. For example, the

FIGURE 5.9

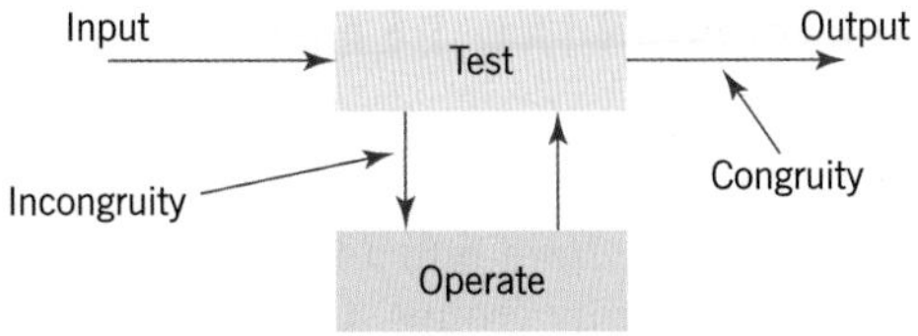

TOTE unit (*source*: Miller, GA, Galanter, E and Pribram, KH (1960) *Plans and the Structure of Behaviour*, Henry Holt and Company. Reprinted 1986, Adams, Bannister, Cox, New York. Reprinted with permission.

FIGURE 5.10

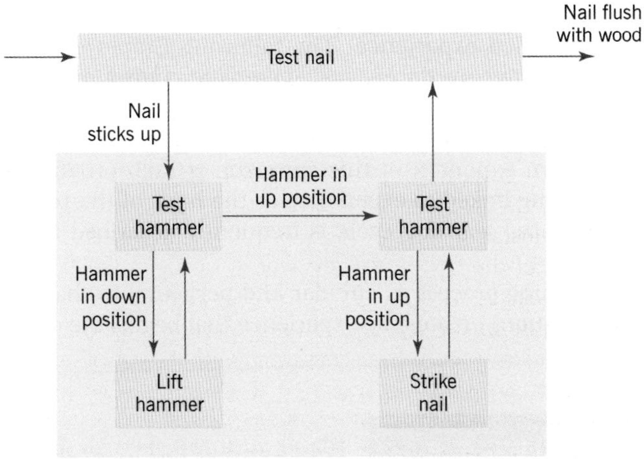

TOTE model of hammering a nail (*source*: Miller, GA, Galanter, E and Pribram, KH (1960) *Plans and the Structure of Behaviour*, Henry Holt and Company. Reprinted 1986, Adams, Bannister, Cox, New York. Reprinted with permission.

particular nail might be part of a tree house for a child or it may be part of the construction of a house for a family. As such the person doing the hammering may be an employee and have as a goal the need to earn a bonus in order to pay for a summer holiday or it may be a father seeking to build the best tree house possible to make his children happy.

The notion of learning based on feedback is central to the cognitive approaches to learning. Take, for example, attempting to learn all the subject matter from your course without any feedback from lecturers before your final exams. The process of linking feedback into a dynamic hierarchical framework provides an important basis for understanding how learning fits into a cognitive-based model. It is also vital underpinning for the practice of performance management within organizations. For example, appraisal systems rely on the provision of feedback on the performance of individuals as a means of identifying training needs, development and career opportunities, as well as future salary or bonus levels. Handled well, feedback can be of significant mutual benefit to the individual and organization. Handled badly, or not undertaken at all, it can lead to people not doing those things which need to be done or personal underachievement. Ineffective feedback can also encourage people to do things that are unnecessary (because they are not told not to do so) and can therefore lead to inefficiency and, in extreme cases, organizational failure.

SOCIAL AND EXPERIENTIAL LEARNING

The social environment (or culture) within which learning takes place is a major influence on the process. Infants are *socialized* into a family unit; young people are *socialized* into various friendship and affinity groups. Often the first lecture in a course is designed as an introduction, the purpose being to let you know what the content is about, how the course will be delivered and what will be expected of students – a process of socialization. In organizations, the process of socialization frequently begins with an induction programme, the main intentions being to ensure that new employees rapidly become effective and (hopefully) stay with the company. This is frequently extended through the structured way in which the new employee is introduced to the work group that they will be part of. The process of socialization can also be regarded as a period of programmed experience. The following Employee Perspective (5.3) demonstrates that management do not have complete control over the induction of new employees.

Social learning attempts to embrace this idea and develop a theoretical base from it. Perhaps the best-known exponent of this approach is Kolb (1985). He proposed a learning cycle of learning linked to experience as the basis of the process (see Figure 5.11). For that reason the learning cycle is frequently described as an experiential learning approach.

Kolb views the learning process as circular and perpetual in that the output from one cycle (experimentation) creates the experience that begins the cycle over again. It

EMPLOYEE PERSPECTIVE 5.3 Orla's induction to work

Orla began a new job as a trainee reporter with a local newspaper after she left university. The newspaper was part of a large chain of similar publications and ultimately owned by a large company quoted on the London Stock Exchange. Consequently, she was very proud to have a start in what she hoped would be a good career in journalism. The company had two levels of induction programme before she began work with the other journalists. The first was with the parent group and intended to introduce professional staff to the way the group functioned, its objectives and policies and the opportunities available should they achieve success in their careers. The second was organized by the company that Orla was working with and intended to introduce individuals to the way it worked and their role within it. It was also intended to introduce new employees to the culture of the company and also the preferred ways of working as determined by management.

Having completed both induction courses, Orla was looking forward to actually starting work. She was assigned to work with an experienced journalist for a few weeks in order to learn the practicalities of the job, before being given some small stories to write under her own name. When she met her new mentor for the first time he was very polite and suggested that she accompany him to interview a local politician about proposed changes to public housing policy in the area. On the drive to the interview the journalist and Orla chattered about the job and what it involved. The journalist concluded by saying to her to ignore what had been said in the induction courses as management didn't have a clue what was involved in getting good stories out of people and meeting the deadlines imposed by publication requirements. The only people that knew how to do the job were the real journalists, not accountants or managers. He also suggested to her that after the meeting with the politician, they should go to a particular pub and meet some of the other journalists, giving Orla the chance to 'get to know' other professionals and to understand how the job was done.

Tasks

1. What would you do if you were Orla?
2. What does this example suggest about induction, socialization and management within organizations?

FIGURE 5.11

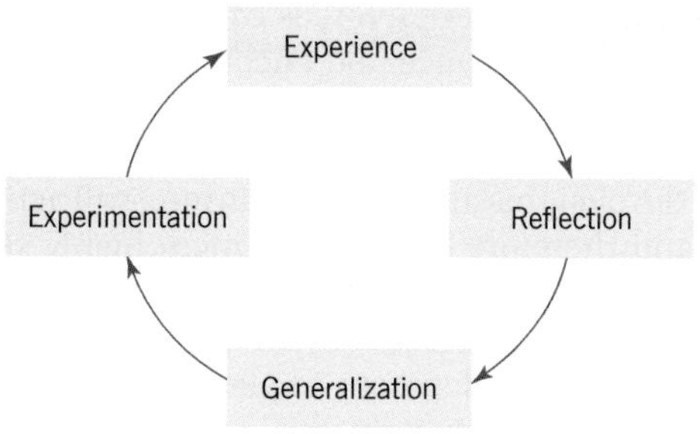

The Kolb learning cycle

firmly locks learning into a developmental cycle in which individual behaviour and its consequences for the individual form the basis of the process. It implies a process of continual adaptation as actual behaviour is followed automatically by reflection and generalized testing out of the lessons learned in new situations. Looking briefly at each stage of the model:

- *Concrete experience.* This refers to an experience of some description which could either be planned or unplanned in nature. In an organizational context this could be an employee being praised by a manager for a job well done.
- *Reflective observation.* This stage in the cycle relates to the cognitive process of thinking about the experience that began the process. This might include the cause of the experience along with the implications of it. For example, how did the employee feel about the praise from the manager? What caused it and was it justified? Was it an unusual event and why?
- *Abstract conceptualization and generalization.* This stage is about the conclusions that emerge from the review process. Issues including the identification of when it may happen again and under what circumstances and so on would be considered. In the example given, would the employee like to be praised in future for good work, and what form of work might trigger the praise?
- *Experimentation in new situations.* For example, transferring the experience to other job situations. In effect, this becomes the basis of new experiences to begin the cycle all over again. In the example given, the employee might seek to change their work behaviours in other situations to see if that also triggered praise from the manager or created other rewards etc.

The Kolb model has many implications for training and development activities within organizations and is the most frequently found basis of course design in that context. For the learning process to be fully effective each of the four stages needs to be provided in training programme design. Individuals need to have the opportunity to reflect on and generalize about the experience if they are to be able to internalize and make future use of the learning points being taught in the classroom. If this is not done adequately then the transfer of learning to workplace behaviour will not happen and much of the potential benefit will be lost. For example, learning to drive only on a simulator would not adequately prepare an individual for actual city and motorway driving.

Social learning is a process which emphasizes the individual in the learning process. In this model, learning is not possible without the active involvement of the individual in reflecting and concluding about the experiences encountered. That is why it is frequently referred to as experiential learning. It places the responsibility for learning on the ability of the individual to establish links between behaviour and experience through evaluation. External forces can only facilitate and encourage the process through provision of experience and encouragement of reflection. The transfer of knowledge from the classroom to the workplace is difficult to achieve in practice without specific actions to encourage it. It also implies that those individuals who are more willing or able to develop this approach to learning will actively seek out developmental opportunities and therefore become the more highly skilled employees. The differential access to self-development opportunities provided by some jobs also influences the process and the relative success of some job holders.

The concept of continuous development implied by the social learning model has been utilized as a major theme within individual and organizational development. For example, the need to foster an organizational culture which values continuous development has been identified as significant to success. Wood *et al.* (1990) suggest a five-stage process of continuous development:

1. *Integration of learning and work*. The use of continuous development as a mechanism of incremental work improvement.
2. *Self-directed learning*. The identification by the individual of their own development needs.
3. *Emphasis on process rather than techniques*. The acquisition of what can be referred to as generalized skills rather than specific task-oriented skills. In other words, to acquire broader skills aimed at developing understanding, potential and commitment.
4. *Continuous development as an attitude*. This reflects the approach to learning through the development of appropriate attitudes to reflection and experience rather than simply technique or skill acquisition. It seeks to develop the attitude that sees learning and development opportunities in everyday events and situations rather than a reliance on formal training events.
5. *Continuous development for organizations as well as individuals*. The objective of continuous development is to achieve organizational objectives through the recognition of the links between learning and performance. As individuals develop, so do the organizations that employ them.

These approaches tend to provide a model of learning that, although strongly tied to the social setting within which the individual functions, are isolationist in practice. Learning as a process is a very personal affair. It is the individual that experiences, reflects and develops as a consequence of the opportunity to experiment with their behaviour patterns. However, individuals are invariably in an interactive relationship with other people and their environment and learning is also influenced by those variables, a point made by Stuart (1986).

OTHER APPROACHES TO LEARNING

Socialization and learning

Some aspects associated with socialization and learning have already been discussed in the previous section in relation to experiential learning. In historical terms one of the most frequent forms of social learning was that which came to be called the 'sitting-by-Nellie' approach. This expression originated in factory environments where a large number of women were employed, hence the use of the name Nellie. This form of training was very simple and relied on one employee teaching a particular skill to another person through demonstration. The employee to be trained literally sat beside

Nellie (the employee who already had the particular skill) to watch and hopefully practice under her guidance. However, as the employee with the skill usually received no training in how to train, it was a very uncertain and inefficient process. Equally, of course, the process assumed that the skilled employee wanted to pass on the skills and also that the trainee employee would learn what management wanted them to learn. Such approaches provided an ideal opportunity for socialization into the employee groups and prevailing practices to be achieved. However, this provided a means through which to reinforce the existing status quo, rather than mould behaviour and attitudes in the way in which management might have wished. Management in Action 5.2 describes one job that demonstrates the effects of employee-dominated socialization linked to the sitting-by-Nellie approach to training.

Learning styles

Another question to consider in relation to learning as an individual process is why it is that not everyone is equally successful at the learning that they are exposed to. For example, not everyone achieves the same marks in an examination yet they will have studied the same course and been taught by the same teacher. Some individuals learn to drive a motor vehicle very quickly, while others need many lessons before they are able to pass the driving test. There are many aspects to the answer to this question, age, motivation, the nature of the relationship with the teacher, interest in the topic and prior experience being just some of them.

Kolb added to this discussion by suggesting that individuals have a preference for activity at one of the four stages in the learning cycle. This, he claimed, reflected the preferred learning style for that individual. The style for an individual could be identified through the administration of a questionnaire based test. Honey and Mumford (1992) further developed the ideas originated by Kolb and produced their own version of his learning styles questionnaire. Using their questionnaire it is possible to determine one's preferred learning style as being one of the following:

- *Activist*. An individual who prefers action, new experiences and will try anything at least once.
- *Reflector*. An individual who prefers to think about things and understand what they are trying to achieve or do before they actually take action.
- *Theorist*. An individual who prefers to understand the linkages and relationships between ideas and events before taking action.
- *Pragmatist*. An individual who prefers to see and understand the how and what related to that which they are expected to do before they take action or decide what to do.

The clear implication in this approach to learning styles is that individuals may not always complete the full cycle of four stages in the Kolb learning cycle if they allow their preferred style to dominate. For example, a theorist might become so locked into thinking about the relationships between variables etc. that they keep putting off changing their actual behaviour on the pretext of not knowing enough to justify a variation in their usual actions. Consequently, it is one of the responsibilities of trainers to encourage individuals with a dominant style to experience the other styles as part of effective learning based on the Kolb cycle.

Studies of personality have also been used to explore the relationship with learning. The results have suggested that personality factors such as extroversion and introversion have an impact on how individuals will respond to aspects such as punishment and reward in the learning process. For example, extroverts respond better to rewards and prefer short term material than do introverts. Other studies have shown the effect

MANAGEMENT IN ACTION 5.2 Who checks the checkers?

This is a true story, only some of the details have been changed to prevent the possibility of identifying the organization and the individuals involved. Some years ago I had the misfortune to be made redundant. I was subsequently offered the job as a bonus checker with the housing maintenance department of a local council. This job was obtained through the good offices of a friend who already worked as a bonus checker in the council and recommended me to his boss. I duly became part of the bonus team (about ten people in total) and started work on the appointed day. I was not given any induction training or other guidance on what was expected of me. I was simply introduced to the other members of the team and handed over to my friend to be 'taught' the duties and responsibilities.

Bonus checkers were required to take a 10 per cent sample of the previous day's completed job cards and then visit the houses in which repair work had been done to check if the maintenance worker had actually done what the job card claimed. The maintenance people were paid bonus in addition to their wages providing they 'earned' more hours than they had worked. Each job to be done had a set time available, but of course, if more work was necessary more time could be claimed. So for example, if a lock was broken and had to be changed the allowed time was (say) one hour, but if the door also needed repairing an additional time of (say) two hours would be claimed by the worker. Naturally the maintenance people worked away from close supervision and they were frequently tempted to claim that additional work had been necessary in order to earn more bonus. The job of the bonus checker was intended to prevent that from happening by 'policing' the system.

When individual's were caught claiming more hours than they should it required the bonus checker to meet with supervisors and managers in order for them to decide if disciplinary action was justified. A disciplinary meeting might then be held which involved the maintenance worker, supervisor, manager, trade union officials and the bonus checker in order to decide on guilt and any punishment. Invariably there was some plausible excuse for the mistake (as the employee described it) on the job card and few people were dismissed or formally disciplined. The job was not popular with any of the workers or managers as it created problems and difficulties for all concerned. Even the bonus checkers themselves thought the work was boring and pointless as workers continued to claim more bonus than they should and management were not totally supportive.

The bonus checkers had slipped into a work pattern in which they collected the 10 per cent sample of the previous day's job cards and then they all disappeared to a cafe to drink coffee, eat snacks, share the sample of job cards out between themselves and chat most of the morning. They would perhaps only visit one job site each before lunch. This process was then repeated with some minor variation in the afternoon! Naturally the full sample of job cards would be signed by the bonus checkers to indicate that they had been checked. Having checked a few job sites a small number of maintenance workers would be found to have cheated significantly and perhaps disciplined. The daily routine for the bonus checkers was varied over the course of the week by engaging in a wide variety of diversions as an alternative to work or by simply driving into the countryside if it was a nice day.

This routine was already established before I joined the section and it was this method of work that I was socialized into by my friend and other colleagues. The system of bonus checking was apparently being followed so management never checked to ensure that we were doing what was expected. Job cards were being signed as having been checked and a few people were caught cheating, so everyone was happy. At first I enjoyed this job, it was easy to learn and we were able to please ourselves most of the time. No one in management was bothered about what we did as, at least superficially, everything was as expected. However, I quickly became bored and so left after a month. The bonus checking section continued as described for about another two years and then it was restructured and changed as part of a reorganization. In the new structure it was not possible for the bonus checkers to continue in the way that they had done as their jobs were also changed.

Stop ↔ Consider

What does this example suggest to you about socialization and 'sitting-by-Nellie' as approaches to learning within organizations?

of the personality of the trainer on the evaluation of trainee performance. For example, extrovert trainers more positively evaluate extrovert trainees. Studies such as these demonstrate the complexity involved in the technical process of learning and also the variety of the interpersonal, process and situational forces acting upon learning as an activity.

Talent, skill and competency

Based on some 120 000 hours of taped interviews with managers collected over many years, Buckingham (1999) suggests that successful managers seek to build on the innate talents that individuals possess rather than simply seeking to develop skills or applying competency models. The author identifies a clear distinction between skills and knowledge (which can be taught) and talent which he describes as, 'the grooved highways of the mind' (which cannot be taught). **Competency** is frequently defined as the behavioural dimensions that lead to performance and in that way is strongly aligned with skill. Boyatsis (1982, p 21) defines a competency in terms of, 'an underlying characteristic of a person which results in effective and/or superior performance in a job'. This view of competency views it as something that delivers extra performance through the application of superior skill levels. The proponents of the competency concept would strongly argue for a distinction with skill, but it is still not clear how they differ. The most common explanation is that competency reflects a broader concept than skill. Certainly, based on the Boyatsis definition, it could be argued that personality and motivation level are aspects of competency.

Competency
The characteristics and capabilities of an individual which directly contribute to superior job performance.

Buckingham argues that managers should seek to capitalize on the innate talents of individual employees by, first, seeking to recruit people with high levels of talent; second, by recognizing that individual difference is important and that it is the end result that is of value, not the process or procedures used to achieve it; third, that people can and should be trained to acquire the skills and knowledge necessary for a particular job; fourth, that individuals should be encouraged to use their innate talents in finding their own path to the desired outcome. It is argued that so much of the training done in organizations is intended to create an environment in which cloning is the desired outcome, rather than improved performance *per se*. Individual difference and talent should be a cause for celebration, not restriction.

Action learning
Group problem solving using an iterative process of progressively understanding the situation and taking action on it.

Action learning

Action learning refers to a form of organizational and individual learning that is also cyclical and experiential in nature. Reavans progressively became disenchanted with management education and suggested that managers did not need education but the ability to be able to solve problems (1972). Action learning generally falls within the OD (**organizational development**) perspectives on organizational functioning and change. From that perspective action learning can be defined in terms of: 'a form of action research in which the focus is helping organizations to learn from their actions how to create entirely new structures, processes and behaviours' (Cummings and Worley, 1993, p 683). Action learning therefore reflects an approach which relies upon the abilities of individuals and the organization to learn how to deal with problems and situations through developing an understanding of them and then creating change. Change is then followed by reassessment and further adaptation as necessary based on the new learning achieved. It is in practice learning through action, a form of continuous development. In individual learning terms it is an approach very much dependent on the same experiential learning process described by Kolb. Action learning also has a very strong association with the concept of the learning organization (to be discussed later). There are different approaches to action research and the Greenwood and

Organizational development (OD)
The systematic application of behavioural science to developing organizational strategies, structures, and processes aimed at improving effectiveness.

Levin (1998) text indicated in the Further Reading section below provides an excellent review of these variations. For a brief but very readable introduction to action learning and its founder, Reg Revans, see Pedler *et al.* (2003). Management in Action 5.3 reflects how this approach is being used within one company to support its senior management development.

Culture

Culture
The acquired and conventionally accepted ways of thinking and behaving among a group or society.

The **culture** of an organization is also a significant determinant of its approach to learning. Some organizations consider that they gain a competitive advantage by engaging significantly in training and development. They perhaps feel that it makes the company seem more attractive to potential employees and therefore eases possible recruitment problems by encouraging high-quality applicants. Equally, individuals keen to learn are generally considered to be keen to apply what they have learned to the benefit of the employer and to be prepared to accept lower salary levels in return for development opportunities. In comparison, some companies regard such activities as an unnecessary expense, something which simply encourages employees to seek promotion and better paid positions elsewhere. It is sometimes suggested that training and development raises expectations among employees that cannot be met in practice. Culture is an imprecise concept, but there are distinct differences in how learning is viewed between organizations and individual managers which are frequently described as reflecting the culture of the organization.

Culture is also something that some would claim can be created or changed through learning activity. New employees will be socialized into the existing culture through the formal and informal induction and training processes they experience. A management decision to seek to change an existing culture will usually be accompanied by considerable quantities of training activity as the new behaviours, values, etc. are explained and taught to employees. Brown (1995) provides a review of a number of the learning-based aspects associated with culture change which demonstrates this breadth of association between culture and learning. Culture is the subject of a full chapter later in the text.

THE LEARNING ORGANIZATION

Learning organization
The facilitation of learning for all employees and the constant adaptation of the organization to new knowledge and capability.

Pedler *et al.* (1989) identify the notion of a **learning organization**. They describe it in terms of the facilitation of learning for all employees and the constant transformation of the organization in response to that new knowledge and ability. In essence, the discussion of learning so far in this chapter has taken the perspective that it is something that people as individuals become involved with. The concept of the learning organization suggests that organizations can also adapt to new circumstances, therefore they can undertake a learning process similar to people. The concept of human learning in an organizational context implies that people should adapt (learn appropriate skills) as determined by managers on behalf of the organization. The learning organization concept suggests that organizations should also adapt to accommodate the humans within it. Mumford (1989) suggests that the main characteristics of a learning organization include:

- Encouragement for managers to accept responsibility for the identification of their own training needs.
- Encouragement for managers to set challenging learning goals for themselves.

MANAGEMENT IN ACTION 5.3 Action learning in action

Westbury, a building firm was growing through acquisition according to Cathy Hipkiss the HR director of the company, and consequently introduced a development programme for senior managers who had the potential to make it to the very top. The strategy being to grow existing people so that they could take on more senior positions as the company grew.

The development programme consists of two parts and lasts about one year. The first being a two-day development centre in order to evaluate managers' skills against the competencies required of senior executives within the company. The second part of the programme begins several months after the development centre and is split into two stages. The first being a two-day workshop run by Richard Hale, a writer and consultant in the area of influence and impact in management activity. The second stage takes place about three months after the Hale workshop and is a skills review process intended to identify what participants got out of the programme.

It is during the impact and influence workshops run by Hale that action learning has been included. The initial plan was to base the workshop on conventional classroom and workshop types of activity. However after a few workshops had been delivered it was felt that they had not achieved the objectives intended. Ashley Hawkins was appointed as training manager of the company and looked afresh at the entire programme and the workshop in particular. It was apparent from the feedback that participants were leaving the programme with a clear idea of the learning points, but no real ideas on how to convert that into practice in the work situation. Hawkins indicated that they also wanted participants to share their learning more.

The result was a change in the focus of the workshop and it is now learning-focused rather than trainer-focused. Hale describes it as moving from role-play to real-play. Individuals come to the workshop clear about their development needs from the initial development centre and they are expected to bring with them real business issues that they need to address. The workshop provides the arena within which participants can explore issues such as how to influence people in that 'problem context', how to deal with conflict, confrontation, managing teams, managing upwards, etc. The other challenge included in the workshop is that Hale requires participants to deliver a tenfold return to the company on the investment in the training for the individual.

For example, Rafiq Tailor, the North-West Technical Director was faced with a particularly difficult dispute with local residents over access to one construction site. Previously he would have viewed these as a matter for the planning authorities and perhaps resorted to legal action if it became necessary. However, he sought to look at the situation from the resident's point of view and made himself available to interact with them over their concerns. The result was the purchase by the company of a strip of land from a local farmer in order to access the site, agreement over access and impact of traffic around the site and the promise to landscape a particular tree valued by the community. Problems did not disappear and people still complain to the council, but the level of problem was significantly lower than might have been expected. Tailor believes that he saved the company £1 million plus as a result of his changes to how the situation was handled. He also believes that the development process improved overall job experience as people were encouraged to share problems and not keep them to themselves.

The adoption of an action learning approach to this development has lead the training team within the company to plan similar programmes for middle managers, graduate trainees and the executive board. It is not however a panacea for all training and development needs. People cannot be forced to learn and must be prepared to accept that they need to invest in their own development if they want to make it to the next level within the company. The company is prepared to invest in its people, but wants a return on that investment. It also requires changes among the training team. They are no longer the experts delivering training, but the facilitator of people's self-development and learning.

Adapted from: Carrington, L (2002) House proud, *People Management*, 5 December, pp 36–8.

Stop ↔ Consider

The process requires participants to return tenfold the cost of their development. Is this realistic and sustainable? What impact might this requirement have on the development of individuals? Does this matter?

- The provision for all employees of regular performance reviews and feedback on learning achieved.
- Encouragement for managers to identify learning opportunities in jobs and to provide new experiences from which employees and managers can learn.
- Encouragement of a questioning attitude to the accepted ways of doing things within the organization.
- The acceptance that, when learning, some mistakes are inevitable, but that individuals should learn from them.
- Encouragement of on-the-job training and other learning activities.

The notion of the learning organization with its constant renewal and adaptation to employees as they continually develop themselves is of fundamental importance in creating a modern, flexible and adaptable organization. It reflects an approach that allows the organization more effectively to meet the needs of all the **stakeholder** groups associated with it and is important in the strategic human resource management perspective adopted by many organizations today (Mabey and Salaman, 1995). A major theme within the learning organization is the notion of single, double and triple loop learning, to which we now turn.

Stakeholder
An individual or group with some form of association or an interest in the organization.

Single, double and triple loop learning

As early as 1973, Bateson was describing different types of learning and demonstrated that not all learning could be considered to be at the same 'level'. He described several levels of learning from the simple receipt or detection of facts at level zero, through reflex learning at level one, skill learning at level two and learning to learn at level four etc.

It was Argyris and Schon (1974) who first linked the notion of Bateson's levels of learning with the cyclical model of learning as expressed by Kolb above and created the single and double loop learning model. The first loop reflects the learning involved in the acquisition of skill, in effect trial and error problem solving involving learning how to make choices from a limited range of options. The second level reflects the decision process in identifying what should be learned during the level one stage of the process. This was further developed by Garratt (1987) into what Hawkins (1994) describes as an 'egg-timer' model of double loop learning (Figure 5.12).

It is clear from Figure 5.12 that the first loop of the model reflects the acquisition of learning at the efficiency end of the spectrum, through skill enhancement and the ability to do things better than previously, even if the plans to so do never quite work out – reflected in the break in the cycle. However, the second loop is perhaps the most important as it deals with effectiveness rather than simply efficiency. It reflects a move towards the need for a strategic dimension in learning in terms of what is done within the organization and the needs of a dynamic environment. This approach to the learning organization seeks to capture the need for an organization to be able to effectively link both operational and strategic aspects of its activities through an integrated learning process. It is of little benefit for an organization to seek to improve efficiency in order to meet current customer need, if that need is changing. Equally, it is of no value to understand the dynamic changes in the environment through strategy processes, if they are not converted into actions at an operational level. Both are needed.

Senge (1990) in a book titled *The Fifth Discipline*, seeks to bring together a number of themes, including the idea of double loop learning as a way of creating the learning organization. He identified five disciplines that he describes as slowly merging to create an integrated approach to how organizations could learn successfully. They are:

FIGURE 5.12

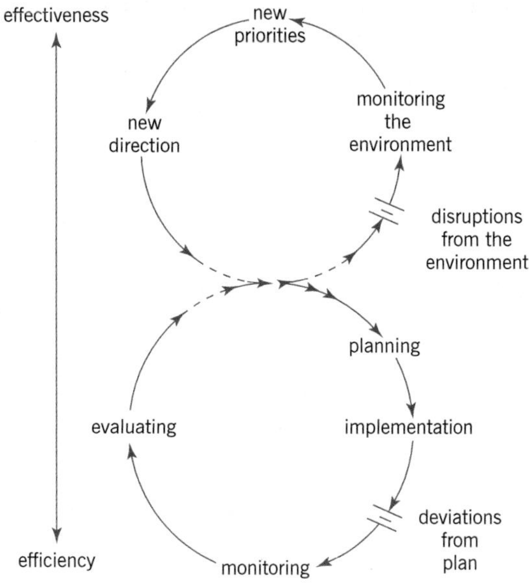

The 'egg-timer' view of double-loop learning. (*source*: Hawkins, P (1994) The Changing view of learning, in Burgoyne, J, Pedlar, M and Boydell, T. eds, *Towards the Learning Company: Concepts and Practices,* McGraw-Hill, Maidenhead. The material is reproduced with the kind permission of the Open University Press/McGraw-Hill Publishing Company

1. *Systems thinking*. The systems perspective on organizations was introduced in Chapter 2 and reflects the fact that many things associated with organizational activity are related in some way or another.
2. *Personal mastery*. Senge regards this as a process of continually clarifying and deepening personal vision and understanding of the world in which we live. Senge describes this as the spiritual foundation of the organization.
3. *Mental models*. These reflect the assumptions or generalizations that we hold about people, the world and how they both function. This reflects the perceptual frameworks and attitudes discussed in Chapter 3.
4. *Building shared vision*. This reflects a common view of the organization and what it stands for. It reflects the ability of some leaders to inspire a common view of the future among all members of the organization. It should not be confused with a vision statement, common in most organizations but which simply reflects management's 'wish-list' of what everyone else is supposed to believe, agree with or support.
5. *Team learning*. In simple terms Senge seeks to describe a situation in which the collective capability of the team is greater than the capability of individual team members.

Flood and Romm (1996) take the idea of double loop learning one stage further and introduce a third loop into the process. In their view, loop one of the model is about the 'how' of organizational activity. They say organizations learn how to arrange their activities in response to the situations that they face. The second loop they describe as the 'what' aspect of organizational functioning. This reflects the need for an organization to understand its environment and identify what should be done. The third loop that they introduce reflects what they see as the missing aspect of most organizational functioning, the 'why' question. They seek to address the fundamental question of the dilemma between might and right in organizational activity. In the context of organizational design, they seek to incorporate issues of power in deciding the management agenda, defining what is 'right or wrong' and defining the reality within which others must function. In the second learning loop as described earlier in this section, the emphasis is about strategy, considering what should be done. But there are many possible interpretations of most situations, that is part of the mental models point made by Senge, and so a common understanding needs to be reached (shared vision in the Senge model). Flood and Romm seek to incorporate the decisions about the underlying reality upon which everything else depends as a distinct stage into the learning process within any organization.

KNOWLEDGE MANAGEMENT

That knowledge is power has long been understood. Knowledge, although invisible, is a commodity, just like any other. It can be stored, sold, bought, traded and stolen. It can also be grown, developed and harvested just like any crop. Organizations contain much information within them and in addition have access to a vast range of information from outside sources. With the development over recent years of computer-based technology, such as database systems and the internet, the opportunity to capitalize on the information available has never been greater. Organizations and the individuals within them now have to learn much more than was the case just a few years ago and also they have to learn how to make effective use of the knowledge that they have actual or potential access to. In short, knowledge is now a significant part of the strategic and competitive activities of every organization.

Knowledge management
The management of all knowledge available to the organization for the benefit of the organization and the individuals within it.

There is another dimension to the concept of **knowledge management**. That is the growing realization that management objectives can be more easily achieved if managers seek to ensure that employees are trained to absorb management's values and norms in addition to technical and job skills. This often finds expression through training and development being driven by business objectives rather than just technical need and delivered through management controlled provision. For example the creation of so-called company universities within Motorola and Unipart (Pickard, 1995), Microsoft, Disney and McDonald's to name just a few, all deliver high-quality learning opportunities but as part of the organization's strategic intentions to enhance its own performance. In other words, the development process being firmly dictated by management and intended to support their objectives. This is the essence of the third loop in the Flood and Romm model of triple loop learning described earlier.

There are different forms of knowledge that exist within a company. For some organizations knowledge represents the purpose of existence as they specialize in selling knowledge to others. There is also the practical knowledge that exists in relation to the products and services provided by the company, there is the business-related knowledge relevant to the industry and how to function within it. There is also the wider knowledge in relation to what might be called market intelligence or understanding what is going on in the world that might be relevant to the organization. In addition, there is the accumulated knowledge and experience of the people who work within the organization in how to make it all work relatively smoothly. This last category of knowledge is rarely, if ever, documented in any form and is dependent on the accumulated experience of the people working in the organization. Nonaka (1996) called this aspect 'tacit knowledge' and suggested that it is just as important to organizational success as the formally classified and captured forms of knowledge, a point reinforced by Baumard (1999).

With the practice of delayering, downsizing or rightsizing, which has become the way of life for many organizations, many of the middle ranks in organizations have been eliminated. Among the effects of that is the loss of much of the stored, unrecorded (tacit) knowledge of the company. Another way of describing this is a loss of organizational memory. The practice of delayering in its many forms means that management must ensure that employee groups are supportive of the business objectives, as without the previous levels of operational management employees have much greater freedom of action and delegated authority. Consequently, if they are not effectively integrated into the business, or feel alienated, there exists a real danger of significant problems or even organizational failure in extreme cases.

Information flows around an organization in ways that are not reflected in any organization chart or other formal document or policy. There are obviously the predictable information paths that are determined by policy and business practice. For example, financial data are collected and disseminated according to set rules and reporting requirements. Customer orders are processed in a way that ensures that orders and invoices are paid as appropriate. However, these forms represent only a small proportion of the total information circulating within a company at any point in time. There will be information about planned orders, proposed new products that some but not everyone, in the organization will be aware of. In addition there will be information about job vacancies, forthcoming training courses and problems that are in the process of being resolved between departments or sections. On top of all of that information there will be the inevitable gossip, rumour, idle chit-chat and thousands of other pieces of relevant and indeed irrelevant information (and misinformation) that circulate in every workplace. In every sense of the phrase, information spreads around the organization as its very lifeblood, carrying with it all manner of necessary items of value (and occasionally malevolent, evil rubbish that can do harm) to every corner. Employee Perspective 5.4 shows just how much informal and negative information circulates around an organization and how damaging it can be to all concerned.

With knowledge carrying with it such a diverse range of meanings and implications for organizations, it is hardly surprising that management seek to control it, and easy to understand why it is so difficult an area to control. It is for that reason that Nonaka (1996) argues that those organizations that will be commercially successful in the future are those that have effectively managed both explicit and tacit aspects of their knowledge. It is also easy to understand under these circumstances why learning as a process becomes vital to encourage commitment, acceptance and internalization of management's objectives among employees. The rationale for company universities and other initiatives in creating a basis for knowledge management becomes obvious as management seeks to embrace the workforce and channel its activities and define its reality in predetermined and acceptable ways. Of course this raises the issue of the extent to which management can determine what defines acceptable and the degree to which it is ethically right to do so.

According to Lloyd (1999) knowledge management strategies need to be grounded in the concept of wisdom. In that context, he defines wisdom as knowledge with a long shelf-life, whereas data are information with a very short shelf-life. In that sense, wisdom in how to manage the control aspects of knowledge forms an important dimension to the development of any effective strategy. This also supports the view that experience and age are of value to an organization, always assuming that wisdom develops with experience etc. Rightsizing, delayering and other cost-cutting processes that remove experience can be a danger to the organization if wisdom is also eliminated. This is not dissimilar to the notion of organizational memory discussed above. Wisdom is also discussed in Chapter 4 in relation to intelligence.

Knowledge management is not just restricted to internal company activities. These days there is a distinct tendency for organizations to form strategic alliances with a

EMPLOYEE PERSPECTIVE 5.4 Mary's indiscretion

Mary, a team leader in the sales department of a particular company was having an affair with someone outside of work. One of her subordinates who was jealous of her and wanted her job wrote several anonymous letters to her husband over about three months. They were on company letter-headed paper and told him about the affair in great detail. When the first letter arrived the husband was furious and after a huge argument at home arrived at work to see Mary's boss. A meeting was called with several senior managers within the company and an internal investigation was held to see if the culprit could be found. Nothing could be proved, but after several more letters the husband was hopping mad and appeared again at the company offices demanding to see the chief executive and shouting at the top of his voice that he would kill whoever was responsible. Naturally his wife continued to deny that the affair was taking place.

The police were called in to investigate and when an unopened letter was received by the husband it was sent for forensic examination, again with no result. People within the company had no sympathy for Mary because she was cheating on her husband, but they also hated the writer (without knowing who was doing it) because everyone was under suspicion and they were being interviewed by both company managers and the police. Mary's husband was regarded as a pathetic figure because he would not accept that his wife was having an affair and kept making a fool of himself at the company (as everyone else became aware of the affair). Mary also tried to keep a low profile as she was highly embarrassed that her affair had become the subject of public gossip. It also became difficult for her to do her normal job. As the investigation could not identify the culprit Mary was moved to another job within the company where she was isolated from other employees and told in no uncertain terms by her manager that she had caused all the problems herself and the company was angry at being put in that position. Shortly after being moved to another job Mary left the company. The letter writer was never found.

Tasks

1. What would you have done if you were Mary?
2. What would you have done if you were Mary's boss?
3. How can management deal (if at all) with personal information, rumour and gossip such as indicated in the above example?

wide variety of other organizations. This can take the form of supply chain management (Slack *et al.*, 1998) in which customers and suppliers form stronger and closer commercial arrangements, often linked together through mutual information systems. Supply chain management can also involve potential competitors working together on common projects to support a particular development, for example the development of industry standards. Each form of collaboration carries with it potential dangers for each partner if mutual respect is not part of the relationship. These points are further developed in relation to the contribution of people management to ensuring an effective network relationship through a study of knowledge-intensive firms by Swart and Kinnie (2003). Tranfield *et al.* (2003) describe knowledge management in relation to innovation projects as consisting of three phases: Discovery, Realization and Nurture. These they then develop into an innovation model consisting of eight stages: Search, Capture, Articulate, Contextualise, Apply, Evaluate, Support and Re-innovate. They discuss the application of this model to the process of managing the knowledge aspects of innovation both within and between organizations.

Mintzberg *et al.* (1998, p 357) describe future successful organizations as amoebas. Such simple creatures are among the most successful on earth as they constantly change shape and adapt to their environment. Their semi-permeable cell walls define them in terms of separation from the environment around them and yet they also allow the relative free movement of 'things' into and out of the amoeba. Using that as an analogy for organizations, it is clear that the free flow of information, skill and capability, etc. forms part of the future as envisaged by Mintzberg and his colleagues, processes that will require ever more effective knowledge management strategies. Schramm (2002) questions the degree to which managers and employees are ready for the challenges of learning in a true knowledge economy. Johnson (2002) offers a more optimistic view in a reported interview with Professor Greenfield from Oxford university, in which she predicts that future changes to the use of technology will influence the way that we use information and think, which will in turn influence the way in which we learn.

LEARNING WITHIN ORGANIZATIONS

Learning through training

Much of the learning within an organization is carried out under the guise of training. Training courses are organized for employees on many topics, usually intended to deliver some benefit to the organization in the form of a capability to undertake a range of tasks more efficiently or productively. Most of this training is based around the notion of the learning curve. It reflects the idea that performance is a function of time and experience, in other words, practice makes perfect. The curve in Figure 5.13 is a very simplified one and should be considered as an ideal type.

In practice, the effectiveness of the training will influence the rate of increase in performance, as will the ability of the trainees along with the impact of situational and emotional factors. Some skills require substantial periods of reinforcement or practice before any increase in performance can be made. In other cases, performance improvement is categorized by a series of jumps and plateaux.

The training process in learning

There are many forms of training used within organizations. They are usually used on the basis of meeting an identified need. Training needs can be identified from a number of sources. For example, a performance appraisal, the existence of low productivity or quality, the introduction of new products or technology, the carrying out of a formal skills audit. What these all have in common is a gap or difference between what is expected and what currently exists (Figure 5.14).

Once the gap has been identified, appropriate mechanisms can be designed to meet the need. Training programmes designed to meet a specific need should be planned around the following issues:

FIGURE 5.13

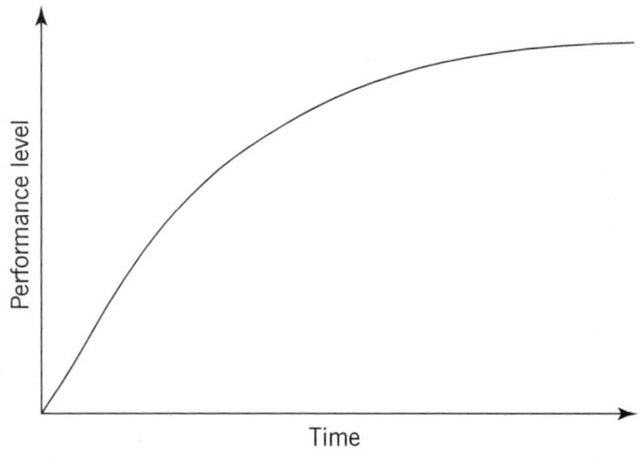

The learning curve

FIGURE 5.14

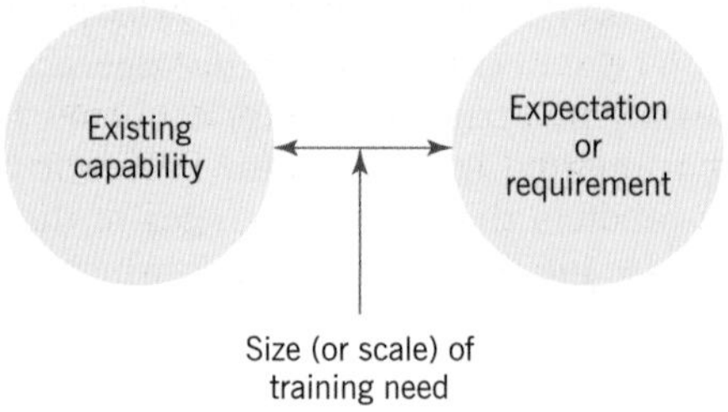

The training need

- *Training objectives*. The objectives should provide a target for measuring performance (or the level of success in training). An example might be: 'On completion of the course the trainee will be able to type at 75 words per minute, with no more than 1 per cent error rate'.
- *Training content*. The content should have been determined by the previous analysis and be a means to close the identified gap.
- *Duration*. The length of the training programme should be determined by the range of material to be covered and the amount of practice required to achieve the effective closure of the identified training gap.

Learning event design

The means through which to deliver an effective learning event will be dependent on a wide range of issues including the preferred style of the trainees, the task to be learned, etc. The options available for the design of training programmes include:

- *Demonstration*. Being shown how to do something and then allowed to get on with it.
- *Coaching*. Provides an interactive, encouragement-based approach to training, includes practice, feedback, reflection, structure and motivational perspectives.
- *Discovery training*. This assumes that people learn more effectively if they discover the answer for themselves through an experiential environment.
- *Job rotation, secondments and special assignments*. Provide for training by systematically moving people between jobs, activities or projects in order to give them experience.
- *Action learning*. Typically a team would be established and expected to solve a specific problem perhaps with the help of an external facilitator.
- *Job instruction*. The systematic application of learning theory to skill acquisition, perhaps using the Kolb model discussed earlier.
- *Lecture*. Process of delivering information with little or no direct involvement from the audience.
- *Talks and discussion*. Informal lectures with higher participation levels based on small groups.
- *Case studies*. Use of predetermined situations to provide opportunities for analysis and presentation of solutions without the risk of failure inherent in 'live' situations.
- *Role play and simulation*. Allow the participants to act out situations as if they were real. Pilots spend a considerable amount of time in flight simulators in order to gain flying experience in a safe environment.

- *Distance learning*. This embraces a wide range of programmes from basic skills acquisition to higher degrees. The process of distance learning includes a variety of instructional approaches, the written word, television, video, audio, electronic, and residential periods offering face-to-face contact.
- *e-learning*. This is short for electronic learning. The process of e-learning involves the use of communications technology as a way of delivering training to people in the workplace and can use telecoms, computer, video and programmed approaches. Some organizations are even delivering some training through mobile phones in order to utilize readily available equipment and remove the need to organize costly off-the-job programmes. As a relatively new field it is still emerging and there are no clear guidelines to follow. Schank (1999) proposes that before any form of what he terms online training can become truly effective a major rethink of teaching methods is needed. He claims that the individual must create a personal journey through the new knowledge and that the technology must be supportive of this process. Reynolds (2002) suggests that the best future for e-learning lies in the ability to provide enhanced learning through technology, not just delivery through that medium. Tulip (2003) reviews the current marketplace for providers of e-learning technology and suggests that it is not yet possible to source all e-learning technology requirements from one vendor. Management in Action 5.4 reflects the use of e-learning within the meteorological services across Europe in response to developing satellite technology.

Training evaluation

Evaluating the benefits of any training is a difficult process. Ultimately, it is an attempt to measure the degree of the transfer of learning to the organizational context. However, there are many complications involved in judging the degree to which this might have happened. For example, trainees can enjoy the training event and therefore judge it to be a success, yet in practice they may gain little practical job-related benefit from it. Conversely, trainees may not enjoy the experience and yet subsequently find the job relevance high. There may be other change initiatives active at the same time as a learning event which restricts the ability to demonstrate that training was the only (or major) source of improvement. It might also take a considerable period of time for any tangible benefits from training to filter through to a measurable benefit. Manocha (2003) reporting from the 2003 Human Resource Development conference outlines the views of Ewart Keep who suggests that it is impossible to measure the effect of training on the bottom line and that the debate should be reversed into a discussion about the effects of not training.

However, training needs to be evaluated if it is to achieve its objectives and be regarded as a resource of value to the organization and employees. It could never be certain that learning as intended has taken place unless some form of evaluation occurs. According to Hamblin (1974) evaluation takes place at a number of levels:

- *Reaction*. This refers to the immediate responses of the trainees on issues such as the perceived benefits, feelings towards the experience and content. It is one form of judging success, on the assumption that if the people enjoyed the learning event (or otherwise feel it was 'good') they will perhaps gain from it. This reflects the so called 'happiness sheet' as it tends to measure the immediate feelings (degree of happiness) towards the process. Evans (2003) reports research carried out by Hatton that few organizations went beyond this stage in measuring the impact of learning events.
- *Learning*. This reflects the actual benefit taken away from the training event in the form of new skills etc. This is frequently reflected in the end of course test

MANAGEMENT IN ACTION 5.4 e-learning

The Meteorological Office is responsible for weather forecasting for military, government, commercial and domestic use across the UK. It is of vital importance to shipping, aircraft, farming, insurance and leisure activities. The same is true for every other country in the world, but with different degrees of emphasis on aspects of weather patterns and activity. For example, much of the UK weather arrives from the Atlantic and is of considerable importance to life here. Germany on the other hand has less need for this information as the Atlantic has less influence on its weather.

The use of satellite technology to observe weather patterns is increasing rapidly and a recent launch of the Meteosat Second Generation (MSG) in the summer of 2002 has lead to the need for new training programmes for up to 5000 meteorologists across Europe. New satellite technology provides access to more and different information. The danger is that forecasters are not able to make effective use of the potential from the new satellite if they are not trained quickly on its data output and how to interpret it. Given the number of people across Europe that need to be trained in the interpretation of MSGs output, the body responsible for operation and exploitation of meteorological satellites, Eumetsat, organized computer based training. The first generation of computer training was developed by a consortium from the UK, French and Dutch meteorological offices, along with the universities of Edinburgh, Berlin and Quebec. Two of the principal project managers subsequently left their organizations and established the e-learning company Intrallect and created a second generation e-learning package.

This new package will allow each country to input its own MSG training information and images onto a standard web page design. So far the company has produced three 45-minute modules that can deliver training via the web. It is also available on CD-Rom for use in remote locations such as parts of Africa where internet access is poor, and also for stand alone PCs to demonstrate the potential of the satellite information. The number of packages is expected to increase as each country introduces its own version and language differences.

The packages allow the learner to work at their own pace and in their own location and at a time of their choosing. This is important given the shift patterns that most forecasters have and the often remote work-locations involved. All members of Eumetsat will have access to the database of material held on the central web server based in Toulouse in France. According to Ian Mills and Julie Turner from the UK meteorological college it will allow the increased use of graphics and interactive material allowing individuals to gain experience of working with the potential from the new satellite technology. Included are multiple choice questions with drag and drop answers, together with animations of satellite imagery and radar pictures to make the learning process more realistic.

Adapted from: Allen, A and Pickard, J (2002) A brighter outlook, *People Management*, 26 December, pp 38–9.

Stop ↔ Consider

To what extent can such approaches deal effectively with the lack of human interaction in the learning process?

and is intended to reflect the exit capability of the people who have been trained. This does not guarantee, however, that they will actually utilize the new skills in the workplace.

- *Job behaviour.* In an organizational context, learning is usually designed to impact on the job that the individual is expected to perform. So seeking to determine if the actual job behaviour of individuals' changes subsequent to the learning event is one way of attempting to judge both the transfer of knowledge to the workplace and the impact of such changes. This can be done through observation of trainees or by interview of trainees and their managers some time after the event.
- *Organization.* At the organizational level training is intended to improve effectiveness in terms of issues such as productivity, quality, output and

customer relations. It might be possible to quantify aspects of this level of evaluation, but it will probably include a significant degree of qualitative evaluation or judgement.

- *Ultimate value.* This refers to the intangible benefits that the organization gains from any training activity. This could be its ability to survive in a hostile market, profitability or even its contribution to society as a whole.

Three features are apparent from a consideration of these evaluation levels:

1. *Measurement.* This becomes increasingly less certain as one moves from the immediate reaction to the ultimate value level. It is relatively easy to assess individual reactions to a particular learning event. It is, however, more difficult to quantify the extent to which a particular learning event impacts on the whole organization.
2. *Time.* This is another variable in the list. Reactions from trainees tend to be determined immediately after the event. Assessment of the impact on the organization as a whole can only be determined after some considerable time has elapsed. By the time organizational value can be determined; other variables will have invariably contaminated any cause and effect links that might have existed.
3. *Hindsight.* The initial assessment of trainee reactions to a particular learning event is useful. But would the reaction be the same six months later when a broader perspective has evolved, perhaps involving an extended opportunity to apply the learning acquired.

The evaluation of training is not a precise science and this results in difficulties for both managers and trainers in identifying the justification for such interventions.

Development

Development can be applied to any category of employee and the term employee development is increasingly finding favour over that of training. It is a process that allows potential to be realized. As such, it places a higher level of responsibility on the individual. The individual must want to be developed and must be prepared to co-operate in development activities. Because of the longer timeframes implicit in development the return is not likely to become apparent for many years. Organizations are increasingly making use of the concept of development centres, which broadly consist of the same type of activity as an assessment centre (Rodger and Mabey, 1987), the emphasis being to identify strengths and weaknesses as the basis of individual and organizational development activity. Development centres were also referred to in Management in Action 5.3.

LEARNING: A MANAGEMENT AND ORGANIZATIONAL PERSPECTIVE

Learning is an important part of organizational activity. It impacts on all aspects of the employment of people, from the induction of new employees to the development of future generations of directors. Unless individuals are exposed to learning opportunities they cannot be expected to undertake the duties that are expected of them, even if they know what they are. The workforce is traditionally male dominated at a senior level and there have been a number of learning initiatives to enhance the development of women and thereby improve their access to these positions. Management in Action 5.5 introduces the debate about the value of separate training for women in this context.

MANAGEMENT IN ACTION 5.5 Trial separation

Given that the workforce in most organizations is male dominated it has been argued by many that special training courses for women provide the kick-start necessary to both meet their needs and boost confidence. However, it has also been argued that women-only training can be counterproductive in advancing their position in the workplace.

Opportunity 2000, an employer-led campaign to boost the status of women, has prompted many large employers to establish action plans to achieve this objective. Companies such as Barclays and Midland banks, the BBC, Lucas and BP have incorporated women-only training into their equal opportunity programmes. Others such as United Biscuits, British Airways and Rank Xerox have not given this type of approach such a high priority within their equal opportunity development. Among those organizations that provide women-only training it is claimed that such courses provide benefits both to the individual and the organization. For example, Ashridge Management College has for many years provided a one-week intensive programme called Business Leadership for Women. From a survey of former students approximately half had subsequently been promoted and more than 90 per cent thought such training was essential. It is not just the career and professional categories of women that have benefited from the provision of such training. Springboard, as a training organization, has developed courses for women at the lower levels of the organization. It reports that individuals perform better after attending their programme and that they frequently take on more responsibility, even if they do not seek promotion.

Among those organizations that have not specifically provided single-sex courses it is suggested that women themselves do not want to be segregated. For example, United Biscuits conducted a survey in one of its divisions that produced a 70 per cent response rate. One of the findings was that if women wanted training it was of a more general nature, not specialized single-sex courses. However, a similar survey within another division found that women did want specialized courses. This suggests that people and circumstances vary and perhaps change over time. As a special needs category it is not appropriate to assume that women will automatically want such provision. Other companies have found that attempting to tackle issues such as organization culture and individual training-need determination for both men and women is a more effective route to influence the role and position of women in the workplace. As the campaign director for Opportunity 2000 said when interviewed, the best time to provide women-only training is when women themselves want it.

Adapted from: Tchiprout, G (1993) Trial separation, *Personnel Today*, 9 February, pp 32–3.

Stop ↔ Consider

Is the provision of women-only training a good thing? Why or why not?

Individuals *per se* are not totally responsible for achieving organizational goals. It is the various groups and teams within the organization that achieve objectives. Therefore, it is a necessary part of organizational life to be able to work as part of a team. Within organizations trainers spend a considerable amount of time on team-building exercises and courses to enhance employee and management ability in this area. Training in group formation and dynamics can provide a basis for shaping the behaviour of groups and so influence the level of effectiveness achieved.

Training and development are usually regarded as internal activities. However, most organizations need to influence the external environment as well. Customers need to be persuaded to buy products and services from the organization. Suppliers need to be persuaded that the organization is a good credit risk. Government needs to be persuaded to follow one set of policies rather than another. The influencing process used to achieve these objectives reflects a form of training. One party seeks to ensure that another party learns certain 'facts' or a particular point of view. Much of the purchasing, marketing, public relations and lobbying activity engaged in by organizations utilize approaches that benefit from material discussed in this chapter.

The challenge facing managers and organizations is how to make cost-effective use of learning within the organization. There are limitless opportunities for the utilization of the principles of learning in the training and development activities carried out in most organizations. If the degree of benefit achieved were the only criterion for success involved, then there would be no decision to take. It is easy to envisage that more training and development activity would solve all management's problems and produce an optimally effective organization. As with many organizational activities, that is too simplistic to be credible. Unfortunately, there is always a cost associated with the provision of learning activity and the benefits are not always easy to identify or quick to materialize. It is necessary therefore to find the appropriate level of activity commensurate with organizational requirements in the short, medium and long term. Consequently, managers are required to exercise judgement in determining the best area for the application of learning, just as with any other resource. One recent study found that managers perceived a clear distinction to exist between their roles as manager and facilitator of learning (Ellinger and Bostrom, 2002) thereby further complicating the relationship between managers and learning within their areas of responsibility, as much of the current literature suggests that coaching represents a sub-set of management.

Organizations are subjected to change in many forms. People join and leave an organization for many reasons. The nature of activity within the organization is subject to change as technology impacts different aspects of operations and new products or services are developed. Consequently, there is a permanent background of training activity to ensure present and anticipated requirements are met. There is also the natural career progression of individuals and appropriate planning is necessary to meet the needs of senior specialists and managers. The failure of many organizations to meet these basic requirements has been a source of criticism in many reports and investigations into the subject. The following Employee Perspective (5.5) seeks to explore the relationship between the actions of an employee outside of work with events at work together with the possible role of training in dealing with potential problems.

EMPLOYEE PERSPECTIVE 5.5 John's fighting and imprisonment

John was a young man in his early 20s, with no family commitments and was a senior industrial engineer within the Polish factory of a large multi-national manufacturing company. He enjoyed an active social life and frequently went out drinking with his friends. He had a reputation for becoming very gregarious when he had been drinking and had been known to get into fights on occasion. The latest of these incidents had involved him getting into a fight with several other men, one of whom had been stabbed so seriously that his life had been in danger for a few days. Although there was no suggestion that John had been involved in the stabbing itself, he was heavily involved in the fracas and had significant cuts and bruises to show for it. The police had been called to the fight and all of the combatants had been arrested after some difficulty. John along with several others was charged with grievous bodily harm and assault on a police officer and bailed to appear in court several weeks later. At the trial he was found guilty on both counts and sentenced to six months imprisonment, partly because he had several previous convictions for minor assault in the past. No mention of John's employer was made in court or the press reports about the fight or the court case.

Tasks

1. If you were John would you expect your employer to keep your job open for you? Why or why not?
2. If you were John's manager, how would you react to this situation? Would you dismiss him or hold his job open for him when he is released from prison? If you hold his job open for him what training provision (or other actions) might you provide to try and ensure that John did not repeat his drunken behaviour again?

Human beings are naturally adaptive and creative in the ways that they approach events around them. Consequently, if no training or development were to take place in the formal sense of the term, individuals would simply 'muddle through'. This is frequently relied upon in times of financial hardship, when organizations cut back on training and development in order to save money in the short term. People are the most flexible, adaptable resource available to an organization and can cope in the short term without clear direction, unlike machines or computers.

Learning is also a process that is part of the management control process within an organization. For example, it is the training provided by management that signals to employees the behaviour considered appropriate within the organization. Employees are socialized into the company and jobs that they undertake. In that sense, management is shaping the behaviour of employees just like Skinner shaped the responses of his laboratory animals. Another dimension of the control aspect associated with learning is control through access. Only those employees who are regarded as a worthy investment will have access to the many development opportunities available through their companies. Consequently, a clear reward for being classified as a good employee is the opportunity to experience development. This also encourages employees to deliver compliant behaviour and acceptable performance to management in return for an appropriate classification and progression through development. Too often the benefits derived from learning activity are undervalued by managers, particularly the potential to socialize employees into management preferred behaviours. However, as with all human behaviour the links between learning and control are not as certain as might be implied from the discussion so far. Individuals do have the freedom of choice to ignore the intentions of managers and indeed to react against these wishes if they so desire. An individual may not value development or may not wish to adopt particular behaviour patterns in response for the returns potentially available.

For the training specialist in the real world of organizations, these are not just interesting issues for debate. Managers under pressure for cost-effective output in the short term and being asked to divert employee time to training activities need to be convinced of the value. Organizations also need to be convinced of the value of the activity, particularly in times of economic stringency. Yet, as has already been suggested, there is no single theory or approach to learning that will guarantee commercial success. Equally, the determination and evaluation of any benefits accruing from any learning event are difficult to ascertain and disentangle from other variables. Managers and trainers must therefore work things out between themselves, taking into account the variables active in the particular situation.

Within organizations learning has many applications. They include:

- *Induction of new employees.* The purpose here is to enable new employees to become effectively integrated into the organization in the shortest possible time.
- *Initial job training.* Not all new employees will possess the necessary skills to perform the tasks expected of them.
- *Subsequent job training.* Over the course of employment the jobs that individuals perform will change. New equipment, new products, etc. all produce a need to acquire new skills.
- *Training on transfer or promotion.* When moving to another job within the same organization different skills will be required. This is particularly true in the case of a first appointment to supervisory or management positions.
- *Training for special groups.* There are a variety of special groups for whom particular training provision needs to be made. They include disabled people, women returning to work following a career break, individuals from ethnic minority groups, employee representatives and employees with responsibility for dealing with customers.

- *Development*. It can be argued that as a distinct activity development has little relevance for most employees, as their responsibilities are tied to the present time. Management has the responsibility for the future and so requires development. Conversely, it can be argued that the commitment of employees is enhanced through development opportunity and that they are therefore more likely to adopt a positive attitude towards work, to the benefit of the individual, management and the organization.
- *Professional development*. Many employees undertake work in which job training is related to professional development. For example, accountants are trained by following a course of study leading to membership of one of the accounting bodies.
- *Specialist career development*. Within many of the specialist areas of an organization there are occupational hierarchies. Examples are common among engineers, computer specialists and accountants. Progression within these jobs often depends on technical competence rather than managerial responsibility. Their regular updating development can be of critical importance to the long term success of the organizations.
- *Managers' career development*. Managers need to be developed in terms of their own specialism, in order to ensure that they keep up to date. They also need some development in other management areas. The purpose being to develop individuals for more senior jobs as well as improved performance in their present job and integration among members of the management team.
- *Development for directors and senior managers*. The nature of senior management work is dramatically different from that of more junior managers. It is not unusual to find separate senior management programmes within large organizations, intended to meet these needs. Indeed, the Institute of Directors now runs a training programme so that new directors can learn about their specific responsibilities.
- *Job termination training*. Every person recruited leaves the organization at some point in time. It could be that they find alternative work; or that they retire; or that they die while in service; they may be dismissed by the company; or they may be made redundant if their job disappears. In some of these cases, the organization may consider providing counselling or training to help the individual adjust to their new circumstances.
- *Special initiative training and development*. Organizations frequently engage in a particular activity that generates a training or development need. Examples include the development of a new product, the need to improve productivity or quality and the introduction of new equipment.

The importance of learning gains increasing significance from the inclusion of a more obvious strategic perspective to the management of the human resource within organizations. Figure 5.15 illustrates the stakeholder approach to strategic training and development (Mabey and Salaman, 1995). It attempts to link together the main elements of the process while reflecting its fluid nature. This model also recognizes that business direction is determined through the stakeholder process and forms part of the generally negotiated balancing between agendas and priorities for the groups involved. It also has many features that would suggest an affinity with the concept of the learning organization. A slightly different approach to strategic learning is reflected in Thomas *et al.* (2001) which incorporates sense-making and knowledge management perspectives into the process.

FIGURE 5.15

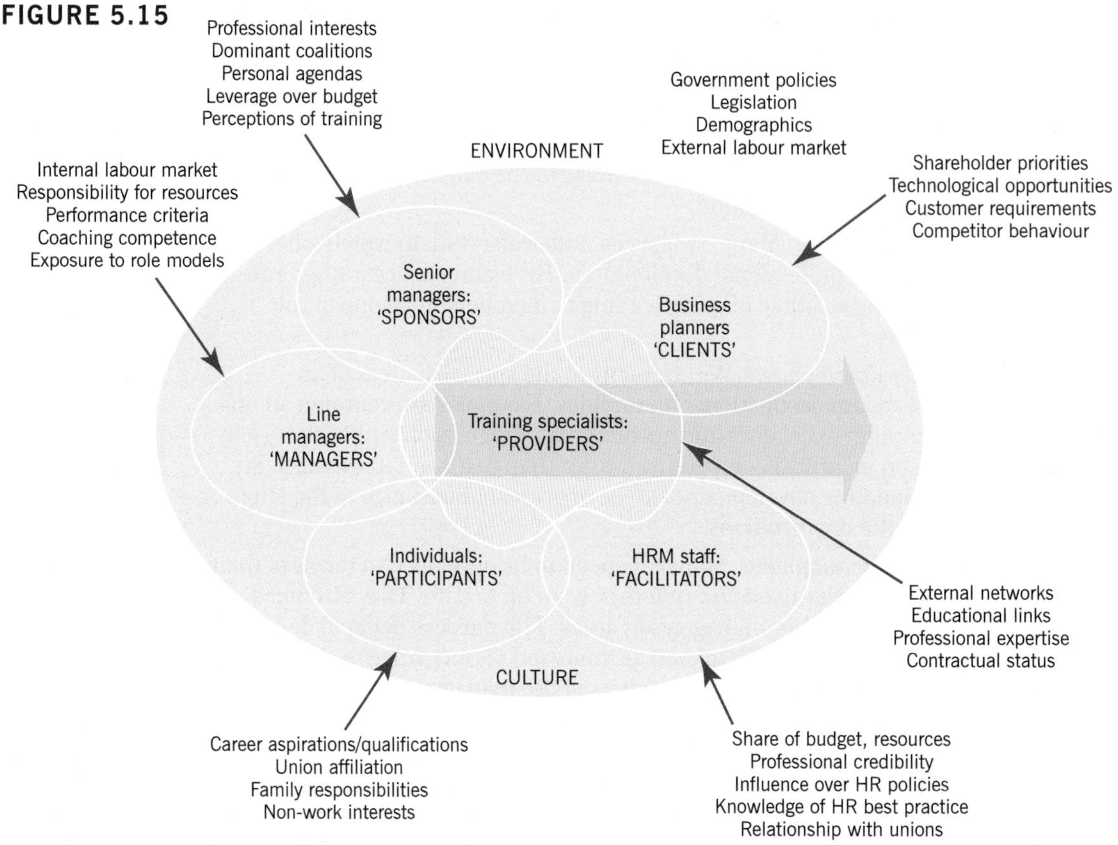

Strategic training and development: a stakeholder approach (*source*: Mabey, C and Salaman, G (1955) *Strategic Human Resource Management*, Blackwell, Oxford)

CONCLUSIONS

Learning is an activity that continues during the entire life of every individual. Human behaviour is also influenced in many ways by the experiences that are encountered in daily life. Psychologists have attempted to understand and explain the processes involved in this phenomenon and in doing so have developed a number of models associated with learning, training and development. Organizations need trained people in order to achieve objectives and they need to develop the talents of individuals in order to make provision for the future. The strategic human resource approach practised by many organizations today places a high priority on the development of employees in order to capture the benefits of the learning organization.

Now to summarize this chapter in terms of the relevant Learning Objectives:

- **Describe the major theoretical approaches to learning.** There are many different approaches to learning. There are the behaviourist theories which one way or another reflect learning through reinforcement schedules. There are the cognitive theories which reflect problem solving approaches to learning, using feedback. The social and experiential approaches to learning are based around the Kolb learning cycle, reflecting a process of stages in a never-ending process. This single loop model has been extended through the addition of the double loop approach to learning. Action learning reflects another variation to the cycle model of learning in which people learn by taking action and then reflecting upon the consequences of those actions, leading to a cycle of continuous learning and action. Issues of competency, talent, culture and socialization are also relevant to understanding how people learn.
- **Outline the concept of a learning organization.** The learning organization is one in which it is not only the individuals that learn but the organizations does as well. It is about the organization adapting in a flexible way to evolving circumstances in the ever changing world around it. It incorporates concepts of double loop learning and the use of continual questioning of the 'how', 'what' and 'why' of organizational activity.
- **Discuss the links between learning and the control of people within organizations.** The control of people can be achieved through the rules and procedures that exist within any organization. However, it can also be achieved if the employees adopt the same values and mindset as management. Employees would therefore internalize the control requirements established by management. Training can help to achieve this through the broader messages that can be contained in any training process. For example, induction training provision provides an opportunity for management to establish itself and its perspectives in the mind of the employee before the work group has the opportunity to do so. Another way in which control can be exercised is through the access to training and development activity made available to those candidates identified as having the capability to succeed at a higher level.
- **Detail the relevance of knowledge management for an organization.** Organizations contain considerable volume and types of knowledge within them. There is the technical knowledge in relation to the products or services. The professional knowledge needed to carry out the correct practice of running an organization – for example how to compile a set of accounts or comply with employment legislation. There is also the knowledge that every employee carries around with them and which is not formally available to the organization and yet is essential for it to run effectively – tacit knowledge. Knowledge flows around an organization in ways not recorded in an organization chart and can be traded, used or withheld just like any other commodity. It is the necessity for organizations to understand the knowledge that they use and in being able to ensure that it is used effectively that the significance arises, as it can easily be misused, or withheld.
- **Explain why the styles of learning are relevant to understanding how people learn.** The significance of the styles of learning reflects the underlying preferences of the individual for how they go about learning in their lives. It is apparent from the styles that individuals tend towards a particular preference, which might imply that the learning achieved is not fully learned, based upon the learning cycle model described by Kolb. Of course this reflects the application of single loop learning to the process and many would argue that for learning to be truly effective the second 'what' loop needs to be incorporated into the process as well.

DISCUSSION QUESTIONS

1. What are the styles of learning that are introduced in this chapter and how might they contribute to the effective design of learning events?
2. Kolb describes learning as a circular process (Figure 5.11). Identify an occasion when you learned something and explain the process using Kolb's model. What conclusions about learning can you draw from the process?
3. 'Each individual should accept responsibility for their own training and development. It is not up to organizations to provide more than essential job-related training.' Discuss.
4. 'Training and development are nothing more than elaborate mechanisms for ensuring worker compliance with management's wishes.' Discuss.
5. How can the effectiveness of any learning event provided by management be evaluated? Justify your answer.
6. How would you recommend to your lecturers that they keep attendance at lectures high and ensure that work is handed in on time? Justify your views based on material presented in this chapter.
7. Describe behavioural modification as an approach to conditioning human behaviour. To what extent does this model provide for a social engineering approach to management control that is doomed to fail because human beings are not animals?
8. What is the learning organization and how does double loop learning relate to it?
9. What is knowledge management and how does learning impact on it?
10. 'Technology can never replace the value of human interaction in training and development.' Discuss this statement and identify under what circumstances e-learning might have an advantage over other forms of training.

CASE STUDY Banking on money!

This case study describes the events as told to me by the former student himself. As far as is known, the activities described in this case would not work today as the banks have changed their procedures since the time that the events occurred, even if they worked then. The events are included here only as an example of learning in action.

Mary was an undergraduate student and in common with most students, always short of money. I interviewed her about six years after she had graduated as part of a research programme exploring how people learned to behave in a work context. During the interview Mary introduced the following story about how she and many other students managed their money whilst at university. Always short of money she said that several students told her abut how to get access to more money from bank accounts than they were strictly entitled to. She said that she used all of the following techniques during her time at university but she never knew if the bank was aware of her actions. She just assumed that they worked. It is possible of course that the bank was well aware of the actions described and prepared to condone them only as long as overdraft limits were not exceeded.

The first rule of managing a student current account was to fold each cheque in half, making sure that the centre crease was well emphasized and sharp. Mary suggested that it was 'common knowledge' among students such cheques took at least a day longer to clear the account, thereby delaying a debit on the current account a while longer.

The second rule of managing a student current account involved having at least two cheque books for the same current account. A cheque could be cashed from the first cheque book in the morning with the relevant hole being punched in the check page at the back of the book. This could be repeated with the second cheque book in the afternoon (and with a different cashier), thereby withdrawing in one day double the cash from the current account than strictly allowed.

The third rule of managing a student current account involved making deliberate mistakes when writing the cheque. If the payee did not notice the mistakes early enough the bank would hopefully refuse payment, thereby causing a delay in payment and a temporary easing of the cash flow.

Mary indicated that she learned these 'scams' from other students and used each of them during her time at university. She admitted that they were wrong and was not even sure if they worked or that she gained any advantage from using them. They did however make her feel that she was getting one over on the system and she thought that it helped her to manage her money more easily and have a good time as well. As indicated above, the bank could have been aware of the actions of students and chose to ignore them as long as the overdraft stayed within manageable bounds.

Tasks

1. Explain the learning involved in this case using one or more models of learning described in this chapter.
2. Mary indicated that she was not sure if the 'scams' actually worked or not, but she still used them. What does this suggest about the relationship between learning and human behaviour?
3. If you were the bank involved how would you go about teaching your customers not to abuse their current account? What does your answer to this question suggest to you about the relationship between organizations and customers in terms of one teaching the other about the products and services offered and the business relationship between them?

FURTHER READING

Clark, H, Chandler, J and Barry, J (1994) *Organization and Identities: Text and Readings in Organizational Behaviour*, International Thomson Business Press, London. Contains a broad range of original articles on relevant material themes and from significant writers referred to in this and other textbooks on management and organizations.

Cohen, MD and Sproul, LS (eds) (1996) *Organizational Learning*, Sage, Thousand Oaks, CA. As an editied work, this text allows the perspectives of a number of leading researchers on organizational learning to be brought together.

Greenwood, DJ and Levin, M (1998) *Introduction to Action Research: Social Research for Social Change*, Sage, Thousand Oakes, CA. Provides an excellent review of the origins of action research as well as its academic positioning and variations in approach.

Hardingham, A (2003) On best behaviour, *People Management*, 17 April, p 50. This is a very brief but interesting review of the reward and punishment principles from behaviourism as used within training and development in organizational practice.

Institute of Personnel Management/Incomes Data Services European Management Guides (1993) *Training and Development*, Institute of Personnel Management, London. This is a practical book that reviews the training and development practices in member states of the European Union.

Lahteenmaki, S (2001) Critical aspects of organizational learning research and proposals for its measurement, *British Journal of Management*, June, Vol 12, No 2, pp 113–30. Provides an extensive review of the current organization learning literature and identifies several gaps which in the view of the writer limit the full understanding of the topic and proposes how these gaps might be filled in order to further understanding of the process.

Russ-Eft, D, Preskill, H and Sleezer, C. (eds) (1997) *Human Resource Development Review; Research and Implications*, Sage, Thousand Oaks, CA. A broad ranging review of research surrounding many aspects of learning in an organizational context.

Zemke, R (2002) Who needs learning theory anyway? *Training*, September, Vol 39, No 9, pp 86–9. A practical review of learning theory applied to workplace training activity. Essentially takes the view that no single theory can explain learning and that a variety of methods of delivery are needed to match the needs of learners. Also includes a 14 point checklist of things to take account of in designing any learning event involving adults.

COMPANION WEBSITE

Online teaching and learning resources:

Visit the companion website for Organizational Behaviour and Management 3rd edition at: *http://www.thomsonlearning.co.uk/businessandmanagement/martin3* to find valuable further teaching and learning material:

Refer to page 35 for full details.

PART THREE

Groups and teams within organizations

The previous section introduced various aspects associated with the individual in a work context. This section extends that approach and moves up one level to consider the nature and functioning of groups in an organizational context.

Groups form a major part of any organizational activity. There are many different types and sizes of group within most organizations, from the board of directors, to the departments and work teams that actually collaborate in making the product or delivering the service. There are also the informal groups that simply exchange gossip or chat over lunch and which can have a significant impact on the attitudes and opinions of employees, as well as exercising an indirect influence over their work activities. Formal groups within an organization do not usually emerge by chance. The people in a department or team are usually selected for some reason and appointed to undertake their particular role. These chapters set out to explore some of the literature and models that can contribute to an understanding of this important facet of organizational activity. This section will also consider the forces that impact on the behaviour of individuals when they come to work in a collaborative environment implied by team activity.

The next section is about management and leadership which in many situations means managing the individuals, groups and teams discussed here and previously. Teams and individuals are fundamental to achieving the organizational objectives that form the purpose of the manager's job – managers cannot achieve these objectives on their own, they need subordinates. In that context it is important to have some understanding of what managers are expected to manage before management itself is considered.

CHAPTER 6

Groups and teams: formation and structure

LEARNING OBJECTIVES

After studying this chapter and working through the associated Management in Action panels, Employee Perspectives, Discussion Questions and Case Study, you should be able to:

- **Outline the concept of a group as distinct from a team or a collection of individuals.**
- **Understand the differences between formal and informal groups.**
- **Describe the Hawthorne Studies and their significance in understanding the nature of groups.**
- **Discuss the nature and value of role theory together with its relevance to the structure of groups and teams.**
- **Explain group development processes and how they might impact on group performance.**

INTRODUCTION

Groups and teams form a significant part of the everyday experience of people. There are many different types of **group** that exist within organizations and most can be categorized under one of three headings:

1. *Organizational.* These are the formal groups and teams that are established by an organization in order to meet its own needs. Examples would include the production, finance and marketing departments.
2. *Self-interest.* People form or join a number of formal and informal groups as a means of protection, or to further their plans and objectives. Examples of the formal groups of this type that exist would include trade union groups and industry pressure groups formed to lobby government about particular policies. Informal groups that emerge in this category include those that meet to gossip and complain to each other about a particular boss, or a new procedure that the company has introduced.
3. *Affinity.* These tend to be informal or friendship groups that offer members the opportunity to meet the basic human need to 'belong' and avoid isolation. Examples would include sports teams, social groups, friendship groups and lunch groups.

Teams are of necessity a group, but that does not mean that every group is a **team**. For example, the finance department of a large company would be classed as a group, but it would contain within it a number of different teams, for example the management accounting team. So in general terms a team comprises a smaller number of people than would be found in a group and would have a more cohesive set of activities to engage in.

Group
Collective of two or more people with purpose, who interact, are psychologically aware and are influenced by the others.

Team
A small cohesive group focused on a common task and working as a single unit.

GROUPS AND TEAMS – ARE THEY DIFFERENT?

Shaw (1981) suggests that a group consists of two or more people who interact with each other in such a way that each influences and is influenced by the others. Schein (1988) suggests that a group can be any number of people who interact with each other, are psychologically aware of each other and think of themselves as a group. Although different in emphasis, both of these definitions have a number of features in common, including:

- *More than one person is involved.* It is not possible to have a one-person group.
- *Interaction must take place.* The people waiting on the railway platform are not a group unless they interact with each other. This may occur in some situations, for example if the train is late in arriving the individuals may begin to talk to each other and collectively protest to the railway staff.
- *Purpose or intention.* Schein suggests that the individuals involved must perceive themselves to be a group. This implies a purpose or intention behind the collectivization of people.
- *Awareness.* It implies that the individuals take cognizance of each other in their psychological processes. It is part of the interaction and influence process as described by Shaw.

This view of groups would also embrace the notion of a team. However, whilst this may be true in a general social context, it is common within an organizational context to refer to teams rather than groups. The notion of a team implies a small, cohesive group that works effectively as a single unit through being focused on a common task. Teamwork is now a common expression in relation to much organizational activity, and many individuals will find themselves being part of a number of different teams in the course of their work. For example, a management accountant in a large company may find themselves being a member of the new product evaluation team, the supplier selection team, the professional development mentoring team and the systems evaluation team in addition to their accounting responsibilities. Belbin (2000) points out that in addition to the size differences between groups and teams, there are crucial differences between the two in how people are selected for membership and the nature of leadership. The basis of the differences between groups and teams becomes apparent in the model of team roles that Belbin developed and which are introduced below and discussed in the next chapter. The logic being that teams should become more effective if they can be designed through the application of selection rules and task allocation based upon individual characteristics.

There are occasions in which groups and teams are formed as a result of circumstances, but they are not necessarily part of the formal plans to achieve organizational objectives. For example, Management in Action 6.1 describes the situation in which volunteer police officers from Britain were brought together and trained to form a United Nations police contingent, along with officers from many other nationalities and expected to contribute to rebuilding war-torn Kosovo. In doing so they were working in an environment that required almost total self-reliance, but the need to be part of a group for emotional and physical support can easily be imagined.

Katzenbach and Smith (1993) draw these ideas together by suggesting that the distinction between groups and teams can be reflected in the relative performance achieved. They describe, as a result of consultancy and research carried out on behalf of McKinsey & Company, that a positive correlation exists between the type of team or group and level of performance. They describe the scale of effectiveness as a reflection of the following changes to the nature of the group or team:

- *Working group*. A collection of individuals working collectively to a limited degree. Performance largely reflects the efforts of individual members.
- *Pseudo-teams*. A collection of individuals who could achieve higher performance if they worked in a more integrated and effective way.
- *Potential teams*. This category is essentially the same as pseudo-teams, but the individuals recognize that they could integrate more effectively and seek to do so.
- *Real teams*. This category of team is committed to the common purpose and has developed appropriate ways of working.
- *High performance teams*. This category are real teams but with the additional features of encouraging personal growth and going beyond performance expectations among members.

From the above discussion it is possible to say that teams are groups within a particular context. The increase in performance that could be achieved in moving from simple work groups to high performance teams, as indicated in the Katzenbach and Smith model, also means that managers have a vested interest in seeking to create them. Boon and Sierksma (2003) developed an interesting model that uses these ideas to identify appropriate new soccer and volleyball players by evaluating their potential to contribute to team success. As all teams are by definition special types of group the distinction between them in this and the next chapter is not of particular significance. Only where there is a clear distinction to be made will the terms be used separately. One area that sometimes causes problems for teamwork within an organization is in the change of title from supervisor to team leader. Employee Perspective 6.1 seeks to explore one aspect of this.

MANAGEMENT IN ACTION 6.1 Keeping the peace

The United Nations (UN) frequently finds itself in the difficult situation of trying to keep the peace and helping to rebuild communities following a war or other national disaster. These can be very dangerous environments and it needs special skills to be able to work in places such as Kosovo. The UN seeks to draw appropriately skilled and qualified personnel on secondment from member nations for this type of work. The individuals are volunteers and often serve for a period of one year in the field. Among other personnel, Britain contributed a number of police officers from the Ministry of Defence Police service (MDP) to the Kosovo region in seeking to restore order and some form of criminal justice system.

The MDP is a specialized civilian police service within Britain looking after Ministry of Defence (MOD) interests and providing a policing capability for dealing with non-military offences on MOD land. They work alongside both the Military Police and the civilian police forces across Britain. When the Kosovan war ended in 1999, the Serbian authorities withdrew from Kosovo leaving it with no civil government or police service and with a badly damaged infrastructure. Water and power supplies were unreliable, refuse collection was non-existent and roads were in an appalling state of repair. Crime was also rife within the country. The country was awash with guns, and had become the route into Europe for the drug trade and was most likely being controlled by the Mafia.

It was into this situation that the UN sought to restore some degree of normality and order, hence the need for teams of people with police skills. The MDP service was particularly well placed to help because of its close association with both military and civilian policing activities and so plans were made to send a detachment to Kosovo. A reconnaissance visit was made in order to assess the logistical and training needs for staff to be posted and advice was also sought from the Police Service of Northern Ireland who already had officers working in Kosovo. A recruitment process was undertaken to select volunteers from within the MDP to be posted to Kosovo for one year. This included careful briefings on the tasks and local conditions so that individuals could judge for themselves their suitability for the role that they would be expected to perform.

One of the key issues for individuals was that they had to be self-reliant and able to sustain themselves physically and emotionally. This was because once in post they would not be part of an MDP team living in barracks, but would be based in local accommodation in the communities to which they had been posted and part of teams made up of personnel drawn up from any of 32 different nationalities. Once selected, officers undertook a four week training course covering issues such as firearms tactics, personal security, UN rules of engagement, mine awareness, environmental hygiene and other organizations working in the area. Once in Kosovo, officers were given further training by local UN staff and then assigned to specific roles. The roles frequently carry more responsibility than the individuals carry in their normal work. For example, some have been appointed to the level of Station Commander, responsible for about 400 other officers; some to close protection for visiting dignitaries; and others to head up specialist police work such as traffic, communications and community relations. Yet others have been given the task of setting up the court system, and establishing the personnel and training departments.

The UN is pleased with the work of the officers from the MDP and the individuals have also gained considerably from the experience. According to Lloyd Clarke, the Chief Constable of the MDP, they bring back to their home force: '... tremendously enhanced skills in areas like negotiation, investigation and management capability. It is a real eye-opening, life-enhancing opportunity which has also given them a greater tolerance of other people and communities.'

However, there has been at least one downside for the MDP says Clarke: 'Many of our staff have wanted to stay out there because of the extra responsibility – and when they come back to a less demanding job – ouch – that's been difficult. But we had to make a management decision that the maximum stay is 18 months, and when they come back they are not automatically promoted. They have to go through the same selection processes and meet the same requirements as everyone else.'

However, this downside is not so serious as to end the commitment. The MDP has made a commitment to the British government that it will provide up to 100 officers each year for postings overseas, wherever they are needed. This represents a new niche for this specialized force of police officers.

Adapted from: Lucas, E (2002) Keeping the peace, *Professional Manager*, November, pp 26–7

Stop ↔ Consider

Identify what problems other than returning to less responsible jobs might arise for the returning police officers?

The process of selecting and training the officers, as well as the overseas posting and nature of the task is likely to reinforce the group identity among individuals. Yet they are reformed into groups with new personnel once they are given their specific roles. What problems might this create, how would you prepare individuals for them and how would you deal with any problems that might arise if you were a senior UN officer in Kosovo?

EMPLOYEE PERSPECTIVE 6.1

David was a team leader, or was he?

David was a production supervisor in a large engineering factory in the Birmingham area. He had served his apprenticeship as a toolmaker and had been promoted to supervisor some five years prior to the incidents described. He was paid slightly more than the employees he supervised but did not earn any production bonus. He was however paid overtime at the same rate as the other workers.

The company for which David worked undertook a restructuring exercise and among the changes made was the elimination of the job of supervisor. This was to be replaced with a team leader who it was intended would work more closely with the work group and lead them rather than manage them. Among the other changes made were an increase in salary for the team leader, but they would not be paid for working overtime.

The changes were introduced without too many difficulties. However, the factory received a large order and had to increase the amount of overtime worked in order to make the products. The workers were very keen to put in the additional hours, but the new team leaders were not as they would not get any extra money. As David said, 'They created the new job of team leader which in practice is no different from the old supervisor's job, stop our overtime pay and then expect us to work all the hours available – for free. We have been conned.'

Tasks

1. What would you do if you were David?
2. What would you do if you were a manager in the same firm?
3. What might you expect the differences between a team leader and a supervisor to be?

GROUPS, TEAMS AND ORGANIZATIONS

Large organizations are made up of many groups. It would not be possible to achieve the objectives of such organizations without the existence of groups. The scale and complexity of activity requires that it be broken down into manageable chunks of activity. For example, sales-related work forms a convenient subgrouping of the overall organizational activity and one that can usefully be separated from the manufacturing and financial processes. However, grouping by function tends to focus the attention of members inwards on the activities, needs and perspectives of their group rather than the overall objectives of the organization. As a result of the creation of such segmented activity it is necessary to also provide integration arrangements in order to ensure that the organization is able to function effectively. An example would be the need for a production planning process to ensure that sales intentions can be realized by the production department. It is because of the need to overcome the compartmentalization of activity that the creation of high performing teams becomes significant in management's attempts to focus efforts on customer service.

Even quite small organizations require groups to be formed. Perhaps the only organization that does not require a grouping-based arrangement of activity is one of fewer than three or four people. Even such very small organizations are likely to have some form of compartmentalization within them, if only between the owner/manager and the workers. Frequently with organizations of five or six people there is a demarcation between administrative and operational activity beginning to emerge. As organizations grow and evolve, the need to create the means of specialization through grouping together the available human resource into convenient units also develops.

There are many types of group that function formally within an organization. Some of the more obvious are indicated as follows:

- *Hierarchical differentiation.* The split of an organization into management, staff and manual worker categories. This can be further subdivided into senior, middle and junior management levels. This form of grouping represents the seniority and status based organization of work. It reflects the decision-making and responsibility scope of work activity commonly used as the basis of payment and reward within organizations.
- *Specialism groupings.* This is the collection of people into the work teams within a function. An example would be the recruitment team within the personnel department or the electricians within the maintenance department. This form of grouping reflects the collection of common activities and responsibilities into a single unit in order to enhance performance and concentrate expertise.
- *Activity groupings.* These are the means through which much organizational activity is co-ordinated, the most common examples being project teams, committees or working parties. They could include the remuneration committee of the board of directors or the regular meeting of a quality circle within one of the departments. This category of group represents one of the primary means of counteracting the functional approach to work. Activity groups typically reflect an attempt to break down the insularity of functional groups; cover activities not specifically the responsibility of one group; and ensure that an appropriate range of perspectives are brought together in dealing with particular issues.
- *Boundary spanning.* In this category, teams are typically formed to span the boundary between one organization and another. One example would be a customer liaison group, intended to provide an interface between customers and the organization. Another would be the regular meetings between senior managers and the organization's bankers to review aspects of company finances. There are internal examples of boundary-spanning groups within organizations. For example, the human resource management department spans the boundary between management and employee groups.
- *Professional.* This could involve the grouping of professionals within the organization into appropriate work-based teams, perhaps even a professional institute or similar association if the company is large enough. It reflects a particular type of work-based grouping commonly found among accountants, engineers, lawyers and doctors.

The approach adopted within an organization to the grouping of people is increasingly being recognized as a basis of competitive advantage. Indeed, this is the basis of the Katzenbach and Smith model described earlier. Traditional organizational hierarchies are focused on functional groupings and hierarchical management responsibility. However the customer experience of an organization is not hierarchical, it is horizontal. Consider shopping at a supermarket, conducting your personal banking or purchasing new equipment for a company. In each of these transactions the customer will encounter the lower level staff that process the order or sale. In meeting the needs of customers a cross-functional approach is inevitably needed. For example any order must pass through sales, finance, warehouse and despatch departments. The boundaries between the various functional groups can act as fences or friction points, preventing a seamless customer-focused experience. In addition the senior managers tend to become remote from the experience of customers as they spend more time 'managing the process' rather than 'doing customer activity' within the organization. This **conflict model of customer experience and organizational functioning** is reflected in Figure 6.1.

Conflict model of customer experience and organizational functioning
This reflects the difficulty of functional groups being able to meet customer needs in a hierarchical organization.

Likert (1961) developed the idea that organizations should be considered as a collection of groups, rather than individuals. In his view individuals would inevitably belong to more than one group and consequently the groups would overlap. This he described as a **linking pin model** and it is shown as Figure 6.2.

Linking pin model
This model reflects the overlapping and connected nature of groups within an organization.

While Figure 6.2 is a simplistic representation of the nature of groups within an organization, it is useful as a means of describing the overlapping memberships of individuals as part of the formal organization structure. Likert recognized that this basic model underestimated the true level and complexity of group activity within an organization. Any individual belongs to many teams and groups at one and the same time. For example, a library assistant in a university library may belong to the issue desk team, the copyright monitoring team, the book repair team, the student debts

FIGURE 6.1

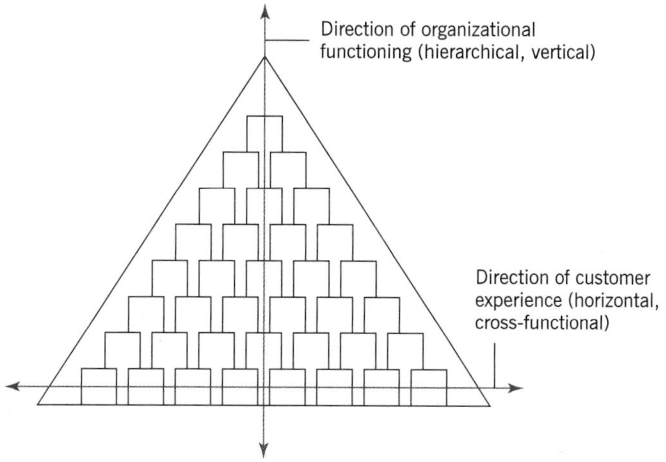

The hierarchical/customer conflict

FIGURE 6.2

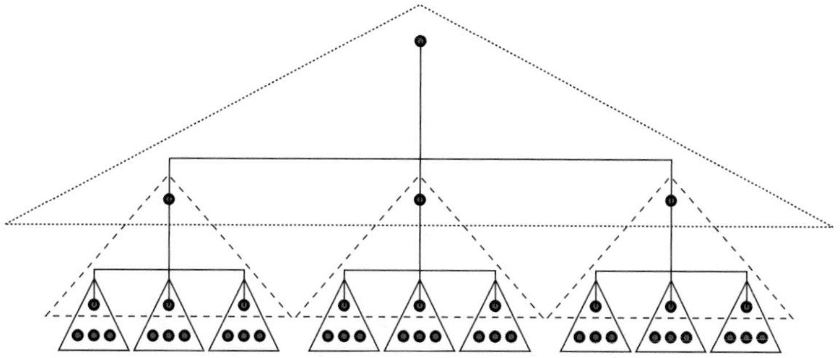

Likert's linking pin model of organizational groups (*source:* Likert, R (1961) *New Patterns of Management*, McGraw-Hill, New York

working group as well as the service development working group. In addition they may have supervisory responsibilities for a number of other staff and be part of a number of friendship and social groupings.

The linking pin model also ignores the instrumental value of groups to individual members. For example, Handy (1993) argues that individuals join and use groups for a number of purposes, including meeting social and affiliation needs and gaining support for their objectives. Groups in organizations are not just imposed on people from above – individuals create groups and vary their level of participation in groups and teams depending upon a range of personal and organizational factors. The concept of the high performing team is one that allows for the possibility of creating a mini-organization within the organization. Were such moves to be successful, teams would be created with the same values and mindset as managers, which would therefore automatically encourage individuals to go beyond their contract in continually giving more than required, reducing conflict and the need for close supervision.

THE SIGNIFICANCE OF GROUPS AND TEAMS

Looked at from a top-down perspective it is senior managers who decide on the form that the organization will take. In doing so they create the formal groupings that will achieve the perceived operational needs. The group structures within the organization therefore represent a given for most people. People are recruited into the particular work group for which their skills and experience have prepared them. Work teams, however, require a closer affinity between the members in order to deliver the high level of effectiveness expected of them. The formation of formal groups and teams is therefore a process of selection and socialization. Call centres are a white-collar equivalent of a factory and many experience high labour turnover. One such organization in the USA (1–800-GOT-JUNK, a specialist in waste disposal) has successfully attempted to impact on this and provide better customer service by adopting the following process; a three stage interview process, a minimum of two days working on trucks hauling waste, classroom training and two weeks of mentoring with an experienced colleague. Royal Caribbean cruise lines went further by extending the mentoring process and even keeping in contact with former employees, as they may wish to return in the future (*Call Center Magazine*, 2003).

In circumstances in which new recruits are chosen to join existing organizations one of the issues is the fit between the existing people and the applicants. Once inside the organization the individual is subjected to an extended process of socialization into the organization and the groups and teams to which they will become affiliated. It is more common to find situations in which a new person joins an existing team than for a totally new group to be formed. Project teams, company reorganizations and the creation of special task forces are common examples of circumstances in which new groups may be formed within an existing organization. The following Employee Perspective (6.2) seeks to explore some of the difficulties for a new employee joining an established group.

The significance of groups within an organizational setting arises from two main factors:

1. *Necessity*. This reflects the need for an organization to arrange for the work to actually get done. It is not physically possible for the chief executive of a large company to personally undertake the full range of work needed. Consequently, devices have to be found which allow the range, scale and volume of work to be undertaken by other people in the most cost-effective way. While there are

EMPLOYEE PERSPECTIVE 6.2 Sarah's first day at work

Sarah described her first day at work. She had graduated from Hull University with a degree in history and had found a job as a trainee personnel officer with a local government organization. She arrived early for her first day and the reception desk called someone from the personnel office to come and collect her. The person who escorted her to the office began to chat about where she had come from and why she wanted to work in personnel. Nothing was said about any of the other staff or the work that she would be expected to do. When they arrived at the office Sarah was handed over to the personnel manager, whom she had already met during the interviews. He greeted her warmly and took her round the rest of the office to meet the existing staff. Sarah found this daunting and could not remember the names, let alone the jobs of everyone that she met. Sarah was told that she had been allocated to the recruitment team and was introduced to them last.

The recruitment team consisted of five people: the manager, two personnel officers and two clerical staff. It was a busy section within the personnel department, always under pressure as line managers always wanted staff instantly, without any fuss or paperwork involved. The team was a cohesive little unit that worked closely together and had not had a trainee allocated to them before. They had been asking for more staff to be able to cope with the volume of work and time pressure they were under, but a trainee was what they had been given. It quickly became apparent to Sarah that the existing team tended to resent that, as it would mean that they would have to take time out of an already pressured job to show her what to do, which would inevitably slow them down.

Just before lunch the manager of the section dumped a dozen bulging files on her desk and said to pick out the five best candidates from the application forms in each file. These would be invited for interview. The details for each of the dozen jobs were kept in a different file and Sarah was told that Richard had these files. Having been introduced to so many people, Sarah was confused, she could not remember who Richard was. All she knew was that he did not work in the recruitment team (as the only male was called John). The manager said that she should be able to do that task by about 3.00 that afternoon and to give the files back to Lucy who would arrange the interviews.

Sarah began to panic. What should she do, who was Richard and how should she select the people for interview? How could so much work be done in such a short time?

Tasks

1. What would you advise Sarah to do in order to get through the work expected and to fit into the recruitment team?
2. Remember, asking for help would be likely to alienate the other staff as they were all very busy and it might show Sarah's lack of experience. Going back to the manager for help would be an admission of failure. Just guessing at which candidates would be the best for the jobs would be likely to result in a disaster. What should she do?

many different ways in which this can actually be achieved they all involve some form of group activity.

2. *Dynamic basis of behaviour.* This will form a significant part of the next chapter and so will only be introduced briefly here. The definition of a group introduced earlier in this chapter makes it apparent that as a social framework it contains a measure of 'togetherness'. Being a member of a group confers personal and social benefits as well as organizational benefits. There is also a personal cost associated with group membership in that individuals have to align their behaviour (conform) to the norms of the groups to which they belong. Groups tend to develop a life of their own in that the very 'togetherness' sought from the existence of a group creates a unity that can subvert the formally intended purpose. All of this reflects **group dynamics**.

Group dynamics
The interactions and patterns of behaviour that occur when groups of people meet.

The significance of groups and teams in terms of the organizational context is that they are necessary for the achievement of the desired objectives and can provide competitive advantage. For example, Hamilton *et al.* (2003) demonstrate that productivity increased by 14 per cent on average as a result of the change from individual piecework to team incentives in a garment factory. But at the same time the creation of groups can lead to other behaviours emerging and because they develop a degree of independence from the organization that created them they can be difficult to direct and control. In extreme cases, they can even become hostile to management and seek to frustrate attempts to direct them.

Equally, from an individual point of view groups are also significant. Human beings belong to many different groups based on family, friendship, location, social grouping and work activities. There are many advantages to being in a group. Sharing responsibility, friendship, support with problems, a feeling of value and comfort in times of distress are just some of them. As many animals find, there is relative safety in numbers. However, there are also individual costs associated with group membership. It is not possible to be an individual within a group. The very essence of a group implies 'togetherness', 'unity' and 'commonality'. From that point of view each member must give up something to become and remain a member. A member who cannot or will not adopt the necessary norms of behaviour and otherwise accept the requirements of membership will probably find themselves subjected to some degree of sanction or, in extreme cases, expulsion. Group membership reflects a social process of give and take, not just take and sometimes the requirement to give (or conform) can outweigh the benefits obtained for the individual.

FORMAL AND INFORMAL GROUPS

The emphasis in the discussion so far has been on those groups and teams that exist as part of the formal activities within an organization. Such groups are established by management and function according to management's rules and standards. From that point of view they are not a naturally occurring social structure. They are designed and imposed by managers on the workforce as a way of achieving the desired objectives in a controlled manner. They also represent an attempt to impose social control on the workforce in encouraging certain behaviours and discouraging others through adopted (or imposed) norms, without the need for large numbers of management 'enforcers'.

Formal group
Designated by management as a way of achieving organizational objectives, they include departments and teams.

It is possible to differentiate between types of **formal group** within an organization on the basis of purpose. Based on the work of Argyle (1989) it is possible to identify formal groups involved in the following activities:

- *Teams*. These are frequently project or activity groups. They are usually given a high degree of freedom in terms of deciding on the processes to be used to achieve the objectives set.
- *Tasks*. The nature of the objectives to be achieved are more clearly set out for this type of group and so there is little discretion available in terms of activity and method to be adopted. Most work groups would fall under this heading.
- *Technology*. The nature of this classification is that the technology or process dictates the work activities and methods involved. There exists little opportunity for the group to exercise discretion in either of these areas. In practice it forms a special type of task category above.
- *Decisions*. Much management time is taken up with meetings associated with decision making. Of course, this form of group activity is not restricted to managers as many specialist and administrative staff would also be involved.

- *Management*. In addition to decision making, management must collectively plan, guide and monitor organizational activity.

Informal groups exist within all organizations and serve a number of functions, both positive and negative. It is usual to describe informal groups in either friendship or interest terms. Membership of an informal group is voluntary and the significance of their existence is frequently understated. In most organizations things get done on the basis of the informal groups and networks that exist. Hofstede (1984) draws attention to the concept of a **marketplace bureaucracy** in his analysis of culture and structure. The essence of this concept is that individuals depend more on personal relationships than formal reporting relationships to get things done. Facilitation in this form of bureaucracy is achieved through the trading of support for mutual advantage. It is based on the assumption of, 'You help me this time and I will help you in future', hence the term marketplace. Hofstede suggests that it would be commonly found in Scandinavian countries, the UK and Ireland.

Informal groups
Arise from friendship, mutual support and dependency needs which cannot be met through the formal organizational groups.

Marketplace bureaucracy
The need to get things done within an organization requires the continuous trading of favours between colleagues outside formal procedures.

However, the negative role of informal relations and networks in excluding women from management positions was also demonstrated by Cooper and Davidson (1982). In response to this form of discrimination there have been moves towards the formation of women-only groups or networks. The purpose being to enhance the ability of women to progress in the male-dominated professions, including management.

Friendship groups form on the basis of relationships within an organization. They are not restricted to level or functional area within the company and frequently act as information channels. In practice much friendship group activity has a social basis and becomes a process of 'mutual looking out for each other'. If friendship groups become too strong, they may attempt to consciously influence events in their favour, perhaps through clandestine means. It is at this point that friendship groups become interest groups. Consequently, there is a danger of friendship groups working against the interests of management. It is also possible for such groups to form the basis of resistance to change. Interest groups could also form as a response to a perceived threat. For example, comments from senior managers that a delayering exercise were being considered might encourage junior managers to band together (or join a trade union) in order to protect their jobs by seeking to influence or frustrate management's intentions.

The existence of informal groups is something that is frequently seen as a matter of concern by managers. Indeed, some writers on the subject refer to them as **shadow organizations** (Stacey, 2000, p 386), the clear implication being that they are something sinister and potentially damaging to the host organization. However, as has already been implied, there is a degree of inevitability about the existence of informal groups and they can be of value to management. For example, the **grapevine** can be a useful means through which to communicate with individuals in the organization, Dalton (1959).

Shadow organizations
Informal groups can form a parallel organization within the host and become a threat to management's ability to control.

Adler *et al.* (1989) report that 66 per cent of their respondents in the People's Republic of China indicated that it was only infrequently necessary to bypass the hierarchical line in order to achieve efficient work relationships. In an earlier study Laurent (1983) found that only 22 per cent of respondents in Sweden responded similarly, but that 75 per cent of Italians did so. The results indicated clearly that there are national differences in the degree to which informal lines of communication would be used. However, it is never possible to be certain of the degree to which respondents answer questions in terms of what they think would be an acceptable answer rather than reflecting actual practice. Katz (1973) also suggests that informal groups can assist the integration of employees into the organization by blurring the distinction between work and non-work activities.

Grapevine
Gossip networks in an organization as a way of passing information, real or imagined around employees at all levels.

Informal groups form the lifeblood of most organizations in that they depend on a level of mutual need and dependency among the members for their existence. Informal groups form because the individuals wish to band together, perhaps for protection against a management decision; perhaps because they enjoy similar leisure interests; or perhaps because there is a work-related dependency. Whatever the reason, many contribute to the effective running of the organization. It is the ability of one employee to speak directly with another and discuss work-related events and problems that is mutually beneficial and keeps things running smoothly. Standard operating procedures provide guidance on what should be done, people in their working relationships actually make this happen. However, as discussed earlier, Hofstede (and others) suggest that this 'bending' of the hierarchical formalities would be more common in certain cultural circumstances.

Many of the recent attempts to increase levels of employee commitment can be interpreted as attempts to tap into already existing informal processes. Management in Action 6.2 provides an indication of the processes involved in reorganizing people into teams and the associated training required.

WHY GROUPS FORM

In an organizational context there are two major reasons why groups are a significant factor for both employers and employees. First, it is necessary to use groups or teams to achieve the organization's objectives. Second, most humans prefer to associate with other people. The main reasons that groups form include:

- *The need to have more than one person to undertake the work.* In organizations of more than one person it is necessary to separate the activities to be done and to allocate people into teams.
- *The need to incorporate the expertise of a number of people in order to achieve the end result.* For example, a project team set up to design a new product may need the skills of designers, engineers, accountants, production and marketing specialists.
- *The need for organizations to match complexity in the environment through the provision of internal operating methods and arrangements.* Ashby (1956) termed this as the **law of requisite variety**. He suggested that only variety could destroy variety. In other words, only organizational complexity could match and offset environmental complexity. Among the implications of this is that the creation of teams can encourage synergy, creativity and innovation through group membership.

Law of requisite variety
see 'Requisite variety'

- *The opportunity to allow employees to minimize the worst aspects of their work by sharing it out or rotating it among the group.* This should enhance job satisfaction or, at the least, minimize dissatisfaction.
- *Groups provide for the social needs of individuals.* Friendships provide a form of social significance for the individual within the work setting. It allows the individual to be more than just a number or a means of production. Such networks and relationships allow for the support of the individual in the work setting by other workers.
- *The groups to which an individual belong provide a basis for socialization into the* **norms** *of behaviour within the organization.* This includes the extent to which official rules are followed and the way in which employees maintain the balance between management demands and employee preference.

Norms
see Group norms.

- *Group membership also provides the individual with a measure of protection from outside threat.* It has been argued that employment conditions and protection have only been improved across Europe as a result of the high levels of trade union membership.

MANAGEMENT IN ACTION 6.2 Sense of involvement

Du Pont's printing and publishing business introduced an annual hours work system in 1992 and as a result moved from four to six-shift working. The 750 workers were organized into 30 self-managed teams. Within the teams employees are trained in all tasks performed by the group, some retaining a core skill function. Each team is responsible for every aspect of the process, including production, costing, productivity, quality, safety and work allocation. This is achieved through a weekly pre-shift meeting supported by one training day every six weeks. The gains achieved are tangible and Pat Tunney, the personnel manager at Du Pont, indicated that productivity rose by 36 per cent in the first year of operation and he predicted a 25 per cent rise the following year.

Team building can be achieved in many different ways. Sue Bradshaw, the dealer development manager with Peugeot, described their approach. In pursuit of accreditation to the BS5750 quality standard an improvement cycle was identified through which continuous change could be made within the dealer network. The company introduced a 'team builder' programme which began with a PC-based questionnaire to generate information for the individual's team profile. This was used to discuss role preferences and team communication style with each individual before a two-day team development workshop. This led naturally into ongoing discussions by the team about how to improve the performance of the business.

Other companies opt for outdoor training as the means to encourage understanding and develop the trust and confidence between individual members. Rank Xerox CSD manager for human resources, Christine Hands, indicated that: 'Group members need mutual trust and respect for each other's skills, knowledge, opinions and commitment. They need to communicate freely and easily with each other.'

The team training at Rank Xerox was provided by a US company and was described by Hands as a mini-Olympics in the following way: 'It went down as a lot of fun. Their style was very un-English – it took some people a while to come to terms with it. But by the end of the week no one wanted to leave.'

Adapted from: Haughton, E (1993) Sense of involvement, *Personnel Today*, 29 June, pp 26–30.

Stop ↔ Consider

To what extent is it possible for management to capture aspects of informal relationships and group membership and formalize them within working practices?
Would such attempts to formalize the informal simply lead to the creation of different types of informal grouping as individuals seek to exert some control over their organizational experience?

- *Groups also emerge as a result of the nature of the work to be undertaken within an organization.* This can be to acquire information, seek clarification of that already obtained, pass work on (or obtain it), cross-reference something or elicit help in undertaking something. The result is that mutual dependency is formed with people either helping (or hindering) each other.

The discussion on groups reflects the complexity in organizational activity. The concept of variety has already been introduced as a useful means of reflecting this state of affairs. Management in Action 6.3 reflects how one organization attempted to deal with the effects of variety.

Formal groups are created by the organization of which they form part. However, the informal groups that exist are created by the people within the host organization. They both feed off and interact with the formal groups around them. Informal groups come into existence for a number of reasons, including:

- *The nature and form of the formal organization.* The way in which the formal organization operates can influence the way that individuals organize themselves and interact.

MANAGEMENT IN ACTION 6.3 Construction on a united front

MW Kellogg is an international construction company employing some 4000 skilled workers. The UK operation specializes in petrochemical design and construction projects that can last from a few weeks to several years. Each project requires a dedicated team of anything up to 100 people from a range of professions and disciplines. Project teams can also involve individuals and groups that are not directly employed by MW Kellogg. This situation can create many difficulties as people have to work effectively together and at the same time look after the interests of the organization they represent. Add to this the cultural, language and professional differences that exist when operating internationally and it is surprising that any project is completed.

Angela Freddi, senior personnel officer for MW Kellogg, attempted to find ways of encouraging the creation of effective teams in this context. Purpose-designed courses were introduced with the help of an outside training company, Arete. The process for each project group follows a similar pattern:

- Once the project group is selected Arete visits each member in order to identify potential problem areas.
- This information is discussed with the personnel department and a three-day course is designed to address the issues identified and create a team.
- Courses have a common theme to them. The first two days are intended to break down barriers and to build team spirit. The third day focuses on issues relevant to the project that the team is to undertake.
- Non-company people who will be part of the project team are encouraged to attend the course.
- Members of the project group will be taken off their current job in groups to go through the course. Participants on each course are from a range of the disciplines and professions represented on the project.

Another aspect of these courses worthy of note is the use of either indoor or outdoor activity, depending upon the background and experience of the participants. These activities involve the solving of problems, where every member of the team has to experience being a team leader as well as operating at the lowest level. This is intended to provide individuals with the experience of what it is like to allow someone else to have the lead role as well as to reflect on their own strengths and weaknesses.

Adapted from: Simons, C (1992) Construction on a united front, *Personnel Today*, 30 June, pp 33–4.

Stop ↔ Consider

Does the approach described reflect an attempt to encourage the rapid development of groups which, of necessity, change frequently? Or does it reflect an organizational need to cope with a complex environment? Does this distinction matter?

- *The need for human beings to function in a social environment and to form relationships of their own choosing.* Schein (1956) describes the manipulation of prisoners of war by the Chinese Communists during the Korean War. The use of rank was dispensed with and groups were reorganized when it became apparent that something approaching an effective structure was emerging.
- *The voluntary nature of many informal groups offsets the involuntary nature of many formal, organizational groups.*
- *The approach adopted by managers to the running of the organization will also influence the formation of informal groups.*
- *The need to run the organization.* Organization structures and procedures are the mechanisms that determine what should be done where and when. However, procedures cannot cater for the interpersonal and dynamic nature of organizational activity. Organizational functioning depends to a significant extent on individuals co-operating in a reciprocal network of activity. Inevitably, in such situations self-help networks of mutual dependency (informal groups)

form. In some cultures informal groups may form for other reasons. For example, cohorts of students recruited by a single organization at the same time may 'keep in touch' during the course of their careers and offer mutual support and advice to each other.

ORGANIZATIONAL RESEARCH APPROACHES

One of the earliest research activities into group activity was reported by Triplett (1897). Triplett observed that racing cyclists performed better when accompanied by a pacemaker than when they were alone. Table 6.1 indicates the results that he observed for two leading racing cyclists to cover a one-mile training 'race'.

The gain from having a pacemaker was an improvement in performance of approximately 20 per cent. This in itself was an interesting result as the experiment was not carried out in a competitive situation. Triplett interpreted these findings in terms of the arousal of the competitive instinct from the presence of the other cyclist. This became known as **social facilitation**, the presence and involvement of others in an activity producing an enhanced performance in an individual.

These co-action effects (changes in behaviour through the presence of others) have been observed in a wide range of species. Table 6.2 has been developed from Zajonc (1965) and demonstrates this. Another form of social facilitation is referred to as the **audience effect**, the mere presence (rather than the active participation) of others producing an enhancement in behavioural activity.

However, there is also evidence of the opposite effect occurring in a group context; referred to as **social loafing**. This effect was originally described by Ringelmann more than 50 years ago according to Kravitz and Martin (1986). Ringelmann gave people a very simple task to do – pull on a rope. What he found was that the more people in a

Social facilitation/ audience effect
Improvements in performance as a result of the participation of others; the mere presence of others produces the audience effect.

Social loafing
The inhibiting effect on the performance of individuals as a result of being part of a group.

	Time to cycle one mile		
	Paced	**Unpaced**	**Gain for pacing**
Person X	99.6 seconds	123.8 seconds	+19.5%
Person Y	102.0 seconds	130.0 seconds	+21.5%

TABLE 6.1 Racing times for one mile

Harlow (1932)	Laboratory rats ate more if fed together than when fed alone
Chen (1937)	A species of ant worked harder at nest building when working in a group than when alone
Rasmussen (1939)	Thirsty laboratory rats would drink more when in the presence of other rats than when alone
Tolman and Wilson (1956)	Repeated the Harlow (1932) findings but with chicks rather than rats

TABLE 6.2 Social facilitation in non-human species

team pulling on a rope, the less effort each person applied to the task. Three people only applied a total of two and a half times the force of a single person, and eight people achieved less than four times the single person's effort. A number of studies have supported aspects of this phenomena (see for example, Zaccaro, 1984; Williams *et al.*, 1981; Jackson and Harkins, 1985; and Mulvey and Klein, 1998). The various explanations include:

- It is more likely to occur when individuals think that other team members will minimize their contribution.
- It is more likely to occur when individuals think that their output is not separately identifiable
- It is more likely to occur when the task was perceived as unimportant, simple or boring.
- It is less likely to occur if individuals think that their contribution will be evaluated.
- People who prefer to work in groups are less likely to engage in loafing than people who prefer to work as an individual.

The British experience

It was during World War I that the British government began a serious interest in the relationship between working conditions, fatigue and output. This is hardly surprising given the demand for military equipment and the social changes at work brought about as a result of the mass conscription of males. This research work continued after the war ended and Wyatt *et al.* (1928) report a study concentrating on women performing a number of jobs, including wrapping soap, folding handkerchiefs, making bicycle chains, weighing and wrapping tobacco, making cigarettes and making rifle bullets. Among the conclusions drawn from their work was that the social conditions within which the work was done held significant consequences for the people. Also, boredom was less likely to arise when people worked in groups rather than on their own.

In the USA work was underway at the same time, that when linked with the ideas from the research activity already described, was to lead to the development of the human relations movement. The significance of the social aspects of work on productivity emerged as a major alternative to the task emphasis in work organization prevalent up to that point.

The Hawthorne Studies

The Western Electric Company in the USA had begun a series of investigations at its Hawthorne Works in 1924. The studies were initially carried out by staff within the company, as it was intended to identify practical productivity improvements. In 1927 researchers from the Harvard Business School became involved in the research and the names of Mayo, Roethlisberger and Dickson are now the most closely associated with it.

It is Mayo who is credited with the leadership of the research team from Harvard. He was an Australian by birth and spent time during and after World War I working with disabled military personnel. It is hardly stretching credibility to imagine that such an experience would have a major impact on his thinking about people, work, organizations and life in general. The significance of people in a collective setting was a predominant theme of the Hawthorne research and the subsequent interpretation of the results.

The studies within the Hawthorne works can be separated into four stages:

1. The illumination experiments
2. The relay assembly test room study
3. The interview programme
4. The bank wiring observation room study.

We now look briefly at each stage of the research in turn. The research process will be discussed in some detail as it represents one of the most detailed and comprehensive studies into the nature and impact of group working.

The illumination experiments The intention of these experiments was to identify the relationship between levels of light and output. The experiment was undertaken by splitting the workers into experimental and control groups. The experimental group was subjected to systematic variation in the level of illumination to measure any changes in output. The control group continued in conditions of normal levels of light with the levels of output also being recorded.

The results of the experiments were inconclusive in that production levels did not appear to vary in relationship to the level of light. The level of output increased even when the level of light was very poor. Output also increased in the control group; which had no change in lighting. The highest level of output recorded was when the experimental group returned to their normal working conditions. This unexpected set of findings led to the conclusion that worker output was in practice influenced by many factors. This prompted subsequent research in an attempt to identify the range and relative impact of these factors.

The relay assembly test room study The work in this room involved female workers assembling a number of small components to make the relay switches used in telephone equipment. The very nature of this work was highly repetitive and boring. To conduct the research, a group of six women were selected from among the regular workforce. Two of the women (who were friends) were selected by the research team. These two women then selected the other four workers. The six women to be studied were transferred to a special room designated for the research study.

Working conditions in the normal department were replicated in the experimental room. The experiment began with a period during which the work practices were identical to those in the normal department. For example, a 48-hour working week with no rest breaks, or provision of refreshment. The normal output on assembling relays was 50 per hour worked. This level of output allowed the research team to detect even relatively small changes in productivity. There followed a research period of almost two years, in which a number of variables associated with the work arrangements were systematically varied as shown in Table 6.3.

The researcher was located in the room with the women workers and by noting all that happened created the records that were used in the subsequent analysis. The women were generally kept informed about the experiment and consulted about events that were to take place. The observer also tried to maintain a friendly atmosphere in the room through his general approach to the staff and the recording of data.

Output increased under each of the experimental manipulations during this phase of the research. Output even increased when the experiment was ended and the women went back to the normal working arrangements operated in the main department. The main reasons put forward as an explanation for the results obtained included:

- The special status accruing to the women as a result of having been selected for involvement in the experiment resulted in an increased motivation to co-operate and perform at their best.

Duration of experiment (weeks)	Experimental condition
8	Incentive introduced to reward increased individual effort
5	A morning and afternoon rest period of five minutes allowed
4	Rest periods extended to 10 minutes each
4	Introduction of six five-minute rest periods
11	Introduction of 15-minute morning and 10-minute afternoon rest periods with the company providing refreshments
7	In addition to the two rest periods immediately above finish work at 4.30 pm (30 minutes early)
4	As previous rest periods but finish work at 4.00 pm (60 minutes early)
9	Saturday working eliminated, plus one 15-minute and one 10-minute rest period allowed each day
11	Introduction of 15-minute morning and 10-minute afternoon rest periods with the company providing refreshments
7	In addition to the two rest periods immediately above finish work at 4.30 pm (30 minutes early)
4	As previous rest periods but finish work at 4.00 pm (60 minutes early)
9	Saturday working eliminated, plus one 15-minute and one 10-minute rest period allowed each day

TABLE 6.3 Examples of the experimental conditions used in the relay assembly test room

- The influence of being consulted and kept informed by the experimenter enhanced output as a result of the increased level of participation.
- Morale improved as a result of the general friendliness of the observer and conditions of the experiment.
- The management approach to supervision during the experiment was different from that experienced normally. The increased freedom experienced by the women within the work setting reduced stress and encouraged higher output.
- The group was self-selected, thereby allowing better than normal relationships to create a climate of mutual dependence and support appropriate to team working.

The results of this stage of the experiment encouraged the researchers to seek out the social and other variables operating in the work setting through an extended interview programme.

The interview programme More than 20 000 interviews were conducted in this phase of the research. Among the earlier findings was the suggestion that output and productivity were related to supervision and working conditions. The interview programme was designed to identify employee attitudes and feelings towards these issues using structured questions. However, it quickly became apparent that workers wanted to talk about other aspects of their work. As a response, the process was changed, involving open-ended and non-directive questions. This allowed interviewees to discuss things that they considered important.

There were a number of findings that emerged from the analysis of this vast amount of research data. Employee views about management in general, the company, even society as a whole were obtained. Indications were also obtained that there was a network of informal groups in existence within the organizationally based work teams. These groups were the primary means by which supervisors and leading employees controlled the productive activities and behaviour of other employees within departments. The techniques developed in this stage of the research programme played a significant part in the subsequent introduction of counselling and attitude surveys as part of human resource management practice.

The existence of informal groups within the formal ones, in effect the existence of an organization within an organization, led to the final stage in the research programme, the bank wiring observation room study. This was intended to discover how these informal groups functioned and exercised control.

The bank wiring observation room study This stage of the research consisted of the observation of 14 men employed in a specific department. The men were organized into three teams each consisting of three wirers and a supervisor. In addition, there were two inspectors checking the work of the department as a whole. The observation of this department also identified the existence of two informal groups. These groups did not coincide with the formal structures within the department. Figure 6.3 reflects the composition of these groups, and is based on Roethlisberger and Dickson (1964, p 504). In this figure it can be seen that one supervisor, one wirer and one inspector were not affiliated to either informal group. In addition, two wirers were only partially integrated to the groups. This suggests that not everyone joins (or is allowed to join) an informal group and that the boundaries of such groups are also somewhat fluid.

Group norms
The patterns of behaviour, attitudes and beliefs held by a group and which members are expected to support.

The two informal groups were found to have developed their own behaviour standards or **group norms** as they came to be called. These norms covered a number of features of the work of the department, including the levels of output to be achieved by each person. Much of the activity of the informal groups was intended to control the behaviour of members with the aim of protecting the group from interference by management while maintaining group cohesion. These informal groups also became adept at being able to 'manage' management by providing an impression of activity

FIGURE 6.3

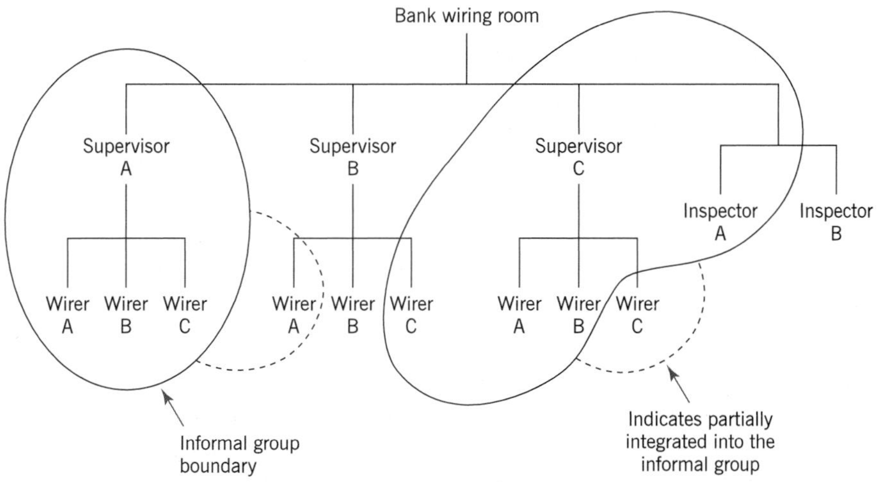

Formal structure and informal groups within the bank wiring observation room

within the department that met the expectations of managers. Output was reported as being constant over the week, even if it had varied on a daily basis. The overall level of output was correctly reported, but the pattern of production was smoothed out. Managers expect consistency (and to achieve what they anticipate) in work activity. Deviation from this expectation becomes a focus of attention and investigation. By 'meeting' that expectation, employees retained effective control over their day-to-day working environment.

The norms of behaviour under which the informal groups operated consisted of a number of rules in which individual workers would be named according to the following criteria:

- *Chisler*. A person who turned out too little work. Someone who was not doing their fair share of work.
- *Rate buster*. A person who produced more than a reasonable volume of work.
- *Squealer*. A person who reported anything to a supervisor that could be to the detriment of a fellow worker.

One rule in the department was that inspectors and supervisors should become part of the informal group structure and not act as part of management. This included an expectation of co-operation with the group in enforcing its norms and not acting in an officious manner. The informal groups reduced the opportunity for members to earn at their maximum level, or at their personally preferred level, in favour of the maintenance of group cohesion. In practice, the group looked after the collective interest of the members, but the price was a loss of individualism and earnings potential.

Within the bank wiring room the group norms and control were enforced through a hierarchy of negative sanctions. These began with light-hearted comments about an individual's output level. If this was not successful in bringing the individual back into line, or if a more serious breach of the norms occurred the comments would become more pointed. This could also include physical contact in the form of tapping on the upper arm, referred to as 'binging'. The inspector who was not part of an informal group in Figure 6.3 considered that he was superior to the wirers and generally acted in an officious manner. The workers played tricks on him with equipment; they ostracized him and generally applied so much social pressure that he asked to be transferred to another department.

There are a number of key findings that emerged from the Hawthorne Studies, including:

- Informal groups inevitably form within formally designated groupings.
- Informal groups will not always match the groupings designated by management.
- Individuals at work are not simply motivated by pay and other tangible benefits.
- Informal groups will seek to manage their managers in order to influence their working environment.
- The rewards that an individual gains from membership of an informal group may be more significant and meaningful to that individual than any benefit that can be obtained from management.
- Informal groups may seek to frustrate management's intentions and objectives.
- The groups to which an individual belongs will have a significant influence on their behaviour and attitudes towards work.
- First-line managers and supervisors are subjected to strong and competing pressures for their affiliations from those above and below.

- Management has little or no influence on the establishment and form or membership of informal groups within the organization.
- Informal groups can engage in activities that are against the interests of the organization as a whole.
- People change their behaviour as a result of being treated differently and observed during research activities – this became known as the Hawthorne effect.

As society changes so too do the forms of control that can be applied successfully. Early approaches to managing relied heavily on coercion and force. This continued, with a small number of notable exceptions, until the time of the Hawthorne Studies, which began a more concerted move towards the humanization of work. The human relations movement, as it became known, was interested in how to adopt a social dimension to work organization and motivation. Another way of thinking about this notion of humanization of work is to consider it as an attempt by managers to maintain control within a changing social environment. It had become apparent that social attitudes and structures were beginning to change and that existing methods of control were not producing levels of output and quality required at an acceptable price. This gap between actual and potential productivity had been demonstrated by Taylor in his application of scientific management. However, given the adverse reaction that his approach generated, alternative ways were needed to achieve improvements in productivity and retain control. The human relations approach offered an opportunity for managers to try and achieve their desired objectives but in a way more acceptable to the workers and therefore more likely to succeed.

GROUP FORMATION AND DEVELOPMENT

Groups do not simply come into existence automatically. If the individuals concerned do not know each other then it is hardly likely that they will be willing or able to immediately perform effectively within the collective context implied by being a member of a group. People need to get to know each other and to determine how they should work together before they can begin to tackle the issues facing the group. This section seeks to review the ways in which groups form and begin to develop the ability to work effectively.

Group formation

Homans (1950) proposed that any group (he used the term social system) existed within an environment consisting of three main elements:

1. *Culture*. The norms, values and goals that make up the shared understandings within which the group will function.
2. *Physical*. The geographical context, involving the actual location and its tangible characteristics, within which the group will operate.
3. *Technological*. This relates to the facilities etc. that the group will have access to in pursuing its activities.

Homans argued that this environment imposed a range of activities and interactions on the individuals and groups within the system. For example, call centre staff are required to interact with customers using the pre-prepared script and prompts held in the computer systems that they use. Homans called this the 'external system'. As a consequence of these impositions, a variety of emotions and attitudes are engendered among the members towards the environment and the other participants. For example, call centre staff may change the tone of their voice to signal frustration rather than maintain the enthusiastic approach demanded by managers. This, Homans called the 'internal system'. He also suggested that frequent interaction between people would lead to a more positive attitude and a better relationship between them. The converse was also true, that is, better attitudes lead to a higher frequency of interaction. This chain of events and reactions leads to the formation of a group (see Figure 6.4).

With an increased level of interaction Homans observed a tendency for individuals to develop attitudes and emotions not dictated by the external system. This led to the development of new frames of reference and norms emerging between the individuals concerned. In turn these embellishments produced new activities not specified by the external system – in effect the development of informal groups within the system. Homans suggested a number of features of these external and internal systems:

- *The external and internal systems are mutually dependent*. A change in one will produce a change in the other. For example, a change in work structure (formal group) can change the patterns of interaction between individuals (informal group). Conversely, attitudes in the internal system can influence the way in which work gets done.
- *The two systems and the environment are mutually dependent*. Individuals will mould and adapt work activities to suit themselves. Multidisciplinary project teams are an example of this process, incorporating the opportunity to tap into the internal system as well as the external.

Homans' theory is an important view of how groups are formed for two reasons. First, it stresses the mutual dependency between the many elements associated with the existence of groups. Second, it exposes the distinction between behaviour required by the environment and external system and the emergence of behaviour not required by the formal system, but equally significant.

FIGURE 6.4

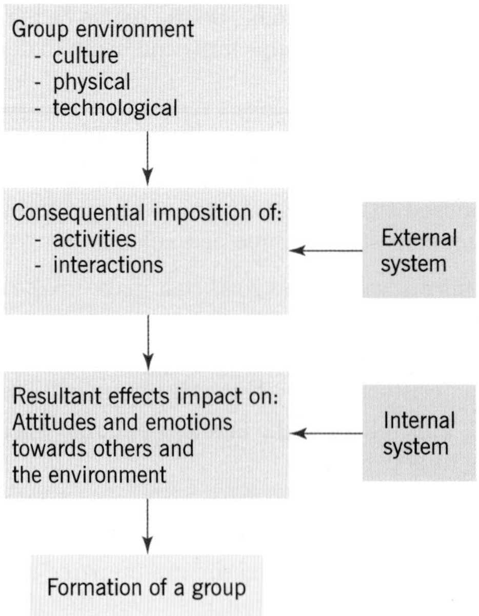

Homan's explanation of group formation

MANAGEMENT IN ACTION 6.4 Family fortunes

Family enterprises account for 76 per cent of all UK companies, but only 30 per cent of family companies make it to the second generation. Although losing a job is a common experience today, it is not often that a son is dismissed by his father. But that was just what happened to Bill Jordan in 1980. Bill was one of the two sons of the chairman, William, working in the company at board level. The company at that time was a cereal maker and flour miller and had been established in 1855 by the same family. The two sons wanted to develop the business further into the breakfast cereal and muesli bar markets and the rest of the family board wanted to remain with the traditional markets of flour milling and animal feed.

The two sons, Bill and Dave were called to a board meeting and were dismissed from the company by the other board members, consisting of their father, mother and another family member. It was a shattering experience for both sides. Once the dust had settled, the two brothers were allowed to buy out the cereal side of the business and run it totally separately. The cereal company has done very well since then, much better than the original company. The cereal company has grown from £4m turnover in 1980 to £50m in 2002. In 2002, the two brothers are stepping down from full-time management, handing the reins over to two non-family executives.

This was a difficult decision for the board to make, but it was the right one for the parties and allowed both sides to subsequently get along much better once the split had been made. This is not a decision that is made easily or frequently enough according to specialists in the field of helping family firms deal with crises. Too often families are intent on keeping power and control within the family, even if this is at the expense of commercial success. However, there are advantages to family firms, according to Professor John Ward of the Kellogg Graduate School of Management in Illinois. Family firms tend to be often able to take decisions quickly and are more resilient in times of recession as they can cut back their own 'profit' in order to help the company survive. They are not hampered by shareholders who may have short term objectives in mind rather than the long term interests of the company, its employees and customers. Family firms also spend more on research and development than externally owned counterparts. The directors of family firms tend to be more loyal to the company and that seeps down through the organization into the entire workforce. Passing the business on to the next generation becomes a prized objective of the current board members, rather than simply making more profit in the short term. There is also a feeling, particularly in the USA that the family model reflects a better corporate model than that implied by a faceless corporation.

Adapted from: Blackhurst, C (2002) Family Fortunes, *Management Today*, May, pp 54–63

Stop ↔ Consider

Are families that run a business a special form of group or team? Justify your views. What special group problems might occur in a family organization and how would you propose that they be dealt with? How would you persuade the family members to support your proposals?

Group development

The existence of a group is no guarantee that it will be an effective or meaningful arrangement for either the organization or individual members. This is clearly demonstrated in Management in Action 6.4, which considers one family firm in which problems at board level between family members caused a total split in the company as it was then.

Groups do not automatically become effective at meeting their objectives and satisfying the needs of the individuals concerned. Consider for a moment an organization that you have encountered. This could be your university or a company that you have worked for. Reflect on the groups that you were part of. It should quickly become apparent that within an organization a number of different groups and collections of individuals exist. For example:

- *There exist a number of units within an organization that would not qualify as a group.* Just because individuals work on similar activities and are classified as part of the same department does not qualify them as a group. For example, it is not uncommon in universities for some lecturing staff in the same department never to meet or even know each other if their academic interests and work commitments never require them to interact.
- *Within formal units in an organization there may exist a number of smaller, formal and informal groups.* For example, a large department may contain a number of sub-sections.
- *Within organizations there will exist a number of informal groups.* Friendship groupings and task-dependent networks across formal boundaries are common examples.
- *Some groups (formal and informal) will be relatively permanent.* For example, a project group may be formed to design and build a new oil refinery, which might take several years.
- *Some groups (formal and informal) will be transient.* Such formal groups are widely used within organizations as task forces or problem-solving groups, usually for specific issues. For example, a task force to report in three months on recommendations for cutting 10 per cent from travel expenses. Informal groups in this category tend to form in response to particular events. For example, employees may form a committee to fight the closure of a particular department.

Each of these possibilities presents different behavioural situations. It is therefore impossible to present a single comprehensive theory of how all groups develop. In some cases it is the existing members of a group who must adapt to new circumstances. In other cases it is individuals who become new members of an existing group. In other situations it is a collection of individuals who must become a group to undertake a particular task. There are two main approaches that offer an insight as to how groups develop, but both assume the creation of a new group. It is not clear the degree to which these stages apply in other situations, for example when a new member joins an existing group.

Group development
Process of individuals coming together to form a group capable of achieving both task and member satisfaction.

Bass and Ryterband (1979) identify a four-stage model of **group development**:

1. *Initial development of trust and membership.* Individuals coming together for the first time need to learn to trust each other and to feel confident enough to contribute to the activities within the group.
2. *Beginning of communication and decision making.* Once trust begins to develop and the individuals are able to communicate more easily mutual dependence emerges. This allows decisions to be made and problems to be solved.
3. *Performance improvement.* In the previous stage conflicts can arise between individuals as the group norms are being developed. In this third stage, these teething problems have been largely overcome and the effectiveness of the group improves. Individuals focus on the work of the group and become collectively motivated to achieve the objectives.
4. *Ongoing maintenance and control.* At this stage individuals have become accustomed to working together on routine group activities. Consequently,

there is a degree of independence between members and flexibility in adapting to new situations.

This model has a number of similarities to the better known work of Tuckman, who in 1965 described a four-stage model of group development. Tuckman and Jensen (1977) subsequently added a stage to the basic model. The five stages are as follows:

- *Stage 1 Forming*. This stage occurs when the individuals first come together. It involves each individual getting to know the others, their attitudes, personalities and backgrounds. Individuals use this stage to make a personal impact within the group. It is also likely that anxiety is felt by the individuals as they attempt to define their position within the group. This process also begins to define the hierarchy and **roles** that will exist within the group.
- *Stage 2 Storming*. As a formal structure begins to emerge and individuals begin to feel more confidence in their position within the group, conflict arises. Individuals begin to bring to the group their own agenda. Issues begin to emerge as the group storms its way towards the next stage. If successfully handled, this stage leads to a more focused group in terms of relationships between the members and the ease with which it can achieve its goals. Not all groups successfully negotiate their way through this stage and lingering problems can continue to inhibit progression. In extreme cases groups can collapse at this stage.
- *Stage 3 Norming*. This stage reflects the process of establishing the norms to be operated within the group. This includes the behavioural standards among members, for example to allow (or prevent) jokes and other diversions. Also the procedural rules that provide the group with its operating framework are developed. Someone with a hidden agenda may also seek to introduce items that allow them to achieve their objectives. This process has recently been explored in terms of the evolution from general to an operational state in small groups involved in computer based teamwork, Graham (2003).
- *Stage 4 Performing*. Only when the group has successfully completed the three previous stages can it make significant progress in its work. In that sense the group is now mature and able to operate effectively.
- *Stage 5 Adjourning*. This stage involves the dissolution of a group, having achieved its objectives. Frequently, at this stage a period of reflection and reorientation is undertaken as individuals consider past glories and anticipate future success.

Roles
The behaviours and job activities undertaken by an individual as a result of their organizational duties and responsibilities.

In practice, a group may not successfully negotiate itself through one of these five stages. Any unresolved difficulties carried forward will result in problems at subsequent stages. For example, a lack of clarity on humour is likely to result in frustration as some people tell jokes while others resent the diversion. The ability of individuals to progress items from a hidden agenda can be another major source of difficulty and friction for a group if it is not dealt with effectively. The consequences of these factors being a reduction in the level of effectiveness or member satisfaction within a group.

Group norms are the means through which a group regulates the behaviour of its members. The norms of behaviour become internalized by the individuals and institutionalized in the accepted patterns of behaviour. They provide a powerful group mechanism through which to release time and energy in order to concentrate on important issues. Imagine if a group had to establish behaviour standards and codes of conduct every time it convened. The goals would never be met. Conversely, the workings of a group can become overly concentrated on establishing norms and regulating the behaviour of its members. Some committees fall into this trap by concentrating on procedural matters and minutes, losing sight of the objectives to be achieved.

Feldman (1984) suggests that groups will adopt a satisficing approach to regulating individual behaviour, unless:

- Group survival is at risk. If the behaviour of an individual threatens the group, then they will be dealt with.
- Lack of clarity in the expected behaviour of group members is creating problems in group activity or performance.
- By taking action the group can avoid bringing into the open things that it would be embarrassing or difficult to resolve.
- The central values held by the group are being threatened. If by allowing something to continue the status of a group might be compromised then action would be taken.

The following Employee Perspective (6.3) reflects life as an employee in a department that is not a cohesive unit and where factionalism has taken hold.

In this section we have described how groups develop to the point that would allow them to function effectively. But that is only one aspect of a group that needs to be considered. Athanasaw (2003) for example, demonstrates that for public sector organizations, individual factors such as years of work experience, frequency of team participation, type of team training received and volunteering for team membership were the key factors for effective team membership in cross-functional teams. In addition, there exist a number of roles within most groups. Formal groups have formal structures, the chair and the secretary etc. Informal groups often have informal roles within them such as an organizer to arrange social events. They are the dominant individuals who lead the activities and direction of the informal group.

EMPLOYEE PERSPECTIVE 6.3 Is it a cohesive department or not?

The industrial engineering department in a medium sized food company in the North of England was responsible for all productivity developments and incentive schemes within the factory. It was a small department of five people, headed by a manager who had been with the company for twenty years and who had drifted into the job after working in several departments within the company. He was aged 60 and was due to retire in about three years. The other members of the department varied in age from 25 years to about 45 years old. They also had differing levels of service within the company ranging from five years to less than three months.

They did not get on well together as a group of people supposed to be working towards common objectives. Some of the staff had considerable experience as industrial engineers and resented the fact that the manager of the department did not have any professional qualifications or experience outside of the company. Some of the staff were serious minded individuals who resented those members who liked to enjoy a laugh and joke at work. The allocation of work projects was also an issue for resentment in the department as it was thought that some individuals were the favourites of the manager and given preferential treatment.

Some individuals would take every opportunity to undermine colleagues by suggesting to people outside the department that their work was not of the highest standard and that better recommendations could have been developed. Senior management of the company tolerated this situation for a while, but eventually decided that something had to be done, but what?

Tasks

1. How would you react and what would you do if you found yourself working in this department?
2. What does your understanding of group development suggest might be wrong and what could be done to correct the situation, if anything?

ROLE THEORY AND GROUP STRUCTURE

In formal groups the structure of the group may be dictated by the situation. For example, a department (or project team) will be created, designed and the members designated by management. The individual members have little direct say in who will be appointed to the team and what role they will perform. In other situations, particularly informal groups, the membership is self-selected and members have a greater influence on both structure and roles. Many groups within an organization are comprised of representatives of other groups or departments, perhaps even from outside the organization itself. Consequently, these representatives are subject to report-back requirements and direction from their sponsoring groups. This can sometimes create conflict between personal, professional and group loyalty for the individuals concerned.

There are a number of ways of considering group structure. For example, Huczynski and Buchanan (2001) identify a number of dimensions on which the structure of a group is dependent:

- *Status*. The reflection of the value placed upon particular positions within the group. Specific roles can also reflect the value of a particular person in the eyes of other people. For example, a major celebrity can perform a useful role in attracting recognition for a charity when appointed as president.
- *Power*. The ability to influence other people. This can either be a function of the position of a person or a reflection of personal influence.
- *Liking*. The personal affiliations among members of a group. It is inevitable that individuals will prefer the company (and ideas) of people they like at a personal level and distance themselves from people that they do not like. This affects the patterns of communication within the group.
- *Role*. This concept refers to the behaviours that accompany a particular function or position within a group. The roles that exist, or that people identify for themselves, determine to a significant extent the behaviour patterns that they engage in.
- *Leadership*. The style adopted by the leader of a group can also have a distinct influence on events within that group.

Belbin (1993) identifies nine **team roles** that, it is suggested, determine the performance of a group. While detailed consideration of this will be held over until the next chapter, it is appropriate to introduce the ideas here because they contain a relevance to the structural aspects of group activity. The roles themselves (see Table 6.4) cover the main requirements of group structure and also provide, according to Belbin, for the achievement of high performance.

Team roles
Model consisting of nine roles that exist within a group including plant, resource investigator, implementer and completer.

It should be apparent that in addition to role definitions, structural issues (as indicated in the Huczynski and Buchanan framework) can be detected in the Belbin views on how a group will function. The Belbin roles also identify the primary weaknesses common within each role. These he describes as allowable weaknesses that are inevitable but can be controlled or tolerated. The Belbin model also allows for the possibility of a mismatch between formal organizational status and group membership role. Management in Action 6.5 includes a review of the Belbin model and how it can be incorporated into a team development approach.

Another way of looking at the notion of roles within an organizational context is to consider the implications in terms of the individual concerned. For most people their primary role within an organization is defined by the job description. This document sets out what tasks and responsibilities are expected from the post-holder. The job

Expected role
The specific role that an individual is to fulfil, frequently specified in a job description.

Perceived role
What the individual understands their role to be.

Enacted role
What the individual actually does in fulfilling their role responsibilities.

Role set
The roles around a focal role.

description therefore defines the **expected role** for the individual, at least as far as the organization, customers, suppliers and other employees are concerned. For example, to know that someone holds a job with the title of personnel manager would immediately convey a range of expectations about what that person should do at work.

However, that is not the end of the matter, because individuals are not simply a function of other people's expectations. Each individual will interpret the expected role in terms of their personality characteristics and a range of other factors such as past experience, beliefs and intentions. In effect they must perceive the expected role and interpret it for themselves. This has been referred to as the **perceived role** in which the individual brings to the job their own understanding of it. Finally, there is the **enacted role**, which reflects what the individual actually does in carrying out the tasks for which they are responsible. It reflects their actual behaviour on the job.

According to Handy (1993) role theory consists of a number of components. They include:

- *Role set*. The **role set** reflects the people, or more accurately the other roles, surrounding the individual forming the basis of the analysis. For example, the

Roles and descriptions – team role contribution	Allowable weaknesses
Plant: Creative, imaginative, unorthodox. Solves difficult problems	Ignores details. Too preoccupied to communicate effectively
Resource investigator: Extrovert, enthusiastic, communicative. Explores opportunities. Develops contacts	Over-optimistic. Loses interest once initial enthusiasm has passed
Co-ordinator: Mature, confident, a good chairperson. Clarifies goals, promotes decision making, delegates well	Can be seen as manipulative. Delegates personal work
Shaper: Challenging, dynamic, thrives on pressure. Has the drive and courage to overcome obstacles	Can provoke others. Hurt people's feelings
Monitor/evaluator: Sober, strategic and discerning. Sees all options. Judges accurately	Lacks drive and ability to inspire others. Overly critical
Teamworker: Co-operative, mild, perceptive and diplomatic. Listens, builds, averts friction, calms the waters	Indecisive in crunch situations. Can be easily influenced
Implementer: Disciplined, reliable, conservative and efficient. Turns ideas into practical actions	Somewhat inflexible. Slow to respond to new possibilities
Completer: Painstaking, conscientious, anxious. Searches out errors and omissions. Delivers on time	Inclined to worry unduly. Reluctant to delegate. Can be a nit-picker
Specialist: Single-minded, self-starting, dedicated. Provides knowledge and skills in rare supply.	Contributes on only a narrow front. Dwells on technicalities. Overlooks the 'big picture'

TABLE 6.4 The nine Belbin team roles (*source*: Belbin, M (1993) *Team Roles at Work*, Butterworth Heinemann, Oxford with permission from Elsevier)

MANAGEMENT IN ACTION 6.5 How to build teams

Based on the work of Belbin, Fowler suggests that ten is a satisfactory number of members in a management or project team. For a complex topic involving intensive work on a clear issue, six members represents a good number. Over 12 members and groups tend to subdivide. With only three or four members any group is unlikely to have the range of team skills necessary and may be dominated by a single personality. Naturally there are many varied and practical reasons why a group may not adhere to these principles. For example, a management group will consist of as many members as report to the chief executive, irrespective of size. The role that specific members adopt in a group will also be determined to a significant extent by their purpose in that group. For example, in a negotiating group a trade union representative is there to represent the interests of members, not to help managers to find ways of meeting their objectives.

The work of Belbin on team roles offers one way of helping to ensure that there is a balance of skill within the group. Managers should be able to display some flexibility in team roles. In some team situations they will be expected to take a lead role, whereas in others they will be subordinate to more senior managers. This requires team training if team membership is to be effective. Fowler identifies two forms of team training:

1. Team theory training. This involves the training of individuals in recognizing their own team style and that of others. It would also involve an understanding of team dynamics. This type of training is an individual approach and need not involve a particular team being trained at the same time.
2. Team-building training. This type of training should involve the entire team. It attempts to create a team from a group of individuals. It should also be specific to the project or purpose for which the group has been established. This approach frequently uses outdoor or simulation training as a means of putting teams into situations in which they must learn to depend on, support and encourage each other.

Team training is not simply restricted to the start of a project; it is something that should be ongoing if the group is to avoid becoming stale. For example, a long-standing management group might take time out every few months to review how well it is performing as a group, perhaps with the support of a skilled consultant.

Adapted from: Fowler, A (1992) How to build teams, *PM Plus*, March, pp 25–7

Stop ↔ Consider

Identify the implications of the Belbin model for the recruitment, selection, training, development and career progression issues within an organization.
What might your analysis of the first question imply about the ability or even desirability of seeking to design groups?

role set for a university lecturer might contain the roles and people reflected in Figure 6.5.

- *Role definition.* The **role definition** is based on the role expectation discussed earlier and sets out what the role of the focal person should be. Job descriptions and common knowledge were introduced as the basis of role expectations but they are not the only signals used to define a particular role. Uniforms, badges of rank, office location, style and equipment are all signals of the expected role of the person occupying the role.
- *Role ambiguity.* This reflects the degree of **role ambiguity** in the minds of the role set as to exactly what their respective roles should be at any point in time. For example, a subordinate going to a meeting with an unpredictable boss might not know their role until the boss makes clear what their respective roles should be on that particular occasion. On one occasion the subordinate might be

Role definition
The sum total of things that define a particular role, including job description, uniforms, badges of rank and office location.

FIGURE 6.5

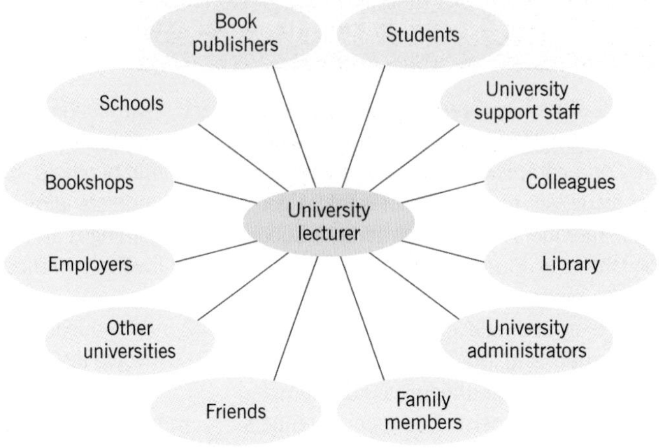

Role set of a university lecturer

Role ambiguity
The degree of ambiguity among individuals as to exactly what their role should be at any point in time.

Role incompatibility
Incompatible expectations between members of the role set about their respective roles.

Role conflict
Arises as a result of a range of conflicting role requirements acting on an individual at the same time.

Role overload/underload
Arise when an individual has either too many roles, or not enough roles for their existing capability.

Role stress
The level of stress experienced by individuals as they act out the various roles allocated to them.

expected to be humble, contrite and accept that the boss was not happy with something and be prepared to be told off without question. On other occasions they might be expected to be outgoing, jovial and prepared to join in the fun that the boss has decided to engage in. Clearly to engage in inappropriate role behaviour (the enacted role) would cause problems for both parties to the encounter.

- *Role incompatibility.* This reflects incompatible expectations between members of the role set about their respective roles. **Role incompatibility** reflects an aspect of the perceived role discussed earlier. A manager might expect subordinates to accept every instruction without question, whereas the subordinates might expect to have a much higher degree of freedom over their work activities. These two expectations are clearly incompatible and need to be resolved if conflict is to be avoided. The following Employee Perspective (6.4) reflects one female's story about being an executive and her treatment at the hands of male colleagues.
- *Role conflict.* This arises as a result of the conflicting role requirements acting on an individual at the same time. For example, a manager is expected to support and help subordinates as well as achieve objectives with a finite level of resources. Clearly, these two realities come into conflict on occasions – **role conflict**. A subordinate may be experiencing personal or medical problems and not be able to perform at full capacity during a prolonged period. However, the manager may not have the budget to allow additional staffing to maintain the output objectives and so need to pressure the individual to do more work, which will conflict with their desire to help the person.
- *Role overload/underload.* These situations arise when an individual is either faced with too many roles, each competing for pre-eminence (**role overload**), or they do not have enough role-demand placed upon them for their existing capability (**role underload**). Many managers (particularly women) faced with the competing demands of work and home roles find that they cannot achieve a satisfactory balance between them and so they experience role stress and other problems. Similarly an individual who considers themselves to be underloaded becomes bored and frustrated because they feel underutilized and undervalued.
- *Role stress.* Each of the role concepts discussed can lead to **role stress** under certain circumstances. It is generally considered that a certain degree of stress is

EMPLOYEE PERSPECTIVE 6.4 The female manager's story

This example is an interview with a senior female executive, quoted by Milwid (1987, p 113). It clearly demonstrates one of the potential difficulties of being a woman, and an executive.

> At one time or another, I've been propositioned by two of the six executives in this company, a couple of times by employees and managers who work for me, and more times than I can count by customers or field people. It's happened frequently enough now that it doesn't bother me.
>
> The first time it happened, it bothered me a lot because then I felt like they were discounting me. I thought that to them I wasn't a whole person anymore. I was just the person in the centrefold. I felt then that somehow their interest in me sexually meant that I wasn't powerful or that I wasn't being professional.
>
> Now, I just think it means they think I'm attractive. And I like that. I don't lead them on, because that's unfair. If I'm not interested in them, I'm not interested. But being a sexually alive person doesn't mean you're not powerful, and it certainly doesn't mean you aren't capable.

Tasks

1. Is this how you would react if you found yourself being propositioned by colleagues or customers? If not, how would you feel and why?
2. To what extent and how could teamwork exclude the sexual aspect of being human?
3. What if anything could be done to deal with this type of experience within an organization?

necessary if effective performance is to be achieved. There is an old saying in organizations that if you want something done give it to a busy person. The logic being that busy people have to be organized and that they develop a level of efficiency which a person who is not busy does not achieve. However, what is not clear is the desirable level of stress either for efficient working or to allow an individual to be able to cope without danger to themselves or others. What is clear, however, is that role stress can result in poor performance, health problems and a host of other difficulties for both individuals and organizations. Stress is a topic which will be covered in detail in a later chapter.

JOB DESIGN, TECHNOLOGY AND TEAMS

Usually jobs are thought to be the preserve of an individual, as reflected in the job description. However, that need not always be the case. There is a specific chapter in this text devoted to the topic of job design and so it will not be explored in detail here. However, group working comes in many different forms and can be found in many different situations. There are many reasons why groups can be used in job design including the reality that in many situations more than one person does the same job and, therefore, it may make sense to group such activities together into teams. Also it may be used as part of a specific organizational design process. For example, management may create multidisciplinary work teams focused on particular customer groups or categories, rather than employ the traditional functional structure.

Autonomous work groups
A team with the freedom to organize its own resources, pace of work and allocation of responsibility within the group.

Teamworking is sometimes described as **autonomous work groups**. This form of team activity is based around the ideas that a group would accept responsibility for a specific part of the overall task to be undertaken and would then have the freedom to organize its internal activities based on the wishes of the members. This freedom can include the sequencing of activity, the pace of work, the arrangement of rest periods, responsibility for supervision and quality monitoring together with the appointment and training of new members. The most famous examples of autonomous work groups in practice are the applications in the motor industry by companies such as Saab and Volvo. Valery (1974) indicates that there have been some 1000 different attempts by Swedish organizations to introduce novel forms of work organization intended to improve productivity and job satisfaction.

Another form of teamworking is to be found in the motor industry in the UK. Garrahan and Stewart (1992) describe the approaches to teamworking in the Nissan car factory in Sunderland. In this approach production teams do not have the opportunity to design the work of the team, but they are expected to co-operate strongly in producing a dynamic and self-regulating group intended to produce at the highest levels of productivity and quality. Within the production groups each member is expected to accept responsibility for the work of other team members and to point out the errors and faults produced by team members in a process of continual improvement.

Of course, there are many forms of simple teamworking that do not go as far as requiring the specific redesign of existing single-person jobs. For example, many college lecturers work as part of a course team. The team might meet to design a degree programme and to determine who should teach which modules. Thereafter, the team members would go their separate ways in designing and delivering each module, only coming together as a group to review progress, solve particular problems and to standardize marks. In a medical context, there are likely to be many professionals involved in developing the treatment plan for a specific patient. They will inevitably function as a group in the process of the determination of the plan, but will function as individuals in delivering specific aspects of the treatment.

Technology is another area in which job design and teamworking is influenced. In many cases the introduction of technology to a work situation fundamentally changes the design of the jobs that people undertake. It also frequently relegates the role of many people to machine minders and monitors of automatic processes. In these situations it can often be the team who decide the task allocation between members in order to reduce the boredom and monotony involved.

GROUP FORMATION AND STRUCTURE: AN APPLIED PERSPECTIVE

Groups are of particular significance to managers and organizations as well as the individuals who belong to them. There are a number of reasons for this, including:

- *The process of management involves the management of groups.* This could be a section, a team, a factory, or even a whole organization made up of many groups. Yet managers cannot directly manage all of the groups for which they are responsible. **Delegated authority** provides for subordinates to take responsibility for the management of specific committees or defined areas of work activity, it involves managers devolving some of their power.

Delegated authority
An action by managers in which they give some of their authority for decision making to subordinates.

- *Managers must be part of some of the groups that they manage.* Recall the Hawthorne Studies. There were supervisors working in the sections within which the research was being conducted. The group pressure on them to conform to group norms placed the individuals in a difficult position because of the potential for divided loyalties. This is a pressure still found in all first-line supervisory jobs. It is common for first-line supervisors to be titled team leaders today. However, their importance is frequently undervalued by senior managers as they are not regarded as completely part of the management team. Neither does the workforce regard them as full members of their groups, but they do recognize the ability of first-line managers to act as a filter between workers and management. This was recognized by the Hawthorne workers in their behaviour towards supervisors.

- *Managers are part of a management group in addition to any others to which they belong.*
- *There are moves towards managers* **empowering** *employees.* This is usually described in terms of pushing decision making and responsibility down to the lowest level possible within the organization. Often this is part of a business process re-engineering or **downsizing** exercise. One form of this process is the **self-managed team**. However, it is a movement that demands different approaches to control, and can lead to new difficulties between groups and managers. For example delegated authority as indicated above is one variant of conventional management responsibility.
- *Individuals spend a considerable proportion of their lives within organizations and much of this time and energy is spent in some form of group activity.* Consequently individuals invest heavily in the organizations and groups to which they belong. Not surprisingly individuals do not like to feel that they are wasting their time and energy and so seek to achieve some return on their investment, whether this is through formal or informal groups depends upon the situation and the individual.

Empowering
Employees are given the freedom (within defined boundaries) to take action without the need to seek approval.

Downsizing
Processes which involve the elimination of jobs or organizational levels to achieve a stronger customer focus.

Self-managed team
A work team in which the team leader is appointed from within the group by the members not management.

It is not uncommon for individuals to seek out personal or career benefits from group membership. Such behaviour is political in that the individual is attempting to manipulate events to their advantage. Promotion opportunities can be enhanced by membership of the 'right' committees and by being seen to be active on successful projects. It is perhaps cynical, but essentially true, that once it becomes apparent that a project is likely to be successful, people previously not involved suddenly want to be associated with it. Conversely, if there is a danger of the failure of a project, people actively begin to distance themselves from it. Management is a political process. Managers are continually in competition with other managers for resources, influence and recognition. Promotion, and, in times of recession (or delayering) continued employment, frequently depends on being able to deliver objectives with reduced resources. The ability to squeeze additional productivity out of subordinates is a prized ability. Indeed one phrase common in management circles these days is the term 'sweating the resource' which refers to the need/ability to get maximum output (more than could be expected) from a particular resource. Resource in this context does not only apply to people, it can also be money, equipment, raw materials, etc. It is from this perspective that the ability to manipulate the use of groups (both formal and informal) to achieve objectives within an organizational setting gains political significance.

The significance of formal groups is self-evident, in that some form of compartmentalization of activity is necessary to carry out the work of an organization. Informal groups are also an inherent part of organizational life, they exist irrespective of management intentions. In situations where management is not trusted by employees, the emergence of a shadow organization (see for example, Stacey, 2000, p 386) might more directly challenge the ability of managers to manage. Managers therefore need to develop an understanding of the importance of groups within an organization as well as an insight into issues such as how they form and function as well as how they can go wrong, a topic for the next chapter.

Within an organization the groups that exist are constantly subject to change. New people join a department; existing members leave or are transferred to other duties; existing groups are reformulated as the tasks for which they were established change; and new groups are created as new tasks emerge. It is within this constantly changing milieu that managers must provide a framework of consistency and stability. Of course, not everything is changing all the time. But there is a steady flow of people and task related change, sufficient to create instability and lack of security, particularly in large organizations. It is partly for these reasons that the autonomous work group has significance as they contain the ability to absorb a significant degree of organizational functioning into the team, thereby reducing the load on managers. It is in an attempt to provide stability within an otherwise changing environment that groups have a significant part to play. Rather like the individual strands of a spider's web the relationships formed within a group can help to provide strength in times of difficulty. If the individual strands in a spider's web become broken, then all is not lost, the damage can quickly be repaired and normality restored. Similarly, within an organization the groups that exist can provide task and personal support to individual members as well as continuity of operational activity. One of the possible implications of this is that the groups so formed become self-sustaining in ways that management would prefer did not happen. For example, Rentsch and Steel (2003) propose research into absence levels, including the effects of culture and work team on the absence behaviour of members.

Managers find themselves in a number of different groups as part of their work. They also manage many groups in order to meet the objectives of their position. It is not uncommon to find that managers ignore the formation and structural aspects of the teams that they create. It is often assumed that the roles within formal groups will naturally overcome any difficulties and deliver what is expected of them. Informal groups are frequently ignored as nothing to do with the organization, irrelevant, an inconvenience, or of little practical impact. Clearly most of these assumptions are questionable, or even false.

The challenge for managers is to provide the formal groupings within the organization that will allow the necessary activities to be undertaken while at the same time retaining some control or influence over the informal groups. Given the nature of informal groups as they have been described in this chapter, it should be apparent that their very nature makes this an almost impossible objective. It could be argued that the very existence of informal groups is a function of management's attempt to maintain control. In other words, an informal group is an employee response to ensure a degree of independence from management domination in what can be described as a coercive employment relationship. The freedom of employees is severely constrained within most organizational situations. They are appointed to particular positions, with a job description that defines the expected role. Consequently the informal group provides a counterbalance to that externally defined behaviour control.

It can be suggested that the informal group is therefore a mechanism through which individuals seek to achieve a personal level of social meaning in a context where so much of the contact and activity is dictated by others. The individual usually has little opportunity to influence events in the working environment and the emergence of social arrangements that meet the needs of the individuals more effectively is hardly surprising. For example, the nature of the job to be done is prescribed by management, the colleagues with whom one works are appointed by management, the physical working environment is designed and provided by management and the standards of performance are set by management. Consequently, the formation of informal groups provides the opportunity for individuals to display a little of themselves in what is a largely prescribed situation. The following Employee Perspective (6.5) demonstrates just how much control informal groups can have over work activities in some situations.

Perhaps, therefore, the challenge facing most managers is not one of how to control the formation of formal and informal groups, but rather how to direct the energies of the groups that do exist in the interests of the organization. In the formal groups that exist management should consider the features of the group that might be expected to influence the outcome. In the context of this chapter, this could include the purpose,

EMPLOYEE PERSPECTIVE 6.5 The team controls the work

Factory work can be boring and monotonous. Employees must work at the pace of the assembly line or machine, with output levels closely prescribed and monitored by management. It is not surprising that factory workers will try anything to break the boredom and relentless grind of the controlled activity in a factory. In a particular factory a large paint-spraying machine was approximately 100 metres long and required a team of 24 people to keep it running. There were only 18 workstations on the machine, but the staffing plan was that six people would float between jobs, thereby allowing everyone to take a break whilst keeping the machine running.

In practice four people would be in the mess room for their entire shift running a card syndicate. Everyone else in the work team would take shorter breaks and simply drop in and out of the card game as their breaks allowed. A different team of four people would be informally 'rostered' each day so that over a period everyone had the total break time allowed by the company. The team achieved their allowed breaks in a way not intended (or approved) by management. Gambling was not allowed by the company either, but this did not bother the workers. Supervisors also turned a blind eye to the process as long as the work was completed and productivity was at acceptable levels.

Tasks

1. As an existing employee, imagine that you had been transferred to a job on the machine described. Would you be happy to go along with the break system described? What would you do if you were not a card player?
2. What would you do if you were a new employee to the company who had been allocated to work on that machine?
3. Should management ignore such adjustments to official policy and intentions? What if an accident occurred and the injured party claimed that they had been working too long and were tired as a consequence?

composition and other group formation issues discussed. If the formal groups are to be effective in achieving their objectives then issues such as the Belbin team roles and the Tuckman and Jensen stages of group development need to be taken into account in order to ensure that the potential for success is provided. In the case of informal groups, managers can to a small extent utilize their existence to the benefit of the organization without appearing to exert covert control. For example, the provision of social facilities for employees can provide an opportunity for interaction among employees that can offset the givens within the organization. The use of group working as the basis of task achievement can also provide an appearance of lack of management control, which if linked with appropriate socialization and training can direct employees' behaviour in company preferred directions.

CONCLUSIONS

This chapter has considered the research into the significance of groups along with the effects of group membership on organizational activity. It is clear that groups, both formal and informal, are significant in terms of organizational activity, employee and management functioning. However, there are still many areas of research to be explored in defining how groups function across all the variables involved. The existence of groups within organizations is closely associated with the need for managers to exercise control over the processes for which they are responsible. It could be argued that informal groups are a natural reaction to that situation. That groups are formed and have structure has been established in this chapter; it is now appropriate to go on to consider issues such as group dynamics and performance in the next chapter.

Now to summarize this chapter in terms of the relevant Learning Objectives:

- **Outline the concept of a group as distinct from a team or a collection of individuals.** This chapter suggests that a group consists of two or more people who are psychologically aware of each other and interact in such a way that each influences and is influenced by the others. The notion of a team implies a small, cohesive group that works effectively as a single unit through being focused on a common task. Belbin also suggests that there are crucial differences between the two in how people are selected for membership and the nature of leadership. Katzenbach and Smith draw these ideas together by suggesting that a positive correlation exists between the type of team or group and the levels of performance achieved.
- **Understand the differences between formal and informal groups.** Formal groups within an organization are created specifically to achieve objectives as part of the need to integrate the skills and capabilities of a number of people and the need to compartmentalize activity. Informal groups emerge naturally as a result of interpersonal, social and common-purpose needs of individuals operating within a largely constrained and formal organizational framework. Informal groups sometimes emerge as a result of the need for individuals to achieve their job objectives by interacting with other employees outside of the formal arrangements provided, or in order to influence the priorities of other people. Management have little influence over the range and type of informal groups that emerge in an organization, yet such groups can be very influential in the way that the organization functions.
- **Describe the Hawthorne Studies and their significance in understanding the nature of groups.** The studies within the Hawthorne works can be separated into four stages and each is described in detail in the appropriate section of the chapter:

  1. The illumination experiments
  2. The relay assembly test room study
  3. The interview programme
  4. The bank wiring observation room study.

  There are a number of key findings that emerged from the Hawthorne Studies, including:

  1. Informal groups inevitably form within formally designated groupings.
  2. Informal groups will not always match the groupings designated by management.
  3. Individuals at work are not simply motivated by pay and other tangible benefits.
  4. Informal groups will seek to manage their managers in order to influence their working environment.
  5. The rewards that an individual gains from membership of an informal group may be more significant and meaningful to that individual than any benefit that can be obtained from management.
  6. Informal groups may seek to frustrate management's intentions and objectives.
  7. The groups to which an individual belongs will have a significant influence on their behaviour and attitudes towards work.
  8. First-line managers and supervisors are subjected to strong and competing pressures for their affiliations from those above and below.
  9. Management has little or no influence on the establishment and form or membership of informal groups within the organization.
  10. Informal groups can engage in competitive activities that are against the interests of the organization as a whole.
- **Discuss the nature and value of role theory together with its relevance to the structure of groups and teams.** There a different ways of thinking about the roles that people perform within a group. One considers role to equate with the formal designation of a job within a group, for example, treasurer or secretary. Another way to think about role is through the work of writers such as Belbin who consider groups in terms of process and take the view that a number of process related roles exist based upon personal characteristics such as being a 'plant' or an 'implementer' for example. The value of role theory is that it allows issues to be considered about how groups set about the activities associated with their purpose and how the individuals taking part in that process are likely to interact and engage with each other and the objectives. This is important for understanding the implications of issues such as role conflict and incompatibility which are introduced in the chapter.
- **Explain group development processes and how they might impact on group performance.** There are two basic possibilities associated with group development. The first is when a completely new

group is formed and must become a unified entity in order to achieve its objectives. The second and more common situation, is when a group already exists and a new member joins the pre-existing group. Other factors that can impact on the development process include the anticipated life-span of the group, whether it is a formal or informal group, and the purpose for which the group has been formed. There are two models discussed in the chapter which related to group development processes. One is the four stage model offered by Bass and Ryterband, the other and better known model proposed by Tuckman and Jensen. This model has the stages of forming, storming, norming, performing and adjourning. These models provide for a process of individuals coming together and over time developing the mechanisms and relationships to be able to work effectively together in pursuit of the objectives to be achieved. The models recognize that there is no certainty in being able to negotiate the passage through each of the stages, and failure, or the creation of an ineffective group is an ever present reality. It is also possible that the members may be able to achieve the objectives but gain no personal satisfaction from the process. The models do not specifically provide for the situation in which a new member joins an existing group. In such situations the degree to which the individual and/or the group adapts to the change in membership is not clear.

DISCUSSION QUESTIONS

1. What is role theory and how might it offer an insight into how groups form and function within an organization?
2. Groups within organizations are different from groups in other contexts. To what extent and why might this statement be true? Do any differences that exist matter in an organizational context?
3. The use of 'team' rather than 'group' in an organizational context represents an attempt by managers to retain control whilst appearing to delegate power and authority to employees. Discuss this statement.
4. To what extent is the distinction between the concept of formal and informal groups a useful one in an organizational context?
5. The bank wiring room observations demonstrate that employees can effectively manage managers without their being aware of it. Give and justify your own views on this statement.
6. Should management do everything it can to prevent informal groups from forming in the organization? Justify your answer.
7. Should individuals be trained in the theories of group formation and structure in order to ensure that they can become effective contributors to group activities? Why or why not?
8. Tuckman and Jensen (1977) describe a model of group development which describes the process that a new group goes through. How might the process differ when a new member joins an existing group?
9. To what extent is the creation of formal groups within an organization an attempt to provide managers with the means of social control?
10. Individuals within an organization belong to so many formal and informal groups as part of their work that it is not possible for managers to control them with any degree of success. Discuss this statement.

CASE STUDY The evolution of a union branch

This case is based in the UK division of an American owned manufacturing company. The main UK manufacturing plant was based in the North West of England and employed about 1500 people engaged in the manufacture of products for the building industry. The factory employed about 1000 of the people in direct manufacturing activities, the rest were administrative staff and managers. This case is based around the staff and management group within the company.

The company had largely adopted the personnel practices from the parent company adapted to meet UK legislation requirements. The major impact of the differences between the UK and USA human resource management was in the field of remunerations practice. The company policy was that no member of staff was allowed to know where their job had been graded, neither were they allowed to know the salary scales for the grade that they had been allocated to. This was classed as confidential to the company. Even managers were not permitted to know anything about the grading or salary structures relevant to their own jobs. However, every manager was allowed access to the grading and salary information relevant to their subordinates. Not surprisingly this situation led to suspicion and a major lack of trust between managers and staff. Each year staff went through a performance appraisal review and were told what percentage salary increase they were to receive, but they had no way of knowing where their salary stood in relation to the salary range for the grade appropriate to their job.

Although it was a disciplinary offence to tell other staff about your salary, or to seek that information about other employees, some staff did just that. Over a number of years it became a major talking point and focus for complaint among the employees in the company. The company had a staff council, membership of which was open to any member of staff by seeking election from their work group. The perceived injustice and mistrust felt by staff about the way that the salary system was managed was frequently raised by staff representatives. However, this only received the standard reply that it was company policy and salary information was confidential to each individual member of staff. That did not deal with the underlying feelings of the staff and slowly people began to feel that something should be done about the lack of openness in the salary system.

Within the larger departments informal groups began to emerge that sought to exchange information about salary levels and how the system worked. Managers would not disclose any information (even informally) as it would be obvious to more senior managers where the leaks had originated from, and serious career and disciplinary consequences were sure to follow. Some of the more assertive individuals even joined a trade union in order to seek to put pressure on the company to take staff views more seriously. Over a period of about five years the number of informal groups grew in number and size, as did the number of trade union members. Management however, chose to ignore the situation and continued with its salary policy and practice. At one stage it even conducted a staff attitude survey to see if it could find out why morale was so low and hostility towards the salary policy so pronounced. The survey was carried out by a senior personnel specialist from the group headquarters in America, who had great difficulty in understanding why the salary policy caused so much controversy when it worked well in factories across the USA.

Not surprisingly, the outcome of the survey was not what management had hoped for and nothing changed as a result. By this stage the trade union felt that it had about 40 per cent of staff members in membership and formally applied to the company for recognition and the right to negotiate terms and conditions of employment. This was rejected by management out of hand. They even refused to meet the officials from the union to discuss matters. Things had reached a stalemate and nothing happened for another couple of years. The informal groups that had formed tended to share what information they could find among each other and the trade union grew slowly in terms of number of members. Every couple of months the union sent letters to the company asking for a meeting to formally discuss recognition. The secretive nature of the salary system was frequently mentioned as a major problem for staff. The need to have access to salary information in order to be able to put people's mind at rest about the fairness of the system was also frequently raised. All of these approaches were rejected and recognition of the trade union refused.

The American head office began to show concern about the situation in the UK and local senior management were replaced by experienced managers from the most successful plants in the USA. However, the new managers were comfortable with the salary policy and saw no reason to change it. They could not understand why British employees were worried by the lack of information about such matters. The line adopted by the new senior managers was essentially, 'To question me about such issues is to show that you do not trust me to have your best interests at heart'. They would not agree with the converse argument that to fail to provide the information suggested that there was something to hide.

The morale within the UK division remained low, labour turnover was higher than the average for the area and productivity and quality began to suffer as the attitudes of the staff towards management deteriorated. Eventually things came to a head when the informal groups within the company arranged a full salary survey covering all staff levels in the company and published the results on company notice boards. Senior management were incandescent with rage and called the staff council together to rant and rave at them about how disloyal they were being. The staff council members had not taken part in the salary survey as they still felt some loyalty to the company. However, the reaction of senior managers soon put paid to that and they resigned from the committee and joined the union. Things happened quickly from that point. Senior management sought to discipline a small number of the people they thought were the union ringleaders. The company discipline procedure allowed for any employee to be represented in the process by someone of their own choosing. Naturally the people being disciplined said that they wanted to be represented by an official from the trade union. This was refused by management, using the argument that it was intended to be another employee within the company. However, that is not what the procedure stated and as management refused to allow the trade union officer to attend the hearings, staff employees walked out on strike.

That sent senior management into a panic as there was no one to deal with customer orders, telephones, etc. There was also a possibility that the press would take an interest in the industrial action, which would reflect badly on the company. After a few hours management called the union office and asked if the officials could come down to the factory immediately and help to get the staff back to work. They also promised to start talks on recognition of the union the next day after people returned to work. That was done and it was only one month later when a formal recognition agreement was signed and pay talks began. The information long kept secret was at last made public and it was apparent that every one of the staff was actually being paid below the minimum of the salary level for their job grade. Management's excuse was that the previous managers had been abusing the system by paying everyone below the minimums allowed by the system and they had been trying to raise salaries over time to the correct levels. The union rejected this view by saying that if they had been open from the beginning a way around the problem could have been found a number of years earlier to the benefit of all concerned.

Tasks

1. Could senior management have used the groups within the organization more effectively to deal with the situation? If so how? Remember that there would be financial and budgetary constraints on what could actually be done in any one year.
2. What would you have done if you had been a senior manager of the company, knowing that the salary system was not working as intended? Could the problems have been avoided? How?

FURTHER READING

Armstrong, P (1984) Competition between the Organizational Professions and the Evolution of Management Control Strategies, in Thompson K (ed.) *Work, Employment and Unemployment*, Open University Press, Milton Keynes. This text considers how professional groups attempt to 'engineer' access to decision making through restrictions on the interpretation of information and what can be described as hostile strategies towards other groups.

Bensman, J and Gerver, I (1973) Crime and Punishment in the Factory: The Function of Deviancy in Maintaining the Social System, in McQueen, DR (ed.) *Understanding Sociology Through Research*, Addison-Wesley, Reading, MA. This text provides an insight into sociological research in general. However, the specific reading indicated describes the use of informal practices within the assembly operations of an aircraft factory. Essentially, 'illegal' practices were condoned by supervisors and inspectors as part of complex web of control and group behaviour. It is therefore worth reading from this perspective alone.

Clark, H, Chandler, J and Barry, J (1994) *Organization and Identities: Text and Readings in Organizational*

Behaviour, International Thomson Business Press, London. Contains a broad range of original articles on relevant material themes from significant writers referred to in this and other textbooks on management and organizations.

Gillespie, R (1991) *Manufacturing Knowledge: A History of the Hawthorne Experiments*, Cambridge University Press, Cambridge. As the title suggests, this work looks at the intellectual and political dynamics of this famous collection of research into work activity. In doing so it examines the way that scientific knowledge itself is produced.

LaFasto, F and Larson, C (2001) *When Teams Work Best: 6,000 Team Members and Leaders Tell What it Takes to Succeed*, Sage, London. This text looks at theory and practice about what it takes to make teams work effectively in an organizational context.

Smith, KK and Berg, DN (1987) *Paradoxes of Group Life*, Jossey-Bass, San Francisco, CA. This text discusses the conflicts that exist for the individual as a result of group membership. Some cultures have a cultural orientation towards the group, others lean towards an emphasis on the individual. In either context, the individual must forgo certain freedoms once within the group. This text introduces the main issues surrounding this debate.

West, M, Tjosvold, D and Smith, K (2003) *International Handbook of Organizational Teamwork and Cooperative Working*, Wiley, Chichester. Explores the psychological and social processes that stimulate successful teamwork for modern competitive situations.

COMPANION WEBSITE

Online teaching and learning resources:

Visit the companion website for Organizational Behaviour and Management 3rd edition at: *http://www.thomsonlearning.co.uk/businessandmanagement/martin3* to find valuable further teaching and learning material:

Refer to page 35 for full details.

CHAPTER 7

Groups and teams: dynamics and effectiveness

LEARNING OBJECTIVES

After studying this chapter and working through the associated Management in Action panels, Employee Perspectives, Discussion Questions and Case Study, you should be able to:

- **Outline the nature of the dynamic processes that occur within and between groups.**
- **Describe the similarities and differences between models of how groups can be made more effective.**
- **Explain how decisions are made in groups and the difficulties that can be encountered in reaching agreement.**
- **Understand how control can be achieved within groups through such mechanisms as socialization and authority.**
- **Assess the implications of issues such as groupthink and the risky shift phenomena on group functioning.**

INTRODUCTION

The previous chapter introduced the basis of group and team activity within an organizational setting. It discussed, among other important topics, what defines a group, how groups and teams differ and their significance within organizations. How groups go through the process of forming, the application of role theory and some of the major research was also introduced. It should be clear from the discussion in the previous chapter that formal groups have purpose within an organizational context. They are part of the managerially determined approach to achieving the desired objectives. Informal groups develop for other reasons and frequently serve the needs of the workforce for a degree of influence in an otherwise managerially created reality. This chapter develops the consideration of group and team activity further and seeks to consider how they function in practice.

All groups and teams within organizations function within a broader **environment**, containing other groups and individuals. Figure 7.1 reflects a simplified view of part of the environment that could be envisaged surrounding the human resource department of a large bank.

The existence of groups and teams within an environment, as reflected in Figure 7.1, carries with it a number of implications for the functioning of any group, including:

- That a need for communication and interaction between the members of a group will exist.
- There will be a need for a group to engage in communication and interaction with other groups both inside and outside the organization.
- Not all groups in an environment will have the same interests or objectives. Relationships will vary from open hostility to active co-operation, depending upon the circumstances. Relationships between groups will also change across time.
- There exists a need for a group to achieve the objectives set for it.
- Invariably groups cannot achieve their desired objectives without the co-operation and support of other individuals and groups.
- That in order to achieve the desired objectives there exists a need to channel and control the activities of members within the group.
- For a group to be successful at both a personal and organizational level there should be the provision of a means through which to meet the social needs and aspirations of group members.
- There exists a need to take account of the potential impact of the social and political dimensions surrounding the activities of a group.

Each of these issues and more will be discussed in the exploration of group functioning in the remainder of this chapter.

Environment
Elements and forces surrounding an organization with which it must interact and which can influence internal events, decisions and processes.

COMMUNICATIONS WITHIN GROUPS AND TEAMS

For any group to function at even the most basic level it is necessary for the members to interact with each other to some degree. There are different patterns of communication that can be identified within a group, each of which has implications for the behaviour of individuals. Figure 7.2 indicates the major communication patterns that can be found, based on the work of a number of writers, including Bavelas (1948), Leavitt (1978) and Shaw (1978).

Group communication
The level and patterns through which individuals within a group communicate with each other.

Each of the **group communication** networks in Figure 7.2 has implications for a number of group features. For example, the style of leadership adopted and the ability of individuals to contribute to **group decision making**. Consider the 'wheel' and 'Y' patterns of communication and the implications for both the flow of communication and group leadership. In both examples there exists a focal person through whom the essentially linear communication channels pass. Such a person might either be a very strong and directive leader seeking to exert total control over the activities of a group or they might be a dominant individual within the group, who in practice has taken control of the process. Clearly, such patterns of communication have significant

FIGURE 7.1

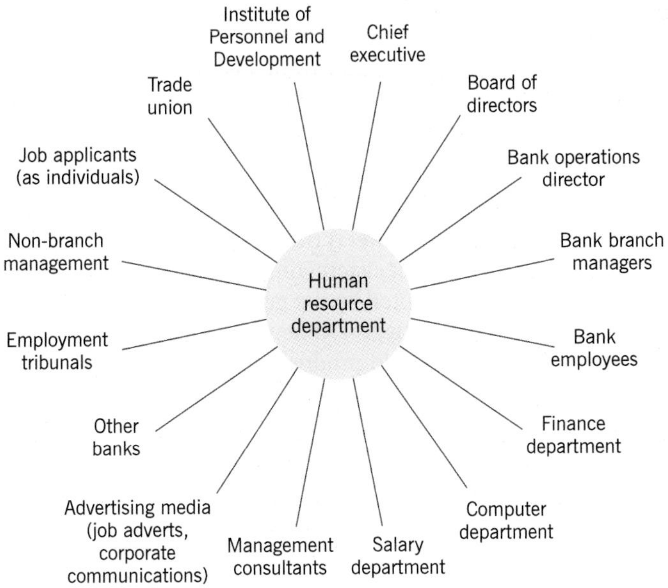

Simplified environment of a bank's HRM department

FIGURE 7.2

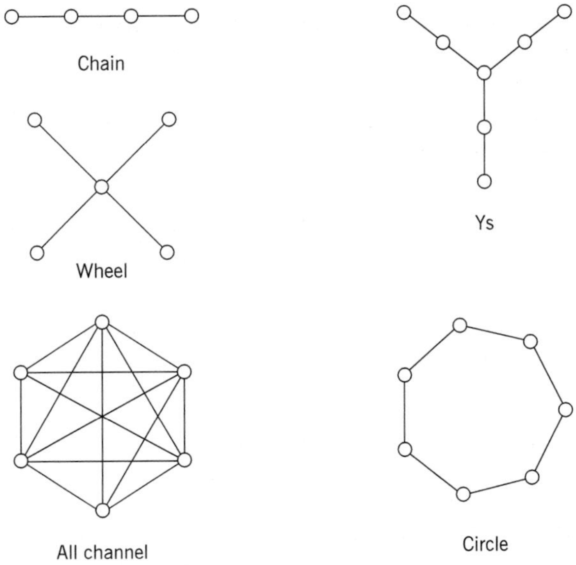

Communication patterns

implications for the work of the group, the degree and quality of debate within the group and the ways in which any decisions would be taken. Compare these implications against the patterns of communication displayed in the 'chain', 'channel' and 'circle' patterns of communication none of which contains a dominant individual.

In organizational group activity not all tasks are equally complex. For example, consider the difference in complexity faced by the production management team within a factory making internal doors for domestic houses when they have to determine:

Group decision making
The processes by which a group will take decisions.

A. If they should make pattern Z before pattern Y when there are enough of both patterns in stock to cover one month's sales.

B. If they should accept a one-off order from a large customer which would require considerable development and tooling costs and from which there would be no repeat business.

In both examples there are different issues and factors to be taken into account in reaching the decision, each with different consequences for the production function and the company. The differences between the types of decision inevitably impacts on the complexity of the process. This decision complexity is also impacted upon through the patterns of communication adopted by the group.

Baron and Greenberg (1990) suggest that where simple tasks are involved the wheel pattern of communication could produce an effective result. The task could be undertaken by the central person alone with the necessary information provided by the peripheral members. They also suggest that the all-channel pattern of communication would produce a poor result in such situations because the flow of information circulates all around the group with no single person collating it in terms of the required decision. Baron and Greenberg also point out that for complex problems the outcome would be reversed. In complex decision situations it is necessary to have the flow of communication around the group to encourage 'richness' in analysis and debate as well as limiting the demands placed on the leader of the group to find a personal solution.

ANALYZING BEHAVIOUR WITHIN GROUPS AND TEAMS

Sociogram
A diagrammatic representation of individual preferences and interactions among group members.

Subgroups
Groups that exist within a larger group.

Cliques
An informal group with a common purpose, frequently the defence of members against other groups and individuals.

Identifying the most common patterns of communication found within groups does not identify the actual interaction patterns within a particular group at a particular point in time. A number of techniques have been developed to allow the patterns of interaction between the members of a group to be charted and analyzed.

Moreno (1953) developed the **sociogram** as a means of charting preferences and interactions between group members. It is based on the positive and negative feelings of individuals towards other members of the group. To construct a sociogram each member of the group is required to express preferences (usually up to three) for other group members in specific situations. For example, who would you most (or least) prefer to work with? The results are displayed in diagrammatic form, illustrating the relationships involved, in Figure 7.3.

A solid line between two individuals indicates that a two-way preference has been identified; a dotted line, that a one-way choice has been expressed – in the direction of the arrow. Examination of Figure 7.3 indicates that there are three **subgroups** (or **cliques**) within the overall group. Person A is a star in that they are a frequent preference among other members, person B however is comparatively isolated, with few preferences being indicated by other members. Sociograms are not without their critics, however. The patterns indicated on a sociogram do not necessarily reflect actual patterns of interaction, they merely represent patterns of preference. The actual behaviour within a specific group context may be completely different from what might be predicted from the preference charts. Relative preference might influence the patterns of communication and the manner of any expression, but the links are tenuous. For example an individual within a group may tend to reject another member, but in a particular group meeting may feel it necessary to interact and support that person against another member over a particular issue.

FIGURE 7.3

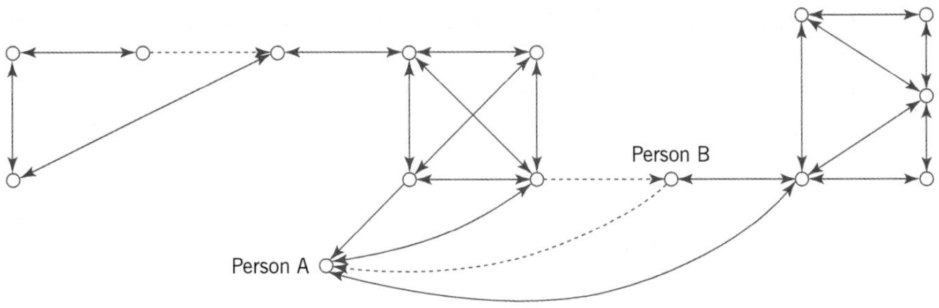

Example of a sociogram

Another approach to describing group activity was that of Bales (1958) who developed **interaction analysis**. He used small group activities such as committees to study how patterns of interaction developed during decision making. He identified 12 categories of activity clustered together under four headings. These can be used to describe the patterns of interaction taking place within a team or group (Table 7.1).

Interaction analysis Contains four categories which can be used for recording interaction patterns within groups.

Bales' work indicates that there are two significant aspects to group activity:

1. *The task to be undertaken and the solution being sought* – referred to as the task function. This reflects interaction oriented towards the purpose of the team activity.
2. *The group atmosphere and member feelings* – referred to as the maintenance function. It describes behaviour intended to preserve relationships, maintain cohesion and minimize the harmful effect of conflict among members.

In addition there is the political dimension to the behaviour of individuals within groups. Individuals may have many reasons for seeking to pursue their own objectives rather than those of the group: a sponsor may have laid down 'things' to be achieved by an individual group member for example. The following Employee Perspective (7.1) is the story of an industrial relations manager (a manager who was also an

A	**Socio-emotional: positive reactions**	
	1	Shows solidarity, raises others' status, gives help, reward
	2	Shows tension release, jokes, laughs, shows satisfaction
	3	Agrees, shows passive acceptance, understands, concurs, complies
B	**Task: attempted answers**	
	4	Gives suggestion, direction, implying autonomy for others
	5	Gives opinion, evaluation, analysis, expresses feeling, wishes
	6	Gives orientation, information, repeats, clarifies, confirms
C	**Task: questions**	
	7	Asks for orientation, information, repetition, confirmation
	8	Asks for opinion, evaluation, analysis, expression of feeling
	9	Asks for suggestion, direction, possible ways of action
D	**Socio-emotional: negative reactions**	
	10	Disagrees, shows passive rejection, formality, withholds help
	11	Shows tension, asks for help, withdraws out of field
	12	Shows antagonism, deflates others' status, defends or asserts self

TABLE 7.1 Bales' categories of interaction

employee responsible to the chief executive) who was given specific targets to achieve in pay negotiations with the trade unions. In that sense they were not completely free to negotiate within the context of a joint management and trade union group. Promotion opportunity could also be enhanced by an individual seeking to be 'noticed' within a particular group – an example of **self-interested behaviour**. A well-balanced group will display the three functions (task, maintenance and political) in proportion appropriate to the purpose of the group, the individuals forming it and the context surrounding its existence.

Self-interested behaviour Behaviour which is designed to serve a particular and personal purpose for the individual.

CONTROLLING BEHAVIOUR WITHIN GROUPS AND TEAMS

When the members of a group or team come together they frequently engage in what would be classed as a meeting. In other words, interaction and communication between the members takes place. Whatever the cause of the gathering it will have purpose, unless it is a chance encounter and interaction is restricted to an exchange of pleasantries. The intended purpose will dictate the intentions of the members, but the actual behaviour will need to be channelled if the purpose is to be achieved. Consequently, there are many parallels between the control of behaviour within formal group situations and the control of meetings. However, it is not just a question of the effective development of an agenda, good leadership and sticking to the point in discussion. There are many other ways in which the behaviour of group members is directed and we will now review some of these.

Perception and attitudes

Groups have the ability to influence the behaviour of the individuals within them by helping to shape the perceptions and attitudes held by members. For example, Sherif (1936) demonstrated that for two and three person groups, individuals could be influenced by the other person(s) present. Subjects were placed in a darkened room and given the task of tracking a light source. The light was stationary, but subjects perceived it to move, an illusion referred to as the **autokinetic phenomenon**. There was a wide variation in the movement reported by individuals 'seeing' this effect. Figure 7.4 shows the results obtained by Sherif.

Autokinetic phenomenon Visual illusion perceiving something to move when in fact it is stationary.

FIGURE 7.4

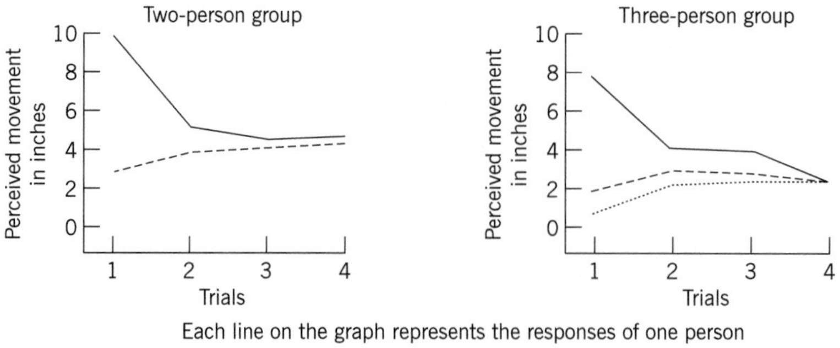

Results of the Sherif experiment

EMPLOYEE PERSPECTIVE 7.1

Negotiating with one hand tied behind your back – part 1

Lauren was the industrial relations manager of a bank in New Zealand and described how her managing director had given her very specific boundaries and targets to work within for the next annual pay negotiations within the company. Previously the managing director had led the management team in the annual negotiation, but this time he wanted to pull back from such a hands-on role and delegate the lead role to the industrial relations manager. Reasonably good relationships had been built up over the previous few years between the management and trade union representatives and no real problems were expected.

The negotiation meeting began with Lauren explaining why the managing director was not present and saying that it would make no difference as the management team had full authority to make whatever decisions were necessary in the negotiation. However, the trade union representatives were not happy at the new negotiation arrangements and they said so very clearly. They saw it as a reduction in their status within the company as they would not now have direct, automatic access to the managing director during negotiations. Lauren said that this was not the case and that the managing director would still meet them in other meetings and would be brought into the negotiations in the unlikely event that a stalemate was reached.

The trade union representatives shrugged their shoulders, looked unhappy and grudgingly started the negotiation meeting. However, it very quickly became apparent that the negotiations were not going to go smoothly and that the trade union wanted more than the management had been allowed to grant. After the first meeting ended Lauren briefed the managing director on how things had gone. He was not happy with the situation and suggested that if he had been running the meeting that he would have handled it differently and so avoided the problems.

At the second negotiation meeting things did not improve and arguments took place between the parties about the management offer being unreasonable. After some time the chief union negotiator called a halt to the meeting and bluntly said to Lauren that she was a coward as she would not negotiate properly, was only a junior manager and had no real authority to reach a reasonable deal. He demanded to speak to the managing director immediately as in the trade union view he was the only person with any authority to deal with them and reach agreement. All of the managers representing the company said that was not the case and that it was disgraceful to suggest it. However, the trade union members rose and left the meeting, saying that they would only deal with the managing director.

Lauren was now in a difficult position. She had been given a clear brief of what she was allowed to offer and the trade union were not going to accept that. Her credibility with the other managers and the managing director were at stake and she was going to have to report back that the union would only deal with the managing director. Not surprisingly the managing director was furious. His plan had gone wrong and he blamed Lauren, telling her so to her face. It was also made clear to Lauren that her future employment with the company was now at risk as she had been unable to deliver on a simple and fundamental element within her job. The managing director arranged to meet with the trade unions and told them in furious tones exactly how he felt about their refusal to reach a settlement. They eventually reached agreement, after a couple of hours argument, within the bounds of the original budget. The final shot by the managing director to Lauren was, 'See that's how to do it!' Later the senior trade union officer told Lauren that their reaction was not personal, but they wanted to continue to deal direct with the managing director.

Tasks

1. What would have done if you had been met with the refusal to negotiate by the trade union if you were Lauren?
2. What would you do now if you were Lauren and why?
3. How could the managing director have handled the situation more effectively in order to achieve his original objective?

There were four trials in the experiment. The first trial recorded the amount of movement reported by each subject independently. Successive trials were reported in the knowledge of the other subjects' responses. The results indicated that personal judgement was influenced by knowledge of the opinion of others. Once established the norm became the basis of subsequent judgement for individuals. It was also noted that few subjects tested were aware that their judgement was being influenced.

This study clearly demonstrates that the groups of subjects developed norms of behavioural response in the common task and that they were generally unaware of the process taking place. From the previous chapter you will recall discussion of the Tuckman and Jensen (1977) model of group development. In this model, stage 3 specifically reflected the process of groups engaging in a process of establishing norms of behaviour. Interestingly, the much earlier Sherif work would seem to suggest that although the process of creating norms exists, it occurs much earlier in group development than implied by Tuckman and Jensen. They suggest that it occurs as part of a sequential process leading towards group performance. Sherif's work implies either that this stage-based group development process occurs very quickly (by the fourth trial) or that the collective shaping of perceptions begins right at the start of the development process.

Conformity
see Group conformity.

Individuals in a group clearly place themselves in a situation in which acceptance by other members is important. A group by definition cannot be a collection of individuals; there is a degree of **conformity** implicit in any group setting. However, it is for each member to take steps to become a member of the group or to remain on the fringes and only partially connected. To become a full member of a group it is necessary for both the individual and the other members to instigate acceptance. One way to become accepted by other people is to become like them, or at least to be acceptable to them. While there are many dimensions to this compatibility process such as personality and the potential to contribute a benefit, one of the key aspects is that of attitude. Behaving in accordance with the expectations of others (displaying approved attitudes and behaviour patterns) is a key aspect of gaining their acceptance and so membership of the group. From that perspective developing particular **attitude sets** that reflect those of the rest of the group is one way of gaining acceptance. It also reflects one way in which the group controls the behaviour of members. It does this by creating a membership which displays particular attitudes supportive of group objectives.

Attitude sets
The totality of attitudes about a particular object held by an individual.

So far the discussion has ignored the opportunity for the potential 'deviant' group member to seek to change the attitudes of the rest of the group towards their position. This possibility introduces political and negotiation perspectives into group behaviour. Factional activity and conflict are possibilities when an individual decides to 'fight back' or 'resist' conformity to group-imposed norms. Observation of this aspect of the control mechanisms active in group situations can most clearly be seen in politics and industrial relations when attempts are made to 'do a deal' involving groups compromising on previously held positions. Frequently, the positions adopted by groups (or individual members) are publicly stated positions and therefore difficult to subsequently change without losing 'face' or credibility. In practice, this arises because of the representative nature of such groups and therefore the need for all parties to negotiate with at least two sets of stakeholders, these being as a minimum the other parties in the negotiation forum and the group from which the representatives originate. For any deal to be successful it must therefore allow for all parties to claim that have gained from the outcome.

For example, a trade union must effectively represent its members to management and in doing so it needs a strong mandate from the members. Inevitably, the expectations that a very good deal can be struck is frequently raised among the members in the process. However, the members are not party to the actual negotiations between management and the trade union. So a separate process then ensues in which the differences between management and the trade union positions are reconciled and a deal agreed. This deal must then be 'sold' to the members. This frequently causes problems for the union negotiators as they will undoubtedly have compromised on some of their initial claims during the negotiation, which the employees may not be happy with. This leads to the need to incorporate the ability to manipulate perceptions and attitudes among the constituents as part of the underlying processes. The following Employee Perspective (7.2) explores some of these issues in relation to negotiation between management and a trade union.

Socialization

Socialization takes place when new people join an existing group and are faced with a process of learning how 'things' are done. Many groups exist for long periods of time and it is individual members who join and leave. An example would be an existing work group with a new employee replacing someone who has left the company. That person is joining an existing set of relationships and interactive networks. The group will seek to ensure that the new member conforms to the established task and maintenance requirements. At the same time, any tendency for self-interested behaviour will elicit a negative response from the rest of the group, at least until full acceptance is granted. Networking represents a key element of business life as individuals seek to 'socialize' with other people and groups to their advantage. Business Clubs UK Limited is a national federation of business clubs, organizations which seek 'to help businesses to help each other', actively encouraging networking in other words. *Management Services* (2003a, p 5) report that the ways of **networking** among managers is changing with the business lunch and corporate hospitality declining in favour of face-to-face meetings and even electronic communications. *Professional Manager* (2003) reports a study which demonstrates that men and women network differently. Women networkers stress the significance of friendship in networking, whereas men tend to opt for more distant, instrumental links in such activities.

> **Networking**
> The development of relationships and contacts that might be useful in the future.

The Hawthorne Studies identified several ways in which groups controlled their members. 'Binging', for example, referred to tapping on the arm. Other sanctions applied could involve a light-hearted joke or sarcastic comment and ridicule of the individual concerned. In effect, a scale of 'punishment' existed. The purpose being to socialize members in the norms of behaviour within the work group. In that context it tended to be directed towards the levels of production achieved by individuals and the group desire to provide management with no more or less than the expected levels. It was also directed towards control of the style of management used within the group – a clear attempt by the group to avoid scrutiny of group activity by managers.

EMPLOYEE PERSPECTIVE 7.2
Negotiating with one hand tied behind your back – part 2

Review the previous Employee Perspective panel about Lauren and her experience during the annual pay negotiations.

Tasks

1. To what extent might the actions of the trade union have been motivated by the need to demonstrate to shop floor members that they were still significant because they dealt with the managing director?
2. To what extent could this have been anticipated by management? How could the views of the trade union have been taken into account within the management strategy?

Social doping
The process of learning how things should be done in a particular context.

Alvesson and Willmott (1996, p103) describe socialization as: 'The process through which humans acquire, and identify with, the values, customs and aspirations of the social groups in which they live'. They also describe it as **social doping** within an organizational context:

> Employees are told – more or less explicitly – how they must perceive and relate to the established organizational reality, and how they should participate in organizational rites where the 'correct' values, virtues and ideals are communicated.

This view clearly sets out the role of socialization as a basis of control within the group context of organizations. The following Employee Perspective (7.3) seeks to demonstrate just how the actions of management in using socialization and group pressure can impact on existing employees and lead to disharmony rather than benefit.

Authority

One feature of decision making within groups (to be discussed next) is the degree to which the group can ensure consistency in the views of the members. This can be achieved either through conforming to the norms of the group or by following the lead of the authority figures within it. Asch (1951) describes an experiment in which subjects were asked to decide upon the relative length of a number of lines. To do this they were presented with a diagram similar to that in Figure 7.5.

EMPLOYEE PERSPECTIVE 7.3 The grey squirrels are taking over!

In one organization, management sought to dramatically change the volume of work and how it was done by employees in a particular department. A new department manager was recruited to replace the previous manager who had been forced into early retirement. The new manager obtained permission to recruit an additional ten staff for the department on the understanding that the work produced would treble within two years. The job adverts were placed in the press and ten new employees were recruited to the department, all from the company that the department manager had previously worked for. They all knew each other and looked forward to leaving their present company as it was slowly losing its place in the market and its profitability.

When they arrived they all had an expectation that they would work as they had done in their previous organization, which was unlike the way that their new company operated. The department was now a total of twenty people, including the ten new employees. Not surprisingly the newcomers mixed socially at work and outside; they also tried to change the way that work was done to match ways that were familiar to them from their previous organization. The department manager supported the new staff in everything that they did and simply brushed aside the complaints of existing staff. The existing employees began to feel threatened and marginalized. One existing employee left the company which unsettled the others even more and so others began to look around for other jobs, anywhere to get out of the department. One of the existing employees likened the situation in the department to that of a forest originally inhabited only by red squirrels. This forest had now been invaded by grey squirrels who were pushing the red squirrels into extinction by forcing them to abandon their natural home.

Tasks

1. How would you react to this story if you were an existing employee of the company described?
2. Does it matter in the long run (and if so to whom) that so many of the existing employees were unhappy and wanted to leave? Why or why not?
3. Was the manager right to encourage the new employees at the expense of existing employees and traditional work practices and if so why?
4. Was the real problem facing the manager his original commitment to treble output over three years? Why might the manager have agreed to this increase and what does that imply about the practice of management?

The subjects were asked to judge which of the three lines (A, B or C) was the same length as line D. The experiment was carried out in groups of about seven people, only one of whom was a true subject. The order of giving the individual judgement was also fixed so that the real subject was near the end of the process and so would be aware of the judgement announced by the others. The 'plants' were instructed to select the wrong answer. Most subjects (about 80 per cent) displayed agreement with the opinions of the rest of the group. Asch suggested three reasons why subjects would adjust their opinions:

1. *Perceptual movement*. Subjects changed their judgements as the result of what they felt to be group pressure. They perceived the majority to be right.
2. *Judgement movement*. Although this category knew that they were reporting incorrectly they believed that their judgement was wrong.
3. *Action movement*. This category simply went along with the majority, but the individuals were aware of what they were doing.

Milgram (1974) also considered response orientation based upon the influence of an authority figure. This experiment involved a simple memory test, the stated intention being to measure the effect of electric shock on memory. A correct response by the subject resulted in progression to another question in the test. Failure to give a correct response resulted in an electric shock being administered, followed by the question being repeated. After each electric shock the voltage was increased for the next repetition of the question. The equipment was clearly marked with a scale of electric shock magnitude. At the top end of the scale was a danger warning, indicating that if it were applied it could be fatal to the subject.

The experimenter in this process was, in fact, the real subject of the experiment, although they were not aware of it at the time. The equipment for generating the electric shock was not connected to the person answering the questions. The supposed subject was strapped into a chair and electrodes were fixed to their body (the experimenter helped to do this), but the electrodes were not wired up to the electric shock generator. The supposed subject for this experiment was 'in' on the subterfuge and deliberately responded to the questions incorrectly. The shock generator was wired up to an electric light and the 'subject' was instructed to respond with cries of pain when it was illuminated and to increase the strength of their cry as the voltage increased. The 'subject' was in a separate room and could not be seen by the 'experimenter'.

When the 'experimenter' began to show signs of resistance to the continuation of the experimental process they were encouraged to go on by Milgram or other senior research confederates. Most of the 'experimenters' continued with the experiment to the point where harm would have been done to the 'subject'. Milgram concluded that the power vested in an authority figure resulted in their being able to pressure individuals to exhibit extreme behaviour. In the group variation of this experiment, it was noted that the reaction of the group tended to determine the reaction of the individual. If the group were rebellious the true subject would be as well; if compliant they tended to react in the same way.

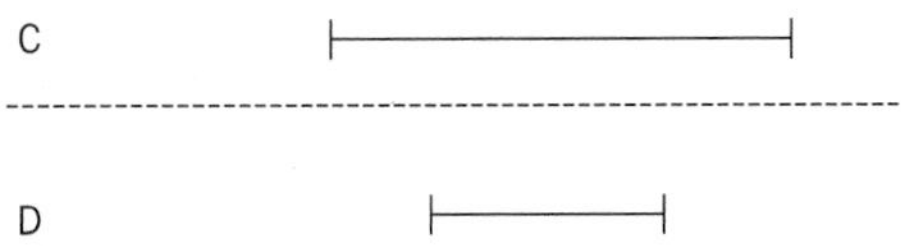

FIGURE 7.5

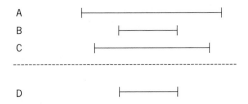

Diagram similar to that used by Asch

MANAGEMENT IN ACTION 7.1 Teams and progress

We trained hard but it seemed that every time we were beginning to form up into teams we would be reorganized.

I was to learn later in life that we tend to meet any new situation by reorganization and a wonderful method it can be for creating the illusion of progress while producing confusion, inefficiency and demoralization.

Petronius Arbiter, 210 BC.

Stop ↔ Consider

What does this suggest about the role of authority and politics in relation to the use of groups in organizations?

Management in Action 7.1 was found pinned to the wall in a personnel department and it is something that reflects both the positive and negative aspects of group formation and activity.

DECISION MAKING WITHIN GROUPS AND TEAMS

Many groups within an organization have a major decision-making aspect to their purpose. This applies whether the group is a manufacturing department seeking ways to assemble toasters, or a board of directors seeking to develop a business strategy. The team roles identified by Belbin, introduced in the previous chapter, are an attempt to provide an effective basis for decision making within the group through the appropriate mixture of personal qualities provided by members. The Belbin model, as well as that of Margerison and McCann will also be discussed later in this chapter. Kretch *et al.* (1962) describe a more comprehensive model of group effectiveness in which the decision-making component forms part of the process. An adaptation of their model is reflected in Figure 7.6.

FIGURE 7.6

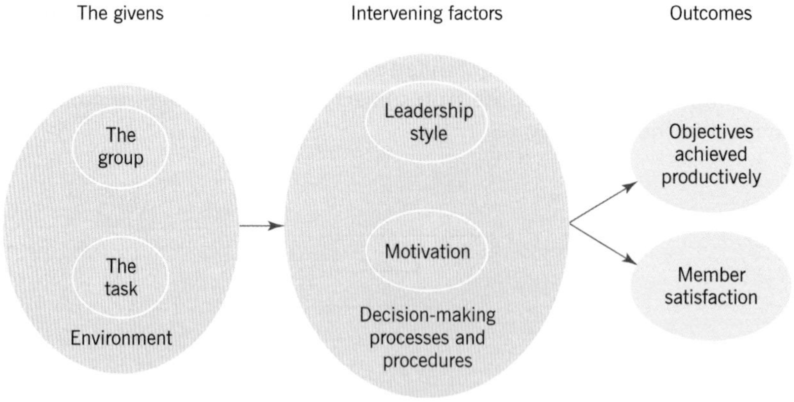

The determinants of group effectiveness (*source*: Kretch, D, Crutchfield, RS and Ballachey, EL (1962) *Individuals in Society*, McGraw-Hill, New York)

In this model the givens provide the constraints within which the group must work. For example, the people who will be in the group and its purpose. Other environmental factors include the size of the group, the difficulty of the task, the physical setting for group meetings together with the frequency and form of interaction with other groups. The intervening factors reflect the decision-making process which includes motivation and the leaders' approach to running the group. The level and type of member participation in the group decision-making process is another aspect of the intervening factors at work in any given context. Athanasaw (2003) suggests that within the public sector it is factors such as years of work experience, frequency of team participation, type of team training provided and the degree of willing participation of individuals in team activities that make for an effective cross-functional group. Thompson (2002) reviews a broad range of material surrounding what she describes as collaborative memory which unlike the work of Asch and others looks at the cognitive effects of collective activity rather than just behavioural issues. The conclusion being that in absolute performance terms collaborative effort is beneficial, but when compared to the predicted performance of individuals within the group, a different picture emerges. This has potential implications for decision making within groups and the development of common understanding among group members.

During World War II, the US government was attempting to encourage the consumption of cheaper cuts of meat among the general population. Lewin argued that the decision on meat purchase was based on group norms, rather than an individual decision at the time of purchase. In 1943 a number of groups of housewives were exposed either to a lecture or engaged in a group discussion on the relative benefits of cheaper cuts of meat (Lewin, 1958). One week after the experiment 32 per cent of those who engaged in the group discussion had tried a cheaper cut of meat, compared with only 3 per cent who had attended the lecture. The group discussion was significant in setting the group norms which encouraged the desired behaviour and in turn influenced future behaviour.

It is clear that in modern management practice the use of teamwork is highly favoured as a means of improving company performance. Indeed, they are held to be central to the success of such initiatives as total quality management (TQM) according to Wilkinson (1993). One of the ways of encouraging managers to recognize the benefits of teamwork and of adopting appropriate behaviour patterns is to expose them to situations where they are forced to take collective decisions in hostile environments. Management in Action 7.2 reviews how one organization sought to transfer from the public sector to the commercial world and successfully achieved this by including teamwork in the changes made.

Whyte (1956) argues, however, that in most cases a group does not produce the best decision. Groups tend, in his words, to mediocrity:

> In your capacity as a group member you feel a strong impulse to seek common ground with the others. Not just out of timidity but out of respect for the sense of the meeting you tend to soft-pedal that which would go against the grain. And that, unfortunately, can include unorthodox ideas. (p 53)

GROUP DYNAMICS

Group dynamics refers to the patterns of behaviour and interaction that actually emerge within a group context. Patterns of communication and related analysis techniques were discussed earlier, but that of itself does not explain what actually takes place when human beings interact across time within a group. It might only explain

MANAGEMENT IN ACTION 7.2 Flying information

The Defence Repair Agency (DARA) in the UK is the part of the Ministry of Defence (MoD) responsible for aircraft maintenance for all of the British armed forces. It was reformed following a review of defence spending in 1999 into a self-funded part of government. In short, it was removed from the protection of automatic government funding and had to compete with the private sector on equal commercial terms. This conversion was achieved on target over two years and DARA has in the process reduced its operating costs by half (including a reduction in the number of employees of 35 per cent) whilst at the same time improving quality, financial and commercial performance.

It recently won a major national people-management award for successfully moving from a traditional military style hierarchical structure, to one based on self-directed teamwork. Bernard Galton, the human resource director and company secretary for DARA said that, 'The [old] culture was hierarchical and risk-averse; there wasn't much of an appreciation of costs beyond what employees were doing. But there was also a clear focus on delivering a high-quality product and staff liked the rules and regulations.' This culture was clearly inappropriate to survival within a commercial environment and so the clear need for change was established. As Galton suggests it was necessary to retain employee pride in the quality of their work and not to 'rubbish' what had existed previously within the organization. 'We wanted people to take far more responsibility for what they were doing, to be far more involved in the decision-making process, to be far more aware of customers and to be looking for business opportunities. We wanted every single person to be a salesperson for the organization.'

Caroline Hose, head of organisation and employee development at DARA developed a programme titled 'New Ways of Working' to facilitate the transition. It involved the introduction of a new, broadbanded pay system to replace the old very hierarchical grade structure and to encourage flexibility. It also included a behavioural competency framework and the introduction of self-directed workteams for shop-floor activities. The trade unions were also involved in the change process through the development of formal working partnership agreements, the first within the MoD. Not everything worked smoothly as many of the engineers felt some fear of the new flat structures within the teamworking process, having spent most of their working lives in the previous military chain of command type of framework. Forces personnel are also seconded to DARA and had to adapt to the new way of working. Rachel Nealon, a production manager, was seconded to DARA and suggested that, 'I have so much freedom in my job – as do the guys on the shopfloor – that going back to a forces environment will be difficult'.

Resistance and reluctance among staff was dealt with though various communication processes, including the chief executive and another director personally addressing groups of staff in an attempt to convince them of the need to change; a regular newsletter allowing staff to air their views; a staff attitude survey; and widespread use of a company intranet. A voluntary early release scheme was also introduced to allow staff who did not want to work in the new environment to leave with dignity. As part of the new working arrangements, managers were required to work on the shop floor for three days doing some of the non-technical work in order to break down barriers with their teams and find out what the real problems were. For some this was a return to their roots, but for some it was a first time experience.

Adapted from: Rana, E (2002) Flying information, *People Management*, 7 November, pp 30–4.

Stop ↔ Consider

To what extent might the success of the changes achieved by DARA be dependent upon the teamwork alone or as a result of the entire range of changes made? What might this suggest about the role of teamworking in success?

what could happen if particular communication patterns are followed. There are many other aspects of group dynamics that impact on the experience of groups for the members as they interact in a dynamic sequence of interlocking behaviours. For example, mood, personality, personal feelings towards other individuals, interest in the agenda items are just some of the issues than can impact on how a group will perform on any particular occasion. Other major topics in this area are discussed below.

Cohesion

According to Piper *et al.* (1983) **group cohesion** refers to the attractiveness of a group to its members, reflected in their motivation to be a part of it, and the degree of resistance to leaving it. In real terms cohesiveness represents the strength of the feelings of togetherness among the members of a group. This can apply to both formal and informal groups. It can be represented as a scale of measurement running from strong to weak.

Group cohesion
Reflects the strength of mutual bonds and attitudes among members.

A group with a weak level of cohesion is effectively a loose combination of people, each person having little or no commitment to the other members or the intended objectives of the group. Conversely, a group with a strong level of cohesion is likely to display behaviour patterns that are tightly focused on the objectives to be achieved and support for each member of the group. Keller (1986) found that cohesive groups more frequently met their objectives. Shaw (1981) suggested that members of cohesive groups displayed more energy (than members of low-cohesion groups) in pursuit of group objectives. The strength of feeling among individual members towards the group is also likely to be evident in the level of commitment shown towards the group and its activities as reflected in levels of attendance at meetings, creating problems within the group etc. (Hodgetts, 1991).

There are a range of factors which contribute to the level of cohesion developed within a group. They are (see Figure 7.7):

- *Environmental factors*. These can include perceived threats to the group and the desire to achieve available rewards.
- *Organizational factors*. These can include the nature of the task to be achieved, the perceived status of the group and the importance of the task to the organization.

FIGURE 7.7

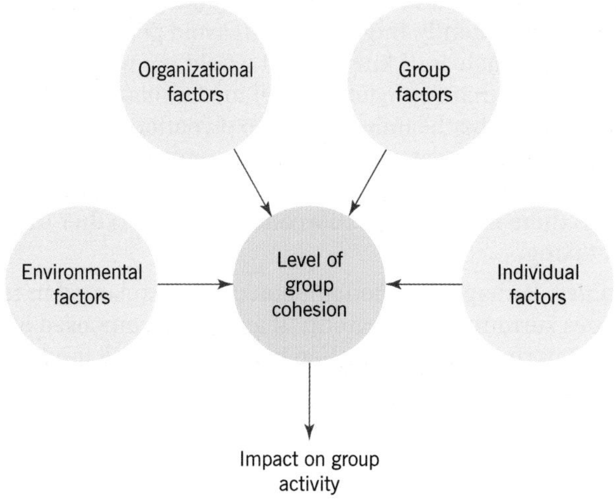

Determinants of group cohesion

- *Group factors*. These can include the size and composition of the group, the personality characteristics of the leader, frequency of interaction and the timescales for achieving the objectives of the group.
- *Individual factors*. These can include the desire (or needs) of individual members to be part of a cohesive group, the level of commitment by individuals to group objectives, the perception of the other members' intentions and the perception of the other forces acting upon the situation.

From a management point of view it would be very useful if all the formal groups within the organization were strongly cohesive, as long as they were supportive of the management determined objectives. There is some research evidence that such groups deliver the highest levels of productivity (Berkowitz, 1954). However, there is a real danger for managers from any strongly cohesive groups that are hostile to their intentions. Such groups can become an organization within an organization or a shadow organization as some writers would describe them. They can be very resistant to the intentions of management if these are perceived to be against the interests of the group. Management in Action 7.3 illustrates this type of situation in graphic terms.

Risks and group decisions

Risky shift phenomenon
The idea that groups tend to take decisions that are more risky than the individual members would take.

Repeated measures experiments
An experimental design which involves subjects attempting the same task on a number of occasions, with only one variable changed.

Stoner (1961) suggested that groups take decisions that involved greater risk than an individual alone would be prepared to take. This became known as the **risky shift phenomenon** and has been identified in a number of different countries and among different groups of subjects. Essentially, the experiment involved the administration of a choice dilemma questionnaire. There were 12 situations described in the questionnaire, all of which required a dilemma to be resolved and a decision to be made. A sample of one of the dilemmas to be addressed is included as Figure 7.8.

The research process involved three stages and two experimental conditions. This is most easily shown as a diagram (Figure 7.9).

Experiments of this type are known as **repeated measures experiments** and for the risky shift reveal that individuals tend to make more risky decisions after group discussion and that groups tend to make more risky decisions than individuals. A number of explanations have been put forward for this, including:

- *Responsibility diffusion*. It is argued that within a group there is less individual responsibility. Consequently, individuals can avoid personal responsibility for any failure. Comments such as, 'I knew that it would not work, but the others insisted on adopting that approach', are all too familiar in most groups. However, this does not seem to be the only possible explanation. Nordhoy (1962) re-examined the original data and found that some of the original questions consistently produced group responses that were more cautious than individual ones. Perhaps there is an exaggeration effect at work, rather than a one-way shift in risk taking.
- *Cultural values*. Perhaps the phenomenon can be explained in terms of the cultural values surrounding the group. If a group is composed of individuals for whom risk is a normal part of life, then perhaps they will tend to favour that approach in their joint decisions.
- *Rational decision making*. It is possible that a group is able to utilize the talents of the members in the discussion process. This increases the opportunity of the group to assess the arguments fully and make a better and more fully informed decision than an individual would be capable of.

MANAGEMENT IN ACTION 7.3 The anti-management workforce

This is a true story told from the perspective of the production director of the company concerned. The organization was a manufacturing company, based in the North of England. It employed about 300 people in the manufacture and sale of industrial containers made from woven polypropylene fabric. Essentially the production process involved cutting the fabric into lengths determined by the design of the container, printing a customer logo on them, sewing the components together to form the container and then packing them according to the customer order quantity. The majority of the workforce were female and had been with the company since it was formed about eight years earlier.

Wages for the factory employees were based on a piecework system of negotiated prices. Because job times were negotiated, rather than being set by the use of time study, attempts were always being made by managers to cut the price of a job. This was resented and caused many arguments over the years. The shop floor workers were a very close-knit group, led by some very dominant personalities. Over the years they had come to distrust management and they had learned that they had to fight for every concession. The piece rates were a constant source of conflict and any new product was refused by the workers unless they were paid average earnings. Then they delayed agreeing a price for the job for as long as possible, years in some cases. In such cases the actual time taken to complete jobs on average earnings was much longer than necessary, but no employee would break with the group norms of working at a very slow pace. Even the piece rates that were agreed were very slack; one job could be actually be done in less than a quarter of the allowed time. So employees on that job could make a decent week's wages in one day.

A new production director was recruited from outside the company, the appointed person being very experienced in industrial relations issues. He was also known by the workforce as he had been engaged in consultancy activity within the company over a couple of years. The task was clear: get away from the traditions of the past, form new working relationships with employees and improve productivity. In short and in financial terms, turn the company around and make it profitable. The appointed production director had the necessary skills and some credibility among the workforce and things began well. He was welcomed into the company at all levels and began to draw up a plan of action, including the design of training programmes, new wage systems and communication with the workers.

To improve productivity, a few redundancies were declared, including a supervisory post. The finances of the company slowly began to improve and the break-even point was reached after about six months. However, the attitude of employees did not change fundamentally. They stalled the negotiations over new wage systems, levels and working practices. They continued to demand average earnings for new products and refused to work on them unless the price was high enough. Progress was stalled. Radical solutions began to be considered by the company directors. After several meetings of the senior management team and an informal meeting with senior trade union officers, it was decided that the problems were simply too great ever to be totally overcome with the existing workforce. It was therefore decided to sell the company, but not as a going concern. The proposal of the company board was to close the company and sell the assets and this was agreed by the group board. It was considered that no one would buy the company as a going concern at a realistic price. Consequently, the chief executive and production director called a factory meeting of all employees and announced the closure, along with the redundancy of all employees.

The workforce cheered! Cries and shouts of 'We have finally beaten management' and 'They have finally had to admit that we are stronger than them' and 'We have shown them that they cannot force us to accept change' were heard from among the employees. The atmosphere among the workforce in those first few days after the announcement was euphoric. Smiles were everywhere and production levels were higher than had ever been achieved before. Employees no longer wanted to work on average earnings jobs and have an easy time. They all wanted to maximize their earnings as this would directly influence the level of redundancy pay to which every employee would be entitled.

However, as the day of closure drew ever nearer one or two people began to recognize that things were not as good as they at first thought. For example, talk of a workers buyout fell apart after one meeting because the trade union would not put up the money and said that employees would have to find the money themselves. Also agreement could not be reached among employees on how many company cars should be provided once they owned the company. Equally, there were no other jobs in the area that would offer the same rates of pay as employees had been earning, without demanding much higher levels of effort.

A few employees began to talk to the production director and suggest that the real problem with the workforce was that a few hard cases had bullied everyone else into agreeing with them. It was also suggested that if these individuals were sacked everyone else would be willing to accept more reasonable work and pay arrangements. It was also said that employees had not believed that the company was actually in a difficult financial position and that the way employees had behaved was not really that bad and had only been intended as fair industrial relations tactics. Had they known how serious things were they would have gone along with management's intentions, it was said. Management took the view that these were empty promises as the individuals concerned had been only too willing to go along with the previous practices and views of the work group. The factory was closed and the assets sold to new owners. The assets were relocated to another part of the country and a new factory opened.

Stop ↔ Consider

Was it inevitable that the factory would close or could it have been saved?
How might you have sought to save the factory if you were the production director?
What problems might you have encountered in doing so and how would you have dealt with them?

FIGURE 7.8

Mr E is president of a light metals corporation in the United States. The corporation is quite prosperous, and has strongly considered possibilities of business expansion by building an additional plant in a new location. The choice is between building a new plant in the United States where there would be a moderate return on the initial investment, or building a plant in a foreign country. Labour costs and easy access to raw materials in that country would mean a much higher return on the initial investment. On the other hand, there is a history of political instability and revolution in the foreign country under consideration. In fact, the leader of the small minority party is committed to nationalization, that is, taking over all foreign investments.

Imagine that you are advising Mr E. Listed below are several probabilities or odds of continued political stability in the foreign country under consideration. Please tick the lowest probability that you would consider acceptable for Mr E's corporation to build in that country.

- ☐ The chances are 1 in 10 that the foreign country will remain politically stable.
- ☐ 3 in 10
- ☐ 5 in 10
- ☐ 7 in 10
- ☐ 9 in 10
- ☐ Please tick here if you think Mr E's corporation should not build a plant in the foreign country, no matter what the probabilities.

Choice dilemma questionnaire, sample questions (*source*: Kogan, N and Wallach, MA (1967) Risk taking as a function of the situation, person and the group. In Newcombe, TM (ed.) *New Directions in Psychology*, Vol. III, Holt, Rinehart & Winston, New York

FIGURE 7.9

Condition	Stages in the experiment		
	1st test (individual)	2nd test (group)	3rd test (individual)
Experimental group	Subjects complete questionnaire as individuals	Group completes same questionnaire (consensus decision)	Individual completes questionnaire (being told that it is a personal decision and to disregard previous group decision)
Control group	As above	No activity	Repeat individual completion of questionnaire

The research process for the risky shift experiment

- *Majority decision making*. If a group relies upon simple majority voting then it is possible for minority views to be overruled. This in turn minimizes the opportunity for full discussion of the points raised, hence limiting consideration of all the necessary aspects, so encouraging more risky decisions.
- *Polarization*. Moscovici and Zavalloni (1969) suggest that groups function in a way which tends to move individual attitudes towards extreme positions. This they describe as a function of the values within the group and an increase in commitment to the decision brought about by discussion.

Groupthink

Groupthink
Tendency of a strongly cohesive group to emphasize unity at the expense of critical evaluation of problems and options.

Janis (1982) reviewed a number of foreign policy decisions involving military planning within the US government and, as a result, coined the word **groupthink**. His research included studying the Bay of Pigs disaster (when the USA invaded Cuba, ignoring information that the Cuban military would actively defend the landing area) and the Vietnam War. As a result, he concluded that such effects were the result of concentrating on harmony and morale to the exclusion of other points of view. In other words highly cohesive groups, particularly those involving very hierarchical memberships such as might be found in the military, were likely to create the very conditions that prevented full discussion and critical evaluation of important issues. Inevitably, this engendered situations which encouraged agreement at any price, unquestioning acceptance of the perspectives of senior members and a lack of critical evaluation of information, thereby producing very poor decision making. Janis identified a number of symptoms which might signify that a group was likely to be suffering from groupthink:

- *Invulnerability*. The group becomes overly optimistic and convinced of its own invulnerability. In the Bay of Pigs fiasco, the US military planners could not envisage that with the military capability at their disposal they could be beaten by Cuba, a country which was much smaller in economic, physical and military terms than the USA.
- *Rationalization*. Such groups find ways to rationalize any evidence or opinion that might suggest an opposing point of view. For example, the Cubans might be defending their homeland, but on this occasion this will not matter because … followed by a range of reasons offered in support of the viewpoint.
- *Morality*. A fundamental belief in the moral correctness of any proposed action. The USA was morally right to seek to overthrow the 'wicked' regime in Cuba – according to the planners.

- *Values*. Individuals with opposing points of view are frequently stereotyped as weak, stupid or evil. Any evidence or information from these sources is therefore automatically disregarded as irrelevant, contaminated or simply of no value.
- *Pressure*. Direct pressure can be used with great subtlety in order to provide an appearance of free speech while preventing active consideration of the views expressed. For example, it is not uncommon in meetings to hear a chairperson state that they are seeking the full agreement of all members for a particular proposal and that they will take lack of disagreement to indicate support. This strategy effectively requires any individual with doubts to speak out and possibly signal opposition to the chairperson. Any individual would have to feel very strongly about an issue and be secure in their position to speak out under such circumstances. Equally, of course, direct pressure can also be used to control individuals through such suggestions as promotion prospects being dependent on 'playing the game' and being openly supportive of organizational objectives.
- *Self-censorship*. Members of the group develop a means of self-censorship in order to hide any doubts and to protect group cohesion. Such a strategy can also be used to the personal advantage of an individual seeking to be viewed by the senior members of a group as supportive of them and their ideas.
- *Unanimity*. A carefully orchestrated unanimity with the equally careful exclusion of divergent views. As indicated earlier silence can be taken as a clear signal that all members are in agreement with the decision, creating an impression of unanimity.
- *Mindguards*. The creation of informal mindguards to filter information flows and to protect the group from adverse comment. Collective responsibility is invoked as justification for supporting a decision and to marginalize any dissent.

Janis also suggested a number of mechanisms through which groups could guard against groupthink, shown in Figure 7.10. They included encouragement for individuals to voice any doubts: the use of subgroups to broaden the search for ideas and to serve as a cross-check on ideas and analysis; encouraging self-criticism among the group and ensuring that junior members are allowed to speak first.

Devil's advocate
A person specifically tasked with challenging the argument or opinion put forward by another person or group.

The role of the **devil's advocate** in Figure 7.10 is based on the idea that someone should be specifically appointed within the group to explore an opposing point of view. It is suggested as a means of preventing a group from simply going along with the accepted case by being forced to consider alternative perspectives. All of the mechanisms suggested by Janis in Figure 7.10 begin with the view that it is the senior members of a group, particularly in an organization, who hold formal power and influence over the careers, lives and development of subordinates. Senior people therefore naturally take the lead in groups and are expected to signal the direction of preferred solutions. This can work to the disadvantage of the group in seeking to deal with complex problems as no one person can hold total understanding, and therefore they should hold back until others have contributed. They can then begin to summarize and bring together the divergent views and perspectives into a solution.

Freud, psychotherapy and group dynamics

Groups must come to terms with their own internal functioning before they can effectively address the tasks facing them. Freud was among the first to address these issues (Strachey, 1953–66) and provided the basis for much of the later work on group dynamics. For Freud, group activity is based on the libidinal impulses of the individual which become transformed through group membership. It is the libidinal (or sexual) impulses that create the links between people and which help to maintain the group.

FIGURE 7.10

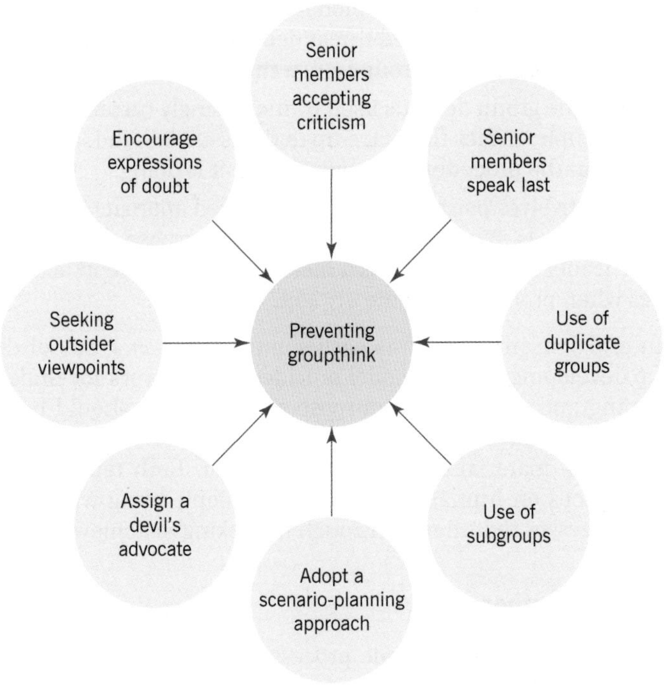

Preventing groupthink

There are other aspects of the group dynamics that Freud seeks to explain. The competition between group members he explains as ambivalence towards the leader who, in effect, becomes a substitute parent. The members compete for supremacy in an attempt to replace the leader. Whatever the views about the value of Freud's work, it does draw attention to the emotional power present in group activity. The ability of a group to create powerful forces in favour of conformity, and indeed rebellion, is without question. Freud's work also points to the clear existence of both a conscious and unconscious level of behaviour in relation to group activities.

Bion (1961) developed a psychotherapy model that relied upon the dynamics of group activity to create changes in individual behaviour. He developed this approach while treating soldiers suffering breakdowns during World War II. As with Freud, Bion was part of the process which he was describing and so his results do not carry the weight of experimentation. Bion concluded that much group experience was the result of conflict between three aspects of group life:

1. *The individual and their needs*. Each individual brought with them their needs and aspirations to the group, which they would expect would be dealt with.
2. *The group mentality*. This related to the feelings and atmosphere within the group.
3. *The group culture*. This Bion described as the need for structure and leadership within the group.

The conflicts and tensions experienced between these three features produce a second level of grouping within the primary one. These second level groupings, or basic assumption groups, act to resolve the tensions for the individuals. It has been suggested that these mechanisms are particularly active when the group is under pressure to achieve results. These effects can be dealt with through:

- *Fight and flight responses*. In this mode, individuals will switch between attack and retreat against the identified threat depending upon the circumstances, the purpose being to protect the group from a threat that might cause it to break up.
- *Dependency*. The group defends itself by increasingly turning inwards upon itself. For example, rather than face up to the issue at hand, a group may concentrate on the procedural aspects of what it is doing.
- *Pairing*. This involves pairing through a ritualized approach to interaction between individuals. It would seem to serve the purpose of providing an alternative leader or objective. It is a metaphorical change in leadership or objectives when problems become evident.

The Tuckman and Jensen model was earlier introduced as a way of describing the stages of group development. This model provides a framework for understanding the process of forming and defining the purpose of a group. It should be apparent that there are points of similarity between the discussion of Freud and Bion and the Tuckman and Jensen material on group development. Both represent an attempt to explain the influences on human behaviour that people bring with them to a group setting and the processes that they go through in seeking to achieve their objectives.

Group dynamics – another view

Another way of describing the dynamic processes within a group is shown in Figure 7.11. This attempts to bring together a number of the elements associated with the internal behaviour of groups.

Within Figure 7.11 there are multiple interactions between all of the elements in the group behaviour box. For example, the style of leadership will influence the process of decision making and the characteristics of the individual members will influence the style of leadership that will be most effective. However Bruinshoofd and ter Weel (2003) found, after studying the effects of forced changes in the management of first division Dutch football clubs, that changes in manager were neither effective nor efficient in improving team performance. There is a feedback loop between the outcome boxes and the other elements within the model. This is because the group

FIGURE 7.11

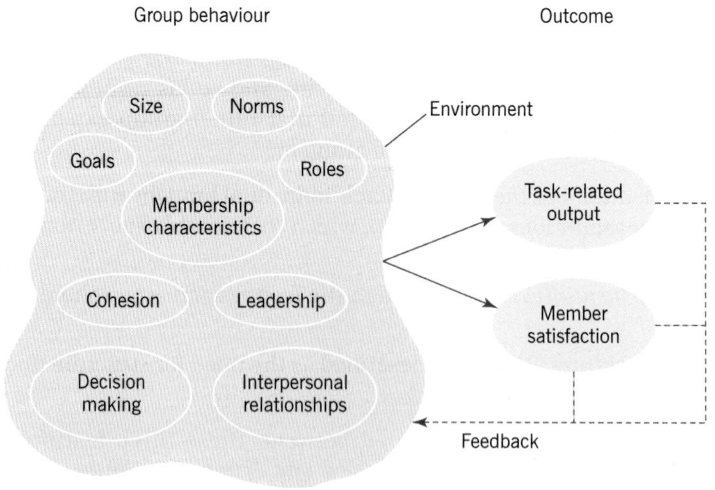

Determinants of dynamic activity within groups

will receive feedback on its progress during its life. For example, if a group produces minutes of meetings, there is likely to be a response from the people who see them. Equally, dissatisfied members are likely to make their dissatisfaction apparent to group leaders at some point in time.

Taking each of the elements within Figure 7.11:

- *Size*. The larger the group the more complex the communication process. Within a group there are trade-offs in relation to the number of participants involved in the process. The larger the number of participants the broader the range of experience that can be brought to bear on the task. By the same token, the more people involved the smaller the contribution any individual can make. Other considerations associated with size of a group include the need for rules and procedures, the potential domination of a group by a subgroup, and the time to reach a decision (and cost) which also increases with size.
- *Norms*. Sanctions can be imposed by the group on those individuals who do not abide by the norms operated by the group. This was clearly demonstrated in the Hawthorne Studies. Some groups can also develop anarchic norms of behaviour, compared to the usual behaviours encountered in a particular setting.
- *Goals*. Group output is made up of two components: the objectives set for the group and the satisfaction level of members (the outcome boxes in Figure 7.11). In most group activity both of these are necessary for success. Imagine a situation where a negotiating group is given the task of agreeing a new pay deal on behalf of workers. If the deal is presented by management as a 'take-it-or-leave-it' situation, the workers may accept it, but morale among members of the negotiating group is likely to drop, along with productivity.
- *Member characteristics*. Individuals differ along a wide range of dimensions, including problem-solving style. A preponderance of one problem-solving style within a group may make it more likely that a result is achieved rapidly, but there are dangers through issues such as the risky shift and groupthink phenomena.
- *Roles*. The Belbin model of group roles has already been introduced along with a discussion of role theory in the previous chapter. Another model was developed by Margerison and McCann (1990) and is called the **Team Management Wheel**. It is reproduced below as Figure 7.12 and attempts to go beyond the Belbin model by 'show[ing] that people have particular work preferences that relate to the roles they play in a team'. This model will be discussed in more detail later in this chapter. There are a number of other role frameworks that attempt to define what happens within a group. Hoffman (1979) provides the following framework clustered around three categories. The main difference between this classification and those of Belbin and Margerison-McCann is that Hoffman is describing what may exist rather than what should exist in order to achieve an effective team:

  1. *Task roles*. These roles encourage the achievement of the objectives of the group. Specific roles include initiator, information givers and seekers, co-ordination and evaluation.
  2. *Relationship roles*. These roles help to maintain the team while it is functioning. Examples include encourager, gatekeeper, follower, standard setter and observer.
  3. *Individual roles*. These concentrate on the needs of the individuals within the group. Examples include blocker, dominator, recognition seeker and avoider.

Team Management Wheel
A model of individual work preferences that relates to the roles that individuals play in a team.

- *Cohesion*. This refers to the degree to which a group feels itself to be a group. At an individual level it is reflected in the desire to stay as part of the group. Although many groups require conformity to group norms, that is not always the case. For example, a group with low conformity to group norms might be high in cohesion if the norms were only loosely structured and enforced. Such an example would be a group unlikely to achieve objectives, but high in member satisfaction.
- *Leadership*. The approach of the leader is important in setting the pattern of behaviour within a group. Informal leaders can emerge over time and tend to be influential in an indirect way. Alternatively, they can directly challenge the nominal leader if that person is weak or seen not to be meeting the needs of members or the objectives being sought.
- *Decision making*. The way in which a group goes about taking decisions can also have an effect on the outcome. Clearly, a group that spends its time talking and arguing without any real sense of purpose is unlikely to produce meaningful results.

FIGURE 7.12

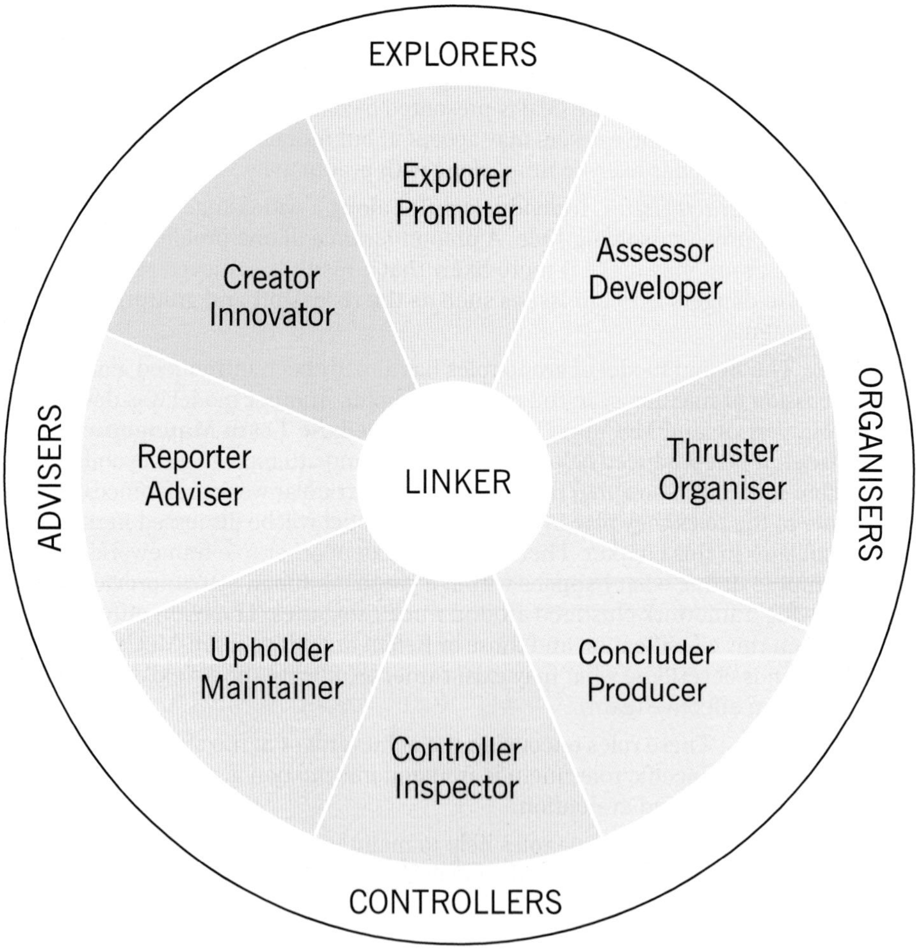

The Margerison–McGann Team Management Wheel (© Prado Systems Ltd. Reproduced by kind permission of TMS Development International Ltd. Tel 01904 641640)

- *Interpersonal relationships*. The way in which the individuals relate to each other within a group can also have a major impact on it. For example, members of a working party who do not like each other at a personal level are less likely to co-operate effectively. The art of sabotaging an 'enemy' within a committee can be carried off with some finesse and become a great source of personal pleasure, even if it is counterproductive in terms of the objectives being sought!

All of the elements in the group behaviour box in Figure 7.11 are surrounded by the environment. All of these features are carried out within a particular organizational, social, cultural and economic environment. Every organization has its own culture and ways of working. In some instances, group activity is seen as very informal and a means of solving problems. In other cases, it is seen as a formal process of communication and decision making. Some groups may even be seen as a mechanism for agreeing to decisions actually taken elsewhere.

DYNAMICS BETWEEN GROUPS

Groups invariably function within a world of groups. Take as an example a joint management trade union negotiating committee. Although this would be a group in itself, it must interact with a number of other groups, which in turn will interact with other groups. Figure 7.13 attempts to reflect this complex situation.

In Figure 7.13, the trade union negotiators have no choice but to consult with the employee group. Similarly, management representatives must consult with the senior managers of the company. Other interactions will be less formal and some only evident as influencing forces. For example, all participants will interact with their family groups and some influence on the overall negotiation process could be expected as a consequence. Interaction with professional or occupational groups could also be expected to have some influence on the primary group's activity. The influences that could be expected to operate between groups are shown in Figure 7.14.

The model reflected in Figure 7.14 assumes that there are several intervening variables that interact on the relationships that exist between groups. Not all of these variables will function all of the time; neither will they have equal potency. The dynamic of the relationship between groups and the behaviours that result are, however, affected by them. Taking each of the factors identified in Figure 7.14 in turn:

- *Objectives*. The objectives that each group has will differ. This affects the relationship between the groups depending how each group perceives its own and the others' objectives. Within an organization it would be the ideal for all groups to perceive their objectives as part of the overall company objectives. However, the nature of conflict between groups is strongly influenced by the perception of the objectives being pursued together with a range of political and power based factors.
- *Task competition*. Groups that are strongly linked together because of the nature of the work are more likely to develop a power basis to the relationship. A typical example of this would be the finance department seeking to control spending at the same time as marketing seek to spend more on advertising to generate future sales. This process can introduce competing objectives into the situation and hence conflict.
- *Resource competition*. Where groups must compete for resources then they could be expected to seek ways of gaining an advantage over the others. Two departments may put forward bids for additional resources to improve

FIGURE 7.13

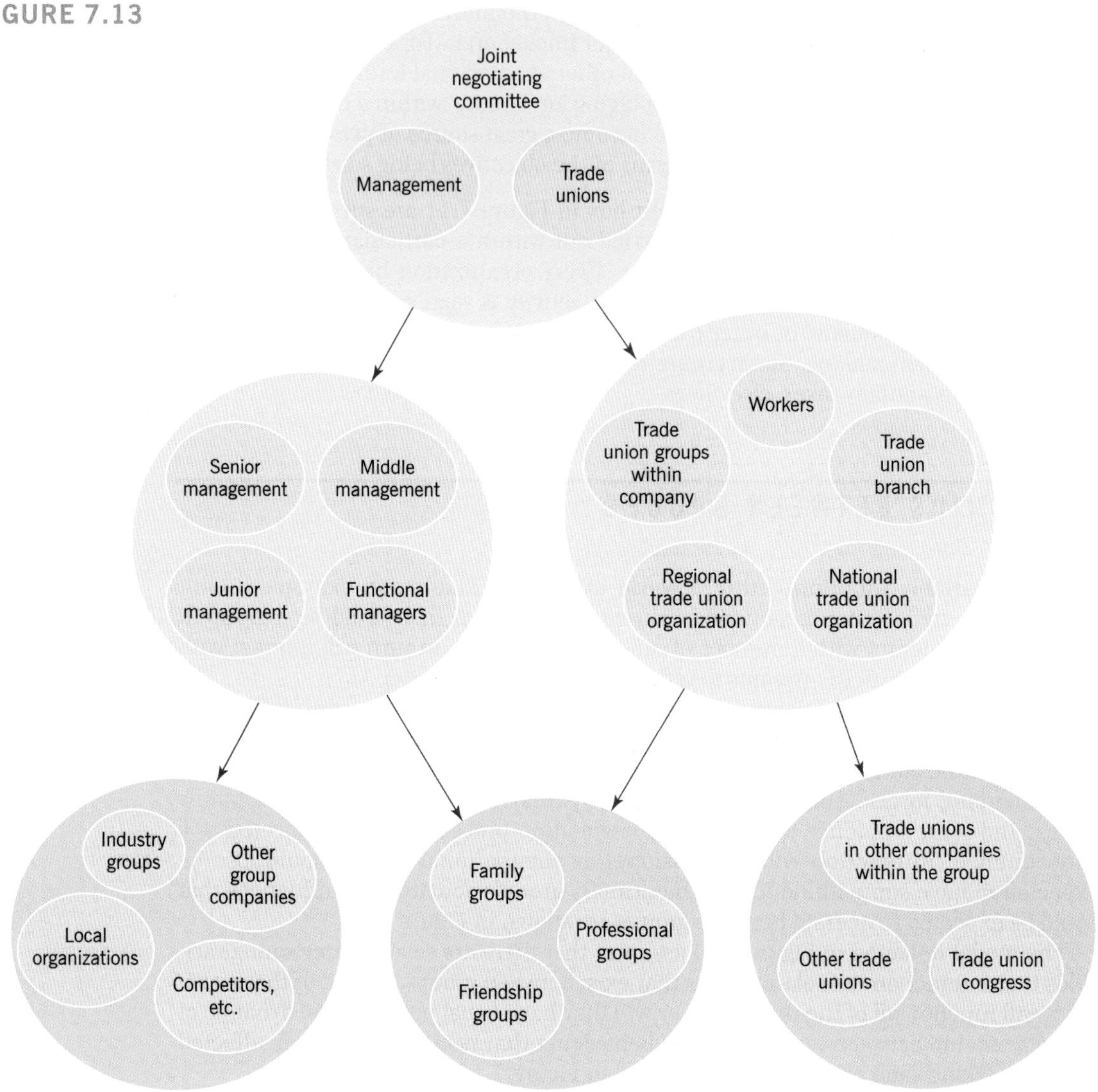

The group hierarchy

productivity, but there may be a limit to the finance available. Under these circumstances the two departments can either fight each other, or find ways of reaching a compromise.

- *Uncertainty*. There is often little opportunity for a group to be certain about another group's motives or intentions. Among the consequences of uncertainty are a lack of trust and an increase in political behaviour towards other groups.
- *Inter-group relations*. Previous experience of interaction with other groups can determine future behaviour. A management that is found to have lied to its workforce will find future interactions tainted by that experience.
- *Attitudes*. Frequently, inter-group relations are based on attitudes established over many years. **McGregor's Theory X and Theory Y** is an example of how the attitudes of individual managers can form the basis of stereotypical inter-group behaviour.

McGregor's Theory X and Theory Y
Considers that managers function on the basis of their beliefs about how employees approach work, irrespective of actual employee behaviour.

FIGURE 7.14

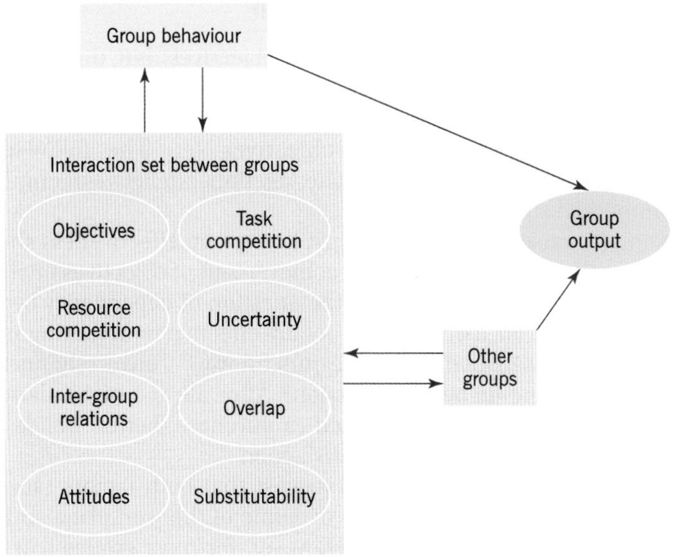

Influences on group behaviour

- *Overlap*. Over the past 200 years many trade unions were formed in the UK, largely based on occupational groupings. As a consequence there was considerable overlap in the claims of individual unions to represent particular groups of workers, which resulted in conflict. Subsequently, a set of rules had to be developed to regulate competition for members.
- *Substitutability*. The opportunity to bypass or circumvent another group provides an opportunity to exercise a degree of control over that group. The threat of buying from alternative suppliers is a classic way for an organization to pressure current suppliers into conceding lower prices.

GROUP EFFECTIVENESS AND SATISFACTION

What makes an effective group? Figures 7.6 and 7.11 suggest that there are two different outputs from group activity:

1. The achievement of objectives in a productive way.
2. Member satisfaction level with the experience.

These models imply that effectiveness should be measured against both of these criteria. Performance is a complex issue to determine. For example, Orlitzky and Benjamin (2003) concluded that mixed sex groups outperformed more homogeneous groups in a business school case competition. They conclude that this could be based on a number of mediators including informational-processing diversity and personality differences between the sexes. But can this finding, based upon a relatively small sample of university students, be taken as representative of all groups operating in an organizational context?

Group effectiveness and member satisfaction

A group could be productive and achieve its objectives, but the members may not enjoy the experience or feel that it was satisfactory for them personally. Conversely, the individuals could have a good time through the group experience, but fail to achieve anything in relation to the objectives set. The following Employee Perspective (7.4) demonstrates the complex relationship between employee satisfaction and commercial success.

These examples raise the question of just how group effectiveness should be measured. Should it only be a reflection of the achievement of objectives or should it reflect the individual perspective? It also raises the question of dependency between the two elements. Is it possible for a group to be totally effective in achieving its objectives if the individuals are not satisfied in any meaningful way? Conversely, does the achievement of objectives create its own satisfaction? After all, the high salaries paid in the insurance company example, can be used to purchase 'better' holidays and leisure services, perhaps improving overall life satisfaction.

Results from the Hawthorne Studies suggest that both factors (achieving results and member satisfaction) interact in the dynamic of the workplace and that satisfaction has a significant effect on output. However, for most groups it is impossible to know what the degree of relationship is because it is not possible to run experiments where the variables are systematically manipulated and results measured. For example, do the results achieved by a group represent the best possible outcome, or do they simply reflect a compromise between the competing views of members? Also in any particular context it is never certain if the objectives set for a group reflect that which could be achieved (optimally) or some defined change to a current situation (for perhaps rational reasons) that gives the appearance of progress in some general way. In crude terms do the shareholders of a company care that they do not achieve the highest returns possible on their investment, as long as the next dividend is the same or better than the previous one, the share price does not deteriorate and the board offers a plausible explanation?

McGregor (1960, p 228) describes the concept of unity of purpose to explain the way that some managerial groups perform effectively. By this term he draws attention to the commitment of individuals to the group and to the achievement of objectives. He goes on to describe the features that differentiate effective from ineffective groups. The main features of his ideas are included as Table 7.2.

EMPLOYEE PERSPECTIVE 7.4 Instrumental approach to work

Mark was a systems analyst working in a large insurance company based in Frankfurt. He described how he worked in an organization where the management style was very autocratic and that senior managers took very little notice of their subordinates. Morale among senior technical specialists throughout the company and particularly in the computer department was very low. Most of the staff at this level felt undervalued and underused in their work. They soon adopted an **instrumental** approach to work in that they showed little initiative and simply followed orders by complying with management requirements. Labour turnover among this group was quite high, but the company paid high salaries and was very profitable.

Tasks

1. What would you do (and why would you do it) if you were Mark and worked in this type of environment?
2. To what extent does this example demonstrate that as long as a group is successful (measured by financial results) other factors (such as low personal satisfaction) are largely irrelevant?

Dimension	Effective group	Ineffective group
1 Atmosphere	Informal, comfortable, relaxed	Indifference, boredom, tension
2 Discussion	Participative, pertinent to task	Dominated by a few people, drifts off point
3 Objectives	Understood and accepted by all	Lack of clarity, not fully accepted by individuals
4 Active listening	Members listen to each other, contribution to debate and ideas	Pushing of own ideas, no evidence of building on others, talking for effect
5 Disagreement	Brought into the open and resolved or accepted	Not resolved, suppressed by leader, perhaps warfare domination is the aim
6 Decision making	By consensus	Premature decisions and actions before full examination. Simple majority voting
7 Criticism	Frank but not personal	Embarrassing, tension producing. Involves personal hostility, destructive approach
8 Feelings	Expressed on group activity as well as ideas. Few hidden agendas	Hidden, not thought appropriate to group activity
9 Action	Clear allocation and acceptance	Unclear in allocation, lack of commitment to achieve result
10 Leadership	Not chair dominated, 'experts' lead depending on circumstances, no power struggles	Chair dominated
11 Reviews	Self-consciousness about present operations, frequent reviews	No discussion of group maintenance issues

TABLE 7.2 Features of effective and ineffective groups (adapted from: McGregor, D (1960) *The Human Side of Enterprise*, McGraw-Hill, New York)

The ideas contained in Table 7.2 could be used to record the way in which a particular group functions. This in turn would allow the members to review their own approach and improve the level of group effectiveness achieved. It does not, however, address the issue of what could be achieved. It simply allows a review in terms of what exists.

The two team systems already introduced in the context of groups seek to define the requirements for a balanced set of abilities and preferences among the members, if success is to be achieved. These ideas were the Belbin model and that of Margerison and McCann. Both of these models also have significant implications for group effectiveness and member satisfaction. It is now to a more detailed consideration of these two approaches that we turn.

Belbin's team roles

Belbin's team roles were outlined in Table 6.4 in Chapter 6, taken from Belbin (1993). These roles are:

- The plant
- The resource investigator
- The co-ordinator
- The shaper
- The monitor evaluator
- The teamworker
- The implementer
- The completer
- The specialist.

For Belbin, each of these roles has an important part to play in achieving an effective group process in terms of the objectives to be achieved. It is the balance between the contributions of each role that delivers the opportunity for the group to make good decisions by allowing individuals to form a complementary dynamic process, not a destructive one. Belbin also suggests that large groups are inefficient and need to be broken down into smaller groups, which would also help enhance the role of women in organizations, Glover (2002a). In his 1981 book, Belbin describes what he considers to be the attributes of successful and unsuccessful teams. These conclusions are based upon his work associated with the application of team roles in training and research contexts.

Successful or winning teams, as Belbin prefers to call them, display the following characteristics:

- An individual in the chair who could make use of the role to ensure an effective process. A person with an ability to work with the talent available within the group.
- A strong plant, essentially a creative and clever person, within the group. Someone able to make an effective contribution.
- A good range of mental ability spread across the individuals within the group in such a way that complemented the team roles present.
- Wide team role coverage within the group. The key team roles within a group provide a basis for effective interaction and balanced decision making.
- A match between team roles and personal attributes. In many groups, activity is allocated on the basis of past experience rather than team role profile. Successful teams were able to achieve a balance between these factors.
- The ability of the team to compensate for role imbalances. This refers to the ability of a team to compensate for its own weaknesses.

According to Belbin the following characteristics are relevant to a lack of success:

- *Morale*. There was only a tenuous link between the level of morale in the group and degree of success in achieving objectives. In other words, groups with a high level of morale are just as likely to fail as those with low morale.
- *Mental ability*. This proved to be a critical factor in that without someone of high ability in a creative or analytical sense, failure was relatively certain.
- *Personality*. Organization culture creates a tendency to encourage the recruitment and promotion of people with a preponderance of particular personality traits. The consequence of this cloning or clustering is a negative impact on group decision-making effectiveness.

- *Team composition*. Some groups will fail because of organizational deficiencies rather than anything specific to the group. For example, senior management may fail to act on the recommendations of one of its specialist functions. However, unless a balance of team roles is achieved within that specialist function then the group is likely to be ineffective in identifying appropriate recommendations.
- *Individuals with no team role*. Belbin identified about 30 per cent of the managers tested as having no clearly defined team role profile. The consequences of the inclusion of such individuals into a team are effectively to destabilize what could otherwise be an effective group.
- *Unknown factors*. Between 10 and 15 per cent of managers in unsuccessful groups failed to take the tests that would determine their team role. This might suggest that individuals that avoid being tested tend to associate with ineffective groups more frequently than would be expected.
- *Corporate influences*. Few groups operate in isolation (as illustrated in Figure 7.13). There are constraints and political influences in all situations. There is also a lack of information, and the existence of imperfect information on occasions which can impact on the quality of any decision. Among the consequences of this are that groups can be channelled in particular directions during their deliberations and suffer interference in their activities, which may result in a poor quality output in objectives terms. For example, Bray (2000) reported that Qantas (the Australian airline) was to raise its domestic fares by an average of 3.5 per cent just as cut-price competition was growing significantly with the entry of Virgin Atlantic into the market and the rapid expansion of an existing local carrier – a decision which may make internal sense to Qantas but might be difficult to sustain if a price war broke out.
- *Role reversal*. Occasionally Belbin found that individuals who displayed a particular team role profile would switch and adopt another role, less suited to their abilities. This switch produced a negative effect on the group activity.

The Margerison–McCann Team Management Wheel

Margerison and McCann (1990) use the analogy of a wheel to describe their team management system (Figure 7.12). Their approach to effective teams is also based on research. The authors claim that they span the psychological and sociological traditions and go further than Belbin in providing an explanatory and practical model. Figure 7.15 reflects the relationship between the Team Management Wheel and other approaches.

The model is based around the **team management profile questionnaire**, which is a forced-choice normative questionnaire. It measures individual work preferences on four dimensions:

Team management profile questionnaire
Tool used in the Team Management Wheel model, allows the team profile of individuals to be identified.

1. *Relationships*. The approach to relationships is measured on an extroversion–introversion scale.
2. *Information*. Measured in terms of the preferences in the way in which information is gathered and used by the individual in analyzing situations.
3. *Decisions*. Measured in terms of the approach adopted by the individual to taking decisions.
4. *Organization*. Measured in terms of structure or flexibility preferences of the individual in approaching tasks to be achieved.

FIGURE 7.15

Psychological approach	**Socio-psychological approach**	**Sociological approach**
Individual differences	Individual role preferences	Role differences
Who am I?	What do I wish to do?	What role do I have?
Jungian and other theories	Psychological and sociological theories	Belbin and other theories
Myer–Briggs® type indicator and other measures	Margerison–McCann Team Management Wheel	Measures of role structure

Different approaches to understanding teams (© Prado Systems Ltd. Reproduced by kind permission of TMS Development International Ltd. Tel 01904 641640)

The information collected provides a profile of the individual in terms that can be translated onto the 'Wheel'. The profile identified falls into the segments on the Wheel, each of which implies the following characteristics:

- *Creator–Innovators*. These individuals are independent and likely to challenge the present ways of doing things. They can generate new ideas.
- *Explorer–Promoters*. Individuals who explore new ideas and sell them to other people.
- *Assessor–Developers*. Individuals good at linking the creative and operational sides of a team. They are good at taking an idea in principle and making it work in practice.
- *Thruster–Organizers*. The people who can get things done. They can organize resources and people to achieve results.
- *Concluder–Producers*. These people can ensure that results are achieved and that the work of the team is effective and efficient.
- *Controller–Inspectors*. These individuals ensure that the details are correct and the output is 'up to standard'.
- *Upholder–Maintainers*. Good at providing support and stability to a team. They support and advise the team.
- *Reporter–Advisers*. The data collection and interpretation specialists. They are the experts in the field and collectors of information.
- *Linker*. This activity is not seen as a preference as such, but as a skill that can be developed by any manager. This activity is central to team activity in that it performs a connecting role in ensuring that the team operates in an effective manner.

The concept of effectiveness in this model is defined in terms of a balance of individuals across the preferences in the Wheel. Most importantly, the writers claim that different situations and team objectives require different combinations of roles from the Wheel. In other words the team composition should be designed to meet the needs of the situation. This implies that the current profile of every manager should be available when the composition of a team is considered and that profile, not just status, politics or function, should be taken into account. What the authors term a 'high-performing team' should:

- Accept that all team members have a responsibility to undertake the linking role.
- Have high expectations and set high targets.
- Gain high levels of job satisfaction.
- Experience high levels of co-operation.
- Provide team managers who lead by example.
- Develop teams that have a balance of roles matched to skills.
- Experience high degrees of autonomy.
- Learn quickly from mistakes.
- Develop teams that are 'customer' oriented.
- Display good problem-solving skills and review group performance.
- Be motivated to perform.

The reasons that teams fail, according to Margerison and McCann, include:

- A lack of balance across the team roles.
- A lack of effective linking between the roles.
- A lack of effective relationship management within the team.
- A lack of effective information management within the team.
- The existence of impoverished decision-making processes.
- The tendency to want to take decisions too early in the process.

GROUPS, TEAMS AND ORGANIZATIONS

The Hawthorne Studies provide the most frequently cited basis for thinking about groups within an organization. However, it has been implied that the studies were 'rigged' in that the process did not achieve the standard of objectivity necessary to be able to isolate the dependent and independent variables. For example, employees were required to participate in the experiments and the researchers became counsellors not only by collecting information but also by seeking to deal with employee dissatisfactions as well (Thompson and McHugh, 1995). The same authors draw attention to the views of Mayo on issues such as trade unions and conflict (see also Gillespie, 1991, for a review of the context). The design of the research and interpretation of the evidence was to a significant extent a function of the individual researchers' attitudes, beliefs and values.

Research in real organizations is not like research in the controlled conditions found in a laboratory. It involves people interacting and behaving in real time and factors not under experimental control impacting on the process. For example, the mood and feelings of people can change depending on a wide range of factors both inside and outside the work setting. Also the researchers are not physically able to observe and record every aspect of behaviour, its determinants and consequences within a multi-person group. There is simply too much going on. Equally, there is always an issue of how much the researcher understands of what is actually going on. Within any situation there is the observable physical behaviour level of activity. That is, the actual movements of the people, their spoken words and other observable events.

However, there is also a shared meaning level of behaviour present that allows the participants to interpret the gross behaviour activity in terms of what it means within the particular group setting. This level of meaning is not easily gained by the researcher and can readily be missed. In some situations deliberate attempts can be made by a group to provide a researcher with the wrong interpretation of events, a problem common among early anthropological studies. So there are many practical and academic difficulties in seeking to achieve what Maslow (1966, p 50) described as **spectator knowledge**.

Spectator knowledge
The knowledge gained as a result of being a spectator rather than a participant in a particular situation.

However, similar criticisms could be made of most research endeavours. In addition to the points already raised, when analyzing the data available, a researcher is looking for patterns, associations and trends. It is inevitable that links will be identified that are not relevant and perhaps do not stand up to subsequent critical scrutiny. This process of research, publication and critical evaluation is all part of the process of creeping forward in the creation of new knowledge. In knowledge terms the Hawthorne Studies are a comparatively recent event. It is hardly surprising that the results are still being questioned and re-examined by modern researchers critically evaluating what the original research team actually did. One interesting research project of recent times is described by Brown (2003) in which standard toy robotic dogs are reprogrammed by students to allow radio communication and therefore collaboration between them. Teams of such robotic dogs compete against each other in a football competition called the 'Robo Cup American Open' organized by Carnegie Mellon University. Such research might eventually allow the mechanisms for effective teamwork to be identified, at least in the robotic world!

As the Hawthorne Studies illustrate, groups can have a significant effect on the behaviour of their members. The balance between output and effort by members of the group described in the bank wiring room study illustrates the power of groups to shape the behaviour of individual members. Other studies, for example, those of Asch, illustrate the ability of groups to produce conformity. Yet, conversely, the same experiment, repeated in the UK by Perrin and Spencer (1981) did not produce a compliance effect. This suggests that the effects demonstrated by Asch could be a function of culture, social or experimental conditions at the time, if we discount the possibility that it was a function of the experimental design as that was common to both experiments.

In a study of informal group practices in maintaining output and control, Bensman and Gerver (1973) studied assembly in an aircraft factory. Company policy stated that if wing parts were not in alignment disassembly and complete rebuilding should follow. This inevitably resulted in a long delay and a loss of production. The 'informal' practice was to use a hard steel screw to force the components together, thus saving time. The company did not allow employees to acquire such screws and anyone found in possession of one was liable to instant dismissal. However, all employees carried one 'for emergencies'. Supervisors and inspectors knew of the practice and would turn a 'blind eye' as long as it was not used too frequently. By allowing specific infringements of the rules a balance of power was maintained which allowed for acceptable outcomes for all parties through tolerance of this **focused deviancy**.

Focused deviancy
Toleration of bending of the rules providing it contributes to objectives and does not become normal practice.

Many groups are influential in the general milieu of organizational life. Interest groups such as trade unions, government and environmental groups have the potential to influence management. The gathering of information about the various interest groups that might impact on operational or business activity is becoming an issue of priority for managers. In a television documentary (BBC 2, 1994) it was reported that during the 1985 British miners' strike the government and coal industry managers employed agents to collect a wide range of information in relation to the underlying views of employees from the various trade union areas. This resulted in management and government initiatives to encourage the formation of groups that were prepared to go through the picket lines and work normally.

The models of Belbin and Margerison and McCann could provide managers with the ability to design teams through the selection and training of individuals. Naturally, such a process could not offer a guarantee that individuals will perform in totally predictable ways. That is why the Margerison and McCann model is specifically intended to be used for development purposes only and not as part of the recruitment or selection process. However, it could allow organizations to review the balance of individual preferences needed or available in particular team contexts, perhaps improving the probability of success (as defined by management) through balance between preferences. It is also likely (assuming that the underlying theory is valid) that such groups will produce a more satisfying experience for the individuals. In some ways this can be described as a form of social engineering; control of group activity and hence corporate results achieved through indirect means. This should be compared with a random natural selection in group membership (within the normal constraints of how group membership is designated) that would allow individuals to apply themselves to the random dynamic of situations that they experience. All management decision making is manipulative in that it seeks to influence events and behaviour in pursuit of particular objectives. So perhaps attempts to make groups more effective through the application of the models available should be described as a form of subtle manipulation, in principle no different from any other form of management.

Training is an attempt by managers to shape the behaviour and attitudes of employees in appropriate ways. Appropriate, that is, as defined by managers. Such an approach attempts to infuse a management-determined perspective and value-set throughout the organization. This inevitably begins at the very top of the organization. The top management team or board of directors is a group, and according to Edmondson *et al.* (2003) it is necessary to integrate aspects of leadership, small group processes and negotiation into the training of top managers if effectiveness of the top team is to be achieved. Group working as a means of continuing to reinforce that perspective is a useful means of providing follow-up and reinforcement of the original socialization. The institutionalization of inter-group and intra-group ways of working and interacting can provide an effective means by which corporate standards can be continually reinforced. Initiatives such as the introduction of total quality management (TQM) and customer focused group working depend for their success to a significant degree on the individual groups accepting delegated responsibility to act with minimal control and direction from above. However, if a particular group (or groups) develop very strong levels of cohesion and they do not support the management agenda then this could present major difficulties. When management set out to introduce widespread use of customer-focused group working within an organization they are undertaking a process that will fundamentally change the balance of power and require management to engage in behaviours that actively create and maintain employee support.

In order to achieve the objectives of an organization, two main conditions are necessary:

1. *There must exist appropriate subgroupings*. This includes the use of groups designed to meet the operational needs of the business and those necessary to ensure co-ordination of resources in pursuit of the common objective.
2. *Within individual groups there need to be appropriate mechanisms to meet the purposes set for them*. This includes the provision of an appropriate composition for the group and also the control of the dynamics of how it will operate in order to achieve its objectives.

The informal groups within an organization should not be hostile to the intentions of management if success is to be achieved. If there is hostility towards the objectives being sought by management, it is unlikely that they will be achieved. Even if they are achieved it will not be done easily, effectively or efficiently. Consequently, the ability of a manager to put together a team of people who are likely to produce the best outcome for both the organization and the individual is equally as important as ensuring that the interactive processes between groups function in a positive way. However, there remains a fundamental difficulty for managers in seeking to control or influence the informal groups that exist in any organization. Any direct attempt to influence such groups would be strongly resisted, yet they cannot be ignored (as they are on an organization chart). In many ways such groups emerge as a reaction to the imposed groupings forced upon employees by managers and so deliberately resist any attempts to direct or control them. One way in which informal groups can interface with management objectives is reflected in Management in Action 7.4

GROUP DYNAMICS AND EFFECTIVENESS: AN APPLIED PERSPECTIVE

In the previous chapter it was suggested that groups are in an almost constant state of flux within an organization as people leave and join, new groups are formed and the objectives for existing groups are subject to change. This affects the way in which groups operate as well as the processes through which they go in undertaking their allotted tasks. Because of the significance of groups within an organization, managers need to develop the ability to make effective use of groups. This includes an understanding of how groups function and the process of achieving the desired outcome from group activity. The failure to understand these issues or make effective use of them in managing group activity is likely to adversely influence the outcome.

The influences arising from the dynamic nature of the environment create a situation for organizations in which both uncertainty and risk are high. For example, employees may have accepted a wage rise below the rate of inflation for the past five years on the basis that it helped to preserve jobs within the company. However, that is no guarantee that they will agree to do so in future. Circumstances change and the range of influences acting upon the situation and individuals involved may well create a shift in collective attitude. So although groups can be used to collectivize things and so reduce uncertainty and risk, they do not eliminate it. Equally, as a result of issues such as cohesion, risky shift and groupthink, other forms and levels of risk can be introduced into a situation.

Because of the risk and uncertainty that remain for an organization from the application of group activity it is tempting to suggest that surplus capability is required within a group in order to be able to deal with crises. For example, members of a group may be unexpectedly taken ill or new developments may come to light which make the task of the group more difficult or complex. In other words, on average any group should be operating at a sub-optimal level. Indeed in an interview with Tyler (1999) Luttwak (a leading consultant) argues that a little inefficiency is inevitable and to be welcomed within organizations as part of the human experience. The surplus capability available at times could be used to absorb some of the **variety** from the environment. However, this runs counter to much of the received wisdom on organizational efficiency, in which the pressure is to minimize input and maximize the output, or as it is frequently put, to **sweat the resources**. In practice, the approach adopted towards this issue depends very much on the purpose for which the group was established and the nature of its operations. In a formal organizational group (say a department) there is frequently a structural means of limiting the dangers from risk. For example, a manager may appoint a deputy to act in his/her absence, thereby minimizing the potential of the department grinding to a halt if the manager is away for any length of time. Groups will make different provision for the need to deal with uncertainty and risk, depending upon the perceived risk and its possible consequences.

Variety
This reflects complexity through the number of different conditions that can arise in any particular system.

Sweat the resources
An attempt to get maximum output from any resource.

MANAGEMENT IN ACTION 7.4 Park life

Informal groups come in many different forms. It is unusual for managers to be able to influence the formation and activities of such groups. Car sharing schemes are one example where managers can seek to facilitate the formation of informal groups to the benefit of the organization. It can also help reduce the demand for car parking spaces at company locations. The internet job site **reed.co.uk** recently published a survey which showed that car sharing schemes can be useful bait for luring and retaining employees. The survey of 3000 people showed that only 5 per cent of employees already use a car sharing scheme, but that 45 per cent would prefer to work for an employer who offered such a perk.

Reed.co.uk director, Paul Rapacioli said that, 'Employees tell us that organizations that set up car sharing schemes would gain through better attraction and retention of staff, as well as strengthening the informal network within the company.' This view is supported by Denise Hollinger, HR manager at Addenbrooke's NHS Trust in Cambridge. She said, 'We state that we have a car sharing scheme in our recruitment adverts, so it is an active recruitment tool.' Hollinger also said that her department was actively involved in running the scheme as part of a cross-departmental transport group that met to tackle staff transport issues. The scheme has been running since 1997 and uses a database of groups for its 9000 employees. It now has 315 groups with 640 people using the scheme and a further 200 waiting to join. There are several incentives for people to join this scheme, such as priority parking near to hospital buildings, and the guarantee of a ride home if a lift falls through.

Adapted from: Davidson, E (2002) Park life, *People Management*, 26 October, pp 44–5.

Stop ↔ Consider

Identify some of the other business benefits that an employer might gain from the introduction of a car sharing scheme?

Groups can be used by individuals towards their own ends. Management is a **political process** as well as being a decision-making one. The achievement of objectives through competitive forces is a necessary feature of organizational life. For example, no company has unlimited supplies of money for expansion and other projects. The allocation of funds to those activities that can provide the best return is more of an art than a science. There are a number of quantitative techniques that exist to make the decision easier, but each requires the inclusion of assumptions about the financial returns possible and future interest rates, etc. The competitive nature of the process of selecting the 'best' activity for investment means that all participants have a vested interest in attempting to make their project the most attractive. This process can colour the way that groups function in decision making, presentational, interactive and political terms, during the preparation and presentation of such cases.

Political process
Any behaviour within an organization which uses political means to achieve a desired objective.

If groups are a key aspect of organizational life then management has a duty to ensure that they perform well, just as there is a responsibility to ensure that other resources are effectively utilized. From that point of view, how groups take decisions and interact and the roles that individuals adopt for themselves are all important issues. The models provided by Belbin and Margerison and McCann seek to assist significantly with this process. A more recent development in seeking to gain effective team results is the creation of the **virtual team**. The use of technology in communicating across time and space, supported by team membership without the need to be physically present in the same room defines the virtual team. Young (1998) demonstrates how several organizations have gained advantage from the application of these ideas. The key feature of the virtual team for Young is the ability to use technology to create and support collaboration at a distance.

Virtual team
A team using mainly electronic rather than face-to-face interaction in order to achieve its objectives.

That organizations perceive an operational advantage from the application of teamwork should be obvious. The difficulty facing managers is how to ensure that they can realize the potential. Within the complex web of organizational activity it is all too easy to create a situation where forces are acting in opposition to each other. One common example is the encouragement of teamwork in operational activity, but reward being determined by individual effort, the pressure on individuals being to maximize individual results in order to optimize their earnings levels. The following Employee Perspective (7.5) considers the difficulties that can arise when personal objectives exist alongside group objectives in a situation when individual objectives are of more value to the employee.

EMPLOYEE PERSPECTIVE 7.5 Richard and his conflicting objectives

Richard worked as a marketing officer within a large frozen food manufacturing company based in Vancouver, Canada. His specific responsibilities were for the marketing activities associated with television advertising. He worked as part of the team involved with all media activity, including press, magazines and radio campaigns as well as television. In practice the television advertising was regarded as the primary media and the other campaigns were based on television adverts adapted for use in the specific media.

Richard's remuneration was based upon a basic salary with in addition a bonus determined from his annual performance appraisal review (carried out by his department manager). The main factors used to measure his performance included, creativity in advert development, audience feedback ratings on campaigns and budgetary control of campaigns. These were all very specific to the television advertising aspects of his job. Group contribution was referred to in the appraisal review, but for development purposes only, it was not used in the calculation of overall performance for bonus purposes.

Richard and his manager both knew that the other members of the media marketing team were younger and with less experience than Richard. The manager suggested to Richard that he should spend more time on tasks which would lead to the development of the other members of the team, thereby enabling them to come up to his standard in capability and performance.

Tasks

1. If you were Richard how would you react to this suggestion and why?
2. How could any potential difficulty for Richard be avoided, without negatively impacting on his performance or bonus?

CONCLUSIONS

In this and the previous chapter we have considered how it is that groups set about structuring themselves; how they function and take decisions. The groups that are relevant to an organization are many and varied, both internally and externally. It is in making effective use of the ideas contained within these chapters that management can attempt to ensure that internal effectiveness is enhanced and external threats from even more effective groups minimized. It is also a means through which some of the social needs of individuals can be provided for within a work setting.

Groups, both formal and informal, are an important part of organizational life. Informal groups within organizations present a particular challenge for managers as they are essential, unavoidable and largely unmanageable. They represent the grease on the wheels of the formal organization as people help, support or hinder each other in practice yet they lie outside the formal organization framework. As the pressure on managers to produce ever higher rates of return from ever fewer resources increases, the significance of achieving a form of self-management within the organization becomes apparent. Group working and the more effective use of groups generally represent ways of seeking to achieve this objective. In this chapter we have introduced some of the main issues surrounding the ways in which groups operate and achieve success. As managers seek to improve the performance of their organizations the levels of effectiveness of the groups within them becomes a more critical factor.

Now to summarize this chapter in terms of the relevant Learning Objectives:

- **Outline the nature of the dynamic processes that occur within and between groups.** There are a number of features associated with group dynamics. For example, groups and teams are made up of individuals, each with a different personality and work background. These factors impact on what will happen between the individuals when they meet in a group context. There are also a range of other factors that impact on how a group will undertake its activities and interactions with other groups, size group norms and leadership being just two of them. The level of cohesion felt by the members of a particular group will also impact on how strongly they feel the need to contribute towards its objectives. The risky-shift phenomenon suggests that there are links between the level of risks associated with group output and the nature of group decision making. Groupthink is another aspect of group activity which suggests that there are a number of forces acting on individual members which influence events. Psychotherapy demonstrates the emotional power present in group activity and how it therefore impacts on how people behave in group settings. The ways in which groups fit together in relationship and influence terms, together with the circumstances prevailing at the time can also influence to a significant degree the dynamic between groups.
- **Describe the similarities and differences between models of how groups can be made more effective.** There are a number of models of group effectiveness, of which the two most common are the Belbin team roles and the Margerison and McCann team management wheel. Figure 7.15 seeks to demonstrate one perspective on how these models differ from each other. It is argued, by Margerison and McCann that their model is based upon a socio-psychological view of individuals, whereas the Belbin model is based on a sociological model of people. In some ways the models are similar in that they explore what it is that people do in a group setting and suggest that an effective team requires an appropriate blend of roles from the spectrum available. Margerison and McCann, however, argue that the balance of people needed will depend upon the circumstances at the time and the purpose of the group. Both of these models offer suggestions about the factors that an effective group displays as compared to an ineffective group. McGregor also makes a general set of recommendations about the eleven factors that differentiate an effective from an ineffective group in Table 7.2.
- **Explain how decisions are made in groups and the difficulties that can be encountered in reaching agreement.** The decision making in any group is similar in many ways to the decisions taken by any individual. There are the criteria that impact on the decision itself. A group might like to recommend a new computer system as a solution to a problem, but the company might not be able to afford it, for example. There are the various decision making models (covered in a subsequent chapter) which encourage particular perspectives on how decisions should be made. Then in addition there are the more general factors that impact on any decision. For example, the political context within organizations can influence group activities in many ways including **hidden agenda (see glossary)** issues that individuals may bring with them to meetings. The interaction that takes place within groups influences, in more ways than the level of expertise brought to bear on the problem, the decisions reached in that forum. For example factors such as the size of a group can influence the degree to which individual contribution can be made.
- **Understand how control can be achieved within groups through such mechanisms as socialization and authority.** The process of socialization involves individuals learning how things are done within a particular context. Control within groups can be achieved through this process as the norms of behaviour established by a group will be passed on formally and informally to new members. All members of a group are expected to adhere to the norms established for the group and sanctions will be applied by other members if these are not followed. This process in action was clearly demonstrated in aspects of the Hawthorne Studies. Authority refers to the ability of a leading or significant figure within a group to directly influence the behaviour of the group. This was demonstrated in both the Asch and Milgram experiments, described in the appropriate section of the chapter, in which pressure from other members of the group or from senior people generally influenced the actions of the subjects. The interesting question is why that happens and to what extent such behaviours occur in the workplace.

- **Assess the implications of issues such as groupthink and the risky shift phenomena on group functioning.** Groupthink reflects a set of processes that were identified in military and bureaucratic committees by Janis. The relevant section of the chapter introduces the major factors that Janis identified as collectively forming groupthink. The danger of groupthink is that inappropriate decisions result because factors occur that disrupt the natural opportunity of a group to draw on the collective capability of members in a free exchange of opinion and information. Because of the hierarchical nature of most organizations it is difficult for junior members of a team to challenge senior members and this can lead to acquiescence in a decision before all the evidence is reviewed effectively. Janis also provided a number of factors that could assist with the minimization of the risk of groupthink occurring. The risky shift phenomena suggests that groups tend to take decisions that are more risky than the individuals acting alone would take. There are a number of possible explanations for this reviewed in the appropriate section of the chapter. Some of the explanations suggest that such a shift is the result of a broader range of appropriate information being available. However, it is also possible that it occurs as individuals can always avoid direct responsibility for the outcome as they were just one of many participants in the decision making process. It is also overly simplistic to suggest that a decision with a higher degree of risk represents an inappropriate decision, as long as the risks are understood and dealt with effectively.

DISCUSSION QUESTIONS

1. Management of an organization is about controlling the formal and informal groups that exist within it. To what extent do you agree with this statement? Justify your answer.
2. What is a sociogram? How might you use it as a means of analyzing group interactions and the dynamics between individual members?
3. Explain in your own words the team roles described by Belbin along with their significance in group activity.
4. Describe the different patterns of communication that might be found in groups and suggest how each might influence subsequent decision making by the group.
5. Define in your own words the team management role preferences described by Margerison and McCann and assess their significance in group activity.
6. Much has been made of the existence of informal groups within organizations. As a manager how might you seek to understand the informal groups that exist within your organization and to what extent might you seek to manage or influence them?
7. What are the factors that might be used by managers to influence and control the behaviour found in organizational groups? How successful would you expect such mechanisms to be and why?
8. What is group cohesiveness? How does it relate to group conformity?
9. What determines the dynamics within a group and how significant are they to the activities of any tutorial or work groups to which you belong?
10. Explore the reasons why managers should be concerned with member satisfaction as a feature of group outcome.

CASE STUDY Employees fighting amongst themselves

This Case Study is based in the same company used in the Case Study at the end of the Chapter 4, on personality. Therefore, you should read that case to refresh your memory of some of the details. In that case it was indicated that John as the production manager was seeking to negotiate new terms and conditions of employment with the trade union representing the factory employees working for the company. As indicated, there was a lack of trust among all levels working at the company and so the negotiation of a new deal was proving very complex and slow progress was being made.

One of the major problems to be addressed was the issue of how easily employees could manufacture overtime for themselves, and hence additional earnings. This was in addition to the productivity bonus scheme which also paid additional money if work was produced more quickly than the previously negotiated targets. Over the years, various production managers had made numerous concessions on these targets and they bore no real relationship to the actual time needed to undertake the work required. This provided some employees with an opportunity to inflate their earnings without too much difficulty. Essentially it was the older products that allowed the earnings levels to be inflated and so it was only a part of the workforce (those with longest service) that could benefit from these weaknesses. This inevitably caused friction and argument between employees, as everyone wanted the lucrative jobs, but once achieved they were not given up willingly or quickly.

This situation led to difficulties for the negotiators from both sides as they sought to deal with the problems. There were essentially two groups within the factory workforce, both of which were represented by the same trade union. One group had the opportunity to inflate earnings quite easily as a result of the slack work standards and also to manufacture the need to work overtime if they chose to do so. This group of employees tended to be the older, longer serving employees and they also had considerable influence in the trade union group within the company. This group was also the largest number of employees within the factory. The other group had some ability to inflate earnings by delaying orders and working overtime. The work standards for their jobs tended to be more accurate and so it was necessary for employees to find ways of delaying work without sacrificing bonus earnings in the process. In doing so they had to balance the additional money earned from overtime, with any potential loss of production bonus, never an easy calculation to make accurately. The number of employees in this group was smaller that the other group and they generally had shorter service with the company. Equally, they were not in such a prominent position within the trade union branch, so it was more difficult for them to get the trade union to take their case seriously and act accordingly.

So the basic position of the parties in the negotiation was that management wanted to develop a new incentive scheme which was consistent and fair to all employees and which would encourage higher productivity. The trade union group had a majority of members on the negotiation committee who had something significant to lose by any changes to the bonus arrangements. But, it also had on it a smaller group who would have liked to see an improved bonus scheme implemented which would provide an opportunity to earn more money without needing to manufacture the overtime as the means of doing so. It was against that background that the management and trade union negotiating committee was seeking to find solutions.

Tasks

1. If you were John, as the senior company representative on the negotiating committee, how would you seek to make progress against this background?
2. If you were the senior trade union representative in this situation how would you seek to make progress against the background of a lack of agreement among the people that you represent?
3. How might an understanding of group dynamics help either of the two leading negotiators in this case?

FURTHER READING

Aranda, EK, Aranda, L and Conlon, K (1998) *Teams: Structure, Process, Culture, and Politics*, Prentice Hall, Upper Saddle River, NJ. Considers how to create effective teams as well as how to deal with some of the problems that can arise in them.

Cartwright, D and Zander, A (1968) *Group Dynamics: Theory and Research*, 3rd edn, Tavistock, London. Although quite old now, this is a research-based text which gives an insight into how these issues can be studied.

Clark, H, Chandler, J and Barry, J (1994) *Organization and Identities: Text and Readings in Organizational Behaviour*, International Thomson Business Press, London. Contains a broad range of original articles on relevant material themes and from significant writers referred to in this and other textbooks on management and organizations.

DuFrene, D and Lehman, CM (2002) *Building High Performance Teams*, South Western. Uses the four stages of the Tuckman and Jensen model to explore how to create effective teams.

Gregory, M (1994) *Dirty Tricks: British Airways' Secret War Against Virgin Atlantic*, Little, Brown & Co, London. An interesting review of some of the main features of the BA campaign against Virgin. It shows how the perception of the activities of groups can form a basis for future action. It also highlights how 'lobbying' can be used to influence decision making in groups.

Hackman, JR and Walton, RE (1986) Leading Groups in Organizations, in Goodman, PS (ed.) *Designing Effective Work Groups*, Jossey-Bass, San Francisco, CA. Part of a larger text (all of which has something to offer) this work considers the group and contextual issues that influence activity.

Shaw, ME (1976) *Group Dynamics*, McGraw-Hill, New York. Covers a number of issues relevant to how groups function and behave in the collective activities.

Stacey, RD (2003) *Complexity and Group Processes: A Radically Social Understanding of Individuals*, Routledge, London. An alternative perspective on the ways in which individuals relate to each other in individual and group contexts.

Zander, A (1983) *Making Groups Effective*, Jossey-Bass, San Francisco, CA. A good review of the subject and related topics.

COMPANION WEBSITE

Online teaching and learning resources:

Visit the companion website for Organizational Behaviour and Management 3rd edition at: *http://www.thomsonlearning.co.uk/businessandmanagement/martin3* to find valuable further teaching and learning material:

Refer to page 35 for full details.

PART FOUR
Managing organizations

The previous section looked at groups, what they are, how they form and how the individuals interact in that context. This section extends that perspective by moving up a level in the organizational framework and considering what management is and how it functions in that context.

One of the issues addressed in this section is the nature of management and the distinction between the formal job of being a manager and the role of a leader. Leaders are not necessarily managers within an organization as there are examples of individuals who have great influence over the attitudes and activities of people and yet who hold no formal position within the organization. Management and leadership are of vital importance in any organization as it is the people who hold those positions that must firstly identify the purpose of the organization; then its strategic objectives; then convert that intention into a functioning reality. In doing so they need the support and co-operation of a wide range of other individuals and groups and also need to ensure that the strategy originally identified remains appropriate and is being achieved. It is also important to realize that managers are also individuals and that they also work in teams and groups and so are subject to the same pressures as ordinary employees in seeking to carry out their special role as manager and leader.

A wide range of perspectives on both management and leadership are introduced in this section in preparation for the next section which involves consideration of what managers actually do in exercising their responsibilities in managing the people under their control.

CHAPTER 8

Management within organizations

LEARNING OBJECTIVES

After studying this chapter and working through the associated Management in Action panels, Employee Perspectives, Discussion Questions and Case Study you should be able to:

- **Understand what management is within an organizational context.**
- **Explain the roles that managers perform and the skills that they need.**
- **Outline the significance of training managers to deal with critical incidents.**
- **Describe the relationship between power and management.**
- **Appreciate the significance of humour in management.**

INTRODUCTION

Management is a common term and almost everyone would be able to provide a very general description of what a manager does. Managers run things; they run companies, they run football clubs, they run shops and restaurants. This chapter will set out to explore just what it is that managers actually do when they run the things that they do. Some of the questions that will be examined include what management actually is, what managers do and if managing is the same in every type of organization? The job of 'running things' is complex and becoming ever more so. As a consequence this chapter reviews much of the nature and form of that complexity in order to provide a better understanding of what is required to perform the task effectively.

One important aspect of the task of management is the question of how managers themselves are trained and developed to undertake their responsibilities. This is an area of organizational activity that is often undervalued by organizations, particularly in Britain (Harrison, 1994). However this situation is changing with the range of undergraduate and postgraduate degrees available in business and management growing every year, in line with the number of students seeking to qualify in this field. Also the volume of in-company training provision is also expanding rapidly as organizations recognize that they need to make provision for the development of their own managers. Frequently, in-company training programmes for managers have been validated by university management departments to improve content credibility and impact. See for example, Hall (1994a) and Merrick (1994) in relation to the training of directors. The directors of any company have particular responsibilities to ensure that the organization for which they hold legal responsibility is managed in accordance with the law and also that it is directed appropriately as a trading entity.

Management
The jobs within an organization charged with running the organization on behalf of the beneficial owner.

WHAT IS MANAGEMENT?

The introduction to this chapter has already given a clue to what management is about – running things. However, that explanation of itself carries very little real meaning and communicates very little of what management actually involves. The *Pocket Oxford Dictionary* (1969) defines the term 'manage' as comprising the following connotations: 'Conduct the working of, have effective control of, bend to one's will, cajole … find a way … contrive to get along … bring about, secure … deal with … skilful handling'.

The term manage can be applied to many different situations. For example, an individual could 'manage' to lose ten kilograms in weight over the course of three months by dieting and taking more exercise. Equally, they could 'manage' to balance their budget over the course of a year so that they did not spend more than they earned in salary. Also, using the term in a negative sense, an individual could 'manage' to make a complete mess of a do-it-yourself project on their home and be forced to call in a builder to repair the damage and complete the project properly. However many of these situations do not specifically relate to the organizational context which is the primary focus of this text.

To manage within an organizational context carries with it several connotations that are based on the dictionary definition already indicated, but which also incorporate other implications. To understand the nature of management within an organizational context it is first necessary to understand the concept of an organization. Any organization is established by someone, or a group of people to achieve particular objectives, including providing benefits for the owners who established it. This generalized view can be applied to almost any type of organization, including those found in the private sector, the public sector, charities, residents associations, the not-for-profit and commercial companies, etc. In the commercial sector the clear objective of the founders is to make profit from an enterprise, through the manufacture of goods or the delivery of a service into the marketplace. In the public sector the government (or ruler) establishes a government department or public utility on behalf of the people to enhance the quality of life in society or to make the functioning of government more effective. In the case of the charity and not-for-profit sectors, organizations are established by groups of people who wish to contribute something to the improvement of standards of living for disadvantaged or excluded groups of people. The main point to recognize is that benefits are created for the founders, through the organization, even if they are not measured in financial terms.

In the early days of any organization it can usually be managed by the founders alone, largely because of the limited size and scale of the operation. However, once it is established and begins to grow, then it needs to have other people brought into the organization. These are, first, worker level personnel but, eventually, other managers are required to assist in managing the organization. Naturally in the public sector as a result of the nature of the way that government works managers would be involved in the process right from the start. That aside, managers are appointed by the beneficial owners to act on their behalf. In principle, it does not matter whether this is a small company with the owners heavily involved and assisted by professional managers, or a large company owned predominantly by institutional investors through the stock market. Managers are appointed by the beneficial owners to act on their behalf in realizing the objectives of the owners.

Managers are in a unique position within an organization in that they are appointed to achieve the objectives set for them and to act *in loco parentis* for the beneficial owners, and yet they are employees. They do not, in most cases, own the company that they manage, although they may in some cases be granted significant blocks of the share capital, yet they are expected to act is if they were the owners. This introduces an element of the complexity in the job of management. Managers are predominantly employees, with the same rights and contract-based relationship with the company as other workers. However, they are expected to act and function as if they were the beneficial owners, on whose behalf they are employed. This can on occasion lead to the existence of double standards as indicated in the following Employee Perspective (8.1).

In effect managers are one of a number of stakeholders linked to an organization. A stakeholder is generally defined as falling into one of two categories implying 'someone who has an interest' (Lynch, 1997, p 427):

1. Those involved in the carrying out of the organization's mission and objectives. For example, managers and employees.
2. Those involved in the outcome of the mission and objectives of the organization. For example, shareholders, customers, government, suppliers, financial institutions, etc.

To this a third category can be added: those groups and individuals with an interest in the by-products of the mission and objectives of the organization. For example, trade unions, the local community, family members of the employees, local shops, etc. These groups will have an interest in the outcomes of the organization's mission and objectives. For example, local shops are keenly interested in the volume of money in the local community, as without money to spend people do not visit shops. It does not matter to the local shopkeeper if a local company is prospering and as a result will move to new premises 500 miles away, or whether it's going bankrupt. What matters to the shopkeeper is that employees from the local community will be made redundant and have less money to spend. A generalized model of the stakeholders surrounding any organization is included as Figure 8.1.

EMPLOYEE PERSPECTIVE 8.1 Do as I say, not as I do!

The following comment was made by an employee about his boss.

My boss is obsessive about timekeeping, presentation and deadlines – for everyone except himself. Although he is always ready to have a go at us for slipping up in any way, he never practises what he preaches. As a result, we're all fairly unmotivated to do as he says. Is it worth having a word with him about his apparent inability to follow his own rules, or will I risk ruining our working relationship?

Task

How would you advise the employee concerned? Compare your advice with that offered by Bullmore, J. in What's your problem? *Management Today*, July 2003, p 81, and reconcile the views expressed with yours.

The value of the stakeholder concept is in offering a means of recognizing the range of groups and individuals with a vested interest in an organization. However, it also provides a means of recognizing the different possible consequences for each category. This allows managers to identify and prioritize appropriate actions for each category. Not all stakeholders have equal power when it comes to influence on the organization and its actions. The level of power held by any particular stakeholder group can also change depending upon the circumstances. For example, the print unions and employees held considerable power in newspaper publishing on Fleet Street, London over many decades. They had the power to stop production instantly and not infrequently did so in pursuit of higher wages and improved working conditions. However, with the introduction of computer-based technologies much of that power evaporated very quickly.

As companies develop it is possible that managers will develop interests different from those of the owners or shareholder of the business. Shareholders are primarily interested in a financial return on their investment. Managers frequently have an interest in growth and reinvestment as with increased size comes professional development, reputation and enhanced salary and benefit levels. Holl (1977) for example suggests that unless managers of large organizations are threatened by takeover or rewarded in particular ways, they may well take a broader view of the organization and

FIGURE 8.1

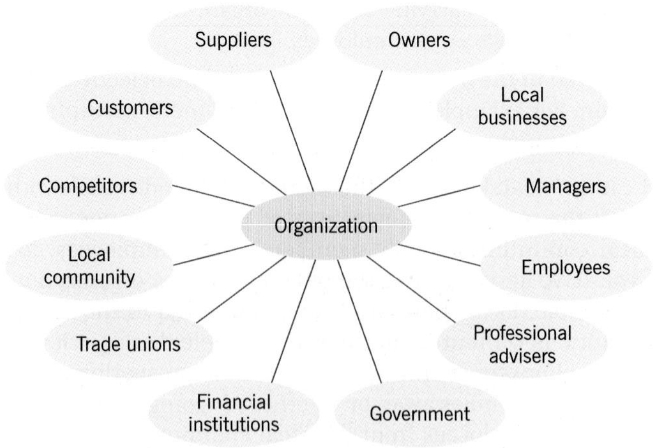

Stakeholder map of an organization

its objectives than the shareholders. This trend to separate ownership from control was detected as far back as the 1930s and can be seen in many corporate battles of today. For example, recent attempts by some members (the owners) of Standard Life, a very large mutual insurance company, to force the company to de-mutualize and so realize their 'locked-in wealth' was fiercely (and expensively) resisted by the senior managers of the organization (Moore, 2000). Managers won the battle (having spent some £10m on the project) on that occasion, but perhaps not for long, at least in the opinion of some investors.

In another perspective on the complexity of management, Cook and Emler (1999) explored the perceptions of subordinate and superior managers in the evaluation of candidates for a middle manager vacancy. This type of research is interesting from many perspectives, including the exploration of who might make a good manager and why. The researchers predicted that senior managers (future boss of the candidate) would evaluate candidates differently to the subordinates of the applicants. The same candidates were evaluated by both groups of evaluators and they used the same criteria (moral, technical and social qualities) to do so. The moral qualities appeared to give the greatest degree of difference, being more significant to subordinates than superiors. Employees want the people with power over them to have high levels of moral responsibility, whereas more senior managers perhaps just want results!

This discussion adds weight to the view expressed earlier that management represents a complex process. Clearly, from the foregoing discussion managing an organization involves achieving objectives. However, it also involves managing the stakeholder environment, managing the power balance between stakeholder groups and harnessing the resources available (including money, equipment, facilities, systems and employees) in pursuit of the desired objectives. There is also more than a suspicion emerging from some of the literature in this area that managers are beginning to exert more influence than the owners of the business in deciding what the organization's objectives should be. It is now appropriate to consider some of the theoretical perspectives on the topic in order to begin to tease out just what management involves.

FAYOL AND THE MANAGEMENT PROCESS

The work of Fayol (1916) is most frequently quoted as offering a foundation in what managing involves. Fayol was a French mining engineer by training and worked for the same company all his working life. He wrote his views on what running an organization involved, for the benefit of other managers rather than as a theoretical model. He began by identifying what he considered to be the main functions of any organization:

- *Technical*. This function represents what would be clearly understood as manufacturing or operations in today's organizations.
- *Commercial*. This function represents what would be clearly understood as purchasing, sales and supply chain or logistics in today's organizations.
- *Financial*. This function represents what would be clearly understood as the provision of financial funds, capital budgeting, project management and risk assessment in today's organizations.
- *Security*. This function represents what would be clearly understood as protection of people, goods and property within the organization. Interestingly, Fayol would also incorporate human resource management activity in this category in the sense of avoiding strikes etc.

- *Accounting*. This function represents what would be clearly understood as the management accounting function together with stocktaking, costing, and statistical analysis in today's organizations.
- *Administrative*. This function represents what would be clearly understood as the management responsibilities in today's organizations.

The management of organizations (administrative functions in Fayol's words) were said to consist of the following activities. In this list of activities Fayol was describing what has become known as the **management process**. In essence, the process that managers must go through in order to manage:

Management process
The view of management developed by Fayol, consists of: Forecasting, Planning, Organizing, Co-ordinating, Commanding, Controlling.

- *Forecasting*. This stage in the management process involves predicting or attempting to foresee the future.
- *Planning*. Having foreseen the future it is then necessary to make provision for dealing with it. This, along with the term forecasting comes from the single French word *prevoyance*; used by Fayol it means to both predict and prepare for the future.
- *Organizing*. Having developed a plan for the future it is then necessary to provide and organize the resources required for the achievement of the plan.
- *Co-ordinating*. This stage of the process is about ensuring that all of the resources available are arranged appropriately, function effectively and are in harmony (co-ordinated) in order that the plan can be realized.
- *Commanding*. This function is about ensuring that everything works as it is intended to in order to achieve the plan. This involves giving instruction to employees and ensuring that the performance of every person is appropriate to the objectives.
- *Controlling*. This function is about ensuring that the plan has been followed. It is about ensuring that everything is done in proper order and in sequence to ensure the achievement of the objectives established in the plan.

Fayol also proposed a set of 14 *principles of management*, which he argued would help to ensure that the process of management was successful. He pointed out that these principles should be used with some flexibility and adapted to the prevailing circumstances for the organization. His 14 principles are described in Table 8.1.

Fayol is not the only person to have a view on the nature of management, although he may be the most widely quoted. For example, FW Taylor (1947) as part of his scientific management approach suggested that the work of the general foreman should be broken down into eight separate functions, each undertaken by a different person. This approach he termed **functional foremanship**. The type of activity identified by Taylor describes a very different job compared to the job of management described by Fayol's functions. However, it must be recognized that Taylor was making these suggestions about a particular type of management job, whereas Fayol was describing management in general and from a top-down perspective. The eight functions identified by Taylor as comprising functional foremanship are included in Table 8.2.

Functional foremanship
The principles of scientific management applied to first line management.

MANAGING IN A SOCIAL WORLD

Managers do not manage in isolation from the forces acting upon society as a whole and, in particular, the reactions to their attempts to control from those being managed. For example, Montgomery (1979) makes the point that the direct challenge to the

1	Authority and responsibility. Authority cannot exist without responsibility. The exercise of authority ensures that the right things are done
2	Unity of command. Each worker should have only one boss
3	Division of work. Breaking the work down into small sets of tasks allows the worker to develop high levels of specialization and efficiency
4	Discipline. This is necessary for efficiency to exist. The manager must exercise appropriate discipline in maintaining order
5	Subordination of individual interest to that of the organization. The organization must be placed above personal or group interest if it is to succeed
6	Equity. Each person should be treated with equity as far as it is possible to do so
7	Scalar chain. There should be a proper hierarchy of grades and responsibilities from the bottom to the top of the organization
8	Remuneration. Payment methods should be fair and benefit both employer and employee
9	Centralization. The degree of centralization appropriate in any organization depends upon the circumstances
10	Order. Material and social order is necessary for the avoidance of loss in goods and people efficiency
11	Esprit de corps. Harmony and unity should be encouraged among the workforce to ensure that everyone works together in the interests of the organization
12	Initiative. This should be encouraged in all levels as a source of strength for the organization
13	Stablility of tenure. Where possible organizations should avoid the 'hire and fire' approach to managing people. With security of employment comes commitment and efficiency
14	Unity of direction. There should be one head and one plan controlling the overall direction of the organization

TABLE 8.1 Fayol's 14 principles of management

Inspector	Repair boss
Time and cost clerk	Instruction card clerk
Gang boss	Order of work and route clerk
Shop disciplinarian	Speed boss

TABLE 8.2 Functional foremanship

power and conditions of work for craft level employees, led to the rejection of scientific management-based attempts at management control on practical and ethical grounds. This reaction emerged originally in the USA when the government attempted to introduce scientific management methods into the military arsenals during World War I. However, as Montgomery also points out, most of the opposition to Taylor's ideas was overcome by the mid-1920s, with some of the unions in the USA supporting its application in return for recognition and union involvement in collective bargaining etc. (Nadworny, 1955).

FIGURE 8.2

On the door hanging section last year, the Superintendent instructed the men to work to their man assignments (i.e. job specifications). Their written instructions were that they were to do 14 two-door cars, 14 estates, and 21 four-door saloon cars. The men accepted – but management couldn't get the cars into correct rotation. The result was chaos, as the workers did just what they had been told to do. Two-door cars were coming down the line with doors for four-cars – 7 inches too short ...estate car doors were being smashed into position on whatever car turned up next! The superintendent begged the men to return to their own patterns of working. But the men insisted on working strictly to their instructions for the rest of the shift. The result of this was that management allowed us to work to our own patterns. They left it to us. The situation is the same today.

Manager always knows best (*source*: *Red Notes* (1976))

Much of the criticism of the methods of management implied by approaches developed by writers such as Fayol and Taylor are that they are inflexible. They imply that managers simply need to apply a formula in order to achieve effectiveness and efficiency. This is not the case. Management reflects a two-way dynamic between the manager and the managed, it is a social process. Figure 8.2 reflects the story of one incident that makes this very clear.

Willmott (1984) points out that management as a reflection of the husbandry of resources must not be confused with what managers actually do in exercising their responsibilities for controlling the work of other people within an organizational framework. For example, corporate planners develop many of the plans to be subsequently approved by managers in a process of selection between options through interactive, but directed activity. In this type of process managers are effectively exercising choice between options developed by other people. It is not the managers themselves who plan or forecast, as implied in the Fayol conception of the management process, they arrange for it to be done, subject to their approval.

It was during the nineteenth and early twentieth centuries that management began to emerge as a distinct occupational category. During that period organizations were growing in scale as they were able to capture the benefits of the then emerging technologies to make and distribute goods and services in vast quantities. Accordingly, as society was changing, so were the organizations within them in terms of size and complexity. This encouraged the **professionalization of management** as an occupational category and the emergence of models underpinning its practice. It was Child (1969, p 225) who pointed this out, by suggesting that management's claim to be a profession could only be plausible if it were supported by a generalized body of knowledge. Therefore models such as the principles of management began to emerge as potential to be such a basis.

Professionalization of management
That management represents more than a job, with its own defined area of work requiring particular skills, knowledge and training.

With the suggestion of the existence of management as a profession a number of writers suggested that a post-capitalist society was emerging with the consequential lack of need to consider political conflict between business owners and labour (see, for example, Dahrendorf, 1959). Such views, however, were not universal, or held across Europe. Fores and Glover (1976), for example, indicate that although the specialist nature of executive jobs was recognized across Europe, the collective category of manager in such activity was not recognized in every country. In a variation on this theme Shireman and Kiuchi (2002) suggest that there exist four seasons within a business cycle and that there is an appropriate management model that can be associated with each. The key to success in this approach lies in the ability of managers to manage the overlap between seasons in the company cycle. The seasons described are essentially thus:

1. *Growth season*. Expanding its physical size with new machines, workers and resources. The application of Scientific Management as developed by FW Taylor would be appropriate here. However, this approach does not work well when the business is faced with change.
2. *Improvement season*. Occurs when an organization is gradually refining its products and processes. The application of quality management principles as developed by writers such as Deming and Juran is appropriate to this season. However, it is not appropriate when the company faces a crisis and must change very quickly.
3. *Pruning season*. A period during which radical action is necessary in order to cut out the dead and diseased material from the organization in order to allow new growth to emerge. The application of Business Process Re-engineering as devised by Hammer and Champy is relevant to this season. That approach can work well once or twice, but if used too often people begin to feel vulnerable as they are under constant threat of being 'pruned' next.
4. *Searching for direction season*. This is a period that allows the organization to remain a cohesive entity during the period in which it searches for a new identity and path of development in an ever changing world. It aligns with the idea of core values management as described by Jim Collins and Jerry Porras in their book, *Built to Last*. However this can be counterproductive if it takes too much time away from the need to grow and develop new products and services as opportunities present themselves.

A sociological perspective on management is provided by Reed (1989). He brings together much of the earlier sociological thinking on management and in doing so identifies four themes on what it is about. They are:

1. *Technical perspective*. Management as, 'a rationally designed and operationalized tool for the realization of predominantly instrumental values concerned with the systematic co-ordination of social action on a massive scale' (pp 2–3).
2. *Political perspective*. Management as, 'a social process geared to the regulation of interest group conflict in an environment characterized by considerable uncertainty over the criteria through which effective organizational performance is assessed' (p 6).
3. *Critical perspective*. Management as, 'a control mechanism that functions to fulfil the economic imperatives imposed by a capitalist mode of production and to disseminate the ideological frameworks through which these structural realities can be obscured' (p 10).
4. *Practice perspective*. Management as, 'a process or activity aimed at the continual recoupling or smoothing over of diverse and complex practices always prone to disengagement and fragmentation' (p 21).

The practice perspective on management as identified by Reed attempts to bring together elements from the other three perspectives into a more holistic framework. Therefore, management looked at from this perspective, contains a number of different themes in describing how it interacts with the social world of which it forms part. What managers actually do is therefore regarded as a function of the dominant perspective in any given situation. A number of writers have sought to modernize the original ideas of Fayol in describing what managers actually do in drawing the distinction between the interests of the beneficial owners and workers in the social environment surrounding the business. For example, Drucker (1977) suggests that there are five activities in managerial work which enable it to be performed effectively within the social environment:

1. Setting objectives and interpreting the implications for each work area.
2. Organizing activities and people in order to be able to meet objectives.
3. Motivating and communicating with employees to ensure an effective work process.
4. Measuring the performance of the organization and the individual's within it and taking action to ensure high achievement.
5. Developing people to enable them to contribute to the achievement of maximum organizational performance.

The point emerging from consideration of the social context within which managers function is that they are subject to a range of forces acting in the social environment and cannot act independently of those pressures. Society is constantly evolving as are the legislative requirements and expectations of the people who form the employees, customers and clients of the organization. Managers must be able to accommodate each of these variables within the dynamic world of business and competition in order to survive and offer value to their employing organizations.

WHAT MANAGERS DO

There is such a wide diversity of management work that it is not possible to specify what range of duties every manager will undertake. There have been a number of reports produced over the years that consider the nature, training and exercise of management responsibilities. Most studies of what managers actually do reflects a view of management not at all like that implied by the Fayol model. They describe a fragmented, hectic job with frequent switches in activity. Handy (1993) summarizes a number of studies (Chapter 11) into the job of managers that clearly demonstrate this, including:

- *Supervisors*. Guest found that each one averaged 583 separate events that required the supervisor to do something in every working day.
- *Managers*. Stewart found that on average each manager enjoyed only nine 30-minute periods without interruption over a four-week period. It is often suggested that managers should adopt an open door policy in which subordinates have open access to their boss. However as the following Employee Perspective (8.2) indicates this can create problems for the boss.
- *Chief executives*. Mintzberg found that many activities for this category of senior manager fitted into ten-minute bursts of time. Meetings were also short, lasting one hour on average.
- *Organization size*. Mintzberg reported differences in activity between the chief executives of large and small organizations.

MacKenzie (1972) classifies the time spent by managers as either managing or operating and identifies the changing balance between these two categories at different levels of the managerial hierarchy. Figure 8.3 illustrates this changing balance of activity between hierarchical levels.

EMPLOYEE PERSPECTIVE 8.2 How can I keep my door open?

The following comment was made by a practising manager about his open door policy.

> I have always kept an open door policy at work and encourage my direct reports to talk to me whenever they need to. Recently, the number of staff reporting directly to me has increased, and I'm finding it really difficult to get on with my own work with all the interruptions. Unfortunately, I've been told by my staff that what they like best about my management style is that I'm always available, unlike some of the other managers. How can I cut down on my 'availability time' without seeming to be letting them all down?

Tasks

1. Is an open door policy a good thing for employees? Why or why not?
2. Is an open door policy a good thing for the boss? Why or why not?
3. What advice would you give to this manager? Compare your answer with that offered by Bullmore, J. What's your problem? *Management Today*, July 2003, p 81, and reconcile the views expressed with yours.

The specific nature, range and pattern of work undertaken by any manager will depend upon a wide range of factors. Stewart (1985) identifies a number of these, including:

- *Industry*. The job of a personnel manager in a national retail chain employing 1000 people would be different to the same job carried out in a heavy engineering company with the same number of employees on one site.
- *Role*. The figurehead role of the senior manager in a large bureaucracy carries with it a different activity pattern compared to that of an entrepreneur at the head of a rapidly growing diverse group of companies.
- *Pattern of work*. Most management jobs contain patterns in the activities involved. For example, the job of a budget accountant is largely determined by the monthly budget cycle. However, a chief executive would focus on the quarterly and annual results reported to investors. Also, project-based jobs are different in activity pattern to line management positions.
- *Level*. The level within the hierarchy clearly influences the tasks performed by the manager. The chief executive generally does different things to the first-line manager.

FIGURE 8.3

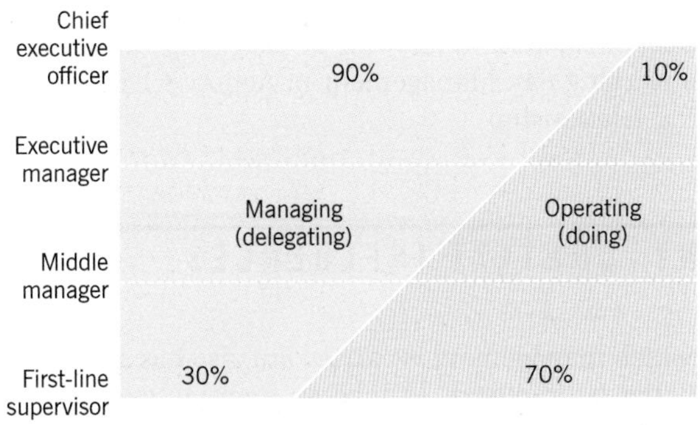

Managerial activity (© Alec MacKenzie. *Source*: MacKenzie, RA (1972) *The Time Trap: How to Get More Done in Less Time*, McGraw-Hill, New York)

- *Exposure*. This aspect of activity reflects the degree of visibility and representation of the organization in the execution of a manager's job. For example, a sales manager is highly exposed (visible) in that much of their time would be spent in contact with customers. This can be compared to the job of a management accountant which would be largely focused on activity within the organization.
- *Contacts*. The nature of interaction with other people is a key factor in work activity. For example, the job of a public relations manager would be expected to be completely different in activity from that of a personnel manager.
- *Personal factors*. Individual difference and preferences encourage variation in work activity to take place at any level within an organization. For example, one manager may prefer to stay in their office and manage through sending memos and e-mails, another may prefer to walk the job and deal with people in person.

Luthans (1995) describes four general types of management activity, along with the approximate proportion of time devoted to it, extracted from the 'Real Managers Study'. However this model does not take account of the range of different types and level of management jobs that exists. Luthans' four types of management activity are as follows:

1. *Traditional management*. Planning, decision making and controlling. This accounts for 32 per cent of management time.
2. *Routine communication*. Exchanging information and handling paperwork. This accounts for 29 per cent of management time.
3. *Networking*. Interacting with outsiders, socializing and politicking. This accounts for 19 per cent of management time.
4. *Human resource management*. Managing conflict, motivating, discipline, staffing and development. This accounts for 20 per cent of management time.

There is another aspect associated with activity to be considered in this discussion. There is a vast difference between activity and effectiveness. Simply doing something does not by itself achieve organizational objectives. Activity has to be effective before it has any value to the organization. Merely rushing around, looking or being busy is not enough. To use a football analogy, it is not the team that runs all over the pitch for 90 minutes that wins; it is the team that scores the most goals. Activity that either scores goals or prevents the other team from doing so is the only effective activity in that situation. This is an aspect of what manager's do that will be discussed later in this chapter. Another important feature of what senior managers actually do revolves around the working relationship with their personal assistant (PA) or secretary. In many ways the PA has as much power as their boss (as perceived by junior level staff) and serves in a gatekeeper capacity by allowing or restricting access and shaping many aspects of the boss's working day. Management in Action 8.1 reflects on a number of aspects of this working relationship.

MANAGEMENT: CONTEXT INFLUENCES

The context within which management is carried out also has an impact on the nature of the management that is practised. To take an extreme example to illustrate this point, the job of the chief executive of a large international organization would be expected to be completely different from the job of the owner of a small manufacturing company employing five people in total. There are many aspects of the context within

MANAGEMENT IN ACTION 8.1 Managing a Personal Assistant (PA)

The relationship between a manager and the personal assistant (PA) is an unusual one in organizational terms. Although technically the boss is the senior person, in salary terms often by many thousands of pounds sterling each year, the PA is very much a force to be reckoned with. They frequently act as an assistant to the boss, performing the duties of gatekeeper, diary manager, researcher, deputizing at meetings and acting as an informal conduit of information on such diverse aspects of company life as employee opinion, morale and gossip. This is a far cry from the traditional secretary role of taking dictation, typing, filing and making the coffee. So how should a boss manage their PA? The suggestions include:

- *Communicate*. Talk things over properly, including your proposed whereabouts.
- *Listen*. Pay attention to what the PA says, it is probably important.
- *Trust*. Trust the PA to do the job that they were appointed to do. If you cannot trust your PA replace them.
- *Don't presume*. Be clear what you expect from your PA from the start. Don't just presume that you can drop any task on the person, such as getting you a coffee; they may not regard that as part of their job.
- *Be accountable*. Accept responsibility for your own mistakes; never try to blame the PA.
- *Respond quickly*. Don't leave questions unanswered for long periods of time. It wastes everyone's time (including yours) chasing answers.
- *Be appreciative*. Remember to say thank you for a job well done. But do not go over the top all the time.
- *Prioritize your tasks*. Make sure that the PA knows the most important jobs to be done and don't class everything as urgent.

However, another aspect of the relationship is the need for the PA to manage the boss if the relationship is to work effectively and the important tasks are to be done. Aspects of this form of upwards management include:

- *Communicate*. Talk things over, especially when there are lots of tasks that need to be done urgently. Explain the problem and its causes clearly.
- *Get to know the boss's way of working*. Try to match the way the boss prefers to work, unless they are completely disorganized.
- *Respect your boss*. If you do not respect your boss and back them in public then it will become apparent and the working relationship will deteriorate rapidly.
- *Be discrete*. Being in a position of great trust and having access to often confidential and sensitive information is a heavy responsibility. Other people will interpret what a PA says as a reflection of the thinking of the boss and that could cause difficulties, so it is easier to stay silent.
- *Never moan about your boss to colleagues*. This is likely to get back to the boss one way or another and destroy any trust between you.
- *Agree on duties*. The role of the PA is to make the boss's working life easier. Over time make sure that a dialogue takes place about the scope of the duties involved in the job and agree on them.
- *Don't be scared of your boss*. If you make a mistake admit it early on and suggest a solution. If the boss has made a mistake and does not realize it tell them discreetly.

Adapted from: Hoar, R (2002) Up close and personal, *Management Today*, December, pp 54–9.

Stop ↔ Consider

The relationship between the boss and PA is an unusual one in organizational terms. In one of the points above it suggests that if the boss cannot trust the PA then they should be replaced. Should this aspect of managing these working relationships be allowed bearing in mind the existence of company employment policies and employment legislation aimed at providing all employees with fair and consistent treatment at work?

which management is carried out that could be explored. Figure 8.4 illustrates a number of the more significant aspects of the context that might be expected to impact on how management is practised within an organization. The following sub-sections will explore each element within Figure 8.4 in greater detail.

Public/private sector organizations

Market testing
Checking the cost of something against market norms.

There are a number of differences between public sector organizations and those in the private sector. It might immediately be assumed that the major distinction lies in the fact that public sector organizations are bureaucratic and do not have the profit motive as the rationale for their existence. While this is undoubtedly true to a significant extent, reality is much more complex than that implies. The public sector is now subjected to many variations on the theme of **market testing** (and charging for services) in an attempt to ensure efficiency and cost minimization. For example, tuition fees have been introduced for students attending English and Welsh universities. This will inevitably change the relationship between institutions, students, staff and government over time. It will in turn also influence the management of universities as they attempt to respond to this changing dynamic. University managers will have to become more commercially aware, rather than simply being the group responsible for allocation of resources and accountable for their use.

Equally, many very large commercial organizations have bureaucratic tendencies and do not match the private sector notional model of lean and fit. The banking sector might serve as an example of bureaucratic organizations in the sense of very large institutions seeking to dominate and dictate to the customer. Ashworth (2000) illustrates this through a discussion of the behaviour of large banks in seeking to enforce disloyalty charges on their own customers for using the cash dispensers of other banks, as well as the continuation of the payment of very low interest rates on current accounts. This has now changed or is being put under severe pressure as a result of consumer reaction, government pressure and the growth in the number of telephone or electronic bank accounts paying relatively high rates of interest, thereby forcing the banks to become more customer responsive or risk losing significant levels of business.

FIGURE 8.4

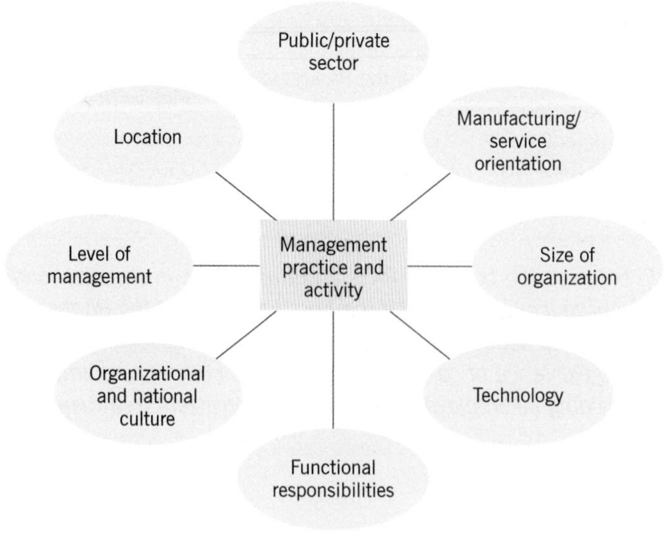

Contextual influences on management

Management in the public sector was regarded as a process of ensuring that the centrally determined policies and procedures were being applied, along with the inevitable checking of the work of subordinates. At a senior level, the job of public sector management was regarded as dealing with the political interface. In local as well as national government, elected politicians inevitably seek to carry out what they regard as their electoral mandate. This inevitably requires public servants to develop new policies and procedures that will impact on the delivery of the public services to the general population. In the private sector it is generally assumed that senior managers must interpret the desires of the owners of the business (often the City) as well as the customers in seeking to achieve the best financial return. However, as has already been suggested, this relationship is more complex and subject to more change than this very simplified model implies.

As with many stereotypes these images hide as much as they reveal about the nature of work and management in both types of organization. Often people work in the public sector because they wish to be involved in some form of public service. People do not only seek to work in the private sector because it pays more money. There are many differences between the public and private sectors, but there are also many similarities (Farnham and Horton, 1996). Therefore it is not possible to generalize about specific differences in management activity between the public and private sectors.

Manufacturing/service orientation

The nature of manufacturing and service organizations are fundamentally different. Pure manufacturing operations do not require the presence of the customer during the process of making something. However, the customer must inevitably be present in some guise during the provision of a service. Of course, there are many examples of mixed approaches. For example, providing designer-made clothes requires the customer to be present for fittings etc., but it also contains a manufacturing aspect in making the clothes. Equally, there are many opportunities for web-based services which at most require an electronic interaction rather than the physical presence of the customer. However, the presence of a customer during part of the organization's activities creates a different dimension to the work of managers. Pak *et al.* (2002) offer guidance on appropriate strategies and tools that can be of assistance in managing geographically dispersed service networks. The basic steps involved in their suggestions are:

- *Know the customer at a local level.* Identify what makes them deal with the local branch.
- *Define the service model and resource needs.* Know how to deliver the service and what resources are needed to ensure that it happens as planned.
- *Map the financial implications at the local level.* Identify the true cost of providing the service as planned, along with any alternative options for delivering the service to customers.

The flow of customers can be unpredictable as can their requirements from the organization. This inevitably leads to a need to be able to manage that uncertainty as well as be available to deal with any crisis as it develops. Service operations have a higher degree of immediacy and susceptibility to customer complaint during the process than manufacturing and this alone can change the nature of the way in which management functions in that environment (Fitzsimmons and Fitzsimmons, 1994).

Size of the organization

The scale of the operation will also have a significant impact on the nature of the management activities within it. For example, the chief executive of a small company with about 50 employees will become involved in a much broader set of managerial activities than the chief executive of a large company with many thousands of employees spread over a number of locations. For the chief executive of a small organization there are many fewer other managers and specialists to whom activity can be delegated than would be found in a very large organization, and so it must be done personally. Also in a very large organization the chief executive would tend to be involved with many more significant players in related fields than would the CEO from a small company. It would not be uncommon for the CEOs of very large organizations to mix with senior banking, City and political figures on a regular basis. The CEO of a small company might meet the local Member of Parliament and bank manager if they are lucky.

Functional responsibilities

The functional responsibilities of a manager will also influence the work they become involved with. For example, the activities of an engineering manager would be different to some extent to the activities of the human resource manager in the same organization. There would be some degree of similarity in these two jobs. Both managers would have to comply with common company procedures and policies; they would both have to attend similar meetings and might become involved in joint projects. However, the emphasis of the two jobs would differ and the expertise and level of general contact might also be different. The engineer would be expected to have a high level of technical knowledge across the engineering disciplines and also to manage stores and maintenance employees, in many ways a specialized line management function. The human resource manager would have to manage their own department, but the staff within it would be at different levels of the organization to the maintenance personnel, which would in itself create differences in activity. Also, the human resource manager might act as a high level adviser and facilitator to the management team in terms of assisting in their personal and professional development, as well as dealing with senior level recruitment and terminations.

Technology

The level of technology used within the organization is another feature which would be expected to impact on the practice of management. For example, in an organization in which computer technology undertakes much of the actual processing of work, then management becomes focused much more strongly on managing the people interface with both the technology and the customer. It is also likely that management will emphasize the creation of novel ways of using the technology available and of developing new applications. Management in Action 8.2 considers one new innovation in this field, the emergence of shared services in human resource management delivery.

Location, organizational and national culture

The topic of culture is explored in Chapter 12 and so will not be developed here. Suffice to say that in this context the cultural context within which management is practised would be expected to have a significant impact on the work of the managers themselves.

MANAGEMENT IN ACTION 8.2 Centre of attention

Re-engineering has been applied to the provision of human resource (HR) management within a number of large organizations. The provision of centralized services is not new, but what is new about the current wave of HR service centre development is, first, the opportunity for the customer (or client) to take as much or as little of the service as they feel necessary and, second, the application of technology to the process.

Research by the Institute for Employment Studies (IES) shows that there are a number of different models for the provision of shared HR services. However, most organize the provision of HR services into three distinct categories. First, the retention of a corporate HR group dealing with high-level strategy, governance and policy. Second, the provision of HR business partners/advisers to work within individual business units, supporting operational managers on issues such as development, change and organizational design. Third, the creation of a shared services unit providing a range of HR advice and support to operational managers via a call centre or intranet. This last category covers the practical, day-to-day HR activity that can take up so much time, particularly when linked to the inevitable administration that occurs with managing people. For example, the paperwork necessary to record employee benefit choices or to advertise a job vacancy.

The IES study identified three main reasons for the introduction of shared services approaches to HR provision:

1. *Cost reduction*. Reducing the number of HR specialists by centralizing activity, saving on accommodation costs and exploiting common purchasing power.
2. *Improving quality*. The approach encourages specialization, consistency through the technology and the development of expertise through repetition. Individual shared service staff become more aware of best practice through involvement and exposure to issues. They also become more focused and sensitive to customer needs (the business units forming the client base of the service). Managers are also more able to monitor the quality of service provision effectively.
3. *Responding to (and leading) organizational change*. This means being able to flex the provision of HR services as the business develops and changes and also to be able to segregate the different client needs appropriately to concentrate on areas of business need.

The development and availability of appropriate technology was an important element in the opportunity to create shared services centres. Some organizations rely heavily on the use of call centre-type operations to deliver the service. For example, IBM has established an 'Ask HR' service covering Europe, the Middle East and Africa from a common base just outside Portsmouth. Although it might appear to be like any other call centre, it employs people who speak 11 different languages and who are conversant with HR practice in their respective countries. Also, unlike most call centres, staff are taken away from the phone desks for about 20 per cent of their time to work on projects. Higher category staff in the centre spend a greater proportion of their time on project work. It is envisaged that employees will progress through the two levels of job within the 'Ask HR' operation, before moving into individual business units at a strategic level.

Although a number of organizations have followed this type of route, not all have. For example, Powergen, a power utility in the UK, has gone down a totally different route in adopting the service centre principle. Splitting the existing HR function into the three categories suggested above, the service centre was located in the same head office building as most of the client business units. This enabled a high degree of human interaction between client and service centre staff and therefore less reliance on communication and computer technology. Customers can actually walk into the service centre and speak to staff face to face, a point which the manager of the unit feels is important to its success.

From a management perspective the issues in running these service centres are described as attracting and retaining appropriate staff, selling the services to the business units and ensuring a high quality of service provision. There is a danger that in a call centre-type of environment staff would not envisage career progression and may become bored quickly. The example from IBM indicated above demonstrates both the opportunity to ensure a career path for such staff and the development of the high-level skills needed to deal with HR work of this type. Even within the Powergen example, where technology does not feature so heavily, the provision of career routes through the service centre are regarded as an important aspect of maintaining an effective service. The manager of one such operation described the service centre as the 'nursery for the development of future HR consultants within the company'.

Adapted from: Reilly, P (2000) Called into question, *People Management*, 6 July, pp 26–30; and Pickard, J (2000) Centre of attention, *People Management*, 6 July, pp 30–6.

Stop ↔ Consider

To what extent might the management of the HR service centres described differ from managing in other contexts?
To what extent might this be as a result of the call centre and intranet technology used?

There are inevitably tensions inherent in international management that do not arise in a single country context. Adler (1991) describes the 'tensions between one's immediate national concerns and the broader interests of humanity and the future' (p 148). She quotes the work of Levinson on the impact of early culture experience which predisposes individuals to particular ways of relating to other people and expectations of power-based relationships. It is suggested that this in turn conditions particular ways of managing or being led in an organizational context. Managers running international operations must, of necessity, be able to reconcile these issues across international borders.

Fenby (2000) reports a study by one overseas employment specialist that suggested that 88 per cent of companies viewed a period spent overseas on assignment as useful for career prospects. This result is particularly important considering the number of organizations, even relatively small ones that now engage in international operations in some form or another. He also quotes a former head of Ford, Alex Trotman as saying:

> Think global, be prepared to work in several different cultures. You'll never get on staying in one place. Speak more than one language; get used to the idea of intensive competition. Be nimble, be courageous and always expect the unexpected.

Adler also quotes an interesting report by Oh (1976) reflecting the application of Theory X and Theory Y to management in China after the 1949 revolution. It identified that managers allied with the communist ideology tended to adopt the Theory Y perspectives in the belief that they were closely aligned with the philosophy of Chairman Mao. Managers with less skill in the ideological areas tended to adopt Theory X principles. This provides an indication that leadership approach may be influenced by political and economic as well as cultural perspectives.

A US-owned company with a subsidiary in South America is likely to face different management scenarios and pressures from those of an indigenous organization. Equally, a foreign organization in any country in the world led by a national from the host country is likely to face different leadership scenarios and pressures from one managed by a parent country expatriate. Figure 8.5 reflects the interaction between the variables active in the international context.

Levels of management

This aspect of the context has already been alluded to on a number of occasions. It is inevitable that the level of a particular manager in the hierarchy will impact on their activities. A branch manager in a bank will become involved in a range of activities different from the regional manager, who will also become involved in different

FIGURE 8.5

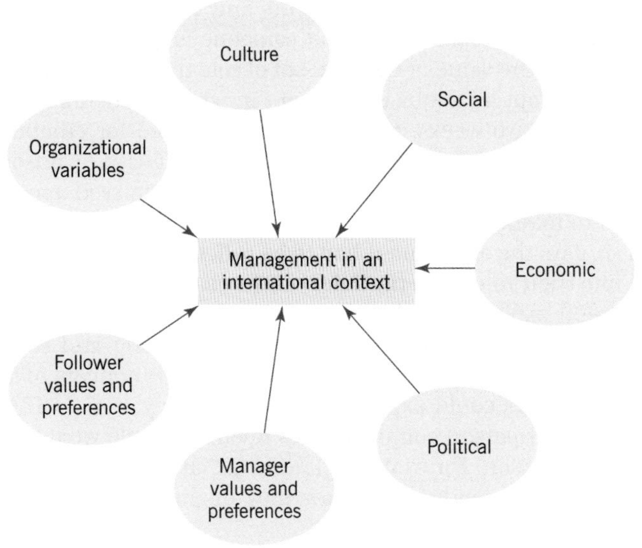

Management in an international context

activities from the branch operations director. Moving up the levels within a large organization requires the individual to become involved in less immediate operational issues and to focus on corporate performance and longer term planning. This point is illustrated clearly in Figure 8.3 in the context of the balance between managing and operating. A junior line manager will spend more time actually joining in the operational work of the organization than would the chief executive. The junior line manager in becoming involved in the work of their subordinates inevitably engages with the basic operations of the organization. However, a chief executive who becomes involved in the work of their subordinates becomes engaged with senior management activity, a different form of managing, not operating.

MANAGEMENT ROLES AND SKILLS

Role theory is based on theatre performance; the actors perform roles as written by the author and as interpreted by the director. The requirements of the part that each actor plays are set out in the script. There is a requirement for each player to behave as expected for the whole theatrical experience to work as intended. Extending this analogy from the theatre to an organizational context implies that there are particular roles (otherwise known as jobs) defining what everyone is expected to undertake. Also that there is a web of requirement and expectation and that everyone in the organization will perform as expected in the specific role that they are performing. The application of this metaphor in practice creates stability and predictability in work activity and relationships within organizations. This area was also introduced in Chapter 6 in relation to group activity.

Role theory
In every job there are several roles to be performed and there are conflicts inherent in the different roles.

The application of role theory provides individuals with a model of what is expected of them in undertaking a particular job or function. The use of **role play** is common in many management training courses as a way of getting the participants to practise (rehearse) behaviour repertoires for use in their daily work. How to tackle 'problem employees' would be one such example, where managers are provided with

Role play
The acting out of a situation which is not real, perhaps for training purposes.

Role model
Someone who is highlighted as a person with desirable qualities to be emulated by others.

the opportunity to role play particular events and explore appropriate management response behaviours. The observation that someone is a good (or bad) **role model** is another indication of the value of the concept of role theory in shaping behaviour.

Zimbardo carried out a famous experiment in which students took part in the role play of a prison over two weeks. Students were screened for emotional stability and maturity before being randomly allocated to the role of guard or prisoner. A basement was transformed into a prison and the volunteers were dressed appropriately. Guards were instructed to maintain order during their shift and left to arrange things on that basis. Within six days the experiment had to be called off. Both sets of 'players' became so integrated into their roles that the safety and well-being of the 'prisoners' was being put at risk. Several explanations have been put forward for this result including the significance of the concept of a role in creating meaning and expectation among participants. Also the direct and powerful influence of the concept of a role on shaping the behaviour of players could explain the result (Haney *et al.*, 1973). Knowledge of the role of a particular person communicates to other people what behaviour patterns to expect from that person. For example, knowing that someone is a prisoner creates a partial picture of that individual and how they might be expected to behave in the mind of the prison guard.

Considering the notion of role in formal terms there are a number of concepts that need to be examined:

- *Role set*. The name given to the group of people with whom a particular person might interact in a particular context. Figure 8.6 is the role set of a personnel manager.
- *Role definition*. The sum of behavioural expectations from the role set surrounding a focal person in a specific context.
- *Role ambiguity*. Refers to the existence of uncertainty among the role set about the precise role that each is expected to play in a specific context.

FIGURE 8.6

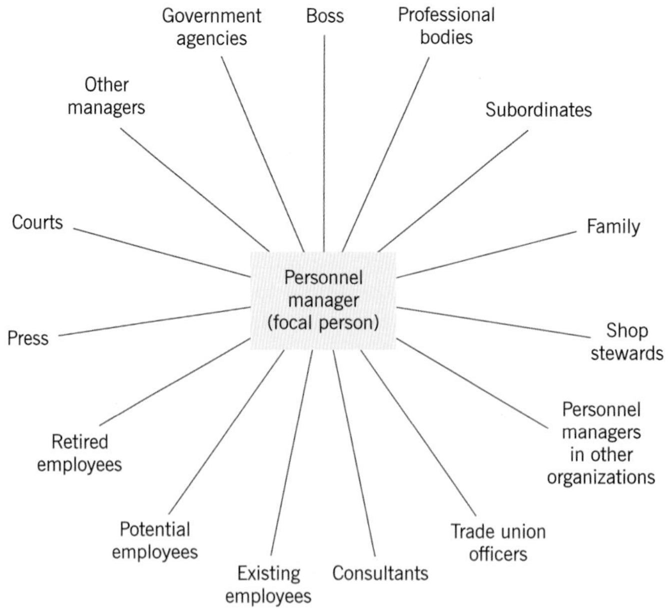

Role set of a personnel manager

- *Role incompatibility*. Where expectations of members of the role set differ with the focal person's view of their role. For example, employees may have been used to an open informal style of management. The subsequent appointment of a manager with an authoritarian style is likely to produce incompatibility in the expectations of both parties in terms of the most appropriate management style to be adopted.
- *Role conflict*. Arises with the dilemmas between the roles that individuals are expected to perform in the same situation. In performance appraisal reviews there is often scope for role conflict as a result of the performance and salary requirements of the system. Managers are expected to 'help' the individual improve their performance at the same time acting as 'judge' in assessing the level of pay rise to be awarded. In a court context it is the equivalent of attempting to be the defence barrister and trial judge at the same time, hence the role conflict!
- *Role stress and strain*. Pressure is placed on individuals as a result of the roles that they are required to undertake in a specific context. For example, where there is role conflict present the individual will inevitably experience stress and feel under pressure. Pressure is not of itself a bad thing, but too much (or too little) can be harmful. This was demonstrated by Weiman (1977) who found that individuals who were at either the low or high end of the stress range displayed more significant medical problems than those who experienced medium stress.

Mintzberg (1973) describes a number of roles undertaken by managers as shown in Figure 8.7. Each of the roles indicated acts in a co-ordinated way to produce a whole job, effectively creating a role profile for the position.

Each of the three categories of role indicated in the Mintzberg model is intended to reflect the following areas of managerial responsibility:

FIGURE 8.7

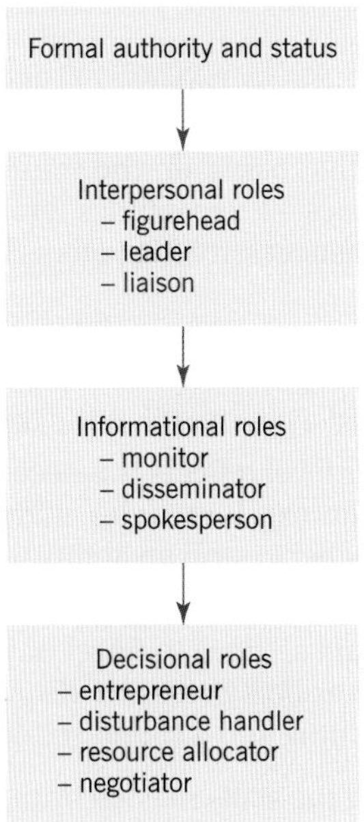

Mintzberg's management roles

1. *Interpersonal roles.* These roles reflect the form that the interaction with other people takes as a consequence of the status and type of managerial job held by a particular manager. For example, the industrial relations manager of a company would be expected to act as a figurehead in representing the company to the employees, the leader of the management–union negotiation body and a liaison between managers and the trade unions. This represents a different role pattern than might be expected to apply to the marketing manager in the same company.
2. *Informational roles.* These roles reflect the nature of the way that information is used in the job of the manager. These are heavily dependent on the dictates of the interpersonal roles of the position. For example, the industrial relations manager indicated above would find it necessary to disseminate particular types of information in particular ways to particular people as a result of their interpersonal roles.
3. *Decisional roles.* These roles reflect the nature of decision-making requirements within a particular managerial job. They are heavily dependent on the previous two categories of role indicated. For example, an industrial relations manager would be expected to play a leading role as a disturbance handler in the company as a consequence of their status and information networks.

Visioning and motivator roles
That part of a manager's job communicating the desired future and encouraging employees to work towards it.

More recent studies have introduced different role titles, including **visioning** and **motivator**. There has been some support for the use of these more recent concepts and their impact on organizational performance (Hart and Quinn, 1993). However, it has also been suggested that much of this is a reflection of a 'pop culture' in management – in other words a transient, shallow perspective offering little of substance.

Over recent years there has been an emergence of the notion of competency as the basis of identifying the abilities needed to perform specific jobs (Armstrong, 1995). Katz (1987) provides one list of the management competencies necessary to undertake a job in this field covering interpersonal skills, conceptual skills and diagnostic skills. Not all management jobs require equal measures of each of the three skill areas. It will vary with seniority and function. There are many other writers who have claimed to identify the competencies necessary for particular managerial jobs. For examples of other competency lists see Dulewicz (1989) and Woodruffe (1990).

One approach to the development of appropriate skills and competencies among managers using role theory is that based on the framework proposed by Pedler *et al.* (1994). This framework identifies 11 capabilities, grouped under three levels, which differentiate successful from unsuccessful managers. They are:

- *Basic knowledge* and information. This level includes those things necessary for taking decisions such as the possession of a relevant professional understanding, an awareness of events and a command of the basic facts.
- *Skills and attributes.* This level reflects the necessary ability to function as a manager in the specific context. It includes analytical and problem solving skills, social skills, emotional resilience and an ability to be proactive in situations.
- *Meta qualities.* This level reflects the ability that some managers have to bring together the other skills and abilities in novel ways in dealing with situations. It includes such capabilities as being creative, displaying mental agility, having a balanced approach to learning and a sound self-knowledge.

Another approach to identifying the skills needed by managers at any level of an organization is proposed through the Management Charter Initiative (MCI). The MCI, established in 1988, is an independent body established with the aim of improving the performance of managers in the UK. One of the objectives of the MCI has been to develop National Management Standards, based on best practice, as a framework for developing managers who are capable of performing effectively. The Management Standards proposed by the scheme fall into seven key roles, each containing a number of units which form the basic competency blocks for being able to perform the role effectively (HMSO, 1997). The seven key roles are indicated in Table 8.3. However, not everyone would support the MCI initiative as reflecting the full range of competencies required of all management jobs. For example, Orbanes (2002) suggests that there are many similarities between designing and playing games such as Monopoly and the skills needed to be an effective manager.

MANAGEMENT AND DIVERSITY

This topic could cover a wide range of perspectives. It is managers who take many of the decisions within organizations, and the lack of diversity (sometimes called discrimination) in an organizational context is in many instances about inappropriate decision making. It is about issues such as selecting an individual to do a job on the basis of the colour of their skin, gender or physical capacity, rather than on the basis of the qualification and skills of the person in relation to the job for which they are being considered. It is about seeking to stay within a narrow (and usually pre-existing) range of human differences to be employed within the organization.

A lack of diversity can occur in promotion decisions, it can arise in areas such as granting access to development and training opportunities or even in the way in which managers speak or deal with other people. For example, the words used by a superior to evaluate the performance of a female subordinate were demonstrated to be different from that used to describe the performance of a man (Thomas, 1987). The

Key role	Example of units within the role
Manage activities	Manage activities to meet customer requirements Contribute to improvements at work Establish strategies to guide the work of your organization
Manage resources	Manage the use of physical resources Manage the use of financial resources Secure financial resources for your organizational plans
Manage people	Manage yourself Create effective working relationships Select personnel for activities
Manage information	Facilitate meetings Chair and participate in meetings Use information to take critical decisions
Manage energy	Promote energy efficiency Identify improvements to energy efficiency
Manage quality	Promote the importance and benefits of quality Manage continuous quality improvement Carry out quality audits
Manage projects	Co-ordinate the running of projects Plan and prepare projects Manage the running of projects

TABLE 8.3 MCI management standards

findings showed that women were described as less competent, logical and mature than men and their performance attracted fewer promotion recommendations and only very general levels of praise as compared to males. This discriminatory behaviour effectively restricted higher performance rankings to men, thereby ultimately limiting the diversity within the more senior levels.

This last research finding reflects the vast majority of discrimination studies in that it is focused on gender. However, it is reasonably safe to assume that much the same would be found with the other forms of discrimination that can arise. Wilson (1995) reviews many aspects of organizational behaviour in terms of the gender issues that arise, including management. She points out that:

> Sex-role identity, which seems to be more of a result of socialization than of basic sex differences, seems to have a substantial effect on the formation of occupational aspirations and expectations. Men are going to aspire to, and succeed in, more male-intensive occupations. (p 115)

Clearly this view, based on research findings, has significant implications for the number of women who would seek to become managers in the first place and who would subsequently achieve the opportunity to function in that capacity. The same can be assumed to be true of many other forms of possible discrimination, such as ethnic origin, age, accent, education, social background, etc. The following Employee Perspective (8.3) reflects the experience one female officer cadet in relation to her spoken accent.

On pages 172–5 Wilson establishes the case for claiming that men and women bring different qualities to the role of management, quoting a wide variety of research sources in the process. Many of the studies reviewed by Wilson suggest that women display what could be described as 'people' orientation in their practice of management, whereas men tend to display a 'task' focus in their management style. While this vastly oversimplifies the discussion, it has been suggested that it might also be a function of laboratory studies of management practice, rather than a function of real gender difference at the workplace (p 175). She concludes with the view that there is much more to learn about how the social world is constructed to the advantage (in terms of pre-eminence) of men, and the ways in which this is perpetuated in both management research and practice.

EMPLOYEE PERSPECTIVE 8.3 Lose the accent if you want to succeed

A female university graduate applied for officer training to serve in the British army. She was born in Newcastle upon Tyne, a fact obvious as soon as she spoke. She had good A level grades as well as a solid upper first class degree and experience in a range of relevant sports and recreation activities. She did very well in her initial officer training and was looking forward to her first positioning. In the final briefing by her senior instructor, she was told that she was very bright and that she had displayed qualities that could take her far in her chosen career; however, there was one problem – her accent. Her instructor (a man) said to her that the best advice that he could give her, if she wanted to be promoted to senior officer rank, was to lose her current accent and cultivate a more appropriate speaking voice.

Tasks

1. What would you do in this situation if you were the lady concerned?
2. Should accent make any difference to promotion in this (or any) situation? Explore both sides of the argument in the context of diversity and the need to manage in a military context. Would the same apply in a commercial company?

Gardiner and Tiggemann (1999) suggest that women face different pressures from men in industries that are male dominated. Also, that in male-dominated industries they face different pressures from both men and women than in industries dominated by women. In male-dominated industries women are reported as adopting male characterized management styles. Research from the Centre for Developing Women Business Leaders at Cranfield University suggests that the strength of the informal organizational culture is what effectively holds women back from reaching the top jobs (Vinnicombe and Harris, 2000). For example, the authors surveyed 100 international organizations and found that 'closed informal' systems existed in many for selection and promotion, involving nomination without candidates' knowledge and appointments being agreed after discussion between line managers and central personnel. Only between 2 per cent and 15 per cent of overseas postings are held by women, indicated elsewhere in this chapter as a key requirement for senior management appointments these days. Another study reported by Vinnicombe and Harris suggests that success as measured by organizations tends to reflect the male view rather than how women might define it. Another study demonstrated also that the concept of commitment is defined differently by both men and women and that as a consequence of the male domination of senior levels, again it is that definition that tends to be recognized and valued.

MANAGEMENT AND ORGANIZATIONAL EFFECTIVENESS

To be effective a manager needs to take account of their own preferences, the preferences of the group being led, the task to be achieved and the context within which it is being carried out. John Adair (1983) describes what a manager has to do in terms of a three-circle model. He emphasizes the notion of leadership rather than the notion of management in his approach, which became known as **action-centred leadership**. Each circle represents a major part of the process of exercising management responsibilities. These are the principal responsibilities for which the leader will be held accountable:

Action-centred leadership
Managing based on three elements – achieving the task, developing the individual, building and maintaining the team.

- Achieving the task
- Developing the individual
- Building and maintaining the team.

In this model achieving the task is self-evident as a significant aspect of management. Adair also suggested that to be successful a leader would also need to recognize the importance of being able to distinguish between the needs of the individual and those of the work group. He argued that it would be very rare when the needs and requirements of all three components were matched. Therefore, it was necessary for the leader to manage the tensions between the three components using a mixture of eight elements of a functional approach to management. These elements are indicated in Table 8.4.

Luthans (1995) also describes two research-based attempts to explore success and effectiveness (pp 384–6) in management activity. Defining success as speed of promotion, networking activities correlated most strongly with it and traditional/human resource management activity the least. The implication of this finding being that promotion depends on socializing and politicking rather than task or subordinate related effectiveness. On the other hand, communication and human resource management activities were most strongly correlated with effectiveness as measured by quality, quantity, employee satisfaction and commitment. One interpretation of this

Defining the task	Evaluating
Planning	Motivating
Briefing	Organizing
Controlling	Setting an example

TABLE 8.4 Adair's eight functional principles of leadership

research is that achieving results does not advance careers! There are a number of other implications that arise from this work including the difficulties in defining and measuring effectiveness and success. Stern (2003) reports the work of Professor Graham Jones of the University of Wales in his research into what he terms 'mental toughness' – the quality that helps elite performers to prevail while others fall by the wayside. This, it is argued, represents the characteristics that are needed by today's successful managers and leaders in seeking to sustain high levels of performance even under extreme pressure. This has links with success in international sports and Lane4 is a consultancy which seeks to link these ideas together on behalf of clients. The ten values of mentally tough people are:

1. *Self-belief*. Being convinced that you possess unique qualities and abilities that enable you to achieve your goals and make you better than your opponents.
2. *Resilience*. Recovering from setbacks as a result of increased determination to succeed.
3. *Focus*. Remaining fully focused on the task in hand in the face of specific, or personal, distractions.
4. *Drive*. Having an insatiable desire and internalized motive to succeed.
5. *Control*. Regaining psychological control following unexpected, uncontrollable events.
6. *Resolve*. Pushing back the boundaries of physical and emotional pain, while still maintaining discipline and effort under distress.
7. *Nerves of steel*. Accepting that anxiety/pressure is inevitable and knowing that you can cope with it.
8. *Independence*. Not being adversely affected by others' good or bad performance.
9. *Competitiveness*. Thriving in the pressure of competition.
10. *Chillability*. Switching the focus on and off as required. Knowing when to relax and stand back from the pressure.

There has been some research support for the view that conscientiousness (as a personality construct) plays a significant part in the achievement of job performance (Barrick and Mount, 1991). Robertson *et al.* (2000) explored this further and found no statistically significant relationship between conscientiousness and current job performance or promotability. They do, however, suggest that conscientiousness does have some links with specific aspects of job performance such as the need for an individual who is organized, and quality driven. In terms of promotability, the significant factors appeared to be articulate, decisive, flexible, innovative, motivated and persuasive, but these same factors were negatively correlated with conscientiousness. The authors suggest the need for a broader view of both personality and what determines job performance. Management in Action 8.3 considers another aspect of this, the effects of having an uncaring manager within the organization.

MANAGEMENT IN ACTION 8.3 Same indifference

The Corporate Advisory Board of Washington DC estimates that the cost of replacing a technical expert in IT, project management or marketing as 1.75 times the individual's salary. Not a cheap process! Even front-line service staff can cost up to 50 per cent of annual salary to replace and train. With some call centres reporting staff turnover in excess of 50 per cent per year, some organizations are spending vast sums of money on replacing staff. Not surprisingly, under such circumstances, it makes sense to find out what makes staff stay put and to try to ensure that they do so.

There are many reasons why staff leave organizations. Better opportunities can present themselves, relocation of the individual or partner, downsizing, re-engineering and merger activity represent just some of them. Among these many reasons some originate from within organizations themselves and add to any insecurity felt by people, encouraging them to take personal responsibility for their careers. However, one significant reason for people leaving an organization is poor management. Buckingham suggests that people do not leave organizations, they leave particular managers. He goes on to report research in one large retail company showing that one in six employees rated their supervisor or manager as the most disliked aspect of the job.

Buckingham reports the results of research carried out by the Gallup Organization, based on 200 000 employees across 12 industries. This found that those organizations demonstrating (through employee survey) high scores on four factors had higher productivity, profit and customer satisfaction levels and lower staff turnover. The four factors on which managers scored highly in these 'successful' organizations were:

1. Having a manager who shows care, interest and concern for each individual.
2. That each employee knows what is expected of them.
3. That each employee has a role that fits their abilities.
4. That each employee regularly receives positive feedback and recognition for work well done.

Buckingham indicates that expectation in organizations is usually shaped by the emphasis on process conformity rather than on the existence of clearly defined objective results for employees to achieve. Also that in recruitment and career planning, emphasis is placed on employee skill and experience, not on natural talent and personal qualities. In addition, recognition and reward for individual employees is usually left to individual managers, leading to inconsistency in the treatment of subordinates. In a recent study it was found that a statistically significant correlation between management talent and level of employee engagement with the work of the organization existed. For example, the most talented managers were those whose subordinates responded positively to the following statement: At work I have the opportunity to do what I do best every day'. This seems to suggest that management should be viewed as the facilitation of employee contribution, not in terms of command and control.

Adapted from: Buckingham, G (2000) Same indifference, *People Management*, 17 February, pp 44–6.

Stop ↔ Consider

Consider the views expressed and seek to reconcile these in terms of the view of management suggested by both Fayol and Taylor.

CRITICAL INCIDENT MANAGEMENT

Crisis management The management task of dealing with unplanned events that pose significant risks to the organization or its stakeholders.

One aspect of management that is just beginning to develop as a result of a number of very high-profile events is that of **crisis management**. Everyone faces the occasional crisis in their lives. For example, a car tyre bursting while travelling along a motorway at high speed, a thief breaking into your house and stealing all your possessions and being sacked from your job without any warning represent some of the difficulties that can erupt and create problems. However, there are some jobs in which the exposure to crisis forms an integral aspect of what might be expected on most days. For example, members of the police, fire and ambulance services are frequently called upon to deal at very short notice with a crisis of some description. A police officer might seek to arrest a thief, only to be faced with a person holding a gun and threatening to kill a hostage. A fire officer may attend a house fire only to be told that people are trapped inside the building. An ambulance crew may attend the scene of a horrific traffic accident and have to deal with terribly mutilated bodies.

These are not the only examples of jobs in which crises can arise. For example, an airline pilot must be prepared for engine failure or other disaster and know how to cope. The senior manager of an oil refinery must anticipate a wide range of possible disasters so that if one happens everyone on site knows what to do. This last example indicates the key theme of this section, that of the management role in preparing for and leading the efforts should a critical incident arise. There is very little literature available on this subject and in terms of the management of critical incidents, Flin (1996) was perhaps the first to bring a number of relevant themes together. Weiner (2001) provides an outline of how to approach the issue of disaster planning and recovery within an organizational setting, including the need to plan ahead, identify an appropriate team and identify the weak points in the organization.

The Home Office (1994), the government department in the UK which is responsible for emergency services, established a three-level incident command structure which has generally been adopted by the relevant services. The three levels within the incident command and control structure are included as Table 8.5.

In many emergency situations it would be the operational level of command that would arrive on the scene first and therefore take initial responsibility. Flin (1996, p 13), quoting Home Office manuals, suggests that the exercise of effective control needs the incident commander to work through the following list of requirements:

Command	Level	Management function
Bronze	Operational	This corresponds to the normal operational response provided by the emergency services where the management is of routine tasks. The initial response to most incidents is at this level. In a major incident the bronze commanders are likely to be in charge of the front-line teams
Silver	Tactical	Their command objective is to determine priority in allocating resources, to plan and co-ordinate actions. At a major incident the silver commander is likely to be the incident commander and located at the incident control post
Gold	Strategic	Their purpose is to formulate the overall policy for the incident response, ensuring that priorities for demands from the tactical commanders are met. They are responsible for government and media liaison. The gold commanders are chief or senior officers, who are likely to be located at a headquarters incident room rather than at the scene. They do not take tactical decisions

TABLE 8.5 Incident command and control structure (source: Home Office (2003) *Dealing with Disaster*, 3rd edn, HMSO, London Crown copyright reproduced with the permission of the Controller of Her Majesty's Stationery Office)

- Prepare
- Assess
- Plan
- Resources
- Implement
- Control
- Evaluate

Similar responsibilities exist within commercial organizations. However, there has been criticism by the Health and Safety Executive and others of the unclear planning and organization for managing critical incidents following rail and other major accidents. One of the difficulties faced by managers of commercial organizations is that the concept of command, particularly in an emergency situation, is very different from the normal practice of management (Larken, 1992, p 31):

> But when time is at a premium and when danger immediately threatens, command has to encompass a wide range of extra skills, mostly concerned with the rapid assessment of people who have changed under pressure and of things which have failed to function as might have been expected. Management is predominantly objective and consultative. ... An important subsidiary conclusion is that the application of conventional management techniques can ironically be quite dangerous in an emergency. (Quoted in Flin, 1996, pp 20–1)

Flin (p 42) goes on to suggest that the necessary personality characteristics for an incident commander are:

- Willingness to accept leadership role
- Emotional stability
- Stress resistance
- Decisiveness
- Controlled risk taking
- Self-confidence
- Self-awareness.

She also identifies (p 44) the skills profile required of an incident commander:

- Leadership ability
- Communication skills (especially briefing and listening)
- Delegating
- Team management
- Decision making under pressure
- Situation awareness
- Planning and implementing actions
- Calm and able to manage stress in self and others
- Pre-planning for possible emergencies.

MANAGEMENT AND POWER – A CRITICAL REFLECTION

Another approach to understanding the nature of management is through an examination of the skills and abilities required to undertake the task. Hellriegel *et al.* (1989, pp 267–71) describe management as a set of activities based on the following characteristics, one of which is power:

- *Relationships*. The quality of the relationship between the manager and subordinates is a major determinant of the ability of the manager to function effectively.
- *Skills*. The skills of self-understanding, visioning, effective communication and empowerment are necessary to achieve effectiveness in group activity.
- **Power**. (model based on French and Raven, 1968). Power is what allows the manager to exercise the function. In the case of management situations these sources of power include:
  - *Legitimate*. Subordinates accept that the manager has the right to be obeyed.
  - *Reward*. The manager controls access and allocation of rewards valued by the subordinates.
  - *Coercive*. The manager controls punishment including disciplinary action, withholding pay or demotion.
  - *Referent*. The personal characteristics of the manager produce in subordinates the desire to follow directions.
  - *Expert*. Subordinates believe that the manager has expertise over and above the others in the team.

Power
Reflects a directing, mobilizing and energizing force in getting people to do what they might not otherwise do.

Each of these sources of power has a number of qualities. First, power in general does not exist as an absolute entity. With the exception of coercive power it is in the gift of the subordinate to accept (or reject) the power used by a manager. For example, if the subordinate does not believe that the manager can deliver desired rewards then that form of power will not function effectively. Even in the case of coercive power the manager does not usually have the power to use physical force and they may not have the freedom to sack the employee without recourse to formal procedures and appeals. That is perhaps why bullying and harassment are becoming more apparent in many organizations. Some writers refer to this as 'downwards' workplace mobbing, Vandekerckhove (2003). This also implies that such behaviour can arise from other directions as well, for example, upwards and sideways. Managers are also employees and can suffer bullying from their subordinates as the following Employee Perspective (8.4) demonstrates.

It is argued that downward mobbing behaviours are a consequence of a failure to work through the effects on management of the changes that are occurring in organizations. Effective managers use most of the sources of power indicated, but the particular one applied at any time would depend on the prevailing circumstances. Pfeffer (1992) explores a wide range of aspects of the use of power and influence within organizations. In his analysis he suggests that managing with power involves the following:

- *Recognizing different interests*. Inevitably, there are a range of stakeholders within any organization and each will have different interests, perspectives and objectives in relation to the business and how things should be done. In any organization it is necessary to understand the political landscape involving the various coalitions and interest groups in order to understand which might be supportive, and which hostile to any management activity.

EMPLOYEE PERSPECTIVE 8.4 Harry's nervous breakdown

Harry was a production manager with about 25 years' experience of working in a range of industrial textile sewing factories within the same group. He had a good reputation among senior managers and was also well liked by his subordinates. He was transferred to a new company bought by the group as it was felt that he had the best range of skills to assist with its integration into the group.

The company that Harry took over as production manager had a largely female workforce but it was dominated by a small number of aggressive individuals. They terrorized their colleagues in many ways and always managed to get their own way with management one way or another. Harry regarded this as unreasonable and set out to change the behaviour of the people concerned. It did not work. On one occasion one of the leading 'terrorists' in the factory kicked Harry's office door off its hinges as he had refused to see her immediately as she had demanded.

Eventually the stress got to Harry and one day the managing director of the company found him in his office sitting in the corner sucking his thumb, having had a complete nervous breakdown. He was hospitalized and soon recovered, but was never again able to take up a managerial position within the group. His confidence had been shattered as had his desire to do the job.

Tasks

1. Could Harry have prevented this happening to himself and how?
2. What if anything could the company have done to prevent this situation developing as it did?
3. What would you do now if you were the managing director of the company and why?

- *Identify the views of the various stakeholder individuals and groups*. This is not just about understanding their views but why they hold them. This is particularly important for those groups and individuals that we do not like personally, as they are the most difficult to take seriously as a threat.
- *Understand the need for power to achieve results*. Power is needed to overcome opposition and it is necessary to understand where it comes from and how to develop greater levels of power held.
- *Understand the strategies and tactics through which power is developed*. Also understand issues such as timing, the use of structure, commitment and interpersonal influence.
- *Being prepared to use power*. It is of no value understanding power if the manager is not prepared (or able) to use it to achieve the desired end result.

The discussion so far presents a very rational and practical view of power in relation to management activity. However, it is one that might imply that power is something that is neutral or which can only exist if all parties agree to it. For example, the French and Raven model implies that employees accept or reject particular forms of power used 'against' them. While there may be some truth in this view, life is never that simple. Employees need the income that jobs (and therefore managers) provide and so the balance of power immediately shifts. Townley (1994) explores the work of Michel Foucault in relation to the practice of human resource management and in doing so examines the concept of power within organizations. One of the conclusions reached in Townley's analysis is that: 'Panopticism is an exercise of power based on analysis and distribution. It operates through hierarchy, surveillance, observation and writing. In this sense power is not located in a person but in practices' (p 139).

Panopticism originates from the design of prisons with a central control tower, from which the guards could observe and control the prisoners in the individual cell blocks radiating from the central hub. A number of people (including Foucault) have likened this design to that of an organization. This incorporates management's attempts to exercise control over the workforce through a wide range of structural, procedural and observational devices. It could be argued that such approaches are an attempt to move the ability to exercise power away from acquiescence by employees in the direction of the 'right of managers to manage'.

Many of the participatory and involvement-based management practices found in organizations today can be viewed through this same lens. Perhaps they function at the level of socializing employees into the ways of thinking preferred by managers? Getting employees involved or engaged in the business encourages workers to see themselves as partners rather than simply employees. As partners they might be expected to adopt patterns of thinking and behaving more like those of managers. By adopting this frame of reference, employees reduce the need for managers to exercise power as employees automatically self-regulate themselves by engaging in approved behaviour patterns.

One of the difficult practical problems faced by managers is how much responsibility they should retain and how much they should delegate to subordinates. This 'problem', or more accurately dilemma, also relates to the issue of power. Many managers feel that in delegating some of their responsibilities they are actually giving away some of their power. In the bureaucratic organizational design, great emphasis is placed on the hierarchy and decision making being carried out at the appropriate level. Exceptions to the normal sphere of responsibility are 'pushed up' the hierarchy for resolution. Inevitably, this can lead to managers becoming overloaded with relatively minor issues and, therefore, not having the time to exercise managerial responsibility. One natural response to this is to increase the number and levels of management, which runs counter to the current trends in downsizing and delayering. These initiatives inevitably reduce the number of levels within an organization because they are grounded in the notion that real effectiveness in operational activity comes from pushing decision making, responsibility and accountability down to the lowest levels possible, that is, **delegation**. It is also argued that giving workers more responsibility increases the quality of the work experience for the individual and, as they are the ones who deal directly with customers it enhances the level of customer service.

Delegation
The passing of some area of responsibility to a subordinate.

Delayering and downsizing are both initiatives that can fall within the approach called business process re-engineering described by Hammer and Champy (1995). Essentially, the authors claim (p 53) that the 'old system' of organizing work was based on the assumptions that the workers did not have the time or inclination to monitor and control work, neither did they have the skills and knowledge to be able to take decisions, therefore managers and many of the specialist functions developed as a response to this. Hammer and Champy argue that these assumptions are now invalid and, moreover, the traditional response creates inefficiency, delay, additional cost and lower levels of customer service. Hence, they argue there is a need fundamentally to re-engineer the organization based on process, not function and as a result (among other things) to compress the vertical dimension of organizations – achieved through delegation.

However, not everyone agrees with this view. For example, McCabe and Knights (2000) argue that Hammer and Champy fail to recognize:

> How power relations in contemporary organizations are bound up with managerial identity. More importantly it [BPR] ignores the way in which power relations are intrinsic to capitalist organizations: hierarchy has not just arisen by accident, it has purpose, being essential to management's control over labour. (p 647)

McCabe and Knights go on to argue that in their view the hierarchy will continue to remain intact because management will be unable to absolve themselves from control through delegation and empowerment. This is because power is relational and inherently part of a capitalist organizational life. They also make the point that in delegating authority and responsibility, managers are not seeking to give away actual control and power. They are simply seeking to ensure that the functioning of the organization more effectively meets customer needs and hence the objectives of management. This, they argue is simply another form of control. Another aspect associated with delegation and control is that of micro management. Management in Action 8.4 introduces some of the issues surrounding these topics.

From this perspective, delegation and empowerment suggest a 'neat trick' perpetrated by senior management on workers. Delegation under this model seeks to integrate workers within the frame of reference determined by managers, thereby allowing middle and junior managers (and the associated cost) to be vastly reduced within the organization through delayering, downsizing or re-engineering. This is achieved through the socialization of employees into the 'new paradigms' maintaining the same overall balance of power and control, while claiming that the quality of work has been improved as well as the level of customer service. It is control achieved through more acceptable social means than the exercise of direct power; covert rather than overt means. Of course, as reduced cost and improved profit levels are likely by-products of these initiatives investors are likely to be satisfied with the outcome.

MEETINGS AND HUMOUR IN MANAGEMENT

Meetings are an inevitable aspect of management. The need to involve other people in decision making as well as persuading them to co-operate in specific courses of action are just two of the reasons for their existence. Other reasons for holding meetings include:

- *Habit.* Holding the regular Monday production meeting, simply because it has always been held, rather than for a specific purpose.
- *Political.* For example, it is possible for managers to convene a meeting simply to be able to say at some future time that everyone was (or had the opportunity to be) involved in (or comment on) a particular project or decision.
- *Courage and risk aversion.* Managers can lack the courage to take a particular decision on their own. This can be a strategy adopted if the decision is risky in business, political or personal terms as it allows the manager to say (if things go wrong) that it was the meeting that decided to take a particular decision. This approach allows the **diffusion of responsibility** to be used as a defence if necessary. This might be expected to occur more frequently in organizations in which a **blame culture** existed. A blame culture describes an organization in which every error (or something not going exactly to the wishes of senior people) must be the fault of an individual or group. Usually the 'blamed' individual or group must be made to 'pay' for their faults as an example to others and to ensure compliance in the future. Not surprisingly, such cultures encourage a 'cover your back at all costs' approach to work.

Diffusion of responsibility
The claim by someone that they were not solely responsible for a decision, thereby avoiding any personal responsibility.

Meetings can therefore be held for rational business-oriented purposes, routine purposes and even defensive or offensive reasons. Just because a meeting is called does not imply that the reason for it is automatically apparent. There may be an agenda which is quite clear, although it is not uncommon to find games being played in terms of what can be included and when, etc. Such events can provide a clear indicator of a hidden agenda at work. This term implies that someone is seeking to manipulate a meeting for some purpose that they do not wish to reveal. However, the existence of a hidden agenda for a meeting can frequently only be guessed at and may only be apparent once the meeting is underway or from comments made (or events that occur) afterwards. The reasons for a hidden agenda frequently fall under the political or courage headings indicated earlier.

Blame culture
Describes an organization in which every error is regarded as the fault of an individual or group.

MANAGEMENT IN ACTION 8.4 Micro management

Every office has one, a boss who is something of a control freak. Always looking over people's shoulders, monitoring their every move, checking tiny, insignificant pieces of work. Working for such people can be demoralizing, demotivating and if left unchecked can crush creativity and innovation across the entire organization.

Organizational psychologist Bruce Katcher suggests that the problem can start right at the top with the chief executive micro managing their immediate subordinates and it then becomes absorbed into the normal ways of working, down through the layers of the hierarchy to the very bottom, becoming part of the company culture. Middle managers who achieve promotion because of their technical expertise often find themselves struggling with the demands of a managerial role and retreat into their comfort zone of familiar technical detail. Poor recruitment can also create difficulties in this area. If companies do not consider the strategic needs of the business they will recruit based on current, not future needs and so the individuals within the organization will experience difficulties in coping with changes in the business as time unfolds. The tendency will then be to fall back on the familiar and begin to micro manage.

However it starts the micro manager spends all their time looking at the detail, fire-fighting and not thinking about the future. This inevitably results in less time for their own development and the development of others. Fresh thinking and enthusiasm are stifled, talented staff get fed up and move on, and both the organization and its staff stagnate. Margaret Gordon, senior consultant with the consultancy Inspiring Performance suggests that organizations need to look at the messages they give out about the sort of work that they value. There is a tendency to reward people for the reactive work that they do and not the proactive work, as the long term is not visible compared to the short term or fire-fighting exercise.

Other reasons for micro management include the egotist who actually considers that their subordinates are not good enough to be able to do the job unchecked, or a boss who is actually frightened for their own job and doesn't trust their subordinates not to undermine their position. The existence of a blame culture also encourages people to act defensively if they consider that they are going to be severely punished for any failure or error that crops up. Feedback from staff is a key element in trying to learn about any tendency to micro manage and the effect it has on staff. Delegating effectively is seen by many as an effective way of breaking the cycle of micro management and its negative consequences. Also finding positive ways of dealing with problems and things that go wrong are important. For example, Laura Parrish a watch leader aboard the LG Flatron (the winning yacht in the BT Global Challenge round the world race) explained that the crew had agreed to look only at the things that went right, not the things that went wrong. If a good sail change occurred, they considered what happened in great detail in order to be able to achieve the same performance every time. Occupational psychologist Peter Honey stresses the need for a coaching approach when things go wrong, rather than pointing the finger and seeking to allocate blame.

Adapted from: Lucas, E (2003) Eye for Minutiae, *Professional Manager*, May, pp 20–2.

Stop ↔ Consider

Is it possible to prevent a blame culture emerging along with micro management as long as mistakes and errors are regarded as bad and something to be avoided in an organization? How can an organization become tolerant of mistakes without encouraging carelessness?

In addition to formal meetings that have been the focus of the discussion so far, there are vast numbers of informal discussions that take place in corridors and over coffee that serve much the same purpose as formal meetings. They can create alliances, sound out opinion and prepare the arguments for a formal meeting. In many large organizations, particularly the public sector, it is common to hold pre-meetings.

These are relatively informal meetings held prior to a formal meeting which in practice allow all the arguments to take place away from the formal setting and so allow the formal meeting simply to ratify the decisions already made. MacKenzie (1972) suggests that many middle managers spend up to 80 per cent of their time in meetings and that approximately 50 per cent of that time may be wasted (p 98).

Humour is a topic that is not formally part of organizational functioning and has therefore been regarded as something incidental to management. It is suggested that organizations are places of rationality and that humour has no place in them. Levity could be a signal that business is not being taken seriously, that there is a lack of respect for the products or senior managers and this is the point of the following Employee Perspective (8.5). Humour is generally considered a trivializing process. However, that is not the only purpose of humour. Consider for example the use of satire as a means of making political points; such insights are frequently far from trivial.

Barsoux (1993) in a book devoted to a consideration of the links between humour, management and culture, suggests that humour in the workplace, 'is rarely neutral, trivial or random. It is deployed for the achievement of quite specific purposes to do with self-preservation, getting things done or getting one's way' (p vii). Barsoux identifies the three main purposes of humour as being:

1. *Sword*. The action aspect of humour. From this perspective it can persuade individuals to particular points of view. It can allow individuals to say those things which otherwise could not be said without causing offence and damage to relationships within the organizational setting.
2. *Shield*. The defensive aspect of humour. It can be used to make criticism more acceptable (by making a joke out of it) and to enable individuals and groups to cope more easily with failure.
3. *Values*. This aspect provides the basis for conditioning individuals into a particular role and contributes to the reinforcement of organizational values. The use of practical jokes and the use of 'in-jokes' – only understandable to the in-group – are the means by which groups can be formed and bonded into cohesive units.

EMPLOYEE PERSPECTIVE 8.5 Don't joke, show respect!

Richard liked a joke and would often tell stories at work in order to lighten the mood and to enjoy a laugh with colleagues. When on occasion someone in authority did something worthy of note it would be turned into a joke or something worthy of a funny story. Peter, his manager on the other hand was a more serious individual who was much more aware of the status of individuals and the need to show what he thought was a proper measure of respect to more senior people. Inevitably, Peter did something which became one of Richard's funny stories and even worse he became aware of it. He called Richard into his office for a serious chat and verbal telling off. During the conversation it was made clear that humour had no part to play in the life of the company or the office and that respect should be shown at all times. Peter actually said to Richard, 'If you can't respect a senior person, then you must respect their position and not make fun of them.' Richard was humbled by the telling off, became rather withdrawn and left about six months later.

Tasks

1. What would you have done (and why) if you were Richard and had just been told off by Peter?
2. Was Peter right in his view about respect and humour? Could an organization function effectively without a 'proper' behaviour pattern existing between senior and junior people? Why or why not? What and who defines 'proper' in this context?

In his book based on a participative research project, Watson (1994) describes a number of aspects of humour during his interviews and observations of managers. In addition to the functions of humour outlined, he describes the role of humour in relation to communication and control. He describes the facilitation of communication being enhanced through a touch of humour in the conversation: 'They [the listener] get something back for giving the speaker their attention' (p 187).

MANAGEMENT: AN APPLIED PERSPECTIVE

The variables associated with the practice of management that have been discussed in this chapter include (see Figure 8.8):

- *The manager*. There are a number of personal variables that influence the approach to management. They include the personality characteristics of the individual together with the training and experience that they have undergone during their lives and careers. Managers' perceptions about the situation and their subordinates (frequently based on past experience) also influence how they respond to situations. It should be remembered that managers are also subordinates, with the exception of those that own their organizations. As such they do not have complete freedom to practise management as they might wish to do. They are constrained by the presence of other and more senior managers as well as company culture and policy. Even the board of directors has to present itself to its shareholders for evaluation and re-election at regular intervals.
- *The managed*. The factors relevant to this aspect of management are generally mirror images of the factors indicated earlier. For example, the personality factors of the subordinates will to some extent predispose them to prefer to be managed in particular ways. Inevitably over time there is a degree of fit that emerges between individuals and job/organization. Individuals that do not fit into a particular situation either because they think or behave differently tend to leave or are pushed out of the group. However, managers can only manage by consent. A manager who seeks to operate in ways totally unacceptable to their subordinates will be unlikely to achieve their objectives and may eventually find themselves being replaced. Management is apparently not held in high esteem in the UK, for example Gwyther (2002) reported a straw poll by BBC Radio Four on the most and least respected professions in Britain. Managers were placed in 65th position, 40 places below road sweeper and 60 places below paramedic. Company director was placed in the 84th position out of 92 categories. Clearly the led do not place much value the contribution of the leaders.
- *The context*. The industry and organization itself will carry some degree of influence on the nature of management practised within it. For example, a context which has been highly confrontational in the past in terms of relationships between managers and workers is unlikely to change quickly to one that could support a participative approach.
- *The situation*. The objectives being sought are a feature of the management process. A military leader seeking to win a battle is faced with a different situation to the manager seeking to process thousands of customer accounts. Consequently there will be differences in the way management would be exercised because of these situations. However, situations can change very quickly, requiring changes to the way in which management operates. A competitor introducing a new product innovation, a price war breaking out and

competition from cheap labour economies all represent real threats in every country. These situations require what exists to be frequently changed in order for the organization to be able to survive; this in turn requires managers to be proactive in 'managing' the organization.

- *The task.* The work of professional or technical specialists requires different approaches to management than work in a factory. The name professional suggests a level of capability and an approach to work that implies that the management of such people is less to do with the content of the work than employee development and the monitoring of their performance. Such professional employees frequently resent (and resist) direct supervision and control. The importance of the task as well as the technology involved are also variables that could be expected to impact on the practice of management. Importance in this context refers to significance for the organization or individuals within it. The more significant the task for the organization, the more likely it is that it will be closely managed.

Management is still a problematic concept to understand and define. For example, which of the variables identified in Figure 8.8 are the most important and which the least? How do the variables interact and how do they influence the approach adopted by particular individuals in particular situations? Would the variation in one variable in Figure 8.8 automatically produce a difference in the way that management is practised? If so, to what degree? Another interesting question, ignored in this chapter, reflects the degree of similarity (or dissimilarity) between the concepts of management, as defined in this chapter, and leadership. This question will be addressed in the next chapter.

FIGURE 8.8

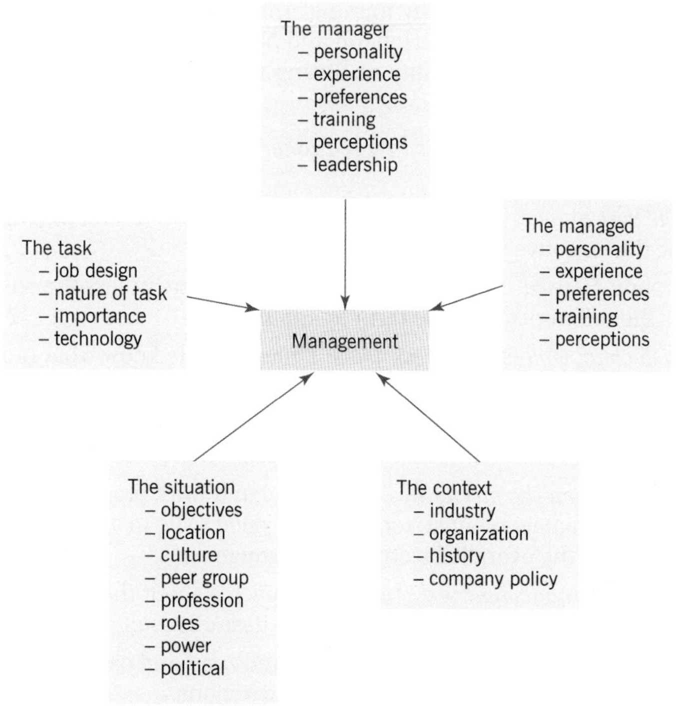

The factors influencing management

To practising managers these issues are very real as they attempt to practise the art and science of management in real time and in real organizations. Senior managers have a responsibility to ensure that their organizations are effectively managed, but before they can make provision for that they need to understand the processes involved. That need creates part of the intuitive attraction for simplifying initiatives such as business process re-engineering introduced earlier. Senior managers also need to be able to make provision for the selection and development of more junior managers. However, if management reflects a situation-specific set of competencies, then a completely different set of criteria apply to the selection, training and careers of managers in every situation. If true, this would seem to fly in the face of much experience common to many management jobs, decision making, working with groups for example, and present insurmountable training problems.

It is not possible to offer definitive models that would ensure that the best match between manager and situation could be provided. It is reasonably safe to assume that the degree of adaptation available through the inherent capabilities of human beings provides a basis for believing that people can learn many of the skills associated with being a manager. Also, that they can adapt their behaviour patterns to achieve at least a workable compromise between anarchy and perfection in specific contexts. The difficulty remains, however, that individuals learn inappropriate habits or become locked into particular behaviour repertoires and so fail to adapt to the changing needs of what is required to be an effective manager in the future. In management there are always new models appearing that appear to suggest new and more effective ways of achieving success. However, if it were that simple then the best model would have been identified and everyone would simply follow that formula. For example a recent model offering a formula on how to achieve success in dealing with major change is called 'red zone management', Holland and Nash (2002). This draws on the idea of the 'red zone' in American Football, which refers to the target to aim for – the desired area in which to score points. Business is said to be constantly aiming for (and frequently missing) this target in being able to capitalize on its plans, intentions and activity. Holland and Nash suggest 10 principles to follow in seeking to maximize the possibility of hitting the red zone and maximizing the results achieved. They are:

1. *Tell employees the company is in a red zone.* Seek commitment to the objective.
2. *Send the best players into the field.* If the best employees and managers are not chasing the objective then it is more likely to fail.
3. *Be customer focused.* Any change will be of little value unless the customer notices the difference in some form or another.
4. *Establish clear, concise business goals.* Unless people know what (and where) the target is they are unlikely to hit it.
5. *Prepare the blueprint for achieving success.* There needs to be a plan of action so that everyone knows what they are supposed to do, when and how.
6. *Focus in detail on the mechanics.* The associated work processes, assets, performance management systems, etc. all need to be in alignment for every employee with the overall objectives being sought.
7. *Programme management is a plus.* This aspect is about the project management aspects of how to achieve the desired result.
8. *Make speed a high priority.* Getting to the red zone and capitalizing on that achievement needs fast responses and rapid actions.
9. *Meet employees' special needs.* In this approach employees are being challenged to deliver what management have identified as the red zone

activity. Consequently, at all levels a high drain will result on everyone's energy levels. Issues such as stress management and workload management flexibility are necessary aspects of the ability to achieve the result.

10. *Reward for performance.* Reward people well for the achievements that they make.

The issue to be considered in relation to this (and many similar) model(s) comes down to this: is it new or is it essentially a restatement of a much older tradition such as the 14 principles of management outlined by Fayol and contained in Figure 8.1 earlier? Unfortunately, you must decide the answer to that question for yourself!

CONCLUSIONS

This chapter has considered many of the variables associated with the practice of management. The chapter began by considering what management actually is and some of the theoretical models developed to explain its function. It also considered what it is that managers actually do and the contextual influences such as the type and size of organization, the culture and international issues that inevitably impact on how management goes about its tasks. The roles that managers adopt while performing their duties was also considered. Diversity and gender issues were introduced into the discussion as a key feature of managerial responsibility. Critical incident management was discussed as it forms part of the major responsibilities of some management positions. Power in relation to management was discussed next and shown to be a major aspect of what management is about and how it can achieve its objectives. The chapter ended with a brief consideration of humour in management and the function of meetings which account for much management time.

Now to summarize this chapter in terms of the relevant Learning Objectives:

- **Understand what management is within an organizational context.** The job of management is intended to direct the organization in the interests of the beneficial owners of the business. From that point of view it is about deciding what should be done and how it should be achieved, subsequently ensuring that the appropriate resources are available and used in the most effective way. There are many different views that reflect aspects of what managers do. For example Fayol used a number of ideas that can be summarized as the management process and the 14 principles of management to describe the nature of the job. However, other research suggests that management is about the exercise of power and the use of politics in order to achieve business objectives. Taylor coined the term functional foremanship as a means of describing the tasks associated with first-line management. Reed identified what he terms the technical, political, critical and practice perspectives on what management is about. These issues allow for the social context within which management is practised to be incorporated into a workable model.
- **Explain the roles that managers perform and the skills that they need.** There are a number of roles that managers perform. For example, Mintzberg identified a number of roles under the headings of interpersonal, informational and decisional activities. There are also a number of factors such as role ambiguity and role stress that were introduced in the chapter that are relevant to how role theory can contribute to an understanding of what management is. The Management Charter Initiative represents one approach to the identification of the skills and competencies needed by managers. It represents a number of areas in which skill is needed under headings such as managing activities, managing resources, managing people, managing information and managing projects.
- **Outline the significance of training managers to deal with critical incidents.** There are some management jobs that encounter critical incidents or crises on a regular basis. These are most easily

identified within the emergency services and high risk operational activities, such as are found in the petro-chemical industry. However, every manager will face a crisis at some point, for example a key subordinate may leave, or be taken ill suddenly and so there is a need to have some preparation in how to deal with these situations. The large-scale disaster plans and emergency control teams may not be necessary for every eventuality, but some forethought and training can prevent a problem becoming a disaster. The relevant section in the chapter considered some of the issues associated with such preparation.

- **Describe the relationship between power and management.** Power is an inevitable aspect of management. At a simple level the ability to acquire and direct the use of resources and people represents an exercise of power. However, power occurs in many different situations and can arise from a number of different sources. The French and Raven model identifies a number of sources and can be used to suggest that power is a commodity that can be used as part of the trading or instrumental approach to work. The sources of power identified by French and Raven also indicate that power is something that in a real sense needs the acquiescence of employees to allow it to be exercised. For example, if an employee does not believe that a manager will deliver promised rewards, then that source of power largely evaporates. However, the power balance between managers and employees is never that simple and employees need a job in order to provide a wage and career options, so the balance of power is not neutral to begin with. Bullying represents another aspect of power in an organizational setting. It can also be exercised upwards and horizontally as well as by a boss on a subordinate.
- **Appreciate the significance of humour in management.** The significance of humour in management is that it can hide other intentions. Barsoux identified the main purposes behind humour as sword (action orientation, intended to achieve something), shield (a defensive purpose) and values (encouraging socialization among the work group). Each of these purposes contains a number of aspects that allow something to be passed off as something else and in a way that does not (normally) give rise to offence or otherwise cause problems.

DISCUSSION QUESTIONS

1. Discuss how the emergence of a critical incident management might impact on the usual activities that a manager undertakes.
2. What is management?
3. Compare and contrast the views on the management process as outlined by Fayol and the four themes on what management is about described by Reed.
4. 'Successful management is about acquiring power and using it to ensure that you achieve your objectives.' Based on the material introduced in this chapter to what extent could this viewpoint be justified?
5. 'Meetings are a complete waste of everyone's time; they are a major source of inefficiency in any organization.' Discuss this statement and in doing so consider how meetings could be made more meaningful?
6. To what extent might the context play a significant part in determining what managers actually do?
7. Does humour have any part to play in management? Justify your answer.
8. 'True equality can never occur in organizations until managers are forced to recruit and promote people not like themselves.' Discuss this statement.
9. To what extent can role theory contribute to an understanding of what management is about?
10. Discuss what it is that managers spend their time doing.

CASE STUDY Mixing the sexes

The situation in this Case Study actually occurred in a large financial organization based in the UK. The institution concerned employed many thousands of employees across the country and at one particular site there were some 500 people employed on a range of administrative and clerical activities not directly associated with customer contact.

One male employee was in fact a transsexual and was undergoing a programme of gender realignment to transform him into the female that he desperately wanted to be. He had worked at the company for about five years and had always been a good worker, with a good attendance record and excellent performance appraisal assessments. There had not been any record of problems with other members of staff and management had no cause for complaint with regard to his work. As the treatment progressed he began to dress as a woman and allowed his hair to grow, so in outward appearance he looked like a woman. The final part of the treatment was the surgery needed to remove the last physical evidence of being a male and to ensure that his transformation to being female was as complete as it was possible to be.

It was at the point that he began to dress as a woman that problems began to emerge. The issue that caused a problem was use of the toilets at work. Now being in outward appearance a female, the individual wanted to use the ladies toilet, rather than the men's toilet as he had done previously. The employee concerned started going into the ladies toilet without first clearing his intentions with management or other employees. The other female employees reacted badly to this and complained to management as soon as they became aware of what was happening. They demanded that the employee concerned be told in no uncertain way that 'he' was not to use the ladies toilet and should use the men's facilities as he was a male, irrespective of how he dressed.

The senior management of the site called on the services of the human resource management department and the employee was called into the office for a meeting. The employee explained the position, which of course management were already aware of and said that as he was almost completely a woman that it was inappropriate for him to continue to use the men's toilet facilities. In a few weeks, after the final surgery had been performed he would have to use the ladies toilets in any case. The senior managers and the human resources manager then went to see the female employees and said that in their view the employee should use the ladies toilets as this was more appropriate to the situation. The women refused to accept this and demanded that 'he' be prevented from going in the ladies toilets permanently. The women threatened to go to the trade union and to the police, press and anyone else who might take up their case.

Management did not know what to do to resolve the situation. The transsexual male refused to continue to use the male toilets and the females refused to let him use theirs. The only suggestion that management came up with (after much consultation with the human resource department) was that the transsexual employee be made to use the unisex disabled person's toilet. This was acceptable to the women, but unacceptable to the employee concerned as 'he' made the point that 'she' was not disabled. Several days of heated discussion between all the parties involved took place but with no real progress being made. Senior management within the company then took the decision that the transsexual employee would have to be dismissed in the interests of harmony among the female employees. Consequently the transsexual employee was dismissed with three months money in lieu of notice.

Tasks

1. Consider how the managers and human resources department responded to this situation.
2. Were managers right to dismiss the employee or could/should another solution been found to the situation?
3. Could the problem have been anticipated and therefore avoided? If so, how?

FURTHER READING

Berkeley Thomas, A (1993) *Controversies in Management*, Routledge, London. This text concentrates on attempting to understand the complexities associated with the study of management.

Clark, H, Chandler, J and Barry, J (1994) *Organization and Identities: Text and Readings in Organizational Behaviour*, International Thomson Business Press, London. Contains a broad range of original articles on relevant material themes and from significant writers referred to in this and other textbooks on management and organizations.

Hartley, RF (2002) *Management Mistakes and Successes*, 7th edn, John Wiley, Chichester. This text has been around for about 25 years now and this latest edition seeks to bring it up to date in terms of episodes introduced and the way that learning material is extracted from the examples.

Heller, R (1985) *The Naked Manager: Games Executives Play*, McGraw-Hill, New York. The behaviours that managers adopt and the political and business reasons that motivate it are the focus of attention.

Holman, D and Thorpe, R (eds) (2002) *Management and Language*, Sage, London. Brings together the work of a number of writers on the use of language in terms of developing arguments, storytelling and metaphor in the application of management.

Luecke, R (1994) *Scuttle Your Ships Before Advancing and Other Lessons from History on Leadership and Change for Today's Managers*, Oxford University Press, New York. This book takes a look back into history at a number of major events involving management, leadership and change. It then attempts to draw lessons from those episodes that can be of value to managers of today.

Maslow, A (1998) *Maslow on Management*, John Wiley, Chichester. The views on management by one of the leading thinkers and researchers of his generation.

Quinn, RE, Faerman, SR, Thompson, MP and McGrath, MR (2002) *Becoming a Master Manager*, John Wiley, Chichester. Considers a number of roles associated with management and sets out to encourage the reader to develop the appropriate competencies necessary to become a 'master manager, in modern business.

Stewart, R and Barsoux, J-L (1994) *The Diversity of Management: Twelve Managers Talking*, Macmillan, Basingstoke. This book is based around interviews with practising managers. Drawn from a wide range of middle- and senior-level jobs in diverse industries the interviewees provide an introspective account of the nature of their work.

Vinnicombe, S and Bank, J (2002) *Women with Attitude: Lessons for Career Management*, Routledge, London. A text which explores the minds and lives of some of the world's top businesswomen. Provides some clear evidence of the experience of real women progressing in real careers in management.

Watson, TJ (2001) *In Search of Management: Culture, Chaos and Control in Managerial Work*, Thomson Learning, London. A research based book based on the observation of real managers working in real organizations. Draws out a wide range of management issues and provides a real 'feel' for the life and work of managers as they struggle to deal with the dynamic environment around them.

COMPANION WEBSITE

Online teaching and learning resources:

Visit the companion website for Organizational Behaviour and Management 3rd edition at: *http://www.thomsonlearning.co.uk/businessandmanagement/martin3* to find valuable further teaching and learning material:

Refer to page 35 for full details.

CHAPTER 9

Leadership in organizations

LEARNING OBJECTIVES

After studying this chapter and working through the associated Management in Action panels, Employee Perspectives, Discussion Questions and Case Study you should be able to:

- **Describe the distinction between leadership and management.**
- **Understand the relationship between leadership and power.**
- **Assess the contribution of the different theoretical approaches to the study of leadership.**
- **Explain the contribution to understanding leadership of the various style approaches.**
- **Discuss the significance of the contingency approaches to the study of leadership.**

INTRODUCTION

Management was introduced in the last chapter as a category of job that was responsible for running things. Managers organize, plan and control in the words of Fayol. They are the category of employee specifically tasked with ensuring that the organization achieves its objectives and flourishes on behalf of the organization's stakeholder groups, including the beneficial owners. However, there is another term which is often used in relation to management, that of **leadership**. This chapter will seek to explore in greater detail what leadership is and how it relates to the job of management.

Consider for a moment the two terms management and leadership. Perhaps they have equivalent meaning, simply reflecting alternative ways of describing the same job or activity? Perhaps they represent completely different ideas about the task of being in charge of organizational activity? Perhaps leadership represent just part of a manager's job – that associated with people management? Is it possible for a manager not to be a leader or is every leader automatically a manager? These are just some of the issues that are not easily answered in exploring the relationship between management and leadership. However, they are fundamental in seeking to establish what it is that leadership is and its value in an organizational context. The starting point for this chapter is to consider these two terms and to draw out the differences and similarities between them.

In research terms there have been many different studies that seek to explain what leadership is and to identify the characteristics of the people who are successful in its practice. For example, the trait approach seeks to identify the characteristics of successful leaders and the style approaches seek to distinguish between the effects of autocratic and democratic leader behaviours on the relative success in achieving the objectives required. But these are not the only theoretical approaches that have been adopted; the contingency models suggest that the leaders' behaviour needs to be appropriate to the circumstances within which it is being exercised. There are also many other approaches offered by writers who do not specifically subscribe to any of the foregoing models. The practice and impact of leadership involves many aspects including the relationship between the leader and the follower, the personality of the leader, the way that power functions within the situation, the stage in the organizational life cycle and the possible entrepreneurial nature of the business or leader. All of these factors impact either directly or indirectly on the way that leadership functions in a particular context and this chapter will seek to explore these issues in a way that encourages the relationships between them to become apparent.

Leadership
A process in which the leader is able to influence the behaviours and actions of those being led.

LEADERS OR MANAGERS?

The terms management and leadership are frequently used interchangeably. But are they the same? Is a manager automatically a leader and do leaders always manage? The study of management and leadership has covered many different aspects of the activity. Most of this work has attempted to identify what it is that managers have to do or the skills and personal qualities that they should display in order to achieve success. Success in this context is usually assumed to reflect benefit to the organization, although there is usually a heavy hint of personal success and career advancement for those who apply the right formula (or have the right characteristics). For example, Rothman (1987) light-heartedly concluded that birthdates formed a key variable in selecting future successful leaders. This emerged because it was found that the senior managers of a number of large organizations shared the same birthday as their predecessors!

The terms management and leadership tend to be used interchangeably on many occasions, for example, Stanley (2002). They clearly involve groups of people and specific functions in relation to the group and its activities. It would be unusual, however, to describe a group of people as having a manager, unless the group was in a specific context. That context invariably lies within an organization and, specifically, a formal part of the structure. An informal, friendship or trade union group would not usually be described as having a manager, but there would inevitably be a formal or informal leader of such groups. A department would, however, have a manager as the formal leader of that particular group. This situation can be made more complex because of the modern company practice of terming many formal group leaders as **team leaders**. An attempt perhaps to recognize that the practice of leadership has certain advantages over the term management, particularly at the first-line supervisor level. For example, *Supervision* (2003) a journal aimed at the first-line manager, contains an article on management which explicitly states that managers are human resource specialists that bring out the best in people. However, it could also be argued that managers are seeking to restrict the use of the term management to the more senior levels and that the introduction of the team leader description gets away from the connotations of the *supervisor* label, without admitting that such individuals are part of management. The two terms of management and leadership therefore have aspects in common, but are synonymous only up to point. Management in Action 9.1 provides an indication of some recent views on the nature of leadership.

Team leader
Person with the task of leading a team, may be appointed by management, or elected by the team.

Leadership and management are two topics that between them generate a vast quantity of published material, training courses and seminars. This material frequently claims to provide a means of delivering increased performance to the organization through the more effective leadership of teams. The assumption underpinning much of this material is that leadership reflects a set of characteristics that can be learned and that ensure that leaders stand out from the ranks of managers, in terms of performance. For the organization this effort (it is claimed) can lead to enhanced commercial success in an increasingly hostile competitive environment. Leaders are said to be the ones with vision who are capable of getting the best performance out of their team, whereas managers are the ones who by concentrating on organizing, planning and controlling activity are unable to get the best out of other people. This simplifies to the view that management equates to little more than bad, inefficient, bureaucratic corporate rule application; compared with leadership which equates to good visionary and people oriented approaches, which motivates staff to scale unimaginable heights of performance and contribution to the organization and its objectives.

However, there is little hard evidence of the sustained gain for any particular formula for identifying leadership (or management) approaches that would guarantee success in every context. The number and complexity of variables active in the organizational environment and therefore involved in achieving success requires an equally complex set of responses in order to lead, manage and achieve it. This is the basis of the law of requisite variety identified by Ashby (1956). This postulates that complexity in the environment can only be managed through equally complex response strategies within the organization. Figure 9.1 attempts to provide an indication of the range and complexity of variables impacting on individuals and organizations. Figure 9.1 demonstrates that leadership (and indeed management) while significant are not enough of themselves to provide the requisite variety to achieve success through overcoming environmental complexity. Leadership and management would be represented as a box within the organization box shown in Figure 9.1.

One of the chief difficulties in measuring organizational success is the meaning of the term success itself. Success is frequently a relative term in that for any organization it is often taken to reflect performance in comparison to other organizations. It can be taken to reflect level of profit or market share compared to competitors, but these are not the only ways in which success could be measured. Survival and contribution to society are other possible measures of success, but are not often used as the

MANAGEMENT IN ACTION 9.1 Taking the lead in leadership

The distinction between leadership and management is explored in a book by Stuart Levine and Michael Crom, of Dale Carnegie & Associates, called *The Leader in You*. It identifies a number of distinctions between management and leadership. For example:

> A leader is a person who can communicate with and motivate people. A manager is someone who doesn't spend enough time recognizing people through a sincere appreciation of what they do. A leader understands that the way to motivate a person is not with a bullwhip and chair – the lion tamer's style of management – but with appreciation.

Leadership is about listening to people, supporting and encouraging them and involving them in decision-making and problem-solving processes, they say. Management involves telling people, what to do, and how, when and where to do it, and then closely supervising their performance. Levine and Crom suggest that no individual can assimilate all the information available to them, so leaders have to start building teams and relying on members of those teams to make the most of what is available and achieve the goals.

In their work they quote Sir Christopher Hogg, chairman of Reuters, as saying:

> Leadership is about getting the best out of people. It is about communicating a vision, and persuading, rather than compelling people. Management, on the other hand, is about an effective performance within an institutional framework, which secures the obedience of a lot of people.

Robert Waterman in his book, *The Frontiers of Excellence,* argues that top-performing companies are better able to meet the needs of their people. Looking after the needs of the people within the organization helps to attract better people in the first place and motivates them to place the needs of the organization and its customers above other interests. In meeting the needs of one's own people it is necessary to understand what motivates them and to have an effective alignment between culture, systems, procedures and leadership. This is far removed from the old idea of manager as one who tells people what to do.

Adapted from: Gretton, I (1995) Taking the lead in leadership, *Professional Manager*, January, pp 20–2.

Stop ↔ Consider

To what extent do these views suggest that leadership represents a subset of management skills?

Do the views expressed imply that the leadership ability of a manager is a major factor on which their performance should be judged?

financial market views tend to dominate thinking about such matters, at least in the private sector. An organization not considered to be successful in terms acceptable to the financial markets will be punished in terms of its share price and perhaps be subjected to takeover and reorganization as a result. Of course, not all organizations are publicly quoted and therefore these 'rules' do not apply universally. There are many organizations in the public sector which have a different basis for measuring success, for example meeting a particular need in society But even here market testing and performance enhancement is being pursued as an attempt to use 'value for money' as the measure of success. The voluntary and charity sectors are generally regarded as areas in which a different measure of success would apply. However, they are also areas which are sometimes regarded as the world of the amateur and the do-gooder, not the professional manager. So, although success is often automatically taken to mean economic success, that is not the only possible meaning of the term in an organizational context.

Most of the factors indicated in Figure 9.1 are self-explanatory. However, the non-specific forces identified would benefit from some explanation. They include:

FIGURE 9.1

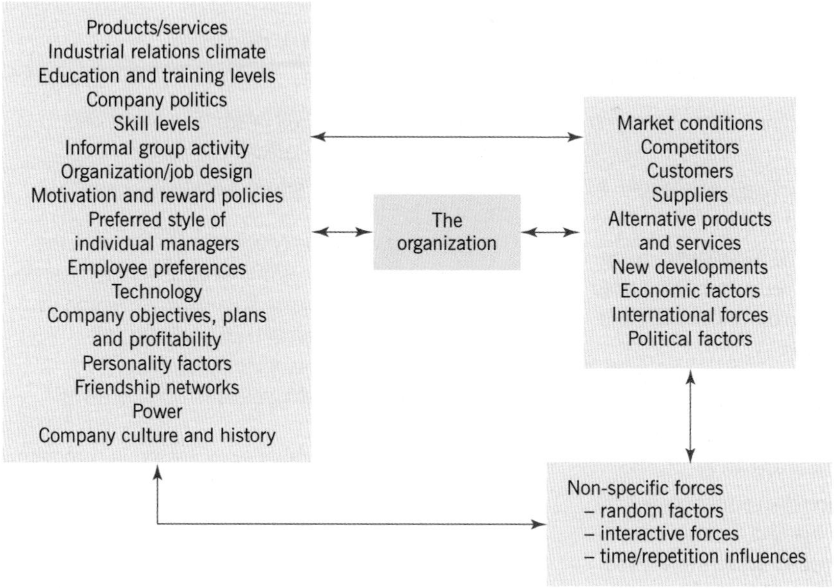

The complexity of the management environment

- *Random factors*. This category reflects those things for which it is difficult to anticipate and plan. For example, an employee being in a bad mood on a particular day or the failure of a supplier to deliver on time can significantly influence events and so impact on the relative success of the organization, at least in the short term.
- *Time and repetitive influences*. These reflect experiential influences that impact on activity. Over time behaviour patterns sometimes change and this influences future activity. Alternatively, behaviour patterns can remain consistent for too long and become outdated and problematic. For example, an international transport company that still used the horse and cart to move goods would not get many major orders in today's world of large lorries and container ships. Response behaviours to situations need to change over time in order to remain appropriate, but this needs to be planned if it is to have any measure of success in an organizational context.
- *Interactive forces*. This reflects the action and reaction nature of experience. An initiative to increase market share is likely to lead to a response from competitors seeking to protect their business. Subordinates are not passive in responding to their experience of being led, thereby creating a dynamic between leader and led. This interactive chain of events leads to situations in which there is an ever present degree of uncertainty in being able to control or shape events in the future.

Leadership and management are complex processes. Simplistic attempts to explain them or train individuals to use a formula are doomed. This view is apparent in Management in Action 9.2.

What, then, provides the distinction between management and leadership? The following list of topics provides some indication of and summarizes the major areas that differentiate them:

- *Role*. Watson (1994) defines management as a process of ensuring that the resources under control are appropriately directed. Leadership, by the same token, is described in terms of people skills and performance. Torrington *et al.*

MANAGEMENT IN ACTION 9.2 The manager's dilemma

The key features of managing in the new millennium include, according to Heller:

- Managers will be concerned with unleashing the potential all around them.
- Managers will need to listen to the messages coming to them from below about what needs to be facilitated to achieve objectives. Those who don't listen will find their basis of authority eliminated.
- Old-style authority frameworks will crumble in an age when success and progress depend on breaking the rules.
- The view of an organization as a system of interrelated parts will grow and the complexity will be dealt with by outsourcing as many of the non-core activities as possible and networking more effectively.
- Success in management will be defined in terms of the ability to work effectively with colleagues from other companies to achieve results for the organization. The distinction between the management and consultancy modes of operation will become blurred.
- The tasks carried out by individual managers will be subject to frequent change in line with the changing perception of customer needs and how those needs should be met through the resources available. Predictable career paths and functional specialisms will erode significantly.
- With the emphasis on task groups and multidisciplinary teamworking and as a consequence of the delayering of recent years, the opportunity for frequent promotion will largely disappear. Beyond the year 2000 managers will progress in status and reward terms by the successful achievement of assignments, rather than vertical progression and changing job titles.
- Theory Y motivation perspectives will dominate the thinking and approaches of managers as they seek to involve as many people as possible in assignments.
- The effective integration of both hard and soft perspectives into their work will also be a characteristic of the next generation of successful manager.
- The ability to live the vision as expressed in corporate values, rather than just pay lip service to them, will also define the new manager.
- Future commercial wars are going to be won with ideas, not whips and chains. As a consequence, managers will not plan, organize, control, etc. They will advise, facilitate, encourage self-management and ensure that adequate resources are available for the groups that actually achieve objectives for the organization.
- The comprehensive growth in various forms of strategic alliance will blur the boundaries between organizations. The consequences are vast for the management of ambiguity and boundary management in the job of the new manager. They become very aware of the true nature of the open organization and job.

Adapted from: Heller, R (1994) The manager's dilemma, *Management Today*, January, pp 42–7.

Stop ↔ Consider

What does this view imply about the distinction between management and leadership in the future?

(2002) describe the role that members of the organization take on in order to exercise formal authority and leadership. From this perspective, leadership is to be understood as a subset of management. Something that managers do in order to be effective. However, leadership as part of a group activity may not be part of the formal structure. The leader of a group designing a new computer system may not be a manager but would be expected to lead the team. There are also informal groups within an organization that will have a leader but not a manager, for example, a trade union, a staff association or a social club. Management can be suggested to be an inwardly focused activity in the sense of formally representing the organization within the work group. Leadership, by way of contrast, represents an outwardly focused activity seeking to optimize performance and maintain cohesion within the group in addressing the externally determined requirements. Leadership would also be expected to actively represent the interests and perspectives of the group within the organization, whereas management seeks to harness the corporate perspective and ensure that is reflected in team activity.

- *Situation*. A manager is appointed by the organization and could hold that position irrespective of the circumstances. Leaders, however, are suggested to be much more situation specific. John Adair illustrates this with examples of shipwreck survivors appointing leaders depending upon the group needs at the time: the soldier for defence, the farmer for food and the builder for shelter (1983, p 15). Situational leadership makes best use of the specialized knowledge available to the group from among the members. For example, the **company doctor** is an individual frequently brought in to replace a senior manager not considered capable of saving a company during a crisis. Such individuals usually stay for a very short period of time. Their leadership approach is invariably based upon the 'do it my way or out' philosophy, an approach which can achieve the desired results in the short term, albeit with much blood on the office carpets.

Company doctor
A senior manager brought into an ailing company in an attempt to turn it around.

- *Context*. The military context is one in which considerable emphasis is laid on leadership rather than management. Constant training and drill leads to a highly capable military machine. There is an interesting contradiction in this situation involving such close and directive management with an emphasis on leadership as the dominant ideology. Much of this can be explained by reference to two unique circumstances peculiar to military activity. First, the chaos and horror of war itself. Second, the need to motivate subordinates to undertake actions which are ultimately life threatening to the individual. Large bureaucratic organizations, conversely, tend to emphasize management rather than leadership. This is inevitably the result of the need to mobilize large quantities of resource in predictable and planned ways over the long term in support of the organization's objectives.
- *Purpose*. Traditionally, jobs and organizations were considered to have permanence into the foreseeable future. Therefore the role of management becomes a routinized and largely symbolic process. In times of turbulence and instability this inevitably and fundamentally changes. This need to change is responsible for the shift in emphasis towards leadership as the dominant ideology in organizations during times of crisis. In times of crisis there is a need to mobilize people to action but in a controlled way. Military and war metaphors and terminology frequently emerge as dominant themes and common forms of expression at such times. Over recent years company trainers have found themselves providing training for leadership more than for other aspects of management (Rowe, 1993, p 65). Scase and Goffee (1989) reported their survey of managers in which 69 per cent of men and 82 per cent of women indicated a need for more human relations and leadership training (p 68).
- *Scope*. The usual differentiation between management jobs is between senior, middle and junior management positions. This distinction is however, a very poor indicator of the type of job involved. For example, a junior manager in a very large organization may have a budgetary responsibility larger than a senior manager in a very small one. Stewart (1976) identified another basis for the classification of management jobs:
  - *Hub*. Jobs that have considerable contact with subordinates, peers and superiors.
  - *Peer dependent*. These jobs contain a high level of emphasis on persuading others to undertake specific actions. Consequently, they are frequently found on the boundaries between groups.

- *People management*. Such jobs emphasize the traditional boss–subordinate types of responsibilities.
- *Solo*. Jobs that require the individual to work alone on assignments but which also require a high level of seniority to do so.

Although the Stewart framework provides a clear indication of the nature of different types of management job, it does not provide any information about the level or seniority in the hierarchy. More than one dimension is therefore required to describe management jobs. Figure 9.2 attempts this by linking together the traditional and Stewart views of management work in such a matrix. This classification suggests that perhaps there are some management jobs in any organization that naturally contain a higher degree of leadership than others.

Breakthrough leadership
An approach emphasizing the personal development that each leader undergoes, includes elements of emotional intelligence and self-knowledge.

In a special edition devoted to leadership, the prestigious *Harvard Business Review* (2001) introduced many perspectives from leading business researchers and thinkers on the theme of what it termed **breakthrough leadership**. It is suggested that this provides a new way of thinking about leadership, effectively providing a means of breaking through the interpersonal barriers; breaking through the cynicism that many people feel towards their jobs and organizations; and breaking thorough the barriers imposed by doubts and fears; all with the purpose of creating more meaning and purpose for people in doing their jobs. It brings together issues of emotional intelligence, mood, self-knowledge in the leader and the need to encourage the same among subordinates. The personal journey in these areas of discovery for each leader is also discussed in this series of articles, as are the experiences and biographies of many significant leaders. Over time as these ideas filter through into research and business practice there will undoubtedly be more to write about the significance of these ideas.

LEADERS, ENTREPRENEURS AND VISION

It is generally accepted that entrepreneurs create – things, new organizations, new products and services and develop new ways of doing existing things. It has been

FIGURE 9.2

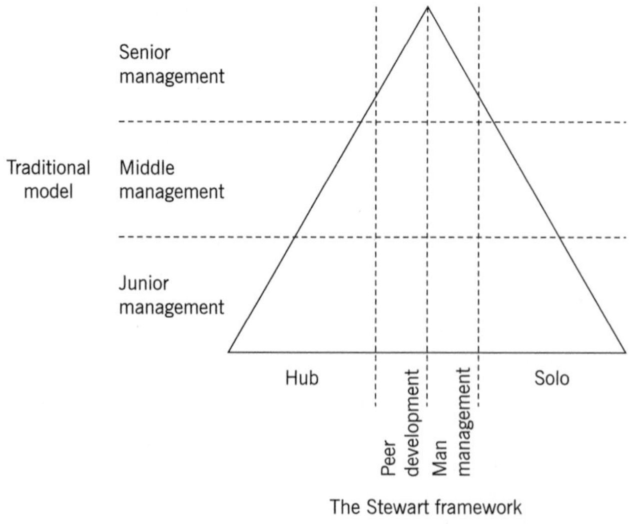

The management job matrix

argued that entrepreneurial behaviour is characterized by a high achievement motivation, with the need for power and affiliation at work (Thompson, 1990). Ettinger (1983) goes further by suggesting that there are two types of entrepreneur:

1. *Independent entrepreneurs*. Such individuals are more concerned with independence than power and therefore are more likely to create, develop and seek to retain control over their own organizations.
2. *Organization makers*. Such individuals have a stronger need to exercise power than to search for independence. Consequently, they tend to search for growth opportunities as this yields both size and power. This form of entrepreneurial activity seeks to take control of organizations with growth potential and develop them. The result for the individual entrepreneur being to float to the top of an ever larger organization as they drive it forward, thereby obtaining ever greater amounts of power.

Clearly, there are different approaches to leadership evident in the two types of entrepreneur in Ettinger's work. Drucker (1985) links together the ideas of innovation and entrepreneurship and suggests that the sources of innovation, on which entrepreneurs depend, include:

- *The unexpected*. For example, the development of computer games subsequently led to the development of opportunities for computer systems and programs to function as home entertainment.
- *Incongruous events*. Differences between what is actually provided and what consumers feel should be provided can lead to the development of more appropriate offerings. For example, the general dissatisfaction with low rates on bank accounts has led many organizations to establish lower cost telephone and Internet banks in order to offer better rates of interest and attract more customers.
- *Improvement and development*. Existing products and services can always be improved upon. For example, the development of digital photography is a development of the traditional film-based technologies and subsequently new opportunities will also become apparent.
- *Changes in industry and market structures*. The opening of the railway links between England and France through the Channel Tunnel has fundamentally challenged the cross-channel ferry business. Volume of traffic on the ferries has reduced and they must seek new ways of developing and retaining business in competition with the trains.
- *Demographic changes*. The population demographics of many countries is changing and this provides opportunities for new products and services. For example, people are generally living longer and many have both time and money to spend. Consequently, holidays and leisure facilities for such people are developing fast.
- *Changes in consumer mood and perceptions*. The general trend among many people for healthier eating and physical fitness provides many opportunities for gymnasium equipment, food supplements and organic food that entrepreneurs could seek to develop.
- *Creation of new knowledge*. Research and invention can provide new opportunities for entrepreneurs to convert ideas into new products and services.
- *Inspiration*. This category reflects the bright idea that turns out to be a winner. Examples include the development of the ballpoint pen and the Post-it Note.

Mintzberg *et al.* (1998) describe the entrepreneurial organization as a very flat structure with a very small number of top managers, one of whom (the entrepreneur) predominates through the need to lead the others. The basic description of such an organization is one of simplified form without elaboration. Everything is determined by the small number of senior people and therefore the middle management and support staff numbers are very small. It is the vision and leadership capabilities of the entrepreneur that enables and energizes the organization. Ensley *et al.* (2003) develop this further through their work in relation to team processes and shared leadership in the success of new ventures.

The concept of the visionary leader is also discussed by Mintzberg *et al.* (1998) and draws on earlier work carried out by Frances Westley at McGill University. Westley sought to explain visionary leadership in terms of two analogies:

1. *Hypodermic needle*. This analogy is based on the notion of vision being the active ingredient loaded into the syringe, which is then injected into the employee by the leader in order to create an energized and directed response.
2. *Drama*. This analogy of visionary leadership is about creating the equivalent of a stage play in which repetition, representation and feedback combine to create a magical moment when fiction and life harmonize. Westley adds a fourth aspect, that of integrity to this basic model. The four key terms represent:
   - *Repetition*. The inspiration of the visionary stems from a depth of experience in a particular context. This is obtained through extended repetition of the needs and practices required to function effectively within that context. It is the equivalent of the actor constantly rehearsing their lines in order to be able to present a professional and realistic show to the audience.
   - *Representation*. This reflects the ability of the visionary to be able to articulate the vision in a way which makes it alive and real for the followers. It is the ability to get others to buy into the vision through language and communication skills. It is the equivalent of the actor being believable in the role they are playing.
   - *Feedback*. Leaders need followers. Actors respond to the feedback that they receive from the audience. Westley argues that leaders become visionary because what they communicate appeals to specific stakeholder groups at particular times. They are therefore given the opportunity to lead by that group, as long as their vision holds and provides benefits to the group.
   - *Integrity*. The problem with the concept of drama is that a play is a particular form of reality; it is a representation or an interpretation of it for the benefit of the audience. An organization, contrariwise, represents a different form of reality. Its function and purpose relative to the principal stakeholders is not only for entertainment or enlightenment, the audience are also the actors, writers, set designers and directors at the same time. In a sense, everyone is performing their own play. Also of course work within an organization has many real implications for those involved for example, wages, status and so on. Therefore, Westley argues that a leader who only relies upon the first three notions will fail. It is the follower's judgement about the integrity of the leader that allows leadership to become visionary and not just about performance, a point considered in the following Employee Perspective (9.1).

LEADERS, POWER AND VIRTUAL WORKING

The notion of power as part of the management of organizations was introduced in the previous chapter. There is also an element of power associated with the exercise of

EMPLOYEE PERSPECTIVE 9.1

What does it take to be an entrepreneur?

Dan David, Chairman of Photo-Me International considers that a major part of being a successful entrepreneur was to learn to believe in himself and what he could do. He says that he is not a ruthless person or a tough businessman. He says that he has been accused of being too soft on occasions. He does not like to dismiss staff and tries to avoid doing it unless they display very poor performance or are dishonest. He claims never to have cheated anyone or to have broken his word (spoken or written). He regards money as a measure of success, not a purpose in itself and each year he donates three $1m prizes in the Dan David Prize for outstanding scientific, technological, cultural or social achievements. One condition of the award is that the winner must give 10 per cent of the prize money to help young scholars or entrepreneurs in their field.

Taken from: Brown, P (2003) First Person, *The Times*, 12 April, p 50.

Task

To what extent does this example suggest that successful entrepreneurs are also visionary leaders?

leadership, so many of the points made there are also relevant in this discussion. Power reflects the ability to influence other people and events. Leadership reflects the ability of one person to direct and control the activities of others, albeit from a slightly different perspective than that of management. It still reflects the process of influence and therefore the exercise of power.

Power is an interesting concept in that it is invisible and largely intangible. Equally, it cannot be felt, tasted or heard. In effect, it exists only in the minds of the user and the people subjected to its effects. It is the recipients who acknowledge that another person holds power over them. Of course, there are situations in which power is obvious and can be easily detected. For example, a thief holding a gun and threatening to use it unless you hand over your money is obviously exerting power over you. However, as the French and Raven (1968) model (introduced in the previous chapter) suggests, leaders and managers have many levers available to use, not all of which incorporate the blatant use of force to achieve influence.

Power in leadership is the achievement of a willing subjugation of subordinates to the will of the leader. The leader is largely given the ability to influence by the followers themselves. This is unlike the position in management when the manager has the right (as a result of their formal organizational role) to demand compliance with their wishes, ultimately through the threat of punishment. The style theories of leadership discussed earlier are based on a continuum running from autocratic to democratic. It would be those styles at the autocratic end of the spectrum that would be least likely to be able to generate a willing response from the followers and therefore be more likely to make use of the overt forms of power indicated in the French and Raven model.

Of course the French and Raven model requires that employees actually believe that the leader has the ability to deliver the rewards and/or punishments implied by the use of those forms of power. For example, a leader who seeks to exercise power through the allocation of rewards, but in a context where the subordinates do not believe that the leader can deliver them, is unlikely to be able to exercise power over that group of followers. It could be argued that recent organizational emphasis on leadership reflects a move to find ways of sharing power that is acceptable to both managers and subordinates. It was Likert (1967) who identified that leaders who engaged and shared responsibility and power with their subordinates achieved the best levels of productivity. The results of his research were developed into the four systems of management discussed in this chapter.

Virtual working
Working remotely and primarily through electronic media and not as part of a conventional team.

In modern organizations there is a growing trend towards **virtual working**. This means working in teams that never meet, perhaps separated by many thousands of miles and many time zones. For example, a task force might be set up within a company to address issues associated with marketing across national and cultural boundaries. This group may draw upon people in several locations to explore and identify the strategies and policies relevant to such circumstances. It is unlikely that the people will ever meet and yet they must form a viable working group under someone's leadership and achieve the objectives set for the group under difficult circumstances. Leading such teams represents a completely different process than leading in a conventional organization where the people have frequent physical contact. One of the major differences in leading a virtual team is the way that power finds expression in the relationship between leaders and the team. In some cases the use of e-mail is appropriate to the activities of the group, but in other situations it might be necessary to use videoconferencing with additional facilities to allow data transfer in real time to aid the process. In such situations, leaders cannot influence through their physical presence and some team members can disengage completely from the process without it becoming apparent for some time (as a consequence of the in-built delays built into e-mail communication). According to Symons (2003) for leadership in virtual teams to be successful it is necessary for mutual trust to be at a high level. He suggests that the main differences between virtual and conventional working and leadership include:

- Virtual working is largely free of race and gender disadvantages.
- The leader should minimize explicitly directive behaviour.
- Hierarchies fade on-line – electronic communication has a levelling effect on hierarchical relationships.
- A democratic approach of shared control and consensual decision making is advisable, particularly in the early stages of a team's existence.
- The leader's role in the virtual team is subtle and focused on the process.
- The virtual leader should adopt the role and style of a coach – helping the group to establish clear procedures and goals, modelling desired behaviours and asking appropriate questions.
- The virtual leader should spend time building the team through electronic socialization.
- The virtual leader should recognize that new attitudes and behaviours are necessary, they should listen more.
- A virtual leader should not assume that they have the same authority as when leading a conventional team.

So far the discussion has ignored those leaders who do not form part of the formal organization. Leadership reflects the ability to lead others and that does not occur only within formal organizations. Many companies have sports and social clubs as part of the welfare and support facilities offered to employees. Such organizations are not usually part of the formal organization and the leaders are frequently non-management employees who have a particular desire to run such associations. Management may have representatives on the management committee of the club but will not run it on a day-to-day basis. Such associations along with the many other informal groups that exist provide opportunities for leadership among people who would not otherwise have the opportunity. Other examples of informal groups include trade union groups, friendship groups and special interest groups all of which will or may seek to influence managers in some way or other and which must be led by people prepared to represent their constituencies. Frequently, the degree of power that such leaders are able to exert over the formal organization is a direct consequence of their leadership qualities and capabilities within the group for which they act as leader. A trade union representative with strong leadership qualities is more likely to be able to achieve and demonstrate solidarity among the members and so achieve greater concessions from management than someone who is simply an average negotiator.

DO LEADERS NEED FOLLOWERS?

In the foregoing discussion about the relationship between management and leadership it was apparent that management reflects a formal position within an organization with particular responsibilities. Leadership, by the same token reflects more of the personal qualities and abilities of the individual as a prerequisite to achieving an enhanced performance from the group. One of the interesting questions about the topic of leadership to emerge from this discussion reflects the degree to which leaders have to be accepted by their group of followers.

The view of management embraced by the previous discussion implies that management is in effect an imposed form of leadership. Managers are appointed by more senior managers to undertake particular responsibilities in relation to a formal group within the organization. The group, or the followers in that sense, have little influence on the process, or alternative other than to abide by the decision. Leaders by comparison are able to capture the imagination and motivation of the group and harness that released energy in the pursuit of organizational objectives. A view which begs the question about whether leadership could exist if the followers did not fully support that individual? The following Employee Perspective (9.2) describes the views of managers in the public sector (as employees) about how more senior managers approach their job.

A manager can manage to a degree against the wishes of the employees through force and direction. Such managers may not achieve the best results, but they can enforce certain standards of performance. The existence of disciplinary procedures within the company, recruitment procedures and the need for employees to earn a

EMPLOYEE PERSPECTIVE 9.2 Manager's views on more senior managers

Much still needs to be done to push real fiscal (financial) freedoms, with appropriate checks and balances down to the lower levels. You need to remove the dead hand of the centre which still controls manpower. (Officer in the armed forces)

We are suffering the syndrome of jumping on every latest bandwagon, often with no clear sense of direction as to where the next journey will take us. (Local government manager)

They're (senior managers) like a group of people at a dinner party when the lights go out. Instead of fumbling for the matches or trying to find the fuse box, they'd rather sit for hours in the dark discussing policy. (Local government manager)

Managers who find innovative ways of doing things tend to get squashed, as that's not the way things have been done in the past. (Local government manager)

Taken from: Public sector managers speak out, *Professional Manager*, July 2003, p 6.

Tasks

1. What might these quotations imply about the relationship between leaders and followers in the public sector?
2. Do these quotes imply that leadership or management is the dominant force at the top of public sector organizations?

living all ensure, as a minimum response, a compliance with managerial dictates. However, the question is can a leader lead under circumstances where resistance exists? Mazlish (1990) identifies a number of characteristics associated with leadership, several of which throw some light on this issue. He points out (pp 251–2) that there is no leader for all situations and that the potential leader must find the right circumstances and the right group to lead. He illustrates his point with the comment that General Ulysses Grant would have remained a failed army officer working in his family's leather business if the American Civil War had not broken out. Mazlish also points out that a leader is 'formed' during interaction with the followers. The potential leader 'discovers a self, forms and takes on an identity as a particular kind of leader, in the course of interacting with the chosen group' (p 252). From that perspective, leadership is as much a function of the followers as it is of the leader.

Leadership appears, therefore, to be a social process in which the leader is able to influence the behaviour of the followers, but only once the followers have accepted their relative position. To integrate this basic view of leadership with the perspective of Mazlish, leadership would seem to describe a mutual adaptation and acceptance process. One in which the leader and followers contribute a willingness to lead and to be led within an adaptable framework in formulating processes which will lead effectively to jointly acceptable styles and the desired end result. In brief, the followers allow the leader to exercise power and influence over them under conditions of acceptability and a degree of co-operation, provided mutual benefits are available. McGregor (1960, p 182) takes this view further (see Figure 9.3) by suggesting that leadership reflects the interaction of four main variables:

1. The characteristics of the leader.
2. The characteristics of the followers, as well as their attitudes and needs.
3. The organizational context including its purpose, structure and tasks to be undertaken.
4. The broader environmental context including social, political and economic forces.

FIGURE 9.3

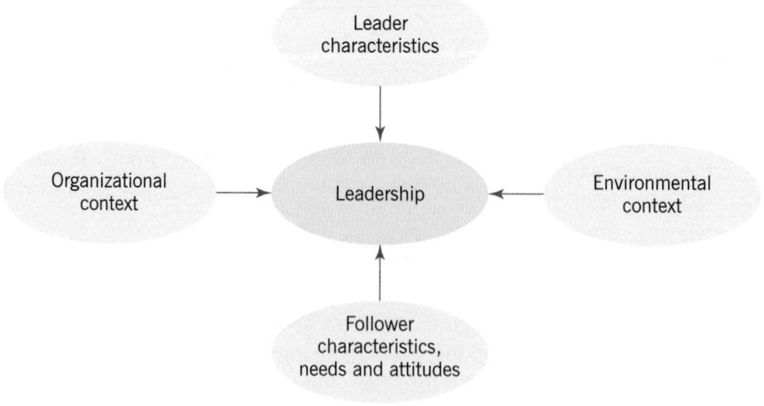

Leadership determinants

LEADERSHIP AS SYMBOLISM

It has been argued that it is the symbolism associated with the leadership role that influences subordinate behaviour (Griffin *et al.*, 1987). For example, the head of state of any country has several official duties to perform, signing new laws, opening parliament, welcoming official visitors, etc. In doing so they act as a symbol representing the entire country and its institutions. In a work context individuals take a lead from the behaviour of their managers. If a leader is thoughtful, caring, concerned and works hard, subordinates will tend to respect that individual and work in a similar manner. The converse is also true.

TRAIT THEORIES OF LEADERSHIP

For much of history it was assumed that leadership was a set of qualities that someone was born with. Adair (1983) quotes from a lecture given to students of St Andrew's University in 1934:

> It is a fact that some men possess an inbred superiority which gives them a dominating influence over their contemporaries, and marks them out unmistakably for leadership. This phenomenon is as certain as it is mysterious. It is apparent in every association of human beings in every variety of circumstances and on every plane of culture. In a school among boys, in a college among the students, in a factory, shipyard, or a mine among the workmen, as certainly as in the church and in the Nation, there are those who, with an assured and unquestioned title, take the leading place, and shape the general conduct. (p 7)

It is being argued in this quotation that good leaders naturally display those characteristics that are required by the position that they hold. The significance of this approach is that leaders cannot be trained and therefore must be selected. It also implies that successful leaders will be situation specific. This view originated from the traditional and aptly named **great man** (as at that time they were all men) view of leadership which suggested that in every situation (particularly in times of crisis) the best leader would emerge from the crowd and lead in such a way that the difficulties would be overcome. As a natural extension of this view future successful leaders could be identified by seeking out people with the same characteristics as existing successful leaders.

Great man
Suggests there are certain people who are born with the characteristics to make them successful leaders.

Handy (1993) suggests that by 1950 there had been over 100 studies attempting to identify appropriate **traits**. Unfortunately, little commonality was identified, with only about 5 per cent of the traits being common. Those traits found to have some association with successful leadership include:

Traits
Holds that there are certain innate characteristics such as intelligence that can determine successful leadership.

- *Intelligence*. A high level of intelligence and good at solving abstract, complex problems.
- *Initiative*. The ability to identify the need for action and to actually initiate appropriate courses of action.
- *Self-assurance*. Confidence in one's ability to do things and to be successful.
- *Overview*. The ability to stand back and take a broader view of situations.
- *Health*. To be of good health.
- *Physique*. To be above average weight and height, alternatively to be significantly below average physique.

- *Social background*. To be born into the higher socio-economic groups within society.

To find a leader with every characteristic (not just those listed here) would seem to be an impossible task. Many successful leaders do not fit the profile implied by the characteristics. There are simply too many exceptions to the identified traits to imply that they are essential for success. The terms used to describe the traits themselves are also imprecise and require judgement rather than allowing absolute measurement. For example, socio-economic grouping is a relative term, peculiar to each generation and society.

Although now largely discredited as an approach to leadership theory, trait approaches are used in the design of many assessment centres for the purposes of recruitment and career development for managers. Assessment centres involve a range of tasks to be undertaken with the behaviour and performance of testees being recorded and evaluated by a team of assessors. The justification for the use of traits in this way is based on the view that there are personal characteristics and behaviour patterns that impact on the effectiveness with which managers will perform their duties. Consequently, identifying individuals with those characteristics will allow improved managerial and organizational performance. The concept of traits has not disappeared from management and leadership thinking; they now appear as skill-based characteristics (or competencies) such as technical skill, conceptual skill and human relations skill, creativity, persuasiveness, tactfulness and ability to speak well. In that sense they have moved away slightly from the notion of inherited, natural or untrainable characteristics. Management in Action 9.3 introduces one such characteristic, that of listening as a factor in effective leadership.

STYLE THEORIES OF LEADERSHIP

Styles
Suggests that successful leadership reflects the style of behaviour towards subordinates, usually described on an autocratic–democratic scale.

Autocratic–democratic
A continuum, with the leader taking all the decisions at one extreme and involving subordinates in decisions at the other.

The basis of this approach to leadership is that subordinates will respond better to some **styles** than others. It is assumed that a positive subordinate response creates the success sought by the leader. There are many studies of this approach, the results mostly capable of interpretation as reflecting an **autocratic–democratic** variation in leadership style. Style theory generally suggests that leaders vary in the degree of involvement allowed to subordinates. At one extreme, leaders direct activity, taking decisions themselves regarding subordinates as a resource to be used – an autocratic style. At the other extreme, leaders can involve subordinates in planning and undertaking the work, delegating some of their responsibility – a democratic style. It is appropriate to consider style theories in chronological sequence, providing an opportunity to reflect on the evolution of such knowledge.

Early studies

The University of Iowa studies were carried out in boys' clubs during the late 1930s by Lippitt and White to study the consequences of leadership differences on aggressive behaviour among 10 year olds. They varied leadership style as follows:

- *Authoritarian*. The leader was directive but friendly or impersonal in style and did not allow participation among the boys.
- *Democratic*. Discussion and group decision making was encouraged by a leader who attempted to be objective but not 'one of the group'.
- *Laissez faire*. The leader gave complete freedom to the group of boys, in effect a lack of leadership rather than a particular style.

MANAGEMENT IN ACTION 9.3 **Leaders listen more**

The cure for poor leadership is to listen – three times as much as you talk. So said Peter Gardonyi a peak performance coach from the SI Group at a conference organized by the Chartered Institute of Personnel and Development.

He also said that leadership required more thinking about the 'we' aspect of organizational activity, which inevitably required more listening to other people. He pointed out the human resource professionals needed to recognize that management dealt with facts and things, whereas leadership centred on feelings and relationships. Neither was right or wrong in itself. But the awareness of these differences and the way that different people thought was necessary to understand the requirements of appropriate and effective leadership.

Adapted from: Management (2003) Top leaders listen more than talk, *People Management*, 12 June, p 12.

Stop ↔ Consider

To what extent could too much listening hinder effective leadership? How might an appropriate level of listening be achieved?

The group of boys subjected to the democratic leadership style contained the lowest levels of aggression and apathy and should therefore have been the most successful. However, there is a vast difference between boys' clubs and complex formal organizations. The original studies did not report other measures of success such as productivity or achievement. The studies are not organizational based and are experimentally weak. They were, however, the first serious examination of different styles of leadership.

The Ohio State University studies began in 1945 and used a questionnaire to examine leadership. Those questioned included officers, other ranks and civilian staff in the army and navy, manufacturing company supervisors, college administrators, teachers and student leaders. Two factors emerged:

1. *Consideration*. Indicating that the leader had respect and a rapport with subordinates as well as concern for their welfare.
2. *Initiating structure*. Reflected the degree to which the leader was task focused, emphasizing the achievement of objectives.

These studies are of important in establishing the task and people dimensions in the achievement of success. It has been argued that these studies do not necessarily identify actual leader behaviour but reflect the perceptions of those completing the form. For example, leaders could answer on the basis of how they think they behave (or would like to), rather than how they actually do. Equally a subordinate might complete the questions on the basis of personal feelings towards their boss rather than based on actual experience.

Likert's four systems of management

Likert developed this approach from the many years of work by a team at the University of Michigan. The four systems (or styles) of leadership identified through the research are:

- *System 1. Exploitative autocratic*. The leader has no confidence or trust in subordinates and does not seek or get ideas from them on work problems.

- *System 2. Benevolent autocratic.* The leader has some confidence and trust in subordinates. Occasionally the leader will seek ideas and opinions on work problems from subordinates. The style of leadership is paternalistic.
- *System 3. Participative.* There is significant confidence and trust in subordinates by the leader. However, the leader still seeks to ultimately control decision making but frequently seeks the opinions of subordinates and makes use of them in the process.
- *System 4. Democratic.* The leader completely trusts subordinates in all areas associated with the activity. The leader actively seeks the opinions of subordinates and always makes use of them.

Research into successful and unsuccessful teams was based on asking thousands of managers about the teams with which they had experience. The most successful departments were described in terms of systems 3 and 4 while the least successful were associated with systems 1 and 2 (Likert, 1967).

However, his work has not been without its critics. It was based on questionnaires and is subject to the common criticisms that such research approaches attract. Also there may be circumstances where it is not appropriate to adopt democratic processes. For example, in a crisis there may not be the time to consult and seek opinion. Muczyk and Reimann (1987) also argue that not every organization has the skill or quality of support to enable participation to be undertaken effectively.

The Tannenbaum and Schmidt continuum

Tannenbaum and Schmidt (1973) utilize concepts of boss-centred leadership and subordinate-centred leadership to represent the essential differences in styles of leadership. The variation in the degree to which each of these factors impacts on the leader behaviour is represented in the continuum that they use as the basis of their model. In this model they express a balance between the two factors as impacting upon the levels of managerial authority and freedom for subordinates in any given context. Figure 9.4 reflects this approach to leadership.

FIGURE 9.4

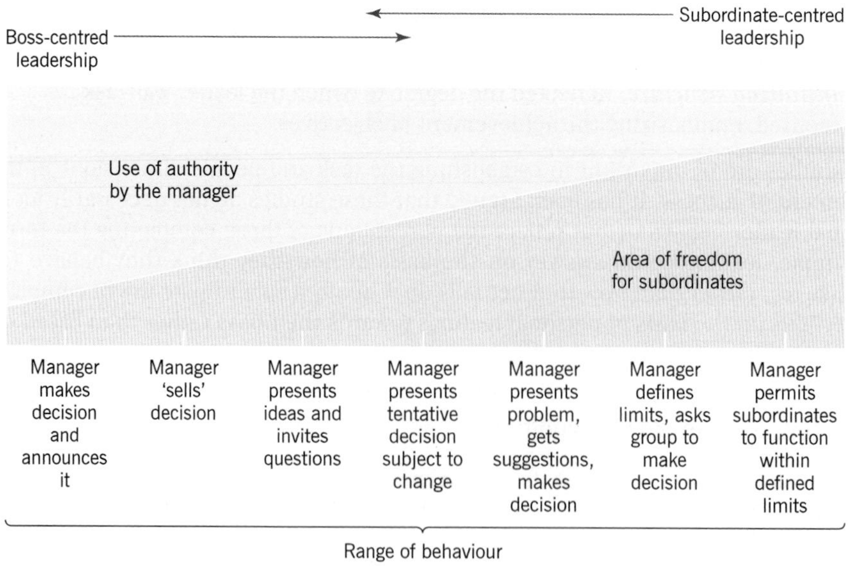

Continuum of leadership behaviour (*source*: Luthans, F (1995) *Organization Behaviour*, 7th edn, McGraw-Hill, New York)

It should be noted that within the model the use of authority or access to freedom never completely disappears. Even at the freedom for subordinates extreme of the continuum the boss still retains the power to say no and to require something to be done in a particular way. However, at the other extreme, employees also retain some freedom, even if it is only the opportunity to display token resistance. Although there are a number of different styles that can be identified within the model (Figure 9.4 indicates seven of them) there are four main categories that are most frequently described:

1. *Tells*. The leader identifies appropriate solutions to problems and the appropriate courses of action and thereafter tells the subordinates what they are supposed to do.
2. *Sells*. The leader still decides upon the appropriate course of action in any given situation but attempts to overcome disagreement and resistance among the workforce by selling the decision to them. Often this involves justifying the decision (taken by the boss) as the best course of action in the circumstances.
3. *Consults*. The leader allows time for subordinates to discuss the problem and present ideas and solutions to the boss. These are then used by the leader to make decisions which are then announced to, and actioned by, the subordinates.
4. *Joins*. The leader defines the nature of the issue to be decided along with any constraints and presents these to the group. The leader then becomes part of the group in finding and implementing acceptable solutions.

The form of leadership that would be appropriate in a particular context depends upon leader preferences, subordinate preferences and situational variables. This model leans towards the contingency approach to leadership in recognizing that success in any particular context depends upon a range of factors, effectively creating the need for an appropriate match between situational need, employee expectation and preferred style of the leader.

Blake and Mouton's grid

This approach emerged during the late 1960s and is based on the idea that differences in leadership approach are a function of two factors:

1. Concern for people
2. Concern for production.

These ideas were not new, being similar to work from the Ohio State University studies discussed earlier. However, Blake and Mouton produced a more systematic approach to the identification of generic styles. A grid is the usual way to represent the relationship between the two factors used in the model. Since it was originally published in 1964, the work has been revised several times, most recently as The Leadership Grid (Blake and McCanse, 1991). Figure 9.5 illustrates the model with the five main leadership styles indicated within it.

The term 'concern' is used in this context as reflecting emphasis in something rather than implying welfare or friendship based perspectives. The score for individuals along each scale would be identified through an analysis to the responses to a questionnaire. Looking at the five leadership styles indicated in the model:

1. *Impoverished management*. This style would be typified by a low concern for both people and production. Such a leader would be considered as remote from their subordinates and with little interest in achieving the business goals set for their department or section.

FIGURE 9.5

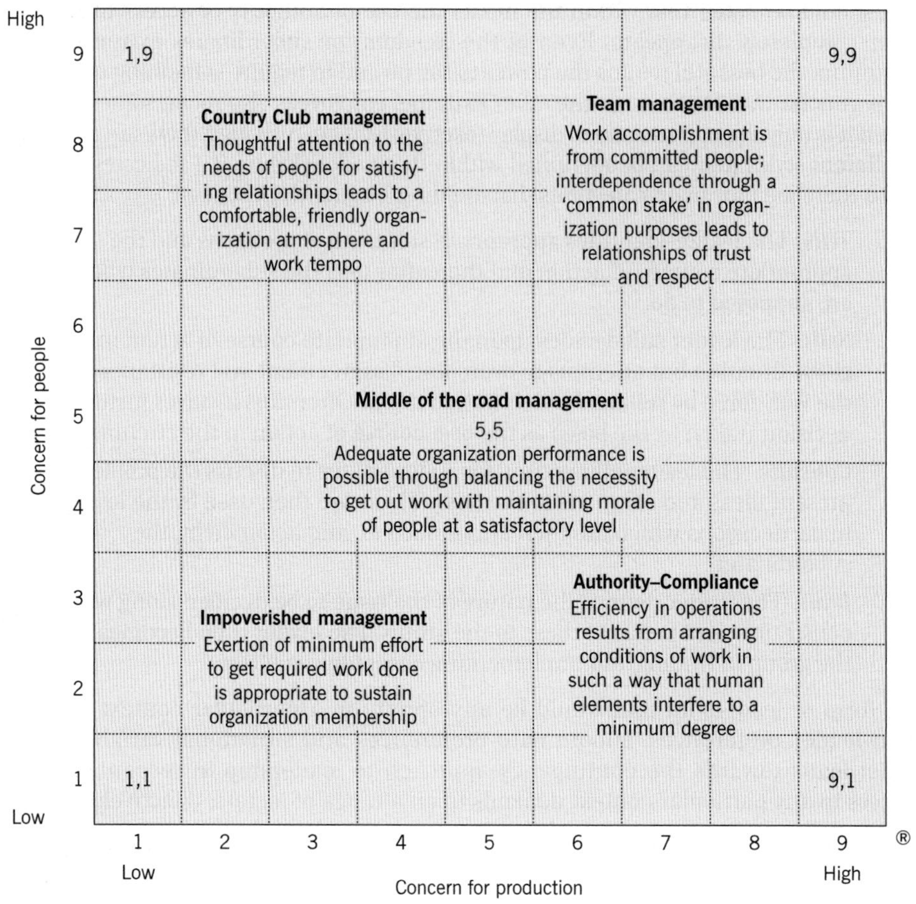

The Leadership Grid® (*source*: Blake, RR and McCanse, AA (1991) *Leadership Dilemmas – Grid Solutions*, Gulf Publishing, New York. All rights reserved)

2. *Authority–compliance management.* This style would be typified through a very high concern for production but very low concern for people. Such a leader would rely on the application of standard procedures and policies to determine action rather than the possible contribution from staff. They would be considered to be drivers of staff in the search for the achievement of objectives.
3. *Country club management.* This style would be typified by a very high concern for people but with low levels of concern for production. Such a leader would be concerned with the need to create harmony and avoid conflict thereby allowing subordinates to get on with the job. They would tend to be regarded as one of the workers by subordinates. They tend to seek a comfortable working environment in relationship terms, often in the belief that this ensures that production will follow automatically.
4. *Middle of the road management.* This style is typified through a medium level of concern for both people and production. Keeping everyone happy is a typical approach of such individuals. Unfortunately, because they are not strong on either index, they tend to underachieve on both, achieving neither good levels of production nor highly integrated work teams.

5. *Team management*. This style is typified by an equally very high concern for both people and production. Managers with this profile seek to create teams in which both the needs of individuals and the search for output become integrated.

Blake and Mouton found that managers tend to have one dominant style but that many have a back-up style if the first proves unsuccessful. They also found that many managers could vary their dominant style to some degree. The factors that influence the style adopted by an individual manager are shown in Figure 9.6.

Hersey and Blanchard's situation approach

This approach was developed by Hersey and Blanchard (1982) and is based on the existence of two different sets of leader behaviour:

1. *Task behaviour*. This approach is based on the degree to which the leader provides an output-focused perspective for the group.
2. *Relationship behaviour*. This approach is based on the amount of support, encouragement and two-way communication that the leader engages in.

There are similarities between this approach and that of Blake and Mouton. The Hersey and Blanchard situation approach adds to the ideas from Blake and Mouton by incorporating additional variables, based on the work of Fiedler (1967). However, not all the situation variables suggested by Fiedler are included, only those related to the readiness of the subordinates to be willing and able to achieve a particular task. From the two basic styles (task and relationship behaviour) emerge four actual styles when the situation variable of subordinate readiness is added to the model as in Figure 9.7.

The four actual styles of leadership are:

1. *Telling*. If the subordinates display a low level of readiness to be willing and able to achieve the task then the leader should adopt a task-oriented style by telling subordinates what is expected from them.
2. *Selling*. This style would be most appropriate where the subordinates display moderate levels of readiness towards the task to be achieved.
3. *Participating*. Where medium levels of subordinate readiness towards the task are found it is possible for the leader to lean towards the relationship aspects of the situation in terms of style.

FIGURE 9.6

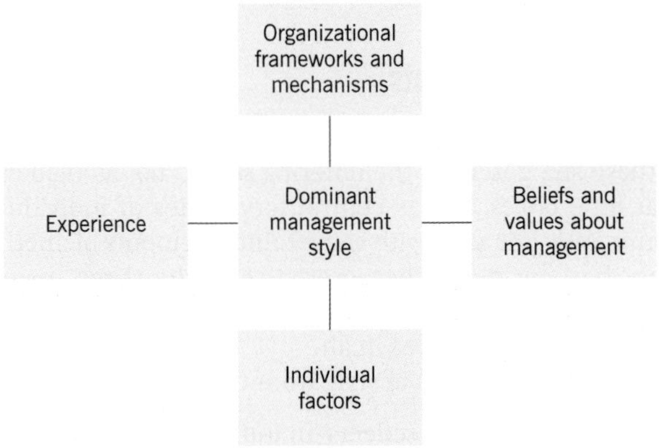

Management style determinants

FIGURE 9.7

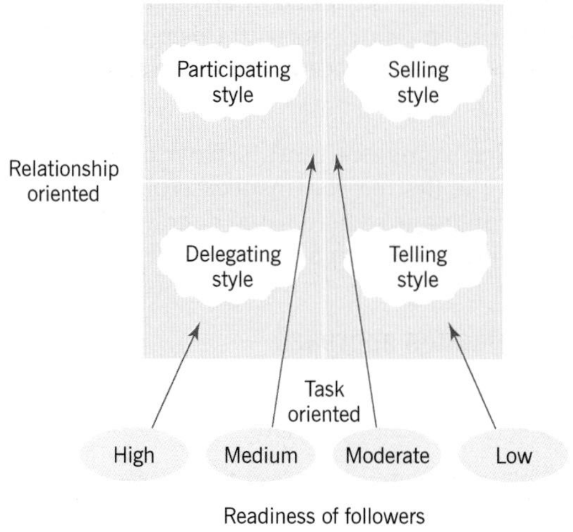

Hersey and Blanchard's situational model of leadership (*adapted from*: Hersey, P and Blanchard, K (1982) *Management Organizational Behaviour*, Prentice Hall, New York)

4. *Delegating.* With high levels of subordinate readiness there is an opportunity to delegate much of the responsibility for both task and relationship dimensions. The leadership role then becomes facilitation rather than managerial.

There are also similarities between the styles suggested here and those from Tannenbaum and Schmidt described earlier. In practice, this model builds on the work of the three sets of earlier writers indicated. There have been a number of criticisms of this model. For example, the theoretical underpinning was argued to be weak because the provision of a rationale for the underlying relationships was neglected. The questionnaire used to determine leader effectiveness was also heavily criticized. Nicholls (1985) argues that the model breaks the three principles of consistency, continuity and conformity. A revised model is offered by Nicholls which, it is suggested, does not break these principles. Naturally Hersey and Blanchard do not agree with the Nicholls' perspective and defended their work in a later publication.

The Hersey and Blanchard model spans the borderline between style and contingency theories of leadership. It emphasizes leadership style but it also introduces situational aspects into the model as being important factors in the determination of which style would be most successful in particular situations.

Artists, craftsmen and technocrats

In her research Pitcher (1997) describes three styles of leadership, each with two further subdivisions. In these she describes the differing styles, 'not as rigid categories, abstract concepts, or neat little boxes, but as central tendencies of individual human beings. People are predominantly one style with some minor elements of another' (p 140).

Table 9.1 identifies the main characteristics of the three major styles of artist, craftsman and technocrat. Each of the three major styles contains three subcategories, giving a total of nine styles in all.

An outline of the nine categories of style from this model are as follows:

- *Pure technocrat.* Such a style reflects an individual who is cerebral, uncompromising, stiff, hard-headed and detail oriented. Individuals displaying this style lack humour, will brook no opposition and remain calmly superior.

Artist	Craftsman	Technocrat
Unpredictable	Well balanced	Cerebral
Funny	Helpful	Difficult
Imaginative	Honest	Uncompromising
Daring	Sensible	Stiff
Intuitive	Responsible	Intense
Exciting	Trustworthy	Detail oriented
Emotional	Realistic	Determined
Visionary	Steady	Fastidious
Entrepreneurial	Reasonable	Hard-headed
Inspiring	Predictable	No-nonsense

TABLE 9.1 Characteristics of artist, craftsman and technocrat

- *Plodding technocrat.* Such a style reflects an individual who is rigid, dogmatic, uncompromising and hard-headed. The major distinction with the pure technocrat is that the plodding technocrat is not as bright!
- *Flashy technocrat.* Such a style reflects an individual who is brilliant in the sense of being able to argue for their point of view and in the use of experts to support it. However, their ideas are not new or original, they are not the true entrepreneur or innovator, they are simply quick witted at being conventional.
- *Pure craftsman.* Such a style reflects an individual who is steady, realistic, trustworthy, calmly intelligent, reflective and tolerant of human error and gives people the benefit of the doubt. It reflects someone who other people love to work with because the pure craftsman genuinely values the contribution of other people.
- *Regimental craftsman.* Such a style reflects an individual who is very methodical, analytical, conservative and controlled. Very similar to the pure craftsman they change their minds more slowly and need more convincing to do so.
- *Creative craftsman.* Such a style reflects an individual who is rather like the gentle artist (described later) but also has the characteristics of the realistic, sensible team player. They also differ from the gentle artist because they prefer to develop new ideas as evolutions from what already exists as opposed to revolutionary innovations. Also, they can deliver more effectively than the gentle artist through their ability to generate team commitment.
- *Pure artist.* Such a style reflects an individual who is unpredictable, imaginative daring, intuitive and exciting. They are the type of individual who is full of nervous energy, constantly on the move, throwing out an idea every minute.
- *Authoritarian artist.* Such a style reflects an individual who is hard to get along with, a poor listener, but brilliant, very determined and analytical. Generally lacking an attractive personality, they are able to take people along with them through the force of their ideas.
- *Gentle artist.* Such a style reflects an individual who is softly spoken, self-effacing, warm, easy-going and people oriented. Like the pure artist they prefer

to develop the big project and lots of them, but they do not have the big ego, do not blame others for failure and do not take themselves too seriously.

Pitcher recognizes that an organization will inevitably consist of many leaders, each of whom will fall into one of the nine categories indicated in her model. Therefore every style will be found in any organization. She also suggests that for any organization its ability to survive and prosper depends to a significant extent on the power struggles carried out between the styles in the dynamic of everyday organizational life. That is not to suggest that open warfare exists between these styles, but is a recognition that tension and conflict exists between people who are in leadership positions and who possess different styles.

The view that Pitcher puts forward is that the technocrat has dominated management thinking and practice over the past few decades. In turn, this has stifled both the opportunity for the artist to create and the ability of the craftsman to deliver the products and services provided by organizations to the benefit of society. It is her view that it is the artist who should be the overall leader, with the other two categories having specific roles to play in support and delivery of the vision.

CONTINGENCY THEORIES OF LEADERSHIP

Contingency theory
Considers that the best style of leadership, motivation, or organizational structure depends upon the factors active in the situation.

Contingency theory attempts to add value by incorporating a wider range of variables into the equation. They suggest that the most appropriate style of leadership is contingent (dependent) on a range of variables from the context within which the leadership will be exercised. These circumstances could include the expectations of the subordinates, the nature of the task to be achieved or the culture.

Fiedler's contingency model

This model attempts to identify situational influences on leadership within a framework that also incorporates the notion of effectiveness in achieving success. Fiedler (1967) brought together three situational aspects for determining the most effective style of leadership. Style was defined as an expression of the leader's personality preferences for either a task or relationship approach. The three situational variables are:

1. *Leader–member relationships*. It would be reflected in the degree of trust between the parties and a willingness to follow the leader's direction on the part of the subordinates.
2. *Task structure*. Tasks are either structured or unstructured in the degree to which the task is capable of being achieved through standard procedures. This is similar to the concept of programmed and non-programmed approaches to decision making as described by Simon (1960).
3. *Position power*. This construct reflects the degree of authority held by the leader.

The model contains two levels for each of these three constructs (for example, position power is either high or low) which produces eight situational combinations. These Fiedler combined into three levels of situational favourableness, each linked with either a task or relationship emphasis in the behaviour of the leader, see Figure 9.8.

Figure 9.8 shows that when the situation is either very favourable or very unfavourable to the leader then a task style would be most effective. When the situation is highly favourable to the leader then task orientation ensures that the objectives

FIGURE 9.8

Leader/member relations	Good				Poor			
Task structure	Structured		Unstructured		Structured		Unstructured	
Position power	High	Low	High	Low	High	Low	High	Low
Situational favourableness	Very favourable			Moderately favourable			Very unfavourable	
Recommended leader behaviour	Task-oriented behaviour			Person-oriented behaviour			Task-oriented behaviour	

Fiedler's contingency model of leadership

are achieved. In such situations it would be all too easy for a 'good time to be had by all' but for nothing to be achieved. When the situation is very unfavourable to the leader then a single-minded, driving approach is necessary in order to achieve the objectives against the balance of forces acting against the leader. When the situation is moderately favourable to the leader a relationship style is necessary in order to gain maximum employee support for the achievement of the objectives.

In determining the orientation of the leader in terms of task or relationship behaviour Fiedler developed a test which he called the Least Preferred Co-worker scale (LPC). Fiedler suggests that the two concepts of task or relationship preference reflect personality characteristics and are therefore relatively stable leader features. There has been criticism of the research studies that were used to support the development of the model. However, there has also been some support for the methodology (Strube and Garcia, 1981).

Fiedler's work reflects the view that success is a function of the interaction between the relationships in the workplace, the task to be achieved, the relative power balance between leader and led and the preferred style of the leader. Fiedler suggests that in attempting to optimize effectiveness, organizations should allow managers to maximize the fit between their preferred style and the other variables. This could be achieved through action plans for improving relationships or perhaps by moving key individuals. This approach has attracted some criticism on the basis that they are not consistent with the original model (Jago and Ragan, 1986).

Fiedler subsequently developed his work into a Cognitive Resource Theory (CRT) (Fiedler, 1986). This model attempts to identify the situational circumstances which interact with the cognitive characteristics of the leader and which impact on group performance. As with all research this approach has not been without its critics (Vecchio, 1992). However, it does offer a broader understanding of the interacting variables involved in leadership.

House's path–goal leadership theory

The path–goal model of leadership links leader behaviour with subordinate motivation, performance and satisfaction (House and Mitchell, 1974). This approach is similar to the **expectancy theory of motivation**. It postulates that subordinate motivation will be improved if the expectation that positive rewards will be forthcoming is likely to be realized. House identified four styles of leader behaviour:

1. *Directive leadership*. Under this style the leader is expected to provide precise instruction on what is required and how it is to be achieved.

Expectancy theory of motivation
Approach suggesting that the desirability of particular outcomes motivates behaviour.

2. *Supportive leadership*. This reflects a style that adopts a friendly, concerned approach to the needs and welfare of subordinates.
3. *Participative leadership*. This reflects a style in which the leader would seek opinions and suggestions from subordinates before making a decision.
4. *Achievement-oriented leadership*. This reflects a style in which the leader is task oriented and sets challenging goals for subordinates.

This contingency approach is based on the notion that individual leaders are capable of changing their style to match the needs of the situation. The two situational factors are:

1. *Subordinate characteristics*. Leader acceptability depends to a significant extent on the degree to which subordinates perceive leader behaviour as a source of present or future satisfaction.
2. *Demands facing subordinates*. Leader behaviour would motivate performance in subordinates if the satisfaction of subordinate need were dependent on their performance in the work itself and/or other aspects of the work environment.

The path–goal model reflects the influence of leader behaviour on subordinate activity within a directional flow of activity towards the goal to be achieved, see Figure 9.9.

There have been some attempts to substantiate the model, with mixed results. A paper which reviewed 48 studies demonstrated mixed levels of support for aspects of the model and suggested the continued testing of it (Indvik, 1986).

The Vroom, Yetton and Jago model of leadership

This model was introduced in 1973 by Vroom and Yetton and expanded by Vroom and Jago (1988). Like the other contingency models, it attempts to identify styles of leadership appropriate in particular situations. It presupposes that leaders can vary their style of behaviour and that only some aspects of the situation are relevant to the type of leadership that would be most effective in that context. The model postulates that it is the degree of subordinate involvement in the decision-making process that is the major variable in leader behaviour. The model is managerial in orientation in that it attempts to offer ways to determine a high-quality decision in relation to the task itself, but at the same time ensure that subordinates will actively support the decision. In application this model uses decision trees as the basis of working through the variables involved in identifying the appropriate style for the circumstances.

There are four decision trees offered by the model, two for group problems and two for individual problems. Each pair contains a decision tree for emergency (or time-pressured) situations and one for less time-sensitive events. The latter variation also

FIGURE 9.9

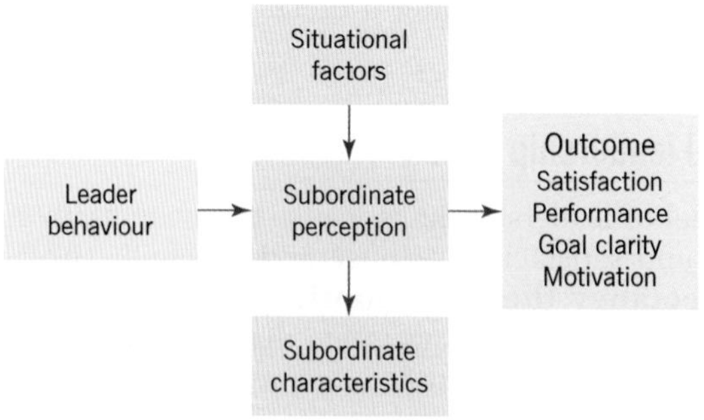

Path–goal model of leadership

allows managers to develop subordinate decision making through their involvement in the process. The decision tree does not provide the answer to the problem itself, but offers a suggestion for a leader style that should generate the best decision in the circumstances, based on levels of subordinate involvement.

There is a potential difficulty in this model for leaders in that changing style dependent on the situation could lead to them being thought inconsistent in their style by subordinates. Equally, for a leader to change style may create conflict, confusion or lower morale and productivity among subordinates. Subordinates may become accustomed to being involved in decision making or become unsure of the degree of involvement that they will enjoy at any given time. That said there is some research evidence that decisions consistent with the model are more effective than those not consistent with it. The following Employee Perspective (9.3) looks at a very specific job, interim management, in terms of the style of management that might be appropriate to the task of one such individual on one assignment.

OTHER APPROACHES TO LEADERSHIP

The vertical dyad linkage model

This approach to leadership was developed by Dansereau *et al.* (1975). It suggests that leaders behave differently with different subordinates. Between the leader and each subordinate is an individual relationship, referred to as a vertical dyad. The model postulates that leaders create an in-group and an out-group around themselves and that these groups receive different treatments from the leader. The in-group is made up of a few special individuals, who are more trusted, and given more preferential treatment and special privileges than the out-group. Figure 9.10 reflects the basis of the vertical dyad linkage model.

EMPLOYEE PERSPECTIVE 9.3 The style of interim managers

Interim management is an evolving area of work for managers. It emerged in Holland during the 1980s as a means of circumventing the strict regulation of employment and labour. It is developing rapidly across some parts of Europe as a way of either tackling a specific issue or filling a gap temporarily. It is however a grey area not yet well understood and is often confused with consulting or contracting. In the UK the market for such services has grown from about £75m in 1995 to around £268m in 2003. It should be seen as less of a reactive, distress purchase and more of a proactive, added value management resource, according to Richard Lambert, chairman of the Interim Management Association.

Alan Charlesworth is one such manager who spent nine months on one assignment seeking to consolidate the business in order to make it profitable. This involved closing either the London or Dublin office. The job involved keeping everyone onside, dealing with people's natural concerns and sensitivities as well as maintaining operations during a period of dramatic change. The job involved split weeks between London and Dublin, living in hotel rooms for much of the time and working long hours trying to overcome initial resistance and concerns.

Adapted from: Mann, S (2003) Working away, *Professional Manager*, May, pp 29–32.

Tasks

1. Which (if any) style of management would it be appropriate for Alan to adopt in this situation and why?
2. Could the contingency approach to leadership offer a better explanation of how to approach leadership in this situation? Why or why not?

FIGURE 9.10

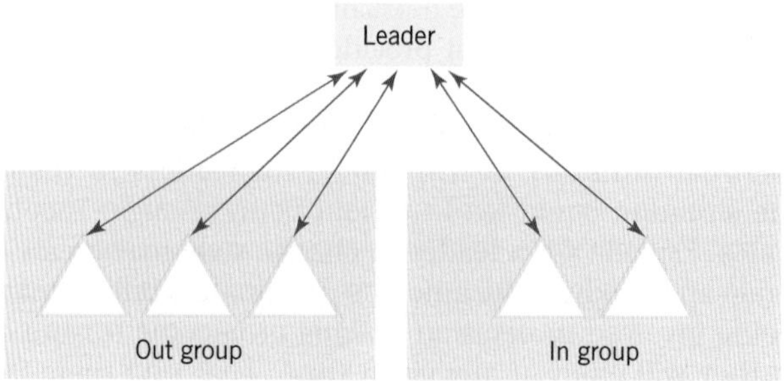

The vertical dyad model of leadership

Transactional and Transformational model

This model was originally developed by Burns (1978) and refined by Kuhnert and Lewis (1987) who suggested that there are two types of management activity, each demanding different skills:

1. *Transactional*. This includes the allocation of work, making routine decisions, monitoring performance and interacting with other functions within the organization.
2. *Transformational*. This is about having the skills and personal qualities to be able to recognize the need for change and being able to identify appropriate courses of action to bring it about. See for example Avolio *et al.* (1999) who suggest that there are a number of sub-components to the concept including charisma, intellectual stimulation and individualized consideration.

Bass (1990) identified the characteristics of both types of leader, (see Table 9.2). He suggests that transactional leaders are a hindrance to change and they foster a climate of mediocrity. Transformational leaders, by the same token, can produce improved performance in situations of uncertainty and change.

Tepper (1993) found transformational leaders more frequently adopted legitimizing tactics than transactional leaders in explaining their decisions and selected courses of action. They were also able to achieve higher acceptance of objectives among subordinates than were transactional leaders. The major issue highlighted through this model is that most leaders are required to engage in both transactional and transformational leadership as part of their responsibilities. If leaders tend to one 'type' then it will be difficult for them to achieve an effective performance across the full range of their responsibilities.

Charismatic leadership

House (1977) characterized charismatic leaders as full of self-confidence, with a high level of confidence in subordinates and high expectations for results. They also have a clear vision of the goal to be achieved, are able to communicate this effectively and lead by example. Charismatic leaders can, however, create problems for organizations. They may not fully understand the business or its environment and so may lead it in the wrong direction. Equally, if they do not make effective provision for succession to the leadership position when they wish to relinquish control the organization can flounder.

It has been argued that the emergence of charismatic leadership could be a function of both leader traits and situational variables (Conger and Kanungo, 1988).

Transactional leaders	
1	Contingent reward: Contracts exhange of rewards for effort, promises rewards for good performance, recognizes accomplishments
2	Management by exception (active): Watches and searches for deviations from rules and standards, takes corrective action
3	Management by exception (passive): Intervenes only if standards are not met
4	Laissez faire: Abdicates responsibilities, avoids making decisions
Transformational leaders	
1	Charisma: Provides vision and sense of mission, instills pride, gains respect and trust
2	Inspiration: Communicates high expectations, uses symbols to focus efforts, expresses important purposes in simple ways
3	Intellectual stimulation Promotes intelligence, rationality, and careful problem solving
4	Individual consideration: Gives personal attention, treats each employee individually, coaches, advises

TABLE 9.2 Characteristics of transactional and transformational leaders (*source*: Bass, BM (1990) From transactional to transformational leadership: learning to share the vision, *Organizational Dynamics*, Winter)

Personal traits that may produce a charismatic approach include self-confidence, skills in impression management and social sensitivity. Contextual variables that could encourage the emergence of a charismatic leader include crisis situations and high levels of subordinate dissatisfaction with the current leadership. Howell and Avolio (1992) introduce an ethical perspective to the discussion, pointing out that it is possible for charismatic individuals to abuse their capabilities in order to achieve an unquestioning following and hence a leadership position.

Conger (1999) suggests that many skills associated with charisma can be developed. For example, speaking skills as part of developing the ability to communicate effectively, and learning how to think critically about the status quo and what could be improved in it. It is also possible to learn how to stage events that send powerful messages to other people. For example, Jim Dawson the newly appointed head of Zebco (the largest fishing tackle producer in the world) quickly recognized the existence of problems with employee relations in the company when he took over. His first act was to abolish managers' reserved parking spaces (one day he got their secretaries to park in them before their bosses arrived) and also personally smashed all the time clocks on the shopfloor (used for employees to record arrival and departure times). Both actions sent out very clear signals about the future style of leadership. It is also possible for the aspiring charismatic leader to learn how to motivate the team on a day-to-day basis. What Conger suggests it is not possible to learn is how to be passionate about what you do – that has to be discovered at a personal level. Passion about what they are doing is a great driver of charismatic leaders and creates enthusiasm in the followers for achieving the vision. It also suggests that it takes courage to become unconventional and a risk taker, the other major skills of a charismatic leader.

Attribution theory

Attribution theory suggests that individuals 'attribute' causes to the behaviour that they observe in others. In a leadership context, the leader observes the behaviour of subordinates, imputes causes to it, and reacts on the basis of those interpretations (Martinko and Gardner, 1987). For example, an employee who is frequently late for work and who will not work overtime may be classified as lazy and not interested in the job. One major problem that can be created by this view of leadership is that assumptions made by the leader may be wrong. In the example of the employee being late, it may be that domestic difficulties mean that the employee is unable to arrive at work any earlier or stay any later, not that they are lazy and do not want to work. In addition, the attribution of causes of behaviour does not automatically result in behavioural responses in the individual. For example, a leader might interpret the cause of employee behaviour as poor working conditions and seek to address those issues rather than change their leadership behaviour, which may be the real issue.

Action-centred leadership

The basis of this approach was developed by John Adair and propounded in many books (see, for example, Adair, 1983). It was also discussed in the previous chapter in relation to management. Essentially he views leadership as a function of three separate, but linked ideas:

1. *Achieving the task*. This includes activities such as planning the work to be done, allocating resources and duties, checking performance and reviewing progress.
2. *Building and maintaining the team*. This includes activities such as building team spirit and maintaining morale, maintaining discipline and the training of the group. It also includes establishing subgroups and appointing section leaders.
3. *Developing the individual*. This includes activities such as dealing with the personal problems of subordinates, reconciling the needs of the group and the individual and the training of individuals.

Although these three areas of leadership are distinct in themselves they do interact with each other in that actions (or inaction) in one area will influence events in the other two. So, for example, a leader who overemphasizes the task aspects of the model at the expense of the team and individual elements is likely to find that morale drops and that individuals become progressively alienated. Adair uses a three-circle model to illustrate the integrated and interdependent relationship between these three aspects of leadership, see Figure 9.11.

Adair suggests that the development of leaders comes through exposure to each of the three aspects of the model. In essence, this reflects a process of being required to take action in each of the dimensions of leadership and also gaining experience in balancing the needs of all three dimensions at the same time. Training courses have been developed to promote personal development in each of the three aspects of the model. Adair also suggests that leaders need the skill to be aware of what is going on within the groups for which they are responsible and the awareness of which component of the leadership model is dominant in any given situation. In a more recent book, Adair discusses what he terms as inspirational leadership which is about those factors and characteristics that mark out very effective leaders. Management in Action 9.4 introduces the basis of this idea.

MANAGEMENT IN ACTION 9.4 The inspirational leader

Radford is in charge of leadership development at the Royal Military Academy, Sandhurst where all future army officers begin their training. Clearly any military establishment has a keen interest in leadership if any war is to be waged successfully. It is a fundamentally dangerous activity to seek to attack or defend a nation's interest through war. Radford reviewed a book by John Adair on the subject of inspirational leadership and in the process made some interesting comments about leadership in general.

Radford suggests that successful military leadership is about the projection of personality, character, intellect and professional skill in order to inspire the led. He also suggests that in essence that is no different to leadership in any other area of endeavour. He describes it as a combination of example, persuasion and compulsion that results in making people do things that they might not otherwise have done. He suggests that the real difference between those who lead and those who are led is the desire for responsibility.

The book that Radford reviews seeks to address the issue of what it is that defines an inspirational leader. Adair in his book of that name suggests that the inspired leader is one who understands the spiritual energy within both leader and led; can think about the big picture rather than the detail; can display a degree of humility and recognize the inspired moment that allows a brief window of opportunity to inspire both leader and led.

Adapted from: Radford, T (2003) A psychological contract, *Management Today*, July, p 37.

Stop ↔ Consider

To what extent does the definition of leadership described by Radford reflect a style as discussed in this chapter or a set of characteristics and skills that could be acquired by any individual seeking to do so?
Are Radford and Adair describing different views about what leadership is, or are they part of the same thing?

Interactive leadership

The notion of the interactive leader is one that emerged over time as a result of the changes that were developing in the ways that people and organizations interact. Burnham (2003) describes research that he has done over more than twenty years into what it is that differentiates effective from ineffective leaders, and how ineffective

FIGURE 9.11

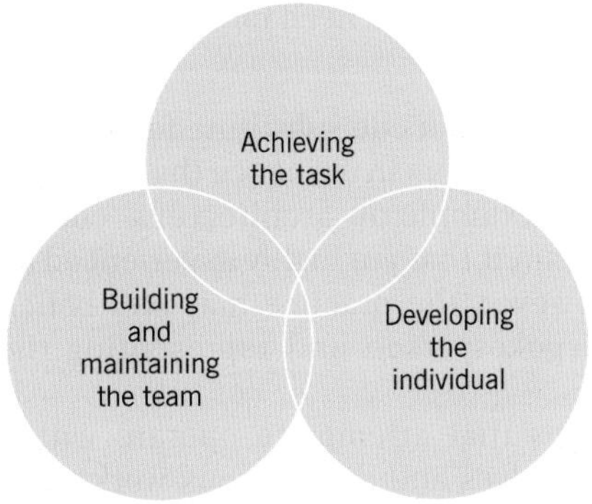

What a leader has to do (*source*: Adair, J (1983) *Effective Leadership: A Self-development Manual*, Gower, Aldershot)

leaders can be encouraged to change their approach. He suggests that since the early 1990s a new leadership paradigm has been emerging in which the inner motivation of the leader feeds the beliefs and attitudes and subsequently behaviour. He describes the interactive leader as he calls such people, as:

- Returning authority to others. Identifying the best decision maker in each situation based on the desire to be involved and assessment of capability. This is more than simple delegation.
- Seeing others as equals, regardless of their position. This requires a high degree of empathy and authenticity in achieving mutuality in the workplace.
- The ability to tolerate ambiguity until the right answer emerges rather than forcing actions based on only partial or misleading information. Requires emotional maturity in dealing with the paradoxes and complexity in such situations.
- Being prepared to modify plans in the light of outcomes achieved and having a high level of pride in their work.

ALTERNATIVES TO LEADERSHIP

Kerr and Jermier (1978) suggest three areas where substitution for leadership is possible:

1. *Subordinate characteristics*. Situations where employees are professionally qualified, highly experienced and very able to undertake the duties expected of them do not need leadership in the conventional sense of the term. Also, where a subordinate is indifferent to the rewards that the leader can offer for co-operating and acceptance of their position there is little scope for the practice of leadership.
2. *Task characteristics*. Where the work is highly routine and contains immediate feedback on performance and achievement there is little scope for the exercise of leadership. The employee is effectively controlled by the job that they undertake and feedback on performance is automatically and quickly received through the work itself. Leadership in such situations becomes restricted to ensuring that work is provided to the employee and that it is taken away when it is complicated.
3. *Organizational characteristics*. An organization that is highly routinized with little flexibility will have limited need for leader activity as it will almost run itself.

Research suggests that these factors do substitute for leadership in certain situations. However, there may be other factors in existence that can influence the level of contribution from a leader. For example an architectural consultancy may have a high number of individuals within it that are highly experienced and capable of doing what is required of them. However, the practice may still benefit from a leader who is capable of acting as a spokesperson and representing the practice to the wider community.

There are some groups that attempt to operate without a formal leader, for example, workers' co-operatives and autonomous work teams. A form of democracy would exist in such groups, replacing the traditional leadership role. These groups tend to abolish the hierarchical status that would be enjoyed by a leader. Instead they distribute the activities and functions among the group in order to create greater involvement for every member and to encourage more effective contribution from everyone. In addition, such groups frequently have a strong desire to practise democracy within an organizational context and therefore seek alternative ways of organizing and running the business.

LEADERSHIP AND THE ORGANIZATIONAL LIFECYCLE

Clarke and Pratt (1985) suggest that there are different requirements from a leader during the various stages in the organization's lifecycle. They identify four different leadership patterns:

1. *Champion*. In the formation stages of an organization a leader is required who can champion the new business, win orders, organize a team of employees and display a broad spectrum of leadership ability.
2. *Tank commander*. In the growth phase of a business new people will be brought into the organization and departments will be established. An individual to bulldoze ideas through and drive the organization towards its future is necessary during this stage of evolution.
3. *Housekeeper*. The maturity phase tends to require an emphasis on the achievement of cost effectiveness. This is the phase when much activity surrounds the development and application of standard procedures to activity – the careful husbandry of what already exists.
4. *Lemon squeezer*. Decline can either result in demise or rejuvenation. A tough leader is required in order to squeeze the maximum out of the situation and attempt to inject new life into the organization at this stage in its evolution.

A variation on this approach is that proposed by Rodrigues (1988). This version is based on the premise that the real experience for most organizations is in attempting to continue to function in a constantly dynamic context. This carries with it implications for problem solving, implementation and stability in a constantly changing environment. This reflects a different form of lifecycle to that just described and so leaders are needed who can cope with the ever changing demands of this type of organizational experience. An alternative view based on these ideas is that the leader should be changed at regular intervals if they cannot adapt to changes in situation. The following Employee Perspective (9.4) describes the very unusual situation facing one individual who felt it necessary to take action in unusual circumstances that involved considerable personal risk and at a time when not everyone in authority felt compelled to do the same.

LEADERSHIP AND SUCCESS

So far in this discussion about leadership the issue of level of leadership has been ignored. The term 'leader' implies a single person at the head of an organization. This may be true for small or entrepreneurial organizations, but many organizations contain large numbers of people and also have many possible leaders across a number of levels. There will be the chief executive officer of the organization, supported by the other executive directors and senior managers. Below those levels will be the departmental and functional managers, with reporting to them section heads, middle managers and technical specialists. Then below that level will be the numerous

EMPLOYEE PERSPECTIVE 9.4 Bill's experience on a sinking ship

This episode was described by Bill, a retired chief engineer who had been at sea most of his working life and who had served in the merchant navy throughout the Second World War. On one voyage the ship in which he was chief engineer was steaming in the Atlantic off the coast of Spain when it was hit by a torpedo. It was a cargo ship and was fully loaded with food supplies destined for the UK. It quickly became apparent that the ship was badly damaged and that it could not stay afloat for more that a couple of hours. So it became necessary to organize everything so that people could abandon the ship and take to the lifeboats safely. The engine room was flooding and there was danger that the boilers could explode so there was a need to shut down the engines and boilers properly in order to give more time to abandon the ship safely. Once power was shut off it would become more difficult to winch the lifeboats down to the sea and impossible to send a distress call to summon assistance and rescue.

This required a number of the engineering crew and officers to stay at their post and follow the emergency drills until given permission to close everything down and take to the lifeboats. Much of this work required people to be in the engine room which was not only flooding but also on fire in places. Clearly this was a dangerous time for all concerned and the loss of life was an ever present risk. Not everyone coped well. Some individuals, deck officers, engineering officers and ordinary crew alike, panicked and just wanted to get into the lifeboats as quickly as possible. Bill said that there were enough people prepared to do their duty to ensure that the emergency shut-down procedures were carried out properly and then it was time to leave the doomed ship and escape in a lifeboat. By then panic had spread and some people became frozen to the spot and could not move or jump over the side into the sea in order to get into a lifeboat. Bill said that he started shouting at people, ordering them to do something, pushing and shoving them towards the rails of the ship. In some cases people were lying down on the deck, huddled up into a ball and crying. He said that he started kicking, punching, dragging and shouting at them to try and get them to move and save themselves. Some roused themselves and made for a lifeboat; some he pushed over the side and they swam to a lifeboat and some just groaned and refused to move. Some would not respond at all. After a while it became obvious that the ship was near to sinking and that Bill would have to take action to save himself. So eventually he jumped into the water and swam to a lifeboat. Some of the officers and crew were drowned, because they would not save themselves.

Tasks

1. To what extent was Bill's behaviour in trying to force individuals to save themselves justifiable in the circumstances?
2. Does the example offered by Bill imply that all leaders are entitled to take drastic steps if the organization is in grave danger? Why or why not?

Downshift
The decision by an individual to seek a job at a lower level, with less responsibility, salary and stress.

supervisory and junior management positions that make up the bulk of the 'management' jobs within any large organization. It would be improbable that any organization could be successful on the strength of a single leader at the top of the managerial hierarchy. The following Employee Perspective (9.5) looks at one employee's decision to **downshift** rather than become like his boss.

By implication, therefore, it is necessary for an organization to have leaders at a number of levels if maximum utility is to be achieved from the notion of leadership as compared to the concept of management. This sounds sensible enough, but it does raise several interesting questions that are not easy to answer. For example, if every manager within an organization were also a leader there might be a danger that this would detract from the ability of the top leader to stand out and so function effectively as the focal point for organizational direction and vision. This line of thinking implies that leadership reflects a graduated scale of ability, with more senior leaders being recognized as more significant than more junior leaders (as reflected in the organizational hierarchy). The existence of multiple leaders within an organization could also lead to the existence of an organization within an organization if they began to compete with each other for expression and supremacy. The conventional response to

EMPLOYEE PERSPECTIVE 9.5 Dropping out of the rat race

Careers are not always based around promotion to more senior positions within management. Downshifting reflects the conscious decision to actively seek a different lifestyle, different career path and usually a lower standard of living. For example, Jamie Evans was a 26 year old derivatives trader in the City of London and was earning about £70k per year in 2001. He was very good at his job, but he decided that he had to get out after his boss called him into the office for a pep talk. He was told that he was very good at his job and that if he continued to work hard he could go far and be just like his boss. The last point was the killer blow. His boss was 32, very overweight and with heart and liver problems. Jamie described him as a nasty piece of work with loads of health problems. The talk had the opposite of the desired effect. It made Jamie think seriously about whether he actually wanted to end up like his boss. He decided no and resigned. Within a few weeks he got a job making cups of tea and running errands for television companies in London which paid about £10k per year. A considerable reduction in status, type of work and lifestyle. But after about 18 months he became an assistant producer for a television programme and is now happier earning much less, but doing something that he enjoys.

Taken from: High-flyers quit the City in Quest for satisfaction, *The Times*, 19 April 2003, p 57.

Task

What might Jamie's experience imply about the nature of career success, leadership and working in organizations?

this being that if such circumstances were to occur (not very likely) then the organization would be highly successful because of the unity of effort and performance achieved, points reinforced by Kedia *et al.* (2002). But it could also be destructive if it were not handled effectively.

What this question also raises is the issue of leadership as a reflection of the personal qualities of the individual, compared to the process of managing an organization. For an organization to be maximally effective is it necessary to have a mixture of routine and vision. In simple terms, the routine processing of orders and the vision to identify future trends in the industry and prepare the organization for them. This implies that such organizations need both managers and leaders, leaders in the sense of the visionary who can, to use the analogy from Westley (as referred to earlier), use drama to energize employees and managers who can adopt an appropriate style to ensure the delivery of performance at the operational level. Such a view would bring the discussion back to the contingency models of leadership which suggest that the most effective style is dependent on the circumstances.

In the case of leaders who achieve that position through charisma a different set of questions arise. For example, how does charisma develop within the individual? Does it reflect natural ability that the individual is born with or do they develop over time? If charisma develops over time, how does that happen, is it guaranteed to happen and does it have a natural limit that might be different between individuals? Given that charismatic leaders make most impact at the very top of whichever organization they inhabit, these are not minor questions. Since the most commonly held view of charisma is that it reflects the ability to lead through the force of personality, this might imply that it develops as the individual's personality forms. Assuming that charismatic leaders do not simply emerge at the top of the organization overnight it is interesting to speculate how they develop within an organization. Consider an organization with a highly charismatic middle manager – could the more senior managers (who may not be charismatic) cope with such a potential threat to their position within their ranks? Such a person may be able to work wonders within their own sphere of responsibility but what of the rest of the organization? Would such a person rise through the ranks very quickly as their ability to achieve results pushed them ever upwards? Or would they be seen as a threat to the existing leadership, as creating an organization within an organization through their attractiveness as a leader to all below them?

What all these questions raise in general terms is how is leadership managed within an organization? Many would argue that leadership qualities can be developed through training and experience. For example, the Blake and Mouton model discussed earlier assumes that having identified the current leadership style as reflecting the balance between concern for people or production, appropriate training can move the individual towards the ideal 9,9 position. However, Pitcher (also discussed earlier) suggests that training, at least as currently undertaken, is unlikely to be successful in moving people's underlying style. Experience suggests that the most likely scenario is that training can provide understanding and experience in different leadership styles, but that the individual may or may not enact them in the normal course of their work. Actually achieving changes in the leadership approach of the individual depends upon a wide range of factors including how they are managed by their own boss, past experience, willingness to experiment, organizational context and feedback on performance. Figure 9.12 reflects a number of these factors.

Another way to consider the issue of success within an organization is in terms of key result areas. Success is one of those terms that can mean different things to different people; therefore it is not always easy to precisely determine the relationship of leadership to it. However, one model that seeks to do just that is the one that under-

FIGURE 9.12

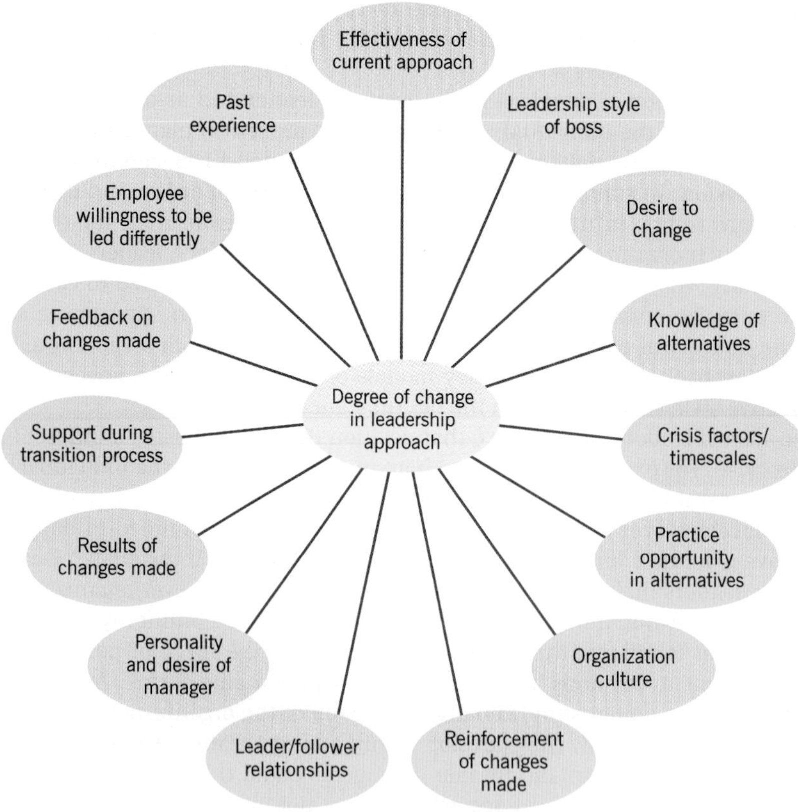

Factors influencing likelihood of changing leadership approach

pins the European Quality Award, introduced in 1992. Established by the European Foundation for Quality Management (EFQM) which was established in 1988 by 14 leading western European companies to encourage quality-based achievements. The essence of the model is that leadership should drive business policy, strategy, people management and resource deployment in the search for business results. The model is shown in Figure 9.13.

The nine elements within the model are classified as either:

- *Enablers*. These include those organizational aspects reflecting how results are achieved. They include the style of leadership and how managers drive quality and continuous improvement, people management policies and practices for energizing staff to improve quality etc.
- *Results*. These areas in the model reflect what the company is achieving in the particular areas indicated. For example, people satisfaction reflects what employees actually think about the company and customer satisfaction reflects the customer perspective on the offerings of the company.

The nine elements in the model are scored by a visiting panel of assessors and the company ranked against others in the competition for the award of the prize. However, it is the relationship of leadership to the achievement of the key performance results for the business that is of prime importance in this discussion. The basis of the model is that leadership is a key driver of activity, but that the effects of this are mediated through many other factors before success can be judged. In other words, it is leadership linked to the context that provides the opportunity to achieve success, not leadership itself. A lack of success, or even worse, failure is usually regarded as a serious thing in a leader. However, Kirwan-Taylor (2003) argues that failure is increasingly being seen as a worthy battle scar. Professor Gretchen Rubin suggests that failure is the price for being at what she calls the 'bleeding edge' of creativity and risk taking. Success comes to those people who don't let failure stop them from trying. For example, Nicholas Beart having been fired from a large company during a recession and then establishing his own business empire now looks at application forms with a keener eye. He actively looks for people with negative experience and how they dealt with it. As Kirwan-Taylor suggests there are 6 tips to 'flopping with flair':

FIGURE 9.13

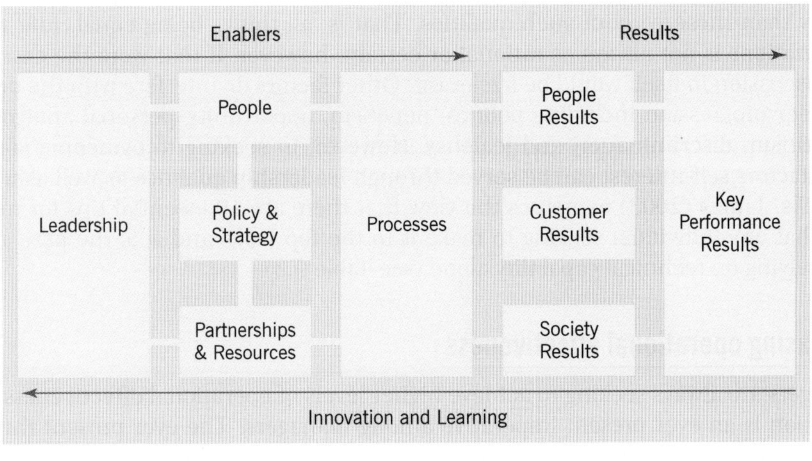

The EFQM Excellence Model (© EFQM, 1999. *Source*: European Foundation for Quality Management 1999–2003)

1. Fail with a bang, not a whimper – if you make enough noise, people will remember you.
2. Reflect on and learn from your disaster.
3. Don't let one flop stop you from trying again – failing doesn't make you 'A failure'.
4. Avoid personal bankruptcy if you can – especially in the UK.
5. Flaunt your scars. They make you more marketable.
6. And remember – 'Only those who dare to fail greatly can ever achieve greatly' – Robert F Kennedy.

LEADERSHIP: AN APPLIED PERSPECTIVE

That leadership and management are not the same has already been established. Management is the exercise of formal authority in an organizational context; leadership is more to do with performance. It is hardly surprising that managers have for a long time been interested in leadership. Gone are the days when leadership could be assumed as a right of birth – at least in many situations. Managers have an interest in the study of the subject from the many perspectives discussed in the following sections.

Enhancing management's position

Consider the choice between a manager or someone with obvious leadership qualities (but with the same technical skills as the manager) who both applied for a particular vacancy that you were seeking to fill. Which would you choose? Given the material discussed in this chapter the answer should be obvious, at least for most situations. At a personal level the person who can demonstrate leadership qualities may be able to achieve better results and higher levels of effectiveness from subordinates and is therefore more commercially attractive. The major problem from a theoretical perspective is identifying what leadership means, as is evident from the vast range of perspectives reviewed in this chapter. However, if they can be identified, such people are more likely to be promoted and rise to senior positions within organizations more rapidly than those without such qualities. That is, all things being equal. Life within organizations is not always as rational or certain, however. If that were the case then this discussion in itself would be irrelevant. Other factors do interfere with the process of career progression including politics, nepotism, opportunity, personal antagonism, favouritism, discrimination and jealousy. However, in seeking to overcome some of these factors self-interest can be served through leadership qualities as well as technical skills. James (2003) expresses the view that there are 10 essential tips for making sure that any individual seeking to make it to the top looks and acts the part, rather than relying on technical capability alone (see Table 9.3).

Increasing operational effectiveness

Managers are always seeking to achieve higher levels of operational effectiveness. Cost reduction is an ever present imperative among managers. The ever present threat of the availability of cheaper labour from somewhere else in the world seems to be a never ending process. Technical capability can achieve so much, but it cannot achieve everything on a continuous basis. It is people who achieve results, predominantly

1. Network at every opportunity.
2. Allow yourself to shine. Make sure that you are up to what you take on.
3. Make a great entrance. First impressions count.
4. Display an air of confidence and energy
5. Learn to listen
6. Learn how to mingle.
7. Offer a good, firm handshake.
8. Never fiddle with your tie or jewellery.
9. Learn to use open gestures and appropriate body language.
10. Dress the part.

TABLE 9.3 Ten top tips for aspiring leaders

non-managers. It is the workers who actually deliver the goods and services to the organization and its customers who deliver real performance and effectiveness. The human being is the most effective of technologies, if it chooses to be so. Feiner (2002) suggests that effective leadership is about managing relationships in a way that motivates and empowers people. It is through the qualities of leadership that the choice process can be influenced to the benefit of management. Employees can be captured, energized and directed through leadership, leading to greater levels of effectiveness in operational activity. In the search for how to identify future leaders, London Business School established the Tomorrow's Leaders Research Group to draw on the experience of major organizations as they worked through these issues for themselves. Among the early conclusions were that managers who actively develop their subordinates become attraction centres that can pull highly capable people towards the organization in the search for improved personal development (Sonsino, 2003). This can assist the organization to shine above its competitors through the talented people at its disposal. However, this aspect of leadership does not feature in the major research approaches reviewed earlier in this chapter and is therefore more akin to a technique than a leadership quality.

Dealing with colleagues

This raises the issues about the scope of leadership. Does leadership reflect a set of characteristics that only function in a vertical direction? Much of the literature discussed in this chapter assumes that to be the case. It is described in terms of being something that operates between leaders and followers. But what about leader-to-leader interaction? A considerable proportion of the activity of leaders involves interacting with other leaders for some purpose. For example, the leader of a trade union group will spend a great deal of time representing members and their interests to management and in so doing be interacting and seeking to influence other leaders. This inevitably raises the question about the impact of leadership qualities on those interactions. One aspect of this is discussed by Pitcher (1997) who believes that it is the interaction between the styles of technocrat, artist and craftsman in a team of management that significantly impacts on the well-being of the organization, thus arguing for a balance between styles across the leaders of a company. For example, the artist is bored with detail and so needs the craftsman and technocrat around them to look after detail and realism. Technocrats, by way of contrast, find it very difficult to do anything other than concentrate on the detail and cannot tolerate the caveats and qualification insisted upon by the other two styles. She suggests (p 166) that, 'the trick is to have the right people in the right place at the right time and to make sure that the technocrat has loads of influence and not a shred of power'. One implication of this quotation being that technocrats should not run organizations. Success (or failure) comes from the type of leadership provided relative to the circumstances and the dynamic between the styles within the organizational context. That is also the essence of the EFQM model discussed earlier.

Increased control

Leadership can also enhance the ability to control. Management has the right to control as a result of the organizational responsibilities given to the role. However, holding that right to control does not automatically achieve it in full measure. Employees may comply with the requirements placed on them by managers for many reasons, some may enjoy their work; some may see the opportunity for advancement as a result of co-operation; others may need the income that the job provides. Yet others may simply go along with whatever is demanded of them because they are within their **zone of indifference** – the demands of the manager do not disturb them enough to create a reaction against the requirement to comply. However, when a leader is directing events then there should be a greater degree of willingness among employees to acquiesce to the requirements dictated by the leader. In that sense through whatever style or form the leader leads they should find it easier (than a manager) to achieve a more effective control over employees. More effective in that context refers to the existence of willingness, co-operation, enhanced performance and general support for the leader-determined objectives. Even in the democratic styles indicated above the leader plays a significant part as one of the team in shaping the group norms and activities and so is influential in determining control mechanisms and behaviour patterns.

Zone of indifference
Situations in which the demands of the organization on the employee do not disturb them enough to create negative reactions.

Atkinson (1999) suggests that without leadership there can be no change and that organizations that do not implement strategies for continued and sustained improvement will not recruit the best people and will be more likely to fail. He argues for a strong blend of transactional and transformational style within the leader and that this should be developed through training and development. In his discussion, he also makes the point that employees inevitably watch their boss, making judgements about their behaviour and the honesty of their leadership style. He uses the expression: 'Do what you say and say what you do'. This makes the point that these judgements are critical in establishing trust among the employees and developing a consistent management style. Management in Action 9.5 sets out some of his views in relation to leadership.

CONCLUSIONS

This chapter has considered many of the variables associated with the subject of leadership. The major theoretical approaches to the study of leadership have been introduced and critically evaluated. In addition, we have discussed a number of other approaches to the subject and related these to features of management activity where appropriate. We have considered alternative approaches to the subject of leadership including charismatic leadership and action-centred leadership. Also considered were the symbolic aspects of leadership and the relevance of it during different stages of the organizational lifecycle. Entrepreneurship and vision and their relationship to leadership were discussed as was the relationship with power and success. The chapter ended with a brief consideration of some of the leadership implications that emerge within the dynamic of organizational experience.

MANAGEMENT IN ACTION 9.5 Without leadership there is no change

Atkinson suggests that the following benefits can be achieved from introducing a strong leadership development programme:

- Behaviours will be clarified which will immediately lead to improved team performance.
- Leadership style will exist by design rather than through default and will signal the preferred ways of leading.
- Development activities will improve as they will be designed and targeted at managers as they undergo the transition.
- Clear signals will be provided to new recruits and newly promoted managers.
- Team morale will improve as new leadership styles transform the old control-based model to new trust-based perspectives.
- Performance management will be taken seriously and cultural measures become measurable and therefore changeable.
- The early adopters of the new styles (the first people through the training) will be able to help the later and slower paced leaders to adapt to the new styles.
- The organizational focus will be on achieving the best from teams.
- The ability to attract and retain top talent will be enhanced through the improved psychological contract with leaders and their newly defined role within the organization.

Atkinson goes on to offer his suggestions as to the main characteristics of effective leaders (he describes them as the top 5 Es):

- *Energy*. The leader must be able to offer high energy levels to demonstrate resilience, ability and stamina in the demanding businesses of the future. Energy in that sense means being positive and able to keep going under pressure.
- *Enthusiasm*. High levels of self-confidence and self-esteem are important to effective leadership. The main block to personal achievement is that individuals do not believe that they can do more. People with low self-esteem are difficult to move from their comfort zone and will usually not challenge the traditional ways of doing things.
- *Energize*. This involves the ability to energize others. It is the leader who can pass on their own enthusiasm and energy who achieves the highest levels of effectiveness within their teams.
- *Execute*. Actually getting on with things is another key aspect of effectiveness for any leader. Forever asking for clarification, more information and greater detail or discussion never produced anything. It is only when a decision is made and acted upon that things change. So prevarication is out for the effective leader. Related to this of course is the need to be able to learn from experience. Making decisions quickly is one thing, but they need to be good ones. Learning from past mistakes is one important aspect of making better decisions quickly.
- *Edge*. Living on the edge by always seeking new ways and challenging the traditional ways of doing things. Never being satisfied with what exists is the key characteristic here.

Adapted from: Atkinson, P (1999) Without leadership there is no change, *Management Services*, August, pp 8–11.

Stop ↔ Consider

To what extent does the material presented by Atkinson reflect the underlying theme of this chapter?

Now to summarize this chapter in terms of the relevant Learning Objectives:

- **Describe the distinction between leadership and management.** Management represents a formal role within an organization. In that sense it is a job which contains particular responsibilities for an area of organizational activity and probably a number of subordinate employees. Leadership tends to be regarded as a set of personal characteristics that reflect the ability to get other people to follow. In organizational terms that includes achieving higher levels of performance from subordinates and having a clear vision of where the organization should be heading and articulating that in such a way that subordinates are energized to achieve the goal.

- **Understand the relationship between leadership and power.** If leadership is regarded as a set of personal characteristics then it implies that followers are automatically drawn to follow the leader's direction. But, this chapter suggests that in doing so it is the followers that grant to particular individuals the right to exercise that form of power over them. In other words the leader cannot automatically have the opportunity to exercise leadership over subordinates. First the subordinate must acquiesce to the claims to leadership status by the person so claiming. Equally a leader cannot lead unless there are followers willing to be led. Consequently, there is a reciprocal relationship between leaders and followers with both needing the other to be able to exercise their relative position. There are also many informal leadership positions that exist and which interact with an organization at many levels; trade unions, pressure groups etc. all provide opportunities for non-management employees to exercise leadership and so exercise a degree of power and influence. The development of virtual working is also changing the ways in which leadership can be expressed and the way that power plays a part in that relationship.
- **Assess the contribution of the different theoretical approaches to the study of leadership.** There are a wide range of theoretical perspectives available on leadership. The trait model seeks to explain the personal characteristics of successful leaders. This proved more difficult than might be expected as so many variables have been identified and there are so many exceptions to the rules found among successful leaders. Equally it is difficult to define success – over how long should it be displayed and what does it mean, share value, profit level, happy employees or customers? These are significant difficulties. The style approaches essentially reflect a continuum between autocratic and democratic and usually claim success for the democratic approach. However this is too simplistic to be credible. For example in a crisis there may not be time to involve everyone and so an autocratic approach may be required. That is where the contingency modules come in, as they suggest that the most appropriate style depends on a range of factors in the context. The range of factors influencing the choice depending upon the individual contingency model. The other approaches to leadership do not reflect a cohesive group in any meaningful sense, they reflect the perspectives of the writer in seeking to explain what leadership is. For example the charismatic approach suggests that successful leadership reflects a particular mix of personality characteristics of the leader and its ability to draw follower responses that are largely unquestioning. However, the existence of the other models should not be taken to imply that style or traits, or contingency views are irrelevant. For example, a charismatic leader may interact with the followers in a mix of autocratic or democratic ways depending upon the people and circumstances, and the vertical dyad linkage model also suggests different leader behaviours towards the two groups which could reflect autocratic or democratic approaches. The transactional and transformational leadership model also distinguishes between two different aspects of leadership and describes them in ways that are not dissimilar to the style perspective. So a grand theory of leadership has not yet been developed that can fully explain what it is, but there are a range of models and theories available that can contribute individually and collectively to an improved understanding of it.
- **Explain the contribution to understanding leadership of the various style approaches.** The various style theories offer an explanation of leadership based on the relative contribution of subordinates to the process of leading. The democratic end of the style spectrum involves leaders delegating some of their authority and power to subordinates through involvement, in seeking to achieve an effective working relationship between them. At the autocratic end of the spectrum the leader retains control of everything and simply requires an unquestioning following by subordinates. Between the two extremes exists a variation in the degree to which involvement and delegation vary and are allowed by the leader. The suggestion is that the democratic end of the spectrum produces a more effective working relationship between leaders and led and hence produces higher levels of productivity. In some ways the contribution of this approach to understanding leadership provides a basis for the contingency models in that the circumstances can be shown to impact on the appropriateness of particular styles of leadership in particular contexts. The style

approaches can also be contrasted with the trait and other approaches to leadership which adopt a different perspective to what it is. For example, the trait approaches emphasize the personal characteristics of the individual and are difficult to justify either in terms of number or exceptions in relation to success. The vast range of other approaches to leadership do not of themselves rule out the existence of style, for example, charisma might find expression in the behaviours of the leader which could be described as relating to their style of interaction with subordinates.

- **Discuss the significance of the contingency approaches to the study of leadership.** The Contingency models reflect approaches that seek to capture a broader range of factors that impact on the ways in which leaders can exercise their responsibilities. Inevitably they work through the factors that each model sees as important and then emerge with the suggestion that one style or other is most appropriate to the circumstances identified. So in that sense they can usually be regarded as extensions of the style theories. What does emerge from the contingency models, however, is that because of the variation in context, variation in style is also needed. That in turn implies that either a leader needs to be able to vary their style, or that the leader should be changed when the circumstances change. This has major implications for the management of organizations. If leadership represents a set of characteristics, then leaders must be trained to vary their style according to the needs of the situation. If on the other hand leadership represents a set of personality characteristics then it may not be possible to vary the style to a significant degree and so the leader should be changed. This has obvious implications for careers and training in the management area. Some of the models suggest that managers have a dominant and backup style and that the necessary qualities of leadership can be acquired through appropriate training.

DISCUSSION QUESTIONS

1. The leaders in an organization are there simply to provide a symbolic focus for the world outside the organization. It is the management in the middle ranks of the organization that actually deliver the level of success achieved. Discuss this statement.
2. Discuss the differences and similarities between the concepts of management and leadership.
3. Is an attempt to identify the most appropriate leadership style simply another attempt to identify a formula which is doomed to failure? Justify your answer.
4. Describe Likert's four systems of management and attempt to make a case for system 1 being the most appropriate style in a particular context. What might this imply about the concept of effectiveness in leadership?
5. 'Come the hour, cometh the leader.' Discuss this statement in the light of the approaches to leadership discussed in this chapter.
6. 'Leaders need to find the right group and context before they are able to exercise their leadership.' Discuss this statement.
7. Do the concepts of artist, craftsman and technocrat reflect leadership styles or personality characteristics? Justify your answer.
8. Fiedler's contingency model suggests that if the situation is very unfavourable to the leader then it is necessary to drive the subordinates towards the objectives by adopting a task-oriented style of leadership. Do you agree with this view? Justify your answer.
9. To what extent is leadership simply a means of expressing management in a way that employees would find more acceptable and therefore be encouraged to work harder?
10. 'Charismatic leaders are not appropriate in the middle ranks of managerial jobs because they could encourage an organization within an organization to develop.' Discuss this statement.

CASE STUDY The supervisor was taking bribes

This case study is based in a medium sized engineering company based in Greece. The company made a wide range of screws, bolts and nuts for use in the engineering, construction and home improvement markets. They employed about 500 people on one site. The company was very traditional in approach having been in existence and owned by the same family for about 100 years. In charge of the factory was a production director who had a production manager, planning manager, stores and warehouse manager and maintenance manager reporting to him. The production department was split into five production units, each responsible for making a particular type of product. Each production department employed around 75 people and was under the control of a production supervisor, assisted by a number of team leaders.

The payment system used within the company was based on piecework. That is each factory worker was paid a basic wage, plus a bonus directly related to the number of units of output achieved over the course of the working week. Each product had a specific price allocated to it which was determined by the production director in discussion with the workers in the factory. For example, cutting the threads on a dozen, size 12, five centimetre wood screws was valued at 0.15 euros. So if an employee produced 100 batches of this size of wood screws in the week, their total pay would be made up of their basic wage, plus 100 times 0.15 euros as a bonus, giving a total bonus of 15 euros.

Because each job had its own time value the supervisor, team leaders and employees had to keep track of many hundreds of prices and also to monitor all production to ensure that only the correct prices were being used and that no employee was claiming more bonus that they were entitled to. The prices for each job had been set over the years and had not been updated as technology and production processes had changed. Consequently, some piecework prices were easy for employees to make good levels of bonus from; whilst others were more realistic and did not produce inflated earnings. There was keen competition among employees to be able to work on those jobs which could produce high bonus earnings. This potentially gave the team leaders and supervisor considerable power over the allocation of work and employee behaviour.

The production director was aware that some of the piecework prices were out of date but did not think that there was any real problem with the bonus scheme. He assumed that everyone had broadly the same opportunity to work on jobs which could produce high bonus payments and that everyone was happy with the situation. He was aware that the wage system was getting old and out of date and had made some suggestions to employees about changing the entire wage system. The discussions had not produced any real progress and the production director was beginning to think that he might have to take a stronger line in the discussions in order to make any changes happen. It was at about this time that the production director picked up a vague hint that some people in some departments were getting more than a fair share of the good bonus jobs. This became apparent when particular individuals began to appear as the top earners in the factory week after week. After a very discreet and low key enquiry, it also became apparent that some individuals were not making high bonus, but were working only three or four days each week but earning the same as many people working the full five days.

The production director became worried as he thought that he could trust each of his supervisors and that they in turn were respected as the leaders of their particular departments. But something needed to be done before chaos and anarchy resulted. Matters came to a head when one of the shop-floor employees resigned and in his exit interview made the suggestion that the main reason that led to him leaving was that he was never given the opportunity to earn high bonus because he would not pay the 'tax'. The personnel officer conducting the interview asked what he meant by the 'tax', but the employee would not elaborate on his comments. After the employee had left the company the production director was shown the interview notes and read the comment about the 'tax'. He too was perplexed and went to see the ex-employee in his home one evening. The employee was reluctant to discuss matters, but it eventually became apparent that one of the supervisors in the factory had invented a money making scam for himself based on the piecework prices. The production director could not believe his ears when he listened to the accusations made by the former employee. It was suggested that each morning the supervisor would auction each of the jobs to be done that day. Essentially the supervisor was giving out the jobs that could make the most bonus to those employees who were prepared to offer him the most money in return – the supervisor was taking bribes from employees for the allocation of work. Employees called this 'paying the tax' for the good jobs.

The production director was very distressed by what he heard and the next day he spoke to the human resource manager and the managing director about the situation. It was decided to carry out an investigation into the issues and the supervisor concerned was suspended on full pay during this process. After the investigation enough evidence was collected to hold a disciplinary hearing in which the supervisor was asked for his response. The supervisor denied all of the charges and said that they were all a figment of management's imagination. The production director concluded that there was enough evidence of wrongdoing and the supervisor concerned was dismissed. However, when the supervisor went to court to seek compensation for unfair dismissal the shop-floor workers in his department wrote a letter in support of his claim. This stated that the director had been unfair in his treatment of the individual, who was in practice a good leader and supervisor. It was said by the workers that the supervisor had always shown a personal interest in his subordinates and concern for their welfare. The issue of giving the best paying jobs to people in return for money was said not to have happened, or if at all only once or twice as a present from a grateful worker to their boss.

The court disregarded the letter in the face of overwhelming evidence to the contrary and the dismissal was upheld. When employees were subsequently asked to explain their actions in writing a letter of support for the supervisor, they replied that the supervisor was a valued member of their group and that managers should not be allowed to victimize individuals. The fact that he had been taking bribes from (or taxing) their colleagues was acceptable to them to the extent that it had actually been done! Individuals could choose to participate or not and so the system was fair to everyone.

The production director interpreted this response as an indication that the employees were beginning to worry that their ability to control events was being threatened. Attitudes towards the production director also began to harden among the workforce as some employees recognized that their ability to earn high bonus easily was being threatened by the management proposed changes to the wage system. Consequently, the discussions over revised wage structures began to stall and agreement could not be reached.

Tasks

1. Explore this case in terms of the management and leadership issues introduced in this and the previous chapters. What does it suggest to you about the role of management and the nature of leadership?
2. Could the supervisor be a good leader under the circumstances of taking bribes from subordinates? Why or why not?
3. What would you have done if you were the production director to try and prevent such abuses of the system occurring?

FURTHER READING

Avolio, B (1999) *Full Leadership Development: Building the Vital Forces in Organizations*, Sage, London. Looks at leadership in terms of a process, not just the individual undertaking it and explores what success means in that context.

Clark, H, Chandler, J and Barry, J (1994) *Organization and Identities: Text and Readings in Organizational Behaviour*, International Thomson Business Press, London. Contains a broad range of original articles on relevant material themes and from significant writers referred to in this and other textbooks on management and organizations.

Cranwell-Ward, J, Bacon, A and Mackie, R (2002) *Inspiring Leadership: Staying Afloat in Turbulent Times*, Thomson Learning, London. Based on the BT Global Challenge Round the World Yacht Race, the authors were given unrivalled behind the scenes access to crew and events. This book brings the lessons learned from such major sporting activity to the reader in the hope that they can learn from such events.

Deering, A, Kearney, AT, Dilts, R and Russell, J (2002) *Alpha Leadership: Tools for Business Leaders Who Want More from Life*, John Wiley, Chichester. A focus on the application of the three concepts of anticipation, alignment and action as the main drivers of successful leadership. The writers provide the tools through which leaders can ensure an effective balance between career and personal success.

de la Billière, P Sir (1994) *Looking for Trouble: SAS to Gulf Command, the Autobiography*, HarperCollins, London. A book which considers leadership from a personal perspective and from the very particular context of the military and special operations.

Fletcher, W (2002) *Beating the 24/7: How Business Leaders Achieve a Successful Work-life Balance*, John Wiley, Chichester. A book in which several of today's most visible business leaders explain how they achieve both business and personal success through an effective work-life balance.

Manzoni, JF and Barsoux, JL (2002) *The Set-Up-To-Fail Syndrome: How Good Managers Cause Great People to Fail*, Harvard Business School Press, Boston MA. Explores how the first impressions and snap judgements of some managers can lock subordinates into a downward spiral of decreasing performance and failure.

Margerison, C (2002) *Team Leadership: A Guide to Success with Team Management Systems*, Thomson Learning, London. Based on the use of the Team Management Wheel introduced earlier in this book in relation to groups, this book applies the lessons learned from practice with that model of group working to the practice of team leadership.

Northouse, PG (2000) *Leadership: Theory and Practice*, Second edn, Sage, London. A textbook which looks in great detail at the latest theory and practice of leadership in organizations.

COMPANION WEBSITE

Online teaching and learning resources:

Visit the companion website for Organizational Behaviour and Management 3rd edition at: *http://www.thomsonlearning.co.uk/businessandmanagement/martin3* to find valuable further teaching and learning material:

Refer to page 35 for full details.

PART FIVE

Managing people within an organization

The previous section explored the issues associated with management and leadership in an organizational context. This section moves on to explore the major aspect of most managers' jobs, that of managing the people. In many organizations, particularly the large ones, there exists a specific department that is charged with supporting line managers in the issues surrounding the employment of people. These days it is often referred to as the human resource management department. It is worth spending a little time, therefore looking at the major areas of concern associated with the management of people from an organizational behaviour perspective. However, it will be apparent by now in your study of organizational behaviour that managing people is fundamentally about the relationship between each manager and their subordinates in the daily dynamic of organizational life. This section sets out to explore some of the major areas associated with managing people some of which have already been introduced and some of which are yet to be developed within this book.

The major people management issues explored in this section begins with stress which is an ever present danger for managers and employees in modern organizations as the pace of life and the demands of work grow in the search for ever higher levels of profit and reduced cost of operations. Managers have a duty and responsibility, as does each employee, for being aware of stress and how it can be dealt with in an organizational context. This is followed by consideration of motivation as the means

through which managers seek to maximize the contribution and performance from employees in pursuit of operational objectives. The management of people brings with it the need to be aware of ethical dilemmas associated with their treatment as well as the entire way that organizations and managers approach the work that they do. Culture is another area in which managers need to operate sensitively in relation to the management of people. Many organizations operate in many countries of the world and employ people from many nationalities at a single location. Equally every organization and indeed work group has its own culture and managers need to ensure that they are aware of the issues implied by that and what it means for the management of cultures and the people who work within them.

The next section builds on this level of analysis and begins to explore the detail of the physical aspects of the organizations within which people work. Managers manage people, but they do so in the context of the jobs that people do, the technology that is used and the structure of the organization.

CHAPTER 10

Managing people and stress

LEARNING OBJECTIVES

After studying this chapter and working through the associated Management in Action panels, Employee Perspectives, Discussion Questions and Case Study you should be able to:

- **Explain the major models and approaches to the study of people management.**
- **Understand the distinction and similarities between stress, PTSD, burnout and pressure.**
- **Describe the physiological effects of stress and the consequent impact on the behaviour of individuals.**
- **Assess the relative contribution of human resource managers and line managers in relation to the management of people.**
- **Discuss the nature of the psychological contract within the context of people management practice.**

INTRODUCTION

People management has always existed within organizations in one form or another. The application of collective effort to the achievement of objectives means that the people best able to undertake particular tasks need to be found and encouraged to contribute effectively to the task in hand. In modern organizations the responsibility for establishing the procedures and processes through which this is achieved falls to human resource management specialists supporting line managers through appropriate policy and practice. The role and responsibilities of the line manager in people management practices varies between organizations and can range from simply accepting and using the people recruited on their behalf, to undertaking the entire task themselves supported by human resource specialist staff.

Modern people management involves much more than the recruitment of new employees by line mangers. It involves the training and development of staff, the design of reward systems, the creation of career development policies, the incorporation of legislative requirement into company policy and practice, encouraging particular behaviour patterns, designing organizational culture and dealing with the inevitable exit of employees from the organization. All of which should be done appropriately, legally and ethically if it is to contribute to business success. This is an aspect of management that draws heavily on much of the organizational behaviour literature in the determination of its practices. Consequently it is useful to incorporate consideration of people management within this context. All of the chapters in this book are of relevance to the management of people at work, but this section of three chapters brings together the major themes. For example, motivation and performance management are necessary in order to sustain the organization in the long term. Organizations these days frequently seek to develop a culture that inspires high performance in order to maximize levels of output and customer service. Ethics represents a key feature of organizational activity and the ways in which people are managed represents one of the key elements of how organizations perform in relation to its social responsibility. This chapter introduces all of these elements of managing people and also pays special attention to stress as a particularly significant aspect of the experience of work for most people – managers and employees alike.

Stress is a major aspect of human life within organizations and so a major concern for employees and managers. There are many possible sources of stress including starting a new job, being required to constantly improve work performance, working long hours, the introduction of new technology or ways of working and being promoted to a more responsible position. There are also events outside of work which create stress for the individual and which can impact on their performance at work. Recent research carried out within the European Union shows that the average number of hours worked each week is falling, but it is generally acknowledged that this overall figure hides the fact that many key employees are working longer and more intensive hours, *Business Europe* (2002). One striking finding reported by the same source is that the use of performance management techniques is increasing at the same time as employee satisfaction with workload issues is decreasing, further contributing to experienced stress.

MODELS OF PEOPLE MANAGEMENT PRACTICE

As with most areas of management theory, there is no one predominant view as to what people management means and how it should be practised within an organization. In terms of human resource management, there are four main approaches that have been developed over recent years. The first, developed by Fombrum *et al.* (1984) begins with the view that human beings are a resource, in principle just like any other resource available to the organization. Any resource is of value to an organization providing that it is appropriate to the needs of the organization, is flexible and reliable in operation and can be used in a cost effective manner. Such approaches begin with the business strategy of the organization setting the parameters within which it will operate; this is then converted into a people resource strategy; followed by the actual policies in order to deliver the results sought.

Another model developed by Beer *et al.* (1984, 1985) takes the stakeholder view of the nature of people management within organizations. It begins with the same strategic perspective as the previous model, but seeks to operationalize it by integrating a human dimension into the role of people in an organization. This is achieved by recognizing that people are more than a simple resource to be used at the whim of management. People represent thinking, dynamic and interactive elements within the organization, not just a static resource waiting to be used. This model recognizes that there are four main areas in which policy is required in order to gain maximum benefit from people. They are employee influence, human resource flows, reward systems and work systems. In general terms this model implies a close relationship between individual objectives and organizational objectives. It is however, achieved through a 'top down' approach dictated by the business strategy.

A third model was suggested by Schuler and Jackson (1987, 1996) which set out to establish an association between the strategy of the organization and the employee behaviours necessary to achieve it. They essentially identify two strategy options, one based on cost minimization, the other based on innovation. Note, these are not business strategies in themselves, but essentially reflect the operational strategy. They do not reflect what activities the business should be in, but how to compete in the market place that they are in. This approach is similar to that developed by Porter (1985) in the generic strategies for competitive advantage, although his model is based on slightly different choices.

Schuler and Jackson, having identified the two basic strategies, then seek to identify the behaviours associated with them. For example, some of the behaviours identified with cost reduction strategies include repetitive, predictable behaviours; high concern with operational process; risk aversive behaviours; narrow skill application; and low job involvement. By contrast the appropriate behaviours associated with an innovative strategy include long term focus; high levels of risk taking; flexible with regard to change; tolerant of ambiguity and uncertainty; and high job involvement. The authors then go on to identify policy areas for planning, staffing, appraising, compensating and development, each containing a number of specific themes appropriate to the two strategy options. For example, under compensation, the cost reduction strategy includes options such as low salary levels, few benefits, lack of job security and limited participation. By contrast the innovation strategy requires high salary levels, a broad range of benefits, high levels of job security together with high levels of participation.

This model is interesting in that it suggests that it is necessary to match the people management policies and practices to the strategy of the business. It also suggests that what could be termed the traditional 'hire and fire' approach to managing people could be appropriate in an extreme cost reduction environment. What maters is not which approach is used, but that the relevant policies and practices are consistent with the desired strategy. Failure to be consistent will result in failure to achieve the desired strategy. This model is also a 'top down' approach in that strategy is determined and the people are then 'fitted' around that process. It is not suggested that the people could actually help to define (either through involvement or capability) the strategy that could be adopted.

A fourth model was developed by researchers at Warwick Business School (Hendry *et al.*, 1989). Unlike the previous models which originated in the USA, this one is based on experience in Britain and was therefore able to explore the subject in terms of the culture, managerial practice and organizational arrangements specific to that context. The model proposes five main interlinked elements as follows:

1. *Outer context.* This represents the broader social, economic and cultural forces impacting on any organization. It also incorporates those issues associated with the organization itself and the industry that it operates in that might be expected to impact on its functioning. For example the history of the organization, its size and the structure of the industry within which it operates.
2. *Inner context.* This represents the organizational factors that could be expected to impact on its functioning. For example, its culture, structure, profitability, technology, products or services, management style and politics.
3. *Business strategy context.* This represents the strategy followed by the business and reflects to a significant extent the earlier discussion in relation to the Schuler and Jackson model.
4. *Human resource management context.* This represents the approach to people management adopted by the organization. It largely represents the philosophy and policy areas associated with how people are expected to contribute to the functioning and success of the organization.
5. *Human resource management content.* This box represents the actual approach to people management adopted within the organization in terms of its practices covering areas such as reward systems, employee relations and work arrangements.

This model demonstrates the complexity of the people management environment for an organization. The five interacting elements above reflect the forces acting upon the situation and which create a dynamic situation which is difficult to manage. This reflects the view of people held by Boxall and Purcell (2003) when they suggest that people management does not 'belong' to specialists because line managers are inevitably responsible for their team. Consequently everyone within the organization is actively involved in people management issues throughout the working day. In their view the human resource specialist is there to 'sell' their technical expertise to those who have need of support in that area. This clearly did not happen in the following Employee Perspective (10.1) when a line manager was left to resolve a difficult issue for himself!

PEOPLE MANAGEMENT – ISSUES AND ACTIVITIES

Although it is the line manager that has ultimate responsibility for managing the people under their control, they must do so within organizational guidelines. In all but the smallest organizations the functional responsibility for providing expertise and support in managing people falls to the human resource management department. This specialism embraces a broad spectrum of activities as shown in Table 10.1. Each of the areas of activity indicated in Table 10.1 represents a major area of work in its own right. It would be impossible to provide more than the briefest of insight into these in the space available in this text. Consequently, only a general introduction to the significant aspects of people management as appropriate to an organizational behaviour perspective will be provided below. The Further Reading section indicates a starting point for in-depth reading in the area of human resource management.

Ethics

The way in which people are managed represents a major aspect of the ethical stance adopted by an organization. Chapter 12 draws together a wide range of relevant

EMPLOYEE PERSPECTIVE 10.1 Anil's experience at work

Anil was in charge of the packing department within a factory that made ceramic wall tiles. He had 30 people working for him covering two shifts, the first starting at 6.00am and the second at 2.00pm. The shifts rotated each week and they worked Monday to Friday only. Each shift was headed by a team leader. Keeping up with the output from the production department was becoming a particular problem for one of the teams and Anil was always behind his schedule of goods packed and despatched as a result.

The production director, in charge of the entire factory was always calling Anil into his office for an explanation and demanding to know when the problems would be solved. Anil felt that he was under considerable pressure as his last performance appraisal with the production director a couple of weeks ago had made specific reference to his significant failings in not being able to resolve the problem in packing and failing to achieve his targets. Anil had looked at the situation and held several discussions with the appropriate team leader and had come to the conclusion that the problem was down to two of the employees who were not doing the job that was expected of them. He had watched the employees concerned and they worked very slowly and just let the work pile up around them. They seemed generally disorganized and not to have a clear idea of what they were supposed to be doing or of the pace of work expected of them.

Anil rang the human resources adviser for the factory for advice and was told that the company discipline procedures were well documented and these should be followed. He was also told to ring back for any advice if he had any more questions. Anil found the appropriate procedures on the company intranet and read them. It all seemed clear. He should first call the people into his office along with their trade union representative to tell them what the problem was, presenting his evidence. The procedure also advised having another management representative present. Anil followed the procedure, even using the pro forma letters provided in the company procedures to inform the employees about the meeting.

The meeting began with Anil explaining the position and presenting his evidence. The trade union representative stopped Anil and said that the entire procedure was a farce as neither employee had received any training on what was expected of them and so they could not be expected to know what they should be doing. They had to pick everything up as they went along and at no point had anyone said to them that they were not doing things properly. Anil was forced to apologize for the confusion and to call a halt to the proceedings. He promised training for the employees and thanked everyone for attending. He then had to go to the production director and explain what had happened.

The production director was furious and said that if that was the best he could do he could now consider himself subject to disciplinary action on the grounds of his being incompetent to undertake his responsibilities. He was told that he was being suspended forthwith and that the factory personnel adviser would be in touch to arrange a formal hearing.

Tasks

1. Try to apportion responsibility in this situation between Anil, the production director, the personnel adviser, the team leader and the employees.
2. Consider what this example suggests about the way that human resource management should be practised within an organization and in particular how line managers should be supported in their need to manage subordinates.

themes associated with the study of ethics in an organizational context. There are of course more facets to ethics than the management of people and the material in Chapter 12 explores the breadth of perspective in that regard. However, the same academic material should inform the basis on which people are managed. At a number of points in this book the potential for exploitation of workers is raised in theoretical terms as a consequence of the capitalist nature of much of the world's economic activity. This inevitably raises ethical issues about the principles and practice of management in this regard. For example, one of the issues discussed below is employee involvement and this can be viewed as a genuine attempt to capture the intellectual and commitment potential of employees for the benefit of all stakeholders. However, viewed from an exploitation perspective it could be argued that involvement

Human resource planning
Human resource strategy
Recruitment
Selection
Induction
Training and development
Performance management
Pay, salary, incentive and benefit systems
Discipline and grievance policy and practice
Diversity, discrimination and equality of opportunity
Health and safety at work
Career progression and development
Compliance with employment legislation
Employee relations
Employee exit planning
Representation of the organization to external bodies such as Employment Tribunals

TABLE 10.1 The disciplines falling within human resource management practice

represents an attempt to persuade employees that they have a real stake in the business, whilst in practice allowing management to retain effective power and control of the major aspects of the business. The same people management practice can therefore be viewed from two totally different perspectives, one positive the other negative. It is difficult, if not impossible, to be absolutely certain of the true reasons and motivations behind the actions of managers (or indeed employees) in any particular context. This is because it is only the actions that are observable, not the underlying reasons for them. It is in trying to understand and resolve this type of dilemma that ethics can offer a means to evaluate the underlying motivations and reasons for particular people management practices. From this limited introduction it should be apparent that all aspects of people management contain significant ethical dimensions.

Culture

Culture is also introduced in Chapter 12 and forms one of the key levers through which management seeks to achieve the necessary conditions for a high performance organization. There are many definitions of culture as will become evident in Chapter 12, however, one common expression is that it represents 'the way that things are done in this organization'. Naturally the people management aspects of the organization form a major element within that expression of culture. For example, if an organization places little value on the long term employment and commitment of its staff, it will tend to employ people on short term contracts and 'high and fire' as the short term needs of the business dictate. Conversely, if it values the people who work in the organization, it will have a high proportion of employees on long term contracts and also it will engage in high levels of training and development in order to encourage maximum usefulness and employability of the people resource. Just using these two extremes as examples, it should be apparent that the two organizations indicated would have very different cultures. Every aspect of people management has an influence on the culture of the organization (and conversely they are influenced by the culture) and hence how the employee behaviour and attitudes align with management objectives. It is hardly surprising therefore that the design of culture, and the ethical dimensions implied by that intention forms a significant part of the totality of people management within an organization. Chapter 12 also explores the nature of international culture as another influence on the management of people within an organization. These days globalization and the existence of the multi-cultural workforce in many organizations require managers to be much more aware of these influences on the management of people.

People planning

Organizations are dynamic in that they are constantly changing in some way or other as they seek to adapt to the ever changing environments that they live within. People join and leave; markets and fashion change; legislative requirements change; technology changes; competitors change their offerings and tactics; economic conditions change; and customers also change. These are just some of the factors that cause change to occur within an organization. However, there is debate about how effectively strategic planning within organizations can deliver competitive advantage because of weaknesses and limitations in the people and processes adopted (Caulkin, 2001). Smith (1996) develops this theme and argues that there is a need for organizations to concentrate on developing a high performance top management team before real progress can be made in formulating effective business strategies. Only after this can objectives be identified and converted into more specific plans for how many and what type of people to seek for employment within the organization.

A major objective of the human resource management function is to provide the best match possible between the current and future needs of the organization and the people working within it (Bennison 1980). This is a very difficult balance to achieve. In practice, organizations recruit new employees for two time horizons. First, there exists a need to be able to do the work of the organization now. Second there is a need to be able to provide the organization with appropriate human resources for its anticipated future requirements. Anticipating the future requirement of the organization is a difficult process which leads writers such as Bowen *et al.* (1996) to suggest that recruitment should be based on the 'fit' between the individual and the organization, not job compatibility. This is because at any point in time a job represents a set of tasks which will change over time. In that context the skills needed to undertake most jobs can easily be taught and so organizational fit becomes the more important selection criteria. There are many variables at work in planning for the people resource of an organization, including the volume of labour required, the location of organizational activity, the nature of operational activity, the future role of technology and the type of products and services offered by the organization, all of which impact significantly on the future role of people within the organization and are also major strategic decision areas. Recent research (Lepak *et al.*, 2003) suggests that there is a relationship between the type of employment flexibility used within the organization and the performance achieved. It is suggested that greater use of a combination of knowledge-based employment and contract work positively impacts on the performance of the firm. This and related research findings demonstrate how complex the relationship is between the variables involved in seeking to identify the correct number and type of employees needed by the organization if it wants to succeed now and in the future.

Organizations can only draw on the talent that is available in a particular location. At the point of seeking to attract potential employees to join the organization the degree of 'fit' must be assessed along with the potential for subsequent development. It may be that within society generally there is not the level of skill or competency available to be able to meet the full requirement that the organization has identified through its demand side planning processes. Consequently, thought needs to be given to the means of overcoming that deficiency. That could be achieved through the use of technology to replace the need for people to undertake certain tasks; the use of training and development to provide employees with the necessary skills and competency; the application of job design processes to change the nature and type of work which employees would be expected to do; and also seeking to influence the provision of education and training provided by the state and other bodies within the environment. Also of course a combination of these processes could be used in order to influence the supply side aspects of the people planning process.

Employer of choice Being a company that people actively seek to join, so contributing to high performance over a long time.

Many organizations seek to achieve the status of being an **employer of choice**. This implies that people will want to seek employment with the company and once there contribute high performance over a long period. For the company it implies that it will be able to attract a high number of well qualified and able candidates from which to select the best. It implies that such employees will be committed to the organization and its objectives, thereby maximizing corporate performance and providing a good place to work. This of course leaves unanswered the questions of what the 'best' mean in this context and also how such people can be identified? Reporting a conference held in America, HR News (2003) points out that a number of speakers suggested that emphasis should be placed on creating what they term 'critical talent pools' by which they mean becoming an employer of choice in areas critical to the development of new products and services as well as those jobs in direct contact with customers. Management in Action 10.1 indicates how one consultant thinks that organizations can achieve the objective of becoming an employer of choice.

Training and development

Once the individual is selected for employment then they have to start work and be shown what it is that they are expected to do. This is generally known as an induction programme. Chapter 5 discussed learning within an organization context and touched on induction and many other forms of training and development as used in practice. Training and development contains an element of socialization which was also discussed in Chapter 5 (and other chapters) in relation to the search for more effectively integrating the individual into a particular group. It represents a 'right of passage' from being an outsider to being a full member of the group. Children are socialized into their family and cultural groups for example. In an organization, training and the ways in which it is accessed can represent strong messages about what is valued in behaviour and attitude terms within that context. In effect it introduces a new member to the culture within the group that they have joined. This is in addition to the job, organizational, technical and practical content of any particular development programme. Of course once a full member of a group or team, there will still be a need for training and development activity and these areas are also discussed in Chapter 5. These represent key areas in the people management activities within any organization.

Reward and performance management

Motivation and reward management will be discussed in detail in the following chapter and so this section will only form a brief introduction to this aspect of people management. The purpose of any reward system is to attract, retain and motivate employees. In order to achieve these apparently simple objectives there are many

MANAGEMENT IN ACTION 10.1 How to become an employer of choice

It is the objective of many human resource departments to be recognized as an employer of choice – an organization that people actually want to work for. This involves creating a culture that keeps people motivated and encourages them to be creative and forthcoming in delivering sustained high performance. Melinda Beckett-Hughes, a director at Portland International Consulting Group, offers the following list of practical suggestions as a way of seeking to become an employer of choice:

1. *Create the right psychological contract.* This reflects the essence of the relationship between employer and employee. Become unreasonable (as defined by the other party) and trust may never be restored.
2. *Know and live your corporate values.* Were the corporate values developed with a wide input from everyone in the organization? If not they can become just another document of little relevance to the vast majority of employees. Decide what behaviours are indicated by the values and how to encourage and reward them.
3. *Assess individuals' values and behavioural styles.* Understand employee motivations and the ways in which they understand the world around them in order to be able to seek to align actual behaviours and attitudes with those desired.
4. *Create a coaching culture.* With flatter structures emerging there is less opportunity for vertical career development. Consequently, there needs to be more emphasis on personal and professional development, including challenging assignments.
5. *Brand your people processes.* Adopt a marketing approach to work within the organization. For example understand the unique selling points of the organization and find out why people join (or leave, or don't accept an offer of work) and build the appropriate material to 'sell' the company.
6. *Offer flexible benefits.* Recognize that not every benefit offered by the company appeals to every employee and be flexible about what range of benefits is available.
7. *Endorse staff needs for a better work-life balance.* Job-sharing, part-time working and various forms of flexibility need to be available so people can find ways of dealing effectively with the different aspects of their life inside and outside work.
8. *Be realistic and market driven.* It is necessary to be creative in reviewing what is actually going on in the marketplace for labour and to find new ways of dealing with problem areas.
9. *Have some fun.* Seeing work as being a 'fun' place to be encourages commitment and a sense of community. Become people oriented and take a real interest in the individuals working for the company. Encourage informal groups to form and encourage social activities, but don't make it compulsory, people can't be made to have fun!
10. *Zap the 'TOLERATIONS'.* Ask each department to identify the ten things that they tolerate, but which they find drain their energy. Then ask them to find ways of eliminating these issues. Done regularly this approach can eliminate the 'drag' factor and so release positive energy

Adapted from: Beckett-Hughes, M (2003) How to become an employer of choice, *People Management*, 28 August, pp 40–1.

Stop ↔ Consider

How would you decide which organizations you would prefer to work for? How does your answer compare to the list above? Explain any differences.

difficulties to be dealt with. These include what competitor organizations offer by way of reward; the history of reward system design within the organization; local cost of living and taxation levels; internal relativities between jobs; company and industry profitability; economic conditions; company policy on its pay position relative to the market; relative balance of negotiating power between company and employee groups; relative skill shortages and surpluses in the labour market and many other factors. Another major element within any reward system is the benefits package offered by the organization. This covers things like pension, health care, company car, child care, holidays, further education policy, canteen arrangements and so on. The benefits offered usually differ at different levels of the organization. The overall reward package needs to be both appropriate to employee needs and employee expectation, but it also needs to be judged against a defined relationship of company practice to the reward practices generally adopted by other organizations in the environment.

There are many different types of reward system available including different approaches to the basis of payment and the ways in which performance management is applied to the payment of additional reward. For example, some jobs have a basic wage paid by the hour and others an annual salary paid in equal monthly instalments. Whatever basis of payment is used it is not uncommon to find that job evaluation provides the means of identifying a rank order of job magnitude, which in turn determines the magnitude of the basic pay. Performance management also finds expression in many different ways. For example, individual or team performance can be used to identify some form of incentive payment that will be paid to the employee as part of, or in addition to their basic wage. For example, sales people are often paid a commission based on the number or value of sales that they achieve. Factory workers can be paid an individual or team productivity bonus for achieving levels of output over and above a set target. Senior managers might be awarded shares for achieving targets for the growth in the value of the company or its share price. Administrative and technical staff might have their performance reviewed by their line manager through an appraisal system each year, the result of which might be used as one of the determinants of their annual pay review, along with cost of living and other factors.

Felt fair
Means that something should be perceived as fair by the people subjected to the system or procedure.

However it is designed and operated in practice, one of the key terms within any reward system is that it should be **felt fair** by the people who are subject to it. This means that individuals should feel that they are being treated fairly within whatever system is used. In essence this reflects the subjective reaction in the individual employee based on how they perceive their treatment compared to other people. It is not something that managers can easily influence as it is always possible to find someone who is paid more (or who appears to be better off in some way or another) than oneself. Therefore it is easy to become convinced that the type and level of reward places the individual employee at a relative disadvantage. It is the job of the human resource management team to try and deal with this possibility when designing reward and performance management policies and practice and in the way that they are communicated to employees.

For a line manager they usually have little control over the design of the reward system, but have to apply it in seeking to motivate and reward employees. Perhaps this requires the manager and subordinate to assess the employee's performance within a centrally determined scheme in order to identify the size of any incentive element within the annual pay award, or likelihood of promotion as a consequence of superior performance. Among the motivation and reward influences inherent in this type of process, there are the ethical dimensions that arise as a consequence of the need to be fair in both the intention as well as in the application of such schemes.

Employee involvement

One of the major practical and ethical issues facing line managers is the degree to which employees should be involved in the running of the business. At one extreme, the view is that employees provide the labour which needs to be directed and channelled by managers. Such views suggest that employees have nothing to contribute other than their skill. The other extreme suggests that employees are an equal stakeholder in the organization and that they have as much right as managers and owners to be involved in deciding how to run the business and to contribute to the strategic

So every employee (and manager) will have a slightly different view about their rights and obligations.

2. *It reaffirms the notion of the employment relationship being based on exchange.* Exchanges in this context are effectively about the future. For example, I will do this now on the understanding that you will do that in return. This implies at some point in the future the reciprocity element becomes due. Research quoted by the authors shows that managers frequently do not keep their promises and so the basis of the psychological contract erodes over time.
3. *The psychological contract is based upon the social and economic context; leadership; communication and human resource practice.* All of these contribute to how the psychological contract functions in practice. It is therefore based on the complex interplay between many forces and factors and can easily fail if they are not all mutually supportive.

Part of the psychological contract reflects the degree to which the employee should give priority to the needs of the employer, this represents the essence of the **work–life balance**. Felstead *et al.* (2002, p 56) define the work–life balance in terms of:

Work-life balance The balance between work, family, personal and leisure activities.

> The relationship between the institutional and cultural times and spaces of work and non-work in societies where income is predominantly generated and distributed through labour markets.

It is a phenomenon that impacts on men as well as women in trying to balance the competing needs of work with the requirements of family and personal life. It does appear however to have a disproportionate impact on the lives of women.

There is considerable pressure on organizations today to deliver more with less, which inevitably reduces the capability of an organization to easily absorb any problems that arise. Inevitably this means that existing employees experience pressure one way or another to contribute more. One impact of this is to increase the amount of work that each individual has to do and also to require them to work longer hours, either at work or at home. This effectively reduces the time and opportunity to fully participate in their family and personal obligations. This raises the need to balance work and personal obligations in some way or other, often to the detriment of non-work activities. Over recent years this is an issue that has had a particular impact on the role of women in the workforce as they try to balance the demands of family and work life. Hochschild (2000) demonstrates that although all working women have experienced this difficulty, it has been those women on low wages that have had the most difficult balancing act to perform. Platt (1997) carried out research at Hewlett-Packard in America and found that professional employees, irrespective of gender spent about 50 hours per week at work, but that women also undertook about 33 hours each week on housework or childcare, compared to only 19 hours each week for men. This shows that women have more committed time and so less time for personal activities compared to men. The outcome of this pressure, irrespective of gender, is additional stress for the individuals concerned and their families.

PEOPLE MANAGEMENT AND THE LINE MANAGER

In the days when personnel management was the term used to describe the specialist function responsible for people management, they tended to take high levels of responsibility away from line managers who were the immediate bosses of the people working in the organization. Under the human resource management term for such specialists it has been recognized that it should be the line manager who is actually responsible for the people that they are in a constant interactive relationship with. Line managers are increasingly regarded as business managers for their particular unit of responsibility. As such they are responsible for the effective use of all resources at their disposal including the people. This brings with it an increased profile for the ethical and other people management dimensions in the job of a line manager, as they are no longer only responsible for output. Thorough training in people management as well as the technical aspects of their job needs to be provided if line managers are to be effective in managing their full range of responsibilities effectively. Equally, line managers need to function effectively as a team if they are to operate as a cohesive entity in pursuit of corporate strategy objectives.

The result of all of this can be increased levels of stress for employees and management alike. So the emphasis of human resource management has shifted to being a strategy and support function for business units. It would be the human resource managers who determine the appropriate policies for the organization in relation to its business strategy. Typically these would focus on issues supporting the need for quality, flexibility and high commitment from the workforce in pursuit of the cost effective use of labour. Culture represents one of the areas in which the organization can be aligned with the more effective use of people, as can the form of motivation and reward practice. There is a developing literature in the area of how human resource and operations management research could be combined in an attempt to more effectively explain the processes involved in running organizations, see for example, Boudreau *et al* (2003), and for European developments, Larsen and Brewster (2003).

There are many ways in which human resource management is used within the organization and many are moving away from the traditional model of having a department staffed by specialists located at the centre of the organization, or from the decentralized structure in which personnel specialists would work in line departments, but would retain a reporting relationship to a centralized personnel department. One recent development is the creation of what has become known as e-HR in which the provision of human resource support to the organization is provided through computer screens and electronic interaction processes (Lengnick-Hall and Moritz, 2003). Arrangements such as call centres and drop-in advice centres are also becoming more common. Management in Action 10.2 describes one such approach at Cable and Wireless.

> **High performance organization**
> The combination of people, technology, management and productivity delivering competitive advantage on a sustainable basis.

> **Intellectual capital**
> The sum total of knowledge, expertise and dedication of the workforce in an organization.

There is much talk within management circles these days about the need to ensure that the status of being a **high performance organization** is achieved. This is achieved by combining many aspects of technology, procedure, product or service design, management, and of particular significance the need to emphasize the **intellectual capital** held within the organization (Ulrich, 1998); together with the need to put people first (Pfeffer, 1998). The psychological contract (introduced earlier) and stress (discussed below) also have relevance to this discussion. Research evidence clearly demonstrates that there is a relationship between people management activity and organizational performance, albeit indirectly through the effect of such activity on work climate (culture) (Gelade and Ivery, 2003). Part of this is also achieved as a result of becoming an employer of choice as discussed earlier. Line managers are the people who have to deliver the high performance organization through the appropriate treatment and use of the people available to them. Line managers have many targets to achieve and responsibilities to exercise, not just the control of people. Hence the danger of the people management issues being undervalued by such managers.

The availability of human resource support should enable line managers to share that responsibility with someone who can concentrate of the various ways in which people function relative to the work environment and how to enhance their

MANAGEMENT IN ACTION 10.2 A global conversion

In 1999, Cable & Wireless decided that it needed to streamline its human resource activities to enable it to function as a strategic partner to the business, in the process removing many administrative tasks and making use of its own web technology. Cable & Wireless Global was formed in 2000 by integrating the many separate operating units into a single global internet service company. The plan involved integrating the human resource database and network with those from the finance and procurement functions within a single computer based system, provided by SAP. This approach is given the general title of an e-HR system, and is based on the idea that line managers (and employees to a lesser extent) have direct control of the web based human resource facilities and they can undertake many of the administrative and routine events associated with managing people through that system without the need for a human resource person being involved. Human resource specialists are therefore free to concentrate on the more strategic and important aspects of human resource activity.

However, in such projects there is considerable resistance to overcome. Line managers can easily resent the imposition on them of a requirement to input data into a computer system which would have previously been undertaken in the human resource department. Line managers are busy people and can accidentally (or deliberately) forget to input data and so the system quickly becomes outdated and of no value. Human resource personnel can also resent these changes as they could foresee job losses and aspects of their work disappearing. This issue was particularly significant at Cable & Wireless as globally the workforce was being reduced from 18 500 to 11 000 as a result of the integration project and the general industry financial crisis. As part of the introduction of the e-HR project it was also decided to outsource its remaining human resource administration for the UK and America to a service provider called Accenture HR Services, based in the UK. During the three years that the e-HR project took to implement, the human resource department within Cable & Wireless has been reduced by more than 40 per cent and 83 people from the department have transferred to Accenture as the new administration service provider. Most of the human resource people left in the company department now undertake very different tasks than they did before and now work as what are termed strategic business partners. The aim being to support the line managers in their search for the most effective use of the people resources available to them.

Adapted from: Pickard, J (2002) A global conversion, *People Management*, 7 November, pp 40–2.

Stop ↔ Consider

To what extent is this type of approach an attempt to save money or a reflection of the adaptation of human resource practice to changes in the social context surrounding work? Justify your views.

contribution. Patterson *et al.* (1997) explored management practice across a large number of manufacturing organizations in Britain over a ten year period. Among their findings were that two particular areas delivered significant impact on company profitability. They were:

1. *Skill.* The acquisition of appropriate skills within the workforce and the continual development of those skills as the organization develops.
2. *Job Design.* The critical evaluation of job design in terms of the application of skill flexibility, task variety, range of responsibilities and team working.

The human resource practitioner should be well placed by training, experience and inclination to offer the means to effectively contribute to both of these areas of significance. However, it could be argued that this is what good line managers have been doing throughout history. Good managers have always valued the contribution that people can make to an organization and this has been operationalized across time according to the prevailing social norms and conditions. It could be argued that in today's world employees are less willing to be controlled and driven to work in particular ways and therefore more subtle and consensual methods have to be developed. The interesting ethical and practical questions arising from this are the degree to which managers are relinquishing their right to manage and control in the process. They could be simply seeking ways to capitalize on more effective ways of getting more from employees whilst not changing the relative power, status and hierarchy by doing so.

STRESS – WHAT IS IT?

Fight or flight response
The process allowing an organism to either stay and fight, or to run away and avoid confrontation.

It is frequently suggested that the reactions to stress are part of the **fight or flight response** capability that humans have in common with many other species. In order to protect itself (and frequently in order to survive) an animal must be able to distinguish between situations in which it is appropriate to stay and fight or from which it is more sensible to withdraw and avoid direct confrontation. One of the formal definitions of stress was provided by Ivancevich and Matteson (1993, p 8) as:

> An adaptive response, mediated by individual characteristics and/or psychological processes, that is a consequence of any external action, situation or event that places special physical and/or psychological demands upon a person.

This definition suggests that stress represents a response that will depend upon a number of characteristics of the individual and will also differ between individuals as to how it finds expression. It also represents a force that originates outside of the individual from either the physical (for example particularly heavy traffic on the way to work) or social (for example a difficult working relationship with the boss) world. It was Selye (1974) who identified the distinction between the potential for stress to have either a positive or negative effect on the individual. He also suggested that the response in the individual to stress can be the same if it is positive or negative in effect. It is the harmful effects of the stress that can produce the damage to the individual. Selye classed the positive effects of stress as eustress and the negative effects as distress. The positive influence of stress (eustress) has an energizing and motivating effect on the individual, whereas the negative impact (distress) has a debilitating and demotivating impact.

Karoshi
A Japanese word meaning sudden death from overwork.

Today, stress is becoming a major problem for individuals, organizations and society. For example in Japan there is now a cause of death known as **karoshi**, sudden death from overwork, that claims the lives of an estimated 10 000 people each year (Dawkins, 1993). The results of a survey carried out in the UK during 1994 revealed that 67 per cent of respondents claimed overwork caused stress, 55 per cent were fearful of being made redundant and suffered stress as a consequence and 54 per cent claimed that they did not get enough support at work which also caused stress. Outside work 88 per cent of respondents claimed that financial pressure was stressful and 84 per cent replied that relationships were also stressful (Hall, 1994b). These figures are broadly supported by later work which shows that more than 10 million Europeans become ill each year as a result of stress and that across the European Union 3 to 4 per cent of the gross national product is spent on the associated mental health problems (Williams, 2000). Other data illustrates the effects in particular countries: including the UK which experiences levels of between 15 to 30 per cent of workers suffering from anxiety and depression; Finland has more than 50 per cent of workers experiencing stress related symptoms; in Germany more than 10 per cent of early retirements are due to stress and 80 million working days are lost each year because of stress (Osborn, 2000). These levels reflect the demands being placed upon individuals today as part of everyday work experience and the reaction among individuals of not being in full control of their lives and what they are required to do.

The normal way in which many humans live does not provide easy opportunities for the individual to run away from or avoid whatever causes them stress. For example, a student under pressure before an exam is not totally able to withdraw from the situation and hence remove the stress. To do so would require a complete change of lifestyle. A fact supported by research carried out in the Netherlands by van Veldhoven *et al.* (2002) which showed (among other things) that psychological job demands were most strongly related to experienced strain in the individual. Human life patterns and experience are now so complex and with so many interrelated facets that to respond on the basis of single episodes is frequently inappropriate. From an organizational point of view this situation is reflected in Management in Action 10.3 which describes the changing patterns of managerial experience of their workload, one of the major causes of stress for the individuals concerned. This evidence supports research carried out by Cooper and Sutherland who report that some 23 per cent of the 118 chief executives surveyed (from major British and European companies) were actively thinking of resigning as a result of the stress (quoted by Arkin, 1991).

Within an organizational context stress can originate from events and circumstances inside or outside that work setting. The effects of stress can also be felt either inside or outside the organization. In simplified form this produces a four-cell matrix of stress contexts (Figure 10.2) that can be used to categorize the events involved and identify appropriate forms of coping strategy.

Taking each of the four cells in turn:

1. *Contextual.* With both the origins and effects of the stress being within the organization the context and everything within it should be the focus of attention. For example, one of the Further Reading texts identified at the end of this chapter is about bullying at work. A report in *Communiqué* (2003) reports about 10 per cent of the working population across Europe claim to have been bullied with another 10 per cent being subjected to physical violence (real or threatened) over the past year. The effect of this is estimated at a reduction in productivity of 2 per cent as a result of the absenteeism and other consequences.
2. *Personal.* Where the source of the stress lies outside the organization but the repercussions are experienced within it different responses are necessary. For example, an employee experiencing domestic problems is unlikely to be reliable or effective while at work. Consequently, counselling might be one option that could assist the individual to identify ways to deal with the domestic problems and thus reduce the level of stress.
3. *Insidious.* Where the stress originates inside the organization but the primary effects on the individual lie outside it there are very real problems for the organization. Consider the subject of bullying again. People who bully usually take great pains to mask their behaviour from those able to take action against them. Victims who seek to complain can easily find themselves subjected to retaliation as inappropriate responses and actions by managers alert the bully to the complaint and also fail to prevent further instances. In such situations, it would not be unexpected to find that the major effects of stress are noticed in the private life of the victim. In such situations it is difficult for an organization to identify the causes of the stress unless all managers and fellow employees are particularly sensitive to employee behaviour. Of course, if that were the situation it would be less likely that bullying would exist in the first place.

MANAGEMENT IN ACTION 10.3 Managers working more than before

A survey of 1250 managers was carried out by the Institute of Management and DHL International (UK) in 1994. It sought to identify the amount of time that managers were at work and the reasons for it. Among the findings were:

- Almost 50 per cent of managers indicated that their workloads had increased 'greatly' over the previous two years.
- The workloads of 20 per cent of managers had increased by more than 15 hours each week over the previous two years.
- Over 40 per cent of respondents worked more than 10 hours extra each week.
- 80 per cent of managers said that they worked more than 6 hours each week in excess of their official working time.
- Almost 50 per cent said that work took priority over everything else in their lives.
- The majority of respondents wanted to spend more time with family and friends.
- More managers than ever did their own typing and basic office tasks that might previously have been done by a secretary.
- Most of the additional workload arose from company restructuring.
- Most managers have fewer staff to support them.

Adapted from: Donkin, R (1995) Managers 'working more than before', *Financial Times*, 6 March, p 9.

Stop ↔ Consider

Can you think of any other possible explanations for the results of the survey besides the 'fact' that everyone is actually working much harder?
How might you test out your ideas?

4. *Peripheral.* This cell in the matrix represents circumstances in which both the source of the stress and its effects lie outside the organization. As such it is peripheral to the functioning of the organization and many managers would argue that it represents an irrelevance to them. However, an alternative view would hold that a caring employer should offer support to employees in attempting to improve the overall quality of life experienced by individuals. In more pragmatic terms, there are few circumstances in which there would be no organizational impact (however small) as a result of stress arising from an outside context.

FIGURE 10.2

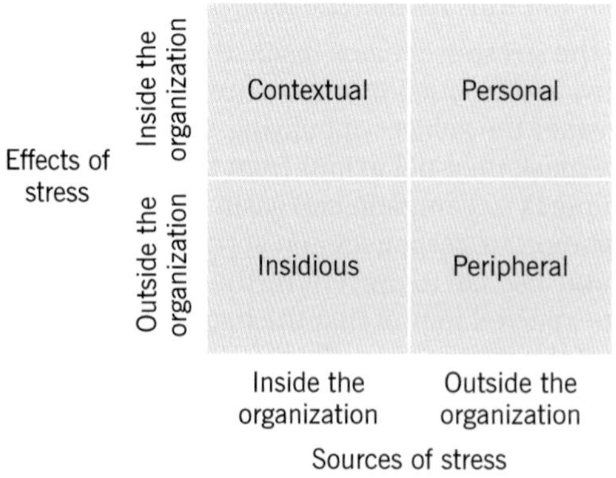

The stress context

Another aspect of stress is that individuals vary in their response to stressful situations. What is stressful for one person another can cope with easily. For example, some people are afraid of spiders and find being near them or even just looking at pictures of them distressing. Some people, however, keep spiders as pets and find them loveable creatures to be played with and held whenever possible. There are many definitions of stress and most of them consider it to be the consequence of events that place high levels of physical and/or psychological demand on individuals. McKenna (1994, p 585) draws the analogy with physics in which, 'stress arises because of the impact of an environmental force on a physical object; the object undergoes strain and this reaction may result in temporary distortion, but equally it could lead to permanent distortion'.

This represents an interesting approach to defining stress in that it reflects many of the salient features of it and yet originates from outside the social sciences. It links the origins of stress to environmental forces. It also introduces a term that is related to stress – strain – which implies that stress can be linked to pressure in one of its many forms. The notion of a distortion also alludes to a consequential change in the stressed object and, perhaps more significantly, that the effect can be either temporary or permanent. However, what this particular definition does not incorporate is a recognition that the effects of the stressor on the individual are to a significant extent dependent upon individual differences and experience. In physical terms distortion is a function of the characteristics of the object under strain. For example some individuals find the thought of flying very stressful irrespective of the number of occasions that they do it. Other individuals find that having flown a number of times the level of stress experienced reduces and they can cope with it more easily.

In relation to the related concepts of pressure and strain, Handy (1993) offers the distinction that pressure represents stimulating stress whilst strain reflects harmful stress. This distinction has a long tradition and originated from work in the 1930s by Selye (see Thompson and McHugh, 1995, p 273). The basis for this differential view of the effects of stress is that a certain level of it is necessary for generating performance, but that too much stress can reduce performance and be harmful to the individual. This perspective is frequently reflected in a diagram, Figure 10.3.

The view of stress implied in diagrams such as Figure 10.3 is a useful way of linking many of the foregoing ideas. In usability terms it does, however, contain one major weakness. The levels of both stress and performance used in the model are not

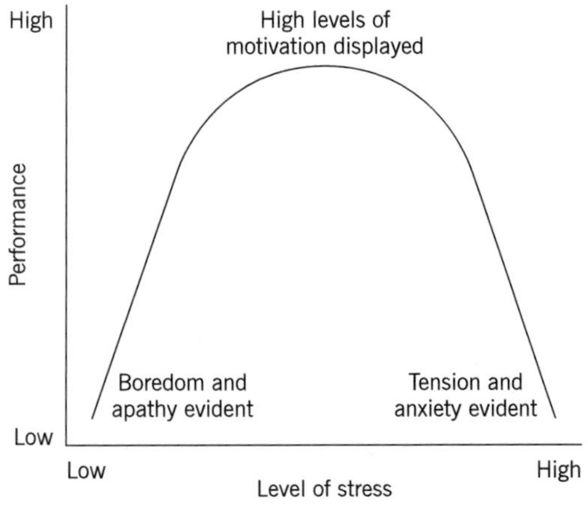

FIGURE 10.3

Stress and performance (*adapted from*: Moorhead, G and Griffin RW (1992) *Organizational Behaviour*, 3rd edn, Houghton Mifflin, Boston, MA)

defined. In short what do high levels of stress and performance mean? It was suggested earlier in this chapter that the effects of stress are dependent on individual difference and experience. This would imply that every individual would have a different curve for each different stress-inducing situation. The model is therefore of general relevance but of limited predictive value. It would not, for example, help managers to determine the optimal level of stress in any specific work context. It could, however, lead them to explore how the variables could be measured and what they mean in that particular context. Even without precise definition, to hold a debate in any specific context about what defines stress and performance could produce a very useful learning experience for the individuals and the organization.

SOURCES OF STRESS

Figure 10.2 identified stress as originating from either inside or outside the organization. Breaking that two-level classification down into greater detail can allow for improved analysis and subsequently the development of more effective coping strategies. For example, a survey carried out in the USA during August 2002 (Brooks, 2002), found that 37 per cent of people with some college education felt their work was stressful, compared to 24 per cent of people with lower educational achievement. Also 38 per cent of salaried employees felt stress compared to 28 per cent of workers paid by the hour. Conversely, only 26 per cent of respondents who felt stressed described their employer as having a strong sense of loyalty towards them, compared to 48 per cent who described their employer as not displaying a strong loyalty towards employees. Nelson (2003) reports a survey which indicated that 41 per cent of people cite workload issues as the biggest source of stress, with another 31 per cent reporting people issues and 28 per cent juggling work and personal life. The most common sources of stress that could be expected to have a measure of impact on organizational activity include:

- *Environmental.* Forces in the environment in general could be expected to create stress for the individuals within an organization. The actual process of getting to work can be stressful for many people. Driving through crowded streets, finding somewhere to park, travelling on a crowded bus or train are all generators of stress.
- *Competitive.* The competitive conditions that exist around all organizations represent a particular form of environmental stressor. In the harsh world of competitive reality no organization is safe from being required to continually improve its performance in an attempt to fight off the threat of closure. Competitors are continually making product improvements and introducing marketing initiatives to attract new business to enhance profit levels and chances of survival. In the public sector there are also initiatives such as privatization and market testing which are intended to significantly influence the performance of those organizations. The net result of all of this activity in the competitive environment of organizations is an instability, uncertainty and unpredictability, in turn leading to a pressure for shorter planning and decision-making horizons. However, when this is linked to cost reduction and efficiency drives, such as business process re-engineering and delayering, additional stress is created as a result of the lower levels of slack available within an organization.
- *Organizational.* The act of having to work in an organization is in itself a stress creating experience. Other chapters in this book examine many features

associated with the nature of an organization making the complexity of this form of social structure obvious. The structure of the organization can create frustration in that hierarchy and compartmentalization introduce a measure of artificial constraint on work activity. The rules, procedures and policies adopted by organizations are another source of stress and frustration. Employees who have significant caring responsibilities outside work frequently find that company rules on attendance, timekeeping, time off, and crèche facilities are unhelpful.

- *Job*. The work that individuals do is also a major source of stress for many of them. The job may be boring and involve many repetitive, short cycle tasks. Many jobs are complex and full of uncertainty with little support and assistance in performing the necessary tasks. Job insecurity is another major source of stress for many individuals. There is also the **survivor syndrome** which reflects the stress experienced by those individuals who do not lose their jobs and yet the individuals mirror the responses among those who have (Hall, 1995). This perhaps originates from a feeling of guilt about being 'spared' compared to colleagues and friends. Handy (1993) identifies a number of role related aspects that can lead to stress for the individual in Table 10.2.
- *Personal*. There are some individuals who appear to be natural worriers. They seem to be pessimistic about most things in life and subject themselves to additional stress as a result. For example, worrying about being punctual for appointments or whether a job will be finished on time. While laudable objectives in themselves, in some people they become major causes of concern and stress.

Survivor syndrome
Reactions of those associated with but not affected by a traumatic event can be identical to those who are.

Role ambiguity	Lack of clarity in what the job entails in terms of evaluation, responsibility, advancement and expectations of performance
Role incompatability	Lack of clarity in expectation of job content between job holder and other people. Perhaps differences between job demands and personal ethics would be an example
Role conflict	The requirement to perform more than one role in the same situation
Role overload	An extreme form of role conflict in which too many roles are expected from one person
Role underload	The opposite of role overload when the role expected is well below that which the individual perceives themselves capable
Responsibility for others	To rely on others to do what is necessary. Achieving results through others
Boundary roles	Those jobs that co-ordinate or integrate two or more groups. Salespeople are a typical example, being the customer representative within the organization
Career uncertainty	Lack of clarity in the future direction of work or career

TABLE 10.2 Job-related sources of stress (*source*: Handy, CB (1985) *Understanding Organizations*, 3rd edn, Penguin, Harmondsworth)

- *Interpersonal.* The quality of interpersonal relationships that exist within the organization can also become major sources of stress. This can arise in all directions and between all groups and individuals.
- *Professional.* Professional bodies frequently have codes of practice and standards to which members are expected to subscribe and adhere in their work activities. There can be occasions when these standards are in conflict with the requirement of the organization for which they work or those of some other business associate. This can create stress for the individual in dealing with the discrepancy.

Each of these major sources of stress can operate together or in different combinations to create a dynamic and ever changing context within which the individual must function and respond. Figure 10.4 attempts to reflect this dynamic relationship.

The moderators identified in Figure 10.4 are the major determinants of the individual's response to the stress experience, and include:

- *Personality.* Personality characteristics can influence how an individual interprets and responds to what happens to them, including the experience of stress.
- *Experience.* Previous experience of situations can raise the tolerance threshold for stress. For example, driving over the same route to work every working day could be expected to produce less stress than driving over the route for the first time.
- *Profile.* The profile of the individual in terms of age, degree of physical fitness, education level and gender could also play a part in determining the way in which stress is dealt with by that person.
- *Support.* The support networks surrounding the individual can also influence the ability to cope with stress. An individual working in an organization that provided easy access to counselling facilities and other forms of social support could be expected to have a higher tolerance for stress.

EFFECTS OF STRESS

Stress could be expected to influence the individual in a number of ways. In addition, it would be expected to produce effects on the people around them and the organization. For example, imagine that an individual reacts to the stress they experience by becoming bad tempered and irritable. The changes in their normal behaviour pattern under such circumstances could be expected to create strains in the family, friendship

FIGURE 10.4

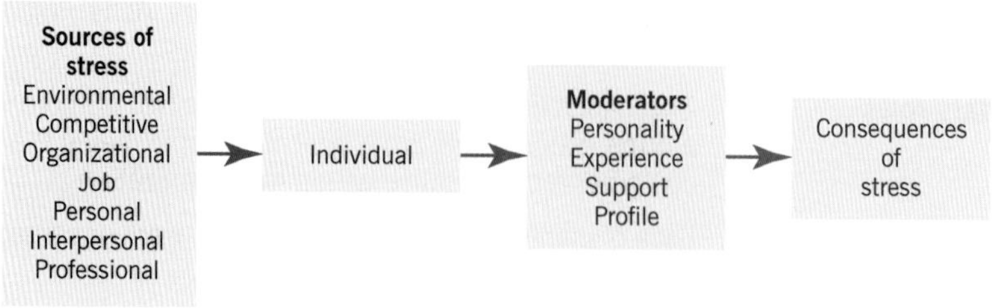

Stress and the individual

and work relationships surrounding the stressed person. Table 10.3 demonstrates some of the effects of stress on the absence levels within organizations.

For the organization the presence of a bad-tempered and irritable employee could have the effect of turning customers away and also there is a strong possibility that the individual concerned would not be effective in their job in other ways. Figure 10.5 reflects these zones of impact for stress. Primarily the consequences impact on the individual themselves, the people around them and those with whom they come into contact, the organization for which they work and possibly other organizations.

The examples just described also provide the basis for suggesting that the effects of stress are interactive, self-reinforcing and cumulative.

- *Interactive*. The behaviour of any individual could be expected to produce responses in the behaviour patterns of those with whom they interact, thereby creating stress for other people and influencing their own behaviour patterns.
- *Self-reinforcing*. The experience of stress and the changes in behaviour that it can produce in the individual and those around them creates a stressful situation in its own right. This effectively reinforces the experience of stress in that context.
- *Cumulative*. It is not just that a particular aspect of work is stressful; the experience of work in total becomes stressful. The effects of the two previous features of stress (interactive and self-reinforcing) produces a situation in which the level of experienced stress begins to rise and feed on itself for everyone. The following Employee Perspective (10.3) demonstrates how some people thrive on this, suggesting that it is not a negative process for everyone.

20% of medium-sized companies report up to 50% of all sick days as being stress related
100 million working days lost each year due to stress (UK only)
30 times as many days lost due to stress as from industrial disputes
Stress related absence has increased by 500% since the mid-1950s

TABLE 10.3 Sample statistics on the effects of stress (*source*: Ward, T (1996) *The Stress Factor*, Institute of Management, Humberside, Newsletter)

FIGURE 10.5

The impact zones of stress

EMPLOYEE PERSPECTIVE 10.3 Stress in the Liffe!

Some people thrive on stress. The trading floor of the London International Financial Futures and Options Exchange (Liffe) was always a dramatic place with more than one thousand people shouting buy and sell orders across the trading floor. It was known as the pit and reflected naked capitalism as billions of pounds moved around the money markets. It was a place of constant stress, noise, chaos and pressure. However, in November 2000, it succumbed to the march of technology and most of the people involved were made redundant. Some people working in the pit actually enjoyed the pressure of the trading environment and Ray Conway was one such person. After he left he was reported as saying, 'I never found the stress unpleasant, I thrived on it. I loved the physicality of it, the interaction. In fact I really miss it.' Another former trader, Duncan Ackery who was Australian, said that, 'My new job is high-pressure, but it's a kind of stress that you can understand and can have some control over. The stress in restaurants (he now manages one) is more comprehensible.'

Adapted from: Hopkins, N (2003) Coping with a matter of Liffe and death of trading floor, *The Times*, 19 April, p 57.

Tasks

1. Should people such as Ray and Duncan be allowed to place themselves under so much stress on a regular basis? Are there some jobs where this should be allowed? If so, identify and justify the list?
2. What do these references to stress suggest about the nature of it and the ability of human beings to cope with it?

Individual consequences of stress

There are three main areas in which stress would impact on the individual; psychological, behavioural and medical. Each of these areas is in practice interactive in that the symptoms and behavioural consequences are not mutually exclusive. A person under stress could be expected to display a range of all three categories. However, the range of symptoms displayed would not be the same for each person and not everyone would display the full range of symptoms. Briefly considering each category in turn:

1. *Psychological.* The psychological consequences of stress can include anxiety, depression, nervousness, irritability, tension, moodiness and boredom. In addition Cox (1978) identifies apathy, low self-esteem, poor decision making, short attention span, hypersensitivity to criticism and mental blocks.
2. *Behavioural.* These are the observable features of the individual's response to stress. Some of the more common behavioural influences include drinking, drug abuse, increased smoking and caffeine intake (Hogg, 1988), violent outbursts, general aggression, moodiness, going absent from work, sickness, demanding perfection from subordinates. In addition to these, Cox (1978) identifies impulsive behaviour, emotional outbursts, excessive eating and nervous laughter as typical examples. However, it is changes to normal behaviour patterns that provide the most reliable indicator of the effects of stress. But such changes can also be the result of many other causes, for example, changes in personal circumstances.
3. *Medical.* The medical consequences of stress are related to the physical effects of it on the individual and resulting medical conditions. These include heart disease, stroke, high blood pressure, headaches, back problems, ulcers, intestinal disorders and skin conditions (Quick and Quick, 1984). Kivimaki (2003) reports that work stress doubles the risk of death from heart disease. Cox (1978) also identifies sweating, dryness of the mouth as well as the effects of alcohol and drug abuse as medical conditions resulting from stress. Hogg (1988) also identifies links with cancer, allergies, rheumatoid arthritis, diabetes, asthma, sleep and sexual disorders.

Having discussed stress in general terms, McKenna (1994) introduces **burnout** and **post-traumatic stress disorder (PTSD)** as forms of it arising in particular situations. Burnout is a term that originated over the last decade or so to describe the situation in which some individuals literally are unable to keep going in their jobs. It was typified by a lack of performance, poor decision making, negative attitudes and exhaustion. It is the equivalent of a fire burning itself out or an engine running out of petrol and simply coming to a complete standstill. Burnout has been described as a form of stress (Ganster and Schaubroeck, 1991) and characterized as emotional exhaustion, depersonalization and diminished personal accomplishment (Cordes and Dougherty, 1993, quoted in Luthans 1995, pp 297–8). Jackson *et al.* (1986) suggest that burnout is more likely among individuals who display high aspirations and who are highly motivated. It is also more likely in situations where the organization restricts the individual's opportunity to use their own initiative while insisting on particular goals being achieved in a particular way.

Burnout
The feeling of helplessness and of being unable to continue experienced by some individuals after prolonged exposure to stress.

Post-traumatic stress disorder (PTSD)
A reaction to major trauma that can lead to a range of negative psychological, medical and social consequences.

There is evidence (Evans and Fisher, 1993) that burnout is particularly evident in the caring professions such as nursing, teachers, social work, and even ministers of religion (Moorhead and Griffin, 1992, p 467). McKenna (1994) suggests that burnout could be viewed as a coping mechanism in that it forces the individual to disconnect themselves one way or another from the situation which is creating and reinforcing the stress. Winstanley and Whittington (2002) suggest a relationship between the aggression (including assaults and abuse) experienced by hospital staff and the levels of burnout among staff. This in turn contributes to higher levels of depersonalization among staff as a coping mechanism, which in turn negatively impacts on behaviour towards patients and so makes staff more vulnerable to more aggression.

There are events that are so stressful in themselves that, fortunately, most of us are spared the trauma of experiencing them and of having to cope with the consequences. For example, there was a recent press report of a fireman who committed suicide because he could not cope with the trauma resulting from having to attend a major road accident and assist in the cutting free and removal of five decapitated bodies from the wreckage. No amount of training can prepare an individual for the sheer horror of having to face such a situation. Also relevant in this context is the notion of critical incident management discussed in Chapter 8. The psychological effects arising from major traumatic events such as already described, or a war, or accidents at work are classified as PTSD. Frost (1990, described in McKenna, 1994) identifies a number of the features of this disorder, including the individual having nightmares and/or flashbacks about the events, sleeplessness, edginess and outbursts of anger. It can also lead to alcohol and drug abuse in an attempt to lessen the anguish involved and to help blank out remembrances of the experience.

The consequences for the lives, work and relationships of individuals suffering from PTSD could be considerable. It is a condition that is beginning to be taken seriously by both the medical profession and employers. Employers have a duty of care towards employees and there are health and safety at work issues that arise from the occurrence of PTSD as a result of events experienced at work. Employers have found themselves being sued for damages when an employee has claimed that the condition resulted from something for which management could be held accountable. It has also lead to the establishment of specialist medical units in an attempt to provide effective treatment for sufferers.

Organizational consequences of stress

The organizational effects of stress can also be categorized under three headings: attitude, performance and withdrawal. These three terms should not be regarded as mutually exclusive. Taking each in turn:

1. *Attitude*. The attitudes of the employee towards the organization could be expected to change as a result of the stress experienced. For example, they may begin to hate the job that they do, or express feelings of hostility towards individuals, departments, managers, customers or suppliers. Attitudes can have significant influence on behaviour, and in this context could be expected to influence **motivation** and willingness to function as an effective employee (at least from a management perspective).

Motivation
A driving force that encourages an individual to behave in particular ways as they seek to achieve a goal.

2. *Performance*. Figure 10.3 provides an indication of the relationship between levels of stress and performance. The difficulty is in identifying the appropriate levels of stress in order to achieve the best result. With inappropriate levels of stress, things within the organization could be expected to deteriorate as a general lethargy and unwillingness to become proactive settle upon the affected employees. Another aspect associated with organizational performance is illness and accident rates. More people are needed on the payroll to cover those people off work ill, thereby increasing the cost of operations. There is also the very real risk of an employer being taken to court and sued for damages by an employee incapacitated in some way because of stress. Welch (1996) reports a record payment (at that time) of £175 000 to a social worker forced to retire on health grounds after two nervous breakdowns brought on by an impossible workload.
3. *Withdrawal*. This can take one of two forms, physical or psychological. Physical withdrawal includes temporary absence due either to sickness or to simply staying away from work. It can also include finding ways of avoiding work while at work. This includes such sanctions as going slow or deliberately restricting the output produced; sabotaging machines to make them break down and thereby 'earn' a rest from the pace of work; going to the toilet for a 'rest' or staying longer than necessary when there. Another form of physical withdrawal is to permanently leave the organization. Psychological withdrawal involves action short of physically doing things to absent oneself from work. It could involve not making an effort to consider the organization's interests or caring about customer views. 'Letting something go' (perhaps a quality defect) instead of doing something positive to correct it would be a typical response in this category. It involves not putting oneself out on behalf of the employer's interests. It indicates that although still at work, the individual does not really care about the organization or its future.

DEALING WITH STRESS

There are many sources that can provide help in developing coping strategies for dealing with stress. However, prevention is inevitably more effective than cure and so some of the techniques have anticipatory or tolerance enhancing dimensions to them. There is a specific managerial responsibility for minimizing the effects of stress on employees. This arises as a result of legislative requirements to provide a safe working environment as well as through the moral obligations to care for employees at work. It also makes commercial sense for organizations to take stress seriously as it can inhibit their ability to achieve the high performance operational environment so prized within human resource management. It should not be forgotten that managers are themselves susceptible to stress, it is not something that just happens to other employees. It is easiest to consider the strategies most frequently encountered as falling into either an individual or organizational classification. In considering the forms of strategy that can be used to deal with stress, the implications of Figure 10.2 should be kept in mind. The actual strategies adopted to meet the needs of particular individuals and situations should be targeted at both source and effect if the intervention is to be successful.

Individual stress management strategies

There are many strategies that individuals can use in order to combat the negative effects of stress. Some approaches such as time management can be totally up to the individual to decide upon and implement. Others such as stress counselling may involve making use of an organizationally (or health service) provided resource. Almost invariably, access to this latter type of stress management approach is directed either by a medical practitioner or by someone within the organization. Management in Action 10.4 demonstrates that a wide range of approaches to provide individuals with the ability to cope with and overcome the effect of stress are being used by organizations.

The more common individual stress management strategies include:

- *Time management.* Time management systems usually contain advice on daily goal setting, prioritization of work and delegation. The argument being that if the main goals and priorities can be achieved then the outstanding issues are of little consequence and so unlikely to produce stress. The work experience of many managers is one of a continual round of very brief activities. Under those circumstances it is easy to lose sight of the main objectives and to fall into the trap of always responding to the latest event – the beginning of stress. The complexity of the relationship between how individuals control their work environment and the effect on stress levels is demonstrated by Troup and Dewe (2002). Goal setting, prioritization and delegation are the recognition that not everything that lands on one's desk has to be dealt with immediately.
- *Relaxation and meditation.* These two approaches come in many forms from the active pursuit of hobbies and activities outside of work to learning meditation or practising yoga. The logic behind these approaches being that stress can become a constant companion of the individual and consequently overwhelm them. By engaging in some from of relaxation activity it breaks the continual feeling of stress and helps to provide balance in the life of the individual.
- *Behaviour control.* This approach involves attempting to manage more effectively the situations that generate stress. It requires the individual to recognize their own behaviour patterns and to be able to anticipate those situations which lead to stress and to develop strategies to deal with them more effectively next time they arise.
- *Counselling.* This provides a mechanism by which individuals can be encouraged to explore their feelings and emotions surrounding the stress. Having the opportunity to talk provides an opportunity for the individual to identify ways of dealing with stress in the future. Employees who have been subjected to traumatic events at work often find it difficult to go back into that same situation without fear or panic attacks. For example the emergency services who must deal with road accident situations and bank employees who have been subjected to armed robbery at work can all experience these difficulties. Counselling can provide a means by which the individual can come to terms with their experiences and cope more easily with the normal work and life experiences. Management in Action 10.5 illustrates a number of aspects of counselling in a stress management context.

MANAGEMENT IN ACTION 10.4 Alternative ways to take out stress

Cable Midlands provides cable TV, telephone and information services in the Midlands region of the UK. It had a staff of about 600 in mid-1996, expected to grow to about 700 by the end of that year. A recent merger with the largest cable operator in the UK as well as constant changes in technology and working practices brought with it rising levels of stress for all employees. Steve Miller, a training consultant with the company, had previous experience of running stress management workshops and was keen to develop similar initiatives within Cable Midlands. His advice was that in addition to topics like time management and assertiveness training as ways to combat stress a number of complementary therapies could offer benefits. The first workshop was titled 'Managing Pressure to Maximize Performance'. It was available only to managers as a pilot programme. Reaction was favourable and so it was made generally available and runs twice each month.

Other pilot programmes developed include a two-day programme to allow managers to assess their own stress levels and develop strategies to manage it more effectively in the future. Other approaches tried or planned within the company include:

- Sessions in clinical hypnosis to teach practical relaxation techniques.
- Aromatherapy advice. It emphasizes the use of massage and aromatic oils to reduce muscular tension.
- Reflexology. Employees are instructed how to use pressure points in the feet to relieve stress.
- Confidential counselling is also available on a one-to-one basis.
- Technical awareness training. In a rapidly changing environment stress arises from not being able to keep up to date and so technical development sessions were provided.
- The company plans to offer yoga and exercise classes.
- A second generation of stress courses is also planned to focus on the psychological aspects of managing stress.
- The managing of perception and general avoidance of negative thought processes as well as maintaining creativity are other areas under consideration for future programmes.

The cost of the initiatives was around £10 000 which, it was hoped, will be recovered through reduced sickness levels and labour turnover. Initial results were positive with about 1 per cent drop in absence being reported and lower labour turnover also being reported by some departments.

Adapted from: Butler, S (1996) Alternative ways to take out stress, *People Management*, 16 May, pp 43–4.

Stop ↔ Consider

Do the approaches described offer an effective response, or should managers be required to find ways of reducing the causes of stress within the organization instead? Justify your views.

- *Role management.* Table 10.2 identifies a number of job-related sources of stress. Role management attempts to manage the stress arising from each of these. For example, managing the stress created from role conflicts might involve an employee with significant domestic responsibilities saying no to the organization when a more senior manager demands that a job be completed immediately. Each of the job-based sources of stress can be managed more effectively if the individuals concerned take the time and trouble to make an assessment of what creates the stress and what alternative response patterns exist.
- *Biofeedback.* Stress creates a number of physiological changes in the body such as heart rate and temperature. It is possible to display physical representations of these changes for the individual and in doing so train them to control particular responses. For example, concentrating on trying to slow the frequency of 'bleep' from a heart monitor as it reflects the experienced levels of stress on

MANAGEMENT IN ACTION 10.5 Cheers all round for employee counselling

Employee assistance programmes (EAPs) are not new. Whitbread introduced its version called Person to Person in response to the large-scale rationalizations taking place in the late 1970s and early 1980s. The degree of change in the business caused stress and other effects among those who worked with the company. The company recognized that stress and tension are common occurrences in everyday organizational life and posed a very real threat to mental, emotional and physical well-being. The EAP offered by Whitbread is provided on an 'arm's length' basis in that counselling is provided by independent specialists who do not work for the company. The company lays down the standard of service required and monitors the delivery of those services, but does not become involved with the process itself.

Complete anonymity is guaranteed by the process. The company receives general information about how many people have made use of the facilities but not who they are. It is a process available 365 days a year from 7.30 every morning until midnight. It is available to the employees and their immediate family living at home. Telephone contact is made initially by the employee or their family and after a discussion a meeting can be arranged at a location selected by the employee. This can be home, work or a hotel for example. Three personal sessions are available through the company; more must be paid for by the employee if they are needed.

Between 5 and 7 per cent of employees use the system each year. Figures for 1994 show that 56 per cent of all problems were discussed and settled on the phone, the remaining 44 per cent receiving one-to-one counselling. Problems fall into four main groups:

1. Work related, 33%
2. Legal, 22%
3. Family/marital, 14%
4. Emotional, 12%.

The calls received were:

- 84% directly from employees
- 8% management referrals
- 3% from employee's partner
- 5% referrals from the occupational health team.

The scheme is promoted on a regular basis so that employees know that they have access to it. Among the benefits from the EAP at Whitbread the following are indicated as the most significant:

- Reduced number of grievances
- Enables better decisions to be made
- Reduced accidents
- Assisted positive approach to drug and alcohol problems
- Demonstrates a caring attitude to employees and their families
- Helps recruitment and retention
- Raised efficiency
- Enhanced the quality of service
- Enable the management to monitor and improve employee well-being
- Provided a good financial investment.

Adapted from: Anderson, I (1996) Cheers all round for employee counselling, *Professional Manager*, January, pp 8–10.

Stop ↔ Consider

In the EAP described, management of the company are told of the volume of use. Should they also be given information on the type of problems etc. so that action can be taken to impact on the causes of stress? Why or why not?

heart rate. By concentrating on such biofeedback the individual learns how to manage the physiological effects of stress.

- *Exercise.* The use of regular exercise can produce a number of benefits in addition to the weight loss and fitness improvement that are the most obvious gains. Exercise can also provide an opportunity to work off some of the aggression and frustration built up during stress. The physical tiredness created by exercise can also encourage better sleeping patterns and create a form of relaxation.

- *Networking*. When under stress an individual tends to feel isolated, think that they are the only one in that position and their focus turns inwards. The value of a network or support group is in providing an outward focus for the individual. The ability to talk with professional colleagues, friends and other support providers (family being the most significant) creates an opportunity to externalize problems and seek ways of dealing with them, perhaps learning new ways to tackle particular tasks. Individuals also frequently place themselves under considerable stress because they have very high expectations. Figure 10.6 reflects the advice given by one anonymous writer on the subject (and benefits) of accepting personal limitations.

Organizational stress management strategies

Morally (and legally) if stress is created within an organizational context then there is an obligation to deal with it because of the potential damage to those exposed to it. It also makes commercial sense. The notion in Figure 10.3 that performance and stress have an inverted 'u' shaped relationship produces a danger of excessive amounts of stress. What is not clear is what level of stress is detrimental to human health and well-being. It could be that the level of stress necessary to create optimal performance is, at a human level, detrimental to the individual if the pressure lasts a long time. Under such circumstances the organization could be creating grounds for legal action concerning the neglect of the health and safety of its workers.

The strategies adopted by organizations in an attempt to manage stress include the following. It will be apparent that many of the following issues are themes that represent major discussion areas throughout this book:

- *Job design*. Careful attention to this can provide a means of minimizing stress for individuals. Ensuring that jobs are not boring with very small cycle times, would be one example, as would careful design of the way that technology interacts with the human worker.
- *Involvement and communication*. Employees, who are involved in the decision-making aspects of work, and who are well informed about what is happening, are more likely to be able to understand their position and what is going on around them. Consequently, as a result of a lower level of ambiguity some of the stress-creating possibilities are eliminated and those that remain lessened.
- *Awareness programmes*. Sensitivity training is a process of making people aware of the existence of stress, its causes and the mechanisms for dealing with it. It is a process of bringing stress out into the open so that it can be dealt with. Individuals who become more aware of the nature of stress and how to deal with it are better able to make informed choices in relation to it and their own lives.

FIGURE 10.6

From tomorrow I will welcome rejection and failure with open arms. I will accept that I am GLORIOUSLY inadequate for the challenges that life places before me. HOWEVER, fortunately or unfortunately, as the case may be, I am the best person currently available!

Anonymous reflection on personal limitations

- *Health programmes.* Health screening and the development of a range of health improvement strategies are the intention of this approach. The logic behind them being to provide an improved medical ability to withstand stress and to introduce a healthier balance into the life of the individual. There is an issue in this context about the use of drug and alcohol screening tests. The results of such tests can be used to identify employees with problems and as a basis of providing assistance to them. However, they can also be used as a possible basis for disciplinary action. As a consequence a number of trade unions and other bodies are reluctant to unilaterally endorse them (Turner, 1995).
- *Organizational design.* Much of the stress within any organization comes from the physical and social arrangements within it. Customers experience an organization horizontally while most organizations function vertically. This conflicting pressure creates stress for the employees subject to them. Therefore, attention to the physical structuring of the organization could be a means of reducing stress.
- *Personal development.* The provision of job and professional training courses is one form of this provision. The more proficient an individual becomes the less stress in doing their normal job will be experienced. The encouragement to develop new skills such as learning another language, or playing a musical instrument all provide an opportunity to relax, and provide a balance in life that allows stress creating situations to be placed in context and the effect reduced.
- *Personnel policies.* There are many personnel policy areas that can be used to influence the stress experienced by employees. The provision of crèche facilities and flexible working arrangements are aspects that can help some people balance work and other parts of their life. The consequence being an employee who is less stressed.
- *Employee assistance programmes (EAP).* The provision of an **employee assistance programme** is intended to provide a broad based support for employees. Often they are provided through external specialist organizations and are accessed by phone at the behest of the employee. Employees are usually entitled to ask for advice or help in dealing with a particular difficulty or problem at work and often a number of face-to-face meetings (or phone discussions) can be arranged with a support worker who will seek to assist the employee to deal with the issue raised. Most schemes have a limit on the number of support interventions available and number of times each year that an employee can access the EAP. The idea of EAPs being that by providing a non-company support service employees are more likely to discuss any problems and consequently the levels of stress and other hindrances to the effectiveness of the employee can be resolved. The result being that a happier, more productive employee emerges from the process to the benefit of all parties.

Employee assistance programme Provision of opportunity to talk over a problem with a support worker.

- *Procedural frameworks.* Procedures are intended to guide activity within the organization. If they are ambiguous or in conflict with each other then they will not be effective, resulting in stress. For example, if it is not clear under what circumstances the sales department can take an emergency order from a valued customer and change the production schedule then the potential for conflict and confusion between all the people involved will exist.
- *Conflict management.* The inclusion of conflict management is not intended to imply that it can be completely eliminated; only that it can be reduced and managed more effectively. One conflict management technique is to recognize the distinction between competition and conflict. Bringing competition into the open as part of the natural decision-making processes within the organization

whilst at the same time restricting conflict is a difficult balance to strike, particularly when organizational politics and power are incorporated into the picture. However, in attempting to do so the levels of stress could be reduced for all concerned. The following Employee Perspective (10.4) shows how conflict can develop and create stress for the people involved.

- *Planning.* The actual organization and planning of work is a means of reducing ambiguity and of providing clarity and predictability into the working life of employees. As a consequence the level of sources of stress should reduce.
- *Culture design.* If a supportive culture can be created as opposed to one based on politics and power, employees are more likely to help and support each other. The consequence being that co-operation would create less opportunity for stress arising from compartmentalization or friction. It would also provide the environment for supporting those individuals who were experiencing stress.

Having introduced a wide range of perspectives on the management of stress it must be remembered that the research links between many of them are weak if not ambiguous. At a common-sense level all of these issues should have a beneficial effect on the level of stress in an organization and the ability of individuals to cope with it. However, organizational life is much more complex than implied by that simplistic relationship. There are too many intervening variables between stress, work and the individual to be able to make trite statements that it can be reduced by simple actions. There are no perfect, guaranteed solutions in attempting to manage stress. Every person is different and responses to stress management strategies will differ, just as with the reaction to the original stress-creating situation. (For an indication of the difficulties involved in attempting to tease out the variables and relationships in stress research refer to Semmer *et al.*, 1996.)

MANAGING PEOPLE AND STRESS: AN APPLIED PERSPECTIVE

Human resource management represents the management function with special responsibility for the management of people within the organization. As such it holds a brief to develop appropriate policies and procedures and to ensure that both line managers and employees meet the formal and informal requirements of the employment relationship. However, the relationships between people within an organizational setting are dynamic and subject to many forces arising from personal and interpersonal events as well as the factors originating from the physical, procedural and operational nature of the organization and the activities within them. In practice every line manager is responsible for the achievement of operational objectives through the effective use of a wide range of resources allocated to them, including employees. Consequently, the human resource department emphasis is to play a key role in providing appropriate organizational frameworks and encouraging effective behaviours among both managers and employees. Yet in practice it is the interaction between all of the people within a specific working environment that determines what will happen and how effectively the objectives will be achieved.

It could be argued very clearly that the human resource department within any organization is the function that addresses all of the issues contained within this book in seeking to develop appropriate policies and practice in the search for the effective use of people. For example, communication, involvement, training and leadership policies are grounded in the belief that the more closely employees are involved in the business the more probable it is that they will align themselves with the perceptions

EMPLOYEE PERSPECTIVE 10.4 Disputes in the office

Guor-Rung was an industrial engineer in a manufacturing company making carpets. His responsibility was to identify projects that could raise productivity and save the company money. He was one of three industrial engineers within the company, each being responsible for proposing productivity projects for a defined area of the company. Each project was presented to management in report form setting out all of the details, including the costs, savings and life expectancy of the improvements. Senior management then reviewed each of the projects proposed, discussed them with the industrial engineers and decided which would be adopted based upon the benefits and budget available.

Guor-Rung and his colleagues although friendly on the surface, were in conflict with each other over the selection of projects for implementation. Promotion and therefore status and salary were dependent on being highly regarded by senior management. Consequently each tried to ensure that their projects were the ones selected for implementation. This led to each industrial engineer adopting a number of behind the scenes tactics to try and influence the decisions. These included lobbying all the relevant managers; exaggerating the positive claims for projects whilst minimizing costs etc; trying to imply in reports and presentations that other proposals were weak and deficient etc. One year open conflict erupted with each industrial engineer making outrageous claims about the other projects, whilst trying to protect their own. The individuals even stopped speaking to each other and made complaints about the professional conduct of the others. Clearly something had to be done; the project selection system would have to change.

Tasks

1. How would you deal with this situation if you were Guor-Rung?
2. Propose how you might achieve the objective of encouraging competition but minimizing conflict in this situation?

and attitudes held by managers and so make the running of the organization easier and the achievement of management determined objectives more likely. Similarly, employee motivation can be addressed through performance management practices, together with the design of salary, incentive and benefits packages.

It is the line manager who holds the responsibility for the application of people management policy. For example, there will probably exist in most organizations a clear policy about how disciplinary problems should be dealt with. This represents a key area of people management in order to ensure that employees failing to work as required are dealt with appropriately, but that managers cannot simply act on personal dislike, or as a result of a desire to hide their own mistakes, with little or no evidence of wrongdoing on the part of the employee. However, there are many examples that exist of discipline procedure being misused by line managers despite the availability of personnel advice. Human resource specialists can only attempt to advise managers, ensure that the procedures are applied correctly and if necessary report their concerns through the chain of command in anticipation of action by senior line managers. A breach of policy could of course make a line manager liable to disciplinary action. Similar restrictions apply to the effective use of every human resource policy and initiative as a consequence of actions being the responsibility of line managers. Therefore one of the key requirements of any human resource practitioner is to be able to persuade, encourage, facilitate, negotiate, use political pressure and where necessary force to be able to ensure that line managers and employees contribute to the effective running of the organization in an ongoing and dynamic way. This means that among all of the responsibilities associated with the management of people, the ethical dimensions are the most complex and difficult to deal with effectively.

One of the other features that influences the nature and sophistication of people management activity within an organization is the size. Large organizations can afford to have large and complex organization structures including the existence of a human resource department. There are many variations in how such departments deliver the service and they are as much subject to the pressure for cost effectiveness as every other functional area within the business. However, small companies face completely different situations. In some cases a company may not be generating enough money to be able to afford the presence of human resource specialists. In other cases the company may simply be too small to warrant such activities existing as a distinct job. In such cases there would simply not be enough work to occupy even a single human resource specialist full time. In such situations the human resource responsibilities are usually added to the existing responsibilities of another employee. Perhaps linking two part-time jobs to make a full-time position; or simply adding the responsibilities to an existing full-time job, say that of a line manager; thereby adding to the levels of stress experienced by that person. This type of approach has advantages and disadvantages in that it is difficult for such people to be fully versed in people management matters as it only forms part of their responsibilities. Also because people management forms part of a portfolio of responsibilities for such managers they are likely to be under-represented in discussions at the senior levels of the company.

However the people management responsibilities are arranged within an organization, one of the major issues that all line managers have to deal with is stress. Equally, employees have to be able to understand and deal with stress as a real issue that impacts on the lives of many people working in organizations these days. Stress is an interesting phenomenon from a management perspective. It has already been suggested in this chapter that it is both necessary in order to create high performance and yet in excessive quantity can be harmful to both individual and organization. Stress cannot be effectively measured or easily controlled at an appropriate level for every individual. It affects everyone from the most senior executive to the most junior employee. It is also such a complex feature of human existence that it is not possible to state with any certainty which jobs and particular individuals are most vulnerable to it. In research terms it has been studied since the beginning of the twentieth century as a cognitive, medical or physiological phenomenon. Thompson and McHugh (1995) provide a brief but very readable summary of the evolution of stress research over this period of time (pp 273–8).

There are so many potential sources of stress and different jobs are susceptible to different forms of it. Equally, individuals vary in their response propensity to it. It has been suggested that one major determinant of individual response to stress is personality type. McKenna (1994) provides a summary of the **Type A personality profile** (p 601) and indicates the tendency of such people to display behaviours making them more prone to a range of conditions including coronary heart disease. It is further suggested that such individuals are prone to suffer excessive levels of stress. The behaviours characterizing a Type A personality are indicated in Table 10.4.

Type A and Type B personality profile
Type A individuals feel under time pressure, impatient and pre-occupied with achievement, Type B individuals are the opposite.

Haste
Aggressiveness
Restlessness
Extreme competitiveness
Impatience
Under pressure
Preoccupied with deadlines

TABLE 10.4 Some of the Type A personality behaviour patterns

By contrast, **Type B personality** characteristics include being relaxed, easy going and not preoccupied with achievement (which tend to be the opposite of Type A characteristics) and therefore less liable to suffer the effects of stress. It has also been argued that those individuals that display an external **locus of control** are more susceptible to the effects of stress. The argument being that such individuals tend to interpret events as being outside their control. The less control that an individual has over their lives and events that they encounter the more they will be stressed by the necessity to respond to and deal with them (McKenna, 1994, p 602).

Locus of control
The degree to which individuals believe they are subject to external or internal control over their behaviour.

Sparks *et al.* (2001) review a number of contemporary issues that face managers in seeking to achieve organizational objectives whilst paying attention to employee well-being, one aspect of which is of course stress. The authors identify four major concerns facing organizations and employees in current operational environments. They are:

1. *Job insecurity.* An ever increasing number of people are employed on short-term or casual contracts of employment which provide little by way of security in the medium to long term. Even people employed under what might be regarded as long term contracts have little security as organizations seek to take advantage of the cost reduction potential available though technology and relocate to areas of cheaper labour.
2. *Work hours.* People are expected to demonstrate good citizenship, their loyalty and commitment to the organization by working longer hours. Also because of rightsizing and other cost reduction initiatives there are fewer people about to do the work that needs to be done and so everyone must absorb extra activity, which often requires them to work more hours.
3. *Control at work.* The ways in which control is exercised are often described as a form of delegation or empowerment in which decision making is passed down to the lowest level possible. This inevitably means that low level employees are given the responsibility of ensuring that everything works as intended by senior management. Employees are controlled closely in various procedural, administrative and managerial ways intended to ensure compliance and the achievement of this objective. The result is more pressure, responsibility and stress for the individuals concerned.
4. *Managerial style.* The style of management practised within the organization needs to be appropriate to the circumstances and to support employees in the work that they do. The increased levels of bullying and harassment reported over the past few years would seem to suggest that this is not happening and, along with the ways in which control is exercised within the organization resulting from inappropriate management styles, can lead to a reduction in the general level of well-being among employees.

The authors identify a number of changes in both the workplace and the people who work in organizations that contribute to the above concerns. For organizations these trends include globalization, the growth in technology use, organizational restructuring and changes to contracts of employment and worktime scheduling. In terms of employees they include increased female participation, growth in dual earner couples, and the level of older worker participation in employment. All of these changes in the workplace impact on how people are managed within the organizations in which they spend a high proportion of their time and energy and also, just as significantly, how they react physically, mentally and emotionally to the working situations that they find themselves in. This in turn creates the significance of the four areas of concern identified above for employee well-being. The writers conclude with points for consideration by both researchers and practitioners in dealing with the emerging reality in terms of employee well-being.

There are a number of reasons why managers take an interest in stress within their organizations. It is not too much of an exaggeration to suggest that this probably is for reasons of self-interest in one form or another. The reasons include:

- *Performance.* If through the more effective management of stress among employees (by reducing it or increasing tolerance capabilities) higher productivity can be achieved then a commercial advantage is gained.
- *Cost.* It has been suggested that between 50 and 75 per cent of all illness is stress related (Brenner, 1978). Some estimate stress-related costs associated with absence and people changing jobs at around £1.3 billion (Summers, 1990). Clearly, improved stress control, providing reductions in cost of this magnitude would significantly improve corporate performance.
- *Protection.* Managers are seeking to protect their organizations from the negative consequences of stress. The most obvious being protection from the threat of litigation and claims for damages from employees who suffer the consequences of stress. In addition there are the public relations issues to be taken into account. Allowing stress to reach excessive levels might suggest to customers that their interests are not being cared for effectively. In addition, the signal to existing and potential employees could make it more difficult to attract and retain good quality staff.
- *Personal.* It would not be unreasonable to suggest that issues that might be expected to impact on managers would be prioritized more highly than issues that do not. Stress is an issue that could have a significant effect on managers; therefore it could be expected to be an issue which they would take an active interest in.
- *Fashion.* There are many organizations who rather than innovate follow the trend set by others. These followers of fashion tend to do things for the sake of appearance. Now, of course, it is not organizations that adopt these strategies but the managers within them. The approach adopted and the 'fashion' to be followed can be used politically within an organization to push particular ideas or functions to the benefit of individual managers.
- *Reputation.* Some organizations pride themselves on being innovators, the leader in particular industries in developing novel approaches to products and the application of management techniques, including dealing with stress.
- *Morality.* There are managers who adopt a moral position in relation to organizational issues, including stress. The moral view of stress would take the approach that as it has the potential to be harmful to employees it should be controlled and minimized.
- *Legislation.* Legislation surrounding health and safety at work is becoming ever tighter. Employers are being increasingly required to identify the areas of risk to employee health and to put in place effective measures to reduce or eliminate them as far as possible.

CONCLUSIONS

The application of people management policies and the ensuing management of practice in this area is the direct responsibility of line managers. As such much of the material contained in this book is relevant to an understanding of the complex array of factors and influences at work in the dynamics of organizational life, with this section being of particular relevance. This chapter seeks to introduce the primary themes associated with this important aspect of organizational behaviour.

People management practice reflects many forces acting upon the social context of an organization. As such it changes and adapts to the prevailing conditions and perspectives on how the relationship between people and work should be enacted in society. However, there are many organizations that do not employ specialists in this area and so line managers have to develop self-sufficiency in being able to manage effectively in this area.

One of the major people management areas faced by all line managers and employees is that of stress. The complexity of stress was identified as was the integrated nature of it with regard to other material in this book. It would appear that some measure of stress is an inevitable by-product of working in an organization, and indeed it has been suggested that a measure of it is essential to securing high performance. However, too much stress is detrimental to those exposed to it and so the problem associated with it from a managerial point of view is one of achieving an effective balance between positive energy and harmful stress. Many of the causes of stress were identified as were many or the mechanisms for dealing with it.

Now to summarize this chapter in terms of the relevant Learning Objectives:

- **Explain the major models and approaches to the study of people management.** There are four models introduced in the chapter. The first, developed by Fombrum *et al.* (1984) begins with the view that human beings are a resource and that it needs to be flexible, reliable and cost effective. This approach begins with the business strategy setting the parameters; this is then converted into a people strategy; followed by the actual people policies. A second model, Beer *et al.* (1984, 1985), takes the stakeholder view of people management. It begins with a strategic perspective, but seeks to operationalize this by integrating a human dimension into the role of people in the organization. People represent thinking, dynamic and interactive elements within the organization, not just a static resource waiting to be used. This model recognizes that there are four main areas in which policy is required, employee influence, human resource flows, reward systems and work systems. A third model was suggested by Schuler and Jackson (1987, 1996) which set out to establish an association between the strategy of the organization and the employee behaviours necessary to achieve it. They identify two operational strategy options, one based on cost minimization, the other based on innovation. As such they do not reflect what activities the business should be in, but how to compete in the marketplace that they are in. A fourth model was developed by Hendry *et al.* (1989). Based on research in Britain it was able to explore the subject in terms of the culture, managerial practice and organizational arrangements specific to that context. The model proposes five main interlinked elements including the environmental context, internal organizational context, business strategy context, human resource management context and content.
- **Understand the distinction and similarities between stress, PTSD, burnout and pressure.** There are many sources of pressure in people's lives. The need to earn enough money to be able to maintain a comfortable lifestyle and the desire to progress in career terms when many other people seek to achieve the same objective represent just two. There are also things that happen at work and which cause pressure. For example the constant pressure to work harder and produce more output with less resource is just one area that if not controlled can lead to stress for the managers involved. So stress can be regarded as an extreme form of pressure which can lead to problems and difficulties for the individuals concerned and the employing organization. PTSD occurs when a particularly stressful event occurs and the individuals involved find difficulty in dealing with the aftermath. For example, the emergency services personnel who attend a particularly horrific motorway crash involving many fatalities are likely to experience such a reaction. Burnout tends to occur in those individuals who place themselves under considerable pressure to succeed for a long period of time and who suddenly find that they cannot cope any longer. So each of these terms are similar in that they are based upon pressure, but they embrace different degrees of it and arise in different circumstances.
- **Describe the physiological effects of stress and the consequent impact on the behaviour of individuals.** The range of psychological consequences of stress include anxiety, depression,

nervousness, irritability, tension, moodiness, boredom, apathy, low self-esteem, poor decision making, short attention span, and hypersensitivity to criticism. The impact of these on the behaviour of individuals can be varied but are usually found in their attitudes, performance, withdrawal and medical condition. For example individuals can become negative, or experience antipathy towards management and the organization. Their work performance may begin to deteriorate as the individuals under stress lose interest and motivation. In terms of withdrawal the individuals can just 'switch off' by not taking an interest in what is occurring at work or they can leave the organization and totally withdraw from the stress-creating context. In medical terms the individual does not choose to experience heart disease or any of the other conditions that can arise, but they can result because of a wide range of factors, including stress.

- **Assess the relative contribution of human resource managers and line managers in relation to the management of people.** The relationship between line managers and human resource managers is a complex one. Every manager is a line manager in that they have line responsibility for the resources under their control, including the people that work for them. Human resource managers are also the line managers of their own departments. It is the human resource function that is responsible for the determination of people management policy and practice that should be used by line managers in pursuit of their operational objectives. The working relationship for every employee is between the individual concerned and the colleagues around them and the managers who are their immediate boss. It is the way that these relationships function in practice that determines the quality of the working life for the people concerned and the level of productivity, customer service, etc. achieved by the company. So in effect the human resource practitioner is seeking to provide the frameworks within which the relationship will be regulated so that the day-to-day relationships between the people within the organization function as intended. The objective being to provide the best chance of a positive experience and outcome for all parties. In that sense they are a facilitator and an influencer, ensuring that the organization runs smoothly. In that context they may at times find the need to criticize and object to the actions of line managers, but they are not usually in a position to order a particular manager to undertake a particular course of action, as the manager is ultimately responsible. Of course breach of procedure by a line manager could make them liable to disciplinary action, should a more senior manager wish to take such action.
- **Discuss the nature of the psychological contract within the context of people management practice.** The psychological contract represents the real working relationship between employer and employee. There is the formal contract of employment which invariable sets out the main rights and obligations available to each party. The psychological contract is the unwritten, mental representation of what each party expects of the other in practice. It does not rely on formally agreed rules, obligations or rights; it embraces the practical and actual ways in which the social relationship between company and employee is operated. For example, employees will have a view about the efforts that the employer will make to protect their jobs, which will partly inform their attitudes towards work in the company. It also encapsulates issues such as how much effort the employees will put in on behalf of the interests of the employer including issues such as personal use of the internet and telephones during company time. In terms of people management practice the psychological contract is important as it guides what is likely to happen in reality, rather than what the employer would like to happen. Today organizations actively seek to go beyond the formal contract in seeking greater levels of contribution and commitment from employees. However, research has suggested that managers cannot always be relied on to meet the future expectations that employees develop under these new psychological contracts.

DISCUSSION QUESTIONS

1. Managing people is the most important part of any line manager's job. Discuss this statement illustrating your answer with examples from your experience.
2. What are the main sources of stress and how might they be controlled?
3. Outline the psychological contract and assess its significance in the management of people within an organization.
4. 'Managers only think they are stressed. It is the factory and office workers tied to boring and monotonous jobs and with low pay who really experience stress.' To what extent do you agree with this statement? Justify your answer.
5. Outline the main effects of stress on the organization.
6. Describe the distinction, if any, between stress, burnout, pressure and PTSD.
7. Outline the main approaches to employee involvement and discuss the circumstances in which each might be most appropriate.
8. Describe the main options available to an individual in attempting to deal with the effects of stress.
9. Some organizations, particularly in the Far East, make all employees do a short period of physical exercise before starting work each day. What general benefits do you think that this might have and to what extent do you think that it would help in managing stress?
10. 'Managing people within an organization is about gripping them warmly by the throat and squeezing gently until they do as management wants. Consequently, human resource management is about finding ways of achieving that objective in ways that are socially acceptable.' Discuss this statement in the light of the material presented in this chapter.

CASE STUDY

Work-life balance, the psychological contract and stress in further education

James is a lecturer in a college of further education in a large town in the south of England. He is thirty-five years old, married and with two children, both under the age of five. He teaches business studies to students on a range of courses leading to nationally recognized qualifications. He has taught at the college for about three years and is well respected by his colleagues and students.

In the academic year 2003/04 he has been given a heavy teaching workload. He has to be at the college to undertake his teaching, marking and other duties from 8.30am until 9.00pm on the Monday, Tuesday and Thursday each week. On a Wednesday he is there from 8.30am until 4.30pm. He is also required to work six hours on each Saturday during the academic year. The three evenings and Saturday that he teaches each week amount to 15 working hours each week, in return for which management have allowed him Friday off work each week.

During the second week of the new academic year, James's head of department (Peter) asked to speak to him. Later the same day they met in Peter's office. Peter explained that due to high student numbers and staff sickness they were short staffed. Consequently, Peter wanted James to come in to work each Friday and take classes to help solve the problem. James said that he did not want to work on a Friday and felt that he was already working enough hours each week. Peter said that he understood James' position but said that he had a big problem in that he needed to allocate a lecturer to teach the students who had now registered. James agreed to think it over and give Peter his answer the next day. The more James thought about the request (or was it a demand) by Peter the more angry he became. He felt that he was already doing more than was expected of him. Management had made no attempt to recruit enough staff to teach the number of students that they expected to register for courses and payment for extra hours worked was not available. Why should James be expected to shoulder the extra work, when management had made no real attempt to manage things properly? He came to the conclusion that he was being asked to do a lot more work and become more stressed in the process. By so doing he was simply making life easier for those who had created the problem in the first place and allowing the college to earn extra income for no extra labour cost.

James eventually went home and described what had taken place to his wife Mary. His wife was exasperated and told him so. With two small children to look after they had taken the joint decision that Mary would take a career break and stay at home to look after the children. James was therefore the only wage earner for the family. Mary said that she saw little enough of James to begin with as he worked such long hours and she admitted to feeling lonely at times without adult company during much of the day and she said that she needed James to be at home more, not less. Also she made the point that the two children did not see James for much of the week as he left for work early and they were in bed asleep by the time he came home in the evening. That only left them with the Friday and Sunday each week to do things as a family. James agreed with the points that Mary was making and this made him feel even angrier at the expectation that Peter seemed to have that he would do as he was told.

The next day James went back to see Peter to give his decision that he was not prepared to do the extra teaching every Friday. When he told Peter his answer, James could see from the look on Peter's face that he was not happy with the decision and had not expected it. Peter responded angrily that that this was not what was expected of his staff and that the spirit of a lecturer's contract of employment at the college meant that everyone was supposed to be flexible in their working arrangements. James lost his temper at that point and said that with his workload he was already being very flexible. He was working 15 extra hours each week and only had 7.5 hours off in lieu each Friday. He hardly saw his wife and family as it was, he was not about to work even more hours. Peter said that everyone in the department was under pressure to take on more work and James was no different to anyone else in that respect. Staff were expected to demonstrate 'good citizenship' when the college was under pressure and help management to deal with the problem. This led to a shouting match between Peter and James. With Peter demanding that James work each Friday and James saying that he had no intention of doing so. Peter finished off by saying that if James expected to get good performance appraisal markings and to become a senior member of the department then he had better work the extra time or else!

James stormed out of the office shouting that he had no intention of working every Friday, did not want to become a senior member of the department and was seriously thinking about looking for another job. He went back to his office, looked for a copy of his CV and picked up the telephone directory to look for the telephone numbers of recruitment agencies.

Tasks:

1. What would you do now if you were James, and why?
2. What would you do now if you were Peter, and why?
3. How could Peter have prevented the problem from arising?
4. To what extent could modern human resource management policy and practice have both contributed to, and prevented, the occurrence of the situation described in this case?
5. What might this case suggest about the reality of people management as experienced by line managers compared to the view of people management adopted by human resource management practitioners?

FURTHER READING

Adams, A (1992) *Bullying At Work: How To Confront and Overcome It,* Virago, London. One of the major forms of stress at work originates from the experience of being managed. It is not an unusual experience to find subordinates at any level being forced to do things or being bullied in other ways. This book attempts to explore this experience and to offer readers an understanding of the root causes and ways of dealing with it.

Clark, H, Chandler, J and Barry, J (1994) *Organization and Identities: Text and Readings in Organizational Behaviour*, International Thomson Business Press, London. Contains a broad range of original articles on relevant material themes and from significant writers referred to in this and other textbooks on management and organizations.

Cooper, CL, Dewe, PJ and O'Driscoll, MP (2001) *Organizational Stress: A Review and Critique of Theory, Research and Applications*, Sage, London. The book reviews the sources and outcomes of job-related stress, along with the ways to measure and deal with it.

Dobschiner, J-R (1969) *Selected To Live*, Pickering & Inglis, London. Not a business text, this book is a very personal and moving real life reflection of Jewish experience during the Second World War. It demonstrates the stress that can arise from events around the individual and which impact on every other aspect of life. It demonstrates how under extreme circumstances individuals can develop ways to cope with considerable levels of stress.

Jackson, T (2002) *International HRM: A Cross Cultural Approach*, Sage, London. Takes a cross-cultural approach to the study and practice of human resource management as experienced in theory and practice. As such it develops the material introduced in this chapter.

Levi, L and Lunde-Jensen, P (1997) *Socio Economic Costs of Work Stress in Two EU Member States: A Model for Assessment of the Costs of Stressors at National Level*, European Foundation for the Improvement of Living and Working Conditions, the Office for Official Publications of the European Communities, Luxembourg. As the title suggests this report attempts to identify a model for the determination of the macro-level costs of stress at work. It also attempts to consider the issues surrounding what causes job stress and how it can be dealt with.

Newton, T with Handy, J and Fineman, S (1995) *Managing Stress: Emotion and Power at Work*, Sage, London. This text takes a different view of stress, seeking to place it into a wider discourse on emotion, power, gender and subjectivity within an organization. In the process a historical review of stress research is undertaken as is an attempt to place the concept into such frameworks as labour process theory and Foucaultian philosophy.

Redman, T and Wilkinson, A (2002) *The Informed Student Guide to Human Resource Management*, Thomson Learning, London. Provides a reference base for much of the ideas and material within HRM. Provides over 300 entries all written by leading HR experts.

COMPANION WEBSITE

Online teaching and learning resources:

Visit the companion website for Organizational Behaviour and Management 3rd edition at: *http://www.thomsonlearning.co.uk/businessandmanagement/martin3* to find valuable further teaching and learning material:

Refer to page 35 for full details.

CHAPTER 11

Motivation and performance management

LEARNING OBJECTIVES

After studying this chapter and working through the associated Management in Action panels, Employee Perspectives, Discussion Questions and Case Study you should be able to:

- **Describe the major motivation theories and the ways in which they can be classified.**
- **Explain the relationship between motivation and employee performance.**
- **Understand what makes the study of motivation difficult.**
- **Discuss the dilemmas and difficulties facing managers in applying motivation theory to a work setting.**
- **Assess the links between motivation, performance management, pay determination, employee participation and job design.**

INTRODUCTION

The term motivation is a familiar one. Reflect on any team sport: the players spend considerable time and effort on the field attempting to exhort the other players to **perform** more effectively. In other words, to **motivate** the individuals to produce better results. Within organizations, managers are constantly seeking ways to improve performance at every level of the business, in order to raise **productivity** and reduce cost. A major element in this process is the application of practices assumed to contain the necessary motivational properties. Clearly, all these terms are closely related and of considerable significance to each of the stakeholder groups associated with organizations.

The *Pocket English Dictionary* defines **motive** as: 'What impels a person to action, e.g. fear, ambition, or love.' This, however, is only part of the richness of the concept as it would be used in organizational behaviour terms. The same source defines perform as: 'Carry into effect ... do (great things, wonders, &c)'. It also contains an unfortunate aspect to the definition of perform: 'Execute tricks at a public show'. Clearly, therefore, **performance** reflects the achievement of results that would be considered extraordinary and motivation is the key to achieving the necessary level of performance. However, the definition of performance also suggests another perspective, that of the manipulation of behaviour at the whim of another for the benefit, pleasure or entertainment of others. This alternative perspective provides a basis for much of the controversy surrounding the application of **performance management** techniques that are popular in organizations today.

Psychologists have long recognized the distinction between **drives** and motives, reflecting the distinction between unconscious physiological reactions and the social process directing controllable behaviour in people. Drives reflect those behaviour forces that are based on the physiological/biological needs of the body. For example, if we are hungry, the smell of food will tend to push our behaviour in the direction of eating. A motive on the other hand, reflects learned patterns of behaviour. For example, we actively seek out situations involving interaction with other people in an attempt to socialize with them rather than spend time on our own. The basic motivational process reflecting these distinctions is shown in Figure 11.1.

Baldamus (1961) introduced the concept of **traction** into this repertoire, to indicate the feeling among some workers of being pulled along by the rhythm of a particular activity. This implies that a highly repetitive job is not automatically boring and could contain some motivational properties as a direct consequence of the nature and pace of the work. Therefore, motivation as an organizational concept reflects a complex process, clearly relating to the willingness or energy with which individuals address their work activities.

Perform
The level of achievement by an individual.

Motivate
To seek to create motivation in another person.

EARLY APPROACHES TO MOTIVATION AND PERFORMANCE MANAGEMENT

In the pre-industrial era communities and individuals were probably motivated by the strong desire to survive and the perishable nature of much of the means of doing so. Much of the available food could not be stored for long periods and so the need was to adopt behaviour patterns that maintained its flow. In addition, the political and social structures were such that individuals had less freedom of choice in their lives. Slavery, bonded or enforced labour meant that individuals could be forced to perform tasks on behalf of others, frequently for a subsistence living in return. However, the discovery over recent years of elaborate and beautifully drawn cave paintings are but one example of the existence of activity beyond the demands of survival even in very ancient times, the implication being that even then life was more complex and richer than might be assumed looking back using today's perspectives, standards and values.

FIGURE 11.1

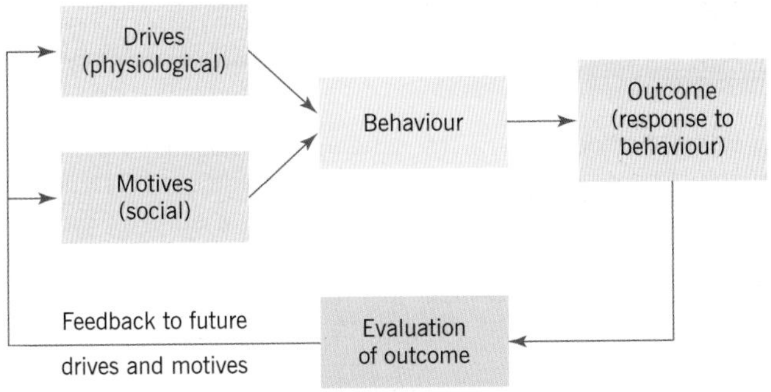

The basic motivational process

The issue of how much work management should expect from employees began to emerge in the Middle Ages. There are examples of the pace of work being set by management at the Arsenal of Venice in the 1400s (George, 1972, Wren, 1987) and of monks estimating the time to build churches and cathedrals at about the same time, (Currie, 1963). Management in Action 11.1 describes one early approach to this subject.

At the beginning of the twentieth century FW Taylor was attempting to develop and introduce scientific management to the companies in which he was working, initially Midvale Steel (1878–98) followed by Bethlehem Iron Company (1898–1901). It involved management identifying the **one best way** to carry out a job and then motivating employees to follow the work method specified through linking the payment of wages (reward) to the output achieved. His initial attempts were successful, the workers' earnings increased, productivity increased and costs reduced, as Table 11.1 (based on Taylor, 1947) indicates.

The level of production increased considerably, but the wages of employees changed very little by comparison. Table 11.2 reflects the changes resulting from the use of Taylor's scientific methods.

Looked at in this way the figures provide a picture of clear benefit for both employer and employee; but the employer gains far outweigh those for the employee. However, Taylor's success was short lived and he was dismissed from the company in 1901 as the result of the growing hostility towards his methods from managers and workers alike.

Chester Barnard described what he saw as the major activities associated with being a senior executive in the 1930s. As a practising manager (the president of a large telephone company) he was writing from experience rather than theory. In terms of motivation he suggests that it was a balancing process:

> The net satisfactions which induce a man to contribute his efforts to an organization result from the positive advantages as against the disadvantages which are entailed. (Barnard, 1938, p 140)

He suggests in a footnote on the same page that the individual was not usually logical in this decision-making process. Logical in this context being defined as an understandable basis for action as perceived by Barnard (as a senior manager) rather than through the frame of reference of the individual. This is also a common mistake among many present-day managers when designing motivational programmes. Managers frequently assume that what they find motivating everyone else within the organization will also find motivating. This is not necessarily so. In his views Barnard was essentially adopting a human relations approach, but also anticipating some of the later theoretical and practical approaches to the question of what motivates people to

Productivity
The relationship between inputs and outputs, expressed as either a conversion or a comparative index.

Motive
Social processes directing controllable behaviour in people.

Performance
The level of achievement by an individual, measured against what they would be expected to achieve.

Performance management
The processes and procedures through which managers seek to manage performance levels within the organization.

Drive
The physiological and biological needs of the human body that direct behaviour.

Traction
The natural rhythm in certain activities that pull people along with the pace of work.

MANAGEMENT IN ACTION 11.1 Early printing in Korea

In sixteenth- and seventeenth-century Korea methods of printing had developed from the carving of pages of individual text to the use of a movable type. As there were literally thousands of characters in the language and the workforce was largely illiterate, good-quality and accurate printing proved to be difficult to achieve.

In order to circulate official documents it was first necessary to have them printed and published. Because of the complexity of the language and the low levels of literacy in the workforce, the composing of the printing blocks and the subsequent printing process were very skilled jobs. In order to ensure the accurate reproduction of documents a motivation scheme was introduced for the printers and supervisors.

The scheme was based on a negative incentive principle, in other words punishment for mistakes rather than reward for accuracy. The punishment was that for every mistake or printed character that was unclear the supervisor, compositor and printer would be flogged 30 times. The consequence, not surprisingly, was very high quality printing, but difficulty in the recruiting and training of people as compositors, printers or supervisors. As with most incentive schemes some benefits were achieved, but other problems were created.

Adapted from: Boorstin, DJ (1983) *The Discoverers*, Random House, New York, pp 505–8.

Stop ↔ Consider

Would you have sought a job as a printer or a supervisor in early Korea (and why)?

One best way
The idea that the application of scientific management could produce the 'one best way' of doing any task.

deliver high performance. For example, *HR Focus* (2003, b) refers to a survey of the leading organizations in America which show that 84 per cent have some form of employee recognition programme aimed at encouraging positive behaviours by rewarding the employee with something that they will value. The range of awards can range from the informal, perhaps a spontaneous gesture of appreciation to the very formal award of gift certificates, cash or jewellery.

THE THEORIES OF MOTIVATION

There is no one theory of motivation that can be claimed to embrace the entire range of organizational and personal circumstances that exist. For example, something that motivates an individual today may not work tomorrow, yet may become viable again the day after, perhaps due to mood swings or factors outside of the work setting. Equally every individual employee is different and will respond to particular

	Pre-scientific management	Using scientific management
Earnings per employee per day (average)	$1.15	$1.88
Tons per employee per day (average)	16	59
Labour cost per ton (average)	$0.072	$0.033
Number of yard labourers	500	140

TABLE 11.1 The effect of scientific management

	Change as a result of scientific management	Percentage change
Earnings per employee	+$0.73	+63.5%
Tons per employee	+43	+268.8%
Labour cost per ton	–$0.039	–54.2%
Number of yard labourers	–360	–72%

TABLE 11.2 The benefits of scientific management

motivation processes differently. For example, the use of recognition and praise for good work may be motivational to one person, but yet have only limited effects for someone seeking to earn additional money to pay a large bank loan. Organizational circumstances also change over time which impacts on motivation practice. For example, the following Employee Perspective (11.1) reflects an example of how employee expectations may not be realized, resulting in an unhappy outcome for both parties to the employment relationship.

In this chapter we will use the convention of classifying theories into **content** or **process** theories wherever possible. Content theories concentrate on identifying the motives that produce behaviour. Process theories emphasize those mechanisms that

Content
These concentrate on identifying the motives that produce behaviour.

Process
These emphasize those mechanisms that encourage (or reward) behaviour in its dynamic context.

EMPLOYEE PERSPECTIVE 11.1 Julia's expectations

Julia is a fully qualified nurse who was born, educated and trained in Indonesia. She was recruited by an agency in 2001 to work as a nurse in the British National Health Service (NHS). She left her family (husband and two children) to take a two year contract to work on a surgical ward in a large general hospital in Manchester. The idea being that by working in Britain she would be able to earn additional money (sending it home to the family), and gain more experience. Julia was happy to be given what she thought was a good opportunity to gain a number of benefits and was looking forward to the challenge, although she was distressed at having to leave her family behind.

In Britain she quickly settled into her new job and began to make friends with the other foreign nurses, most of whom were in a similar position to herself. However, it was soon after she arrived that problems began to surface and Julia found that she was increasingly unhappy with the job and working in Britain. She also missed her family and friends terribly. The hospital was short of staff and everyone was forced to work very hard. Staff shortages were invariably covered by the use of agency staff who had only limited knowledge of the ward, patients or hospital procedures. A number of British nurses had left the NHS to work for agencies and as a result more responsibility was placed on the shoulders of Julia and her colleagues. Agency nurses were also paid considerably more money than Julia. This Julia felt to be unfair. Also the culture was different to what she had been used to in Indonesia and that made it difficult for Julia to know what was expected of her in a wide variety of situations, including how to respond to her managers.

Julia became increasingly frustrated and disenchanted with her job. She also found that because of the cost of living in Manchester and being away from her family she was not able to send as much money home as she had intended. Because of the conditions attached to her work permit, she was not allowed to resign and seek work as an agency nurse thereby earning additional money. After six months she resigned and went back to Indonesia.

Tasks

1. Was the outcome for both Julia and the hospital inevitable or could it have been avoided? If so how?
2. Could Julia have been motivated to stay longer? How?

encourage (or reward) behaviour in the dynamic context. Figure 11.2 provides an overview of the way that these approaches emerged from the earlier work in this area.

Intrinsic motivator Originates inside the individual as a response to the job itself and the circumstances surrounding it.

Extrinsic motivator Represents motivation that originates outside of the individual.

Another important concept in relation to motivation at work is that of an **intrinsic motivator**. This represents a source of motivation that originates inside the individual as a response to the job itself and the circumstances surrounding its execution. For example, an architect may be motivated to produce exciting buildings because of the satisfaction gained from having the opportunity to realize their ideas and also through avenues such as professional and peer recognition of their work. An **extrinsic motivator**, by way of contrast, is one that originates outside the individual worker and which influences their behaviour. For example, Taylor was prepared to reward employees with higher wages providing they worked to his prescribed methods. Figure 11.3 reflects the relationships between extrinsic and intrinsic motivation and the resulting work activity. It also clearly demonstrates the existence of feedback in the process. If the rewards obtained by an individual do not meet their expectations either in terms of the level received or the impact on their lives then a reassessment of the rewards offered would be made and perhaps future behaviour adjusted accordingly.

Both intrinsic and extrinsic concepts can be used with some effect in designing motivational practice within organizations. The self-regulation implied through intrinsic motivation could provide managers with lower costs and higher quality along with a reduced need for close supervision, than would a reliance on extrinsic motivators

FIGURE 11.2

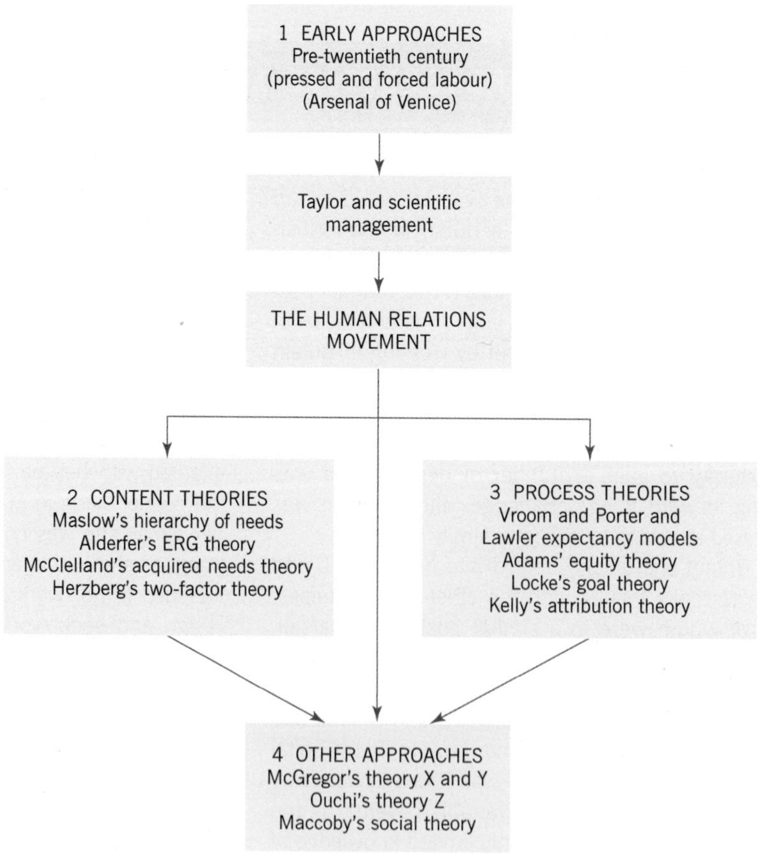

Evolution of motivation theory

FIGURE 11.3

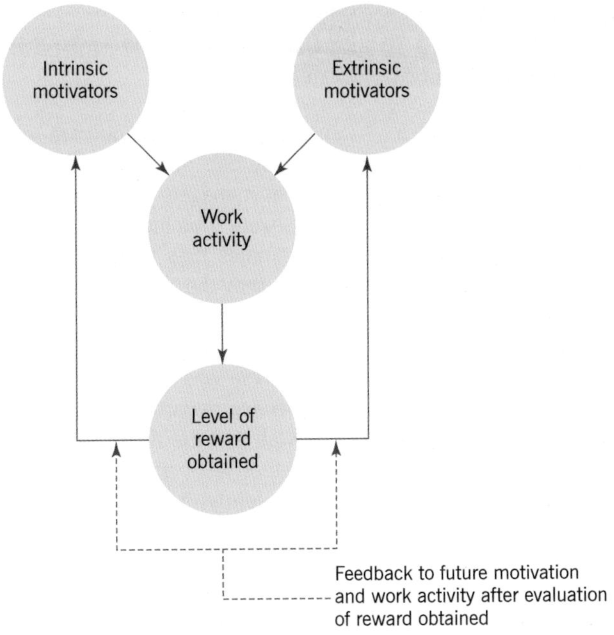

Intrinsic and extrinsic motivation

alone. Writers such as Foucault (1977), Hollway (1991) and Townley (1994) criticize much management theory, including motivation. They describe it as an attempt to seek to describe employees as 'objects' to be subjected to theory development, the ultimate intention of which is to place them within models supportive of management control and power (Townley, p 92). In effect this argues that employee performance is delivered within a reality defined and measured by managers; consequently the underlying motivational models are judged on the basis of this perspective. This point is illustrated in the following Employee Perspective (11.2).

CONTENT THEORIES

Content theories emphasize particular aspects of an individual's needs or the goals that they seek to achieve as the basis for motivated behaviour. The major theories falling into this classification include:

- *Maslow's hierarchy of needs theory*
- *Alderfer's existence, relatedness and growth (ERG) theory*
- *McClelland's acquired needs theory*
- *Herzberg's two-factor theory.*

Maslow's hierarchy of needs

Maslow was an American psychologist who produced the idea that a hierarchy of needs could explain purposeful behaviour (Maslow, 1943, 1987). The basis of the model is that individuals have innate needs or wants which they will seek to satisfy. In addition, these needs have an in-built prioritizing system. Figure 11.4 shows the model, indicating the hierarchical nature of the innate needs.

EMPLOYEE PERSPECTIVE 11.2 Time-sheet compliance

James worked for a large government department in Spain. The department in question had considerable contact with representatives of public companies in dealing with tax matters. Specifically, James had to visit the finance managers of a number of companies to deal with queries about the tax affairs of the company. The idea being that he should seek to determine if the stated accounts of the business were a true and fair reflection of the tax position of that company so that the government could collect its full tax entitlement.

James was a relatively junior grade member of staff and so was subject to a civil service requirement to account for his time whilst at work. He was expected to complete a time-sheet each day on which there were a number of categories of activity listed and against which he had to put the hours worked and also provide a list of companies that he had visited and what had been done. The form had to be filled in on the basis of an eight hour day, but his actual working hours were contracted as 7.5 each day, and in practice he often worked between nine and ten hours. He was not paid overtime, but on occasions he could take time off work in order to compensate him for some of the additional hours he worked. The consequence of all of this was that the time-sheet bore little resemblance to his actual activity over the course of each week. Each week all of the time-sheets were analyzed and the totals for each office calculated. On a monthly basis these weekly statistics were summarized and submitted to the national headquarters of the civil service department. Each year the manager of each regional office within the department had the performance of their region reviewed and the summary information from the time-sheets played a significant part in this process. Naturally one of the consequences of this was that regional managers reviewed very carefully the weekly time-sheets submitted by their staff and made it clear to subordinates how time should be booked in order to ensure that the manager's performance would look good when it was reviewed at the end of the year.

About three years after these time-sheets were introduced there was a national audit of every aspect of the civil service department's operations. One of the findings was that the time-sheets bore no resemblance to the actual work activities of the staff filling them in. Consequently it was recommended that they be dropped or significantly changed. The national director of the civil service department held a meeting with his senior colleagues and was very annoyed and demanded to know how the system could have been allowed to drift to such an extent. He said that he had always viewed the time-sheets as a key part of the performance management of the department and showed that collective performance was increasing year on year. He made it clear that he felt that he had been let down by his colleagues.

Task

The time-sheet system had been designed to be simple and easy to complete and to provide management with an overview of how time was being spent within the department. Do you think it is possible to ever have a simple but effective measure of performance that does not become meaningless by diverting attention away from the real objectives being sought? Why or why not?

The five levels included in this hierarchy can be defined in the following way:

1. *Physiological needs*. These include the wide range of basic needs that every human requires in order to stay alive and function normally. Examples would include the need for food, air to breathe, water to drink and sleep. In an organizational context this would also include the need for wages.
2. *Safety needs*. This category incorporates needs that provide for the security of the individual in their normal environment. Examples would include the need to be free from harm and to have shelter from the elements. In an organizational context this would also include the need for job security.
3. *Social needs*. From this category individuals would look to draw on social support necessary to life. Examples would include friendship and a sense of belonging. In an organizational context this might include the need to work as part of a team.

FIGURE 11.4

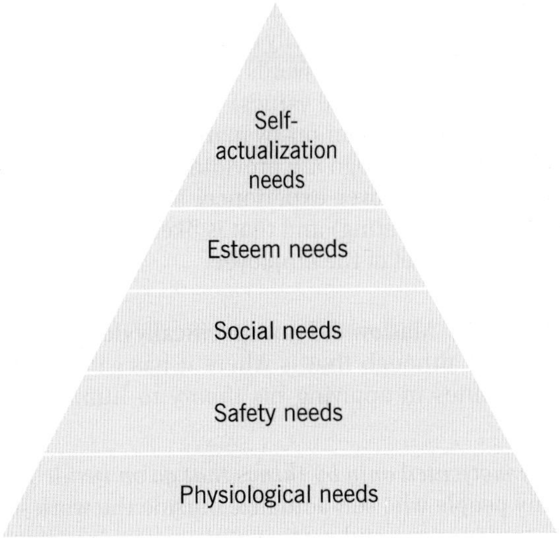

Maslow's hierarchy of needs

4. *Esteem needs*. This would include individuals having self-respect. Also incorporated in this category are concepts of achievement, adequacy, recognition and reputation. In an organizational context this could include the formal recognition by management of useful ideas originating from employees or employee of the month awards.
5. *Self-actualization needs*. This category is related to the opportunity to realize one's full potential. That is, the ability to have a significant influence over one's own life. In an organizational context this could include the freedom to organize one's job to suit personal preferences and circumstances and also to be managed on the basis of ends not means.

Maslow suggests that these elements in the hierarchy are not to be considered as a rigid framework, within which individuals move in a totally fixed and predictable way. He suggests that the hierarchy displays the following properties:

- *A need once satisfied is no longer a motivator.* For example, once employees become accustomed to being consulted by the employer on matters of company policy, it becomes the norm and therefore loses some of its motivational properties. In effect, the basis of comparison shifts to match the new circumstances.
- *A need cannot be effective as a motivator until those before it in the hierarchy have been satisfied.* For example, it would be of little value to offer employees who are currently very poorly paid the opportunity to work in teams in an attempt to increase productivity.
- *If deprived of the source of satisfaction from a lower order need it will again become a motivator.* For example, if a self-actualizing employee is given notice of redundancy, their natural reaction would be to start looking for another job (reversion to a lower level need for security).
- *There is an innate desire to work up the hierarchy.* Employees working in a team may begin to plan and organize their work without management involvement.
- *Self-actualization is not like the other needs; the opportunities presented by it cannot be exhausted.* A marketing manager who has just enjoyed a successful sales campaign may also have a number of similar campaigns at earlier stages of

development to form the basis of future motivation. However, Maclagan (2003) argues that self-actualization can only be properly understood as the realization of personal moral ideals. In other words it is for the individual to decide for themselves (based on their moral values) what provides self-actualization opportunity. Consequently, attempts by management to impose participation schemes or particular job design are providing at best a vicarious experience of self-actualization (the employee experiences self-actualization in ways that the manager would find motivating) and that is likely to have a very limited effect on the actual motivation level of the employee.

Assessment of the theory Maslow did not specifically describe his theory as applicable to the work situation, although that is where it has gained most exposure. There are a number of difficulties in applying his theory to humans in an organizational context, including:

- *Not everyone is motivated only by things that go on inside the organization.* There are many people who self-actualize outside the work setting, running youth groups, trade unions and participating in a wide variety of other leisure activities. Even the time of year can have an impact on the behaviour of a significant number of people, as indicated in Management in Action 11.2.
- *People at different stages of their lives will be motivated by different things.* For example, a young employee saving up to buy a motor car will be motivated by factors different from an employee five years away from retirement.
- The amount of satisfaction needed at a specific level before a higher level need is activated is unknown.
- *The theory cannot explain all behaviour.* For example, how can it explain that many actors and artists are prepared to endure personal hardship in order to pursue their art?
- To what extent can a theory developed in the USA during the 1940s, reflecting the values and culture of that time, be relevant to today's organizations and other countries?
- *Organizational events can impact on satisfaction at more than one level in the hierarchy.* For example, money can be used to satisfy needs at every level in the hierarchy. However, the use of money by employees is not under the control of managers, it is for the individual to determine the level of the hierarchy that is being met through the money given. This represents a very indirect motivational process.
- *Individuals will place different values on each need.* For example, some people prefer to work in relative security but with lower pay. It is just this issue that has over recent years been creating difficulties within public sector employment. Traditionally public sector employment has been very secure and some degree of advancement almost guaranteed. However, over recent years most countries have struggled with the desire to cut public spending and have as a consequence changed the basis of the psychological contract with employees. A not surprising reaction to that situation is that public sector employees now consider themselves to be just as vulnerable to high work demands and low security as those in the private sector and are demanding higher wages and better rewards in return.

Having said all that, Maslow's theory has been very influential over the years in assisting managers to prioritize elements in their attempts to motivate employees. It is an approach which encourages managers to 'get the basics right' before they attempt to

MANAGEMENT IN ACTION 11.2 SAD syndrome assistance at Capital One

A significant proportion of the population (estimated at 5 per cent – 2.5 million people) are claimed to suffer from 'SAD' syndrome (Seasonal Affective Disorder). In addition, some 90 per cent of the population are said to experience subtle changes in mood, energy levels and sleeping patterns when the seasons change.

Catherine Hope, Human Resource Director in the UK for Capital One reported that the company regularly undertook staff surveys to find out how the working environment for their 2000 staff could be improved. The actions taken by the company to ensure that the working environment is as positive as possible include:

- *Fun Budget*. Managers are allocated £50 per person per quarter to enjoy on inside or outside work activities. Associates (the company term for employees) are encouraged to be as creative as possible in deciding how to spend the money. Examples have included line dancing, hosting a medieval banquet and overseas city breaks.
- *Listen to the staff*. Regular staff surveys on what they think about the work environment and how it could be improved.
- *The right use of colour*. Using colour co-ordination to blend internal and external themes with the style of the building helps to keep it fresh and energizing. The building is mainly glass in its external fabric and white with splashes of colour was chosen to harmonize with the outside. Dark colours such as brown, purple or dark green have been avoided as too depressing.
- *A view to the world outside*. The design of workspace is such that Associates work in the offices next to the windows facing the outside of the building so that they always have a view of the surrounding environment and weather. The windows are all floor to ceiling to allow maximum light into the building as well as creating a feeling that the outside is part of the workspace. Managers' offices are deliberately placed towards the centre of the building so that Associates can have the best views.
- *Staff interaction*. The company has provided comfortable lounge areas, meeting rooms, coffee shops and restaurants for informal meetings. This alongside the opportunity for staff to work in groups at desk stations so that people can mix with each other, providing a happy working atmosphere.

Catherine Hope argues that people are the most important resource available to any organization and it is therefore important to keep them happy and motivated. The working environment is a key aspect of creating a place of work that Associates enjoy working in.

Adapted from: Newsdesk (2002) Capital One helps staff avoid 'SAD' syndrome, *Management Services*, December, p 5.

Stop ↔ Consider

If you were a manager working at Capital One how would you feel knowing that your subordinates needs in terms of working in an office with good light and views of the surrounding area were considered more important than your needs?

How might you approach this issue of work environment design to deal with SAD if you were a senior manager working in an old office block with only old buildings or factories surrounding you?

As a senior manager would you be persuaded to accept lower levels of productivity in the autumn and winter moths because of SAD? How might you seek to maximize motivation levels during those months?

undertake complex motivational initiatives. It should force managers to examine motivation from the employee perspective and to seek out how they perceive the situation. It also provides a basis for managers to reinforce what they already provide through benefit and support programmes as part of the employee reward package. For example, reminding employees of the existence and value of counselling and pension schemes.

Overall, there are many potential advantages to managers seeking to apply the Maslow model to the design of motivation within the organization – which is why it has much popularity as a topic on management courses. However, that alone does not make it a good theory. There have been studies carried out that have shown limited support for it as well as studies that have not supported the model. However, as a theory it must be seen in the context of the strong desire among managers for control of the process and outcome of work. It is in that context that, although originating outside the organizational context, it gains its significance, as suggested by Townley (1994).

Alderfer's ERG theory

Alderfer (1972) describes a three-level hierarchy, compared to the five levels proposed by Maslow. They are:

1. *Existence needs*. This category is grounded in the survival, or continued existence, of the person. As such it would include many of the issues covered by the physiological and safety needs identified by Maslow.
2. *Relatedness needs*. This category is based on the need for people to live and function in a social environment. It would embrace the need to be part of a group and belong to a valued organization. It would incorporate many of the issues covered by the safety, belonging and esteem needs described by Maslow.
3. *Growth needs*. This category is grounded in the need for people to develop their potential. As such it would cover the self-actualization and much of the esteem needs described by Maslow.

Assessment of the theory Having described the Alderfer model as being strongly related to the Maslow framework, that does not imply that Alderfer merely simplified the original material. For example he suggests that individuals move from existence needs to relatedness needs to growth needs, as each becomes satisfied. However, he does make more than Maslow of the variability inherent in all motivational situations. For example, he suggests that more than one need could be functioning at the same time. Also that individuals may regress back down the hierarchy as the result of a frustration – regression mechanism – if they were prevented from meeting their needs at any level. The following Employee Perspective (11.3) demonstrates just how complex motivation can be at a personal level.

EMPLOYEE PERSPECTIVE 11.3 Edith's time off for a new career

Edith Tsang lived and worked in Hong Kong. She did not like school and left at the earliest opportunity with no real academic qualifications. She was however, a bright girl and quickly got a job in a sewing factory near to her home. At first she enjoyed the work and companionship of the other girls who worked beside her. All the employees were friendly and she frequently socialized with them during any free time that they had. The money was also good and she was able to save a little and also pay her mother a contribution towards the cost of running their home. However, after about one year Edith began to feel that the work was boring. She did the same job every day and could do it without thinking. Her mind began to wander and she began to observe the more senior and technical people within the company, the lifestyle that they had and the fact that they were not tied to a specific machine all day doing the same job over and over again. Therefore she began to look for opportunities to change her job. However, she quickly began to realize that without qualifications her chances of getting promotion or a transfer to a better job in another department were severely restricted.

She talked to her mother and father about being bored at work and her desire to find a better job, possibly one with career prospects. Her parents said that she should go to college in her spare time and try to get some qualifications. She thought this was a good idea and began to explore the range of course available to her. Her first thoughts were to try and acquire some of the general education subjects that she missed out on at school, but quickly realised that this might not be the best route for her. She had always been interested in drawing and so she thought that perhaps if she did an art and design course she might be able to become a textile designer, working for her present employer. The more she thought about this the better plan it seemed. Her parents agreed, but suggested that she talk to her supervisor at work about it as the company might help her. She tentatively mentioned the possibility to her supervisor one day and was told that the company had never allowed anyone to transfer from the shop-floor to the design office in the past. So she did not push the idea. She thought that if she developed a portfolio of her work that this might impress them sufficiently to allow her to transfer. She began the course and really enjoyed the experience. She clearly had a talent for textile design and was doing well, frequently getting praise from her teachers and being encouraged to show her work to other students. The time came to take the exam for the course and Edith discovered that part of the assessment was during the day and she would have to take time off work.

Edith spoke to her supervisor to ask for the time off and was told that it was not normally allowed, but that the relevant manager would be consulted. The next day Edith was told that the company personnel manager wanted to see her about the time off request. The personnel manager asked why she needed the day off work and so Edith told her. The personnel manager said that such a course was not relevant to the company as they employed trainee graduate designers only from a particular university. Also they did not have any vacancies at that level and were unlikely to have any for the next couple of years. So her request for time off work was being denied. Edith was clearly disappointed and said that she had decided to do the course to further her career prospects and that she would not be at work on the day of the exam, whether management approved it or not. She did take the time off work and did well in her assessment. When she returned to work the next day she was called into the supervisor's office and given a formal warning for taking time off work without permission. Edith was clearly hurt by the reaction of the company and she became very disheartened by the experience. The amount of effort that Edith put in at work reduced significantly, although not enough to make her liable to further disciplinary action.

She continued on the second year of her course and did so well that she was offered a place at a local university to study for a degree in design which she accepted. She resigned from work and joined the university. When she graduated her previous employer offered her a job in their design department. She was interviewed by the same personnel manager who had turned down her request for time off five years earlier. Edith turned them down and told the personnel manager that it was because of their attitude towards her search to improve her career chances all those years before. The personnel manager apologized and said that they had not believed that she was serious in her aim and they did not want to set a precedent for the other workers to seek days off for trivial reasons.

Tasks

1. How would you react (and why) if you were Edith?
2. What does this example of motivation at an individual level suggest about the ability of managers to be able to motivate employees effectively to achieve management determined objectives?

Maslow's theory was not specifically work related. Alderfer, by the same token, contains a more direct organizational basis in grouping together categories of need into a more usable framework (at least as might be perceived by managers). It is also a stronger or more robust theory than Maslow's. It postulates that managers should seek to motivate by addressing all three levels of need, but that if one (say growth) cannot be met then additional effort will need to be put into providing for the others as they will increase in significance for the individual. However, it suffers from the same criticisms as the Maslow theory in its evident cultural positioning, underlying assumptions and managerialist perspective.

McClelland's acquired needs theory

This theory develops a different set of needs as the basis of motivation (McClelland, 1961):

- *Achievement*. He abbreviates this to nAch.
- *Affiliation*. He abbreviates this to nAff.
- *Power*. He abbreviates this to nPow.

Projective techniques
Ambiguous images are presented to an individual for interpretation; responses provide an insight into attitudes and personality.

To some extent these categories can be regarded as elements within the higher order needs described by Maslow. His ideas were developed by using **projective techniques** (introduced in Chapter 4 in relation to personality). He also suggests that needs are acquired through the social process of individuals interacting with the environment. McClelland suggests that all people have these three needs to some extent although there is a tendency for only one of them to be dominant at any point in time. Questionnaires similar to that included as Figure 11.5 are suggested to be able to identify the existence of individual needs as well as their relative dominance.

Assessment of the theory Questionnaires have been developed that it is claimed, can be of use to managers in attempting to identify the basic need profile of employees. This could then be used by managers to motivate employees by linking individual needs with job demands. Table 11.3 reflects this by providing an indication of the work preference associated with each need and a job example for each category. One

FIGURE 11.5

1. Do you like situations where you personally must find solutions to problems?
2. Do you tend to set moderate goals and take moderate thought-out risks?
3. Do you want specific feedback about how well you are doing?
4. Do you spend time considering how to advance your career, how to do your job better or how to accomplish something important?

If you responded yes to questions 1–4, then you probably have a high need for achievement.

5. Do you look for jobs or seek situations that provide an opportunity for social relationships?
6. Do you often think about the personal relationships you have?
7. Do you consider the feelings of others very important?
8. Do you try to restore disrupted relationships when they occur?

If you responded yes to questions 5–8, then you probably have a high need for affiliation.

9. Do you try to influence and control others?
10. Do you seek leadership positions in groups?
11. Do you enjoy persuading others?
12. Are you perceived by others as outspoken, forceful and demanding?

If you responded yes to questions 9–12, then you probably have a high need for power.

How to identify McClelland's needs (*source*: Steers, RM and Porter, LW (1979) *Motivation and Work Behaviour*, McGraw-Hill, New York)

difficulty associated with such tables is the generalized nature of the preferences and examples. Also, if needs provide a basis for job suitability, how can this be linked with the fluid nature of the needs themselves? For example, nAch tends to emphasize those aspects of work typified by the job of a sales representative. However, if a person classed as nAch and working as a sales representative then moves towards nAff as the dominant need this may suggest the necessity to change jobs, but there may be no suitable job opportunities available, carrying with it a variety of consequences for all concerned (from underperformance to job termination).

Herzberg's two-factor theory

The original research carried out by Herzberg involved interviews with 203 accountants and engineers from organizations around Pittsburgh in the USA (Herzberg, 1974a; Herzberg *et al.*, 1959). He used the **critical incidents** approach by asking questions about what had made the individual feel good or bad about their work. The answers were then subjected to a content analysis which identified that those factors that led to satisfaction were fundamentally different from those issues that lead to dissatisfaction. This he labelled the two-factor theory of motivation and named the categories motivators and hygiene factors. The theory offers some insight into the relationship between motivation and job satisfaction.

Critical incidents
Involves asking what makes an individual feel good or bad about something, subsequent content analysis identifies the important issues.

The hygiene factors were those that, if absent, caused dissatisfaction. They are predominantly concerned with the context within which the job is carried out and other extrinsic issues. The presence of these factors will not motivate individuals as such, but their absence will serve to create dissatisfaction with the job and organization. They included:

- Salary
- Working conditions
- Job security
- Level and quality of supervision
- Company policies and administrative procedures
- Interpersonal relationships at work.

Individual need	Work preferences	Example
High nArch	Individual responsibility Challenging but achievable goals Feedback on performance	Field salesperson with challenging quota and opportunity to earn individual bonus
High nAff	Interpersonal relationships Opportunities to communicate	Customer service representative; member of work unit subject to group wage bonus plan
High nPow	Control over others Attention Recognition	Formal position of supervisory responsibility; appointment as head of special task force or committee

TABLE 11.3 Work preferences based on McClelland's needs theory (*source*: Schermerhorn, JR, Hunt, JG and Osborn, RN (1982) *Managing Organizational Behaviour*, John Wiley, New York)

The motivating factors were those that could motivate the individual to improve their work performance. They were primarily concerned with the content of the work, together with the way in which it formed a meaningful whole (intrinsic factors). They included:

- Recognition
- Sense of achievement
- Responsibility
- Nature of the work itself
- Growth
- Advancement

Although Herzberg did not claim a hierarchical relationship for the two factors, it is possible to compare this theory with those of Maslow, Alderfer and McClelland. This is most easily illustrated with a diagram, Figure 11.6.

The significance of Herzberg's model is that the two factors are not opposite ends of a continuum. Lack of positive levels in the hygiene factors does not lead to demotivation, but to dissatisfaction. High levels in the hygiene factors do not lead to motivation, but to non-dissatisfaction. High levels among the motivation factors will however, lead to positive motivation. Conversely, low levels of motivating influences will reduce the overall level of motivation, but not create dissatisfaction; it would create feelings of non-satisfaction. So in effect there is a non-overlapping middle ground between these two factors, as shown in Figure 11.7.

FIGURE 11.6

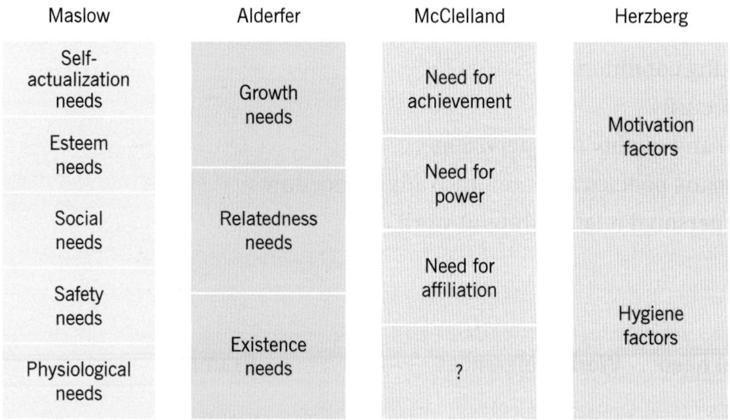

Maslow
Alderfer
McClelland
Herzberg
Self-actualization needs
Esteem needs
Social needs
Safety needs
Physiological needs
Growth needs
Relatedness needs
Existence needs
Need for achievement
Need for power
Need for affiliation
?
Motivation factors
Hygiene factors

Comparison of the need theories

FIGURE 11.7

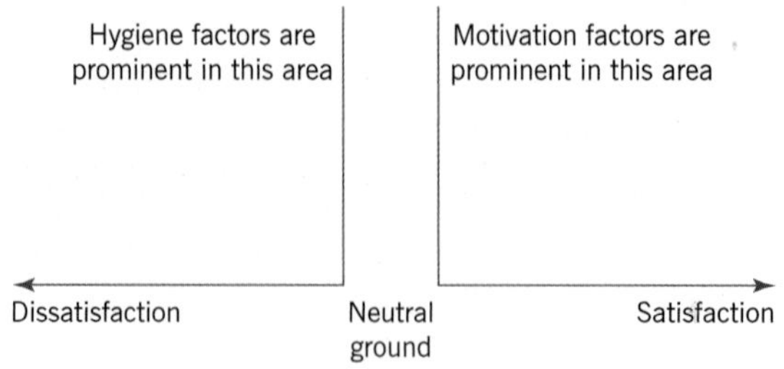

Satisfaction and Herzberg's two factors

The major implication of this theory for anyone seeking to make use of it in designing motivational practices is that they need to concentrate on two sets of factors at the same time if motivation and satisfaction are to be maintained.

Assessment of the theory There have been a number of criticisms of Herzberg's work. They include:

- *The results obtained are research method dependent.* Studies which use the same research methodology as Herzberg tend to arrive at broadly similar conclusions. Research using different methods is less supportive of the conclusions.
- *The results obtained by Herzberg are capable of different interpretations.* This is the line developed by Vroom (1964). Also, the theory is not clearly set out which has resulted in different interpretations when replicating his work (King, 1970).
- *It does not provide for individual difference.* For example, close supervision may be resented by some and yet welcomed by others.
- *In an organizational context the application of the principles implied by the model is often restricted to manual or unskilled workers.* This is surprising, given that it was developed from a research base drawn from accountants and engineers. It is often claimed that manual workers adopt an instrumental approach, concentrating on pay and security rather than the intrinsic aspects of the work. Work by Blackburn and Mann (1979) however, suggests that people in low-skilled jobs adopt a wide range of work approaches, not just economic factors, a result that reinforces the traction aspects associated with highly repetitive work referred to earlier.
- As with all content theories the universal application of Herzberg's work has been criticized because of the underlying assumptions about people and work as well as the cultural basis of the work context.

PROCESS THEORIES

Process theories attempt to provide a model of the interactions between the variables involved in the motivation process. The major process theories include:

- *Vroom/Porter and Lawler expectancy models*
- *Adams' equity theory*
- *Locke's goal theory*
- *Kelly's attribution theory.*

The Vroom/Porter and Lawler expectancy models

Vroom's expectancy model. The basis of expectancy models is that motivation is a function of the desirability of the outcome of behaviour. In other words, if an individual believes that behaving in a particular way will generate rewards that the individual values and seeks, they will be motivated to produce those behaviours. This is also referred to as **path–goal theory**, because it is possible to identify a distinct path leading to particular goals, Figure 11.8.

Path–goal theory
A model suggesting that it is possible to identify a motivational sequence leading to the achievement of particular goals.

This model implies that individual behaviour will be moulded by what is perceived as the available rewards on offer and their importance to the individual. For example, offered the opportunity to attend training courses leading to a professional qualification

FIGURE 11.8

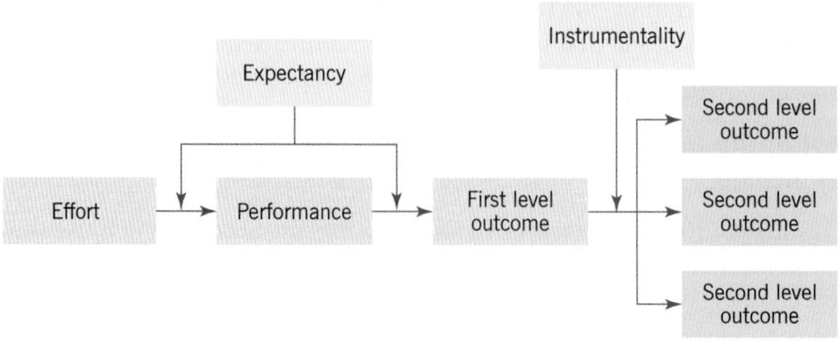

Vroom's expectancy model

in return for higher performance, an employee seeking such an opportunity will be motivated. If, however, an employee was not interested in becoming professionally qualified, it would have no effect on their behaviour. Also, an offer of such training would not motivate the employee even if they were interested in becoming qualified, if they did not believe that the manager could or would deliver the opportunity.

Vroom (1964) was the first person to link expectancy theory to work motivation. The model contains three key elements:

1. *Valance.* This refers to the importance of the outcome for the individual. Valance can either be positive or negative. It is positive if the individual wants to acquire or achieve the outcome. Negative valance refers to something that the individual would wish to avoid. Valance should be distinguished from value. Valance is based on anticipation; value implies the satisfaction from actually possessing something. In deciding whether to work overtime, an individual may take into account the family wish to go to the cinema that night. If the individual does not want to see the film, working late will allow them to achieve that objective (the valance). Subsequently, if the individual finds that the family could not get seats and so went to a restaurant instead, the value gained (realized valance) through working overtime may be altered.
2. *Instrumentality.* This concept links together the ideas of first and second level outcomes. It is necessary to become familiar with the notions of first and second level outcomes before instrumentality can be fully understood. First level outcomes are those things that emerge directly from behaviour and are related to the work itself. Examples include productivity, labour turnover, absenteeism, quality and 'doing a good job'. While these results may hold valance for the individual, it is the opportunities that these first level outcomes provide that contain the highest levels of it. For example, higher levels of productivity (first level outcome) may generate a financial bonus which is therefore a second level outcome. The bonus is a function of the additional output produced, not the level of motivation and as such tends to be need related. The importance of second level outcomes is that they are dependent on the first level outcomes, not on the original effort. For example, working harder may increase productivity (first level outcome), but if the company did not have an incentive scheme then no financial bonus would be paid (no second level outcome). Equally, individuals are usually rewarded for actual achievements not for the amount of effort expended.
3. *Expectancy.* This is about the probability that a particular first level outcome will be achieved. Machines are liable to break down, parts may not arrive when required and other workers may not work hard. The result of these and other

sources of variability is that the achievement of a first level outcome may not be certain.

The model can also be described in an equation. The use of an equation has the advantage of reflecting the motivational process in the way that it would be experienced by an individual. The equation allows a wide range of forces acting on the behaviour of an individual to be identified and the positive and negative influences taken into account, also the cumulative effect of the interactions within and between forces can be determined:

$$M = \Sigma (E \times V)$$

where M refers to the motivational force resulting from the sum of all the expectancy and valance elements in the equation, E refers to the expectancy measure reflecting the probability that effort will result in a particular first level outcome and V refers to the valance (or attractiveness) of a particular outcome for the individual.

The Porter and Lawler extension Porter and Lawler (1968) develop the model by attempting to link motivation and performance. In their model they draw attention to the fact that it is not just motivation that produces performance, but a range of variables such as the individual's view of work. Figure 11.9 gives a diagrammatic view of the extended model.

Assessment of the theory According to the expectancy model, individuals always seek to optimize the return on their effort investment. One illustration of this concept is to consider a manager faced with a crisis needing the staff to work late one night. Individuals will have completed their basic work commitments for the day and will have plans for the evening. If the manager is to achieve the objective it would be necessary to work through the path–goal for each person involved. For some, it might be the extra money, for others, it could be the thought of helping the boss out of a

FIGURE 11.9

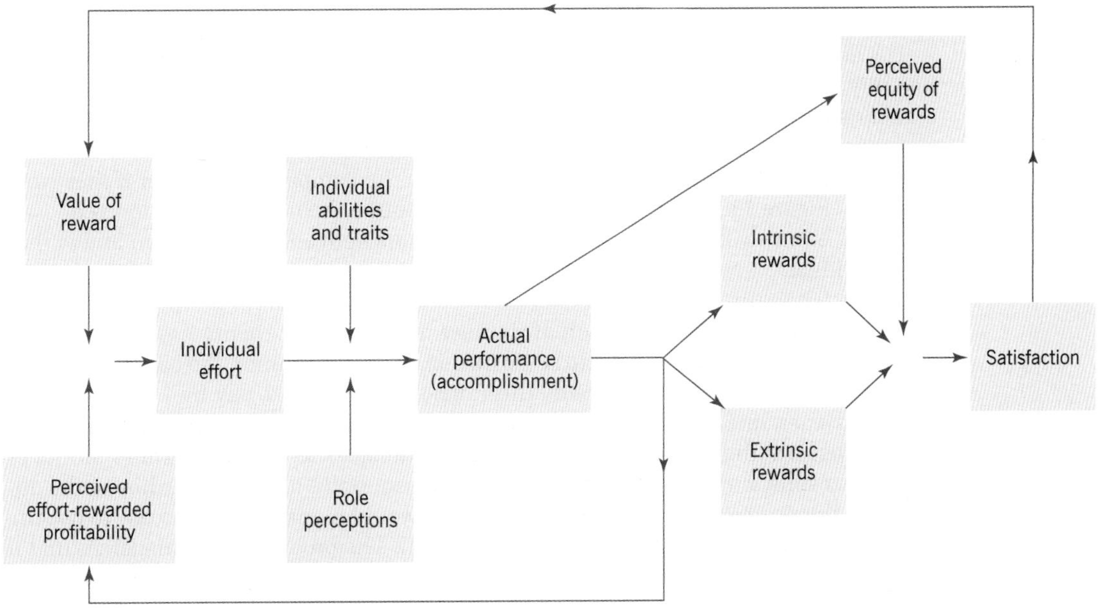

Porter and Lawler expectancy model

difficult position, for yet others, it could be ensuring that the department maintains a high reputation with customers, the point being that it will vary for every person, and every person will evaluate for themselves the balance of rewards, effort and probability of receipt. This represents a complex process for both managers and employees.

One of the implications of this theory is that managers must seek ways of strengthening the links between effort, performance and reward. Rewards should be linked to the things that employees value. In order to apply this approach, managers need to be able to identify the employee calculus in order to be able to design appropriate arrangements. Because of the many and varied components in the equation, together with the changeable nature of it, this would become an almost impossible task to achieve with any accuracy. The complexity in attempting to apply the theory is reflected by Hollenback (1979) in which matrix algebra was needed to deal with the number and combination of variables.

Adams' equity theory

People develop strong feelings about the relative fairness of the treatment that they receive at work. When reaching a conclusion on fairness, individuals need a point of reference against which to judge what they actually experience. The main source of such comparisons being the perceived treatment of other people. This formed the basis of the equity approach to motivation (Adams, 1965), based on social exchange theory. This model suggests that individuals operate social interactions as a form of trading. In effect, balance sheet approaches in which individuals invest in relationships to the extent that they anticipate an equitable return.

Equity theory in motivation is therefore part of an evaluation and investment process. The most obvious application of these ideas lies in the field of financial reward. Every employee is paid a wage or salary together with a range of additional benefits and these provide many opportunities for comparison. Examples of the different opportunities that exist for making comparisons include other employees performing the same job, the same job in other companies, friends, neighbours and professional colleagues. Industrial relations specialists are well aware of the issue of equity in pay comparisons. Management in Action 11.3 illustrates the concept of equity in a particular context.

For Adams, the process of comparing can produce two possible outcomes, equity or inequity. Equity is achieved when a perceived balance between the individual and the comparison target is achieved. Inequity arises when the balance is disturbed in either a positive or negative direction. The individual would feel that an inequitable situation existed if, for example, they were paid more than the comparator, not just if they were paid less. Figure 11.10 reflects the operation of equity theory. Which option is chosen to restore equity will depend on a number of factors active in the situation and within the individual.

Assessment of the theory Much of the research on equity theory has concentrated on its application to pay and rewards. Dornstein (1989) examined the basis of comparison in people's judgements about the fairness of received pay and found that it changed depending on a number of factors. Research in Hong Kong by Law and Wong (1998) suggests that the use of different methodologies to explore fairness produces differing results, further clouding the issue. Consequently, it is not clear how individuals apply the principles of equity theory; neither would managers find it easy to be sure that equity was being achieved for each individual. The problem for managers is that it is for each employee to undertake the evaluation of what 'equity' means for them. Managers are not in a position to judge on behalf of employees what determines an equitable situation, they cannot know against what or whom the comparison is being

MANAGEMENT IN ACTION 11.3 Moving tale of a fair day's work

Furnham reports the experience of a group of underwriters in the USA who were forced to move offices during a refurbishment programme. Among the group of underwriters were varying degrees of seniority, yet all performed at approximately the same level before the move. As a result of the reassigned work places some staff moved into an office previously allocated to someone of a higher grade, some moved into offices previously inhabited by staff of a lower grade and others were allocated offices appropriate to their seniority. The productivity of staff allocated lower status offices dropped dramatically. Conversely, staff allocated offices of a higher status dramatically increased their productivity. Staff allocated to appropriate office accommodation stayed at the pre-move levels of productivity.

Furnham provides one explanation for this phenomenon through the concept of equity. He suggests that there are three possible approaches to the determination of what it is right to expect in relation to exchanging work and reward:

- *Equality*. Imagine a group of friends who go out for a meal and order what they wish from the menu and drink as they see fit. The bill at the end of the meal could be split equally between all the friends irrespective of what each individual actually spent. Those who choose modestly subsidize those who have expensive inclinations.
- *Taxation*. This would suggest that food and drink consumption should be separated from payment responsibilities. The greediest (or hungriest) should order as they wish. The bill, however, would be split according to ability to pay, the wealthiest having to bear the heaviest responsibility for their contribution.
- *Equity*. This approach requires each individual to show restraint in ordering both food and drink to comply with the desires of the group to fund the evening. Equity requires that no individual is markedly out of line compared to the others in both consumption of food and drink and payment of an equal share.

Of the three approaches the equity view tends to be the most commonly found. The taxation option is the least popular – apart from those individuals who deliberately seek advantage from a situation. In the case of the underwriters moving offices it is suggested that they each reviewed the rewards received (the office allocated) for the input of work expected and adjusted their work activity to match the perceived value of the offices provided.

Adapted from: Furnham, A (1993) Moving tale of a fair day's work, *Financial Times*, 24 March, p 14.

Stop ↔ Consider

Attempt to interpret the results described above using each of the motivation theories so far discussed. To what extent could they provide equally satisfactory explanations for the behaviour of the underwriters? What might this suggest about motivation theory in general?

made. However, more recent work in this area suggests that individuals use both instrumental and value-expressive standards when evaluating the fairness of pay procedures (Jones *et al.*, 1999), a clear implication of this being that not only does pay need to be allocated fairly, but the pay allocation procedures need to be perceived to be fair by those subject to them.

Working relationships are much less personal than those based on friendship and it is less likely that the same level of commitment to work based relationships exists (Campbell and Pritchard, 1974). Consequently, it is argued that the perception of inequity will be reduced in a work context when overpayment is involved. It is more likely that in their own work context individuals will change the basis of their view of what forms an equitable payment (Locke, 1976).

FIGURE 11.10

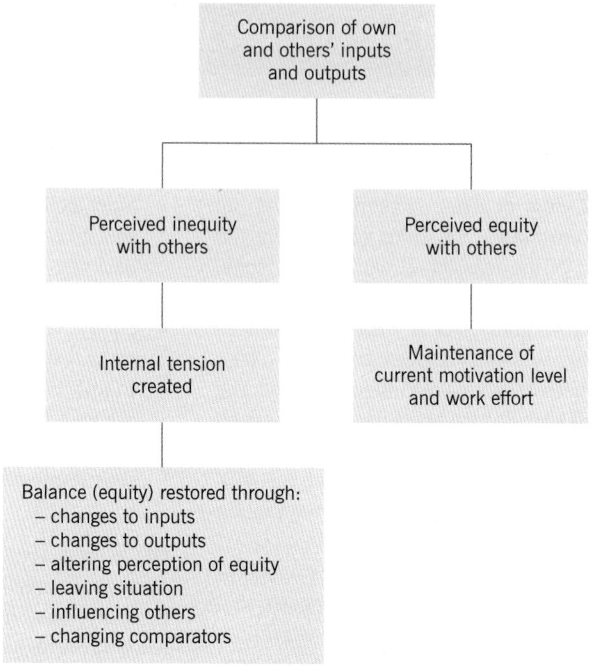

Adams' equity theory

Even with the limitations described, the model provides a useful mechanism for considering the significance of equity between employees along with the implications for motivation and performance of failing to achieve a perception of it. These points are particularly relevant to the subject of pay and other tangible rewards. The theory implies that organizations should give close attention to the comparison process when designing pay structures, incentive schemes, merit awards and even promotion, the key being that perceived equity exists for the individual, which is not the same as the actual equity. The earlier chapter on perception (Chapter 3) provides enough basis for understanding the significance of it as a personal and largely subjective interpretation process rather than a simple registration of facts or reality.

Locke's goal theory

Locke (1968) suggested that people's objectives play a significant part in formulating their behavioural patterns. In a work context, this can be used as a mechanism to motivate people to deliver desired behaviours. For the process to work it is necessary that organizations are able to deliver the objectives that employee's desire. It is used as the basis of performance appraisal systems which attempt to shape employee behaviour and achieve improved performance. The essence of the process being that employees who meet the performance standards expected by management are likely to be rewarded with higher salary, career development opportunities or promotion. These are all objectives that most people value (the reason why that might be so represents an interesting question in its own right, but is beyond the scope of this discussion). Performance appraisal systems are a formal feedback mechanism to direct employee behaviour towards the achievement of management determined objectives. A generalized model of goal theory is shown as Figure 11.11. Note 'goal deficiency' in the model refers to the level of desire in the individual to achieve the goal.

FIGURE 11.11

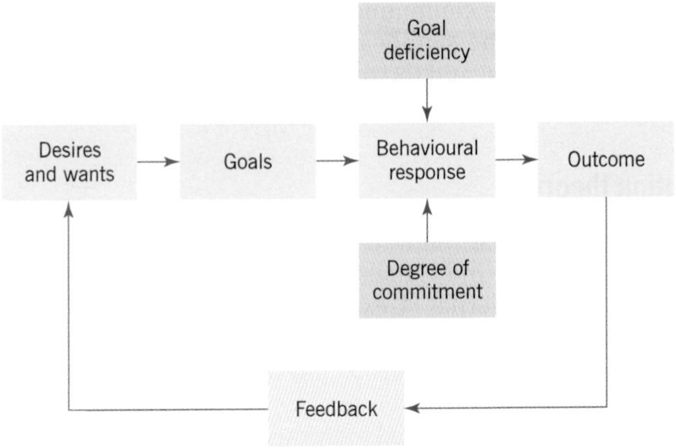

Goal theory

Within the model there are a number of issues surrounding the notion of goal setting and feedback that can significantly influence the outcome. They include:

- The more specific the goal the more likely it is to be achieved.
- The completion requirement (finish date) should be specific.
- Goals that are difficult to achieve are more likely to be achieved than easy ones.

In modern performance appraisal use these ideas have been refined into the so-called **SMART objectives** that form the basis of determining performance objectives. The acronym SMART stands for setting objectives that are **s**pecific, **m**easurable, **a**ttainable, **r**ealistic and **t**ime bounded (Armstrong and Murliss, 1998, p 247).

SMART objectives
Refers to objectives that are Specific, Measurable, Attainable, Realistic and Time bounded.

Assessment of the theory There have been a number of studies of goal-setting approaches to motivation (for example Early *et al.*, 1990; Erez *et al.*, 1985 and Shalley *et al.*, 1987). This idea has also been studied in relation to personal motivation to learn through educational or work based training programmes, see for example Little (2003). Generally the results have been supportive of the approach, but raise questions that remain unanswered. For example, what degree of subordinate involvement is required in setting goals to achieve optimal results? Another outstanding issue is the need to understand the process through which the behavioural impetus of the employee is maintained once the goals have been agreed.

Issues such as individual difference, personality, previous experience, education and training and career path are among the factors that could be assumed to have an effect on the validity of the goal-setting model. These aspects also remain to be researched in any depth. The approach is widely used as the basis of performance appraisal systems, particularly where projects, tangible results or change are features of the job. However, the model does have limitations. Some jobs are not amenable to goal setting (for example, assembly line tasks and call centre activities). With an increasingly turbulent operating environment being common for many organizations, goals are subject to frequent change. This makes it increasingly difficult for individuals to maintain performance targeted at specific goals over an extended period. Goal setting represents an individual level process, but most tasks within an organization require groups of people to co-operate in order to achieve them. This reality of organizational life means that it is frequently difficult to provide enough individual control over work activity to be certain that goal theory is effectively motivating behaviour. One area where this might be more effective is in the sales area. Evenson (2003) proposes a number of actions that are necessary for the effective motivation of sales personnel including the need for effective communication between manager and sales personnel so that the goals are clear; the significance of positive feedback in directing their efforts towards particular goals; and the use of rewards to focus on the achievement of objectives.

Kelly's attribution theory

Attribution theory suggests that motivation is a response by the individual to a self-perception of their behaviour. Individuals decide (through perception) whether their behaviour is responding to internal or external influences. On the basis of this decision, the individual will decide whether or not they prefer to be intrinsically or extrinsically motivated. The result of this decision affects the form of motivation that will be effective for that individual (Kelly, 1971).

The effect of an intrinsically motivated individual being managed within a regime that was based on extrinsic motivation was studied by Deci (1971). He found that such individuals subsequently became extrinsically motivated. Wiersma (1992) concluded that the links between extrinsic and intrinsic motivation were complex and could work against each other in particular situations. It is argued that intrinsic motivation provides the 'best' approach to obtaining a totally effective employee, one who will perform well and take pride in producing good quality work. However, many motivation strategies rely on incentive schemes or other extrinsic principles to motivate employees through tangible rewards. The criticism of such approaches being that they purchase output, generating at best an instrumental or compliance response. The earlier points made in relation to employee control by management and framing the reality within which performance is defined in this context are also pertinent to this discussion.

ADDITIONAL PERSPECTIVES ON MOTIVATION

McGregor's Theory X and Theory Y

McGregor (1960) explicitly introduced a particular set of underlying assumptions concerning human nature into motivation when he proposed the notion of Theory X and Theory Y. His claim was that managers tend to hold beliefs that classify employees into either a Theory X or Theory Y category. Consequently, managers operate policies and practices (including motivation) that are based on one or other of these sets of assumptions (see Figure 11.12).

In essence McGregor implies that motivational practice is in real danger of becoming a self-fulfilling prophecy as employees respond to the reality created for them, points that would be supported by the work of Deci (1971) and Townley (1994), already introduced.

Ouchi's Theory Z

Ouchi investigated the ways in which Japanese and US managers managed their subordinates. In doing so he identified a number of cultural differences between the two:

- American organizations
  - short-term employment
  - explicit control processes
  - individual decision making

FIGURE 11.12

Theory X

1 The average man is by nature indolent – he works as little as possible.
2 He lacks ambition, dislikes responsibility, prefers to be led.
3 He is inherently self-centred, indifferent to organizational needs.
4 He is by nature resistant to change.
5 He is gullible, not very bright, the ready dupe of the charlatan and the demagogue.

The implications for management are:

1 Management is responsible for organizing the elements of productive enterprise – money, materials, equipment, people – in the interests of economic ends.
2 With respect to people, this is a process of directing their efforts, motivating them, controlling their actions, modifying their behaviour to fit the needs of the organization.
3 People must be persuaded, rewarded, punished, controlled, their activities must be directed.

Theory Y

1 People are not by nature passive or resistant to organizational needs. They have become so as a result of experience in organizations.
2 The motivation. The potential for development, the capacity to assume responsibility, the readiness to direct behaviour towards organizational goals, are all present in people. It is a responsibility of management to make it possible for people to reorganize and develop the human characteristics for themselves.
3 Management is responsible for organizing the elements of productive enterprise in the interest of economic ends. Their essential task is to arrange the conditions and methods of operation so that people can achieve their own goals best by directing their own efforts towards organizational objectives.

McGregor's Theory X and Theory Y (*source*: McGregor, D (1960) *The Human Side of Enterprise*, McGraw-Hill, New York)

  - individual responsibility
  - segmented concern
  - quick promotion
  - specialized careers.
- Japanese organizations
  - lifetime employment
  - implicit control processes
  - collective decision making
  - collective responsibility
  - holistic concern
  - slow promotion
  - generalist careers.

From these profiles it is possible to identify a number of implications for motivational practice. Ouchi developed his Theory Z on motivation from the work of McGregor on Theories X and Y, suggesting that it would tend towards the Japanese profile, for example, adopting longer term employment contracts, but not as long as the Japanese version (Ouchi, 1981).

Hofstede, Trompenaars and cultural influences on motivation

Hofstede (1980) introduced the impact of national culture into the debate about motivation. In his research he used the following framework to study the differences between 40 countries:

- *Power distance.* Reflects the degree to which a society accepts that organizational power is distributed unequally.
- *Uncertainty avoidance.* Reflects the extent to which a society feels threatened by uncertainty and ambiguity and actively seeks to minimize these situations.
- *Individualism–collectivism.* This reflects the underlying arrangement of society into a loose (everyone is responsible for themselves) framework; or an integrated, tight social arrangement involving collective responsibility.
- *Masculinity.* This reflects the degree of domination of society's values by 'masculine' characteristics.

In his research he put forward the idea that each of the theories of motivation reflected a particular set of cultural norms. As such they could be expected to be most effective in situations reflecting that particular cultural orientation. This introduces into the debate on motivation the notion that the wide range of theories available may not be mutually exclusive. His work has been subjected to heavy criticism recently, largely because his research was based on employees from a single company (IBM). The argument being that all being from a single very large company, the people would have a high degree of commonality across all countries, compared with people from the different national groups researched. A more recent cultural perspective is offered by Trompenaars (1993) in which he offers seven different dimensions of national culture which could impact on organizational behaviour, including motivation. For example, some societies rely on achievement as a measure of success, whereas others prefer an emphasis on age, experience, etc.

Maccoby's social theory

A different approach to the concept of motivation is offered by Maccoby (1988). He argues that the social and work environments have changed over recent years, particularly as a result of the growth of new technology. The effect of this has in practice invalidated the relevance of traditional approaches to motivation. He argues that a new motivation theory is needed, based not upon the partial man assumptions of Maslow, but specifically including concepts of trust, caring, meaning, self-knowledge and dignity. Emerging is a new type of worker it is argued, interested in self-development and motivated by opportunities for self-expression and career development, combined with a fair share of profit. In a variation of this theme, Qubein (2003) puts forward ten ideas that are intended to enhance motivation levels which are based on recognition that motivation does not exist in isolation from other aspects of the social environment at work. His ideas are:

1. *All people are motivated.* The manager has to provide the opportunity to express it and also clear direction.
2. *People do things for their own reasons.* The manager has to show people the personal benefits that will accrue as a result of doing things that benefit the company.

3. *People change because of pain.* People don't generally like change, but will change when the 'pain' of staying the same outweighs the 'pain' associated with change.
4. *The key to effective communication is identification.* Managers need to identify with the employees in order to understand their perspective and to be able to explain to them what is needed and why it is the appropriate course of action for company and employee.
5. *The best way to get people to pay attention to you is to pay attention to them.* Paying attention is about listening, not just hearing. Hearing is a passive process, listening means to engage with the other person and what they are saying. Listening leads to understanding and hence to the ability to develop appropriate motivation strategies.
6. *Pride is a powerful motivator.* Pride and self-esteem go together. Giving employees self-esteem and pride in what they do will ultimately result in them providing improved services to customers.
7. *You can't change people; you can only change their behaviour.* Managers cannot change the people at a fundamental level, all they can hope to achieve is to direct the behaviour of employees into appropriate patterns. This implies that attitudes and beliefs need to be addressed as part of the process of seeking to establish suitable behaviour patterns.
8. *The employee's perception becomes the executive's reality.* People react to the world around them, including other people and management, on the basis of their perception and interpretation of what they see. These perceptions are not likely to be the same as those held by managers. Consequently, managers need to understand the employee's frame of reference and seek to work with that reality in developing appropriate motivational strategies.
9. *You consistently get the behaviours you consistently expect and reinforce.* Managers should seek ways to reinforce those behaviours that they want to occur.
10. *We judge ourselves by our motives or intentions; but we judge others by their behaviours or actions.* If a manager is late for work they would tend to justify it on the basis of urgent tasks at home, or heavy traffic etc. If an employee is late for work it tends to be judged as a reflection of a poor attitude or they are being irresponsible. Managers should try to deal only with what occurs – the actual behaviour – not impute reasons and causes that are essentially irrelevant. It is desirable behaviour that delivers motivation through actual achievement.

This approach to motivation, put more directly as getting the best out of employees, gains some credence in a review of business and management practice in *Management Today* in 1999. The main themes and arguments from that article are outlined in Management in Action 11.4.

PERFORMANCE MANAGEMENT AND MOTIVATION

The management of performance is a major issue for managers in the search for stable and high levels of productivity. One way of achieving this is through the achievement of a controlled performance from individuals. To see this in context, imagine a team sport where each member of the team played at their own speed, not delivering a consistent effort. The result would be a team that did not win many games. It is the

MANAGEMENT IN ACTION 11.4 Can nice guys finish first?

The most common perspective on management is that it reflects hard-nosed, ruthless, aggressive and brutal decision making in pursuit of the highest level of profit that can be achieved. In effect business leaders are regarded as driven individuals determined to succeed at any cost.

However, most chief executives when they are interviewed or provide material for research or magazine articles tend to describe their duties in terms of providing good working environments and looking after staff. For example, Peter Mead of Abbot Mead Vickers (a leading advertising agency) refused to retrench staff during the last recession and also refuses work associated with cigarette promotion. The idea of niceness is not new. For example in the 1970s JW Marriot, who founded the hotel chain of that name, was saying: 'You can't make happy guests with unhappy employees'.

There is even support from the sciences for the idea that niceness or co-operation between organisms could create advantage. Novak (a zoologist) and Sigmund (a mathematician) put forward the notion that doing good etc., even with no expectation of return (indirect reciprocity as they called it) could glean an advantage over more ruthless rivals. This was tested through a computer model that explored the ways in which groups developed, based on variation in co-operation and altruism levels. The model postulated that the level of niceness would be reflected in the reputation of the individual among peers which would result in stored positive or negative goodwill. This would then be capable of being cashed in at some time in the future to the benefit (or detriment) of the individual. Those with a good reputation would gain benefit. Conversely those with a bad reputation would suffer in the long run.

However, there is also research that suggests that organizations need to be tough to survive. Silvestro reviewed the performance of a number of stores in a large grocery chain. She found that at individual store level employee satisfaction and loyalty were positively correlated. However, low employee satisfaction correlated with high profitability and vice versa. Profit in stores is also strongly related to the size of the unit and this could also impact on a range of issues such as management style, closeness of supervision, workload, customer relationships, etc, all of which would be expected to impact on expressed loyalty and happiness. This research suggests that commercial reality might force niceness out of the situation. Add to this the effects of downsizing and delayering on morale, trust and commitment and the scene is set for what Lynn refers to the senior management attitude as being: 'Do what you can, but look after yourself first'. He concludes (rather cynically) with the view that perhaps the best strategy is to use public relations more effectively to bridge the gap between (or put a spin on) the two opposing realities.

Adapted from: Lynn, M (1999) Can nice guys finish first?, *Management Today*, February, pp 48–51.

Stop ↔ Consider

How would you reconcile the different points of view evident above? Is the answer to utilize PR techniques in an attempt to disguise (or put a spin on) the real management purpose behind seeking to achieve high levels of motivation and performance?

same within organizations; managers continually seek to achieve operational consistency. Naquin and Holton (2003) build on this by suggesting that motivation should include being motivated to use learning as a way of improving performance. In other words motivation can operate directly and indirectly on many aspects of human behaviour, including learning how to do things in a way which increases performance. This represents a view that implies an indirect relationship between motivation and behaviour. Looked at as a model this can be seen as a process of managing a number of variables concerned with motivation, performance management and rewards (see Figure 11.13).

Performance management as a process can be described as the links between a number of the boxes included in Figure 11.13. For example it seeks to provide

FIGURE 11.13

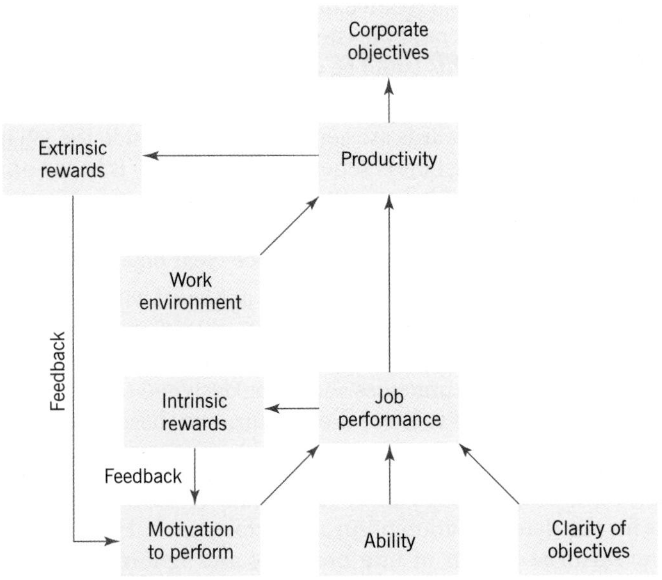

The links between motivation, performance and rewards

feedback on actual performance achieved while impacting on factors such as ability (through the identification of development needs) and setting clear objectives about what is expected from the employee in the future (clarity of objectives). It is also important to recognize that the situation and purpose of the performance measurement requires different measures of it to be adopted, Behn (2003). The model also reflects the cyclical process between motivation, reward, productivity and objectives. Taking each of the elements within the model in turn:

- *Work environment*. This refers to the physical circumstances in which the activities take place. The level of technology, methods of work used and equipment provided being examples.
- *Ability*. The skills and abilities that individual employees possess. This also reflects the organization's recruitment and selection processes along with its training and development provision.
- *Clarity of objectives*. If individuals are to be expected to achieve high levels of job performance they need to be provided with clear objectives. If the employee does not know what they are trying to achieve then anything will seem to be acceptable.
- *Motivation to perform*. This refers to the behavioural influences known as motivation. The precise content of which depends upon the particular drivers, needs and motives active at the time.
- *Job performance*. This relates to the observable activity level delivered by the individual. It would encompass not only the pace of work but also the quality of output produced. Job performance is a function of individual level activity. This has to be linked with environmental elements (such as machines and computer systems actually working as intended) in order to produce achieved productivity.
- *Intrinsic rewards*. Intrinsic rewards are those that accrue to the individual as a direct result of the job itself. Rewards obtained in this way act as internal reinforcement. Consequently, there is a feedback loop to motivation from intrinsic rewards.

- *Productivity*. Productivity is a relative or comparative term, a measure of conversion. For example it could measure the amount of goods produced for a particular input of labour, this could be compared with a figure from a previous time period to see if productivity was increasing or decreasing.
- *Extrinsic rewards*. Such rewards are generated from outside the job itself. The most obvious example being bonus schemes in which pay is based on output. These rewards are also intended to influence motivation and objectives. For an extrinsic reward system to be effective the individual must have a good knowledge of the basis of any reward, and hence clear objectives.
- *Corporate objectives*. The level of productivity achieved will determine to a significant extent the degree to which corporate objectives are achieved. This last element also refers to the guiding principles within the model. Consequently, motivational practices should be designed to encourage the delivery of things that are of value to the organization, based on corporate goals.

Organizations vary in the degree to which they attempt to plan for future performance. At the simplest level the use of work study techniques to develop incentive schemes provides a basis for the determination of future performance. However this approach is based on the Taylorist notion of one best way and ignores the possibilities of **continuous improvement**. Other organizations use performance appraisal techniques in one form or another to assess individual contribution. Examples include 360° and team appraisal systems which seek to embrace a broad spectrum of measures in relation to individual or group performance. However, concern about the use of 360° feedback as part of a performance management process rather than as pure development has been expressed by writers such as Fletcher (1998). Whatever the approach adopted it is necessary that the employee can clearly see the links between the effort they put into work and the rewards that they obtain. This Lawler (1995) described as the line of sight model. The 'line of sight' beginning with the effort delivered by the employee, leading to job performance; in turn leading to results being achieved; leading to those results being measured and resulting in the reward being obtained by the employee. The following Employee Perspective (11.4) reflects one situation in which the organization seems to have lost sight of motivation, leadership and the effects on performance.

Continuous improvement
An approach based on incremental and frequent changes aimed at improving effectiveness over a long period of time.

Another approach found in many organizations over recent years is that based upon the concept of competencies (defined as 'behavioural dimensions that affect job performance' (Woodruffe, 1990, p 47). This approach seeks to encourage the consid-

EMPLOYEE PERSPECTIVE 11.4 Practise what you preach

The following comments were made by an employee about their company:

> I work for a management consultancy that gives great advice to its clients but cannot seem to take its own medicine. Our offices are riddled with communication problems, clashing agendas, and backstabbing. It's becoming increasingly hard for some of us who work there to give clients sane advice before returning to the chaos of the office. How can I nudge my senior colleagues into practising what they preach, without rocking the boat still further?

Tasks

1. What advice would you give the employee and why?
2. What does this situation suggest about motivation, leadership and performance within this organization?
3. You might like to compare your advice with that given by Bullmore, J in What's your problem?, *Management Today*, November (2003), p 125.

eration of personal development as the basis of future performance enhancement. Dulewicz (1989) indicates one set of competency clusters for middle management jobs based upon intellectual, interpersonal, adaptability and results orientation factors. Other writers suggest different competencies as the basis of what determines effective capability and performance for particular jobs. The application of competency frameworks seeks to identify and monitor the actual behaviours necessary for an individual to carry out their allotted tasks effectively. As such it retains the traditional (Taylorist) perspective of seeking to optimize the whole through optimizing the performance of the individual. Many of the motivation theories discussed in this chapter could be used in support of such approaches.

Although the competency approach has the advantage of being behaviour based, if not carefully designed it could ignore the creative and team aspects of many jobs. However these aspects or work are now generally incorporated into the competency frameworks of organizations for which these represent important aspects of work. Motivation is consequently integral to the process of review and development as a means of the individual being encouraged to deliver what is expected of them. It is managers who determine what behaviour is expected and also they who evaluate delivery. Subsequent access to career development opportunities is also a function of management sponsorship, which in turn is dependent upon being evaluated as a 'worthy person' for such investment. As a consequence there are power, political and control (as well as performance and development) aspects to performance management processes. Figure 11.14 reflects the competency process in action along with an indication of the areas of motivational influence. Kaplan and Norton (1996) proposed the use of a **balanced business scorecard** as the means to enable a review four major aspects of organizational performance. They are:

Balanced business scorecard
Reflection of business performance in four major areas: Financial; Innovation and learning; Internal processes; and Customers.

1. Financial
2. Innovation and learning
3. Internal processes
4. Customers.

These macro level dimensions can form the basis of assessing the organization's performance relative to its objectives. This could subsequently form the basis of cascading downwards the organization level goals (with appropriate measures) and actual performance as part of the performance management process. In short, the performance of individuals needs to be seen as part of a broader process of organizational performance. There are different ways in which this can be interpreted. For example, Clarke (2003) proposes a list of seven core measures of business activity (demand-forecast accuracy, lead time reduction, and on-time delivery of new product introduction, for example). The seven measures are based around business activities and do not directly address the human issues, although they are implicit in the actual performance achieved. An alternative approach was developed through research carried out by the Tavistock Institute which demonstrates that global pressure influences both organizational frameworks and the moves towards the need for high performance working (Stern and Somerlad, 1999). The Institute of Personnel and Development in association with the International Labour Organization (part of the UN) suggests that high performance working can be defined in the following terms (Stevens and Ashton, 1999):

- Sustained market success (or achievement of organizational objectives).
- Innovation in quality and customer satisfaction (or product or service differentiation).
- Customer and continuous improvement focus.

FIGURE 11.14

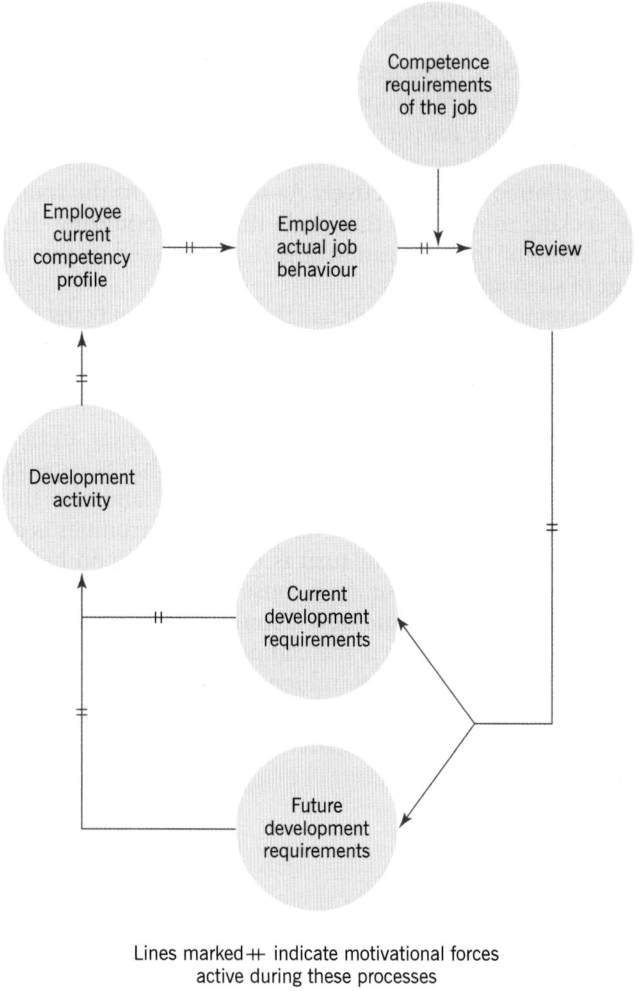

Competency processes and motivation

- Use of self-managed work teams.
- Viewing the workplace as a source of added value.
- Clear links between training and development and organizational objectives.
- Support for organizational and individual learning.

More recent developments in performance management systems and techniques are moving a considerable distance from the original notion of Taylor and the earlier motivation theorists. Also a richer, more complex understanding about the nature of work and what performance actually means is slowly emerging. The definition of high performance working described earlier is based on completely different assumptions about what performance means for the organization compared to that based on individual performance. The more recent work described seeks to take a more obviously holistic and top-down view of performance and the links with motivation. However, that in itself does not eliminate difficulties or problems. For example, improved understanding of motivation could provide managers with more control over employees, leading towards that aspect of the definition of the word perform introduced at the beginning of this chapter which talks of it being to 'execute tricks at a public show'!

MOTIVATION AND PERFORMANCE MANAGEMENT: AN APPLIED PERSPECTIVE

Motivation is an individual level phenomenon, but the level of it is influenced by many factors. The level of motivation that people hold can be reflected on a scale running from not motivated to highly motivated as in Figure 11.15.

All motivation theories allow for the existence of cognitive processes. Content theories adopt the needs and wants perspective and process theories concentrate on the decision making that guides behaviour. The common factor with both categories is that individual behaviour is motivated towards the achievement of goals. From an organizational perspective it is the goals that are important, not the level of motivation that delivers them. Motivation is the means through which performance is achieved. It reflects how effectively the goals will be achieved and in that sense is the basis of the corporate desire to maximize performance through various management techniques.

Motivation is grounded in internal cognitive processes that are not available for direct inspection. Consequently in order to assess the level of individual motivation, inferences must be drawn from observable activity. Human beings are employed to achieve organizationally determined objectives, irrespective of any personal wants or desires that might determine the level of motivation. In that sense their behaviour is subject to direction and manipulation in pursuit of those objectives. This adds additional complexity to the use of the concepts of motivation and performance for a number of reasons:

- *Managerial assumptions*. Managers cannot be aware of why individuals are behaving as they are, so wrong assumptions may be made. For example, work behaviour will be subject to motivational forces from outside the organization as well as inside it.
- *Situational context*. Employees who have never been given any degree of involvement in the organizational decision making may find participative management styles motivating. However, when memories begin to fade the basis of comparison will change. Employees will see participation as the norm and it will become a frame of reference against which to interpret future events.
- *Personal preference*. Not all individuals actively seek increased levels of motivation at work. Some employees will see work as instrumental to the support of other aspects of their life. Lee and Lawrence (1985) suggest a four-factor model of decision-based motivation based on the goals sought, strategies adopted, coalitions formed and the power available through which to achieve the desired goals.
- *Instrumentality*. Managers can mistake instrumental behaviour for motivated behaviour. One survey showed that more than 40 per cent of workers were worried about losing their jobs during the following 12 months (Summers, 1993). This might imply a compliant workforce, adopting an instrumental approach to work in co-operating with managers, and thereby (hopefully) avoid losing their jobs. Managers on the other hand might think that the workforce is highly motivated and keen to achieve success.

FIGURE 11.15

The motivation scale

- *Bio-social basis of behaviour.* The needs and wants held to underpin motivation are not themselves constructs that are problem free. In order to function biologically humans need certain things such as food and sleep. However, beyond these basic requirements, many needs are socially determined. For example, what type of food, how much quantity, how should it be cooked and served? This makes it difficult to know why individuals are motivated by certain things and how long that form of motivation might last.
- *Motivated to do what?* What are employees being motivated to achieve? It could be argued that the organizational purpose of motivation is to provide the highest levels of customer service, but is that so? The customer is simply one of many stakeholders linked to an organization each with expectations and degrees of influence. Consequently, they are motivated to do what is usually a reflection of that which has been determined by management. This is particularly true when it comes to the issue of performance management as the process though which to measure the level of motivation delivered.
- *What is performance?* Again this appears to be an easy question to answer, at least superficially. However, consider the university experience of students. What defines a high-performing lecturer? One who produces the highest marks among students, one who gives the most entertaining lectures, one who teaches the most students, or one who produces the most research? The answer lies in the minds of the many different people interested in some aspect of lecturer activity. In other words there can be many different definitions of performance. However in most organizations it is management that creates the definition of performance that will be used to measure employee activity. Performance as defined by managers is not always the same as performance as defined by the employee.

Society determines many aspects of life that are classified as a basic need. For example, televisions are now essential to life compared with 40 years ago. A Marxist analysis would bring into question motivation grounded on needs that are socially derived and which are then used as the basis of forcing individuals to increase their effort within the capitalist system. The argument is approximately thus: individuals need money to live, they are forced (in a capitalist system) to earn that money by working for the owners of capital who exploit them through various management control devices. They are then persuaded by clever sales and marketing processes into believing that they should desire particular goods and services, thereby the money that they earn is diverted back into the hands of the capital owners further enriching them. This, it would be argued, is a circular process in which the individual is trapped into meeting the ever increasing demands of the capital owners. This reflects the manipulation of both consumption and work practice by the owners of capital to their own advantage. It has been argued that motivation only became an organizational issue when meaning was lost from work: 'In consequence, motivation theories have become surrogates for the search for meaning' (Seivers, 1986). This point becomes more apparent in the motivational ideas expressed in Management in Action 11.5.

It is reasonable to suggest that a motivated individual will feel a higher level of commitment to work; sometimes this is described as ownership of a particular set of tasks. Many recent management writers suggest that higher levels of ownership are desirable. However, in that context ownership is taken (by managers at least) to refer to the task and a responsibility to produce high quality; not company ownership. Even when share options exist only a very small proportion is usually owned by employees. In effect managers expect employees to act as if they actually owned part of the process, even though that is clearly not the case. The potential problem for managers with ownership in this context is that individuals might begin to claim ownership of

MANAGEMENT IN ACTION 11.5 A cold feat

Rupert (bear) Grylls was the youngest person to have climbed Mount Everest at the age of 23. Grylls nearly died twice on that climb, once when a massive sheet of ice over a ravine gave way and secondly when his oxygen ran out on the descent when he was still in the 'death zone' above 26 000 feet. Four people in his party of climbers died during that expedition. He is well used to danger and having the need for motivation having spent three years with the British Special Forces during which he broke his back in three places when a parachute failed. He spent 18 months in rehabilitation as a consequence and only the dogged determination of himself, his family and friends meant that he regained the ability to walk. His latest adventure was to sail round the arctic circle in an inflatable boat with four other people. To fund this adventure he has had to raise £300 000 in sponsorship money, which he has done in nine months.

In a talk to the Chartered Institute of Personnel and Development's Annual Conference and Exhibition in October 2003, he will pass on his key message about motivation and superior team performance in difficult conditions as being:

- Look after each other.
- By giving a little extra you can turn the ordinary into the extraordinary.
- Give your whole heart to the project.
- Using your passion you can create magic.

Grylls believes that we live in a culture in which people are afraid to take risks in any area of our lives and that it is taking risks that brings the highest rewards.

Adapted from: Glover, C (2003) A cold feat, *People Management*, 28 August, pp 22–3.

Stop ↔ Consider

How might the ideas of Grylls be turned into motivational practice by managers working in conventional organizations?
To what extent do the views of Grylls suggest a search for deeper meaning from life and the activities engaged in during life and not just those in relation to work?

the total activity and attempt to divest management of its presumed right of overall control. Garrahan and Stewart (1992) provide a review of more recent motivational practices, such as teamworking, quality circles and company culture. These are practices frequently associated with Japanese organizations or European and US organizations attempting to emulate them. In their description, the negative impact on the individuals can clearly be identified through increased stress reported by some employees and descriptions of a take it or leave it style on management's part.

Increased productivity is the major management objective sought in an attempt to achieve corporate goals (at least according to the rational model of organizations). Motivation is a mechanism through which this is achieved and rewards are the device through which motivation can be triggered. In this way motivation can be seen as a manipulation device in pursuit of management's goals. For managers there is a wide range of motivational options available. It could be argued that every aspect of the experience (real or perceived) in the workplace influences the motivation level of the people within it. Indeed this could be expanded to encompass events and situations outside the immediate working environment including:

- *Family relationships and events.* Crises at home can easily divert the energies of individuals away from work activities for example.
- *The local community.* A win by the local football team can have beneficial effects, although the effect is far from certain, as Moreton (1993) suggests.

- *Commercial environment*. The closure of a competitor can help to secure the jobs in other organizations. Equally a negative change in the exchange rate could make jobs less secure for a company heavily dependent on exports.

Most of these would only be expected to have an indirect effect on motivation within an organization and then for only a relatively brief period. This illustrates the dynamic nature of much human behaviour and the circumstances within which it takes place, an issue not always apparent from specific motivation theories. Motivation is not something that is achieved and then fixed at that level. It is fluid, being subject to variation through the vast range of dynamic forces acting on the individual. This makes managing motivation difficult, as managers must be permanently sensitive to (and understand) their employees as individuals and adjust their own behaviour accordingly. Figure 11.16 seeks to reflect the processes involved in this circular and dynamic process. It also illustrates that managers are limited in the range of levers available to them in seeking to impact on the performance of employees.

Managers face major difficulties in attempting to motivate employees. To begin with, the construct of motivation is an abstract one. There are a number of theories offering a view on the nature and process of motivation but not all offer a realistic option for being able to motivate employees. Imagine attempting to apply the expectancy model calculation for each employee on a regular basis! Finally, managers individually do not have complete freedom to change company policy to a significant extent in order to personalize motivational opportunities. Although motivation is an individual level response, managers must maintain consistency in the treatment of employees across groups. It was to address this issue that the so-called **cafeteria or flexible benefits** approach was developed, the idea being that individuals are able to pick and mix a personal benefits package, up to a set limit, from

Cafeteria or flexible benefits
An approach that allows individuals to select items to a set limit from the total range available.

FIGURE 11.16

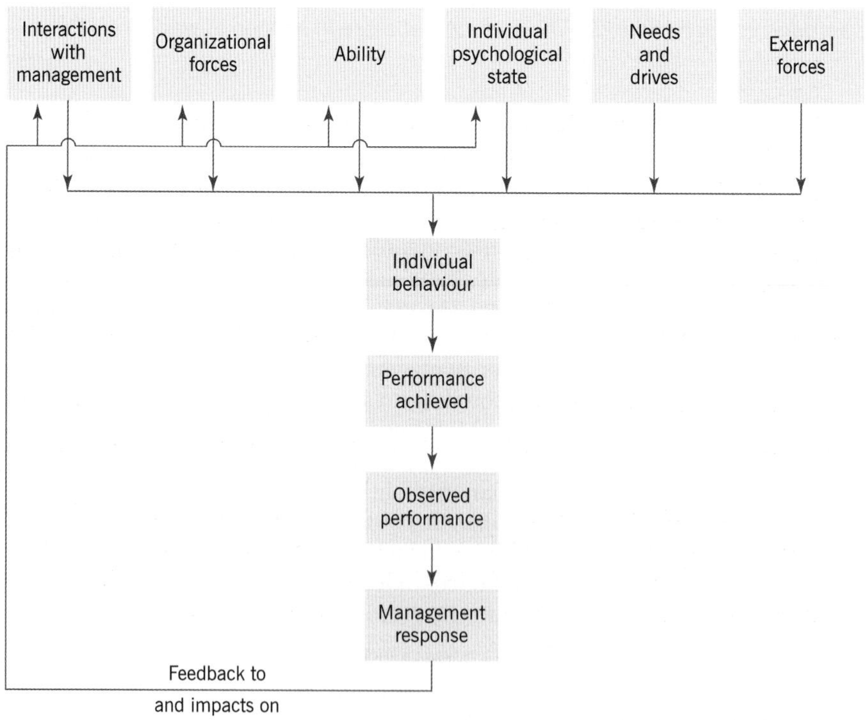

Management influence on motivation and performance

the total range available (Stock, 1992). In effect, a personalized benefits package, intended to optimize the motivational effect from collective arrangements, was established.

Another difficulty facing managers is deciding which theory to follow. Each has something to offer and brings a slightly different perspective to bear on the subject. The theories discussed predominantly originate from a western (USA) culture and may not be valid in other cultural settings. The meaning of work, acceptance of ambiguity and power distance could all be expected to play a part in determining a cultural perspective to motivation, according to Hodgetts and Luthans (1990). Because it can be difficult for managers to decide what theory to follow, this tends to provide a market for books and articles offering practical guidance on how to motivate people. One such article is offered by Browning (2003a) suggesting nine ways through which to motivate employees. Many of the ideas in this list have been introduced earlier in this (or other) chapters:

- *Be motivated yourself.* If the leader is enthusiastic then that is likely to rub off on employees.
- *Each to their own.* Each person is different and will be motivated by different things. Managers should find out what these are and use them.
- *Give them a challenge.* Targets should be hard, require effort but be achievable. Failure can be de-motivating.
- *Treat them with respect.* Demonstrating to people that you value them and their efforts is the bedrock of motivation.
- *Listen to them.* This is more than just hearing what people say, it involves understanding them and their views.
- *Help them learn.* Most people like learning something new, particularly if they think that it will be valuable to them in some way or other.
- *Welcome difficulty.* Solving problems can be a challenge and interesting. This can be motivating if the people involved gain a benefit (not necessarily financial) as a result of solving a work related problem.
- *Recognition.* Acknowledging that people have made a contribution is an important part of any reward system.
- *Raise the bar.* Try to eliminate (or reduce) the frequency of repetition of the same things every day. This is about setting new, interesting and more difficult challenges in order to motivate employees through keeping their interest and commitment.

The options (or levers) available to managers with which to influence levels of motivation include:

- *Pay levels and structures.* Also the other terms and conditions of employment.
- *Incentive schemes.* Including monetary, gift and prizes. Hilton (1992) reviews the use of non-financial incentives as a motivation facilitator.
- *Organizational factors.* The structure, job design and the way in which employees are integrated into the business processes (for example, decision making) can be adjusted to influence motivation levels.
- *Performance appraisal.* There are many of these systems, including management by objectives – MBO techniques.
- *Management style.*
- *Feedback, praise and punishment.*
- *Management by example.*

- *Company policies*. Issues such as compassionate leave, equal opportunities, study and further education possibilities can all affect employee motivation.

The wide range of motivation levers indicated above is another reason why it is difficult for managers to optimize motivational strategies and hence maximize performance. This basic complexity is increased further when interaction between the elements is taken into account. Managers do not have the opportunity to adjust all the levers potentially available, for the following reasons (see also Figure 11.16 in relation to this point):

- *Availability*. Not all organizations employ every option. Not every organization uses incentive schemes to reward higher output, for example.
- *Freedom of action*. Some levers are centrally determined and so individual managers do not have the discretion over how (or to whom) they are applied.
- *Personal preference*. Not every employee is equally amenable to the rewards on offer. For example, a young employee may be more interested in higher wages or career opportunities, whereas an older employee may be interested in pension and health related benefits.
- *Variability*. Employees vary each day in what will motivate them. These personal factors can be as simple as feeling unwell or perhaps feeling hostile to the organization as a result of a 'telling off' from the boss.
- *Group norms*. This and peer pressure can significantly influence the behaviour patterns of employees, irrespective of management's hopes and desires.
- *Procedural difficulties*. It is likely that a company will use a single performance management process for a particular group of employees, irrespective of the differences between the jobs within that group. So even though the set procedure might not completely match the performance realities of each job, the procedure will have to be used. This might mean that because of the process the true contribution of the employee might be undervalued or remain unrecorded and so directed towards 'appropriate performance' rather than 'true performance'.
- *Scale of effect not anticipated*. In situations in which it is intended to increase performance it is usual to reward people for the achievement of particular objectives. However, in some cases individuals can considerably exceed the expected output. This can cause difficulties for the individual, other employees and managers alike as it illustrated in the following Employee Perspective (11.5).

Another area of complexity in seeking to motivate employees is in the possible differences between the various generations within a particular society. Cordeniz (2002) suggests that within the UK the recruitment of nurses born between 1943 and 1960 (so called baby boomers) needs to be approached differently compared with nurses born between 1963 and 1977 (the so called generation X'ers). The main reason for the different recruitment emphasis being differences in the factors that motivate these two groups of people. According to Cordeniz, baby boomers value a collective, teamwork-based work environment and are motivated by independence, general goals and creativity. Generation X'ers on the other hand are individualists who care little about what others think and are motivated by recognition, opportunities to learn new things and constant stimulation. Not everyone accepts the existence of such sweeping classifications, but there are serious issues for managers to address if motivation does vary between people in this way as within any organization there are likely to be people from many different generations. The last point to make is that the approach to motivation and performance management within the organization needs to be reviewed and adapted in line with current needs on a regular basis. *HR Focus* (2003, a) suggests

EMPLOYEE PERSPECTIVE 11.5 Should I earn more than my boss?

The following question was posed by an employee:

> When I joined this company six months ago, I negotiated a deal where part of my pay would be performance-related, depending on new business I brought in. I've been more successful in this than expected, and my pay will soon top that of my boss. He doesn't know I know this, and has asked me to if I'll agree to decrease the proportion of my salary that is performance-related so it's more in line with other employees. I'm sure that it's actually because he doesn't want anyone to earn more than him. Should I confront him with this and refuse to change my set-up? The money itself is not important to me – it's the principle.

Tasks

1. What would you advise the employee to do and why?
2. What does this suggest about the design of incentive schemes and their relationship to motivation?
3. You might like to compare your advice with that of Bullmore, J in What's your problem?, *Management Today*, June (2003), p 85.

ten ways (developed by Mercer Human Resource Consulting) to improve the results achieved through performance management systems. They include:

- Secure the commitment and active participation of all company executives.
- Find appropriate metrics (what to measure and how to measure it).
- Build in the accountability of managers for effective use of the system.
- Integrate performance management with other business and human resource processes.
- Minimize the administrative burden of the system.
- Provide the necessary training and communication.
- Monitor results.
- Don't sit back. Seek to continuously improve the process.

CONCLUSIONS

Motivation is essentially an individual level response and yet managers must operate most of the time at a group level. Company policies and procedures have to be applied consistently if claims of inequity or injustice are to be avoided. This places a heavy burden on most managers as they attempt to increase the levels of performance among their employees by adopting individual, collective and personalized collective methods.

The general conclusion, therefore, seems to be that motivation is a concept that may be intuitively attractive in explanatory terms and offer some opportunity for managers to enhance the nature and meaning of work for individuals. However, it is not possible to offer a definitive definition of the concepts of motivation or performance, how they relate to each other, or how they should be used in practice. They are social and political concepts as well as being psychological and technical in nature. Their application represents another opportunity for creativity in the lives of managers as they seek to optimize corporate performance.

Now to summarize this chapter in terms of the relevant Learning Objectives:

- **Describe the major motivation theories and the ways in which they can be classified.** Motivation theories are usually split into two main groups, content and process types. Content theories concentrate on identifying the motives that produce behaviour, whereas process theories emphasize those mechanisms that encourage (or reward) behaviour in the dynamic context. There is a third group of motivation theories that is not really a group as such because they represent individual contributions to how motivation functions and do not fall neatly into either of the other two categories. The major content theories include those developed by Maslow, Alderfer, McClelland and Herzberg. The major process theories include those developed by Vroom, Porter and Lawler, Adams, Locke and Kelly. Among the other theories of motivation are models by McGregor, Ouchi, Hofstede and Trompenaars and Maccoby. Space precludes a description of each of these models, but they are summarized within the chapter.
- **Explain the relationship between motivation and employee performance.** The nature of the relationship between these two concepts is complex. It is generally assumed that higher performance is the result of higher levels of motivation, but the relationship is more complex than suggested by that simple equation. For example an employee might be motivated to work against the interests of the organization under some circumstances. If an employee feels that the company does not value their contribution or that they are being taken advantage of, then they might actively seek ways to frustrate the effective working of the company. Equally an employee might be highly motivated to work very hard and earn high bonuses in order to leave at the earliest opportunity to travel the world. As for performance, it is not always certain that management define the term in the same way that employees might. Therefore delivering high performance actually means delivering it as it would be recognized by management. It is about meeting management expectations rather than delivering performance *per se*. Also managers do not have complete freedom to personalize motivational practice; they must work within corporate policies to ensure collective consistency between employees. Although the two concepts of motivation and performance should strongly align, that is not automatically so and it is up to individual managers to find ways of working within the organizational constraints and ambiguities to ensure that the best match is found for the benefit of all parties.
- **Understand what makes the study of motivation difficult.** The fundamental reason that makes the study of motivation difficult is that it is a cognitive process that cannot be seen and therefore inference must be drawn from observable behaviour or answers to questions. Motivation is not something that can be physically taken apart and examined under a microscope in a laboratory. It is also subject to variation between individuals, groups, cultures and organizational experience. Because of the vast array of influences on how individuals relate to the work that they are expected to do and what it is that conditions them to produce particular behaviours in that context it is very difficult to identify through a single research approach how these processes function within each individual. Consequently, different approaches to the study of motivation can produce different models and also different cultures relate to the role of work in society differently all of which impacts on how motivation is thought to work.
- **Discuss the dilemmas and difficulties facing managers in applying motivation theory to a work setting.** The major dilemma facing managers as they seek to apply motivation theory is that of trying to personalize the approach adopted whilst staying within the boundaries of collective consistency required by corporate policy. A major difficulty for managers is which theory of motivation they should follow. There are many different models of motivation available and each has something to offer in relation to what it is and how it operates. Deciding which approach is most appropriate to the circumstances and individuals is no easy task. The manager's personal beliefs also play a significant part in their preference for which approach to motivation would offer the most effective way to capture high performance from employees – the essence of McGregor's Theory X and Theory Y model. Another area of difficulty is the variable meaning of performance for each of the stakeholders within the organization. This begs the question as to what performance the manager is seeking to maximize and what processes are they provided with in order achieve that objective.

- **Assess the links between motivation, performance management, pay determination, employee participation and job design.** The links between all of these variables are complex and yet they all contribute to the level of effectiveness that will be achieved by the employees in question. High performance is the overall objective being sought and it has already been seen just how problematic this concept can be. Therefore it is not clear that there would be a universally accepted view as to what high performance means in any particular work setting to begin with. Motivation is the process by which employees are encouraged to deliver high performance behaviours whilst actually at work. Again the complexity of motivation as a cognitive process has been demonstrated, further adding to the complexity of the relationship. Pay determination, employee participation and job design are specific areas which can contribute to levels of motivation in a positive or negative way. They are however only three of the many areas or work related experience that contribute to the motivation demonstrated by employees. They are however significant areas of activity for managers in seeking to achieve high and consistent levels of motivation. Pay determination represents one of the most significant areas of motivation practice. Wage and salary levels associated with incentive payments and performance based wage reviews are a major lever though which managers send signals to employees about their performance as judged by the manager. These judgements can have a major impact on the future level of motivation displayed by an employee. The level of employee participation in decision making allowed by the company can also impact on a wide range of reactions including motivation level and performance. Employees who do not understand what is going on within the company and why certain things take place are not in the best position to respond positively to management decisions. Equally employees are capable of offering a unique perspective on many aspects of company operations and therefore can play a useful part in the decision making of the company. Not every employee would wish to be involved in such processes, but those that do are likely to find them motivating. There is of course the danger that such involvement could be used to further the personal or political objectives of the individual and so it does not represent a panacea. Job design is of interest to all employees as most spend about eight hours each day on the tasks associated with it. Boring jobs can drag the levels of motivation down, but of course there is the issue of traction that it was suggested could deliver performance in such situations.

DISCUSSION QUESTIONS

1. Content theories offer a more realistic view of motivation compared to process theories in an organizational setting. Discuss.
2. If you were a manager, would you prefer to have your team extrinsically or intrinsically motivated? Why?
3. Motivation is best achieved through offering employees a monetary reward for working harder. Discuss this statement.
4. Are human needs socially, physiologically or psychologically determined? What are the implications for motivation?
5. Discuss what performance means to the 'job' of being a student. If you were a lecturer how would you measure student performance and why?
6. What is motivation? Describe two theories of motivation and suggest where you think they might be most useful. Justify your answer.
7. To what extent would you agree that the concepts of motivation and performance simply reflect management processes intended to exercise more effective control over employees in support of a managerialist agenda? Justify your answer.
8. It would be impossible for an organization fully to motivate all employees all the time. Discuss.
9. Compare and contrast one content theory of motivation and one process theory of motivation.
10. Motivation is an individual level phenomenon, yet managers must operate at a collective level in following company policies. Therefore because motivational practice cannot be personalized it is not possible to fully motivate every individual. Consequently it is not possible for organizations to achieve the highest levels of performance from all employees. Discuss this statement.

CASE STUDY Changes to the management of police services

The following case study in based upon the changes to how one divisional commander sought to arrange the provision of police services in her area. The events described took place in a large semi-rural police division based in Germany. The divisional commander was in charge of all police activity within the geographic area. Their job invariably required them to work a normal day shift pattern of 9.00 till 5.00 Monday to Friday. In addition to these hours they would be called out to take charge of serious incidents as necessary. The area included four medium sized towns with populations of between 50 000 and 200 000 each. It also included large areas of agricultural land and about 65 small to medium villages, each with less than 10 000 inhabitants. It was a large area with the problems that might be associated with trying to provide effective police cover over such a diverse community with the relatively small number of police officers allocated to the division. Being semi-rural it was not seen as attractive in career terms by many promotion minded officers, who preferred to be attached to the large cities and high profile specialist crime squads that sought to deal with large-scale crime and major inquiries.

Staff within the division were allocated to one of four shifts, each under the control of a shift commander. Each shift was in charge of all policing activity in the division for the duration of their shift. Within each shift team there were a number of sub-teams each under the leadership of a sergeant. The divisional commander would be called out if a significant event happened that needed a more senior officer to co-ordinate the police response, even if they were off duty at the time. This practice meant that the divisional commander had to be available 24 hours every day, 365 days each year, unless they appointed a deputy to cover for longer periods of absence, holidays or other reasons. This requirement was resented by the divisional commander because she found it disruptive and it often curtailed her private and social life. Consequently, she began to think how the system could be changed in order to maintain an effective policing service whilst reducing the demands on herself.

Eventually she identified what she thought was a workable staffing plan that would reduce the demands on herself and, she thought, improve the level of motivation among her subordinates. It would also, she thought assist junior officers to gain more managerial and strategic policing experience and so assist their promotion chances. The plan was based around the four sub-divisional shift teams that already existed and involved no changes to the shift patterns or management structures that were in place. The change involved introducing a geographic split of the division into four sub-divisions. Each of the four shift commanders was then given responsibility for primary policing within a specific geographic sub-division. The objective being to encourage each shift commander to develop a detailed knowledge of their allocated sub-division. This was a 24 hour, 365 day responsibility and in addition to their being in total charge of the division when their particular shift was on duty. The rules for calling out a senior officer were also changed. Instead of the divisional commander being called out when a serious problem arose, the shift commander was instructed to turn first to the particular shift commander responsible for that sub-division. That individual (which could be the shift commander if the incident occurred in their sub-division) then had a duty to deal with the incident using their expert knowledge of the area and its people. The divisional commander was only to be called if the incident was of a very serious nature and needed inter-agency or department co-ordination; a murder or major traffic accident for example. The first question asked by the divisional commander when she was called was, 'What has the shift commander for that area done to deal with the incident and why am I being called?'

The divisional commander thought that this approach would give the shift commanders some real responsibility and an opportunity to gain useful experience, thereby motivating them to enhance the performance of the entire division and enhance their career prospects. However, the practical effect was that the number of occasions on which the divisional commander was called out reduced, but the shift commanders now found that they would be called out at any hour of the day or night, in addition to having to work their normal rotating shift pattern. They found this very tiring and disruptive on top of an already disrupted work and private life. They resented this change and interpreted it as a cynical attempt by the divisional commander to make her own life easier at the expense of the shift commanders.

In response to the changes implemented by the divisional commander the shift commanders became demotivated and began to grumble amongst themselves. After a period of time one of them developed an idea through which to make the changes more bearable. It was suggested that each shift commander should break down their geographic area into sub-units and make a sergeant responsible for each. This would mean that instead of the shift commander being called immediately a problem in their area was identified, it would be allocated to the appropriate sergeant to deal with. The shift commander with special responsibility for that area would only be called upon to become involved if the sergeant could not do so. The intention being to reduce the number of times that each shift commander would be called out, by requiring each sergeant to make themselves available at all times. Not surprisingly, this made the shift commanders feel better, but had the effect of de-motivating the sergeants.

Tasks

1. Was the divisional commander ever going to be able to motivate the shift commanders by making the changes that she did? Justify your answer.
2. How might the divisional commander have been able to motivate her subordinates and still reduce the demands on herself? Justify your views in terms of the motivation theories and performance management material introduced in this chapter.

FURTHER READING

Clark, H, Chandler, J and Barry, J (1994) *Organization and Identities: Text and Readings in Organizational Behaviour*, International Thomson Business Press, London. Contains a broad range of original articles on relevant material themes and from significant writers referred to in this and other textbooks on management and organizations.

Flannery, TP, Hofrichter, DA and Platten, PE (1996) *People, Performance and Pay: Dynamic Compensation for Changing Organizations*, The Free Press, New York. Intended to review how pay and performance practices can be lined up with modern organizational culture. Being practitioner oriented it does not explicitly analyze the underlying assumptions about motivation included in the discussion.

Hartle, F (1995) *How to Re-Engineer your Performance Management Process*, Kogan Page, London. Seeks to explore the nature of performance management and its application across Europe and the USA as well as how to align the process with changing organizational frameworks and cultures. The text does not make explicit the links between motivation and performance, but assumes that the objective is to improve performance.

Kouzes, J and Posner, B (2003) *Encouraging the Heart: A Leaders Guide to Rewarding and Recognizing Others*, revised edition, Wiley, Chichester. This is an unusual book in that it focuses on an aspect of motivation and performance that is not directly addressed in this text, that of caring. The authors argue that people will aspire to achieve higher performance when they are genuinely appreciated for their dedication and publicly recognized for their achievements.

Meyer, MW (2003) *Rethinking Performance Measurement: Beyond the Balanced Scorecard*, Cambridge University Press, Cambridge. Explores what performance management means in the light of the balanced business scorecard approach and the weaknesses that have been identified within it.

Pinder, CC (1998) *Work Motivation in Organizational Behaviour*, Prentice Hall, Upper Saddle River, NJ. Provides a current and research oriented approach to why people work in its broadest sense. Concentrates on the motivations for working rather than general work motivation theory.

Weiner, B (1992) *Human Motivation: Metaphors, Theories and Research*, Sage, Thousand Oaks, CA. This text is described as a source book in the sphere of motivation theory. In that sense it incorporates a much greater level of detail than is possible in a single chapter. It offers an approach to motivation that places it in a social context.

Williams, RS (2002) *Managing Employee Performance: Design and Implementation in Organizations*, Thomson Learning, London. This text takes a practical approach to the design and implementation of the key mechanisms for performance management systems as used within organizations.

COMPANION WEBSITE

Online teaching and learning resources:

Visit the companion website for Organizational Behaviour and Management 3rd edition at: *http://www.thomsonlearning.co.uk/businessandmanagement/martin3* to find valuable further teaching and learning material:

Refer to page 35 for full details.

- Let the manager know that they have been found out.
- Send an anonymous letter to the chief executive.
- Report the manager to the subordinates' trade union.
- Write a letter to the press.
- Write a letter to the largest shareholder.
- Report the manager to their professional association (if they belong to one).

Each of these options has a range of costs and benefits for the individuals involved in the situation. In identifying the most appropriate course of action the subordinate can adopt one of two approaches. First, they could take the decision based on their judgement of the rightness or wrongness of the act that they have encountered. In doing so they would be acting irrespective of any consequences for the manager involved, themselves or the organization. Second, they could form a judgement based on the possible consequences for the principal stakeholders. For example, if they had an extremely good working relationship with the manager and felt a high degree of personal loyalty towards them, an approach that ran counter to that would be likely to cause distress to the subordinate.

Cederblom and Dougherty (1990) use these ideas as the basis for deciding between alternative courses of action. They refer to the two approaches as utilitarianism and contractarianism. **Utilitarian approaches** are summarized as benevolence and **contract approaches** are about fairness. Within each model there are two versions, giving four different options which form the basis of choosing an appropriate course of action.

Utilitarian approaches
Requires evaluation of the options available in terms of the impact on those likely to be affected by the consequences.

Contract approaches
An approach to ethics grounded in the notion that agreements whether they be explicit or tacit should be honoured.

Utilitarian approach

This approach is grounded in the concept of utility or usefulness. In determining the right course of action in any given context a key feature should be the level of valued results produced. The approach to be adopted is one of benevolence towards the needs of others in determining one's own behaviour. This approach looks forward in assessing the ethical perspectives on any particular situation. It requires an evaluation of options on the basis of the future impact on those that are likely to be affected by the consequences.

Act utilitarianism This version suggests that every dilemma should be regarded on its own merits. For example, telling a lie could be justified if it created happiness for the people involved. It would appear to run contrary to all the norms of society to be able to justify actions such as lying, cheating and even murder under some circumstances. For an interesting discussion on this area of ethics see Keep (2003).

Rule utilitarianism This approach takes the view that act utilitarianism might be a good thing to do in a specific instance, but still wrong if society is to operate in a consistent way. The rule approach to utilitarianism requires rule frameworks to be created which can allow individuals to identify appropriate courses of action in specific contexts.

Contract approach

This approach to resolving ethical dilemmas is grounded in the notion that agreements whether they be explicit or tacit should be honoured. Because of the social environment, co-operation between human beings is a necessity. As a consequence of the web of interaction formed many mutual obligations (contracts) are created. In the execution of these contractual relationships, individuals are required to apply the general test of fairness to their behaviour. However, circumstances can create an inequality in the balance of power between individuals and so fairness is difficult to achieve. For example, inside knowledge of an impending takeover bid could allow certain individuals to buy shares cheaply before they rise sharply when the announcement is made. A contract view is one that looks backward at the obligations that have been entered into and assesses the implications of these for future behaviour.

Restricted contractarianism This approach takes the view that every agreement entered into should be assessed through the veil of ignorance (Rawls, 1971). This forces an individual to consider the rightness of any proposed action without knowing the outcome for themselves. Cutting a cake is frequently used to illustrate the need for fairness in this context. The person agreeing to cut the cake should be the last person to select a piece to eat. By so doing they cannot know which piece of cake will be left for them to eat, and so every piece will be equal!

Libertarian contractarianism This approach holds that the parties should be bound by any agreement voluntarily entered into as long as it does not conflict with the broader rules of a just society or cause harm to others. It is an approach that accepts the limitations on the concept of fairness in the dynamic nature of the social world. It implies that once a contract is entered into, individuals have an obligation to abide by the terms of that relationship and not to take action to terminate (or change) the contract. For example, an employee should fulfil their contractual obligations to their employer in following the instructions of management, unless they are being expected to break the law of the country in which they work, say to falsify the company accounts. That is because the 'contract' between each citizen and their country has a higher status than the contract with the employer. In the case described the employee would be acting ethically by upholding the rule of law. Of course this can lead to many difficulties in the area of whistleblowing in which the organization would argue that there was no conflict of 'contract' and that loyalty to the company should be upheld and the employee argues otherwise.

Considerable management and employee activity is associated with making choices or taking decisions. Manual workers on an assembly line have to make decisions about the quality of work that they are undertaking; administrative employees have decisions to make with regard to dealing with customer queries or complaints and so on. Often there are competing pressures in these decisions that make the identification of the right thing to do difficult. Leys (1962) produced a diagram in which a number of moral standards are identified which conflict with the standards in the opposite side of the model (see Figure 12.2).

This model is useful in identifying many of the conflicts and dilemmas associated with decision making. For example, an employee faced with a boss who is attempting to increase efficiency and reduce the cost of operations will span the dilemmas of loyalty and institutional trends at one side of the model and integrity/self-respect at the opposite side. In such a situation an employee may well feel that loyalty to the organization is important and that increased efficiency represents an institutional trend that cannot be stopped. At the same time, however, these feelings are likely to be in conflict with the need for personal integrity in performing a good job to high standards of quality, and self-respect in not being subject to every whim of the boss. This model does not provide a basis for identifying a course of action to resolve the moral dilemma facing the individual. It simply helps to identify some of the conflicting areas in the decision. At best this model should be regarded as a simplification of the complexity of situations involving ethical conflicts. It is, however, a useful starting point for thinking about the issues involved in a specific situation.

FIGURE 12.2

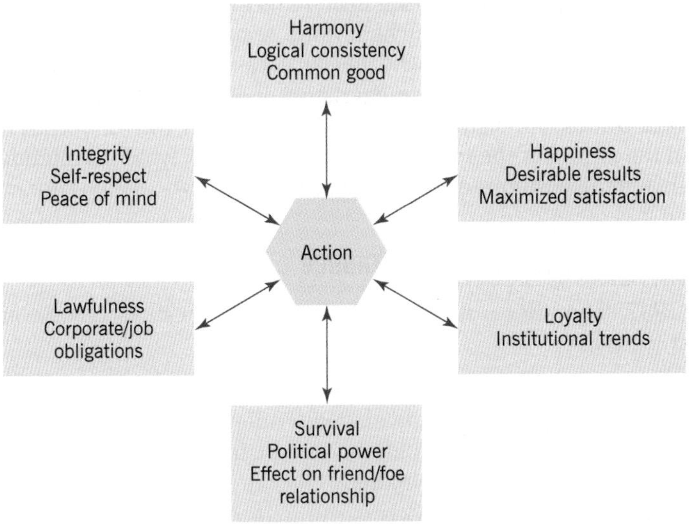

Conflicts between moral values (*adapted from*: Leys, WAR (1962) *The Value Framework of Decision Making,* Prentice Hall, Englewood Cliffs)

ETHICS AND RESEARCH

Ethics is not just about how people should behave within an organizational context. There are ethical issues associated with the development of knowledge about organizations and the people who work within them. Whatever the form of research there are potential ethical issues to consider. Hornsby-Smith (1993, p 62) describes the role of codes of practice in the area of research as a means of seeking, 'to control unethical methods of investigation … by professional bodies'. Implying that research can be 'slanted' in some way or another if it is not carefully protected from the pressure of vested interest.

Fielding (1993, p 169) highlights the ethical dilemma facing researchers engaging in ethnographic studies by referring to the earlier work of Rosenhan. The research led by Rosenhan required that 'pseudo-patients' be placed in mental hospitals as a way of checking on the diagnosis activities of medical staff. When they arrived at the hospital each 'pseudo-patient':

> Feigned hearing voices, but once admitted they ceased simulating any symptoms. All but one was admitted with a diagnosis of schizophrenia. Not one was caught out. … Nor were their diagnoses changed when they switched to normal behaviour, despite many of their fellow patients guessing.

This research demonstrated the unreliability of psychiatric diagnosis as well as the institutional and professional consequences of 'labelling' patients. A different outcome would be very likely to have emerged had informed consent (to be investigated) by the medical staff been required as part of the research process. Indeed Rosehan adopted such a policy in a subsequent study, resulting in 23 out of 193 admissions being 'listed' as 'pseudo-patients' when none had been sent to that particular hospital. These studies, important as they are, clearly highlight the ethical difficulties facing researchers in seeking to advance knowledge. It is not possible to know the impact of the particular ethical standards adopted by researchers on the models and theories developed. It does, however, reflect the need to be aware of ethical aspects of research in seeking to explain and understand behaviour. Another aspect of ethics in research is demonstrated by Yurtsever (2003) who developed a moral entrepreneur measurement scale to identify the personality characteristics of such people. In this context there are the ethical issues associated with how the research was undertaken running in parallel with the nature of the measurement device itself, which is intended to identify persons with a predisposition to operate ethically.

Business ethics and corporate governance

Mahoney (1997) identifies a number of reasons why businesses take an interest in ethics. They include:

- *Following fashion.* This approach regards ethics as something that is useful in the short term, until the fashion changes. Adopting the current fashion represents something that would not become integrated into business operations or management thinking.
- *Response to pressure.* There are many pressure groups that seek to influence business activities and by adopting appropriate ethical codes and policies organizations can demonstrate that they seek to meet their obligations.
- *Pursuit of profit.* It is possible that by being ethical in pursuit of business goals customers would be attracted to doing business with the organization. This is demonstrated in the following Employee Perspective (12.1).
- *Stakeholders consider that it is right.* Such individuals would probably behave and manage organizations in an ethical way irrespective of other considerations as a matter of personal belief. Therefore the cost or benefit to be gained becomes irrelevant to such business leaders. However, if such a business made huge losses it would still go bankrupt or be taken over!
- *Mixture of the reasons already given.* In many cases, the reasons that businesses engage in ethical activity is for a mixture of the reasons indicated, the proportion of each reason active in the specific context depending upon the individuals and situation.

Corporate governance
The systems through which ethics are expressed in business activities, the basis of company direction and control.

Although there are many ways of defining **corporate governance**, the Cadbury Committee (1992) defined it in terms of the systems through which companies are directed and controlled. The need for a review of corporate governance arose as the result of a number of high profile scandals in the business world involving fraud and the abuse of power by senior managers and directors in the UK and USA. In the UK the Cadbury Committee produced a number of recommendations (the main ones are listed in Table 12.3) and received a mixed response. The general reaction was that it should have incorporated a broader set of recommendations including environmental and social responsibility aspects of business activity. This has subsequently been developed to some extent as a result of the work of the Hample Committee, which reported on corporate governance during 1998.

Codes of practice

In an attempt to provide guidance on ethical standards and behaviour many organizations and professional bodies have produced codes of practice. Most establish what the approved (ethical) courses of action are in particular circumstances, for example, what to do if faced with a demand for a bribe. They also attempt to provide an indication of the procedure to be adopted if a breach of the code is suspected as a result of someone not following established procedures.

EMPLOYEE PERSPECTIVE 12.1 Ethical can be profitable

Mark was a civil engineer with a water utility based in Austria. One of his tasks was to update a number of the treatment plants that were scattered around the water distribution network. The treatment plants tended to be in semi-rural areas, often areas of natural beauty or of high ecological importance. The bulk of the water was however used in industry and heavily populated cities far distant to where the work was being done. The updating work involved taking out old and out of date machinery, building new facilities and installing new, modern equipment. Not surprisingly this involved considerable disruption for the people living around the water treatment plants as well as noise and mess as heavy earth moving machines and trucks came back and forth to the construction sites over many months. Not surprisingly environmentalists and local inhabitants protested strongly about the effect that the work had on their lives and communities.

Over time James developed a strategy for each construction site that involved talking to local residents and environmentalists to find the best way of doing the work with minimal effect on life around the treatment plant. The solution at each location was slightly different although as more experience was gained it became apparent that a number of common themes could be identified. James was able to incorporate these ideas into the plans for each location at a very early stage which effectively reduced the potential for disputes at each new location to be upgraded. At first the cost of doing the work increased by taking account of the local views. However as new ways of work developed, costs began to fall back to just above the previous levels.

The company for which James worked began to see this new capability as a commercial opportunity and began to market itself as having a particular skill at civil engineering in partnership with local communities. Prospective clients from outside Austria began to hear about the company and enquires resulted which resulted in invitations to tender for work in locations and areas that had not been readily available to the company in the past. James and other senior managers in the company were asked to make presentations at international conferences on how to undertake civil engineering projects based on partnership. The levels of business undertaken by the company increased by about 20 per cent year on year and the profit generated by the company also increased significantly.

Task

Is it ethical to make extra profit by developing ethical business models approaches as James did? Justify your views.

The codes of practice for professional bodies only direct themselves to issues associated with that particular area of work and how it should be conducted. There can be occasions when the code of practice for a professional body is in conflict with the practices within the organization employing the member. Such eventualities pose difficulties for the individual in deciding which to follow. For example, a doctor employed by a company may interpret their professional responsibility as a duty to provide the highest standards of care for employees, but the company may interpret its requirement is to provide the most cost-effective level of care. Verpeet *et al.* (2003) for example point out the difficulties that exist for nurses in Belgium where there is no code of practice to guide their professional practice and seek to demonstrate the benefits of developing such a tool.

SOCIAL RESPONSIBILITY

Social responsibility
Seeks to explore the responsibility of business towards society and the various stakeholder groups that surround it.

The notion of **social responsibility** stems from asking what responsibility any business has towards society. Responsibility is generally taken to imply a duty of care or a set of obligations. Society, however, is a difficult concept to define, particularly in relation to a specific business. At one level of interpretation it could imply the government

The board of directors should have separate audit and remuneration committees, comprised only of independent directors
The audit committee should meet with the external auditors of the company at least once each year and without an executive director present
The total remuneration package of directors should be fully disclosed in the annual report of the company
The term of office for a director should be no more than three years in between shareholder votes on appointment to the office held
Non-executive directors must have funds available to them to pay for independent professional advice
The board must meet at regular intervals
Non-executive directors should be appointed through a formal process
Non-executive directors should enjoy a standing in society or the business community that ensures that their views carry weight
Non-executive directors should be completely independent of the company other than in relation to their fees and any shareholdings
No one person should have total power at the top of the company. The jobs of chief executive and chairman of the board should be split wherever possible.

TABLE 12.3 Major recommendations of the Cadbury Committee

of the country or region in which the business is located. In a narrower sense, it implies the stakeholders linked with a particular business. There are benefits from taking the narrower view as any business impacts on each of the stakeholder groups in different ways. For example, taking such a view would allow the relative benefits to all parties to be evaluated (along with any negative consequences) in the desire of a particular organization to reduce its expenditure on pollution control.

Johnson and Scholes (1993, p 192) discuss a report produced in 1981 which identifies ten roles that seek to reflect the range of underlying approaches to business activity and social responsibility. At one extreme there are organizations that only seek to maximize profit, whilst at the other extreme there are those that actively engage with the social and political aspects of the environments within which they operate. Of course, this engagement does not disbar interest in making profit if the organization is commercially based. However, not all organizations are commercially based, some are created to deliver public services. This classification process can assist in identifying the different attitudes among organizations towards social responsibility, but it does not provide a basis for condoning particular expressions of it. Johnson and Scholes go on (p 195) to identify some of the internal and external aspects of social responsibility:

- *Internal aspects.* These include issues such as employee welfare provision, working conditions and job design.
- *External aspects.* These include issues such as 'green policies', product design and possible use/abuse, marketing and advertising, dealing with suppliers, employment policies and community activity.

There are, of course, many other aspects of social responsibility that can be identified. For example, which locations to enter in operational and selling terms (and why) together with the degree of political influence sought and exercised in them.

The difficulty associated with establishing, maintaining and enforcing social responsibility within the business and management community lies in the very nature of the stakeholder concept. Each stakeholder group has a particular relationship with the organization. This is perhaps more accurately described as a **web of relationships** as it is very rarely a single element relationship. For example, employees can be assumed in general terms to want interesting work that does not damage their health and with high pay (among other things). Governments seek high levels of employment, high taxation income, industrial relations (and social) stability, international prestige and a low cost of social support to the population. Even in these two simple examples it is possible to identify the conflicts that could exist between the individual stakeholders. If employees and governments cannot be relied upon to seek the common good, how much less could business leaders in search of the best financial return be expected to follow such an emphasis? Therefore the role of pressure groups, investigative journalists, professional bodies and individuals is crucial in pursuit of social responsibility among organizations. Zwetsloot (2003) reviews the trends in social responsibility over recent years and concludes that a new approach is evolving. It is one that extends the management science approach to decision making in seeking to identify what it is right to do, not just what should be done.

Web of relationships
In any social situation relationships are complex and involve a web of multiple people and groups rather than linear interactions.

A recent survey found that 87 per cent of respondents felt that business leaders had a responsibility to take into account the impact of decisions on the local communities; 77 per cent felt that directors should set an example as responsible and involved members of their local communities; 87 per cent of respondents felt that organizations could differentiate themselves in marketing terms through their social responsibility activities; and 73 per cent felt that organizations should encourage employee development so that they can more easily find alternative employment as it is no longer guaranteed (Butcher and Harvey, 1999, p 39). However just because such strong feelings exist, it does not ensure that appropriate polices will emerge or be effectively implemented. It takes time to organize a synthesis between society and business, especially when there is little tradition of social responsibility being an organizational imperative.

CROSS-CULTURAL PERSPECTIVES ON ETHICS

The starting point for understanding ethics in an international context is, according to Stewart and White (1995), to understand the major religious and philosophical teachings. These writers suggest that such reviews identify a common thread in the concepts of mutuality and the common good. However, as the economic development of regions and individual countries evolve then the nature of ethical problems also changes. It is, they suggest, much too simplistic to contemplate the standards applied in developed Western countries as the ideal to be achieved by developing countries. The developed economies of the West do not offer an ideal; they experience new situations requiring different ethical discussions and solutions to those relevant in other cultures.

Leisinger (1995) quotes the earlier work of Goodpaster in identifying the following 'moral common sense' rules:

- Avoid harming others
- Respect the rights of others
- Do not lie or cheat
- Keep promises and contracts
- Obey the law
- Prevent harm to others

- Help those in need
- Be fair
- Reinforce these imperatives in others.

He goes on to explore the difficulties in applying such standards in a largely unequal world. One aspect of ethical concern on a global scale is that of bribery and extortion. Mahoney (1995) discusses several aspects associated with these phenomena and the impact on commodity and financial markets as well as the diversion of resources away from more effective use within society. He describes several initiatives under the auspices of the United Nations and individual governments to limit the occurrence of such behaviour through the policing of business activity and company reporting requirements.

Mahoney discusses the difficult issue of the degree to which companies should engage with cultures in which corruption is rife and offers a number of suggestions based on the view that there is more than one ethical response to an unethical situation. This discussion uses the apartheid era in South Africa and the widespread bribery found in Italy prior to the 1990s as examples. He argues that it is the justification for engagement with a particular unethical practice as well as the stance adopted by the organization that changes situations. Working in such environments can be justified providing:

- It is unavoidable, at least in the short term.
- The reason for so doing is grounded in good business and social reasons.
- The business endeavours to change the unethical features of the particular culture.

The ability to influence events in a particular location depends upon the opportunity for a company to do so and a willingness within the society to change. Official complaints, the use of the media to publicize such activity or providing opportunities for local people that would not otherwise be available can all begin to improve a situation. Other measures include the need for education, the creation of specific legal frameworks penalizing such behaviour and requiring company self-regulation. In some cases (Russia being one example) even allowing the government to engage in what would otherwise be regarded as unethical behaviour in order to create order from chaos. However, at the end of the day success in controlling bribery and corruption can only be achieved if individuals have the moral courage to follow through with courses of action that change the situation.

ETHICS AND ANTISOCIAL BEHAVIOUR

The previous discussion touched on bribery and extortion as unethical practices and these are examples of what could be described as antisocial behaviour. There are, however, many other occurrences that would fall into this category. Giacalone and Greenburg (1997) identify a number of events that they classify as falling, at least potentially, within the classification of antisocial behaviour (Table 12.4).

Some of the items in Table 12.4 have already been discussed and some have an obvious ethical dimension, for example lying and theft. However, some are not so obvious and need further consideration. For example, the threat of lawsuits can be a good thing in improving the standards of ethical behaviour within a company, say following the occurrence of an episode of sexual harassment. However it can also be a process that is used unethically. For example, a dismissed employee threatening to go to court to sue the employer as a way of obtaining a 'pay-off', because they know that it

Arson	Fraud	Sabotage
Blackmail	Interpersonal violence	Sexual harassment
Bribery	Kickbacks	Theft
Discrimination	Lawsuits	Violation of confidentiality
Espionage	Lying	Whistleblowing
Extortion		

TABLE 12.4 Examples of antisocial behaviour

would be cheaper for the company to pay money rather than defend their case. Equally, whistleblowing can be used maliciously to cause trouble if the grounds for so doing are not well founded or truthful.

Espionage is another rather shady area of activity which few organizations would admit to being involved with. The equipment to enable espionage to be carried out exists but it is not clear as to the true extent of the potential problem. It is, however, an area of ethical concern. It is possible for the governments of most countries to arrange for listening devices to be placed on telephones etc. providing they (sometimes) follow strict guidelines. Countries also make a practice of collecting commercial information on other countries as part of international diplomacy. Companies collect information on markets, competitors, customers, suppliers, potential and actual employees, etc. In the commercial world it is not a large step from collecting information otherwise in the public domain and going one step further and seeking information that would not otherwise be available – espionage. Croft (1994) provides an interesting look at a range of information sources available as well as the electronic and other devices that can be used to engage in 'corporate cloak and dagger', as his book is titled.

Punch (1996) explores another aspect of antisocial behaviour which he terms 'dirty business', 'corporate misconduct' or 'organizational deviance'. His examples range from nuns in a Belgian convent diverting approximately $5 million from a hospital project to build an indoor swimming pool and placing TV sets in each cell of a new convent (p i), to the global BCCI and Maxwell scandals (pp 5–15). His work claims that misconduct is endemic to business and that to understand such behaviour it is necessary to understand, 'the nature of business, the realities of organizational life, the dilemmas of management, and the manners and morals of managers in their daily working lives' (p 213). In seeking to explain why it is that managers engage in deviant practices, Punch identifies three categories of variable:

1. *Structure*. This category covers such features as the competitive nature of markets; that the size and complexity of businesses can create 'obfuscation of authority' (p 222); the emphasis placed on goals with the associated opportunity and rewards available.
2. *Culture*. The opportunity for deviance to become ingrained in corporate culture is ever present.
3. *Personality/identity*. The depersonalization of corporate activity can result in managers feeling removed from the consequences of their actions or seeking to rationalize them through denial, claiming that business is an analogy for war, following a role model or simply for the fun or excitement. It is even possible that companies have a need at times for 'dirty work' to be undertaken and that some managers are willing to undertake such duties. It is even suggested that the huge rewards that can be achieved by people at the top of

business encourage people to cut corners and take risks to achieve promotion and success.

Much of this antisocial behaviour depends upon individuals being willing to engage in it. It was Kohlberg who first proposed a model of the stages of moral reasoning in humans (see, for example, Kohlberg and Ryncarz, 1990). This model contained six stages which each person moved through in a fixed sequence. The model states that a person operates at each stage until progression in moral reasoning occurs and that propels the individual on to the next stage. Snell (1995) reviews this model and proposes his own version of it, based on research among practising managers. The six stages in the development of ethical reasoning in Snell's model are (pp 148–9):

1. Avoid punishment; obey those in authority.
2. Seek personal gain; avoid losing out.
3. Earn the approval of others around you or attached to you by being nice to them and by fitting in with their expectations.
4. Conform to rules, laws, codes and conventions.
5. Follow principles based on respect for people and their rights, other organisms, the greater good, a strong sense of empathy and compassion for the human condition.
6. Continually question your own actions and principles.

Snell argues, based on his research, that there are four 'psychic prisons' (incorporating one of the metaphors identified by Morgan, 1986) that restrict the ability of managers to deal effectively with ethical dilemmas. The first two are within the individual and the second two are based in the environment. They are:

1. Being in possession of a limited ethical reasoning capacity.
2. Having stereotypical assumptions about the nature of organizational structures, responsibilities and power relationships.
3. Holding restricted levels of organizational responsibility or power.
4. Being constrained in the actions possible by a particular moral ethos dominant in a particular context.

Among the implications of this research are that an individual chooses to act in particular ways either as a consequence of their own internal cognitive processes and/or as a result of external, contextual forces. This view generally supports the ideas of Punch in his view that organizational and personal factors can influence the occurrence of antisocial behaviour. For example, Ronald (2003) demonstrates that the managerial bullying of subordinates (downward workplace mobbing as it is also termed) reflects the inability of organizations to deal effectively with the consequences of change impacting on areas such as creativity, excellence and responsibility.

ETHICS AND MANAGEMENT

The role of people in an organization is somewhat ambiguous. What is expected of employees by the organization and what they as individuals and groups should expect from the organization are based on a complex wheel of interdependent factors. Figure 12.3 reflects the interaction between these influences and the role of people within the organization. There are number of ethical dilemmas that emerge from the need for organization and control within a business. The more significant ones are introduced in the following sub-sections.

The role of work in society

Work plays a number of important roles in society. It provides the basis for individuals to earn money and thereby purchase the goods and services necessary for life and recreation. There are indirect benefits through the payment of taxes so that common services such as healthcare and education can be provided. Work also provides individuals with social meaning in their lives through the careers and work activities that they engage in. For example, those with appropriate leadership talents could become senior managers and find ways of creating wealth and jobs for the benefit of society. It also provides an opportunity for social encounters with other people as employees interact with other human beings.

Should work and the organizations that provide it be seen as the dominant force within society? Should any organization have the power to dictate to the members of a society how they should live and work? Is work a basic human right in society? How much time should be devoted to work, how much payment should be received and so on? In short, should we as humans work to live or live to work? There are a number of organizations who have an income larger than many of the poorer countries of the world. This could provide opportunities for big business to pressure some countries to organize things in a way that supports business objectives, rather than for the benefit of society. These and many other aspects of the role of work in society create ethical dilemmas that are not easy to resolve, yet politicians and business leaders must develop policies and practices which match the expectations of society to some degree if social conflict is to be avoided.

Corporate and public interest

There is a fundamental conflict between organizations and the public at large. In very crude terms, all organizations would like to sell cheap products at very high prices. Consumers, by the same token, would like very expensive products at very low prices.

FIGURE 12.3

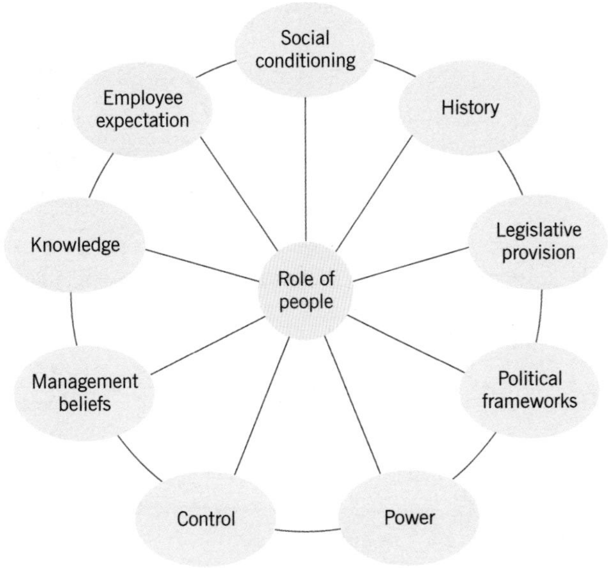

The wheel of people role determinants within organizations

This is a vast simplification of a complex process associated with purchase and ownership. It is well known among marketing people that there are circumstances in which charging low prices actually undervalues the product or service in the eyes of potential customers therefore reducing the likelihood of purchase. This market and value-based form of conflict can lead to ethical issues arising as organizations seek to maximize their profits.

One of the illustrations that can be used to illustrate potential conflicts in this area is contained in Management in Action 12.1. The conflicts in this example are associated with the company need to reduce the cost of operations and customer demands for a reasonably priced toy. The moral issues include the deliberate payment of low wages (by European standards) as a management policy. There is also the issue of customers preferring low priced products when they in turn seek high wages for their own work, thereby encouraging the export of jobs to areas with cheap labour. Countering this is the provision of economic development in areas that need it. There are also the issues of export profit from, and technology/skill transfer to, areas of cheap labour. This begins to open up economic arguments that are well beyond the scope of this text. Goldsmith (1995) however, puts forward a spirited defence of his views that by not protecting jobs and production at home, countries are sowing the seeds of their own destruction.

Obligations at work

There are a number of areas of obligation that impact on employees. Figure 12.4 attempts to reflect many of these.

Not all of the categories identified in Figure 12.4 will apply to every employee and there are areas relevant to some jobs that not represented. The ethical dilemmas arising from obligations at work arise as a result of the potential conflicts in demands placed on the individual from the range of responsibilities that they have in their lives.

FIGURE 12.4

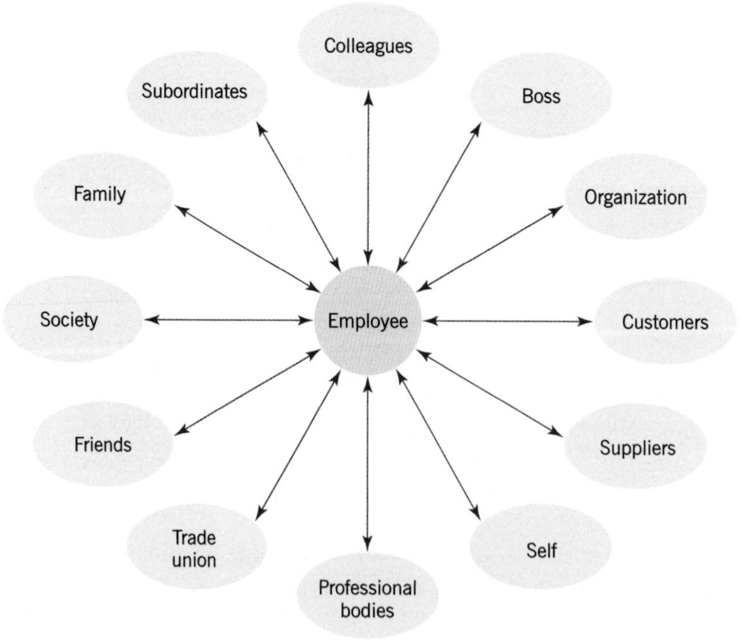

Employee obligation map

MANAGEMENT IN ACTION 12.1 Poverty pay of Barbie doll workers

A report produced by the World Development Movement, the Catholic Institute for International Relations and the Trades Union Congress show that poverty wages are frequently paid to workers in Asia making toys for sale in the west.

The findings of the research indicated that many leading toy companies use subcontracted factories in Asia which fail to meet basic internationally agreed standards. The average person works a shift of at least ten hours each day for six days per week. For example, Chinese workers were paid less than £2 per day to make Barbie dolls. The Mattel Company which makes the Barbie doll spends about £1.80 per doll sold on advertising, about the same as the daily wage for each factory worker.

In Bangkok the research team interviewed factory workers and reported the following comments:

> Barbie doll is more expensive than our wages. We lost a lot of sweat to produce those dolls.

Another worker explained that overtime was compulsory,

> We have to do it otherwise we would be dismissed... . One month the management gives 60 dolls for one worker to produce but when we finish the 60 dolls per month they will increase it another 10 to 70 dolls; if we finish 70 dolls they will increase it again.

The group sponsoring the research pressed the British Toy and Hobby Association, which represents companies responsible for 90 per cent of all sales of these products in the UK market, to adopt a new charter in this area. It seeks to establish an independently monitored code of practice for the safe production of toys. It requires companies to undertake spot checks on subcontractors and to take action if any violations were found.

Mattel, as a leading maker of toys, welcomed the charter and suggested that it would enhance its own existing code of practice which required subcontractors to comply with local labour and safety laws. It also required staff to report any violation of the laws.

Adapted from: Garner, C (1995) Poverty pay of Barbie doll workers, *The Independent*, 23 December, p 2.

Stop ↔ Consider

Based on your reading of this story and this chapter to what extent do you think (and why) that ethical considerations should outweigh economic and market forces?

For example, balancing the demands of organization and family can create problems in many situations, as can the demands of ever higher productivity on the self-respect of the individual.

Privacy

The right to privacy for the individual has been eroded in a number of areas over recent years and in turn raises a number of ethical dilemmas. For example, the use of information technology has created an opportunity to collect and retain more information about employees than was previously possible. The organization is able to 'know' its employees more fully. However, this should not be overstated as large bureaucracies such as the civil service have had effective and comprehensive personnel files on staff for many years.

Another aspect of privacy in today's world is that associated with medical screening. Testing for drug use and for HIV are just two of the more recent areas to emerge. How far medical screening should be allowed to go before it moves from being necessary to being intrusive is a difficult balance to strike.

Working at home and work-life balance

There are many situations that arise which require the individual to take work home with them. A report may be required at short notice and it may be necessary for a manager to finish it at home in the evening. There are however, a wide range of aspects of work that go home with the employee, as demonstrated by the following Employee Perspective (12.2).

The ethical issues surrounding the practice of working at home are many and depend on the circumstances creating the situation. The dilemmas and issues involved in the two examples just quoted are different. In the first case, they surround the rights and obligations of both parties. Does a senior manager have the right to expect subordinates to put in more hours than contractually agreed, particularly at short notice? Equally, does a manager have an obligation to 'do what is necessary' in pursuing corporate objectives? In the second case, the ethical issues are of a completely different nature as the employee is not being required to think about work at home, it is a result of the threat of redundancy and the relative opportunity of alternative work.

To refuse to take work home could be regarded as an act of disloyalty and have implications for the career and promotion prospects of the individual concerned. There may also be others only too willing to take advantage of the situation to advance their own careers. The demands of work in terms of the balance with other aspects of life have long been recognized as a major problem for women with caring roles at

EMPLOYEE PERSPECTIVE 12.2 What counts as taking work home?

John worked on an assembly line in a factory making washing machines along with a range of other white goods. There had been rumours for a while that management were thinking about moving the factory to the Far East in order to cut the cost of manufacturing, but nothing had been said officially. One day management called all of the employees in the factory together in order to hear an important announcement. The rumours began to circulate, all based on the same theme, redundancy and job losses.

The factory came to a standstill before the meeting time as people began to gather in groups to talk about what might be going on. At the appointed time for the meeting a group of senior managers came onto the factory floor and climbed onto a platform so that everyone could see and hear them. The production director said that the biggest customer for washing machines had said that it was not going to place any further orders with the company and that this meant that production would have to be cut by 25 per cent starting in three months time.

The production director said that talks would start immediately with the trade unions and that is was hoped that compulsory redundancy could be avoided, but that inevitably less labour would be required, unless additional orders were forthcoming. He said that this was a very sorry day for all concerned and asked for patience while all the options were considered. He then closed the meeting and asked everyone to go back to work. Not surprisingly, very little work was done that day, or for the next few days as people huddled together in little groups talking about the consequences of the loss of the work and the possible effects on everyone working at the company.

John was obviously worried as was everyone working at the factory and found that he was not able to stop thinking about work when he was at home. Naturally he talked about the situation to his wife and family on a regular basis and he also talked to his colleagues at work. This did nothing to lessen the worry that he felt about the future of his job and the income that went with it.

Tasks

1. What are the ethical issues implied by John's situation?
2. In what ways if at all, does this example of taking work home differ to that of a manager having to finish a report at home? Justify your answer.

home as well as careers. In many organizations there is a phenomenon which has become known as 'presentism' that impacts on all employees. Presentism is simply a reflection of the usually unstated expectation of being 'at work' for long periods of time as proof of commitment. One survey in 1998 among BT's senior managers found that 38 per cent would not accept promotion because of the perceived damage to home lives (Cooper, 2000 a, p 35).

Whistleblowing

Whistleblowing involves an employee bringing into the public arena acts that the organization would prefer to keep hidden. Such individuals frequently try unsuccessfully to use internal methods to bring about change within the organization and stop unethical or illegal activities. In frustration at what they see as the intransigence and wrongdoing of individuals within the organization they find themselves going public to blow the whistle on the situation. Whistleblowing has generally been thought of as an ethical issue, but Rothschild and Miethe (1994) prefer to place it into a broader context as an aspect of political resistance. They define whistleblowing as, 'the disclosure of illegal, unethical or harmful practices in the workplace to parties who might take action' (p 254). This definition invariably implies that the 'issues' are taken to a higher level within the organization and/or outside it. This distinguishes it from other forms of worker protest which might be horizontal, by involving colleagues or family members in listening to explanations of the 'problem'.

In whistleblowing the individuals often leave themselves open to retaliation on the part of managers and other employees who think that their job or profit levels might be at risk. They are often dismissed, subjected to abuse and threats of violence to themselves their families or property. When the employer is the government it can also lead to imprisonment for revealing secrets. The following Employee Perspective (12.3) demonstrates differing ways in which whistleblowing can find expression together with the consequences for the individuals.

Codes of practice are a way of institutionalizing whistleblowing, allowing senior managers to take action on problems as they emerge. However, it is not only managers who try to prevent the truth from coming into the public domain. Rothschild and Miethe point out, as do Giacalone and Greenburg, that whistleblowing can be abused

EMPLOYEE PERSPECTIVE 12.3 Whistleblowing can get you dismissed!

Lynn (1998) describes the totally different experience of two people who found themselves in whistleblowing situations. The first individual worked in marketing at the Abbey National (a large bank) and discovered that his boss was putting false invoices through the system. He collected the information, left the company for another job and then gave his information to the board of the company. They investigated the allegations, found them to be true and involved the police. The individual was given £25 000 as a reward for the stress and invited back to the company with a promotion. The second individual was the managing director of an advertising agency and sought to 'straighten out' a few financial irregularities. Five months later he was sacked for incompetence. The parent group would not investigate his claims that a more senior executive within the group was fiddling and that this was the cause of his dismissal. It took the next five years of his life to collect enough evidence to prove his case, eventually winning large sums of money in compensation and an apology.

Task

What would you do if you came across evidence that your boss was cheating the system as indicated in the above examples? Justify your decision.

for purely political reasons and so become a different type of ethical problem. Rothschild and Miethe (1994) describe a case in which one employee was fired because she began to ask questions about the chemicals she worked with, only to find that she was suffering life-threatening conditions as a consequence of her work. Yet other employees tried to keep her quiet and 'turned their backs on her' because their jobs were at risk (p 263).

DEFINING ORGANIZATIONAL CULTURE

As far back as 1952 Kroeber and Kluckhohn reported that culture had 164 different meanings, a figure which must have been well exceeded in the intervening 50 years. This has led some writers to suggest that the concept has no real value because the variety of meaning is so diverse and largely contradictory that it is impossible for it to offer any value as a research idea (Kraut, 1975). Culture seeks to describe those facets of human experience and behaviour that contribute to the differences and similarities in how people engage with their perceived world. In that sense culture retains its value as a meta construct with metaphorical and descriptive power, even if it is imprecise and problematic.

Some writers raise questions over the value of culture as a construct with the ability to reflect meaningful differences between situations. For example, Ashkanasy and Nicholson (2003) imply that in Australia, a construct which they term 'climate of fear' has more discriminative power than culture (measured by innovative leadership culture, and communication culture) in its ability to differentiate between work sites within the same organisation. The same construct would not vary between organizations, whereas culture measures would vary between organizations, implying that it simply reflects variability on particular scales of measurement within a particular context.

Kilman *et al.* (1985) suggest that culture reflects the ideologies, shared philosophies, values, beliefs, assumptions, attitudes, expectations and norms of an organization. An early definition offered by Jaques (1952) suggests that culture is the:

> Customary and traditional way of thinking and doing things, which is shared to a greater or lesser degree by all members, and which the new members must learn and at least partially accept, in order to be accepted into the services of the firm. (p 251)

Deal and Kennedy (1982) suggest that culture includes a range of elements, including symbolism and leadership, as a means of achieving employee commitment. Sciarelli (2002) demonstrates this by suggesting that the quality achieved by a business is a reflection of its culture. Consequently, any attempt to change quality requires that the culture be changed as well. Thompson and McHugh (1995) suggest that personnel management is of particular significance in designing and maintaining new and more appropriate (from a management perspective) cultures. They also review a considerable body of evidence to demonstrate that, as far as the excellence view of culture (based on Peters and Waterman – reviewed below) is concerned, it has little to offer by way of an explanation for the significance of culture in an organizational context.

The two definitions of culture provided so far can be seen as supportive of each other. The Kilman *et al.* (1985) view of the factors that compose culture can be seen to provide the basis of the earlier definition of Jaques (1952) and through which the learning of it could be achieved. In other words, the later definition considers content and the earlier definition process. However, the process as described by Jaques is one of acquisition by individuals. It assumes that the individuals will either possess the same culture as the organization before joining it or that they will subsequently acquire it through the various forms of training and socialization. This implies it is something that it is in management's interest to design or engineer on the premise that particular cultures may be more supportive of management's objectives than others. Interest in the so-called Japanese management phenomenon fuelled interest in this issue through the perceived need to build strong teams through what Thompson and McHugh call **compulsory sociability.**

Compulsory sociability
The achievement of strong team cultures by requiring individuals to join group activities and adopt particular behaviours or risk sanction.

Levels of analysis

It is possible to identify three different levels of cultural analysis from the literature (see Figure 12.5).

Taking each level in turn:

1. *Perceived culture.* This reflects the most apparent level of culture. It is based upon the 'way things get done around here' view of culture. Typically, it would incorporate the rituals, stories and ceremonies that describe the group in action.
2. *Common values, and so on.* This level attempts to get behind that which is observable and identify the factors that determine the perceived culture. Typically this would incorporate the factors identified in the Kilman *et al.* definition.
3. *Underlying assumptions.* Behind the common values are the underlying assumptions that individuals hold about the world and how it functions. It is often very difficult to identify these hidden assumptions as they are not directly articulated in the behaviour and attitudes that people display.

There are other ways in which approaches to the study of culture have been categorized. For example, Adler (1984) categorized studies of culture in terms of the research perspective adopted, including parochial, polycentric and synergistic. The main distinguishing features between these categories being the number of cultures studied and the research methodology adopted. Redding (1994) proposes a two-dimensional classification scheme for research in this area based upon the degree of interpretation or description in the study, with the second scale reflecting micro to macro levels of analysis. More recently Cray and Mallory (1998) suggest that it is possible to address many of the earlier criticisms of research in this field by classifying studies according to their relationship to theory. In doing so they offer three approaches that can be identified from the literature:

FIGURE 12.5

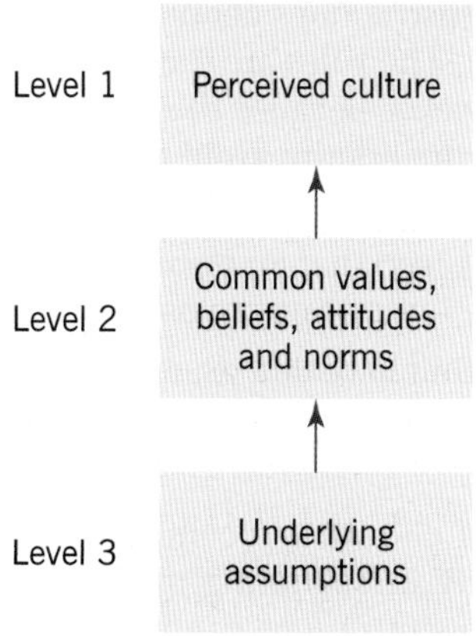

Levels of cultural analysis

1. *Naive comparative.* This approach regards culture as the explanatory variable for any differences observed. The writers use the term naive to reflect the lack of any theoretical basis to the work. The emphasis in such studies being to compare issues such as how managerial functions differ between cultures.
2. *Culture free.* An approach taking contingency theory as the basis of seeking to explore the differences and similarities between cultures. The notion of contingency allows the perspective of cross-cultural studies to be undertaken and the impact on a variety of structural dimensions associated with organizing and managing to be explored.
3. *Culture bound.* This approach draws on a broad range of theoretical models to explore and explain differences between cultures.

Each of these categorization approaches has its own strength and they are not automatically mutually exclusive. Each could be used for different purposes, for example, the Cray and Mallory approach sets out to provide the basis for their cognitive model of international management. This uncertainty in how to classify studies of culture reflects the relatively recent exploration of this concept, together with the growing complexity of international operational activity and human multicultural experience which inevitably frustrates attempts to theorize in this field.

THE DIMENSIONS OF CULTURE

Schein (1985) identified six dimensions that, he suggests, reflect the composition of culture within an organizational context:

1. *Behavioural regularities.* This reflects observable patterns of behaviour. It might include induction ceremonies, in-group language and the ritualized behaviour that reflects membership of particular organizations.
2. *Dominant values.* These are the specific beliefs expressed by groups and organizations. For example, an organization might attempt to create a 'quality image' by adopting a number of specific initiatives, including publishing a policy.
3. *Norms.* These are general patterns of behaviour that all members of a group are expected to follow. For example, many retail chains encourage employees to use specific customer greetings including smiling and making eye contact.
4. *Rules.* Rules are specific instructions about what must be done, whereas norms are sometimes unwritten. The rules are the 'must dos' of the organization set out by management. However, because they must be followed employees may simply comply with them in order to avoid punishment.
5. *Philosophy.* In this context these reflect the underlying beliefs that people hold about people in general. Given that an organization is controlled by the managers who run it, the underlying philosophy tends to reflect their values.
6. *Climate.* The physical layout of buildings, recreation facilities, management style and the design of public areas all help to create the atmosphere or climate within the company.

Each of these six dimensions of culture is a complex idea in its own right. They do, however, offer descriptive ability in beginning to tease out how culture influences organizations and how in turn organizations can influence culture. This circularity is reflected in Figure 12.6.

FIGURE 12.6

The cycle of culture

The circularity displayed in Figure 12.6 indicates that culture produces particular behaviour and associated belief patterns, which in turn influences what actually happens within the organization. Actual events are then measured against management objectives with the consequences feeding back into culture. The implication being that if management perceive that a particular culture achieves the objectives being pursued it will be reinforced. If it does not contribute to the achievement of objectives then management will attempt to change it.

CULTURAL FRAMEWORKS

The previous discussion concentrated on the dimensions of culture evident at level two of the model included as Figure 12.5. It is now appropriate to describe how culture manifests itself at level one. In other words, how is culture experienced, observed and detected? The different approaches to this question are reviewed below.

Handy's four types

Based on the earlier work of Harrison (1972), Handy (1993) describes four manifestations of culture:

1. *Power culture*. Typically found in small organizations, everything revolves around the focal person. All important decisions are made by them and they retain absolute authority in all matters. As a diagram Handy describes this culture as a web (Figure 12.7). The success of power culture depends on the capabilities of the focal person in technical, business and management terms.
2. *Role culture*. This type of culture is based firmly on the existence of procedure and rule frameworks. It is typified by a Greek temple diagram (Figure 12.8). The hierarchy and bureaucracy dominate this type of organization, with instructions coming down the organization and information going back up to the senior levels.
3. *Task culture*. The expertise within this type of organization is vested in the individuals within it and it is they who must be organized in a way that meets the needs of the business. The description used by Handy to illustrate this

FIGURE 12.7

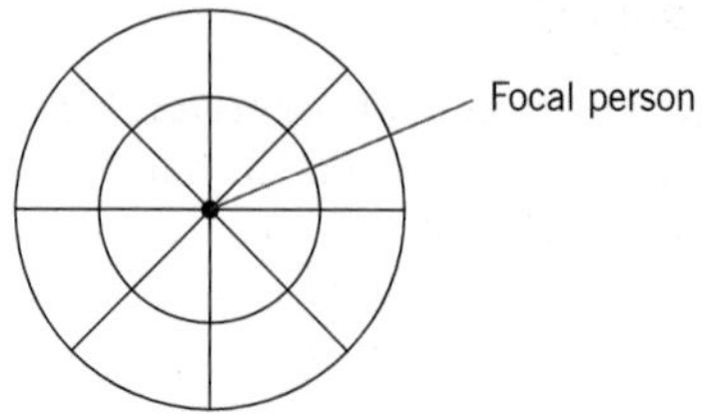

Power culture

FIGURE 12.8

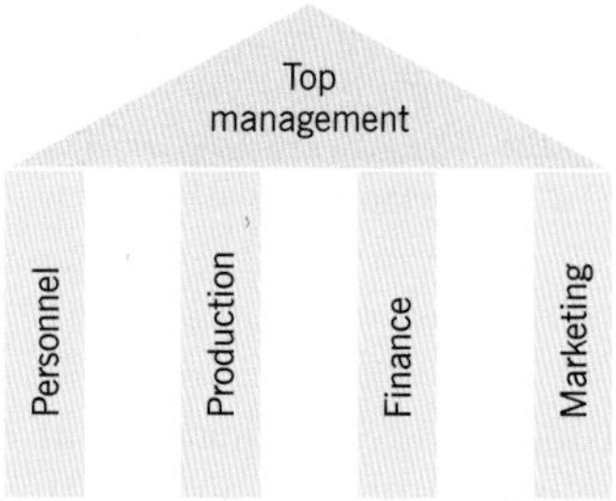

Role culture

culture is that of a net (Figure 12.9). This type of culture is supportive of a team organization. Decision making is frequently distributed throughout the 'net' dependent on the needs of the task. Organizations involved in project-based operations such as consultancy and civil engineering might be expected to adopt this cultural framework.

4. *Person culture*. This is based upon the individual and should not be confused with the power culture. The power culture is based around a single focal point. The person culture allows each person to be a focal point depending on the circumstances. A consultancy practice and barristers' chambers are used by Handy to illustrate this type of culture.

There are obvious links between the concept of culture as described here and the structural issues discussed in other chapters. Some of the links have been made obvious, as in the case of bureaucracy, while others have only been hinted at. For example, the task culture has a number of associations with the matrix form of structure, with its emphasis on teams and dual reporting relationships.

FIGURE 12.9

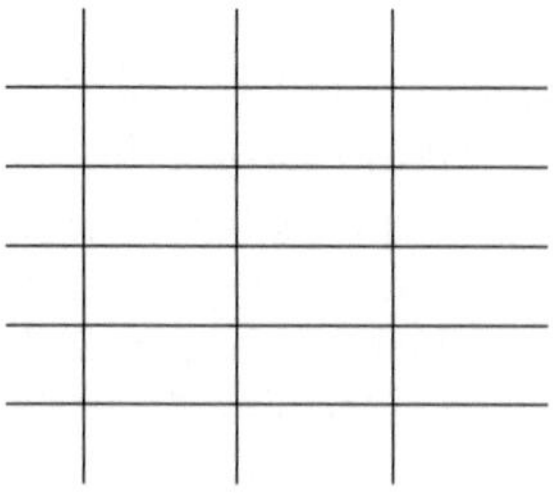

Task culture

Ouchi's type Z companies

Ouchi suggested that Japanese firms operated from a different cultural base to that of Western organizations. He also suggested that this difference originated from the societal culture in Japan and that it offered a likelihood of higher levels of productivity than found in Western cultures. In his 1981 work he identified a number of key differences between Japanese and American organizations (see Table 12.5).

Ouchi gave his idea the title Theory Z because it extended McGregor's Theory X and Theory Y (see Chapter 11) as a stereotypical organizational type. Ouchi suggests that some American organizations contained some of the features described in Table 12.5, but not to the extent found in Japanese organizations.

A number of the claims made by Ouchi have been brought into question by later researchers. For example, the notion of lifetime employment in Japan applies to only a small proportion of employees in a few larger organizations. It is also suggested that far from being a more participative approach to organizing work activity, the Japanese approach produces a more tightly controlled approach to work. Little personal discretion exists and employees are pitted against each other in the relentless search for ever higher productivity and quality (Garrahan and Stewart, 1992).

Peters and Waterman's excellence and culture

Peters and Waterman (1982) attempted to identify what it was that made some American organizations excellent. The research included reviews of the published data over a 25-year period on each of the 43 companies in the sample. This was supported by a range of interviews with senior executives. From this research (and in collaboration with Pascale and Athos) the **McKinsey 7-S Framework** was developed.

McKinsey 7-S Framework
A model consisting of seven interacting elements Structure, Strategy, Systems, Style, Skill, Staff, and Shared values (culture).

The seventh item in the list (shared values) relates specifically to organizational culture. From the 7-S Framework emerged a set of eight features that Peters and Waterman suggest are commonly found among excellent organizations. As such, these features prescribe the cultural dimensions of an excellence oriented organization from the perspective of 'the way things are done around here':

1. *Bias for action.* Based on the recognition that delay can be fatal. Managers should be action rather than analysis oriented.
2. *Being close to the customer.* Success requires a desire to get close to the customer in order to understand their needs.

Japanese organizations	American organizations
Lifetime employment	Short-term employment
Slow evaluation and promotion	Rapid evaluation and promotion
Non-specialized career paths	Specialized career paths
Implicit control mechanisms	Explicit control mechanism
Collective decision making	Individual responsibility
Holistic concern	Segmented concern

TABLE 12.5 Ouchi's cultural differences (*source*: Pugh, DS and Hickson, DJ (1989) *Writers on Organizations*, 4th edn, Penguin, London)

3. *Autonomy and entrepreneurship.* Everyone should be encouraged to contribute to company performance and to take risks in pursuit of the development of products and services that effectively meet the needs of customers.
4. *Productivity through people.* Acceptance that it is individual employees who deliver productivity in the dynamic, real-time world of organizations.
5. *Hands on, value driven.* The philosophy of the organization needs to be seen by all employees as a clear set of values that they can subscribe to. The hands-on perspective allows managers to personally experience all aspects of the organization through their presence where the work is done.
6. *Stick to the knitting.* By staying close to products and services that the organization has experience of, the degree of risk is reduced. Moves into unfamiliar territory reduce the relevance of the knowledge available, making the risk of failure higher.
7. *Simple form, lean staff.* The temptation to elaborate organizational design and the accompanying systems and procedures should be resisted. There is a tendency to seek to incorporate new functions and specialisms as finance allows and perceived need dictates. In addition there is always the political temptation for managers to build empires as a means of increasing their own status and influence.
8. *Simultaneous loose–tight control.* This reflects the ability to achieve a balance between effective control and the freedom of action necessary to take advantage of circumstances as they develop.

The ideas developed by Peters and Waterman have been subjected to considerable criticism. A number of the organizations they identified as excellent very quickly ran into problems in the recessionary markets of the early to mid-1980s. Peters himself produced work which he claimed superseded these ideas. For example, in *Thriving on Chaos* (1989) he describes even more radical approaches to dealing with the turbulence from market uncertainty. However, as suggested earlier, Thompson and McHugh (1995) claim that the excellence literature has little to offer in the debate on organizational culture. It is possible to reconcile these two positions in that the excellence literature reflects a number of organizational practices which in themselves do not define culture, but reflect the first level in Figure 12.5, whereas Thompson and McHugh reflect on issues pertinent to levels two and three.

Management in Action 12.2 provides an insight into the ideas of a senior manager and writer who wants to encourage radical approaches to how culture can be used to influence corporate activity.

Deal and Kennedy's cultural profile

The work of Deal and Kennedy (1982) developed two particular aspects of organizational culture. First, they describe four types of culture based on the approach to risk and the speed of feedback from the environment on decision making:

1. *Work and play hard culture.* This culture is grounded in cohesive groups that attack both work and play enthusiastically. This category would be typically found in organizations with low risk but rapid feedback loops, for example fast-food restaurants.
2. *Process culture.* This culture emphasizes the systems and procedures because success comes from attention to detail. It is typified by a low-risk environment with a slow feedback response, for example local government and large insurance companies.

MANAGEMENT IN ACTION 12.2 Secrets of the Semler effect

Semco is a company based in Brazil headed by Ricardo Semler who took over the company from his father at the beginning of the 1980s when he was just 21 years old. Since then he has taken the manufacturer of pumps, mixers and other industrial equipment to new heights, with sales growing by a factor of six and profits by 500 per cent. In many ways the company is a vast test bed for new and different ideas in managing and organizing.

The most startling impact of Semco from the outside is that employees are able to set their own working hours, some are even able to set their own salary levels and everyone from the highest to the lowest has open access to company financial information. The intention is to create a self-sustaining organization which can carry on without an obvious leader. For example, five people share the position of chief executive officer on a six-month rotating basis. Semler takes his turn along with the others.

Semler takes the view that: 'The main goal of a company should be to create an entity which everyone involved in feels is worthwhile. That will then manifest itself in good quality and good customer service.' He also considers that the company is an ongoing project and that change is not a once-for-all effect: 'Semco is an ongoing project and we think we are only halfway there. We need another 10–15 years to finish the job.'

In setting the approach for Semco, Semler picked aspects from many other organizations and systems: personal freedom, individualism and competition from capitalism; control of greed and sharing of information and power from socialism. The flexibility of the Japanese was also added, although not the veneration of elders or strong ties to the company. The company was about to enter a consolidation phase in its evolution he suggested. For example, only about 25 per cent of employees set their own salaries. Semler would like to see everyone undertaking that role as well as being involved with the financial analysis programmes. He would also like to see the level of working from home increased from the 20 per cent of people who currently do so for between one and three days each week.

Clearly a sea change is under way at Semco that influences the way work is organized and managed. Many other companies, researchers and students have sought Semler's advice on how to achieve the same level of success. This advice can now be acquired from his book on his approach at Semco, but Ricardo Semler claims not to be about to become a consultant, selling his vision to others!

Adapted from: Dickson, T (1993) Secrets of the Semler effect, *Financial Times*, 25 June, p 13.

Stop ↔ Consider

Is the approach adopted by Semler an attempt to allow culture to develop as preferred by the employees or an attempt to impose one preferred by himself?
To what extent does the answer to this question matter to employees, managers or customers?
To what extent do you consider that because the company culture indicated is so different from any other that particular types of people would be encouraged to join it and they therefore become highly motivated by these differences?
If more companies were to follow this example would the lack of uniqueness limit the success? Why or why not?

3. *Macho culture.* This type of culture is associated with high risk and rapid feedback. It implies similar features to the power and person cultures identified earlier. It is based on the ability of the focal person to be able to achieve objectives, for example small entrepreneurial organizations and specialized consultancies.
4. *Bet your company culture.* The emphasis in this culture is on the technical skill to 'get it right' within directional guidelines. The risks are very high but the feedback is slow in coming from the environment.

The second perspective added by the work of Deal and Kennedy is that of the existence of strong and weak cultures. A strong culture would be evident if almost all members supported it or if it were composed of deeply held values and beliefs. Table 12.6 indicates those features associated with a strong culture. A weak culture by comparison is one that is not strongly supported or rooted in the activities and value systems of the group.

From the items included in Table 12.6 two are of particular interest. The hero is a person who personifies the values and actions expected of the true believer in that particular culture. They are used as role models for the population at large. The use of ritual and ceremony as the basis of reinforcement of the desired culture is also part of the mechanism for ensuring that it is internalized by individuals. The importance of ritual and ceremony was demonstrated by Wright (1979) in a story about retirement parties and included as the Employee Perspective (12.4) following.

Managers frequently seek to inculcate a strong culture in order to achieve the simple form, lean staff type of organization identified by Peters and Waterman. A strong culture which is highly supportive of management's objectives makes the organization easier to manage as more of the collective effort and energy is channelled towards meeting business objectives. However, there is a conflict inherent in this situation in that strong cultures become difficult to change as a result of the very depth of commitment and unity created by them.

Trice and Beyer's organizational culture

Trice and Beyer (1984) describe culture in terms of it being a device for providing common meaning for a particular group. This was developed into an approach described as a **cultural web** by writers such as Johnson (1992). Trice and Beyer describe a number of elements that go to make up an organizational culture, grouped together under four categories as follows.

Cultural web
The routines, rituals, stories, symbols, power structures, control systems and organization structure that contribute to a particular culture.

1. Company communications The means through which culture is described, communicated to the group and continually reinforced across time:

- *Stories.* Reflections of the past but elaborated in the retelling.
- *Myths, sagas and legends.* Including real and fictional events from the past reinforcing the 'greatness' of the group. Often involving the founders and heroes.
- *Folk tales.* Fictional stories which carry meaning and reinforcement for existing and new members.
- *Symbols.* The outward and visible signs that express the underlying values of the group and which individuals are expected to uphold.

- Widely shared philosophy
- Concern for individuals
- Recognition of heroes
- Belief in ritual and ceremony
- Well-understood informal rules and expectations
- Importance of individual contribution to whole

TABLE 12.6 Deal and Kennedy's strong cultural elements

EMPLOYEE PERSPECTIVE 12.4 Breaking the conventions

One of the purposes of retirement parties is to provide an opportunity for employees to say goodbye to the 'old guard' and to demonstrate their allegiance to the remaining team and the firm as a whole. They also represent an opportunity for the retiree to show that there is a smooth transition and that the 'baton' of office has been safely handed on to the next generation. As such the speeches and events are usually carefully scripted and choreographed to meet these demands. At one such event a retiring General Motors executive in America broke the unwritten rules by openly criticizing a senior manager much to the visible embarrassment of the others in the room.

Task

Is it always wrong to break the conventions surrounding such ceremonial events? Why or why not? Under what circumstances might it be acceptable to do so and why?

2. Company practice These reflect the activities that organizations engage in demonstrating the culture in operation and reinforcement of its importance:

- *Rites*. This might involve a public reward for some noteworthy behaviour by an employee which demonstrated the cultural norms.
- *Ritual*. Refers to behaviour that helps to reinforce group cohesion. Company outings and team building activities can often serve this purpose.
- *Ceremonial*. The official visit of a head of state to another country is accompanied by much ceremony. Company milestones also offer similar opportunities, for example celebrating 50 years of operation.

3. Common language Every organization has its own terminology to describe events and activities. A major part of the socialization of new members into a new group involves their learning the common language for that group. For example, engineers must learn the technical terms for their area of engineering. This serves to separate them from non-engineers as well as providing an effective form of communication. It also serves to reinforce group cohesion in that it helps to bind together the individuals through common forms of expression.

4. Physical culture This reflects the physical nature of organizations and is the tangible reflection of the culture.

- *Artefacts*. The equipment and facilities provided are a strong signal about the culture. For example, the presence of director-only car parking and dining rooms provides a reflection of the underlying culture.
- *Layout*. The physical layout of the buildings and offices provides a reflection of the aims, intentions and operating preferences prevalent within the organization.

Sub- and countercultures

In the discussion so far culture has been described as a unifying or integrating concept, which binds together the individuals within the organization. However, that is not the only view of culture. It is also possible to see culture as a differentiating feature of organizational life. This differentiation view of culture concentrates on the different groups that exist within the organization. At this level of analysis it becomes possible to identify inconsistencies between the culture of the organization and that of different groups within it (Meyerson and Martin, 1987). The existence of different

Sub-cultures
Refers to a sub-set of the dominant culture within a specific context.

Counter-cultures
The existence of one or more groups that have objectives running counter to those of the dominant group.

groups within a single organization forces consideration of disunity and even conflict as part of the cultural milieu. These groups within an organization are usually referred to as either **sub-cultures** or **countercultures**. This means that there will be differences in the cultures operating across the organization and not a single, common one. For example, Haugh and McKee (2003) studied small family firms in north-east Scotland. They found that in some cases the group adopting the culture of the dominant family formed an inner team, the rest of the employees (sharing a different value system) forming a peripheral team. This raises several issues in relation to the notion of a single organizational culture and how layers of slightly varying culture meld together within a common context (the organization). It would not be surprising to find that the organizational culture was a blend of subgroup cultures (subcultures) or even the imposition of a dominant culture on a collection of suppressed minority ones.

Countercultures exist where one or more groups are disaffected and have objectives that run counter to those of the dominant group. Within an organization, countercultures can exist in parts of the company and can create hostility and anti-management sentiments. For example, countercultures can develop following a company takeover. Some managers and groups may feel that their contribution is undervalued by the acquiring company and that they are being forced to accept new procedures and ways of working. Consequently resentment, resistance behaviours and attitudes begin to emerge. Such resistance is often self-perpetuating in that it begins to isolate the individuals from the main groups and increases the value of the counterculture to the deviants – as they become regarded.

It can also be argued that as the culture within society changes the dominant culture within an organization comes under pressure to change. This can be described as cultural diversity or, perhaps more accurately, cultural fragmentation. This can be clearly illustrated through recent reviews of the Metropolitan Police service in London and its continued lack of ability effectively to accommodate women and people from ethnic communities into its ranks (Cooper, 2000 b). This report finds that appropriate policies exist but that the operationalization of them fails because of an inability to gain understanding or commitment to them at the lower levels of the organization, perhaps because of the existence of sub- or countercultures. Another major problem was identified as training because it was not effectively tied to the achievement of the intended objectives and so failed clearly to support them or be grounded in the identified training 'gap'. The nature of culture and associated tensions within international organizations and the role of human resource managers in attempting to achieve appropriate cultures are illustrated in Management in Action 12.3.

THE DETERMINANTS OF CULTURE

In the early days of an organization the culture is very much dependent upon the founders, their personalities and preferred ways of doing things. Employees must learn the culture, a process Herskovitts (1948) termed as enculturation, a process similar to learning by assimilation. Handy (1993) indicates a number of influences on the apparent culture of an organization:

- *History and ownership.* Culture is something that is partly independent of individuals within the organization. In most cases the company existed before particular employees joined it, and it will continue to exist after they leave. From that perspective, the culture of an organization could be subject to accommodation as people flow through it and interact with the culture that exists. The type of ownership will also have an impact on the culture of the

MANAGEMENT IN ACTION 12.3 Winning ways with culture

In a research project, the Institute of Personnel and Development sought to find out how personnel professionals could function in relation to the development and change of corporate cultures within international organizations. For international organizations there are two cultures active in any given context; the national culture and the organizational culture, and tension can exist between them.

The study concentrated on cross-border management and was based upon 15 international organizations at different stages of cultural 'management'. At one extreme there was a major bank undergoing a culture change programme and at the other a French retail company attempting to retain its 40 year old 'family' culture. As a working definition of culture the study recognized that it is largely determined by the environment, including national values, business and customer characteristics as well as economic considerations. The four main determinants of corporate culture were identified as strategy, structure and technology, values and systems, and policies.

Managing tension was one of the key skills in relation to the management or change of corporate culture. Tension arises when the existing culture is being challenged during a change process or when the components within an existing culture are incompatible. A four-cell matrix was created, based on the closeness of the relationship between home base and local site, and an organization being either people or systems driven. The four cells (cultures) in the matrix were:

- *Value driven*. People driven and a close relationship with home base, this cell implies that some common policies and practices would exist, but individual locations retain considerable freedom to adapt to local circumstances.
- *Centralist*. A close relationship with a home base and systems driven, this cell implies that policies and procedures are determined by the home country with little local discretion.
- *Local autonomous*. People driven and with a loose connection to the home base, this cell implies considerable freedom to allow separate cultures to coexist within the company.
- *Pioneer*. Systems driven with a loose relationship with the home base, this cell implies a use of expatriate managers to run local organizations in line with centrally determined systems, with limited discretion to adapt to local conditions.

In terms of the role of personnel managers towards corporate culture the study identified several areas of initiative, including:

- *Strategic development*. The identification of appropriate cultural components and the associated personnel policies.
- *Communication*. Of policies and procedures in such a way that the cultural norms are reinforced at every location and at all levels.
- *Implementation*. Of flexible personnel practices and appropriate training to encourage people to cope with change and to reinforce the desired culture.
- *Review*. Constantly review the people management strategies, policies and practices to ensure that they support the desired culture.

The research concluded with the view that diversity represented an important organizational strength not a weakness and that some organizations were making effective commercial use of this.

Adapted from: Baron, A (1994) Winning ways with culture, *Personnel Management,* October, pp 64–8.

Stop ↔ Consider

How could human resource managers contribute to the development of each of the four cultures indicated in this research?

How might human resource managers seek to change the culture within an organization from (say) the pioneer culture to (say) the value-driven culture?

organization. For example, a small company owned by an authoritarian figure will be managed in a totally different way from that owned by a humane bureaucrat. The Haugh and McKee study above is also relevant in this context.

- *Size.* Size influences culture if for no other reason than the formality required in the operation of larger organizations. This does not imply that large organizations have cultures that are 'better' or 'worse' than small organizations, simply that they differ.
- *Technology.* An organization that specializes in the use of high technology will emphasize the technical skills of employees in the values that govern its culture. Contrast that situation with a company where the emphasis is on personal service which would value a completely different set of characteristics and values.
- *Goals and objectives.* What the organization sets out to achieve will also influence the culture. For example, the organization that seeks to become the best in customer service within its industry will seek to incorporate values inherent in that idea into the culture.
- *Environment.* The organizational environment is made up of several elements. There are the customer markets, the supplier markets, the financial markets, governmental influences, competitors and the environmental lobby, to name just a few. The way in which an organization chooses to interact with its environment will influence its culture.
- *People.* Manager's preferred approach to the management of their subordinates helps to form the organization culture. Employee preferences as to how they wish to be managed also influences the way that culture develops. If management attempt to enforce a culture that is unacceptable to employees there will undoubtedly be a reaction, examples being industrial action, sabotage, high labour turnover, low productivity, low quality and a need for tight supervision and control.

Management in Action 12.4 outlines some of the strategies that may be necessary if a change in culture is desired, perhaps in difficult circumstances.

NATIONAL CULTURE

Organizations operate within a national setting. In that sense they are subject to the same cultural forces that act upon every other aspect of life in that situation. The majority of employees of an organization will come from the national setting into the organization bringing their culture with them. It would be natural to expect, therefore, that the culture of an organization would be based largely on the predominant local culture. However, that is an assumption that proves very difficult to refute or substantiate as a result of the number of factors acting upon any given situation. For example, within any national or organizational culture there exists sub- and countercultures that introduce variety; there is the growing movement of people around the world introducing cultural diversity into any particular setting. There is also the growing globalization of business which introduces another element of variety into the cultural milieu.

The convergence perspective on the relationship between national and organizational culture suggests that within an organization the national culture is subservient. This implies that organizations are able to identify and separate culture into two distinct forms (internal and external). Also, that they are able to manage the internal form as necessary to support business objectives as distinct from the surrounding

MANAGEMENT IN ACTION 12.4 Cultivate your culture

Egan argues that there are often two levels of culture operational in any organizational setting. The 'culture-in-use' represents the dominant culture in any particular context. There is also a 'culture behind-the-culture' that represents the real beliefs, values and norms that underpin behaviour patterns within the company. These cultures can either add cost or benefit to the organization depending on the degree to which they support effective operational activity.

Egan proposes a number of strategies for dealing with culture change:

1. Strategies based on business reality:
   - A change in business strategy can provide the necessary leverage for changing culture.
   - The use of total quality management and business process re-engineering are just two recent examples of approaches that can be used to lever culture change.
   - Restructuring and reorganizing work also provides opportunities for culture change.
   - Using levers such as training and promotion to reinforce the message and move people into other jobs can assist cultural change.
2. Change-linked strategies:
   - Direct action in areas not apparently associated with culture can produce changes in culture as a consequence.
   - Financial or other crisis situations are opportunities to change the culture as people are more likely to adopt different behaviours and accept change across a broad front.
3. Frontal attacks:
   - The use of guerrilla tactics such as the use of roving 'hit squads' (individuals with the power to turn up and ask difficult questions) to begin a culture change process.
   - Simply flooding the organization with training courses and other programmes to promote the new values can be an effective (if costly) way of 'forcing' the new culture into the system by 'swamping' the old one.
   - The use of symbols to convey powerful messages about both the demise of the old culture and emergence of the new. For example, it is reported that Lee Iacocca, former chairman of Chrysler, turned down the car presented to him by the workforce and asked for the next one off the assembly line, the symbolism being that every car should be capable of being presented to the chairman.
   - Constantly pointing out that the dominant culture is not beneficial can become so annoying that people change, just to stop the constant annoyance.
   - Form a critical mass of people who can champion the new culture and encourage them to work on the others in the organization who need to be convinced.
   - Simply announcing 'what-will-be' might just achieve the change in culture. It is possible that others are simply waiting for positive direction.

Adapted from: Egan, G (1994) Cultivate your culture, *Management Today*, April, pp 39–42.

Stop ↔ Consider

Culture emerges naturally over time in any given situation. Consequently, any attempt to change or manage culture represents management attempts to manipulate employees in the search for higher levels of control and profit.

Discuss this statement in the light of the advice given by Egan.

national culture. In practice this view holds that employees leave their national culture at the door when they arrive at work and automatically adopt the cultural values of the workplace without difficulty.

The divergence view holds that national culture takes preference and that organizational culture will adapt to local cultural patterns (Lammers and Hickson, 1979). This view holds that it is organizations that need to adapt to local circumstances otherwise the corporate culture will be out of synchronization with the local norms and will be ignored or even create problems. It is not difficult to envisage that both views could be correct in appropriate circumstances. For example, large international organizations that operate according to centralized styles could well display convergence characteristics, while, conversely, organizations predominantly based in a specific country are more likely to demonstrate divergence. The problems that can result from the clash of cultures in a joint venture situation (based on a case study in China) are demonstrated by Xiaoli (2001).

It is also possible that there will be a middle line. That organizational culture will adapt to meet the needs of both head office and the local situation. It has even been suggested to me by postgraduate students from many parts of the world with practice of working in companies headquartered in other countries that a form of what was described as innocent deception is frequently practised. This implies that local staff give the superficial appearance (officially and upwards) of complying with the requirements of head office, while in practice doing things as dictated by the local culture. This, of course, is anecdotal evidence and therefore of limited value, but it is heard frequently and it always sounds credible. For a review of the convergence and divergence debate in relation to the ethnic and organizational circumstances in South Africa see Herselman (2001).

Hofstede's perspectives

Hofstede (1983, 1984) carried out an extensive series of studies into culture over some 13 years. He defines culture as mental programming because it predisposes individuals to particular ways of thinking, perceiving and behaving. That is not to say that everyone within a particular culture is identical, simply that there is a tendency for similarity to exist. He developed four dimensions of culture from a factor analysis of his questionnaire research:

1. *Individualism–collectivism.* This factor relates to the degree of integration between individuals in a society. At one extreme, individuals concentrate on looking after their own interests and those of their family. The other extreme emphasizes collective responsibility to the extended family and the community.
2. *Power distance.* The degree of centralization of authority. The higher the concentration of power in a few people at the top, the higher the power distance score. A low power distance score implies a closer link between those with power and 'ordinary' people.
3. *Uncertainty avoidance.* How the members of a society deal with uncertainty. Societies in which individuals are relatively secure do not feel threatened by the views of others and tend to take risk in their stride (weak uncertainty avoidance). Strong uncertainty avoidance requires policies, procedures and institutions to control and minimize the effects of uncertainty and risk.
4. *Masculinity–femininity.* In societies classified as 'masculine' activity tends to be gender based, stressing achievement, making money, generation of tangible outputs and largeness of scale. Societies classified as feminine tended to be those putting people before money, seeking a high quality of life, helping others, preservation of the environment and smallness of scale.

Table 12.7 provides an indication of those countries that exhibit high and low levels of each of the four dimensions identified by Hofstede.

Hofstede considered that power distance and uncertainty avoidance were the 'decisive dimensions' of organizational culture (1990, p 403). This view clearly links organizational and national culture by implying that the preferred ways of managing and organizing in a specific context will be based upon the national tendencies. This

	Individualism	Power distance	Uncertainty avoidance	Masculinity
High	USA	Philippines	Greece	Japan
	UK	Mexico	Portugal	Australia
	Australia	India	Japan	Italy
	Canada	Brazil	France	Mexico
Low	Mexico	Australia	Denmark	Sweden
	Greece	Israel	Sweden	Denmark
	Taiwan	Denmark	UK	Thailand
	Colombia	Sweden	USA	Finland
			India	

TABLE 12.7 Illustration of Hofstede's classification

assumption is not, however, directly tested in his work. It is possible that organizational culture is composed of different dimensions from national culture.

The research itself can be criticized on the basis of its emphasis on description rather than analysis. Categorization of cultures is inevitably a simplification process based on frameworks and interpretation imposed by the researcher. Although there are statistical methods that can be used to identify clusters of related data (Hofstede used this approach) it is still left to the researcher to interpret the findings. By adopting this approach, Hofstede omits a more detailed consideration of how cultures form, change and are maintained (Furnham and Gunter, 1993). As presented, the dimensions give no clue as to the degree of difference that could be expected in any context (Tyson and Jackson, 1992). Hofstede tends to regard culture as relatively consistent across time, changing only slowly, a view based upon anthropological perspectives. More recent work from a sociological perspective prefers the view of culture as a much more dynamic process representing the balance between contradictory social and economic pressures constantly acting on a society in real time (Alvesson, 1993).

Trompenaars' perspective

Frans Trompenaars, worked for Shell in nine countries before becoming a consultant. He built up a database of the cultural characteristics of 15 000 managers and staff from 30 companies in 50 different countries. In his book (1993) he discusses several aspects of cultural difference and its relationship with organizational life based on his database.

His views contrast sharply with those that suggest that the world is becoming a 'global village', in that he argues firmly that what works in one culture will seldom do so in another. Included in his observations are the following examples:

- *Performance pay.* He suggests that people in France, Germany, Italy and many parts of Asia tend not to accept that 'individual members of the group should excel in a way that reveals the shortcomings of other members'.
- *Two-way communications.* Americans may be motivated by feedback sessions, Germans, however, find them, 'enforced admissions of failure'.

- *Decentralization and delegation*. These approaches might work well in Anglo-Saxon cultures, Scandinavia, the Netherlands and Germany, but are likely to fail in Belgium, France and Spain.

Trompenaars identifies seven dimensions of culture. Five deal with the way in which people interact with each other. A sixth deals with people's perspective on time and the seventh concerns the approach to moulding the environment. These combine to create different corporate cultures including:

- *Family*. Typically found in Japan, India, Belgium, Italy, Spain and among small French companies. Hierarchical in structure with the leader playing a 'father figure' within the organization. Praise can frequently be a better motivator than money in such cultures.
- *Eiffel Tower*. Large French companies typify this culture, as might be expected. It also embraces some German and Dutch companies. Hierarchical in structure, very impersonal, rule driven and slow to adapt to change are the dominant characteristics.
- *Guided missile*. Typical of American companies, and to a lesser extent those in the UK. They are typified as egalitarian and strongly individualistic in nature with a measure of impersonality. They tend to be capable of adjusting the established course of action quickly but not completely to new situations.

Trompenaars advises companies to avoid a blanket approach to culture, based on the dominant head office variety. Instead he argues that a transnational approach should be adopted, in which the best elements from several cultures are brought together and applied differently in each country. Managers should also be trained in cross-cultural awareness and respect and how to avoid seeing other people's cultural perspective as stubbornness.

GLOBALIZATION AND CULTURE

Globalization is a term that has a relatively recent history in relation to the ways in which business operates. According to Yip (1989) globalization consists of a three-stage evolutionary process:

- Developing a core strategy as the basis of competitive advantage, usually home country based.
- Internationalization of the home country strategy. A multinational organization.
- Globalization through integration of largely separate country-based international strategies.

The third stage of this model is what differentiates globalization from international business activity. Bartlett and Ghoshal (1989) identify two forms of global organization:

- *International organization*. The global company seeks to capitalize on the advantages of the global scale in a centralized way; whereas the international organization seeks to function more like a co-ordinated federation. They seek a balance between the needs and contribution of the centre and local units.
- *Transnational organization*. This type of organization seeks to blend together the three major themes of global integration, local differentiation and worldwide innovation. In practice an integrated network of all available resources and products used to the best advantage of the organization as a whole.

One of the difficulties facing any organization operating internationally is that of culture. Every country is made up of different cultural groups, with varying degrees of similarity and difference. Equally, cultural groupings frequently span national boundaries. Even today there are several major trouble spots in the world where ethnicity (as an expression of culture) is linked to attempts to break up an existing country into individual self-ruled autonomous units. So 'nation' is only a poor reflection of the cultural boundaries that exist among the people who inhabit the world.

There are two basic options available to an organization in its approach to culture:

- *Polycentric*. This approach takes the view that it is not possible to operate in a consistent way around the world as a consequence of the cultural differences that exist. Therefore each unit within the company should be allowed to operate appropriately within its cultural context. The danger with this approach is that the organization becomes overwhelmed with the impact of the number and scale of cultural differences that must be accommodated. Not every cultural difference needs to be incorporated into the ways of doing things across the organization. Bribes are a common experience for many organizations as illustrated in the following Employee Perspective (12.5).
- *Ethnocentric*. This assumes the superiority of the culture of the globalizing organization and holds that every other culture must be subservient to it. This view holds that it is a business imperative to have worldwide consistency in policy, procedure and practice to make it easier to run the company. The potential danger of this approach is that it may prevent the company getting close to the local community and so lose competitive advantage. Also local staff must tread a difficult line between following orders and meeting the needs of the situation which can also cause problems.

Ulrich and Black (1999) reflect upon the process of globalization in terms of the often quoted mantra of acting globally and thinking locally. This requires the organization to consider its capability of meeting these demands if they are to function successfully in the global market. They suggest that six areas of capability arise from this need, included as Table 12.8.

It should be obvious from the list in Table 12.8 that each of the capabilities listed involves managing a tension. It is through this tension that culture makes its impact evident. In seeking to organize on a global scale it is necessary for senior managers to retain control and to be able to extract ever greater levels of value from the operations.

EMPLOYEE PERSPECTIVE 12.5 Bribes as a way of life?

Most western companies would seek to avoid becoming involved in bribes as a way of doing business, but in some parts of the world this practice is a way of life. In some countries it is difficult for the government to raise enough tax to be able to pay for an effective public service. Consequently, paying money to public servants can be a form of local tax collection as they seek to make a living wage. For example, it has been reported (Stockton, 1986) that in Mexico it is common practice for businesses to 'tip' the local postman once a month, otherwise the post simply gets lost in the system.

Tasks

1. If you delivered the post to business premises in Mexico how do you think you might feel about the 'tips' that you receive from business premises?
2. Imagine that you worked for a large British or American company and had been posted to run the office in Mexico. You have been asked to sign a petty cash voucher authorizing the 'tips' for the post delivery person when company policy specifically states that bribes should not be paid. How would you react and why?

1	To determine core activities and separate them from non-core activities
2	To achieve consistency while encouraging flexibility
3	To obtain leverage in the market (bigger is better) at the same time as focus (smaller is better)
4	To share learning throughout the organization and to encourage the creation of new knowledge
5	To build a global brand that respects and honours local custom
6	To engender a global perspective at the same time as ensuring local accountability

TABLE 12.8 The six global capabilities

This involves the inevitable and never ending search for economies of scale. In the search for control and cost effectiveness uniformity in all things is an inevitable first port of call. However, cultural (and other) differences around the world simply will not allow such simple solutions. For example, Colgate-Palmolive found that its large tubes of toothpaste were not selling well in Latin America and was forced to introduce much smaller tube sizes. The reason for this was that most people simply could not afford the price of a large tube.

There is another form of globalization with a direct impact on cultural issues in organizations. That is the growing tendency for organizations to experience multicultural issues within a single operational unit. With an increasing number of people from different ethnic traditions being found in most countries it is common to have to deal with cultural diversity in an organization's home territory. It is possible to adopt either a polycentric or ethnocentric approach to these issues, although European legislation in relation to equality prefers the polycentric approach.

MANAGING CULTURE

In seeking to address the issue of how culture impacts on behaviour in an organizational context, Cray and Mallory (1998, pp 89–112) propose a cognitive model. The essence being that actual behaviour is based on many forces acting on that individual, including culture. Their model of the cognitive approach to cultural influences on behaviour is included as Figure 12.10.

In offering a basis for being able to manage cultural issues more effectively the model allows an improved understanding of why contrasting behaviours occur between cultural boundaries. As such it should allow those cognitive features which are deep seated and thus less amenable to change to be identified and separated out from those cognitive components that may be easier to manipulate (Cray and Mallory, 1998, p 107). The writers illustrate the potential of the model through the work of Calori *et al.* (1992). This found differences between French and British managers in their cognitive maps of the dynamic competitive forces in their organization's environment. The differences, it is argued, are based on educational system and cultural differences between the two countries. Similar differences in the cognitions of managers between the industries included were also found, suggesting support for the organizational cognitive framework element included in the model.

A number of tools have been developed over recent years that seek to measure aspects of culture within an organization, making it easier to manage those aspects

FIGURE 12.10

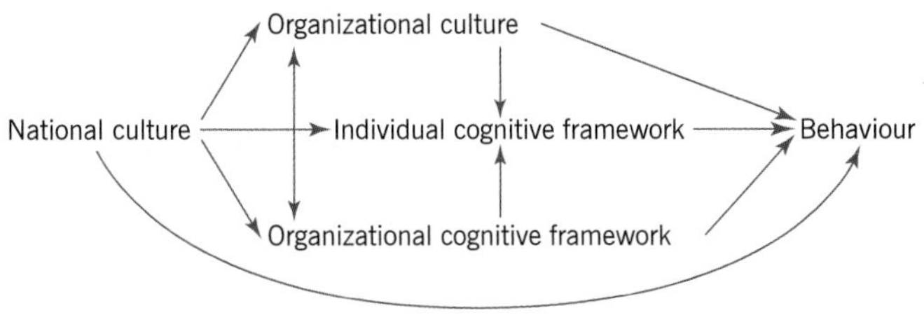

The impact of culture on behaviour: a cognitive model (*source*: Cray, D and Mallory, G (1998) *Making Sense of Managing Culture*, International Thomson Business, London)

that need attention. For example Littlefield (1999) uses a nine-factor test developed by Cartwright from the University of Exeter in a case study of Kerry Foods, a large direct sales company with a turnover of £70m per year that had been formed as a result of several mergers and which employed 500 people. A number of problem areas were identified from the case study, including the need to address the way in which head office initiatives were communicated and implemented; together with the style of management adopted by first-line managers. There was also a need to integrate the staff from the various merged companies into one unit. As a result of various initiatives over a year, senior managers of the company felt that it had been possible to manage the culture by beginning to understand and change it. It was intended that an annual survey based on the nine factors (shown in Table 12.9) would help to measure cultural shifts across the company.

Trompenaars and Woolliams (1999) elaborate on Trompenaars' earlier work on culture and link it with that of Charles Hampden-Turner. In doing so they identify seven dimensions reflecting ways that values differ between cultures:

1. *Universalism v participation.* This reflects the distinction between cultures which value allegiance to rules and those which value loyalty to relationships and other people.
2. *Individualism v communitarianism.* This reflects the distinction between cultures that favour individual fulfilment compared to those which value behaviour in support of the group as a whole.
3. *Specific v diffuses.* This reflects the distinction between cultures which favour facts and impersonal business relationships compared to those which prefer personal relationships within business.
4. *Neutrality v affectivity.* This reflects the differences between cultures in which it is common to hide emotions or where it is acceptable to be open with personal emotions.
5. *Inner directed v outer directed.* This reflects the differences between cultures in the degree to which individuals feel that they are in control of their environment.

Acceptance	Trust/agreement	Development
Fairness	Expectation	Team spirit
Respect	Balance	Ownership

TABLE 12.9 The nine key factors

6. *Achieved status v ascribed status.* In some cultures success confirms status and delivers promotion. In others status is a function of position, which subsequently motivates the individual who then delivers success.
7. *Sequential time v synchronic time.* This dimension reflects the differences between cultures in orientation to the passage of time, the varying focus on timescales and ability to handle more than one thing at a time.

The writers argue that each of these dimensions reflects an aspect of managing in what they call a transcultural manner. Each of the dimensions reflects a tension between the two juxtaposed concepts that must be reconciled in some way or other by managers operating across cultures. The conflicts that arise in seeking to deal with the differences in cultural preference evident in each dimension must involve actions such as compromise, reconciliation of the different perspectives or allowing one cultural norm to dominate. In some situations their research shows that women appear to exhibit a higher ability to be able to reconcile opposing values than do their male counterparts. Also some men begin by starting from their own cultural perspective and then move towards the opposing values as they seek to resolve the dilemma. They have also found in their preliminary research that those managers who recognize, respect and are able to reconcile the dilemmas arising under each one of these seven dimensions perform better than those who do not.

CHANGING ORGANIZATIONAL CULTURE

Turner (1986) criticizes the view that culture can be managed, suggesting that it would not be possible to manipulate it accurately because it becomes such an integral part of the organization's fabric. The definition of culture in relatively superficial terms also ensures that it is more amenable to change (Berg, 1985). For example, if culture were defined only in terms of the symbols used to reinforce it, changing the symbols would change the culture. Lundberg (1985) argues that it is possible to change culture and provides a six-stage programme for achieving this objective:

1. *External.* Identify external conditions that may encourage a change to the existing culture.
2. *Internal.* Identify internal circumstances and individuals that would support change.
3. *Pressures.* Identify those forces pressing for change in the culture.
4. *Visioning.* Identify key stakeholders and create in them a vision of the proposed changes, the needs and benefits.
5. *Strategy.* Develop a strategy for achieving the implementation of the new culture.
6. *Action.* Develop and implement a range of action plans based on the strategy as a means of achieving movement to the desired culture.

There are a number of problems with this view. It is rather simplistic about what defines culture and also the nature of change. To suggest that there is only one culture within an organization is to deny the existence of sub- and countercultures. Consequently, there are political, power and control perspectives to take into account. Perhaps the 'problem' is not one of how to ensure that change happens, but one of ensuring that it moves in the right direction. Grugulis and Wilkinson (2002) for example review the very significant changes that took place in British Airways during the 1980s and 1990s and which were frequently cited as exemplars of how culture change could deliver significant commercial advantage. Whilst not denying that significant change took place the writers make a compelling case for the impact of the environment and structural change rather than culture itself being significant factors in the results achieved. Looked at from this point of view it is possible to reconcile the two apparently opposing perspectives concerning culture change. Perhaps culture can be described as very difficult to change in the short term, but viewed as a continually changing phenomenon it can be manipulated in appropriate directions over time. It could also be amenable to rapid change in times of crisis when survival becomes an issue on which to focus the attention of everyone in the organization. Hursthouse and Kolb (2001) demonstrate that a new and different culture can be achieved in greenfield situations within the same company through the adoption of different strategies. This study was undertaken in a food processing plant in New Zealand. Management in Action 12.5 demonstrates how one service industry organization went about changing its culture.

ETHICS AND ORGANIZATIONAL CULTURE: AN APPLIED PERSPECTIVE

A considerable proportion of management activity is about taking decisions. Implicit in that view is the notion that managers are faced with options and choices. In many situations facing managers there are dilemmas and conflicts between aspects of the decision facing them, to offer a bribe or not for example. How should they decide what it is right to do in any particular circumstance? Equally, it is not only managers that are faced with ethical dilemmas. Employees are also exposed to decisions that are difficult. What should employees do when they find that an organization has been cheating its customers? There is no single approach that will allow individuals to resolve these types of dilemma.

This chapter introduced some of the distinctive approaches based on moral philosophy that exist to guide decision making. Each approach offers a particular view of what defines right and wrong in any particular context and against which decisions should be judged. Elliott (1998) makes the point that there are both internal and external organizational forces that impact on any individual at the time that they are faced with an ethical dilemma and which will impact on the decision made. He uses the example (p 22) in which: 'An Operations Manager has to decide on a sensitive staffing issue, at a time when there is internal competition for his/her job, some family trauma, he/she feels rather demotivated by the reward system and there is the threat of law if things go wrong!' Clearly, the balance of particular forces impacting on the individual is likely to influence their decision to some degree, even if it should not.

From a management point of view culture occurs naturally, it is not something that has to be designed or implemented as such. However, that is not to say that managers should adopt a passive stance towards it. Neither does it imply that they should not, and do not, attempt to create specific cultures – a process which itself can create ethical dilemmas. The discussion in this chapter has taken the view that there is an active relationship between managers, employees, ethics and culture.

The culture that emerges over time within an organization may not be an appropriate one for the achievement of the identified objectives. For example, it could be that the dominant culture within an organization is hostile to management's intentions; or that managers are trying to force employees to work in ways that are alien to their preferences. These would make it very difficult for managers to achieve their goals. Of course this does assume that the goals being sought by managers are the 'right' ones

MANAGEMENT IN ACTION 12.5 Real change dealer

Lindsay Levin took over as managing director of Whites (a motor dealership) in 1994 and became one of the few women in this traditionally male-dominated industry. The dealership is located in the south-east of England and was founded by her great-grandfather in 1908. It enjoys a turnover of about £82 million per year with 350 staff. There is overcapacity in the industry generally and a heavily incentivized commission culture permeated all levels of payment, right from the deal with the manufacturer to eventual sales to a customer. Consequently, a hard 'push-at-any-cost' approach is apparent in any motor dealership. There were also clear distinctions between managers, technicians and customers and a feeling that the customer was an intrusion into the process who was not to be allowed to see or understand what was going on in the servicing or repair of their cars.

The starting point for the culture change programme was an analysis of the attitudes of both staff and customers, including 15 hours of video interviews from customers who were less than satisfied with the service provided. A harrowing experience for staff and managers alike, who saw for the first time what customers actually thought of their work and how they were treated. The second major tactic in seeking to change aspects of the culture occurred when Levin declared that she would be prepared to see a drop in revenue while the changes were being introduced. Volunteers were sought to train as continuous improvement facilitators and 20 completed the training and formed the basis of subsequent action teams.

The pace of change was slow to begin with as staff were not convinced that managers actually wanted to hear what was being proposed and feared that they would not implement their proposals. As encouragement each team was 'given' £500 to spend on anything that they felt would benefit the business, but many teams had to be pushed into spending it. To become successful, the process of change required a change to the existing culture in which staff (and managers) expected staff to report a problem to a manager and then wait for a decision. The intention was to change this to a culture of expecting initiative to be shown at all levels. This change took some time to work its way through to the people in the company.

The other changes introduced within the company include:

- Self-selected multifunctional teams have been formed incorporating sales, after-sales and technical staff.
- A change in the pay structure for sales staff to 25 per cent dependent upon team performance and 75 per cent dependent upon competencies.
- The introduction of a shift system covering six-day working for sales staff to allow seven day week sales cover.
- Technicians work 12-hour shifts over three days, followed by four days off.
- Introduction of salaried status for technicians.
- Introduction of continuous improvement groups led by the specially trained change champions.
- Introduction of team leader training over ten one-day sessions over the year.
- Technicians receive one day's training each month.
- Role-playing exercises on customer care have been introduced into the induction training for new employees.

After some three years of the change process the attention of Levin can now be turned to considering the future of the business. The motor manufacturers themselves are closely monitoring Levin's work and using it as the basis of encouraging other dealers to make change. Academic interest in Levin's achievements is also growing with the Lean Enterprise Research Centre at Cardiff Business School suggesting that her model reflects the future for motor retailing.

Adapted from: Littlefield, D (1999) Real change dealer, *People Management*, 29 July, pp 44–6.

Stop ↔ Consider

To what extent do the change processes described reflect cultural issues and to what extent the practice of good management?
To what extent does this imply that an effective organizational culture will automatically follow from the exercise of 'good' management?

and that they are the only ones worth pursuing. Culture provides managers with a number of opportunities. For example, a culture supportive of management's objectives should make it easier and cheaper to manage the organization as a result of the acceptance and internalization of the goals by employees. This opportunity manifests itself in three main ways:

- *Control.* The existence of a strong managerially-based culture should enable control mechanisms to be audit oriented. Such an approach would be evident in organizations operating a **just-in-time** approach for example. Emphasis on 'right first time' means a reduced need to constantly check operational activity. Consequently, a high level of trust in employees and suppliers 'to do what is necessary' is required. An appropriate culture can help achieve this.
- *Norms.* Culture provides the norms which underpin how individuals go about their tasks. A management-supportive culture should ensure that these are favourable and automatically enforced through the group dynamics. An example would be the existence of a 'work until the job is complete' norm. The existence of such a norm among employees would give managers the confidence that orders would be despatched on time, unless a real crisis occurred.
- *Commitment.* This last example also serves to demonstrate the third advantage of culture for managers, that of commitment. A strong management-based culture would produce a situation where employees were generally committed to and supportive of management's aims and objectives. This goes beyond simple compliance with instructions by employees in creating positive support for management's objectives. Some organizations have begun to use the term 'good citizenship' to describe and reward supportive behaviour from employees that goes beyond the requirements of the job.

Just-in-time
An approach linking processes together to ensure that good quality components are delivered just when they are needed.

From a managerial perspective the main problem arises in attempting to create an appropriate culture. It is too simplistic to suggest that managers can decide, design, implement and maintain particular cultures. There are many other features and processes that need to be in place as well. For example, the decision to move towards a more participative culture in which employees are given greater autonomy and authority will fail if it is not supported by appropriate training, encouragement and tolerance of mistakes. Similarly, to attempt to change the culture of an organization without taking into account the structural and procedural dimensions is also likely to fail.

The maintenance of a culture once installed is also problematic. It has already been suggested that culture is subject to continuous adaptation. Consequently, the question of attempting to maintain a static position with regard to culture does not arise as it will change anyway. The problem is therefore one of how to retain direction and alignment with organizational objectives. Assuming that a culture change has been made this process becomes one of preventing the new culture from slipping back towards the old or even drifting towards an undesirable one. Assuming that the culture has been introduced effectively then it should not 'slip' as everyone would be convinced of the benefits to be gained from the new one. This is not always done fully or effectively however.

Watson (1994) studied one company in depth at a time when it was undergoing considerable change, including attempts to modify its culture. He describes a number of reactions to this process from people within the organization (pp 109–34):

- Resistance from all levels.
- A lack of confidence in the commitment, understanding and ability of senior managers.
- Confusion about what culture was.
- A cynical view of culture change as being just another initiative designed by senior managers to further their own careers.

This reflects the political and situational reality within which culture exists and evolves. Indeed, it could be argued that culture makes this 'reality' more complex. The creation of groups each with a culture slightly different to the organizational culture produces the very boundaries that create differentiated and cohesive units. These other groups are considered different, and in extreme cases the enemy. Also, anything from outside a group that seeks to impact on the way things are currently done represents an infringement of its independence and therefore something to be resisted. So management seeking to change the culture of the various work groups frequently encounter resistance. These are not conducive conditions to the notion of culture as a managerially supportive concept.

Reference has been made earlier to the existence of strong and weak cultures. A strong managerial-based culture is the easiest situation to manage in that everyone has internalized the objectives sought by managers and will therefore function in the desired way. There is unity of purpose and intent which makes them less amenable to change. Because of the internalization by individuals of the beliefs and values underpinning the group, ownership and a strong feeling of unity is dispersed among them. Consequently, the level of ownership (and hence control) in the hands of managers is that much less. Therefore, the ability of managers to direct the behaviour within such cultures is also reduced. Strong cultures often have a figurehead or leader in an attempt to retain a measure of control and influence through common support for that person.

Managing internationally describes the need to manage across cultures in one form or another. Differences between national cultures, ethical values, distances in both time and space, and the increased scale of operations all produce a need to manage differently. This need is further complicated as a result of the interaction between organization culture (which will have emerged within a compatible national culture) and local organizational cultures (produced by different national cultures). It is too simplistic to suggest that an effective mixing of different national and organizational culture can be achieved, but neither can they be ignored. People's approach to work and organizational responsibilities are developed within a particular national culture. For an organization to superimpose its own cultural norms on that situation and expect that employees will adapt underestimates the strength of existing values and beliefs. This is evident from the work of both Hofstede and Trompenaars discussed earlier. It is likely that some form of accommodation will take place and that compliance will emerge on the surface, with local preference being met in the reality of activity. For the managers of large international organizations the need to maintain some form of consistency in culture while at the same time recognizing local differences is a major task. It is also one which requires particular sensitivity if problems are to be avoided. Expatriate managers find it particularly difficult to adjust to local conditions and can sometimes fail in their assignments through not being able to balance these conflicting requirements.

CONCLUSIONS

The material included in this chapter provides a basis on which ethical dilemmas can be resolved. It considered the different approaches that have emerged over the years and how they might link to organizational activity. A number of the more common areas of conflicting moral obligation were discussed. The subject of culture is one that influences a wide range of ethical issues and behaviour both within society and organizations. It is not a precisely defined concept and is capable of being misinterpreted and manipulated by the managers who must attempt to make use of it in their work activities.

New employees must be effectively integrated into the organization if they are to become useful members of the team (as defined by management). It is not possible to manage every person all the time that they are at work. Some internalization of responsibility and knowledge of requirements must be handed over if efficiency in management is to be achieved. Culture is able to offer a meaningful way of accounting for these phenomena. However, the notion that culture, particularly strong culture, provides a conflict-free way for managers to ensure harmony and the achievement of objectives is simplistic and does not reflect experience (Thompson and McHugh, 1995).

Now to summarize this chapter in terms of the relevant Learning Objectives:

- **Understand the different approaches to ethics.** There are a number of different approaches to the study of ethics. In an organizational context, the model adopted in this chapter is that proposed by Cederblom and Dougherty (1990) of the utilitarian and contract approaches. The utilitarian approach is based on the notion of usefulness and is split into act and rule sub-sets. Act utilitarianism is based on the idea that every dilemma should be regarded on its merits. For example, telling a lie could be justified in some circumstances. Rule utilitarianism suggests that taking each act separately might not be the best way to provide for the effective running of society as a whole and so a set of rules should be developed. The contract approach is based on the idea that all social relationships are based on a contract (or agreement) of some description. All agreements should be honoured, it is argued. Restricted contractarianism suggests that every act should be viewed through a 'veil of ignorance' in terms of possible impact on the individual making the decision. Libertarian contractarianism argues that individuals should abide by the agreements entered into as long as they don't conflict with the broader rules of society or cause harm to others.
- **Outline the links between culture and ethics.** Ethics reflects the values and standards that an individual adopts in relation to their behaviour. Culture reflects at its most simple level, the 'way things are done around here'. Therefore culture and ethics link through their common interest in what and how things are done by people in a particular context. Particular cultural contexts can accept as normal behaviour (bribery being an obvious example) that which would be unacceptable in another cultural context. Within an organization there may also be issues associated with events such as whistleblowing and working at home that can also be a reflection of a particular culture that might cause ethical dilemmas for the individuals concerned.
- **Assess some of the ethical dilemmas facing managers.** There are a wide range of possible ethical dilemmas facing managers, only some of which are represented in this chapter. How much value is actually provided to customers in return for doing business with the organization represents a fundamental ethical dilemma. Most companies seek the highest price for their products and services and the highest level of profit, and so there is a potential danger of seeking ways to 'cheat' the customer by providing inferior products and services at inflated prices. There are also areas associated with the management of people and how much they might be exploited in the search for lower cost and higher profit by the organization. This area includes a number of more specific dilemmas such as the role of work in society; the level of obligation to work by individuals and rights of the individual to privacy. Other ethical dilemmas include the area of corporate social responsibility and the degree to which organizations should be expected to put effort into the communities of which they form part. It could be argued that this is achieved by the payment of wages and taxes in any location, but there is a view that says that there should also be additional contributions to the community to cover the degree of interference in the local environment.
- **Explain why the concept of culture is problematic when applied to organizations.** Culture is a problematic concept because it is difficult to define in precise terms. It is an easy term to recognize in that it is relatively obvious how organizations differ. When visiting an organization a feeling is generated in the visitor which provides some measure of reflection of the culture. For example, one organization might feel busy with a buzz of activity and a feeling of purpose; whilst another might feel relaxed with a feeling of calmness in its approach to

work. However, these are not the only facets of organizational activity that reflect culture. There are a number of models that seek to define what culture is and how it can be measured and these are introduced at appropriate points in the chapter.

- **Appreciate the forms through which organizational culture finds expression.** Culture finds expression in a number of ways within an organization. It is reflected in the way that the organization does business and in the style of management used by the organization. It is reflected in the approach to work and how it is organized within the organization. It is reflected in the ways in which decisions are made and the ways in which ethical dilemmas are dealt with by the organization. It is reflected in the ways in which communications, company practice, language and the physical artefacts such as layout are organized (based on Trice and Beyer's model introduced earlier). In short culture influences just about every aspect of organizational activity either directly or indirectly.
- **Discuss the possibilities for the management and change of organizational culture, together with the means of doing so.** It can be argued that it is very difficult if not impossible to change an organization's culture. It can also be argued that an organization's culture is constantly adapting to the prevailing circumstances and so it is not a question of changing it, but of steering it in appropriate directions. At a simple level it could be argued that changing any of the features of culture will change the culture itself. However, this is too simplistic and does not recognize the sometimes deeply entrenched cultures that can exist in some situations. For example, a strong culture can be particularly resistant to change, as can the cultures of some subgroups, particularly if they are hostile to management's intentions. It has been argued by writers such as Lundberg (1985) that it is possible to change cultures provided a particular process is undertaken. The approach proposed by Lundberg is discussed in the appropriate section of this chapter. The notion that changing culture can be achieved is also pertinent to the issue of being able to manage a culture, a topic which is also discussed in the chapter, including the nine-factor test used by Littlefield (1999) discussed earlier in this chapter.

DISCUSSION QUESTIONS

1. 'Ethics has no part to play in managerial activities.' Discuss this statement.
2. Discuss employee rights to privacy in the light of management's need to maintain good public and customer relations.
3. The primary responsibility of employees is to the organization that pays their wages. Whistleblowing should therefore result in the dismissal of the employee. Discuss.
4. 'Business is about making money and anything lawful and within reason that achieves that objective is ethical.' Discuss.
5. 'The concept of culture is of little practical value to managers because it simply describes tendencies and ignores the variation between individuals.' Discuss this statement.
6. It has been suggested that strong organizational cultures are essential to the achievement of success. It has also been suggested that strong cultures could predispose an organization to failure. Can you find an argument that could reconcile these two positions?
7. How would you set about achieving a change in an organization's culture?
8. 'The concept of culture is intended to provide managers with an opportunity to increase the level of control without increasing the level of management.' Discuss.
9. Do you think that a code of practice could provide adequate guidance for individuals in deciding upon the right course of action in any particular situation? Justify your answer.
10. 'Culture is such an imprecise term that it is not possible to measure it let alone change it within an organization.' Comment on this statement.

CASE STUDY Breakfast cereal games at the supermarket

This is a story of two organizations, a small breakfast cereal manufacturing company and a large supermarket group. The small breakfast cereal company was based in Switzerland and had an excellent reputation in the industry for making innovative products. They were very keen on new product development and were always searching out new ways of processing the various grains that were traditionally used in the making of breakfast cereals and of linking these with fruits, nuts and other ingredients in various combinations to produce novel products with high customer attraction. They were particularly good at identifying the health and nutrition potential for their products and their products always sold well in the supermarkets.

One of the major UK based, but international supermarket chains that already took a number of products from this particular cereal manufacturer introduced a new quality scheme within their operations. It was based on the ISO 9000 programme which sought to ensure that quality procedures were in place at all levels and in all aspects of the supermarket's operations. This process included the requirement for all suppliers to become involved in a partnership arrangement with the supermarket with regard to the quality of the products that were being supplied. The ISO 9000 approach to quality essentially requires that every aspect of the company processes must be documented and that detailed records of actual work undertaken along with the quality standards expected and achieved must be kept for customer inspection. The cereal manufacturer accepted the need to comply with the supermarket's requirement, although they did regard the amount of paperwork involved as rather excessive and not particularly helpful to their own ways of ensuring quality which had built up over many years of practical experience in the industry. Also it was not cheap to implement and maintain the systems required and the supermarket would not increase the price they paid for the breakfast cereal products that they bought to compensate for the requirement to adopt the new system.

Regular meetings took place between supermarket representatives and the senior management from the breakfast cereal manufacturer to discuss progress, order levels and possible new products. At one such meeting after the new quality system had been running for about one year, managers from the breakfast cereal maker were asked by the supermarket to provide them with all the relevant documents in relation to the quality of the products that were supplied. It was said that a quality audit was being undertaken and that all the records were needed in order to determine whether or not the cereal maker had been using the system correctly and ensure that their quality was of an acceptable standard. The cereal manufacturer complied and handed over all the relevant documentation. This included the recipe data and processing methods for their best selling product. Generally this information had been kept secret prior to this time as it was commercially sensitive and could allow a competitor to copy their products. About one month later, managers from the cereal maker were called to a meeting at the supermarket headquarters and were told that the shelf space allocated to their range of products was being reduced as the supermarket had introduced a new range of 'own brand' breakfast cereals of a similar type to those supplied by the company.

The Swiss managers were clearly disappointed by the decision and tried to persuade the supermarket to change its mind. This was without success and when they asked for more information on the new range of products they were fobbed off with a vague answer that left them no better informed. They asked for information on who was to make the new products as they might like the chance to tender for the work and were told that this would not be possible as they were to be made by a company in which the supermarket had part ownership and the contract had already been placed. They asked for the name of the new supplier and learned that it was one of their competitors. The order level for the breakfast cereals was reduced, the Swiss senior managers were furious. A few weeks later they flew to England specifically to visit to one of the supermarket branches in the UK to look at the new range of own label cereals and found that they looked almost identical to their existing range, but at a cheaper price under the supermarket's brand name. They bought a few packets and took them back to the factory in Switzerland for analysis and found that for all practical purposes they were identical. The

Swiss managing director called the senior management at the supermarket and said that they felt cheated and that they thought that it was no coincidence that this had occurred shortly after the detailed information on the product had been supplied to them under the new quality scheme. The supermarket denied it saying that the product development staff had not had access to any information supplied by the cereal manufacturer and had developed their own brand version by trial and error only. The managing director was very depressed at the news, but realized that trying to prove anything untoward had taken place would be very difficult.

Tasks

1. Identify the ethical issues present in this case study from both the supermarket and cereal makers' perspective. How could you establish whether anything untoward had happened from the perspective of the cereal manufacturer? How might the supermarket defend itself against such claims?
2. Could organizational culture have influenced the supermarket's approach to this situation? If so how? What about the culture within the cereal maker, were they too trusting and could they have prevented the situation getting to this stage by adopting a different culture or ethical perspective?

FURTHER READING

Alatas, SH (1991) *Corruption: Its Nature, Causes and Functions*, S Abdul Majeed, Kuala Lumpur, in association with Gower, London. As the title suggests, this book reviews the history and causes of corruption. It is set primarily within an Asian context and so provides a less usual reflection on aspects associated with ethics.

Alvesson, M (2002) *Understanding Organizational Culture*, Sage, London. Looks at what culture is and the ways in which it interacts with a wide range of other organizational activities such as performance, administrative activities and leadership.

Clark, H, Chandler, J and Barry, J (1994) *Organization and Identities: Text and Readings in Organizational Behaviour*, International Thomson Business Press, London. Contains a broad range of original articles on relevant material themes and from significant writers referred to in this and other textbooks on management and organizations.

Crane, A and Matten, D (2003) *Business Ethics: A European Perspective*, Oxford University Press, Oxford. Includes consideration of corporate citizenship and sustainability as well as ethical models and decision making.

Hampden-Turner, C (1990) *Corporate Cultures: From Vicious to Virtuous Circles*, Random Century, London. Provides a readable review of culture in an organizational context.

Kotter, JP and Heskett, JL (1992) *Corporate Culture and Performance*, The Free Press, New York. Considers the general issue of culture and its relationship with organizational performance.

Maclagan, P (1998) *Management and Morality: A Developmental Perspective*, Sage, London. This text is concerned with the realization of individual moral potential and the development of ethically responsive organizations.

Mallin, C (2004) *Corporate Governance*, Oxford University Press, Oxford. Explores a wide range of issues surrounding corporate governance and how it relates to legal and capital structure issues as well as the role of directors in monitoring corporate activity.

Martin, J (1992) *Cultures in Organizations*, Oxford University Press, New York. A well-argued and comprehensive review of the subject.

Semler, R (2003) *The Seven-Day Weekend*, Century Books, London. This text provides a more recent and updated review (compared to Management in Action panel 12.2) of the way that Ricardo Semler runs his group of companies and is challenging and controversial in a number of areas covered within organizational behaviour.

COMPANION WEBSITE

Online teaching and learning resources:

Visit the companion website for Organizational Behaviour and Management 3rd edition at: *http://www.thomsonlearning.co.uk/businessandmanagement/martin3* to find valuable further teaching and learning material:

Refer to page 35 for full details.

PART SIX

Managing work design, technology and structure

The previous section explored some of the key aspects associated with the management of people as part of a manager's job. This section explores other aspects of managerial responsibility in the form of the physical aspects of the organization including the technology and work activity that takes place within its structure.

It is commonly understood what a job is. But there is more to it than might at first appear to be the case. In earlier chapters many aspects of the individual, groups and associated features of human interaction have been discussed. It should be apparent that there are many influences on what goes on within an organization as a result of human participation in work. This complexity of influence and effect is also apparent in the jobs that people do. Individuals and groups will shape to some degree the jobs that they do as a consequence of the variables operating in any situation; and conversely the design of jobs can help or hinder the effective use of people in achieving the objectives of the organization. Job design should therefore represent a major consideration for all managers and employees in the search for meaningful work and high productivity. The technology used is also a major influence on the activities engaged in by the people who work in an organization. Usually technology is regarded as the machines and computers that most people use in their work, but there are administrative and social technologies that also impact on the jobs that individuals do and the performance that they achieve. The structure of the organization provides the main

framework that allows the technology and jobs to be integrated in pursuit of the objectives being sought. There are many different structural forms available and each has advantages and disadvantages in relation to the nature and type of business as well as the way that people are accommodated into the process.

This section prepares the way for the consideration of the material in the final section of this organizational behaviour book. The final section seeks to identify and bring together many of the themes addressed in earlier sections in exploring the dynamics of organizational activity. In short the discussion of what actually goes on within most organizations and what interaction and pressures are placed on managers and employees as they seek to deal with the implications of their ongoing relationship within the dynamic context of organizational life.

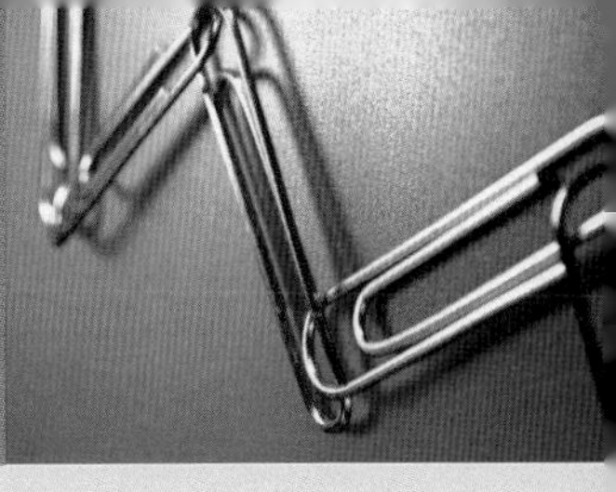

CHAPTER 13

Work design and organization

LEARNING OBJECTIVES

After studying the chapter content and working through the associated Management in Action panels, Employee Perspectives, Discussion Questions and Case Study, you should be able to:

- **Understand the main approaches to the design of work within an organizational setting.**
- **Explain how work study attempts to influence job design activities and how changing the design of jobs can be a difficult process.**
- **Outline the interrelationship between technology and work organization.**
- **Assess the quality of working life movement and the use of quality circles as an influence on work organization.**
- **Discuss the Fordist and post-Fordist approaches to work organization.**

INTRODUCTION

It is inevitable that the business that an organization is engaged in, together with its structure will determine to a significant degree the types of jobs that exist within it. The configuration of activity into personnel, finance, marketing and production departments determines the broad area of specialism in the work to be performed. However, the purpose and structure of an organization do not of themselves fully prescribe the nature of jobs that will be created. For example, within a personnel department it would be possible to arrange for the work to be undertaken by generalists (individuals being involved with all personnel activity), or to split the overall activity into a range of specialist groups (a recruitment team, an industrial relations team, etc.). Also issues such as technology, culture and the pattern of work activity (shift-work etc.) could all be expected to have an impact on the ways in which work is actually organized within any particular context.

The design of jobs is frequently based on what has always existed in that situation, the traditional work arrangements simply being perpetuated. However, increasingly the formal design of jobs is being seen as a means of improving levels of quality, employee motivation and commitment to the objectives of the organization. This chapter brings together much of the thinking around these ideas in a review of how work is organized and the possible consequences of the choices made.

THE NATURE OF A JOB

Job
A collection of tasks brought together as a practical 'chunk' of activity serving a particular purpose within an organization.

It may seem obvious what a **job** is. People hold jobs, careers are made up of jobs and jobs form the basis of many stories on television, in films and in books. It is widely understood what the job of a police officer or doctor involves. However, not all police officers do the same job; some specialize in traffic duties, others in the detection of crime, while others patrol the streets or manage the service. In short, there are many different forms of police officer job. In much of the academic literature there is discussion of management as a job (a discrete set of activities) without any real recognition that there are many different types and levels of management job. For example, the job of an engineering manager is different in many respects from the job of an accounting manager. Equally, the job of a first-level production manager is completely different from the job of the chief executive.

Add to this the opportunity for individuals to adapt jobs to their own preferences and jobs can become unique, even if they are performed by many people. For example, Roy (1960) described the use of informal breaks and playing 'games' with fruit as devices through which employees in one factory coped with the high level of monotony in the production tasks. Through these informal practices employees maintained some influence over their work activities and were therefore able to reduce the experienced levels of boredom and monotony. The nature of jobs changes over time and it has even been suggested that the concept of work is a relatively new one. Management in Action 13.1 reflects the views of Professor Alain Cotta on this.

It is now appropriate to consider what defines a job. A job can be considered to be a collection of tasks brought together within a single convenient overall activity. The work of an organization has to be broken down into the tasks to be achieved, which then have to be grouped together and allocated to an appropriate number of people in a set of arrangements referred to as jobs. There is nothing sacrosanct about a job; it is a social construction created and adapted by people, for people. However, within an organization the chief beneficiary should be management, as it is they who determine the design of jobs, theoretically at least in pursuit of operational objectives. Therefore

MANAGEMENT IN ACTION 13.1 Why not simply stop working?

Professor Alain Cotta from the Dauphine University in Paris argues that the notion of work as conveying social status is only about 200 years old. Before the Industrial Revolution only people with no other option worked. The more an individual worked, the lower their social status. The Industrial Revolution changed the social standing of work and introduced a meritocracy based upon work having moral value. The change in the perception of work created a situation in which people became part of a new type of 'machine state'.

Cotta builds on the ideas of Elias Canetti, a Nobel Prize winner who predicted that the machine would replace muscle. Cotta refers to this as the 'neuron prosthesis'. It is based on the reality that:

> More than half of the people are now employed in sectors where they create, release, transfer, receive and utilize information. The crossing of the frontier between muscle and neuron may have as many consequences as the rise of industry.
>
> People are now looking forward to filling their time instead of producing. Man is trying to free himself from the original painful constraints of work.

Cotta points out that arguments against work today tend to focus not so much on the duration, but on the subordination of individuals to orders. However, as Donkin points out, in practice delayering and empowerment over the past few years have had a major impact on management. Middle ranks see themselves as having been emasculated and senior levels as having been challenged as a result of these developments.

Cotta describes the emergence of three groups within society, differentiated by their relations with work:

- *Middle class*. Defined as those for whom work remains to be endured as their only way to make a living.
- *Excluded from work*. Excluded as a result of the ever rising skills needed. Also includes those individuals who have retired, have a private income or voluntarily absent themselves.
- *Those who choose to work*. This includes individuals who opt into work without the need to do so.

Cotta does not have a category for the traditional working class. Equally, he asks whether progress will create extremes in the approach to work, exclusion and predilection. The pressure on the middle class as their need to work is challenged by technology might well be simply to give up work and opt out. The alternatives being the never ending drudge of work, or the assertion that it can be the reason for living.

Adapted from: Donkin, R (1994) Why not simply stop working?, *Financial Times*, 16 November, p 14.

Stop ↔ Consider

To what extent (and why) do you agree with Cotta's view that three groups of people (or classes) will emerge based on their relationship to work?

If you disagree with his analysis, to what extent, how and why do you consider that the nature of work in society is changing over time?

the design of jobs can serve particular interests. However once created, changing the design of jobs can be very difficult as job holders are likely to resist attempts to make them adopt different work practices.

Whilst it is generally true that managers are the main beneficiaries of a particular job design, there are examples where jobs have been designed for the benefit of the job holder. Examples include the professions such as the law and medicine. Traditionally, it has been argued by the bodies representing the interests of the professions that entry to these jobs should be carefully controlled in order to ensure the perpetuation of the superior status (and often income levels) associated with these areas of work. Such bodies have similar objectives to the trade unions which represent other classes of employee, but they are able to exercise control over job design through different means.

The design of jobs reflects a series of compromises that create benefits and problems for both managers and employees. If a manager decides to create a new type of job within their organization (by grouping together the tasks to be done in a novel way) then it is unlikely that they will find an employee already having the necessary skills and the company will be forced to undertake extensive training. This will inevitably increase the cost of operations and will also make it more difficult to recruit new people quickly. It also means that the employer becomes vulnerable to problems if they do not ensure that they 'keep their employees happy'. Employees would not be easy to replace if they left. Alternatively, when using standard jobs that exist across society labour is more likely to be readily available, training (and labour) costs would be reduced and an increased clarity in work activity would exist.

From an employee's perspective both approaches to job design have advantages and disadvantages. Having skills that are widely used means that it becomes easier to find alternative work, but it is more likely that the jobs will be repetitive and attract lower wages. A higher level of uniqueness in job skill, by way of contrast, might attract higher wages and provide more interesting work. However, such employees would be more vulnerable to competition from those prepared to accept lower pay for greater transferability of skill and hence a greater chance of work.

How do jobs vary? Jobs are usually described as varying in two dimensions,vertical and horizontal, Figure 13.1.

Taking each dimension of Figure 13.1 in turn:

- *Vertical.* This reflects the responsibility incorporated into a job. For example, an assembly line job with no responsibility for checking quality would contain very little vertical responsibility. Contrariwise, the job of an owner–manager in a small company incorporates considerable vertical loading as they would be involved at every level of the organization. One moment they may be helping to pack an order, the next they may be dealing with the bank concerning overdraft facilities.
- *Horizontal.* This reflects the breadth of activity in a job. Jobs with a narrow range of tasks are limited in scope and highly routine. Jobs with a broad range of tasks contain variety which can minimize levels of monotony and boredom. At the narrow end of the spectrum simple repetitive assembly line jobs would be found. At the other extreme for example, a cabinet maker may undertake the full range of tasks from the design to the complete manufacture of a piece of furniture.

A job is not something that is static and incapable of being manipulated by either management or the job holder. Jobs are things that can be consciously designed, providing managers with a vehicle through which they can control employees and harness energy in pursuit of their objectives. Jobs also provide employees with a basis

FIGURE 13.1

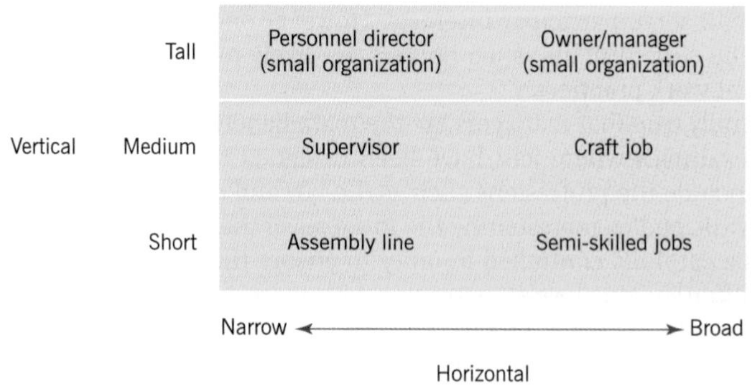

Job dimensions

for protecting a defined area of work, thereby gaining a degree of power and independence in an otherwise defined context.

WORK STUDY, ERGONOMICS AND JOB ANALYSIS

Work study

Work study is commonly thought to have emerged through the work of FW Taylor in developing scientific management in the early years of the twentieth century. The search by Taylor for the one best way produced techniques to analyze and define the work methods and pace of work that should be expected from employees. He encouraged compliance with these requirements through the payment of output-based bonuses. However, the work study has a much longer tradition. For example, there is some evidence that medieval monks used job times to determine the duration of monastery and cathedral projects. Currie (1963, p 2) also describes an extract from an employment contract in which an individual undertook secretly to time jobs in a factory and report the outcome to the owner:

> I Thomas Mason, this 22nd day of December, 1792 solemnly pledge myself to use my utmost caution at all times to prevent the knowledge transpiring that I am employed to use a stop watch to make observation of work done in Mr. Duesbry's manufactory; and to take such observations with the utmost truth and accuracy in my power and to give the results thereof faithfully to Mr. Duesbry.

It was Adam Smith (1776) who is first credited with coining the phrase **division of labour** in the context of the study of work. The term described the detailed job design used in a pin manufacturing factory to increase the output of pins per person, achieved by breaking up the overall task into specialized and smaller activities. This represents the essence of work study. The study of work activity in order to identify the component parts involved, then to critically evaluate them in order to identify the most efficient methods of work that could be used and subsequently determine the time to undertake these duties. Essentially, work study contains as its core activity two distinct elements: **method study** and **work measurement**. The contribution associated with each is reflected in Figure 13.2.

The extract from the employment contract just quoted provides some indication of the secrecy with which work study activity had to be undertaken. It can be assumed from the tone of the document that employees in the late 1700s did not generally respond positively or with enthusiasm to having their jobs studied. By the time Taylor had developed his scientific management techniques at the turn of the twentieth

Work study
A management discipline aimed at maximizing productivity through the application of method study and work measurement.

Division of labour
The search for higher levels of productivity and job specialization by breaking up the overall task into small tasks.

Method study
A process involving the critical examination of work in order to identify the most efficient work methods.

Work measurement
Uses timing devices and techniques to identify how long particular tasks should take to perform.

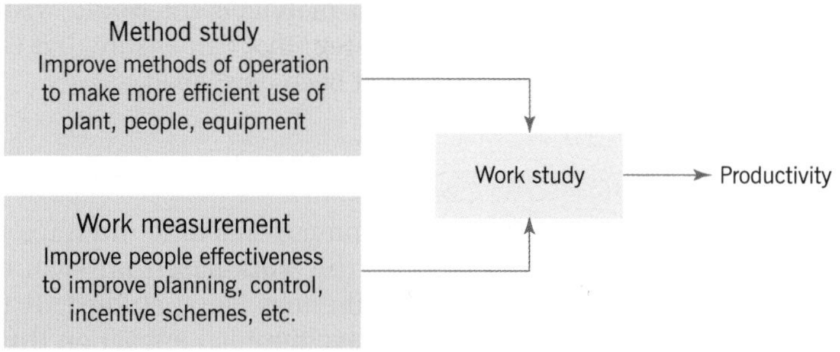

FIGURE 13.2

Work study (*adapted from*: Currie, RM (1963) *Work Study*, Pitman, London)

century this had changed little, leading to the following criticisms of it being presented to a commission on industrial relations in the USA (Hoxie, 1915):

- That it formed the basis of a cunningly devised speeding-up and sweating system.
- That it furthered the trend towards task specialization.
- That it condemned the worker to monotonous and routine work activities.
- That it transferred to managers the traditional knowledge, skill and judgement of the workers.
- It emphasized quantity at the expense of quality.
- That it placed at management's disposal a wealth of information that could be used unscrupulously to the detriment of workers.
- That it allowed ever tighter control and discipline of worker activity, beyond a level at which this should be necessary.

The application of work study techniques to job design provides management with an opportunity to control not only the design of work but also its delivery. This is part of what Torrington *et al.* (2002) identify as the disciplinary aspect of management – management ensuring they are satisfied that the employee is delivering what is expected under the contract of employment. One way of achieving compliance is through the threat of sanction unless behaviour is appropriate. However, that relies upon negative reward – punishment for a failure to do that which is required. A more effective approach is to reward positive behaviours through the award of things such as bonus payments for increased output. This is what scientific management attempted to achieve. That it failed to do so was largely because of the negative reaction to being spied upon and controlled – as workers perceived it. This was often with some justification as such initiatives were frequently followed by job cuts, demands to work harder for the same or less pay and a generally tighter control of work.

Discipline in the sense of control over behaviour is most effective if the underlying values and standards are internalized by employees. If they could be persuaded to adopt the same values, standards and norms as management then the job of management would become that much easier. Employees would require less supervision and would naturally function in ways that were supportive of management's objectives. They would be committed to the management's objectives. That was what Taylor sought to achieve through scientific management, but he completely missed the point that such commitment cannot be engineered.

Compliance can be required, but commitment is an individual level response and in the gift of employees to withhold if they wish to do so. Compliance involves the employee following the rules precisely, for which they cannot be punished. But equally the rules cannot cover every eventuality in precise detail, so failure to achieve objectives (or systems breakdown) is almost inevitable. Commitment involves the employee going beyond the contract and doing what management would wish them to do without being asked to do so. The control system that can ensure that employees give full commitment against their will has not yet been developed.

Ergonomics
Sets out to identify how humans interact with the work-based physical environment and to design appropriate equipment.

Ergonomics

Ergonomics is frequently defined as the human–machine interface. It sets out to identify how human beings interact with the work-based physical environment, particularly the equipment to be used in the jobs being studied. It then seeks to design the equipment in such a way as to have minimal impact on the people using it, thereby generating maximum efficiency with minimal effort and stress being experienced by workers.

Ergonomics is one of a range of specialist areas including physical anthropology which specializes in seeking to develop anthropometric profiles of human beings. So, for example, it has been found in America that 25 per cent of the population has an arm reach of less than 21 inches. Therefore 75 per cent have a reach longer than 21 inches (Kennedy and Filler, 1966). Other specialist fields include work physiology and biomechanics both of which seek to understand the actual impact of work on the human body. For example, jobs which require considerable energy expenditure perhaps need more rest periods built into them or the design of specialized mechanical handling equipment to take away the strain on muscles and joints. All of this data can be used to design the jobs that people undertake within organizations.

Job analysis

Job analysis is a systematic approach to the identification of the content of a job. It can be used to support a wide range of activities, including:

- *Resourcing*. A detailed knowledge of the jobs to be undertaken within the organization provides the basis for human resource planning in terms of the numbers employed, succession planning and career development. Knowing the jobs to be done provides a means of being able to identify the most suitable candidates. In a *downsizing* exercise it is essential (to management) to retain the most competent employees; a job analysis would enable the skills required to be identified and matched against the profile of existing employees.
- *Training*. Knowing the content of jobs allows the skills required to be matched against employee capability. This allows training plans to be developed to ensure that employees are competent to deliver the tasks expected of them.
- *Career development*. Knowing the jobs that people have done (and the content) allows career development paths to be identified. Career moves can be planned to provide additional experience and responsibility in order to ensure the appropriate development of senior staff.
- *Payment*. Job analysis provides the information required for the preparation of a **job description**. These can then be used to determine the relative magnitude of jobs through a **job evaluation scheme**. The rank order (or scale) of jobs produced through job evaluation can in turn form the basis of a pay structure.
- *Performance evaluation*. Knowing the tasks that are to be performed by an employee provides a basis for understanding how much work should be produced by an average worker. Both of these pieces of information are necessary to determine the performance achieved by an employee.
- *Equality*. The systematic analysis of a job provides a basis for decision making about jobs and people that is not dependent on gender, race or any other irrelevant criteria. One definition of equality is inappropriate decision making and this is much easier to perpetuate and justify without clear information. Job analysis forces attention onto the tasks and activity involved in a job, rather than who undertakes the work.

There are two main approaches to job analysis according to Ivancevich (1992):

1. *Functional job analysis*. This approach requires consideration of four aspects of the work:
   - Employee activities relevant to data, people and other jobs.
   - The methods and techniques used by the worker.
   - The machines, tools and equipment used by the worker.
   - What outputs are produced by the worker.

Job analysis
A systematic approach to the identification of the content and responsibilities of a job.

Job description
A document setting out the duties and other requirements of a job.

Job evaluation scheme
A process by which job descriptions can be used to identify the relative magnitude of jobs in an organization.

The first three of these categories require an assessment of the tasks undertaken within the job and how they are achieved. The fourth requires the type and level of output expected from the employee to be identified. It is easy to see both method study and work measurement perspectives at work within this approach to job analysis. In addition to issues relating to the work to be done, the position analysis questionnaire incorporates an assessment of the people dimension of the work:

2. *Position analysis questionnaire*. This approach requires consideration of six aspects of the work:
   - Sources of information necessary to the job.
   - Decision making associated with the job activity.
   - Physical aspects associated with the job.
   - Interpersonal and communication necessary to the job.
   - Working conditions and their impact on the job.
   - Impact of work schedules, responsibility etc.

Job analysis plays a significant part in the identification of what tasks should be contained within a job. It is, however, only one part of the process. Figure 13.3 reflects the nature of work as a function of both organizational and individual factors.

Although Figure 13.3 is largely self-explanatory, two points are worth highlighting. First, management intentions are indicated as an influence on both job analysis and job design. This is intended to reflect the iterative nature of decision-making in this area of management. For example the job analysis of an existing job may raise questions in relation to the design of a particular job that leads to a further round of job analysis and job design. Second, whatever the nature of a job as defined on paper, employees perceive and interpret the work expected of them and respond accordingly. This process is further filtered by such forces as motivation, training etc. For example, a workforce suffering from low levels of morale is unlikely to enthusiastically undertake the full range of duties expected of them. This will inevitably lead to inefficiencies somewhere in the operational system and problems for management.

FIGURE 13.3

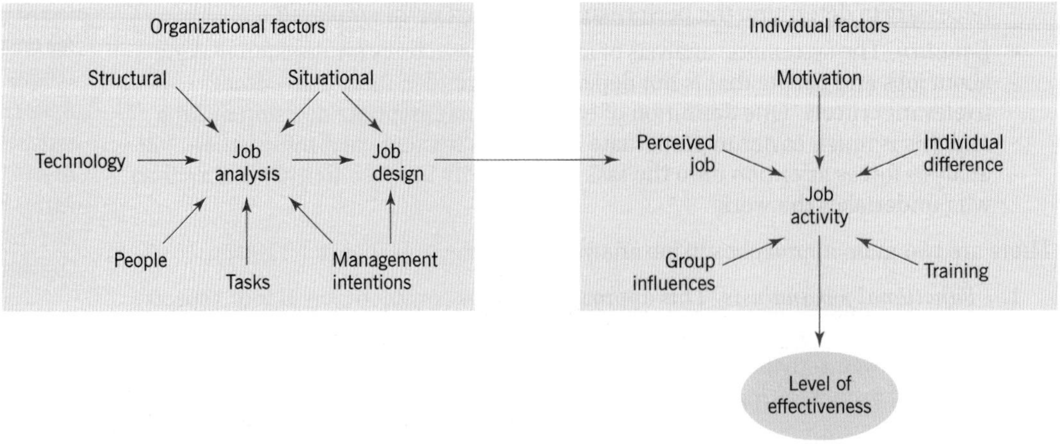

Job analysis and job effectiveness

APPROACHES TO DESIGNING JOBS

The tasks to be undertaken in an organization need to be combined into specific jobs that make sense for people to undertake. In most situations job design is about changing jobs that already exist. The design of totally new jobs (perhaps resulting from opening a new factory or department) does exist but to a lesser extent. The reasons for job redesign can be many. For example, the introduction of new equipment, or an attempt to improve productivity, or as the result of high labour turnover, or simply to cut cost. There are a number of approaches to the ways in which jobs have been designed and these will be reviewed in the following sections.

Simplification and job engineering

With the introduction of the factory system of manufacture opportunities emerged to increase the output per worker through the division of labour. This was observed by Babbage (1832) to reduce training times, increase skill through constant repetition of a small range of tasks and also reduce waste as a result of the higher skill level achieved. Fewer tool changes and machine set-ups were also required as a result of the batch nature of production and the specialized nature of equipment to support it. This approach represents the essence of **job simplification** or job engineering as it is sometimes called. It was FW Taylor who further developed this through the introduction of the scientific management approach to job simplification.

Job simplification
An approach to work organization which involves minimizing the complexity and range of tasks in a job.

Job simplification involves minimizing the range of tasks into the smallest convenient job size to make an efficient contribution to the overall process. It is an approach seen in many production and assembly line jobs. In assembly line approaches to production the workers stay in a fixed position and the item being made moves down the line until it is completed. The number of workstations and workers must be carefully balanced to provide an efficient assembly process with minimal idle time. The assembly of motor vehicles is the most obvious example of this process in action.

The aim of job simplification is to maximize output and minimize labour input. Consequently, this approach lends itself to the application of technology in seeking to match human activity to the needs of production. The difficulties associated with job simplification were recognized very early. It can be argued that the founding of the human relations movement was a direct consequence of the dehumanizing effect of such work. As far back as 1952 Walker and Guest identified a number of causes of dissatisfaction among assembly workers in a car factory, including:

- Lack of control over the pace of work as a result of the management-determined speed of the assembly line.
- Repetitiveness (short cycle-time) of the work being undertaken.
- Low skill levels required to undertake the jobs on the line.
- Limited social interaction with fellow workers because of the physical spacing between workstations and pace of work required.
- No employee control over the tools used or the methods of work adopted on the line.
- No involvement in a total product, employees only ever see and work on part-completed goods passing down the line.

This approach to job design is not restricted to work in factories. It can also be found in administrative jobs. For example, in accounting departments, someone has to open the post, sort the invoices from the payments and enter the details into a computer system. Such jobs bear all the classic symptoms of job simplification, including monotony, boredom, high labour turnover, alienation and lack of commitment. The same is true in education in which the job of teachers and lecturers is being ever more closely prescribed through national and local initiatives in schools and universities. This is usually justified in the name of providing quality and consistency in educational experience for students. However, in the process, the opportunity for the exercise of professional judgement and skill at an individual level is increasingly minimized, just as it is for an assembly line worker in a factory.

Job rotation

Job rotation
An approach to work organization involving the combination of two (or more) simplified jobs into a rotating pattern of work.

Job rotation as an approach to work organization accepts that simplified jobs provide the most efficient method of work. However, it also recognizes the shortcomings that limit the achievement of the full potential from that approach to job design. For example, the effects of boredom and monotony on employee commitment levels. One solution to this problem is for job designers to seek to limit the adverse effects of job simplification while retaining the benefits of specialization.

The simplest solution to this (so the argument goes) is to combine two (or more) simplified jobs into a pattern of work rotation. Job rotation requires that each person be trained to undertake a range of simplified jobs and then to spend a proportion of time on each. This provides some relief from the mind-numbing effects of performing a narrow range of tasks all day, every day. Job rotation does not have to be based on a daily cycle; it could be weekly or monthly.

The rotation of jobs does not produce all the expected benefits and can reduce the efficiency gained through job simplification. The argument follows thus:

- Employees must learn a wider range of skills in order to undertake a broader range of tasks, increasing the time and cost involved in training. Also employees can claim that more responsibility and skill is needed than to undertake a simplified job and so demand higher pay.
- With the reduced practice opportunity as a result of job rotation employees do not build up the same level of skill, speed or proficiency as when performing single, simplified jobs.
- Rotation round a series of simplified jobs does not change the fact that the work is basically mundane, boring and monotonous.

Conversely, job rotation can provide a benefit through the ability of employees to take on a wider range of duties at short notice. This provides management with an increased degree of flexibility in labour utilization and an opportunity to cope with unforeseen situations.

Job enlargement

Job enlargement adopts a slightly different approach to job design in that it seeks to build up a job by adding more tasks into it to form a larger job. In effect it seeks to move a job along the horizontal axis in Figure 13.1 towards the broad end of the scale. It adds a wider range of similar duties to create an enlarged job. The potential advantage is that the perceived meaningfulness of the work is increased for the employee as a result of the broader range of tasks involved. It is argued that productivity may increase as employees are likely to be motivated and have more interest in their work than if simplified job design is used.

It is not always easy to introduce enlarged jobs into a factory as it requires a different approach to the pattern of interaction between the tasks to be achieved, machines and people to be adopted. As an approach this can conflict with the basic view of work study as to what should be happening at the task level of work. Work study attempts to eliminate or control activity considered to be irrelevant or unnecessary to the main purpose of the job. In many situations this is unrealistic, but it can be difficult to change the desire for tight control among managers. Hence the persistent drive to keep trying to apply the principles of work study.

Conant and Kilbridge (1965) provide an early description of the application of job enlargement to the assembly of water pumps in washing machines. The assembly of the pump had been done on a production line with each worker adding components as the pump body went past. After redesign the enlarged job allowed each worker to assemble the entire pump, but still on an assembly line with no loss of productivity. The major problem with enlargement as a design option is that it is frequently restricted to simple assembly line jobs, which even when enlarged remain relatively small jobs. Consequently, the benefits to employees quickly dissipate and the job becomes monotonous once again.

Job enrichment

Job enrichment requires that activity and responsibility be added to a job in a vertical direction (as defined in Figure 13.1). It is a process intended to integrate responsibility and control over the tasks performed by the employee. Herzberg (1968, 1974b) identified six forms of enrichment that designers should seek to include in jobs:

1. *Accountability*. Provide a level of responsibility and support for employees that requires them to accept accountability for their actions and performance.
2. *Achievement*. Provide employees with an understanding and belief in the significance of their work.
3. *Feedback*. Superiors should provide feedback to employees on their performance and work activities.
4. *Work pace*. Employees should be able to exercise discretion over the pace of work that they adopt and be able to vary that pace.
5. *Control over resources*. Employees should have high levels of control over the resources needed to perform their duties.
6. *Personal growth and development*. Opportunities should be found to encourage employees to acquire and practise new skills and develop themselves through their work.

Another approach to **job enrichment** was developed by Hackman and Oldham (1980). They suggest that there are five core job dimensions, which in turn combine and produce psychological responses, which in turn produce work and personal outcomes (Figure 13.4). This they termed the **job characteristics model** of job enrichment.

Taking each of the core job dimensions in turn:

- *Skill variety*. This reflects the idea that a job should contain a wide range of activities requiring a broad range of skills and talents from the employee. The broader the range of skill required the more significant the job will be to both the employee and employer. This is because it will have a longer training period and ensure that the individual is considered as a major contributor to the organization. Individuals vary in their need and ability to cope with skill variety. Too little variety will produce boring and monotonous work; too much will produce fragmented work activity with stress and uncertainty for the employee.

Job enrichment
An approach to work organization which involves adding a range of more complex tasks and responsibilities to a job.

Job characteristics model
A model of job enrichment based on the need to incorporate a number of core job dimensions into job design.

FIGURE 13.4

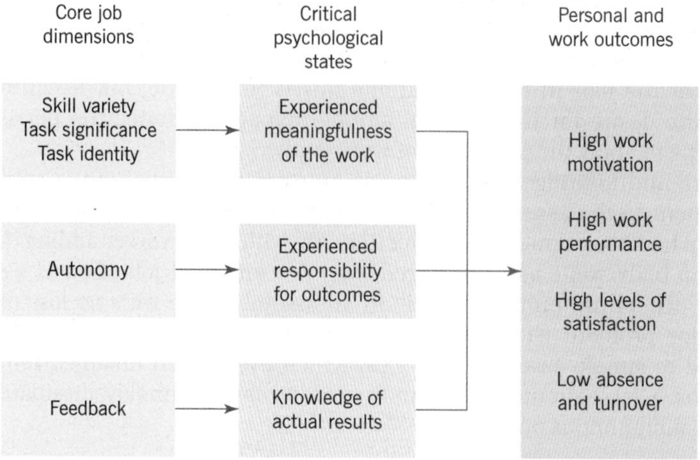

Job characteristics approach to job enrichment (*source*: Hackman, J and Oldham R (1980) *Work Redesign*, Addison-Wesley, Reading, MA)

- *Task identity*. This element is about the degree of wholeness in a job. It reflects the degree to which the employee undertakes a complete job. If the employee only undertakes a small number of tasks on part of a whole product then they are unlikely to relate to the finished article. Neither are they likely to think that they make a meaningful contribution to the organization.
- *Task significance*. The importance of the job being done creates significance for the employee. This is often reflected in the degree of impact on the lives or work of other people. Very few people would be happy or conscientious in their work if it was felt to be of no consequence to anyone, a point relevant in the following Employee Perspective (13.1).
- *Autonomy*. This reflects the degree of individual freedom to schedule and adapt work methods. A closely prescribed job – working on an assembly line – has very little scope for autonomy compared with the job of a sculptor, who has considerable freedom in the artistic interpretation of the subject and pace of work. Autonomy makes the individual responsible for their actions, thus providing a sense of ownership. An interesting study of this aspect of work organization was provided by Sadler-Smith *et al.* (2003) who found some association between autonomy and the cultural environment in Egypt.
- *Feedback*. This allows an employee to know how well they are doing in the eyes of others; it also provides an indication of how effectively they fit into the organization. This can be achieved through a number of routes from giving employees customer contact, to formal performance appraisal systems, etc. The purpose being to provide a learning opportunity for the individual in terms of performance, quality, integration and contribution.

The first three core job dimensions are linked together in Figure 13.4 because they lead to a feeling of relative meaningfulness in the job. Hackman and Oldham developed a means of being able to measure the level of job enrichment present in any job, the motivating potential score (MPS). The score produced through the application of the MPS is essentially a subjective response by the job holder, based upon their ability to compare with other jobs that they have experienced. It is a useful, although not altogether objective measure. There is evidence of general empirical support for the MPS, although not strong support for the causal linkages suggested by it (Wall *et al.*, 1985).

EMPLOYEE PERSPECTIVE 13.1 Cleaning in the factory

Marjorie was a general worker in a garment factory in Thailand which employed about 600 people (almost all women) on making various shirts and jackets for customers around the world. Her principal job was to sweep the floor and to move bins of part completed garments between work areas. The sweeping accounted for about 30 per cent of her working time and was intended to make sure that no small pieces of fabric or thread were left lying about to cause people to slip and hurt themselves. The rest of the time was taken up with moving bins of part completed garments between work areas. She was one of a team of twenty people constantly sweeping up and pushing garment bins around the factory. The factory only worked Monday to Friday each week and for half a day every two weeks Marjorie had to take her turn in cleaning the toilets. All of the cleaners hated this part of their job.

Generally the women engaged in sewing jobs regarded themselves as superior to the general workers. The sewing machinists tended to talk down to the general workers and frequently tried to order them about as if they were in charge. The general workers such as Marjorie were made to feel inferior in every way and it was also apparent to them that their work was not appreciated by either the sewing machinists or the managers. The managers in the factory also treated the general workers as inferior, in practice ignoring them most of the time. The only time that a manager spoke to Marjorie was to shout an order or to tell her off for apparently doing something wrong or not responding to an order quickly enough.

Most of the general workers hated their job. They only stayed with the company as long as they had to and were constantly on the look-out for other job opportunities, preferably in other companies. Labour turnover was very high among the general workers and the standard of work that they produced was very low. They only half-heartedly undertook their duties and if they thought that they could get away with not doing something they would. This was particularly true when it came to cleaning the toilets. This particular job was the most hated by all the general workers as it did not matter how often they were cleaned, they quickly became filthy again. Most of the workers paid no attention to the state of the toilet facilities, for example, just throwing paper towels onto the floor rather than crumple them up and put them in the bin provided.

Marjorie was always looking for another job and after six months at the factory she found one with another company and resigned. The personnel officer of the company asked why she was leaving and she said that she felt her present job did not matter to anyone and that she did not feel that anyone valued her work.

Tasks

1. Would you have done any different if you were Marjorie and if so why?
2. If you were the personnel manager of this factory what changes to the job of the general worker might you seek to introduce and why.

Work designed using the enrichment approach might be expected to provide higher levels of stimulation than the other approaches to job design. There is some suggestion for example that normal aging processes such as brain decay can be slowed by undertaking stimulating work (Rawlins, 2003).

Based on a social information-processing view of job design, Salancik and Pfeffer (1978) argue that the assumptions behind the job characteristics approach were open to question. Individuals have basic and stable needs that can be met through work and jobs display stable characteristics that people respond to in evaluating work. They argue that the process of evaluating the value of work for an individual is a more complex process than recognized by the Hackman and Oldham model. It is a process based upon the social reality of work experience for the individual and as a consequence dependent upon the personal perspective of each individual. Writers such as Morgeson and Campion (2002) pick up on this idea and begin to develop a model of job design that seeks to minimize the trade-offs between what they term as the motivational and mechanistic aspects of job design whilst maximizing the benefits achieved in terms of factors such as satisfaction.

TECHNOLOGY AND WORK ORGANIZATION

Technology influences the organization of work through a number of routes. There is the technology used in the work itself. There are the administrative and procedural technologies that must be complied with. There are the social technologies that influence how people interact with the other technologies that impact on their work. In addition, there is the impact of new technology on the range of products and services that can be provided, hence allowing the creation of new job and organizational arrangements.

The major advantage to organizations from the employment of people over machines (how technology invariably manifests itself) is the flexibility that they provide. They are cheaper to acquire (no capital costs); can be dispensed with quickly and more cheaply if necessary; and they are adaptable and can solve problems in a dynamic environment. However, there are disadvantages with the employment of people: they are not as consistent as machines in work output or quality; they cannot work every hour that exists without a break; and maintenance costs (wages and benefits) are high. In addition, the major difficulty involved with the employment of people is that they have free will and expectations. Seeking to achieve an effective balance between the use of people and technology within an organizational context is not easy to achieve and inevitably raises many ethical issues. The uses to which technology can be put combine to produce the form that jobs and organizations take. For example:

- *Equipment*. This category includes the machines, tools and work methods required by the process itself. To extract ore from a deep mine requires tunnelling equipment, conveyors for removing the ore and crushing/filtering equipment to extract the minerals. It is not possible to operate a mine with the equipment required for building aircraft. There will however, be some equipment common to most organizations. For example, fork lift trucks exist in almost all organizations. In addition, the relative cost of labour is an influence on the technology that can be justified, as is the need for high volume, consistent quality and the business that the organization is in. Management in Action 13.2 provides an insight into one aspect of this, namely the relationship between people and the advanced manufacturing technology increasingly appearing in factory operations.
- *Administrative*. Every organization needs procedures to control operational processes and cost. Although there are legal and professional standards to follow in many accounting and employment fields, there is considerable freedom of choice in how these are implemented in practice. For example, developments such as just-in-time seek to eliminate much administrative activity. Considerable savings in physical stock, time, space and money have been reported by such methods (see for example, Evans *et al.* (1990), pp 712–13 and 715–19). Such approaches directly influence the design of jobs for the workers who administer and manage organizations as well as manual employees.
- *Social*. Through the two forces indicated above, a considerable degree of the constraint in the job design process is established. However, there are also opportunities for influencing the job design through the ways that people are fitted around these constraints. Examples include the use of teamwork and job sharing. The history of the organization and the way that it has used its employees in the past influences both the choices available for the future and employee preferences. For example, employees who perceive a history of employer exploitation are more likely to be suspicious of new initiatives.

MANAGEMENT IN ACTION 13.2 Matching AMT jobs to people

The starting point for considering the design of jobs involving advanced manufacturing technology (AMT) is the level of human intervention necessary. Many systems designers attempt to eliminate human intervention in the running of systems, but this has not been completely successful. There are two forms of human intervention with AMT:

- *Production intervention*. This is a necessary part of the production process. It involves such tasks as changing tools, loading and unloading materials. These occur at predictable times and are necessary because it is not cost effective to fully automate a process.
- *Corrective intervention*. This is necessary because the system may make a mistake during the production process. These can be machine faults, human error, programming faults or material problems. These categories of fault are impossible to predict and so the impact on automatic processes is difficult to define, hence the need for human intervention.

It is in the field of corrective interventions that most scope for job design exists. When a fault arises there are essentially two options available. First, call a specialist to diagnose and correct the fault. Second, allow the operator to deal with some or all of the implications of the problem. Each option has its own advantages and disadvantages. For example, calling an expert wastes time when the problem may be easily rectified by the operator. Equally, allowing operators to deal with problems may result in reduced downtime, but no operator can be expert in all aspects of the process or technology. To design a two-stage process allowing the operator to diagnose and rectify the problem if possible, only calling for support if necessary, might save time in some cases but could considerably lengthen delays in others.

In one case where many corrective interventions were necessary a working party identified job changes which improved overall efficiency. Breakdowns reduced by about 40 per cent and machine downtime reduced by about 28 per cent after the changes to job design. This demonstrated that allowing operators greater control over corrective interventions had a direct impact on performance. In another case poor communications and low involvement in the planning of work caused problems for the workers. Regular communication meetings were introduced and workers were given responsibility for planning daily work priorities. Following some resistance from technical staff and supervisors the changes began to pay dividends in higher productivity and job satisfaction. Senior staff were freed from routine decisions and were thus more able to think and plan ahead, while the workers concentrated on achieving the objectives for the current work period.

Adapted from: Martin, R and Jackson, P (1988) Matching AMT jobs to people, *Personnel Management*, December, pp 48–51.

Stop ↔ Consider

Speculate on the future impact of technology on work organization. To what extent is it likely that technology can eliminate the need for most people to do jobs as we currently understand the term?

What are the arguments (for and against) suggesting that technology should be restricted if it begins to impact on the ability of society to maintain reasonably high levels of employment?

- *New activity*. As technology changes over time so the need for some jobs disappears and new jobs and organizations are created. Such change is not restricted to the arrival of a new technology. Even new technologies change as they become more accessible and integrated. For example with the arrival of the computer on a commercial scale in the 1960s came the job of a punched card operator. In those days the only way to input information in significant volume was to first create a card with the data punched into it as a series of holes.

> Batches of these cards were then fed into a card reader and the computer could then process the data. Such jobs were in high demand and commanded high salaries. However, with the development of direct keyboard input such jobs disappeared almost overnight.

The relationship between the first three of these forms of technology and job design can be shown as a diagram, Figure 13.5.

GROUPS AND WORK ORGANIZATION

The work of the Tavistock Institute brought together the scientific management tradition and the human relations movement into a single perspective on job design. Trist and Bamforth (1951) studied the impact of the mechanization of coal mining on the work of miners. Traditionally, coal was extracted from short faces (a seam of coal being worked on) by teams of skilled miners working in small groups supported by labourers. The introduction of machines and conveyor belts allowed much longer faces to be worked (referred to as the longwall method). Jobs had to be changed to allow the machines to be used efficiently. The small teams were combined into larger groups organized around the machinery and with a new supervisory structure. As a consequence a number of other non-work behaviours changed as well. These included a deterioration in the quality and effectiveness of communications between workers and across shifts; an increase in blaming other shifts for problems; increased absenteeism; increased number of accidents; increased stress. The result being a generally poor employee relations situation.

Through their research Trist and his colleagues demonstrated that it was possible for a particular technology to support different types of work structure. They also demonstrated that the social and technical aspects of work needed to be integrated into a unified socio-technical system. In addition the work also needed to be undertaken in an economically viable way. The Tavistock Institute has been involved in many similar studies and has reinforced the application of the open systems model (see Figure 13.6) view of organizations and the role of job design in achieving effective operations. The open systems view seeks to introduce into the concept of an organization the dynamic, interactive and dependent nature of its relationship with the environment. Job design therefore needs to support this relationship if success is to be achieved.

Autonomous work groups are an extension of the socio-technical approach to job design. The job to be done is effectively contracted to a work group which then decides

FIGURE 13.5

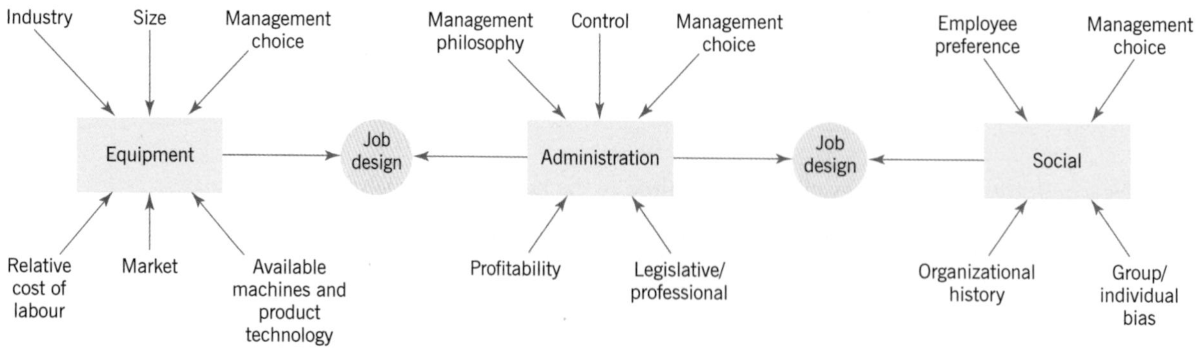

Technological influences on job design

FIGURE 13.6

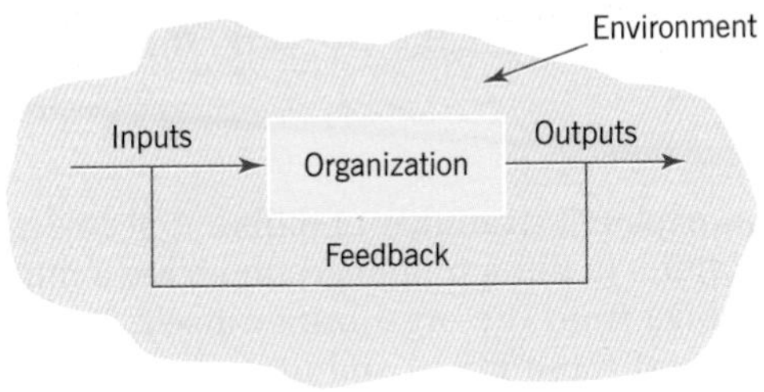

Open systems model of an organization

for itself how to undertake it. It essentially becomes responsible to management for the output and cost of operations. This allows control of job design, work allocation, work rates and work schedules to remain within the group. There have been a number of variations of the basic autonomous work group concept. For example, the group can either have a leader appointed by management or it can elect its own leader as a permanent or rotating job. Emery and Thorsrud (1976) suggest that there is more to take into account than the linking of the physical aspects of the tasks into the desired social organization. They also suggest that the psychological job demands on human beings should also be taken into account. Table 13.1 reflects a number of the psychological demands identified as essential if job design is to be effective.

The most famous application of these ideas on job design has been in the Kalmar plant of Volvo, the Swedish car maker. It began operations in 1974 and used teams of between 15–20 people in car-building activities. Socio-technical job design is also associated with concepts such as the quality of working life. Management in Action 13.2, above, reflects some of the more recent ideas on the integration of teamwork in car industry activities.

- Optimal level of work cycle – to avoid short cycle, repetitive activity
- The inclusion of supplementary tasks in relation to the main job
- The inclusion of opportunity to determine own performance in terms of quality and quantity of output
- The job should contribute to the value of the product as far as the customer is concerned
- There should be provision for job rotation and involvement in a broad range of facets of the overall job
- Provision of communication opportunities so that employees' requirements can be incorporated into job and product design
- The job should consist of a meaningful pattern of tasks providing a feeling of a complete whole
- The job should comprise degrees of skill, knowledge, care or effort that is worthy of respect in society
- Wherever possible, jobs that interlock should be grouped to allow for teamwork

TABLE 13.1 Psychological job demands (*adapted from*: Emery, F and Thorsrud, E (1976) *Democracy at Work: The Report of the Norwegian Industrial Democracy Program,* Martinus Nijhoff, Leiden, with the kind permission of Kluwer Academic Publishers)

ORGANIZATIONAL INFLUENCES ON WORK ORGANIZATION

The discussion so far has explored a number of different perspectives associated with the design of work. In addition to these influences there are a number of forces acting on the situation that emerge from the organization itself. It is the intention of this section to review a number of these forces and to explore the links with the ways in which work is organized and jobs designed. However, some of this discussion will inevitably involve consideration of organization structure, frameworks and culture as topics. These issues are discussed more fully in Chapters 12 and 15 of the book. In this chapter they are being introduced as relevant as influences on the way in which work may be organized.

Bureaucracy

Bureaucracy is a term used to describe an approach to organizational design that is particularly relevant to large-scale public and private sector organizations. Weber (1947) is the earliest and most frequently quoted source of material in relation to the notion of bureaucracy. Weber was a sociologist working at Heidelberg University in Germany at the beginning of the last century. He was interested in the concepts of power and authority, how they differed and found expression within society. He concluded that the nature of authority changed as society developed and that what he termed as rational–legal authority was emerging. This was based on the creation of formal written rules which enjoyed a legal status within the organization. These rules governed the appointment of those empowered to lead as well as the way in which their leadership was to be exercised. For example, employees follow the instructions of managers because they accept that managers have the legal power to exercise that authority.

At the time Weber was writing he was surrounded by organizations that were growing rapidly in size, complexity and sophistication. International trade was developing rapidly as was the public sector and growth in domestic consumption. There was no computer based technology to assist with the running of the large-scale organizations and all records, documents, etc. had to be produced by hand. This required armies of people to undertake the range of duties involved, all of whom had to be organized and directed in their work activities. Bureaucracy was therefore regarded by Weber as the principles suggesting the best way to organize activity in order to achieve the objectives necessary. The main principles of bureaucracy as set out by Weber are included in Table 13.2.

In this type of organizational arrangement Weber was describing the application of impersonality and rationality as guiding principles. In other words he was suggesting that as an ideal type of organization such an organization would be run in the best interests of its customers and according to rational rules. Authority would be exercised according to these principles and not based on whim, nepotism or favouritism. In using the term ideal type, Weber was recognizing that this may not be found in precise form in specific organizations, but that the general principles would be found in most organizations to a greater or lesser extent. Other writers have criticized this notion and suggested that rules do not necessarily create order and stability. Gouldner (1954), for example, draws attention to the fact that within organizations rules are created by managers and that employees usually do not have any say in their development. In short, rules are drawn up for the benefit of those creating them. In his analysis, Gouldner identified different classes of rules, each of which elicited a different response from those subjected to them.

- Specialization. Each job specializes in a particular set of tasks
- Rules. That rules should govern the conduct of business and the tasks being undertaken
- Hierarchy. That there should be an ordered system of reporting relationships
- Impersonality. The duties of each office should be conducted without fear or favour
- Appointed officials. Individuals should be appointed based on qualification and capability
- Full-time officials. The job should be the main occupation of the individual
- Career officials. Promotion should be based on merit
- Private-public split. The private life of an employee has no part to play in the job

TABLE 13.2 Bureaucratic principles

Having said that, the concept of bureaucracy has been very influential over the years in providing the basis upon which organizations arrange their activities and design the jobs to be undertaken. While bureaucracy should, if followed closely, allow for the design of jobs which all fit together into a cohesive organizational framework it does have certain drawbacks. For example it does not allow for the employee to be able to exercise judgement in the course of their work. They are required simply and unthinkingly to follow the rules. Any exceptions should be referred to a higher authority for resolution. In a very real sense the human employee exists within the organization as a substitute for a machine. They are there to follow set procedures mechanistically and channel their energies as directed by the rationally–legally appointed superior. Creativity, ingenuity and individuality are all to be eschewed, if not forced out of the organization. It is an approach to organization that encourages a compliance response from employees, not the commitment so often sought in today's environment.

Taylorism

FW Taylor developed his views on work organization, which he termed scientific management, during his working life as a manager in the steel industry in the USA during the late 1800s and early 1900s. His approach was very much task oriented and he used work study techniques to review actual working methods and identify the one best way of performing each task. He set out to achieve three main objectives through his approach to work organization:

1. *High productivity*. Through the identification of the one best way of doing each task and applying the use of monetary incentives workers would be encouraged to produce efficiently. This would benefit both company and employee financially and in other ways.
2. *Standardization of work activity*. Through the application of work study techniques the one best way would be identified and each employee would be carefully selected to match the needs of the task. This would standardize both work activity across employees and the performance they achieved (through incentive payments).
3. *Discipline at work*. He also attempted to introduce an improved hierarchical approach to authority which would allow the decisions of managers to be cascaded throughout the organization. This would allow a more effective control of workforce activity, which the 'scientifically' designed jobs would then covert into cost-effective output.

Systematic soldiering
A deliberate restriction on the amount of work done by employees to protect their jobs and future income.

As with Weber, Taylor was working in a particular social context and responding to the needs of management as he perceived and understood them. For example, workers were liable to engage in what he termed **systematic soldiering**, a deliberate restriction on the amount of work done by employees to protect their jobs and income levels. The context at the time consisted of a workforce with relatively low levels of education, with a lack of a factory work-ethos (many workers were immigrants to America with limited language skills and predominantly from an agricultural background). As he saw it he was seeking to organize work around the limitations that existed at the time through the development of a science of work and the introduction of an appropriate distinction between management and worker responsibilities.

As with many attempts to introduce work study techniques as the basis of work organization since, he encountered significant problems. The workers resisted his attempts at the close control of activity, managers resisted the attempts to reorganize their jobs as well and eventually Taylor was dismissed by the company. During World War I the American government became so concerned at worker hostility to scientific management as a way of designing jobs and work output (following a strike) that they banned its use in the defence industry.

However, the widespread use of the approach to determine how jobs should be designed and the level of output that should be expected from each worker has continued across the world. For example, Pean (1989) describes the results of applying work study to eye surgery carried out in a Moscow hospital. The procedure was studied and broken down into five discrete workstations, each staffed by a medically qualified person. The patient is laid out on a bed attached to a conveyor belt, has the anaesthetic given to them and then moves automatically between workstations where the surgeon performs the specific tasks appropriate to that stage of the surgery. By the end of the ten minutes 'processing' time the patient leaves the operating theatre conveyor belt as one of the 15 per hour who can be treated in this way.

Classical management view

Although the main name in this context is that of Fayol a number of other individuals have been influential in developing the approach to organizing that became known as the classical management view. Essentially the classical view holds that there are a number of guiding principles that should be followed in creating an organization and the jobs within it. It was Lussato (1976) who brought together these ideas within the classical model (Table 13.3).

The application of these principles creates a basis for the organization of work within the business. However, as with the other approaches introduced it relies upon the application of rules etc. to be able to function. Just like the other approaches it ignores several important aspects associated with human nature in a work context. It assumes that the application of rules and authority creates order and predictability. It ignores the human qualities of the people employed in the organization and does not allow for the application of individuality or creativity in the exercise of work responsibility. In brief, it is represents a top-down approach to how work should be organized.

Contingency view

The contingency view of organization essentially holds that structure and the design of the work within it should be driven by the circumstances surrounding the organization. From that perspective the external and internal forces acting upon the organization would be interpreted by management and appropriate working arrangements created. Figure 13.7 reflects the contingency chain of events leading to the design of work activity within the organization.

- Scalar concept. This literally means the hierarchy or chain of command
- Exception. Only exceptions to the norm should be referred upwards. This encourages delegation and management by exception
- Span of control. The number of subordinates reporting to any boss should not be excessive, as this causes work overload and management and communication problems
- Specialization. The specialization of work principle should also be applied to management jobs
- Unity of command. Each person should have only one boss

TABLE 13.3 Classic management principles

The advantage of the contingency view of organization is that it specifically allows for the existence of variation between organizations. The sum total of the circumstances impacting on any two organizations, even of similar size, location and industry is never identical. Therefore the application of contingency principles would recognize this and allow for the development of different organizational responses. The difficulty with the concept of contingency is that it relies heavily on the ability and/or willingness of managers to acknowledge the existence and significance of the forces acting upon the situation. Equally, it depends on their being prepared and/or able to take action on work organization elements as part of the response strategy.

Culture

In Chapter 12 a range of models of organizational culture were introduced. Each of the models of culture discussed there has general implications for the organization of work. In more specific terms, Spender (1989) described organizations as bodies of knowledge, used and created by managers. He also considered that each body of knowledge was specific to a particular industry. They constitute the received wisdom of each industry and comprised the shared beliefs, judgements and underlying knowledge about the nature and functioning of the industry, its markets and networks. Spender termed this common understanding the industry recipe. In that sense his views are very close to the Deal and Kennedy (1982) view of culture as 'the way we do things around here'. Spender was working at the level of industry commonalities that impact on how organizations function through the inherited recipes. In that sense one aspect of the recipe would be an understanding of how to arrange the organization's work to be able to function effectively in a particular industry.

At an organizational level one of the earliest studies of the transfer of working practices between cultures was that carried out by Rice (1958). A new weaving technology developed in Britain had been exported to an existing textile mill in Ahmadabad in India. The new machinery, designed and built in Britain, was based around Western conceptions of how jobs should support the operation of the machine. This required a complete change to the ways in which weaving jobs had been undertaken previously in

FIGURE 13.7

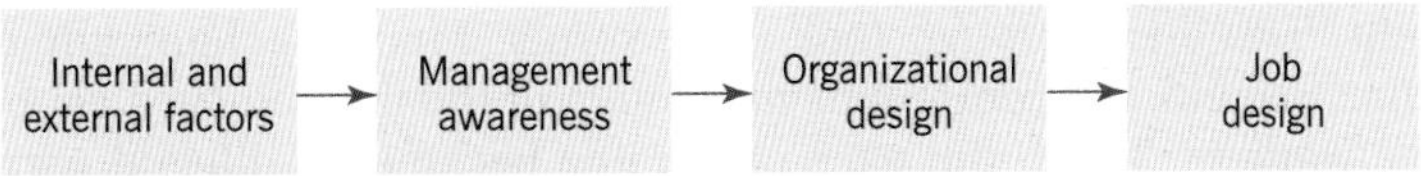

Contingency approach to work organization

the Indian factory. Twelve specialized jobs with a total of 29 operators were necessary to run the new machine, whereas with the previous machines each worker would have had a specific job to undertake. The new arrangement of work required completely different job structures to be introduced. This caused confusion among the workers and productivity and quality both suffered as a consequence. The result was not a function of low morale or poor management–worker relations, which had all been good previously. It was simply that the culture of the organization within its national context was not in alignment with the cultural basis of the job design as built into the machine. In seeking to overcome the difficulties it was decided to develop a group approach to work organization, thus allowing teams to develop and design job structures that they would feel were most suitable. This was adopted and found to impact positively on quality and productivity.

Gomez (2003) illustrates this point more recently through her work with MBA students from Hispanic and Anglo-American backgrounds. She found that the Hispanic students were collectively oriented and so preferred jobs which incorporated these features as compared to Anglo-American students who preferred jobs which contained more individualistic dimensions. There are clear job design issues that emerge in relation to the cultural preferences of the organization and its employees. A recent workspace satisfaction survey carried out by *Management Today* in conjunction with Stanhope and ICM Research (Myerson, 2003) found that 85 per cent of respondents thought that the workplace was a key indicator of a company's corporate culture and the following Employee Perspective (13.2) reflects some of the other findings from that survey.

FORDISM AND POST-FORDISM

The terms Fordism and post-Fordism reflect the application of scientific management principles to the running of manufacturing and other organizations, largely developed and refined by Ford in the early years of the twentieth century.

Fordism

It was the fledgling motor car industry in which the ideas and principles which became known as Fordism were first developed. At the turn of the twentieth century motor cars were traditionally made by teams of craftsmen. The process of manufacture was so detailed that it could take anything up to 13 weeks to complete each vehicle. Even in volume car production there was much skilled work. Partly assembled vehicles remained in one position while teams of workers moved around the factory building up the product as they went. This process was relatively inefficient.

Early attempts to increase productivity included building vehicles on a trestle that could be pushed between teams. This was refined into a simple production line in which employees remained in one position and the vehicles moved between workstations. Early attempts required the workers to push each vehicle to the next workstation as they completed their task. This left control over the pace of work to the employee. It was Henry Ford who made a breakthrough in the early years of the twentieth century by mechanically driving an assembly line at a speed determined by management. The breakthrough took three forms. First, mechanically driving the assembly line. Second, the continuous movement of the line removed control of activity from the workers. Third, the pace of the line became an integral part of the job design process.

EMPLOYEE PERSPECTIVE 13.2 Workplace satisfaction survey

Among the workspace satisfaction survey results were:

- Only 47 per cent of respondents were proud to bring clients or contacts to their place of work.
- 56 per cent of staff actually wanted relaxation/thinking space, but only 20 per cent had it available.
- 53 per cent of staff wanted a gym, but only 14 per cent had one on site.
- 41 per cent wanted a restaurant, but only 31% had one available.
- 27 per cent wanted childcare or eldercare to be available, but only 6 per cent had it available.
- 94 per cent of respondents think that the workplace reflects the employers' attitudes to their staff, but only 39 per cent think their place of work was designed with people in mind.

Tasks

1. As an employee how might you interpret these results in relation to work organization?
2. From a management perspective what might these findings indicate about the ways in which organizational culture impacts on work organization in its broadest sense? How might these factors impact on the way that work should be organized?

The combination of mechanically paced assembly lines, scientific management-based job design and piecework payment was the mixture that managers had been seeking in order to control production. Because of the pivotal role of Henry Ford and the Ford Motor Company in this process it has become known as Fordism. In employee terms, it is frequently associated with alienated workers performing boring tasks with no interest whatsoever in the end product of their labours. An indication of the benefits of assembly line technology can be found within data published by Ford itself in Table 13.4 (taken from Ford Motor Company, 1918).

It did not take long for the benefits of Fordism to become established across a wide range of industries and countries. The principles were introduced to the manufacturing of a wide range of household goods, including radios and vacuum cleaners. The River Rouge factory of Ford in the USA became the biggest factory in the world, employing some 80 000 people in the assembly of the Model 'T' car. The factory received raw material in the form of metal, rubber and wood and through its own foundries, tyre factories, machine shops and assembly lines a new car was spewed out every few seconds.

However, not everything was perfect. Many employees were not able to tolerate the noise, pace of work, boredom and sheer scale of operation, consequently, labour turnover was very high. The response of Ford was to raise wages, thereby retaining labour and allowing employees to become consumers of the goods being produced, for example it was possible to save for a car through a company savings scheme. Money

Pre-assembly line	Post-assembly line
1100 men assemble 1000 car engines in a 9-hour day	1400 men assemble 3000 car engines in an 8-hour day
Each engine = 9.9 labour hours	Each engine = 3.37 labour hours
	A reduction in labour content of 6.17 hours or 62.3%

TABLE 13.4 The effect of an assembly line on car engine production (*source*: Ford Motor Company (1918) *Facts from Ford*)

Golden handcuff
An attempt to lock the employee into the company through the use of some incentive to stay.

was used as a **golden handcuff** in an attempt to lock the employee into the company. Ford also engaged a private police force to ensure that workers were committed to the company and did not join trade unions. It was in principle and practice very much a top-down process with decisions and policies being formulated by managers. Employees were regarded as an extension of the machines that were used to drive the factory system.

Managers were not able to realize the full potential from the Fordist approach. The relentless pressure of an assembly line introduced an additional cause of stress into a delicately balanced system. Supervisors were continually pressed for increases in line speed, jobs were deskilled to the level of the banal and the opportunity for social interaction eliminated. The human dimension of the organization was something that Ford actively discouraged: 'A big business is really too big to be human. It grows so large as to supplant the personality of the man' (Ford, 1923, p 263). So conscious was Ford of the need to maintain order and control that several unique features were present in the factories. Under the influence of the sociological department within the company great emphasis was placed on the 'quality' of the working environment. Walls and roofs of factory buildings at the River Rouge factory were painted regularly and windows washed, by the team of 700 cleaners and painters. Welfare provision included a school, a hospital, cut price shops and a newspaper. However, there was a strong element of paternalism and attempts to achieve control over workers' lives through this provision.

Industrial disputes began to emerge as employees found ways of resisting the inevitable control and alienation from working on the assembly line. In structuring production into a stream of activity greater output and reduced cost had been achieved at the expense of vulnerability. A break in any part of the production process brought the entire system to a standstill. This placed a considerable degree of power in the hands of employees. Blauner (1964) describes it thus:

> The social personality of the auto worker, a product of metropolitan residence and exposure to large, impersonal bureaucracies, is expressed in a characteristic attitude of cynicism toward authority and institutional systems, and a volatility revealed in aggressive response to infringement on personal rights and occasional militant collective action. Lacking meaningful work and occupational function, the automobile worker's dignity lies in his peculiarly individualistic freedom from organizational commitments. (p 177)

Goffee and Scase (1995) summarize a number of weaknesses associated with the Fordist model (pp 78–9), including:

- *Alienation*. The organizational consequences of alienation can include high labour turnover, absenteeism, the production of poor quality products and even sabotage.
- *Product change*. The original Ford model depended on a single product with no variation. However, with increased competition and customer ability to exercise choice this becomes difficult to sustain.
- *Managing and doing distinction*. Taylor envisaged a strict distinction between managerial and operational activity. The danger of this view is that it separates parts of the organization that need to co-operate, creating low trust relationships.
- *Inhibition of creativity*. The imposition of managerial control can actively inhibit levels of creativity and desire for change, even among those charged with pursuing them.
- *Potential not fully realized*. Because of the need to plan ahead for specific levels of capacity in production, variation in market demand can frequently lead to an underutilization of resource. In addition, many of the issues discussed above also have the effect of reducing output.

These difficulties soon became apparent and led initially to tighter control of the process and work methods in an attempt to manage out the undesirable influences. Considerable effort was put into method study and similar approaches to critically examine problems and identify solutions.

Post-Fordism

There are immense benefits potentially available through the application of scientific management to the running of an organization. However, there are a number of forces that conspire to offset these benefits and they tend to be one-off in effect. Once the workers produce a car engine in 3.73 hours instead of 9.9 hours (from Table 13.4) this becomes the norm over which improvement must be achieved in successive years. Different and more radical approaches become necessary to obtain the next generation of leaps in productivity.

Post-Fordism attempted to retain the advantages of Fordism, but to overcome the major weaknesses. There are three areas in which post-Fordism sought to address the difficulties identified:

- *Market*. Marketing trends and competition demand increasingly fragmented product ranges, updated products and new products to be introduced at regular intervals.
- *Methods*. The clearest illustration of just how adaptability can be incorporated into production processes comes from the motor car industry. For example, any of the large car makers can produce a large number of end product variations within the basic body-shell design for any particular model.
- *Management*. In attempting to overcome the Fordist problems it is managers who must decide what must be done. They need to be prepared to change their own practices to more effectively capture the potential from employees. Ford tried paying higher wages to handcuff employees to his factory. This worked for a while, but it does not take long for the new conditions to become the base against which future comparisons are made, as well as becoming ordinary by virtue of familiarity. So a circular process is established in which regular 'treats' are necessary on a regular basis to maintain interest. Early work from the Human Relations School and the Tavistock Institute began to suggest that employees could become more involved through developments such as empowerment (delegation of responsibility).

Figure 13.8 reflects the phasing process between Fordism and post-Fordism with the three forces just outlined.

There are a number of forces that produce a reticence in moving away from the principles embedded in Fordism. The efficiencies potentially available through Fordism retain their attraction. The difficulty is it cannot be achieved in its pure form in the long run. Humans are not machines and they react to being controlled by an inflexible assembly line. Roy (1960) describes the rituals and routines of four factory workers over the course of a working day as they attempt to cope with the demands of production. Fordist managers would regard such behaviour as deviant and as creating a loss of efficiency for the system and therefore something to be eliminated. The underlying problem however is that it is not possible to completely separate the worker from the human.

Other pressures in the environment also tend to encourage the retention of Fordist principles, including:

- *Risk*. Every person within a Fordist organization is familiar with their role and the types of problem that will be encountered. To introduce change carries with it risk and a lower certainty that events can be dealt with effectively or quickly.

FIGURE 13.8

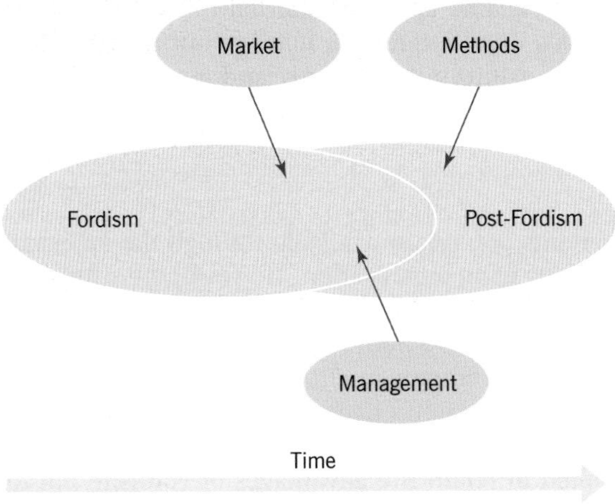

The evidence of post-Fordism

- *Training*. The training and experience of most managers is in organizations which originate and espouse the Fordist perspective. Managers make use of what they know and believe in running organizations. It takes time for new ideas, thinking and knowledge to filter through and become an accepted part of their skill base.
- *Systems*. The systems and procedures adopted within organizations tend to reinforce the status quo. Many organizations reward executives based upon short-term financial gains rather than long-term measures of corporate performance.
- *Preference*. Managers with careers to develop are not likely to deliver things not valued by those in a position to allocate rewards. Also, as Kanter (1989) points out, management skills have developed in specific organizational settings and to change these makes many of these skills redundant. The maintenance of the distinction between managed and manager could also be brought into question if radical organizational change were to be pursued.

Goffee and Scase (1995) identify a number of distinguishing features which the authors describe as paradigm shifts in management, reflecting the evolution of organizations from Fordist to post-Fordist models (see Table 13.5).

FLEXIBILITY, EMPOWERMENT AND PATTERNS OF WORK

Flexible firm
Organizing approach based on job, location, temporal, numerical, financial flexibility, or based on the use of core and peripheral employees.

The notion of the **flexible firm** will be introduced in Chapter 15 in relation to organization structure. However, as an approach to work organization it also contains a strong association to job design. It is also a way of organizing work that has a very long tradition in some industries, as shown by Haunschild (2003) using as a case example German repertory theatre. The approach to flexibility adopted by the organization could be expected to significantly impact on the way that jobs were arranged within the organization. For example:

- *Flexibility*. There are a number of forms that flexibility can take. Flexibility could be job flexibility, location flexibility or temporal flexibility. The opportunity

From: Fordist	To: Post-fordist
◆ Precisely-defined job roles	◆ Broadly-defined job roles
◆ Specialist skills	◆ Transferable skills
◆ Tight control	◆ Loose control
◆ Bounded responsibilities	◆ Autonomy and discretion
◆ Rules and procedures	◆ Guidelines for behaviour
◆ Closed communication	◆ Open/fluid communication
◆ High status differences	◆ Low status differences
◆ Low-trust relationships	◆ High-trust relationships
◆ Prevailing custom and practice	◆ Innovation and change
◆ Colleagues as individuals	◆ Colleagues as team members
◆ Invisible management	◆ Visible leadership

TABLE 13.5 Paradigm shifts in management (*source*: Goffee, R and Scase, R (1995) *Corporate Realities*, Routledge, London)

to undertake a different job can help to develop the individual by introducing them to new skills, or old skills in a new setting, or it can simply introduce a fresh location to add variety to an otherwise predictable work routine. Temporal flexibility refers to changing the times of work. Schultz *et al.* (2003) however point out that there can be some negative consequences arising from some forms of worker flexibility perhaps as a result of work interruption and performance feedback difficulties. They provide some ideas on how the effect of these difficulties might be dealt with. Management in Action 13.3 provides a survey indicating many forms of flexibility and some indication of their value as seen by managers.

- *Empowerment*. Employee involvement in decision making is generally what describes empowerment. It could incorporate, at its lowest level, consultation with a trade union over issues of common concern or, at the other end of the spectrum, worker representatives on the board of directors. Whatever the particular form, the purpose is to involve employees in decisions relating to the direction of the business and allowing them to take more decisions about operational issues. If nothing else, empowerment should provide employees with a stronger view of the whole organization and their part in it. It should also encourage a closer connection between the employee and the customer as employees are sometimes empowered to take whatever actions become necessary to meet the needs of the customer. Empowerment addresses most of the core job dimensions identified by Hackman and Oldham (1980) (Figure 13.4).
- *Patterns of work*. There are many different patterns of work. For example, shiftwork as compared to a daytime-only pattern. Curson (1986) identifies a broad range of alternative patterns. Among the options are:
  - *Annual hours*. Based on variable hours worked each week, accumulated towards an annual total.
  - *Compressed week*. This provides for a smaller number of working days to be worked, but of longer duration. For example, four days at ten hours worked compared to five days at eight hours.

MANAGEMENT IN ACTION 13.3 Juggling act

Personnel Today and Plantime conducted a survey to find out more about flexible working. Among the flexibility practices identified were part-time working, annualized hours, flexible hours, job sharing, telecommuting and homeworking. For example, Earl's Court Olympia, an exhibitions and catering company, has a number of flexible practices and systems in order to be able to meet the needs of its clients. Jim Black, group personnel director, points out that many exhibition facilities are used out of normal working hours and clients frequently make many last-minute demands. So the company needs the maximum level of flexibility possible. For example, within the catering division of the company a database of all staff skill areas and work location and hours preferences is held to allow managers to match individuals to the tasks in hand. The maintenance department uses an annualized hours system (which allows for peaks and troughs in work demand within a total working time for the year) to allocate staff to particular projects.

Some of the findings from the survey include:

- 90 per cent of organizations use part-time working.
- 50 per cent of organizations use flexitime.
- 26 per cent of organizations use job sharing.
- 14 per cent of organizations use annualized hours.
- 11 per cent of organizations use telecommuting.

The advantages of flexible working include:

- 40 per cent of organizations report it helps to recruit and retain certain staff.
- 39 per cent of organizations report that it improves the ability to deal with peaks and troughs in demand.
- 34 per cent of organizations report that it improves flexibility from a management perspective.
- 31 per cent of organizations report that it reduces company costs.
- 28 per cent of organizations report that flexibility improves morale and is popular among staff.
- 16 per cent of organizations report that it reduces overtime costs.

Some of the barriers to introducing flexibility include:

- 44 per cent of organizations report management resistance.
- 30 per cent of organizations report administrative difficulties.
- 24 per cent of organizations report trade union resistance.
- 24 per cent of organizations report employee resistance because of fears over remuneration.
- 18 per cent of organizations report the costs of introducing flexibility.
- 15 per cent of organizations report practical problems such as fragmented workforce locations.

Adapted from: Hall, L (1994) Juggling act, *Personnel Today*, 8 February, pp 21–4.

Stop ↔ Consider

Forty-four per cent of organizations reported management resistance and 24 per cent reported trade union resistance to flexibility. Identify the reasons that might lead to this level of resistance as well as how they might be overcome.

The report is largely silent on the employee perspective on the use of flexible working practices. Identify what you believe different categories of employee might think about these approaches. For example, a new graduate just starting work, a single mother with two children, a junior manager aged 48 years old. What does this add to your understanding of the advantages and disadvantages associated with flexible working and its impact on work design, from both management and employee perspectives

EMPLOYEE PERSPECTIVE 13.3

To work from home or not, that is the question?

Consider the following request for advice from an employee working from home:

> I am pioneering working from home in our small company – but it's patently not working. Decisions are made without me, colleagues insist on calling me 'part-timer', and the boss keeps making heavy hints about things I've missed 'because you're never in the office'. I'm reluctant to admit defeat but the concept isn't exactly catching on. Will working from home irretrievably damage my standing at work?

Tasks

1. Consider the nature of homeworking and the way it might be organized. Is the reaction of this employee inevitable given the circumstances and the fact that it is a small company?
2. What advice would you give the employee and why?

You might like to compare your advice with that offered by: Bullmore, J (2003) What's your problem? *Management Today*, August, p 63.

- *Overtime restrictions*. This can be achieved by providing time off as an alternative to pay, flexing working hours or simply restricting overtime working.
- *Temporary and part-time working*. Allows individuals to choose the amount of time that they want to devote to a particular employer (or job).
- *Job sharing and homeworking*. Job sharing allows two (or more) people to share a specific job, by agreement taking a proportion each. Homeworking allows individuals to work at home utilizing computer-based technology to communicate with clients or other employees. But there is another side to working from home as indicated in the above Employee Perspective (13.3).
- *Sabbaticals and career breaks*. A university lecturer may apply for a sabbatical in order to undertake some research that would otherwise be difficult to complete. Career breaks are a gap in employment that can provide a means for an employee with other responsibilities to retain a career while meeting their other obligations.

The links between each of these aspects of work experience and job design are not direct. Each could influence the ways in which tasks are combined into jobs. They are also an influence on how the job is interpreted by the employee. For example, employees in a supportive environment in which they have some opportunity to balance their work and other commitments are more likely to interpret a boring job in a positive light because of the overall context.

CHANGING THE DESIGN OF JOBS

Change is the subject of a detailed review in Chapter 19 and so will not be explored in depth here. However, much of the change activity within organizations is intended to impact on the way in which work is undertaken. The approach to changing in the design of jobs within the organization will depend on many factors, many of which are indicated in Figure 13.9.

In certain situations the use of method study techniques would be used in order to develop alternative job content. This would perhaps then form the basis of a negotiation between management and trade unions representing the job holders about the nature of the new job, appropriate rates of pay, etc. In more coercive organizational

FIGURE 13.9

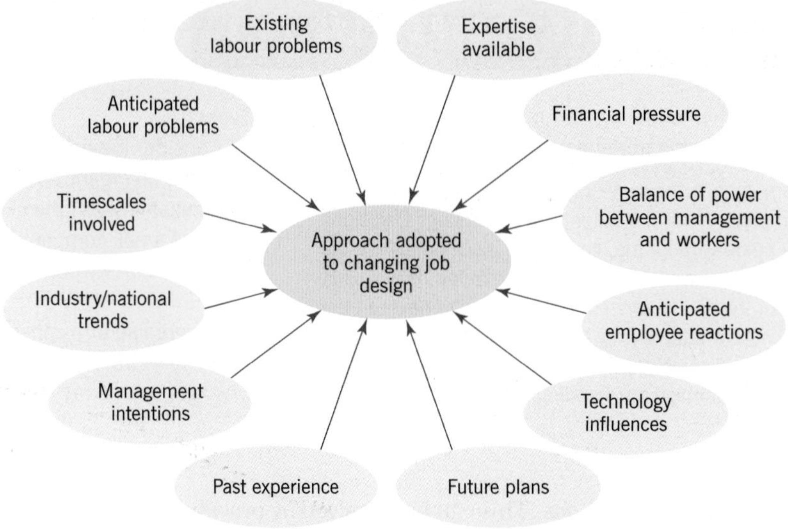

Factors influencing changes in job design

situations it could involve the manager deciding that a change was in order and what form it should take. This new requirement would then be given to the employee as an instruction on the basis of 'comply or be dismissed'. Clearly, there could be employment legislation in existence that might have a bearing on the ability of management either to get away with such actions or which would allow the employee to claim a measure of compensation if they were dismissed, but that is outside the scope of this discussion. Equally, there could be a legal restriction on management in terms of the degree of freedom to change the content of a job. For example, it is not legal for anyone without the appropriate qualifications to work as a medical doctor and consequently it is difficult to change the nature of medical practitioner jobs.

The approach adopted by management in seeking to change the design of jobs within an organization will inevitably have a major impact on the reaction of employees. An imposed job change is at best likely to generate a compliance response from them. A response hardly likely to engender a spirit of co-operation or high levels of productivity, quality or customer service. However, when the senior managers of organizations decide that they need to downsize in some form or other in order to reduce cost, then little can be done to make the wholesale job losses and work reorganization palatable to everyone. Early retirement and voluntary severance deals give people some degree of financial protection or compensation for the loss of their job. But for those who remain inside the organization it is sometimes a case of having to accept more work and longer hours for the same money (or resign and look for another job).

Taking large numbers of people out of an organization without also simplifying the operational processes and procedures simply means that fewer people must do more work. The essence of business process re-engineering (BPR) concept was to encourage managers to go back to first principles and redesign the organization and its processes from the ground upwards (Hammer, 1990). The demand to fundamentally redesign all aspects of work and organization as well as cutting numbers employed is perhaps a significant reason why BPR has been less than successful in achieving the intended widespread recognition and success originally expected.

ALIENATION, SATISFACTION AND PRODUCTIVITY THROUGH WORK ORGANIZATION

Alienation has been described as an expression of human independence. Managers cannot force employees to fully join in and become part of their reality. Compliance is not the same as commitment. People are not completely malleable to the will of others. Even in the most difficult of circumstances individuals will find ways of expressing individuality and freedom from total domination. The story of Lomax (1995) demonstrates how prisoners of war can maintain some measure of independence even in the most hostile of conditions. Also from literature, the classic *Brave New World* by Huxley, first published in 1932, provides insights into how a number of the characters are able to resist the all embracing control of society in the future world. From management's perspective the advantages of employing people must outweigh the disadvantages for it to be worth the effort and cost. Therefore, ways of directing and controlling the people resource are important aspects of management activity. Managers continually seek devices or techniques to generate additional benefits from the **social capital** that they employ.

Alienation
Detachment of the individual from the work that they do; feelings of powerlessness, meaninglessness, isolation or self-estrangement.

Social capital
A way of describing people which emphasizes their financial value to an organization in terms comparable to machinery or buildings.

From an employee perspective their experience of work includes the ever growing demands of industrialization. Some of these include ever tighter control, reduced ability to adjust the pace of work and subservience to the needs of technology. Mills (1959) described most work experience as a number of traps, a theme common to many later sociological studies. Traps in this context imply that employees become 'locked into' particular patterns of contribution and reward within an organization. Consequently as a reaction, employees actively seek to increase the significance and value obtained through their work. Managers seek controlled behaviour from their employees, which in this context means predictable, expected and directed. However, this search for control does not automatically mean that it can be achieved. Human beings inevitably retain a measure of independence. The existence of negative power introduced elsewhere in this book is just one example of free will in an organizational context. It is not possible to completely control the essential nature of human beings simply because management would like to do so.

Alienation represents a concept that emerged in the work of Marx and describes, 'the condition of humanity under capitalism' (Sims *et al.*, 1993, p 228). It originally reflected the inevitable (for Marx) separation between the worker as a human being and the person with the skill to provide the capitalist with the means of production; from a specific connection with the actual end product, other people and any control over the application of their labour. Sims *et al.* go on to point out that the meaning of the term alienation has changed over the years and now is generally taken to infer frustration and separation. Blauner (1964) suggested that as organizations moved towards mass production the level of alienation would increase, but that as high-technology operations began to take over the level would reduce as the human being became the master of technology and drudgery became a thing of the past. Not surprisingly this view has been heavily criticized for being overly simplistic and a reflection of the view of technology at the time (see for example, Thompson, 1989, pp 19–23). However, the concept of alienation forces a consideration of the design of work, particularly the way in which technology is integrated into it, and the impact of it on the worker.

Productivity is an organizational imperative and significant driver of management activity. Job design is about grouping the tasks that need to be undertaken into convenient chunks of work, which in turn contributes significantly to the level of productivity achieved. The basis of this design process can be subject to a number of forces including organization structure, historical job structure, and employee or managerial preference. Productivity is a reflection of conversion efficiency and therefore cost, hence, a concept strongly tied to the nature of work organization within the company. The continued existence of an organization is largely a function of its relative productivity within the competitive environment.

The search for productivity and control leads naturally to the job simplification approach to job design, based on the machine metaphor of organizational functioning. This view ignores the perhaps rather obvious truth that people are not machines. The recognition of this led to the adoption of other job design approaches in the search to capture the most effective way to organize work. In the service industries, for example, the nature and level of contact between employees and customers is a particular feature of the design of both jobs and the service encounter itself. Considerable training effort in most service companies goes into trying to drum into staff the desired (as defined by management) form of customer greeting and processing procedures. What much of this ignores is that most customers are aware of the relative insincerity of these trained-in exchanges and are not taken in by them. This cynicism arises for many reasons including the fact that most people have experienced such processing technologies supporting very poor real customer care. Indeed, many customers will work in other organizations that preach customer care but cannot deliver it and so employees become cynical about such programmes as is evident from the following Employee Perspective (13.4).

A number of job design approaches attempt to incorporate satisfaction into work. This is based on the assumption that workers contribute more if they are happy and feel that they are contributing something of value to something of value. There are three possible links between performance and satisfaction (Petty *et al.*, 1984):

1. *Satisfaction generates performance*. This would reflect the view that job design should aim to produce high levels of satisfaction as this in turn will optimize worker performance.
2. *Performance generates satisfaction*. The converse view is that achievement generates satisfaction. Therefore, every effort should be made to improve performance as this in turn will increase satisfaction.
3. *Satisfaction and performance link indirectly*. This holds that the two are linked, but only under certain conditions. Intervening variables such as management style, pressure, personality factors, job design, equity and rewards are examples of the factors that could mediate between the two. Figure 13.10 illustrates this relationship.

In his book on motivation, Vroom (1964) provides a clear indication that a satisfied worker is not automatically a high performer. It could be that at one extreme a very happy worker is enjoying work so much that they spend most of their time socializing, while at the other extreme a productive worker hates the job so much that working hard makes the time pass quicker. The relationship between satisfaction and

FIGURE 13.10

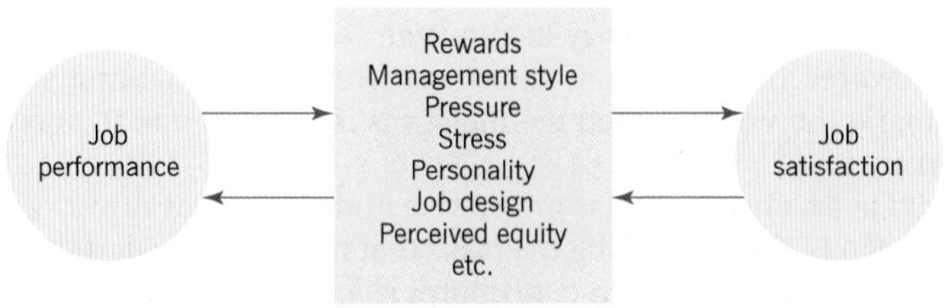

Relationship between performance and satisfaction

EMPLOYEE PERSPECTIVE 13.4 David was furious with his bank

David was in his mid-50s and had worked in the insurance industry since leaving school. He was used to dealing with customers at all levels in the industry from the individual looking for car insurance, to the large insurance companies in preparing quotations and claim documentation. Over the years he had become aware of the changes in the industry, particularly in relation to the use of call centres by the large insurance companies. He was also aware of the reduced levels of personal service provided by these organizations in dealing with both new business and claims. For example the reliance on computer systems and speaking to a different agent each time it was necessary to contact a particular company about a specific client. The number of mistakes in relation to each client contact, the reliance on standard and formulaic answers to questions and the inability of first contact customer agents to deal with anything out of the ordinary or complex was also an issue of frustration to David and his clients. The end result of all of this was frustration and more work for David in trying to provide his clients with a good level of service.

David was less than impressed with the impact of the changes within the insurance companies and its impact on his work. However, this frustration also became apparent to him in relation to his personal banking. David had a small loan and decided to pay it off early within the terms of his agreement with the bank. He contacted the call centre to make arrangements to pay a cheque into his account in order to clear it. He was given the details by the customer service agent and consequently paid the cheque to the bank. Nothing happened. Further calls to the call centre followed, all to no avail. The money paid in was withdrawn from his current account, but did not appear in his loan account and no one seemed able to resolve the problem. After four unsuccessful calls to the call centre David went to see his local branch of the bank in question and spoke to one of the cashiers. The cashier called his account up on the computer screen and found out what had happened. Whilst David was there the cashier wrote an e-mail to the particular department responsible for loan administration to explain what had happened and what should be done to correct matters. David was shown the e-mail and agreed with everything that it contained. This was sent and David waited for something to happen. About two weeks later he received a letter apologizing for the mistake and telling him that it had now been put right and that the additional loan that he was requesting had been approved and the money transferred to his current account the previous day! The new payment required from him would be an additional £50 per month and would be taken by direct debit the following week.

David was obviously furious. He was telling his friends at work about his experience and everyone laughed and had something similar to describe, either through personal experience or from the experiences of friends. David stormed off to his local branch again and spoke to a cashier. The cashier was only partly interested in what David was trying to explain and was only interested in trying to tell him that the bank had introduced a new account that very week that would pay him more interest if he would transfer all his existing accounts to the new one. After a few minutes of making no progress David stormed out of the branch and wrote a letter of complaint to the chief executive explaining in great detail exactly what he thought of the services offered by the bank and the mistakes that had been made. About a week later he received a reply from the chief executive saying that he was sorry about the problem and that his letter had been passed on to the head of customer services to deal with. The chief executive also pointed out that the particular bank was well known in the industry for delivering a consistently high world class service and therefore they were looking forward to his continued custom. A couple of days later he received a phone call from the head of customer service from the bank to apologize and to say that everything had now been sorted out correctly. A letter followed confirming that this was the case. David was not happy and there had been no mention of any redress for the inconvenience and stress that he had experienced. However he began to relax, at least everything had been sorted out satisfactorily. Then his bank statement arrived and he found that a direct debit payment had been taken from his account and paid to his now completed loan account!

He was incandescent with rage!

Tasks

1. What would you do next if you were David?
2. To what extent can organizations make effective use of technology, standard operating procedures and job design to be able to provide call-centre based mass service provision more reliably and efficiently? Or is it simply a reflection of a basically flawed business model; because service implies personal contact and continuity, it cannot function with anonymity and remote technology-based operations. Justify your views.

productivity is less direct, more complex and a function of a variety of forces acting upon the situation (Bassett, 1994). These include the individual, the job, working environment, management and the personal relationships involved.

QUALITY OF WORKING LIFE AND QUALITY CIRCLES

Quality of working life
An approach seeking to enhance the dignity of work, improve an organization's culture, the physical and emotional well-being of employees.

The **quality of working life** (QWL) movement emerged from a belief in the need to improve the experience of work for all employees. There is no single definition of QWL, but one which captures the breadth of the approach is Kopelman (1985, p 239):

> A philosophy of management that enhances the dignity of all workers, introduces changes in an organization's culture, and improves the physical and emotional wellbeing of employees.

Implicit in this definition is a broad approach to work activity, including job design and the other factors identified in Figure 13.10. It attempts to integrate both organizational needs for a productive workforce and the late twentieth-century expectations that individuals have in relation to work. James (1991, p 16) describes QWL as being composed of:

- *A goal*. The creation of more involving, satisfying, effective jobs and work environments at all levels.
- *A process*. Achievement of the goal through employee involvement. Bringing together the needs and development of people with the needs and development of the organization.
- *A philosophy*. Viewing people as assets to be released and developed, rather than costs to be controlled.

QWL activity tends to be concentrated into eight areas of working life experience (Walton, 1973):

1. *Compensation*. The rewards for work should be above a minimum standard for life and should also be equitable.
2. *Health and safety*. The working environment should reduce the adverse effects of danger and pollution that can impact on the physical, mental and emotional state of employees.
3. *Job design*. The design of jobs should be capable of meeting the needs of the organization for production and the individual for satisfying and interesting work.
4. *Job security*. Employees should not have to work under a constant concern for their future stability of work and income.
5. *Social integration*. The elimination of anything that could lead to individuals not identifying with the groups to which they belong. This includes the elimination of discrimination and individualism, while encouraging teams and social groups to form.
6. *Protection of individual rights*. The introduction of specific procedures aimed at guaranteeing the rights of employees at work.
7. *Respect for non-work activities*. Respect for the activities that people engage in outside work. Recognize the impact of work activities on private life.
8. *Social relevance of work*. Initiatives to increase the understanding among employees of the objectives of the organization and the importance of their part in them.

QWL initiatives have enjoyed mixed results, partly as a result of the complexity of the issues involved. There are external forces that influence how employees react to company initiatives. For example, the economic climate can either be hostile or favourable to the security of employment aspects of QWL. The activities of other organizations can also influence the perceptions of employees about the actions of their own employer, for example, the arrival in an area of a new employer offering better terms and conditions of employment. The wider social environment and attitudes can also influence events. For example, sex discrimination is largely a function of the prevailing social attitudes among predominantly male power holders which no longer matches changing social expectations. One aspect of this is the changing expectations of fathers in trying to meet the needs of their families and of their careers. Management in Action 13.4 introduces the findings of some research into how fathers can be categorized in relation to their approach to family responsibilities.

From the perspective of QWL, job design is an important part of the overall experience of individuals at work. It should be undertaken in such a way so as to ensure that the other seven aspects are not compromised. The use of quality circles has been associated with attempts at continuous improvement. While not part of job design as such, circles can play a significant part in shaping people's experience of work. A quality circle is described as (Department of Trade and Industry, 1985):

> A group of four to 12 people coming from the same work area, performing similar work, who voluntarily meet on a regular basis to identify, investigate, analyse and solve their own work-related problems. The circle presents solutions to management and is usually involved in implementing and later monitoring them.

Quality circles originated in the USA but gained wide acceptance in Japan during the 1960s, since when they have been re-exported to the west as a result of their success in improving quality, commitment and productivity. For circles to be successful the members need to be trained in problem solving, communication and teamworking. They also need to be taken seriously by managers. There has been some hostility to the concept from trade unions, managers and employees for a number of reasons, including a perceived erosion of power, the need to give up free time and the suspicion that it was a management attempt to reduce cost.

In introducing quality circles management need to demonstrate their commitment as well as recognizing that by allowing employees to solve problems, a shift in control takes place. A quality circle approach can be suggested to impose a parallel set of structures onto the existing formal hierarchy (Bushe, 1988; Goldstein, 1985). These dual frameworks can become a problem if commitment to the quality circle begins to take precedence over commitment to the formal organization. Potentially they become a struggle for power, circle members seeking to increase their influence over their working life and managers seeking to retain power over both activity and agenda.

WORK ORGANIZATION: AN APPLIED PERSPECTIVE

Not all jobs are in the gift of managers to design. The professions including the law, medicine, etc. ensure through qualification schemes, training and work demarcation that individuals are prepared in a nationally, or even internationally, consistent way. This limits the ability of managers to change these jobs or impose their own structure on them within particular organizational settings. Even with non-professional jobs, the more a particular organization personalizes its jobs (designs jobs without reference to what is generally the case in society) the more it is necessary to train employees to do the work. This increases the cost of recruitment,

MANAGEMENT IN ACTION 13.4 Work-life balance for men

Management Today together with BT and the Work Foundation polled 500 fathers to identify their attitudes towards work as the basis of a comparison with previous generations. They identified five distinctive types of father from their research:

- *21st century dad*. Typified by the view that this generation and type of father feel far more responsibility for their children's happiness.
- *Step-dad*. Part of the growing number of second family groupings that arise along with 40 per cent marriages ending in divorce. Care is needed to adapt to the existence of step-children as well as natural children into a family unit.
- *Happy dad*. Typified by someone who feels that they have their life in balance and being confident enough to decide what is important and give that priority when necessary.
- *Juggling dad*. Typified by someone who has a job in which it is difficult to balance the needs of home and work, perhaps being away from home for several days at a time.
- *Career dad*. A more extreme version of the 'juggling dad' concept. One in which the needs of career and work come first with family falling into a distinct second place.

Adapted from: Gwyther, M (2003) Working dads who want it all, *Management Today*, April, pp 44–53.

Stop ↔ Consider

What effect should this type of research have on the design of jobs, if any? Justify your views. How could such results be included in the design of jobs and quality of working life initiatives in a way that is fair to all employees (male and female, including those without children) and the organization?

training and wages which would need to be offset by productivity improvement if commercial disadvantage were to be avoided.

The more enlightened management approaches recognize that it is not possible to force or restrict the human qualities that employees possess. Indeed, it might even be possible to harness (or manipulate) those very qualities to provide added value to the organization. One manager described this as recognizing that with every pair of hands recruited a free brain was provided as well! However, some individuals would be happy to simply sell their labour and achieve self-actualization and personal meaning though other routes. For example, a young person may view a job as providing the money to allow them to subsequently take a year out and travel the world.

Boring and mundane aspects of work exist in all levels of job. They can be simplified, automated, incorporated into other activities or simply reduced in volume, but they are a certain aspect of organizational life. One difficulty with such activities is that personal preference plays a significant part in their definition. What is boring and mundane to one person is not so to another. Some people are able to cope with such jobs in a way which minimizes the negative impact of them. Every job becomes boring at some point in time. No matter how much an individual enjoys their work there are times when it is undertaken less than willingly and a change welcomed. These issues further complicate the design process as it is not possible to say that any particular job design will be 'good' for every person all of the time. Managers also have multiple objectives to achieve which influences the design of the jobs for which they are responsible. Cost reduction, efficiency and City expectation all tend to push managers towards job simplification in the search for maximum output and minimal cost.

To persuade managers to divert employee time from productive activity to the use of quality circles as an aid to subsequent improvement is not always easy, particularly if the result is to be an erosion of managerial decision making, control and power. The Taylorist notion that managers think and decide and workers labour is still evident in many operational situations. Many managers are less than comfortable with the notion that employees can and should be empowered to organize themselves through such initiatives as self-managed teams. The use of such approaches can be seen to bring into question the very need for managerial jobs to exist. It also introduces a need to consider the design of management jobs. There tends to be an assumption in much of the discussion of job design that it is about the work of employees other than managers. However, managerial jobs also need to be designed and created. A significant aspect of such initiatives as quality circles, delayering, downsizing and business process re-engineering calls into question the traditional view of what management work should be about and how it should be exercised. In the language of metaphor, perhaps the job of management should be seen as conducting an orchestra, not policing a football crowd. This is also perhaps what differentiates management from leadership.

Figure 13.11 reflects the range of factors that have a significant impact on job design. These influencing factors impact on the design of jobs in both direct and indirect ways that are not always recognized by the participants. The main factors are:

- *Operations*. These reflect the activities to be undertaken and which define to a significant extent the types of jobs that will exist within the organization.
- *Philosophy*. This guides the organization. Views on empowerment and quality of working life, for example, will impact on the way in which work is organized. For example, Guest (2002) suggests that job design is one of the elements within the practice of human resource management that positively impacts on higher work and life satisfaction. A result confirmed in research carried out in India by Paul and Anantharaman (2003).
- *Technology*. The level and type of technology available within the organization influences the job design to support it.
- *Market*. A service industry company will place significant emphasis on the interaction between employees and customers. This influences the design of the

FIGURE 13.11

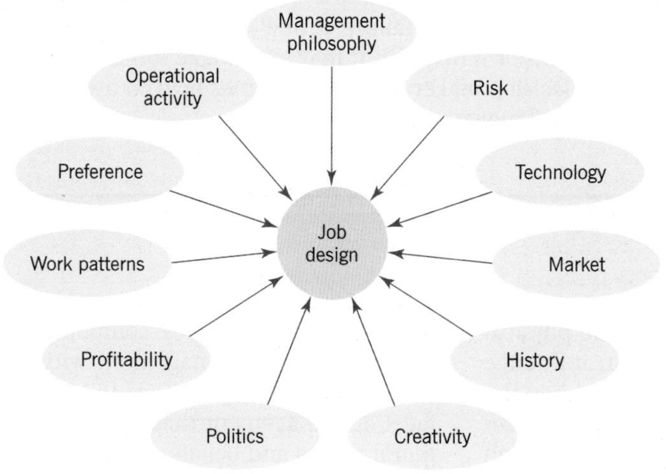

Factors influencing job design

jobs in question as well as the standards of behaviour expected. Also, education and training prior to employee entry to the labour market provides the skills and abilities that recruits bring with them to any job.

- *History*. The evolution of the company and how it has approached job design and managed its employee relations in the past will influence what is likely to be achieved in the future.
- *Creativity*. The ability to create jobs that are interesting, stimulating, rewarding and deliver high levels of productivity is a function of the creativity of the people involved. It is easy to adopt other organizations' ideas; equally it is not possible to create something new and original every time. Therefore, job design becomes a balancing process between these two extremes.
- *Political*. Managers can use job design as a political tool in reinforcing the rights and status of managers, or it can be used to attempt to capture the commitment of employees.
- *Profitability*. A highly profitable organization has the ability to direct resources towards experimentation and the development of alternative ways of working. An organization with little money available will have less freedom to concentrate on anything other than survival. There is an interesting paradox here because it is organizations with little money that actually need the best response from everyone to maximize the chance of survival. Situations of scarcity require the highest ability and creative responses from managers and employees in order to break the cycle of crisis. Yet this is usually when it is least visible.
- *Work patterns*. Job sharing and shiftwork have an influence on the design of jobs. It is not uncommon in factories to find shiftworkers being trained to undertake minor repairs in order to reduce the total number of engineers required.
- *Preference*. If the particular design of a job does not sit comfortably with either managers or workers then something will happen. Managers can specifically initiate a redesign process. Employees can simply adapt their work activity informally or they can formally press for change. Employees can also resign, seek alternative work, the level of quality could drop or there may be increased industrial relations problems. The relationship between motivation and job design is explored in a study carried out in a parks and recreation department setting within a local government organization (William and Lankford, 2003).
- *Risk*. The level of risk aversion is also a factor in the job design process. With any new idea there is a risk of failure. A new job design may deliver the anticipated benefits or it may not. It may even make some things worse. The attitude of the decision maker to risk determines how far away from the tried and tested they will move.

CONCLUSIONS

Job design is something that influences a considerable range of aspects of work, not just the physical execution of the necessary tasks. It can influence the way in which the organization approaches the very nature of employment within it. Job design can reflect a belief about the rights of employees to high level involvement in the activities of the company or it can reflect the view that workers provide a flexible (or necessary) alternative to machines.

Job design is also something that can be used to draw out from employees' additional commitment to the objectives of management without any reward other than job satisfaction. In other words, it is a facet of management that can be used to reflect the moral values and beliefs of the people involved or it can be a form of cynical manipulation. The difficulty lies in being able to identify the proportion of each active in any given context. Anyone who is seeking to manipulate employee commitment for commercial or personal gain is unlikely to admit it.

Consequently, a high level of trust is required if radical approaches to job design are to be adopted; trust that managers are not going to abuse employee commitment; and trust that employees will not abuse the additional power that they would be given to self-determine work activities (if that were the option chosen). Trust is something that is hard to gain but easy to lose. Unfortunately, managers generally do not have a good track record maintaining trust – at least as far as employees perceive it.

Now to summarize this chapter in terms of the relevant Learning Objectives:

- **Understand the main approaches to the design of work within an organizational setting.** The main approaches to job design are the use of job simplification (or job engineering as it is sometimes known); job rotation; job enlargement; job enrichment and the socio-technical approach (developed by Trist and Bamforth). Each of these approaches has advantages and disadvantages and involves seeking to offset the weaknesses in the simpler models. For example, job rotation seeks to offset the weaknesses in job simplification by incorporating a wider range of basic jobs within a rotating pattern of work. The socio-technical approach seeks to utilize the open systems model of an organization in identifying the need to incorporate the social, technical aspects of work into an integrated package of activity relevant to the economic and other forces in a particular context. One of the best known models of job design is that proposed by Hackman and Oldham, which utilizes task significance, skill variety, task identity, autonomy, and feedback as the necessary core job dimensions to take into account when designing work.
- **Explain how work study attempts to influence job design activities and how changing the design of jobs can be a difficult process.** Work study consists of two main themes, method study and work measurement. Method study seeks to critically examine the way in which work is carried out in order to eliminate unnecessary movement and activity, then to design the 'one best way' of efficiently undertaking the job. Work measurement seeks to establish, based on the prescribed method of work, how much work a qualified worker should be able to produce in a given period of time. Both of these aspects combine to produce an approach to job design based on scientific management principles. Changing the design of jobs is a complex process for many reasons. Resistance to change among managers and employees can arise for many reasons including the desire to defend a specific area of expertise or to maintain current levels of power or control. Change brings with it an element of risk that things may not work as intended. There are also cost implications associated with radical change if the new design of jobs requires skills that may not be widely available in society.
- **Outline the interrelationship between technology and work organization.** The relationship between technology and job design is both positive and negative. In some instances the nature of work has been relegated to that of machine minding, ensuring that the technology does what it is supposed to do. In other cases jobs have been eliminated as a new technology has developed and removed the need for people to undertake particular tasks. On the other hand technology can make some jobs easier by removing guesswork, hard physical labour and drudgery. Machines can do much of the routine processing that once required human effort to spend many hours copying data from one document to another. Technology also creates new jobs as the ways in which people are required to interact with the machines evolves and also the machines themselves need to be built and operated. Of course technology in its broadest sense is more than just machines and this is a topic that will be covered in the next chapter in relation to its impact on jobs.
- **Assess the quality of working life movement and the use of quality circles as an influence on work organization.** The quality of life (QWL) movement seeks to enhance the ways in which people are used within an organization. James (1991) describes it as consisting of a goal, process and philosophy. The intention of QWL is to enhance the dignity of workers in connection with the ways in which the organization makes use of the human qualities necessary for work. Job design is therefore

just one element in this broad approach to delivering a high quality of work experience as well as effective operations to the organization. The other elements in QWL include (among other things) effective compensation systems, health and safety, job security and respect for non-work activities. Quality circles involve groups of workers getting together to identify and solve work related problems. It is premised on the notion that it is the actual workers that suffer the consequences of problems at work and they who can most easily identify what could be done to put them right. The basic model of a quality circle involves people meeting voluntarily in their own time to work on these issues. It is the group that makes the presentation to management on what should be done, how and how much it might cost. Management can then agree or otherwise with the proposal. Of course if they disagree they must have a real justification or employee morale and commitment will suffer considerably. Quality circles came to prominence in Japan, but have not been as successful in the west. There is some suggestion that all of the major groups within an organization have some reason to resist their use. For example, employees were expected to give up their own time to participate, management could lose some degree of control if the groups became too successful and the trade unions thought that it could undermine their traditional role as the representatives of employees.

- **Discuss the Fordist and post-Fordist approaches to work organization.** The Fordist approach to work is grounded in scientific management and the application of work study. It takes its name from the wholehearted adoption of these principles by the Ford Motor Company in the early twentieth century. In is basic form it represents the traditional assembly line approach to mass production of motor cars and other factory made products. Whilst the approach did deliver vast improvements in productivity and so made many products available to mass markets, this came at a price. The work involved was boring, demanding and heavy. There were constant demands from the company to increase the speed of the production lines in order to maximize the output and minimize the cost of production and this led to high labour turnover and industrial unrest. As an approach however, it is still widely used within factory operations and in many service activities. Post-Fordism as an approach seeks to retain the advantages of Fordism, but to overcome the weaknesses inherent in it. There are three ways in which this approach sought to influence the work carried out within organizations. Firstly, markets changed over time and now demand individualized products rather than identical mass produced versions. This has led to ways having to be found to produce the maximum number of end product variations with a minimum number of basic operational changes. Consider the motor industry in this regard with the vast number of variations in car types, styling devices, colours, etc. within each product type as a prime example. Methods of work represent the second approach within post-Fordism. This is also represented by the motor vehicle example just given. The methods of manufacturing the vast array of end product variations in an efficient way has forced the design of different production methods, still based on scientific management, but with innovations in order to meet the needs of production. The third area of difference is in management and the ways in which it makes use of its human resource in pursuit of operational objectives. Scientific management suggested that managers decided and workers worked. This has now developed into what managers would claim as a more partnership-based use of people at work in order to ensure that the highest levels of employee commitment are achieved in pursuit of the world class status title that many organizations claim. Table 13.5 illustrates some of the changes in moving from a Fordist to a post-Fordist operational process.

DISCUSSION QUESTIONS

1. Explain and consider the implications for job design of autonomous work groups and consider how the role of management might change under this approach to work.
2. Why should managers be concerned with job design?
3. What is a job and why is job design such a complex concept?
4. If job design is a function of the many factors identified in Figure 13.9 how can work study techniques offer any real value in identifying the most effective design?
5. Compare and contrast the Hackman and Oldham job characteristics approach to job enrichment with the ideas associated with the socio-technical perspective.
6. Why might a satisfied employee not be the most productive?
7. Describe what the quality of working life approach to work organization involves and outline the role of job design in it.
8. How does technology influence the organization of work?
9. In the section 'Quality of working life and quality circles' it was suggested that the introduction of quality circles introduced a 'parallel organization' onto the existing hierarchy. Explain why this might be so, identify the consequences of this for management and suggest how the problems can be overcome.
10. Describe the main organizational influences on work organization and explain how each would impact on the design of jobs.

CASE STUDY Job simplification on a slicing line

This case provides an illustration of job simplification on an assembly line designed for the slicing and packing of bacon. Imagine a factory in which sides of bacon (weighing about 20Kg) are cut into slices and vacuum packed into pack sizes ranging from 500 grams to 3Kg. The small sizes are sold to supermarkets for domestic purchases and the larger packs are sold directly to hotel and catering outlets for commercial use. The bacon curing process leaves the meat wet and slippery and it has to be kept at low temperature in order to preserve it. In practice before a side of bacon is sliced by the machine it has to be frozen in order to make it cut easily and retain its shape during the packing process. This makes the working conditions cold, damp and unpleasant to work in.

The overall process involves the slicing and packing of bacon, and includes the following jobs and activities:

- A frozen side of bacon needs to be fed into a machine which then cuts it into slices.
- The slices need to be separated and stacked into the pack quantity on a moving conveyor belt.
- The individual stacks of bacon need to be placed into a packing machine.
- The packing machine needs to be set up for the type of pack to be produced and needs to be monitored during the packing process.
- The packed bacon needs to be weighed, priced and labelled.
- The packs need to be checked for presentation, label accuracy and quality.
- Individual packs of bacon need to be put into cardboard boxes ready for cold storage and despatch to customers.
- The cardboard boxes need to be labelled with the contents and customer details.
- The cardboard boxes need to be stacked onto wooden pallets and moved to the cold store for despatch to customers.

The layout diagram below represents the machine layout and people workstations identified using a work study based job simplification exercise. The simplified tasks in this job involved:

1. Slicing. One person responsible for obtaining the bacon, setting and cleaning the slicing machine and pacing the slicing processes to keep the other workstations fully utilized. This operator could wear gloves to keep their hands warm when picking up

the frozen sides of bacon and feeding them into the machine.

2. Stacking. Four people working on either side of a conveyor belt splitting the cut bacon into stacks of the right quantity as it passes them by. The conveyor belt speed and rate of slicing sets the pace the work for these operators. This operation was rather like separating out a specific number of pages from a sheaf of papers. It required dexterity and the ability to use the fingers and finger nails to separate out the correct number of frozen slices of bacon. It was difficult to do this wearing gloves and so the work was very cold and not the most pleasant of tasks.
3. Packing. One person responsible for setting the machine, placing individual stacks of bacon into it and generally ensuring a smooth operation. They would also monitor the quality of the packed product.
4. Pricing and boxing. One person responsible for setting the automatic weighing and pricing machine, boxing the packs of bacon, sealing and labelling the boxes, stacking the cartons on a pallet ready for transport to the cold store. This person would also monitor pack quality, rejecting faulty packs and stopping the line to reset the machine if necessary.
5. Transport. Someone else would remove loaded pallets and bring empty ones as part of a similar job for other packing stations.

In addition to these direct production activities there would be a need to keep records of output and quality. Also the group would need to ensure that the whole process worked smoothly with individuals working as a team.

Using work measurement techniques the number of operators (and tasks) needed at each workstation illustrated in the diagram would be determined in order to produce the highest possible levels of output. In this case it is suggested in the diagram that a balanced line contains eight people (including one shared with other lines). However, it could be that the slicer operator is only working for 50 per cent of the time. Under these circumstances it would be common to recalculate the line speeds or redesign the jobs to keep worker utilization as high as possible.

Task

In practice the process described was not very efficient. It did not prove possible to balance the line effectively so that each workstation was fully occupied and each machine fully utilized. How might this process and the jobs associated with it be more effectively designed for the benefit of employees and maximization of output?

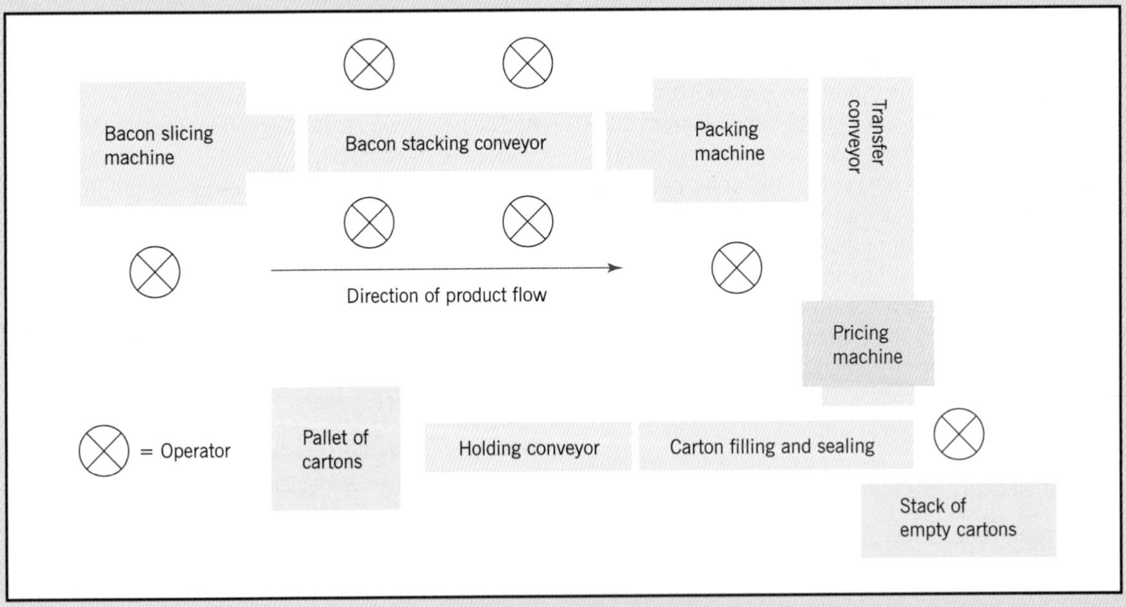

FURTHER READING

There are a number of occasional papers published by the ACAS Work Research Unit that have relevance to the ideas contained in this chapter. For example:

- No. 27 December 1983. Effective and satisfactory work systems, Geoff White.
- No. 29 February 1984. Employee involvement in work redesign, Geoff White.
- No. 43 May 1989. Quality circles – a broader perspective, Sean Russell and Barrie Dale.
- No. 46 July 1990. Self-regulating work groups, David Grayson.
- No. 50 November 1991. Quality of working life and total quality management, Graham James.

Barling, J (1994) Work and Family: In Search of More Effective Workplace Interventions,. in Cooper, CL and Rousseau, DM (eds) *Trends in Organizational Behaviour*, John Wiley, Chichester. Considers the links between family and work roles and examines the assumptions surrounding the interrelationship between job design on family 'well-being'.

Clark, H, Chandler, J and Barry, J (1994) *Organization and Identities: Text and Readings in Organizational Behaviour*, International Thomson Business Press, London. Contains a broad range of original articles on relevant material themes and from significant writers referred to in this and other textbooks on management and organizations.

Marchington, M, Grimshaw, D, Rubery, J and Wilmott, H (2004) *Fragmenting Work: Blurring Organizational Boundaries and Disordering Hierarchies*, Oxford University Press, Oxford. Considers the reality and complexity of modern organizational functioning and supply chain operations together with the structural and job related issues that emerge from that reality.

Siddons, S (2003) *Remote Working: Linking people and organizations*, Elsevier, Oxford. Considers the forms that remote working can take and what is necessary to support the people engaged in that form of employment.

Whitaker, A (1992) The Transformation in Work: Post-Fordism Revisited, In Reed, M and Hughes, M (eds) *Rethinking Organizations: New Directions in Organization Theory and Analysis*, Sage, London. This chapter reviews much of the debate surrounding the notion of post-Fordism in its broader social and organizational context.

COMPANION WEBSITE

Online teaching and learning resources:

Visit the companion website for Organizational Behaviour and Management 3rd edition at: *http://www.thomsonlearning.co.uk/businessandmanagement/martin3* to find valuable further teaching and learning material:

Refer to page 35 for full details.

CHAPTER 14

Technology and work

LEARNING OBJECTIVES

After studying the chapter content and working through the associated Management in Action panels, Employee Perspectives, Discussion Questions and Case Study, you should be able to:

- **Understand what is meant by the term technology and how it influences both the operational activities found within organizations and jobs that people undertake.**
- **Explain the impact of technology on the organizations that employ it.**
- **Outline the relationship between technology, politics and change in managerial decision making.**
- **Discuss the relationship between technology and control.**
- **Appreciate how the application of technology can result in alienation and the degradation of labour.**

INTRODUCTION

The concept of technology is most frequently associated with the application of computers and automation to work activities. However, there are other perspectives about technology and how it impacts upon the operation of organizations that are important to consider. In the past, technology literally referred to the machines and the methods of production associated with them. However, today it can be regarded as a rather vague term which alludes to a broad spectrum of organizational influences, together with the related social connotations. It is appropriate to begin this chapter by attempting to examine the meaning of technology a little more closely.

TECHNOLOGY – A DEFINITION

Technology is a broad term incorporating the equipment, procedural and social perspectives associated with how work is undertaken. From a historical perspective technology reflects a process in which human endeavour is oriented towards solving real problems, experimenting with new ways of doing familiar things or simply finding out new knowledge.

Technology
A broad term incorporating the equipment, procedural and social aspects of how work is undertaken.

This outline of **technology** is based on the work of Winner (1977) who points out clearly the changing view of the concept. According to his analysis technology has gone from being a relatively precise term with little significance to a rather vague term with a considerable degree of importance in terms of its value to organizations and society. Winner (p 10) identifies three general applications of the term technology:

- *Apparatus*. This category of technology refers to the physical apparatus or materials that are necessary for the achievement of tasks. It includes the tools, machines and instruments needed to undertake work either in support of people's actions or as an automatic means of producing goods and services.
- *Technique*. This refers to the purposive aspects of human activity through the application of skills, methods, procedures or routines as a means of achieving objectives.
- *Organization*. This use of the term refers to social arrangements including factories, bureaucracies and teams established to achieve particular goals. It is the framework within which the apparatus and techniques are practised.

Fox (1974) introduces an attempt to define technology from the perspective of the industrial sociologist, and distinguishes between:

- *Material technology*. This refers to the tangible aspects of technology that can be seen, touched or heard.
- *Social technology*. This refers to the social and behaviour shaping devices of structure, control, co-ordination, motivation and reward systems. In other words it is the means through which individuals are managed to ensure that the desired objectives are achieved.

The material technology described by Fox clearly aligns with the apparatus concept as identified by Winner. The social technology of Fox would also match the organization category described by Winner. However, the technique classification identified by Winner is not so easy to incorporate into the work of Fox. It could be argued that the purposive nature of technique makes it part of the material technology described by Fox. A similar argument would be based on the physical aspects of skill etc., which can be expressed and therefore experienced by others. However, the execution of skill requires routines and procedures to be followed in achieving the set objectives and therefore it could also be classed as a social aspect from Fox's classification.

The problem with both of these definitions of technology is that any specific example is likely to contain elements of each classification. For example, the introduction of new equipment in a factory is likely to influence both the techniques used and the social organization within which it is carried out. In terms of Fox's classification scheme there is also likely to be an interaction between the 'hard' aspects of the material technologies and the 'soft' aspects of social order and behaviour within which the tangible aspects will be operated.

Clark *et al.* (1988) introduced an alternative approach, based on the notion of an engineering system. Their definition offers a relatively narrow view of technology, but adds complexity and sophistication through the incorporation of engineering principles. Their definition begins with the view that technology encompasses aspects of hardware, software, engineering principles and the functional configuration of components categorized under two headings:

- *Primary elements*. The two elements within this category are the architecture (design and structure) and the technology (hardware and software).
- *Secondary elements*. The two elements within this category are the dimensioning (adaptation for specific use) and appearance (ergonomic and aesthetic features).

This approach has the advantage of overcoming the potential conflicts inherent in the earlier definitions because of the inclusion of variability within it. The earlier definitions saw the significance of technology as a function of its attributes. Not all examples found can be fitted neatly into this framework. The model of Clark *et al.* incorporates a wider number of variables into a single model. Consequently, additional richness and complexity can be accommodated without violating the essential unity of the framework. Within this model it is easy to accommodate the findings that there are both imperatives and constraints that exist and which operate on the choice of technologies used:

> First, they [the technologies] eliminate or reduce the amount of complex tasks requiring manual skills and abilities; second, they generate more complex tasks which require mental problem-solving and interpretative skills and abilities and an understanding of system interdependencies; third, in order that many tasks can be performed effectively, tacit skills and abilities associated with the performance of work with the old technology are still required; fourth, they involve a fundamentally different relationship between the user and the technology compared to [older] technologies. (McLoughlin and Clark, 1988, pp 116–17)

In order to understand technology and the impact of it in an organizational context the approach of Clark *et al.* has much to commend it. It adopts a clear view of technology as being the hardware and the software associated with the physical representation of it. However, it also allows for the introduction of contextual and social dimensions through the dimensions of architecture, dimensioning and appearance within a single model.

The approach adopted to the study of technology will depend on the purpose for which it is to be used. For example, engineers are concerned with the equipment aspects; industrial engineers with the efficiency of use; product designers with the implications for the physical end result; managers with control, levels of throughput and cost; and social scientists with the social, political and control aspects of it. Braverman (1974) incorporated these into two broad categories of approach to technology:

- *Engineering approach*. Regards technology as a representation of machines and equipment. Emphasizes the physical aspects and internal relationships between these components.

- *Social approach*. Considers technology from the perspective of the impact on labour and views it as a social construction serving the needs of particular groups within society. This is an issue that will be developed further in the subsequent discussion of alienation.

This approach to technology is very much a function of whether it is considered to be a collection of hardware or as part of the structure and social ordering of society. The particular metaphor adopted will significantly influence the subsequent view of its impact. What emerges from this review of the definition of technology is that it reflects much more than simply machine- and computer-based approaches to work. Management in Action 14.1 demonstrates one aspect of this by reviewing how the use of the wide range of technology and communication devices available can lead to stress if it is not integrated with the needs of people as they seek to do their jobs. The latest predictions for networking through digital technology are also described by Law (2003) which demonstrate some of the benefits though productivity improvement as well as some of the problems such as stress and security.

THE EVOLUTION OF TECHNOLOGY

Technology is not static. The ability of the ancient Greeks to provide an automatically opening temple door when a particular altar fire was lit must have seemed like pure magic to the people of the day (Klemm, 1959). It was certainly an example of a new technology in its time. There would appear to be four major implications that emerge from a historical perspective on technology:

- *Experience*. All technology is new technology at some point. What we refer to as new technology today will not be so classified in the future.
- *Loss*. Political, military, religious and social events can conspire to lose a particular technology. The Roman occupiers of Britain (around 200 AD) had central heating for their houses. Because such systems would be operated by slaves some of the aboriginal inhabitants would have developed appropriate skills in utilizing that technology. However, when the Romans left Britain, the use of central heating died out, not to become widely available until the mid-1900s.
- *Erratic*. The development of technology does not follow a smooth or continuous pattern across time and location. Military need plays a significant role in technological advancement. One of the effects of the end of the Cold War – the peace dividend – has been a reduction in size of defence-sponsored development as well as the military itself.
- *Human*. Decisions relating to technology are taken by people and it can support their objectives. The development of a machine-based factory technology could be used to replace human labour and reduce the power of trade unions. Conversely, the higher skills needed to operate and maintain sophisticated technology increases the power and value of the remaining employees.

There are a number of perspectives that could be adopted in reviewing the evolution of technology. It appears from even the most cursory reading of the history of the subject that there was a considerable movement of technology around the world even in ancient times. For example, the windmill appears to have been brought to the Islamic cultures of the Middle East from countries in the Far East before the tenth century and into parts of Europe by the twelfth century. The following sections will attempt to provide a brief insight into the evolution of technology from a predominantly European perspective, based on Klemm (1959).

MANAGEMENT IN ACTION 14.1 Digital depression

Research undertaken by Priority Management, an international personal productivity training company, shows that a new form of stress is emerging within organizations. Called 'Digital Depression' it is caused by the profusion of technological and communication devices that people need to use in their daily work. The irony being that this wide range of devices is designed to make their working life simpler. One in three people say that the technology (mobiles, e-mail, blueberries, wireless PDAs and laptops) that they use in their jobs contributes directly to the stress that they experience in their jobs.

Priority Management's research identifies seven signs of digital depression:

1. *Digital Darwinism*. Anxiousness caused by the feeling of being left behind as technology develops. It can be perceived that career advancement and status is threatened by a lack of systems and program knowledge – skills often taken for granted by younger employees.
2. *Access stress*. An inability to detach from working life as a result of the continual contact achieved through the use of portable communication devices.
3. *Cognitive interruptions*. A state of permanent interruption at work as a result of the unpredictable demands arising through the wide range of communication devices used in the working environment. Leads to a feeling of being out of control.
4. *Continuous Partial attention*. The 24-hour work activity and society that is increasingly the norm for many employees means that it is very difficult to concentrate on one task alone or at any particular time. Shorter deadlines, faster working environment and the increase in multi-tasking all mean that urgent items take priority over important items. Time for reflection, thought and consideration are lost in the race for action.
5. *Device creep*. The pressure to adopt the latest technology, device, gadget or toy to demonstrate that they are at the forefront of the IT revolution
6. *IT rage*. The frustration felt by employees dealing with the behaviour or workings of their desk-top computers. The seemingly illogical behaviour of a PC combined with pressure to meet deadlines is a key stress-creator in this area.
7. *The technological treadmill*. The constant stream of communication, information and data landing on employees creates a feeling that work never ends. There are always more e-mails in the inbox, queries to answer and more problems to solve. Often at its peak when returning to work after a few days holiday when the first days back are spent clearing the huge volume of e-mails in the inbox.

Director of Priority Management South East, Glynn Gatrix says,

> Technology does make people's lives easier if used correctly but this is rarely the case. UK employees work some of the longest hours in Europe but we are still 13 per cent and 20 per cent behind Germany and France respectively in terms of productivity.

Adapted from: *Management Services* (2003) 'Digital depression' identified as a new form of stress, May, p 7.

Stop ↔ Consider

Gatrix also says, 'If emptying your inbox is your daily big achievement, you're working to other people's priorities, not your own and the likelihood is that you will succumb to one or other of the digital depression categories.' In using new technology how would you seek to ensure that digital depression did not arise?

Ancient history

Cave drawings in southern France dating from the later Palaeolithic period (Stone Age) indicate the use of traps for catching bison and mammoth. Examples of the very first machines were based on a lever to release tree trunks onto the trapped animal. Around 1000 BC the pyramids and civil engineering works (to harness river flood waters) were being built in Egypt through the ability of the state to organize and control the necessary resources. Much of the technological activity during this period seems to have been driven by a small range of forces:

- *Subjugation of nature*. In this context the main purpose of technology was to overcome the difficulties in controlling the world in which people lived. For example, understanding and explaining the principles of leverage in general and as used to row a ship in particular. The use of screw mechanisms to drain water from mines was something that the Romans had achieved in Spain before 200 AD.
- *Religious and political representations*. The building of the pyramids, temples and the use of technology to open doors automatically when particular sacrificial fires were lit are examples of the ingenuity to which technology could be put. The use of aqueducts to carry water to cities was an example of politically based civil engineering used for the benefit of citizens.
- *Military*. The need for weapons of defence or attack was a significant driver to the application of technology in this period. The slingshot, catapult and other engines of war were developed as the understanding of maths, geometry and proportion grew alongside an ability to work with the raw materials of wood, rope and metal.
- *Curiosity*. The simple exercise of curiosity and the resultant development of mechanical devices and amusements for the citizens of the day created more technological development. A water organ and water pump are but two examples of this form of mechanical artwork.

It is worth noting that the Romans had an understanding of the water wheel and its potential for grinding corn etc. However, the ready availability of slaves made it an uneconomic and unnecessary proposition at the time. This and the earlier point about the presence of central heating in Roman houses, which was 'lost' for almost 2000 years illustrate the relative nature of technology – its development depends significantly on its perceived value relative to other options. This clearly illustrates social and contextual influences on technology.

The Middle Ages

Klemm summarizes the achievements of this period as, 'utilizing the elemental forces of beast, water and wind to a far greater degree than was possible for Antiquity' (p 79). Developments in ship technology through the introduction of the stern rudder and improved rigging arrangements allowed the easier transport of goods and people over larger distances. In military terms the development of the gun provided an opportunity for both improved defence and attack strategies.

The Renaissance

This period of history is typified by the recognition that developments in the future could be based on an understanding of what had gone before. In essence, the evolution of the scientific method. The ability of various craft-based occupations (builders, stonemasons, sculptors, goldsmiths, etc.) to create ever more sophisticated results was largely a function of the development of rules for their work, based on an analysis of what had gone before, rather than the application of rules of thumb. Social development went hand in hand with technological development. The success of craft and commercial activity began to break down the privilege, ownership and power of the feudal lords. The work of Leonardo da Vinci would typify this period. His careful analysis of such things as anatomy, architecture and flight provide the clearest picture possible of the new spirit of development and a desire to understand the workings of nature. In many ways this period can be described as a time of consolidation in areas of mechanics (leverage, pulleys, etc.) in an attempt to harness the technology more effectively.

The baroque period

The formalization of research is what typifies this period of history. The emergence of scientific instruments such as the microscope and the calculating machine created the opportunity for scientific research to develop. The emergence of the first scientific societies and journals led to the possibility of the exchange of knowledge and the testing/replication of conclusions. The application of technology was directed towards increases in the volume of production through the division of labour and improved organization of work activity.

The development of an effective means of protecting the interests of those individuals who developed new ways of doing things was crucial to the further development of technology. Allowing individuals to reap the benefits for their inventions was a means not only of encouraging the creation of new technologies but of allowing the commercial exploitation of them.

The age of rationalism

This period saw the transformation from small-scale industrial operation based on craft to the industrialization model found in the Industrial Revolution. Improvements in the design of the steam engine by Watt in the middle of the eighteenth century were the basis for developments in mining, metal processing and manufacturing. This went hand in hand with the development of machines and chemicals for the textile industry. In essence, this period saw the emergence of the skilled engineer as the person capable of converting new technologies into practical applications through a mixture of theory and practice.

In terms of trade this period saw the publication (in 1776) of *The Wealth of Nations* by Adam Smith in which the notion of free trade and competition as the basis of a strong economy were first put forward, ideas which further encouraged the development of technology as an aid to competitive advantage supported by the free market. Indeed, it can be said that the division of labour described by Smith set the scene for the later work of Taylor and scientific management. In France the Polytechnic was opened in Paris in 1794 as an institution for the scientific study and the teaching of technology.

The period of industrialization

Continuous improvements to the ability of engines to meet the power needs of the emerging factory system typified the early part of this period. The development of the railway engine also allowed the rapid and easy movement of people and goods, further allowing markets and industry to develop. It was during this period that the first claims that machines were replacing workers appeared. It was said that 150 000 people operating factory-based spinning machines could produce more yarn than 40 million people using the old-fashioned hand wheel (Baines, 1835).

The machine pacing of work in a factory and its effects on jobs also emerged at the same time (Ure, 1835). This aspect of technology began to make a more direct appearance in the thinking of the day with a number of writers making reference to the dismal conditions for the workers, low pay, grinding pace of work and the emergence of the trade unions, strikes and riots. However, by the middle of the nineteenth century improvements in technology and organization were seen as the main means of increasing output.

During the latter part of the nineteenth century and the early years of the twentieth century the technologies developed in the Western world were transported to other countries, notably America, Japan and Russia. The development of the internal combustion and diesel engines allowed the introduction of more efficient forms of machine and transport. It was in the early years of that century that Henry Ford began to experiment with mass production methods in the assembly of motor vehicles. This signalled the introduction of production-based technology on a large scale and was grounded in the availability of electrical power, dating from the 1880s.

Since the early years of the last century there have been many more technological developments that have contributed to the world as we know it today. For example, flight, computers, radio and television, the nuclear industry and medical technology are all examples of recent and significant developments. The development of such technologies has led many people to argue that the world has now entered a post-industrial or information era.

PERSPECTIVES ON TECHNOLOGY

The impact of technology on an organization has been studied from a number of different perspectives and based on a differing view of what technology actually is. There are six different approaches that are worthy of review in this context.

Woodward and production technology

In a study of 100 manufacturing organizations in the electronics, chemical and engineering industries Woodward (1965) defined technology in terms of the approach to production. This she split into:

- *Unit or small batch*. This indicates that items are made in very small quantities, perhaps even being made individually, specifically to a customer order.
- *Large batch or mass production*. This reflects the manufacture of large quantities, perhaps on an assembly line as in the manufacture of motor cars.
- *Continuous process*. This reflects operations where the raw material is taken from its initial state and subjected to a continuous sequence of processes until it is in its final form ready for sale. Typical examples are oil refineries and chemical plants.

Woodward found that there was a definite tendency for a number of organizational characteristics to vary depending upon the classification of the production process (Table 14.1).

Although there were differences between the organizations in the sample there was a clear tendency for the production technology to influence a number of aspects of structure. It also became apparent that those organizations that were the most commercially successful were closer to the norm for their particular production technology than those firms that were less successful. The definition of production technology used in this study is very broad and there are many differences in operational activity between large batch and mass production environments. Consequently it has been argued that the categories adopted were simplistic and may have reflected continuity in the operational process rather than technological complexity (Bedeian, 1984).

Burns and Stalker – stability and change

From their study of electronics and traditional manufacturing organizations (1961) they identified:

Unit or small batch	Lowest number of levels of management and span of control of chief executive Highest ratio of direct to indirect staff and total labour cost
Large batch or mass production	Lowest number of verbal communications and skilled employees Highest number of written communications, sanction procedures and span of control of supervisors
Continuous process	Lowest number of written communications and span of control of supervisor Highest number of levels of management and ratio of managers to other staff

TABLE 14.1 Conclusions from Woodward's study

- *Mechanistic structures*. Close definition of jobs and procedures to be followed. Clear lines of authority and levels within the hierarchy. Work organization best suited to stable environments with a slowly changing technology.
- *Organismic structures*. Lack of definition of jobs and hierarchy. Continuous adaptation of hierarchy and jobs as the prevailing technology undergoes rapid change.

Technology in the context of the Burns and Stalker study is one of the environmental factors within which the organization operates. It is, therefore, something to which the organization must adapt if it is to be successful. This view was supported by the work of Lawrence and Lorsch (1967), but has been criticized by writers such as Hughes (1985) who claim that political activity and government policy also play a significant part in the success of organizations.

Perrow – a continuum from routine to non-routine

A slightly different approach to the notion of technology was introduced by Perrow (1967, 1970). He created a view of technology based on a continuum from routine to non-routine in terms of the approach to operational activity. This view allowed the concept to be applied to all organizations not just manufacturing operations. Used in this way technology is an integral part of the processes involved in the work of the organization. It relates to the ways that problems (or exceptions to the normal routine) are dealt with and the integrative approaches to functional interdependence. In this way the notion of technology is broadened into a concept that reflects social, structural, procedural and relationship perspectives as well as the hardware associated with machines and production processes.

Thompson – resource and technology matching

In this view it is argued that the organization attempts to arrange its resources and processes in such a way as to match its natural technological tendency. Thompson (1967) identified three categories of technology:

- *Long linked*. This approach describes the sequential processes most obviously found in assembly line factory operations. The technologies used in this type of process are designed to ensure that each part of the process fits together effectively in producing the end result.

- *Mediating*. This form of operational technology seeks to bring together (mediate) what would otherwise be independent activities or needs. For example, a bank brings together borrowers and lenders; the human resource department within a company seeks to meet the needs of both management and workforce. The process begins with a need, followed by the development of appropriate transactions intended to meet the identified need. The technology in this context comprises the operating procedures, rules, etc. that allow the transactions to be effectively executed.
- *Intensive*. This definition of technology revolves around skill. It attempts to provide a personal level of service within a standardized framework. Typical examples include a medical treatment, where the doctor will need to personalize the treatment regime within a standard process of consultation and care.

This view of technology reflects organizational attempts to achieve objectives as described in the above three categories, with an ability to deal effectively with problems and at minimal operating cost. Features of this approach include the structure and design of the organization in which, for example, a warehouse can help absorb some of the variability in sales levels or the human resource function can assist in resolving some of the people problems quickly or train employees to a high level of skill and proficiency.

The Aston studies

In terms of technology these studies utilized three categories:

1. *Operations*. This type of technology reflected the nature of the transformation process, the techniques used.
2. *Materials*. This aspect of technology reflected the nature and characteristics of the things that were being processed. For example, different metals have different properties and need to be processed differently. Equally, in a service organization each customer's needs are slightly different (the various patients visiting a doctor) and therefore the processing (treatment) would differ accordingly.
3. *Knowledge*. This reflects the skill and ability required to undertake the tasks necessary to achieve the objectives. For example, a nuclear power station would not be capable of operating at full capacity unless the employees, specialists and managers were trained and skilled at the tasks expected of them.

Blumer and industrialization

Industrialization
Refers to the use of technology in a particular location, moving it away from agricultural to a factory based economy.

In a work published after his death, Herbert Blumer considered the nature of **industrialization** (the application of technology to a particular context) and its influence as an agent of social change (Maines and Morrione, 1990). In this work Blumer suggests that the term industrialization is frequently used in a way which conjures up the stereotypic image of the development of the factory system, urbanization of residence, the use of machines, the dilution of skilled work and the formation of a managerial class, etc. To this framework is added an emotional veneer as the result of, 'inadequate study, partisan interests, doctrinaire concerns, and agitation on behalf of social reforms' (p 15). To Blumer this view of industrialization emerged largely from Great Britain as a reflection of the particular historical process.

Blumer makes several points of distinction between industrialization and technological change, including (pp 18–20):

- *Non-industrial technological change*. There are a number of technological developments that have no impact on the level of industrialization. For example, the introduction of the steel axe as a replacement for the stone axe is an example of technological development that need not directly impact on the level or type of industrialization within which it is used.
- *Industrialization as one form of technological development*. Industrialization brings with it many changes other than those based on the technology. For example, the increased use of female labour, the emergence of a managerial class, factory-based work, and the development of organized labour are just some of the consequences of industrialization that are not, of themselves, technologically based.
- *Transplanted industrialization*. It does not automatically follow that technology evolves as part of the process of industrialization. Many of the developing countries of the world have received transplanted technologies as part of packages of industrialization.
- *Causal relationships*. It is frequently implied that there is a direct link between technology and society. For example, it can be suggested that the introduction of high technology creates social problems in society by increasing alienation. This approach tends to underestimate the complexity and chain of events involved in such relationships.
- *Ambiguity*. The term technological development contains a higher level of ambiguity in terms of its interrelationship with social change than does the concept of industrialization. In other words, technology contains a wide variety of meaning which it is difficult to restrict in attempting to tease out the social implications.

In terms of the relationship between the terms 'industrialization' and 'technology', Blumer is approaching the question from the perspective of social change. In dealing with social science concepts it is inevitable that definitions will not have the precision of the natural sciences. In terms of how these two concepts impact on social change it is apparent that for Blumer there are differences between them. They can be considered to be overlapping circles in a Venn diagram. On occasions, they will meet and be very similar, but on other occasions they will differ. Blumer does not spell out in detail his view of technology, but it is clear that he adopts a mechanical view rather like the apparatus concept of Winner.

Each of the six approaches to technology discussed contains different perspectives on the subject. Whatever approach to the concept is adopted it is clearly much too simplistic to consider technology as equivalent to computers and automation. From the studies reviewed it is clear that there are links between technology and structure, work organization, hierarchy, people management, customer needs, operational strategy and organizational success. In addition there is also the suggestion that with some forms of technology there are opportunities to become more sensitive and adaptive to the environmental pressures surrounding the organization. In being able to adapt to the changing environments surrounding the organization there is assumed to be a greater likelihood of commercial success in the short term and survival in the long term. Clearly, therefore, a view of technology that generally provides an opportunity to support managerial objectives is emerging from these studies.

JAPANIZATION, TECHNOLOGY AND WORK

That organizations reflect the broader social context in which they exist cannot be denied. These relationships become even more complex when cross-cultural perspectives impinge on the situation. This was highlighted with particular force during the late 1970s and early 1980s when the impact of Japanese manufactured goods suddenly became apparent throughout the Western world. The quality and reliability of Japanese products and the perceived value for money decimated the market share of many long-established producers. For example, by 1986 Japanese manufacturers held 84 per cent of the world market for 35mm cameras, 71 per cent of microwave ovens and 55 per cent of motorcycles (BBC/OU, 1986). Oliver and Wilkinson (1992) provide many similar statistics which indicate the significance and magnitude of the Japanese threat. Table 14.2 is a summary of some of this data.

The threat to jobs and even whole industries quickly became apparent and a search for an explanation undertaken. The original view was that there had to be a new way of managing to provide such impressive results. It was thought to be a reflection of the Japanese culture and religion as well as the emphasis on the group rather than individual prowess. Oliver and Wilkinson (1992) identify a number of features of Japanese production methods that collectively provide the scale of benefit achieved, including:

- *Quality*. The view that quality is integral to the production process and reduces cost was proposed by US consultants during the 1940s and adopted by Japanese managers in the 1950s. The common view of quality in the west was that it was inspected into a product after it was made, repairs being carried out if necessary. In Japan, quality was seen as a feature of the manufacturing process and a reflection of control within the organization. One of the ways that this can be achieved is by solving problems as they arise rather than tolerating them.
- *Just-in-time*. This approach requires the elimination of inventory, items needed in production arriving at the point of use just-in-time (JIT). The traditional Western approach to planning is to push items into the system in the belief that if all the parts are available production flow will be maintained. Just-in-time operates on the basis that usage should dictate when components are pulled forward into the production process. Operating just-in-time requires inventory to be progressively reduced. It also requires the problems resulting from the lack of inventory to be dealt with so that they do not restrict operational activity in future. Ahmad *et al.* (2003) show in a study that spanned 110 plants across the US, Italy and Japan that organizational infrastructure factors such as product

	Japan	West	America	Toyota
Set-up time (hours)*			6.0	0.2
Number of set-ups per day*			1.0	3.0
Sales per annum per employee†	$150K	$85K		

*Based on the work of Burbridge (1982)
†Based on the work of Parnaby (1987)

TABLE 14.2 Japanese and Western productivity comparisons (adapted from: Oliver, N and Wilkinson, B (1992) *The Japanization of British Industry: New Developments in the 1990s*, 2nd edition, Blackwell, Oxford) technology, people policies and work integration systems impact on the ability to use JIT to achieve competitive advantage.

- *Continuous improvement.* It is never possible to achieve perfection, but improvement can always be achieved. This is the philosophy behind continual improvement (frequently achieved through **quality circles**). In Japan the culture expects individuals to participate in problem solving (usually in their own time). Failure to do so to an acceptable level would be held against an individual in pay and promotion terms.
- *Work organization.* The use of cellular manufacturing methods and U-shaped production lines allows for greater employee flexibility as well as improved control of the product and process. According to Gaither (1992, p 294) the benefits of a cell approach to production are:
  - Machine changeovers are simplified.
  - Training periods for workers are shortened.
  - Materials-handling costs are reduced.
  - Parts can be made faster and shipped more quickly.
  - Less in-process inventory is required.
  - Production is easier to automate.

Quality circles
Small groups of people from the same work area who voluntarily meet to solve work-related problems.

A cell becomes a micro production unit dedicated to the production of a small range of products, thereby allowing a high level of expertise, flexibility and efficiency to develop. U-shaped assembly lines are assembly lines that have been shaped to encourage team commitment to develop. In straight assembly lines the linear approach ties workers to specific workstations and their only contact would be with adjacent work activities. U-shaped assembly lines simply bend the straight line to create involvement opportunities. Figure 14.1 shows a U-shaped production line, based upon the principles developed by Toyota.

A team provides an opportunity for people to work together and adds a social perspective to their work. In the Japanese approach the possibility for flexibility through teams is taken much further. Oliver and Wilkinson (1992) quote Sayer (1986) who indicates that one Toyota worker performed 35 different jobs in one day and walked six miles. They also quote Domingo (1985) who suggests that the system deliberately introduces tension into the system which turns every day into a challenge.

FIGURE 14.1

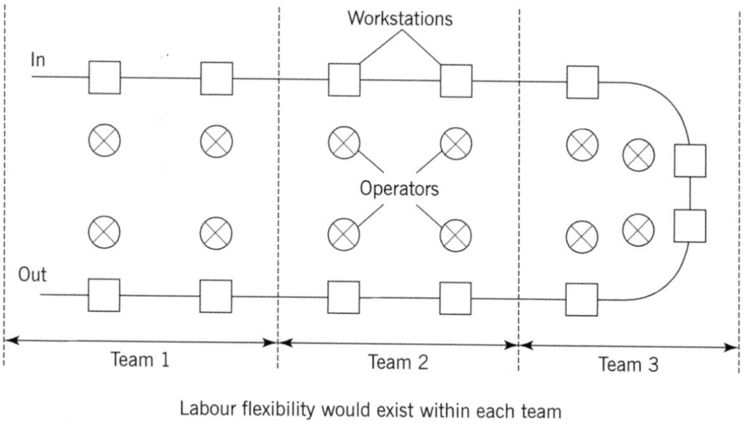

'U'-shaped assembly line production

An alternative view of teamwork is provided by Garrahan and Stewart (1992) who describe a control and conflict perspective on teamwork. They suggest that teamwork provides a more effective form of management control and sets one worker against another in the drive to identify problems and seek continual improvement. Each worker is expected to report problems immediately. Failure to do so makes the individual rather than the 'creator' of the problem liable to punishment.

- *Structure and system*. Japanese organization structure was researched by Lincoln and Kalleburg (1990) who show that they generally contained more hierarchical levels and incorporated a greater measure of formality. Oliver and Wilkinson describe the Japanese outside-in approach to accounting as providing a strong market focus. This approach involves identifying a market price and then managing costs within that constraint. The Western inside-out approach tends to be based on identifying costs and then attempting to ensure that price can cover these needs. Similar strengths in product development activities can also be identified. Smaller teams, with greater power and forced by the system to face up to the requirement to get it right first time are able to respond more quickly to changing market trends.

  The relationship between buyers and suppliers has been frequently described as an adversarial one in the West. Buyers would frequently have many suppliers and would play one off against the other in terms of price and delivery. The Japanese approach is based upon co-operation and long-term relationships with a small number of suppliers. This leads to the inevitable development of dependence relationships. Neither party can afford to abuse the relationship. The location of suppliers is frequently adjacent to the customer so that just-in-time principles can be more effectively applied. It is also common to find companies part owning their suppliers.
- *Personnel practice*. There are many features of personnel practice that it has been suggested differ between the West and Japan. Practices such as lifetime employment; high levels of company welfare benefit; selection for employment based on degree of fit with company values and norms; promotion and reward based upon seniority and service and excessively long working hours have all been identified as major points of distinction. However, the experience of employment in Japan would appear to be somewhat more complex. Lifetime employment has not been available to all workers and organizations have made use of large numbers of temporary or short-term contract workers.
- *Social, political and economic factors*. Organizations and management practice emerge in a specific cultural context, therefore it should not be surprising to discover differences in how organizations are structured and function. There are a number of features of the Japanese environment that are worthy of note. It is not uncommon to find executives in a Japanese company who have spent time as union officials in that same company as part of their career. The education system is very competitive and forces very young people to study extremely hard for long periods of time. Entrance to the best universities is very competitive and demands considerable sacrifice on the part of students and their families.

Fuelled by the inroads made by Japanese products into home markets Western manufacturers have found it necessary to respond or be eliminated. One way of responding is to emulate. It has not always been possible to change working practices quickly (or successfully) as employees and trade unions have sometimes perceived initiatives as a threat to established rights and benefits. Most of the major motor manufacturers have experienced years of frustration, negotiation and dispute in order to introduce some of the Japanese practices into UK factories (see, for example, Giles and Starkey, 1987; Turnbull, 1986).

In order better to serve their export markets and to placate any suggestion of unfair competition, Japanese producers began to build factories in the West. Garrahan and Stewart (1992) describe this process in general terms, with particular emphasis on the role of the decision of Nissan to build a car assembly plant in Washington, near Sunderland. In this situation there was an opportunity to import Japanese management methods by Japanese companies and to impose them onto **greenfield** sites. Clearly, in a greenfield location there are no established practices to change and management have a relatively free hand to set their own agenda and methods of work. This must, of course, be tempered with the knowledge that there will be the established norms, expectations and behaviour patterns that exist in the surrounding environment. The Garrahan and Stewart text provides a very vivid description of this process and is a useful point of comparison with the authorized management views expressed by Wickens (1987). Wickens was at the time the head of personnel and administration at the company and the first British appointment to be made.

Greenfield
A new previously undeveloped location as compared to a Brownfield site which describes a redevelopment location.

The arrival of Japanese companies in the UK provided an opportunity to observe some of the ideas on Japanese management at first hand. Of course, many Japanese home country practices could not be translated directly. Essentially, the notion of a flexible workforce committed to teamwork and getting it right first time were introduced along with single union agreements (the nearest form of enterprise unions that could be achieved in the UK). There is the suggestion that transplanted Japanese operations are little more than warehouses (screwdriver factories) and that the full transfer of all manufacturing activity is far from the intention (Williams *et al.*, 1992). This aspect also has a major impact on the work activities and approach to management adopted by such organizations.

The work reviewed so far clearly reflects that Japanese companies have found ways of organizing themselves that produce very effective organizations. However, there are a number of questions that emerge. First, it is necessary to consider whether or not Japanization reflects an approach to management that is fundamentally different from Fordism and scientific management, or whether it simply reflects a refinement of those principles. Second, it raises a question about the purpose of effectiveness. In whose benefit is effectiveness being pursued and why? This in turn leads to a consideration of the purpose of organizations and the goods and services that they produce. Whose benefit are they intended to serve and why? Also emerging are questions related to the purpose of work itself.

It is clear that the purpose of the Japanese approach to management is not intended to benefit the employees. It has been suggested elsewhere in this text that stress is a common experience (even leading to early death) among Japanese workers. The references already identified indicate the low levels of satisfaction of Japanese workers compared with Western counterparts. The pressures to conform to the needs of the group are considerable and individuality is not encouraged and indeed considered a threat to group cohesion. Therefore one is left with the conclusion that Japanese management practices are grounded in the same principles of power and control as Fordism, but that they are a considerably more effective from management's perspective.

ASSUMPTIONS ABOUT TECHNOLOGY

There are a number of commonly held assumptions that relate to the nature of technology, its impact on organizational functioning and operation:

- *Neutrality*. The first assumption is the view that technology is a neutral process. That is not so. It is management who determine the organizational objectives that are being sought and the way that they will be operationalized through technology. Technology is, therefore, something that is part of the 'design and achieve' aspects of management and can be used by managers in an attempt to control and direct employees. It can also be used to ensure that the entire organizational process works to a management-determined agenda. In that sense, technology is under the control of management, to use as they consider appropriate.

- *Impact*. Taking a very limited view of technology, it is frequently asserted that it is only in the production areas of an organization that technology has any impact. This may be where technology has its most obvious impact, but it is not the only area of involvement. For example, administrative and accounting procedures, control reports and quality-control data are just some of the specialist areas where technology has made an impact. In addition opportunities to integrate islands of manufacturing activity or stages in service delivery have also been evident over the past few years. These approaches take a broader view of technology and incorporate the people, material, flexibility, adaptability and political aspects into the concept.
- *Modernism*. There is a general tendency to see new things as better than those that went before. Nowhere is this more evident than in advertising of consumer products. Television and static advertising campaigns are forever attempting to persuade customers that a reformulated product such as a cleaning agent is a considerable improvement over the previous product. The same is true of many aspects associated with technology. Components produced by computer-controlled machines are said to be more accurate, reliable and better than those produced by skilled employees. While this may be true in some circumstances, not everything can be so easily fitted into this perspective. For example recent research has shown that although dealing with bank call-centres represents the third most frequently used method, it is the least popular among customers. Internet banking is by contrast proving more popular (*Management Services*, 2003 b).
- *De-skilling*. It is often assumed that the introduction of higher levels of technology will allow the level of skill required from employees to be reduced. This should provide two main benefits for management. First, reduced labour cost as skill is positively correlated with pay. Second, reduced training times and cost as it is quicker and cheaper to train people to a lower level of skill. However, offsetting these claimed advantages are the higher skill levels needed to operate more complex equipment and processes as well as the new jobs created as a result of the different technologies adopted. It is also apparent that this assumption is based upon a relatively narrow definition of technology in that not all forms provide for de-skilling among employees.
- *Structure*. The studies described earlier tend to emphasize the structural aspects of technology. This is not the only area of impact for technology. It also affects the control processes; it reinforces the dominance of managers and technical specialists over general employees. It is part of the political process of management and provides the opportunity for new products and services. Structure is also influenced by technology in very complex ways that tend to be understated by the earlier theories.
- *Efficiency*. It is assumed that the application of technology will increase efficiency in operational activity. While his may hold true in a very narrow sense, it does depend how broad a measure of efficiency and productivity is used. For example, the cost of the acquisition of the technology, retraining the workforce and the cost of the new jobs created are just some of the additional costs to take into account in determining the balance of benefit. This approach is also based

upon a narrow conception of technology and from the implications referred to earlier; efficiency could be one of the least important variables involved in the adoption of technology. For example, the application of new process technologies as a means of demonstrating to customers a commitment to consistent and high quality as well as a means of forcing change in working practices can have many benefits in addition to efficiency. In addition when a new technology is introduced into an organization it is not unusual to find additional work being created as the organization learns to deal with the new situation.

THE POLITICS OF TECHNOLOGY

Among the many professional facets to management activity it is also a political process. Individual managers are in competition with each other for scarce resources, there is never enough money to fully invest in each department or function. Managers also seek to achieve personal, professional and functional goals within their organizations in order to develop their careers. Management is also political in that the pursuit of objectives requires interaction and co-operation with many other stakeholders who may have conflicting objectives. For example, employees may want much higher pay and managers may want to reduce labour cost. Part of this process involves using technology as a political tool in order to achieve control or influence. For example, the power of head office administrative departments to dictate work routines in bank branches can be achieved by the introduction of computer systems which require branch staff to follow prescribed routines in processing customer transactions and queries.

There is another form of people control achieved through the political use of events and activities that engage with their lives. It is this form of control to which Braverman (1974) refers when he began what became known as the **labour process debate**. Essentially, this debate turns on the use to which human labour is put in the transformation of raw material into commodities for capitalist markets and the part played by managers in the organization of that work. It is management that determines the nature of any technology in any given context. Consequently, it is a management agenda that determines the use of technology and how human labour will be accommodated around it. The application of technology can provide managers with a number of direct benefits including tighter control over the work process, pace of work, skill levels required and the design of work. All of these lead to a reinforcement of the dominant position of managerial control over organizational functioning and cost of operational activity. Howcroft and Wilson (2003) make the point that employee participation in information systems development is frequently justified on the basis of achieving a better, more effective end result that will result in an empowered workforce. These they term as foreground rational assumptions. However their research claims that underlying these are instrumental politically motivated justifications that drive the need to involve users in the process.

Labour process debate
Seeks to explain management's relationship to workers (and their role) in capitalist economies and in relation to capital owners.

This debate revolves around the degree of malice aforethought that managers use in taking those decisions. Is it done to control labour and reinforce management's position, is it done to further the commercial objectives of the organization, or for the benefit of employees and society? One of the key problems in researching in this area is that of being able to find out the true causes of particular managerial actions. A manager who is attempting to manipulate workers is unlikely to admit it! Many writers prefer to limit consideration of decision making to a form of rationality. Schon (1994) for example talks of a technical rationality (p 243) in which the search for solutions to problems follows a logical pattern and competence can be measured through the degree to which the intended effects are achieved. Also Child (1985) argues that the social and organizational aspects of decisions are generally subordinate to the financial imperatives. He goes as far as suggesting that the broader aspects are essentially consequences of the financial perspectives, not objectives in their own right. This theme will be developed further in Chapter 16.

TECHNOLOGY AND ALIENATION

At a common sense level alienation is a form of switching off. In a work context that would be the equivalent of not feeling part of (connected to) the department or the organization and not engaging with anything at a significant level. It can be argued that the only reason organizations employ human beings is that there are some tasks for which an effective machine has yet to be developed. Looked at from this perspective, people are simply a substitute for machines. This is, of course, a simplistic argument as it ignores the social, political and economic aspects associated with human work. It does however; provide a very stark introduction to the nature of alienation.

Thompson (1989) provides a definition of alienation as follows:

> Work performed under conditions in which the worker is estranged from his or her own activity in the act of production, through the sale of labour power and the subordination of skills and knowledge to the capitalist, or other external social forces. (p xiii)

This definition picks up a number of aspects from the earlier sociological viewpoints of writers such as Blauner, Braverman and Marx. Essentially attempting to assess the nature of work within the context in which it is carried out, the labour process debate brings together a number of traditions in considering issues such as the degradation of work and de-skilling. It is within this paradigm that the notion of alienation as defined earlier is set.

Alienation is about separation, ownership and the rights of workers as stakeholders. It is argued that alienation occurs as an inevitable reaction to the control of work by managers and that technology plays a significant part in the support of that process. It has already been suggested that technology is not neutral; it is utilized by managers as part of their attempts to achieve business objectives. Blauner (1964) made this assertion in relation to continuous process industries on the basis of his research in a number of different (technologically speaking) operations. In doing so, his approach to alienation was based on the feelings of workers formed in response to the dominant technology. It was defined in terms of:

- *Powerlessness*. A lack of control or influence over the pace and methods of work, as well as the general working conditions and the processes involved in carrying it out.
- *Meaninglessness*. A feeling of being a very small part of a large process and that the individual's contribution had little real significance in terms of the finished product or service.
- *Isolation*. A lack of belonging, or a feeling of not being part of a team or group.
- *Self-estrangement*. A reduced feeling of self-worth as a consequence of being reduced to a number within a crowd and a lack of work being a significant focus for life.

The degree to which continuous process technologies can achieve the type of work envisaged by Blauner must be open to question from a number of perspectives, at least in the short term. For example, the number of jobs available in continuous process operations tends to be much smaller than in most other forms of technology applications. Not all products and services are amenable to continuous process technologies, a hospital can never function like a chemical factory. It does, however, have its own version of continuous process technology – it functions 24 hours a day and for 365 days a year and it contains some highly skilled personnel. As such a hospital should be a low alienation environment containing high skill, high discretion jobs in a human-based caring environment.

Alienation is clearly an aspect of the human experience of work in some contexts and technology impacts on that experience. There are clearly differences in the way that alienation can be experienced and therefore the impact of technology can be expected to be different for each variation. However, what is not in question is that the two concepts are linked and that alienation can adversely affect behaviour with the organization. It can be argued that a significant aspect of some of the features of more recent approaches to job design are attempts to reintroduce elements of ownership and reduce the feelings of separation arising from the use of technology. Perhaps an attempt by managers to balance the people issues with the procedural, production and social technologies available in the search for efficiency.

DETERMINISM, RATIONALITY AND CONTROL

There are compelling arguments that technology, particularly new technology, is independent of any particular organizational context and universally applied. However, Friedman and Cornford (1989) use the term autogenerative to suggest that computer innovations are as much a function of the user as they are the original designer. Taken in isolation, this view could support the deterministic perspective in that the development of technology is part of a cyclical relationship with the designer and user both developing the technology for each other's benefit. However, it can also be used to support the opposing point of view. If the user can influence the innovation process they are in a position to shape it and can control it to a significant extent. The economic imperative provides organizations with a basis for attempting to match (or better) competitor activity in the search for competitive advantage and so seek the maximum capability that technology can provide.

Management objectives play a significant part in the way in which the environment is perceived and interpreted. The objectives that management seek also colour the way in which the situation is interpreted and decisions taken. Decision making is a political process and can be used for reasons other than the benefit of the organization. For example, the director in charge of a computer department may seek to ensure that the company takes decisions that enhance the reputation and standing of the department. In that sense it is more effective to consider not a technological imperative as such, but to see things in terms of cause and effect, with technology being a major determinant of the options available. Figure 14.2 reflects this role of technology as a driver of options as well as being a feature of managerial interpretation.

This view is perhaps closer to the conclusion reached by McLoughlin and Clark (1988) in which they argue for a complex definition of determinism rather than the simple linear process suggested by many writers. So far rationality has been assumed. This suggests that managers take decisions based on a rational process in the best interests of the organization. That is a major assumption. The word rational might be implied in many decisions, but rational from whose point of view? Rationality is an illusive concept and is not necessarily obvious or apparent to everyone. It depends on the points of view and perceptions of the individuals involved.

FIGURE 14.2

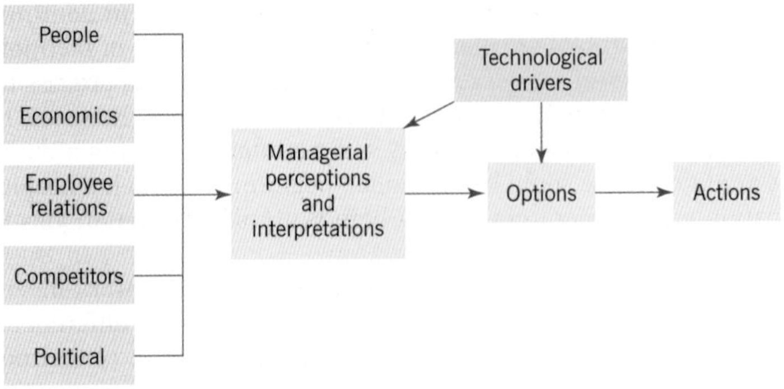

Technological change and decision making

The justification for new technology is frequently based upon improvements in control in one form or another. Control of cost; control of a process; control of quality; or control of employees being among the most commonly used. Control can become a self-perpetuating process of management finding ways to improve control involving tighter control over employee behaviour, leading to adverse employee reaction, confirming the need for ever tighter control. Clegg and Dunkerley (1980) describe this as a **vicious cycle of control** (Figure 14.3).

> **Vicious cycle of control**
> A counterproductive cycle of management control, producing negative employee reactions and failure to achieve objectives, resulting in tighter control.

The application of any technology can be easily justified in control terms as it ensures a consistency of operation not possible through human beings. In addition, it is easier to fit people around the technology than adapt the technology to the people. Conversely, even sophisticated new technology is comparatively stupid by human standards. It is not very flexible in that it can only operate within program parameters and certain narrow climatic conditions. It has been argued that the 'office of the future' is being significantly held back because of poor new-building design and the limited availability of appropriate facilities in existing buildings (air conditioning and cable ducts etc.). People, by way of contrast, are flexible, they can adapt to changes in circumstances and are capable of solving problems for which they have not been programmed or trained. Even with the development of expert systems, computers are not as adaptable as people. It is this constriction in the way in which computers operate that provides control possibilities through the structuring of time, space and activity of the humans with whom they come into contact.

There are several aspects to the relationship between control and technology. For example:

FIGURE 14.3

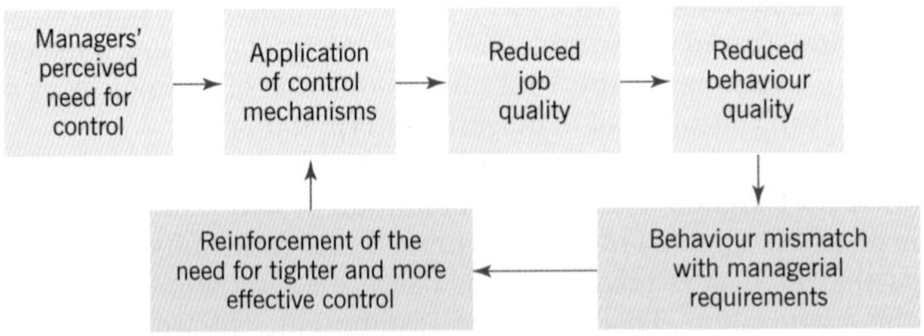

The vicious cycle of control (*adapted from*: Clegg, S and Dunkerley, D (1980) *Organization, Class and Control*, Routledge & Kegan Paul, London)

- *Adoption*. It is a management decision which technologies are introduced into an organization. This provides managers with the opportunity to target particular technologies, particular applications or particular intentions. Each of these objectives provides a basis to reinforce the control aspects of management through an agenda-setting process. This can cause conflict to emerge if the technical rationality of the technology designer conflicts with the work rationality of employees. This was demonstrated by Hagedorn-Rasmussen and Vogelius (2003) in a study of the implementation of business process re-engineering in the social service administration department of a Danish municipality.
- *Development*. The majority of technological development (at least as far as organizations are concerned) is funded by management for purposes identified by them. This allows control of the organizational environment to be exercised through channelling and directing the evolution of technology.
- *Access*. It is again a management decision to whom and how access to technology should be granted. For example, in using computer-controlled machines in a factory the design of the computer programming could be the responsibility of the machine operators or it could be done by a separate group of specialists. Which option is chosen is a management decision in which control of the skill levels, and hence, power are part of the process.
- *Application*. There are always more opportunities to use technology than there is money available to fund them. This requires management to ration its resources and therefore select which parts of the organization have access to which technologies. This allows management to selectively target parts of its operations for the application of technology. This threat of having technology introduced (or developed) is part of the control balance in any context. It also allows for people problems – as defined by management – to be solved by the application of technological solutions, a form of direct control. For example, poor quality of work on an assembly line (perhaps as a result of boring, monotonous jobs of very short duration at a high pace) can be improved by the application of robot technology to replace the people.
- *Intention*. Most of the issues discussed so far in relation to control have an indirect link with technology. In other words, control is achieved largely as a by-product of the main or stated purpose. By its intention, management, as a policy, can use technology to increase its control over events and people. This comes through the overt or covert justification of the technology. Frequently, technology is justified on the basis of a reduced cost of operation for a specified quality and quantity. Through covert intention management can seek to achieve objectives which improve its control as a first priority and subordinate cost to an incidental benefit. For example, an improved level of quality achieved through the application of technology provides management with improved control of the process (and indirectly the people operating it).

THE IMPACT OF TECHNOLOGY

Structure

Technology can affect structure in a number of ways. The impact will depend upon management discretion and the ways in which the technology is used within the organization. The impact influences three areas of structural design:

1. *Scale*. Technology can impact on the number of jobs provided by an organization. Organization structure is a means of compartmentalization based upon the need to manage human activity. If the operation is automated a significant rationale for the existing structure changes.
2. *Function*. The introduction of a new technology produces a need to accommodate new jobs or even functions within a structure. Also it is not unusual to find new jobs springing up within existing departments, for example, computer accountant, a job responsible for seeking ways of using computer technology within accounting.
3. *Integration*. The integration of technology into existing jobs also influences the structure. For example, the use of CAD/CAM allows the integration of designers with production, logistics and marketing specialists. Under such operating circumstances it becomes increasingly difficult to justify the traditional separation of activity into functional compartments. This can be used as the justification for reviewing the structure of an organization.

Adhocracy
Organization structures with few management levels; little formal control; decentralized decision making; few rules, policies and procedures.

Where new technology has been integrated into an organization to the extent that it dominates operational activity, Mintzberg (1983) describes the emerging structure as an **adhocracy**. This form of structure is typified by:

- Few levels of management
- Little formal control
- Decentralized decision making
- Few rules, policies and procedures
- Specialization of work function.

This form of structure can be particularly useful when the nature of the work facing the organization does not fall into regular patterns and the work itself is complex. Typical areas where this form of organization might be seen are in a hospital casualty area or a consultancy organization where no two client problems are identical or amenable to the same solution. The introduction of expert systems is an attempt to harness some of the decision rules and diagnostic skill involved in such situations.

Job design

New jobs are created by technology; computer programmer is a job that did not exist 40 years ago, for example. Some jobs have also disappeared from organizations. For example, punched card operator was an essential job with early data-processing computers. It came into existence with a particular technology and existed only as long as direct keyboard entry was not possible. At that time the only way to enter information was to convert data into machine-readable punched cards. Many thousands of these were required for every processing operation. A change in computer technology eliminated the need for this job to be done and it disappeared virtually overnight.

Other jobs have been changed as a result of the application of technology to the work. For example, secretaries, 'as a group, have been affected by the introduction of word processing and their jobs look set to change further with the spread of computer systems offering electronic mail, diary management, graphics, spreadsheets and desk-top publishing' (Thompson, 1989, p 1). This source goes on to examine a number of options for the ways in which the job of a secretary could be changed to make use of technology in becoming a personal assistant. In effect, having delegated authority to act on their own initiative on behalf of the superior. The possibility of remote working sometimes called homeworking or teleworking has also emerged through the technological developments available. Simpson *et al.* (2003) explore a particular aspect of this in reviewing the impact of teleworking on rural communities in Australia and how the experience in these situations differs from that found in urban environments.

Job performance has been changed through the application of new technology to the training of individuals. Management in Action 14.2 indicates the impact of simulation machines on the training of pilots, ships' officers and power engineers.

Managerialism

Managerialism refers to the ability of managers to maintain control of the organization through the imposition of their perspective on activity. It is management that determines the technology that will be used by the organization and how it will be utilized. There are organizational differences in the degree to which new technology is utilized. Some organizations pride themselves on being at the forefront of technological applications; others prefer to be followers, allowing the cost and risk of development to be carried by others. Pries (2003) explores one aspect of this in reviewing the effect on production systems of a German car manufacturer engaging in international operations. The intention was to identify any reciprocal impact on production systems when specific German manufacturing operations were exported to other countries. It is suggested that a model involving interest-driven organizational learning provides the best basis for understanding such exchanges.

Management also decides the degree of employee involvement in determining the human interface with new technology. There are a range of options from full involvement in the design and selection of new technology to simply being told what will be. Terry Molloy, the Deputy General Secretary of the Banking, Insurance and Finance Union, writing on behalf of the trade union movement in a government report in 1984 is quoted (Thompson, 1985, p 5) as saying:

> To get the maximum benefit from IT, it is necessary to involve the workforce. This is not only right in principle, but right in practice, since the people who perform the tasks that will be changed by IT understand the practicalities better than any systems analyst or departmental manager. In our recommendations we lay great stress on the need for proper consultative mechanisms when introducing IT, and indeed, for consultation to start at the earliest planning stage.

Thompson goes on to illustrate the problems for management if they do not take into consideration the employee point of view. Also demonstrated is the crucial effect of the attitudes of middle managers. A case study regarding the implementation of a new computer system to the freight operations of British Rail (undated but presumably during the early 1970s) illustrates the problems. A top-down approach was adopted, with middle managers and employees given a new system to operate with very little involvement. All was well in the early stages until it became apparent that with implementation would come job loss and change. Resistance to implementing the system meant that only after ten years was significant change beginning to happen.

This example clearly illustrates the exercise of **negative power**. Management have a controlling interest and can determine to a significant extent the form and direction of the agenda. They also have the resources to provide a higher-than-chance probability of success. However, they are vulnerable to the withdrawal of co-operation in achieving their intentions. That is one reason why the trade union movement is always sensitive to the removal of the right to strike or take industrial action. Ultimately, the withdrawal of labour or cooperation is the most powerful weapon in employee relations. This is the exercise of negative power – not doing something with the intent to influence.

Negative power
The ability to influence another party by not doing something that would normally be done.

MANAGEMENT IN ACTION 14.2 Tournament of the skies and other simulations

In Japan, Ishikawajima-Harima Heavy Industry (IHI) developed a simulator that reproduced a ship's bridge and could be used from the safety of a warehouse. To adapt the £6m simulator to any location all that is needed is a set of images and data about local tides and currents. The simulator screens stretch 225°, providing realistic day or night visual imagery. Sound equipment reflects engine vibrations through the floor as well as noises such as metal tearing on impact. The performance of trainees is monitored for later feedback and analysis. In addition to its training use, the simulator can be used to recreate accidents, allowing an investigation team the opportunity to understand what happened.

In the UK electricity supply industry coping with emergency situations that disrupt power distribution is an important requirement. Staff controlling the system can work for many years without experiencing an emergency and so never develop the expertise in handling crises. They have to rely on general training, skill and manuals to assist in dealing with emergencies. With the introduction of a simulator, realistic situations can be created that provide exposure to the more likely events. In the North this may be the effects of snow and in the South the effects of a power failure from France or high winds from the channel.

The Royal Air Force has introduced a simulator that can replicate battles. It is impossible to obtain and uses the aircraft of possible enemies for practice work in the sky. The development of a combat simulator called 'Joust' was intended to be able to replicate many different flying situations and aircraft types. It is possible to train pilots how to fly in battle conditions and in different flying circumstances without the risk of losing planes or pilots. The increase in skill, reaction times and the ability to fly planes creatively in battle could make the difference between life and death for a pilot facing hostile action. Multiple aircraft can be simulated at the same time, pitting pilots against the machine or other pilots in group flying and bomber protection duties, etc.

Flight simulators are being used not just to train pilots but to examine how they interact with the technology. Monitoring the use of flight controls, reactions to equipment layouts and the medical consequences of flying are all possible with the new £15m simulator shared by Lufthansa and Berlin University's Institute of Aerospace.

Adapted from: Thomson, R and Fisher, A (1994) All at sea from the safety of a warehouse. The human factor. Collapsing the system without getting the sack, *Financial Times*, 3 February, p 12; and Boggis, D (1995) Tournament of the skies, *Financial Times*, 10 March, p 17.

Stop ↔ Consider

Given that every trainee in a simulator knows that it is not for real, can such training ever replace real experience? Why or why not?

TECHNOLOGY, INNOVATION AND DIVERSITY

Innovation is about creating new things or creating new ways of doing existing things. New technology is, by definition, an innovation. Technology can also help organizations to innovate in the design of new products and it can assist in improving existing operations. Betz (1987) describes innovation as falling into one of three categories (Table 14.3):

1. *Radical*. This represents the initial development of a technology; the major breakthrough that allows the subsequent transformation of an industry or the creation of a new one. The development of the first computer during the 1940s is an example. The highest level of risk is associated with this type of innovation as much cost and time is needed. Many innovative ideas are developed but most do not achieve subsequent commercial realization.

2. *System*. This represents the commercialization of a technology. A computer by itself is simply a calculating and storage machine. However, linked to a typewriter and telephone it developed into the multifunction workstation of today. The level of risk is lower than with the radical level as it tends to involve the combination of existing technologies, rather than the creation of something completely new.
3. *Incremental*. This contains the lowest risk of the three levels and is a process of refinement. It represents the upgrading of a computer system through the miniaturization of components or improvements to a word-processing package. It is the level of innovation that aims to extract the maximum capability and potential out of a particular technology.

There are many ways in which innovation occurs. There are the research activities in universities that create many of the first radical versions of a particular technology. For example, my own university in Hull, played a pioneering role in the development of the liquid crystal, now an essential element of calculators and other forms of display screen. There are military laboratories specifically looking at technology of value in that context. There are science parks located near to universities intended to encourage the transfer and exploitation of pure research through commercial expertise. Within large organizations there is frequently research and development activity engaged on projects spanning the three categories we have examined.

Organizations need conformity in many guises in order to achieve success. Products and services must consistently conform to the appropriate specification. One of the major benefits of technology is that it can produce conformity to a much higher level than human beings. People must conform to behavioural and procedural requirements to ensure that the organization functions consistently and as expected. The use of company uniforms, dress codes, rules and training are all part of the process of engineering (or socializing) the behaviour of people. However, Herriot and Pemberton (1995) argue that uniformity (the consistency achieved through conformity) is a weakness and only through diversity comes strength.

They argue that uniformity leads to situations where inappropriate decisions are taken. The Bay of Pigs (Janis, 1982) is one of many decisions used to illustrate the point. This decision was about a group of people being so close in type and perspective that they could not entertain different points of view. The result was military failure and embarrassment for the American government. By encouraging diversity and establishing learning processes based on its incorporation into normal decision making, higher levels of innovation are encouraged. In turn a higher success rate should be achieved. They link their argument to the Myers–Briggs indicator of personality in order to create balanced and effective teams. You will recall the Belbin and Margerison and McCann team roles introduced in an earlier chapter. These provide a similar perspective on the need for a balance of personality and work preference if a team is to be successful.

Category	Example
Radical	Development of computer
System	Linking computer to typewriter technology
Incremental	Improvement in word processing package

TABLE 14.3 Categories of innovation

TECHNOLOGY AND CHANGE

Major differences between old and new technologies will inevitably create more change than if the differences are relatively small. Another aspect of the relationship between new technology and change is a reflection of the cause and effect process. Does the need to make change create developments in technology? Or could it be that a technology emerges which then allows change to take place through the utilization of that technology? It is possible that both could occur depending upon the circumstances. It is also possible that the relationship between technology and change is complex involving a range of intervening variables.

The impact of change on the ways that technology and work interact is experienced in a number of areas of organizational activity, for example:

- *Employment*. To build cars using manual labour obviously provides more jobs than would be the case if a fully automated process were employed. However, if cars made on an automated assembly line are of a higher quality and cheaper to purchase, then the organization may be able to employ more people as a result of increased sales. Equally, there will be employment opportunities that emerge as a result of the new technology itself. So some employment opportunities will disappear and others will emerge. For example, Table 14.4 based on research carried out by Business Software Alliance (*Management Today*, 2003) shows significant increases are being predicted in IT jobs for many countries.
- *Careers*. Some careers change as technology changes the jobs within them. For example, to be a maintenance engineer today demands a working knowledge of computer-based equipment and electronics, as well as the traditional electrical and mechanical specialisms. Other career paths will disappear as the traditional types of work are replaced by computers. New careers will emerge out of the work opportunities that are created by the adoption of a technology. For example, computer specialisms have emerged over the past 30 years as that form of technology has evolved.
- *Products and services*. New products and services emerge as technologies change and develop, for example, the building and selling of robot machines and computers. In the service sector the introduction of ATMs has provided a completely new range of service opportunities for banking customers. This provides for the creation of two distinct forms of new product and service. First, those associated with the technology itself. Second, the products and services that can be developed as a consequence of the technology.
- *Economic activity*. Economic activity is both influenced by and influences technology. Companies not profitable enough to raise capital will find it difficult

India	97.6%	Ireland	33.3%
China	92.9%	France	31.9%
Poland	50.6%	Spain	31.8%
Italy	34.6%	Sweden	31.7%
UK	31.6%	Denmark	29.6%
Germany	27.5%	USA	20.4%

TABLE 14.4 Growth in IT jobs 2002–2006

to invest in new technologies, which in turn may affect their chances of survival. The economic health of nations also influences the ability to be able to acquire new technologies.

- *Risk*. Every new venture carries with it an element of risk. With the introduction of computer technology comes particular risk as much of the processing is obscured from view. Earlier in this chapter it was argued that one of the benefits of information technology was the visibility that it provided. Managers are able to see in great detail (through reports and systems) what is going on. However, before that is possible much information processing takes place within the computer and is, therefore, not observable. It is the end result rather than the process that is visible. Lengthy commissioning and debugging processes are necessary in order to ensure that the system delivers what is required. Apocryphal stories are legion about new computer systems that send the wrong products to customers or that keep sending an order over and over again.
- *Internationalism*. Companies of all sizes and types now compete in international markets and new technology plays a significant part in this. There is also the international trade in high technology itself. Companies and governments are constantly seeking ways to capture new developments for the benefit of their organizations or citizens. Companies buy competitors' products and services and deconstruct them to learn about manufacturing processes, cost, etc., a process known as reverse engineering.
- *Fashion*. Inevitably what significant organizations do becomes an aspiration for many others. This is one means by which risk can be reduced. The first adopters of a particular technology will encounter and solve most of the problems. Following also gives managers confidence (real and political) that something will work and produce benefits. Conversely, there is an element of being less than creative as a result of simply following what others do. By simply following the trend and not working things out for themselves managers can be missing opportunities. The trick, if there is one, is to achieve an effective balance between following and innovating. The following Employee Perspective (14.1) reflects how one senior employee sought to deal with this issue.
- *Transition*. It is never possible to move from one state to another instantaneously and without consequence. Change takes time to achieve. In implementing a new technology there are a series of time lags between the initial ideas and commissioning the equipment and systems that can successfully meet the need. The transition period from one technology to another can be fraught with problems and difficulties. It is a time of running with two systems while a phased changeover takes place. Figure 14.4 reflects this transition period.

There are the cost, space and process-based implications associated with the need to keep old and new systems running in parallel. There are also people-related problems associated with technology change. Frustration is a common experience as replacement technologies begin to encroach onto the work of employees. Employees who consider that they have no future in the new order are less likely to willingly co-operate in solving the problems that emerge. They are more likely to engage in **Luddite** behaviour and further slow the change process.

Luddite
People resistant to change, originated in the early 1800s to describe workers who damaged machinery which replaced workers.

- *Limitations*. New technology is not always capable of living up to its image or the claims of its designers and salespeople. Neither is it always the best solution to every operational need. An electric typewriter (or handwriting) can be a quicker way of producing a short letter than a word processor. Perhaps speaking directly to a colleague could be a more effective way of dealing with a problem

EMPLOYEE PERSPECTIVE 14.1 Changing an industry

Richard had spent most of his career as a mining engineer working in many parts of the world. He had gained his experience in deep-mine coal extraction in the UK but had gone on to work in gold and copper mining in various countries in Africa. He had gained considerable experience as a result and at the age of 45 was regional operations director of a collection of coal mines in England. He was getting bored with his job as he found it becoming routine administrative work and seeking ways to cut cost, rather than developing new seams of coal to work on. He began to look around for another job and was eventually offered the position of director of maintenance projects with a major contract company working with railway companies around the world. The emphasis in his work would be track and signalling new and upgrade projects. Richard saw this new job as a challenge as both the railway and mining industries are similar in many ways. Safety is a major concern in both industries; geological factors can create problems and significantly influence the way that work is undertaken; both industries are very traditional in approach and people tend to make a lifelong career in whichever industry they join as young people.

This traditional approach also covered the ways in which people worked and the technology that they used in running their respective operations. There were recognized ways of doing things in both industries and change was slow to make any inroad into them. That is not to say that new technology was not used, simply that it took a while to find acceptance and wide use as a result of the traditional views prevalent at all levels and the imperative not to increase the risk of safety problems. Among the consequences of this for both industries were the slow pace of change and the tendency to adapt existing technology rather than risk what appeared to be unproven technologies.

In looking around his new organization and watching his teams of employees at work on major upgrading projects, Richard was struck by the many similarities between the tasks in mining and railway construction. For example laying, renovating and moving railway lines were tasks common to both industries and yet they were done in completely different ways in both industries. Richard began to ponder the implications of this for his work and quickly realized that it could be possible to adapt many of the technologies used in mining operations to the work of railway contracting. The question being how to introduce people to his ideas in a way which would encourage them to consider the possibilities, rather than react negatively. A further complication being the need to persuade the equipment manufactures to consider the redesign of large and very expensive machines that they had invested many millions of dollars developing and marketing.

Task

How would you go about this task if you were Richard?

than exchanging e-mail. Therefore a combination of old and new technologies integrated into a well thought out partnership could offer the most effective option. The following Employee Perspective (14.2) demonstrates the need to consider simple technological solutions as well as complex, high technology approaches in seeking to improve work methods.

FIGURE 14.4

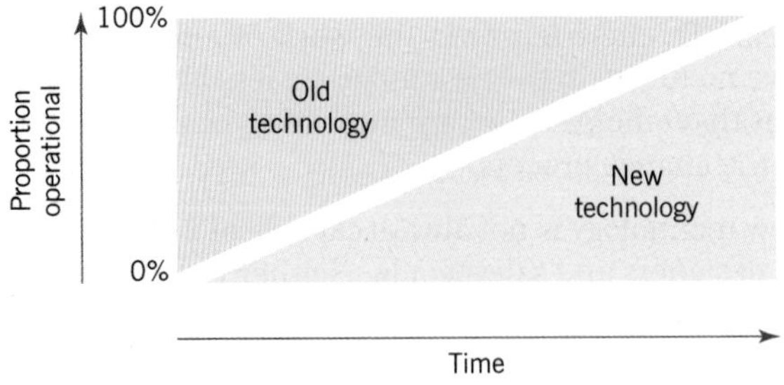

Technology transfer

EMPLOYEE PERSPECTIVE 14.2 Technology can be simple

John was the industrial engineer in a factory that made motor car tyres. His job was to find the most efficient methods of work for each of the manufacturing tasks. One of the operations in the factory was known as bead creeling. The bead on a car tyre is the part that fits onto the metal rim. The bead is made of rubber coated wire wrapped around (creeled) several times to create the strength to grip the rim and prevent the tyre from slipping or the air escaping. The machine that performed this particular task was essentially a rubber extruder which coated a number of copper wires as they passed through the die of the extruder. The rubber coated wires were then gripped in the jaws of a circular metal disc which then spun several times wrapping (creeling) the bead the correct number of times before a guillotine cut the now circular bead to the required length. It was then pushed from the circular metal disc by four spring loaded fingers. The circular disc was now clear to grip the now free end of the rubber coated wires and start spinning again to form the next bead.

In engineering terms this machine was relatively simple as the process contained few components and few operations. It was efficient and did not require much maintenance to keep the process running. However, there was one problem with the process. The bead was made with freshly extruded rubber which was hot and sticky. This was necessary as it helped the layers of rubber coated wire to stick together forming a solid component which performed better in the final tyre. Unfortunately as a consequence the creeled bead had a habit of sticking to the metal disc and not being ejected when the spring loaded fingers tried to push it off so that the cycle could begin again. This problem had been recognized since the machine had first been developed several years earlier and no solution had been found. Many engineers and rubber technologists within the company had sought to find a solution involving such innovations as Teflon coating the disc (caused a bad reaction in the rubber); making the disc out of stainless steel (the rubber still tended to stick); changing the rubber compound (caused problems with performance in the finished tyre) and changing the speed of the machine (no impact at all). Nothing worked; but the operator had developed a solution that did, but unfortunately it damaged the machine and made a mess around the workstation. It was a very low technology solution in the extreme. The operator filled a bucket with water and kept a plastic cup by the metal disc. After a bead was ejected from the disc and before the next spinning cycle began the operator part filled the cup with water and literally threw it over the disc, coating it with water and cooling it. Over time the operator found that if he did this every second bead that was creeled the machine worked as intended. Unfortunately the machine was being doused with water on a regular basis and it was damaging the mechanical and electrical components. Still the various specialists worked on the problem but to no avail.

The solutions being proposed became ever more elaborate and complex as desperation began to find its way into the professionals trying to come up with a solution. Eventually a major research programme was launched and a team of experts identified that if the machine were to be computer controlled it should be possible to constantly monitor variables such as extruder temperature, rubber stickiness, metal disc temperature and size of the bead being produced. As a consequence it was identified that if these variables were controlled within a very narrow range the incidence of beads failing to be ejected from the metal disc could be reduced by 80 per cent. This was felt to be the best option available but it would cost something in the region of £2 million to develop and £4 million to build the new machine. The decision was reluctantly taken to propose a major new development programme and to seek funding for it.

As the factory industrial engineer John was involved in a routine review of the work practices in the department which included the bead creeling machine. One day he was watching the operator at work and saw him throwing cups of water over the metal disc. He spoke to the operator and asked why he was doing it. The operator explained the problem and John began to chat to him about how the machine worked and how the operator had stumbled across the idea. The operator complained that it was a messy process and that by the end of his shift he went home soaking wet as he only had a very short period of time to throw water on the metal disc and it inevitably splashed back onto his clothes and went all over the machine. As a consequence the operator had to cover the machine in oil to prevent it rusting up, this further added to the mess around the workstation.

That weekend at home John was in his garden spraying the weeds with weedkiller from a hand held spray gun and he had a flash of inspiration. He wondered if it would be possible to use a simple hand spray to spray water onto the metal disc on the bead machine? On Monday he took his hand spray bottle into work with him and filled it with water. He took it onto the factory floor and showed it to the operator. The operator quickly grasped the idea and showed enthusiasm for trying it out. This he did and found that it could work, but that it was not quick enough to cover the full circumference of the metal disc in-between production cycles. John went and found the maintenance manager and brought him to the machine to explain the problem. The maintenance manager scratched his head and thought for a while and then said that he thought that it should be possible to put a couple of spray heads around the circumference of the metal disc, linked to a simple trip switch, water pump and tank. He went away and got one of the maintenance engineers and explained roughly what he thought would work and asked him to try to develop the device. After two days of tinkering about with various bits of tubing, switches and spray heads a working system was running on the machine. It ran for two weeks with no problems and so at that stage the project engineers were brought to see the new solution to the problem and they were amazed that such a simple approach could achieve a satisfactory solution, when their combined technological expertise had not been able to do so. Everyone was happy at the solution. The operator avoided getting wet at work and having to work in damp and unpleasant conditions; the machine was in better condition by not having water thrown over it every few seconds and the beads themselves were not as wet, which meant that they could be used in the next stage of the production process more quickly.

Task

What does this example suggest about the nature of technology and the ways in which it relates to the job of technical specialists such as John in an organization?

INFORMATION TECHNOLOGY

Forester (1987) suggests that it is high (computer-based) technology that allows the development of new techniques that impact directly on work. Much of the computer-based technology is intended to provide improvements in the ability of organizations to process information in one form or another.

Information technology, argues Zuboff (1988), differs from the technology used in the nineteenth century in one respect only: it combines the replacement of people with machines and it provides a higher level of transparency through the ability of computer technology to process information. 'Activities, events, and objects are translated into and made visible by information when a technology informates as well as automates' (p 10). It is the control potential from the transparency achieved via the technology that is the new dimension to the technology. It brings employee activity into the public domain. With knowledge comes the opportunity to control.

Buchanan and Boddy (1983) suggest four aspects of information-handling capabilities that differentiate computer systems from other forms of technology:

1. *Capture*. Computer systems are able to capture data passively or actively in a number of ways. The collection of vehicle density through sensors placed on a road reflects an active collection of data.
2. *Storage*. There are two types of storage in computer systems. First, the program that governs the activities of the machine itself. Second, the information captured by the system as directed by the program.
3. *Manipulation*. Computer systems are capable of manipulating the information captured and stored. A production line computer system could capture volume and dimension data on items passing across a sensor. It could then automatically calculate a range of quality-control data for the production batch.

4. *Distribution*. The information collated can be automatically distributed to anyone with access to the system and entitled to the information. In the case of a quality control analysis, the results could be displayed on a monitor at the worksite for all to see.

It has been argued (Konsynski and Sviokla, 1994) that the failure by management to obtain the full value and potential from information technology is a consequence of the continued use of outdated paradigms of organizational functioning. They claim that cognitive reapportionment is necessary if managers are to obtain full advantage. The new paradigm sees organizations as bundles of decisions: decision making being based on an appropriate allocation of bundles between humans, systems or a combination of the two.

Information technology is not restricted to computer applications. The portable telephone has made an impact on a number of job functions. Sales staff can be in constant contact with the office and can phone orders directly into a computer system or e-mail it directly from their car. For a review of the latest 3G mobile phone technology see Payton and Bowen (2003). Compact discs and DVDs store vast quantities of data for subsequent retrieval and analysis. Electronic mail (e-mail) can eliminate the need for the traditional memo and provide senior managers with immediate access to all employees, bypassing the normal hierarchy. This last point has a number of connotations for open door management policies.

The development of neural networks, imitating human brain functioning, leads the way for the next generation of information processing. For example, the development of expert systems that solve problems in ways that reflect human activity can help to detect credit card fraud by scanning many thousands of transactions on a daily basis.

NEW TECHNOLOGY APPLICATIONS

The growth in new technology jobs within emerging economies reflects a process that has major implications for jobs and organizations in the West, as illustrated by Management in Action 14.3.

The approach for the following discussion is to examine the major organizational classifications of manufacturing and service and administration. Few organizations are purely manufacturing or service, most contain elements of both. A theatre falls firmly within the service sector. However, within a theatre, groups of people will be engaged in manufacturing scenery, costumes and the preparation of food for the restaurant. Hill (1983) describes manufacturing as being about the production of goods for purchase and subsequent consumption. Service, by comparison, involves the production of intangibles consumed at the time of provision, with the customer taking away the benefit of the service. Whatever the type of organization however, it will contain administrative activities of some degree. One of the more recent innovations has been in the area of e-business which brings with it particular problems, particularly in relation to the potential for fraud (Corbitt, 2002).

Manufacturing

Manufacturing is about making tangible items for subsequent sale. Motor cars, washing machines and toasters for example. New technology has impacted on this type of operation in a number of ways. Machines and robots can now process information and therefore demonstrate a relatively low level of thinking ability. This takes many forms and leads to more integration of activity as computers talk to each other.

MANAGEMENT IN ACTION 14.3 Jobs for all in the global market?

Various predictions have been offered about the high-tech future. Recently Sir James Goldsmith argued that some 4 billion people had recently entered the world labour markets from China, India, Indochina, Bangladesh and the countries that originally formed the Soviet Union, their labour cost being 90–95 per cent lower than European workers.

Crabb reviewed developments in India to find out more about the possible impact on jobs within the UK. India has relaxed its closed economy, tariffs have fallen dramatically and returning graduates with experience of working in the USA have brought a new focus back with them. Salaries for highly skilled new graduates are very low by comparison with the West. For example, software engineers can start on as little as £1000 per year. At about five hours' time difference there is sufficient overlap time to be able to engage in telephone communication with clients. There is also a sufficient period of non-overlap to allow uninterrupted access to computer systems on the client's premises. The level of business between the West and India has risen from about $39 million in 1986/87 to $14 200 million in 1993/4.

There are typically three routes for software developed in India to arrive in the West:

1. *Outsourcing*. Western companies outsourcing some or all of their IT operations to India. This route is the basis of the scenario that predicts the wholesale loss of IT jobs to India. Companies using this approach include Swissair and Lufthansa.
2. *Joint venture*. A variation of exporting with products developed by 'partners' being taken back to home locations. Examples include Mahindra–British Telecom, Tata–Unisys and IBM–Tata.
3. *Exporting*. The normal exporting of software products to the West by Indian companies. For example, London Underground commissioned CMC in India to develop a new train scheduling, signalling and timetabling system. Priced at around £200 000, the 18-month project cost was well below that proposed by European suppliers.

Robert Reich in his 1991 book *The Work of Nations* sums up the situation and implications of high-tech development in countries such as India by suggesting that there are three types of worker in the modern world:

1. *Routine production worker*. The person whose job is moving to ever cheaper parts of the world.
2. *In-person servers*. Retail workers, domestic helpers, security guards, etc. This category of worker finds that they are being squeezed in wage terms due to competition for jobs and the application of technology to their work.
3. *Symbolic analyzers*. In the UK these workers would be referred to as 'knowledge workers'. This category is the real winner according to Reich. 'If you are well educated, if you have skills, if you are a problem solver, you have a larger and larger market within which to sell your problem-solving skills. International trade is working to your advantage.'

Adapted from: Crabb, S (1995) Jobs for all in the global market?, *People Management*, 26 January, pp 22–7.

Stop ↔ Consider

To what extent does the process described above reflect similar processes to that applicable to the transfer and globalization of technologies in the past?

Robots with the ability to pick up, move and position items began to appear in the 1960s. They were used predominantly for paint spraying, spot welding and stacking operations. Automatic trains could also follow a predetermined path around a factory collecting and delivering pallets of components or finished goods. These driverless trains followed a magnetic strip buried in the floor and as computer technology developed were able to integrate a broader range of functions such as self-loading. From these early days there are many apocryphal stories of managers being pinned against walls or run-over by runaway trains or robots. These stories, usually told by shop-floor employees, often demonstrate that even the robots and computers have a certain attitude towards management.

With the incorporation of vision- and touch-sensitive devices robots can be used for a wide range of tasks within the manufacturing process. For example, the quality and quantity of glass bottles can be determined as they travel down a conveyor belt and pass an electronic eye (sensor) linked to a computer. The dimensions of the bottles can be checked against a model held in the memory of the computer and the quality of the glass can be reflected in light patterns passing through the glass and checked against the norms anticipated. Pass/fail decisions can then be made by the computer about individual bottles and they can be channelled to either packing or recycling accordingly. In addition, records and analysis of quality data can be generated for subsequent interpretation by management.

Advanced manufacturing technologies (AMT) and flexible manufacturing systems (FMS) have also incorporated the computer to create more flexible and consistent products. The purpose of such systems is to link together a number of machines so that items can be automatically transferred between them in successive stages of production. They also allow groups of machines to be linked together so that smaller batches of product can be made efficiently. These systems attempt to replicate the economy of large-scale production but for small quantities. Small batch sizes with frequent deliveries is a function of what began as a very low technology approach to production – just-in-time production.

The design of manufactured items has also been subjected to computer technology. Designs can be drawn directly onto a computer screen through a mouse, drawing palette, etc. These can be interpreted by the computer and converted into three-dimensional representations, parts lists, detailed drawings, etc. The combination of computer-aided design (CAD) with computer-aided manufacture (CAM) provides a very powerful approach for technology to create and produce products automatically. This can be totally amalgamated into computer integrated manufacture (CIM). However, this is very difficult and has yet to be achieved on a significant scale with any degree of success.

Evidence concerning the impact of new technology on work in manufacturing organizations is not consistent. Forester (1987, Chapter 6) reviews a number of texts and reports from Europe, the USA and Japan that reflect this ambiguity. The major perspectives include:

- *Take-up*. The adoption of high technology has not been as dramatic as might be expected. In the USA in 1983 only 4.7 per cent of machine tools were numerically controlled – remember these were the first generation new technology machines!
- *Cost*. Integrated systems are expensive to develop and install. Organizations that have opted for high levels of new technology have not generally enjoyed significant financial benefit over other organizations. However, there are some amazing results claimed: Normalair-Garrett in the UK achieved some very significant cost savings using FMS – labour down from £400 000 to £150 000; output per worker up from £70 000 to £210 000; work in progress held at any time reduced from £690 000 to £90 000.
- *Reliability*. Very high levels of reliability are required within integrated production systems as the failure of a single component can stop a whole assembly line or island of production. Production systems become more vulnerable than if they consist of individual machines not linked together.
- *Government policy*. Governments in the major industrialized nations adopt different policies towards new technology. In the UK a form of passive facilitation is the best description of the approach adopted up to 1981, at which

time the crisis in the machine tool industry as a consequence of Japanese penetration of the market became impossible to ignore. The result was a more positive encouragement of the adoption of high technology through conferences, grants and consultancy support.

- *Employee impact*. There can be a considerable saving on labour with the adoption of new technology. Yamazaki (a Japanese machine tool manufacturer) claim that using FMS 12 day workers plus a night watchman can produce as much as 215 workers and four times as many machines using traditional methods. Also, lead times (time to make the product) reduced from three months to three days. New jobs are also created by technology. Also some jobs change as a result of the application of technology.
- *Managerialism*. Part of the lower take-up of high technology in the USA and Europe could be the result of low levels of technological expertise among managers. They don't understand the complexity involved and so resist adopting new systems. It is also suggested that where new technology is adopted the full benefit is not achieved because Western managers do not understand how to obtain maximum flexibility from it. An emphasis on short-term results also works against the introduction of integrated technology which requires long time-frames to become fully operational.
- *Social factors*. The social factors associated with high technology influence general attitudes towards it. Braverman (1974) discussed alienation and the managerial imperative for control over workers. Shaiken (1985) introduces similar arguments in connection with work in a high-technology factory and the demeaning effect on people's lives. Overall the evidence is somewhat contradictory, with other studies reporting employee satisfaction with the use of CNC equipment.

Forester argues the negative arguments towards new technology are not proved because of the existence of some positive comments about it and because engineers design systems to achieve tasks, not control desires. There are three weaknesses in this argument. First, engineers design systems to a management agenda – they never have a completely free hand as management funds the process and has influence over it. Second, opinion surveys can be unreliable – is an employee seeing many fellow workers made redundant likely to be critical of new technology provided by management? If so, they may be regarded as unreliable or not demonstrating commitment and so be more liable to lose their job. Also there is no way of knowing that what interviewees say is what they actually believe. The third weakness is that technology can be neutral in principle, but biased in practice. It is managers who decide how new technology will be used to meet their needs. The political, power and control justifications may never be articulated, but that does not mean that they do not exist.

Service

The effect of new technology on employment in services has been noticeably different from that in manufacturing. Although there has always been a service sector, for example, doctors and market traders, it was just beginning to develop in scale and significance when computer technologies arrived. The rapid growth of the service sector was largely enabled because of the release of labour from manufacturing as a result of the use of technology in that sector. People also had the money to spend on more than the essentials of life. Jobs have not been obviously lost in the service sector, growth having outstripped this tendency.

There is unevenness in the effect of new technology on different categories and levels of job across the service sector (Reed, 1989). For example, the history and control of work within the medical profession gives practitioners a much greater say in the application and job impact of new technology than would be available to the staff in a bank. Some occupational groups are more able to control the impact on their jobs and working conditions than others. The employee relations implications of greater supply chain integration in grocery distribution across the United States of America as a result of technological advances are discussed by Lund and Wright (2003). The potential for increasing business vulnerability through the greater levels of union bargaining power are discussed along with the need to identify strategies which offset that risk.

Administrative

By the early 1960s most large companies had a mainframe computer undertaking routine processing of accounting and payroll information. Most computer departments began as data processing departments, often within the accounting section. Forester (1987) reviews a 1985 UK survey indicating that less than 50 per cent of office workers had direct access to any electronic equipment other than a phone or calculator.

The development of new technology in administrative activity has concentrated on three main areas:

1. *Convergence*. Much of the technology available began as separate pieces of equipment with different functions. This distinction is disappearing with the inclusion of microprocessors in much equipment. The multimedia workstation is rapidly making an entry as the major application of new technology.
2. *Visibility*. The use of networks and data-analysis packages allows greater visibility of information among managers. Once the raw data are entered into the system it can be analyzed and reported on much more quickly. It is also possible for managers to experiment with the information available to them. Considering questions such as: 'If we reduced the expenditure on x, what would the consequences be?'
3. *Integration*. Integration is not the same as convergence. Convergence is the bringing together of technological difference. Integration is about creating an office system as a single set of processes not a separate set of tasks. It is about being able to undertake several activities at the same time, accessing information sources as necessary to achieve the objective. It might be a budgetary control system as a single process, being able to access, analyze and extrapolate historical records, current information and future plans, all this being carried out at a single electronic workstation, perhaps even remotely as a teleworking exercise.

The effects of new technology on administrative work can be summarized under four headings (Forester, 1987):

1. *Employment*. In any reduction in the overall numbers of administrative jobs it is difficult to separate out the effects of technology, economic downturns and cost cutting. There is also the need to take into account the creation of jobs in the computer and systems areas.
2. *Job quality*. There is a common view that most administrative jobs involve sitting at a computer screen, typing information into the system for hours. This view sees people being required only because the technology has not developed to the extent that they can be eliminated altogether. While this view of

technology is true to an extent, previously armies of clerical staff would have sat at rows of desks making entries in ledgers all day long. It is not clear which job would have the lower quality in job design terms. Data-entry duties can often be automated thus releasing time for analysis, interpretation and action at a lower level in the organization.

3. *Health and safety*. There have been fears expressed about the impact of prolonged use of computers on the health of workers. This has included the effects of radiation from the computer screen; the impact of constant use of a keyboard on joints and muscles and back problems from continually sitting in one position. Research into these issues is ongoing. The problems can be resolved to a significant extent by the use of correct seating and lighting, the introduction of regular breaks away from screens or through keyboard design and usage techniques. Management in Action 14.4 looks at one aspect of this, the use of a keyboard.
4. *Social relations*. Communication with or through a computer system inevitably reduces or eliminates the opportunity for people to interact with each other at work. There are, however, organizational benefits to be gained from human interaction, problem solving and innovation being among the more obvious. A lack of human interaction can be used as a form of control – the divide and rule principle – leading to alienation and lack of commitment. The relationship between technology and the way in which it is used is not automatic; managers ultimately determine how the technology will be integrated with employees.

One of the ways in which technology is impacting on administrative activity is through the introduction of e-HR processes, including online recruitment. Welch (2003) reviews technology-based hiring processes and concludes that as yet they have made only limited impact. Recruiters seem reluctant to make use of the potential of technology to deliver a cost effective full service activity. Out of 500 of Britain's top companies 164 had no recruitment section in their web sites and only 9 of 33 who claimed to allow job seekers to register for e-mail alerts had sent any out after three months.

TECHNOLOGY: AN APPLIED PERSPECTIVE

In this chapter technology has been introduced as a broad ranging concept, not just the application of computer technology to operational activity. This breadth of meaning provides a major benefit to managers as they seek to run organizations – that of control. With the introduction of computer-based technologies management control has been developed further through automation and integration of activity. Technology in its broadest sense provides a number of potential benefits to the management of any organization:

- *Control of process*. Management is able to more easily control the design of operational layouts, machine configurations and the methods of work.
- *Control of work*. Management is able to more easily control the design of jobs and issues such as work rate, quality and product design. Through these aspects management is also able to control social relationships at the workplace. For example, Garrahan and Stewart (1992) describe an attempt to achieve high quality by requiring employees to report the mistakes of others in the team.
- *Control of people*. Management is able to more closely define and control the activities and behaviour of the people in the workplace through the application

MANAGEMENT IN ACTION 14.4 Piano gives a lesson for the workplace

The use of computer keyboards has dramatically changed the nature of much work within organizations. It has also increased the risk of injury for those using a keyboard inappropriately. Tenosynovitis, tendonitis and carpal tunnel syndrome are just some of the injuries that can be found in this context. Stephanie Brown, a New York-based professor of piano, noted similar injuries among those piano players who did not develop effective keyboard skills. She first noted these problems in relation to computers when she began to use a computer keyboard for the first time. She commented: 'It's well known that certain positions and motions can cause injury in practically every sport. Everyone has had the experience of watching someone swing a tennis racquet or golf club and think "ouch!". It just looks wrong. Using a computer keyboard is no different. It's a vigorous micro-athletic workout for the hands and fingers. Do it wrong and you're asking for trouble.'

Brown published a book, *The Hand Book*, to publicize 14 lessons in how to avoid some of the pitfalls to which she gave names such as the 'the cobra', 'the spider' and 'the Flying Pinky'. Athletes warm up before a race and so should computer users. There are also issues associated with injury, such as workstation adjustment that are given recognition in her book. Some of the dos and don'ts when using a computer keyboard identified in her book include:

- Keep the natural wrist line.
- Let the wrists float.
- Let the elbows hang free.
- Relax the ring and little finger.
- Don't squeeze the mouse.
- Rest the hands when not keying.

Adapted from: Boyling, J (1994) Piano gives a lesson for the workplace, *Financial Times*, 12 January, p 21.

Stop ↔ Consider

Can you think of any other areas of life that could offer benefits to computer users? If so, what are they and how might they be used?

of technology. This can be through the subordination of people to machine processes, the application of administrative technologies or the application of scientific management-based technologies. Each of these opportunities restricts the freedom of influence over, and ownership of, their work by individuals.

- *Control of cost*. Management is able to control the cost of operations through a number of technologically based devices. For example, they control the design of the work itself and they control the pace of work. However, through the development of administrative technologies and procedures there is an improved level of visibility among managers about how costs are influenced and, therefore, how they can be managed.
- *Control of agenda*. Management is able to control the technological agenda within the organization, within society and among competitors. It is management that decides on the technology to be used and on its preferred options for future developments. Management also shapes the future of much pure research through funding assistance.
- *Control of resistance*. Management is able to control the level of resistance to the use of technology through a number of routes. The creation of jobs, career opportunities and fashion creates a view of technology that can become attractive to those seeking to create a future in organizational life. The threat of the loss of a job can reduce overt resistance (particularly if jobs are scarce). The use of people technologies can encourage employees to become an active part of

the process itself. For example, employee involvement, matrix structures, teamwork and profit-share options are just some of the ways in which employees are encouraged to identify with management's objectives.

- *Control of skill*. Management is able to control the level and type of skill that exists through the design of jobs and the nature of technology itself and how it is adopted within the organization.
- *Control of organization*. Management is able to control the design of the organization itself through the use of technology. The number of people employed, the type of work and the compartmentalization of activity are all amenable to the influence of technology. These issues influence the size and shape of the organization's hierarchy, structure and approach to bureaucratization/formality etc.
- *Control of location*. Management is able to control the location of an organization as a result of the ease with which activity can be transferred between locations. For example, Management in Action 14.5 reports how one publishing organization in Singapore dealt with a labour shortage by transferring some of its activities to other parts of the world.

It is easy to understand how and why organizations are tempted to rush into adopting new technology if it improves control, thereby reducing a number of existing operational problems and the perceived level of risk. However, there are broader considerations that need to be taken into account regarding the application of technology. During the transition period associated with the emergence of a new technology there are usually significant labour imbalances. Individuals with the old skills are displaced from the opportunity to work and there is a shortage of people with the new skills. This creates difficulties for organizations, governments, trade unions and individual workers. For example, removing employees with outdated skills results in having to meet redundancy costs, whilst at the same time the cost of recruiting labour with scarce skills increases. Inevitably, the level of employment in an economy reduces, with a reduction in revenue for a government at a time when state benefits may be needed to support the displaced employees and to pump prime training initiatives to equip people with the emerging skills. The trade unions also face a loss of members as individuals leave jobs and perhaps move into other areas of work. They also face difficulties as members (or potential members) question the value of belonging to a trade union that claims to represent their interests but which finds it difficult to prevent job losses and change being forced upon workers.

Risk of failure is one of the problems that technology brings. It is developing at such a rapid rate that no sooner has a particular technology been introduced than it has been superseded, the danger here being that competitors adopt the next generation of new technology and steal an advantage. The cost of the adoption of a particular technology can be prohibitive and is not something that can be undertaken every year. Flexibility and keeping future options open is a key requirement of new technology. However, technology suppliers make this very difficult by seeking to lock customers into their own product range in order to protect future business. Variations in product and technology standards prevent the easy switching from one supplier to another. Consequently, the successful adoption of new technology comes not so much from the technology itself but from its effective integration with other work activities and existing technologies.

Very few managers have an in-depth understanding of the technologies available. In developing their careers managers progressively move away from the operational levels of activity. Increasingly, technology becomes something that other people use regularly. Managers inevitably rise through a particular discipline – accounting, personnel or production for example. They will have some knowledge of new

MANAGEMENT IN ACTION 14.5 Singapore dials long distance to find staff

The island of Singapore has an enviable growth rate (approximately 10 per cent per year). The island is booming and jobs are relatively easy to find. This poses problems for many employers who find it necessary to recruit labour from overseas in order to be able to function efficiently. Another way of attacking this issue using technology has been developed by the island's main newspaper publishers, Singapore Press Holdings (SPH).

Mr Cheong Yip Seng, an editor-in-chief at SPH, indicated that about 80 per cent of the graduate intake to SPH has left by the end of their fourth year, to earn higher wages in stockbroking and other professions. Recruitment teams have been sent as far afield as South Africa in an attempt to recruit sub-editors and business writers. About 17 per cent of the staff at SPH are from overseas. Mr Cheong commented: 'We have never been able to bring our staffing levels up to full strength. Journalists, subs, photographers and graphics people – we just can't find enough of them.'

In a unique experiment in newspaper publishing a proportion of the sub-editing, layout and graphics work is being undertaken by satellite offices in Sydney and Manila. In Sydney, there is a team of 12 people, about six of whom are Singaporeans and Malaysians who had settled in Australia. These staff provide the sub-editing and layout expertise for sections of the *Straits Times* (the main SPH English language newspaper). The Asian employees provide the local knowledge about style and related aspects to ensure that the paper retains a local feel and conforms to local needs. In Manila there are five graphic artists who feed artwork between Singapore and Sydney on a regular basis. Only about 5 per cent of the *Straits Times* is 'subbed' offshore in this way. Plans exist to extend that to about 40 per cent over time, if the experiment is successful.

One of the difficulties experienced in the experiment is that Sydney is two hours ahead of Singapore and consequently it is not possible to leave the later aspects of the newspaper to be produced there. The group are considering opening offices in Bombay, because it is two hours behind Singapore time and many good journalists live there. However, communication links with India remain a difficulty in getting the project off the ground. The telephone lines must be of top quality to ensure the best transmission between the two locations.

Adapted from: Cooke, K (1995) Singapore dials long distance to find staff, *Financial Times*, 31 May, p 3.

Stop ↔ Consider

Identify some of the problems that might be expected in setting up operations of the type described above. How might they be overcome?

technology applications within their own areas of expertise but less in other areas. At some point in their careers, managers have to take responsibility for disciplines of which they have no direct experience. At the same time, technology continues to develop within their original profession, the danger being that managers become reactionary and resist technology applications, or they become prey to the claims of vested interests. In most organizations senior managers have enough experience to be able to tread this line with some considerable skill, but it is a danger that continues to exist. Effective measures are needed to ensure that senior managers are not left behind in understanding new technology.

Another element of new technology for managers is the effect on jobs and employees within the organization. It is easy to see technology as an end in itself rather than a means to an end. Technology is not capable of running a company without input and support from that most capable and flexible of all technologies (an old technology at that), the human being. The true success of new technology comes from the effective integration of these two totally different expressions of creativity. After all it is technology that is intended to support people not the other way round!

Buchanan and McCalman (1988) studied the effects of computerized information systems in hotels and concluded that they offered a number of advantages, which they describe as a visibility theory. These five items perhaps best summarize the general impact of information technology on the role of management in any modern organization, perhaps with the exception of the last, which appears to optimistically suggest that conflict and political activity would be reduced:

- *Sharing*. Computer-based systems encouraged managers to share information more readily than manual systems.
- *Confidence*. The more widely available information encouraged and motivated managers, thus increasing confidence levels.
- *Pressure*. The wider and timely availability of information as a result of computerization puts pressure on managers to react quickly and effectively in pursuing business objectives.
- *Visibility*. Improved information flows bring into the open the relative performance of individual managers.
- *Co-operation*. These four previous elements combine to produce a situation where managers find it easier to work together and reduce levels of conflict generally.

CONCLUSIONS

This chapter has introduced the concept of technology in its broadest sense as it impacts on organizations and those who work in them. It has shown that technology has been evolving for as long as people have been attempting to improve their ability to survive and raise living standards. In doing so technology as it impacts on an organization has a particular part to play. It influences both the way in which employees experience work and the rewards that they accrue from it, also, the level, cost and type of goods and services that are available to be acquired by consumers. As a consequence, humans are victim, beneficiary and creator of the technology that has such a fundamental impact on their work experience. It is inevitable that any discussion of new technology will quickly become dated as new technologies and different applications for existing ones emerge. The risk associated with any new technology is that it takes a predominant position in organizational thinking and diverts attention away from the potential available through human capability and diversity as important elements in success.

Now to summarize this chapter in terms of the relevant Learning Objectives:

- **Understand what is meant by the term technology and how it influences both the operational activities found within organizations and jobs that people undertake.** At its simplest level technology refers to the machines, computers and equipment that people use in the work that they undertake. However, there are other forms of technology that exist and which impact on the people in a work context. There are the procedural devices, skills and methods of work that are also technologies in their own right. In addition there are the social technologies that refer to the ways in which people are managed and their behaviours directed within an organizational framework. It is this last form of technology, that integrates the earlier two definitions of it into a cohesive framework, that we refer to as an organization. In its broadest sense technology is a fundamental expression of organization. The equipment, procedures and social arrangements all determine to a significant degree how employees and managers will be accommodated around the various technologies in order to contribute to the pursuit of organizational objectives. At a more specific level, technology in the sense of machines, equipment and computers define to a significant degree the jobs that people undertake through the design of the technology itself. As part of the design process for the technology, the designer is required to define how users will be required to interact with it, in so doing effectively creating the jobs for those employees. In operational terms a technology can determine to a significant extent what the organization can actually do. For example, the development of computer based educational technology has allowed increasing development of the virtual campus approach to university education. Increasingly students will be able to study a particular topic at any location with computer and web-based access through the provision of video lectures, chat-room tutorials, electronic library facilities and electronic assessment submission.

- **Explain the impact of technology on the organizations that employ it.** There are a number of perspectives on the relationship between technology and organization. Six approaches are introduced within the relevant section of the text. They include Woodward, who described the relationship between production technology (batch size, mass production, etc.) and a number of organizational features. Perrow describes the relationship between technology in its broadest sense and the ways that problems are dealt with. Burns and Stalker discussed the ways in which technology linked to the type of industry in terms of its degree of market stability and which found expression in the approach to organizational activity. Another approach discussed in the text is that of Japanization. The success of Japanese manufacturing companies in making rapid and significant inroads into Western markets forced a serious consideration of how this had been achieved. A number of features were identified as relevant to the levels of success that had been achieved. They included different approaches to quality, the introduction of just-in-time and continuous improvement, the organization of work and organizational structure differences. All of this developed within a specific cultural, political and economic context which was not easily transferred to other situations.
- **Outline the relationship between technology, politics and change in managerial decision making.** The existence of politics within management activity is inevitable. Resources are always in scarce supply and every manager is in competition for whatever additional resources are available. This inevitably encourages competition which if not managed effectively can easily turn into conflict and political activity. Technology is one area of resource which can contribute to this through the political potential for decision areas associated with the development and acquisition of particular technologies. For example, pressure for higher pay among employees can be countered by the threat of the introduction of automation and the elimination of jobs. The development and adoption of technology is a managerial decision area and is not therefore a neutral process, it can be used to the relative advantage of that group as a political process. The relationship between technology and change is also a complex one. At a simple level the introduction of technology can signal job loss as people are replaced by machines. However there are other changes that take place including the creation of new jobs through the need to employ new skills in support of a particular technology; the new jobs that are created as a consequence of the making of the new technology equipment and systems; the new jobs that emerge as a result of the enhancements in products and services available through technology applications. There are other issues associated with technology and change. For example, the influence of economics on technology development and uptake; the growth in internationalism through the ability of information technology to reduce distance between customer and supplier; the role of fashion in managerial thinking and decision making, etc.
- **Discuss the relationship between technology and control.** The ways in which technology and control link together includes a wide range of forces and factors. For example, the development and adoption of technology. It is managers who determine to a significant degree how technology develops and its use within any organization; therefore it can assist in their desire to achieve greater levels of control over processes and people in the pursuit of operational or other objectives. The issue of who should be allowed access to a particular technology is also part of the control processes within an organization. For example, who should hold primary responsibility for the design and running of a particular system impacts directly on relative power balance between groups and therefore how these

groups will either exercise control over others or be controlled by other groups. The use of technology determines to a significant extent the jobs of those employees interacting with it. This effectively controls their behaviour in a number of ways. It determines their work activity in terms of tasks, sequencing and pace of work, but it also determines deadlines, priority and even work patterns. Through covert intention managers can claim to be seeking improvements in quality or customer service through the application of a particular technology, but in practice the achievement of tighter control of the operational process (including employee activity) may be the real objective.

- **Appreciate how the application of technology can result in alienation and the degradation of labour.** In general terms, alienation reflects a feeling in the individual of not being part of the organization that employs them. It has been summarized as containing aspects of self-estrangement, powerlessness, meaninglessness and isolation in the experience of work. It was originally envisaged by writers in this area that the increasing use of technology would de-skill and dehumanize work to the extent that the human employee would be little more than a machine minder, necessary only because the machine could not perform the full range of tasks needed to convert the raw materials into finished production and transfer it to a warehouse. Humans were envisaged to be nothing more than service operators, destined for the boring, menial and degraded work to support the machines that would undertake the real work of the organization. The reality however has proved to be more complex than implied by that stark perspective of the impact of technology on the experience of human beings at work. There are undoubtedly many examples of boring and mundane work using technology which result in a feeling of alienation among employees. However, it is also possible to use the creativity and ingenuity of designers to create technology that supports human activity in an organization, rather than the other way around. Of course that is not to say that boring work can be completely eliminated, but the human being is nothing if not adaptable and any organization that ignores the potential of the human employee is surely doomed to mediocrity if not long term failure. Some of the approaches to job design discussed in the previous chapter, along with initiatives such as employee involvement introduced in previous chapters can contribute to the development of meaningful work that does not offer a degraded or alienated experience for those engaged in it.

DISCUSSION QUESTIONS

1. Japanization as a phenomenon reflects the effective integration and application of technology in its broadest sense. Discuss this statement.
2. Identify the ways in which new technology has influenced the traditional ways of exercising control within organizations.
3. How are technology, diversity and innovation linked together?
4. Does technology manage managers or do managers manage technology? Justify your answer.
5. Discuss the relationship between technology, organization structure and job design.
6. Managers are as much victims of technology as those employees with skills that are superseded by technology. Comment on this statement.
7. Discuss the view that understanding how technology has unfolded across history provides an improved picture of its benefits and problems today.
8. Technology provides the means of support for the values and objectives of managers. Discuss.
9. Does technology inevitably lead to alienation? Justify your answer.
10. The main reason for managers to seek to utilize technology is to increase their control over the processes for which they are responsible. Technology is, therefore, a political tool in the service of capital. Discuss this statement.

CASE STUDY Martha the 'Martini' employee

Martha was an employee development associate with a large international bank. She was based in Hong Kong, but was expected to work anywhere in the world that the bank needed her to. Her particular area of development activity was in providing support for branch and regional managers in the use of technology to enable them to more effectively meet the ever more difficult targets that were set for business development. As a consequence, Martha was away from her office and home for an average of three days each week most of the year. Although Martha was used to living out of a suitcase and enjoyed her job, her family resented the amount of time that she spent away from home. Most of the time Martha and her family communicated via e-mail as it was easier than trying to make voice or personal contact when she was away.

Within the bank, there were a large number of employees in a similar position to Martha; they were generally technical specialists in finance, IT, marketing or HR working away from their base office to provide the operational parts of the business with the necessary support. They were generally referred to as 'Martini' workers, because they were prepared to work and talk anytime, anyplace, anywhere. This was a reference to an advert for that particular drink in which it was suggested that it could contribute to a certain lifestyle by being available and acceptable 'anytime, anyplace, anywhere'.

Standard basic equipment for employees like Martha included a laptop computer and mobile phone. Each day wherever they worked they would hook-up to the company communication system and check their e-mail inbox. It was never empty! Martha, like most people within the company received something like 60 e-mails every working day, most with no direct relevance to the projects that they were involved with. Each e-mail had to be read, just in case, but Martha tended to find that she was one of about 30–50 people who had been copied into a particular e-mail in what could only be described as electronic back-covering by the originator. Such people could not be bothered to identify who actually needed to know what they were saying; or thought it better to tell everyone to prevent any comeback in the future; or wanted to play politics by getting their name known as widely as possible or perhaps by trying to show how clever and important they were. It was frustrating for Martha to have to go through all of this material and she frequently became annoyed and frustrated with the process, but could not find a way of avoiding the need to work through her e-mails every day. It took at least an hour out of her working day, and when she was away from home she tended to leave it until she was back in her hotel in the evening as there was little to do then and it minimized the need to take time out of her busy schedule during the day.

However the mobile telephone was a different technological wonder. Martha was forever getting text messages and phone calls about work and projects that she was working on. The people ringing her took no account of the current project that Martha was engaged on; they simply rang when it suited them. When she was engaged in a meeting or development programme, Martha always turned her phone off so that she could not be disturbed. However, this meant that she always had a number of messages waiting for her when she switched it back on. This gave her more tasks to perform when she was able to return the calls; sometimes people e-mailed as well as phoned, leading to some confusion and duplication. Inevitably Martha tended to deal with many of her phone messages in the evening when she returned to her hotel. However, depending on the time differences between Martha's location and the location of the message originator this could be difficult. On occasions, Martha rang a colleague's mobile only to find that they were at home, resentful of the fact that their free time had been interrupted with work matters, let alone that they may not have the appropriate information to hand. Not surprisingly this led to some friction between colleagues as Martha also complained that she was working much longer hours and away from home and had no choice but to call when she did. If a colleague did not answer their phone in person then it inevitably led to messages going back and forward, perhaps even e-mails being used to communicate whatever the message was about.

This was the reality of the work experience for Martha and many of her colleagues. It was wasteful of their time and energy and added considerably to their working hours. It also reduced the time they had to talk to their families when they were away from home which placed a strain of that most important of relationships. But what could Martha do? Her specialist area involved helping other people to use technology more effectively in support of their lives, yet she could not help herself with her own technology-driven overload problem!

Tasks

1. What would you do if you were Martha and faced with this situation?
2. What advice would you offer Martha about how to deal with the demands of technology-based communication if you were her boss?
3. What should organizations do to ensure the effective use of technology within their organizations?

FURTHER READING

Castells, M (2002) *The Internet Galaxy: Reflections on the Internet, Business and Society*, Oxford University Press, Oxford. Makes the case that the internet is more than just a technology, reflecting the backbone of the future economy and what we need to understand in order to make it contribute to business and personal success.

Clark, H, Chandler, J and Barry, J (1994) *Organization and Identities: Text and Readings in Organizational Behaviour*, International Thomson Business Press, London. Contains a broad range of original articles on relevant material themes and from significant writers referred to in this and other textbooks on management and organizations.

Clark, J (ed.) (1993) *Human Resource Management and Technical Change*, Sage, London. This text does not consider specifically the organizational behaviour issues associated with new technology, but it does reflect on the nature of technical change in its broadest sense and the human resource issues that emerge.

Haddad, CJ (2002) *Managing Technological Change: A Strategic Partnership Approach*, Sage, London. Looks at the successful (and unsuccessful) implementation of technological change and factors such as the involvement of key stakeholders that can increase the probability of success.

Haydu, J (1988) *Between Craft and Class: Skilled Workers and Factory Politics in the United States and Britain, 1890–1922*, University of California Press, Berkeley. Considers the reaction of skilled metalworkers to the economic changes surrounding them as a result of new production methods emerging in the early twentieth century. The author places this process in the context of the emergence of different approaches to collective effort as a means of attempting to achieve greater influence on management decision making.

Stair, R and Reynolds, G (2001) *Principles of Information Systems*, Thomson Learning, New York. Introduces the basics of technology in relation to the business uses to which it can be put.

van Slyke, C and Belanger, F (2002) *Electronic Business Technologies*, Wiley, New York. Provides an introduction to e-business and the technologies used to support it.

Woolgar, S (ed.) (2002) *Virtual Society? Technology, Cyberbole, Reality*, Oxford University Press, Oxford. Considers the effect on society of the developing electronic technologies.

COMPANION WEBSITE

Online teaching and learning resources:

Visit the companion website for Organizational Behaviour and Management 3rd edition at: *http://www.thomsonlearning.co.uk/businessandmanagement/martin3* to find valuable further teaching and learning material:

Refer to page 35 for full details.

CHAPTER 15

Organizational structure and design

LEARNING OBJECTIVES

After studying the chapter content and working through the associated Management in Action panels, Employee Perspectives, Discussion Questions and Case Study, you should be able to:

- **Outline the main structural choices available to organizations.**
- **Detail how the need to compartmentalize the work of an organization is at variance with the need to integrate activities.**
- **Assess the significance of the development of more recent approaches to structure such as the shamrock and federal organization.**
- **Explain the limitations of the standard organization chart in describing activity within an organization.**
- **Discuss the contingency model and its relationship to organizational structure.**

INTRODUCTION

There has always existed a need to arrange the resources of an organization in such a way that will achieve the objectives set for it, in the most effective manner possible. Imagine the organization structure necessary to build the great pyramid of Cheops in Egypt. It covers an area of 13 acres and was constructed from approximately 2.5 million blocks of stone, each weighing an average of 2.5 tons. Construction is estimated to have lasted some 20 years involving a total labour force of 100 000 men (George, 1972, p 4).

Obviously, there are many differences between the way work was organized in ancient Egypt and the way in which it is organized today, but organizational design decisions had to be made even then. The framework of an organization in any age represents the way the designers interpret, in the light of prevailing models and fashion, the objectives to be achieved matched together with the human and technological resources available. That such decisions can have an impact on the performance of the firm is illustrated through the recent study of the two largely parallel stock markets within India, the Bombay Stock Exchange (BSE) and the National Stock Exchange (NSE). These organizations are involved in the same activities and trade essentially identical stocks, but are owned differently and have different organization structures. Using a standard industry measure of market quality the NSE was found to provide a superior quality market compared to BSE (Krishnamurti *et al.* 2003). Most organizational designers are faced with adapting that which already exists – in many ways a more complex process than creating a new organization. Changing an existing organization structure requires a major effort by all concerned, particularly if it is a large and complex entity.

PERSPECTIVES ON ORGANIZATIONAL STRUCTURE

Traditional approaches to organizing emphasized the task aspects of the work being undertaken in the structure of the organization. In essence it represented an approach to organization which reinforced hierarchical control and segmented responsibilities. This section will explore a number of the major views in relation to the nature and significance of structure, from a range of theoretical, applied and symbolic perspectives.

Three perspectives on determinism

What is it that determines the structure that an organization adopts? One view (the deterministic approach) holds that structure is a function of one of two possibilities. First, that technology is the main determination of structure. The second holds that it is situational or other environmental factors that determine structure. The third, non-deterministic perspective, holds that organization structure is a function of managerial choice. The topic of technology and its relationship with structure was discussed in the previous chapter. Environmental determinism is based on the view of an organization as an interactive part of its own environment and will be more fully explored below. Figure 15.1 reflects a number of the environmental factors that impact on any organization. Managerial choice in the process is reflected in the ways in which these forces are interpreted and subsequently acted upon by managers.

It is possible to reconcile the different approaches to organizational structure in that managerial choice does not totally negate the influence of determinism. For example, Woodward (1965) pointed out that there was a tendency for organizations to be more successful if they followed the norms for their industry and technology. This suggests that managers interpret situations, the outcome of which results in different structural forms. This view is also evident in the work of Lawrence and Lorsch (1967).

FIGURE 15.1

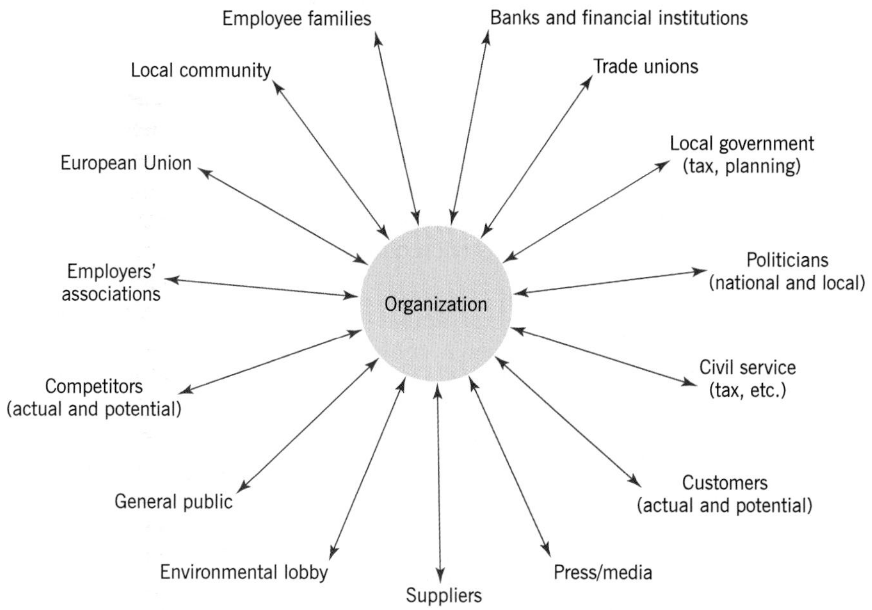

Organizational environments

For a more recent review of the relationship between technology and structure see Mukherji (2002). However, given Woodward's findings, managerial choice is perhaps an intervening variable between environment and structure, with the consequences being apparent in the level of success achieved by the organization.

Weber and bureaucracy

The essence of bureaucracy with its hierarchy of control, rule frameworks and task specialization was first articulated by Weber (1947). His ideas were developed in the early years of the twentieth century, a time when organizations were generally becoming much larger and more complex but did not have the benefits of technology to aid the process. The consequence was a need to develop the human equivalent of the computer in administering large organizations efficiently – the bureaucracy. Weber described this need in terms of a machine analogy. He likened the benefits available from bureaucracy to the advantages to be gained in manufacturing through the application of machines and factory-based technology. Weber's main areas of research interest were in the sociology of religion and the sociology of economic activity. One of his major contributions was his study of the power and authority relationships within organizations. He postulated three types of organizational form differentiated through the way in which authority was legitimized within them. He described these organizational forms as ideal types – not necessarily found in the precise form described. He also suggested that any combination, or even all three might exist within parts of the same organization. The three types of organization were:

1. *Charismatic*. In the charismatic form of organization authority is based around the personal qualities of the leader. Frequently found in religious or political movements, this type of organization might also be found among small owner-managed companies in the commercial world. However, as a result of the strong reliance on the charismatic qualities and authority of the leader the issue of succession is invariably a problem that is not easy to resolve. If the

succession process can be institutionalized then the organization invariably transforms into one of the two remaining categories.

2. *Traditional*. The traditional form of organization relies on accepted precedent as the dominant form of authority. The leader in such an organization relies on tradition and accepted custom as the basis of being obeyed. It maintains the status quo by constantly referring back to precedent or position as the ultimate arbiter of the legitimacy of a rule or instruction. Many family-owned organizations rely on this form of organization as leadership and authority are restricted to family members, irrespective of ability or experience.
3. *Rational–legal*. The rational–legal notion of authority forms the basis of the bureaucratic form of organization according to Weber. This approach is termed rational because the organization is established to achieve specific (rational) objectives. It is also legal in the sense that it adopts a rule- and procedure-based approach to the exercise of authority. The exercise of authority is prescribed by the rule frameworks and is therefore independent of the individual post-holder. Weber argued that this allowed precision, speed, continuity, unity, strict subordination and the minimization of labour cost, etc. All of the resources of the organization are effectively directed at the objectives being sought, without undue interference or whim.

The basis of a bureaucratic form of organization is reflected in Table 15.1, adapted from Scott (1992). The points included do not individually or collectively suggest a specific structural form in itself, but more an approach to the process of arranging the resources, including people. If these principles and guidelines are followed whatever the framework adopted actually looks like, it will be bureaucratic in essence and approach. It reflects an attempt to provide a sound basis for a factory-based analogy to efficiency at a time when neither computer nor administrative technology was well developed. Weber also linked his ideas on bureaucracy to his views in relation to economic development and the emergence of Protestantism with its associated work ethic.

Gouldner (1954) introduced the idea that there existed different types of bureaucracy. He suggested that the three types of bureaucracy were:

Characteristics of bureaucracy
Fixed division of labour
Postholders selected on the basis of capability
Postholders appointed and not elected
Administrative basis for keeping files and records
Separation of business and private affairs
Postholders paid by salary paid in money
Work in the organization is primarily occupation of postholder
Promotion based on achievement or seniority
Rules govern work routines
Depersonalization of decision making
Disciplined approach to work required

TABLE 15.1 Bureaucratic form of organization

1. *Mock*. The rules and procedures in a **mock bureaucracy** are largely ignored by all inside the bureaucracy, having been imposed on them by an outside agency.
2. *Punishment*. In practice the **punishment bureaucracy** represents a variant on the mock bureaucracy in that the rules are imposed on the workers inside the organization. However, the difference is that in the punishment bureaucracy it is management alone that develops the rules and procedures and then imposes them on the other groups. Not surprisingly, Gouldner felt that this approach would not encourage the full commitment and support of the employees because they did not accept the legitimate basis of the authority implied under these circumstances. Some of the issues that arise in situations in which management seeks to impose control within a university are described in the following Employee Perspective (15.1).
3. *Representative*. In a **representative bureaucracy** the rules and procedures are generally supported by those inside the organization having been developed by managers with the involvement of the other worker and stakeholder groups.

Mock bureaucracy
Organizational rules and procedures are largely ignored by all inside, having been imposed by an outside agency.

Punishment bureaucracy
A variant on the mock bureaucracy in that rules are imposed on the workers by management.

Representative bureaucracy
The rules and procedures are generally supported within the organization having been developed by managers with employee involvement.

A number of criticisms have been levelled at bureaucracy, based on the negative impact on people. Weber himself recognized the potential negative effect of boring, routine and monotonous jobs on the people who did them, but insisted that it was the only way to create efficient administrative and organizational structures. It is also the basis of work by Merton (1968) who describes the development of a bureaucratic personality as a result of being tied to the application of rules and fixed procedures. This is similar to the notion of the 'organization man phenomenon' described by Whyte (1956) in which he describes in graphic detail the implications of working and succeeding in a bureaucracy. Another view of bureaucracy is that the tight structures and procedures that are evident in the principles of it cannot eliminate the political and interactive human behaviour. Crozier (1964) studied a number of bureaucracies and described them in terms of dynamic social systems. He identified individuals who sought ways to achieve their own goals and position in the overall scheme of things through capitalizing on areas of uncertainty or ambiguity in the rules, procedures and responsibilities of individuals and groups within the organization.

In recent years the concept of bureaucracy has become a term of derision. This is as a result partly of the inability of bureaucracies to change with the times and partly of the frequently perceived unwillingness of staff in such organizations (at least from the customer perspective) to bend the rules and accommodate non-standard events. Equally, the notion of a bureaucratic form of organization is not appropriate to all situations. For example, organizations that operate in an industry or market in which flexibility or adaptability represent key factors for success will not do well if they are bureaucratic in structure. Also organizations that employ large numbers of professional employees (accountancy or legal practices being examples) would not get the best out of the staff if they relied on bureaucratic structuring. As Hatch (1997, p 172) suggests professionals are highly trained and socialized to adopt high standards of both work quality and performance and so rules and procedures seeking closely to direct such employees are redundant and offensive to them. The previous Employee Perspective panel addresses just this issue.

Organ and Greene (1981) carried out a study among research scientists and engineers in an attempt to measure the tension between the control inherent within a bureaucracy and the desires of such professionals to operate under self-actualization conditions in their work. Their conclusions suggested that bureaucratic structures can assist in the management of such professionals through the formalized structures and the resulting clarity in role expectations that exist. Also, a higher degree of clarity in the position (and contribution) of the individual in the total organizational context

EMPLOYEE PERSPECTIVE 15.1 Control through workload models

Pam worked as a lecturer at a university in England that had originally been a polytechnic. It recruited large numbers of students and the teaching was done in large groups often involving a teaching team of six people delivering a module to about 500 students. The management of the university were short of money and sought to reduce the cost of teaching by increasing the average class size and by forcing lecturers to follow standardized procedures in doing their work.

Among the processes introduced by management was a workload model which sought to apply work measurement to the activities that lecturers were engaged in. For every task to be undertaken a time value was allocated and each lecturer had to account for a given number of work hours each year. Standard forms were also introduced for providing written feedback to students and also for recording the comments of staff on batches of scripts (for external examiner review and quality assessment purposes). Procedures for dealing with students were prescribed and forms were introduced to record all such interactions. Most of the changes made were introduced with little or no consultation with lecturers. The style of the university moved away from a collegiate approach with staff being heavily involved in all decision areas, to a managerial one in which managers decided what should be done which was then communicated to lecturers as an instruction. Lecturing staff including Pam began to feel that they were not valued and were being taken for granted by not being treated as the professionals that they were supposed to be.

Naturally over time resentment began to arise among Pam and her colleagues and they sought to retain some degree of control over their work, careers and what they perceived as the standards of university education. Inevitably staff began to cut corners (as management would describe it) in seeking to retain some degree of control over their work environment and to be able to get through the volume of work demanded of them. For example, forms might not be completed in the timescale prescribed, or they might not be filled in as fully as required by management. Pam undertook a range of activities for which she was not allowed any time in her workload hours and so she stopped attending the many meetings that became part of the management control process. Also she became less available to students after lectures to deal with their questions. Pam always fulfilled the minimum requirements of her job and did not place herself in a position where management could discipline her for not doing her job properly, but she (along with most other lecturers) resented the ways in which they were being managed by the university. Consequently, she (along with everyone else) sought ways to cope as effectively she could in the circumstances by giving priority to those things that she judged to be important.

Inevitably over time the number and severity of student complaints began to increase. Also most lecturers were constantly looking for other jobs or thinking of ways to change careers in an attempt to escape the pressure of working in that particular environment. The only staff to remain for any length of time were those who could not get a job elsewhere, those who were trapped in that location for family or other personal reasons and those who for whatever reason aligned themselves to the management approach and supported the changes made. Pam concentrated on work and activities that supported her personal career plans irrespective of the workload and other requirements imposed on her. She avoided as much work as it was possible to and moved to another university after about two years.

Tasks

1. How would you react to this situation (and why) if you were Pam?
2. Could such an approach to running a university ever provide an appropriate experience for students in higher education? Why or why not?
3. Can management ever effectively manage professional staff such as lecturers through conventional bureaucracy approaches and top-down management practice? Why or why not?
4. How could professional services such as a university be managed to ensure the best result for all stakeholders within a cost effective process?

exists, which helps them judge their value relative to others. This has led some writers to suggest a differentiation between a machine bureaucracy in which the objective is to manage an administrative operation which is relatively stable and predictable and a professional bureaucracy in which the control processes need to be different in focus and intention in the management of professionals.

Fayol and classical management

Fayol was a practising manager who wrote from his experience in running the mining company in which he spent his entire working life, eventually becoming general manager. In his 1916 book he identified the operations necessary to run a company as:

- *Technical*. The production and manufacturing activities.
- *Commercial*. Purchasing and sales activities.
- *Financial*. Funding and control of capital.
- *Security*. Protection of goods, people and the organization.
- *Accounting*. Stockholding, costing and statistical information.
- *Managerial*. The management process of organizing, co-ordinating, commanding, controlling, forecasting and planning.

Fayol also identified a number of principles associated with the management process which he considered impacted on the structure of the organization. They included centralization and decentralization, the division of work into compartments and the unity of command, principles still important in today's organizations. The basic approach to organizing described by Fayol has been developed by a number of people over the years and has become known as classical management theory. Names such as Mary Parker Follett, Oliver Sheldon, Lyndall Urwick and James Mooney are all commonly linked to these ideas. That is not to suggest that they all worked together (or even in the same country), but their ideas were broadly similar and so common themes between them could be identified. Lussato (1976) described his views on what were the main principles associated with classical management theory (see Table 15.2). In a real sense, the classical approach to organizing adapted and went beyond the administrative and control emphasis of bureaucracy and emphasized the need to consider the whole organization in structural and process terms.

The size of an organization and the complexity of operational activity create the need for the work to be compartmentalized in order to ensure that it can be done.

Scalar chain	Hierarchy of grades seniority
Exception principle	Delegation of decision making to the lowest level possible
Unity of command	Each employee should have only one boss
Organizational specialization	Creation of appropriate departments and functions
Span of control	The achievment of an optimal number of subordinates for each boss
Application of scientific management	The application of FW Taylor's ideas in running organizations through the use of work study techniques and principles

TABLE 15.2 Classic form of management

Kanter (1983) described this as segmentalism in which individuals restrict themselves to the 'boxes' implicit within bureaucratic frameworks. This she contrasted with the entrepreneurial spirit found in successful organizations. The dilemma facing managers when they contemplate the design and structure of an organization is that structure creates differentiation and task-based efficiency, because it segments, often on the basis of function. For example, the production department is separated from the marketing department. This represents the classic structural configuration of an organization (Figure 15.2). On the other hand, following segmentation there is a need for the integration of activity and effort in order to be able to deliver the whole product or service. The work of the marketing department must be integrated with that of the production department if customer needs are to be met. Bureaucracy seeks to achieve this balance through procedure and work routines, but at the cost of responsiveness. Innovative organizations seek to avoid the dilemma by adopting other structural approaches.

The main advantage of this classical type of structure is that a high degree of expertise and efficiency can be achieved as a result of the opportunity for individuals to concentrate on a relatively small range of duties. The main problem with such structural arrangements is that they encourage the achievement of functional and personal objectives as opposed to the overall objectives of the organization. This view can be identified in the research interviews carried out by Watson (1994) in which one manager reported:

> They [managers] are far more interested in steam-rollering in these new things [changes to work practices] so that they can move on in their careers than they are in trying to understand people and show them how these new ideas will advantage everybody. (p 155)

Watson's research demonstrates the extensive processes used to balance segmentation with integration when one of his interviewees reported that a customer order passed through 14 different pairs of hands before arriving in the manufacturing department (p 149). The relative slowness of the decision making within this type of framework, together with the potential for interfunctional conflict, is easy to envisage.

Foucault – power and control through structure

From a philosophical perspective Michael Foucault considers many issues associated with the need for co-ordination and differentiation. He does this through a wide range of publications not specifically associated with commercial organizations, but in such a way that pertinent themes and critical evaluations can be identified. Townley (1994) provides an insightful analysis of his work from an organizational perspective. Among the relevant features identified from his work on the nature of structure are:

- *Enclosure.* In creating an enclosure, boundaries are created allowing distinctions to be drawn between distinct entities. This compartmentalization

FIGURE 15.2

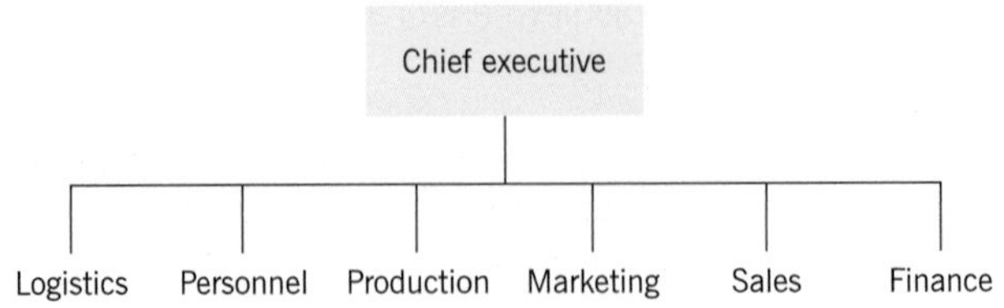

Functional organization structure

together circumstances and structure, but in a different way from the traditional view. The traditional view seeks to impose a cause and effect relationship between circumstances and structure. The contingency model takes a more holistic view and suggests that structure is the result of a range of forces impacting upon the situation, management's interpretation of them and the identified business objectives. Figure 15.4 illustrates the contingency model.

Taking each element in the model illustrated in Figure 15.4 in turn:

- *External contingency factors*. There are a wide range of external factors that impact on the situation. For example, the activities of competitors, the industry in which the organization operates and the location will all impact on the structural arrangements adopted. Burns and Stalker (1961) developed the concepts of mechanistic and organismic to describe the way in which an organization is organized relative to its environment. Mechanistic refers to organizational forms that tend to emerge in stable and predictable conditions. In essence it reflects the application of clear hierarchical structures and specialization of tasks. In that sense it holds many similarities to the bureaucratic form of organization. Organismic reflects an organizational form emerging in fluid and relatively unpredictable situations. It is typified by a high level of flexibility in job responsibilities, also incorporating high levels of technical expertise at the lower levels of the organization and recognition of the value of individual contribution.

  Lawrence and Lorsch (1967) extended the work of Burns and Stalker through what they termed integration and differentiation. Integration reflects how co-ordination between departments was brought about. They viewed this as mediation to incorporate the genuinely different qualities and perspectives existing in different functions. Differentiation reflects the variety of perspectives and approaches adopted by managers to such issues as formality of structure, interpersonal relationships, etc. Their conclusions were that in complex, uncertain environments high levels of both differentiation and integration were needed for success. In more stable environments, while it was necessary to have high degrees of integration, lower levels of differentiation could produce success.
- *Internal contingency factors*. There are a wide range of internal forces that influence structure. For example, production technology and the size of the

FIGURE 15.4

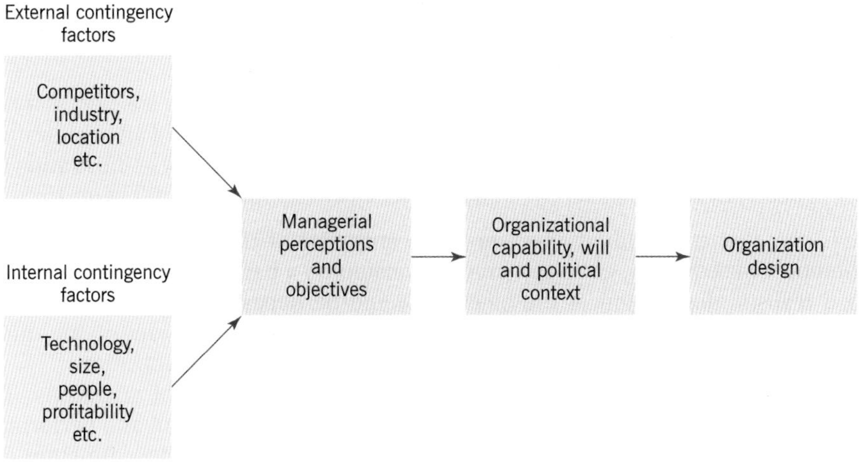

Contingency model of organization design

organization. Child (1988) argues that in very large organizations those adopting a bureaucratic approach to organizing were likely to be more profitable and grow faster than less bureaucratic organizations. Birkinshaw *et al.* (2002) demonstrate that the knowledge base within an organization is one of the variables that impacts on the structural arrangements adopted.

- *Managerial perceptions and objectives*. There are few situations where a manager is given the opportunity to create an organization from first principles; it usually involves changing an existing design. This can involve adapting to circumstances such as a new product introduction or competitive threat. Personal preference and preconceptions about how things should be organized influence the basis of responding to circumstances. Culturally determined perspectives and preferences also influence the way in which managers exercise their roles (Child and Kieser, 1979).
- *Organizational capability, will and politics*. The organization needs to have the capability to achieve its desired objectives. If an organization does not possess the expertise to do something or the will to make changes happen then it is likely to fail to match the needs of its situation. To succeed in adapting or changing an organization the political realities must be taken into account and appropriate strategies developed.

The contingency model is very useful for explaining the diversity in organizational design that is found to exist. It provides for the forces external to the organization to be mixed with forces internal to the company. These are interpreted by managers and filtered through capability etc. to produce a structure that will be specific to that organization at a particular point in time.

It was during the 1960s that the Industrial Administration Research Unit emerged at Aston University as a leading multidisciplinary research group. They developed a research approach which examined three elements (Pugh and Hickson, 1989, pp 9–15):

1. *Change and complexity*. Because of the degree of change to which organizations are subjected, it is necessary to develop theories that are incremental rather than discrete. The structure of an organization is the result of a number of forces acting upon (and interacting with) the situation.
2. *Institutional arrangements*. These include the control, hierarchical and work arrangements that exist. In many organizations these arrangements exist before employees join and will be there after they leave. Consequently, individuals are slightly detached from total ownership as they are in practice custodians of these features during their employment.
3. *Multiple perspectives*. In order to create a full understanding it is necessary to consider more than one point of view. Different perceptions of an organization might exist among the different stakeholder groups. One way of illustrating this necessity is to consider the notion of perspective, illustrated in Figure 15.5.

Each one of the individual observers sees only part of the shape and each view is different. Consequently, each can only be considered a partial reflection of the whole. For a realistic description of the object it would be necessary to integrate the three individual reports into a cohesive framework. The approach of identifying multiple perspectives is much more complex for social entities such as organizations.

The contingency model has been the subject of a number of criticisms. These include the fact that it assumes a relationship between organization and performance. The achievement of organizational performance is assumed to be a function of the structure and degree of fit with the environmental forces acting upon the situation. This ignores the ability and performance of managers at a personal level together with

FIGURE 15.5

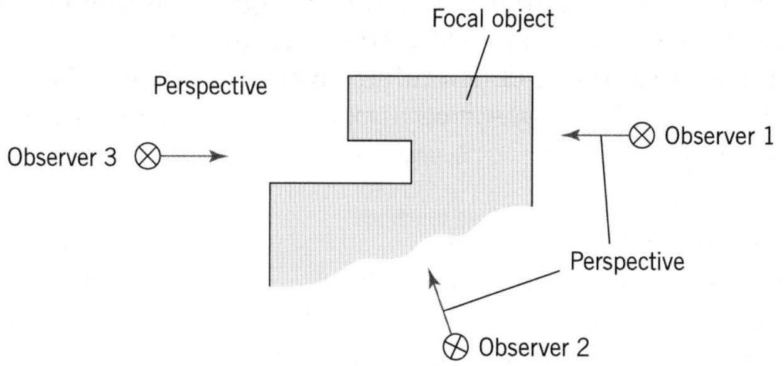

Multiple perspectives of an object

a range of other factors independent of structure. For example, an incompetent sales person is unlikely to win many orders irrespective of the structure of the sales department. Legge (1978) suggests that the contingency model is intuitively attractive because it contains powerful normative connotations. It encourages the view that effectiveness could be achieved if only the context could be interpreted properly, retaining the essence of a formulaic approach to success. The contingency model does not take account of the role of power or control in dynamic work relationships. In addition, technology, for example, is not a neutral force within an organization. Managers decide that they will utilize a particular form of technology and they decide upon its use and application in order to achieve particular objectives, including control over operational processes. They therefore determine to a significant extent how a range of factors will impact on the process of organizing.

Systems views of an organization

The notion of a system originated in the physical sciences as a means of reflecting how a number of elements or subsystems interact within a cohesive whole. It has since been integrated into the social sciences and with particular success in the explanation of how organizations function. The open systems view of an organization is profound, yet in essence very simple (see Figure 15.6) and is based on the work of Katz and Kahn (1966). As an open system the organization is in an interactive relationship with its environment. It is very much a cyclical and interactive process. For example, the Ford Motor Company makes motor vehicles which it sells to its customers for money. The money thus obtained is recycled in the form of wages, tax payments and the purchase of raw materials. Information is also part of this process. For example, if a particular model is not selling, or is selling very quickly, the manufacturing process (or pricing policy) can be adjusted very quickly to respond to the new situation.

The basis of the open systems model is that a company starts life with only the essential core of the business present (along with minimal levels of support). This is essential to the creation of the organization as without it the organization could not achieve its intended purpose. It is only later, according to Katz and Kahn, that the organization begins to elaborate itself by adding adaptive or buffering functions, thereby creating more elaborate structural frameworks. These adaptive functions can include personnel, accounting, public relations, marketing and research and development for example.

The process of elaboration goes through a number of stages as follows:

- Activities such as purchasing and marketing become structurally separated from the core operations tasks. This forms the start of the buffering of the main operations process in order to protect it from the instability of the market and suppliers.

FIGURE 15.6

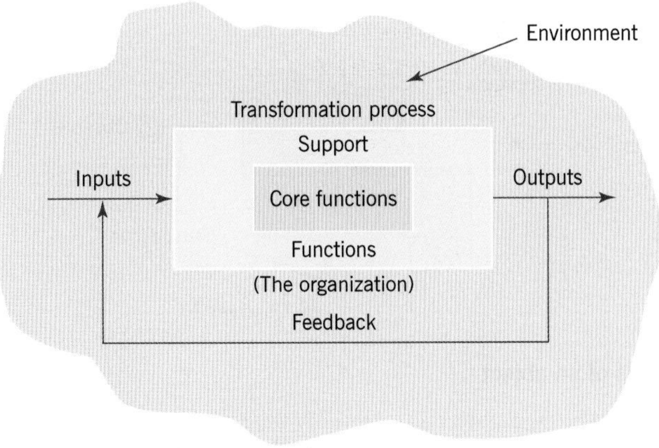

Open systems model of an organization

- Pressure to integrate the already established functions begins to arise in order to prevent the tendency to compartmentalize and fragment effort.
- The growth in the organization by this stage in its development frequently brings a number of needs not previously encountered, which must be dealt with. For example, improved equipment maintenance, the recruitment of staff and the demands of local and national government for information and tax revenues. The inclusion of these activities reflects a second tier of support to the organization. They become necessary to prepare and preserve aspects of the organization's environment so that the core functions can concentrate on the main purpose of the business. The inclusion of these less direct activities is usually accompanied by the arrival of new levels of managers, some of whom supervise the work of other managers.
- The next stage of the organization's evolution is likely to bring with it the need to be able to deal with product diversity and increasing sales volume. There emerges a need for higher levels in the sophistication of the approach to production planning, raw materials and supplies management and customer satisfaction issues in order to protect cashflow and reputation.
- As the company further evolves it will encounter new situations and will inevitably respond by further elaborating itself and its social structures and organizational framework.

This last stage is likely to continue until the organization is faced with the need to take stock of its position. Perhaps this might be forced on the organization as a result of economic downturn; competitor pressure; rising cost of labour; or perhaps the arrival of alternative products or services onto the market. Whatever the cause, the process of elaboration will cease and a redesign will be undertaken in order to take account of the new circumstances. This model is not dissimilar to the model proposed by Greiner (1972) introduced later in this chapter.

Strategy and structure

Figure 15.7 illustrates a strategic management perspective, intended to produce alignment between the organization and its identified objectives. Decisions resulting from this process have a significant impact on organizational design considerations. Structure in this context is the means by which effort is co-ordinated and through which results are achieved. Indeed, Porter (1985, p 23) argues that: 'Each generic

FIGURE 15.7

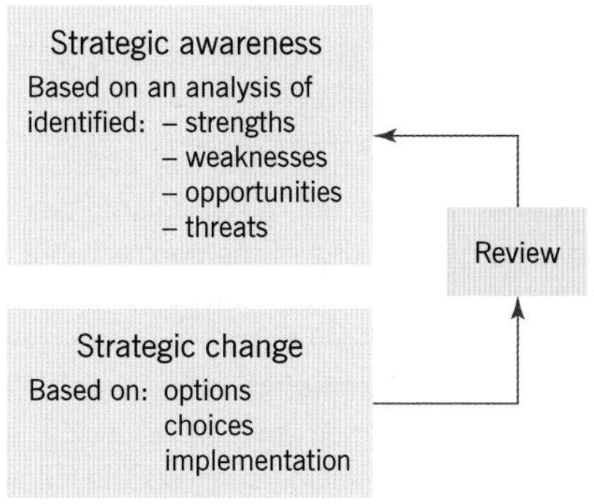

Strategic management approach (*adapted from:* Thompson, JL (1990) *Strategic Management Awareness and Change International,* International Thomson Publishing, London)

[competitive] strategy implies different skills and requirements for success, which commonly translate into differences in organizational structure and culture.'

The strategic approach to structure begins with an intention to create understanding of the environment within which the organization is functioning. Once in an understandable form this then becomes amenable to manipulation through the decision-making process. Management in Action 15.2 illustrates the strategic links with structure in attempts by local government to improve service delivery and reduce cost. This involves not only reorganizing activities but outsourcing whole departments to specialist providers. From this brief review of the significance of structure it is apparent that it is management that defines the boundaries and content of organizations. They also construct the reality which determines what employees must adapt to. This provides management with a range of benefits other than an ability to meet operational objectives. It is also clear from Management in Action 15.1 that these are difficult objectives to achieve.

ORGANIZATIONAL LIFECYCLE

It is well understood that products go through a lifecycle. A new product is designed and introduced to the marketplace. If it is successful then sales will begin to grow rapidly. Eventually, the level of sales will stabilize as the product becomes mature. Thereafter, sales will decline as the market changes and newer products emerge. Eventually, the product will be withdrawn as it no longer meets the need for which it was intended. Occasionally, a new lease of life will be generated for old products based on fashion or changes in taste.

The Greiner (1972) model of organizational growth (Figure 15.8) reflects this lifecycle perspective. Also see the Katz and Kahn discussion above. But is organizational growth always followed by death or even contraction in size? The creation of large numbers of new companies each year is inevitably followed by the failure of a large number early in their existence. In that sense there is a lifecycle. However, a number of companies will change form and many will be taken over and absorbed into other organizations. Have such companies died or ceased to exist in any meaningful way? Equally, companies that go into receivership and have their assets sold, only to reappear in another guise or under new ownership could be said to have died or survived, depending upon the definition of 'death'.

MANAGEMENT IN ACTION 15.1 Outsourcing service departments

Outsourcing is now a common feature of everyday life in organizations as they increasingly seek better value for money. This occurs in areas either not regarded as core business activity, or those determined as being capable of being delivered more effectively by specialists in the field. Capita is the largest provider of outsourced professional services to the public sector. For the first seven months of 2002, it won new contracts to the value of £1.1 billion, including a single 10-year contract worth £500 million to administer TV licensing in Britain. It is not uncommon for example, to find this company running a broad range of services, including the entire human resource function within district councils.

However, not every contract runs smoothly. For example, in the late 1990s, the London Borough of Lambeth transferred its housing benefit service to Capita, as it was seen as being expensive and not offering a good service when under council management. The contract was valued at £48 million, about half of the then cost of providing the service in-house. Instead of improving, the service deteriorated further and the Local Government Ombudsman and Benefit Fraud Inspectorate became involved, following many complaints from the public. Claims, which by law had to be processed in 14 days, were taking 87 days to complete and there were some 35 000 pieces of unopened mail waiting to be dealt with. The subsequent investigation identified that there were as many problems with the council as with the contractor in running the contract which led to the problems not being dealt with effectively. The council had failed to invoke penalty clauses in the contract when the problems deteriorated, and had no person responsible for ensuring that the contract was being delivered as expected. A partnership board was set up to review the working of the contract, but all this did was avoid any adversarial dimension to the relationship.

So what are the key points to be able to utilize outsourcing effectively? Philip Vernon, European Partner and outsourcing specialist at Mercer HR Consulting suggests the following:

- *Be clear why you are going into outsourcing.* Simply doing so to offload problems will inevitably cause difficulties.
- Ensure that both parties have a common view of what the client wants out of the relationship, and the delivery objectives.
- *Check the contractor's track-record.* Have they the ability to deliver what they claim to be able to do?
- *Do the calculations.* What exactly is the cost of the present service, and what exactly are the parameters and what does it deliver? Remember, extra services (not in the original service agreement) will be charged at extra cost.
- *Ask the question, "Can we work with this contractor"?* You need to be able to trust and have confidence in them over the life of the contract.
- *Manage the contract.* Outsourcing is not the same as handing over complete responsibility. You need to manage the contractor, just as closely (if not closer) as an internal department would be managed. Potential problems and difficulties need to be identified and dealt with early in the relationship.

Adapted from: Hammond, D (2002) It shouldn't happen to a vetting, *People Management,* 21 November, p 32–7.

Stop ↔ Consider

Why might outsourcing provide a more effective and cheaper way of delivering a service than an in-house department?

Why might it not be possible for these advantages to be achieved through in-house provision?

Who is the employer as far as the employees would be concerned? What impact might that have on how they go about their job? What might the implications of this have on organization structure and how such employees should be managed?

FIGURE 15.8

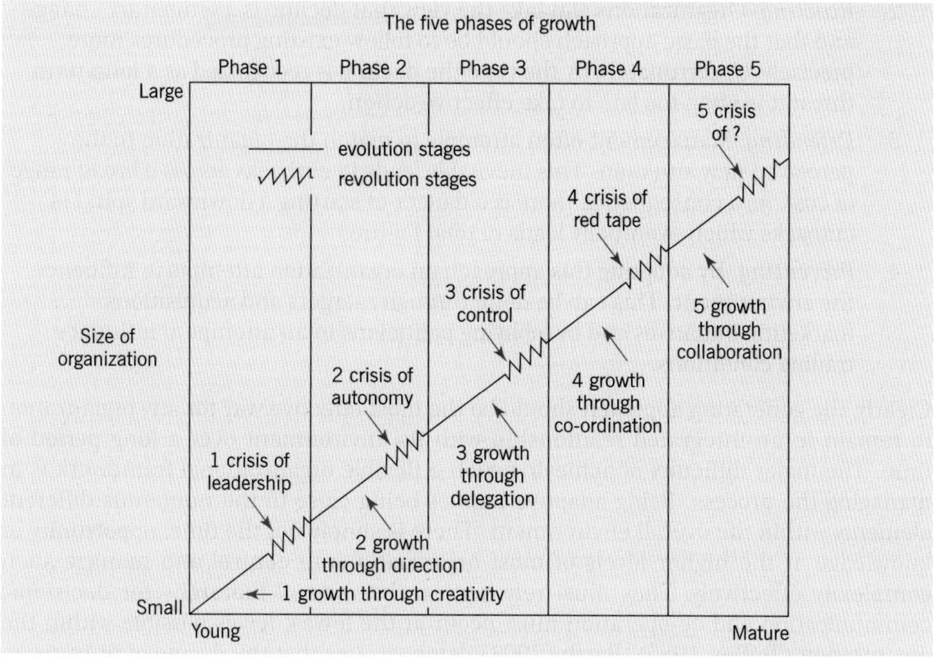

The growing pains of an organization (adapted and reprinted by permission of *Harvard Business Review*. The Growing Pains of an Organization, from *Evolution, revolution as organizations grow*, by Greiner, L, May/June 1978, p 58. Copyright by the Harvard Business School Publishing Corporation, all rights reserved)

Quinn and Cameron (1983) describe four organizational lifecycle phases:

1. *Entrepreneurial phase*. This stage is typified by the presence of an owner/manager, little formal control and an emphasis on survival.
2. *Collectivity phase*. During this phase it becomes less easy for the owner/manager to control every aspect of the business and delegation becomes a key part of the process.
3. *Formalization phase*. During this phase an organization is mature, stable and predictable. Achieved through the development of rules, procedures, meetings and communication between people.
4. *Elaboration phase*. The next phase introduces a process of differentiation into the organization as it attempts to fight stagnation. It could include the introduction of a holding-company concept or of a divisionalized structure in an attempt to allow innovation and increase motivation and performance.

To these four stages a fifth can be added based on the work of writers such as Cameron *et al.* (1988):

5. *Organizational decline*. There are two forms of decline. The first is a decline in absolute terms, a reduction in the physical size of the organization. The second relates to what could be described as relative decline, through stagnation. The lethargy brought on as a result of age, size, bureaucracy and passivity towards the competitive environment allows competitors to dominate the market.

Whetten (1980) identified four response options to decline:

1. *Generating*. This is about anticipation and continual adjustment of the organization in retaining its relationship with the markets etc.

2. *Reacting*. Organizations can take the view that decline is a temporary change and that the basic approach should be to follow existing procedures more precisely. Unfortunately, by the time the decline is recognized as a long-term threat it is often too late to take effective action.
3. *Defending*. Management often attempts to match the organization to the perceived new situation. This inevitably leads to cutbacks across a broad range of cost. As a consequence there is a danger of starting a downward spiral of cutbacks which eventually leads to total failure.
4. *Preventing*. By adopting this approach an organization attempts to influence the environment. This can be done through mergers and acquisitions, marketing initiatives and by lobbying politicians in an attempt to influence trading conditions.

Clearly, the generating approach should be the most effective way for any organization to remain in an integrated relationship with its environment over a long period of time. The major difficulty of achieving such a flexible organizational framework is in managing the process. Being adaptive implies being close to the numerous different elements within the overall environment. There is simply not the time, opportunity or knowledge at the higher levels of most organizations to control and manage such complexity effectively. They must rely less on the vertical hierarchy for decisions, communication and co-operation must occur at the lowest levels possible within the organization (Toffler, 1985). Barth (2003) demonstrates that the degree of fit between the strategies followed, management skills, organization structure and the performance of the firm are related to industry maturity.

STRUCTURAL FRAMEWORKS

Among the most important decision areas that can influence the structure of an organization are:

- *Formalization*. This relates to the notion of the formality and degree of prescription involved with the way in which the organization undertakes its activities.
- *Job design*. The way individual tasks are combined together to create specific jobs influences the structure of the organization.
- *Height*. A tall structure will have different structural frameworks from one that is relatively flat. This is frequently reflected as the size and shape of the pyramid used to diagram most organizations (Figure 15.9).
- *Orientation*. An organization that is designed around the functional activities (personnel, finance, marketing, etc.) will have different structural arrangements from one organized along product lines (all activities involved with a specific product grouped together).
- *Centralization*. The degree to which an organization operates in a centralized or decentralized manner in terms of decision making and delegated authority will also influence the structural design.
- *Co-ordination*. The mechanisms for ensuring that whatever form of segmentation is adopted, the various sub-units are integrated in an effective way.

Taking these points into account we now examine the most frequently found forms of organizational structure.

FIGURE 15.9

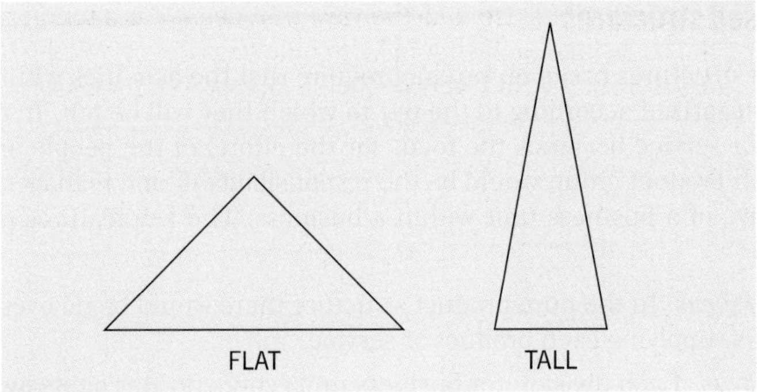

Organizational height

Entrepreneurial structures

The entrepreneurial structure is typically found in small organizations where the owner also plays an active and dominant role in running them. In the early years there may not be enough work to justify employing many staff. The simplest form of an entrepreneurial structure is shown in Figure 15.10.

In running an entrepreneurial organization all decisions of any significance are taken by the owner/manager, with employees being the resource to implement them. In this form of organization the management activities are largely inseparable from the personalities and personal preferences of the owners. Decision making is very often based on personal feelings and needs, rather than those of the business. Personal relationships feature very heavily as an important feature of the activities within this type of organization. The relative lack of size together with the direct involvement of the owner creates a scenario where everyone needs to be able to work together effectively if major problems are to be avoided. Individuals typically become involved with a wide range of tasks in order to deliver the service or complete orders on time. It is not uncommon to find the owner 'rolling up their sleeves' and undertaking the most menial tasks when necessary. In a very real sense power and authority within the organization lie with the owner/manager.

There are a considerable number of entrepreneurial organizations in both the manufacturing and service sectors. In the service sector many small partnerships exist in the field of personal services. For example, legal firms, accountancy practices, travel agencies, retail shops and restaurants. Indeed, it was part of the job creation strategy of the UK government during the 1980s to encourage the establishment of many small enterprises, the intention being to encourage unemployed people to create their own jobs and in addition to create a number of jobs for other people. The failure rate of new businesses is very high, with something like 30 per cent going into liquidation within two years. Figures for the UK for 1994 indicated that 127 482 new businesses were formed, the highest number since 1989 (*Financial Times*, 1995).

FIGURE 15.10

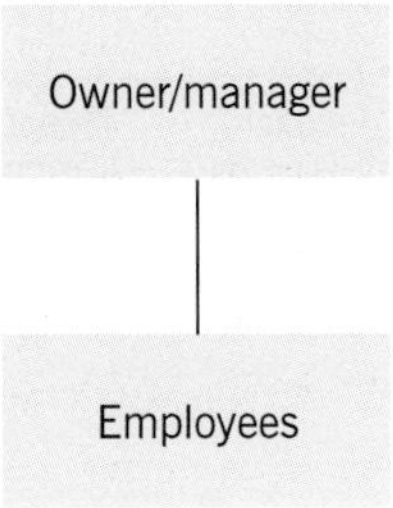

Entrepreneurial organization structure

Product-based structures

Organization structures based on product require that the activities within the organization are categorized according to the use to which they will be put. In this approach the product or service becomes the focus for the efforts of the people and resources. Typically, each product group would be the responsibility of one manager, in effect the chief executive of a business unit within a business. The key features of this type of structure are:

- *Product focus*. In the pure product structure there would be no overlap between divisions supplying each product or service.
- *Single head*. Each division (or business unit) concentrates on its own product or service range and deals with its own customers. There is invariably a manager responsible for each business unit usually with the title of divisional director or general manager.
- *Limited autonomy*. Each divisional manager will be accountable to the head office for the running of their business unit. Because there is a need to retain an overall consistency across the whole company each division will enjoy only limited autonomy. Restriction exists to maintain overall consistency, otherwise anarchy and financial disaster could result if each attempted to operate independently.

Product-based structures are advantageous when there is a need to get close to customers and the company offers a range of products, each serving a specific market. It is an option when there is instability in the various markets, requiring the organization to be proactive across a broad front. Splitting the product range into groups, each the responsibility of a separate business unit, provides the opportunity to concentrate on part of the overall problem. This achieves the advantages of specialization, without losing the benefits of being a large organization. An example of a product-based structure is included as Figure 15.11.

The main advantages of a product structure include:

- *Risk*. This approach spreads the risk of particular products failing and dragging the whole organization down with them. Operational decision making can be left to the business units and strategic decision making to head office.
- *Evaluation*. Those business units that are successful will be more visible through the cost and profit evaluation processes used. Equally, problem operations are more easily detected.

FIGURE 15.11

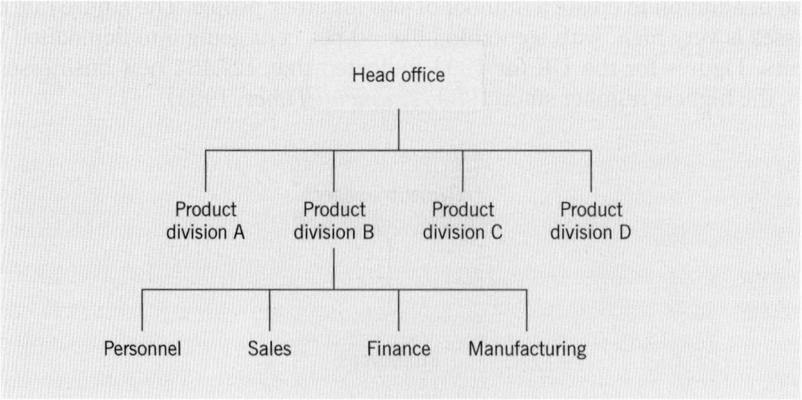

Product structure

- *Motivation and development*. Being responsible for a specific business unit should increase motivation among managers. Business unit managers should develop 'general manager' skills at an earlier stage of their careers.
- *Support*. Support services will be available within head office. These could be utilized to support and enhance the resources available in business units that experience difficulties or need particular skills.
- *Acquisition and divestment*. The integration of acquired companies should become easier if they are to be absorbed into an existing business unit structure. Divestment can also be more easily achieved as the closure or sale of one division should have minimal impact on the others.
- *Change*. It is assumed that because each business unit will be closer to its customers and the market for its products it will be more adaptable and responsive to the need for change.

The disadvantages of a product-based structure include:

- *Responsibility*. There may be confusion or lack of clarity between the responsibilities and rights of head office to interfere with business unit activity.
- *Conflict*. It is likely that there will be conflict between business units as a result of competition for resources. No company can support every demand for additional resources and must prioritize them.
- *Short-term perspective*. Depending upon career development patterns and budgetary and incentive arrangements, it is possible that business unit managers will concentrate on short-term results. This is apparent in the following Employee Perspective (15.2).
- *Relative size*. Smaller business units often feel forgotten and dominated by the larger ones, which can lead to frustration, underperformance and missed business opportunities.
- *Customer confusion*. It is possible that a single customer may have contact with more than one business unit. This leads to duplication and frustration for both parties.

Process-based structures

Process-based structures split the organization according to the manufacturing or service activities involved. Another way of describing this type of structure is as a functional approach. For example, the typical process-based structure of a manufacturing company would group together the resources under production, personnel, marketing, finance and engineering (see Figure 15.12).

Typically, process would be the structural form that an entrepreneurial organization would first evolve into when growth required change. It is also likely that the separate business units within a product-based structure would adopt a process orientation as the basis of grouping the sub-tasks.

The advantages of the process-based structure are:

- *Specialization*. Individuals develop a high level of expertise in their particular discipline. Support is also readily available because all the specialists work in one department. However, with specialization comes loyalty to the functional group rather than business objectives.
- *Stability*. Such structures are able to deal more effectively with circumstances in which there is continuity across time.

EMPLOYEE PERSPECTIVE 15.2 Short term only please

Julia was the training officer responsible for the training and development of head office-based junior management personnel within a major airline based in the Middle East. It employed many thousands of people from 30 nationalities many of whom were based at airports and regional offices around the world. Julia was Australian by nationality and was on a standard expatriate contract with the airline. The location of the company head office was in a country that traditionally had used a very high proportion of expatriate staff across all levels, but recently had begun a process of localization in which the government required companies to give priority to local personnel when recruitment or promotion decisions were being considered. Among the intentions being to provide career opportunities for local people and to reduce the reliance on expatriate labour. Julia had held her job for about three years and was one of 50 training officers involved in broadly similar duties across the company.

Julia reported to a training manager who was responsible for the training of all junior managers across the company. In turn the training manager reported to the director of training and development along with five other training managers. Julia's immediate boss was from the USA and had been in post for seven years. His career development plan meant that he would be moved on from his current job in about six months, probably to another training manager's job in the company for a maximum of one year. After that he would be required to leave the company and return to the USA. Julia had been in discussion with an Australian university about the possibility of gaining accreditation for the training that she provided for her client group. This would mean that the training programmes would need to be adapted to the satisfaction of the university, delegates would have to undertake some form of assessment and if successful they would be awarded a postgraduate diploma or master's degree in business. Julia thought that this was a good idea and that it would contribute to personal, organizational and national development objectives. It would however mean a considerable amount of work and take between two and three years to fully develop and achieve accreditation.

Julia took her ideas to her boss. He thought it was interesting as an idea, but that it required too much time and commitment. He told her to forget the idea and to concentrate on developing new short courses to be available in three months time for a major relaunch of the junior manager development programme. She was told to concentrate on a number of 'hot topics' such as time management, leadership skills, performance management and managing across cultures. He wanted to see her proposals in two weeks as he had a meeting with the director of training and development the following week about his annual review and his next career move, which would provide a good opportunity to present the revised training programme. Julia left the meeting disappointed and to think about her next move.

Tasks

1. If you were Julia what would you do next and why?
2. Why do you think Julia's manager reacted as he did?
3. Could such difficulties be avoided in this type of organization and if so how?

- *Centralization*. At the lower levels of process-based organizations there is little integration of activity across the functions. Consequently, it is only at the higher levels that any form of holistic picture of the organization, its objectives and strategies is possible. This inevitably leads to a centralized approach to running the organization. Management in Action 15.2 illustrates recent moves in a number of large complex organizations to recentralize aspects of their operations, having felt that decentralization had gone too far.
- *Clarity*. Because of the compartmentalized nature of this approach, job holders just concentrate on part of the overall operation, providing clarity of purpose.

The disadvantages of the process-based structure are:

- *Co-ordination*. Specialization requires co-ordination between functions. If co-ordination does not take place, or if it is ineffective, then the potential benefits will not be realized.

MANAGEMENT IN ACTION 15.2 Return to the centre

Many organizations are seeking to move away from the decentralized structures carefully created over the past decade or so. They are attempting to create a new unified corporate brand through seeking to provide a 'glue' to hold the entire organization together. There is a danger that in any decentralized organization the sub-units inevitably begin to question the purpose of head office and its value in terms of the overhead required to pay for it. Equally the sub-units tend to develop their own ways of doing things, some of which may be appropriate, but many will be done for expediency and may cut across the need for a corporate consistency in policy.

In a survey carried out by the Institute of Personnel and Development among 153 chief executives from multi-site organizations employing between 500 and 5000 people, 85 per cent were providing more leadership and direction from the centre. About 33 per cent were also taking decision making away from divisional sub-units. These findings were equally applicable to public as well as private sector organizations. In interpreting the findings, Professor Andrew Kakabadse from Cranfield School of Management suggests that many companies are never completely centralized or decentralized and remain in a state of semi-flux most of the time. He also made the point that the over the past decade many companies became decentralized in order to get closer to the customer. However so many organizations did this that it was no longer of competitive advantage and so strategy driven by the centre was finding favour again.

For example, Hampshire County Council devolved personnel responsibility to individual departments during the late 1980s and early 1990s, retaining a small central department to develop policy and support departments with specialized advice. By 1997, however, it was apparent that personnel practice across the departments was beginning to differ in significant ways. For example, some departments offered relocation expenses to new staff, while others did not. It was described by Rita Sammons (the head of personnel and training) as people with the available expertise working in silos not being available to the entire council. The solution developed involved a reduction in the number of personnel units to six, still physically located in departments but part of the central personnel function which has also been strengthened by the creation of new senior posts.

IBM has also changed its approach to personnel management through the creation of a pan-European call centre to offer guidance and support to managers across the continent. This means that the service is more consistent in its advice, but the relationship between personnel and the operations that it serves are not direct. The provision operates through telephone or electronically. The business need was to seek to orient all the front-line services of the company towards a consistent approach to customers. To do that it was argued a stronger line was needed from the centre as well as consistency from the various support services. It is seeking to globalize within the company in line with the globalization of its products and customers. Local country personnel managers are increasingly concentrating on those issues that cannot easily be carried out on a global scale, industrial relations being the most obvious example.

Adapted from: Arkin, A (1999) Return to centre, *People Management*, 6 May, pp 34–41.

Stop ↔ Consider

Consider the extent to which you would expect the changes described to have any positive effect on the effectiveness of the organizations indicated. Also to what extent might they reflect the desire of the people at the top to exercise more power and control?

- *Budget orientation.* No one function is responsible for the profitability of the organization. That responsibility rests with the chief executive. The achievement of a budgeted level of expenditure by a function does not guarantee that the profit achieved will be maximized.
- *Succession.* Functional managers are not responsible for the activities beyond their expertise and do not gain experience of general management until they are very senior within the organization. Problems can therefore be created in career development and succession planning.

FIGURE 15.12

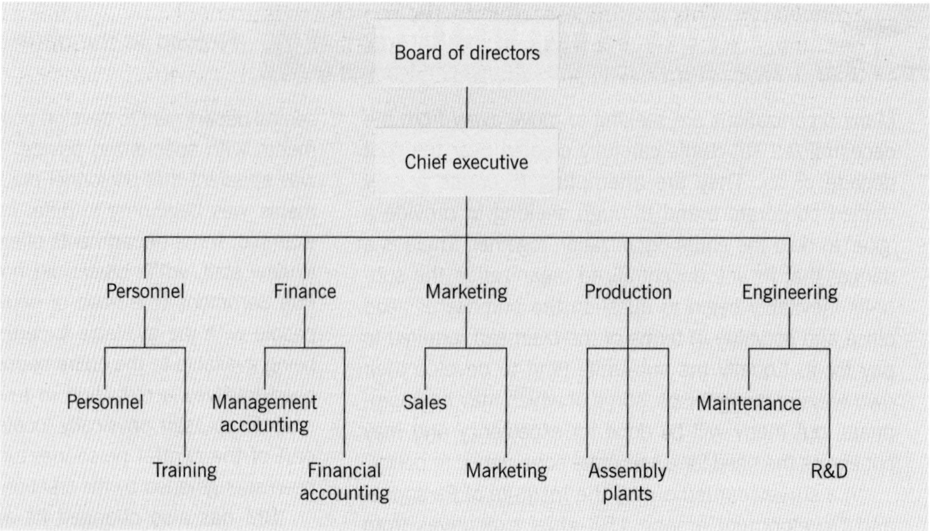

Process structure

- *Growth.* Growth in the complexity of the organization as the product range develops can create problems of co-ordination which restricts performance.
- *Political.* An emphasis on the department as the main focus of activity creates a primary loyalty to that group. This can lead to empire building and political behaviour as managers seek to enhance their influence and careers.

International organizations

One of the difficulties in attempting to identify the types of structure used by international organizations is the range of size and type of such organizations. The most commonly found forms of international activity include:

- *Exporting.* The essence of exporting is that a company based in one country sells its products or services in other countries through sales offices or directly in response to customer orders. The use of the post or an international freight company is the usual means of shipping orders to the customer. In the service sector this could involve sending a management consultant to undertake an assignment for example.
- *Agents.* A variation of the exporting approach is to sell through a number of agents in other countries. Typically, the agent would be self-employed, perhaps dealing with a number of suppliers across a broad range of similar products. The main advantage is that they have a better knowledge of foreign markets than the company itself. However, sales are in the hands of someone who may not be fully committed to selling only one company's products. In addition, the organization does not build up any direct expertise in the foreign markets covered by the agent, and it is in the interests of the agent to keep the company at arm's length.
- *Licensing.* This involves a company granting a licence to another company to produce and sell something the first company has exclusive rights over. In return a fee would be paid to the original company. This can be an effective means of generating money for the original company without the risks and costs of setting up in other countries. However, it is also creating an opportunity for other organizations to obtain production technologies, design specifications and market information in a way that could be damaging to the original company.

- *Franchising*. This is a process whereby the franchisee is granted a right to use a trademark in return for a payment to the franchisor. The franchisee is required to find a sum of money to start the franchise and is given help with the process. The franchisor would continue to support the franchisee in the running of the business in return for a fee. There are many franchise operations – hotel chains, fast food restaurants, business and domestic services being among the most common.
- *Direct investment*. This could embrace the total ownership of a company in another country or part ownership through a joint venture or partnership.
- *Multinational enterprise*. Often referred to as an MNE for short, such organizations engage in a truly international scale and type of operation. They engage in an integrated approach to the manufacture and marketing of products and services across a number of countries. In organizational design terms they can vary considerably in structure depending upon the nature of the business and the strategies adopted.

There are a number of ways in which international activities can be incorporated into the organization. Following is a description of the main options for dealing with international activities, at least of those organizations that have a physical presence in more than one country:

- *International division*. The creation of an international division as a separate business unit within the company is a way of coping with relatively small international activities. A simple example of an international division is shown in Figure 15.13.
- *Product-based business units*. This type of structure groups together international activities by product type, thus allowing for the development of appropriate expertise within each location. Product-based expertise is also spread across the spectrum of international activity for each product group (Figure 15.14).
- *Geographic business units*. This approach compartmentalizes operational activity by location (Figure 15.15).
- *Functional orientation*. The functional approach to international operations differentiates activity by purpose and location. For example, the personnel people, wherever they are based, report through their line managers to head office rather than to any specific country general manager (Figure 15.16).

FIGURE 15.13

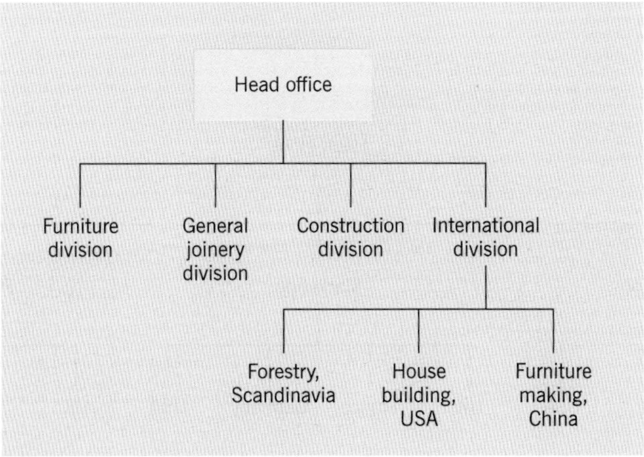

International operations as separate division

FIGURE 15.14

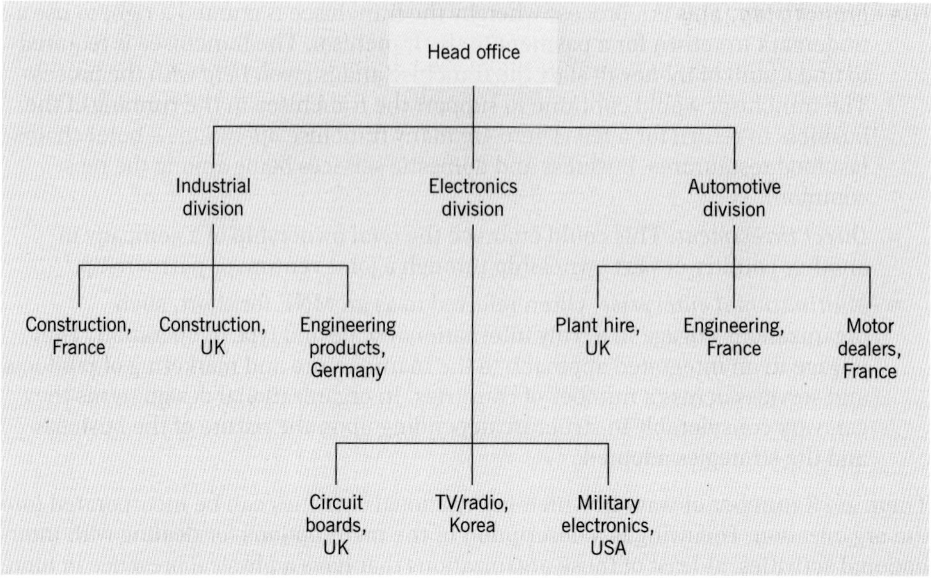

Product-based international operations

FIGURE 15.15

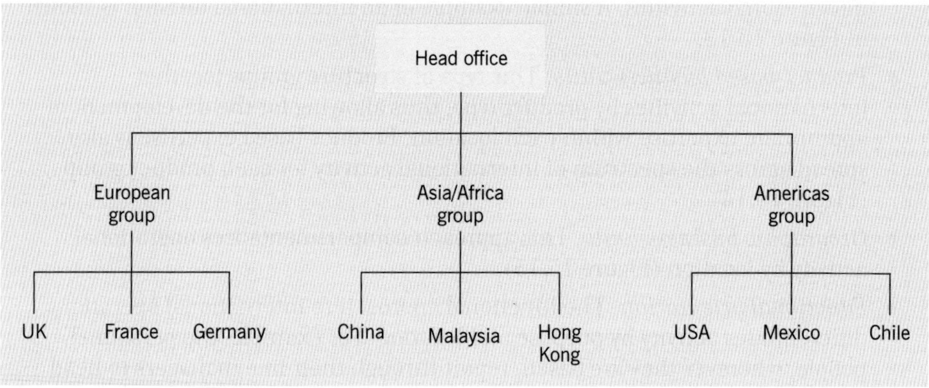

Place-based international operations

FIGURE 15.16

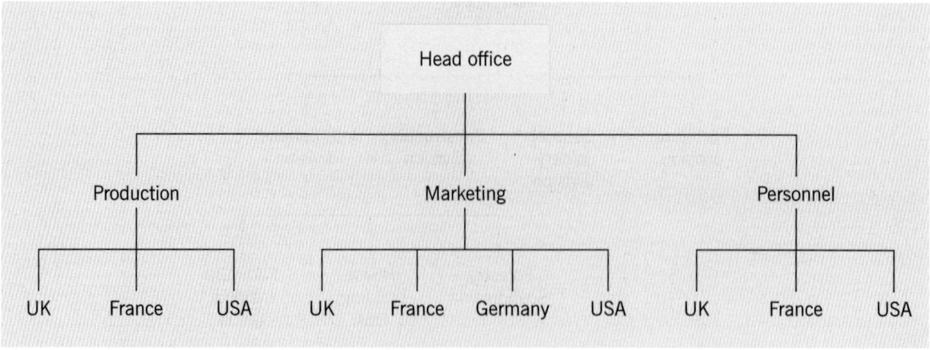

Functional basis for international operations

The holding company

The holding-company framework is one in which the head office is a company in its own right and owns (fully or partly) a number of separate businesses which are legally constituted companies in their own right. Within each of the subsidiary companies, the structure adopted could be any one of the frameworks previously described. In its pure form the holding company acts as a banker to the group. It brings together organizations that create a synergy within the group as a whole and divests those companies that do not fit with the plan or that otherwise fail to live up to profit potential. In that sense the parent company is acting as an investment house on behalf of its shareholders.

One response to the desire for size in a commercial organization is to create a structure in which integration and diversification exist at the same time. The holding-company concept can help to achieve that requirement. The existence of separate companies within the holding company provides the potential to manage according to profit (or contribution) returned to the parent company. This should result in each organization within the group displaying the following characteristics:

- *Objectives*. Being relatively free to pursue its own objectives.
- *Market*. Being able to get closer to the markets in which it operates.
- *Motivation and development*. Management being responsible for a company with its own profit targets, without the stock market risks.
- *Funding*. It should be possible to fund growth and development from within the group.

Matrix and project-based structures

The matrix approach is based on the notion that vertical reporting relationships limit involvement in the overall activity of the organization. The matrix emerges as an attempt to integrate both functional and product responsibilities into the activities of individual managers and employees. It is not a new concept. For example, management consultants frequently work in multifunctional teams to undertake specific projects. Members retain a working relationship within their individual disciplines at the same time as reporting to a project leader for the specific project in hand. The same is true of large-scale construction projects where civil engineers and other specialists will report professionally to someone other than the manager in charge of a specific project. Lampel and Shamsie (2003) discuss the changes that have taken place in the Hollywood movie industry when it changed from the studio system in which everyone was directly employed, to the project based approach in which specific largely self-employed teams are assembled to make a particular movie and then they all go their separate ways. Among the issues identified in their study is that it is harder and takes more managerial skill to assemble a project team and that it becomes harder to transmit the creative lessons learned from one project to the next because of the dissipation effect of assembling and disassembling teams.

Matrix ideas have been implemented in manufacturing and service organizations in an attempt to enhance the integration of functional specialization with more effective design, manufacturing and marketing of products and services (see Figure 15.17). The 'manager product A' shown in Figure 15.17 would be specifically responsible for that product and for bringing together a team drawn from the appropriate functions that would have an influence and impact on the product. That team is then responsible for optimizing the capability of the product to contribute to the company's profit etc.

Essentially, a matrix organization utilizes a twin reporting framework in an attempt to provide a more complex application of resource. It reflects the principles of the

FIGURE 15.17

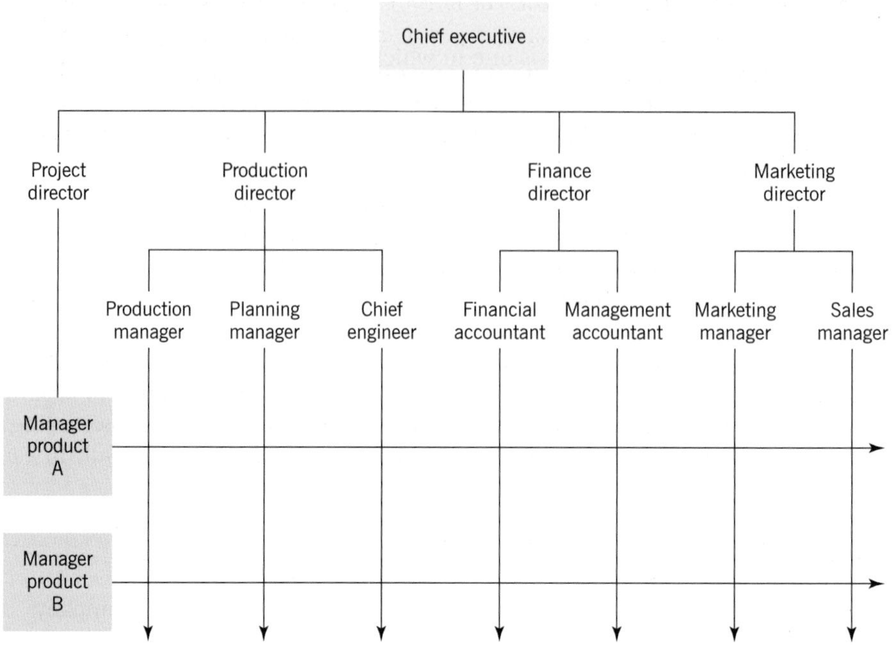

Matrix structure

contingency approach to design in that it allows a duality of emphasis. This should enable the organization to capture and use a greater amount of environmental detail in its operational activity. Atkinson (2003) suggests that a matrix should be regarded as a process rather than a structure and as such it should evolve and self-renew based on feedback from the members and the environment. He also suggests that for success to be achieved an appropriate and supportive culture needs to be in existence. There are a number of difficulties inherent with the matrix structure, including:

- *Complexity of operation*. A matrix structure can add complexity to what may already be a complex organizational framework.
- *Split accountabilities*. Employees find that they have more than one superior. This can be difficult for both managers and employees as evident from the following Employee Perspective (15.3).

EMPLOYEE PERSPECTIVE 15.3 How can I work for more than one boss?

The following situation was described by an employee who reported to more than one boss:

> My job has expanded and I now have three bosses to report to rather than one. I have tried to point out that I can only do a limited amount for each boss, but they don't seem to understand the difficulties involved in reporting to three different masters. My initial idea was to get them all together to discuss what each can reasonably expect of me, but they don't get on with one another and have found excuses to miss the meetings. How can I tackle this?

Tasks

1. What advice would you give to this employee?
2. How might such difficulties be avoided in a matrix structure?
3. You might like to check your views with the advice given by: Bullmore, J (2003) What's your problem? *Management Today*, December, p 75.

- *Increased political opportunity*. For example, it would be possible for a line manager to blame mistakes on a project team and thus avoid responsibility.
- *Lack of clear focus*. Because of split responsibilities it is possible that a lack of focus creeps into organizational activities. Unless great care is taken in setting out individual responsibilities, it is possible that things of importance may be missed with everyone assuming that they are someone else's responsibility.
- *Requires specific skills*. It is not easy to work effectively for two different people, each with different priorities and demands, particularly when accustomed to traditional organizations. The pressure on individuals is much greater and they need resilience, appropriate personality characteristics and training to be able to cope effectively.
- *Conversion*. Most organizations seeking to employ a matrix structure will already be in existence and hence find themselves needing to convert to that model. The process of being able to move from one framework to another, together with the time and resources involved, should not be underestimated.

BPR, FLEXIBLE AND FLATTER ORGANIZATIONS

It was Ashby (1956) who first suggested the law of requisite variety. In order to ensure that the variability (variety) experienced by any system can be controlled, it is necessary for the controller to match the complexity of the environment. The example often used to illustrate the notion of variety is a motor vehicle. Imagine there are 5000 possible causes for a motor vehicle not starting. If a repair technician has knowledge of only 4999 of these and the unknown cause occurs, then they will not be able to repair the vehicle. In that sense any organization structure attempts to improve the level of requisite variety by providing a higher level of internal complexity to more effectively match that found in the environment. Many of the less conventional and innovative approaches to organizational design are intended to achieve that objective and this section looks at three such approaches.

The flexible firm is an idea based around the premise that an organization should have the capability to adapt itself easily to its prevailing circumstances. This can include approaches such as location and temporal flexibility. Another is the notion of the flexible organization described by Atkinson (1984). In this approach the flexible firm could be created through any combination of the three areas of flexibility identified below:

1. *Numerical flexibility*. This allows the number of people employed to grow and shrink rapidly in line with business needs. Only a small proportion of employees would be regarded as core or established employees. The rest (peripheral employees) would be employed under a range of short-term, part-time or sub-contractual arrangements.
2. *Functional flexibility*. This involves the ability of the organization to achieve multiskilling and non-demarcated working practices, thus ensuring that core employees could be used across a range of jobs, reducing non-working time and the need for additional staff.
3. *Financial flexibility*. This provides for expenditure variability through pay systems alignment with company performance, reducing the amount of fixed cost carried by the organization.

Flexibility in the form of increasing employee detachment from access to permanent employment is very common today. Many organizations contain high levels of casual and temporary employees on a range of employment contracts lasting from a few weeks to a few years. It is described by many trade unions as the increasing casualization of work. However, some employees (particularly those with key or readily transferable skills) prefer the benefits of freelance working for several reasons including the relative freedom of not being tied to one organization.

Business process re-engineering (BPR) is a recent approach to organizing activity in its broadest sense based around the essential processes to meet customer needs and improve productivity. It assumes that the application of scientific management principles can support the achievement of organizational objectives. In essence, the structure of an organization should be a function of its objectives, technology and environmental forces – a form of contingency model. A summary of the business process re-engineering approach is included as Management in Action 15.3.

The essence of BPR is a move from the traditional hierarchy towards a horizontal focus for the organization as part of the search for a stronger alignment with the core process of meeting customer need. In that sense every aspect of an organization should add value. The challenge facing managers is how to emphasize the horizontal while accommodating the inevitable vertical dimension. There are many ways in which this can be achieved depending upon the company objectives and form. This can involve developing matrix type structures or, 'integration of the supply chain with disciplines acting as centres of excellence. [As]... in companies like Kodak and Ericsson' (Armistead and Rowland, 1996, p 52). They also point out that BPR can be about finding ways of more effectively managing the boundaries between processes to, 'minimise the disconnects in flows of information, materials or people' (p 53). However, the concept of BPR is heavily criticized, even by its originators, as the level of failed applications is high, it can be too complex to apply easily and the costs can outweigh the benefits.

Flatter organizations are those with relatively few levels in the hierarchy. The intention is to improve the focus on customer needs and the speed of response and to reduce the levels of bureaucracy in the organization. It is usually the middle ranks of management and technical specialist within the organization that are removed in the delayering, downsizing or rightsizing of an organization that is seeking to become flatter. In creating a flatter organization it is necessary to recognize that more needs to be changed than simply the removal of layers of management. Systems, procedures and working practices need to adapt to the new situation if it is to function. Simply taking levels and people out of the organization and expecting the remaining employees and managers to absorb the consequences is unrealistic and a recipe for disaster. Such an approach effectively suggests that the jobs removed did not contribute anything to the organization or duplicated what others did and can safely be eliminated.

Corporate anorexic
Describes organizations that cut employee numbers to the point of extinction out of a fear of becoming fat.

However, there is also a danger of becoming what has been termed a **corporate anorexic**. This was first described by the Canadian Stress Institute to reflect those organizations that cut employee numbers out of fear of becoming fat. Just as with human anorexics the managers of such companies think that they look unhealthy and fat, when outsiders can see that they look unhealthy and painfully thin. The bosses of such organizations are in danger of cutting and cutting numbers employed, making it more and more anorexic until it goes bankrupt because it is too thin to sustain its own life. JP Morgan was recently accused of being a corporate anorexic as it was cutting large numbers of staff. One internal e-mail circulating among staff suggested that by the end of 2002, 120 per cent of staff would have been cut, more staff than it actually employed (Kirwan-Taylor, 2002).

If a flatter organization removes slack from the system there will be less spare capacity to deal with any crises that arise. Everyone can become so busy concentrating on the immediate task that they do not communicate with others above, below or alongside themselves. This can mean that jobs do not get done; questions are not

MANAGEMENT IN ACTION 15.3 Business process re-engineering (BPR)

The term BPR emerged around 1990 following the work of two distinct sets of authors. Management consultant Mike Hammer wrote an article in the *Harvard Business Review* titled 'Reengineering work: don't automate, obliterate'. This article talked about the need to re-engineer at both the business and process level. At about the same time an article appeared in the *Sloan Management Review* with the title 'The new industrial engineering: information technology and business process redesign'. Written by Thomas Davenport and James Short it talked of business process redesign, but not of re-engineering as such. The Hammer approach tended to suggest a fundamental review and change process whereas Davenport and Short adopted a more cautious and structured approach through the application of technology and industrial engineering principles. In practice the term business process re-engineering was not used by either set of writers and appeared only after the publication of both articles.

There are a number of definitions of BPR but that offered by Hammer and Champey in a 1993 publication is a useful starting point:

> The fundamental rethinking and radical redesign of business processes to achieve dramatic improvements in critical contemporary measures of performance, such as cost, quality, service and speed.

Some organizations claim to have made considerable savings and improvements through the application of BPR. For example:

- Ford Motor Company reduced the number of people in the accounts payable department by 75 per cent, with no reduction in service level.
- The Bank of America and Italy reduced cashier closing time by 91 per cent, opened 50 new branches and doubled revenue without any increase in staff.
- Kodak reduced new product development time by 50 per cent and reduced tool and manufacturing costs by 25 per cent.

However, not all companies that attempt BPR achieve the success intended. Hammer estimates that 70 per cent of organizations that attempt BPR do not achieve any benefits. Conventional organization structure gets in the way of effective working as it compartmentalizes activity and creates the need to hand over work and split responsibility. Hammer and Champey illustrate this through the example of IBM Credit Corporation. In arranging finance on behalf of customers five steps were necessary (each in a different department) and the processing time for each application was about six days, although it could take two weeks. After 'walking the process' it became apparent that the actual work time for each application was about 1.5 hours. The whole operation was re-engineered with a new job of 'deal structurer' being created to process each application from beginning to end. Supported by new technology and database systems the turnaround time fell to four hours with a small reduction in staff numbers and the capability to handle many more transactions.

Adapted from: Patching, D (1994) Business process re-engineering: getting to the heart of the matter, *Management Services*, June, pp 10–13; and Patching, D (1994) Business process re-engineering: what's in a name? *Management Services*, November, pp 8–11.

Stop ↔ Consider

To what extent does BPR consist of the application of scientific management techniques, the contingency approach to organizing, or simply innovative and radical thinking? Justify your views.

asked or remain unanswered. It also means that the steps between levels of management become greater. One implication of this is that managers do not develop the experience of taking decisions appropriate to the many relatively small steps within the hierarchy as their careers progress, with those above them checking before the organization commits to the decision. In a flatter organization this safety and development process is significantly reduced or absent and so there is a greater risk of inappropriate or wrong decisions being made.

In flattened organizations managers who feel that the organization cannot be trusted to look after them will take the initiative and look after their own interests. This in turn weakens the commitment of an individual to the organization. It introduces the danger of an instrumental approach to work emerging among the people who are charged with seeking to motivate and lead the rest of the employees within the organization (Gretton, 1993). Flatter or horizontal organizations are an attempt to overcome the complexity generated by the matrix organization. In the matrix structure the dual reporting relationships can create complexity, confusion and conflict in operational activity. One way to resolve this problem would be to remove one of the reporting relationships. Rationality would suggest that the one to be sacrificed should be the one contributing least to the overall success of the organization. The flatter or horizontal organization is based on the view that the customer experience and need is the most important therefore every effort should be made to reduce the vertical and less significant processes within the organization. This structural form is organized around a number of key features, including:

- *Flat hierarchy*. Fewer managers and organizational levels.
- *Process organization*. The structural basis for activity should be the customer experience – horizontal not hierarchical.
- *Team activity*. Everyone depends upon other people for some part of their job so work groups should become the norm for organizing activity.

Bringing these ideas together should enable an organization to operate horizontally. Activities would be organized around the customer experience of the company and work teams ensure that all aspects of the delivery of the product or service are integrated effectively towards meeting those needs. An example of one horizontal organization is shown in Management in Action 15.4.

THE VIRTUAL, FEDERAL AND NETWORKED ORGANIZATION

The term virtual organization appeared towards the end of the 1980s and is a metaphor for an organization that is capable of delivering more than its resources would allow. Such organizations have been in existence in some industries for many years. For example, small consultancies use networks of associates to pool resources when additional capacity is needed. The basis of the virtual organization is that it is a temporary network of otherwise independent organizations for a specific purpose. It could include suppliers, competitors and specialists in design, engineering and finance. The purpose being to capture the strengths of each member of the alliance in achieving a specific objective, from which each would benefit.

Clearly, the main advantages of the virtual organization include the opportunity to provide a response to opportunities that would otherwise be beyond the capability of the individual members. There are potential dangers with this type of approach including the risk of providing potential competitors with commercially sensitive information and expertise. Also, a failure to manage the dynamics of the relationship effectively could lead to a collapse of the venture.

In terms of structure, there should be opportunities to reduce hierarchical frameworks to a minimum as each member of the alliance concentrates on only part of the process. However, there is a need for the integration of activity across the member organizations which would not exist in other forms of structure. Byrne *et al.* (1993) quote a number of key lessons (based on data supplied by Booz Allen & Hamilton Inc.,

MANAGEMENT IN ACTION 15.4 What a way to run a company!

Orticon is a Danish company that makes hearing aids; it employs about 1200 people. Lars Kolind has been the president of the company since 1988. The company was very traditional in its approach to the ways in which it went about its business, having been in existence for about 90 years. It had, however, lost touch with developments in technology and changes in the market. Having realized that the situation could not continue, Kolind set about changing how it functioned in order to be able to compete with its larger rivals such as Siemens and Philips. He suggested that: 'We did not have the same resources as our big competitors so we were forced to look for a different way to get ahead. We set out to create a company that doesn't work like a machine but functions like a brain.'

Out went the traditional organizational hierarchy and specific job titles. Office walls were removed and so was the right to work at a specific desk. Desks were provided for people to work at, but they were available on a first-come, first-served basis. If a junior was at a desk normally used by the boss then it would be the boss who would have to find somewhere else to work. Each person has a mobile phone and a personal trolley for their files and they tow it around with them as they go from task to task. People do whatever tasks are necessary without pre-allocation or thought of structure or status. There is also a high degree of freedom to come and go as the individual pleases, with no set hours or time-off constraints. The same degree of flexibility does not exist within the factory operations of the company, because of the higher need for control and in order to be able to produce efficiently.

The effect on the business has been dramatic. New product development has improved as a result of the greater degree of interaction between staff. Lounges, coffee bars and meeting rooms are provided to function as places for staff to mix and talk freely with each other away from the workplace. For example, the company was able to introduce a new product that was years ahead of the competition very quickly because of the recognition that the technology already existed. The technology had been available within the company since the late 1970s but the potential had not been recognized until people began to interact in different ways following the restructuring.

Profits also increased dramatically as a result of the changes. In 1990 pre-tax profit was 13.1m Danish Kroner, the forecast for 1994 was 124.8m Danish Kroner. People have not let the team down since the introduction of the much more relaxed approach to work. People do not appear to have taken advantage of the situation. Each employee is allocated a mentor within the company who would help to guide the work and behaviour of the individual. The mentor would also be involved with salary discussions about the employee with project leaders. Salary proposals are then put to the management committee for final approval.

It is a matter of debate whether the success of Orticon could be replicated in other countries and social settings or whether it is situation specific. It is also necessary to consider the role of Lars Kolind in achieving success. He holds strong beliefs about human nature and how people function best together. Equally, the same structural and organizational flexibility is not possible in the manufacturing parts of the company. So it is not a universal panacea for achieving higher staff contribution. It does nevertheless represent a significant innovation and many large businesses and consultancies have shown interest in attempting to understand it by making visits to the company.

Adapted from: Piper, A (1994) What a way to run a company!, *The Mail On Sunday,* 11 September, pp 76–7.

Stop ↔ Consider

To what extent would it be possible to retain in the long term the horizontal design in part of the organization and conventional structures in other parts of the organization? Would those employees not allowed the benefits of such working resent those that were and would those differences become a source of problems?

a large consultancy practice) for organizations attempting to develop virtual relationships, including:

- *Marry well*. It is necessary to select members of the network for the right reasons. Success depends upon high trust and dependability between the members.
- *Play fair*. Each partner needs to feel that membership is in their interests. If the members cannot trust each other then information and contribution will be withheld which could result in failure.
- *Offer the best*. Committing the best employees to collaborative activities provides a clear signal of commitment to the project and also increases the probability of success.
- *Define objectives*. It should be clear to each member of the network what the ultimate objective is and their part in it. To fail to identify the objectives will result in a lack of direction and targets against which to measure progress.
- *Common infrastructure*. Each of the members needs to communicate with each other in a meaningful way. This requires some commonality in procedures and perhaps computer systems.

The federal organization described by Handy (1989) reflects the joining together of separate groups under a common identity for a specific purpose. It seeks to reflect the need for market impact and economies of scale along with flexibility inherent in small organizations. It is different from the virtual or decentralized organization. Virtual implies a temporary coalition for a specific project. Decentralization implies delegated power being passed to the subordinate operational units, with the centre retaining absolute control. Federalism, by way of contrast, reflects a reverse form of delegation in which it is the individual groups which specify the limits and purpose of the overarching body, not the other way around. Handy makes much of the political analogy in describing the approach to federalism in such countries as Switzerland and the role of the president as the chairman of the co-ordinating committee. It is a simultaneous tight–loose arrangement in which the centre holds some power (perhaps to channel money into specific projects etc.) aimed at the long-term strategy of the whole organization, but the main driving force for activity comes from the individual units themselves.

These are both examples of different forms of networking in the ways in which organizational arrangements are realized in practice. Gould and Campbell (2003) review one form of networking in which the co-operating units retain considerable autonomy whilst relying on extensive collaboration through voluntary networking. The objective of such organizations being to retain the benefits of interdependence achieved through the matrix approach to structure, but to avoid the difficulties often found in such arrangements. The network arrangement seeks to retain clear responsibility, managerial initiative and accountability, speed of decision making and lean hierarchy. It is about promoting co-operation without creating unnecessary and redundant overheads or introducing processes which interfere with the otherwise effective running of operational units. It is about creating enough, but not too much structure. In all of these forms of organization it is the boundaries between people, jobs and even organizations that are becoming fluid and even non-existent. Rubery *et al.* (2002) review the implications of this type of development on the practice of conventional human resource management. Among the issues that they identify are that it is increasingly likely that people will be working together under different contractual and procedural arrangements and that confidentiality and conflicts of interest are more likely. The practice of human resource management needs to develop strategies and approaches to how to deal with these situations effectively as well as how to integrate high trust and an appropriate psychological contract into working arrangements in new organizational forms.

ALTERNATIVE ORGANIZATIONS

Organizations are social creations and there are as many variations as human ingenuity can create. What follows is a brief introduction to some of the other major alternatives that exist.

Shamrock and triple I organizations

Charles Handy (1989) introduced the idea that an organization could be represented as a shamrock (a small three-leaved plant). In the picture of a shamrock (Figure 15.18) are the three different categories of employee, each of whom are organized, managed and rewarded differently:

- *Professional core*. This category of employee represents the professional worker such as engineers, managers and specialists who direct the organization in its technical and professional endeavours.
- *Contractual fringe*. These are the subcontractors of various descriptions who provide the necessary but not essential services to the host organization. Typically, paid for results; much of the low-skill, and monotonous work falls into this category.
- *Flexible labour force*. The part-time, casual and freelance workers found in many organizations that come and go as needed and are rewarded accordingly. For example, many university or college lecturers and management consultants are employed on a casual basis.

The model is an extension of the flexible firm model discussed earlier and its purpose is to encourage managers to consider organizational purpose along with the nature of the staff relationship to the organization. There are organizational structure implications in that the three categories of worker engage with the organization differently and need to be managed and integrated differently to conventional employees. For example, integration between the three main categories becomes very difficult in the short term as the working patterns vary so dramatically and are not easily changed.

Handy also discusses using the customer as a worker, which can impact on structure. Consider self-service restaurants, self-assembly furniture and the wide use of

FIGURE 15.18

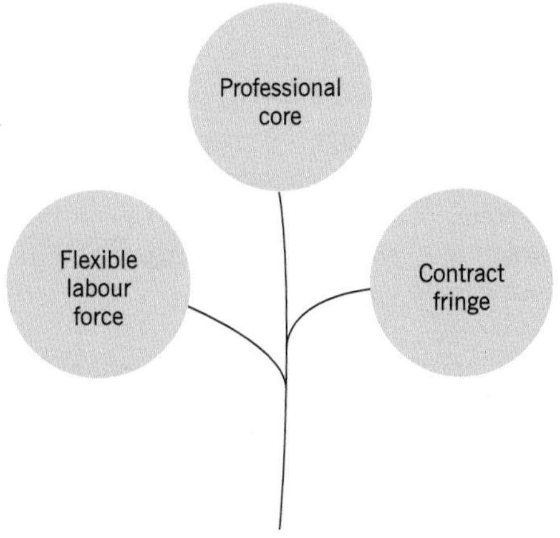

The shamrock organization

automated teller machines (ATMs) by the banks for example. In each of these cases work that would have at one time been done by a company employee is now widely accepted as part of the customer's responsibility. The following Employee Perspective (15.4) demonstrates that control over the customer as a part of the organizational framework is not as easy as control over conventional employees.

Triple I organization
An organizational form that recognizes that future success will depend upon intelligence, information and ideas.

The **triple I organization** is an organization, according to Handy, that recognizes that in the future success will depend upon **i**ntelligence, **i**nformation and **i**deas, hence the triple I name. Handy recognizes that not every part of the organization needs these three concepts in full measure, for example the mail will still need to be sorted and offices cleaned. However, it is at the core of the business that these three concepts will be essential for survival and effectiveness. If the key factors for success do become the triple I factors then structural (and leadership) forms which do not support it will lead to failure.

The human service organization

This type of organization includes schools, hospitals, social work/welfare departments and public assistance providers. They are often organized along bureaucratic lines because they are part of a public sector organization. However, there are differences that make them useful for considering non-standard organizations. Hasenfeld (1992) suggests that for the recipients of the services provided by these organizations they often evoke a mixture of 'hope and fear, caring and victimization, dignity and abuse' (p 4). He also proposes that employees of these organizations suffer a conflict between a personal need to provide the services based on need and professional standards and the restrictions imposed by managers of the organization. He identifies a number of reasons that could account for this pattern of contradiction (pp 4–9):

- *People as 'raw material'*. Such organizations act in a very direct way upon the people who come to them for whatever purpose. This makes these organizations uniquely different from others.

EMPLOYEE PERSPECTIVE 15.4 Customers replace employees

Littlewood and Ashworth (1999) describe the very hostile and public reaction of customers when the banks in the UK generally sought to charge more frequently and at a higher level for using cash dispensing machines (ATMs). The banks have sought to encourage the widespread use of ATM machines as a cheaper and more efficient way of dispensing cash than customers going into a branch to cash a cheque. They are also available 24 hours each day, which a bank could never afford to be. ATMs can be put into virtually any location including supermarkets and other retail outlets, which reduces the cost of providing branch networks and cashiers for the bank. The customer becomes a replacement bank employee in that by using the appropriate card and computer technology they can undertake many of the routine transactions formerly done by employees.

However, by seeking to derive income from these 'new employees' a negative reaction resulted. 'Employees' are used to being paid, not to having to pay for the privilege of being allowed to work. The banks eventually withdrew their plans for higher charges. Perhaps customers are aware of their status in such situations, and of how far their 'employer' should be allowed to push them before they react in a way which could damage the business.

Tasks

1. To what extent does the introduction of the customer as employee introduce a different power balance to the relationship between customer and supplier?
2. How if at all might it be possible to encourage such developments whilst minimizing the potential risk to the company?

- *Human services as moral work*. This reflects the 'social worth' and 'self-identity' of the people on whose behalf the service is being performed. Defining clients as being either objects or subjects also reflects the moral dilemma facing the providers. If they are objects then the professional knows best. If they are subjects then the individual should be involved in determining their own processing.
- *Human services as gendered work*. Caring and nurturing activities within society have traditionally been undertaken by females. It has been argued (Hasenfeld, 1992, p 7) that this creates organizations with a tendency towards feminine qualities (collectivism and participation) compared to the typically male dominated commercial organizations reflecting bureaucracy, authority and control.

Consensual organizations

Examples of the consensual organization are the co-operative and the kibbutz (Iannello, 1992, p 27). The writer quotes a definition from Rothschild and Whitt (1986) as, 'any enterprise in which control rests ultimately and overwhelmingly with the member–employees–owners, regardless of the particular legal framework through which this is achieved'. This work identifies the following aspects that differentiate consensual organizations:

- *Authority*. This is retained by the collective body and is not a function of position. Authority may be temporarily vested in a particular individual but is subject to recall and control by the whole group.
- *Rules*. These emerge from the norms and ethical values associated with the founders and members of the group.
- *Social control*. This is based on group dynamics and the value frameworks of the individuals involved. In managerial organizations it is based on supervision, disciplinary sanction and the socialization of individuals.
- *Social relations*. These are also based on the values and ideals espoused by the collective.
- *Recruitment and advancement*. This is based on friendship networks rather than the formalized assessment of qualification and skill. Compatibility with the ideals of the organization is a significant requirement for employment in such organizations.
- *Incentive structures*. It is the social, collective involvement and ideological aspects of the activities that are suggested to motivate and reward individuals.
- *Social stratification*. Consensual organizations seek to function under egalitarian principles and therefore avoid differences resulting from hierarchical stratification.
- *Differentiation of labour*. Emphasizes integration, flexibility and contribution with differences between jobs and 'manual' and 'mental' work being less pronounced.

Rothschild and Whitt also imply that in attempting to achieve a non-hierarchical structure, a number of issues restrict the possibility of its achievement. They include the additional time required for decision making in a non-hierarchical setting. Another is the difficulty in moving away from non-democratic habits, values and work practices. The environmental constraints arising from the conventionally organized world around the consensual organization also affect structure and design.

Iannello indicates that the primary goal of consensual organizations is the humanization of the workplace in an attempt to re-establish the relationship between workers and society by minimizing the effect of hierarchy on the organization. In discussing research into this type of organization, studies of the kibbutz, Yugoslavian worker organizations and the Mondragon operations in Spain are frequently quoted. Summarizing the work of Greenberg (1986), Iannello identifies the characteristic of a number of consensual organizations:

- *Kibbutz*. Originating in Israel, the kibbutz is an attempt to combine work, social and family life into an integrated whole. Decisions are agreed at a weekly meeting of the whole organization. The leadership positions are elected and carry no special privileges or reward. Formal hierarchy is actively discouraged and control is achieved through a system of committees and the weekly meeting. Of the three types of organization described, only the kibbutz achieves any significant degree of employee influence over the sub-society.
- *The former Yugoslavia*. A national system of employee-governed organizations evolved. Legislation required organizations of more than ten people to establish a works council, its function being to determine the main company policies. The council also elected (and could remove) the management board and the plant director. It was the job of the management board to run the company on a day-to-day basis under the general direction of the works council. Given the recent major political and social upheavals in this part of the world it can only be assumed that this organizational approach has largely ceased to function and that it did not engender any depth of harmony between the peoples involved.
- *Mondragon*. This type of consensual organization originated in Spain and consists of some 80–90 individual co-operatives, employing approximately 19 000 people. Responsibility in each of the separate co-operative organizations lies with the general meeting of all members, which meets once each year. Its function is to elect the board of directors and senior managers. Managers below this level are appointed in the conventional way. The organization seeks to function on the basis of shared ownership and egalitarian principles of operation.

FACTORS INFLUENCING ORGANIZATIONAL DESIGN

In attempting to design an organization there are a number of departments, functions, activities or components to be fitted together within a framework. Whatever the purpose or size of the organization it is necessary to integrate these components effectively so that the desired objectives can be achieved. The structure of the organization is only one part of this integration process. Other important elements are the systems and procedures that the organization utilizes in support of its activities. For example, the use of financial reporting can help to ensure that each operational unit within the organization knows how it is contributing to the overall financial well-being of the organization.

Integration processes to support particular organizational designs include the communication, consultative and reporting mechanisms adopted, the purpose being to ensure that separate parts of the organization keep each other informed about their activities, problems and requirements so that effective integration of effort takes place. Company policies on issues such as secondment and career development can also influence the degree of unanimity within the structure as a whole. This view of design suggests that structure alone will not guarantee the success or failure of an organization. The weaknesses and deficiencies of a particular structural configuration can be offset to a significant degree by the support mechanisms introduced by management. Naturally, the converse is also applicable – that an effective structure can be weakened through poor support infrastructure.

It was Mintzberg (1979, 1981) who provided a simple view of the structural components that needed to be fitted together in the design of any organization. Figure 15.19 is adapted from his work.

Each of the components in Figure 15.19 has a different set of functions to perform:

- *Senior management*. Responsible for the direction of the organization and setting appropriate objectives.
- *Middle management*. Responsible for ensuring that resources are effectively utilized in pursuit of the objectives set by senior management.
- *Technical support staff*. These provide expertise across a number of necessary disciplines. For example, designers, engineers, lawyers and computer specialists.
- *Administrative support staff*. These provide indirect support through clerical and administrative activities, maintenance of the production equipment etc.
- *Functional core employees*. These actually work on the products and services offered by the organization.

A slightly different view of how to categorize organizational activity was described by Handy (1993). He adopted a classification based on the type of activity undertaken by different parts of the organization:

- *Policy*. This guides the direction of the organization. In addition, allocating resources and setting of priorities are important features of this category.
- *Innovation*. This is about the development of new products and services, changing the organization itself and finding new ways to meet the needs of customers.
- *Steady state*. This describes those parts of the business that function best in a predetermined, stable mode. For example, production facilities are most efficient when they are able to plan ahead and organize their resources effectively.

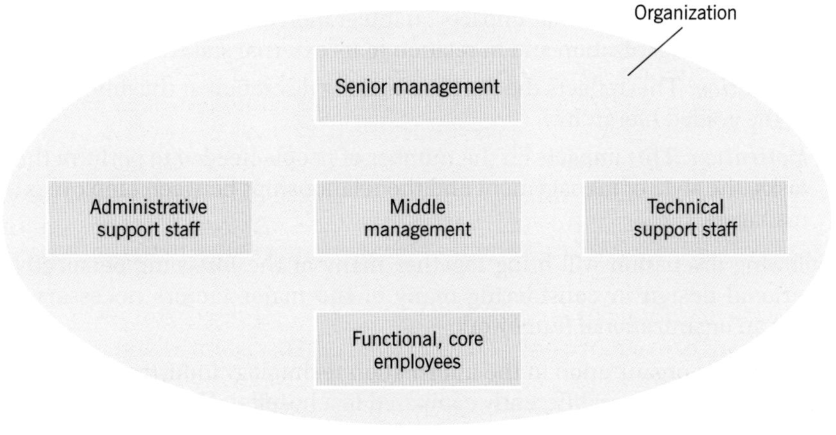

FIGURE 15.19

Organizational components (*adapted from*: Mintzberg, H (1979) *The Structuring of Organizations*, Prentice Hall, Englewood Cliffs, NJ)

- *Crisis*. These deal with unexpected events, for example the repair of machines. However, responding to the needs of a customer who is experiencing a sudden upsurge in demand is also an example of a crisis.

Handy stresses in his work that the 'activity types' are not the same as functional groupings. Many of the functional groups will incorporate a number of the four types of activity described here. For example, a personnel department could be described in the following terms:

- *Policy*. The senior personnel team that has the responsibility for the determination of personnel policy and the integration of personnel activities.
- *Innovation*. The development of new personnel initiatives such as the design of a new pay deal intended to encourage teamwork and flexibility.
- *Steady state*. This would be the routine processing of personnel data and statistical information such as reporting on absence levels.
- *Crisis*. This could be the industrial relations section having to respond to a walkout by factory employees.

These examples indicate the complex nature of organizational activity and the difficulty in prescribing brief, though intuitively attractive descriptions of how organizations function. Handy does recognize this constraint but suggests that functions will tend towards one or the other 'activity types' as a dominant orientation. Harris and Raviv (2002) develop a model that seeks to explain organization structure based on identifying the optimal co-ordination of interaction between managerial activities. In doing so, they evaluate the trade-off decisions between the various costs, and benefits of various configurations between individual manager expertise and the CEO company-wide co-ordination.

Child (1988) suggested six components necessary for the creation of an organization structure. They are:

1. *Task*. This reflects the way in which the actual tasks that need to be performed within the organization are bundled together in order to create jobs.
2. *Reporting relationships*. This reflects the way in which management will be imposed on the organization in a graded hierarchy of responsibility.
3. *Clustering*. This reflects how the groups of activity will be clustered together in a recognizable organizational pattern.
4. *Procedures*. This reflects the systems, procedures, communication networks and information flow that impacts on integration and co-ordination both within the organization and in relation to its external stakeholders.
5. *Delegation*. This reflects the decision making discretion at the different levels in the graded hierarchy.
6. *Motivation*. This impacts on the number of people needed to perform the tasks, the style of management and the relationships between employees and managers.

The following discussion will bring together many of the foregoing perspectives on organizational design in considering many of the major factors necessary to the creation of an organizational framework:

- *Purpose*. An organization in the information technology industry is likely to arrange its resources differently compared to a hospital. However, it is more complex than that simple example might suggest. For example, a hospital that specializes in accident and emergency will structure itself differently from one that will specialize in care of the elderly.

- *Levels*. Any organization with more than one person in it comprises more than one level. This might be as simple as two levels if the organization consists of two people, the owner–manager and one employee. However, within organizations such as the civil service and very large private sector companies there might be many levels. Levels reflect the graded hierarchy associated with the magnitude of decision making together with responsibility for resources and areas of the business. It reflects a top-down view of how things should be.
- *Division of labour*. This reflects the need to group together the tasks that need to be done into the meaningful 'chunks' of activity that are called jobs. Division of labour is therefore about how work is organized and there are many ways in which that can be done. At one extreme lies the scientific management approach with job enrichment at the other. Enrichment in the form of empowerment has been argued to reflect attempts by managers to control employees through more subtle means than Taylorism. If employees will engage with managers in the running of the enterprise then, it is argued, they will become like managers and will automatically perform their allotted duties (and more) in the best interests of the capital owners, what Thompson (1989) refers to as 'the manufacture of consent' (p 159).
- *Centralization and decentralization*. This is an old problem that is still evident, even in the political world. Michael Heseltine (1999), reflecting on the role of the British prime minister points out the temptation for political leaders to centralize power and control on themselves in order to drive change in public policy. But at the same time, he notes, it is impossible for the individual to cope with the demands of having done so. There is an almost inevitable circularity in the centralization–decentralization approach to organizational design. In a decentralized organization, there will be pressure to seek the maximum level of in-house collaboration between units and to minimize the level of duplicated effort. More effective integration leads the organization towards centralization. Centralization leads to slowness of reaction and decision making as well as the growth in central functions that do not contribute directly to operational performance. Very few organizations seem able to achieve the full potential from either decentralization or centralization.
- *Line and staff functions*. It is unfortunate that these terms are used in different ways which can confuse. The first way in which the term line is used is to refer to a **line manager**. Every employee reports to a line manager – their boss. Another way in which the terms are used is in referring to **line and staff functions**. A line function is involved with the main purposes of the organization – the operational functions. For example, in a major bank the line functions would be those associated with direct banking activities, including the branch network, commercial loans, insurance services, etc. The staff functions refer to the activities which although necessary are supportive of the main operational functions. Examples would include personnel, marketing, computer services, etc. However the definition of staff function differs between organizations and depending upon the main business. So a bank might class the computer function as a line department in its internet division. The terms line and staff potentially become more confusing because employees within staff functions all have line managers!

Line manager
Every employee reports to a line manager – their boss.

Line and staff functions
Line functions deliver the main purposes of the organization – operations departments; staff functions are the support activities.

The distinction between line and staff functions is becoming less meaningful as the commercial activities of organizations diversify. All functions are now expected to add value to the organization or they become prospects for closure or outsourcing. For example, Merrick (1999) reviews the experience of Westminster City Council which outsourced most of its personnel department. The remaining in-house personnel function concentrated on strategic issues, leaving the day-to-day provision of the service to the subcontractor. The outsourced personnel function is a staff function of the Council, but at the same time a line function within the company providing the service. Equally, companies can sometimes see the opportunity for turning their own staff functions into a commercial activity. For example, British Airways advertises the services of Chameleon Training and Consulting, the commercial organization created from the development of customer care training for its own staff (see their advertisement in *People Management*, 1999, p 90).

Span of control
Refers to the number of subordinates reporting to a single boss.

- *Span of control*. This refers to the number of subordinates reporting to a single boss. The significance of the concept of the **span of control** lies in its relationship with the diversity of responsibility and interaction requirements. The more people reporting to a single boss the more likely it is that the boss is responsible for a broad range of disparate activities. It is not usual for a single person to be equally knowledgeable and experienced across a wide range of job functions. Therefore the wider their responsibilities the more likely it is that they will underperform in some aspect of them. This also provides opportunities for subgroups and informal leaders to emerge which can lead to fragmentation of authority and other problems. Equally, the number of interaction channels increases with the number of people reporting to each boss, which means that each person gets a smaller proportion of the boss's time and less opportunity to contribute to group discussions etc. This can result in significant aspects of situations being missed and the potential contribution from particular specialisms being under-represented in critical discussions. Some writers and consultants such as Urwick suggest that the span of control should be a specific number, usually five or six people. This is perhaps unrealistic and not supported by the work of Collins and Hull (1986) who suggest that the debate has now changed because of the flexibility created through the use of new technology. Also the personal characteristics of the individuals concerned, morale, motivation and other situation factors impact on the number of subordinates that can be managed effectively.
- *Scalar chain*. This aspect of organizational design reflects the height of an organization in terms of the number of levels from the top to the bottom. As such it does not reflect the number of grades of staff, but the number of reporting levels. So in the case of a production factory, a shopfloor worker might report to a supervisor, who in turn reports to the production manager, who in turn reports to the production director, who in turn reports to the chief executive. This example reflects an organization with five levels in it. Putting the span of control together with the **scalar chain** gives a common way of describing an organization as either tall or flat (Figure 15.9). A tall organization would be one with many levels in it. A flat organization would be one with relatively few levels in it. Over the past few years many organizations have been engaging in delayering to strip out levels to make the organization more responsive to its customers and less reliant on the scalar chain.

Scalar chain
This reflects the height of an organization in terms of the number of levels from the top to the bottom.

- *Organizational metaphors*. The term metaphor conjures up a generalized picture from which more specific meaning can be gleaned. When we say 'the man is a lion', we use the image of a lion to draw attention to the lion-like aspects of the man. The metaphor frames our understanding of the man in a distinctive yet partial way (Morgan, 1986, p 13). What the metaphor provides is an insight through an efficient form of communication: the lion conjures up a complex picture that needs few words to express it – provided that the receiver has the same understanding. To know that the man is like a lion provides a basis for both understanding and action towards that person without having to have a detailed knowledge of him.

In the same way, we use **organization** as a metaphor to describe individual entities, to disguise difference and simplify complexity arising from the existence of individual variation. This perspective adds a dimension to the contingency approach to organization design. If humans understand through the use of metaphor then perhaps the metaphors managers use to relate to organizations determines how they subsequently structure them. Morgan identifies a number of metaphors that illustrates this point in Table 15.3. Metaphor becomes the basis of belief about how organizations should function. The 'facts' encountered are 'fitted' into the metaphorical image. The importance of metaphor in contingency thinking is that it provides a means through which humans understand organizations and how they function in a specific context. That understanding can provide a basis for deciding how the organization could be structured. Oliver (2002) uses biological and gene structure metaphors to demonstrate that survival in the long term is achieved by what he terms organic organizations using strategies that mimic biological, complex, self-regulating development rather than mechanistic strategy models.

Organization
Social arrangements of people and other resources working together in consciously created structured arrangements in pursuit of collective objectives.

CHARTING ORGANIZATIONS

The **organization chart** is a means by which organizations describe the structure and reporting relationships that exist. The organization chart can also be an effective means of tracking formal lines of communication, levels of responsibility and audit trails. Reproduced as Figure 15.20 is an example of an organization chart for a hypothetical medium-sized company in the fast food industry.

There are, however, severe limitations in the ability of the organization chart to reflect what actually happens within an organization. Not included are the cross-functional relationships that are necessary to ensure that information flows around the organization in an appropriate way. Nor does it reflect the decision-making processes that exist. Frequently, organization charts do not reflect the levels of responsibility held by the individual posts indicated in them. For example, in Figure 15.20 the

Organization chart
A diagrammatic means by which organizations describe structure and reporting relationships.

Machine	A network of parts: functional departments ... which are further specified as networks of precisely defined jobs (p 27)
Organisms	Living systems, existing in a wider environment on which they depend for the satisfaction of various needs (p 39)
Brains	Utilizes the concepts of intelligence, feedback and information processing to model organizational functioning
Culture	Directs attention to the symbolic or even 'magical' significance of even the most rational aspects of organizational life (p 135)
Political	Managers frequently talk about authority, power and superior–subordinate relations ... Organizations as systems of the government that vary according to the political principles employed (p 142)

TABLE 15.3 Organizational metaphors (*source*: Morgan, G (1986) *Images of Organization*, Sage, Newbury Park, CA)

FIGURE 15.20

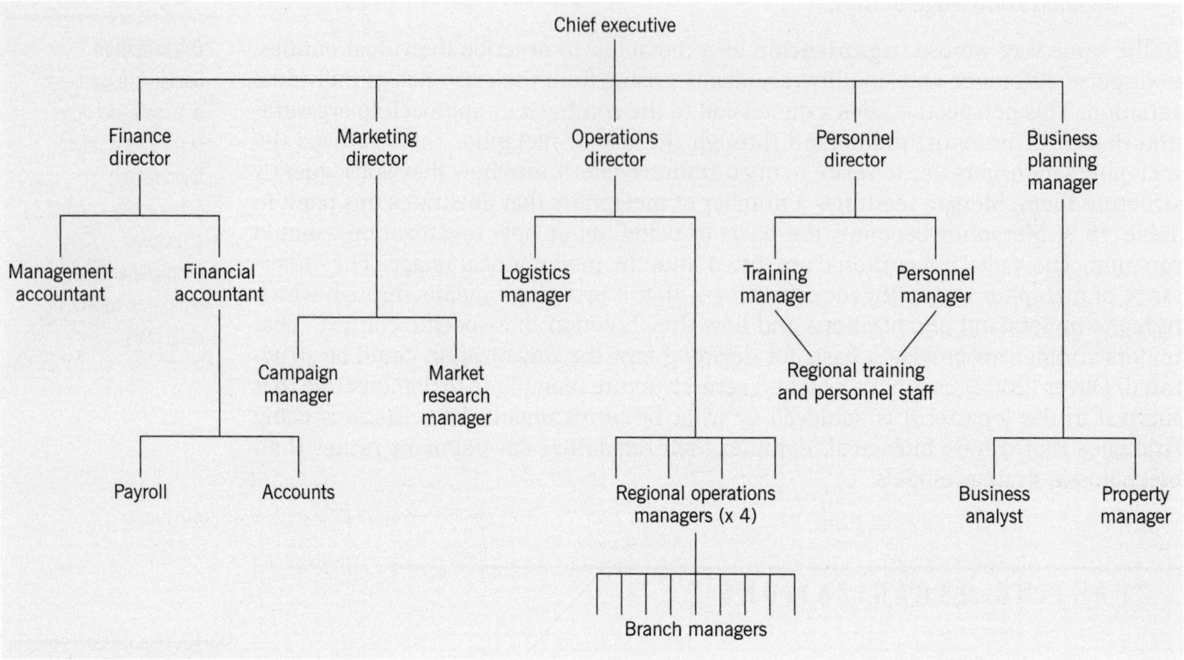

Organization chart for a fast-food chain

senior managers are all shown at the same level, reporting to the chief executive. But there are four directors and one manager in the job titles at that level. Does this imply that the business planning manager has less responsibility than the others, or that the postholder does not have a seat on the board of directors? There have been attempts to reflect the relative seniority of people within an organization chart by scaling the vertical dimension of it, see Figure 15.21.

The solid lines drawn between job titles on an organization chart reflect direct reporting relationships. These reflect the line manager relationships discussed earlier. In addition, it is not uncommon to see dotted lines between positions in a chart. These indicate high levels of influence and consultation based relationships. For example, the production planner in a manufacturing company may report to the logistics manager as their line manager, but have a dotted-line relationship with the production manager. The production planner does not work for the production manager, but can significantly impact on the effective running of the production department, so it makes sense for the semi-formal relationship between the two to be recognized.

Rich picture
A drawing reflecting a dynamic situation in a manner meaningful to the participants.

There are other ways of reflecting how an organization functions. For example, the concept of a **rich picture** provides a mechanism through which a dynamic situation can be reflected in a manner meaningful to the participants. Figure 15.22 is an example that illustrates the problems and influences acting upon a particular situation. The picture is reasonably self-explanatory in that the swords represent conflict and the joined hands areas of agreement. In effect, an organization chart describes the formal appearance of an organization but a rich picture can reflect how the organization actually works. It can reflect how the processes function as well as people interaction and behaviour patterns within the organization.

Influence diagram
Illustration of the influences and relationships that exist between individuals and groups interacting with an organization.

Another means of reflecting activity within an organization is through an **influence diagram**. This can illustrate the relationships and influences that exist between individuals and groups within and outside the organization. Figure 15.23 is a

FIGURE 15.21

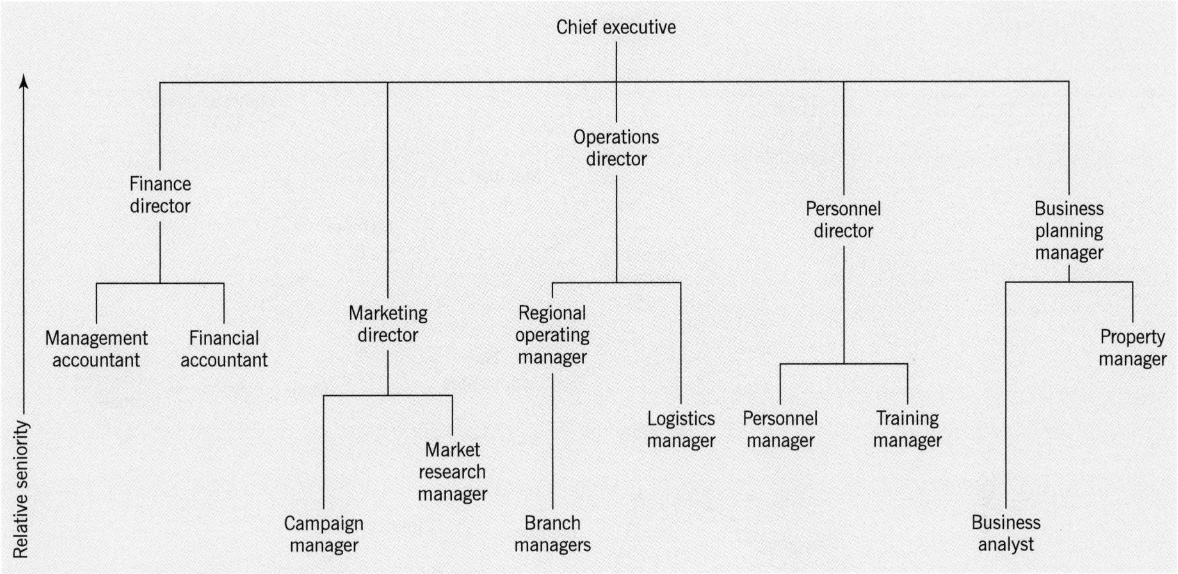

Organization chart scaled to show relative seniority

FIGURE 15.22

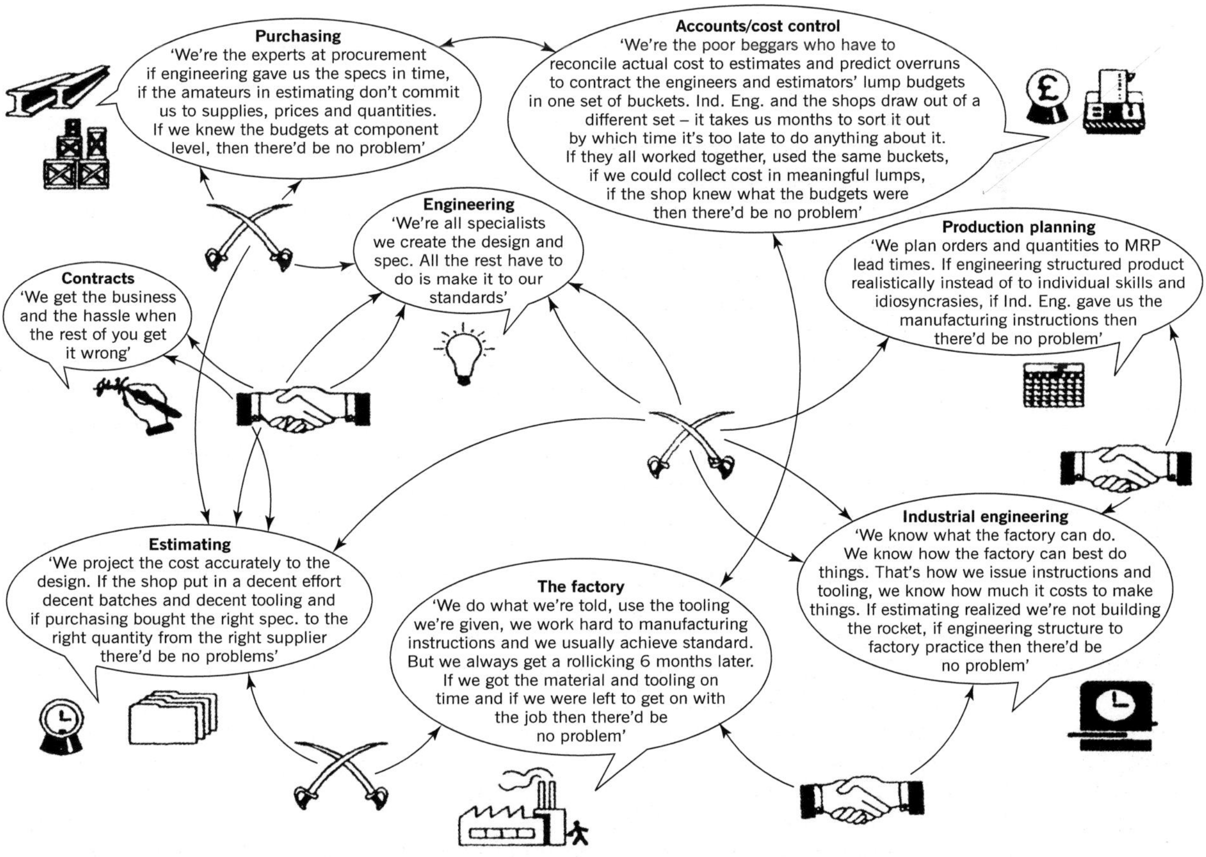

A rich picture of a situation in an engineering company (*source*: Checkland, P and Scholes, J (1990) *Soft Systems Methodology in Action*, John Wiley, Chichester).

FIGURE 15.23

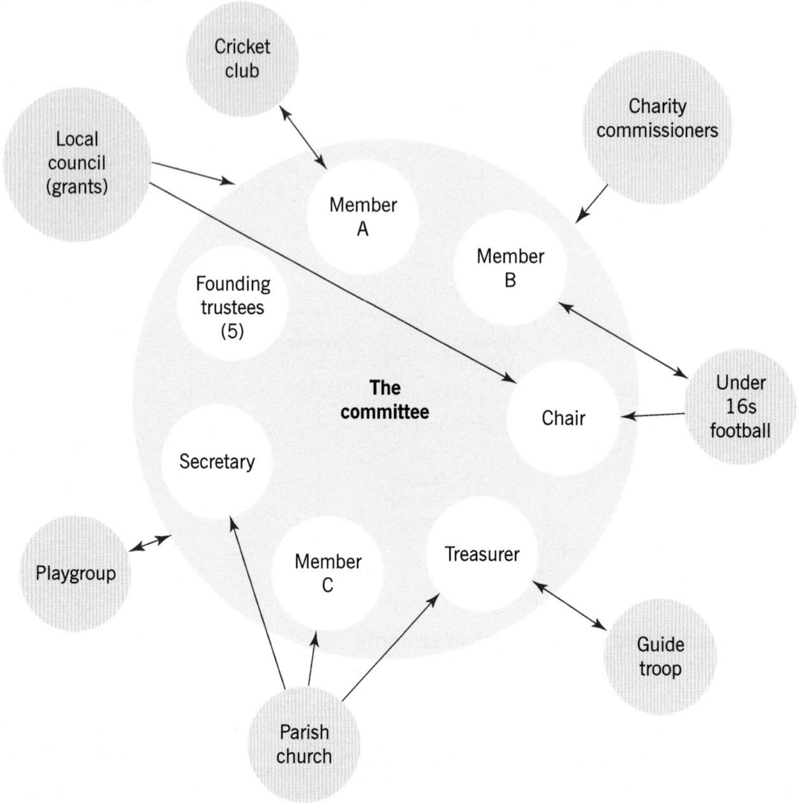

Influence diagram (*source*: Giles, K and Hedge, N (1994) *The Manager's Good Study Guide*, Open University, Milton Keynes)

simple influence diagram based around a village playing fields committee (the organization). The type of arrow used between elements in the diagram reflects the form and/or frequency that interaction takes.

Organizations are continually subjected to change. This can include individuals leaving or joining; jobs being declared redundant or new jobs created; promotions and changes in reporting relationships; acquisitions and divestments. Consequently, the organization chart needs to be updated frequently in order to maintain its relevance and value. Townsend (1985) goes so far as to suggest that organization charts can demoralize people as they reflect how far from the top most people actually are and the number of bosses that exist above each individual. The organization chart reflects how management wish the organization to look and function. This is not necessarily the same as the way the employees (and customers) think that the organization looks or functions, based on their experience, a point made by Heller (1997). The validity of an organization chart is a function of a number of factors, including:

- *Age*. The older an organization chart is, the less likely it is to reflect current structure and reporting relationships.
- *Detail*. It is not unusual to find larger organizations having several organization charts, covering different levels and divisions within the organization.
- *Purpose*. A chart drawn up to reflect the main functional splits within the organization would be of little value in identifying who deals with customer queries.

- *Need*. Organization charts have limitations in being able to describe how an organization functions. This need might be more effectively met through the use of rich pictures and influence diagrams.

ORGANIZATIONAL STRUCTURE AND DESIGN: AN APPLIED PERSPECTIVE

The relevance of the foregoing discussion for organizational design lies in the decision making process around the options available. It is managers who make the decisions about the organization, its size and structure. It is therefore a process that is based upon the same perceptual, political and self-interest factors that exist in every other area of managerial work. That is not to suggest that there are no rational or business-related reasons for the choices that are made. It is simply to suggest that in making a choice, factors other than the 'facts' can influence decisions. Equally, this is not the place to begin to consider just how many things that are taken as 'facts' stand up to scrutiny as objective and essential influences on structure. In this context it is relevant to point out that the reasons that justify the choice of a particular design configuration are just as vulnerable to perceptual 'interpretation' as any other stimuli. However, making choices with regard to organizational design is what managers are required to do. For example, Schminke *et al.* (2002) demonstrate a relationship between the structural arrangements of an organization and the employee's level within that structure on the perception of fairness as experienced by that individual. This idea is developed further by Ambrose and Schminke (2003) who suggest that different forms of organizational justice were dominant in mechanistic and organic organizations.

In the discussion so far the different frameworks have been introduced as discrete types. The impression is easily gained that organizations consider at frequent intervals the structure that is best suited to their circumstances and then implement that form. Rarely does the process operate in that simple way. It has been suggested earlier in this chapter that organizations evolve and change over time in response to the success achieved and the desires of the owners. This process is reflected in the Greiner model included as Figure 15.8. However, the process is less well defined and less certain than is implied by that model. For example, a company may be taken over by another and integrated into an existing operation and structure. An owner/manager may decide to restrict the size of the organization deliberately in order to retain effective control. Partners may decide to break up a company if they find that they can no longer work together. A sudden expansion opportunity may present itself as a result of a large order. All of these situations will force some rethinking of the organizational design, but they are far from the simple and linear growth model implied in Figure 15.8.

Organizations evolve and in moving from one 'stage' to another in the lifecycle the structure tends to adjust. It is frequently only when a significant crisis occurs that a fundamental rethink of major activity, including structure, is undertaken. Radically to change the way in which work is undertaken within an organization requires time and additional resources. It also carries with it the risk of failure – it lowers performance until employees become accustomed to the new work patterns and reporting arrangements. It may also disrupt the service to the customer as mistakes inevitably occur. Consequently, it is hardly surprising that evolutionary change is preferred to revolutionary change. However, evolution also carries significant risk; the lack of clarity in responsibilities during the transition period for example. The effect of evolutionary change in organization design produces a degree of mismatch between the structure in existence at any point in time and that desired.

The technology utilized within an organization is an influencing factor in structural decisions. It is also true that technology is not a neutral factor in management activity. Management pays for the development of technology through the purchase decision. The decision to use a particular technology can be based on the desire to control activity within the organization as much as through a need to increase efficiency and reduce cost. In that context it influences both the design of jobs within the organization and the configuration of the units that make up the organization itself. Technology can also be used as the justification for a change in the structure of an organization. In short, a change in structure can be deliberately brought about through the introduction, adaptation or elimination of particular technologies. Structure can be both the driving force for technological development or driven by it.

Some views on the determinants of structure assume a restricted metaphor on the nature of organizations and how they operate. Simple views of organizational hierarchy and structure create the very conditions that make it difficult for organizations to meet the needs of their customers. The creation of an authority-based hierarchy forces everyone inside the organization to focus on the boss, their needs and interpretation of events. Continued employment, promotion and performance assessment are dependent on the views of superiors. Therefore, in practice, what the boss does not see does not exist. Inevitably this directs the attention of employees inwards and upwards, not in the direction of the customer as reflected in the following Employee Perspective (15.5).

The customer experiences any organization horizontally, not vertically. Consider your experiences of a bank, supermarket, university, church or any other organization. You are very unlikely to meet anyone other than the lower levels of the organization as it is they who deal with your transactions. Senior levels usually see their role as strategic and as running the organization, not dealing with the customers. A view which perhaps contributes to the reaction described in the previous Employee Perspective. Figure 15.24 seeks to reflect this through the conflicting forces originating from customer and hierarchical needs acting on any organization. Because of this fundamental clash between the verticality of focus and horizontalness of activity it is hardly surprising that senior managers become detached from an understanding of the real needs of customers. Everything on which they base their decisions is processed and filtered as it moves up the hierarchy to them, and they do not have regular contact with customers to keep them in touch with that perspective.

EMPLOYEE PERSPECTIVE 15.5

How do you know when you have 'made it'?

Mei-Wei worked in a large bank in Melbourne, Australia. She described how her organization worked in practice, rather than as the management, advertising, service standards, employee handbooks and staff training suggested that it worked.

She said that every employee aspired to reach the first level of seniority within the bank – the first 'level' at it which it could be said that the individual had 'made it'. When this level was reached it meant that the individual no longer had to deal with customers every day. Once at that level, employees then aspired to achieve the next level of seniority at the bank – this reflected a post in which the individual *really had* 'made it' to the big time! This meant that as well as not having to deal with ordinary customers, it was no longer necessary to deal with employees either!

Tasks

1. What effect might such views have on the performance of the bank and its customer service?
2. How would you seek to deal with such a cynical view of the organization if you were the Chief Executive Officer of such a bank? Recall that you have probably worked your way through the ranks of the bank and might have held such views yourself in the past!
3. What part might structure play in such attitudes and how might it be used to break them down?

FIGURE 15.24

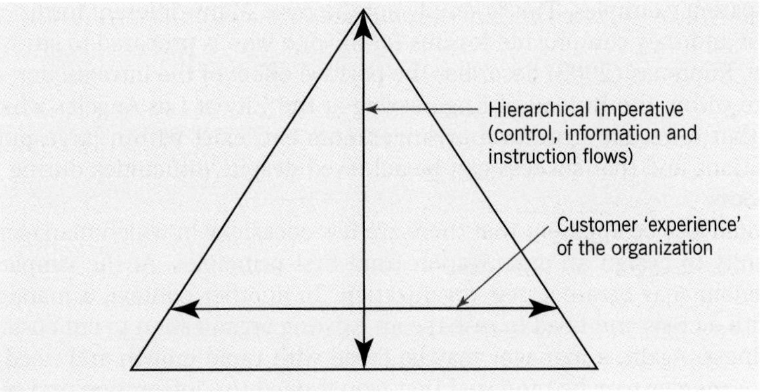

Conflict between customer and hierarchical needs

The appeal of contingency theory is the potential to determine the significance and number of forces acting on the situation and therefore to account for them (at least superficially) in the design of the organization. This emphasis on a normative perspective delivers high levels of usability benefit to managers but perhaps offers little by way of fundamental explanation of what it is that creates structure (Legge, 1978). Organizations are composed of a number of smaller groups or departments and these can have very different perspectives and interactions with the environment around them. For example, the personnel department will interact with a number of the same groups and individuals as the production department, but a largely different set to those appropriate to the research and development function.

Another way of considering how organizations evolve over time has been the application of population ecology to the process. Using what can be described as Darwinian theories this approach emerged in the late 1970s, but it has not yet produced a significant alternative explanation in relation to organizational evolution. It attempts to utilize the notion of selection to the way in which structures evolve over time. It is an approach which suggests that the most appropriate organizations are 'selected' for survival based on environmental fit and adaptation (Thompson and McHugh, 1995). However, the discussion above in relation to the biological metaphor used by Oliver (2002) is illuminating and more positive in this respect.

While it may be an interesting academic debate to consider the nature of structure, its determinants and evolutionary forces, managers must function in real time in a dynamic context. Consequently, a contingency model can provide managers with an improved opportunity to influence design and perhaps increase the probability of organizational survival. The notion of selection in ecology would imply that the environments are in some way rewarding the most effectively adapted organizations with continued existence. In that context, managers are only one aspect of the environment and can only facilitate, not determine survival. If this approach could be shown to have relevance then it would have profound implications for the role and purpose of management in relation to organizational functioning.

Structure is the means of organizing within the enterprise. It is the vehicle for ensuring that the necessary work can be done without overloading individuals. It also allows specialization to be introduced in order to reduce the skill and training required within the organization. However, it also provides the simplified and repetitive tasks that can create alienation and a lack of commitment to the objectives being sought. It is a double-edged sword, providing benefits and disadvantages. It is in an attempt to offset some of the disadvantages arising from conventional structural forms that the alternative organizational forms are important. It is easy to assume that the only structural forms that exist are the large private and public sector organizations that are the most apparent examples. This is simply not the case. Many different forms of organization exist and they can provide lessons for anyone who is prepared to study them. For example, Kuprenas (2003) describes the positive effect of the introduction of a matrix structure within the Bureau of Engineering at the City of Los Angeles which demonstrates that different structural arrangements can exist within large public sector organizations and that success can be achieved despite difficulties during the transition process.

It should also be apparent that there are few occasions in which managers have the opportunity to design an organization from first principles. At the simplest level an entrepreneur may create a new organization. In another context, a manager may be faced with a crisis and need to reshape an existing organization to cut costs or refocus the business. Again, a manager may be faced with rapid growth and need to expand quickly. A merger may be proposed that would need the integration and reshaping of two or more overlapping organizations. An organization may seek to develop new product lines (or close existing ones) the implications of which need to be integrated into an existing framework. A new manager may decide that reorganization is necessary in order that they might strengthen their own position relative to a group of long-serving subordinates. These all reflect examples of situations where changes to an existing structure are likely to occur. Gowland and Aiken (2003) review the structural and cultural changes that took place in a number of privatized organizations in both New Zealand and Australia during the 1990s. In doing so they drew on the experiences of senior executives who had detailed knowledge of pre- and post-privatization conditions. Although limited areas of no change were identified, significant change generally followed privatization.

With the need (or desire) to change an existing structure comes a range of factors that need to be taken into account which are not present in creating something for the first time. For example, existing staff will be familiar, experienced and may be comfortable with the status quo and may resent and resist any imposed changes. Equally, procedures and systems may need to be redesigned to accommodate the proposed changes. Even customers and suppliers may not be happy with the impact of proposed changes. All of this suggests that adapting an organizational design to changed circumstances is a much more complex process than designing a new company.

CONCLUSIONS

This chapter reviewed the major themes associated with the design of organizations. It demonstrated that there are a considerable number of options available with regard to the design of an organization and that each has advantages and disadvantages. The structural form of an organization shapes to a considerable degree the behaviour of the individuals within it. It determines the jobs that people do as well as the nature of interaction within and outside the organization. It also determines the nature of any reporting and control relationships. At several points in the discussion in this chapter the notion of an interactive relationship with the environment was also introduced.

The design and structure of an organization is an area in which managers make choices. The form of the organization is not something that occurs by chance, or as a result of some dictat from shareholders. It is appropriate to view an organization as something over which people have stewardship for a period of time. They are therefore constrained by a number of forces when moulding the organization. These constraints include the industry, size, history, technology, markets, legal requirement, profitability as well as the will, ability and objectives of individuals within the organization.

The notion of a direct cause and effect link between a number of environmental forces and the structure of an organization is overly simplistic. It ignores the interactive nature of external and internal forces and managerial responses. The use of metaphor was introduced as a means of accounting for the understanding that managers have of what an organization is and how it should function relative to its circumstances. It is not the intention to suggest that contingency approaches offer perfect explanations and applied options for understanding organization design. They do, however, offer a richer means of attempting to understand the processes involved.

Now to summarize this chapter in terms of the relevant Learning Objectives:

- **Outline the main structural choices available to organizations.** There are a number of distinct organizational frameworks that exist. The simplest being an entrepreneurial structure which would tend to be found in smaller organizations. Also introduced were the product and process based structures in which the focus of activity is either functional departments or the products or services produced. Other common organizational frameworks introduced include the approach to international organizations, the holding company concept, matrix and project based structures. Other less frequently found organizational frameworks such as the virtual and flexible organization were introduced as were alternative organizational forms such as the shamrock organization and consensual organizations such as the co-op and kibbutz. Descriptions about each of these forms of organization are included in the appropriate sections of this chapter.
- **Detail how the need to compartmentalize the work of an organization is at variance with the need to integrate activities.** The process of structuring an organization is necessary in order to achieve a number of objectives including the need to break down the overall activity into discrete jobs and areas of responsibility. However, the customer experience does not neatly break down into such compartments. The customer inevitably wants to be able to deal with a streamlined process that involves minimal inconvenience and necessity to interact with more than one person. In all organizations the customer process invariably involves some form of (as a very simplified process) placing an order, receiving the goods or service and paying the bill. This invariably involves several 'compartments' within any organization working together. So the compartments created by the structure must interact effectively if the customer experience is to be achieved in a way which would encourage further business exchanges. This is the basis of the vertical and horizontal conflicts model included as Figure 15.24. The structure of an organization tends to emphasize the vertical reporting relationships and departmental loyalty at the expense of effective integration across functions in support of customer service and this is what any integrative procedures and practices are designed to achieve. It is also what some of the structural frameworks are intended to achieve through an emphasis on the matrix, delayered, flexible and virtual forms.
- **Assess the significance of the development of more recent approaches to structure such as the shamrock and federal organization.** Organization structure reflects the ways in which the physical arrangements are organized in seeking to achieve operational objectives. As such it reflects a social process involving how managers seek to position their organizations relative to the environment in achieving commercial success. The more recent approaches to organizational design are a reflection of some of the trends apparent in seeking to find ways of differentiating organizations and seeking to capture an advantage in the marketplace. In some industries change is very fast and it is sometimes not possible for a single conventional organization to be capable of keeping up with the changes occurring and at the same time convert these into products and services for customers. Consequently the virtual organization allows coalitions to be formed that enable various contributing parties to utilize their particular strengths in conjunction with other organizations in order to become capable of achieving more that they could individually. Other forms of structure such as the shamrock approach the issue of structure from a different perspective and suggest that it is the essence of flexibility that will allow organizations to respond more effectively in the future and so arrangements need to reflect the various forms of labour flexibility available into differently managed business approaches that can better match the changing needs of the marketplace. The significance of these approaches is that they demonstrate that the issue of structure is not one of the application of a formula seeking to provide a guaranteed match between product, size and intention, but one of creativity and the development of innovative ways of looking at the needs of customers and how these can be met within a social arrangement that needs to function internally, not just externally.

- **Explain the limitations of the standard organization chart in describing activity within an organization.** The standard organization chart reflects little more than reporting arrangements. It shows the major compartments that exist and the job titles that exist within those departments. It usually gives no indication of the relative seniority of the people or jobs indicated in the chart or of the cross-functional interactions and process relationships that exist. There are charts that seek to compensate for these deficiencies, by seeking to incorporate relative seniority and other factors; however these are generally limited in scope as their inclusion can quickly make any chart look a mess as a result of the number of lines included. The almost continual movement of people into and out of jobs, departments and the organization itself, combined with job changes and other activity changes also means that any organization chart is out of date almost as soon as it is published. There are other charting devices that are intended to reflect other aspects of activity within an organization and these are discussed in the chapter.
- **Discuss the contingency model and its relationship to organizational structure.** The contingency model of structure is an approach which suggests that structure reflects an interactive relationship with the environment. Figure 15.4 provides an indication of the contingency approach to structure. It suggests that there are two categories of contingency variable, external and internal contingency factors. Both of which include a range of elements particular to the specific organization and its context. These factors are detected to a greater or lesser extent by managers who must also interpret them in seeking to understand them in relation to their business (and personal) objectives. This in turn produces an intention which is filtered through a number of factors such as the capability and willingness of the organization to change or adapt (if that is the intended course of action). Out of all of these processes emerges the actual organizational form that exists for the particular organization in question. It is an approach to organization structure that allows for differences between the structures of organizations of common size, in the same industry and in the same location as common environmental forces (external and internal) can be interpreted differently by the managers. Equally factors such as the will to make changes, or the capability to make the necessary changes might differ between organizations. The contingency approach captures all of this complexity by simply suggesting that structure depends upon the circumstances!

DISCUSSION QUESTIONS

1. What is a virtual organization and how does it differ (if at all) from the federal form?
2. Is the concept of a horizontal organization the same as the matrix organization? Identify the differences and similarities. Which would you prefer to work in and why?
3. To what extent does the view that theatre can be used as a metaphor for organization offer any value in understanding structural issues?
4. 'Organizations with fewer layers of management will face significant problems in the future as their managers will not have the opportunity to gain experience of major decision making before they have that responsibility.' Discuss the implications of this statement for organizational structure.
5. Describe bureaucracy and its various forms. In what ways and to what extent does bureaucracy have a part to play in modern organizational design?
6. Is it inevitable that centralization and decentralization will be cyclical trends in organizational design? Why or why not?
7. Business process re-engineering offers nothing new in seeking to simplify organizational structure; it simply reflects the application of scientific management. Discuss this statement.
8. Describe the contingency approach to designing an organization. How does it differ from the traditional views on structure?
9. Structure reflects nothing more than the means through which power and control over employees can be exercised by managers. Discuss this statement, justifying your views
10. What is a flexible firm and to what extent does it reflect the contingency approach to organizational design?

CASE STUDY Premium bonding

In February 1998 Commercial Union and General Accident, both general insurance businesses on a global scale merged, forming the £18 billion insurance company CGU Insurance. One of the key features of the process was the heavy involvement of staff in creating the design of the combined organization. Cees Schrauwers, managing director of Commercial Union indicated when he announced the merger:

> We wanted to avoid the infighting that is so often associated with takeovers, especially as the two companies were of almost equal size. We have all seen examples of mergers where the internal warfare has carried on for years after the event. That was something we wanted to avoid.

The merger was announced on 25 February 1998. All local managers were contacted by telephone overnight and asked to be in their office by 7am the next morning to receive a faxed briefing document. Presentation materials were delivered to each branch by 9am that morning. Included in the briefing was a commitment to design the new organization according to a set of principles:

- Structures would have the fewest possible number of levels (maximum of 5).
- Decision making would be delegated to the lowest appropriate level.
- Positions would have clear accountabilities, outputs and measures of performance.

It was some four months before the legal and financial merger was completed. In between the initial briefing and formal merger both companies worked hard to retain the loyalty of existing staff. Research was conducted to identify what the new company (CGU) needed to do in order to maintain the high levels of contribution from the staff. This was followed by the creation of a 'Discovery' programme. Large groups of first-line supervisors and technical specialists were nominated by staff in both companies to be trained to undertake a culture survey. First-line supervisors were chosen as the people to undertake the culture survey because they were close to staff, management and customers. Each person on the Discovery programme was paired up with someone from the other company in order to allow a cross-examination of each other's organization. In effect a 'visitors eye view' was created for each company and its way of doing things.

The second stage followed in June 1998 shortly after the Discovery process, when the two trade unions represented within CGU Insurance helped to organize a two-day conference for about 500 junior managers and technical specialists. It was the employees who nominated their first-line supervisors for inclusion in the process, which was given the title 'Being One'. The 500 delegates and trade union representatives were split into four smaller cohorts within the conference hall and asked to work on one aspect of the programme. In addition an employee survey and brand research was undertaken. This was all seeking to answer the basic question: 'What would make CGU Insurance the best place to work for employees?'

Each of the four cohorts within the conference worked on one topic from the themes for the conference which were:

- Getting the work done
- Leading and managing people
- Developing and rewarding people
- Working atmosphere and environment.

The activity in the hall was constantly televised on huge screens around the hall in order to give the two days the vibrancy, atmosphere and feeling of a major sporting event. During the latter part of the two days three-quarters of the delegates would circulate around the hall finding out what the other groups were deciding as part of developing their own group's work. The remaining quarter would stay behind and answer questions from the other groups seeking information. Strong feelings were surfaced over the course of the event. For example there was anger at the lack of an engaging style of leadership in both companies and the acceptance by managers of poor performance.

At the end of the event the directors undertook a commitment to build the type of organization that would meet the mandate emerging from the two-day conference. The areas of commitment undertaken were:

- To incorporate an empowered branch network, with appropriate support processes and profit accountability.
- To create high-performing teams that recognize success based on a 'can-do' attitude and supported by training, multiskilling and rewards
- To develop an appropriate supportive, open, relaxed and performance-oriented management style based on competence.

- To encourage staff through personal development, succession planning and provision of open access to opportunity.
- To value staff through consultation and a recognition of individuality.
- To support staff by valuing their contribution and rewarding it through performance pay.

The next (third) stage was to use a series of focus groups among senior managers in order to translate the directors' commitments into what became known as 'the best place to work blueprint'. This contained three main strands:

- Alignment of employee aspiration and company practice in terms of issues such as key result areas and knowing where each person fitted into the organization.
- Performance management practice to include issues such as managerial support for fair dealing and acknowledgement of success, along with customer-focused teams and well trained managers.
- Support from leaders who inspire confidence and trust; provide the technical and administrative support for front-line staff; provide an informal working environment and a respect for home- and work-life separation.

This blueprint now forms the basis for an annual employee survey to monitor employee expectation and company performance. The third stage created the basis for the fourth major involvement exercise, which took place in September 1998 and involved about 80 people from the trade unions, technical specialists and all levels of management. They were brought together to undertake an organizational design process. To aid this they had the output from a small team that had spent several months collecting data from around the group on aspects of best practice and operational effectiveness. At the end of the four-day design process the group had provided an outline of the new organization in terms of its relationship with its customers, its services and cost drivers. The main structural frameworks were also designated at that time including the size of business units (between 30–50 people), the size of work teams (between 10–12 people) and which locations would remain and which would be closed.

The result of the design process was piloted in a number of offices that were converted into CGU Insurance locations during April 1999. The final touches were put on the design framework during that pilot experience. It was at this stage that outside management support was introduced to the change process when PricewaterhouseCoopers provided members for a programme management team. The new structures were then rolled out to the other locations within the new company and the process of integration gathered pace. It also initiated the beginning of an attempt to continue to capture the potential of all employees in making the company a leader through employee involvement in decision making.

Adapted from: Clarry, T (1999) Premium bonding, *People Management*, 2 September, pp 34–9.

Tasks

1. To what extent does the process described indicate the application of a contingency approach to organizational design or simply the application of techniques intended to smooth over or avoid the potential problems associated with the merger? Does this distinction matter?
2. Using the internet and any documentary sources such as annual reports, press coverage that you can find, see if you can identify what happened to CGU after this merger process took place. Attempt to evaluate the success of the process described above. What conclusions can you draw about organization structure and the ways in which it develops over time, particularly following major events such as a merger?

FURTHER READING

Armistead, C and Rowland, P (1996) *Managing Business Processes: BPR and Beyond*, Wiley, Chichester. This is an edited book with contributors drawn from a wide range of organizations and academic disciplines. It seeks to review the basis of process approaches to organizations and what it means to manage from that paradigm. As such it does intersect with the design of organizations at a number of levels.

Brown, H (1992) *Women Organizing*, Routledge, London. Chapter 3 is worth reading in the context of the contingency and systems approaches as it provides a detailed review of social context within which organizations function and the basis of women creating organizations for their own needs.

Clark, H, Chandler, J and Barry, J (1994) *Organization and Identities: Text and Readings in Organizational Behaviour*, International Thomson Business Press, London. Contains a broad range of original articles on relevant material themes and from significant writers referred to in this and other textbooks on management and organizations.

Daniels, JD and Radebaugh, LH (1989) *International Business: Environments and Operations*, 5th edn, Addison-Wesley, Reading, MA. This text covers a considerable amount of material relevant to international operations, their finance and management. It also incorporates a broad review of the structural and design choices facing organizations.

Goold, M and Campbell, A (2002) *Designing Effective Organizations: How to Create Structured Networks*, John Wiley, Chichester. Seeks to explore the virtual organization and how to achieve it without destroying what already exists.

Handy, CB (1989) *The Age of Unreason*, Arrow Books, London. This text takes a view of organizations and their relationship with the environment as its core. It explores how this relationship has changed and the potential for future design frameworks.

Josserand, E (2004) *The Network Organisation: The Experience of French World Leaders*, Edward Elgar, Cheltenham. Reviews the French experience of four industries in which decentralization and cross functional relationships became essential for success.

Martin, S (2001) *Industrial Organization: A European Perspective*, Oxford University Press, Oxford. Considers a range of business factors including the structure of the firm, market structures and innovation in relation to the integration of the EU.

Mintzberg, H (1979) *The Structure of Organizations*, Prentice Hall, Englewood Cliffs, NJ. This text provides a broad review of the issues surrounding the topic of organizational design.

COMPANION WEBSITE

Online teaching and learning resources:

Visit the companion website for Organizational Behaviour and Management 3rd edition at: *http://www.thomsonlearning.co.uk/businessandmanagement/martin3* to find valuable further teaching and learning material:

Refer to page 35 for full details.

PART SEVEN

Managing the processes and dynamics of organizations

The previous section explored the physical aspects of an organization and sought to reflect some of the issues identified earlier in the book in relation to what work is and how it, along with technology is accommodated into the structure of an organization. This section develops that theme further by exploring the dynamic elements within the organizational milieu.

Communications, decision making and negotiation are the lifeblood of any organization in that instructions and information needs to be available to the right people at the right time in order that they can make appropriate decisions. But there are many influences on the decisions that are taken within an organization and people do not necessarily act in a rational way, at least as it might be defined by the owners or customers of a business. Negotiation is a key skill in many management jobs as objectives must be achieved and many people persuaded to co-operate in helping to achieve them. But of course it is not only managers that engage in negotiation, a group of colleagues need to co-operate with each other in achieving the collective task and so the work must be prioritized and shared out in some way or other. Power, control, politics and conflict are all things that arise in an organization as a result of the individuals and groups that exist and the personal, professional, perceptual and personality based

interactions that influence what people do in interacting with each other. Managers have the right to expect their subordinates to follow their instructions and as such have the power to enforce that right. But life is never that simple and employees have many opportunities to react to the exercise of power. It is important for any student of organizational behaviour to have some acquaintance with the power and political nature of human behaviour within an organization, just as they need to be aware of the effects of such behaviour on issues such as control and conflict.

The final chapter in this section explores the fundamental reality for all organizations, that of change. It is often said that nothing ever stays the same and that organizations are changing at an ever increasing rate. Change and organizational development are key trends in modern organization that involves all managers and employees in finding new ways of doing new things, and of finding news ways of doing existing things. It requires every aspect of organizational behaviour discussed in this book to be integrated in the search for ongoing survival and effectiveness. It is therefore an appropriate point at which to end this journey of discovery and learning.

CHAPTER 16

Communication, decision making and negotiation

LEARNING OBJECTIVES

After studying the chapter content and working through the associated Management in Action panels, Employee Perspectives, Discussion Questions and Role Play, you should be able to:

- **Outline the concepts of communication, decision making and negotiation.**
- **Explain the major models of decision making processes.**
- **Assess the organizational significance of communication, decision making and negotiation.**
- **Discuss how principled negotiation is intended to achieve a satisfactory and consistent result for all parties.**
- **Understand the main influences on interpersonal communication.**

INTRODUCTION

Communication, decision making and negotiation are fundamental aspects of everyday life for all employees and all organizations. **Communications** is a process involving information and influence. One definition states that communication in an organizational context, 'is an evolutionary, culturally dependent process of sharing information and creating relationships in environments designed for manageable, goal-oriented behaviour' (Wilson *et al*., 1986, p 6). **Decision making** as a process represents a means of selecting a particular course of action from among the options available. **Negotiation**, by the same token, broadly reflects a process of difference reduction through agreement between individuals and groups who have mutually dependent needs and desires. Kennedy (1999) defines negotiation as, 'the process by which we obtain what we want from somebody who wants something from us' (p 14). The notion of compromise as the basis of negotiation is something that Kennedy argues against because it obscures the essential 'exchange' purpose of the process.

There are strong links between these three activities in a very particular way within an organizational context. Not every act of communication involves decision making or negotiation. Decision making, however, requires information and communication to make it effective, but does not automatically involve negotiation. Every negotiation however requires communication and decision making as part of the process. For example, a company may automatically communicate its annual results to employees without a specific decision being required as a consequence. However, a production manager cannot make a decision on the production sequence for orders without communication between appropriate departments and specialists on issues including priority, capacity and raw material availability. During the annual wage negotiations between managers and trade unions communication between the parties on issues such as desires, expectations and ability to pay are the basis of exploring possible solutions and ultimately decisions on what will create an acceptable agreement. The one-way hierarchical relationship between these concepts implied by this discussion is reflected in Figure 16.1.

Communication
A process of sharing information and creating relationships in environments intended for manageable, goal-oriented behaviour.

Decision making
A process through which a course of action or solution is identified from the evidence and options available.

COMMUNICATION WITHIN ORGANIZATIONS

Communication differs from the simple passing of information from one person to another in that it implies the two-way process. Sitting in front of a television set watching a news programme is not a process of communication, it reflects information transmission because there is no direct interaction involved. Individuals may think about, or discuss some of the news items with other people, or even shout at the television screen, but the direct link with the presenters and producers does not exist. The purpose of each of the main communication flows within organizations is reflected in Figure 16.2.

Figure 16.2 includes external as well as internal communications within the model. This is because many people within an organization engage in a considerable degree of communication with other organizations and groups. For example, suppliers, government departments, customers, professional associations and competitors all have business-related communications links with an organization. In addition to the formal links implied in Figure 16.2, there exists a wide range of other formal and informal communication networks that exist both in and around any organization. For example, all employees communicate with family members and friends and some of this interaction will contain an organizational dimension or relevance. In one form, this could involve an employee describing their feelings about work to family or friends; in another, it could involve an employee selling company secrets to a competitor. More

FIGURE 16.1

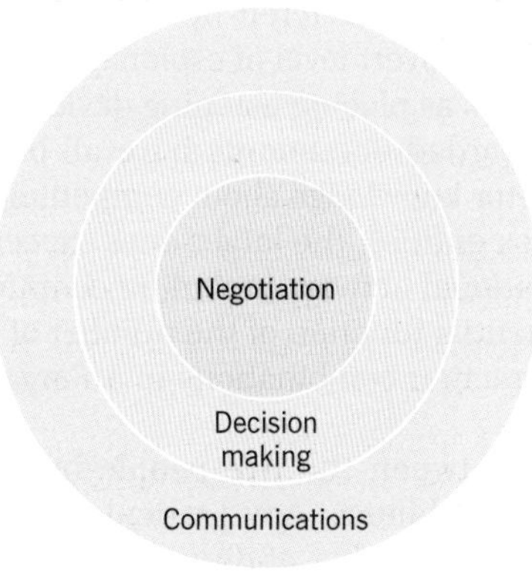

The one-way hierarchy

> **Negotiation**
> Reflects a process of forming agreements between individuals and groups who have mutually dependent needs and desires.

FIGURE 16.2

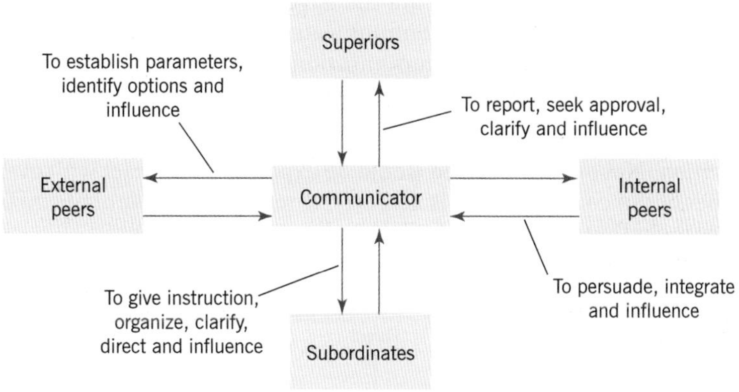

Organizational communications

formal links could involve an employee filling in a tax return setting out their earnings. All of the communication links indicated may contain various degrees of association with organizations, both formal and informal.

From an organizational perspective it is possible to summarize communication in two dimensions. One relates to the degree of formality involved, broadly reflecting the degree of business need. Formal being associated with the commercial activities of the organization and informal to do with matters involving the organization but not in a specifically business sense (perhaps public relations in a very general sense). The second dimension relates to direct and indirect aspects of the purpose of the communication process. So, for example, the organization would be directly involved in communicating to its customers, but only indirectly involved with an individual's tax affairs. These two dimensions can be reflected as a diagram (Figure 16.3) along with an illustration of what form of communication might fall in each quadrant. Espionage is an interesting phenomenon in relation to organizational activity in that all organizations engage in it to some degree. It reflects the processes of seeking to understand the environment and competitor activity. Obtaining company accounts and other publicly available information represents one form of trying to understand what competitors are doing, as does reverse engineering (the purchase of competitor products and stripping them down to establish manufacturing methods, technology uses and costs). Recruiting key employees from competitors represents another way of seeking to gain understanding, albeit potentially restricted by contractual or legal requirements. There is however, a much more covert level of espionage that it is possible to engage in and occasionally such practices as placing listening devices in offices or searching the refuse of executives for discarded documents have all been used by unscrupulous people in the search for greater knowledge about competitor activity.

Organizations are complex entities, the larger ones exceedingly so. This is reflected in many aspects of organizational activity, including communications. Complexity in communication is an exponential function of the number of people involved. Consider the possible number of interaction combinations in an organization consisting of just five people in Figure 16.4.

There are ten channels between the five people in Figure 16.4, reflecting the number of communication possibilities. Any particular episode could be initiated by either party which increases the number of directional channels to 20. Now consider the number of channels of communication possible in a company of 2000 people, even recognizing that not every individual needs (or even desires or has the opportunity) to communicate with every other individual! In addition to the vast number of individual communication links there are the large number of groups that exist within an organization and which need to communicate with other individuals and groups. Clearly, in large organizations the communication process needs to be managed carefully if total chaos is to be avoided. There are many ways in which organizations seek to achieve this in practice, including:

- *Limitation*. Not every employee would be expected to interact with every other member of the company. This is achieved through a number of organizational devices including hierarchical and departmental structures.

FIGURE 16.3

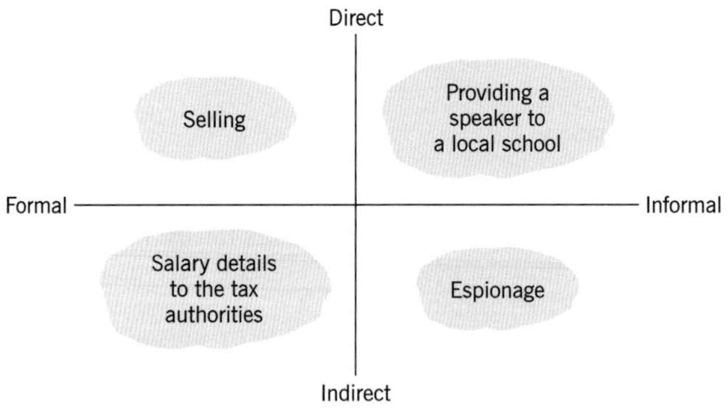

The two dimensions of communications

FIGURE 16.4

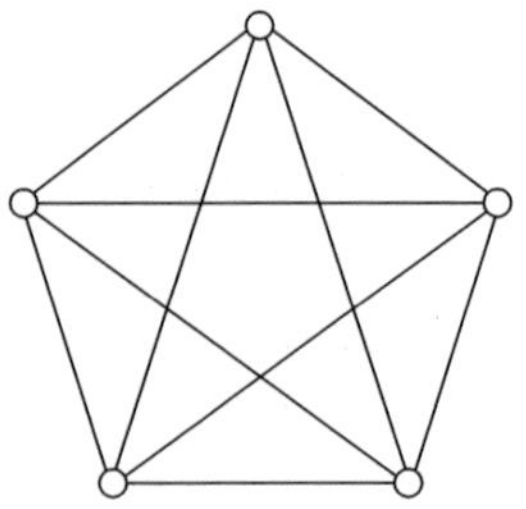

Communication channels

- *Procedure*. The development of appropriate procedural arrangements sets out to ensure that information is circulated only to those individuals needing it (or with a presumed right to access it).
- *Teamwork*. The use of teams and committees allows a degree of informality to facilitate communication between members; also the use of group representatives ensures that not every member is involved in communicating with every other group; group activity also concentrates communications on relevant issues at specific times.
- *Automation*. The use of electronic media should increase the opportunity for easier communications as individuals can access parts of the overall information available as necessary to their jobs and at a time appropriate to them. They can then process and transmit transformed data through the same media, allowing others flexibility in reacting to it.
- *Separation*. The identification of activities that require communication and those which can be designated as information flow. For example, employee communications is often separated into categories such as newsletters (one-way) and formal meetings between employee representatives and human resource managers (two-way).

COMMUNICATION PROCESSES

Figure 16.5 reflects the main interaction networks that form the basis of communication for managers. In addition to the work-related internal and external network reflected in Figure 16.5, managers will (in common with other employees) be part of friendship and family-based communication networks.

Communication serves four general functions within an organization:

FIGURE 16.5

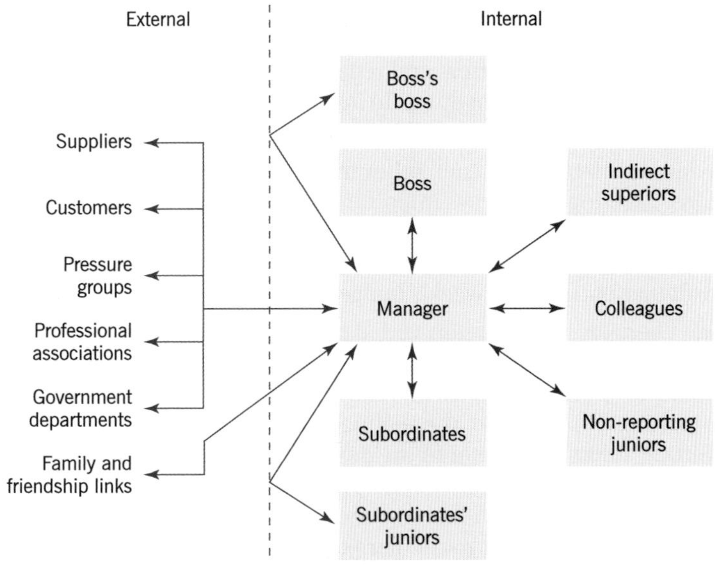

The manager's communication network (*adapted from*: Hellriegel, D, Slocum, JW and Woodman, RW (1989) *Organizational Behaviour*, 5th edn, West Publishing, St Paul, MN)

1. *Information processing*. Communication is more than the simple transmission of information. Data will be collected and turned into information that has meaning and purpose. The ability of individuals to create and share information is what generates effective activity. It is on the basis of information that decisions and planning can be undertaken.
2. *Co-ordination*. Communication also allows the integration of activity within the organization. For example, if a sudden drop in sales is identified, all departments can be alerted to take action. This could include reducing expenditure, cutting output, product review, speaking to customers and bankers, etc.
3. *Visioning*. Through the exchange of thoughts and ideas communication is a process that can develop and convey the vision, mission and strategies to employees throughout the organization. It contributes to commitment and the shaping of organizational culture by creating shared understandings.
4. *Personal expression*. Everyone in an organization will have their own views and opinions about work and non-work issues. These include opinions about the products and services offered, the individuals that manage the organization and how the company compares with other employers. Individuals at all levels will also have opinions on the way in which the company is run. Understanding these attitudes and feelings is an important aspect of management activity. Indeed attempts to shape employee attitudes and feelings form a significant focus for much internal company communications. This is the basis of the social partnership approach to engaging employees in a form of management–worker relationship supposedly based on mutual commitment, understanding and respect so much talked about today. For a review of this process in action within the Rover Group see Whitehead (1999). For a review of the trade union perspective on this process and the associated so-called sweetheart deals (in which employers select the trade union to which their employees will belong) see Walsh (1999). It has been argued that this dimension to communications provides managers with an ability to manage (or manipulate) employee attitudes and hence their behaviour more effectively.

The methods of communication that occur within organizations include:

- *Written*. The use of memos, letters and reports are the chief means of communicating through this medium. In addition, there are the company procedures, the majority of which will be committed to writing.
- *Oral*. Individuals interact with each other in a variety of ways within organizations. Meetings to discuss important items involve considerable oral communication. Less formal interactions also take place frequently. For example, an administration assistant may telephone the accounts department to query a particular entry in the weekly budget report.
- *Non-verbal*. There are a host of non-verbal communication signals that accompany interaction and which provide interpretative information between the individuals involved. Examples include tone of voice, body posture and spatial positioning. For example, the seating arrangements can set the tone for a meeting. Sitting across the corner of the desk (Figure 16.6A) provides a less threatening layout than sitting across the desk (Figure 16.6B). The physical environment in which an individual works can also provide powerful clues to the status and authority of that particular person
- *Electronic*. With an increase in the availability and sophistication of electronic devices the opportunity to communicate in new ways has emerged. The ability to use e-mail instead of written memos, teleconferencing in place of face-to-face

FIGURE 16.6

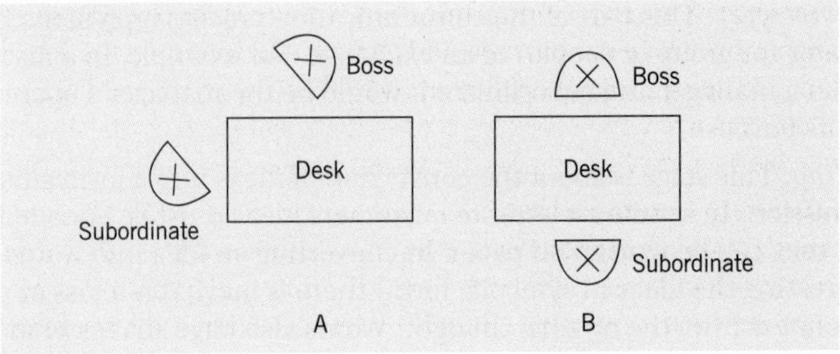

Seating arrangements for effect

meetings and the use of the fax machine to send written information have all changed the nature of much communication. The internet and intranet facilities have also developed very rapidly and allow organizations to allow employees, managers and other stakeholders to access and transmit large quantities of information at times appropriate to the recipient, rather than at times dictated by the sender. It can also be easier to hold information necessary for reference purposes (reports, procedures and background information for example) in electronic form than as a paper copy in a filing cabinet. However, there is a negative element to the large and growing quantity of electronic information that employees and managers are being presented with. For example, mail rage is emerging as a reaction in individuals who find themselves being overwhelmed, abused or threatened through the volume and nature of e-mails.

The communication model

The process of communication is a social activity involving two or more people across time. Figure 16.7 reflects the essential nature of this process and it should be noted that it is circular. The process involves the sender initiating a communication sequence with the receiver responding and providing feedback to the originator, thus beginning an iterative process.

Taking each element described in the model:

FIGURE 16.7

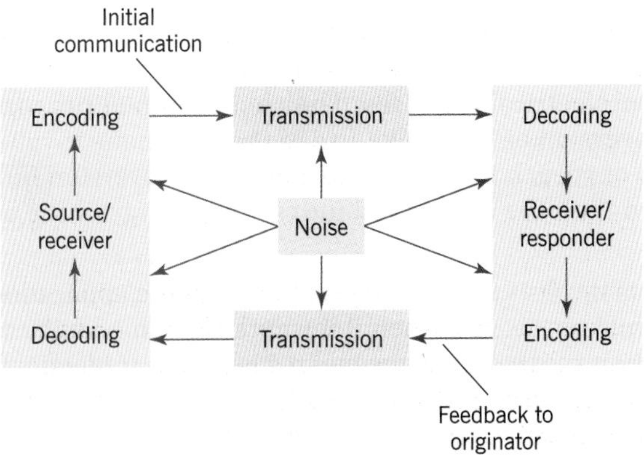

The communication loop (*adapted from*: Moorhead, G and Griffin, RW (1992) *Organizational Behaviour*, 3rd edn, Houghton Mifflin, Boston, MA)

- *Source/receiver*. This part of the communication process represents the originator (or group of people) of an exchange. For example, in a discussion between a manager and subordinate it would be the manager's opening remarks about its purpose.
- *Encoding*. This stage is about the conversion of ideas into a form suitable for transmission. In sending a letter to customers ideas must be encoded into words before they can be written on paper. In converting an idea into words (encoding or expressing the ideas in symbolic form) there is inevitably a loss of precision and richness from the original thought. Words also have shades of meaning and can convey different things to different people. This is particularly true when the sender and receiver come from different cultures and therefore have a different frame of reference against which to judge meaning. The following letter from a newspaper illustrates just this point. Spoken words also take on meaning from the context in which they are used and the non-verbal cues that accompany them. For example, 'can I help you?' said with a sneer conveys a totally different meaning from when it is said with a smile.

As an Australian writer living in Malaysia, I am well aware of the sensitivities of language and language translation. Take the Malaysian-English expression, 'to run away' for example. Here in Malaysia I find it a rather quaint expression meaning to leave a place in a hurry. In Australian-English it is taken far more literally and it is rarely applied to adult behaviour. There, it means to drop everything and run. If used in a military context, it would mean desertion of duty and absolute cowardice.

Unfortunately, this expression has found its way into the nightly English-language Sound and Light performance in Malacca. It is used to describe the withdrawal of British and Australian troops from Malaya to Singapore during World War II. While that military manoeuvre (withdrawal, recall, regrouping, etc.) is indeed a very sensitive issue in British–Australian–Malaysian historical relations it cannot be described as 'running away'. To call it that is deeply offensive to the dozens of Australian and British tourists who come to watch this show each night.

There is every chance that the older tourists that this show attracts may even have been here during the war. Almost every elderly Australian knows people who were in Changi Prison, on the Burma Railway or who died in Borneo.

On behalf of the disgruntled group that I happened to join last week, I'd like to ask the organizers to change those two words, so as not to offend the very people for whom the show is designed. (Pauline Bruce, Kuantan, *New Straits Times*, Malaysia, 13 May (1994))

- *Transmission channel*. This reflects the actual channel of communication chosen to convey the message from sender to receiver. In speaking it is sound waves, in written communication it is words on paper and electronically it is radio waves or electrical impulses. The choice of medium may involve more than one conversion of form. The use of the telephone involves the transmission of speech into the mouthpiece, a conversion into electrical impulses, and then the conversion into sound energy in the ear piece at the other end.
- *Decoding*. This involves the receipt of signals and the application of prior experience and knowledge to their interpretation. This can be an automatic process, as when speaking to someone in a language understood by both sender and receiver; or it can require interpretation, as with the need to refer to a phrase book if translation between languages is necessary. The meaning attached to a signal by the receiver may not be that intended by the sender as is apparent in the following Employee Perspective (16.1).

EMPLOYEE PERSPECTIVE 16.1 Reading between the lines

John worked as a joiner in a factory making doors and windows for sale through large stores and directly to house builders. The work was cyclical and it was not uncommon to find that people were laid off work for two or three months at a time when order levels reduced significantly. In September 2004, management of the company sent out a newsletter to all employees intended to reassure them by signifying that although orders were down and that costs would have to be reduced, no job cuts were being planned unless orders dropped even further over the following four months. John had worked in the company for five years and had not seen a newsletter of this type before.

The newsletter caused a stir among John and his colleagues and it became the topic of many conversations in the canteen and during coffee breaks. People were generally not sure how to interpret the message contained in the newsletter. Some said it was good news and provided a clear indication of management's intentions to keep the current workforce in jobs as long as possible. Others said that management were being devious in trying to hide their real intentions. They pointed out that in the past when orders had dropped no newsletter had been sent out so they asked, what was different this time? In essence this view suggested that something was going on behind the scenes which had prompted management to send out the letter and it was only safe to assume that whatever it was it would not benefit the employees. John did not know what to make of the two different interpretations of the newsletter. Management became aware of the negative interpretation of the newsletter circulating around the company and so issued another newsletter making it clear that there was nothing going on behind the scenes and that the first letter was factual in setting out management's intention with regard to jobs. Those employees who thought that the negative interpretation of the first newsletter was correct were not persuaded or reassured by the second letter and management did not know what to do next to convince employees that their intentions were genuine.

Tasks

1. What would you do next if you were John and why?
2. What would you do next if you were a manager in that company?
3. Could the negative reaction to the first newsletter have been prevented and if so how?

- *Feedback*. The receiver may become a sender by providing a signal to the originator that conveys a response on how the original message was interpreted. For example, an employee about to step off a walkway into the path of a truck may stop walking in response to a shouted warning. It is possible that a response to a message is conveyed through body language, an expression of boredom for example. Communication without feedback does not allow the sender to know if the recipient has received or understood the message. Imagine a manager issuing instructions for the day's production activities without having any idea if they have been received, understood or are being actioned.
- *Noise*. This refers to the contamination of the signal as a result of interference surrounding the process. In an organizational setting it could be the background **noise** in a busy office that makes it difficult to hear a telephone conversation. In electronic terms it could refer to the volume of e-mails received by an employee resulting in an important message from a customer being overlooked.

Noise
Background contamination surrounding communication that interferes with the clear reception of the message sent.

Interpersonal communication

At its most basic level, interpersonal communication involves two people in a dyadic interaction utilizing all of the elements of the process described in Figure 16.7. Of the communication channels open to individuals, non-verbal signals are the least obvious and yet carry much information. Table 16.1 provides a summary of the main non-verbal communication categories used to support other forms of communication. An emerging theme referred to as the theory of equivocation is beginning to offer explanations on how individuals such as politicians interact with interviewers and members of the public when direct answers to questions might prove embarrassing or involve loss of face (Bull, 2003). This invariably involves seeking to understand how question and answer types of interaction develop and how they are managed in the dynamic context in order to convey a particular message.

Taking each category in turn:

- *Body language*. An individual can stop speaking but their body keeps on sending signals through gesture, touch, posture, facial expression and eye contact for example. The following quote illustrates this process: 'In 20 minutes Mr Roosevelt's features had expressed amazement, curiosity, mock alarm, genuine interest, worry, rhetorical playing for suspense, sympathy, decision, playfulness, dignity and surpassing charm. Yet he said almost nothing' (Gunther, 1950, p 22). There are also cultural differences in the meaning of many of the signals given (Pease, 1984).
- *Paralanguage*. This aspect of verbal communication conveys a number of clues and can be split into four separate areas (Trager, 1958). Voice quality (pitch, range, resonance, etc.), vocal characteristics (whispering, groaning, coughing, etc.), vocal qualifiers (momentary variations in volume or pitch) and vocal segregates (pauses, interruptions such as 'ah', 'um', etc.).
- *Proxemics*. This refers to the spatial needs of people and their environment. This links together communication distance and the type of message. Seeing two people physically very close, heads almost touching would tend to suggest that a secret was being shared, whereas the same individuals separated by several feet could be discussing the weather.
- *Environment*. The layout of a room can have a powerful effect on the communication process. A meeting between a boss and a subordinate over a pay rise will be more likely to take place in the boss's office (or territory), a home base to give support to the boss's views. The following describes the feelings of a lawyer summoned to appear before the US Justice Department to explain why criminal proceedings against a client should not be instituted:

  > They were immediately shown to the criminal division's coldly utilitarian conference room. 'It's the most perfect government room you ever saw,' Trott says. 'It's nothing but a table, some chairs, a picture of the president and the attorney general on the walls.' 'It was,' he adds, 'an icebox, a meat locker.' (Carpenter and Feloni, 1989, p 74)

- *Temporal*. The use of time to create an impression is well understood by most effective communicators. Calling all employees together for a meeting at a time which requires them to interrupt their normal work will give the message

Body language	touching, eye contact, gestures, dress, etc.
Paralanguage	voice tone, speed, pitch, etc.
Proxemics	seating arrangements and personal distance, etc.
Environmental	room design and facilities, etc.
Temporal	the use of time to create effect and influence

TABLE 16.1 Non-verbal communications

greater impact. A manager making someone wait outside their office a few minutes before a meeting creates pressure and can destabilize the person kept waiting. In addition to the time pressure Sengupta *et al.* (2002) suggest that care is needed because the need to create a particular impression can lead to misrepresentation of the message itself. Management in Action 16.1 is a true story of how one manager used time to control an industrial relations situation.

Electronic communication

In today's organization the use of computer-based technology to communicate is widespread and becoming increasingly commonplace. The fax machine is now a basic piece of 'old technology' equipment for sending messages and documents between locations. The more recent introduction and use of intranet and e-mail systems allows information to be circulated more widely and more rapidly than ever before. In manufacturing companies, the ability to design products on computer systems that produce parts lists and production schedules makes the task of ordering and invoicing that much easier. In service organizations the ability to call up a client file on computer allows the transaction to be more effectively tailored to client needs.

Organizations can design computer systems that allow designated individuals access to appropriate information from a database. For example, a computerized personnel system can hold information on each employee's career history, references, performance markings, pay progression, attendance record, disciplinary warnings and so forth. Access to the available information can be restricted in various ways. For example, job history, references and previous performance markings could be available to the department head but not the immediate supervisor of the person. The same principles can be applied to any of the company information systems including finance, budgets and marketing data.

As with all areas of management activity the potential of electronic communication needs to be balanced with the other forms of communication available in order to produce an effective process at a cost that the organization can afford. This forms part of what is referred to as the knowledge management activities within an organization. For example, there is little to be gained from introducing teleconferencing between two locations only five miles apart when the usual communication between them is twice each year. However, with more frequent need to visit and/or seek technical support or assistance it may be justified.

Communication and the law

It has long been realized within organizations that information is a source of power and that there is unequal access to it between managers and employees. Indeed, there also exists unequal access to information between levels of management and across functions. In an attempt to redress the balance between employers and employees European employment legislation requires managers to communicate certain information to trade unions in specific industrial relations circumstances. This includes areas of collective bargaining and proposals to declare redundancies. Where trade unions have a need for particular types of information they can reasonably expect employers to disclose these so that they can undertake their responsibilities for representing members more effectively. Recent research has shown support for the view that consultation does help to save jobs in such situations (Edwards and Hall, 1999).

Additionally, limited liability organizations with more than 250 employees have to include a statement in their annual reports identifying any actions taken over the year to introduce, maintain or develop communication with employees. Within the European

MANAGEMENT IN ACTION 16.1 The power of time

The industrial relations manager of a large privately owned manufacturing company told the following story, which he claimed was true. Industrial relations within the company were difficult at the best of times. For example, whenever management attempted to introduce a new machine into the factory a dispute with one or more of the trade unions would result. From a management point of view everything was an uphill battle. It was not uncommon for the senior shop stewards to refuse to accept a piece of equipment unless manning levels and outputs were agreed before it was commissioned. Not infrequently threats of strike action were also used to force management into conceding to employee demands.

In one instance (on a Friday), the shop stewards had threatened that unless a particular manning level could be agreed immediately a strike would be called. The factory finished work at 12.30 lunch time each Friday and so any strike would mean an early finish and Monday off work (effectively a long weekend). The managing director (who had decided to deal with the matter) said to the shop stewards that he had been called to a meeting with the group chief executive, but that he would be back as soon as possible. The shop stewards were asked to wait in the managing director's office and they were given coffee.

The managing director had a short meeting with his boss and sent for the industrial relations manager to meet him in the head office complex. The two managers then had lunch together at the instigation of the managing director. Protestations by the industrial relations manager that a strike was imminent drew little reaction and a leisurely lunch resulted. By this time the factory employees had gone home, having finished work, but the shop stewards were still waiting in the managing director's office. A strike could not be called as management had not refused a meeting, so all the shop stewards could do was wait. They became increasingly frustrated and made several attempts to contact the managing director to press for the meeting, as they could see their original advantage slipping away. Responses from the managing director were that the senior managers were still meeting and would be back in the factory as soon as possible.

After a very leisurely lunch, which lasted until about 4.30 in the afternoon, the managing director decided that it was time to return to the factory. Not surprisingly, the shop stewards had left by then, refusing to wait any longer. Consequently, the two managers also went home for the weekend. First thing the following Monday morning the shop stewards stormed into the managing director's office to demand an explanation of the events from Friday. The response of the managing director was calm and he asked if they would have preferred him to have left the group chief executive and a discussion that could influence the future of the factory. He had the long-term interest of the factory and its employees at heart, even if they could not see beyond today. In any case, he had returned as early as he could, only to find that the shop stewards had gone home. Clearly, the problem that they wished to discuss was not important enough to make them want to give up some of their free time to solve it. There was no response from the shop stewards and the dispute ended. Management had 'won' this time, through the effect of using time to their advantage. However, this was not a tactic that could be used often as the shop stewards would find ways to counteract it. In this particular company it was a continual battle of wits between management and employees.

Stop ↔ Consider

Is the situation described an example of good communication, effective communication or good or bad negotiation practice? Or does it simply reflect a pragmatic approach to issues of power and control? Justify your answers.

How would you have dealt with such situations if you were the senior manager involved?

How would you deal with such situations if you were a trade union representative?

Union there are expectations that employee participation will go further than simply being entitled to information and regular communication. The introduction of works councils is now built into employment legislation within the European Union.

DECISION MAKING WITHIN ORGANIZATIONS

There are many levels of decision making from the minor short-term purchase of more paper-clips, to the major long-term commitment of capital resources. Decisions are taken by all levels of employee within the organization. For example, word-processor operators have to decide upon the sequence for processing allotted tasks. At the other extreme, the board of directors will have to consider issues such as the construction of new factories and launching of new products. The major distinction between these two decisions being their magnitude and the timeframe for their impact.

At the lower levels within the organization, decisions tend to be focused on immediate events involving the sequence of activities and the use of current resources in order to achieve the desired daily/weekly output. For example, a supervisor in a factory will constantly monitor the flow of work in order to divert people to bottlenecks or to adjust production to achieve the best output every day. At a senior level, the directors may only review the financial results of the company every quarter. The rest of the time they may consider issues such as the implications of industry news about trends etc. on the strategic plans of the company. However, even senior managers are involved in relatively small decisions, for example what information about the company to allow into the press. Many such decisions are small by comparison to some of the large financial decisions made, but they could have significant and fundamental consequences if they go wrong. The following Employee Perspective (16.2) is frequently quoted in this context, even though the employee in this case was the chief executive! It demonstrates that very senior managers have a responsibility to carefully consider their actions and comments in terms of the implications for employees and the organization before they speak.

EMPLOYEE PERSPECTIVE 16.2 Mouth in gear, brain in neutral

Gerald Ratner was the owner and chief executive of a jewellery chain in the UK which bore his family name. It specialized in selling value for money products to the mass market and had a shop in most large towns. It was also a very profitable company. Mr Ratner was invited to give an after-dinner speech to senior members of London's financial institutions on why his company was so successful.

During his speech he made the throw-away comment that, 'Many people ask me how my company can sell its products so cheaply. My reply is always the same; it is because we sell total crap!' He then laughed at his own joke, as did most of the people in the room at the time.

Naturally the press picked up on his comments and it made the headlines the next day. A public relations nightmare erupted instantly. Customers deserted his shops and many demanded their money back. Sales and the share price slumped overnight and the company had to close all its shops resulting in thousands of job losses, including Mr Ratner. The company was eventually bought out, and merged into another retail jewellery chain.

Tasks

1. Could Mr Ratner have anticipated the reaction to his throw-away joke?
2. Could he have made the same point in a way that did not provoke the negative reaction, how?
3. Could the situation have been salvaged once the storm had erupted and if so how?

At senior levels business decision making can involve many facets and take considerable time. It is reported that Margaret Thatcher began to court Japanese business leaders in the mid-1970s, well before she became British prime minister in the late 1970s. Her approach to them being that when (in the future) she was elected prime minister she could be trusted to create an appropriate business climate for them in Britain. It was approximately ten years after this approach that Nissan became one of the first Japanese companies to invest in large-scale production facilities in the north-east of England (Garrahan and Stewart, 1992).

The foregoing discussion also illustrates the third property associated with decision making within organizations, that of risk. Generally speaking, the larger the decision and the longer timescale involved the greater the degree of risk associated with it. For example, consider the options facing a medium-sized bank if it wants to become a large organization. Although there are many options available, the main ones are either to open a large number of new branches or to take over a competitor and gain size through the additional resources acquired. There are considerable dangers in either approach. The cost and refurbishment of new outlets will be high and training of new staff will take time. The level of additional business gained may not justify the additional expenditure, but this may not become apparent for some considerable time. With a takeover (or merger) there are also many difficulties to be resolved. For example, overlap in customers and retail outlets, duplication in management and incompatible computer systems are just some of the issues to be addressed. The end result may be that the growth achieved will not equal the business levels of the two separate organizations or cover the cost of the merger.

The three elements associated with decision making introduced in this section are reflected in Figure 16.8.

It is frequently suggested that the decision making engaged in by front-line staff (manual workers, sales assistants, etc.) is short term and therefore of limited impact. That is an oversimplification of their potential to significantly influence the future well-being of any business. It is the front-line staff who interact with customers or make the products that the customer will use. In doing so they are the ones who deliver (or fail to do so) the company objectives. It is the ability of front-line staff to decide for themselves the extent to which they will 'delight the customer' (an often heard phrase used to describe the objectives of many organizations) which will directly impact on company reputation and future sales. Recent trends in delayering, downsizing and rightsizing place greater emphasis on the ability of front-line staff to take decisions (empowerment) and thereby vastly increase the vulnerability of the organization to their actions (both positive and negative). Consequently, there exists an ever greater need for employers to communicate and engage staff effectively if they are to minimize the potential negative consequences of employee ability to take important

FIGURE 16.8

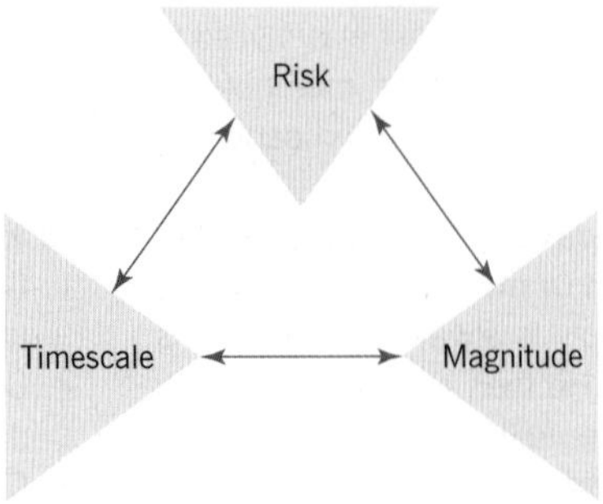

Dimensions of decision making

decisions. The following Employee Perspective (16.3) is one example where employee involvement, based on their experience saved the company significant cost.

Research carried out by Van Y peren *et al.* (1999) in the Netherlands also suggests that involvement in decision making resulted in employees feeling that they were more positively supported by their immediate supervisor. This in turn increased what the authors describe as **organizational citizenship** behaviours. Organizational citizenship is generally defined in terms of voluntary behaviour, 'not directly or explicitly recognized by the formal reward system that, nevertheless, generally contributes to organizational effectiveness' (p 377). As such, it incorporates behaviours categorized as conscientiousness, courtesy, sportsmanship and civic virtue in going beyond the basic job description requirements and supporting colleagues and the organization's goals. The authors claim that through involvement in decision making employees are given a clear signal of respect by the employing organization as well as close collaborative involvement with the supervisor. This in turn encourages employees to reciprocate by displaying high levels of organizational citizenship to the benefit of the organization.

Organizational citizenship
Voluntary behaviour that contributes to organizational effectiveness but not explicitly recognized by the formal reward system.

Approaches to decision making

Decisions are about choice. If there were no choices then decisions would not be necessary. For example, a production manager may have had a machine out of service for two days and as a consequence be late in the delivery of orders to some customers. The choices facing the manager are to cancel some of the orders, increase the speed of the machine (when it is working again), work overtime, subcontract some of the orders, or continue to deliver late on existing work and reschedule future orders. The problem facing the manager is identifying which option provides the most appropriate course of action. Each possibility has advantages and disadvantages. Customers would seek to encourage a decision which delivers their product on time. The maintenance team would prefer a decision which is less likely to result in future damage to the equipment. The quality specialists and designers within the company would be keen to maintain product standards and the finance people would wish to see costs not exceed revenue. In addition, employees and other managers will have views that could influence the solution actually adopted. For example, the sales manager may have favourite customers that they would not wish to upset. The difficulty facing the production manager is that many of these viewpoints and expectations are in conflict. For example, if employees work overtime and get paid extra for doing so, unit cost will inevitably increase. However, the customer will be happy and may provide further orders as a result of the service provided. It is finding ways to balance these competing pressures that forms the basis of decision making.

EMPLOYEE PERSPECTIVE 16.3 Looking after the pennies

During the 1980s Robert L Crandall encouraged staff in American Airlines to come up with cost-saving ideas. In 1987, two flight attendants working in first class put forward the suggestion to reduce the number of olives in the mealtime salad from two to one. This was because they had noticed that many passengers ate only one of the two olives that garnished the meal. An inconsequential thing you might argue, the cost of one olive not worth worrying about. Crandall did not agree, he implemented the change and as a result saved American Airlines a whopping $40 000 in food costs each year.

Source: Nightingale, V (2003) Looking after the pennies, *Management Today*, December, p 13.

Brainstorming has long been described as an effective means of maximizing creative solutions to problems. It was developed in the 1950s by advertising executive Alan Osborn who concluded that traditional group decision making processes inhibited the level of creativity displayed by members. Generally, groups for brainstorming sessions are between five and seven people. All ideas and suggestions are welcomed, the more outlandish the better as it is easier to discard or modify ideas than create them in the first place. Brainstorming should be undertaken in a supportive, non-threatening environment intended to encourage the maximum number and variety of ideas generated in a non-critical context. There are claimed benefits for brainstorming usually summarized as improved decisions which reflect higher levels of creativity than would be possible using more conventional approaches. However, the research evidence does not support that conclusion. Glover (2002b) reports an interview with Adrian Furnham in which he identifies several research studies that identify the limitations in brainstorming. For example, when individuals brainstormed alone and then used a group to undergo a process of combining and developing the ideas it consistently outperformed a conventional brainstorming group. Later studies show that the use of computer-facilitated brainstorming also outperforms the conventional approach. Gumble (2003) reviews technology-based approaches in this area with an introduction to web based programs from a company called 'BrainJuicer' which seeks to encourage idea development among employees or customers in an interactive and enjoyable context.

Decision making takes time, is resource demanding and carries with it a degree of risk. In situations where the problem has not occurred before it is necessary to work out the options and relative benefits for each before deciding which to follow. If the problem is new then there is no experience on which to judge the likely success of any course of action. The decision is taken before the result can be known. The actual chain of events that will follow from any decision cannot be fully anticipated and there are frequently extraneous factors that emerge as time passes. The D-day landings of the allied forces in France in June 1944 were the culmination of considerable planning and training activity. However, by chance a crack German armoured regiment was on exercise in the area of one of the landing zones and so was able to reinforce the defence of the area more effectively than had been anticipated. In that situation, there was no opportunity for the allied military commanders to take another decision in the light of the new information. It simply had to be dealt with as the landings progressed. In other words, only subsequent decisions could take account of the new situation. This perspective has led commentators to describe decisions as a stream rather than a series of single activities. This type of approach has led to the development of models intended to assist in the ability to learn from experience. For example, Franco *et al.* (2004) consider the use of problem structuring methods in managing non-routine problems in projects within the construction industry. The aim being to allow the partners in a particular project to learn from the experience in order to improve future collaboration.

Mistakes and failure can arise if the wrong decisions are made. It is personally, commercially and organizationally dangerous to make too many mistakes. However, they can also provide an effective learning experience. The trick, if there is one, appears to be to encourage risk taking while minimizing the dangers. Coca-Cola attempted to achieve this balance by celebrating failure as an opportunity to learn. Penny Hughes is quoted as saying mistakes were actually applauded in Coca-Cola and, that people were aware that they could take a decision from a position of safety (1999, p 61).

Problem-solving preferences

Another way to think about decision making is to consider the preferences that individuals have for approaching the process. In Chapter 4 the views of Jung in describing information gathering and evaluation approaches were outlined. The information-gathering approach is defined in terms of either sensing (preference for facts) or intuition (preference for possibilities). The information evaluation approach is defined in terms of thinking (preference for logic) or feeling (preference for values) in analyzing available information. This view of the individual preferences in problem solving can be reflected in a diagram (Figure 16.9), each cell in the matrix reflecting a different approach to solving problems.

Another approach to individual problem solving is that described by Thompson and Tuden (1959). Their model is based upon two dimensions:

1. *Preferences for outcomes*. This is about the goals that are being sought and is measured along a continuum from clear to unclear. So if the end result is known (fix the photocopier) then it would fall at the clear end of the spectrum. If, however, the end result is not clear (design a new product) then a different set of choices emerge.
2. *Beliefs about causation*. This is also measured along a clear/unclear continuum. It refers to the understanding that the individual has about the relationship between cause and effect in that specific situation. For example, in original research there can be little clarity as to how the variables will interact. Conversely, a knowledge that clearing a paper jam will allow the copier to function properly would fall at the 'clear' end of the spectrum.

This model goes further than the model described in Figure 16.9 by providing an indication of the problem-solving approaches that arise from these dimensions. Each of the four cells in Figure 16.10 implies a different approach to the problem-solving process. For example, where the outcome and the relationship between the variables are clearly understood, then a logical approach will achieve the best result. By the same token, where neither variable is clear, inspiration is the best guide to dealing with the problem.

However it is necessary to recognize that there are differences between decision making and problem solving. Jones (1999, p 71) reports on a symposium at the 1998 British Psychological Society London conference which explored aspects of decision making. One speaker (Nigel Harvey) pointed out that a good decision can still result in a bad outcome, whereas problem solving cannot. Problem solving implies that a right answer exists; but decisions are frequently made in conditions where considerable uncertainty exists and the aim is to reach the 'best' or optimal decision possible. Emma Soane suggested that City traders reported that emotion played an important

FIGURE 16.9

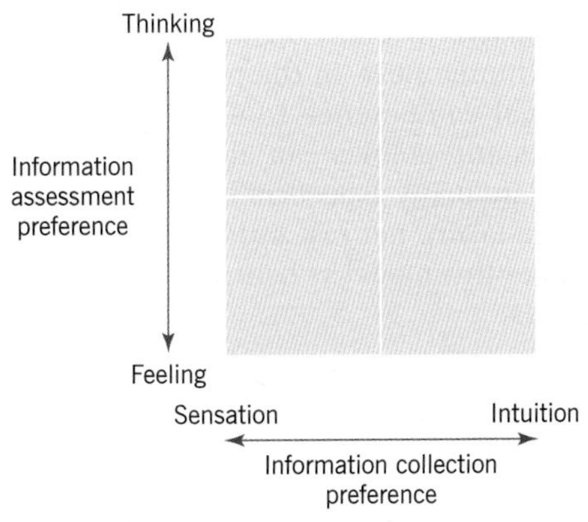

Problem-solving preferences (adapted from: Hellriegel, D, Slocum, JW and Woodman, RW (1989) *Organizational Behaviour*, 5th edn, West Publishing, St. Paul, MN)

FIGURE 16.10

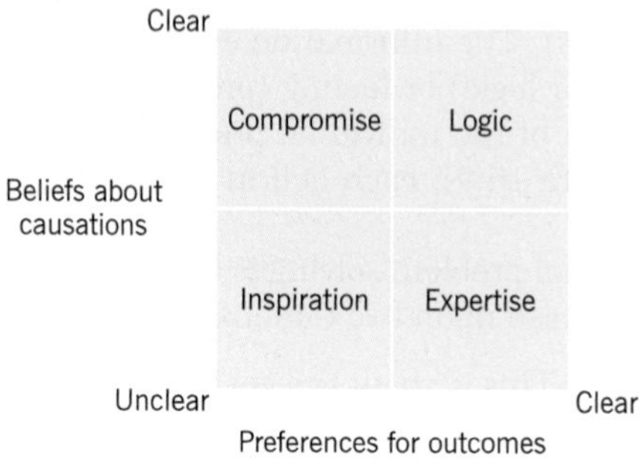

Two dimensions of decision making (*source*: Thompson, TE and Tuden, A (1959) *Comparative Studies in Administration*, University of Pittsburgh Press, Pittsburgh)

part in their decisions as they often carry great risk and uncertainty. There is also some suggestion of cultural influences on this issue. For example, Kosaka (2004) examined the approach adopted in the strategic decision making of major Japanese firms and found that compared to the approach adopted by Western firms there was a higher degree of similarity between the approaches of Japanese managers across different firms.

DECISION-MAKING MODELS

There are a number of models that attempt to describe how decisions are made within organizations and the following sub-sections will review a number of the major perspectives.

Rational and restricted rationality models

Rational decision making model
Suggests that the best interests of the organization are used in data collection, analysis and the evaluation of alternatives.

The rational model assumes that decision makers always follow a **rational** approach. Actions would be based on data collection and analysis, along with evaluation of alternatives. Appropriateness of the decision would be measured against the benefit to the organization as a whole, rather than any specific group or individual (Harrison, 1987).

Although the rational model may offer an ideal or preferred model, it may even be claimed to be the basis of all decisions by many organizations. However, as a model of decision making, it ignores the 'humanness' in the process. Individuals may lack the intellectual capacity or technical competence to evaluate every option rationally. Perceptual bias, group dynamics and politics can also play a significant part in the decision-making process. There are many aspects of behaviour within an organization that influence how decisions are taken, not just rational aspects (March and Simon, 1958). McKenna (1994) describes this model as bounded rationality and suggests that it comprises three main processes:

1. Sequential consideration of alternatives.
2. Using heuristics (rules which guide a search) to identify the most appropriate alternatives.
3. Satisficing, choosing on the basis of the identification of the first acceptable solution.

Political model

In this model, decision making becomes a process intended to achieve personal objectives through organizational activity. As such, information that supports this objective forms the basis of the **political model** process. One form of this was described as a **garbage can model** by Cohen *et al.* (1972). This is based on the idea that organizations are essentially comprised of solutions looking for problems. For example, a company may purchase a number of components from sub-contractors which the production manager may wish to have made in the main factory. Consequently, they are likely to continuously seek to demonstrate that the company would be 'better off' producing the items in-house. Quality problems with suppliers' products will be highlighted, as will late delivery and so on. In effect, the solution already exists (expand the production department) all that is necessary is for the 'problem' to occur. Cohen *et al.* see the garbage can model as a receptacle for solutions and situations, both waiting to be matched up.

Political model
Decision making as a process intended to achieve personal or short term objectives.

Garbage can model
The idea that organizations comprise bundles of available solutions looking for problems to attach to.

Another approach to the political model describes decision making in terms of managers looking after their own short-term interests. Powell and Mainiero (1999) carried out an experiment in which managers were asked to take a decision about which employees they would allow to adopt non-standard working arrangements. Generally, the basis of the decision was that employees would be refused permission to change their working arrangements if it would cause inconvenience to the manager. Within the results four different clusters were identified representing managers who adopted different criteria to the decision. So the same decision basis is not used by every manager even though self-interest is apparent in the overall process. Management in Action 16.2 illustrates just how far the political model can contribute to achieving personal objectives.

Conflict model

Janis and Mann (1977) describe a model based on five assumptions. First, it is applicable to important life decisions only. Second, procrastination and rationalization are part of difficult decisions as they allow individuals to deal with stress. Third, some decisions will be wrong and this can affect future decisions. Fourth, that alternative options will be compared against personal moral standards. Finally, individuals will be ambivalent towards the alternative decision options, making it difficult to choose between them. Figure 16.11 describes the algorithmic nature of this approach.

Programmed and non-programmed decision making

Programmed decision making
This refers to situations in which pre-planned steps lead from problem to solution.

Simon (1960) describes decisions as falling along a continuum from **programmed** to **non-programmed**. Programmed in this context refers to the existence of decision rules that lead from the problem to the solution. If a photocopier stops reproducing copies part way through a print run then a code number on a control panel often indicates the type of problem and the machine manual indicates how to repair the machine. The programmed aspects of this process are created through the design of the machine, the inclusion of sensors to detect certain malfunctions and the development of an operator's manual. Similar effects can be seen in the training of airline pilots using flight simulators. The purpose is to expose the pilot to a wide variety of flying experiences and train them how to respond effectively without putting lives and expensive aeroplanes at risk. Programmed decisions, therefore, reflect a form of problem solving in which a solution exists which simply needs to be determined.

Non-programmed decision making
These are new, complex situations that cannot be anticipated, or do not have pre-existing methods for resolving them.

Non-programmed decisions, however are new, cannot be anticipated or do not have pre-existing methods of resolving them. A recent example of this is the situation facing

MANAGEMENT IN ACTION 16.2 Getting a better company car

This event was described to me by the chief executive of a large successful company who thought it was rather funny and demonstrated how personal interest influenced decisions and how easily senior managers can be manipulated politically.

Essentially, the story was as follows. The head of the reward systems department within the company decided that he wanted a bigger, more expensive company car than the existing policy allowed. Having thought about this for a while he decided upon the following course of action. At the next annual review of pay and benefits for the company the reward manager proposed (having consulted with sales managers first) that it would be in the company's interest for sales staff to be given a more prestigious car. This (he argued) would enhance their status internally and with customers, and also motivate them to sell more. The cost of the bigger cars was justified financially on the basis of additional sales and reduction of labour turnover among sales staff. After some discussion the company car policy was changed and the new cars were provided. This was stage one of the reward manager's plan.

Stage two was to wait a while (a few months) and then informally and on the quiet to 'remind' a number of head office managers and other company car drivers that junior level sales staff now had bigger cars and to ask if they were happy about this situation. Naturally, a few responded that this change to the car policy lowered their own perceived internal status by lifting the level of benefit given to sales staff. This effectively 'planted the seed' of an attitude among company car drivers that implied a problem might be emerging. The next move by the reward manager was to raise the issue more directly with the manager responsible for organizing and running the company car fleet. This was where the reward manager ran the most risk of failure as he effectively had to pass the problem over to another manager, who might have reported the reward manager's intentions to higher management. However, by implying that every manager (including the car fleet manager himself) could achieve a car upgrade if the 'problem' were addressed, he was soon convinced. The car fleet manager was persuaded that by carrying out a user survey among company car drivers he would soon detect significant resentment towards the new policy. Not surprisingly this was found to be the case and the car fleet manager wrote a report to his manager and the head of personnel to that effect.

The reward manager was then brought back into the 'problem' and asked to find a solution that could be accommodated within the company's overall reward strategy. This was done. The reward manager essentially proposed that as the company had enjoyed a couple of good financial years additional money could be made available, any change could be phased in over a number of years as company cars were replaced (which would reduce the cost) and direct pay increases could be shaved back a fraction over the whole company to reduce the overall cost. Equally it was argued that managers eligible for a company car might start to look for other jobs if this problem were not addressed. Not surprisingly, the head of personnel supported this proposed plan as the overall cost was marginal and it would avoid a morale and industrial relations problem. The fact that he would also get a bigger car as a result of the change in policy was never formally part of the discussion or decision. The proposal was put to the chief executive who agreed with it (how surprising) and it was put formally to the board (who all agreed with it). So the company car policy was changed and all managers (including the reward manager) gained by getting a bigger car.

This process was not a fast one, taking over two years from the original idea to the reward manager actually getting his new and bigger car. He did, however, manipulate the entire process to meet his particular objective.

Stop ↔ Consider

Once it was formulated could the reward manager's plan have been prevented and, if so, how and by whom?

FIGURE 16.11

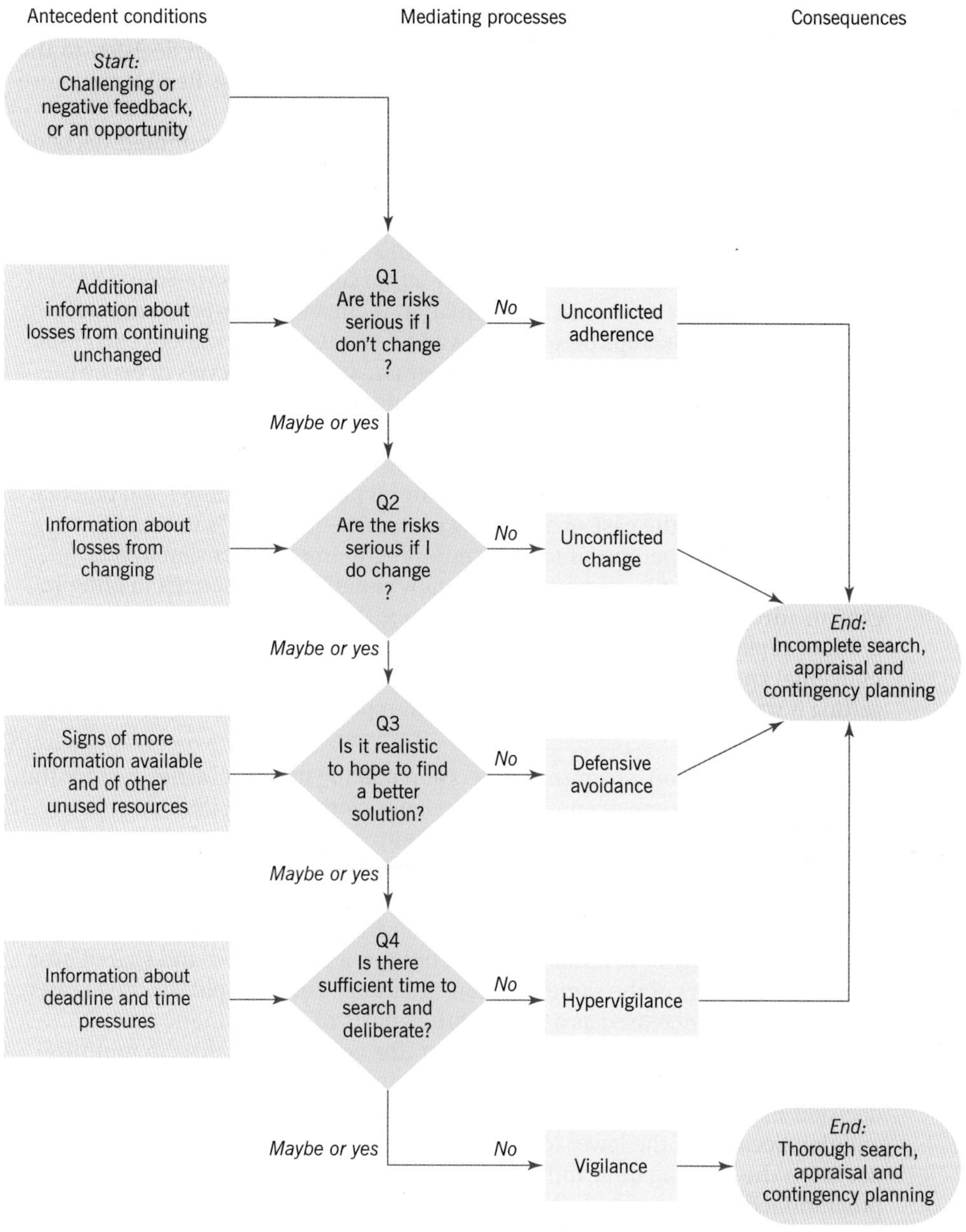

Conflict model of decision making (*source*: Janis, IL and Mann, L (1977) *Decision Making: A Psychological Analysis of Conflict, Choice and Commitment*, The Free Press, New York)

the cross-channel ferry companies on the opening of the Channel Tunnel rail links between the UK and France. Although not a rapid emergence of a new product (the tunnel took several years to design and build) the effect on the ferry companies was dramatic. The ferry companies had never experienced this situation before (at least not across the English Channel) and so they were forced to rely on their internal ability to define and solve problems intelligently. Only time will tell how successful they are in achieving this. Tom Bentley, a director of Demos, suggests that timing is the most difficult aspect of any decision. Acting too early or too late can turn an otherwise good decision into a mistake or failure. In his view the best approach to decision making combines early thought and planning with leaving the actual decision to the last moment. An approach which, in his view, provides the most flexible response capability (Bentley, 1999, p 61).

Comparing the two approaches of programmed and non-programmed decision making a number of conclusions should be apparent, including:

- *Risk*. There is less risk of failure in a decision which is based on the programmed approach. Decisions based on this approach are familiar, there is considerable experience of the 'behaviour' of variables and the outcome has a higher predictability as a result. In a situation requiring a non-programmed response the relationships between the variables must be worked out each time. This invariably involves anticipation, judgement and higher levels of expertise. This approach inevitably contains a higher potential for failure as a result of the increased uncertainty. The distinction between these approaches can be compared to the difference between a sporting event and a theatrical performance. In both of these situations careful planning, training and practice occur. However, in the case of a sporting event, the intention is to beat the opposing side and that introduces the non-programmed dimension to the process. Each side will attempt to create new situations and actions in order to gain an advantage. In a theatrical performance the rehearsal is intended to produce replication for each performance. The aim is to ensure that each individual knows what they must do at every stage in the show. The risk of getting it wrong (in not producing equivalent repeat performances) is thereby greatly reduced.
- *Cost*. Reliance on non-programmed decision making incurs a higher cost for the organization. In a company producing designer clothing each item must be different and tailored specifically to each client. The cost of producing each item is therefore high because there is no opportunity for economies of scale. Conversely, the development of programmed decision approaches significantly reduces the cost of operations. The cost of solving the programmed problem might be much higher in absolute terms, but it is a one-off cost and shared over very large numbers of the same decision situations. For example, air travel safety has been greatly increased as a result of the efforts of pilot trainers, aircraft designers, maintenance planners and air traffic control specialists to routinize much of the process, learn from experience and programme all of this into decision-making covering all aspects of aircraft design and functioning. In addition because of the lower levels of skill necessary to implement programmed decisions the training time and cost of labour is lower than needed for non-programmed decision situations.
- *Performance*. Measured in units of output per person, the performance of an organization using a high proportion of programmed decisions will be greater. Programmed decisions need less processing time and therefore individuals can take more of them. Consider, for example, the lending policies of banks and financial institutions. If a programmed decision approach is adopted the resulting 'formula' can be applied to each application and an answer produced quickly. The process can be speeded up to the extent that it becomes a marketing advantage and is used as such by a number of banks.
- *Variety*. End product variation incorporating programmed and non-programmed decision making to ensure maximum customer product individuality has been developed by the motor industry. Having anything made to a personal specification is expensive and takes time. High volume cars would all have to be identical (like the Model T Ford) if that were the only possibility.

However motor car design and manufacture is an excellent example of the ability to combine programmed and non-programmed aspects into one process. The designers of a motor car will begin with a small number of variations for a particular model, engine size, number of doors and body style. However, from the basic model there are a wide range of optional extras available so that customers can design a vast number of end product variations. The use of computer technology along with process technologies such as just-in-time allows the appropriate components to be made available to the factory at the correct time to provide cost effective assembly, with the illusion of relative uniqueness built into the product.

- *Complexity*. Unique situations cannot be dealt with in a programmed mode of operation; they must be channelled out and dealt with separately. In order to cope with the complexity that this implies for organizations a number of initiatives have been undertaken. For example, in the motor industry it was necessary for a highly skilled mechanic to diagnose a problem with a car and then to be able to rectify the problem. As cars have become more complex this diagnostic process has also become more difficult. However, the use of technology has helped to contribute to a resolution to these difficulties. So the inclusion of diagnostic programmes in many cars these days allows a computer in the workshop to identify the area of the fault, if not the actual cause of the problem. The mechanic can then take the information provided and either change the part identified or explore further the possible causes before correcting the fault. This approach combines both programmed and non-programmed decision making into a single process that reduces the complexity arising from modern motor vehicle design.
- *Employee skill*. Where non-programmed decisions are the norm, the skill level of employees must be of a higher order than required for programmed decisions. For non-programmed decisions, the employees involved must be capable of high level analysis and trained in a wide range of techniques to cope with the uncertainties inherent in the process. For example, imagine the level of knowledge and skill required to deal with a computer crash if there were no handbooks or self-diagnosis programs available.
- *Organization design*. The structure of the organization in terms of the number of departments and their function will be affected by the approach to decision making. The lower skill levels implied by the programmed approach to operational decision making requires fewer specialists and larger numbers of people at the lower levels of the organization. For example, the design of a company specializing in designer clothing will be very different to one specializing in ready-to-wear apparel.

Pragmatic model

Pragmatism is a means of combining both rationality and the reality of human behaviour into a systematic approach aimed at achieving the best decision in the circumstances. Figure 16.12 reflects the main elements of this approach.

Cycle model

This approach to decision making proposes a nine-step process based upon research carried out by Arucher (1980) in which the decision-making stages used by some 2000 managers were explored. The steps identified in the process of decision making were as follows:

FIGURE 16.12

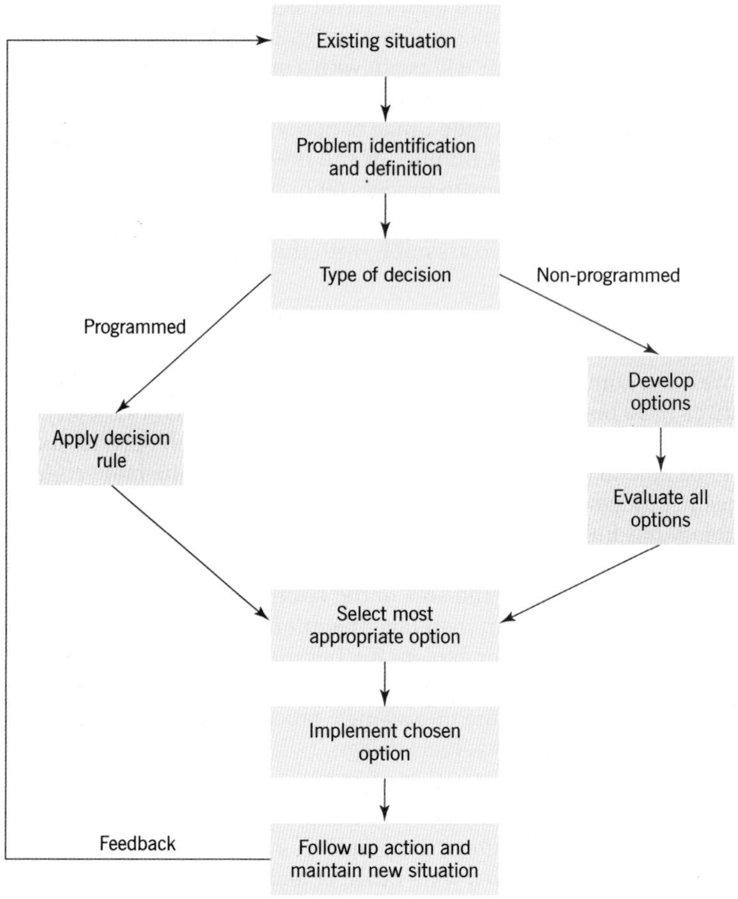

Pragmatic decision-making model

1. Monitor the environment for issues that need to be decided and for feedback on the consequences of previous decisions.
2. Define the issue(s) or problems(s) that need to be decided. Separate symptoms from problems.
3. Specify the risks, constraints and objectives for the decision.
4. Diagnose the problem(s) more thoroughly.
5. Develop the possible options or alternative courses of action available.
6. Establish the criteria against which any decision will be made and success judged.
7. Appraise the options in terms of the established criteria.
8. Choose the option which best meets the needs of the situation.
9. Implement the selected solution. This would be followed by another iteration of the model, beginning with step 1, monitor.

NEGOTIATING WITHIN ORGANIZATIONS

Negotiations are frequently considered to only take place in circumstances when employee relations problems are to be solved or commercial contracts arranged. In the employee relations context it is an area that has close association with issues such as consultation and employee involvement. For example, managers may well consult with employee representatives over a broad range of issues including how they might expect their pay and benefits to develop in the future before deciding upon an initial pay review proposal or the actual negotiation tactics. However, if negotiation is defined in terms of the resolution of difference, the basis for exchanging something mutually sought by two or more parties, or the making of agreements, then it assumes a much broader significance in organizational activity. Consequently, many of the employees within an organization are involved in negotiations in one form or another for much of their time.

Negotiations can take place either formally or informally. The annual negotiations between managers and trade unions over rates of pay and negotiations over the terms to be included in a sales contract are typical formal negotiations. Technically, a superior is empowered to give 'instructions' to subordinates, who must then carry them out. In practice, however, any manager who relied on giving orders as the only way to lead would not achieve the best result from their subordinates. Consequently, informal negotiations take place every day between people at all levels within the organization. For example, the sales director of a company might seek to persuade the production director to change the priority on a particular order. To do so an informal negotiation might take place in which mutually acceptable compromises (often involving the exchange of something of value to both parties, or perhaps an exchange based on favours) would be explored and agreed over a cup of coffee. Equally, two colleagues may negotiate informally every day over who should collect the post from the main office. Other tasks to be done over the day might be traded as part of the process. Each instance of negotiation will involve the need for communication to take place between the parties involved. It will also involve taking decisions both jointly and individually as part of the negotiation process. Negotiation is, therefore, best seen as an interactive process of making mutually agreeable bargains in situations where one party needs to influence the activities of another.

A negotiating framework

Formal negotiation is a means through which differences can be resolved and agreement reached; thereby providing the basis for the future relationship and providing all parties with a record of their rights and obligations. In all relationships there is a power dimension and negotiation can be a reflection of the balance of power that exists within the relationship. For example, if a company has many suppliers for a particular raw material and each source is equivalent in terms of quality, the suppliers are individually very weak compared to the customer and it would be almost impossible for individual suppliers to raise prices. The customer would simply switch to another supplier. This process has also been apparent historically in the employment field as employers traditionally exploited the ready availability of labour and the need for people to earn money in order to live. Over time this led to the emergence of trade unions as a means of providing a balance in the power between employers and employees. Figure 16.13 provides a framework for understanding the formal negotiation process within employee relations. The basic principles incorporated into this model are also relevant to all forms of negotiation.

FIGURE 16.13

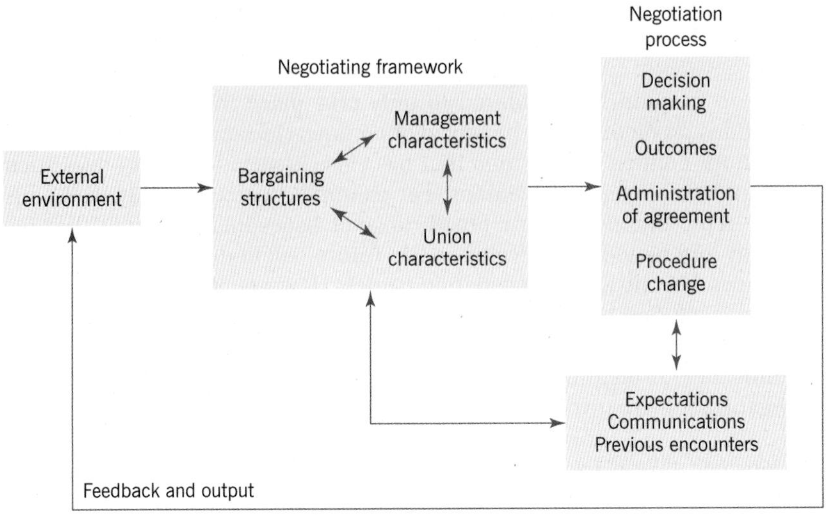

A negotiating framework (*adapted from*: Kochan, TA (1980) *Collective Bargaining and Industrial Relations*, Irwin, Homewood, IL)

It is clear from Figure 16.13 that negotiations are a process dependent to a significant extent upon previous encounters, expectations and external forces. It should also be apparent how communications and decision making fit into this model of the process.

Negotiating tactics

There are a number of approaches to dealing with conflict that are relevant to negotiations. They include according to Torrington *et al.* (2002, 632–3):

- *Avoidance*. This approach simply ignores the problem on the basis that most simply disappear. However, if problems are simply repressed or ignored they can be much more difficult to deal with when they eventually surface and have to be dealt with.
- *Smoothing*. This approach to conflict seeks to 'patch up' a rift through calming actions to get through the 'problem'. It can frequently include calls to stay loyal or stick together or show support for the leadership, etc. However, this approach can leave the real problem unresolved by these actions.
- *Forcing*. This is about imposing one's own point of view onto others by trying to stamp out any signs of conflict or dissent. It can work in the short term but invariably leads to resentment and a desire to seek revenge in some form or other when the opportunity presents itself.
- *Compromise*. This approach seeks to resolve conflict by finding an acceptable middle ground. It represents the best worst solution to any problem. For example, if employees demand a £20 per week pay rise and the company claim to be only able to afford £10 per week, then a compromise of £15 per week may achieve a solution and save face for both parties. But it means that neither side won and both will leave the process dissatisfied.
- *Confrontation*. This approach to conflict requires all parties to confront the problem. It requires an acceptance that there exists a conflict of opinion and interest which can only be resolved by exploring the issues in some depth from all perspectives and by so doing seek to develop an accommodation of the

differences in whatever solution is agreed. This approach should deliver a greater level of satisfaction among the parties that overall their objectives have been recognized as far as it is possible to do so within the eventual solution.

The tactics that negotiators are likely to adopt during a formal negotiation process depend on a number of factors surrounding the process itself. They include the preferred style of the individuals involved; the relative power balance between the parties; the degree of change involved in the topics covered by the negotiation; the willingness of the parties to accept change; previous encounters; environmental and contextual influences; the expectations of and pressure from the constituents of the negotiators; training and experience in negotiation along with the dynamics of the process itself (see Figure 16.14). Less formal negotiations will also be less likely to exhibit the clear patterns of behaviour implied by many of the tactics discussed. For example, deciding whose turn it is to make the coffee is likely to be treated as a bit of fun, unless someone never makes it and then the approach is likely to change significantly.

It is naive to suggest that all negotiations are a means by which both parties can discuss differences and reach mutually acceptable compromise. Many negotiations are undertaken from a win–lose perspective. In other words, if one side 'wins', then the other must, of necessity, 'lose'. This is based upon the notion that the issues are fixed and can only be shared out like cutting a cake into pieces. In this analogy, a piece once cut and allocated is no longer available for the other party. In extreme cases, the tactics employed by individuals using this approach can become very aggressive. Typically, a deep diving approach is taken on each item to be covered until a win is recorded and then moving on to the next issue. There are many fighting tactics that can be used in pursuit of this approach, including (based on Scott, 1981):

- *Probing*. From the outset seeking information of value, without giving anything away that may help the other side.
- *Get/give*. Seeking to gain something before conceding anything. Matching what is given to what was gained.
- *Emotion*. The use of voice tone and other body language signals to create emotion in the process. The following Employee Perspective (16.4) shows how the use of anger could be used to influence a negotiation meeting.

FIGURE 16.14

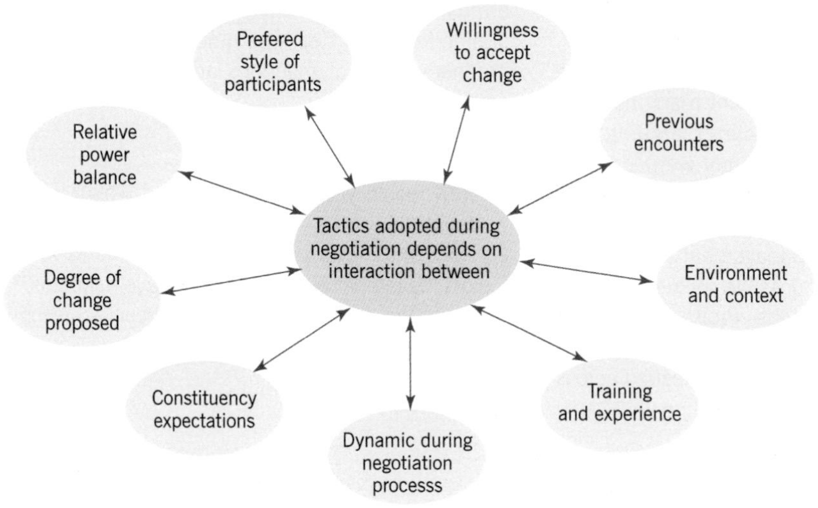

Factors influencing negotiation tactics

EMPLOYEE PERSPECTIVE 16.4 The boss who lost his temper

Janet worked as the production manager in a medium sized manufacturing company in Spain. The company employed 300 people, mostly women engaged in making printed circuit boards used in the engine management systems of motor cars. The company recognized a trade union for the employees and terms and conditions of employment including wages were negotiated each year between the senior factory managers and the trade union representatives.

The relationship between the parties had always been cordial and few real problems had been experienced over the years. The chief executive of the company, Bernard, had been in post for about two years and was keen to see the unit labour cost reduced as customers were beginning to suggest that much cheaper options were easily available from competitors in Korea. Consequently, Bernard and the other managers had decided that at the next annual negotiations new productivity schemes would have to be implemented in order to raise productivity and reduce cost.

A package of measures was designed by management which included minimal increases in basic pay, a new bonus scheme, profit share scheme and next year's pay increase to be determined by the reduction in unit labour cost over the next twelve months. This represented a completely new way of deciding pay for the employees and when the document was presented to the trade union representatives they were shocked by the changes proposed. Management had expected such a reaction and were prepared to discuss the ideas in considerable depth and over an extended period of time.

The trade union were not sure how to react to the negotiation package offered and spent many hours of time during the negotiation meetings arguing and discussing the proposals. They simply wanted a rise in the basic wage which exceeded the cost of living increase over the past year, which was how things had been done in the past. Management kept repeating that this was no longer possible in the changing economic and trading conditions. Progress was very slow and at one meeting Janet said that her boss Bernard, who was chairing the meeting, leaned across to her and whispered, 'Watch what happens next!' Janet became worried about what Bernard might do and the possible consequences of his actions.

A few seconds later Bernard exploded. He jumped up, banged the table with his fists, shouted at the trade union side that they were not interested in the long term survival of the company and that their attitude would inevitably result in the closure of the company in a few years time as cheaper sources of printed circuit boards were available. During this tirade his face went bright red with anger; he was waving his arms around, shaking his fists and stabbing his finger at the trade union officer leading the employee side. The trade union side were shocked into silence, never having heard Bernard react so violently before. They then began to shout at him to sit down and to be calm or he was in danger of having a heart attack. Everyone began to talk at once and the meeting soon became a chaotic mix of noise and confusion.

Bernard sat down, leaned across to Janet and whispered to her, 'I enjoyed that, I was getting bored. Let's see what happens now!' Janet was shocked. Bernard then just sat back and watched the people in the meeting shouting and arguing with each other. After a few minutes, the trade union officer leading the employee side called a halt to the confusion and began to restore order to the proceedings. The trade union side suggested an adjournment until the next day for tempers to cool and to restore a sense of order to the process. This was agreed and the meeting ended. The next day a much more constructive atmosphere was evident in the meeting and the outline for a new deal was quickly identified and after another couple of meetings agreement was reached on a new pay deal.

Tasks

1. How would you have reacted and why if you were Janet?
2. How much of a risk was Bernard taking when he lost his temper and what might have happened?
3. Could the same end result have been achieved in a different way and if so how?

- *Good guy/bad guy*. The 'reasonable' member follows the 'aggressive' and 'unreasonable' one and builds on the advantage gained by the threat of more to follow. This is a very familiar theme from many police movies.
- *Poker face*. The ability to manage the body language and verbal cues allows the fighter to cloak their feelings and intentions.
- *Managing the minutes*. The person producing the minutes is in a strong position to slant the official record. The careful choice of words and phrasing can be used to great effect, as can the selective inclusion (or exclusion) of items discussed.
- *Understanding not agreement*. One side may claim to understand the other's position throughout the negotiations, only to fail to accept that agreement has been reached at the end of the negotiations. A customer may say that they understand the need for the supplier to raise prices, but may not agree to pay it. This approach gives apparent comfort to the party being 'set-up' as they begin to believe that their arguments are being accepted and so they relax. When the failure to accept the agreement becomes apparent it destabilizes them, throws them into a panic and frequently encourages further last minute concessions to be made. Invariably these last minute concessions are not in the best interests of the party making them – the purpose all along.
- *Getting upstairs*. Going over the head of the negotiating team to the boss is a threat that can be used with effect. No one likes to have their boss think that they are incapable of meeting their objectives and so it can encourage the team to concede something in order to reach a settlement. Invariably such settlements work to the disadvantage of the party being forced to make the concessions.
- *Forcing*. There are various forms of force that can be used. Threats of withdrawing from the relationship (strikes or stopping of supplies) is one form, but bribes, blackmail and dirty tricks are other options that have been used.

The fighting tactics described here are intended to gain and retain control of the process. There are various ways in which these tactics can be dealt with, but essentially it comes down to remaining in control of temper, emotions, content and process.

There are few occasions in which the power balance is completely one-sided during a negotiation and therefore negotiation should be regarded as a joint process of identifying the best outcome for all concerned. Often this comes down to understanding what the best alternative to a negotiated agreement is. In other words, what will happen if no agreement is reached? This is a point made by Fisher and Ury (1986) in their description of **principled negotiations**. This requires negotiators to concentrate on four elements within a negotiation process:

Principled negotiations
Negotiation based on four elements – the participants, their interests, the options available and the evaluation criteria.

1. *Separate the people from the problem*. It is the issues that are important, not the people discussing them. By forcing attention onto the issues, the people involved on all sides become focused on finding mutually acceptable solutions rather than the personalities of other negotiators.
2. *Focus on interests, not positions*. The purpose of a negotiation is to reach agreement. All parties have interests relative to the negotiation which may not be reflected in the position that they adopt at the start of the process. For example, a trade union may demand a 20 per cent pay rise (their position), but their interests may include having secure, well paid and interesting jobs with long holidays. By identifying and focusing on these it should force an emphasis on finding mutually acceptable real solutions of long term benefit to all parties.
3. *Invent options for mutual gain*. This is the major difference from the win–lose approach. There is usually no single cake to be split into a fixed number of

pieces. For example, in negotiations over price increases, the discussions need not be about profit, loss and cost alone. It is possible that an increase in price may be acceptable if conditions regarding guaranteed delivery, quality and packaging can be met. It is up to the negotiators to seek out ways by which they can both win from the process.

4. *Insist on objective criteria*. The means by which success and failure should be judged needs to be objective and sound in the circumstances. Often a negotiation can degenerate into a horse trading event in which issues are traded so that each party wins some and loses some. 'Objective criteria' means a decision basis that is independent of either side. This approach should ensure that it is the merits of the case that decide the outcome, not pressure or trading tactics.

The authors recognized that not every negotiator operates by these principles and they include in their work a number of tactics for dealing with such situations, including knowing what the alternatives to agreement are. After all, it may be in the best interests of one party to walk away from a particular negotiation, rather than create an unacceptable agreement.

NEGOTIATOR CHARACTERISTICS

The Huthwaite Research Group is a specialized marketing and sales consultancy and has studied negotiating behaviours for approximately 30 years. As a consequence of their work they have identified a number of ways in which successful negotiators distinguish themselves from less successful negotiators, which they have generously allowed to be summarized below (© Huthwaite Research Group). Successful negotiators have a tendency to:

- *Seek information*. Skilled negotiators spend about 30 per cent of their time asking questions during negotiations, compared to only 10 per cent by average negotiators. This is thought to give a degree of control over the discussion and avoid direct disagreement.
- *Test understanding*. Skilled negotiators spend twice as much time as average negotiators testing that they understand what the other party is saying. This aspect is about the clarity of the issues under discussion and how each party understands the other's point of view. It is about statements such as: 'Let me see if I have understood what you are saying.'
- *Summarize*. The same degree of difference is detected between skilled and less skilled negotiators in terms of summarizing the negotiation and the points made as the process unfolds. This reflects an attempt on the part of the skilled negotiator to build on their understanding of the perspective of the other party and of ensuring that everyone holds a common understanding of the stage of agreement (or disagreement) reached. Summarizing flows naturally from testing understanding. It is about statements such as: 'Can I just take a few minutes to review where we have got to?'
- *Label behaviour*. This aspect of effective negotiation is about providing advance indication of what is to be said next. For example, rather than simply saying, 'What is your best discount for bulk orders?' the skilled negotiator might first say, 'Can I ask you a question? What is your best discount for bulk orders?' It is suggested that labelling the following behaviour in this way takes some of the surprise out of the process, slows the whole process down, focuses attention on

the second sentence rather than the label and so is more likely to gain a positive reaction and response.

Huthwaite's research has also showed that successful negotiators tend to avoid the following behaviours:

- *Irritators*. By avoiding saying unpleasant and offensive things about opponents arguments can obviously be avoided. However, average negotiators are more likely to offer favourable comments about themselves and their case. For example: 'This represents a very favourable offer.'
- *Defend/attack spirals*. By directly avoiding the use of attack or defend behaviours a spiral of deteriorating quality of discussion and argument can be avoided.
- *Counterproposals*. Simply using counterproposals avoids the opportunity to explore the merits in the other party's case or to find ways for mutual benefit to be developed. Skilled negotiators make significantly fewer counterproposals.
- *Argument dilution*. Skilled negotiators use many fewer justification claims to back up their case. This runs counter to the argument that the more reasons to back up a case the stronger it becomes. However, more reasons provide more potential points of disagreement if the other party holds a different perspective. This can dilute the strength of the underlying argument.

It has also been found that there are gender differences in the involvement in negotiation activities. Linda Babcock, a professor of economics at Carnegie Mellon University was asked by the Dean of her School why it was that more male graduate students taught their own courses than female graduate students and she was told that women just didn't ask! So with colleague Sara Laschever, she began to investigate how women relate to, and become involved with, negotiation across a broad spectrum of business situations. The result published in their book titled, *Women Don't Ask: Negotiation and the Gender Divide* reviews the results of their research (*Potentials*, 2004). Two of their findings were that men initiate negotiations about four times as often as women and about 20 per cent of adult women say they never negotiate at all. Among the reasons that contribute to the gender differences identified by the writers are that more women need to be liked than men and they place a higher value on personal relationships than do men. Also assertiveness, one of the key traits for negotiators (according to the writers) was found to be more desirable in men than women. Babcock and Laschever also point out that women can use some of their natural characteristics to advantage when negotiating, what is needed they argue is a desire on the part of women to engage in negotiation and the opportunity to practise doing so.

COMMUNICATION, DECISION MAKING AND NEGOTIATION: AN APPLIED PERSPECTIVE

There are many applications of communication, decision making and negotiating in the field of management. Managers must therefore develop appropriate policies and practices with regard to these issues. For example, some organizations adopt a high profile and, consequently, court publicity at every opportunity. Other organizations adopt the opposite approach, preferring to stay out of the public eye and seeking to operate in private. There is, however, a fine line between simply avoiding publicity and actively seeking to divert attention from something that should be brought into the open. The first case is an example of not using communication to its fullest potential, the second a potentially sinister and manipulative approach in order to hide something. This latter approach provides the opportunity for corruption to develop and flourish through obscurity. It is not therefore in the long-term interest of any individual, company or society. Corruption in all its forms has a long history and has affected human behaviour in organizations in every continent, its effect being to wear down the fabric of society (Alatas, 1991). The challenge facing managers is how to achieve operational effectiveness without directly abusing the resources available to them (or encouraging such behaviour in others by default or indolence) through the unethical and inappropriate use of communication, decision making or negotiation.

Most communication within an organizational context takes place between individuals and groups. The more formal external contact tends to be restricted to specialist departments and senior managers acting on behalf of the organization. However, word of mouth and accidental communication should not be underestimated as active sources of information and influence. Employees and managers invariably talk to other people as part of their social life outside work. The views and opinions expressed in that context can have a significant impact on public perception of an organization, sales levels and its standing in the local and business community. Rumours originating from such interaction can easily build pictures that form the basis of investigative journalism and City speculation, both of which can have adverse (or positive) impacts. Not everyone is a good communicator and not all channels offer equal effectiveness in getting the message across. For example see Table 16.2, indicating the relative effectiveness of various forms of internal company communications.

Many of the situations relating to communication will also involve decision making and negotiation. These will form part of the negotiations with trade unions, government departments, customers or banks for example. It is a management responsibility to establish who can negotiate what with whom in relation to company operations. Also, it is necessary to establish who can take what level and type of decision. Not to establish these frameworks can result in major difficulties for the organization. It is reported (Carpenter and Feloni, 1989) that a respected Wall Street financial institution had little by way of formal financial accountability at the top of the organization and so was unable to control and monitor the level of 'cheque-kiting' (a complex process of moving cheques around various bank accounts to obtain loans). As a result of these fundamental weaknesses in communication and decision making, together with the resulting lack of control, the organization eventually collapsed and had to be absorbed into another Wall Street firm. This example shows the complex interactions between communication, decision making, negotiation (local managers were free to negotiate deals with local banks), management structure, accountability and operational activity.

Team briefing	57%
Roadshows/staff meetings	11%
Newsletters	7%
Noticeboards	6%
House journal/newsletter	6%
Other	5%
E-mail	4%
Video	1%

TABLE 16.2 Effectiveness of employee communication channels (*source*: *Personnel Today*, 3 May, 1994)

There is a significant difference between a manager communicating the technical features of a product to customers and the same manager attempting to convince employees to work harder because of a reduction in the number of people employed following a delayering exercise. The intended audiences are different, as is the purpose of the message, but so are the relative power relationships that will influence subsequent events. The political nature of decision making was well described by Pettigrew (1973) in linking a hierarchy of power to control of resources. Regent (2003) identifies a number of points that should be taken into account when breaking bad news to staff, including:

- *Keep it personal.* Don't use e-mail, voice mail or text messages to do your dirty work. Tell people face-to-face either individually or in groups.
- *Beware of the rumour mill.* People are likely to have some idea that a problem exists, whatever it is, and so the rumours will probably be circulating. Rumours are often wrong and so it pays to get the correct news out into the open sooner rather than later.
- *Time it carefully.* In an ideal world bad news would be broken at the same time both internally and externally, or perhaps even slightly earlier internally. Employees should not have to hear bad news from the media. Although there is a legal requirement to tell shareholders first careful planning needs to be done to ensure that employees are also told as early as possible.
- *Plan for business as usual.* Unless the bad news is closure make contingency plans to ensure that normal running of the company returns as soon as possible.
- *Tell it like it is.* Don't sugar-coat the news as this may give the impression that things are not as bad as they seem. Also try to offer a way forward through the problem so that people support the organization and think that it has a future worth working for.
- *Offer support.* Bad news about work can be like bereavement and send people into shock. Letting the dust settle and then holding a follow-up session; or perhaps the use of a helpline or counselling can assist by offering support.

In decision-making processes the potential dangers arising from the emergence of the groupthink phenomenon is of particular importance (Janis, 1982). Also the decision to establish a group to take a decision could itself be flawed. It is often assumed that a group will take a better decision than an individual, the justification being the inclusion of a range of expertise and opinions and skills. Unfortunately, this view assumes that such a group will undertake its tasks without the wide range of potential interference factors corrupting the process. There are many pressures acting on the members of a group, even when it is made up of senior people. Many of these factors have already been introduced and include personal, political, interpersonal and capability issues. In decision making there are number of approaches which seek to improve the creative dimensions (and hence the overall quality) of it. Of the approaches developed, those created by Edward De Bono are perhaps the best known. Management in Action 16.3 indicates some of his views on how to improve decision making.

Managers are collectively and individually responsible for the actions carried out within the organization. They may not personally take a decision but they have a responsibility to ensure that those who undertake these activities do so to the highest levels of professionalism. That is not to say that perfection should be expected on every occasion, that would be unrealistic. What it does imply is that managers have a responsibility to ensure that it is done to the highest standard in the circumstances. There is the potential to have access to a variety of sources of information to help managers in decision making, see Table 16.3.

MANAGEMENT IN ACTION 16.3 Put on your thinking caps

In an interview with Lucy Kellaway, Edward De Bono, the person who developed 'lateral thinking', talked about his latest approach to creative thinking – the six thinking hats. He argues that approaches to thinking adopted in the West are too rigid and lock creative process into patterns that are no longer appropriate to the fast changing world of today. In making this claim he refers to Socrates, Plato and Aristotle as the 'Gang of Three', who developed the approach to thought still dominant today.

His latest approach to making people more effective in their lives and work is to adopt the perspectives and processes of the six thinking hats. Each hat is a different colour and represents a different thought process. The colours are:

- *White*. This hat is used to denominate the information-gathering stage of thought.
- *Red*. This hat represents the feelings and emotions towards the thought object.
- *Black*. This hat incorporates the evaluation of risk, critical appraisal and the adopting of a cautious approach to the focus issue.
- *Yellow*. This hat requires the wearer to concentrate on issues associated with the feasibility of solutions and the benefits to be gained from them.
- *Green*. This hat is the one that emphasizes the development of new ideas, options and possibilities.
- *Blue*. This hat is described as the 'meta' one. It is intended to concentrate on the total process, ensuring that the end result takes all hats into account.

In a meeting context, everyone would wear the same colour hat at the same time and would examine the issue or problem from that perspective. The meeting would work through each of the hats in sequence, considering the issue or problem from every angle.

Companies in the USA which have already used his 'six hats' approach include IBM, Rothmans, Du Pont, Federal Express and the Mormon Church. The approach has spread to other parts of the world, including Canada, Japan, South Africa, Italy and the UK.

De Bono argues that by adopting the logical and concentrated approach to creative thinking implied by the six hats, the chemical actions in the brain change compared to when an undifferentiated approach is being used. The result is a more efficient thinking process in which each person concentrates on the same perspective at the same time thereby eliminating the political and ego-based 'contaminants' that otherwise disrupt effective thought and decision making. By everyone emphasizing the same aspect at the same time he suggests that a much more effective inclusion of each perspective occurs. He claims that meeting times can be reduced by approximately 50 per cent, saving some executives the equivalent of about one day each week in wasted time.

Adapted from: Kellaway, L (1994) Put on your thinking caps, *Financial Times*, 17 June, p 17.

Stop ↔ Consider

Could you envisage using the thinking hats approach in practical decision making? Why or why not?

What do you think the effect would be if you tried it with a group of fellow students in order to decide on the answer to this activity?

How would you persuade other people to join a decision-making process based upon the thinking hats approach?

The notion of programmed decisions should encourage organizations to channel many of the decision-making areas towards the routine (and controlled) end of the spectrum, thereby freeing time and resources to concentrate on strategic and non-programmed decision areas. However, as Child (1973) points out, this approach further differentiates the organization on the basis of technical expertise as a prerequisite for access to and interpretation of information relevant to non-programmed decisions. Those who deal with programmed decisions have the scientific management

Newspapers, journals and magazines	98%
Word of mouth	95%
Market reports	86%
Company reports	83%
TV/radio	75%
Online information sources	59%
Microfiche	34%
CD-ROM	19%

TABLE 16.3 Sources of information available to managers (*source*: *Personnel Today*, 3 May, 1994)

approach to their work imposed upon them. Their jobs are de-skilled, routinized and generally regarded as inferior and menial. Whereas those who deal with non-programmed decisions develop a wide range of skills, are likely to have enriched jobs and be regarded as highly valuable by their employing organizations. They are also likely to be the ones who have careers and access to promotion to the most senior levels within organizations.

The view of limited rationality introduced in the context of decision-making models leads to a notion of satisficing rather than a selection between optimal choices. This leads to a short-term approach to control, based on frequent reviews of performance against target, rather than a strategic approach based on the longer term achievement of goals. Lindblom (1959) describes this as the **science of muddling through**. In other words, a continuous process of readjustment of actions in line with perceived deviation from a short-term objective in an attempt to achieve what Cyert and March (1964) call uncertainty absorption. Decision making can be a career-limiting event if the decision turns out to be wrong, costly or embarrassing for the organization. There are many ways in which individuals attempt to deal with this aspect of organizational life and which have been touched on in various chapters in the book. For example, the holding of meetings can be used as an attempt to improve decision making and share responsibility as can the use of project teams and taskforces. Management in Action 16.4 illustrates how meetings and decisions are frequently seen by individuals within organizations.

Science of muddling through
A short-term approach to control, rather than a strategic approach based on the long term achievement of goals.

Decisions can be placed into one of three categories: operational, tactical and strategic. Each category contains variation in the timeframes and consequences for the decision. For example, operational decisions represent the day-to-day activities involved in meeting the immediate needs of the organization. As such they tend to be the low-cost, small impact and low-risk decisions, perhaps more akin to problem solving. At the other extreme, strategic decisions involve issues such as the direction of the business, acquisition or divestment of divisions or even entire companies. These, together with the development of new products and new facilities tend to be at the high-cost, high-risk end of the spectrum. The decision to build a new factory may take five years from first idea to post-commissioning hand-over, by which time both the market and product may have changed considerably. Strategic decisions are expensive to correct if they turn out to be wrong. Tactical decisions tend to reflect the means through which a strategy will be achieved; as such they lie between the short term focus of operational decisions and the long term focus of strategic decisions.

People can experience the theories that underpin communications, decision making and negotiation through training courses and degree programmes. Experience

MANAGEMENT IN ACTION 16.4 On the road to procrastination

There are many light-hearted observations found on company notice boards and office walls about the benefits or otherwise of meetings. The following is not uncommon:

> Are you lonely? Work on your own? Hate making decisions? Hold a meeting! You can see other people, draw flowcharts, feel important and impress your colleagues. All in work time. **Meetings** – the practical alternative to work.

It has long been established that making decisions is stressful. The well-known 'executive monkey' studies from the 1960s demonstrated that forcing the animals to decide between options, the results of which determined if an electric shock would be applied, caused the animals to become ill. There are many parallels between these experiments and the work experience of modern managers. Under pressure from many quarters to cut costs and at the same time enhance customer service it is hardly surprising that many attempt to slow down the rate of change and decision making. In his light-hearted review, Furnham draws attention to the decision-avoidance possibilities of committees and individuals.

Committees, claims Furnham, represent the most popular decision-avoidance technique. He goes on to explain that the best committees at this process are those that include individuals who prefer to do nothing who can then legitimately meet and decide that nothing can be done. At an individual level, the more popular decision avoidance (or procrastination) techniques are claimed to be:

- *The temper tantrum*. Adopting the behaviour typical of a spoilt two-year-old child can frequently manipulate the reactions of others to the extent that any decision becomes unnecessary or at least favourable.
- *The hush-hush approach*. Pointing out to a colleague that information exists that they could not possible be party to can effectively halt any decision that is about to be made. Such comment means that any progress on the problem would result in severe embarrassment or even worse at either a personal or professional level.
- *The clarification method*. This approach can also be classed as elaboration. It adopts the approach that continually referring back an issue for further information or clarification or for the delineation of decision boundaries can simply exhaust the person being targeted and so halt a project.
- *The double-talk method*. This approach is much beloved of those individuals with the ability to use long words and complex sentences. It is a jargon-based approach intended to confuse others and to make them look inadequate as the basis of controlling their behaviour.
- *The denial approach*. Simply stating over and over again that no decision is necessary can frequently be used to avoid having to take one.
- *The 'that's your problem' response*. Simply handing the problem back to the originator can be an effective way of avoiding a decision. It can involve trying to make them feel that they should be adapting to a situation or be capable of taking the decision themselves without the need to refer it to other people.

Furnham finishes with two quotes demonstrating opposite perspectives on procrastination. Victor Kiam is reputed to have said that: 'Procrastination is opportunity's natural assassin.' James Thurber, by way of contrast, suggested that: 'He who hesitates is often saved.' A view which perhaps explains the popularity of decision avoidance techniques.

Adapted from: Furnham, A (1994) On the road to procrastination, *Financial Times*, 4 May, p 17; original source for the meetings quotation unknown, but this version taken from the *Australian Family Physician*, 1992, 21, p 904.

Stop ↔ Consider

In the light of this is, 'a decision not to take a decision, actually a decision'? Justify your answer.

within organizations adds to this by providing practice opportunity in live situations. The hierarchical structure of organizations can be seen as allowing experience in these skills to be gained by individuals in a structured and relatively risk-free environment. Junior staff are allowed to take comparatively small decisions and are usually monitored by supervisors or junior managers. Promotion brings with it the opportunity to become experienced in dealing with ever larger communications, decision-making and negotiation issues. One of the consequences of delayering over recent years has been the reduction in the amount of practice opportunity available. This is particularly evident in the opportunity for graded decision-making and negotiating experience, with a possible increase in the level of risk and failure for both individuals and organizations. Essentially, the steps between levels in a delayered organization are much larger and there are fewer checks on activity (pushing decision making down the hierarchy to the lowest level possible is a prime objective of such schemes) and, consequently, there is less room for error or incremental learning. The issues associated with learning how to engage effectively with other people become even more relevant when doing business in other countries. The need to engage in international business has spawned a range of publications that offer help in understanding the cultural implications and differences between business locations, see for example, Rice (2004) for an indication of the requirements for doing business in Saudi Arabia. Also see *New Straits Times* (2004) for an indication of how public sector procurement systems should include negotiation and other processes in an attempt to avoid corruption creeping into the system.

There is a unique relationship between the three concepts of communication, decision making and negotiation that is not often found in management theory. There is a cumulative relationship between them. Communication can take place isolated from the other two. The simple exchange of information and related interaction does not imply either decision making or negotiation. Decision making, however, cannot take place without communication, but it can take place without negotiation. The chief executive reviewing the financial performance of the company can decide on an appropriate course of action based upon the financial reports available and other information communicated by and discussed with senior managers. This does not necessarily require that the chief executive must negotiate with anyone over the intended course of action. Negotiation, however, can only take place in conjunction with the other two. In order to negotiate the parties must communicate and take decisions. This complexity is evident in the context of nursing as shown by Antai-Otong (2004). Antai-Otong identifies: being positive and optimistic; choosing the battle carefully; understanding what is negotiable (and what is not); the promotion of win-win strategies and being flexible as important features of the process of successful negotiations.

CONCLUSIONS

Communications, decision making and negotiation are three of the most important aspects of managerial activity. They are interlinked in a way that makes them difficult to separate and consider in isolation. From the point of view of anyone connected with organizations they are all about the process of influencing others in some way or other. For example, communication has as one of its main features the persuasion of others to a particular point of view. Decision making has as one of its main objectives the selection of a course of action that will inevitably impact on others. Negotiation has as one of its main features the persuasion of others to reach agreement (or an exchange) on a mutually acceptable basis.

Now to summarize this chapter in terms of the relevant Learning Objectives:

- **Outline the concepts of communication, decision making and negotiation.** The three concepts are linked together in a particular one-way relationship. Negotiation cannot take place without some form of decision making and communications being present. Decision making needs communication to occur, but is not necessarily associated with negotiation. Communication forms part of the other two concepts, but not all communication is related to decision making or negotiation. Communications is more than the simple passing of information; it implies an interactive process involving more than one person. As a process it is about the exchange and development of ideas. It is also a difficult thing in that there are limitations of the human ability to express ideas in any observable form of expression and the interpretation of transmitted information is also subject to similar difficulties. Decision making represents a process of selecting between options. There are many decision sciences that can contribute to the mechanical process of making a decision, but that said it still represents a human process and consequently becomes subject to many of the tendencies found in other areas of human activity. There are a number of models that can help to understand the ways in which human beings approach decision making and these are reviewed at the appropriate point in the chapter. Negotiation represents a process of seeking to resolve differences, or the making of agreements. It can occur formally or informally within an organization. Formal negotiations are likely to have a greater degree of structure to them than informal negotiations between colleagues. There are a number of tactics that are likely to be encountered during a negotiation process and the principled negotiations approach has been proposed as a means to avoid many of them.
- **Explain the major models of decision making processes.** One of the major decision making models is the programmed and non-programmed approach. This suggests that it is cheaper and easier to function more effectively if programmed approaches to decisions can be developed. Programmed decision areas have a known path between the problem and the solution. Non-programmed decision areas are new, novel or different and the solution has to be worked out from scratch. That takes time, costs money and contains a high risk of failure. There are also approaches to decision making based on rationality. These assume that the person making the decision acts in a rational manner as befits their status and job responsibilities. In other words that they will act in the best interest of the organization. However, that is not always the case; there are a number of personal, political and capability issues that can limit rational actions being taken. The political or garbage can model of decision making reflects that in practical terms the political processes within organizations can influence the decisions taken. For example, managers may seek to enhance their careers or functional status through the decisions that they make. Equally it could be argued that many specialist functions have a range of solutions already available that need problems to exist in order to attach themselves to. Consequently, problems can be created or interpreted in particular ways in order to allow this expertise to be applied. Other models introduced in the chapter include the pragmatic model, conflict model and cycle model, all of which are described in the appropriate section of the chapter.
- **Assess the organizational significance of communication, decision making and negotiation.** The significance of the three concepts that form the basis of this chapter emerges from their importance in managerial and organizational activity. An organization that cannot communicate with its customers or employees effectively is unlikely to survive for long. It is not enough for an organization to simply tell its customers what is available without listening to what they need or want. Such an approach would increasingly separate the company from its customers and lead to loss of sales. Equally an organization that did not take effective decisions would soon find itself going into liquidation and financial ruin. To understand how and why decisions are made is important in positioning the company appropriately to its market and customers. Of course it is not possible to take appropriate decisions without effective communication to provide appropriate information and interaction between people in reaching the conclusions forming the output of the decision making process. Negotiation is significant to an organization as it will inevitably need to arrange a number of contracts right from its early days. For example, the rent

charged for premises, the purchase and delivery arrangements with suppliers and contracts of employment for employees are all areas which involve negotiation. As organizations grow the number and level of negotiation becomes more complex and there are many elements within the actual processes of negotiation that can influence the quality and value of the result achieved.

- **Discuss how principled negotiation is intended to achieve a satisfactory and consistent result for all parties.** Principled negotiation contains four elements within it:
  1. *Separate the people from the problem*. It is the issue at the heart of the negotiation that is important, not the people representing the parties to the process. Concentrate on the issue not the people.
  2. *Focus on interests, not positions*. Negotiations often begin with all parties setting out their position. These positions are indented to place a mark in the ground about what will be acceptable. These pointers usually bear little relationship to the underlying interests of the parties. For example, an employee may demand a 20 per cent pay rise, but actually be interested in secure employment, with good wages and career development opportunities. Seek to identify what the underlying interests of all the parties are.
  3. *Invent options for mutual gain*. This aspect is about seeking to create a win-win basis for finding solutions to the problem. A 20 per cent pay rise represents additional cost with no return for the employer, so it is worth seeking to identify how the employee can deliver something of value to the employer in return for the rise expected. That way a good rise is more likely to be awarded as both sides can gain something through the process.
  4. *Insist on objective criteria*. How can the value or benefit from the negotiation be measured? How is it possible for any party to the negotiations to know when a deal is a good deal? These are the questions that this element seeks to answer. If the measures used to determine the value of a deal are objective and neutral to all parties then the result is likely to be more appropriate and acceptable to everyone.

  Each of these elements is designed to achieve a particular benefit in a consistent manner for all of the participants.

- **Understand the main influences on interpersonal communication.** These include body language, paralanguage, proxemics, the environment and time. Each of these aspects of non-verbal communication adds meaning to the basic words used in any communication. They are largely automatic and individuals usually have little control over them in that they represent an unconscious element in the communication process. Table 16.1 sets out what many of these terms mean and the associated discussion in the chapter sets out how they impact on the communication with which they are linked.

DISCUSSION QUESTIONS

1. The garbage can approach to decision making suggests that bundles of decisions exist within organizations just looking for problems to attach themselves to. To what extent does that suggest that functions such as the human resource management department have no real contribution to make to an organization? Justify your answer.
2. Explain the differences between programmed and non-programmed decision making providing examples of each. To what extent can all decisions within an organization be said to fall within this framework?
3. Describe some of the tactics used in negotiation. How do you think that you could counter some of the aggressive tactics described?
4. Describe how communications can be thought of as a perceptual process.
5. Is rationality the only basis on which decisions are taken? Illustrate your answer from your own experience.
6. Is negotiation group dynamics in a particular situation? Justify your answer.
7. What is interpersonal communication and why is it important for an organization?
8. 'Negotiation is nothing more than a power struggle between two unequal parties.' Discuss this statement.
9. Would it be possible for managers to operate in such a way that negotiation with trade unions could be avoided?
10. 'Communication, decision making and negotiation skills are so closely linked to the personality of the individuals that they cannot be learned.' Discuss this statement.

ROLE PLAY The missing nurse

This exercise involves a role play involving two people. You will either play the part of the manager or the nurse. Consequently, you should only read the role brief for the appropriate position. After you have read the pre-meeting brief and the appropriate role brief you should begin the meeting playing the role that you have been allocated.

There is also a task section at the end of this role play exercise that will tell what to do when the meeting has ended.

Pre-meeting brief

Each of the two participants will be playing one role. Take a few minutes to read and absorb the role to which you have been allocated. There will not be enough information in either role play to fully reflect the situation facing the manager (Valerie) or the nurse (Julie) so be prepared to go beyond the basic information provided, providing it is appropriate to the general situation and spirit of the exercise.

The manager has called the meeting and so it is for the person playing Valerie to take the initiative and organize the seating arrangement and any other physical aspects surrounding the context within which the role play is to take place. The meeting begins when the manager (Valerie) calls Julie into her office. At that point you should take on the role that you are playing and act out the part in an interactive process as if you were actually that person in that situation. The meeting should last until it reaches a natural conclusion when either the problem is resolved or some other event results in it ending.

Role 1: Valerie Jacques – Ward Manager

You are in charge of a general surgery ward within a large district general hospital in the North of England. The general atmosphere within the ward has always been very positive and generally, it has the lowest rate of absence and lateness within any of the departments within the hospital. You pride yourself on the fact that you have encouraged staff to contribute to the running of the ward, which along with the level of outside social interaction among staff, has helped create a positive approach to work and a caring patient environment.

Julie Marshall is a 33-year-old D grade nurse who has worked on permanent day shift within your ward for the past 4 years. Julie's work has always been very good and she has never been one for turning up late for work or taking days off. She was always willing to join in work or social activities within the department and she could be relied on to work overtime or put in additional late shifts if required. However, things have changed over recent months. Reviewing her records for the past few months, you have noticed that she is not as reliable as she used to be, and you have noticed that she is not as willing to work overtime as she used to be.

Other members of staff on the ward have commented that she no longer comes out for a drink after work, or mixes with them at the social events organized. They have also noticed her poor timekeeping and the other changes already indicated. In missing the social events, she always comes up with an excuse about prior engagements or a family event. Although none of the other members of staff on the ward have made any complaint against Julie as a result of having to cover for her, it has been noticed and you get the feeling that they feel let down, bemused and irritated by her actions. One or two patients have also begun to refer to her as 'old misery' and so you decide now is the time for action.

You don't want to lose Julie as she has proved herself as a good worker over a long period of time, but you want things to be back the way they were and her present behaviour is unacceptable. You have spoken to the Human Resource Department and they suggest that the appropriate way to deal with this type of situation is set out in the hospital disciplinary procedure. The procedure allows for a preliminary discussion to be held with the member of staff in order to identify the scope of the problem and determine if the formal stage of the disciplinary procedure is necessary. The Human Resource Officer also indicated that unless you deal with the issue correctly it could prevent any formal action being taken against Julie about this matter in the future. Consequently, you have asked Julie to come to a meeting in your office for a preliminary discussion.

Role 2: Julie Marshall – D grade nurse

Your name is Julie Marshall and you are a 33-year-old D grade nurse who has worked within your current ward for 4 years. You work permanent day shift on a general surgery ward within a large district general hospital in the North of England. You have always enjoyed nursing and you have worked hard over the past 4 years to create a happy, professional atmosphere around your job, as a consequence you have contributed considerably to the positive team spirit within your ward. The entire team takes great pride in their work and have a very good timekeeping and attendance record. The nursing team on your ward often spends time socializing together after work, frequently involving other family members in social activities. Your active social life is largely supported by the overtime payments that you earn from the frequent opportunity to put in additional shifts on your ward and sometimes on other wards within the hospital.

Everything was going well until about 4 months ago when your partner of 8 years walked out on you, leaving you to care for the two children aged 5 and 2 years respectively. You have considerable help from your mother and various friends in taking the older child to school and to nursery for the younger child. They are also very useful in collecting the children from school and nursery and in looking after them if you have to work overtime or a late shift. However, it is in relation to the potential to work overtime that most problems arise. It is very difficult to arrange for someone to pick up the children at short notice, and of course the nursery cannot accept children at short notice, or during the late evening or night. Your mother has to get a bus from her home to your house each time she looks after the children and she cannot guarantee an arrival time because of the unreliability of the service and the variability of traffic volume. When friends look after the children it can be relatively easy to arrange as they live locally and the school for the 5 year old is within walking distance. The nursery for the younger child is near to the hospital where you work and is open from 7.00am to 7.00pm Monday to Friday. As a consequence of these difficulties you have not been as consistently punctual as previously and you have had to ring in sick a couple of times as a result of the stress, or when one of the children was ill etc. Also, you have not been able to work much overtime and have missed most of the after work socializing and social events that have been organized since your partner left.

Although you have been a very active member of the ward staff in the past, you do not like to talk about private matters or to have your private life talked about, or to be the focus of gossip and rumour. Consequently, you haven't told anyone at work about your problems or difficulties at home and have tried to hide the real situation. Equally, your problems at home have been compounded as a result of the reduction in your income because of the lack of overtime pay and the loss of your partner's income. You feel tired all the time and alienated from your colleagues, for whom everything seems to be going on as normal. You do not know what to do next in order to improve your situation. The ward manager has asked you to attend a meeting with her, and you can guess what the discussion will be about. You can't afford to lose your job now, or to go part-time, so you approach the meeting with a defensive/aggressive attitude in order (as you see it) to better protect your position.

Post-meeting brief

After the meeting has ended discuss the events that have taken place in the meeting and how they relate to the communication, decision making and negotiation material presented in this chapter. Also discuss these issues with other groups that have taken part in the exercise and any observers that were present during the process. For example how difficult was it for Valerie to persuade Julie to openly discuss her situation? What might this suggest about the way in which the interaction took place and the preconceived ideas that both parties entered the process with? How were any decisions reached? To what extent did the meeting become a negotiation process intended to 'force' Julie to return to her previous behaviour patterns or face formal disciplinary action? There will inevitably be other issues that emerge from the role play that will arise during this discussion process. Identify the general implications in relation to communication, decision making and negotiation that you have learned from this exercise.

FURTHER READING

Cialdini, RB (1988) *Influence: Science and Practice*, HarperCollins, New York. A highly readable text on the general topic of persuasion in all its forms. It includes consideration of all three topics covered in this chapter, but from a different perspective.

Clark, H, Chandler, J and Barry, J (1994) *Organization and Identities: Text and Readings in Organizational Behaviour*, International Thomson Business Press, London. Contains a broad range of original articles on relevant material themes and from significant writers referred to in this and other textbooks on management and organizations.

Fisher, D (1993) *Communications in Organizations*, 2nd edn, West Publishing, St Paul, MN. This text considers communication from many perspectives relevant to material within the organizational behaviour field.

Fisher, R and Ury, W (1986) *Getting To Yes: Negotiating Agreement Without Giving In*, Penguin, New York. This book describes the principled negotiation approach developed by the authors. The subtitle for the book is 'negotiating agreement without giving in', and this effectively describes the approach adopted by the authors. It was followed by a second text (*Getting Past No*, W Ury, 1991, Business Books, London) which outlines how to deal with difficult people in a negotiation context.

Hickson, DJ, Butler, RJ, Cray, D, Malory, GR and Wilson, DC (1986) *Top Decisions: Strategic Decision Making in Organizations*, Basil Blackwell, Oxford. This book describes the decision-making activities across organizations ranging in size from very small to very large. Among its strengths is that it shows how the political dimension of organizations manifests itself in the decision-making process.

Kennedy, G (1999) *The New Negotiating Edge*, Nicholas Brealey, London. A recent addition to the wide range of texts on negotiation. Written by a professor at Edinburgh Business School it provides a good balance between theory and practice.

Rosenhead, J and Mingers, J (2001) *Rational Analysis for a Problematic World Revisited: Problem Structuring Methods for Complexity, Uncertainty and Conflict*, 2nd edn, Wiley, Chichester. Explores a broad range of approaches to problem solving and uses a case study to demonstrate the application of each model.

Scott, W (1981) *The Skills of Negotiating*, Gower, Aldershot. This is a practical 'how to' type of book which covers many of the facets of negotiating in a range of situations. It is readable and sets out to improve the capability to carry out negotiations as well as describing the process itself.

Spitzer, Q and Evans, R (1999) *Heads You Win: How the Best Companies Think*, Touchstone Books, London. Based on a specific problem-solving approach the authors review the practical implementation issues around the model. It is intended as a practitioner text and is supported by the consultancy experience of the authors.

COMPANION WEBSITE

Online teaching and learning resources:

Visit the companion website for Organizational Behaviour and Management 3rd edition at: *http://www.thomsonlearning.co.uk/businessandmanagement/martin3* to find valuable further teaching and learning material:

Refer to page 35 for full details.

CHAPTER 17

Power and control

LEARNING OBJECTIVES

After studying the chapter content and working through the associated Management in Action panels, Employee Perspectives, Discussion Questions and Case Study, you should be able to:

- **Understand the major perspectives on power as experienced within an organization.**
- **Describe the sources of power within an organization.**
- **Explain the differences and similarities between the concepts of power, influence and authority.**
- **Outline the characteristic features of control systems as found in organizations.**
- **Discuss the significance of the 'zone of indifference' in relation to the use of power and control within an organization.**

INTRODUCTION

The notion of power is endemic in organizational relationships. Managers exercise power over subordinates in directing their endeavours towards the objectives being sought. Industrial relations activity within organizations is largely directed towards a redistribution of the prevailing power balance between managers and employees. For example, one view of the annual negotiation over wages is that it represents an attempt to influence unilateral management decisions about the use of company finances.

A concept that has strong association with power is that of **control**. This can be used to refer to a range of actions, including the processes associated with the control of machine activity. It can also refer to the control of organizational activity on behalf of the objectives identified by the principle stakeholders. However, it can also be used to reflect more sinister processes. It can be taken to reflect the manipulation of employee behaviour by managers. Some managers for example resort to bullying in order to force subordinates to comply with their wishes. Bullying goes beyond the need to ensure that employees follow the instructions that they are given and reflects the desire of some individuals to exercise power and control (or domination) over others (Adams, 1992).

Both power and control contain positive as well as negative connotations. For example, an effective power balance between capital and labour should allow both to function effectively without damage to the interests of either. That is in essence the basis of a free market. Controlled activity within an organization can also be of benefit to the various stakeholders. For example if through the control of the production process within the organization, product changes are brought about which in turn provide commercial advantage, then it could be argued that such activity was advantageous and of benefit to customers, employees and shareholders. The difficulty with both concepts however is that very often the positive and negative aspects function in parallel, or they are not used solely for the benefit of the stakeholder groups. In other words they can be used for personal advantage or for political reasons by individuals or groups. Politics is a subject to which we shall return in the next chapter.

Control
Processes intended to deliver the outcome desired by the designer of the system.

POWER, INFLUENCE AND AUTHORITY

Power is a concept related to ideas of influence, force, manipulation and providing the means through which objectives can be realized. In that sense it reflects a directing, mobilizing and energizing force. For example, managers have the power to require subordinates to follow their instructions, the ultimate sanction being dismissal if they refuse. This is based on the view that managers do the thinking and act in the best interests of the organization, whereas employees are there to follow orders in doing the work considered necessary. This view has predominated throughout history and has been reinforced through such approaches as scientific management.

Influence
The ability to direct the behaviour of another person involving persuasion rather than force.

Power also reflects a process of being able to **influence** the behaviour of others either formally or informally, Peiró and Meliá (2003). Influence being generally viewed as a softer process compared to that of power. For example, a manager exercising power could order an employee to do something. A manager exercising influence may, through recruitment, training, reward and socialization practices encourage employees to align their working habits and attitudes to those of management, therefore avoiding the need to give orders. The same end result is achieved, but through different mechanisms.

Power is also something that is an accompaniment to the concept of **authority**. Generally, those in authority would be expected to have power. However, this is only relatively accurate as there are those who hold power irrespective of their position.

The elected prime minister of a country has considerable power by virtue of their electoral mandate. With a large parliamentary majority they are able to ensure that particular legislation is enacted and enforced. However, they are also at the whim of the population when it comes to election time. The subjects of the power displayed by politicians (the population) hold the power to take away from the prime minister the position that is the source of their power. At election time the ordinary voter holds considerable power over those in authority under normal circumstances.

Authority
The ability of someone to require certain actions or behaviours from another.

Management in Action 17.1 outlines how influence is becoming more important than power in an organizational context as a means of achieving commercial success. It also explores ways in which influence can be achieved and used to advantage when formal authority and power is absent.

Power has been defined in many different ways. Perhaps the most effective definition is that provided by Pfeffer (1992) who brings together a number of views on it as, 'the potential ability to influence behaviour, to change the course of events, to overcome resistance, and to get people to do things that they would not otherwise do' (p 30). In this definition the linkage between power, influence and authority is evident. Within an organizational context it is easy to envisage the hierarchical linkage between power, influence and authority. There is no purpose to the position of a line manager unless it is the exercise of authority over others. However, some management positions exist because of the high technical skill and status necessary to undertake the job; the direct management of others may not be a major part of such activity. However, by virtue of their position within the hierarchy, authority and the ability to influence others will still exist.

There are also many positions within an organization that do not have any formal authority yet the individuals concerned are able to exercise considerable influence. The secretary or personal assistant to a chief executive is frequently in such a position. Working closely with the person with formal authority allows them a considerable degree of influence beyond their formal status. In a very real sense they are gatekeepers and the power behind the throne. The gatekeeper role within an organization is very important in that, as the title suggests, such a postholder can grant or restrict access. For example, the secretary to the personnel manager has the power to make and prioritize appointments, pass on messages or direct enquiries to lower status personnel staff. To a real extent they are in a position to shape the work experience of their boss, as well as the access granted (and hence fortunes of) people wanting to engage with the boss for some purpose. Many salespeople and consultants make a point of getting to know the secretaries and personal assistants of senior managers in client organizations for just this reason.

Authority has been described as the legitimate expression of power (Handy, 1993, p 124). In this context, it reflects power used by someone who is accepted as having the legitimate right to exercise it in that context. Employees generally accept the rights of managers to exercise authority over their activities and behaviour by virtue of the position conveyed formally by the organization. The work of Milgram (1965), introduced in an earlier chapter, is important in this context. His experiments with fake electric shocks demonstrated just how far people can be pushed and how easy it is for individuals in authority to achieve compliance with their wishes. It was Chester Barnard who was among the first to write about the notion of authority in an organizational context. In 1938 he described authority in the following terms:

> The character of a communication (order) in a formal organization by virtue of which it is accepted by a contributor to or 'member' of the organization as governing the action he contributes; that is, as governing or determining what he does or is not to do so far as the organization is concerned. (p 163)

MANAGEMENT IN ACTION 17.1 Influence without authority

Cohen and Bradford describe that 'the crutch of authority' is missing from modern organizations. However, the inhabitants of modern organizations still need to be able to influence others. Northrop, an American aircraft manufacturer, decided that manufacturing specialists should be involved from the beginning of the design process, the intention being to improve the ability to build aircraft more efficiently and with fewer problems. The cost and time involved in making engineering changes during production were excessive and reduced the commercial viability of the company. The ability of the manufacturing people to veto the design engineer's specifications at first caused some problems and resentment. However, when the benefits became obvious in the form of fewer in-process problems it began to function more easily. The results speak for themselves in that 97 per cent of all parts fitted perfectly first time (the previous best was 50 per cent) and engineering changes were reduced to one-sixth of their previous levels and implemented five times faster. The same applies in many service sector companies, including banks, which must share information between separate parts of the organization to target customers more effectively.

Effective influence begins with the ways in which individuals think about the people that they must influence. Regarding them as a partner or strategic ally involves a different approach to working relationships. It moves away from the old win–lose approach to interpersonal relationships with an emphasis on obligations and exchange. After all the person who wants help from you today might be in a position to help you next week. It matters little if they are your boss or a subordinate; the network of relationships is about mutual benefit. Cohen and Bradford make the following suggestions for individuals seeking to achieve influence over others:

- *Mutual respect*. Assume that others are competent and smart.
- *Openness*. It is not possible to know everything, so sharing information helps you as well as them.
- *Trust*. Assume that individuals will not purposely hurt or undermine you and so there is no reason to hold back information.
- *Mutual benefit*. Plan win–win strategies.

Adapted from: Cohen, AR and Bradford, DL (1993) Influence without authority, *World Executives Digest*, December, pp 28–32.

Stop ↔ Consider

To what extent does influence reflect a recognition that traditional ways of exercising power no longer work effectively and therefore its application needs to be appropriate to the dominant social conditions?
Justify your views.

Barnard goes on to explain that a requirement to act in a particular way is evaluated by the recipient in terms of its legitimacy. Acceptance of the requirement to follow the order also acknowledges the authority of the giver of that order. Conversely, denial of the order also denies the legitimacy of the giver to issue it. So, much as those in authority might deny it, the classification of an order as legitimate or otherwise is not in their gift, it is for the recipient to decide. This is what Luthans (1995) describes as an acceptance theory of authority intended to support group cohesion and goals. The inability of those in authority to guarantee that subordinates accept every instruction as legitimate remains a potential source of difficulty for them. There have been many disciplinary cases within organizations based on the refusal of an employee to carry out what was classified by managers as a reasonable instruction. Inevitably, whatever the context, the refusal to obey a reasonable instruction (as defined by management) would be regarded as a threat to the established order and as such something to be dealt with severely.

Influence is an interesting word in English and Handy (1993) introduces it as both noun and verb to explain some of the confusion with power. He attempts to clarify its use by restricting its use to that of a verb in the sense of, 'the use of power' (p 124). In that connection power is only one of the sources of the ability to influence others. Influence can therefore be regarded as a broader concept than power. Influence is also a softer term than power. It implies a willing acquiescence on the part of the subject and more subtle processes at work than would be expected if power was being applied. Influence implies persuasion, co-operation and relationship-based mechanisms for achieving the desired behaviour. In essence implying more of a two-way process compared to power which is unidirectional and predominantly top down.

It would be tempting to restrict the distinction between power and influence to this rather cosy view based around the notion of persuasion. However, these terms are more complex than that would allow. Overt attempts to use power and force are likely to be met with resistance. Consequently, it is not uncommon to find more subtle mechanisms being used in order to obtain compliance with the will of another. For example, as a result of management encouraging employees to become shareholders of the company it might become easier to implement initiatives on issues such as flexible working and lower pay rises. Thus, encouraging shareholding could be an attempt by managers to manipulate employees, making the use of direct power unnecessary. Rothschild and Miethe (1994) (quoting Forsyth, 1993) identify, in the context of whistleblowing, a number of influence strategies that they suggest are used in order to obtain compliance from employees. These are identified in Table 17.1.

Eight of these nine tactics, bullying being the odd one out, represent the indirect application of practices intended to persuade the individual to offer compliance to the will of the perpetrator. In each of these cases it could be suggested that a deliberate attempt to avoid resistance is being made and hence the underlying notion of power is being hidden or disguised. For example, the person initiating a negotiation is seeking to move the other person (or group) towards their position, recognizing that they may not get all they wish for, but it will represent some movement and possibly the exercise of power disguised as compromise.

Where power is a feature of a particular relationship there is also dependency. Power can be exercised if there is no dependency present but it achieves compliance at best. In an organization for example, if an individual employee does not value money, promotion or any of the other 'benefits' provided there is little dependency present and the opportunity for power to be used as a source of influence is strictly limited. In effect managers have few levers (influencing tactics) with which to control

Promising	to do something for the individual in the future
Bullying	the use of threat (real or implied)
Discussion	the use of rational argument and explanation
Negotiation	making compromises
Manipulation	the use of lies and deceit
Demand	insistence on compliance
Claiming expertise	reliance on superior knowledge or skill
Ingratiation	reliance on flattery
Evasion	avoidance of revealing aspects of the situation

TABLE 17.1 Influencing tactics (*source*: Forsyth, GDR (1993) *Group Dynamics*, Brooks/Cole Publishing Company, Pacific Grove, CA)

and direct the behaviour of the individual. Employees that need the job and/or the money for some reason are dependent and thus amenable to the exercise of power. The Employee Perspective (17.1) that follows provides an example in which the impact of a lack of dependency is clearly demonstrated.

PERSPECTIVES ON POWER

The study of power within organizations has generally been neglected by the mainstream disciplines. It is in the field of organization theory that it has gained most prominence as part of the fundamental relationships between organizations and the social structures of which they form part. Ackroyd (1994, p 287) points out that:

EMPLOYEE PERSPECTIVE 17.1 You know what you can do with the job!

Maurice had been a middle manager within the French public sector for about 30 years before taking early retirement. He had plenty of time on his hands after he retired and thought that it would be a good idea to get a part-time job to provide an interest and to enhance his pension. He looked around and eventually found a job as the driver for a medical practice. The job involved working two nights each week driving a doctor to visit patients who had asked to see someone urgently in their home as they could not wait until the normal surgery next day.

Maurice knew the area well and was soon able to get quickly from one patient to another. However, he was quite a lot older than many of the doctors he was transporting around. He indicated that some of the doctors were very friendly and liked to chat as the night passed, while others were remote and viewed themselves as superior to a humble driver. Claude was one such doctor; he was in his mid-30s and acted as though his education, job and status gave him the right to treat Maurice as a servant.

One night the pair had been visiting patients for about two hours and Claude was clearly in a bad mood. For example, he ordered Maurice to take him home as he wanted to pick up a book to read between visits. This done he demanded that Maurice speed up so that they could make up for lost time. Maurice did so, but said that he was not prepared to break the speed limit as he would have to pay a fine if he was caught by the police. Claude told him to shut up and drive as instructed or he would report him to the practice manager for insubordination. Maurice lost his temper at this and stopped the car. He asked Claude who he thought he was talking to. Claude replied that Maurice was only a driver and because such people needed the job he had better keep quiet and start driving. Claude sneered as he made the following point, 'What would you do if I threatened you with dismissal for not following orders? You need the money don't you?'

Maurice shouted back that he did not need the money. He also shouted that if Claude did not change his attitude he would drive out into the countryside near to his own home, stop the car, get out and throw the keys into a field. Then he would walk home to bed, leaving Claude to try and do his job on his own. Claude was lost for words. He had obviously never been spoken to like that before. His reaction after a couple of minutes of embarrassed silence was to laugh and say that he had only been joking and could they go now please. He was never rude to Maurice after that. He adopted a friendly, polite approach to Maurice but tended to keep a distance between them.

Tasks

1. Why do you think Maurice reacted to Claude as he did?
2. To what extent would it be an impossible task to manage employees who are not dependent upon the job or the organization for an income or meaning in their lives?
3. How might you attempt to manage such employees?

> The dominant view in the UK has emphasized the place of organization in the social structure and so makes power and authority central to the analysis. Social structures are structures of power and the organization is a vital part of the mechanism sustaining and perpetuating the social structure.

Much of the emphasis within organization theory therefore has explored the nature of power relationships and the ways in which organizations interact with other organizations within a social context. The other major focus for the study of power has been that of its association with resistance within the notion of the agency concept of organization. This debate forms much of the basis of labour process theory (Braverman, 1974). In subsequent sections some of the major themes associated with the study of power will be explored.

Traditional perspectives on power

Within much of the traditional management literature power was assumed to reflect the nature of the hierarchical relationships endemic to organizations. Management was described as an activity that involved the determination of what needed to be done and then the direction of the necessary resources to meeting that objective. Within that paradigm management had the power to ensure that what was necessary was actually done. Non-management people within the organization existed solely to provide the means of achieving the objectives, there to have power exercised over them. In that sense power is a reflection of the natural social order and as such only one element within the study of leadership and control.

The traditional perspective on power and its relationship with existing social structures was also evident in the views of the early trade unions. For example, during the great building dispute of 1859–60, when carpenters, masons and bricklayers struck in London for (among other things) the right to have their working day reduced to nine-hours, the trade unions told the Central Master Builders Association:

> That our society shall be governed by laws, and that the members shall be requested to conform to those laws is but natural, and we believe that such is the case in all corporations and every club among the upper classes in Pall Mall and St James's. (Quoted in Briggs, 1955, pp 176–7)

They accepted without question that the rule of law in both society and organizations was 'natural' and that if individuals did not follow the 'rules' they could not expect the support of the trade union.

Some of the models used within the literature, particularly that of leadership, capture aspects of power as a normal dimension to be used by managers in the determination of appropriate courses of action. For example, Likert's (1967) four systems of management contain at one extreme an approach titled 'exploitative autocratic' and at the other 'democratic' – the distinction between them largely being grounded in the way in which power is used by the leader concerned. At the autocratic end of the spectrum, leadership is purely top down, akin to the giving of orders. At the other end, democracy is based on trust on the part of the leader that subordinates can effectively contribute through involvement (in management-approved ways) to the achievement of management determined objectives. Also managers retain the ultimate right to say 'no' even within a democratic process.

Fiedler (1967) developed his contingency model of leadership which specifically incorporated a power dimension into his work. Through the leader 'position power' concept Fiedler was reflecting the degree of authority held by the leader. It was scaled as either high or low, reflecting the degree to which the group would follow the leader's wishes. This model is interesting in that it only recognizes the possibility of 'low' as the smallest amount of power held by a leader. Yet in the previous Employee Perspective

(17.1) (Maurice and Claude) a specific example was given whereby the ultimate sanction of dismissal carried little weight in supporting the conventional conception of hierarchical power. The conventional views of power in management do not generally acknowledge the possibility that a leader may not hold power or influence in a particular situation. Schwarzwald *et al.*(2001) studied the relationship between leadership and employee compliance with instructions in conflict situations involving police captains and their subordinates. They found a greater willingness among subordinates to comply with 'soft' rather than 'hard' power base superiors. Police captains who were identified as transformational in leadership style were also more likely to be able to achieve compliance under all power base variations. These results were also broadly supported by Koslowsky (2001) in a hospital context.

The conception of power within an organization in this way is generally based on the existence of three features:

1. Humans have needs, wants and desires that can only be met by the individual engaging with an organization.
2. The existence of resources through which these needs and wants can be met.
3. The existence of a manager who is prepared to act as the go-between in facilitating the 'deal' between the individual and the organization and subsequently managing its realization in practice.

A slightly broader view of power emerges from the work of Pfeffer (1992) when it is linked to the concept of politics (the topic of the next chapter). Pfeffer essentially argues that power is a commodity for managers and that political activity is the means through which it is obtained and traded. He suggests that power within the organization is needed if a particular manager is to gain influence and advance their department, function, professional capabilities, significance (to the organization), personal standing, wealth and career. In that context power is not just a top-down concept, it reflects a 360° process endemic to the experience of managers and non-managers alike.

Lower level employees can also gain and exercise power in a number of ways. Strikes and other forms of industrial action are intended to demonstrate that employees can force management to concede to their demands if they will not willingly agree to do so. Also within the economy of any country a scarcity of labour or particular skills will cause wage rates to rise as companies compete for scarce resources, reflecting a different form of power. Management in Action 17.2 reflects one example of this diffuse concept of power as it can actually function within an organizational context.

Foucault and power

For Foucault, power represented something different from the idea of a commodity. He considered that power was a condition that existed within society as a whole. It was ingrained in the language used and so created the knowledge accepted by a particular society and reflected in its social practices (Linstead, 1993, p 63). Power in this context uses discourse (language) to create the rules which in turn creates and classifies the available knowledge in particular ways. In an organizational context this allows the classification of activity (and people, jobs skill, etc.) into differentiated packages of management and non-management compartments, and so allows the hierarchical framework to be perpetuated as legitimate.

Foucault reminds us in his work that the boundaries around the things that we see, understand and take for granted are in fact artificial and socially created. In that sense our stock of knowledge is created for us out of the discourses that exist within society. By creating these boundaries and compartments our attention is channelled in certain directions and it is automatically directed away from other things. We are effectively

MANAGEMENT IN ACTION 17.2 Promoting the function?

This story was told to me by the human resource director involved in the situation. The company employed about 4000 people and was a medium sized bank with the usual branch network and range of head office functions. Up to the late 1980s the personnel function had been a small department led by a senior manager (not director level). Below that level were a personnel manager and training manager who looked after the entire company. In turn they were supported by a personnel manager for the branches, one for the head office functions and a couple of training officers. There were also a small number of personnel officers and clerical support staff. The department employed a total of about 17 people. The head of the department reported directly to the chief executive, although he did not sit on the board of the company.

The finance sector was changing rapidly by the late 1980s and many companies began to develop new business strategies to take advantage of the new opportunities available. In the bank concerned a major firm of business consultants was retained to assist in the development of new strategies and the subsequent reorganization of the company to enable it to realize its objectives. Clearly a major part of this process involved reorganizing the jobs that people did, training, the development of new pay structures etc., all of which fell under the personnel department's remit.

Not surprisingly under these circumstances the head of personnel argued that major changes were also required within his function. He argued that a range of things should change, including a rebranding of the function under the title of human resource management department, that he should be elevated to director status (to better advise the board on people issues) and that more staff were needed to operationalize the people strategies needed within the new business plan. This view was supported by the retained consultants. This was agreed by the board of directors and the department was totally transformed.

The senior manager became director of human resource management. Integrated into the function were the existing salary administration and pensions functions and a number of new sections were created. A reward management department was established as was an employee relations and safety unit. The training function was expanded and a number of regional human resource managers were recruited. In total the number of people employed in the new human resource management department grew to about 70, approximately 30 of whom were new to the company at senior specialist or manager level.

The payroll cost of the department jumped by considerably more than the rise in numbers might suggest. The number of people in the department rose from about 17 to about 70 suggesting a rise of just over four times. However, the new posts accounted for about 30 positions in the new department, the rest being transfers from other functions within the company. This might suggest an additional payroll cost to the company of about double its original cost. However, the new positions were predominantly at the senior specialist and manager levels and so the new cost was that much higher. The total new cost to the company was an increase in salary and benefits of approximately seven times its previous magnitude. It should also be noted that this additional cost did not include any company employee-based taxes, training, equipment or other costs. It only reflected salary and benefit costs.

From the new director of human resource management's perspective the changes contained a number of benefits. He now had a seat on the board. That gave him the power to influence strategy and policy more easily, at the same time as giving him the status to influence other managers more directly. Personnel activity in the company increased dramatically because there were more people carrying it out. However, it was said that company performance in terms of the bottom line did not improve as a consequence of this additional activity. But the main advantage to the director was that as a consequence of his elevation to the board and the growth in size of his department he personally trebled his salary because he had become responsible for a much bigger (and more significant) department!

Stop ↔ Consider

To what extent does the outcome reflect either the exercise of politics as a way of gaining power within an organization, or simply opportunism in taking advantage of circumstances (for personal gain) as they arise?
Does this distinction matter? Why or why not?

socialized into seeing and understanding the world in which we live through the discourses that we experience and these are a reflection of the distribution of power as it exists in society. However, once formed these foundations for behaviour can become difficult to change and so create a power base for resisting attempts to create alternative organizational frameworks. For example, the provision of central government services in any country is achieved through the diverse range of civil service departments. The current British Prime Minister (Tony Blair) has been frequently reported as wanting to encourage 'joined-up government' to blur these boundaries and encourage the more effective delivery of public services. However, see, for example, Brooks *et al.* (2000, p 10) for one instance of just how difficult this can be to achieve in practice, demonstrating the power of existing and dominant organizational forces.

Foucault demonstrates the association between power and knowledge through a number of examples. In one (Foucault, 1975) outlined in Townley (1994, p 5) he describes how the authorities define an individual accused of murdering his mother, sister and brother through the reports of the police, doctors and presiding judge. These reports are then used by the authorities as the means of knowing the accused and then deciding his fate, thereby exercising power over him. Similar arguments are made in terms of the nature of power within an organizational setting. He suggested that factories have many similarities to institutions such as prisons, monasteries, the military, schools and hospitals. In each of these institutions the prime objective is to know the subject effectively and fully as a basis for being able to ensure, 'that they operate as one wishes' Foucault (1977, p 138). O'Neill (1986, pp 51–2) describes the outcome of power as a form of socialization in social institutions (including organizations) as, 'places where the system can project its conception of the disciplinary society in the reformed criminal, the good worker, student, loyal soldier and committed citizen'.

Labour process theory and Lukes' views on power

Labour process theory originated from the Marxist tradition and attempts to explain the nature of work. It has been defined as, 'the means by which raw materials are transformed by human labour, acting on the objects with tools and machinery: first into products for use and, under capitalism, into commodities to be exchanged on the market' (Thompson, 1989, p xv). As an area of study it began with Braverman, who in 1974 published *Labour and Monopoly Capital,* which stimulated the rediscovery of the earlier Marxist material on the nature of labour. Within this tradition there is the view that management protects itself from the consequences arising from excessive use of authority by allowing practices such as collective bargaining and the legal definition of workers rights to develop, thereby retaining the pre-eminence of capital over labour (Burawoy, 1979). By so allowing some of its power to be dissipated, capital retains effective control over labour activity and use, leading some writers to talk of the **manufacture of consent**. This describes how workers are encouraged to continue to support (to give their consent) to the relative imbalance of power in a capitalist society.

> **Manufacture of consent**
> The manipulation by managers of employee acceptance of control through practices including collective bargaining, although managers retain effective control.

Lukes (1982) attempts to provide a more radical perspective on power. He develops a three-dimensional model which seeks to explain a wider view of its function within an organizational context. The first dimension is suggested to reflect the nature of power as it would be commonly described in much of the literature. In that sense it is a view of power based on its observable and measurable effects. As such it is detected in the behaviour of individuals, who are analyzed in terms of the relative degrees of power that they hold in a particular context. Decision making and conflict are common examples of situations that are interpreted and dissected for the relative quantities of power evident.

The second dimension according to Lukes, reflects the exercise of power over what might be classed as the agenda. For example, the management of a company may recognize a trade union as the representative body for shop-floor employees. However, the scope of involvement for the trade union (and hence employees) in the decision making and running of the company will be governed by the recognition agreement. Management, therefore, have a mechanism to retain control over the agenda for employee involvement. Brannen (1983), for example, describes how worker–director schemes such as that run by British Steel in the 1970s were effectively manipulated through careful scheme design, adulteration of the rules of engagement and the socialization of the representatives involved. As a consequence the rights and power of management over the agenda and activity were never seriously challenged. In this example, the socialization process effectively shaped the views, attitudes and desires of those subjected to it. This reflects a form of covert activity intended to retain the status quo in terms of the relative power balance and its associated structures. However, this second dimension of power has been challenged as still requiring definition in observable terms.

The third dimension in Lukes' model suggests that concepts of hegemony, incorporation, dependency and inaction underpin power. In that context it reflects the essential structural inequalities that exist between groups. For example, management have in their gift the jobs that provide economic and other necessities for the workers, so there is an inevitable asymmetrical power basis to the employment relationship. The major problem with Lukes' model is that it requires the unseen to be incorporated into the analysis. For example, to what extent is power being used and what are its consequences in a situation where a company receives 150 applications for five jobs? Clearly, there is an element of power implicit in such situations as management must choose the lucky five and the remaining 145 will be rejected. But a wide range of forces could impact on these decisions. Managers could take bribes in appointing particular individuals, they may also pick (or reject) people with certain physical characteristics or people from a particular ethnic group or gender. But, having done so what are the likely consequences for the relationship in the future? Managers would like to ensure subsequent compliance, but it is not guaranteed. These represent fundamental difficulties that Lukes does not effectively address.

SOURCES OF ORGANIZATIONAL POWER

In practical terms power is invisible. It has never been seen, unless that is, someone points a gun at you and demands that you hand over your money or that you do as instructed. It cannot be held, touched and it is not detectable by any mechanical or electronic sensor. However, as apparent from the previous discussion, power is a very real and potent force in any organization. It is important to distinguish between power and the associated trappings which are detectable. For example, wealth is frequently associated with power. Stereotypical assumptions lead to implying that an individual holds power simply because they dress in expensive clothing or behave as if they were superior. False claims to power through such outward signs (if uncovered) can leave the individual concerned subject to ridicule or marginalization. Equally, of course, the opposite is also true. There are individuals and groups who are not obviously powerful and yet in practice they might be described as the power behind the throne. These are people with the real power to influence, decide, and direct events and other people.

Power is something that only lives in the minds, attitudes, behaviours, expectations and perceptions of individuals. Once established in society the prevailing forms of power are supported by a wide range of structural devices. The laws, culture, status, work and educational systems are aligned in support and reinforcement of a particular power framework. However, individuals and groups who for various reasons do not wish to accept the prevailing power framework can seek to change the situation or if all else fails seek to overturn it through revolution. Of course, situations where direct force (or the threat of it) is used to obtain results represent the application of a particular form of power.

Revolution can also occur within an organizational environment. If enough shareholders consider that the management is failing then they could be removed and changed. Equally, a management that becomes disaffected with its position relative to the owners may seek to leave or achieve a buyout in order to gain more power over events. It is also employee acceptance of the fact that managers have the power to direct endeavours that allows managers to exercise it. If the employees were not willing to accept management direction then managers would have no ability to influence events, other than by changing the entire workforce. This is the dependency aspect of power described earlier.

If power is not a tangible entity and is dependent upon the recipients to create its significance where does it originate? French and Raven (1968), Raven (1993) identified a number of sources of power within a social context. These are based on the commodity or resource dependency view of power indicated earlier and are discussed in the following sections.

Coercive power

This form of power is based on the ability of the power holder to enforce the threat of direct control. In the mind of the receiver of this form of power is the fear that they may be punished if they do not comply with the directions of the power holder. In any organization there is a degree of coercive power implied in the managerial relationship with subordinates. Historically, this power source was much stronger than it is today. The emergence of trade unions, improved management practices and employment legislation have all provided counterbalance to the freedom of managers to take unilateral action. However, as was indicated earlier, by accepting these limited restrictions managers are able to effectively retain their relative power advantage. Ogbonna and Harris (2002) report a two year study in a UK food retailing company and show that the cultural change programme implemented by management resulted in different behaviours being adopted by 95 per cent of employees at all levels. However, they also found that these were the result of coercion rather than willingness on the part of employees. Extensive redundancies and demotions among store managers resulted in those remaining learning to put on an act in front of their colleagues and work more than 80 hours each week to safeguard their jobs. All levels within the organization were cynical about the purpose, intention and effect of the culture change programme.

Coercive power is also evident in many of the episodes of bullying that are reported. For example, a report based on research across Europe found that 10 per cent of workers claimed to be the victim of bullying or harassment, while another 10 per cent had been subjected to the threat of, actual physical violence in the workplace (*Communiqué*, 2003). Roberts (2003) reports a wide range of bullying episodes and research which demonstrates that women are just as likely as men to be a bully and that much of it stems from the stress, overload or inadequacy experienced by the bully. Management in Action 17.3 provides one writer's views on how to deal with bullying.

Reward power

Managers have the power to award pay increases, promote and otherwise reward individuals who perform as desired. In most organizations there are limitations on the

MANAGEMENT IN ACTION 17.3 How to cure bullying at work

The writer suggests that a number of measures are needed to deal effectively with bullies at work. They are:

1. *Understand the problem*. Bullying is not easy to define and can be hard to distinguish from tough, hands-on management. It is an abuse of power or position that involves persistent personal attacks involving the criticism, open condemnation or humiliation of a person on an ongoing basis.
2. *Draw up a policy*. Say clearly that bullying is unacceptable; indicate what it is and how complaints will be handled. For it to work it must have the support of the chief executive and the human resource management staff need to be trained in how to recognize and deal with it.
3. *Set a good example*. Bullying thrives in autocratic environments so set a good example as a manager.
4. *Appoint counsellors*. It is useful to provide people to whom staff can turn to for advice and support if they think they are being bullied.
5. *Don't wait for a claim to be made*. Look out for the warning signs in all sections and departments such as high levels of absence, high labour turnover, reduced productivity and low morale.
6. *Don't look for bruises*. Bullying is invariably psychological so there may be no physical signs. Investigators need to be trained to look for patterns of behaviour over months or even years.
7. *Investigate thoroughly*. Get the complainant to write down each incident with times, dates, including any witnesses. Investigators should also be trained to deal with the strategies frequently adopted by serial bullies such as claiming that they were the victim in the situation.
8. *Don't look for the easy way out*. Don't just move the victim. Health and safety legislation provides a duty of care in psychological as well as physical matters. The company could be liable for damages to the victim resulting from bullying and if suicide occurs, charges of corporate manslaughter might follow.
9. *Do say*. 'Persistent attempts to undermine a colleague's self-confidence will be regarded as bullying and disciplined accordingly.'
10. *Don't say*. 'It's a dog-eat-dog world. We've no time for cry babies here.'

Adapted from: Garrett, A (2003) How to cure bullying at work, *Management Today*. May, p 80.

Stop ↔ Consider

To what extent should it be possible to eliminate bullying from an organization, or is it simply a reflection of power being applied at a personal level and therefore it will surface in other ways if attempts are made to control it?

opportunity for individual managers to control the full range of rewards potentially available. For example, individual managers do not have total freedom on issues such as promotion. Company procedures are also designed to limit the ability of individual managers to create inconsistencies in reward allocation across the organization. However, such requirements do not automatically remove favouritism; it simply requires it to be justified in terms acceptable to the system. In that procedures and policies can drive the use of reward power underground, cloaked in a veil of half-truth and thinly disguised justification.

Managers can easily send the wrong signals about what behaviours are valued by inadvertently rewarding inappropriate behaviours. Paying considerable attention to difficult or troublesome employees can indicate to good employees that it does not pay to be well behaved. Managers who occasionally allow poor quality work to be despatched clearly indicate that good quality is not always important. In general terms such inadvertent rewarding of undesirable behaviour reinforces the idea that individuals should play the system, taking an instrumental view to the work that they do.

Legitimate power

In any organization most people accept that managers have legitimate authority to exercise power. There are three main sources of this form of authority (Luthans, 1995, p 323). First, the accepted social structures within a society provide certain groups with a legitimate basis for exercising power. It might be a ruling family or a class of people that perform that role. Second, cultural values can also create a basis for claiming **legitimate power** through the veneration of particular classes or individuals. For example, old people often become significant leaders, or men play a dominant role in society. Third, legitimate power can be delegated. Managers act on behalf of the owners of an organization in running the business on their behalf. In doing so they hold delegated power from the owners.

Legitimate power
The ability to exercise power as a consequence of having the accepted right to do so.

Handy (1993) suggests that holding legitimate power provides automatic access to three invisible assets. First, information, which as a commodity can be directed, channelled and traded by power holders. Second, the right of access to a number of different networks. The significance of networking cannot be underestimated. Heald (1984) examines many different networks along with the principles and practices that guide them. The value and growth of women-only networks (using the Internet) is described by Ashley (2000). Third, the right to organize. The following Employee Perspective (17.2) illustrates some of the implications of networks between academics and the organizations that fund jobs within universities.

Expert power

This source of power originates from the knowledge, skill and expertise of the holder. The pilot of an aeroplane is the one with the appropriate skills to fly it and consequently everyone goes where the pilot decides. Within management, technical specialists often have greater knowledge than the line managers that they are supposed to be supporting and so have considerable influence. Claims to be an expert are however subject to validation by the group over whom the expertise is being claimed. Failure to deliver the results of claimed expertise can be dealt with severely by the group who will feel that their trust has been violated, that they have been conned and let down badly.

EMPLOYEE PERSPECTIVE 17.2 Independence has a price

David Cooper was Price Waterhouse professor of accounting at UMIST in the mid-1980s. During the 1984 year-long national miners' strike in the UK, he published an article alleging 'misinformation' in the National Coal Board's (NCB) assessment of the viability of its coal mines. One senior member of the NCB expressed indignation and the editorial practice of the journal in which the article appeared was reviewed. Cooper also claims to have been telephoned by one of the partners at Price Waterhouse (they had also been appointed sequestrators to the National Union of Mineworkers). Cooper recalls the conversation with the partner thus: 'He screamed at me about causing the firm severe embarrassment and how could we bite the hand that fed us and how Price Waterhouse would continue to fund the chair over his dead body.' The partner concerned (by now retired) was asked for a response by Jack and he said: 'I did have words. It was an irritation. We were just concerned that he didn't start impinging on our activities. We were trying to keep a low profile.'

Based on: Jack, A (1993) Dons learn that 'freedom' has a bottom line, *Financial Times*, 9 December, p 14.

Tasks

1. What would you have done in this situation (and why) if you had been David Cooper?
2. What might this example suggest about the boundaries between legitimate and coercive power?

Information as power

This source of power is based on the possession of knowledge or information that is not generally available. The phrase, 'Information is power' is frequently heard in many organizations and reflects the significance of this source of it. For example, the lecturer who writes the exam paper for a particular module (assuming that it is to be examined by an unseen exam) has the questions and also the outline answers, the students do not. That places the lecturer in a relative position of power over the students. In most organizations some people are in possession of information that could be used to advantage because not everyone has access to it. For example, the employee representatives seeking to negotiate the annual pay rise for employees may not know the level of profit achieved by the company which if high levels of profit are being achieved might give them more power. Managers might try to hide information about the high levels of profit actually being made, but would be only too willing to tell the employee representatives about the losses being made as that might lower expectations among employees.

Referent power

This source of power is based on the characteristics of an individual. It could be that the individual is of celebrity status and so attracts others to join them and follow their wishes. Religious and political leaders are frequently charismatic and so attract many followers only too willing to follow every word and instruction. Advertisers continually utilize this perspective in using models, stars and personality figures to sell products through association and/or emulation.

Negative power

There is also a seventh form of power that is different in nature from the others, but can have a significant impact on events. Handy (1993, p 131) calls this negative power. This form of power impacts through not doing something that should be done. For example, a post room employee who is dissatisfied with their job could quickly cause confusion throughout the organization by deliberately misdirecting the post for a few days. It reflects the ability of the lower level people within an organization to take revenge on the senior people within the organization by withholding something necessary to the effective running of the organization. It may not be anything as obvious as going on strike, as that reflects an attempt to exercise coercive power, but is likely to consist of small events which quickly interrupt the effective running of the business.

These sources of power provide the basis of the ability to influence the behaviour and actions of others. What they do not do is provide an indication of how that power is converted into influence. It is the mechanisms or tactics described previously in Table 17.1 that provide an indication of how power is operationalized.

POWER AND DECISION MAKING

Decision making and politics are inextricably entwined within organizational activity. Many decision-making approaches assume rational behaviour on the part of the participants. Politics also influences the ability to implement a solution. Former President of the USA Richard Nixon wrote in 1982: 'It is not enough for a leader to *know* the right thing. He must be able to *do* the right thing. ... The great leader needs ... the capacity to achieve' (p 5).

Being able to ensure that a particular course of action is followed requires both power and political expertise. This is most clearly identified in the sphere of national and local politics. The hugely successful British television and book series under the titles of 'Yes, Minister' and 'Yes, Prime Minister' found much of their appeal in illustrating the political management by civil servants of the decisions made by the elected politicians. Pfeffer (1992) identifies three aspects of decision making that provide for the concept of power to be incorporated into the processes. They are:

1. *Decisions change nothing*. Taking a decision does not automatically imply that it will be acted upon. New Year resolutions are a clear example of decisions to change part of one's life, intentions which invariably last about one week. In addition to the decision sciences which help to identify what to do, there exists a need to understand implementation processes in order to be able to realize the decision.
2. *Decision quality requires retrospective assessment*. It is not possible to judge the value of a decision until after the event. It is only with the benefit of hindsight that any realistic evaluation can be made. However, it is very difficult to isolate the effect of any decision from the vast array of other things that will have changed by the time evaluation takes place. For example, a company may decide to redesign a particular product and yet sales continue to decline. It could be argued that the failure to improve sales was a function of changes in the market, not as a result of a 'bad' decision in the first place.
3. *Significance duration*. Pfeffer points out that the impact of any decision invariably lasts longer than the time taken to reach the decision in the first place. For example, it may take a company five years to decide to build a new factory and bring it on line, but the consequences of that decision will be with the company for the life-span of the factory (perhaps 40 years) and possibly beyond that. This perspective has led some psychologists to suggest that human beings are rationalizing rather than rational (Aronson, 1972). This also provides a link with cognitive dissonance as discussed in an earlier chapter.

One of the consequences of this perspective on decision making is that it reflects a stream – rather than a discrete process. A decision is taken and then implemented. Consequences then flow from that. Some of the results will be desired, others will be undesirable or were not anticipated and so further decisions are required. In addition, circumstances around the decision change, or the decision could have been wrong in the first place. Whatever the cause, there are many reasons which require decision-making to be regarded as a continuous process. Because the social environment surrounding the decision making process is dynamic, complex and subject to change this also allows power to constantly influence this stream activity.

So far this discussion has been about decision science aspects and has largely ignored the implementation issues. Within commercial organizations it is largely assumed that power is directly correlated with level in the hierarchy. While that may be true to some extent it reflects a vast oversimplification of the nature of organizational power and its practice. The trade union representatives in some organizations hold more power than many of the line managers, at least reflected in the ability to influence employees. The other sources of power identified earlier also form part of the dynamic of organizational behaviour and its influence on decision making. For example, managers rarely work in isolation, it is necessary for other people to be involved on many occasions. For instance, an accounting department may create a policy on expense claims, but it is other individuals who must comply with the system if it is to work. The following Employee Perspective (17.3) illustrates this and the use of negative power with regard to the completion of expense claims within one large organization.

EMPLOYEE PERSPECTIVE 17.3 Reasonable expenses

Louise worked for a large management consultancy based in Holland which employed several hundred field-based staff and associates. The primary duties of these staff involved travelling to client organizations and carrying out consultancy projects at those locations. This could involve a short visit of about two hours or anything up to two weeks of travelling daily to the same location. Clearly this process involved considerable amounts of travelling and high levels of expense claims.

Louise's employer paid staff a mileage allowance for each mile travelled on company business. The distance used as the basis of payment was the smaller of either the actual distance travelled or the distance to the visit from the office at which the member of staff was normally based. This was generally regarded as a fair system by staff as it allowed for the normal travel to work distance each day.

In an attempt to save money the senior management decided that any distance travelled to visit a client which involved the individual travelling over part of their normal route to the office would also be discounted for expense purposes. This was seen as both complex and unfair by the staff concerned. It also involved keeping more records of distance and routes travelled. Managers were also expected to know each consultant's normal route to the office and also the best route to each client visit.

As a consequence staff (including Louise) adopted a number of strategies in response to this instruction. One of the most effective was to find and use minor roads when visiting clients in areas near to the normal route to the office, justifying this with excuses such as traffic congestion. Another involved changing work routines to find reasons to attend the office when visits involved distances which would be longer than if done directly from home. Managers became confused about the new rules and would sign expense claims only to have them rejected by the accounts department on a technicality. This led to severe delays in payment until queries were resolved.

Very quickly senior management recognized that the cost of administration for the scheme was increasing rapidly, as was the level of expense claims. Eventually the old rule was reinstated. In other words, by following the rules of new scheme together with some ingenuity Louise and her colleagues were able to exercise negative power and frustrate the intentions of senior management.

Tasks

1. Were Louise's (and her colleagues) actions justified? Why or why not?
2. Does this example illustrate negative power, incompetent management, the desire for tighter control just for the sake of it; or does it reflect a group of staff seeking to retain a practice that was able to provide them with higher levels of expenses than they should have been entitled to? Does this distinction matter? Why or why not?

Managers must engage in co-operative behaviour in ensuring that their decisions are acted upon. The personnel department of a company would find it hard to implement a new remuneration system if other managers refused to allow employees time to write job descriptions or attend meetings to evaluate jobs for example. Competing priorities are frequently cited as the reason for one department or manager not being able to help another, the net result being that a particular decision may not be implemented, irrespective of the intentions of senior managers. An opposing view is that managers should always follow orders, as in the military. However, what if the orders are deficient? The danger in highly centralized structures in which real power is restricted to a few people at the top of the organization is that it can be abused. The late Robert Maxwell was an illustration of the ability of one individual to use various forms of power and bullying to centralize control for their own purposes. Pfeffer (1992) identifies seven decision issues that should be considered as part of the power process within decision making (see Table 17.2). Of course, not every decision requires the exercise of power in order to be successfully implemented. However, if the contributors are actively in favour of the decision or even if it is within their zone of indifference it is unlikely to require much application of power to influence events.

1 Decide what your goals are, what you are trying to accomplish
2 Diagnose patterns of dependence and interdependence; what individuals are influential and important in your achieving your goal?
3 What are their points of view likely to be? How will they feel about what you are trying to do?
4 What are their power bases? Which of them is more influential in the decision?
5 What are your bases of power and influence? What bases of influence can you develop to gain more control over the situation?
6 Which of the various strategies and tactics for exercising power seem most appropriate and are likely to be effective, given the situation you confront?
7 Based on the above, choose a course of action to get something done

TABLE 17.2 Power and decision making, reprinted by permission of Harvard Business School Press, from *Managing with Power*, Pfeffer, J (1992) Boston, MA. Copyright © 1992 by Jeffrey Pfeffer, all rights reserved

There have been attempts to create a contingency model of power by bringing together the work of French and Raven as already described and the work of Kelman. Luthans (1995) brings together these ideas in a model, to which has been added the levels of analysis perspective of Fincham (1992). The resulting contingency model is reflected in a simplified form in Figure 17.1.

In the contingency approach to power there exists a relationship between the sources of power and the responses generated as a consequence of specific conditions and motivation to respond in particular ways. For example, with a power source based on reward, a compliance reaction is likely to be created if the target person seeks to avoid punishment or to make a favourable impression. To be successful the power holder must have the ability to deliver the reward as well as the punishment for failure.

It is argued elsewhere that empowerment and other forms of involvement contain elements of power and control. One possibility in situations where power is an obvious element within the employment relationship is that employees will simply comply or conform. In Etzioni's (1975) terms they might adopt an alienative or calculative (instrumental) response. Clearly in today's world of lean, delayered and

FIGURE 17.1

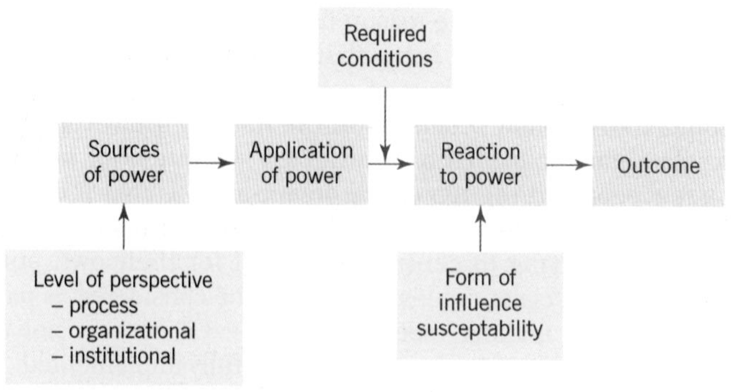

Contingency model of power

high-performing organizations these responses are not desirable. Empowering and otherwise involving employees can be an attempt to encourage them to buy into or adopt the underlying values of management. Employees with the same value set as managers would be easier to manage and would think in the same terms as managers. This can be thought of as eliminating the need for power in the employment relationship. Equally, it can be described in terms of substituting internalized forms of self-control for the less effective outward forms. In effect, relying on covert rather than overt forms of power application – power by socialization.

Power as part of the decision-making process is frequently associated with political behaviour. Individual managers frequently seek power as a means to further their careers and enhance the position of their departments. This relationship was also identified in the work of McClelland on motivation. This was reviewed in an earlier chapter when the nPow concept associated with the need for power within the individual was discussed. The acquisition of power is something that some managers seek and is associated strongly with a tendency to function politically.

CONTROL WITHIN ORGANIZATIONS

There are many definitions of control. One of the simplest is that provided by Dunford (1992), in which it is described as a process which, 'involves attempts to bring about desired outcomes' (p 243). This definition should immediately suggest a connection with the subject of power. Power is frequently used as the means through which to be able to exercise control over something or someone. Within an organization there are two distinct and opposite aspects to the existence of control. First, it provides the basis of order and predictability in operational activity. Processes need to be 'under control' if the product or service is to be delivered consistently to the customer with acceptable quality and at a realistic price.

Second, there is the opposing perspective that control is restrictive, lacks flexibility, is manipulative and greedy with regard to the abolition of personal freedom. It could be argued that many initiatives on employee involvement and participative management are covert attempts to find ways of retaining control within an illusion of freedom for the individual. These initiatives are frequently expressed as an encouragement to go beyond the contract and enjoy a new partnership with managers in developing a mutually prosperous and fulfilling future. The net effect, however, being the exercise of more subtle forms of control intended to minimize the risk of conflict and maximize contribution. This is related to the view of power indicated earlier which suggested that by allowing some controlled erosion of total power, effective control is retained by management.

It has been suggested by Huczynski and Buchanan (1991, p 579) that control has three connotations. First, it is necessary as an economic activity, critical to the success of the organization. Second, it represents a psychological necessity in order to eliminate the ambiguity, unpredictability and disorder that would prevent individuals from operating effectively within the organization. Third, it represents a political process in which some individuals and groups are able to exercise control over less fortunate groups. It is possible to identify a fourth purpose that control serves in addition to the three just identified, that is its physical connotations. A brief description of each is provided below:

- *Physical*. At the detailed control level, jobs, processes and machines need to be organized and controlled effectively if they are to combine to produce the goods and services required (Edwards, 1986). Frequently, the physical level of control involves record keeping, measuring activity and checking actual performance against that intended.

- *Economic*. As an economic process control is geared towards achieving the financial objectives of the organization. It is not just the detailed control described above. It represents the micro level co-ordination and planning of activity along with the macro level directional planning necessary to achieve the financial returns to ensure that investors and other stakeholders remain satisfied.
- *Psychological*. This process represents both the need among individuals to function within a predictable environment and the inherent need that some individuals have to either control or be controlled. In its broadest sense management can be described as a controlling activity. That some individuals seek elevation to these positions can be taken as evidence of their desire to exercise control over resources. There are individuals who for many reasons do not gain promotion within organizations. Some do not have the opportunity; others do not have the confidence or the inclination. Still others perceive promotion as selling out to the owning 'classes' or perhaps they achieve fulfilment through other aspects of their life. Whatever the reason subordinates psychologically accept the right to be controlled by others.
- *Political*. Control provides the means by which existing structures and social conditions can be reinforced. Xinyi Xu (1994) demonstrates the political impact through the complex and politically based control processes and structural features inherent in all levels of organizational and social life within China. Owners of capital insist on their pre-eminent right to ultimate determination of organizational existence. If an organization does not make money then the owners, creditors and banks retain the right to liquidate the assets irrespective of the impact on the non-owning stakeholders. That represents the ultimate political control. Of course accountants would argue that an uneconomic business must fail, but this represents the exercise of a particular perspective and the case could be argued otherwise. A different economic picture might emerge if the social costs of closure were to be taken into account, for example.

There are other political perspectives to control. For example, through the exercise of political skill a departmental manager may be able to increase their own significance and importance within an organization, thereby being able to exercise control over a greater range of resources. Management in Action 17.4 illustrates this and other aspects of control within an unusual context.

FORM AND CHARACTERISTICS OF CONTROL

Control and organization are inextricably linked. It has been argued (Thompson, 1989) that it was a desire for increased control by owners that formed a significant part of the movement towards the factory system of production in the eighteenth century. Under the putting-out system owners could not directly and closely control the activities of workers and the development of the factory system was intended to change that situation. Table 17.3 reflects some of the major levers of control that functioned under the putting-out system. It can be seen from that information that although the owners had considerable power in the process, it tended to be retrospective. So, for example, they could withhold work, but this would only be done if there was a reason, such as a lack of orders or the quality of work was poor. But by the time

MANAGEMENT IN ACTION 17.4 Thou shalt not cook the books

The finances of English cathedrals provides a fascinating opportunity to study accountancy practice. The Cathedrals Measure of 1963 required the accounts of the 42 Anglican cathedrals to be published each year. However, it provided little guidance on the form that the accounts should take and the Church Commissioners do not examine them in any detail. Most cathedrals operate as charities and need considerable sums of money to maintain them. But as Malcolm Hoskins of Touche Ross suggested: 'Like any other charity, if anything the incentive is not to appear too financially healthy'. He should know, he has audited cathedral accounts and serves on a working party set up by the Association of English Cathedrals to identify how to present financial information fairly and consistently.

One member of a commission set up in 1992 by the Archbishop of Canterbury to examine the management of church resources said: 'Cathedral accounting is disgraceful. It's a fascinating aspect of medieval life. They get up to every trick in the book.' He described the use of off-balance sheet finance and undeclared trusts as ways to conceal the true wealth of cathedrals from the church hierarchy. Deans and canons are in an impregnable position in a cathedral as, once appointed, they become a 'corporation spiritual' and immune to any earthly power but God. Perhaps, that is, until the controlling power of the accounting profession reaches out and lays its hand on them!

Adapted from: Jack, A (1993) Thou shalt not cook the books, *Financial Times,* 17 December, p 9.

Stop ↔ Consider

To what extent do the accounting practices of cathedrals raise ethical issues about power and control, or do they simply reflect shrewd management practice in seeking to maximize income?
Does the answer to the previous question matter and if so in what ways?

that action had been taken the owner would have given out raw material and perhaps machines etc. so incurring cost or delay. The factory system was designed to provide greater levels of control and predictability in the production process and in a way which minimizes loss and the cost of operations.

So although the control levers indicated in Table 17.3 would appear to provide a sound basis for the effective operation of a business this is not so compared with factory-based systems of production. A factory system provided the owners with an opportunity to exercise an immediate in-process level of control. For example, it became possible to break the manufacturing process down into small parts and to create jobs requiring low skill levels. Lower skill levels are directly associated with

Allocation	the ability to allocate or withhold work
Price	the ability to reduce the price paid to workers in order to pressure them into producing more in order to maintain earnings
Quality	the ability to reject (and therefore not pay) for work not of an acceptable standard
Machine	in some instances owners provided workers with the equipment necessary to perform the tasks and so controlled production methods

TABLE 17.3 Control under the 'putting-out' system

cheaper labour and reduced unit labour costs. Equally, the pace and methods of work could be directly controlled in a factory, increasing the output per worker and further reducing labour costs. The factory system also increased the level of dependency of the workers on the owners, so providing greater social control as well. The factory as a building provided what Foucault describes as an opportunity for managers to observe, know and therefore control, effectively creating the reality within which the workers should work and live.

Very little control takes the overt form of force or pressure. It is usually incorporated into the fabric of the organization, management practice and indeed society. Becoming part of the experience of what would be considered normal it is not subjected to question by those to whom it is being applied. If control is defined in terms of the ability to determine the behaviour of others it makes sense to exercise it in such a way that obviates the likelihood of conflict. Creating an acceptance of the normality and necessity for control mechanisms is one way of achieving this. However, as Baker and Jennings (1999) demonstrate, control mechanisms are not always effective in achieving their objectives as a consequence of both systemic difficulties and inappropriate behavioural reactions (as defined by control system designers). The main forms of organizational control are now discussed.

Output control

This is based on the premise that if the output achieved is as predicted, then the system is under control. It is the **management-by-exception** process that posits that managers should function on the basis of defining in advance what should occur, provide the resource to deliver that requirement and subsequently manage the deviations from that intention. It is argued that it is a waste of valuable time and resource to monitor and review things that are going according to plan. The difficulty is that reports can be falsified or presented in such a way as to disguise the true situation. Upwards management and the tendency of groups to meet the reality of current operational activity in a way which meets management expectations were among the findings from the Hawthorne studies, discussed in an earlier chapter.

Management by exception
An approach to managing that intervenes only where an exception or deviation from a plan is identified.

Process control

This form of control reflects a mirror image of the previous approach in that it relies on monitoring and controlling the means rather than the ends. It is premised on the view that it is necessary to control the detail and process aspects of operational activity in order to ensure that the objectives are achieved. It represents the traditional bureaucratic approach to organizational activity. Procedures determine in detail what should be done within the system and yet more procedures determine and report on events as they occur. In practice this can be an expensive approach to control and it provides fertile ground for business process re-engineering and other techniques to eliminate what inevitably comes to be seen as non-value adding activity.

Work design

In terms of the ability to control activity in the workplace the design of jobs is a key determinant. The way that the tasks to be undertaken are clustered together into jobs reflects a major feature of organizational life. However, it is also a reflection of the intentions of management in relation to how they view the business and the need to control activity in relation to the desired objectives. For example, the specialization of work in a hospital into such categories as nursing, physiotherapy, hotel services and administration allows high skill levels to be developed across a relatively narrow range of tasks. Thereby productivity can be achieved in a factory-type hospital configuration. As such it provides the possibility of tighter control of the overall process and its associated cost. The paradigm adopted by management significantly determines the approach to issues of control and work organization according to writers such as Morgan (1986).

Structure

Much of the work design issues follow from and contribute to the way in which the organization is structured. It is the approach to compartmentalization of activity that provides the opportunity to control through specialization. It also allows managers to be able to simplify complex activity into meaningful and understandable units. For example, the creation of an accounting department provides the opportunity for the development of efficient, specialized accounting control systems as a consequence of grouping together experts in a particular field. It also provides the more senior managers with the knowledge that accounting issues are the responsibility of that department and that they have (in theory) no bias towards other functions in reporting accounting data. The compartments provide clarity in relating to the complexity of organizational activity, particularly from a top-down perspective. Consider the difficulty of attempting to understand and manage a university if it were not compartmentalized into student records, library, teaching, etc. Unfortunately, as effective as this top-down perspective might be for the senior people within the organization, they are not the customers. Tighter and more effective vertical control can therefore be achieved at the cost of customer experience and satisfaction. These two often conflicting requirements represent a difficult balance to achieve, a point already demonstrated in previous chapters.

Hierarchy and authority

The owners of the business are held to be the people who have the ultimate right to determine what happens within an organization. Much of that right is delegated to the board of directors. Within large organizations some form of delegation below that level must also be introduced. In practice a power-sharing process must be entered into in order to define the responsibilities and relationships between the principal players. As a consequence of these processes a hierarchical arrangement of responsibility and control is introduced into the organization. Individuals explicitly acquiesce to these arrangements when they agree to join the organization. Managers know that they have certain rights to exercise control over their subordinates, again subject to policies and procedures. They are part of a complex web of hierarchy and authority that allows control over activity to be exercised in support of the objectives being sought.

It has long been recognized that the direct exercise of authority is not always the most effective way to achieve the desired result. It can create a compliance- and dependency-based cultural environment. Being conditioned to expect that someone in authority will direct every move can result in individuals failing to exercise discretion and common sense in performing their duties. An employee who continued to produce components knowing them to be substandard, because they had not been told to stop would serve as an example.

Unless it is a specific requirement of a particular situation, then the exercise of direct authority is likely to be resented by subordinates and produce a compliance response (or conflict). It is therefore desirable from a management point of view to avoid these potential difficulties by softening the application of authority-based control. There are many ways of attempting to achieve this, for example the use of training courses allows managers to inculcate employees with the preferred value and attitude sets, thereby seeking to internalize among employees the managerial norms that underpin control. Employees consequently become self-regulating (if the process is successful). Only if employees show dissent in adopting the preferred value sets would it be likely that formal authority (direct control) became the means of achieving the desired result.

In commercial organizations it is increasingly being claimed that with every pair of hands recruited comes a free brain, and that this represents the most valuable of the human assets. To capitalize on this, managers need to ensure that individuals are liberated from constraint and prepared to contribute to the maximum of their capability. This can frequently be introduced as empowerment or **employee involvement** in one form or another. Under such operational situations the direct application of control is likely to be counterproductive. It is hardly surprising that middle managers have not always been enthusiastic supporters of employee empowerment as it can be viewed as undermining their traditional authority base. It is also possible that increased control through this route can be achieved by accident. If employees push for greater involvement and as a consequence become more understanding and amenable to management perspectives, greater managerial influence (control) over events will have been achieved indirectly (Fells, 1989).

Employee involvement
An opportunity to become involved in decision making beyond the requirements of the job.

Skill

There are many jobs in which skill or professional status provides an opportunity to exercise control in one form or another. To know more than others in the same context is a basis for acquiring power and exercising control. Only chartered accountants are able to sign the audit of a set of company accounts. This requirement is intended to provide confidence to investors and the authorities that the accounts are a true and realistic reflection of the financial position of the company. Such auditors hold considerable power. The degree to which this is a double edged sword in practice is evident from the number of major accounting practices that are being sued by investors for large sums of money when events come to light not previously identified through an audit. However, where skill is an important feature of a particular job it can also lead to problems as the following Employee Perspective (17.4) demonstrates.

EMPLOYEE PERSPECTIVE 17.4 I won't apologize!

The following letter was published by the problem page in a management magazine:

> One of my brightest employees has made an enormous cock-up on a client's account. I would normally support my team, but in this case I can see the client's point of view. Unfortunately, my employee can't and has refused to apologize. The client has now demanded that I fire or demote the employee, but he's too good to let go. We're a small company and very dependent on this one client, so I can't afford to lose them either. Any suggestions?

Tasks

1. To what extent does the fault lie with the employee or the manager (because of their responsibilities as a manager and the way they exercised control) and why?
2. As the manager how would you deal with the situation?
3. Would you deal with the situation differently if the client was not so important and just one of many that you did work for? Why should this make a difference and what does it suggest about power and control in such situations?

You might like to check your views with the advice offered by Bullmore, J (2003) What's your problem? *Management Today*, October, p 81.

Technology

Machines can work at a predictable and stable pace until they break down or are switched off. People are not so programmable. As a consequence of the desire of managers to justify the introduction of technology humans are frequently relegated to second place in consideration. It is the technology that determines (controls) the human participation in the production process. The work that humans undertake is determined by what the technology cannot tackle and by what is needed to service the ability of the technology to maintain continuous production. This provides a very real form of control over human endeavour.

It is not just factory work that has been subjected to the influence of control through technology. Clerical, administrative, technical and managerial work has all been influenced and is therefore subject to different forms of control than in the past. For example, in customer service teams it is common to find that the technology providing improved ability to serve the customer also provides the opportunity to manage the performance of staff more effectively. Telephone calls are recorded for subsequent analysis, call rates and queue waiting statistics are automatically generated.

Social control

There are many forms of social control, including those institutions provided by the state including the police, and other government agencies. In addition, and of particular relevance to an organizational setting, are institutions such as the education system which is intended to prepare children and young people for the world of work. Within an organization there are the induction, training, development, performance appraisal, pay, promotion and career development activities which all provide a basis for shaping behaviour patterns in management preferred ways.

Clegg and Dunkerley (1980) describe the impact of control as provoking a vicious cycle reinforcing the need for ever tighter means of control. This arises as a consequence of the continually constricting influence on employees of control and of their negative reaction to it in terms of increased dissatisfaction. This response to management's attempt to tighten control reinforces their perceptions of the need for more effective control, so creating a perpetual cycle of tighter control leading to increasingly negative reactions among employees. This model was also discussed in Chapter 14. It is the danger of creating the downward spiral of ever tighter control leading to less real or meaningful contribution from employees that leads to organizations attempting to introduce involvement strategies. The hope being that involved employees would internalize the need for the level of control being sought by managers and so respond positively.

POWER, CONTROL AND RESISTANCE

Resistance to the exercise of power is not new. It was Marx who linked the ideas of revolution and the overthrow of capitalism as the natural response of workers to the unequal power and levels of control inherent in society. The exploitation of labour in the capitalist system of production would inevitably result in revolution as the workers sought to resist and so would bring about a socialist state. Conflict as a concept will be covered in the next chapter and so will not be fully developed here. However, it represents only one form of resistance found within any organization.

It has already been suggested that overt forms of control and attempts to exert power would be likely to be met with some form of resistance. However, resistance is not something that might find expression immediately. Braverman (1974, p 151) suggested in the context of developing the labour process theory, that the reaction of workers to the degradation of work forced upon them would, 'continue[s] as a subterranean stream that makes its way to the surface when employment conditions permit, or when the capitalist drive for a greater intensity of labor oversteps the bounds of physical and mental capacity'.

In short, the workers will pick their time for reacting to the exercise of power and control. When that will be depends either on the existence of the right economic conditions (e.g. low unemployment levels or an urgent order needing special treatment) or if the level of pressure gets too great. Of course this view of resistance is based upon the existence of what Marx and others call class consciousness. In other words, a natural working-class reaction to their exploitation under capitalist forms of production once they become aware of it. There are however other forms of resistance reflecting the day-to-day reactions of employees and managers to their experience of work.

There are many apocryphal as well as true stories of resistance in many forms and in many organizations, some of which enter the realms of folk history and legend. For example just about everyone who has worked in an office must have been told of the secretary of the rude and difficult boss who sought revenge by spitting in his (they usually were male) coffee and smiling sweetly at the praise for it being made perfectly! More formally, managers can resist the implementation of instructions from more senior managers by claiming that they don't have the necessary resources or other tasks have a higher priority. Workers can strike or even leave an organization if they do not like the way it is run or the way in which power and control are exercised. Sabotage and whistleblowing are other forms of resistance to the effects of how power and control are exercised within the organization.

LaNuez and Jermier (1994) review episodes of sabotage by managers and technocrats and suggest that it could be significantly linked to reduced levels of power and privileges in managerial and technical specialist types of work. In essence they argue that such job holders are moving away from alignment with the objectives of the capital owners who are generally in search of profit maximization, whereas managers want security, career progression and growth.

POWER AND CONTROL: AN APPLIED PERSPECTIVE

The way in which power and control functions within an organizational context is very complex. Power and authority are closely aligned and are integral to aspects of management. With organizational status and formal position in the hierarchy comes the right to have others follow your instructions. Managers without power are likely to have little influence on the organization for which they work. It is the close relationship between power and influence within a management context that provides a perfect breeding ground for the political behaviour that forms a major theme in the next chapter.

Etzioni (1975) first provided a categorization for the basis of power as normative (based on legitimacy of authority), utilitarian (based on the payment of inducements) or coercive (based on the ability to apply sanction). It is through the application of the last two categories that the potential for the use of politics and the misuse of power is created. However, it is also important to recognize that there are three caveats to the use of power in an organization. They are:

1. *Balance*. Only on very rare occasions is there a complete imbalance in the power held between the parties to a particular situation. Pushed too hard employees may feel that they have nothing to lose by going on strike or leaving

the company. The degree of care and attention that an employee pays to their work is largely a matter for them to decide. Managers are not in a position to control every aspect of work all of the time. Employees who feel they have no meaningful stake in an organization are likely to become alienated, to resist and to apply negative power to the disadvantage of management.

2. *Domain*. Few sources of power are likely to be valid across time and in every context. For example, an employer may be able to force down the price of labour when there is little alternative work for employees. However cheap labour will attract new organizations into the area. As a result of the increased availability of jobs, labour costs will inevitably rise as employees with transferable skills move to the highest bidder.
3. *Relativity*. The acquisition and application of power is only possible if there exists a lever that is of value to the target person or group. For example, an organization that does not value personnel management skills is unlikely to listen to the advice offered by such specialists and therefore the function would have little power in that situation.

Kotter (1977) identified a number of characteristics shared by those managers who were able to use and manage power effectively, including:

- *Sensitivity*. They are able to understand the feelings of others in relation to how power is obtained and used.
- *Intuitive*. They have an intuitive feel for how to acquire and use power across a wide range of contexts. They also recognize that in making use of power it is people not objects that are influenced by it.
- *Repertoire*. They have a wide range of power sources on which to call.
- *Career*. Some jobs are naturally more powerful than others and people who are able to use power effectively actively seek these positions.
- *Investment*. Managers who are able to make effective use of power tend to regard it as an investment. Power is not a static resource; it can be grown, harvested and squandered. Through careful husbandry all the resources available to an individual can be used to develop the power available to them.
- *Maturity*. Crude attempts to acquire power and the blatant use of it are quickly transparent to most people, who then resist its application to themselves. To be most effective power needs some support (or at least little resistance – the zone of indifference) from those exposed to it and so a mature approach to it is more likely to produce positive results for the individual applying it.

It has been argued (Braverman, 1974) that the organizational history of the twentieth century can be described in terms of increasing management control and the potential for conflict and alienation that flows from it. This neatly encapsulates the fundamental dilemma that exists from a management perspective. The scale of international business, the level of competition, the differential costs of operations around the world and many other forces all create conditions in which there is continual pressure for improved organizational performance. Inevitably, this dynamic leads managers to seek ever greater levels of control over every aspect of the enterprise in order to achieve greater added value from it. Braverman makes it clear that the price for this increased control is that employees experience greater levels of alienation. They are increasingly treated as just one of the resources available to managers and, consequently subject to the same degree of manipulation and control. However, Courpasson and Dany (2003) suggest that in the post-bureaucratic organizational world now evolving that a different form of power is emerging. The power–based employment relationship unfolding in modern organizations is described in their terms as moral obedience. The thrust of their argument being that in the post-bureaucratic organization different forms of employment based around loosened coalitions of people require individuals to hold a sense of duty to their immediate task and organization, and this expression of morality will increasingly become part of the political and power-based frameworks in the future. In essence they argue that it reflects management's attempt to introduce a different basis for the employment relationship, intended to offset the alienation from the less secure employment now prevalent.

For managers, control contains different connotations depending upon such factors as the seniority and job function of the individual. For example, a chief executive should not be concerned with control over the purchase of pens. They should, however, assure themselves that someone is exercising control over the purchase and use of consumables. A production supervisor would be expected to exercise detailed control over day-to-day production activities. They would not be expected to opine on the strategic direction of the business, that would be regarded as the preserve of senior managers. Control in an organization is a fragmented function, distributed across the members according to level and function. This could be taken to imply a rational and planned process, determined by some all-seeing and omnipotent senior manager applying appropriate models to achieve effective control. Such models do indeed exist. Figure 17.2 is representative of this view, based upon Dent and Ezzamel (1995).

However, even within models such as included as Figure 17.2 there is limited recognition of the realities of organizational life. The data essential for control purposes may not exist; even if they do exist they may not be accurate or available at the appropriate time. The style of management and decision making are also variables that influence control activities. In addition, there are the power and political processes that operate and which can influence both the control processes themselves and the interpretation of the data emerging from them. Like all aspects of management the design of control systems, the interpretation of data and the subsequent actions following from the analysis are social processes. As a consequence they are subject to all of the foibles, idiosyncrasies and other influences associated with individual and collective human behaviour.

Wage–work bargain Subjective balance between what represents a fair exchange in the amount of work done for the wages paid.

Drawing on the earlier work of Edwards (1986), Blyton and Turnbull (1994) identify a major problem for employers in relation to the **wage–work bargain** with employees. It is the last vestige of the ability of employees to resist the attempts of employers to exercise absolute control and to be able to adjust the level of effort

FIGURE 17.2

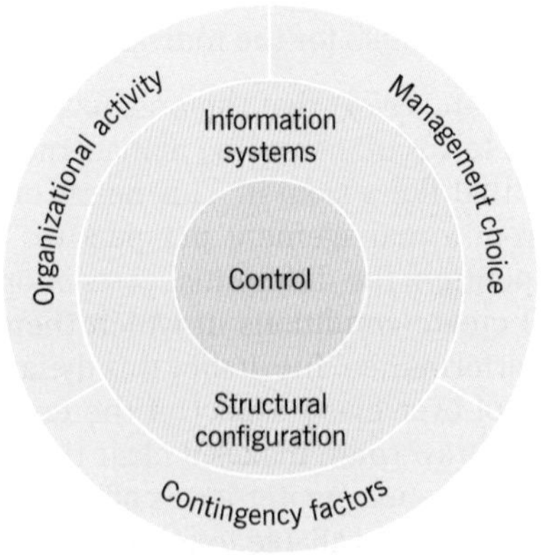

The organizational control 'onion' (*adapted from*: Dent, J and Ezzamel, M (1995) Organizational control and management activity. In Holloway, J, Lewis, J and Mallory, G (eds) *Performance Measurement and Evaluation*, Sage, London)

expended in the service of the master. The extended tea break, pace and diligence of work are some of the variables at the disposal of the employee in demonstrating independence from total subjugation to the will of another. Recent managerial approaches can be categorized as attempts to delegate control in such a way as to provide the illusion of independence and encourage self-control. Torrington *et al.* (2002) use a hierarchical model of discipline in an organizational context to describe the level of responsibility for ensuring appropriate behaviour (Figure 17.3).

There are many implications that emerge from considering the nature of discipline as described in Figure 17.3. Defined in terms of behaving in expected ways, discipline can be seen as a means of control. Management discipline is behaviour control achieved through a superior, team discipline is achieved through group norms and influence and self-discipline is achieved through accepting and internalizing the desired behaviours. At the self-discipline level of the hierarchy in Figure 17.3 very little management effort is required as employees effectively police themselves by delivering automatically that which is expected of them. If this level of the hierarchy can be achieved then the benefits to managers in terms of the reduced cost of management, an improved performance from employees and reduced levels of conflict are considerable. From this perspective, it is hardly surprising that managers have made considerable efforts to ensnare employees into adopting self-managed practices across a wide range of facets of employment. It also leads to the accusation of deceit and manipulation by those who interpret such events as a cynical attempt to take advantage of employees in the pursuit of higher profit levels.

CONCLUSIONS

Power and control are important aspects of organizational behaviour. They are inseparable from the needs of organization and the needs, aspirations and inclinations of the individuals that work within them. Power is endemic to the employment relationship. Employers have work that they need done; individuals need to work for economic, psychological and social reasons. Interestingly, managers are also employees and subject to these same pressures, but within the particular context of acting for the largely absent owners of the organization. Control is needed to ensure that objectives are met. However, as with most other aspects of organizational behaviour they contain the seeds of danger and risk that can cause damage to either individuals or the organization if they are not handled carefully and with respect.

FIGURE 17.3

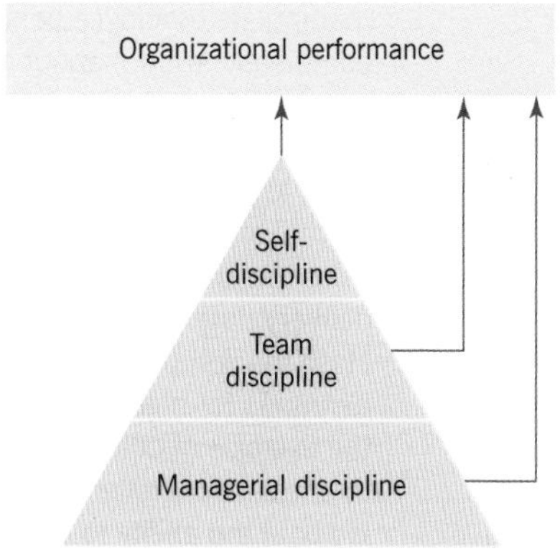

The discipline hierarchy (*adapted from*: Torrington, D and Hall, L (1991) *Personnel Management: A New Approach*, 2nd edn, Prentice Hall, Hemel Hempstead)

Now to summarize this chapter in terms of the relevant learning objectives:

- **Understand the major perspectives on power as experienced within an organization.** There were three major perspectives on power that were introduced within the chapter. The first was the traditional view which tended to describe power as a natural function of the formal position in the hierarchy and as a natural part of the leadership process. In that context, power was regarded as something that went with position and so was available to the post-holder to use (or abuse) as they saw fit. It also implies to a degree that it is a commodity that could be traded, acquired, divested or squandered depending upon the circumstances and how the individual acted in that context. It is also apparent that it has close association with organizational politics as the means through which power could be acquired, lost or traded. Politics is the main topic of the next chapter. The second perspective on power was that based on the work of Foucault. He was interested in how power operated in society as a whole and considered that it was a fundamental element in the way in which language was used to construct and maintain existing social structures. In his view language was the means through which boundaries between the things that are taken for granted in society are created and that effectively reinforces the relative status and position of the 'rulers' (compared to the 'ruled') and hence defines where the power lies. A major part of his work was that the authorities in a social system spend considerable time and money in seeking to 'know' the people who are their subjects, because by knowing them more fully it becomes possible to control them more effectively through the application of power that 'knowing' creates. The third perspective on power was that falling under the labour process and Lukes' views. The basis of this approach to power is that originally developed by Marx in relation to the exploitation of labour in support of capitalist objectives. Lukes developed a three dimensional model to reflect his views of power. The first dimension consisting of the measurable effects of power. The second reflects the agenda aspect of power by reflecting the process of engagement with others and how that impacts on control of the way in which the relationship functions in practice. The third dimension reflects the underlying reaction modes available to those subjected to power. These approaches to power are discussed in greater detail in the appropriate sections of the text.
- **Describe the sources of power within an organization.** The sources of power that exist within an organization include coercive, reward, legitimate, expert, information, referent and negative. Coercive power emerges in situations in which force is used (or threatened) in order to make someone do something that they would not otherwise do. For example, to be threatened with dismissal if they don't do a particular job immediately. Reward power is about achieving control by offering someone a benefit or reward in return for their submission. Legitimate reward is the acquiescence by an individual that someone else has the right to exert power over them. Expert power is the ability to exert control because of the knowledge or ability that an individual has. For example, if a water pipe bursts in your house, the emergency plumber has expert power in the situation and can charge a high price as a consequence. Information refers to the way that access to information not generally available can enhance the ability to exercise power in that context. Referent power is achieved through the force of a charismatic personality, a characteristic which people tend to follow willingly. Negative power is the ability to achieve some measure of control or influence by not doing or withdrawing something. For example, a post room operator could send the mail to the wrong departments and slow the flow of orders and money into the company.
- **Explain the differences and similarities between the concepts of power, influence and authority.** Power can mean a number of different things within an organizational context, but generally relates to the ability to get other people to do what they might not otherwise do. In that sense it can involve each or all of the processes of manipulation, force, and influence. For example, managers might seek to manipulate employee behaviour by not being completely truthful about a situation in order to gain co-operation. They might say that a particular order is vital to the commercial success of the business in order to encourage employees to work harder than normal and get it out on time simply because the sales department miscalculated an appropriate delivery date. Force might be used by threatening to close the company if employees do not scale-back demands for higher pay. These examples illustrate the exercise of different forms of influence, therefore in one sense it reflects the exercise of power. Power is about the ability to influence the behaviour of others through various devices. However, generally speaking influence implies a softer term than power.

The use of power implies the use of some degree of force or coercion in being able to influence the behaviour of the target. On its own, influence implies a friendlier, less directive approach to encouraging or persuading the target to do as the controller desires. As an approach it is less likely to generate a hostile or negative response in the target than the application of power itself. Authority notionally reflects status within an organization and is consequently a reflection of where the formal power lies. Employees generally accept that managers have the right (the authority) to exercise power and control over them in a work context. It is a recognition and acceptance by employees that they will to a significant degree subjugate themselves to the wishes of those given authority (formal power) over them. Of course this authority-based right to exercise power has limitations and an employee pushed too far will react negatively and reject the attempt to control their behaviour if the boundary is crossed.

- **Outline the characteristic features of control systems as found in organizations.** Control has at least two meanings within an organization. Firstly it can mean that order and predictability exists within the organization, used in the expression 'everything is under control'. Secondly it can also be regarded as a restrictive term which implies that people are being manipulated for some purpose or other. For example a company might introduce a training course on financial awareness in order to prompt employees to identify cost saving ideas in order to maintain profitability levels so that the senior mangers do not have to take actions that might create conflict. Little control takes the direct form of orders or force which might produce a negative response. Control is usually built into the fabric, hierarchy, procedures and policies of an organization and can be achieved through a number of devices including output control which it is the planned output that is monitored and assuming the plan is met then no intervention is necessary. This represents the management-by-exception approach to control. The opposite approach requires the operational process to be monitored on the assumption that if every part of the process is functioning as planned then the output will be as desired. Other levers that are used to achieve control within an organization include work design, structure, hierarchy and authority frameworks, expertise and skill in the way that work is organized and structured, the use of technology and social control in the ways in which people are socialized and trained into their work roles, etc. Each of these issues is discussed in greater detail in the appropriate sections of this chapter and many are also covered in other chapters.
- **Discuss the significance of the 'zone of indifference' in relation to the use of power and control within an organization.** The zone of indifference refers to the level of something that does not create a negative reaction in an individual. For example, many organizations seek to achieve more output with lower levels of resource, particularly people. This inevitably leads to people being put under pressure to produce more work. It is argued that the intention is to 'sweat the resource' by forcing people to cut out the slack from their activities and concentrate on those aspects of their job that add value. This, it is often suggested, is about working smarter, not working harder. However, many people find it stressful. So, the pressure to work 'smarter' can be applied and if the employee is still within their 'zone of indifference' they may grumble, but they will try and meet the expectation placed on them. However, after being under constant (and increasing) levels of pressure for some considerable time an employee may suddenly snap and refuse to do any more. They might tell the manager 'where to go', they may simply slow down or switch off, or they might organize a formal grievance or dispute thorough their representative or trade union. They might even go off on sick leave, or resign from their job. Whatever they do they have reacted. They are no longer in their 'zone of indifference'. It is a personal and subjective reaction in each individual to the circumstances surrounding them. It is difficult for any manager to know the boundary for each individual, but it is an important element in the process of managing. Clearly it makes sense for a manager to operate within the employee's 'zone of indifference' as that means that a negative reaction will not be forthcoming as the employee will go along with whatever is being proposed. If a negative reaction does emerge then it will have to be responded to in some way or other. That will divert time, energy and resources away from what was being planned and may mean that it becomes more difficult to make further changes in the future. It might also require the use of direct force or power to be able to retain some control of the situation which again means that a compliance response is what might be achieved from the employee – not the most effective basis for a long term employment relationship.

DISCUSSION QUESTIONS

1. Describe the main ways in which control is exercised within an organization and provide examples from your experience to illustrate them.
2. Can compliance as an employee response to power and control ever form a basis for the creation of an effective organization? Justify your answer.
3. 'Ultimately everyone has free will and can resist control by others. Consequently power does not exist in reality. Control is therefore a device that provides at best the illusion of order and structure.' Discuss this statement.
4. It is suggested that there is an inevitable power imbalance in the employment relationship and that this can lead to the development of self-defence groups such as trade unions. Why might this power imbalance exist, is it inevitable and how might it be limited?
5. Describe the main sources of organizational power and provide examples of each from an organization with which you are familiar.
6. 'Employee participation is nothing more than the worst type of confidence trick, played on people who have no opportunity to resist by those who have everything to gain.' Discuss this statement in the light of the material presented in this chapter.
7. Identify the differences and similarities between the concepts of power and influence.
8. Why is the 'zone of indifference' important to the notion of how power and control operate within an organization? Justify your answer.
9. 'The trick in management is to find ways of control that are socially acceptable.' Discuss this statement.
10. Management is ultimately about acquiring and using power successfully. What might this suggest about the scope of training and development programmes for managers?

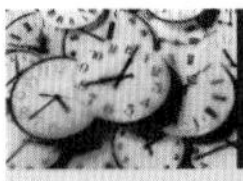

CASE STUDY Controlling the invisible?

This story describes events that occurred in a meat processing factory in Oman. The process involved the preparation of beef carcasses into joints, steaks and products suitable for curing as beef bacon. James was from Scotland and was the management accountant at the factory. He was responsible for the determination of product costing and he asked for a full breakdown of material and labour data for each process within the factory. The work study department were tasked with the job of obtaining and collating the wide variety of data needed for this. A number of studies were undertaken to determine the time taken to perform the work and product weight was checked at each stage of the process. The data collection phase of this exercise lasted for several weeks.

The data were collated and among the various findings was the rather surprising one that each carcass lost weight at each stage of the production process. Every beef carcass and joint was weighed before each process and all processed meat was also weighed (including the small trimmings, bones, etc.). There was always a slight difference between the total after-processed weight and the original weight. When this was first discovered it was thought to be due to careless weighing. The factory was staffed by people from many nationalities and it was first thought that perhaps misunderstanding or poor communications were to blame. Considerable effort was made to tighten up on the weighing process and this part of the project was put under the specific direction of Lafi, the chief work study engineer who originated from Kuwait. As a result of this special initiative everyone in the production and work study departments was satisfied that the weighing process was as accurate as it could possibly be. The difference in weight between production stages became known as the invisible loss and was about 4 per cent on average of the original weight. The food technologists and production specialists within the company thought that it was probably due to moisture leaching out as the meat was being cut. This was included in the findings presented in a report to James as the management accountant.

James was not happy with the idea of having something that could not be properly accounted for and, even worse, with no physical evidence to see. This went against every belief and his professional training and he refused to accept the report as the basis of product costing. Something had to be wrong. For James, meat did not and could not simply become invisible. Of course, the fact that meat is a valuable commodity and the temptation to divert it to non-company use is an ever present risk in the trade was another factor in his thinking. He was being asked to price the company product on the basis that some 4 per cent was disappearing. Over a full year that represented a considerable volume and value of meat. James created a scene within the senior management team of the company and demanded that the data be rejected and more tests be done. He even refused to believe the evidence of his own eyes when he was present at a demonstration of the effect.

Clearly, there was a problem associated with the ability to control the processing of meat within this factory that needed to be addressed. It was at this stage that the politics and relative power of the key players began to influence events. James was not popular as an individual and had upset the production director (Ameer an Omani national) in the past. He was considered to be pedantic, rude, unhelpful and not fully part of the multi-national senior management team. And that was on a good day! The finance director (Yousef, another Omani national) was a very quiet individual but he was connected by marriage to the owners of the business. Consequently, he had considerable status and influence in the business. So the stage was set for a battle of who would win the argument about the invisible loss. The accountants had a natural advantage in that they determined the product costing upon which sales prices and profitability depended. They also had to satisfy the owners that the company was being well run. But James was in a difficult political position as he had alienated the key players from the operational functions and did not have strong support from his own superior.

After considerable behind the scenes discussion and lobbying by all concerned together with discussion with various other organizations in the meat industry James was overruled and the invisible loss became a feature of the costing process.

Tasks

1. To what extent does this case demonstrate that it is not possible to control through numbers and systems, but that it is a social process involving shared frames of reference between all the parties involved? Justify your answer.
2. What might your answer to the previous question imply about the processes of management, power and control within organizations?
3. What should James learn from this experience and how might he regain his credibility in the situation?

FURTHER READING

Adams, A (1992) *Bullying At Work: How to Confront and Overcome It*, Virago, London. This review of the experiences of individuals at work being bullied provides an insight into the darker side of control. The book is written as a guide to the subject and also offers some advice on how to deal with the subject of being bullied at work.

Buchanan, D and Badham, R (1999) *Power, Politics and Organizational Change: Winning the Turf Game*, Sage, Chichester. Reviews the relationship between the themes indicated in the title and so provides a direct link between theory and practice in this area.

Clark, H, Chandler, J and Barry, J (1994) *Organization and Identities: Text and Readings in Organizational Behaviour*, International Thomson Business Press, London. Contains a broad range of original articles on relevant material themes and from significant writers referred to in this and other textbooks on management and organizations.

Jay, A (1987) *Management and Machiavelli*, revised edn, Hutchinson Business, London. A humorous text which considers many aspects associated with power and authority in management. It does not take Machiavelli's work specifically as its basis, but his spirit is evident. A translation of Machiavelli's original work, which is very accessible and available as a 1981 Penguin book, is also well worth reading.

Jermier, JM, Knights, D and Nord, WR (eds) (1994) *Resistance and Power in Organizations*, Routledge, London. Provides a review of how attempts to use power as a basis of control inevitably leads to resistance in one form or another. It is grounded in the labour process perspective and attempts to interpret the arguments from the perspectives implied by that model.

McMahon, P (2002) *Global Control: Information Technology and Globalization*. Edward Elgar, Cheltenham. A solid review of information systems as the means of providing control in the cycles of capitalist reorganization and globalization.

Monks, RAG and Minow, N (1991) *Power and Accountability*, HarperCollins, London. This book attempts to show some of the consequences of power when large organizations can operate without the effective means of holding them accountable for their actions. As such it is a chilling reminder of the many ways that power can be abused and trust violated.

COMPANION WEBSITE

Online teaching and learning resources:

Visit the companion website for Organizational Behaviour and Management 3rd edition at: *http://www.thomsonlearning.co.uk/businessandmanagement/martin3* to find valuable further teaching and learning material:

Refer to page 35 for full details.

CHAPTER 18

Conflict and organizational politics

LEARNING OBJECTIVES

After studying the chapter content and working through the associated Management in Action panels, Employee Perspectives, Discussion Questions and Case Study, you should be able to:

- **Understand the different perspectives on the concept of conflict.**
- **Describe the sources of conflict within an organization.**
- **Explain the major conflict handling strategies used within organizations.**
- **Outline the concept of organizational politics.**
- **Discuss how political behaviour can be managed within an organization.**

INTRODUCTION

Conflict frequently arises when the differences between two or more groups or individuals become apparent. In industrial relations situations this might occur if a trade union makes a demand for a 10 per cent pay increase and management make an equally forceful case for a 2 per cent increase. However, the existence of differences such as these does not automatically lead to open conflict. It depends what happens. The large difference in the pay claims of the trade union and the management would be subject to negotiation between the parties in an attempt to reach an agreement or acceptable compromise. Only if open argument, disagreement or some form of industrial action resulted would it be said that real conflict existed. However, some writers would argue that latent conflict is ever present as a result of the exploitation of labour within a capitalist system of production.

Therefore, normal use of the term conflict implies a negative and openly hostile situation. Indeed, the first definition of the term in the *Pocket Oxford Dictionary* (1969) is, 'trial of strength between opposed parties or principles'. In an organizational context it is perhaps more appropriate to consider conflict in terms of its potential or as representing a scale of activity. In industrial relations terms the need to take into account the potential for conflict in the relationships between managers and employees requires anticipatory behaviour in seeking to develop strategies and practices that minimize the risk. This requirement often leads to forms of partnership and involvement being developed as a means of avoiding the open conflict which could lead to strikes and other industrial action intended to force a change in behaviour in the other party.

Concepts that have strong associations with **conflict** are those of power, control and **politics**. Power and control were covered in the previous chapter and politics reflects the purposes for some of the behaviour of individuals in the workplace. Politicking is frequently described as behaviour outside the accepted procedures and norms of a particular context, intended to further the position of an individual or group at the expense of others. As such it is often identified with undesirable behaviour not intended to advance the interests of the organization. It is most often associated with the attempts of individuals to advance their own careers or to undermine the status and reputation of other departments and people to their personal advantage.

Both concepts of conflict and politics do however contain positive dimensions. For example, the resolution of conflict can allow for genuine differences to be resolved in a dynamic way which strengthens the working relationships involved. Political activity can also be of benefit to the organization. For example, if through the politicking of the marketing manager the reluctance of the other functions in a company to adapt the product range were overcome and changes are brought about which prove successful, then it could be argued that such behaviour was of benefit. It is the 'Janus-faced' or 'double-edged' nature of both conflict and politics that encourages some writers to describe them as being part of the **shadow themes** within an organization. Stacey (2000, pp 386–7) for example, describes these as being the point of fusion between the legitimate and the illegitimate in human behaviour.

SOURCES OF ORGANIZATIONAL CONFLICT

Conflict
This frequently arises when the differences between two or more groups or individuals become apparent.

Conflict can be considered as something that disrupts the normal and desirable states of stability and harmony within an organization. Under this definition it is something to be avoided and if possible eliminated from the operation. However, it is also possible to consider conflict as an inevitable feature of human interaction and perhaps something that if managed constructively could offer positive value in ensuring an effective performance within the organization.

There are six major areas within an organization that can give rise to conflict (see Figure 18.1). Each of these sources of conflict will be discussed in the following subsections.

Politics
Behaviour outside the accepted norms of a particular context, intended to further the interests of an individual or group.

Shadow themes
These reflect the area of contact between the legitimate and the illegitimate in human behaviour within an organization.

Intrapersonal

This represents the conflicts that arise within the individual. There are many forms in which this can arise, but essentially it stems from the choices or decisions that each individual must make. For example, the ethical dilemmas facing individuals in their work were discussed in Chapter 12. These represent one potential area of conflict for the individual to resolve within themselves. Others' internal conflicts are of a less complex nature, for example, to go to work or stay at home when feeling unwell, how much effort to put into the job, etc.

Interpersonal

Whetten and Cameron (1991) identify four sources of interpersonal conflict. They are:

1. *Personal difference*. No two people are exactly alike. It is not possible to like everyone with whom one works and personalities frequently clash. For example, Jensen-Campbell *et al.* (2003) suggest that agreeableness as a personality factor in individuals plays a large part in minimizing the risk of conflict and also its easy resolution in children.
2. *Role incompatibility*. The functional nature of work activity creates very real potential for interpersonal conflict. For example, a personnel manager may seek to organize training courses for employees. However, an operations manager with tight production schedules to meet and with no spare labour may resent the efforts of the personnel manager. There exists a high probability of conflict between the two managers in this type of situation.

FIGURE 18.1

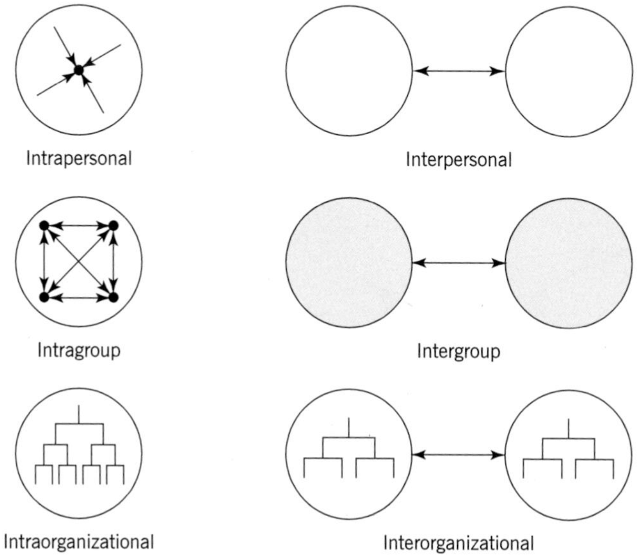

The major sources of conflict

3. *Information deficiency*. An individual with access to information is better able to perform more effectively. They also know more in Foucault's (1975) terms and are therefore better able to exercise power over the situation and other people. Consequently, information (or at least the imbalance in access to it) can provoke conflictual relationships between individuals. At a less political level the quality of information provided to a computer system designer could easily become the subject of conflict if the system does not subsequently meet user expectations.
4. *Environmental stress*. Conflict can become more likely in times of severe competitive pressure. Most organizations have been going through significant periods of downsizing, re-engineering and change over the past decade. As a consequence individuals can find that their ability to retain a job and career is continually under threat. Because the individuals within such organizations feel under constant threat the environmental conditions exist for fractious relationships and open conflict to emerge.

Intragroup

One particular context within which interpersonal conflict can be found occurs within a group. The models proposed by Belbin and Margerison and McCann, discussed in the chapters dealing with groups, claim to offer a basis for minimizing the potential for harmful conflict between group members. These models argue that careful selection should provide balance between the necessary skills and personal qualities among group members to allow the task to be achieved effectively without unnecessary friction or conflict. Group activity inevitably brings the differing characteristics, attitudes and opinions of individual members into focus. The interaction of these variables on the group decision making process and conflict can be reflected in a diagram, Figure 18.2. Research by De Dreu and Weingart (2003) demonstrates the contradictory and complex links between task and relationship conflict within groups and the effects on team performance and member satisfaction with the team process.

FIGURE 18.2

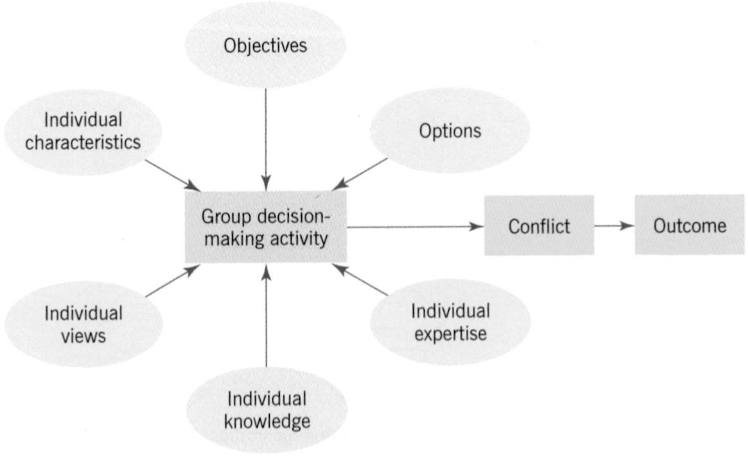

Group decision making and conflict

Intergroup

Many different groups exist within an organization and inevitably they will experience differences and conflict at some point in time. Employees seek to earn as much money as possible, employers, of course, want labour to be as cheap as possible. There is an inherent basis for conflict in this situation. Marketing departments may press hard for a diversified product range with regular changes in order to compete in turbulent markets. The production department may demand stability to be able to achieve economies of scale. Again there is the potential for interdepartmental friction and conflict in this type of situation, created by the functional nature of organizational structure.

Intraorganizational

Individuals and groups play such a significant part in organizational activity that they inevitably account for much of the incidence of conflict. However, there are other features of organization that favour the emergence of conflict (Figure 18.3).

The physical realization of an organization in terms of structure, hierarchy, information flows, together with career development, reward and information flows are all ways of compartmentalizing activity. Link these with the inevitable limitations of resource availability and a basis for competition is created. There is a very narrow line between competition and conflict. If one party considers that it has not been fairly treated in the competitive process or attempts to influence outcomes in its favour then conflict can arise. There are also propensities to conflict in the nature of organizational ownership and the relative exclusion of employees. The impact of technology on jobs linked to the concepts of power, control and politics are other endemic features of organizational functioning that allow conflict to emerge.

Interorganizational

Markets provide a scenario in which organizations are inevitably in conflict with each other. All of the competitors in a particular industry attempt to meet the needs of the customer in such ways as to maximize profit and market share for themselves. The

FIGURE 18.3

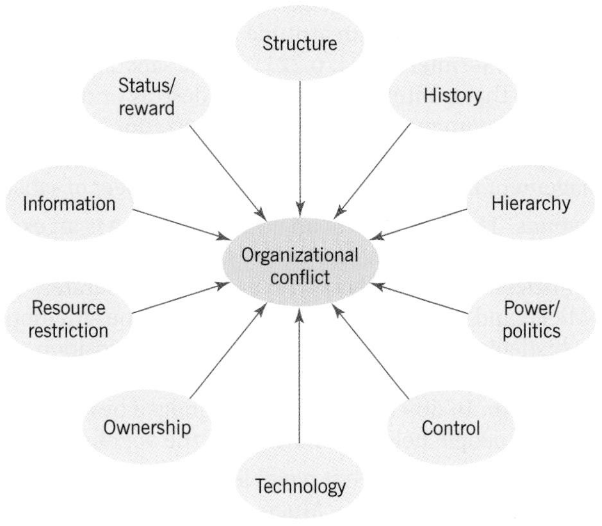

Organization and the determinants of conflict

unfair use of state subsidy can support otherwise uneconomic organizations to the disadvantage of organizations that do not have access to those funds. In a variation of interorganizational conflict there is considerable unease in some quarters at the potential for it to exist in relation to how the large accountancy practices function and interact with the large banks, all of which offer a wide range of services. The essence of this debate is reflected in Management in Action 18.1.

FORMS OF ORGANIZATIONAL CONFLICT

This section explores how conflict finds expression within an organizational setting. Disagreement that escalates to the level of conflict could become apparent in many forms including arguments, adversarial attitudes, antagonistic and other forms of hostile behaviour for example. Within an organization there are two distinct levels for differentiating the form that conflict can take. They are the individual and group levels of analysis. These forms of conflict are now discussed further, taking each level of conflict in turn. Conflict from a managerial perspective has the potential to create disruption within the organization and hence lower output levels, quality and profit. As a result most organizations attempt to institutionalize the mechanisms for seeking to minimize the risk of its occurring and dealing with it quickly if it should arise. However, this is not the only way of thinking about conflict within an organization and some of the other perspectives will be discussed in a later section.

Individual

Some of the ways in which conflict can find its way into observable behaviour include:

Sabotage
An attempt to damage the interests of an organization by an individual or group seeking a benefit or revenge.

- *Sabotage*. The deliberate interruption of company operations is the broad definition of **sabotage** (Brown, 1977). At one extreme, it involves causing machines to breakdown by deliberately causing a malfunction. At the other extreme, it is simply not working as effectively as would be considered reasonable by management. Sabotage arises through the deliberate intent to damage the interests of another by an individual who considers that they have some reason to feel aggrieved by the actions of that party. Sabotage is not part of the conflict itself, but it reflects an attitude and an attempt to get even with the target. LaNuez and Jermier (1994, p 221) define sabotage to be, 'deliberate action or inaction that is intended to damage, destroy or disrupt some aspect of the workplace environment, including the organization's property, product, processes or reputation, with the net effect of undermining [the] goals of capital elites'. Management in Action 18.2 illustrates one aspect of sabotage in a factory.
- *Ethical dilemmas*. The existence of an ethical dilemma is an example of a conflict, usually between alternative courses of action. For example, should an individual whistleblow on their boss who has been deliberately over-claiming expenses? Miceli and Near (1997) suggest that in some situations the main purpose of whistleblowers can be to further their own position at the expense of others. One measure of the antisocial use of whistleblowing is reflected in the concept of net harm. In other words, it can be judged by the balance between the proportions of people helped or harmed by the act of whistleblowing.
- *Interpersonal disputes*. It is just not possible for all human beings to live in peace and harmony all of the time. Much as we might strive for such an ideal and even function as if it were the norm, the weight of history and human nature would suggest otherwise. For example, a manager may perceive that a

MANAGEMENT IN ACTION 18.1 For what we are about to receive

Many large accounting practices have a range of services they offer to clients. Such firms claim that there are 'Chinese walls' between the various component parts of the practice, particularly in the sensitive areas of audit, support and insolvency. However, not everyone is convinced that the inevitable tensions are dealt with as they should be. This situation becomes even more complex when the role of bankers in company financial management is taken into account.

Jack describes one case that illustrates some of these potential conflicts. It involves a north London textile company, a bank, the accountants that it hired and the eventual fall into receivership of the business. In 1992 the company lost its largest customer. The bank pressed the owner of the business to consider the implications of this loss of revenue and he agreed to pay £18 000 to a large firm of accountants to write a report on the viability of the company. As a result of the report all parties agreed that the company should stay in business, but that the position should be reviewed six months later. During that time the business paid the accountants £3000 each week to monitor the financial health of the company.

At the end of the six months the company overdraft had been reduced to within a few thousand pounds of the owner's forecast. The owner and his independent auditors made repeated proposals for the restructuring of the company which were turned down by the bank and the accountants. Instead the bank appointed the firm of accountants as receivers and closed the business down. The underlying issue from this case (and many others) is the probity of banks using the same accountants to investigate troubled companies as would be appointed as receivers should the company fail. The potential conflict of interest that arises in these situations emerges from the pressure on the accountants to generate fee earning opportunities. There is a danger that the information on a company may be 'slanted' to 'encourage' its closure in order to gain the additional fees for the accountants were they appointed as receiver.

Not all firms of accountants undertake insolvency work as some believe that the potential for a conflict of interest does not serve their clients well. Mr Michael Snyder, senior partner at accountants Kingston Smith indicated that they did not conduct any insolvency work because he believed that it did not sit happily with its work as investigating accountants. He went on to say: 'What is required is a wholly independent review. The investigators appointed [from large firms] are most likely to be insolvency experts with the prospect of a future receivership in their minds.'

However, not surprisingly, these claims are vigorously denied by the large firms. Allan Griffiths, a partner with Grant Thornton and vice-president of the Society of Practitioners of Insolvency, said: 'It's a bit hard to stomach people doubting my professional integrity. I get my enjoyment from saving companies, not closing them down.' He also suggested that most of the companies that he is asked to investigate emerge intact with existing management in place and with the creditors none the wiser. He also pointed out that to appoint another firm as receivers would add to the cost as they would have to learn about the business. Word would spread and the value of the remaining assets would drop further. The banks are also divided on the issue. The Royal Bank of Scotland has taken positive steps to control the situation by reducing the number of people who can approve receivership from 300 to three. By this action, and by deliberately not appointing investigating accountants as receivers, it claims to have greatly reduced the number of companies put into receivership.

Adapted from: Jack, A (1994) For what we are about to receive, *Financial Times*, 24 June, p 18.

Stop ↔ Consider

Based on the views expressed, should there be restrictions on the range of products and services that a company can offer? Should this apply to any industry or just financial services? Justify your views.

How would you ensure compliance with any restriction requirement?

MANAGEMENT IN ACTION 18.2 Time for a break

This story was described by the factory industrial engineer who was a member of the task force charged with solving the problem described. The particular factory in question was located in Germany and made fibreboard ceiling panels. These were made in sizes of approximately 3 metres by 2 metres and then cut down to smaller panels as dictated by the specific customer order. It was possible to have a number of textured finishes pressed into the surface of the panels and all would then be finished off with several paint coatings as dictated by the order. These panels would be used in offices, banks, retail outlets or any number of similar buildings. Given the nature of the product and production process, considerable quantities of dust were created by the cutting and sanding processes involved. Much of the dust was removed by the dust extraction and air conditioning systems, but some still found its way into the factory environment.

The machine in question was the final painting and packing line which was about 100 metres in length with a normal crew of 24. This allowed for the machine to run continuously during the production shift. Each employee took turns on a rota to have a break and so the machine only actually required about 18 people to operate it at any point in time. The other six people were on a break lasting about 20 minutes at a time. The machine was loaded with finished ceiling panels and a final coat of paint was applied automatically in a spray booth. The panels then went through a drying oven, to be followed by a quality check before being packed into boxes at the packing stations. The finished boxes were then stacked on pallets and moved into the finished goods warehouse.

The process was not technically complex, consisting of conveyor belts; spray booths with moving arms, fed by paint pumped from large containers; drying ovens, which were heated by gas; a cooling section with cold air circulated by fans. The quality checks were done on a large flat conveyor and the boxes were packed by picking tiles off the same conveyor belt. The production process contained a number of elements that needed to be co-ordinated if the end product were to be acceptable. For example, if the spray heads were not cleaned regularly they tended to clog and if the oven temperature was not appropriate burnt or wet paint resulted. The machine had a record of inconsistent production and had to be stopped several times each shift for corrections and adjustments to be made.

The production manager set up a task force to explore what was happening on this machine and to find solutions to the problems. Many weeks of investigation by the industrial engineer, maintenance engineer, quality inspector, etc., all produced minor changes to the process but not the significant improvement sought. During the investigation it was noticed that mechanical breakdowns began to increase. The safety trips on the motors driving the conveyor belts began to cut in and stop the motors from working. The electricians were called out to examine the motors and found that they were very hot to the touch, but once cooled down they started and worked as expected. No electrical or mechanical fault could be found either on the equipment or as a result of the way in which operators were using it.

This lasted for several weeks and neither cause nor solution seemed any clearer. Until that is, one day purely by chance, the industrial engineer appeared by the machine and found the cause. A pile of dust had built up around one of the conveyor belt motors. An investigation followed. It transpired that the operators had been building piles of dust around the electric motors, effectively insulating them and allowing the heat to build up to the extent that the safety trip cut in and switched them off. When the electricians were called in the operators quickly disposed of the dust, leaving a very hot motor to be examined by the electricians.

The operators claimed the jobs they did were so boring that 'playing this game' added a bit of interest to their daily routine and gave them more time in the mess room chatting to their friends and playing cards etc. The management view was that this represented sabotage and formal disciplinary hearings were held. No employee was actually dismissed as a result, partly because it was not clear just how much the supervisors had known about this 'game'. However, it was made clear that if it happened again dismissal would result. Productivity on the machine did improve after this situation was dealt with. However, the jobs were not changed in any way in an attempt to improve job satisfaction.

Stop ↔ Consider

Does this demonstrate sabotage, or does it reflect alienation, frustration, resistance, boredom or bad job design? Justify your views.
It is suggested that the supervisors might have known what was happening. Why do you think that they may have known but chosen to ignore it?
How would you have dealt with the situation if you had been the production manager responsible for the machine?

subordinate is lazy and inefficient. The manager may as a result of that perception make life difficult for the individual as an encouragement to them to leave. This would inevitably create a conflictual and antagonistic relationship between them.

- *Work manipulation*. It is not unknown for new work procedures to be followed to the letter by those onto whom they have been forced, even though they recognize that problems will occur. The intention being to exact a measure of revenge on the managers concerned. Thompson (1989, p 137) quotes an example from Chrysler in which the assembly line operators had been given precise instructions on what sequence of car doors to hang. Unfortunately, management could not provide the sequence of cars to correctly match the doors. The workers continued to do exactly as they had been instructed and chaos resulted. Managers begged the workers to go back to the ways of working that the workers themselves had developed – in practice they had developed the skills and common sense to know what job to do next. The workers however refused and insisted on following the way of working demanded by management for the rest of the shift. Management then withdrew the new job instructions and allowed the workers some discretion over the process.
- *Misuse of resources*. The appropriating of resources for personal use can be rationalized by individuals on the basis of correcting a perceived injustice and by so doing reduce the possibility of conflict. Examples include making private phone calls at work, use of the Internet and e-mail systems at work and taking pens and paper clips home. Many organizations now consider such theft as a major cost and attempt to clamp down on it. The procedures involved have included random searches of people and property, which can create new opportunities for conflict to emerge!
- *Choice*. A virtually limitless opportunity for choice exists within an organization. Promotion; access to career development opportunities; pay increases; interesting work; the giving or withholding of friendship; co-operation and assistance are just some of the more obvious. For example, to fall out with a boss may result in open conflict over duties, or it may result in certain opportunities not being made available. Discrimination in all its forms falls clearly into this type of behaviour.
- *Politicking and power*. There is an ability to experience conflict through power and political behaviour. For example, the personal conflict between two managers could lead to an attempt by one to undermine the position and authority of the other through political activity.
- *Rumour and gossip*. This can be regarded as a milder form of political behaviour and power. That is not to suggest that rumour and gossip in themselves are mild. There are occasions when they form very powerful and damaging weapons in their own right. The creating and spreading of rumours about someone with whom one is in conflict can represent effective ways of undermining their position and credibility. Management in Action 18.3 describes the impact of one such situation.

MANAGEMENT IN ACTION 18.3 Getting rid of the boss

This event was described by the personnel director of the organization concerned and only names and incidental details have been changed. There was one small department within a large company that dealt with a single product for a particular market. This department was for all practical purposes independent of other activities within the company. Over the years it had gained the reputation for being a problem area, containing difficult staff, and ineffective management. The standard of service was continually slipping downwards. Eventually the manager was moved sideways and replaced by one of the staff who up to that point had enjoyed a good reputation for attempting to do things correctly.

Unfortunately, this action created a number of additional and unforeseen problems within the department. The previous boss resented being moved to another job. The staff began to see that change was about to be forced upon them and began to side with the old boss. The new manager was not experienced; neither did he receive any training. Senior managers did not make any obvious attempt to ensure that everyone would take the new situation seriously. The result was an escalating cycle of resentment, frustration and a sense of grievance and unresolved conflict at a personal, group and job level.

Eventually, rumours began to spread about the new boss and staff would not talk directly to the individual. In short, life became difficult; a hostile (bad) atmosphere developed and work began to suffer even more. After some time anonymous letters were sent to senior managers purporting to demonstrate the wild excesses in behaviour and general lack of ability of the boss. Investigations failed to reveal the source of these letters but the situation continued to deteriorate. Eventually, after about a year, the boss asked to be moved to another job and this was done. After another three months the boss resigned and left the company altogether.

A new boss was recruited from outside the organization but he was not given the resources necessary to change the situation. Things did not deteriorate much further but neither did they get any better. The department did not develop the full potential of its product or market and was eventually closed down.

Stop ↔ Consider

Imagine that you had been brought in from outside the company and put in charge of the department described. How would you deal with the situation?
Justify your intended plan of action and outline any contingency plans that you would develop?

- *Attitude.* It is possible to identify how attitudes can be influenced by conflict and indeed vice versa. Individuals who experience conflict and for whom it is not effectively resolved retain a sense of grievance and hostility towards the other party. It is against that background that attitudes towards and about other people are formed.
- *Absence and leaving.* In extreme instances conflict can result in one or more parties withdrawing from the situation. This can result in absenteeism or in leaving the company, as was the case in Management in Action 18.3.

Group

Some of the forms of conflict identified under the individual classification can also find expression at the group level. For example, if bad attitudes develop between workers and management, strikes and other forms of industrial action will become more likely as trust and mutual respect diminish. The major forms of group conflict include:

- *Strikes and lock-outs*. The withdrawal of labour by employees or the prevention of work activity by management are two sides of the same coin. During a collective dispute between managers and trade unions the final lever that either party holds is to restrict the activities of the other. If all employees go on strike they effectively prevent management from running the business. If managers lock out the workers they prevent them from working or earning any wages. The intention of both courses of action is to force one side to concede to the demands of the other or at least to negotiate further to find an acceptable compromise.
- *Work-to-rule*. The loss of income can be significant during a strike, even if it only lasts for a brief period. It is clearly more effective to attempt to find ways of putting pressure on an employer without the consequent loss of income. One way of achieving this is through the notion of a work-to-rule. The rationale of such a course of action is that employees are inevitably encouraged to go beyond the contract and rules in the normal course of their jobs. No rule book, job description or procedure manual can ever fully provide for how a job needs to be done effectively, efficiently or to overcome the inevitable difficulties that arise every day. These emerge as the result of mistakes, errors or delays in deliveries, distribution, breakdowns or elsewhere in the company's operations. If it were not so then the practice of working-to-rule would not have the potential to produce an impact. Employees are able to undermine the manufacturing process or quality of service provided merely by doing exactly and precisely as they are required, rather than exercising discretion in bending or not following the rules when appropriate. Essentially, then, management usually require workers to follow the spirit, not the letter of the rules (Blyton and Turnbull, 1994, p 31).

  It is interesting to contemplate why it is that organizations are making themselves increasingly vulnerable to this form of action through delayering and empowering employees. Clearly, the greater responsibility that is delegated to employees the greater the risk of susceptibility to action of this type should conflict erupt. This is perhaps why many organizations seek to adopt what have been described as progressive personnel policies in an attempt to reduce (through socialization, empowerment and association) the divergence of attitude between managers and workers. It is a trend that parallels (but in the opposite direction) the diminution in the power to influence events of the British trade union movement since the late 1970s as a result in political and economic forces in the UK.
- *Work restriction*. Groups are capable of determining the level of effort that they are prepared to invest on the employer's behalf. This was evident in the Hawthorne studies discussed in the chapters on groups. Consequently employees slow down a little and less gets done. A frustrated group of employees who feel some sense of grievance with an employer are not likely to perform at their best.
- *Factionalism*. There are a wide range of means by which groups can demonstrate some degree of conflict in their relationships with other groups. The circumstances that gave rise to the British tradition of trade unions being occupationally based also gave rise to union strategies that attempted to protect the interests of those groups against the interests of others workers. This created a number of opportunities to display factional behaviour including demarcation disputes between unions and employers, and membership disputes between unions. Within a company it is possible that the sales department may be hostile to the production department as a consequence of the historical lack of

co-operation between them. Consequently, this may lead to factional behaviour at every opportunity including 'bad-mouthing' each other at meetings and blaming each other for mistakes etc.

THE CONSEQUENCES OF CONFLICT

There are a number of consequences that arise from the existence of conflict. The potential for conflict between individuals and groups in the work context produces a situation in which co-operation cannot be taken for granted. Everyone within the organization must work on the quality of relationships, or conflict is likely to arise. In essence where trust is absent or at a very low level, conflict is almost inevitable. For example, Sheppard and Tuchinsky (1996, pp 153–61) reflect on the role of negotiation as a means of building trust within an organization through its ability to reconcile differences and build partnerships. One of the outcomes of such approaches would be to reduce the level of open hostility or conflict present in a particular situation.

That is not to suggest that conflict can be eliminated completely. There will always be individuals who do not get along at a personal level. For example, Lewicki and Bunker (1996, pp 126–8) develop a model which reflects the possible outcomes for a relationship in which trust has been violated. Included among the active variables are the possible responses by the violator, one of which is disagreement with the violated person's perceptions. Clearly under such circumstances repair to the relationship will be impossible and conflict or a break-up will result. Equally, the motivations that cause one group to act in a particular way are potentially subject to different perceptions and interpretations by another group. Graffiti-art is seen as an expression of freedom and skill by those that do it, but as an eyesore and a nuisance by many other people in society. However, to minimize conflict (assuming that represents a desirable state) is something that requires positive action rather than passivity. Miller and Bedford (2003) suggest the following five step process as the way to re-establish trust at a company level based on the establishment of core values:

1. *Identify the core values*. Core values define the make-up of the organization and should reflect its culture.
2. *Bring the core values to life*. For each core value develop behavioural statements that contribute to shared understandings for all members of the organization.
3. *Spell out the do and don't aspects of each value*. Elaborate each of the behavioural statements with specific examples of do and don't aspects of the behaviour so that everyone is clear about what is expected of them.
4. *Weave values into the fabric of the organization*. Ensure that the core values and associated behaviours are reflected in all aspects of operational activity. This should also be reinforced through training and development programmes intended to reinforce the new core values and implications for behaviour.
5. *Ensure accountability and model the way*. Ensure that senior managers set a good example in all that they do; they should act as a model for all staff. Hold all employees accountable for their behaviour. Reward good behaviour that reflects the core values and deal firmly with behaviours that do not support them.

Conflict is a concept that, it can be argued, is either a negative or positive force. Interpreted as a negative force it is therefore something to be driven out, or at least minimized. Conflict from this perspective is regarded as something that disrupts effective relationships or company operations. It follows, therefore that if employees can be persuaded, or forced, to see things as managers do then conflict would largely disappear because there would be only minor differences between them. As a positive force, it can be described as a means of challenging the status quo and any other form of ineffectiveness within the system. By so doing it would force all parties within an organization to seek the most effective compromises in making full use of all available resources in pursuit of objectives. This is the basis of the **pluralist** perspective on conflict to be discussed later.

Pluralism
A perspective of organizations as collections of groups which have common and competitive objectives but also a desire to compromise.

Another viewpoint suggests that conflict represents a force that can either be negative or positive depending upon the circumstances. Too much or too little conflict is harmful. However, just the right amount of conflict can contribute to the optimization of performance. This view is represented in Figure 18.4.

Essentially in this view, conflict is being defined as a pressurizing force. Using the analogy of a domestic water pipe, too little pressure in the system and no water will come out of the tap. Too much pressure and the pipe is likely to burst. Just the right amount of pressure is needed in order to make the system function effectively as intended. Conflict in this model is regarded as a force that can be harnessed to ensure that slackness is kept out of the workings of the organization. For example, if management cannot take for granted the loyalty and commitment of employees they will find it necessary to ensure that they keep in touch with the thinking and aspirations of the workers. In so doing, a continual reassessment of the working relationship will be undertaken and the potential for major conflict minimized.

With no conflict in existence a form of amnesia would result. People and groups would begin to act as if they were operating on automatic pilot, simply going through the motions at work without thinking about them and taking everyone else for granted. In this view such an organization would become slack and desensitized to the activities going on around it. Equally, at the other extreme, excessive conflict, for example a protracted labour stoppage, would bring the organization to a standstill and thereby reduce performance to zero. In practice there are a number of consequences of conflict within an organization. They range from the harmful to the beneficial. Not all would be active in every situation. They include the items identified in Figure 18.5.

Most of the consequences identified in Figure 18.5 are self-explanatory, but some need further elaboration. Items such as stress, high labour turnover and difficult relationships can easily be understood as a direct consequence of conflict. However, items such as training and involvement will be better understood if they are considered further:

FIGURE 18.4

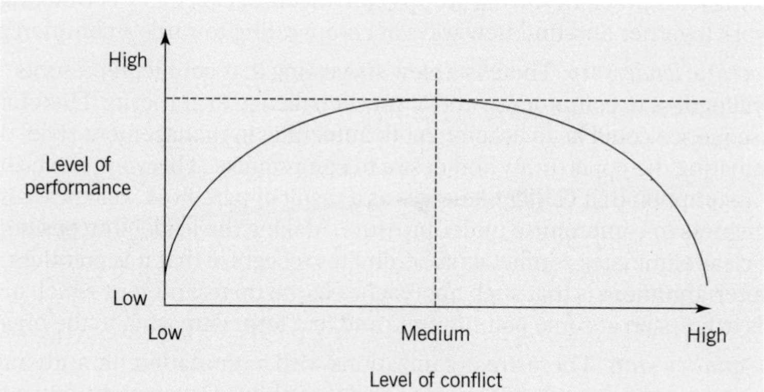

Conflict impact on performance (*adapted from*: Ivancevich, JM and Matteson, MT (1993) *Organizational Behaviour and Management*, 3rd edn, Irwin, Homewood, IL)

FIGURE 18.5

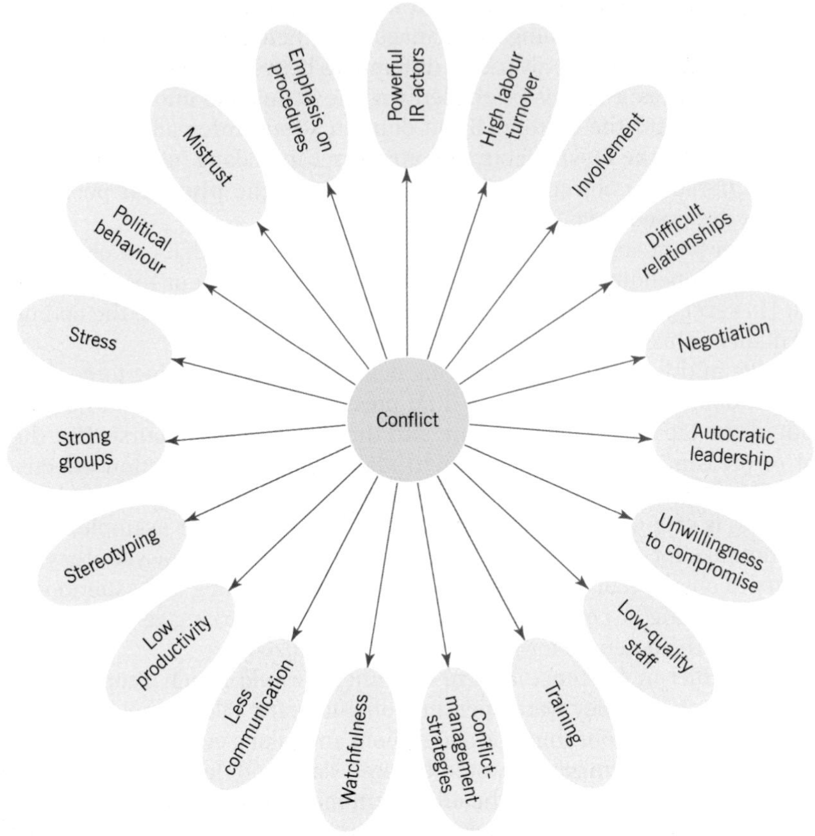

Some consequences of conflict

- *Training*. Where conflict is a real possibility, training and related activities can be effective means of exploring and resolving the difficulties. Training can therefore emerge as a direct consequence of the perceived conflict. Conflict can be reduced through many training initiatives. For example, socialization achieved through training could help to integrate groups by developing a common framework and culture as the basis of the relationship. Equally, forming joint problem solving groups can encourage formally conflicting groups to work together and find new ways of co-operating towards a common goal.
- *Autocratic leadership*. There is a view suggesting that conflict represents unwillingness to compromise and a direct challenge to authority. Therefore, one consequence could be to become more autocratic in management style, thereby eliminating the opportunity and desire to compromise. This view can be based on the assumption that conflict emerges as a result of perceived weakness and willingness to compromise under pressure. Making the leadership position strong and clear eliminates conflict as subordinates recognize that it is pointless. The counter-argument is that such approaches bottle up resentment which always finds expression at some point in time and in a form damaging to the organization.
- *Low-quality staff*. There are organizations with a reputation for autocratic management and conflictual working relationships. Consequently, in a local labour market potential employees tend to regard such employers as a last resort and only remain until something better comes along. High labour turnover, poor quality products and services typify such organizations.

- *Less communication*. When people are in conflict the level and quality of communication drops. This can be seen in any industrial dispute, or even a family argument. There are also consequences such as the emergence of strong subgroups along with increased political behaviour among the groups and individuals concerned. As a consequence of this there is a tendency to attempt to institutionalize the procedures and processes by which conflict is resolved.

Many of the items incorporated into Figure 18.5 reflect the negative consequences of conflict and it might be argued that this should be taken to imply that the view represented in Figure 18.4 is invalid. If there are very few positive consequences of conflict it cannot be helpful to performance. This need not be so as it should be possible to achieve medium levels of overall conflict through strategies such as negotiation and socialization. Offsetting the negative consequences of conflict should also improve performance through the removal of barriers to performance. The process of conflict resolution should also provide greater levels of unity within the organization thereby improving performance. One potential weakness implied by Figure 18.4 is that to be effective organizations should encourage a certain degree of conflict. This is not a view that would sit comfortably with many managers, who usually prefer to see performance achieved through more conventional mechanisms.

PERSPECTIVES ON CONFLICT

There are a number of perspectives on the topic of conflict and this section will begin by reviewing the traditional points of view. The labour process theory perspectives will then be discussed. Labour process theory has already been introduced in this text and so will not be fully developed in this chapter. The traditional views on conflict were encapsulated by Fox (1966) who describes three major perspectives on organizations, each of which has a different underpinning based on the nature of conflict.

Pluralism

Pluralism holds that an organization comprises a collection of groups each with their own objectives, aspirations and agenda to follow. Inevitably, the diversity of groups involved will have divergent interests in some areas, but convergent views in others. Employees seek to maximize earnings and organizations seek the lowest labour costs. These different perspectives are irreconcilable and are therefore a basis for conflict between the groups involved. However, such differences do not automatically result in a failure of the ability of the organization to function. All of the groups recognize that compromise is essential if they are to stand any chance of partially achieving their objectives. For example, if the cost of labour becomes too expensive the company may become uncompetitive and close down, resulting in everyone losing their jobs. So the wage–work bargain becomes a major area of potential conflict in the search for balance between these conflicting interests.

In the pluralist model conflict provides an indication of the issues on which there are fundamental differences between the various stakeholders. In effect, it provides a relationship regulation mechanism, surfacing problems while preventing major fracture (through the recognition of the need to compromise) which would be to every group's disadvantage. However, remember that managers are also employees and as the following Employee Perspective (18.1) shows there are situations in which the opportunity to bridge the gap in seeking a solution does not exist.

EMPLOYEE PERSPECTIVE 18.1 A boss's life at the sharp end

Life for Alberto Morales, general manager of the Gillette manufacturing subsidiary near Seville in Spain, changed completely on 18 March 1994 when he told the works council that the company had decided to close the factory. His home had to be put under 24-hour guard, he had to be accompanied by two bodyguards and he could not leave his office to walk around the factory.

About 250 people were employed at the factory, but the parent company wanted to concentrate European razor-blade manufacture in England and Germany. Reaction to the proposed closure was very hostile at a number of levels. The regional government challenged the decision in the courts and the industry minister for the country described the move as 'a provocation'. A consumer boycott of Gillette products was suggested as a reaction to the closure. Spanish labour law allows for collective redundancy on certain grounds, including the reorganization of production. However, these were intended to cover situations within Spain, not the cross-border transfer of work. Globally, Gillette was seeking to realign its operations, which involved the loss of about 2000 jobs, mostly outside the USA, and the creation of new jobs in countries such as China, Russia and Poland where new ventures were planned. The justification for the factory closure, according to Morales, 'is not that it is unprofitable, but that it is superfluous'.

To avoid lengthy administrative procedure, Spanish employers frequently offer the maximum redundancy compensation of 45 days' pay for each year of service. Morales suggested that the company might even go beyond that level in order to achieve a negotiated settlement. This enhancement consisted of a retirement plan, outplacement services and a range of resettlement policies. The works council at the Seville factory would not listen to the initial offer from management for two months. Future negotiations were also likely to be 'conflictual' in nature. The future for Morales at a personal level was also bleak. He was 54 and had been at the factory for 20 years, the last six as general manager. He felt that there were not many suitable alternative positions for him within the company. As a factory manager, the possible locations were likely to be India or somewhere else in the world, not a prospect that he relished. Once the factory was closed down he expected to be out of work just like the other workers.

Adapted from: White, D (1994) A boss's life at the sharp end, *Financial Times*, 8 June, p 20.

Tasks

1. What would you do if you were Alberto Morales trying to deal with this situation?
2. To what extent could the conflicting views of employees and the government on one hand and the company on the other be reconciled?
3. To what degree might the reactions of the workers be recognition of the inevitable and therefore an attempt to increase the 'price of going quietly'? Could you ever determine if this was actually the case? How?

Unitarianism

Unitarianism suggests that the whole organization is the natural unit of consideration. The organization is frequently likened to a family unit in which different branches and factions might exist but the family unit is the unit of concern for all members. Conflict in that sense is something that reflects a major breakdown in the normal and desirable state of affairs. From that perspective conflict is suggested to reflect something that should be avoided if possible and if it arises eliminated. It is viewed as emanating from members classed as deviant, so they should be dealt with severely as they put at risk the overall harmony of the group.

Marxist or radical perspective on conflict
Suggests that conflict is an inevitable function of the exploitation of employees within a capitalist system.

Marxism

The **Marxist** or **radical** perspective as it is sometimes called suggests that conflict is an inevitable function of capitalism. Under this view, employees are fundamentally exploited by the controllers of the means of production. One of the consequences of this is resistance to the will of management in the form of conflict. Not only is this inevitable, but it is desirable in the Marxist tradition as it assists the breakdown of capitalism in the revolutionary creation of socialism.

Labour process theory and conflict

The concept of the labour process developed out of the Marxist tradition and has been defined in the following terms:

> The means by which raw materials are transformed by human labour, acting on the objects with tools and machinery: first into products for use and, under capitalism, into commodities to be exchanged on the market. (Thompson 1989, p xv)

As an area of study it began with Braverman, who in 1974 published *Labour and Monopoly Capital* which stimulated the rediscovery of the earlier Marxist material on the nature of labour.

Labour process theory, therefore, seeks to explore the nature of work relations within a specific system of production. In most analyses this is reflected in the way in which capitalism acquires labour as a commodity and uses it to produce other commodities to the benefit of the capital owners. Within this analysis conflict between workers and managers (or more accurately capital owners represented by managers) is inevitable as more and more control is exercised in the search for increased efficiency in the value extracted from the labour process. Of course, the workers are not passive in this process and are well able to resist this search for ever more profitable use of their labour. For example, McKinlay (2002) demonstrates that the approach to enhancing the contribution of employees through knowledge management practices does not usually take account of organizational politics or the impact of such initiatives on the labour process. The effect of even passive resistance brought about by negative reactions among employees could significantly limit the success of such programmes. Thompson and McHugh (1995) indicate that the twin pressures on any capitalist organization of market competition and conflict within the employment relationship requires managers to continually reappraise the production capabilities. This inevitably places more pressure in the system, resulting in ever greater levels of potential conflict.

Thompson and McHugh (1995, pp 373–4) also identify a number of consequences that flow from the capitalist nature of the labour process, including:

- Work organizations are distinct from other organizations and can only be understood within a theory of capital accumulation and labour process.
- Organizations are structures of control in the broadest sense of the term. The concept of management as the agent of capital owners as the means of achieving control arises in this context.
- In advanced capitalist societies large scale organizations act as mechanisms which integrate economic, political, administrative and ideological structures.
- Organizational structures and processes involve political issues, decisions and choices on such matters as job design, control systems, etc.
- Organizations do not embody a universal rationality, but rather a contested rationality arising from the antagonistic and conflictual relationships between capital and labour.
- Organizational change reflects the balance between control and resistance expressed in the daily dynamic of experience.

There would appear to be five core elements to a theory of labour process identified by Thompson (1989) and which are relevant to an understanding of organizational conflict. These are now discussed.

Labour as a unique commodity

In seeking to create profit capitalists acquire a number of resources which they control in pursuit of bringing goods and services to market. Many of the resources are totally malleable at the discretion of the owner. For example, raw material will allow itself to be moulded and worked into any shape or product for which it has a capacity to become. However, the human resource has a high degree of restriction in its level of such malleability. Humans have free will; they have understanding; they have communication abilities; they can answer back; and most importantly they can resist management's direction. Many of these human capacities are of potential value to the capitalist. The vast majority of managers are paid employees and are paid to organize, take decisions and use what have been described as the higher level human qualities in support of capitalist objectives. Humans employed to produce the goods and services, however, have generally been regarded as little more than a flexible machine.

Because human labour has the qualities necessary for the achievement of capitalist intentions it is an essential part of the process of converting the other resources into the goods and services intended for sale. However, it is a mixed blessing as it automatically brings with it other undesirable qualities and obligations (from a capitalist point of view). For example, a surplus of cash within a capitalist organization has a very different set of connotations and ramifications compared with a surplus of people. It is the range and nature of these relative contrasts between the human and other resources that give it a unique quality within capitalism.

Labour as a special focus of attention

It is the nature of capitalism to create surplus. The notion of profit is a surplus – the extra money obtained through the market system over the cost of production. From that perspective every resource used within the capitalist organization must provide an opportunity for a contribution to the surplus obtained. This is the basis of the concept of added value used in accounting. In the Japanese management approaches anything that does not add value represents waste and should be eliminated. Consequently, there is a requirement for labour to create surplus as its basis for existence. In short, labour value must be higher than its cost for it to be viable as a resource. It is argued that this predisposes the participants to a conflictual relationship.

Capitalism forces minimization

It should be apparent from the previous discussion that there are two pressures in a capitalist system. The first is the notion of surplus as the objective of the whole process. The second is the volatility and unpredictability of the market system. In a truly free market there is no possibility of an individual being able to dictate price. It is simple economics that high profits attract new supplies and hence cause price reductions. The converse is also true, Low profits (or losses) result in some suppliers leaving the market either voluntarily or through financial failure. The resulting cycles once begun are ongoing in one form or another.

It is the unpredictability of markets that has created attempts over the years to try and 'fix' them through one form of intervention or another. Cartels, restraint of trade clauses in employment contracts and holding back supplies are some of the manipulations used to control risk (and keep prices high). The other side of this particular coin is to minimize the cost of operations so that it is possible to achieve the maximum surplus from a particular market price. This is more directly amenable to management action than some of the other options. It also provides a differentiating feature between organizations. Market price affects all suppliers equally (ignoring the potential effects of scale or bulk purchase effects) but internal costs influence only one organization. It is also possible to use this approach as the basis of price reduction to force out some of the rivals and achieve a stronger position over market conditions. This invariably forces capitalist organizations into a perpetual search for lower costs and the minimization of disruption to the ability of management to achieve its objectives. Once begun capitalism is a competitive process and forces all such organizations to minimize or demise unless the market can be controlled, hence its potential to create conflict.

Control as an imperative

There are several perspectives to this feature of the labour process theory. First, in order to ensure that profit is obtained the process must be controlled. If the capitalist does not control the process then one of the other stakeholders will. Second, because there are conflicting objectives between the stakeholders in an organization, control is the means by which these are regulated. Third, control is something that is associated with power and the ability to have other people do what the controller wants. Control is something that people seek in order to be able to exercise it at a personal level. Fourth, there are differences between operational and strategic control. Because of the size and complexity of most large organizations the owners of capital delegate much of the operational control decisions to employees designated as managers. By allowing employees a financial stake in the performance of the business through such arrangements as profit share or share options, it is argued that they will be more committed to the objectives of the capital owners. However, the proportion of ownership divested in this way tends to be very small in comparison to the total. Consequently, the degree of control devolved is also of little real significance and so liable to fuel conflict. There are many examples in which the interests of managers (even directors) have become openly separated from those of the capital owner with conflict being the result. For example, the so called 'fat-cat' arguments which are about shareholders and others, vociferously complaining about the very large salary and bonus arrangements for directors which appear not to serve the interests of investors is one such area of conflict.

Institutionalized conflict

The classic Marxist view of the class struggle is also part of the labour process. Much of the foregoing discussion has created a picture of the exploitation of workers. It can be argued that because of the notion of a requirement for added value from every aspect of the resource base it is by nature an exploitative process. Employees are paid less in wages than the true value of their labour; this is the basis of the wage–work bargain. Managers permanently attempt to seek better value from the employee resource and employees attempt to balance their contribution with the reward achieved. Employees are also dependent upon the owners of capital for the ability to earn money and acquire the necessities of life. This represents a low-trust conflictual approach to organizing.

Working in an organization is a relationship that includes a degree of mutual dependence as well as control. Capitalists need workers to provide the cost effective goods and services that will be sold for a profit. However there must be someone to purchase the goods and services available. This implies that ways of resolving the conflict that emerges within an organization must be found if continuity of supply and demand is to be achieved. Conflict resolution must therefore become institutionalized if its potentially harmful effects are to be minimized. Inevitably the goods produced are consumed in some degree by the workers that produce them. It is a feature of modern capitalist organization that as part of the search for minimization much production is carried out in locations remote from consumption. But even in these situations consumerism is beginning to emerge in developing countries to fuel the cycle of dependence.

As Thompson readily admits, there are many who would argue with the views put forward by labour process theorists. They include those who would see it as moving away from a traditional Marxist view of the common ownership and those who would prefer to see an emphasis on management study as a traditional social science. It does, however, provide a way of considering the nature of labour in capitalist organizations and perhaps placing conflict into a broader context. It is also an inescapable fact that not all organizations are capitalist, even in a predominantly capitalist society. There are the public services, voluntary organizations and charities. Each of these institutions makes use of modern management techniques and would be indistinguishable from capitalist organizations apart from the profit motive. So perhaps the labour process approach is fundamentally flawed as a means of being able to provide an all-embracing perspective on every type of organization.

CONFLICT AS RESISTANCE TO CONTROL

The previous chapter discussed the nature of resistance within the context of power and control. This chapter has touched on the nature of resistance within the concept of conflict and perspectives such as the labour process theory. Resistance has been described in this chapter as a reaction by workers to the attempt by managers to exercise control as part of the capitalist search for domination of the labour resource. Equally, resistance can be seen as a cause of conflict as workers reject management attempts to create the reality and frame of reference that employees are supposed to adopt. In short, if workers always agreed with managers there would be no conflict. That is because it is worker resistance to control that creates it – at least that is what many managers would like to believe! But as we have already seen there are other points of view about the nature and role of resistance in relation to power, control and conflict.

Traditionally within the field of management, resistance has been studied as a reaction to the exploitation of labour within a capitalist system which is subject to both economic and political control (Hyman, 1987). There are also perspectives on resistance as a cultural issue (for example, Clarke *et al.* (1976), Willis (1990)), all of which are based on the view encapsulated by Salaman (1979, p 145):

> Despite the major efforts of senior executives to legitimize the activities, structures and inequalities of the organization and to design and install 'foolproof' and reliable systems of surveillance and direction, there is always some dissension, some dissatisfaction, some effort to achieve a degree of freedom from hierarchical control – some resistance to the organization's domination and direction.

Collinson (1994) identifies two distinct and very different forms of resistance, both of which he illustrates through case study examples. The first is described as resistance through distance. This reflects the strategies adopted by workers to escape control and the demands of authority through physical or symbolic distance from the existing power structures. The second is described as resistance through persistence. This reflects resistance through the dogged and persistent demands of employees to become better informed, therefore being better equipped to challenge management decision making. It holds management to account, whereas resistance through distance holds firm to the absolute position of managers as responsible for everything.

Resistance through distance is a form of resistance as it seeks to, 'deny any involvement in or responsibility for the running of the organization' (p 37). It is an approach to work which recognizes a clear distinction between work and non-work lives as separate spheres and also refuses to accept the dilution of the capital/labour split in responsibility and role. In that sense it resists the attempts of managers to achieve control through involvement and integration. However, as the discussion by Collinson shows, such approaches can create conflict among colleagues as it can be regarded as simply complying with management intentions. As a perspective, resistance through distance accepts the managerial prerogative in a wide range of areas including decision making and technical expertise, therefore adherents simply respond to management's intended actions.

Resistance through persistence, by way of contrast, challenges the managerial prerogative at every opportunity. As the title suggests it persists in pushing managerial decision making and information flows as a way of resisting the imposition of a management created agenda and frame of reference. By constantly challenging the management perspective, ultimately the underlying assumptions, prejudices, inconsistencies and irrationalities are exposed. This can lead to changes in management intentions and a better deal for workers. However, it is possible that such approaches can create conflict between workers, as well as the conflict that arises when managers are persistently challenged. Not all workers will support such persistence, for example those who believe in resistance through distance will not support such engagement. Also colleagues who fear that they have something to lose as a result of the engagement may become conflictual in attitude. For example, they may fear that persistently questioning the financial data released by the company during annual negotiations may make management hostile to the entire factory and perhaps lead to it being closed down.

CONFLICT-HANDLING STRATEGIES

There are a number of ways in which conflict can be managed within an organizational setting. They include:

- *Clarity and openness*. This is based on the notion that conflict can arise when there is a lack of clarity about the intentions of management or other people. For example, when managers suddenly spend considerable amounts of time away on business and groups of visitors are shown around the facilities it is only natural that doubts about the future of the company will begin to be voiced. This in turn is only a short step away from people actively questioning what is going on and conflict emerging. A commitment to ensure a clarity and openness within the organization can go some considerable way to providing a climate of trust which in turn minimizes the possibility for misunderstandings and conflict.
- *Signals*. The signals and messages that managers and other individuals within the organization give also contribute to the likelihood of conflict breaking out. For example, if managers only speak to employees when there is a real threat of industrial action taking place, then they are sending out a clear signal of what they think about the workers. It becomes apparent that the only way to attract the attention of management is to threaten to take industrial action. Appropriate signals can be used to encourage different behaviour patterns. For example, it would be possible to encourage openness and discussion by involving employees on a regular basis. This would also signal that it was not necessary to threaten conflict in order to gain attention.

- *Training and socialization*. The development of training courses can help to reinforce the management's perspective. For example, a training course on customer care is a signal that managers are interested in customers, as well as providing an opportunity to explain why managers adopt those views and thereby providing staff with an opportunity to internalize those same views. This provides an opportunity for employees to be socialized into particular behaviour patterns and beliefs as defined by management, thereby reducing the potential for conflict. Conversely employees who display inappropriate behaviours are less likely to be promoted or gain access to training.
- *Style and structure*. Autocratic managers with dictatorial styles are more likely to create resentment and hostility. Employees inevitably seek the means to deal with this and conflict in one form or another may result. The structure of an organization can also encourage conflict if there are unclear boundaries between work and decision-making responsibilities. For example, if it is not clear that the sales department must agree any urgent delivery orders with the production department before they are confirmed then a basis for departmental conflict exists.
- *Procedure*. There are many different forms of procedural mechanism that can be utilized to either prevent conflict from arising or to minimize its potential for disruption and negative effects. Among the more common procedural devices used are:
  - *Operating policy and procedures*. Every organization uses policy and procedural frameworks to guide their functioning. The purpose being to provide clarity of operational responsibility, prevent duplication of effort and to establish ground rules for activity. In large organizations such policies and procedures would be committed to writing in the form of procedures manuals. However, in smaller companies they may be more informal and only reflected in the normal ways of working.
  - *Communication and consultation procedures*. Conflict can arise through a lack of knowledge or the misunderstanding of the actions and intentions of others. Communication and consultation between the various groups that exist within an organization should facilitate an improved level of understanding and knowledge which in turn should reduce the prospect of conflict.
  - *Decision-making practices*. Involvement in decision making can reduce the opportunity for conflict. For example, a department that is involved in taking a decision will have little scope for subsequently engaging in conflict over the outcome. Of course, this assumes that the decision-making process is both rational and fair. In most organizations power and political behaviour is present in decision-making and if not kept in check these can create scope for conflict arising.
  - *Negotiation*. This was a topic covered in detail in Chapter 16 (along with decision making). Negotiation provides a process by which individuals and groups can directly resolve their differences. However, it assumes that all parties are prepared to negotiate and reach a compromise which although less than ideal would be acceptable. Oetzel and Ting-Toomey (2003) demonstrate that the cultural factor referred to as 'face' played a significant part in the approach to negotiation as a conflict resolving strategy.
  - *Discipline and grievance procedures*. Torrington *et al.* (2002) introduce the notion of organizational justice in relation to discipline and grievance procedures (p 532). The employment contract determines the duties and

responsibilities to which both employer and employee commit themselves during the employment relationship. The discipline and grievance procedures are the vehicles through which both parties have the opportunity to ensure satisfaction with the operation of the contract. For example, if an employee arrives late for work the employer is not receiving the input of time required by the contract. One way to redress this conflict is through the application of the disciplinary procedure by management. Equally, if an employee feels that they are being unfairly treated by a manager they have the grievance procedure through which to seek redress for this conflict. The following Employee Perspective (18.2) demonstrates the potential for conflict in relation to anti-smoking policies at work.

EMPLOYEE PERSPECTIVE 18.2

To smoke or not to smoke, that is the question?

Joanne worked in the Brussels-based European regional headquarters of a large multi-national bank. Her employer had been trying to encourage staff to give up smoking and had introduced a range of policies and support facilities to encourage this. For example, smokers had their own rest room where they could go whenever they felt the desperate need to light-up. The occupational health department in the bank also provided a number of support services aimed at encouraging people to quit smoking such as nicotine patches and gum and counselling sessions together with regular health checks.

Joanne was not a smoker, and along with several of her non-smoking colleagues began to notice that some of the smokers with whom they worked disappeared from their work places a number of times each day for periods of up to twenty minutes at a time. Officially employees were allowed two fifteen minute coffee breaks each day, one each in the morning and afternoon. Smokers inevitably took these breaks, along with Joanne and her non-smoking colleagues, however, they also tended to disappear in between these official breaks, usually saying as they left, 'I need a quick smoke, I won't be long'. Soon comments began to circulate about how these unofficial smoke breaks happened just when something urgent needed to be done or the office became busy. Joanne tackled Mike about this one day when she was feeling a little irritated by his third smoke break in as many hours. Mike just laughed and said that she had no idea how difficult it was to be addicted to smoking and she should have some sympathy for him as he was not allowed to smoke at his desk. The company were punishing him enough for being a smoker and the privilege of being allowed to go for a smoke when he needed it was only fair.

Joanne however felt that she and the other non-smokers were being taken advantage of and made to do more than their fair share of the work, whilst the smokers such as Mike were taking advantage of the situation. Joanne and a few of her colleagues spoke to their boss Lydia about the situation. Lydia was sympathetic as she herself had noticed the effects of the smoke breaks on the work of the department. However she said that there was little she could do as it was company policy to help smokers to quit and to offer them as much support as possible in the process. Joanne pointed out that Mike (as an example) showed no signs of wanting to give up smoking and it was unfair that the non-smokers had to do more work as a result. Lydia promised to speak to the smokers about the situation. When she did so Mike and the other smokers just laughed and said that the company allowed them to take smoke breaks when they needed them and that they would continue to do so. Lydia's appeal for them to pull their weight in the department for the sake of fairness and harmony also made no impact on them. Joanne was furious at this response and lack of willingness to be fair among the smokers. She and a few of her colleagues went to their staff association representative and demanded that management be formally made aware of the situation through the raising of a grievance and that the only acceptable solution was that non-smokers be allowed additional breaks to compensate for the extra time away from work that smokers were allowed.

Tasks

1. If you were Joanne would you have reacted as she did? Why or why not?
2. How would you react (and why) to this situation if you were the management of the bank?
3. What would be the fairest solution to this problem for all parties?

– *Industrial relations procedures*. One definition of industrial relations is that it 'is concerned with the formal and informal relationships which exist between employers and trade unions and their members' (Armstrong, 1995, p 667). The same source (p 665) indicates that: 'The primary aims of [industrial relations] policies and procedures are to improve co-operation, to minimize unnecessary conflict, to enable employees to play an appropriate part in decision making, and to keep them informed on matters that concern them'. Most countries in the world recognize the significance of this aspect of organizational activity and provide some form of state sponsored dispute resolution service in order to deal with conflict that may not be resolved otherwise. In Britain this service is provided by the Advisory, Conciliation and Arbitration Service (ACAS) who have at their disposal specialists in dealing with employment based conflict situations.

All these strategies provide an indication of the devices that are available through which to manage conflict but not how to respond to it in behavioural terms. Equally, they do not specifically take into account the labour process or Marxist views on the nature of conflict between capital and labour. Thomas (1976) identified five generic conflict-handling styles based on the balance between two dimensions; the need to satisfy the concerns of the self, and those of the other party. These dimensions he termed self-assertion and co-operation respectively (Figure 18.6).

The five conflict-handling styles identified in Figure 18.6 are:

- *Smoothing or accommodating*. This approach reflects a style that would allow the other party to achieve what they desire from the situation. It is an attempt to maintain unity and harmony though subjugating one's own wishes to those of the other party. This could be as a consequence of indifference towards any personal needs in the situation. However it could also reflect a fear of the consequences of not allowing the other party to have their way.
- *Avoidance*. This style reflects a minimalist approach and the avoidance of any open confrontation or hostility in the situation. It constitutes a desire to ignore

FIGURE 18.6

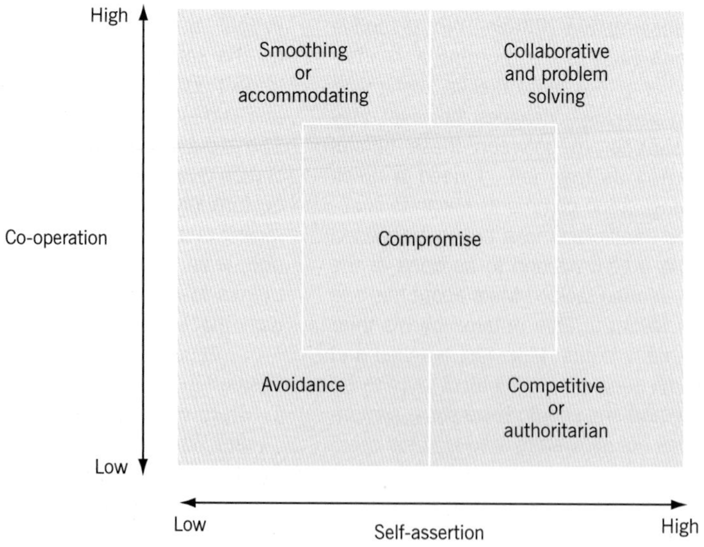

Five conflict-handling styles (*source*: Thomas, K (1976) Conflict management. In Dunnette, MD (ed.) *Handbook of Industrial and Organizational Psychology*, Rand McNally, New York)

the problem and hope that it will go away. Common responses include ignoring the problem, evading specific attempts to deal with it and prolonging the use of any procedural devices invoked to deal with it.

- *Collaboration and problem solving*. This represents an approach to conflict resolution which seeks to maximize the possibility of all parties working effectively together in the search for a viable outcome. It reflects the win–win approach to negotiation and problem solving (Fisher and Ury, 1986). This style gives equal recognition to the need to resolve conflict through meeting the objectives and desires of both parties if a lasting settlement is to be achieved. Leaving one party disadvantaged is a recipe for future conflict.
- *Competitive or authoritarian*. This style reflects the win-at-all-costs approach to conflict resolution. It contains no consideration of the other parties' interests in the situation and simply concentrates on the desires of the 'self' in the process. In negotiation terms it represents the view that anything conceded is something lost.
- *Compromise*. This is the search for the acceptable. It represents the satisficing approach to conflict resolution. It is the search for the acceptable middle ground between two points of view so that no one completely wins or loses.

The style adopted in a particular conflict situation will be a reflection of a number of forces. For example, the preferences of the individuals will play a part. Prior experience will also create a tendency towards a particular style. For example, a trade union which encountered an aggressive style from managers during previous negotiations is more likely to begin meetings using the same style in future. Also in an emergency situation, where little time is available to seek mutually acceptable solutions, it is more likely that a directive/authoritarian style would be adopted.

POLITICS WITHIN ORGANIZATIONS

The quotation from Richard Nixon used in the previous chapter indicated that an effective leader must be able to implement the decisions made as well as know what should be done. In doing so the significance of political perspectives becomes apparent. There are two different perspectives on organizational politics. One views politics as a negative process that actively inhibits the effective running of an organization. The other views politics in a more positive light, considering it as an inevitable part of conflict resolution.

It is not possible to offer a definitive view of all political behaviour, it can only be judged on a case-by-case basis. For example, managers who seek to advance their own careers by engaging in politicking might engage in some unpleasant tactics. However, assuming that they subsequently perform very well as senior managers, how should they be judged? Of course there are a range of criteria that could be used to evaluate this situation and the material on ethics in Chapter 12 has relevance to this. One of the major difficulties in assessing political activity is that it is not possible to know what might have happened in the same situation but under different circumstances.

One of the earliest works on the subject of politics was that of Machiavelli on the subject of serving princes and other rulers. His work titled *The Prince* was written in the period of fifteenth-century Renaissance Italy when politics was frequently a life-or-death business. Essentially, the argument put forward by Machiavelli was that the ends justified the means and anything was acceptable in the pursuit of the protection of the state. In short, it reflected on the mechanisms and strategies necessary to obtain and hold onto power through political activity.

The negative view of politics imposes a definition that considers it to be outside normal practice, used to enhance existing power or to offset the power of another, the purpose being to increase the certainty that a particular and preferred course of action (as defined by the person engaging in politics) will be followed (Mayes and Allen, 1977). The difficulty in practice is that it is not always possible to categorize acts of political behaviour as clearly as this definition might imply. Imagine a situation in which a manager attempts to influence a forthcoming decision by lobbying for support for their preferred plan. Just how far this should go before it would be considered wrong or political is a difficult matter to judge, particularly if the result were beneficial to the organization.

The more positive view of political behaviour regards it as an inevitable part of the need for individuals and groups to function in a collective context. Organizations are run by a mixture of individuals, departments and interest groupings. Whatever the nature of a job it involves interaction with other people and politics is a means of achieving collaboration between them and other sub-units within the organization. Every individual is part of a number of formal and informal groups within the organization. There are professional as well as friendship and departmental groups to identify just some of the more obvious. Each of these levels and collections within the organization will have objectives to achieve and preferences for how the organization should function. For example, the marketing department frequently finds itself in conflict with the production department because of the different perceptions on product design and, how best to prioritize, sequence and process customer orders. However, co-operation is needed between these groups when it comes to production planning and so a political balance must be struck, during which each side will actively seek a greater degree of influence on the process.

Split departments are another form of grouping within organizations that can become embroiled in the political process. The manufacturing division of a company might include a personnel department which is separate from the head office personnel function. It is not uncommon in these situations to find that a divisional personnel department identifies more strongly with the plans and objectives of its manufacturing division than with its professional grouping in head office. This can lead to problems within professional groupings and result in political manoeuvrings in order to influence loyalties and events. As a positive process, politics allows for these groupings to find ways of accommodating each other's perspective in a competitive framework which limits real damage to relationships, the individuals, groups or the organization. Underlying this model of political behaviour is its association with success and failure. Imagine a situation in which a manager presses for a preferred course of action which is then followed but which is not successful. The perceived status if not the actual job of the individual concerned would be severely reduced.

Most managers recognize the dual nature of politics within an organization. They intuitively understand that it contains elements of both good and bad and that it can be an important, indeed inevitable part of the experience of work. Gandz and Murray (1980) carried out a survey among over 400 managers in an attempt to identify how they perceived politics in their working lives. Table 18.1 reflects some of the more interesting findings from this research.

It is clear from the findings illustrated in Table 18.1 that politics is regarded as common, more prevalent in senior positions and linked with success and promotion. It is also regarded as something that individuals undertake if they have no other source of power and that it is the cause of inefficiency and unhappiness. These findings reflect the duality of politics in its positive and negative connotations. These findings have broadly been confirmed by later studies (Ashforth and Lee, 1990; for example).

The positive view of organizational politics suggests that it will be rewarded if it is linked to success for the organization in some way. Imagine that a marketing manager

Statement	Strong or moderate agreement %
(a) The existence of workplace politics is common to most organizations	93.2
(b) Successful executives must be good politicians	89.0
(c) The higher you go in organizations, the more political the climate becomes	76.2
(d) Only organizationally weak people play politics	68.5
(e) Organizations free of politics are happier than those where there is a lot of politics	59.1
(f) You have to be political to get ahead in organizations	69.8
(g) Politics in organizations are detrimental to efficiency	55.1
(h) Top management should try to get rid of politics within the organization	48.6
(i) Politics help organizations function effectively	42.1
(j) Powerful executives don't act politically	15.7

TABLE 18.1 Perceptions about politics among managers (*source*: Gandz, J and Murray, V (1980) The experience of workplace politics, *Academy of Management Journal*, June)

of a company were to set out to change the existing power balance of the organization from one which favoured the production department to one which favoured marketing. The strategies adopted might include attempting to get close to the chief executive, using every opportunity to make adverse comments about problems in production and indicating how competitors were gaining market share through the adoption of marketing strategies. Strengthening alliances with departments that might be favourable to the cause of marketing would also be another likely strategy. As a consequence of these strategies further imagine that a change in the power of the production department occurred as the company became marketing driven. If as a result the company found its reputation, market share and profits rose then it is likely that the company would pay more attention to advice from the marketing department in the future and less attention to the needs of production. That is until the marketing department succumbed to the political activity of other departments or failed to deliver success. This can be reflected in diagrammatic form as in Figure 18.7.

The point made by Figure 18.7 is that from an organizational point of view rewarding political behaviour (if it delivers success) encourages functions to compete in this way without harming the whole. In effect this approach allows for a process of providing an effective match between the needs of the market and the capability of the organization. Political activity that helps the organization ultimately benefits everyone and should be allowed free rein or so it would be argued within this conception of it. It is the harsh world of the market that is the ultimate judge of politics, not the impact on particular individuals or groups. If the market reacts badly to the consequences of political behaviour then one way or another punishment of the perpetrators will follow. This view of political behaviour could be criticized because it ignores the personal and ethical perspectives on why people engage in it. It is clear from the negative perspective on politics that there are individuals who use it for their own ends, rather than for

FIGURE 18.7

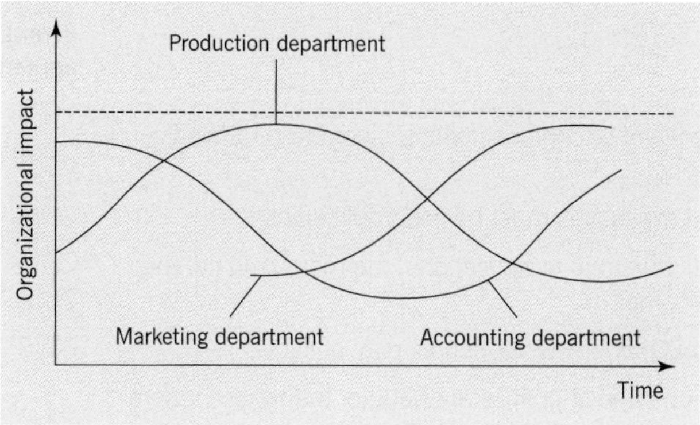

Organizational politics: impact and success

the benefit of the organization. It can be used to help or harm individuals just as it can be a process of attempting to acquire power to enable decisions to be implemented that could be beneficial to everyone.

POLITICAL STRATEGIES

The use of politics within an organizational setting involves adopting one of three strategies. These will be discussed in the subsections that follow.

Offensive strategies

These political strategies are effectively initiating behaviours. They represent the attacking behaviours that are intended to gain advantage over another individual or group. In military terms these are the equivalent of one army going on the offensive and attacking another before it has time to marshal its defences. An example of this form of political behaviour is described in the following Employee Perspective (18.3), in which a senior manager victimized one of his subordinates, also a manager.

Frequently political behaviour contains a high degree of normal or allowable behaviour but applied in ways that produce a particular end result. In the previous Employee Perspective (18.2) it can be reasonably inferred that James' manager wanted rid of him as he was perceived to be a threat to William's position. However, prioritizing work and reallocating resources are all perfectly legitimate practices in running a department. It is the intent behind such actions that indicates a political motive. In reality, James was set up to fail by his boss who used political strategies and company procedures in a way which cloaked the real intention and allowed it to take place.

There is another type of offensive strategy based on the view that: 'If it is not possible to look good oneself, then make the others look bad.' This is an undermining strategy. It covers many different types of behaviour all intended to weaken the position of another individual or group. Examples include making disparaging comments about the target at either a personal or professional level. It can involve recalling with gusto any past mistakes as evidence of continued weakness. This can also include 'whispering campaigns' which involve the spreading of rumour often based on half truth or even total fabrication in order to discredit the target. The spreading of rumour without

EMPLOYEE PERSPECTIVE 18.3 Getting rid of a subordinate

James was an experienced manager and had a particular expertise in personnel management, having worked for a number of years with one of the major consultancy practices in Australia. He was recruited by a large manufacturing company in Adelaide to act as deputy manager to the head of the personnel department (William) in preparation for the head of department's promotion about six months later. It was intended that James would then take over as head of department. The personnel department also had an employee relations manager, training manager and resourcing manager as well as James as the deputy to the head of department. William had not worked in any other organization since leaving university some 15 years earlier.

Shortly after James joined the company it became apparent that it was entering a difficult period and that restructuring was a real possibility. It was at that time that the head of department's behaviour and attitude changed towards a number of people including James. It had become apparent that William was not going to be promoted under the changing circumstances facing the company and therefore James would have to remain as the deputy manager. James and a number of other managers in the department who had expectations (and the capability for promotion) were therefore a potential threat to William's position.

The political campaign included deliberately holding back the start date for jobs that James was to undertake and reallocating staff and other resources away from supporting him. Performance was, however, still to be judged against the original objectives and timescales for the work allocated to James. Eventually, after about seven months, it was time to review James' salary. His manager produced an annual report that claimed that James was underperforming, incompetent and should be downgraded, perhaps even dismissed. Such performance certainly did not justify receiving any pay increase that year. James, having suspected what was to happen, had found another job and so tendered his resignation on the spot.

Tasks

1. How could James have reacted to the situation other than by resigning and what might the consequences of that have been?
2. What does this tell you about political behaviour among managers?

evidence can be a very effective means of undermining other people without the need for evidence to support the assertions.

Defensive strategies

Defensive strategies are those that are not intended to harm others but are destined to prevent harm being done by them. In the previous Employee Perspective James decided not to defend himself as such but to find another job and leave. He could have attempted to fight fire with fire and engage in a range of political behaviours to protect himself. For example, he could have made a number of alliances with more senior managers who may have been prepared to defend him against his boss. He could have set out to undermine the position of William with other managers. James could also have attempted to set his manager up for a fall by deliberately doing something wrong that would directly reflect on his boss. It should not be inferred that defensive political behaviour is weak or less aggressive than the offensive form. It can be just as effective and equally nasty in execution. It is the intention, not the content that differentiates it.

Neutral strategies

This approach to political behaviour reflects a stance that does not actively engage in it for either of the two purposes so far described. It reflects an actively protectionist approach to politics. It is an approach that attempts to keep out of political battles but one which will defend itself if absolutely necessary. It is an appeasing approach to the existence of politics. It is easiest to use offensive politics against a neutral strategy as it takes considerable pressure to begin to force the other party to retaliate. James could be described as adopting a neutral strategy in response to his manager's attack. He did not defend himself other than by attempting to do the best job that he could and by attempting to be considered as a non-threatening subordinate by his manager. In the end rather than take on William in a battle, he side-stepped the problem by leaving the organization.

Some of the tactics that are used politically within an organization are identified in Table 17.1 (in the previous chapter) as influencing tactics. Behaving politically is a process of attempting to influence other people towards a decision, viewpoint or course of action favoured by the initiator. Consequently, many of the strategies adopted can be categorized under the headings in that table. Other researchers have identified categories that are framed slightly differently. For example, Yukl and Falbe (1990) identified the tactics described in Table 18.2.

Tactics	Description
Pressure tactics	The use of demands, threats, or intimidation to convince you to comply with a request or to support a proposal
Upward appeals	Persuading you that the request is approved by higher management or appealing to higher management for assistance in gaining your compliance with the request
Exchange tactics	Making explicit or implicit promises that you will receive rewards or tangible benefits if you comply with a request or support a proposal or reminding you of a prior favour to be reciprocated
Coalition tactics	Seeking the aid of others to persuade you to do something or using the support of others as an argument for you to agree also
Ingratiating tactics	Seeking to get you in a good mood or making you think favourably of the influence agent before asking you to do something
Rational persuasion	Using logical arguments and factual evidence to persuade you that a proposal or request is viable and likely to result in the attainment of task objectives
Inspirational appeals	Making an emotional request or proposal that arouses enthusiasm by appealing to your values and ideals or by increasing your confidence that you can do it
Consultation tactics	Seeking your participation in making a decision or planning how to implement a proposed policy, strategy or change

TABLE 18.2 Political tactics (*adapted from* Yuki, G and Falbe, CM (1990) influence tactics and objectives in upward, downward, and lateral influence attempts *Journal of Applied Psychology*, 75)

USING POLITICAL BEHAVIOUR

It can be seen by comparing Tables 17.1 (influencing tactics) from the previous chapter and 18.2 (political tactics) from this chapter that although the terms used are different, they are broadly similar in flavour and content. These behaviours reflect the purpose of much political behaviour as an intention to influence other people in some way or another. Moorhead and Griffin (1992) bring together the work of a number of other writers in order to identify the main techniques associated with political behaviour. Table 18.3 lists the main techniques identified. The following sections consider each technique briefly.

Control of information

There is a saying that information is power. The ability to determine who has access to what information provides a particularly powerful opportunity to influence events. Decision making requires information. The individual with access to the best range and quality of information is the one most likely to be in a strong position to plan effective strategies for the future. In relation to the stock market, access to inside information on company plans could make anyone privy to it rich as they could either buy or sell shares at the most advantageous price. That is why insider dealing, as it is called, is regarded as a serious offence and market authorities are constantly monitoring market activity in order to detect and prevent it.

Control of communication channels

The control of who has access to whom, who communicates with whom, etc. can significantly influence events. During the 1960s, 1970s and early 1980s most trade unions regarded communication with employees as their prerogative. In situations where particularly militant trade union representatives were present, threats of strike action would be used if managers proposed addressing their workforce directly. In such situations whoever actually communicated with the workforce was likely to put their particular perspective on the message being communicated. This trade union control over the communication channels within organizations is now rare as more joint or parallel processes now exist. However, there are many examples that can be found within the management levels of an organization. Simple

- Controlling information
- Control of communication channels
- Using outside specialists
- Control of the work and/or meetings agenda
- Game playing
- Impression and image management
- Creating coalitions
- Control of decision-making criteria

TABLE 18.3 Political techniques (*adapted from*: Moorhead, G and Griffin RW (1992) *Organizational Behaviour*, 3rd edn, Houghton Mifflin, Boston, MA) examples include who is invited to attend particular meetings and who might be left off the distribution list for a report.

Use of outside specialists

The use of external specialists can be a powerful lever to ensuring that one's point of view is favoured. The selection of a particular consultant or expert is a difficult process as there are many thousands of potential candidates available. It is relatively easy to select one who might be expected (or told) to support a particular point of view as most consultancy practices have an active interest in generating follow-on or repeat business. The careful selection, creation of terms of reference and briefing of consultants ensures that they are able to deliver an appropriate report and recommendations. The question is 'appropriate' from whose perspective? This can reflect a process that adds weight to the position of those insiders who also lean towards that proposed viewpoint, as outside experts are assumed to be independent, and expert. The politically based misuse of outside specialists is something that most consultants are aware of and indeed internal consultants also need to understand if they are to succeed. Writers such as Gilbert (2003) offer guidelines for such people, in managing the potential for political manipulation.

Control over work and meeting agendas

Being able to influence events directly is another useful political technique. The individual who determines the agenda for a meeting determines what can (and frequently of more significance what cannot) be discussed. This allows the direction of decision making to be determined and channelled to the advantage of the person setting the agenda. For example, the role of technology in change programmes can be used politically to the advantage of some groups and the complexity involved in this is reflected in Koch (2001). A related political technique is to accept responsibility for writing the minutes of a meeting. Very few meeting records are verbatim and so the writer has considerable discretion over what is recorded and more importantly how the content of the record should be phrased. Naturally it is usual for the minutes to be verified at a subsequent meeting but a skilled political operator would not find that a particular problem. In the following Employee Perspective (18.4) employee involvement in the decision-making processes is used by a manager for political and control reasons in an attempt to avoid open conflict. Or if a cynical view of the manager's actions were adopted, to make life easier by avoiding responsibility for a difficult decision!

Game playing

There are individuals who appear to enjoy the 'sport' of playing politics just to see what happens and to demonstrate their ability to control events. Employee Perspective 18.3 described the events surrounding James and his eventual departure from the organization. The department manager in that situation was playing games in that he was using established procedure and practice to achieve a particular objective that would not have been officially sanctioned. As an individual he also enjoyed engaging in political activity as he tried similar 'games' with other people and his colleagues. He was however ultimately dismissed when this behaviour became too frequent.

Impression and image management

This represents a less direct approach to politics as it involves creating an image that in turn could be expected to influence events. Simple examples include attempting to

EMPLOYEE PERSPECTIVE 18.4 Sharing out the overtime!

Pam worked in the customer service department of a water utility company in Canada. The department was small, employing eight people all engaged on the same task. The department was the first point of contact for customers with a query over their bill, reporting some problem with water supply such as a burst pipe or contamination in the water, or simply seeking advice on changing their water supply in some way or another. The office was staffed during normal office hours every Monday to Friday. The management of the company wanted to provide an additional service facility out of normal office hours, but was not sure what would provide the most effective option without increasing the number of staff considerably and therefore its costs. Consequently, it wanted to experiment with the provision of additional service availability at different times of the week over a two year period before deciding what to do in the longer term. A schedule of additional customer service department availability slots was drawn up to test out the customer response preferences with the intention of showing this to staff before asking for volunteers to work overtime to fill the available slots.

The manager of the customer service department was called Terri and she was presented with the plan for additional working and asked for her view and who would be the most appropriate people to work the overtime. The plan called for the office to be staffed by one person every Saturday morning for the first five months of the experiment. Terri quickly realized that it would be useful to have the same person working each Saturday as it would provide the basis for an in-depth review of the experience of extra service. She also recognized that each one of the employees in the department, including Pam, would jump at the chance to work overtime as they each needed extra money because of their personal circumstance. Management accepted the need to have the same person working each week and Terri was told to go ahead and organize the overtime. However, the dilemma between one person working all the overtime for five months and every employee wanting the additional money presented Terri with a problem.

Terri recognized that by simply nominating one person to work overtime for the following five months conflict would be likely, so she tried to think of how this could be avoided. Whilst retaining the constraint that it had to be the same person each week Terri hit upon what she thought was a good idea. She called Pam and her colleagues into a meeting and told them about the need for the office to be staffed by one person every Saturday morning and that it had to be the same person each week. She also explained that as every employee had a need for the extra money that would be earned management had thought that it would be best if the employees decided among themselves who should work the overtime. Terri then told the employees to talk about the issues among themselves and decide who would work the extra Saturday morning each week. Once everyone had agreed amongst themselves who it should be they should give the name to Terri who would then make appropriate arrangements to start the overtime the following week.

Tasks

1. If you were Pam how would you react to this requirement and why?
2. As an employee in this situation on what basis would you seek to decide who worked the overtime and why?
3. Does this attempt to share out the overtime by management reflect real employee involvement in decision making? Or is it simply an attempt to avoid management responsibility for a difficult decision which would inevitably cause conflict and resentment among employees? Justify your views.
4. What would you have done in this situation if you were Terri and why?

become associated with successful projects or to distance oneself from failing ones. It is not unusual for a manager to sit on the sidelines of a particular programme of work and to suddenly seek to take a high profile near to completion when success is more certain. Claiming major involvement in particular projects is another common example of overstating reality in order to enhance one's reputation. Of course, this must be done carefully as a number of people will know the truth about such claims. Once exposed as false claims they can undermine every other claim made by that individual. Bromley (1993) provides an analysis of many aspects of impression management which collectively demonstrate the complexity of these psychological constructs.

Creating coalitions

Political alliances are another means of achieving desired objectives. Imagine a situation in which a personnel manager wishes to introduce a new payment system into a company. The sales manager may not see any benefit or problems with such a scheme and so may be neutral towards it. The production manager may be in favour of the new scheme if higher productivity and reduced cost is a likely result. The finance director may be openly hostile towards the idea as it would create additional work for his department. The employees may also be against the idea because higher productivity could result in job losses and having to work harder. Clearly the personnel manager needs to ensure that all the managers are supportive of the plan before attempting to convince the employees of its merits. The finance director is presumably more senior to the other managers and as a result would carry 'more weight' in collective decision-making. Perhaps if the sales manager could be persuaded actively to support the scheme and ways could be found to lessen the burden on the finance department then open hostility might be reduced. The personnel manager would probably begin to lobby the sales manager for support, perhaps using the argument that the higher productivity achieved would benefit the sales department through pricing and delivery benefits. This together with a scheme redesign to reduce administrative requirements might be enough to sway the finance director to either support the scheme, or at least not reject it.

Taken to an extreme this approach to political behaviour can be little more than 'horse trading'. This approach to politics attempts to operate on the basis of buying cooperation for past favours or seeking support in return for promises of future help on matters of value to the courted individual. At an organizational level this approach reflects the cartel approach to fixing markets in favour of particular suppliers.

Control over decision-making criteria

It is sometimes possible for a manager to set down the criteria against which decisions will be made and in so doing they do not have to be directly involved in order to influence the outcome. It is not uncommon for industrial relations specialists facing the annual negotiation round with the trade unions to initially hold meetings with other managers to determine the negotiating strategy. In doing so it could be that a chief executive would set out in very clear terms what they expect to happen and in effect write the script for the negotiators. Clearly, in this situation very little scope is available to the negotiation team to respond creatively to the dynamics of the situation and create a settlement acceptable to all sides. The 'dead-hand' of the chief executive rests over the situation and effectively controls events in absentia. In a more general context such approaches can allow a leader to claim non-involvement in a situation, distancing themselves from events both physically and psychologically while in reality retaining control.

MANAGING POLITICAL BEHAVIOUR

The degree to which it is possible to manage political behaviour in others is difficult to specify. It depends on so many factors. For example, the style of management within the organization can determine the level and volume of politicking that takes place. The personality of individuals is also likely to influence their predisposition for playing games and other forms of politics. The skill level and networks of the individuals concerned can also influence events. Indeed Butcher and Clarke (1999) make the point that political activity is central to making things happen in a change process and so should be taught as a mainstream management discipline.

Managers are inevitably in competition with each other for resources and power. There are never enough resources to meet every possible demand within an organization. Every manager would like to feel that they could make a positive contribution to the organization given a completely free hand in spending unlimited amounts of money. However, it is just not possible for any organization to be in that position and therefore a process of rationing must exist. Rationing implies deciding between competing options for allocating scarce resources and finding ways to prioritize alternative options. This creates a context where managers must justify proposed actions and find ways to gain support for their plans. Politicking can be used to influence these processes and increase the probability of success. Browning and James (2003) offer general advice on how to deal with and manage politics in an organization from the two different perspectives of getting involved and trying to stay above it all. They provide an illuminating array of techniques and practices that could be followed with more or less light hearted or serious enthusiasm.

In order to attempt to control and minimize the harmful effects associated with politics it is necessary to find ways to encourage competition without allowing hidden agendas to flourish. Specifying in advance how decisions will be made and by not allowing power to become a means of acquiring resources are just some of the ways that this can be encouraged. By separating the evaluation of resource allocation from issues associated with performance evaluation and promotion some control of politics can also be achieved. The sending of very clear signals that politicking will not be tolerated by dealing severely with obvious cases and encouraging examples to be openly discussed are other means of minimizing its impact. Browning (2003b) suggests ten ways to manage the office politics (Table 18.4).

CONFLICT AND ORGANIZATIONAL POLITICS: AN APPLIED PERSPECTIVE

In the previous chapter it was pointed out that Braverman (1974) considered that the organizational history of the twentieth century could be described in terms of

1. Be transparent in your actions
2. Communicate with all sides
3. Network extensively
4. Keep well informed
5. Identify and watch the politicians
6. Never get personal
7. Maintain good upwards contacts
8. Anticipate and manage the others' reactions
9. Be clearly good at your job
10. Get it in writing

TABLE 18.4 Ten tips for managing the office politics

increasing management control and the potential for conflict and alienation that flowed from that situation. Workers are increasingly treated as just one of the resources available to organizations and consequently subject to management attempts at manipulation in the search for ever higher cost effective operations. It is against that background that the concept of resistance is an important counterbalance to the domination of capital. However, it is also interesting to remember that managers also are workers, they are not the real owners of capital, and as such are subjected to many of the same constraints as workers. They are of course in a privileged position and, acting *in loco-parentis* for the absent owners, are able to pass on down the line attempts to achieve ever tighter control, perpetuating the opportunity for power, conflict and politics to function within an organization. Against this backdrop much management activity over the past few years has been an attempt to reframe organizational reality for employees so that effective (and tighter) control can be exercised but in ways that minimize the risk and consequences of conflict.

Conflict is regarded by most managers as something to be avoided within their organization. It is thought to be a distraction; a sign of dissension or disloyalty; an indication that their 'message' is not getting through; even an indication that their capabilities as a manager are being challenged or questioned. It is also thought by many managers to be a reflection of the natural attitudes of workers to work and the role of management. The following Employee Perspective (18.5) is an apocryphal story but is one which invariably resonates with the managers who keep this and its many variations alive. Many managers think that the worker opinion represented is how most, if not all, workers think. Consequently for them the risk of conflict is ever present as they try to force productivity, quality and commitment from what they regard as an intransigent, unwilling and lazy workforce.

Conversely, some workers regard managers as the enemy and as deliberately seeking to take advantage at any opportunity. Consequently a lack of trust can exist and form fertile ground for conflict to erupt. Many practising managers and writers would subscribe to the pluralist or unitarist perspective on conflict discussed earlier. They would argue that attempts at employee involvement and participation over recent years have represented attempts to move away from what has been described as the old-style confrontational basis to the employment relationship. Cynics might argue that such approaches do not represent a new paradigm in management. They simply represent a recognition that the social conditions within which work is carried out have changed and that managers have found it necessary to soften their approach in

EMPLOYEE PERSPECTIVE 18.5 How many days do I have to work?

This story results from the visit of chairman of the then British Coal Board to a coal mine in the north-east of England in the early 1960s. The particular coal mine visited had a high absence level even by industry standards and the chairman asked one miner why he only worked four days each week. The answer came back without hesitation: 'Because I can't earn enough money in three days!'

Tasks

1. Was the miner simply being cheeky when he made his reply to the chairman; was he being disloyal; or was he potentially expressing a valid point of view in suggesting that people should be able to work as many days as they felt earned them as much money as they needed? Justify your views.
2. Could a company function effectively if employees chose freely how many days they worked, their working hours and times of work each week? Discuss some of the practical issues that this possibility raises as well as the implications for power, control, politics and conflict.

order to find more convenient ways to continue to enact the ongoing struggle between capital and labour.

The use of political behaviour can enhance the relative level of power and influence held by an individual or group, thereby increasing their status and perhaps their ability to exercise control and avoid conflict. Or alternatively, increased power relative to an adversary might provide a basis for winning if conflict actually erupts into hostility, strikes or other industrial action. Of course, resistance reflects another major concept that forms part of the latent conflict within an organization. As indicated in the earlier discussion it can find expression in many ways; going slow, withholding effort and sabotage all reflecting ways; that workers can engage in forms of conflict without open hostility.

Politics, by way of contrast, can be seen as the process by which power is shared among a number of interested groups and individuals. At an organizational level it can provide a mechanism for allowing the relative power of the various departments and subsidiary companies to rise and fall without adversely affecting the structure and performance of the overall organization. It is, however, possible for political behaviour to be misused to the personal advantage of those perpetrating it. In such situations it is not uncommon to find the existence of special interest groups that are informal, perhaps temporary, but definitely outside the formal organizational framework.

Cliques are one form of group whose prime motivation is the defence of the members against the interests of other groups and individuals. Trade unions exist to advance and protect the interests of members against the inevitable power imbalance in the employment relationship. Hau and Tung (2003) demonstrate the need for managers to deal carefully with employee groups when changes which may break the existing *psychological contract* are being planned if conflict is to be avoided. Another example would be a coffee-break group that attempted to provide member support against the behaviour of a dictatorial and inconsistent boss. **Cabals** are another form of group that attempt to take the initiative within an organization to the positive advantage of its members (Burns, 1955). The phrase 'Young Turks' is frequently used to describe the activities of young executives who attempt to force the organization to adopt policies supportive of their wishes. In that sense it represents a proactive approach to the acquisition and use of power through political means.

Cabal
An informal group that attempts to push views supported by members to enhance their status and position.

Political behaviour is encouraged to exist in situations where the formal roles and authority are unclear. If the designated roles and lines of authority are clearly specified then it is easy for breaches and deviations to be identified. In addition it is also easy to appeal to the formal structural mechanisms as ways of combating the politicking. There are a number of issues that emerge from this view of political behaviour and organizational informality or lack of clarity. A number of new structural forms of organization attempt to take out the formality and rigidity of structure originating from bureaucracy. The informality and lack of clear role definition implied by these recent innovations could provide the very basis on which political behaviour flourishes. It is possible that without very clear attempts to manage out these aspects of organizational activity they could offset the advantages available through the informality and ability to respond rapidly to market conditions. There are also managerial benefits from being political. Over the past few years organizations have been delayering and downsizing, all of which impacts directly on the number of management jobs available. This has had a major impact on management careers and job opportunity. No longer can managers expect to be protected from the harsh realities that have faced many other occupational groups. As a consequence they find it necessary to take a more active role in managing their own careers and survival. This can lead to political behaviour as a means of influencing decisions about job security and career development. Being considered a good employee is now as important for every manager as it is for every other employee. Politics can be used to enhance the probability of success by tipping the balance one way rather than another. Trust and loyalty between employer and employee has always been a valued part of the employment relationship and yet in the emerging world of personal careers writers such as Charles Heckscher suggest that it should be eliminated. This view is outlined in Management in Action 18.4.

There is also a link between the type of organization and the form that politics takes within it. For example, in bureaucratic organizations it is the audit functions that enjoy a high degree of power and influence. The predominance of rules and procedures encourages the policing role in an attempt to prevent fraud. In organic types of organization it is the advisory functions that have most power as they attempt to maintain consistency of operation across a range of relatively segregated operating units. In this type of situation the organizational politics would tend to be aimed at holding or changing the power balance between line and staff functions.

MANAGEMENT IN ACTION 18.4 The importance of stamping out loyalty

In a book review of *White Collar Blues: Management Loyalties in an Age of Corporate Restructuring* by Charles Heckscher (1995), published by HarperCollins, Jackson identifies some interesting ideas. In the USA, middle managers account for 8 per cent of the workforce, yet between 1988 and 1993 they accounted for 19 per cent of the job losses. The old middle-class ethos of commitment to the organization was based on a two-way commitment. In return for security, managers worked extra hours, took risks and allowed inroads into their personal lives. Heckscher suggests (as have others) that this two-way commitment has been broken by employers and so they cannot expect middle managers to continue to support a one-sided deal.

The existence of communal trust and loyalty between the members of an organization developed as a means of allowing the bureaucratic forms of organization to function effectively. However, Heckscher argues that this is now too rigid and does not allow change to happen at the necessary rate. Heckscher goes on to argue that it should not be a question of how to regain the loyalty of middle managers, but how to stamp it out once and for all. While managers cling to the debris of the old order, fundamental change cannot happen and continuous decline becomes inevitable. This creates a cycle of yet more drudgery, further resentment and less likelihood that change will be successful.

Some of Heckscher's work has revealed that change was least successful in organizations in which loyalty was strongest and managers were most overworked. Conversely, change was most effective in those organizations in which the level of loyalty was the weakest. A different form of loyalty is proposed by Heckscher, that of loyalty not to the organization, but to the project on which the individual is working. This may last for three to five years and then the individual moves on to another project, perhaps even to a different company.

There are, of course, many implications of this form of working. Individuals would have to accept greater levels of responsibility for their own career, job networking and training. Equally, organizational issues such as pension portability and commitment to making individuals more marketable on a wider scale would need to be introduced. But for those organizations and individuals who have been able to make this change the benefits in being more relaxed and confident about the future and their place in it are available.

Adapted from: Jackson, T (1995) The importance of stamping out loyalty, *Financial Times*, 30 March, p 18.

Stop ↔ Consider

Reflect on the implications of the views of Heckscher on the nature and form of loyalty as it should be developed. What implications might this approach to loyalty have for conflict and political activity within organizations? How could this be managed effectively?

CONCLUSIONS

This chapter has attempted to consider the related topics of conflict and politics. These subjects have strong links with negotiation, power and control which were introduced in previous chapters. Both conflict and politics can be argued to be endemic to organizational life. There are also individuals who introduce an element of game playing intended to enhance their power base and as a means of making work more interesting. Politics and conflict can also introduce a source of fun and enjoyment to the observers of this behaviour in others. However, there is a danger of trivializing these concepts if this aspect is overplayed. Being the subject of political activity is no joke for most people and conflict can only result in a dissipating effect on corporate and individual performance. The difficulty is that, following the Marxist and labour process perspectives, and much common experience, they are ever present within the employment situation.

Now to summarize this chapter in terms of the relevant learning objectives:

- **Understand the different perspectives on the concept of conflict.** The major perspectives on conflict introduced in this chapter were pluralist, unitarist and Marxist. The pluralist perspective holds that different groups exist within an organization and their interests and objectives inevitably conflict on occasion. However all parties recognize that compromise is necessary if their objectives are to have any chance of even partial achievement. The unitarist perspective holds that different groups exist but that an ultimate loyalty to the larger collective group to which they all belong takes precedence, and so it is that group's perspective that determines the nature of any compromise or solution to the conflict. The Marxist tradition holds that conflict within an organization is an inevitable reaction to the nature of capitalism and the exploitation of labour that exists within that form of political economy. It also holds that such conflict is to be welcomed in the pursuit of the demise of capitalism and the emergence of a socialist based political economy involving public ownership of all resources.
- **Describe the sources of conflict within an organization.** There are several major sources of conflict that exist which arise between individuals and groups within an organization. Intrapersonal conflict involves the inevitable conflict that arises within each individual over matters such as how much work to do for their employer. Interpersonal conflict describes the conflict that arises between individuals, perhaps as a consequence of personality clashes. Intragroup conflict is a special form of interpersonal conflict in that it emerges among the members of a particular group. For example the conflicts that might arise over what the objectives of a particular group should be. Intergroup conflict reflects the conflict that can arise between groups. For example, management might experience conflict with the employee group within a company over the annual pay award. Intraorganizational conflict emerges within an organization and reflects situations in which the groups, departments and individuals are fighting each other in some way or another. Effectively it represents the breakdown of order and control within the organization. Interorganizational conflict represents the expressions of conflict that can arise between organizations. In a free market economy, organizations are in competition with each other for sales and market share. This inevitably puts them in conflict with each other, but such activity is usually described as marketing. However it can sometimes lead to other forms of conflict which can result in legal action or open hostility.
- **Explain the major conflict handling strategies used within organizations.** The main conflict handling strategies available within organizations include the following. Clarity and openness in making sure that everyone knows what is going on within the organization and why. The signals and messages that managers send out to employees is another area that can significantly reduce the level of potential conflict. By rewarding appropriate behaviour and not responding to threats and argument, management make clear what it values and how it operates. The use of training in an organization can help to reinforce the appropriate

perspectives of management and what is valued. This can contribute to employees being clear about what is going on within the organization, but it also assists with socialization processes and encourages employees to deliver appropriate attitudes and behaviours in order to gain development opportunity. The management style and organization structure can also contribute to or hinder the likelihood of conflict. An autocratic style of management or an ineffective structure will create operational problems and employees will react negatively probably causing conflict. Procedures can contribute to the management of conflict by helping to institutionalize the means of dealing with it or of minimizing the risk of its emergence. Figure 18.6 also identifies a number of conflict handling styles with are further described in the associated text and which have relevance in this context.

- **Outline the concept of organizational politics.** Organizational politics represents one of the ways in which power can be obtained and subsequently retained. It reflects particular types of activity intended to influence events and make particular occurrences more or less likely to occur. In an organizational context it can be described as having either positive or negative connotations. For example, it can be seen in terms of the means though which power, control and conflict can be managed in order to bring about particular results. If as a consequence of such behaviours the result is beneficial for the organization and individuals within it then it is likely that the individuals engaging in it will be rewarded. If however it does not bring benefit then it is likely that they will be punished, if through no other sanction than losing influence. So in positive terms politics can be viewed as the means that allows each function or specialism to seek to maximise its contribution and influence in the constant dynamic of the adaptation of the organization to its environment. In its negative guise politics is viewed as outside normal and acceptable practice and as such something that can only create difficulty and conflict within the organization. This view sees politics as something to be avoided and driven out of an organization in the search for ever more effective operational activity. The negative view of politics regards it as something that specific people engage in when they are seeking to advance their own position at the expense of others, or to manipulate some particular situation supportive of their intended objective. The problem in practice is that politics can contain elements of both positive and negative perspectives at the same time. It is not always easy to judge what is happening in any specific situation. People who engage in political behaviour are unlikely to admit that they are doing so for personal reasons and will inevitably justify their actions in terms of organizational benefit. The relevant sections in the chapter also discuss the offensive, defensive and neutral strategies that can be adopted with regard to political activity. The chapter also discusses a number of devices such as the control of information and the use of outside specialists that can be used politically within an organization.

- **Discuss how political behaviour can be managed within an organization.** The management of political behaviour within an organization is difficult as it involves such a fundamental part of much management and interpersonal activity. For example managers are in competition with each other for resources and the ability to influence organizational direction and functioning. That very competition if not appropriately channelled and managed can lead to political behaviour being used in a negative way in order to attempt to shape decisions. Consequently, the decision making processes in an organization need to be clear and open so that hidden agendas and behind the scenes activity is minimized and brought out into the open. In essence the management of politics requires that its practice is not rewarded and that when discovered it is punished if it is shown to have been used negatively. Some of the earlier approaches to handling conflict and power within an organization are also relevant to the management of political behaviour.

DISCUSSION QUESTIONS

1. Discuss the pluralist, unitarist and Marxist perspectives on conflict, using examples from organizations with which you are familiar to illustrate your answer.
2. What are the major forms of conflict that might be expected to arise in a group context? How do these differ from individual expressions of conflict?
3. Managers must compete for scarce resources. Political behaviour can influence decisions. In what ways might it be possible to encourage competition while minimizing the potentially harmful effects of political behaviour?
4. What does the term resistance mean and how does it relate to the concepts of power, control and conflict? Illustrate your ideas with examples from organizations with which you are familiar.
5. Describe the various sources of conflict that exist within an organizational context. To what extent can any of them be eliminated?
6. Outline some of the consequences that might be expected to arise from the existence of conflict, illustrating them where appropriate with examples from your experience.
7. Identify and provide an analysis of the procedural devices that can be used to minimize and resolve conflict within an organization.
8. 'Conflict management represents the biggest challenge for every manager.' To what extent and why do you agree with this statement?
9. Outline the labour process theory and explain how it can inform an understanding of the concept of conflict within an organizational context.
10. 'Politics is a process which cannot be eliminated from an organization therefore it should be ignored in running a business.' Discuss this statement.

CASE STUDY Not paying the wages and conflict

Lowsling was a small company based in a small market town in the North of England. It had been in existence for about four years and made one-trip bags for the transport of sand, gravel and fertilizer-type raw materials used in the construction, farming and related industries. Each of the bags was designed to hold a maximum of 1000Kg of material and to be capable of being lifted by fork-lift truck when full. The design of the product had been developed by the owners of the business who had then set up a small factory to make the products. The business had been very successful and had grown rapidly over the four years of its existence. At the time of the case study it employed 100 people in the factory and twelve people in the administrative, sales and management areas.

The company had always had a difficult financial time in terms of cashflow and the quality of management had never been high in terms of leadership or its ability to control the business. Employees generally did as they thought best with little or no supervision or direction from managers. The owners of the business were more interested in the technical aspects of the design of the product, and in looking for new markets and increased sales volume than in running the factory efficiently. The three production supervisors essentially organized things as they thought appropriate, for example they scheduled work on the basis of the easy jobs first. The production manager was also in charge of maintenance and had very little idea of either activity, but being the brother-in-law of the chief executive his position was relatively secure. The workforce was not highly paid, but the working atmosphere was generally good and people were not expected to work too hard and they could work overtime on a frequent basis to supplement their wages. The payment system was based on individual piecework, in which a bonus was paid over and above the basic wage for each unit of production produced. The price for each job was negotiated between the workers' representatives and the production manager. Any job which did not have an agreed price paid bonus based on the average bonus earnings of the worker over the past three months for the time spent on that particular job. Not surprisingly, this system had been compromised over the time it had been in place and so although the total wages paid were not high, the amount of work done was also relatively low.

Orders were frequently late in being delivered and high levels of overtime became the norm. Attempts by the production manager to negotiate reasonable prices for jobs were met with strong resistance and threats of conflict. Similar reactions resulted when attempts were made to deal with the large number of jobs which attracted average earnings. People would try and find out what jobs were being planned in order to be able to keep their average pay high and then they tried to be allocated jobs which required average earnings to be applied which they then took a long time to produce. Naturally in this environment the supervisors held considerable power and they took advantage of the situation to enhance their own position and earnings. For example, one supervisor was known to auction off jobs which were regarded as 'good' bonus earners by shop-floor employees. In other words he was taking bribes from employees for allocating jobs. Having said all of that the factory was regarded as a happy place to work and one which produced a reasonable wage for a reasonable amount of work. Labour turnover was low and absence levels average for the area.

The company could best be described as one in which a game of 'cat and mouse' was constantly played out between the various groups and individuals that worked in it. Management would occasionally try and regain the initiative over some aspect of operational activity, only to have this strongly resisted by one group or another. The workers would constantly try and push the boundaries of what they could get away with only to find that if they went too far they would meet resistance from management. It was the difficulties from the tight company cashflow that ultimately caused most problems.

Wages were paid in cash to shop floor workers every Friday for the previous week's work. Time sheets would be filled in every day and passed back to the wages office by the supervisors, who were supposed to check and authorize the information on them for each worker. On a Monday morning the task of collating all the previous week's wages information was undertaken and the wage bill worked out by Tuesday afternoon. This was a tight schedule as all queries had to be resolved by then for the wages to be paid correctly on the following Friday. On the Wednesday morning a cheque would be made out for the total wages bill and this would be taken to the bank for collection. The cash would be brought back to the factory and the task of making up individual wage packets would begin. The individual wage packets would be collected by employees when they finished work on the Friday afternoon.

Within Lowsling cashflow was always a difficult balance to manage and there was often just enough money in the bank to be able to pay the wages. Whilst the employees were not aware of this problem, occasionally they were made aware of the parlous financial position of the company in the most direct manner. Occasionally they did not get paid on a Friday! This did not happen often, perhaps only once every three months, and when it did the chief executive always came down into the factory late on a Friday and told the workforce about it, apologizing and saying that it would all be sorted out on Monday. Invariably the employees were paid on the Tuesday, usually with a few extra pounds in the packet to 'compensate' them for the problem. However, although unusual this became such a regular occurrence that staff began to look out for which senior managers were at work on a Wednesday morning.

The banking arrangements for the company required that cheques be signed by the two directors of the company before they could be cashed. There were in practice only two directors, the chief executive and the finance director. So if one of these people was absent then no cheques could be signed or cashed. For most purposes this was not critical as invoices were cleared on set days each month when both people were always around, and if one or other was going to be away arrangements could be made to sign the cheques early. However, this practice was not followed with regard to the wages cheque. If one or other director was not at work then the cheque was not completed or sent to the bank for cashing. Equally the directors would not sign the blank cheque early if they were going to be absent on the Wednesday as the sum of money involved was comparatively large and so they argued that close control was needed.

Over time the directors began to realize that delaying paying the wages could be a useful way of managing the cashflow more effectively and so the incidence of late payment began to rise. It did not rise significantly but became about once every ten weeks rather than every three months. The chief executive also began to resent the abuse that he had to take every time that he went onto the shop floor to break the bad news and so he started to delegate the task to the production manager. Staff gave him an even harder time as they did not really respect him as a manager and recognized that being the brother-in-law of the chief executive he held his job because of family connections rather than ability. Consequently, the production manager missed some occasions of telling the staff which meant that it was the wages office that had to tell staff that no pay was available. This made matters deteriorate even more; complaints began to surface and morale and working atmosphere dropped significantly. That was when the workforce began to pay more attention to whether the directors were at work on a Wednesday morning. Working relationships began to deteriorate, quality began to suffer and orders were further delayed. People began to join a trade union to try and fight management over a range of problems that had become the focus of attention in the working arrangements and the company began to experience higher labour turnover.

Tasks

1. Analyze this case using the material included in this chapter on conflict and organizational politics.
2. What are the key problems and how might they be tackled assuming that the position of the parties is as indicated at the conclusion of the case?
3. Given that the basic arrangements, personalities and financial position of the company cannot be changed, could the deterioration in the state of the company have been prevented, and if so how?

FURTHER READING

Bazerman, MH (ed.) (2004) *Negotiation, Decision Making and Conflict Management*, Edward Elgar, Cheltenham. A three volume set that explores themes from a number of significant publications covering these themes over the past fifty years.

Clark, H, Chandler, J and Barry, J (1994) *Organization and Identities: Text and Readings in Organizational Behaviour*, International Thomson Business Press, London. Contains a broad range of original articles on relevant material themes and from significant writers referred to in this and other textbooks on management and organizations.

Cooper, C, Einarsen, S, Hoel, H and Zapf, D (eds) (2002) *Bullying and Emotional Abuse in the Workplace: International Perspectives in Research and Practice*, Taylor and Francis, London. This text looks at one aspect of politics and conflict which is also relevant to power and control, that of bullying at work. The edited work considers the research approach in Europe which emphasizes the 'mobbing' or 'bullying' approach and also that emerging in the USA, which emphasizes 'emotional abuse' and 'mistreatment' perspectives.

Edelmann, RJ (1993) *Interpersonal Conflicts at Work*, British Psychological Society, Leicester. This small book is intended to help the reader to understand the causes of a range of interpersonal conflicts that can arise in a work setting and to be able to develop strategies to cope with them more effectively.

Heller, R (1985) *The Naked Manager: Games Executives Play*, McGraw-Hill, New York. Considers a broad range of the games that are played within organizations. They are not directly political in the negative sense of the term. Nevertheless it is possible to gain a flavour of the complexity and subtlety of much of this activity.

Jay, A (1987) *Management and Machiavelli*, revised edn, Hutchinson Business, London. A humorous text which considers many aspects associated with power and authority in management. It does not take Machiavelli's work specifically as its basis, but his spirit is evident. A translation of Machiavelli's original work, which is very accessible and available as a 1981 Penguin book, is also well worth reading.

Kolb, DM and Bartunek, JM (eds) (1992) *Hidden Conflict in Organizations: Uncovering Behind-the-Scenes Disputes*, Sage, Newbury Park, CA. This book provides an insight into a wide range of dispute and conflict situations that are not at first glance formally part of organizational life. The book surfaces many otherwise hidden or cloaked features of conflict and its resolution.

Pascale, RT (1991) *Managing on the Edge: How Successful Companies Use Conflict to Stay Ahead*, Penguin, London. This book takes the view that conflict is an aspect of human behaviour which is to be welcomed within an organizational setting. It encourages a healthy tension between the individuals and functional groupings which can be used to the benefit of the business through the synergy generated.

Vigoda-Gadot, E (2003) *How Political Dynamics affect Employee Performance in Modern Worksites*, Edward Elgar, Cheltenham. This text reviews a broad spectrum of perspectives on organizational politics in order to identify the impact of employee performance in the broadest sense of the term.

COMPANION WEBSITE

Online teaching and learning resources:

Visit the companion website for Organizational Behaviour and Management 3rd edition at: *http://www.thomsonlearning.co.uk/businessandmanagement/martin3* to find valuable further teaching and learning material:

Refer to page 35 for full details.

CHAPTER 19

Organizational development and change

LEARNING OBJECTIVES

After studying the chapter content and working through the associated Management in Action panels, Employee Perspectives, Discussion Questions and Case Study, you should be able to:

- **Describe the major change models available and explain how they contribute to the management of it.**
- **Explain the approach and value of organizational development (OD) as a change strategy.**
- **Appreciate why people frequently resist change.**
- **Discuss the forces acting on an organization which push for change to be undertaken.**
- **Detail what is meant by term 'change agent' in relation to change management.**

INTRODUCTION

The world in which we live is changing, as are the organizations within which we work, and the jobs that we undertake. The world has always changed and people, plants and animals have either evolved and adapted to new environmental circumstances, or died out if they could not. However, the rate of change that is being experienced now is much greater than ever before. Table 19.1 has been extracted from Pritchett (1996) to demonstrate this rate of change together with some of the ways in which it can influence the working environment.

Given that change has always existed and that it requires adaptation among those exposed to it, it should be a feature of life that humans can easily cope with. However, this does not appear to be the case. Resistance and reluctance to adapt to change appear to be a common reaction among adult human beings within an organizational environment. There would appear to be a desire, if not a predisposition, among significant numbers of humans to remain with the familiar and to avoid the challenge and uncertainty that accompanies change. Predictability in life appears to be a valued condition for many people. There are likely to be many reasons underlying this response. It is, however, a different reaction from that evident among young children. Young children are very keen to learn and acquire new skills and, once learned, they become desperate to demonstrate them to adults who will probably applaud and positively reward such behaviour. For example, consider the joy and pleasure on a child's face when it has just learned to walk and it stumbles about seeking (and achieving) the attention of its parents and other adults. This willingness to change current behaviour capabilities in children is something that seems to disappear in many adults or at least among people who work in organizations.

It is interesting to contemplate why this reluctance to change emerges. Is it 'taught out' of people as a result of formal education; or because of the natural slowing of the cognitive processes underlying learning; or as a result of the organizational experiences that people encounter? Change in an organizational context for most people invariably means having to take on more work, experiencing additional stress or even losing one's job, hardly positive reward for accepting change. It is because of the dilemma created by the requirement to change within an organization and a general reluctance to willingly embrace it by people that managers must pay special attention to the subject.

Organization development (OD) as an approach to dealing with change incorporates aspects of culture, working atmosphere, employee commitment, conflict, power, politics and particular change techniques in seeking to achieve organizational effectiveness for all members and stakeholders. Many of these themes have already been introduced in earlier chapters and so will not be fully developed here. There are however a number of change models and approaches to OD that need to be explored in order to understand it as part of the change processes frequently encountered within organizations. The values that the members of any organization hold is an important aspect of its culture and Arnold (2003) sets out to demonstrate how one Australian hospital sought to focus on its distinctive values, those that would most support employee commitment to the changed organization, as part of the change process itself.

PRESSURE FOR CHANGE

For organizations there are particular events and experiences that are the instigators of change. Some of these forces arise from outside the organization and some from inside it. These forces can be changes brought about by the organization or events to which the organization must respond by making changes. However, it is somewhat misleading to talk of organizations in this context, because organizations as such cannot do anything. It is the managers who run organizations who must determine the courses of action to be followed. Management in Action 19.1 illustrates that

1. The number of mobile telephones sold was zero in 1982 and 4 million in 1995
2. The cost of computing power drops approximately 30% every year and microchips are doubling in performance power every 18 months
3. The first industrial robot was introduced during the 1960s. By 1982 there were approximately 32,000 in use in the USA. Today there are over 20 million
4. Of the largest 100 UK companies in 1965 only 32 remained on that list in 1995
5. In 1954, 45% of UK employees worked in manufacturing. Now it accounts for less than 22%.

TABLE 19.1 Five changes over recent years (*source*: Pritchett, P (1994) *The Employee Handbook of New Work Habits for a Radically Changing World*, Pritchett & Associates, Washington, Tyne and Wear)

organizational change can originate from any or all of the political, cultural and fashion connotations of management.

Change within an organization can affect many different aspects of it. For example an individual might find that a change to the technology used might impact on their traditional methods of work or might eliminate the need for their job altogether. Change can affect a group through, say, the introduction of teamwork. Change could also affect the entire organization. For example, the development and introduction of a new product range might involve the building of a new factory in a location with cheaper labour and the reallocation of work across existing locations, as well as structural and other changes to the organization.

There are also changes that impact on society and which in turn cascade back into organizations. For example, the taxation levels applied to products such as alcohol and tobacco by governments are often designed to influence consumption rates in a downwards direction. Consequently, the organizations producing these products experience reductions in business. Also, with products such as tobacco there is an attempt to influence the health of the population through taxation levels and so impact on the need for public health provision and other government spending. This also impacts on the public sector in a variety of ways.

There is another factor to be taken into account when considering the nature of, and complexity inherent in, change. That is the occurrence of random or chance factors. For example, in some parts of the world earthquakes and storms are natural hazards occurring on an annual basis. An earthquake could physically destroy buildings and disrupt communications in seconds, the effects of which could last for months. The high probability and severity of such factors can cause sudden and dramatic change and also they require mechanisms to be developed that can more easily tolerate these factors and when they occur, recover more easily. Political instability can disrupt trade very quickly and so benefit or destroy business activity depending on the nature of the business and its relationship to the area affected. This brings into the discussion the fields of risk assessment along with emergency and recovery planning, all of which are beyond the scope of this chapter.

FORCES ACTING ON ORGANIZATIONS

There are many and varied forces acting on organizations which create, directly or indirectly, the need for change. There are many ways that these forces can be

MANAGEMENT IN ACTION 19.1 Off with their overheads

Cutting the number of employees may be a necessary course of action in difficult situations but it has the potential to damage future prospects. As Trapp says:

> It is not a lesson that British or US managers have yet fully learned. The cut, cut, cut mentality is now deeply embedded in Anglo-Saxon corporate culture – every company says people are its greatest asset, but when life starts to get tough, again and again those 'assets' are unceremonially heaved over the side.

Fortune magazine suggested in the early 1990s that companies were caught in the grip of 'wee-ness envy', a desire to emulate other companies that were of the same size but smaller in numbers. Russell Baker commented that the scale of dismissals by a manager was a measure of the right to membership of the CEO club. Two examples of the cut, cut, cut mentality identified by Trapp include:

- During 1995 British Gas experienced a 150 per cent increase in complaints. At the same time it was in the process of shedding 25 000 jobs.
- Ever Ready the battery manufacturer was acquired by Hanson in the early 1980s. It shed 900 of the 2900 jobs at the R & D centre. This began what one commentator described as an attempt to make the decline of the company as long and profitable as possible. When it was sold in 1993 its market share had dropped from 80 per cent to 30 per cent. Its technology was by then ten years behind the industry.

Professor Gary Hamel, visiting professor of international and strategic management at London Business School, compiled a 'Downsizing Hall of Fame' which included such names as Westinghouse, Kodak, General Motors, Union Carbide and DuPont, all of which had aggressively reduced the numbers employed over recent years. In the UK, companies such as Hanson, GEC, British Coal (which cut itself out of existence) and the clearing banks would all appear on the list. This has produced a generation of what Hamel describes as 'lowest common denominator managers' in the USA and the UK. Managers who are able to delayer, downsize, declutter and divest better than managers in other countries. As evidence of this, from 1987 to 1991 (a period of economic growth) more than 85 per cent of the *Fortune* 500 companies reduced the size of their white-collar staff. Hamel describes the process as one of 'corporate anorexia'.

Business process re-engineering (BPR) has most frequently been linked with downsizing and has largely been discredited as a consequence. It has been suggested that some 75 per cent of all attempts to apply BPR fail. The main intention behind BPR, to focus the business on what it should be attempting to achieve, has been overshadowed by its potential to cut cost and numbers of employees. Surveys in the USA have shown that only 22–34 per cent of companies that restructure increase productivity to their satisfaction. This invariably leads to a downward spiral of cutting and failure to achieve success. Similar results on profitability have also been observed. In a survey of 210 companies not one reported a post-redundancy profit performance that matched previous figures.

Hamel suggests that companies continue to adopt the cutting approach because it has become an organizational norm. Organizations are 'forced' by various means to follow the conventional wisdom of the day. This includes pressure from institutional shareholders, following the fashions of the moment, pressure from City analysts, a desire to be like other organizations and a wish to follow the lead of those organizations that are regarded as the most prestigious in their industry. It does not, however, guarantee commercial success or benefit for customers or society.

Adapted from: Trapp, R (1995) Off with their overheads, *Independent on Sunday, Business section*, 10 December, pp 1–2.

Stop ↔ Consider

One implication of these views is that organizational change is a self-inflicted problem to a significant extent. It simply occurs because it is described as a good thing in conventional wisdom and therefore, a necessary thing.

To what extent and why do you support this view of change? In addition, what might this imply about the ways that society should seek to control (if at all) organizational and managerial activity?

classified. For example, Johnson and Scholes (1999) use the PESTLE model (introduced in Chapter 1) as the basis of the categorization of the forces active in any situation; another is to categorize forces as originating from either outside or inside the organization. Table 19.2 represents some of the external sources of pressure for change (Open University, 1990).

In addition to these sources of change, Hellriegel *et al.* (1989) identify the following:

- *Rapid product obsolescence.* This refers to the increasing rapidity of product change necessitated by fashion and technology etc. It reflects the pace of change in what organizations offer to the marketplace and what customers demand by way of products and services.
- *Knowledge explosion.* Information and knowledge are rapidly becoming commodities in their own right. This creates both new organizations and also impacts on those not directly involved in the creation of information. This knowledge explosion can influence an organization in many different ways. For example, the growth of the internet allows potential customers to find and compare a range of possible suppliers much more easily than would have been possible without that technology. Another trend among organizations is to **benchmark** themselves against other organizations as a means of judging their performance against nominated targets. This requires the collection and analysis of large quantities of data; usually on a reciprocal basis between organizations or through management consultancies. Management in Action 19.2 reflects a number of aspects associated with this trend.
- *Demographics.* The demographics and nature of both customers and the workforce is changing which inevitably impacts on many aspects of organizational functioning. Education levels are generally rising, with more people now entering higher and further education than ever before. Whatever else advanced education achieves it appears to significantly influence expectations about the role of work in people's lives. Individuals with more qualifications develop an expectation that their work experience will reflect that achievement and the delayed start to their working life. In economic terms they seek a return for their investment of staying later in the educational system. Also, the growth of the dual career family along with the emergence of an older

Benchmark(ing)
A process of comparing company operations with other organizations in order to measure relative performance and effectiveness.

Source of change	Examples
Market demand	Decline in demand for particular products/services, for example, monochrome television sets
Market supply	Mergers in retail companies
Economic	Overall fall in retail companies; changes in exchange rates
Social	Changes in taste, for example, increase in health consciousness in 1980s
Technological	Increased availability of new production technologies and information systems
Political	Change in leadership of local authority or government
Chance	Earthquake, fire, flood, storm

TABLE 19.2 External pressure for change (*source: Managing Change*, Book 9, B784, The effective manager, Open University)

MANAGEMENT IN ACTION 19.2 A measure of success

Benchmarking encourages an organization to identify others against which it can measure its own performance and from which it can learn new ways of improving its effectiveness. For example:

- South-West Airlines in the USA studied the performance of the pit crews at the Indy 500 motor car race and learned how to reduce the turnaround time of its aircraft at an airport gate from 30 minutes to 15.
- The Granite Rock Company studied the use of ATMs in banking. The upshot was that the company introduced a system of ATM-like cards for its drivers to make the weighing and record keeping simpler, faster and more reliable.

Benchmarking is not new but it has only become established as an essential management technique over the past few years. It could be argued that it was Walter Chrysler who began the idea many years ago when he bought and stripped down an Oldsmobile. He was intent in finding out what went into the competitor's car, how it was made and how much it cost to make. It is frequently seen alongside business process re-engineering and total quality management as a trilogy of efficiency improvement techniques. The British government also uses the technique as part of its market-testing programme for public sector efficiency.

In a survey of the top 10 000 UK companies by Coopers & Lybrand and the Confederation of British Industry it was revealed that 66 per cent of the respondents across all sectors practised benchmarking and that 85 per cent felt that it had been successful. Of the *Fortune* 500 companies, 80 per cent used the technique and 60 per cent intended to increase investment in its application. In the early 1980s it was Xerox that began to use benchmarking to seek ways of combating competition from the Far East in copier products. In doing so it recognized that the best ways of doing things could be identified from parallel but not identical operations in other companies and sectors.

In recent times the emphasis in benchmarking has moved away from performance measurement and concentrated on what gives leading companies their competitive edge. The emphasis should not be 90 per cent on the development of measurements and 10 per cent on change, but the other way around, according to Victor Luck, head of commerce and industry consulting services at Coopers & Lybrand. Arthur Andersen, an international accounting and consultancy firm, has invested over £6.4m in developing the Global Best Practices Knowledge Base. This represents its proprietary benchmarking database, built up from a wide variety of sources and intended for use by its consultants in helping clients. It should be noted that since this was originally written, Arthur Andersen has been dismantled and swallowed up by other major consultancy practices.

Adapted from: Dickson, T (1993) A measure of success, *Financial Times*, 5 May, p 14.

Stop ↔ Consider

Why would any organization help another to study its operational activities and performance in detail, would it not simply lead to misinformation and half-truths being divulged? How would you persuade another company to co-operate with a benchmarking exercise that you were responsible for?

population with disposable wealth has created opportunities for new products and services to be developed.

The internal forces for change that arise within an organization include:

- *Efficiency*. There is an ever present drive for minimalism in organizations. The increased level of competition evident today forces every organization to enter a spiral of cost reduction. The finance markets seek ever higher profit levels on behalf of investors. Managers themselves have careers to manage through being better than their peer group. Better in this context implies being able to demonstrate that they can deliver that which more senior managers expect – minimalism and higher profit!

- *Fashion.* Change for the sake of change is another force acting upon internal change processes. There are organizations (and managers) who pride themselves on being cutting edge in this respect. This creates a pressure for change as others follow and adopt yesterday's innovation.
- *Control.* New managers frequently make changes simply to demonstrate that the previous incumbent has gone, thereby allowing the new manager to be seen as the one in control. Employees frequently refer to, 'the way it has always been'. This might be accurate, but it also represents an attempt to socialize the new manager into employee preferred work practices. Employees have the upper hand in such situations as they inevitably know the established ways better than the new manager. If the new manager changes everything around then it neutralizes that potential benefit, allowing the new manager to demonstrate that they are 'in control'.
- *Internal pressure.* Change can be forced on an organization as a result of the internal pressure from various stakeholder groups. For example, changes to the wage structure and working practices could be brought about as a result of industrial action by the workforce. The social pressure from women and ethnic minority groups for a greater degree of equality at work has forced organizations to respond by changing previously white-male-dominated employment and work practices.

Stewart (1991) identifies a number of changes that specifically influence managerial careers in addition to other aspects of organizational life. They include, in addition to the points already made:

- *Business structure.* This would include more frequent changes in business ownership; growth in multinational and foreign ownership; privatization of the public sector and the globalization of business activity. These changes inevitably impact on the ways that predominantly middle and junior managers can progress their careers. For example, the takeover of one company by another inevitably creates overlap in many areas. Inevitably as a consequence a number of positions (and therefore people) will be surplus to requirements at the same time as new career opportunities are created.
- *Business functioning.* This factor reflects the growth of flexibility as a means of matching resources to requirement through self-employment, contracting and the need to seek new business opportunities. More and more aspects of company activity are being 'contracted out' to other organizations in the search for cost reduction and efficiency. The house building industry in the UK provides a clear example of this. Years ago each building company would directly employ the joiners, bricklayers, plumbers and other craftspeople needed to build the houses. Today they directly employ only a very small number of workers, the bricklaying, plumbing, joinery and electrical work being subcontracted to independent companies or teams of self-employed people. Consequently, the opportunities for people to work their way up from worker to manager within the same company are much reduced and the job of site managers is one of project management rather than the direct control of workers.

IMPACT OF CHANGE ON ORGANIZATIONS

The discussion so far has demonstrated that a wide range of forces act on organizations and directly or indirectly result in change. It is now appropriate to consider how these are experienced within an organization. The way in which change impacts on an organization is dependent on two factors, the scale of the change impact and the degree of planning for change involved. Figure 19.1 illustrates these as two axes in a matrix, which consequently generates four categories of change impact.

Each of the four cells in Figure 19.1 reflects a different basis for deferent response scenarios to the experienced situation. The two axes of the model will be discussed in the following subsections, but it is appropriate at this point to briefly consider each of the change impact cells in the matrix:

- *Surprise*. This reflects situations that are both unplanned and relatively minor in nature. For example, interest rates might unexpectedly change and require the finance managers of a company to adjust loan repayment schedules.
- *Incremental*. This could reflect situations which are anticipated and are relatively minor in nature. For example, the implementation of quality circle recommendations may require that small changes be made to the design of a particular component to make it easier to fit during the assembly operations. However, this will be only one of a series of changes planned by the circle to make the production process more effective.
- *Crisis*. This represents both the unexpected and the serious. An extreme example might be the destruction of a factory as the result of a gas explosion or terrorist attack. It contains the potential to destroy the organization unless the response is appropriate and effective.
- *Strategic*. This represents major planned events that attempt to position the organization more effectively in relationship to its environment. For example, a company making manual typewriters anticipating the growth of computer-based systems may seek to acquire a business systems or computer division.

Adaptive change

The vertical axis of Figure 19.1 represents a scale of change impact. Those changes categorized as adaptive are relatively small in scale and as a consequence can be accommodated without major disruption and danger to the organization. It represents the many thousands of small adaptive movements in absorbing and responding to day-to-day events, balancing and integrating operations with the environment within which they take place. However, small in scale as such changes may be in organizational terms, that does not mean that they will be small in impact for individual employees or managers.

FIGURE 19.1

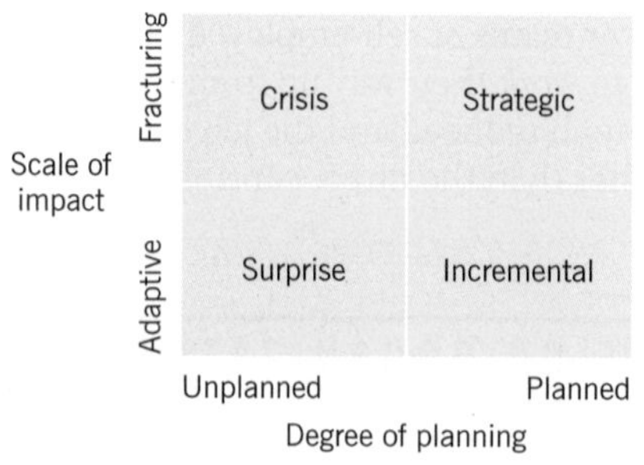

The change matrix

There are many possible examples of this type of change that exist. For example, a flu epidemic occurs and the level of sickness absence suddenly and unexpectedly rises. This type of change can be accommodated relatively easily, but not without some measure of increased cost. Employees at work could be asked to stay behind and work overtime. Alternatively, temporary labour could be hired to cover for the absent employees. Allowing production to fall behind schedule is another option. These represent the tactical levels of decision that line managers engage in all the time in responding to the ever changing circumstances that they are exposed to.

Other adaptive changes are more permanent, but nevertheless minor in scale. For example, minor modifications to the external features of product design on an annual basis. The intention of such change being to keep the product fresh and respond to marketing initiatives among competitors. The introduction of a new computer package for personnel records would serve as another example. The new system might require changes to the design of a number of personnel forms and procedures as well as the transfer of much existing data from one computer system to another. Overall however, important as such systems are they represent changes that are relatively small in comparison to everything that the organization does.

Fracturing change

This scale of change impact in Figure 19.1 represents the major events that occur within the experience of all organizations. The scale of change represented by this category is very large and of such significance that it could seriously damage or destroy the organization. In other words, it has the potential to fracture or break it.

Products and services are all designed to meet particular needs among their consumers. There is always a danger that these needs can be met in different ways and thus eliminate the market for a particular product. In recent years the changes to political structures have fundamentally changed the military balance that existed for the previous 40 years. The so-called peace dividend has produced a number of major changes, including the possibility for a massive reduction in business for those companies making military equipment. Such organizations have had to adjust rapidly to this dangerous situation (for their survival and profit) or face severe contraction in size or even their demise.

Another example of the possibility of fracturing change would be the natural disasters that can strike any organization at any time. For example, a gas explosion could destroy a building and so potentially destroy the company. A major area of managerial responsibility over recent years has been the field of risk and disaster planning in an attempt to minimize the consequence of such events.

There is a scale of magnitude reflecting the level of real or potential threat to an organization. Equally, some issues which might be major in one context may be considered minor in another. For example, in a company with a poor industrial relations record frequent strikes may be the norm. Therefore, it may be part of the management planning process to build an allowance into their operations, schedules and costs to reduce the impact. Also, there are situations in which relatively minor events can slip out of control and become life threatening if they are not handled effectively. For example, the new computerized personnel system referred to in the previous subsection could be inappropriate or faulty in some respect. Its introduction could also be resisted by personnel staff. Employees might also interpret its introduction as an attempt by managers to tighten control and intrude into their lives. The consequences of any of these could be a slide into a major disaster for the organization if they were not effectively managed.

Planned change

The horizontal axis of Figure 19.1 reflects the degree of planning that can be brought to bear on the situation. It is about the level of anticipation concerning the events which are forcing change to occur. Planned change represents those events that management either intend to occur or those for which they have the opportunity to provide a thought-through response.

There are many examples of planned change. Management may identify that its ability to retain market share is being threatened by competitors with much lower labour costs. Consequently, a package of measures could be developed including the introduction of automation and high technology; the development of flexibility and teamwork practices among the workforce; the linking of wages to performance; the redesign of the product to make it more attractive to the customer; along with the development of a range of customer inducements and support measures.

It also represents the strategic moves made by organizations in order to position themselves to minimize the overall impact of declining markets and to capture the potential of expanding businesses. This refers to the merger, acquisition and divestment strategies that many large organizations engage in as they search for higher returns, market dominance and growth. Planning for the many small changes that occur is also part of normal managerial experience. For example, the introduction of **total quality management** (TQM) initiatives is an attempt to capture and routinize the process of continuous improvement.

Total quality management (TQM)
An approach involving everyone in seeking continuous improvement in the product, service and customer experience.

Unplanned change

This category within Figure 19.1 represents the unexpected events that arise and which can never be completely eliminated from an organization's environment. Parts of California are known to be subject to earthquakes as they lie along faults in the earth's crust. Knowing this, measures can be taken to minimize the consequences through building design and emergency planning. However, it is not yet possible to predict with any certainty when or how strong a particular tremor will be. They remain random factors and so when they occur pre-prepared recovery plans must be activated. It can be argued that it is one of the primary responsibilities of management to anticipate events and to minimize the possibility of the unexpected arising. Also they have a responsibility for the development of plans for dealing with such eventualities that cannot be eliminated or totally controlled. This contingency planning approach to change attempts to scan the internal and external environment and develop response scenarios for what might be expected to occur.

Over recent years many organizations have engaged a reductionist approach to managing. The ability to cut back the numbers of employees and to rationalize operational activity has been a much prized management skill. This was the point made earlier in Management in Action 19.1. This is achieved by eliminating slack from the system as a whole and by concentrating on doing rather than thinking. One of the potential dangers of this minimalist approach is that it removes the ability to anticipate and plan as a result of the emphasis on producing to standardized plans in the current and future time periods. The inherent risk in this approach is that there is a higher potential to miss intelligence and important signals from the environment, which in turn creates the risk of more unplanned events arising with the consummate risk of crisis being higher. Crisis in Figure 19.1, being the least desirable and most dangerous cell in the matrix, naturally carries with it the greater risk for the survival of the organization.

ORGANIZATIONAL DEVELOPMENT AND CHANGE

Organizational development (OD) can be defined as, 'a systematic application of behavioural science knowledge to the planned development and reinforcement of organizational strategies, structures, and processes for improving an organization's effectiveness' (Cummings and Worley, 1993, p 2). Table 19.3 reflects Robbins' (1998) views on the five key values that should underpin any OD intervention.

Organizational development
The systematic application of behavioural science to organizational process in order to improve effectiveness.

The strands of theory and practice within OD include:

- *Encounter groups*. Sometimes these groups are called sensitivity or 'T' groups (the 'T' stands for training or therapy). The purpose of these small unstructured groups is to meet and, without a formal leader, purpose or agenda, to begin exploring personal and interactive behaviour within the group. As a consequence of the depth of emotional involvement, interaction and feedback generated during the process, members learn about themselves and their behaviour. The intention being for the individuals within the group to be able to use the understanding gained to connect with each other in a more meaningful way and so be able to engage in a participative change process more effectively. This could be used as the first stage in a major team-building and group development project.
- *Process consultation*. This approach advocates the use of an external consultant as someone who can help the organizational members better understand organizational problems and facilitate a process allowing them to find context-acceptable workable solutions. The usual consultancy intervention is based on the application of technical expertise to bring an already existing solution to the problem. Schein (1969) is worth reading in this context as he has always been a major advocate of **process consultation**.
- *Survey feedback*. Attitude and opinion surveys are a way for organizations to find out what employees think about some aspect of working in the company. This might include how they react to the management style or it could be about communications and consultation practices, or perhaps about some planned change or the future direction of the company. The findings from these surveys (once they have been analyzed and made anonymous) can be communicated back to the participants in a way that creates learning opportunities and also contribute to the way that change is dealt with. However, honest feedback can be a problem, particularly if it contains bad news, as is evident in the following Employee Perspective (19.1) in which James had some negative feedback to give to his senior managers. Feedback is a sensitive issue in any context, particularly if it contains negative aspects.

Process consultation
An approach to organization development in which the consultant seeks to facilitate clients in problem exploration and solution identification.

1. An organization's culture should be based on trust, openness and mutual support among members.
2. Individuals should be treated with respect and dignity within the organization.
3. Authority and control based only on hierarchical position are not usually effective.
4. The people who are going to be affected by change should be involved in its design and implementation.
5. Problems and conflict should be addressed and not hidden or ignored.

TABLE 19.3 The five core values of OD interventions

EMPLOYEE PERSPECTIVE 19.1 The attitude survey negative feedback

James was a senior industrial engineer in a large manufacturing company in the North of England. He had worked for the company for about 18 months and his current project was as manager of a company-wide attitude survey of all staff. The company employed about 500 factory staff plus about 150 administrative, sales, technical and managerial employees. The attitude survey had covered everyone below management level and had been undertaken through a questionnaire completed anonymously. Employees could either opt to fill in a paper copy or to complete it on-line. The response rate was high at about 68 per cent and James and his team of two analysts had spent over two weeks analyzing the data and drawing conclusions from it.

Unfortunately (as James saw it) there were many negative comments about managers and how the company was run in the survey. For example, something like 80 per cent of respondents had indicated that the style of management in the company was aggressive, unhelpful and uncaring. Just over 73 per cent of respondents felt that their specific line manager did not have the necessary technical skills to run the section effectively. Sixty two per cent of respondents suggested that the company made profit despite the efforts of managers and that it was only the employees who knew how to get things done efficiently. It was going to be difficult to feed back this type of information to management as senior managers and directors all thought that they did a good job and that they were respected by all employees. The senior managers were expecting a glowing endorsement of their stewardship of the company from employees and had already suggested to James that particularly good comments might be useful in public relations and marketing terms. James was worried about how to deal with this.

Tasks

1. If you were James what would you do in preparing to feed back this type of information to management?
2. What might James have done to prevent this situation from arising in the first place, and what does that imply about the value of attitude surveys?
3. Can employees be relied upon to tell the truth about managers, or is it likely that they will always be negative in their opinions, or will they take the chance to 'stick the knife in' given the opportunity? Why or why not?
4. How can bad news be fed back to people in a way which might allow for positive outcomes?

- *Action research*. This reflects an active and iterative approach to research and change. Action research is based upon a cyclical process beginning with research into identified problems. This in turn leads to conclusions and the development of action plans in relation to the target 'problem'. Opportunities for further study and problem solving are also identified, and so the cycle begins again. For a more extensive introduction to action research see Greenwood and Levin (1998).
- *Planned approach to OD interventions*. This reflects a seven stage process as reflected in Table 19.4.
- *Quality of working life*. The quality of working life (QWL) movement has already been discussed in an earlier chapter and it has now been incorporated into the OD practitioner's toolkit. This can include the use of teamwork and seeking the improvement of interpersonal and intergroup relationships.
- *Strategic change*. This reflects an attempt to integrate all organizational variables into a common purpose. A vision or strategy is needed to create this unified purpose. The change aspect of the process arises through the need to integrate all activity into a cohesive (strategic) whole. This frequently involves the need to change the organization structure or other aspects of operational activity (including job design, systems or procedures) in order to achieve the cohesion required by the strategy. Huntington *et al.* (2000) demonstrate the

1. *Scouting.* This involves the client and the consultant exploring ideas on the nature and scope of the proposed intervention.
2. *Entry.* This reflects the establishment of the basis of the consulting relationship with all of the parties involved.
3. *Diagnosis.* This reflects the data gathering phase of the process in relation to the nature of the 'problem', its origins and any causal relationships.
4. *Planning.* This involves the process through which all participants come to agree with the objectives of the intervention and how it will be undertaken.
5. *Action.* This phase represents the actual intervention strategies being applied and the necessary actions implemented.
6. *Stabilization.* The newly implemented actions need to be locked in place and stabilized if the situation is to be permanently changed and slipping back to the old state is to be prevented.
7. *Termination.* This represents the closing down of the OD intervention during which the consultant will negotiate their withdrawal.

TABLE 19.4 The seven step planning model of OD

need for integration of several elements from OD such as leadership, control of risk management and the learning organization through their assessment of the contribution of it to the clinical governance of quality assurance in British medical care.

The basis and practice of OD has been criticized for a number of reasons. It is a practice that assumes incrementalism as the best way to achieve change. This is fine as long as the organization is at a high level of effectiveness to begin with. Dunphy and Stace (1988) argue that not all situations allow for the slow process of evolutionary change. Time and the political climate may be against the application of OD as an approach. This debate also reflects a major distinction between the business process re-engineering (BPR) and TQM approaches discussed below. OD as a process requires participation which, as Stephenson (1985) suggests, is not the panacea often claimed. Individuals or groups intent on resisting change, perhaps as a consequence of being disadvantaged by the outcome, may not be persuaded by involvement and might slow down the process itself. Involvement can expose but not necessarily solve problems. Compromise may not be the best option and changing opinions may not deliver the results sought and intended. For example, the case study used at the end of this chapter reflects a situation where the attempts at involvement did not work to the advantage of any of the stakeholders. Also a company faced with a competitor's product that serves as a replacement for their own may not have the time or financial resource to allow an OD approach to finding a solution.

Figure 19.5 (below) and also the following section make specific reference to the notion of power as part of the change process. This is lacking in the classic OD approach. Recognizing this weakness Schein (1985) makes several suggestions for including a power and political perspective to OD interventions. Identifying with powerful stakeholders and attempting small projects first to gain credibility before tackling the more complex and risky projects, for example. A number of the specific change models identified in subsequent sections originate from the OD tradition, or have found value in the toolkit of the OD practitioner.

POWER, POLITICS AND CHANGE

There are two major ways in which power and politics interact with change:

1. *Process*. If change is to be successful support and commitment must be maximized with resistance and opposition being minimized. Power and politics can be used to facilitate this. For example, offering to provide help in the future in return for support now would constitute recognition of the political dimension to decision making. Many of the power and political tactics discussed in the previous two chapters would also be relevant in this process. Munduate and Bennebroek Gravenhorst (2003) specifically review the complex and dynamic relationship between several aspects of power and change processes.
2. *Purpose*. There is a saying about not getting mad but getting even as a means of extracting revenge. Change can therefore be used as the means to achieve another purpose. For example, the following Employee Perspective (19.2) demonstrates that it is possible to engineer a change in order to deal with employees defined (by management) as a problem.

Stephenson (1985) identifies the following tactics useful in the introduction of change, the application of which should minimize the risk of power or politics impacting on the process in a negative way:

- *Simple first*. 'Nothing succeeds like success.' Beginning with small projects that are successful creates confidence and encouragement to go on and tackle more difficult problems.
- *Adaptation*. Being flexible and adaptable in modifying planned changes improves the chances of success. It provides a means of dealing with unplanned events and resistance.
- *Incorporation*. People feel less threatened and more comfortable with minor change. Consequently incorporating as much as possible from an existing situation in a change programme gives the appearance of continuity and stability.
- *Structure*. Attitudes can be used to influence the structural and physical aspects of change, or vice versa. Product and service quality ultimately depends upon employee commitment. This in turn depends upon their underlying attitudes to a significant extent. Improvements to quality could be attempted by engaging in widespread training to try and ensure that employees understood its importance. Subsequently changes to the relevant work routines would be introduced, hopefully supported by the appropriate employee attitudes. However, by changing working practices, subsequently reinforced through training and reward systems, etc. quality is addressed directly and changes in attitude could be brought about over time. Eventually the changed employee attitude supports the higher quality (because quality is seen to deliver positive results) without the need for the structural props such as training and other reinforcements.
- *Ceremony*. The use of ceremonial events provides a clear signal of what defines success in a particular context. It also has the effect of institutionalizing change through the ceremonies attached to it. The razzamatazz around new product launches are as much about rewarding the changes adopted to bring them about as they are marketing initiatives.

EMPLOYEE PERSPECTIVE 19.2 Reorganizing to get rid of a problem?

Sandra joined the administration department of a large manufacturing company based in Detroit in the USA. She was ambitious and tried to demonstrate in her work and attitude that she wanted to be taken seriously and to move into a more senior position. She was a very able employee and quickly came to the attention of senior managers as someone who could be relied upon to achieve results quickly. She was soon promoted, to the dismay of some of her former colleagues who resented what they saw as her pushy and abrasive manner. However, she continued with her approach to work and as office supervisor, anyone who would not comply with her requirements was quickly and forcibly told to 'shape up or ship out'. This caused further friction among employees and one or two left. However senior management were happy with Sandra's work and she was soon promoted to administration manager when the incumbent died suddenly of a heart attack at the age of 50.

Sandra now felt that she had achieved the status that she was entitled to as a result of her capabilities and this went to her head a little. She now had a number of supervisors reporting to her and she sat on the management committee. She was now only one step below the board of directors. Rapid promotion for a 35 year old that had only been with the company for four years. Not surprisingly a number of longer service employees and supervisors resented her rapid promotion and also her style of working. The other managers within the company also began to feel the sting of her words as she began to tell everyone how she thought that they should run their departments in the efficient and effective way that she ran hers. The board of directors began to hear complaints from a wide range of sources, including customers and suppliers who also encountered her from time-to-time over late payments or incorrect invoices. She was said to never admit a fault even when it was blatantly her responsibility and that she always claimed personal credit for things that she had not been indirectly involved with. More of her subordinates left as they felt undervalued by Sandra, being constantly told that they were not good enough.

The managing director and the director of administration held a meeting and decided that something had to be done, but what? They had appointed her and simply dismissing Sandra would be an admission that they had made a bad decision, something that they wanted to avoid. Eventually they hit on the idea of a restructuring exercise in which the prime purpose of the administration department would be changed to that of financial services and therefore a professionally qualified accountant would be needed to head it. The director of administration was himself a chartered financial accountant, and it was decided that if they replaced Sandra with a management accountant they would benefit in a number of ways and it would also limit her ability to sue the company for unfair dismissal.

So the new structure was designed in greater detail and Sandra was dismissed. She was told that it was nothing personal, but that she did not have the qualifications or experience to provide the finance department, as it would become, with the appropriate leadership or technical skill. She was devastated by the news and let her director know in no uncertain terms about her feelings on the situation. She also told him that he was making a terrible mistake and that the company would lose its administrative efficiency as a result, plus of course she was intent on suing them for considerable compensation.

Tasks

1. What would you do in this situation if you were Sandra and why?
2. Does this situation reflect a 'proper' or ethical use of change to achieve a different objective, why or why not?
3. What might the company have done to deal with the situation and Sandra more effectively?

- *Assurances*. How people perceive that they will be treated as the result of change is important to how they react to it. Previous experience of the value of assurances (on say fair treatment) is an important part of creating future responses.
- *Timescales*. As a general rule the more time available to make change the more likely it is to be successful. However, there are situations in which time is not available and rapid change must take place. Crises can become a focus for successful change.

- *Support*. Adapting to change causes stress and individuals often feel threatened. This requires support in order to maintain momentum and to avoid encouraging resistance.
- *Transition*. There are three different contexts active at the same time in change processes. The existing situation, the desired situation and the transitional situation. They overlap and are not discrete categories of event. This creates uncertainty, ambiguity and complexity, all of which must be managed.
- *Unexpected*. Unexpected things can and will occur. Some preparation for these situations can be done and not all are hostile to change.

Another way of considering the political and power dynamics associated with change were identified by Nadler and Tushman (1988). In this view there are three mechanisms required to manage the problems associated with the power, anxiety and transitional situations found in all change situations:

1. *Mobilizing political support*. This mechanism is all about preparing the ground for the change process. It involves gaining the support of key sponsors and of forming supportive alliances with those likely to be influential in or affected by the process. It is about attempting to maximize support and minimize resistance to the proposed changes.
2. *Encouraging supportive behaviour*. This mechanism uses a variety of devices to build support among those more directly involved with the change. For example, the participation of employees in designing changes to working practices might help them understand existing problems and identify appropriate alternatives. Change as a social process within a social construction (the organization) is very dependent upon the discourses that are used to describe events in the search for the creation of specific perceptions and frames of reference through which stakeholders are encouraged to understand the processes. Doolin (2003) demonstrates the significance of discourse as an influence on the level of support for change within a hospital in New Zealand which took place during a period of general public sector change.
3. *Managing the transitional process*. Having identified what is to be done, it then has to be achieved in practice. The difficulties associated with transition are the uncertainty of the new state – because it has not yet arrived; the familiarity of the old – because it has not yet gone; and the complexity of temporary arrangements – designed to facilitate movement from one situation to another. The transition period is a dangerous one for any change process as things can go horribly wrong and threaten the achievement of the ultimate objective.

While power and politics are very important aspects of any change process that does not provide the only reason for managing them. It could be argued for example, that by acting in an overtly political way management could be encouraging others to act in a similar way, creating a deteriorating cycle of behaviour into a pit of intrigue and politics. In this situation power and politics become the masters not the servants.

APPROACHES TO ORGANIZATIONAL CHANGE

It has already been established that change is both endemic to management and an issue which can generate resistance from a wide range of sources. The major responsibility of managers is to enable the organization to function effectively and so it is they who have a prime responsibility for both creating change and responding to it in pursuit of their objectives. However, not all large-scale change can be planned and even senior managers have to respond to the situations that they find themselves in. For example, Bichard (1996) describes what happened following an announcement of the merger of the UK government departments of employment and education employing a total of some 52 000 people between them. The civil servants and politicians in charge of the two departments did not know about the planned merger until one hour before it was due to take place. It was not until some six months later that a common framework had been decided for the merged departments and the top 110 posts filled. Work could then begin on merging the lower level functions and activities.

Leavitt's organizational variables and change

One model of a company, the work of Leavitt (1965), reflects the major constituent parts of an organization within its environment. This can be used as the basis for change management initiatives to be identified as well as providing a means of identifying the consequences of any planned changes (Figure 19.2).

Leavitt argues that change can affect any (or all) of the variables identified in Figure 19.2. Alternatively, change can be applied to any single element (or combination of them) within the model in an attempt to influence the other elements within the organization. So for example, the technology used by a company could be changed in order to impact on the structure, people, and task aspects of it. Because of the integrated nature of these elements changes to one of them will have consequential effects on the others. As another example, the change of some of the key managers in an organization could well create a number of subsequent changes to the structure of the organization, its technology and some of the tasks to be undertaken. This aspect is also evident in the previous Employee Perspective (19.2) involving the removal of Sandra through changes to the structure and task elements of the organization.

Mergers, acquisition and change

Already introduced in this discussion are the opportunities to achieve change within an organization through adaptations to aspects of it such as structure, technology, etc. Another major creator of change within an organization is the merger and acquisition activity commonly found as part of the strategic planning intended to achieve growth and/or cost reduction. Johnson and Scholes (1999) suggest that development by acquisition tends to occur in waves. They quote such periods of high acquisition activity in the UK as 1898–1900, 1926–29, 1967–73 and 1985–87. They also point out that

FIGURE 19.2

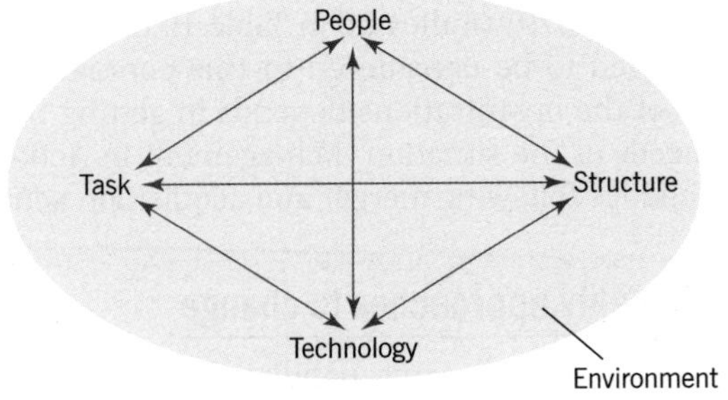

Leavitt's organization variables (*source*: Huczynski, A and Buchanan, D (1991) *Organizational Behaviour*, Prentice Hall, Hemel Hempstead)

each of these periods showed a tendency for particularly high activity in specific industries. For example, in the period 1985–87 there was a considerable volume of high street retailing takeover activity taking place in the UK.

Whether the purpose of the acquisition, merger or takeover is growth or cost reduction, change is an inevitable consequence. Two or more sometimes very different organizations must be brought together and from that total pool of capability, a new unified organization must be forged with the potential to return greater shareholder wealth, growth and/or cost reduction. It is the task of the managers in that situation to realize that potential. Among the many problems of duplication of resources, product range, customer lists and procedural/systems incompatibilities that must be resolved, often the major difficulties lie among the people and organizational culture areas.

Organizational culture is discussed in detail in an earlier chapter in this text and much of that material is relevant to this discussion. Johnson and Scholes explore the process of managing strategic change, including the cultural dimensions. They suggest that the important cultural blockages to change can be:

- *Routines*. By this term they refer to the, 'ways that things get done around here'. It reflects the normal ways of operating and functioning, which inevitably differ to some degree between any two organizations.
- *Control systems*. These refer to the reporting and procedural ways of working within the organization.
- *Structures*. This reflects the arrangement of tasks and jobs into sections, departments and a hierarchy of responsibility.
- *Symbols*. These they describe as the symbolic acts and artefacts of an organization that help to preserve the original model. This reflects those aspects of an organization that help to create its identity and sense of difference from other organizations. Inevitably, therefore, these symbols can become a major source of difficulty for achieving cultural amalgamation between organizations following a merger or takeover.
- *Power and dependency relationships*. The ways in which power and political activity finds expression in the separate organizations will inevitably be disturbed by attempts to combine them. New relationships, alliances and power structures will have to be formed and inevitably this gives rise to new political activity as integration takes place. It is commonplace to hear stories in such situations about the old days, references to us and them and how the 'other lot' are not as good as we were. In some ways this reflects the process of establishing a new 'pecking order', behaviour found among chickens and other animals when forming a flock or group.

Johnson and Scholes suggest that the role of the change agent is vital in seeking to achieve success in changing culture. They suggest that the each of the options offered by Kotter and Schlesinger (1979) (indicated in Table 19.6 below) have advantages and disadvantages which need to be considered in this context. Success in achieving change in the culture of the organizations depends in getting the style of the change agent to match the needs of the situation. Management in Action 19.3 reflects some recent research into change following merger and acquisition activity.

Re-engineering and quality approaches to change

Business process re-engineering became popular during the early 1990s. It was an approach to the design of organizational activity that required managers to go back to first principles and recreate the organization with a complete emphasis on meeting the needs of customers. Most organizations are organized vertically. Reports are

MANAGEMENT IN ACTION 19.3 Executive action for acquisition success

Angwin describes a number of changes that surround the takeover process. He suggests that as many as one in seven executives will experience a takeover during their working lives and that this might be expected to be higher for MBA-qualified managers. He also points out that most takeovers fail (about 44 per cent subsequently split up) and that many of those involved find it a negative experience. In America consultants recommend a formal grieving period for staff in the acquired company, perhaps incorporating the use of mock funerals and coffins!

The research conducted by Angwin suggests that immediately following the takeover a high level of change-related initiatives occur but that this quickly tails off. He reports levels of 500 changes initiated in the first month following a takeover dropping steadily to fewer than 50 changes by month 19. This process reflects the new owners being seen to 'take control' and making everyone in the company understand that they 'mean business'. The speed of making such changes is a little surprising given that the new owners cannot know everything about the acquired company before they take charge. It might be expected that extensive pre-takeover planning would identify what changes were to be made following acquisition. However, Angwin's research, carried out in conjunction with Ernst & Young, did not find this in practice. Many executives described the process as running into a wall, as senior managers who organized the deal frequently go on to work on new deals leaving the actual merger of the acquired company to executives not involved in the negotiations.

Some of the immediate change can be accounted for as a result of the need to introduce standardized procedures and practice in the finance areas. Equally there is the expectation that change will be made and anything already planned in the acquired company might be implemented in order to demonstrate progress. If a senior executive is appointed from outside of the acquired company to run it, they will need to 'stamp' their authority on both organizations for many political, control and business reasons. Doing nothing following an acquisition was not regarded as a realistic option by the respondents in Angwin's study.

The research shows the phasing of change with the initial thrust on finance and marketing noticeable in the early stages, but by the end of the first year this is replaced by human resource issues. This was suggested to be a necessary refinement on what inevitably was a crude process immediately following a takeover. Subsequent changes also tend to be more complex and difficult to achieve. Perhaps the 'skeletons in the cupboard' of the acquired company finally surface and need to be dealt with. The post-takeover period is highly stressful for everyone concerned, particularly because job security is always at risk. It is not uncommon to find that companies put together teams from each company to integrate activity. Over the period of the integration it becomes apparent which team members will be 'released'.

After an acquisition there can be strong feelings of 'winners and losers', but it is frequently forgotten that it can be a two-way process. The acquiring company can also be changed as a result of exposure to the purchased one. This interactive development is the best possibility to emerge from a takeover and can be a driver for strategic renewal. However, for this to be achieved, takeovers must be change processes and that means careful, sensitive management.

Adapted from: Angwin, D (1996) Executive action for acquisition success, *Warwick Nexus*, Spring, pp 4–5.

Stop ↔ Consider

To what extent do you consider that the ideas put forward by Johnson and Scholes offer a means of achieving the, 'careful and sensitive management' of integration, suggested as necessary by Angwin?

created and transmitted upwards to more senior managers; instructions are determined at a senior level and communicated downwards. Careers are developed in a vertical direction as promotion takes the individuals up the organization. However, the customer experience of any organization is horizontal. Very few customers of an organization ever meet or deal with people at a senior level. Consequently, it is hardly surprising to find that much human effort within any organization is directed at meeting the needs of the hierarchy, rather than being totally focused on the needs of the customer. Hammer and Champy (1995) took this idea one stage further and proposed that any company should be organized around the notion of a business process and that each process should be re-engineered so that it added maximum customer value and minimized non-value adding administrative activity. This they termed business process re-engineering (BPR).

The concept of a process is fundamental to BPR. A process in this context refers to a series of actions or proceedings used in the manufacturing, creation or achievement of something (Malhotra, 1998). Harrington (1991, p 9) defines a process as any activity that adds value to an input in converting it into an output for an internal or external customer. However a process is defined, the message from BPR is clear, only things that add value to the customer requirement should be considered important. Hammer and Champy describe re-engineering as an approach to change and efficiency that capitalizes on the American strengths of, 'individualism, self-reliance, a willingness to accept risk and a propensity for change' (p 3). They also describe it as an approach which requires discontinuous thinking in challenging the existing thinking and ways of undertaking business operations. It proposes a revolutionary way to identify and implement change. BPR requires the rapid identification of major change issues followed by the rapid implementation of the changes required.

The rapid, revolutionary and top-down driven BPR approach to change can be compared with approaches that emerge out of thinking about quality and how to maximize it. For example, total quality management (TQM) is one such approach which according to Slack *et al.* (1998, p 763) evolved from the earlier inspection approach to quality. TQM is an approach to quality which seeks to:

- Meet the needs and expectations of customers.
- Cover all parts of the organization.
- Include every person in the organization.
- Examine all costs associated with quality (especially the cost of failure).
- Emphasize 'right first time' in quality.
- Develop the systems and procedures that support quality improvement.
- Develop continuous improvement.

Dale (1999, p 231) suggests that it can take up to ten years to implement TQM fully through the: 'Fundamental principles, practices, procedures and systems, [to] create an organizational culture that is conducive to continuous improvement and [to] change the values and attitudes of its people'. Clearly there are a number of major differences in the approach to change offered between BPR and TQM. BPR is intended to be revolutionary, rapid, top-down driven and a single-shot process. TQM, conversely, is slow, evolutionary, bottom-up in emphasis and incremental in its approach to change. Indeed, Hammer and Champy argue (p 216) that TQM should be used in-between the major upheavals created through a BPR exercise.

Both BPR and TQM are about change although the methods of achieving it are radically different. However, Hammer and Champy admit in subsequent work (as do many other writers) that most BPR initiatives fail to work or deliver the sustained benefits intended by senior managers, the speed and scale of change being too disruptive perhaps. The time distinction for the implementation of change between these two initiatives is interesting in that BPR argues that very rapid change is most easily accommodated. In effect, frenetic periods of disruption followed by relatively quiet and stable periods when TQM approaches may be followed. TQM, however, claims that perfection can never be completely achieved and that the search for it reflects a journey through continuous improvement, not an end state. Unlike BPR, TQM also posits that it is the people who carry out the work of the organization who know what creates the difficulties and they should be the ones to drive change in order to raise the level of quality achieved and solve the operational problems.

The approach adopted in TQM is that a problem once resolved has disappeared forever, but there are always more problems to tackle. However, TQM takes such a long time to become truly integrated within an organization's fabric and culture that it too can fail, particularly if people think that it does not deliver results or improve operational activity. Being driven by its bottom-up philosophy it contains a very heavy demand on the time of many ordinary employees which can cost significant sums of money if it is done in company time. One of the criticisms of TQM has been that some companies have tried to make involvement in it voluntary and in private rather than company time, so avoiding the cost of its operation, but consequently limiting its impact.

Having discussed some of the major organizational variables and initiatives that can create change, it is now appropriate to consider the approaches and models that have been proposed as reflecting the change process itself.

Lewin's forcefield model of change

Lewin (1951) developed a change model which states that any situation exists as the result of a balance between the forces acting upon it. These forces occur in opposing directions, some driving for change while others are restraining that change by pressing in the opposite direction. It is known as the **forcefield analysis model**, intended to guide the identification of the forces acting upon the situation (Figure 19.3).

Forcefield analysis model
A change model proposing that situations are locked in place by the balance of change and restraining forces.

The model is very simple to understand and can easily be applied to a wide range of situations. For example, assume the current level of absence within a company to be 500 hours per month. An analysis of the situation might reveal the driving and restraining forces indicated in Table 19.5.

The absence level of 500 hours per month is the balance point between the sum of driving and restraining forces. It follows that if a change is desired in that situation then either the magnitude of the driving forces needs to be increased and/or the magnitude of the restraining forces reduced.

FIGURE 19.3

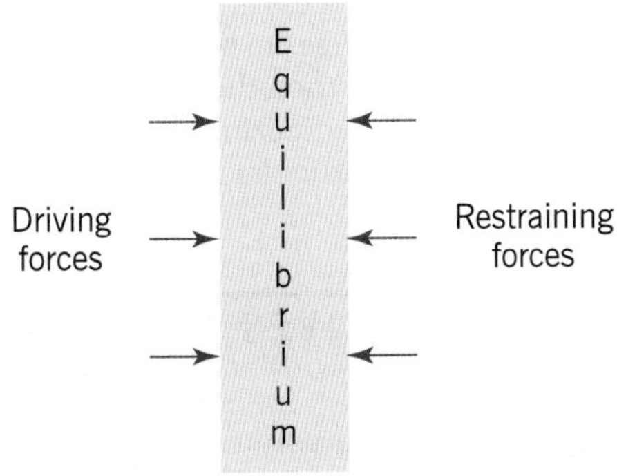

Lewin's forcefield analysis model

Driving forces	Restraining forces
Management need for higher productivity	Laziness
Need to reduce high levels of payment for sickness absence	Past practice
Management desire for control	Boring and monotonous work
Employee commitment to the company	Lack of car ownership
Employee travel to work distance	Poor public transport
Employee loss of income	Road congestion
Employee desire to do a good job	Domestic difficulties
Career development and promotion desire	Illness
	Inconvenient work starting time
	Habit

TABLE 19.5 Examples of driving and restraining forces acting on absence levels

Lewin identified three stages of change associated with his forcefield analysis model:

- *Stage 1 Unfreezing*. The first stage requires the current situation to be unfrozen. The current level of absence is frozen at 500 hours as a result of the balance between the two opposing forcefields. A desire to change that requires the current situation to be unfrozen in preparation for change to be made. It is a difficult period in any change process as the intentions for the future become clear and as resistance to that intention surfaces. In the example used, this could involve a statement by management of the problems associated with absence and the beginning of negotiations with the trade unions on how to deal with the problem.
- *Stage 2 Changing*. Having unfrozen the situation it is then time to make appropriate changes. This could involve introducing mandatory counselling after every period of absence; changing the working hours; introducing flexitime; introducing nursery provision and many more initiatives. These changes could be in either or both of the driving and restraining force categories. The level of absence should be seen to reduce if the changes have been successful.
- *Stage 3 Refreezing*. The change process is one of movement. The third stage of the Lewin model requires the changes to be refrozen or consolidated in a new state of balance. If this is not done then the balance will not be fixed and it will slip back to its previous position. Refreezing implies that the changes made become the new norms for that particular situation.

CONTINGENCY PERSPECTIVES ON CHANGE

Contingency approaches to change incorporate a broader range of elements into the process than political or OD perspectives. They represent a directly managerial approach to the subject of change compared with OD, which tends to be directed at incremental and self-directed methods. However, under the OD methodology managers still retain control of the agenda and context. It could therefore be argued that it also represents a manipulative device intended to find ways of achieving acceptance of managerial perspectives.

Kotter and Schlesinger's model

One of the earlier approaches to the contingency view of change is reflected in the work of Kotter and Schlesinger (1979). They identified a number of change management strategies along with the contexts to which they could be applied (see Table 19.6).

Approach	Commonly used in situations	Advantages	Drawbacks
Education + communication	Where there is a lack of information or inaccurate information or inaccurate information and analysis	Once persuaded, people will often help with the implementation of change	Can be very time consuming if many people are involved
Participation + involvement	Where the initiators do not have all the information they need to design the change, and where others have considerable power to resist	People who participate will be committed to implementing change, and any relevant information they have will be integrated into the change plan	Can be very time consuming if participators design an inappropriate change
Facilitation + support	Where people are resisting because of adjustment problems	No other approach works as well with adjustment problems	Can be time consuming, expensive and still fail
Negotiation + agreement	Where someone or some group will clearly lose out in a change, and where that group has considerable power to resist	Sometimes it is a relatively easy way to avoid major resistance	Can be too expensive in many cases if it alerts others to negotiate for compliance
Manipulation + co-option	Where other tactics will not work or are too expensive	It can be a relatively quick and inexpensive solution to resistance problems	Can lead to future problems if people feel manipulated
Explicit + implicit coercion	Where speed is essential and the change initiators possess considerable power	It is speedy and can overcome any kind of resistance	Can be risky if it leaves people mad at the initiators

TABLE 19.6 Methods of managing change, reprinted by permission of *Harvard Business Review*. Methods of managing change, from *Choosing Strategies for Change*, Kotter, JP and Schlesinger, CA (March/April 1979, p111).

Taking each of the strategies for change in turn:

- *Education plus communication*. This strategy represents an approach to change based on understanding and rationality. If employees can be shown the reason behind a proposed change they are more likely to accept the need for it and support the programme. It is a slow process and can allow potential opposition to develop through access to information. The value of communication in change was supported by more recent work by Hau and Tung (2003).
- *Participation plus involvement*. This strategy is based on the notion that if people are actively involved in change they will go along with it. This point is reinforced by Holbeche (2003), head of research at Roffey Park. It can be useful where resistance is likely to exist. Also by working together improvements to interpersonal relationships could occur and the ground be prepared for more effective change in the future. There is however, a danger of participation producing inappropriate outcomes if a new power balance emerges.
- *Facilitation plus support*. This would be suitable in situations where the difficulty was one of being able to cope with the change process or the new situation. It is an approach in which the strategy is one of providing an opportunity to come to terms with the change and to grow in confidence during the transition.
- *Negotiation plus agreement*. Negotiation is a strategy aimed at resolving difference though agreement. It is usually associated with problem solving and situations in which a trade-off possibility exists. Changing working patterns in return for higher pay, for example.
- *Manipulation plus co-option*. The political aspects of change provide a clear indication of situations in which some form of arranging of events and alliances are undertaken in order to make more certain a particular outcome. In a very real sense this represents a manipulation of events. Co-option can be used as a means of diverting resistance through direct involvement. For example, the promotion of an active trade union representative to a supervisory position might reduce conflict and allow a more moderate individual to take over the trade union position. The major problems with manipulation and co-option are in being discovered or the acts undertaken being misinterpreted.
- *Explicit plus implicit coercion*. This strategy towards change is all about force and threat. It is not intended to create commitment; it is intended to achieve compliance. It is a 'take it or else' approach. As an example it is the strategy that makes it quite clear that the company will relocate to areas of cheap labour unless the workforce accept lower wages and higher output targets. Implicit coercion is a more subtle form of that force. As a strategy this can offer success for a while – as a result of the compliance achieved. For example, the threat to close a factory if employees do not accept low pay might work for a while but as soon as higher paid work becomes available they will leave. The quality and quantity of output might also be expected to drop or if the spending power of the employees becomes very low they may call the bluff of managers and strike.

Dunphy and Stace's model

Dunphy and Stace (1990) introduce a two-dimensional matrix as another way of identifying strategies for the management of change. One axis describes the scale of change involved and the other the style of change management in the situation (Figure 19.4).

FIGURE 19.4

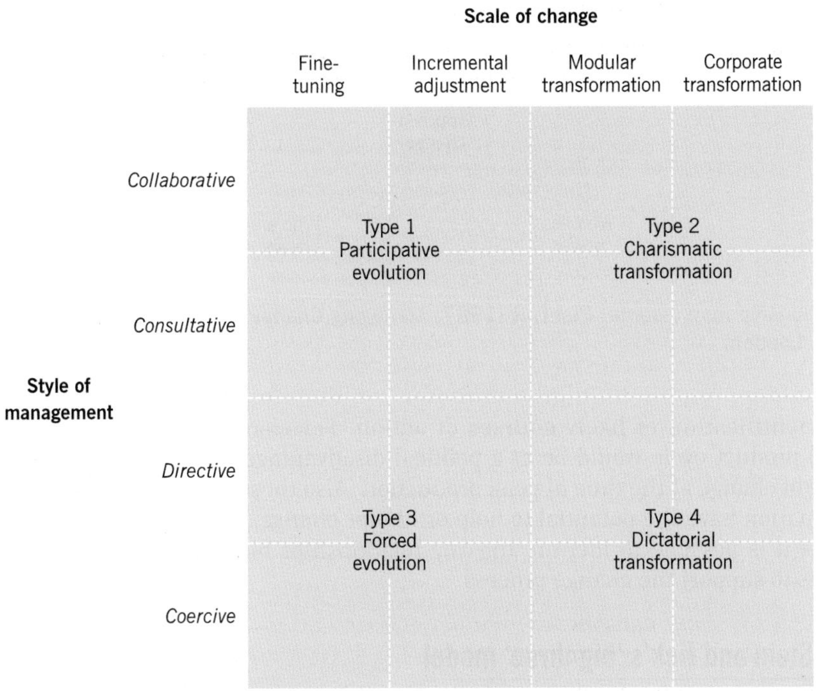

Dunphy and Stace's change strategies (*source*: Dunphy, D and Stace, D (1990) *Under New Management: Australian Organizations in Transition*, McGraw-Hill, Sydney)

The four change strategies in Figure 19.4 are as follows:

1. *Participative evolution*. This strategy involves relatively small changes achieved through involvement.
2. *Forced evolution*. This strategy forces change onto the participants, but the changes themselves are relatively small.
3. *Charismatic transformation*. This strategy is used for large-scale change of a one-off nature. Frequently such changes are initiated and driven by a charismatic leader or sponsor.
4. *Dictatorial transformation*. This strategy relies on force or coercion to make large-scale changes of a one-off nature. This could be most successful as a one-time emergency response to a crisis. Here time is of the essence and significant resistance might be expected.

Plant's model

In seeking to manage change Plant (1987) advocates key relationship mapping in attempting to identify appropriate change strategies. The model requires consideration of four key elements associated with change: winners, losers, power and information (Figure 19.5).

Winners would not normally be expected to resist proposed changes, whereas losers would. If a company reorganizes its wage structures those employees who receive a pay rise are likely to consider it a good scheme and those who are likely to lose money under the new scheme would consider it a bad one. In this type of situation the power balance between management and trade unions might be important

FIGURE 19.5

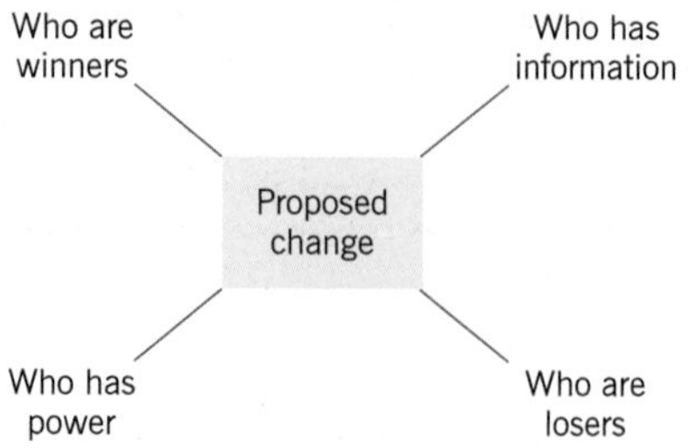

Key relationship map (*source*: Plant, R (1987) *Managing Change and Making It Stick*, Fontana, London)

in the identification of likely courses of action. For example, a company with a seasonal product cycle would be at a political disadvantage if it sought to introduce this type of change at the time of peak production. Also those who hold or have access to information have the potential to help or hinder change. In considering these four elements it is possible to identify the key relationships between them and to plan strategies to support the change process.

Kanter, Stein and Jick's 'big three' model

This model of change (Kanter *et al.*, 1992) proposes that change is multidirectional and continuous. Stability as it is usually experienced within organizations does not reflect the absence of change. It reflects levels of change that are not noticed by the participants, or it reflects change that goes unchallenged by them. From that perspective stability is regarded as a state of predictability when the interests of the various stakeholder groups are broadly in alignment.

Change as conceived by this model occurs when there is a lack of predictability or harmony within the situation. For example, the organization may lose its close connection with the environment if it becomes complacent and does not monitor competitor activity or the needs of its customers. Equally, the organization may need to change radically if its physical structure is no longer able to organize the delivery of goods and services in ways that effectively meet the customer needs. In that sense this model of change offers an attempt to capture a very broad concept of change tied into human experience within an organizational setting. The authors suggest that at the societal level it is macro evolutionary forces that act upon the situation, emerging from other organizations and social change generally. At the organizational level the authors argue that it is micro evolutionary forces emerging from factors such as the stage in the organizational lifecycle, age, history, etc. that influence change. At the individual level within an organization, it is suggested that it is the political forces associated with power and control that influence the change process. Change as experienced within the organization will depend on the balance of each of the individual forces acting upon the situation at any particular moment.

Although this model offers an attempt to describe change as a complex social process, it is difficult to identify how it could be used to manage the process. It suggests that there are many possible forces acting upon the situation at many different levels, but that simply identifies potential change forces and does not offer explanation or clues as to its management in any particular context. An analyst or manager seeking to use the model is left to identify the particular forces acting upon the situation for themselves, and so different interpretations are possible between people. The big picture may be useful in identifying general trends, but is of little value to the specific manager or employee seeking to deal with their own situation.

Each of the contingency models reflects a simplification of the complex circumstances that exist at the time of change. Simplification represents a mechanism for aiding understanding and therefore the ability to control. It is searching for and imposing the familiar onto stimuli to create meaning. In doing so the signals can be misinterpreted, clues missed and inaccurate interpretations made. Inevitably, if this happens as part of a change programme there is a danger of a failure in the process, or in the ability to generate the result intended.

The potential limitations in contingency models have been recognized by a number of writers and Dunford (1992) reviews some of them in relation to the Dunphy and Stace model outlined earlier. Examples include the complexity of the organization and environment relationship and the political nature of managerial self-interest. Managers have particular ways of relating to organizations, workers and the rights and responsibilities of the other stakeholder groups. This leads to the creation of particular interpretative schemes, the existence of which play a determining role in strategy formulation. So as with all aspects of management, caution is necessary in accepting any model of change management as offering a totally valid explanation of the processes involved and how to manage them.

SYSTEMS PERSPECTIVES ON CHANGE

There are a number of systems approaches that have something to offer as a basis for problem solving. One approach is specifically worthy of mention in the context of managing change. Total systems intervention (TSI) is grounded in the philosophy of critical systems thinking. This philosophy is itself based upon three principles: complementarism, social awareness, and human well-being/emancipation. These principles reflect the view that techniques should be selected according to their appropriateness, that the social context plays a major part in determining the approach adopted and that the human dimension to work should contribute to the process of problem solving. The original source for this perspective is Flood and Jackson (1991). A more recent review of this subject (Flood, 1996) is referenced as Further reading.

The TSI approach is a problem-solving approach and has a wider application than the management of change. It is included here because of its relevance to managing some change processes. TSI comprises three phases:

1. *Creativity*. 'The task during the creativity phase is to use systems metaphors as organizing structures to help managers think creatively about their enterprises' (p 50).
2. *Choice*. 'The task during the choice phase is to choose an appropriate systems-based intervention methodology (or set of methodologies) to suit particular characteristics of the organization's situation as revealed by the examination conducted in the creativity phase' (p 51).
3. *Implementation*. 'The task during the implementation phase is to employ a particular systems methodology to translate the dominant vision of the organization, its structure, and the general orientation adopted to concerns and problems, into specific proposals for change' (p 52).

Although there are three stages to the TSI methodology it is intended to function as an iterative process with movement back and forth through reference to earlier and later stages during the process. Within the TSI approach there is the opportunity to utilize one or more specific systems methodologies. Each of the systems methodologies available is claimed to be of benefit in particular contextual conditions.

The benefits of the systems approaches are that a range of techniques can be accessed that offer the opportunity to tailor actions to locally defined analysis. It offers the ability for wide involvement in creating a creative picture of the situation and of finding mechanisms for resolving the competing points of view about those situations, in the process finding ways of surfacing and managing the power and political aspects of change.

CHAOS AND CHANGE

There is a widespread view in human society that advancing knowledge is about seeking to impose order onto chaos. From that perspective, chaos is regarded as something that is random, of no value, with no order or apparent pattern evident. Indeed the *Pocket Oxford Dictionary* (1969) defines chaos as: 'Formless welter of matter conceived as preceding creation; utter confusion … utterly without order or arrangement'. Clearly chaos is something to be avoided and the role of science and research has generally been seen as the main mechanism through which knowledge can be created and so order imposed on what would otherwise be simply a chaotic mess. However, a relatively recent branch of science has begun to develop an interest in what has become known as chaos and complexity theory. The point of interest in essence lies largely in the distinction between unpredictability and chaos. The weather is frequently quoted as an example in this context. Weather patterns are largely unpredictable, but that does not mean that they are chaotic in the broadest sense of the term. They are unpredictable systems, but they are quite ordered in a very complex way. Another analogy is that of the so-called butterfly effect. A butterfly flaps its wings in Australia and this sets in motion a chain of events that creates a tidal wave on the east coast of South America. Most times this does not happen, but it might under the right circumstances. The same can be said of much of the reality of organizational experience. There exists a massive array of variables in an equally complex dynamic environment impacting on every organization. This forms the basis of the application of chaos theory to the organizational situation.

Waldrop (1992, pp 9–10) summed these issues up when he wrote:

> Why did the Soviet Union's forty year hegemony over Eastern Europe collapse within a few months in 1989? Why did the stock market crash more than 500 points on a single Monday in October 1987? … If evolution (or free-market capitalism) is really just a matter of the survival of the fittest, then why should it ever produce anything other than ruthless competition among individuals? In a world where nice guys all too often finish last, why should there be any such thing as trust and cooperation?

Marion (1999, p 15) suggests that:

> Mathematically, Chaos happens when equations used to describe seemingly simple systems just won't behave as expected. They will not yield a stable response, or the answers they give jump wildly when the quantity of an input variable is even lightly perturbed. These equations are called 'nonlinear' because their inputs are not predictably related to their output.

Hopefully, the potential for such models to be of value in an organizational context begins to become apparent with these quotations. Managing within an organizational environment would clearly be seen to qualify as falling within the chaotic concept as described by Marion.

The point to emerge from the work of Marion and others is that any organization is essentially a complex adaptive system (CAS). As such, it is forever perched on the edge of change, susceptible to the 'slightest breath of wind [which] can topple them. Most breezes – even gales – have no effect, however, because CAS are, by definition, vast networks of interdependent structures, and such interdependency gives strength to a structure' (p 270). However because of the relationships between the elements within the CAS, change has the potential to reverberate throughout the system, providing the impact is in the right place, at the right time, with the right force and the system itself is in the right state. This is again where the butterfly analogy makes sense even within an organizational context. However, change and chaos are never far apart and many employees experience change weariness as the result of too many changes being required too quickly, this is illustrated in the following Employee Perspective (19.3).

THE CHANGE AGENT

Another feature of the management of change touched on earlier is the role of the **change agent** in the process. A change agent is someone who plays a leading part in sponsoring the need for change or in its implementation. There have been a number of frameworks describing the forms of change agent activity. One of the more recent is

Change agent
Someone who plays a leading part in sponsoring the need for change or its implementation.

EMPLOYEE PERSPECTIVE 19.3 The effects of reorganization

A large retail company based in Edinburgh decided to engage in a major restructuring exercise in its head office. The number of staff was to be reduced by 35 per cent and the number of levels was also to be reduced. A voluntary redundancy/early retirement scheme was offered to employees and the company was able to achieve its planned reduction in numbers without any difficulty. Louise, one of the team leaders in the accounts payable section of the finance department had been with the company for 25 years and had seen many changes in operational procedure and work organization over that time.

Following the redundancies and reorganization changes to work organization and procedure began to filter through as instructions from senior managers, supported by outside consultants. Some of the changes did not make sense to Louise and seemed to make many of the jobs more difficult and complex than they had been. She frequently made the point to her manager and was told that the new systems had been designed to comply with the revised way of running the company and she should simply get on with her job. Yet Louise was sure that some of the revised procedures would not work as intended as similar ideas had been tried in the past and failed. Still she persisted in making what she considered to be useful points, only to be told time and time again to get on with the job as directed.

She began to become more and more disillusioned with the way that the company was now operating and after about two years of working in the revised arrangements her manager offered her early retirement on very generous terms. She gratefully accepted the offer and prepared to leave. On her last day she was chatting with her manager, with whom she had a good personal relationship, and said that she was sad to be leaving after so many happy years, only to have it spoiled in recent times. Her manager said that it was inevitable that she would have to go one way or another because the company did not want to be reminded of the past so often. Even if things had been tried before the outcome might be different this time and her reaction had suggested disloyalty. Also the senior management wanted to be seen to be in charge and to organize things their way.

Tasks

1. What would you have done if you were Louise and why?
2. What does this example suggest about the number and rate of changes that can take place within an organization?
3. What might the implications of Louise's experience contribute to understanding how organizations should go about making change?

that of Ottaway (1982) who produced a taxonomy linked to a particular model of change – that of Lewin (1951). However, in general terms it has a much broader relevance than its grounding in one model might suggest. Three types of change agent are identified:

1. *Change generators*. These are linked with the unfreezing process. They are the individuals or groups who identify areas of potential change and convince others of the need to take action. This could include a charismatic leader who is able to create a movement willing to adopt the changes expressed in the leader's vision. It could also include a special project team who are given the task of reviewing a particular aspect of company operations.
2. *Change implementers*. These deliver actual change to the organization. They can be charismatic leaders who are able to persuade subordinates to accept change. They can be sponsors from senior management who lend their position to the call for change and so encourage others to see it as important or inevitable. They can be industrial relations specialists who have the task of making agreements with employee representatives and thereby bring about change proposals.
3. *Change adopters*. These represent the refreezing stage of the Lewin model. They are the individuals who make the changes work in practice and by so doing ensure that they become the norms within that particular context. They are inevitably the line managers, supervisors and employees who get on with the job and make sure that it does not slip back to what existed before.

RESISTANCE TO CHANGE

The starting point for considering resistance to change is the image conjured up by the phrase itself. It implies that an individual or group has determined to frustrate the intentions of another to implement a particular course of action. In a managerial context, that inevitably reflects the decision of the employer to change some aspect of the organization and in so doing influence the work activities and/or employment of workers. Kahn (1982) suggests that resistance behaviour during times of change is frequently indistinguishable from normal behaviour patterns. The difference being a function of the perspective of the person classifying the behaviour rather than the behaviour itself.

The following material has been compiled from a number of sources including Armstrong (1995), Hellriegel *et al*., (1989), Kanter (1983), Kotter and Schlesinger (1979), Moorhead and Griffin (1992), Mullins (1996) and Plant (1987).

Individual resistance to change

Individuals resist change for a number of reasons, including those indicated in Figure 19.6.

Many of the reasons indicated in Figure 19.6 are self-explanatory and easily understood. For example, fear of the unknown infers that the individual would prefer to remain with existing arrangements. Change can be a negative experience for many employees. Organizational experience soon indicates that managers do not always have the best interests of employees at heart, particularly when cutbacks are the norm! However, some of the reasons identified in Figure 19.6 need further explanation:

FIGURE 19.6

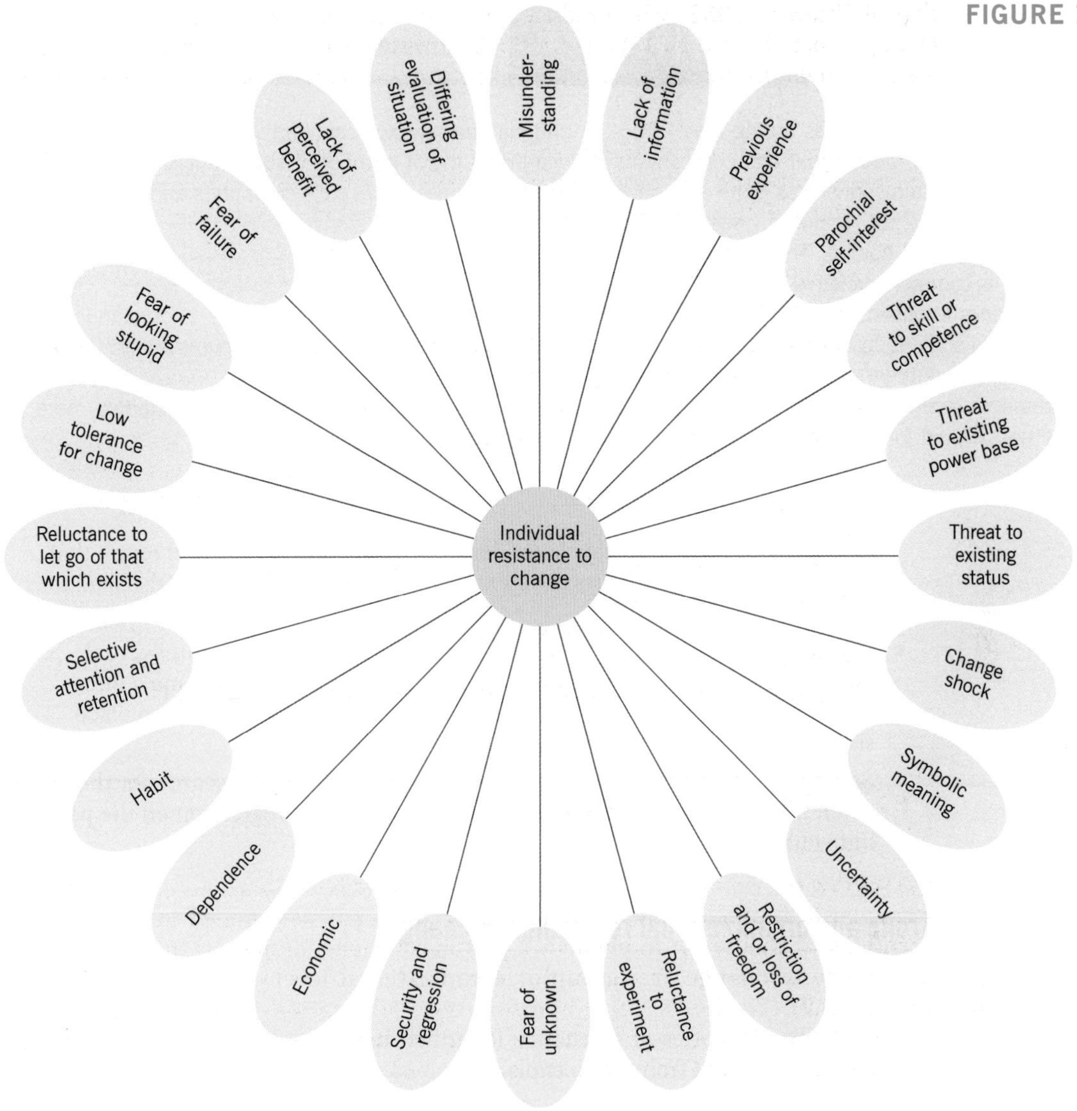

Individual reasons for resisting change

- *Symbolic meaning*. The entitlement to benefits such as a company car or the use of a private office rather than an area separated by partitions all provide symbols of status within the organization. Changes which impact on such visible signs can be fiercely resisted even if they are incidental.
- *Change shock*. The previous routine will have been familiar and individuals will have known instinctively what they were supposed to do. Change can destroy that level of familiarity and create situations in which predictability is reduced, thus creating an experience of shock for the individual. The following Employee Perspective (19.4) demonstrates the reaction of angry employees in shock at their treatment over a major change in their working lives.
- *Selective attention and retention*. Individuals define reality for themselves based upon their perception of the world as they experience and understand it. Change can call into question these frames of reference and as a consequence

EMPLOYEE PERSPECTIVE 19.4 **Dismissed by text message!**

It was widely reported in the press during May 2003 (see for example, Jones, 2003) that one company in the personal injury claims business (The Accident Group) dismissed all its 2500 workers by text message when it suddenly ceased trading. The personal injury claims industry is commonly referred to as 'ambulance chasing' as it seeks to obtain compensation for people who have suffered some form of accident. Its advertising slogan was, 'Where there's blame, there's a claim'. The text messages received by the staff told them that they would not be paid for the previous month's work and that their employment had ceased immediately. On hearing of this a number of staff went to local offices and either smashed or stole computers and other office equipment.

Tasks

1. Is this response from employees understandable, excusable or tolerable in the circumstances? Justify your views.
2. How could the situation have been handled more effectively?

be rejected. Individuals have a tendency to only pay attention and retain that information which supports their existing world views which can also lead to resistance.

- *Dependence*. Students are dependent upon lecturers for their intellectual development. However, taken to extreme, dependence can become a force which resists change as security is threatened. Dependence can also place significant power in the hands of those who are relied upon.
- *Security and regression*. The need for security can lead to a search for the past when things appeared simpler and more familiar. This regression on the part of individuals can be a potent force for resisting change.

Group and organizational resistance to change

Resistance to change at a group or organizational level comes in many forms (Figure 19.7).

Most of the categories of resistance identified in Figure 19.7 are self-explanatory, but a few could benefit from some explanation:

- *Misinformation*. Control over communication provides opportunities for a group to impart particular interpretations to information and so engineer resistance. Sometimes rumour and gossip can fall into this category. For example Bordia *et al.* (2003) identify five different categories of rumour and gossip. They also classified individual examples as either positive or negative depending on the content relative to the change. Not surprisingly, negative rumours were more prevalent during change than positive ones. The five categories of rumour identified were:
  1. Those about changes to jobs and working conditions
  2. Those about the nature of organizational change
  3. Those about poor change management
  4. Those about change and its consequences on organizational performance
  5. Interpersonal gossip about change and its impact.
- *Organization structure*. The bureaucratic form of organization was designed to deliver consistency and predictability of operations. Consequently, it is a structure that does not cope easily with change.

FIGURE 19.7

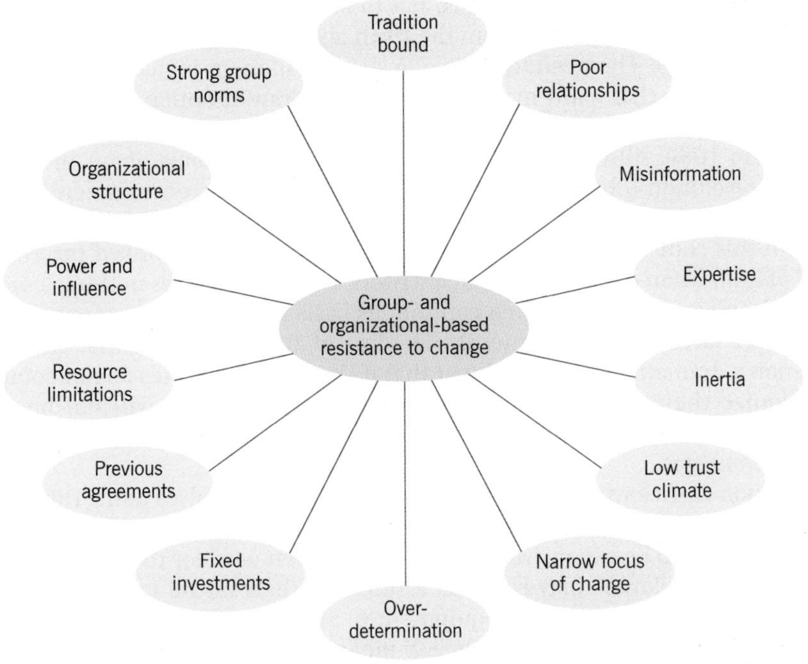

Group and organizational reasons for resisting change

- *Previous agreements*. Arrangements entered into with another group or organization are designed to control events in the future. This restricts the ability to make changes in the interaction between these groups over the period of such agreements.
- *Fixed investments*. The investments that an organization makes in buildings, land and equipment place considerable restriction on what can be done in the future. In practice, they limit the ability to change because they represent assets that are not easy to liquidate in the short term.
- *Overdetermination*. The systems and procedures that organizations create to provide control can also restrict the ability to introduce change.
- *Narrow focus of change*. In considering change an organization very often takes the immediate zone of impact into account. It is possible for situations to arise in which groups not immediately affected by change resist involvement and so limit the benefits ultimately gained. For example, in addressing the production problems in one department management may introduce team working and in the process replace supervisors with team leaders. Supervisors in other departments may see this as an attempt to erode their status and indeed job security. If they are not involved in the original exercise and supportive of the changes, then they may well resist any attempts to introduce change in the future.

INNOVATION AS A CHANGE STRATEGY

Innovation and change are areas of activity that are strongly tied together. One dictionary definition of innovation is to bring in novelties and to make changes. This conveys a feeling of something that is frivolous, not to be taken seriously and of little importance. Nothing could be further from the truth about the experience of innovation in many organizations. The need to be able to stay ahead in an increasingly competitive world is something that many management writers draw attention to. Tom Peters, for example, has produced a stream of books that began with *Thriving On Chaos* published in 1989. All were intended to drive a message home about the need for continual revolution (change) in responding to the operating environment, the basic message being innovate or die.

It is in this context that innovation and change are strongly linked together. The degree of innovation demanded by such writers as Peters requires nothing less than a total and complete revolution on a continuous basis in the running of organizations. Change on a large scale, permanently. The line of argument being that competition poses such a dramatic and global threat that if Western companies do not completely revolutionize their strategies and operational activities they will not be able to compete with companies that make those changes and operate from a base with natural advantages.

Innovation carries with it a measure of risk because it involves doing things differently. Consider the decision to innovate through the introduction of high technology. The equipment will be expensive; it may not have been used for that particular application before; employees may see it as a threat to their future employment; and it will take time to commission the equipment to an acceptable standard of reliability. Each of these features carries with it a measure of risk which when combined produce an even greater danger of failure. There are some industries that are particularly prone to the risks associated with innovation. For example, restaurants and clothing are subjected to rapid and frequent changes in fashion and taste. Unless they continually innovate and update their offerings to the market they will lose trade. Piva and Vivarelli (2004) demonstrate a link between the increases in proportion of jobs classified as skilled as a result of change from research in some 488 Italian manufacturing companies. But the same statistical support was not there for the links between skill upgrading and innovation (defined as R&D). This is an interesting result and one which runs counter to what might be expected. Further research in this area is clearly needed.

Just as with change itself, innovation is an issue that finds resistance in many organizations for a number of reasons. There is a significant degree of inertia built into most organizations. Control and operational effectiveness come from the predictability, repeated practice and consistency available through standardized products and services. Changing anything can create uncertainty, unfamiliarity and problems. Pascale (1990) points to a number of organizational features that restrict the ability to innovate and change in Table 19.7. These were identified from a comparison between Honda and General Motors.

There are different forms that innovation can take. Betz (1987) identifies three levels of innovative activity:

1. *Radical*. This represents the invention of something new. This is frequently the application of fundamental science. It carries with it the greatest level of risk, highest cost and longest timescale for development.
2. *Systems*. This level represents the application of existing science and technology in a novel way. It tends to be the combination of radical-level innovations once they become established and less vulnerable to failure. The combination of the internal combustion engine and carriage-building technologies to create the motor car for example. The timescales involved in the introduction of innovations at this level are shorter.
3. *Incremental*. This level of innovation represents the adaptation of existing technologies and products etc. It is the fine tuning of that which already exists.

Now to summarize this chapter in terms of the relevant learning objectives:

- **Describe the major change models available and explain how they contribute to the management of it.** There are a number of models associated with change that can contribute to the management of it. For example, Lewin's forcefield model is based around the notion that any situation is held in its current state as a result of the balance between opposing forces. In order to make change it is therefore necessary to increase the pressure on one side of the opposing forces relative to the other side. The assumption being that the increased relative pressure in one direction will move the situation in the desired direction. The change process consists of three stages: unfreezing, change and refreezing. The stages are intended to prepare the situation for change, make the changes and lock the new situation into the normal behaviour patterns in that context. Organizational development is also introduced in the chapter but as this is discussed below it will not be expanded here. A number of contingency models of change were discussed including that proposed by Kotter and Schlesinger, which is based around the use of strategies to bring about change. This is described in Table 19.6. Dunphy and Stace's model is based around the style of management present in the situation and the scale of change that needs to be made. The variations possible in the matrix resulting from these two dimensions produces four change strategies including participative evolution, and dictatorial transformation. Katner, Stein and Jick developed what is called the 'big three model' which proposes that change exists when there is a lack of predictability or harmony between the stakeholders. This model is of more descriptive than management benefit as it tends towards the explanation of the circumstances surrounding change rather than how to deal with it. Plant offers a model of change that is based on the need to identify a number of key relationships in any change process. They are who wins, who loses, who has power and who has information, all of which need to be taken into account if change is to be managed successfully. The chapter also introduces very briefly one of the systems approaches to managing change which also has relevance in this context. The McKinsey 7-S framework was introduced in this chapter as being of relevance to change management.
- **Explain the approach and value of organizational development (OD) as a change strategy.** Organizational development contains a number of elements and is therefore a broad-based approach to change and the management of it. For example, it makes use of action research, attitude surveys, encounter groups, process consultation, quality of working life principles and an integrated or strategic approach to making change in a planned and systematic way. The underlying perspective of organizational development is that incremental change is the best way forward and that the people in the situation know best how to tackle change if only they can be prepared and supported effectively. For example, process consultation as an approach seeks to facilitate problem solving rather than introduce expertise into a situation as this take away ownership from the members. In terms of its value, OD has much to offer providing the parties are prepared to work together and allow a high degree of empowerment in the identification and process of making change. It also assumes that time exists to make the necessary change as a high degree of learning through experience and discovery is implicit in the process. It may not be an appropriate methodology if a crisis exists or if the political climate is hostile to such involvement. Equally, participation may not always deliver the best solution to a change requirement as the parties involved may actively seek to resist the change if it is perceived to be against their interests.
- **Appreciate why people frequently resist change.** People resist change for a wide range of reasons, many of which are identified in Figure 19.6. These include being familiar with one way of doing things and not wanting to do anything differently; self-interest; threat to skill or competence; threat to status within the organization and the uncertainty associated with making change. In addition, there are group and organizational level factors which influence resistance to change and these are identified in Figure 19.7. For example; misinformation by one group or another can be used as a means of encouraging individuals or groups to resist; the existence of a low trust environment can also work against change being accepted. These figures and the associated text should be consulted for more detail on this objective.
- **Discuss the forces acting on an organization which push for change to be undertaken.** The major forces acting on any organization which push

change onto the agenda include rapid product obsolescence, which is the constant pressure to adapt what is already produced and offer new products or services to the market in order to keep up with customer taste and competitor activity. Information and knowledge creation and availability are important. Information is a commodity and has created its own market through the internet, also it is relatively easy and cheap to use the information available to develop new products and services or identify different ways of doing existing things. This increases competition possibilities and reduces the security of any dominant player in a market. Changing demographics means that different products and services are in demand across time. There also internal forces acting on an organization and which require change to become a constant feature of life. The need for efficiency in order to keep shareholders happy through higher profits, and retain customers through lower process is an ever present pressure in organizational life. Fashion also encourages managers with careers and reputations to create or protect to be seen as leading edge in the change process. Control is a management imperative and as such they inevitably see the increased need for it as one way of achieving their other objectives. Consequently, the perceived need for control can be a major driver of change. Internal pressure from one of the stakeholder groups can force change. For example, workers might strike in support of higher wages and if successful may force higher labour cost onto the company. Stewart uses the terms business structure and business functioning to describe managerial careers which it is argued have relevance to the existence of change.

- **Detail what is meant by the term 'change agent' in relation to change management.** The change agent is the person who plays a leading part in sponsoring the need for change or in the change process itself. In practice they represent the figurehead that forms the focus for the importance of the change process; it is usually a senior manager or other significant figure within the organization. Three type of change agent are identified in the text. The first is a change generator. These people are the ones who are mostly associated with the need for change and the early stages of it, the unfreezing stage in Lewin's model. The second type of change agent is the change implementer. These people are associated with the actual change process and are often charismatic leaders who can rally people behind a particular idea. They may not be a management representative as it is possible for employee representatives to hold the status necessary to provide this type of leadership. The third type of change agent is the change adopter. These people make the changes work in practice. They are associated with the refreezing aspect of the Lewin model. As is implied by this discussion, not all change processes have the same change agent for each stage of the process, and they may not all be formally appointed by management. Employees will however, take their lead on change from the (formal and informal) change agents that they see around them and how they respond to the processes that are being experienced at work.

DISCUSSION QUESTIONS

1. 'Human beings are their own worst enemy as they demand high quality products and services at very low prices whilst at the same time demanding high quality jobs and high wages. These demands are incompatible and change which negatively impacts on jobs and people is therefore inevitable.' Discuss this statement.
2. Describe the McKinsey 7-S framework and explain how it could be used to inform a change management programme.
3. Outline the links between power, politics and change and explain why they are necessary to the management of a change programme.
4. Provide a brief explanation for six of the individual reasons for resisting change.
5. Distinguish between planned and unplanned change, adaptive and fracturing change. What are the consequences of these distinctions?
6. Discuss how BPR and TQM could be used separately and in an integrated way to support change processes.
7. Describe the contingency approach to organizational change and distinguish it from the OD approach.
8. Provide a brief explanation for six of the group and organizational reasons for resisting change.
9. 'The true skill in management is to keep change happening so that everyone has to pay attention to what they are doing and they do not have any spare time to cause trouble for managers.' Discuss this statement in the light of the material in this chapter on power and politics in relation to change.
10. Describe the five elements in the innovation process. How might innovation be used as part of a change process?

CASE STUDY Involvement and failure

This case study is based on Lowsling, the company that was introduced in the case study for Chapter 18. This case study describes one of the other areas of difficulty that existed within the company and how it was handled by the people involved. The production process involved the cutting of rolls of polypropylene fabric to particular lengths and sewing them together to make large sacks and single-trip industrial containers. The work was physically demanding.

Prior to the operations director joining the company some attempt at increasing factory productivity had been made through the introduction of work-measurement based incentive schemes. The production manager of the company (the brother-in-law of the chief executive) when this was being done had suggested that it would be cheaper to estimate the job times and then to negotiate these with the trade union representatives. This would, he argued, also allow some degree of participation of employees in the process. In practice it produced a situation in which many of the job times were generous and an effective employee veto existed on attempts to raise productivity as once agreed job times could not be changed. If a job time could not be agreed for a new product then average earnings were paid until agreement was reached, resulting in significant delays in implementing true incentive conditions. Inevitably, over a couple of years employee earnings rose steeply and productivity dropped. For example, on some jobs, employees could earn what would be classed as a week's wage in one day. On other jobs it was a struggle for employees to make a decent wage. This also led to some supervisors taking bribes from employees for allocating them jobs with the highest earnings potential. So overall although wages in the company were not high, not much work was being done either.

Clearly this situation could not continue and the production manager was eventually moved sideways to the newly created position of production planning manager. An operations director with experience in employee relations and factory management was appointed with the remit of sorting the problems out and restoring a sound basis for factory operations. He began by reviewing the current situation and as a result he came to the conclusion that fundamental change was needed in the way that the factory operated and the ways in which employees were paid. The employees and their representatives also considered the existing pay scheme to be unfair and inequitable. Also they wanted better benefits such as a pension scheme and longer holidays to be included in their reward package. As the company was losing money, all parties accepted that fundamental change was necessary if it were to survive. The operations director considered that as a consequence the basis existed for a joint management–employee approach to finding solutions to the many problems.

A joint management–employee group was established and agreed that a completely new way of determining a fair day's work for a fair day's pay was needed. A professionally qualified work study engineer with considerable experience in the same industry was recruited to identify accurate job times for the full range of jobs in the factory and also to act as a consultant to the joint management–employee group. It was after the consultant had carried out his measurement of the time that it should take to do each job in the factory that problems began to emerge. When the real level of productivity was established through conventional work measurement techniques the employees on the joint group began to realize the degree of change that was going to be required. They expressed concern that the times were wrong and that no human could be expected to work at the rate implied by the figures. It became clear that this perception would be a major sticking point in achieving change, but the operations director was determined to maintain the involvement of employees in finding a solution.

Meetings were held over a period of eight months in an attempt to find ways around the problems identified by the work study exercise. A number of options were considered involving many different wage structures and transitional arrangements (to give employees time to adjust to the new requirements as well as allow them to maintain their earnings levels during the change). Essentially the new arrangements required that employees raise average productivity by 25 per cent over a two year period in order to retain current earnings levels. Of course that average figure hid a wide range of individual job variation. Also some employees would be more significantly affected than others. For example, the wife of one of the supervisors was always among the highest earners, as was one of the employee representatives, because they had been 'bought-off' in the past with easy jobs that paid a high bonus.

Over time it became apparent to the operations director that the employees on the group were not really interested in finding a solution. They were simply prolonging their involvement in the process in order to maintain the status quo for as long as possible. A comprehensive package was put together by management which included elements of transitional protection for one extra year, profit-share payments, improved holidays, the introduction of a company pension scheme and other benefits, in return for agreeing to the new work study arrangements. The employee group did not feel that they could support this package as they admitted that it would create problems for them personally with their colleagues. The package was therefore put formally to the trade union for negotiation but was rejected. The trade union representatives said that it was completely unacceptable as it required them to work harder for the same money. They wanted to retain the current wage system but to accept the other benefits in the proposed package. Naturally this was unacceptable to management. The trade union would not negotiate with managers on any other basis and so management called a factory meeting and put the plan to all employees. The proposals were noisily shouted down and rejected in a mass vote.

Management had one more attempt at negotiating with the trade union over the proposed package, even suggesting a longer phasing-in of the new work study arrangement, but this, too, was rejected. The events were reported to the main board at its next meeting and the decision was taken to close the company down at that location and start again in another part of the UK. When the closure was announced to the factory a small group of people (not employee representatives) approached the operations director for a meeting. They claimed to represent many of the workers and said that they had not realized that the situation would end in closure. They also said that they had not been serious in rejecting the company proposals, they simply wanted to retain the status quo as long as possible and that if management had said that it was either accept the deal or the factory would close, then they would have accepted. Management rejected the points made by this group of workers as being too little, too late. Management also took the view that it would be difficult to get everyone to work to the new scheme and that things would quickly slip back to how they had been. Management wanted a new start completely. The factory closed three months later and everyone lost their jobs.

Tasks

1. How would you have dealt with the original problems if you were:
   a) management
   b) an employee representative?
2. Would any of the change models outlined in this chapter have helped to achieve the changes intended at Lowsling? Why or why not?
3. Do the events described in this case study suggest that employee involvement in change:

- is not a good idea;
- may only work in certain situations;
- cannot be separated from the political and power structures that exist;
- should be used only as a means of manipulating opinion and attitudes to a management desired perspective; or,
- should be used because ultimately all stakeholders have to accept some responsibility for the circumstances that they create?

4. Justify your views in terms of the material presented in this and other chapters in this book.

FURTHER READING

Clark, H, Chandler, J and Barry, J (1994) *Organization and Identities: Text and Readings in Organizational Behaviour*, International Thomson Business Press, London. Contains a broad range of original articles on relevant material themes and from significant writers referred to in this and other textbooks on management and organizations.

Cummings, T and Worley, C (2001) *Organizational Development and Change* (with Infotrack) 7th edn, South Western, New York. A comprehensive text covering both areas of this chapter in great detail. Has the advantage of providing access to Infotrack, a fully searchable library resource provided by the publisher.

Flood, RL (1996) *Solving Problem Solving*, John Wiley, Chichester. This text takes a new look at a number of systems approaches to problem solving and updates the approach to the TSI perspective introduced earlier. In that context problem solving is being equated with the management of change. It should be recognized that there are distinctions between these two concepts in particular situations.

Hamlin, B, Keep, J and Ash, K (2001) *Organizational Change and Development*, Financial Times/Prentice Hall, Harlow. A balanced, practical and academic book on both of the major topics covered by this chapter.

Lee, WW and Krayer, JK (2003) *Organizing Change: An Inclusive, Systematic Approach to Maintain Productivity and Achieve Results*, Wiley, Chichester. Explores the use of teams in a practical approach to change activity.

Mabey, C and Mayon-White, B (1993) *Managing Change*, 2nd edn, Paul Chapman Publishing, London. This book is intended to be a reader for one of the Open University courses that deals with managing change. It brings together a wide range of research-based perspectives on change and how to manage it, as well as examples of it in practice.

McCalman, J and Paton, RA (1992) *Change Management: A Guide to Effective Implementation*, Paul Chapman, London. As the title suggests, this book is about how to manage change processes. In doing so it concentrates on the two approaches to managing change, the systems approach and the organizational development model.

Oswick, C and Grant, D (eds) (1996) *Organization Development: Metaphorical Explorations*, Pitman, London. This text attempts to provide a basis for the critical evaluation of organizational development, rather than the more usual practitioner perspective. It also uses the metaphor as a basis of enhancing understanding of organizational development in general and specific terms.

Tidd, J, Bessant, J and Pavitt, K (2001) *Managing Innovation: Integrating Technological, Market and Organizational Change*, Wiley, Chichester. A text which covers many aspects of innovation and how it impacts on change within an organization.

COMPANION WEBSITE

Online teaching and learning resources:

Visit the companion website for Organizational Behaviour and Management 3rd edition at: *http://www.thomsonlearning.co.uk/businessandmanagement/martin3* to find valuable further teaching and learning material:

Refer to page 35 for full details.

Glossary

Action-centred leadership An approach to managing which consists of three elements – achieving the task, developing the individual and building and maintaining the team.

Action research (or learning) A problem solving process in which a group defines the problem to be examined and then uses their combined skill and experience to understand it in order to then take action to deal with it. An iterative and dynamic process of learning about problems by trying to solve them.

Adhocracy A form of organization structure typified by few levels of management; little formal control; decentralized decision making; few rules, policies and procedures; specialization of work function.

Administrative management Considers management as activities aimed at running the organization as a whole. Also see Classical management theory and Bureaucracy.

Alienation The detachment of the individual from the work that they do and/or the organization for which they work. Sometimes described as feelings of powerlessness, meaninglessness, isolation or self-estrangement in which the person no longer feels part of, or involved with, the work that they do.

Assessment centre A group recruitment or development process using a series of tests, interviews, group and individual exercises that are scored by a team of assessors in order to evaluate the candidates.

Attitude A predisposed feeling, thought or behavioural response to a particular stimulus. Acquired through socialization, education, training and previous experience of the stimulus.

Attitude set The totality of attitudes about a particular object held by an individual.

Attribution theory (of leadership) Suggests that leaders observe the behaviours of individual subordinates and vary their reactions accordingly.

Authority The ability of someone in a job or position to be able to require certain actions or behaviours to be undertaken by another person.

Autocratic–democratic style of leadership A continuum view of leadership with one extreme involving the leader taking all the decisions, and at the other the leader involving subordinates in decision making.

Autokinetic phenomenon Visually perceiving something to move when in fact it is stationary, a visual illusion.

Autonomous work groups A work team with delegated responsibility for a defined part of an organization's activities with the freedom to organize its own resources, pace of work and allocate responsibilities within the group.

Balanced business scorecard Developed by Kaplan and Norton as the means to measure the performance in four major areas of organizational activity: Financial; Innovation and learning; Internal processes; and Customers.

Benchmark A process in which aspects of company operations are compared with other organizations in order to measure relative performance and effectiveness.

Blame culture Describes an organization in which every error is regarded as the fault of an individual or group. Such cultures encourage a 'cover your back at all costs' approach to work.

Breakthrough leadership An approach to leadership which emphasizes the personal journey of discovery that each leader undergoes, includes elements of emotional intelligence and self-knowledge.

Brownfield site A term used to describe a location which already contains an operational unit, which may be about to undergo reconstruction or some form of transition or change. See also Greenfield site.

Bullying and harassment The act of intimidating or seeking to force someone to do something by subjecting them to persecution intended to undermine their confidence and self-esteem.

Bureaucracy see Bureaucratic.

Bureaucratic An approach to organizing the activities within an organization which involves specialization of task, plus a hierarchy of authority and decision making. See also Classical Management Theory and Administrative management.

Burnout The feeling of helplessness and of being unable to continue experienced by some individuals under prolonged exposure to stress.

Business process re-engineering (BPR) An approach to reorganization in which the key business processes are identified, followed by the elimination of other activity and the rapid transformation of the organization to the desired process orientation.

Cabal An informal group that attempts to take the initiative within an organization to further views supported by members or enhance their status and position.

Cafeteria or flexible benefits An approach to employee benefits that allows individuals to select a personal benefits package up to a set limit, from the total range available.

Change agent Someone who plays a leading part in sponsoring the need for change or its implementation.

Charismatic leadership The ability to exercise leadership through the power of the leader's personality.

Classical conditioning An approach to learning developed by Pavlov in which he used dogs to demonstrate that when the conditioned stimulus (bell) was associated with an unconditioned stimulus (food) over several repetitions a conditioned response resulted (salivation to the sound of the bell).

Classical management theory An approach to organizing described by writers including Fayol, Mary Parker Follett, Oliver Sheldon, Lyndall Urwick and

James Mooney. See also Administrative management and Bureaucracy.

Cliques A particular type of informal group in which individuals have a common interest and purpose; frequently the defence of members against the interests of other groups and individuals.

Coercive power The ability of a holder of such power to achieve control over another person through the threat of direct action, force or violence.

Cognitive dissonance Used to explain behaviour in an individual in situations where conflict exists between attitudes or beliefs.

Commitment This involves the employee internalizing the underlying values and norms held by management and in so doing committing themselves to management's aims and objectives.

Communication A process of sharing information and creating relationships in environments designed for manageable, goal-oriented behaviour.

Company doctor A senior manager brought into an ailing company in an attempt to turn it around.

Competency The characteristics and capabilities of an individual which directly contribute to superior job performance.

Compliance This involves the employee following the rules precisely, paying only 'lip service' to the aims and objectives determined by management.

Compulsory sociability An approach to building teams with a strong culture by requiring individuals to join in group activities and follow particular patterns of behaviour or face sanctions.

Conditioned The behaviour of an individual which results from the application of behaviourism techniques.

Conflict This frequently arises when the differences between two or more groups or individuals become apparent.

Conflict model of customer experience and organizational functioning This reflects the difficulty of functional groups being able to meet customer needs within a hierarchical organization.

Conflict model of decision making An algorithmic approach to taking decisions which is only intended to apply to life decisions and when certain other conditions can be met.

Conformity see Group conformity.

Content theories of motivation These concentrate on identifying the motives that produce behaviour.

Contingency theory Applies to the leadership, motivation and structure areas within organizational behaviour. Takes the view that the best style of leadership, form of motivation, or organizational structure depends upon the factors active in the situation.

Continuous improvement An approach to improvement adopting incremental and frequent changes aimed at improving operational effectiveness over a long period of time. It is often described as a journey without end.

Contract approach to ethics An approach to resolving ethical dilemmas grounded in the notion that agreements whether they be explicit or tacit should be honoured. It comes in two variations, Restricted contractarianism and Libertarian contractarianism.

Control Processes intended to achieve the outcome desired by the designer of the system.

Corporate anorexia Describes those organizations that cut employee numbers, out of a fear of becoming fat, perhaps to the point of extinction.

Corporate governance Defined by the Cadbury Committee as the systems through which companies are directed and controlled. It is about the ways in which ethics finds expression in business activities.

Corporate social responsibility This refers to the rights and responsibilities of an organization relative to its social context.

Countercultures These reflect a situation where one or more groups have objectives that run counter to those of the dominant group.

Crisis management The aspect of management that deals with major unplanned events that pose significant risk to the organization, its employees or other stakeholders.

Critical incidents research An approach involving asking what makes an individual feel good or bad about something, subsequent content analysis identifies the important issues.

Cultural web Based on the notion that the routines, rituals, stories, symbols, power structures, control systems and organization structure all contribute to the form of a particular culture.

Culture The acquired and conventionally accepted ways of thinking and behaving among a group or society.

Cycle model of decision making An iterative approach to decision making based on a nine step process.

Decision making A process through which a particular course of action is selected or solution identified from among the many options available.

Delayering The act of removing layers from an organization, thereby making it 'shorter' in the vertical dimension.

Delegated authority An action by managers in which they give some of their authority for decision making to subordinates.

Delegation The passing of some area of responsibility to a subordinate.

Devil's advocate A person specifically tasked with trying to disprove or challenge the argument or opinion put forward by another person or group.

Diffusion of responsibility The claim by someone (usually within a group) that they were not solely responsible for a particular decision or act, thereby avoiding any personal responsibility.

Division of labour The term describes breaking up the overall task into specialized and smaller activities in the search for higher levels of productivity and job specialization.

Downshift The decision by an individual to seek to move jobs to one at a lower level, with less responsibility, salary and stress.

Downsizing/rightsizing/delayering Processes which involve the elimination of jobs or entire levels within the organization on the assumption that unnecessary activity will be eliminated and a closer customer focus will result.

Drives The physiological and biological needs of the human body that direct behaviour. See also Motivation.

Emotional intelligence An approach to intelligence which describes it in terms of the ability to perceive, to integrate, to understand and reflectively manage one's own and other people's feelings.

Employee assistance programme A scheme provided by an employer (usually through a specialist consultancy) to offer assistance to employees who experience a problem and who might find it beneficial to have the opportunity to talk it through with a support worker. The intention being to assist the employee to find a way of dealing positively with the difficulty.

Employee involvement Represents an opportunity for employees to become involved beyond the normal scope of their job in decision making and/or running the business.

Employer of choice This implies that people will actively seek employment with the company and so contribute high performance over a long period of time.

Empowerment Means that employees are given the freedom to take action (within defined boundaries) without the need to have specific approval.

Enacted role What the individual actually does in fulfilling their role responsibilities.

Environment The elements and forces surrounding an organization with which it must interact and which can influence events, decisions and processes within the organization.

Ergonomics It sets out to identify how humans interact with the work-based physical environment and then to design the equipment in such a way as to have minimal negative impact on the people using it.

Ethics Takes as its focus of interest right, wrong, good and bad in relation to behaviour in an organizational context.

Expectancy theory of motivation A view of motivation that suggests that the desirability of particular outcomes is what motivates behaviour.

Expected role The specific role that an individual is expected to fulfil according to the organization, frequently specified in a job description.

Expert power This source of power originates from the knowledge, skill and expertise of an individual in a particular context.

Extrinsic motivator This represents a source of motivation that originates outside the individual worker and which influences their behaviour. See also Intrinsic motivation.

Extroversion One aspect of personality. The extrovert likes excitement, is sociable and lively. An introvert, by comparison, has a quiet and retiring aspect to their personality.

Federal organization Reflects the joining together of separate groups under a common identity for a specific purpose.

Felt fair A term used within reward management and employee relations that means that something should be 'felt to be fair' by the people subjected to the system or procedure.

Fight or flight response The process which allows a living organism to either stay and fight, or to run away and avoid confrontation.

Flexible firm There are a number of forms that flexibility can take, job, location, temporal, numerical and financial. It also relates to a specific organizational model which includes core and various forms of peripheral employee.

Focused deviancy The toleration of bending of the official rules as long as it contributes to the overall objective and does not become normal practice.

Forcefield analysis model A change model which proposes that any situation is held in place as the result of the balance of change and restraining forces acting upon it.

Fordism An alternative term for Scientific management.

Fordism and post-Fordism Refers to ways in which Scientific management principles are used in the running of manufacturing and other organizations.

Formal group Designed and imposed by managers on the workforce as a way of achieving organizational objectives through structure, departments and teams.

Frame of reference The internal frameworks held by an individual that informs their understanding of the world and how to relate to it.

Free association Refers to the right of employees to associate with whom they choose, perhaps against the wishes of management. It has a different meaning in psychoanalysis in that it reflects the process of allowing a patient to respond freely to a particular stimulus without prompting by the analyst.

Functional foremanship The principles of Scientific management as applied to first line management.

Garbage can model of decision making This is based on the idea that organizations are comprised of bundles of available solutions looking for problems. The garbage can is a receptacle for solutions and situations, both waiting to be matched up.

Gatekeeper Person (or post) within an organization able to grant or restrict access to a more senior person.

Golden handcuff An attempt to lock the employee into the company through the use of some incentive to stay, usually high wages or an incentive payment based on service.

Grapevine The rumour mill or gossip networks that exist in all organizations as a way of passing information, real or imagined around employees at all levels.

Graphology The study of handwriting.

Great man view of leadership This view suggests that there are certain people who are born with the appropriate characteristics to make them successful leaders.

Greenfield site A term used to describe a brand new operational location as compared to a Brownfield site which describes an existing site.

Groups Consists of two or more people who have some purpose and interact with each other in such a way that they are psychologically aware of each other and are influenced by each other.

Group cohesion Reflects the strength of mutual bonds and attitudes among members.

Group communication The patterns through which individuals within a group communicate with each other.

Group conformity The degree of compliance to the group norms by individual members.

Group decision making The processes by which a group will take decisions.

Group development Process of individuals coming together to form a group capable of achieving task objectives and member satisfaction.

Group dynamics The behavioural interactions and patterns of behaviour that occur when groups of people meet.

Groups, instrumental value of The benefits that an individual gains from joining a group, including meeting social and affiliation needs and gaining support for their objectives.

Group norms The patterns of behaviour, attitudes and beliefs that are held by a particular group and to which members are expected to subscribe.

Groupthink The tendency of a strongly cohesive group to emphasize unanimity at the expense of critical evaluation of a problem and available options.

Groups types within an organization

- Hierarchical differentiation.
- Specialism groupings.
- Activity groupings.
- Boundary spanning.
- Professional.

Habituation Constant repetition of a stimulus can lead to the senses turning off from the awareness of it.

Halo (or horns) effect The bias introduced when attributing all of the characteristics of a person (or object) to a single attribute. When this is positive it is a 'halo' effect, when negative a 'horns' effect.

Hawthorne effect The tendency of people to change their behaviour as a result of being subjected to research and observation, first identified during the Hawthorne studies.

Hawthorne studies A series of four research studies exploring aspects of group working within the Western Electric Company in the USA during the late 1920s and early 1930s.

Helicopter perspective The ability to take an overview of a situation.

Hidden agenda An intention that is not apparent but forms a significant motivation for an individual's behaviour in a particular context.

High performance organization An organization in which the combination of people, technology, management and productivity are integrated effectively to provide competitive advantage on a sustainable basis.

Human relations movement The school of management thinking that originated from the work of Elton Mayo in which the significance of social groups and processes was emphasized.

Human resource management An approach to the management of people that supposedly represents a more central strategic management activity than personnel management.

Human resource planning The process of seeking to match present and future human availability to the needs of the organization.

Ideal type An example or typical model which would not be found in practice in its exact form, but would be identifiable to a greater or lesser extent from what is found.

Idiographic theories of personality These offer an approach to describing personality based upon the uniqueness of each individual and in so doing do not rely on psychometric tests.

Individual difference See Personality.

Individualism–collectivism A cultural dimension reflecting the underlying arrangement of society into a loose collective framework; or an integrated, tight social arrangement involving collective responsibility.

Industrialization Refers to the application of technology in a particular location, moving it away from agricultural to a factory based economy.

Influence The ability to direct the behaviour of another person involving persuasion rather than force.

Influence diagram These seek to illustrate the influences and relationships that exist between individuals and groups within and outside an organization.

Informal groups Formed from employee friendship, mutual support and dependency needs which cannot be met through the formal groups provided by an organization.

Instrumental approach to work An approach to work which is based on a trading and value approach to relationships and the determination of contribution.

Instrumental conditioning An approach to learning based on the reinforcement of particular behaviours by a trainer which consequently shapes it into the desired pattern.

Interaction analysis This contains four categories of interaction which can be used for recording interaction patterns within groups.

Intelligence Often described in terms of a number of primary mental abilities such as verbal comprehension, number ability, or a capacity for learning.

Intellectual capital The sum total of knowledge, expertise and dedication of the workforce in an organization.

Interpersonal, Informational and Decisional roles Three categories of role used to describe the main features of a managers job.

Intrinsic motivator Motivation that originates inside the individual as a response to the job itself and the circumstances surrounding its execution. See also Extrinsic motivation.

Introversion See Extroversion.

Job Essentially a collection of tasks brought together as a practical 'chunk' of activity, created and adapted by people, for a particular purpose within an organization.

Job analysis A systematic approach to the identification of the content and responsibilities of a job, results in a job description being written. See also Job description.

Job characteristics model A model of job enrichment based on the need to incorporate a number of core job dimensions (Skill variety, Task identity, Task significance, Autonomy and Feedback) into the design of a job.

Job description A document based on job analysis that sets out the duties and other requirements associated with a job.

Job enlargement An approach to work organization which combines a range of tasks together that would add breadth to the design of a job.

Job enrichment An approach to job design that requires activities and responsibilities to be added to the design of a job.

Job evaluation A process by which job descriptions can be used to identify the rank order (or relative magnitude) of jobs in an organization.

Job rotation An approach to work organization which proposes that two (or more) simplified jobs are combined into a pattern of employee rotation.

Job simplification An approach to job design based on a minimization of the range of tasks into the smallest convenient size to make the job efficient and cost effective.

Just-in-time An approach in which processes are linked together in an extended chain to ensure that good quality components are delivered to the user just-in-time for them to be used.

Karoshi A Japanese word meaning sudden death from overwork.

Knowledge management The management of the knowledge available to the organization from all sources in such a way as to allow the creation of new knowledge and the sharing of existing knowledge; together with the manipulation of that knowledge in such a way as to benefit the organization and the individuals working within it.

Labour process theory Essentially, this seeks to explain the use to which human labour is put in capitalist organizations and the part played by managers in the organization of that work for the benefit of capital owners.

Laissez faire An approach to leadership in which the leader effectively abdicates responsibility for the decision making within the group.

Law of requisite variety see 'Requisite variety'.

Leadership A process in which the leader is able to influence the behaviours and actions of those being led.

Learning The relatively permanent change in behaviour or potential behaviour that results from direct or indirect experience.

Learning organization The facilitation of learning for all employees and the constant transformation of the organization in response to that new knowledge and ability.

Legitimate power The ability to exercise power as a consequence of having the legitimate right to claim to be able to do so.

Line manager Every employee reports to a line manager – their boss.

Line and staff functions A line function is involved with the main purposes of the organization – the operational functions. The staff functions refer to the activities which although necessary are supportive of the main operational functions.

Linking pin model This model reflects the overlapping and connected nature of groups within an organization.

Loco parentis Having the right to act as though you were the parent of another person.

Locus of control The degree to which an individual believes that they are subjected to outside control as opposed to having internal control over the forces influencing their behaviour.

Luddite The term originated from the bands of workers who roamed England in the early 1800s breaking up machinery and destroying the factories which they perceived would cost them their jobs. These days used to describe people who are resistant to change.

Management The jobs within an organization charged with running the organization on behalf of the beneficial owner.

Management by exception An approach to managing that assumes that only where an exception or deviation from a plan is identified does any action need to be taken.

Management, principles of 14 elements of what being a manager involved, developed by Fayol and included as Table 8.1.

Management process The view of management developed by Fayol, consists of: Forecasting, Planning, Organizing, Co-ordinating, Commanding, Controlling.

Manpower planning See Human resource planning.

Manufacture of consent The achievement of employee consent to control by managers through such practices as collective bargaining, although managers retain effective control over labour use, which perpetuates the relative imbalance of power in a capitalist society.

Marketplace bureaucracy In practice, the need to get things done within an organization requires the continuous trading of favours between colleagues over and above formal reporting relationships or procedures.

Market testing Checking the cost of something against market norms.

Marxist or radical perspective on conflict This suggests that conflict is an inevitable function of the exploitation of employees within a capitalist system.

Masculinity A cultural dimension reflecting the degree of domination of society's values by 'masculine' characteristics.

McGregor's Theory X and Theory Y Theory X managers consider workers as lazy and having to be driven to achieve performance. Theory Y managers consider workers enjoy the experience of work and have a desire to achieve high performance. McGregor believed that managers managed their staff on the basis of these beliefs, irrespective of actual employee approach to work.

McKinsey 7-S Framework A model consisting of seven interacting elements Structure, Strategy, Systems, Style, Skill, Staff, and Shared values (culture).

Metaphor The explanation of something complex through reference to something simpler, but in a way which conveys additional meaning in the process.

Method study The application of a range of techniques which allow the critical examination of work activity in order to facilitate the search for the most efficient methods of work.

Mock bureaucracy The rules and procedures are largely ignored by all inside the bureaucracy, having been imposed on them by an outside agency.

Modernism An approach to management based on the understanding of the social and natural world revealed through the application of reason and science. See also postmodernism.

Moral philosophy A branch of philosophy that takes as its sphere of interest the norms or values, ideas of right and wrong, good or bad, what should and what should not be done.

Motivate To seek to create motivation in another person.

Motivation A driving force that encourages an individual to behave in particular ways as they seek to achieve a goal. The willingness or energy with which individuals perform their work.

Motive –Social processes directing controllable behaviour in people. See also Motivation.

Negative power The ability to influence another party by not doing something that would normally be done.

Negotiation Broadly reflects a process of difference reduction through the forming of agreements between individuals and groups who have mutually dependent needs and desires.

Networking The development of relationships and contacts that are not of immediate necessity, but which might be useful in the future.

Neuroticism An aspect of personality reflecting a person who worries, is anxious, moody and unstable. The stable person by comparison tends to be calm, even tempered, carefree and reliable.

Noise The peripheral and background contamination surrounding a communication that interferes with the ability of the recipient receiving the complete message sent. For example, noise from a television playing in the background can prevent someone hearing every word spoken during a phone conversation.

Nomothetic theories of personality These offer an approach based upon the identification and measurement of characteristics through psychometric tests.

Norms see Group norms.

One best way The idea that through the application of scientific management the 'one best way' of doing any task could be identified by management.

Open systems model A model of an organization which represents it in terms of inputs being transformed into outputs, in turn leading to feedback to the organization, all taking place within a dynamic and interactive environment.

Organization Social arrangements of people and other resources working together in consciously created structured arrangements in pursuit of collective objectives.

Organizational behaviour A mainstream approach to the study of management and organizations incorporating anything relevant to the design, management and effectiveness of an organization, together with the dynamic and interactive relationships that exist within them.

Organization chart A diagrammatic means by which organizations describe the structure and reporting relationships that exist.

Organizational citizenship Defined in terms of voluntary behaviour that generally contributes to organizational effectiveness but not directly or explicitly recognized by the formal reward system.

Organizational development (OD) The systematic application of behavioural science knowledge to the planned development and reinforcement of organizational strategies, structures, and processes for improving an organization's effectiveness.

Paradigm A model based on the theoretical assumptions made in creating an understanding of the nature of social science and the nature of society.

Path–goal theory A model based on the idea that it is possible to identify a distinct path leading to the achievement of particular goals.

Perceived role what the individual understands their role to be.

Perception A generally subconscious psychological process which enables individuals to understand the vast range of 'things' that are external to themselves, necessary so that individuals can determine appropriate response behaviours.

Perceptual defence A process that provides a measure of protection for the individual against information, ideas or situations that are threatening to an existing perception or attitude.

Perceptual errors These reflect the mistakes of judgement or understanding that can occur during the process of making sense of perceptual information.

Perceptual set The predisposition to perceive what an individual expects to perceive.

Perform see Performance.

Performance In human terms this reflects the level of achievement by an individual, measured against what they would be expected to achieve.

Performance management The many processes through which managers seek to manage performance levels within the organization.

Personality The personal characteristics such as extroversion and stability that result in consistent patterns of behaviour over time.

Personnel management See human resource management.

Pluralism A perspective that regards organizations as collections of groups which have some objectives in common and some in competition. Conflict results but can be usually resolved as all parties recognize the need to compromise in order to achieve some of their objectives.

Political decision making model Decision making as a process intended to achieve personal or short term objectives through organizational activity. One form of this was described as the garbage can model.

Political process Any behaviour within an organization which uses political means to achieve a desired objective.

Politics This is defined as behaviour outside the accepted procedures and norms of a particular context, intended to further the position of an individual or group at the expense of others.

Postmodernism An approach to management based on the view that reality is a composite of many differing realities and that it is constructed through the human ability to express these realities.

Post-traumatic stress disorder (PTSD) A reaction among individuals subjected to major trauma that can lead to a range of negative psychological, medical and social consequences.

Power A concept that reflects a directing, mobilizing and energizing force in getting people to do what they might not otherwise do and is related to force, influence and manipulation.

Power distance A cultural dimension reflecting the degree to which a society accepts that organizational power is distributed unequally.

Principled negotiations An approach to negotiation based on four elements: Separate the people from the problem; Focus on interests, not positions; Invent options for mutual gain; and Insist on objective criteria.

Process consultation An approach to organization development in which the role of the consultant is to facilitate understanding of how to explore problems and find workable solutions.

Process theories of motivation These emphasize those mechanisms that encourage (or reward) behaviour in its dynamic context.

Productivity The relationship between inputs and outputs, expressed as either a conversion index reflecting (for example) the organization's sales for each unit of labour, or a comparative index measuring changes across time.

Professionalization of management The idea that management is not just another job, but represents a defined area of work with its own skills, knowledge base and training requirements.

Programmed and non-programmed decision making models Programmed decision making refers to the situations in which known steps lead from problem to solution. Non-programmed decisions are new, cannot be anticipated, or do not have pre-existing methods for resolving them.

Projection A psychological process of projecting onto others characteristics that we see in ourselves.

Projective techniques (or test) A process based on ambiguous images being presented to an individual who is then asked to interpret the image; thought to provide some insight into attitudes and personality characteristics.

Psychological contract The actual nature and boundaries of the relationship between employer and employee prescribed through the unwritten and unstated rights and obligations of both parties.

Psychometrics The process of mental measurement through the application of tests that claim to measure aspects of personality or other characteristics such as ability or aptitude.

Punishment bureaucracy Represents a variant on the mock bureaucracy in that rules are imposed on the workers (who try to ignore them) by management.

Quality circle Small groups of people from the same work area who voluntarily meet on a regular basis to identify, investigate, analyse and solve their own work-related problems.

Quality of working life An approach to management that seeks to enhance the dignity of workers, improve an organization's culture, and improve the physical and emotional well-being of employees.

Quantitative school A mathematical approach to management that seeks to find ways of modelling relationships between variables so that causal relationships can be identified and predictions made.

Rational decision making model This assumes that decisions are made in the best interests of the organization on the basis of data collection and analysis, along with evaluation of alternatives.

Re-engineering See Business process re-engineering.

Referent power This source of power is based on the characteristics of an individual, usually based on a charismatic personality.

Reinforcement The encouragement of particular behaviours through the application of positive and/or negative rewards, based on the application of four schedules; Fixed ratio, Variable ratio, Fixed interval, Variable interval.

Repeated measures experiments An experimental design which involves subjects attempting the same task on a number of occasions, with only one variable changed.

Representative bureaucracy The rules and procedures are generally supported by those inside the organization having been developed by managers with the involvement of the workers.

Requisite variety The view that only variety can destroy variety implying that complex situations require equally complex processes to deal with them.

Restricted rationality decision making model Also termed the 'bounded rationality' model, this implies that group dynamics and politics can influence decisions and also individuals may lack the intellectual or technical capacity to evaluate decisions rationally.

Reward power This is about achieving control over another person by offering them something that they desire. It represents the trading basis of power, exchanging a willingness to be controlled for desirable rewards.

Rich picture A drawing that provides a mechanism through which a dynamic situation can be reflected in a manner meaningful to the participants. It can reflect how the processes function and how the people interact within the organization.

Rightsizing See Downsizing.

Risky shift phenomenon The idea that groups tend to take decisions that are more risky than the individual members would take.

Role The behaviours and job activities undertaken by an individual as a result of their organizational duties and responsibilities.

Role ambiguity The degree of ambiguity in the minds of individuals forming the role set as to exactly what their respective roles should be at any point in time.

Role conflict This arises as a result of the conflicting role requirements acting on an individual at the same time.